Attention!
To access the premium website for this textbook, please vis
www.cengage.com/login
Your unique access code can be found on the back of this c

QUANTITATIVE METHODS FOR BUSINESS 11e

David R. Anderson
University of Cincinnati

Dennis J. Sweeney
University of Cincinnati

Thomas A. Williams
Rochester Institute of Technology

Jeffrey D. Camm
University of Cincinnati

Kipp Martin
University of Chicago

SOUTH-WESTERN
CENGAGE Learning

Australia • Brazil • Japan • Korea • Mexico • Singapore • Spain • United Kingdom • United States

SOUTH-WESTERN
CENGAGE Learning™

Quantitative Methods for Business, Eleventh Edition
David R. Anderson, Dennis J. Sweeney, Thomas A. Williams, Jeffrey D. Camm, & Kipp Martin

Editorial Director: Jack W. Calhoun

Editor-in-Chief: Alex von Rosenberg

Senior Acquisitions Editor: Charles McCormick, Jr.

Developmental Editor: Margaret Kubale

Editorial Assistant: Bryn Lathrop

Marketing Communications Manager: Libby Shipp

Marketing Manager: Bryant Chrzan

Content Project Manager: Jacquelyn K Featherly

Media Editor: Chris Valentine

Senior Manufacturing Coordinator: Bev Breslin

Production House/Compositor: Macmillan Publishing Solutions

Art Director: Stacy Jenkins Shirley

Internal Designer: Michael Stratton/ cmiller design

Cover Designer: Craig Ramsdell

Cover Images: Getty Images/GlowImages

Photo Manager: John Hill

For product information and technology assistance, contact us at **Cengage Learning Customer & Sales Support, 1-800-354-9706**

For permission to use material from this text or product, submit all requests online at **www.cengage.com/permissions** Further permissions questions can be emailed to **permissionrequest@cengage.com**

ExamView® and ExamView Pro® are registered trademarks of FSCreations, Inc. Windows is a registered trademark of the Microsoft Corporation used herein under license. Macintosh and Power Macintosh are registered trademarks of Apple Computer, Inc. used herein under license.

Library of Congress Control Number: 2008936407

Student Edition Package 13: 978-0-324-65181-2

Student Edition Package 10: 0-324-65181-3

Student Edition ISBN 13: 978-0-324-65175-1

Student Edition ISBN 10: 0-324-65175-9

South-Western Cengage Learning
5191 Natorp Boulevard
Mason, OH 45040
USA

Cengage Learning products are represented in Canada by Nelson Education, Ltd.

For your course and learning solutions, visit **www.cengage.com**

Purchase any of our products at your local college store or at our preferred online store **www.ichapters.com**

Printed in Canada
1 2 3 4 5 6 7 12 11 10 09 08

To My Children
Krista, Justin, Mark, and Colleen
DRA

To My Children
Mark, Linda, Brad, Tim, Scott, and Lisa
DJS

To My Children
Cathy, David, and Kristin
TAW

To My Wife
Karen Camm
JDC

To My Parents
Bruce and Phyllis Martin
KM

Brief Contents

Contents

Chapter 15 Waiting Line Models 655

Preface

The purpose of this eleventh edition, as with previous editions, is to provide undergraduate and graduate students with a conceptual understanding of the role that quantitative methods play in the decision-making process. The text describes the many quantitative methods developed over the years, explains how they work, and shows how the decision maker can apply and interpret them.

This book is written with the nonmathematician in mind. It is applications-oriented and uses our problem scenario approach. In each chapter a problem is described in conjunction with the quantitative procedure being introduced. Development of the quantitative technique or model includes applying it to the problem to generate a solution or recommendation. This approach can help to motivate the student by demonstrating not only how the procedure works, but also how it contributes to the decision-making process.

The mathematical prerequisite for this text is a course in algebra. The two chapters on probability and probability distributions will provide the necessary background for the use of probability in subsequent chapters. Throughout the text we use generally accepted notation for the topic being covered. As a result, students who pursue study beyond the level of this text will generally experience little difficulty reading more advanced material. To also assist in further study, a bibliography is included at the end of this book.

CHANGES IN THE ELEVENTH EDITION

The eleventh edition of QMB is a major revision. We are very excited about it and want to tell you about some of the changes we have made and why.

New Members of the ASW Team

Prior to getting into the content changes, we want to announce that we have added two new authors to the ASW author team for QMB. The new authors are Jeff Camm and Kipp Martin. Jeff received his Ph.D. from Clemson University. He has been at the University of Cincinnati since 1984, and has been a visiting scholar at Stanford University and a visiting professor of business administration at the Tuck School of Business at Dartmouth College. Jeff has published over 30 papers in the general area of optimization applied to problems in operations management. At the University of Cincinnati, he was named the Dornoff Fellow of Teaching Excellence and he was the 2006 recipient of the INFORMS Prize for the Teaching of Operations Research Practice. He currently serves as editor-in-chief of *Interfaces,* and is on the editorial board of *INFORMS Transactions on Education.* Kipp received his Ph.D. from the University of Cincinnati in 1981 and studied there with the current authors: David Anderson, Dennis Sweeney, and Thomas Williams. Dennis Sweeney was his dissertation advisor. Kipp is currently a Professor at the University of Chicago and does research in the fields of management science and computer technology. He has authored or coauthored three books and published research articles in various academic journals. We welcome Jeff and Kipp to the new ASWCM team and expect the new ideas they bring to make the text even better in the years to come.

New Chapter 12: Advanced Optimization Applications

A new chapter on optimization applications has been added. Applications include portfolio selection, a nonlinear extension of the RMC problem, and selecting stocks to go into an index mutual fund. This chapter introduces the idea of a nonlinear optimization model, but strictly from an applications standpoint. The Management Scientist cannot be used for nonlinear problems, and LINGO or Premium Solver are required.

New Documented Solutions

The Management Scientist will not be used in future editions of this book. We encourage adopters of this edition to use either LINGO or Premium Solver when solving optimization problems. To make it easy for new users of LINGO or Excel Premium Solver, we provide both LINGO and Excel files with the model formulation for every optimization problem that appears in the body of the text in Chapters 7 through 12. The model files are well-documented and should make it easy for the user to understand the model formulation.

New Appendix A: Building Spreadsheet Models

This is not a book on spreadsheet modeling. However, spreadsheets are a very valuable modeling tool. This Appendix will prove useful to professors and students wishing to solve optimization models with Premium Solver. The appendix also contains a section on the principles of good spreadsheet modeling and a section on auditing tips. Exercises are also provided.

Updated Chapter 10: Distribution and Network Models

This replaces the old Chapter 10, "Transportation, Assignment, and Transshipment Problems" from the tenth edition. We have added sections on the shortest route problem and the maximal flow problem. However, in keeping with the theme of the book, we do not burden the student with any algorithms. All of the models in the chapter are presented under the unifying theme of linear programming.

New Q.M. in Action, Cases, and Problems

Q.M. in Action is the name of the short summaries that describe how the quantitative methods being covered in the chapter have been used in practice. In this edition you will find numerous Q.M. in Action vignettes, cases, and homework problems.

COMPUTER SOFTWARE INTEGRATION

We made every effort to write the text so that it is not dependent on any particular software package. However, the software described in the various chapter appendices is available for download; an access code is included with each new copy of the text on the premium Web site access card in an envelope in the back of the book. The software packages available for download are LINGO for simulation, The Management Scientist v6.0, the TreePlan add-in for decision analysis, Crystal Ball for simulation, and the Premium Solver add-in for solving linear and integer programs with Microsoft Excel. If you plan to have your students use Premium Solver, please visit the Instructor Companion Web site for instructions to obtain a Course Code for your students. The students will not be able to download the software without it. Excel worksheets and LINGO models are available on the premium website as well.

All of the computer output shown in Chapters 7 through 11 (linear and integer programming) is from The Management Scientist v6.0 software. Users of LINGO should not experience difficulty interpreting this output. For instructors who prefer to use Excel Solver, we include chapter appendixes describing how to formulate and solve linear and integer programs. In Chapters 14 through 16 (Inventory Models, Waiting Line Models, and Simulation), we integrate Excel worksheets into the body of the chapter, and show how these worksheets can be used to perform the analysis.

FEATURES AND PEDAGOGY

We continued many of the features that appeared in previous editions. Some of the important ones are noted here.

- Annotations: Annotations that highlight key points and provide additional insights for the student are a continuing feature of this edition. These annotations, which appear in the margins, are designed to provide emphasis and enhance understanding of the terms and concepts presented in the text.
- Notes and Comments: At the end of many sections, we provide Notes and Comments to give the student additional insights about the methodology being discussed and its application. These insights include warnings about or limitations of the methodology, recommendations for application, brief descriptions of additional technical considerations, and other matters.
- Self-Test Exercises: Certain exercises are identified as self-test exercises. Completely worked-out solutions for these exercises are provided in Appendix G, entitled Self-Test Solutions and Answers to Even-Numbered Problems, located at the end of the book. Students can attempt the self-test problems and immediately check the solutions to evaluate their understanding of the concepts presented in the chapter. At the request of professors using our textbooks, we now provide the answers to even-numbered problems in this same appendix.
- Q.M. in Action: These articles are presented throughout the text and provide a summary of an application of quantitative methods found in business today. Adaptations of materials from *Interfaces* and *OR/MS Today* articles and write-ups provided by practitioners provide the basis for the applications in this feature.

ANCILLARY LEARNING AND TEACHING MATERIALS

For Students

Print and online resources are available to help the student work more efficiently as well as learn how to use Excel.

- LINGO: An educational version of the latest version of the LINGO software is sold at a discounted price when it is packaged with a new text. Instructor support materials are available to adopters from the Cengage Learning Academic Resource Center at 800-423-0563 or through http://www.swlearning.com.

For Instructors

Instructor support materials are available to adopters from the Cengage Learning Academic Resource Center at 800-423-0563 or through http://www.cengage.com/southwestern.

- Instructor ancillaries are now provided on an Instructors Resource CD (ISBN: 0-324-65177-5). Included in this convenient format are:

  Solutions Manual: The Solutions Manual, prepared by the authors, includes solutions for all problems in the text. At the request of the instructor, a printed version of the Solutions Manual can be packaged with the text for student purchase.

Solutions to Case Problems: Also prepared by the authors, it contains solutions to all case problems presented in the text.

PowerPoint Presentation Slides: Prepared by John Loucks of St. Edwards University, the presentation slides contain a teaching outline that incorporates graphics to help instructors create even more stimulating lectures. The slides may be adapted using PowerPoint software to facilitate classroom use.

Test Bank: Also prepared by John Loucks, the Test Bank in Microsoft Word files includes multiple choice, true/false, short-answer questions, and problems for each chapter.

ExamView Computerized Testing Software: A separate version of the Test Bank in ExamView allows instructors to create, edit, store, and print exams.

- WebTutor for Blackboard or WebCT: This online tool provides Web-based learning resources for students as well as powerful communication, testing, and other course management tools for the instructor. More information may be found at www.cengage.com

COURSE OUTLINE FLEXIBILITY

The text provides instructors substantial flexibility in selecting topics to meet specific course needs. Although many variations are possible, the single-semester and single-quarter outlines that follow are illustrative of the options available.

Suggested One-Semester Course Outline

Introduction (Chapter 1)

Probability Concepts (Chapters 2 and 3)

Decision Analysis (Chapters 4 and 5)

Forecasting (Chapter 6)

Linear Programming (Chapters 7, 8, and 9)

Transportation, Assignment, and Transshipment Problems (Chapter 10)

Integer Linear Programming (Chapter 11)

Advanced Optimization Applications (Chapter 12)

Project Scheduling: PERT/CPM (Chapter 13)

Simulation (Chapter 15)

Suggested One-Quarter Course Outline

Introduction (Chapter 1)

Decision Analysis (Chapters 4 and 5)

Linear Programming (Chapters 7, 8, and 9)

Transportation, Assignment, and Transshipment Problems (Chapter 10)

Integer Linear Programming (Chapter 11)

Advanced Optimization Applications (Chapter 12)

Project Scheduling: PERT/CPM (Chapter 13)

Simulation (Chapter 15)

Many other possibilities exist for one-term courses, depending on time available, course objectives, and backgrounds of the students.

ACKNOWLEDGMENTS

We were fortunate in having the thoughts and comments of a number of colleagues as we began our work on this eleventh edition of *Quantitative Methods for Business*. Our appreciation and thanks go to:

Ellen Parker Allen,
Southern Methodist
University

Gopesh Anand, The Ohio
State University

Daniel Asera, University of
Nevada, Las Vegas

Stephen Baglione, Saint
Leo University

Ardith Baker, Oral Roberts
University

Robert T. Barrett, Francis
Marion University

Gary Blau,
Purdue University

William Bleuel, Pepperdine
University

Richard G. Bradford,
Avila University

Thomas Bundt,
Hillsdale College

Heidi Burgiel, Bridgewater
State College

Ron Craig, Wilfrid Laurier
University

Swarna D. Dutt, State
University of West Georgia

Charlie Edmonson,
University of Dayton

Paul Ewell, Bridgewater
College

Ephrem Eyob, Virginia
State University

Christian V. Fugar,
Dillard University

Alfredo Gomez, Florida
Atlantic University

Bob Gregory,
Bellevue University

Leland Gustafson, State
University of West Georgia

Joseph Haimowitz,
Avila University

John Hanson, University of
San Diego

William V. Harper,
Otterbein College

Harry G. Henderson,
Davis & Elkins College

Carl H. Hess,
Marymount University

Woodrow W. Hughes, Jr.,
Converse College

M. S. Krishnamoorthy,
Alliant International
University

Melvin H. Kuhbander,
Sullivan University

Anil Kukreja, Xavier
University of Louisiana

Alireza Lari, Fayetteville
State University

Jodey Lingg,
City University

Donald R. MacRitchie,
Framingham State College

Larry Maes,
Davenport University

Timothy McDaniel,
Buena Vista University

John R. Miller,
Mercer University

Saeed Mohaghegh,
Assumption College

Herbert Moskowitz,
Purdue University

Shahriar Mostashari,
Campbell
University–School of
Business

V. R. Nemani,
Trinity College

William C. O'Connor,
University of
Montana–Western

Donald A. Ostasiewski,
Thomas More College

John E. Powell, University
of South Dakota

Avuthu Rami Reddy,
University of Wisconsin

Kazim Ruhi, University of
Maryland

Susan D. Sandblom,
Scottsdale Community
College

Tom Schmidt,
Simpson College

Rajesh Srivastava,
Florida Gulf Coast
University

Donald E. Stout, Jr., Saint
Martin's College

Minghe Sun, University
of Texas at San Antonio

Rahmat Tavallali,
Walsh University

Dothang Truong,
Fayetteville State
University

William Vasbinder,
Becker College

Elizabeth J. Wark,
Springfield College

Robert P. Wells, Becker
College

Kefeng Xu, University of
Texas at San Antonio

John F. Wellington,
Indiana University–
Purdue University,
Fort Wayne

Laura J. White, University
of West Florida

Mari Yetimyan, San Jose
State University

Cynthia Woodburn,
Pittsburg State University

Writing and revising a textbook is a continuing process. We owe a debt to many of our colleagues and friends for their helpful comments and suggestions during the development of earlier editions. Among these are:

Robert L. Armacost,
University of Central
Florida

Uttarayan Bagchi,
University of Texas at
Austin

Edward Baker,
University of Miami

Norman Baker,
University of Cincinnati

David Bakuli,
Westfield State College

Oded Berman,
University of Toronto

Rodger D. Carlson,
Morehead State University

Ying Chien,
University of Scranton

Renato Clavijo, Robert
Morris University

Mary M. Danaher, Florida
Atlantic University

Stanley Dick,
Babson College

John Eatman, University of
North Carolina–Greensboro

Ronald Ebert, University of
Missouri–Columbia

Don Edwards, University
of South Carolina

Ronald Ehresman,
Baldwin-Wallace College

Peter Ellis,
Utah State University

Lawrence Ettkin,
University of Tennessee at
Chattanooga

James Evans,
University of Cincinnati

Michael Ford, Rochester
Institute of Technology

Terri Friel, Eastern
Kentucky University

Phil Fry, Boise State
University

Robert Garfinkel,
University of Connecticut

Nicholas G. Hall, The Ohio
State University

Michael E. Hanna,
University of Houston–
Clear Lake

Melanie Hatch,
Miami University

Daniel G. Hotard,
Southeastern Louisiana
University

David Hott, Florida
Institute of Technology

Christine Irujo,
Westfield State College

Barry Kadets,
Bryant College

Birsen Karpak, Youngstown
State University

William C. Keller, Webb
Institute of the University
of Phoenix

Christos Koulamas, Florida
International University

John Lawrence, Jr.,
California State
University–Fullerton

John S. Loucks,
St. Edwards University

Constantine Loucopoulos,
Emporia State University

Ka-sing Man,
Georgetown University

William G. Marchal,
University of Toledo

Barbara J. Mardis,
University of Northern
Iowa

Kamlesh Mathur, Case
Western Reserve University

Joseph Mazzola,
Duke University

Patrick McKeown,
University of Georgia

Constance McLaren,
Indiana State University

Mohammad Meybodi,
Indiana University–
Kokomo

John Miller, Jr.,
Mercer University

Mario Miranda, The Ohio
State University

Joe Moffitt, University of
Massachusetts

Alan Neebe, University of
North Carolina

Donald A. Ostasiewski,
Thomas More College

David Pentico,
Duquesne University

B. Madhusudan Rao,
Bowling Green State
University

Handanhal V. Ravinder,
University of New Mexico

Donna Retzlaff-Roberts,
University of Memphis

Don R. Robinson,
Illinois State University

Richard Rosenthal, Naval
Postgraduate School

Antoinette Somers, Wayne
State University

Christopher S. Tang,
University of California–
Los Angeles

Giri Kumar Tayi, State
University of New York–
Albany

Willban Terpening,
Gonzaga University

Vicente A. Vargas,
University of San Diego

Emre Veral, City
University of New York–
Baruch

Edward P. Winkofsky,
University of Cincinnati

Neba LAbbe Wu, Eastern
Michigan University

Our associates from organizations who provided application write-ups made a major contribution to the text. These individuals are cited in a credit line on the associated Q.M. in Action.

We are also indebted to our senior acquisitions editor, Charles McCormick, Jr.; our marketing manager, Bryant Chrzan; our developmental editor, Maggie Kubale; our content project manager, Jacquelyn K Featherly; our media editor, Chris Valentine; and others at Cengage Business and Economics for their counsel and support during the preparation of this text.

David R. Anderson
Dennis J. Sweeney
Thomas A. Williams
Jeffrey D. Camm
Kipp Martin

About the Authors

David R. Anderson   David R. Anderson is Professor of Quantitative Analysis in the College of Business Administration at the University of Cincinnati. Born in Grand Forks, North Dakota, he earned his B.S., M.S., and Ph.D. degrees from Purdue University. Professor Anderson has served as Head of the Department of Quantitative Analysis and Operations Management and as Associate Dean of the College of Business Administration. In addition, he was the coordinator of the College's first Executive Program.

At the University of Cincinnati, Professor Anderson has taught introductory statistics for business students as well as graduate-level courses in regression analysis, multivariate analysis, and management science. He has also taught statistical courses at the Department of Labor in Washington, D.C. He has been honored with nominations and awards for excellence in teaching and excellence in service to student organizations.

Professor Anderson has coauthored 10 textbooks in the areas of statistics, management science, linear programming, and production and operations management. He is an active consultant in the field of sampling and statistical methods.

Dennis J. Sweeney   Dennis J. Sweeney is Professor of Quantitative Analysis and Founder of the Center for Productivity Improvement at the University of Cincinnati. Born in Des Moines, Iowa, he earned a B.S.B.A. degree from Drake University and his M.B.A. and D.B.A. degrees from Indiana University, where he was an NDEA Fellow. During 1978–79, Professor Sweeney worked in the management science group at Procter & Gamble; during 1981–82, he was a visiting professor at Duke University. Professor Sweeney served as Head of the Department of Quantitative Analysis and as Associate Dean of the College of Business Administration at the University of Cincinnati.

Professor Sweeney has published more than 30 articles and monographs in the area of management science and statistics. The National Science Foundation, IBM, Procter & Gamble, Federated Department Stores, Kroger, and Cincinnati Gas & Electric have funded his research, which has been published in *Management Science*, *Operations Research*, *Mathematical Programming*, *Decision Sciences*, and other journals.

Professor Sweeney has coauthored 10 textbooks in the areas of statistics, management science, linear programming, and production and operations management.

Thomas A. Williams   Thomas A. Williams is Professor of Management Science in the College of Business at Rochester Institute of Technology. Born in Elmira, New York, he earned his B.S. degree at Clarkson University. He did his graduate work at Rensselaer Polytechnic Institute, where he received his M.S. and Ph.D. degrees.

Before joining the College of Business at RIT, Professor Williams served for seven years as a faculty member in the College of Business Administration at the University of Cincinnati, where he developed the undergraduate program in Information Systems and then served as its coordinator. At RIT he was the first chairman of the Decision Sciences Department. He teaches courses in management science and statistics, as well as graduate courses in regression and decision analysis.

Professor Williams is the coauthor of 11 textbooks in the areas of management science, statistics, production and operations management, and mathematics. He has been a consultant for numerous *Fortune* 500 companies and has worked on projects ranging from the use of data analysis to the development of large-scale regression models.

Jeffrey D. Camm   Jeffrey D. Camm is Professor of Quantitative Analysis, Head of the Department of Quantitative Analysis and Operations Management, and College of Business Research Fellow in the College of Business at the University of Cincinnati. Born in Cincinnati, Ohio, he holds a B.S. from Xavier University and a Ph.D. from Clemson University. He has been at the University of Cincinnati since 1984, and has been a visiting scholar at Stanford University and a visiting professor of business administration at the Tuck School of Business at Dartmouth College.

Dr. Camm has published over 30 papers in the general area of optimization applied to problems in operations management. He has published his research in *Science*, *Management Science*, *Operations Research*, *Interfaces* and other professional journals. At the University of Cincinnati, he was named the Dornoff Fellow of Teaching Excellence and he was the 2006 recipient of the INFORMS Prize for the Teaching of Operations Research Practice. A firm believer in practicing what he preaches, he has served as an operations research consultant to numerous companies and government agencies. He currently serves as editor-in-chief of *Interfaces*, and is on the editorial board of *INFORMS Transactions on Education*.

Kipp Martin   Kipp Martin is Professor of Operations Research and Computing Technology at the Graduate School of Business, University of Chicago. Born in St. Bernard, Ohio, he earned a B.A. in Mathematics, an M.B.A., and a Ph.D. in Management Science from the University of Cincinnati. While at the University of Chicago, Professor Martin has taught courses in Management Science, Operations Management, Business Mathematics, and Information Systems.

Research interests include incorporating Web technologies such as XML, XSLT, XQuery, and Web Services into the mathematical modeling process; the theory of how to construct good mixed integer linear programming models; symbolic optimization; polyhedral combinatorics; methods for large scale optimization; bundle pricing models; computing technology and database theory. Professor Martin has published in *INFORMS Journal of Computing*, *Management Science*, *Mathematical Programming*, *Operations Research*, *The Journal of Accounting Research*, and other professional journals. He is also the author of *The Essential Guide to Internet Business Technology* (with Gail Honda) and *Large Scale Linear and Integer Optimization*.

CHAPTER 1

Introduction

CONTENTS

This book is concerned with the use of quantitative methods to assist in decision making. It emphasizes not the methods themselves, but rather how they can contribute to better decisions. A variety of names exists for the body of knowledge involving quantitative approaches to decision making. Today, the terms most commonly used—*management science* (MS), *operations research* (OR), and *decision science*—are often used interchangeably.

The scientific management revolution of the early 1900s, initiated by Frederic W. Taylor, provided the foundation for the use of quantitative methods in management. Modern research in the use of quantitative methods in decision making, for the most part, however, originated during the World War II period. At that time, teams consisting of people with diverse specialties (e.g., mathematicians, engineers, and behavioral scientists) were formed to deal with strategic and tactical problems faced by the military. After the war, many of these team members continued their research into quantitative approaches to decision making.

Two developments that occurred during the post–World War II period led to the growth and use of quantitative methods in nonmilitary applications. First, continued research resulted in numerous methodological developments. Probably the most significant development was the discovery by George Dantzig, in 1947, of the simplex method for solving linear programming problems. At the same time these methodological developments were taking place, digital computers prompted a virtual explosion in computing power. Computers enabled practitioners to use the methodological advances to solve a large variety of problems. The computer technology explosion continues, and personal computers can now be used to solve problems larger than those solved on mainframe computers in the 1990s.

According to Irv Lustig of ILOG, Inc., solution methods developed today are 10,000 times faster than the ones used 15 years ago.

Q.M. *in* ACTION

REVENUE MANAGEMENT AT AMERICAN AIRLINES *

One of the great success stories in quantitative methods involves the work done by the operations research (OR) group at American Airlines. In 1982, Thomas M. Cook joined a group of 12 operations research analysts at American Airlines. Under Cook's guidance, the OR group quickly grew to a staff of 75 professionals who developed models and conducted studies to support senior management decision making. Today the OR group is called Sabre, and employs 10,000 professionals worldwide.

One of the most significant applications developed by the OR group came about because of the deregulation of the airline industry in the late 1970s. As a result of deregulation, a number of low-cost airlines were able to move into the market by selling seats at a fraction of the price charged by established carriers such as American Airlines. Facing the question of how to compete, the OR group suggested offering different fare classes (discount and full fare) and in the process created a new area of quantitative methods referred to as yield or revenue management.

The OR group used forecasting and optimization techniques to determine how many seats to sell at a discount and how many seats to hold for full fare. Although the initial implementation was relatively crude, the group continued to improve the forecasting and optimization models that drive the system to obtain better data. Tom Cook counts at least four basic generations of revenue management during his tenure. Each produced in excess of $100 million in incremental profitability over its predecessor. Today, the revenue management system at American Airlines generates nearly $1 billion annually in incremental revenue.

Today, virtually every airline uses some sort of revenue management system. The cruise, hotel, and car rental industries also now apply revenue management methods, a further tribute to the pioneering efforts of the OR group at American Airlines and its leader, Thomas M. Cook.

*Based on Peter Horner, "The Sabre Story," *OR/MS Today* (June 2000).

As stated in the Preface, the purpose of the text is to provide students with a sound conceptual understanding of the role that quantitative methods play in the decision-making process. The text is applications oriented. To reinforce the applications nature of the text and to provide a better understanding of the variety of applications in which *quantitative methods* (Q.M.) have been used successfully, Q.M. in Action articles are presented throughout the text. Each Q.M. in Action article summarizes an application of quantitative methods in practice. The first Q.M. in Action, Revenue Management at American Airlines, describes one of the most significant applications of quantitative methods in the airline industry.

1.1   Problem Solving and Decision Making

Problem solving can be defined as the process of identifying a difference between the actual and the desired state of affairs and then taking action to resolve the difference. For problems important enough to justify the time and effort of careful analysis, the problem-solving process involves the following seven steps:

1. Identify and define the problem.
2. Determine the set of alternative solutions.
3. Determine the criterion or criteria that will be used to evaluate the alternatives.
4. Evaluate the alternatives.
5. Choose an alternative.
6. Implement the selected alternative.
7. Evaluate the results to determine whether a satisfactory solution has been obtained.

Decision making is the term generally associated with the first five steps of the problem-solving process. Thus, the first step of decision making is to identify and define the problem. Decision making ends with the choosing of an alternative, which is the act of making the decision.

Let us consider the following example of the decision-making process. For the moment, assume that you are currently unemployed and that you would like a position that will lead to a satisfying career. Suppose that your job search results in offers from companies in Rochester, New York; Dallas, Texas; Greensboro, North Carolina; and Pittsburgh, Pennsylvania. Thus, the alternatives for your decision problem can be stated as follows:

1. Accept the position in Rochester.
2. Accept the position in Dallas.
3. Accept the position in Greensboro.
4. Accept the position in Pittsburgh.

The next step of the problem-solving process involves determining the criteria that will be used to evaluate the four alternatives. Obviously, the starting salary is a factor of some importance. If salary were the only criterion important to you, the alternative selected as "best" would be the one with the highest starting salary. Problems in which the objective is to find the best solution with respect to one criterion are referred to as **single-criterion decision problems**.

Suppose that you also conclude that the potential for advancement and the location of the job are two other criteria of major importance. Thus, the three criteria in your decision problem are starting salary, potential for advancement, and location. Problems that involve more than one criterion are referred to as **multicriteria decision problems**.

The next step of the decision-making process is to evaluate each of the alternatives with respect to each criterion. For example, evaluating each alternative relative to the starting

TABLE 1.1   DATA FOR THE JOB EVALUATION DECISION-MAKING PROBLEM

Alternative	Starting Salary	Potential for Advancement	Job Location
1. Rochester	$48,500	Average	Average
2. Dallas	$46,000	Excellent	Good
3. Greensboro	$46,000	Good	Excellent
4. Pittsburgh	$47,000	Average	Good

salary criterion is done simply by recording the starting salary for each job alternative. Evaluating each alternative with respect to the potential for advancement and the location of the job is more difficult to do, however, because these evaluations are based primarily on subjective factors that are often difficult to quantify. Suppose for now that you decide to measure potential for advancement and job location by rating each of these criteria as poor, fair, average, good, or excellent. The data you compile are shown in Table 1.1.

You are now ready to make a choice from the available alternatives. What makes this choice phase so difficult is that the criteria are probably not all equally important, and no one alternative is "best" with regard to all criteria. Although we will present a method for dealing with situations like this one later in the text, for now let us suppose that after a careful evaluation of the data in Table 1.1, you decide to select alternative 3. Alternative 3 is thus referred to as the **decision**.

At this point in time, the decision-making process is complete. In summary, we see that this process involves five steps:

1. Define the problem.
2. Identify the alternatives.
3. Determine the criteria.
4. Evaluate the alternatives.
5. Choose an alternative.

Note that missing from this list are the last two steps in the problem-solving process: implementing the selected alternative and evaluating the results to determine whether a satisfactory solution has been obtained. This omission is not meant to diminish the importance of each of these activities, but to emphasize the more limited scope of the term *decision making* as compared to the term *problem solving*. Figure 1.1 summarizes the relationship between these two concepts.

 ## **1.2** Quantitative Analysis and Decision Making

Consider the flowchart presented in Figure 1.2. Note that we combined the first three steps of the decision-making process under the heading of "Structuring the Problem" and the latter two steps under the heading "Analyzing the Problem." Let us now consider in greater detail how to carry out the activities that make up the decision-making process.

Figure 1.3 shows that the analysis phase of the decision-making process may take two basic forms: qualitative and quantitative. Qualitative analysis is based primarily on the manager's judgment and experience; it includes the manager's intuitive "feel" for the problem and is more an art than a science. If the manager has had experience with similar problems, or if the problem is relatively simple, heavy emphasis may be placed upon a qualitative

FIGURE 1.1   THE RELATIONSHIP BETWEEN PROBLEM SOLVING
AND DECISION MAKING

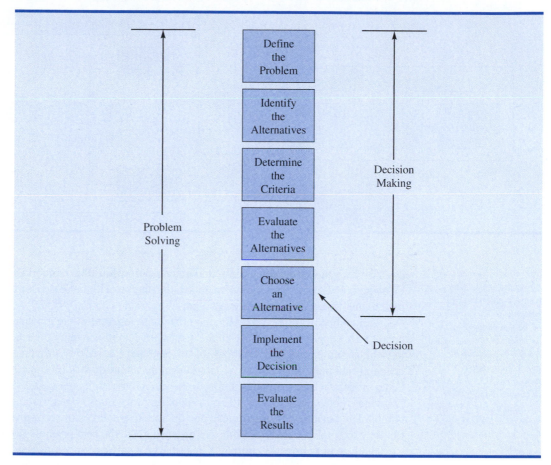

FIGURE 1.2   A SUBCLASSIFICATION OF THE DECISION-MAKING PROCESS

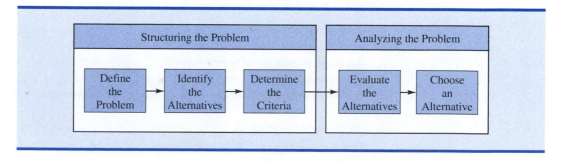

analysis. However, if the manager has had little experience with similar problems, or if the problem is sufficiently complex, then a quantitative analysis of the problem can be an especially important consideration in the manager's final decision.

When using the quantitative approach, an analyst will concentrate on the quantitative facts or data associated with the problem and develop mathematical expressions that

FIGURE 1.3   THE ROLE OF QUALITATIVE AND QUANTITATIVE ANALYSIS

Quantitative methods are especially helpful with large, complex problems. For example, in the coordination of the thousands of tasks associated with landing the Apollo 11 safely on the moon, quantitative techniques helped to ensure that more than 300,000 pieces of work performed by more than 400,000 people were integrated smoothly.

describe the objectives, constraints, and other relationships that exist in the problem. Then, by using one or more quantitative methods, the analyst will make a recommendation based on the quantitative aspects of the problem.

Although skills in the qualitative approach are inherent in the manager and usually increase with experience, the skills of the quantitative approach can be learned only by studying the assumptions and methods of management science. A manager can increase decision-making effectiveness by learning more about quantitative methodology and by better understanding its contribution to the decision-making process. A manager who is knowledgeable in quantitative decision-making procedures is in a much better position to compare and evaluate the qualitative and quantitative sources of recommendations and ultimately to combine the two sources in order to make the best possible decision.

The box in Figure 1.3 entitled "Quantitative Analysis" encompasses most of the subject matter of this text. We will consider a managerial problem, introduce the appropriate quantitative methodology, and then develop the recommended decision.

Some of the reasons why a quantitative approach might be used in the decision-making process include the following:

Try Problem 4 to test your understanding of why quantitative approaches might be needed in a particular problem.

1. **The problem is complex**, and the manager cannot develop a good solution without the aid of quantitative analysis.
2. **The problem is especially important** (e.g., a great deal of money is involved), and the manager desires a thorough analysis before attempting to make a decision.
3. **The problem is new**, and the manager has no previous experience from which to draw.
4. **The problem is repetitive**, and the manager saves time and effort by relying on quantitative procedures to make routine decision recommendations.

(1.3) Quantitative Analysis

From Figure 1.3 we see that quantitative analysis begins once the problem has been structured. It usually takes imagination, teamwork, and considerable effort to transform a rather general problem description into a well-defined problem that can be approached via quantitative analysis. The more the analyst is involved in the process of structuring the problem, the more likely it is that the ensuing quantitative analysis will make an important contribution to the decision-making process.

To successfully apply quantitative analysis to decision making, the analyst must work closely with the manager or user of the results. When both the quantitative analyst and the manager agree that the problem has been adequately structured, work can begin on developing a model to represent the problem mathematically. Solution procedures can then be employed to find the best solution for the model. This best solution for the model then becomes a recommendation to the decision maker. The process of developing and solving models is the essence of the quantitative analysis process.

Model Development

Models are representations of real objects or situations and can be presented in various forms. For example, a scale model of an airplane is a representation of a real airplane. Similarly, a child's toy truck is a model of a real truck. The model airplane and toy truck are examples of models that are physical replicas of real objects. In modeling terminology, physical replicas are referred to as iconic models.

A second classification includes models that are physical in form but do not have the same physical appearance as the object being modeled. Such models are referred to as analog models. The speedometer of an automobile is an analog model; the position of the needle on the dial represents the speed of the automobile. A thermometer is another analog model representing temperature.

A third classification of models—the type we will primarily be studying—includes representations of a problem by a system of symbols and mathematical relationships or expressions. Such models are referred to as mathematical models and are a critical part of any quantitative approach to decision making. For example, the total profit from the sale of a product can be determined by multiplying the profit per unit by the quantity sold. Let x represent the number of units produced and sold, and P the total profit. With a profit of $10 per unit, the following mathematical model defines the total profit earned by producing and selling x units:

$$P = 10x \qquad \qquad \textbf{(1.1)}$$

The purpose, or value, of any model is that it enables us to make inferences about the real situation by studying and analyzing the model. For example, an airplane designer might test an iconic model of a new airplane in a wind tunnel to learn about the potential flying characteristics of the full-size airplane. Similarly, a mathematical model may be used to make inferences about how much profit will be earned if a specified quantity of a particular product is sold. According to the mathematical model of equation (1.1), we would expect selling three units of the product ($x = 3$) would provide a profit of $P = 10(3) = \$30$.

In general, experimenting with models requires less time and is less expensive than experimenting with the real object or situation. A model airplane is certainly quicker and less expensive to build and study than the full-size airplane. Similarly, the mathematical model in equation (1.1) allows a quick identification of profit expectations without actually requiring the manager to produce and sell x units. Models also reduce the risks associated with experimenting with the real situation. In particular, bad designs or bad decisions that cause the model airplane to crash or a mathematical model to project a $10,000 loss can be avoided in the real situation.

The value of model-based conclusions and decisions depends on how well the model represents the real situation. The more closely the model airplane represents the real airplane, the more accurate will be the conclusions and predictions. Similarly, the more closely the mathematical model represents the company's true profit–volume relationship, the more accurate will be the profit projections.

Because this text deals with quantitative analysis based on mathematical models, let us look more closely at the mathematical modeling process. When initially considering a managerial problem, we usually find that the problem definition phase leads to a specific objective, such as maximization of profit or minimization of cost, and possibly a set of restrictions or **constraints**, such as production capacities. The success of the mathematical model and quantitative approach will depend heavily on how accurately the objective and constraints can be expressed in mathematical equations or relationships.

The mathematical expression that defines the quantity to be maximized or minimized is referred to as the **objective function**. For example, suppose x denotes the number of units produced and sold each week, and the firm's objective is to maximize total weekly profit. With a profit of \$10 per unit, the objective function is $10x$. A production capacity constraint would be necessary if, for instance, 5 hours are required to produce each unit and only 40 hours are available per week. The production capacity constraint is given by

$$5x \leq 40 \tag{1.2}$$

The value of $5x$ is the total time required to produce x units; the symbol $\leq$ indicates that the production time required must be less than or equal to the 40 hours available.

The decision problem or question is the following: How many units of the product should be produced each week to maximize profit? A complete mathematical model for this simple production problem is

$$\text{Maximize} \quad 10x \quad \text{objective function}$$
$$\text{subject to (s.t.)}$$
$$\left. \begin{array}{r} 5x \leq 40 \\ x \geq 0 \end{array} \right\} \text{constraints}$$

The $x \geq 0$ constraint requires the production quantity x to be greater than or equal to zero, which simply recognizes the fact that it is not possible to manufacture a negative number of units. The optimal solution to this model can be easily calculated and is given by $x = 8$, with an associated profit of \$80. This model is an example of a linear programming model. In subsequent chapters we will discuss more complicated mathematical models and learn how to solve them in situations where the answers are not nearly so obvious.

In the preceding mathematical model, the profit per unit (\$10), the production time per unit (5 hours), and the production capacity (40 hours) are environmental factors not under the control of the manager or decision maker. Such environmental factors, which can affect both the objective function and the constraints, are referred to as **uncontrollable inputs** to the model. Inputs that are controlled or determined by the decision maker are referred to as **controllable inputs** to the model. In the example given, the production quantity x is the controllable input to the model. Controllable inputs are the decision alternatives specified by the manager and thus are also referred to as the **decision variables** of the model.

Once all controllable and uncontrollable inputs are specified, the objective function and constraints can be evaluated and the output of the model determined. In this sense, the output of the model is simply the projection of what would happen if those particular environmental factors and decisions occurred in the real situation. A flowchart of how controllable and uncontrollable inputs are transformed by the mathematical model into

FIGURE 1.4   FLOWCHART OF THE PROCESS OF TRANSFORMING MODEL INPUTS INTO OUTPUT

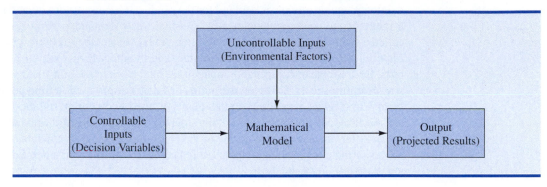

output is shown in Figure 1.4. A similar flowchart showing the specific details for the production model is shown in Figure 1.5. Note that we have used "Max" as an abbreviation for maximize.

As stated earlier, the uncontrollable inputs are those the decision maker cannot influence. The specific controllable and uncontrollable inputs of a model depend on the particular problem or decision-making situation. In the production problem, the production time available (40) is an uncontrollable input. However, if it were possible to hire more employees or use overtime, the number of hours of production time would become a controllable input and therefore a decision variable in the model.

Uncontrollable inputs can either be known exactly or be uncertain and subject to variation. If all uncontrollable inputs to a model are known and cannot vary, the model is referred to as a **deterministic model**. Corporate income tax rates are not under the influence of the manager and thus constitute an uncontrollable input in many decision models. Because these rates are known and fixed (at least in the short run), a mathematical model with corporate income tax rates as the only uncontrollable input would be a deterministic model. The distinguishing feature of a deterministic model is that the uncontrollable input values are known in advance.

FIGURE 1.5   FLOWCHART FOR THE PRODUCTION MODEL

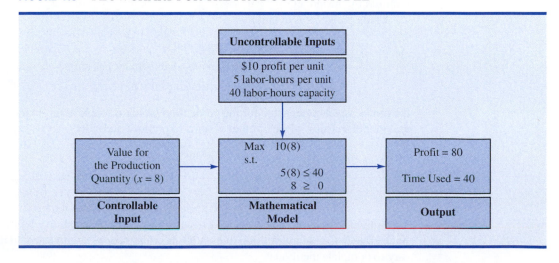

If any of the uncontrollable inputs are uncertain and subject to variation, the model is referred to as a **stochastic** or **probabilistic model**. An uncontrollable input in many production planning models is demand for the product. Because future demand may be any of a range of values, a mathematical model that treats demand with uncertainty would be called a stochastic model. In the production model, the number of hours of production time required per unit, the total hours available, and the unit profit were all uncontrollable inputs. Because the uncontrollable inputs were all known to take on fixed values, the model was deterministic. If, however, the number of hours of production time per unit could vary from 3 to 6 hours depending on the quality of the raw material, the model would be stochastic. The distinguishing feature of a stochastic model is that the value of the output cannot be determined even if the value of the controllable input is known because the specific values of the uncontrollable inputs are unknown. In this respect, stochastic models are often more difficult to analyze.

Data Preparation

Another step in the quantitative analysis of a problem is the preparation of the data required by the model. Data in this sense refer to the values of the uncontrollable inputs to the model. All uncontrollable inputs or data must be specified before we can analyze the model and recommend a decision or solution for the problem.

In the production model, the values of the uncontrollable inputs or data were $10 per unit for profit, 5 hours per unit for production time, and 40 hours for production capacity. In the development of the model, these data values were known and incorporated into the model as it was being developed. If the model is relatively small and the uncontrollable input values or data required are few, the quantitative analyst will probably combine model development and data preparation into one step. In these situations the data values are inserted as the equations of the mathematical model are developed.

However, in many mathematical modeling situations, the data or uncontrollable input values are not readily available. In these situations the analyst may know that the model will need profit per unit, production time, and production capacity data, but the values will not be known until the accounting, production, and engineering departments can be consulted. Rather than attempting to collect the required data as the model is being developed, the analyst will usually adopt a general notation for the model development step and then a separate data preparation step will be performed to obtain the uncontrollable input values required by the model.

Using the general notation

$$c = \text{profit per unit}$$

$$a = \text{production time in hours per unit}$$

$$b = \text{production capacity in hours}$$

the model development step for the production problem would result in the following general model (recall $x =$ the number of units to produce and sell):

$$\text{Max } cx$$
$$\text{s.t.}$$
$$ax \leq b$$
$$x \geq 0$$

A separate data preparation step to identify the values for c, a, and b would then be necessary to complete the model.

Many inexperienced quantitative analysts assume that once the problem is defined and a general model developed, the problem is essentially solved. These individuals tend to believe that data preparation is a trivial step in the process and can be easily handled by clerical staff. Actually, this assumption could not be further from the truth, especially with large-scale models that have numerous data input values. For example, a moderate-sized linear programming model with 50 decision variables and 25 constraints could have more than 1300 data elements that must be identified in the data preparation step. The time required to prepare these data and the possibility of data collection errors will make the data preparation step a critical part of the quantitative analysis process. Often, a fairly large database is needed to support a mathematical model, and information systems specialists also become involved in the data preparation step.

Model Solution

Once the model development and data preparation steps are completed, we proceed to the model solution step. In this step, the analyst attempts to identify the values of the decision variables that provide the "best" output for the model. The specific decision-variable value or values providing the "best" output are referred to as the **optimal solution** for the model. For the production problem, the model solution step involves finding the value of the production quantity decision variable x that maximizes profit while not causing a violation of the production capacity constraint.

One procedure that might be used in the model solution step involves a trial-and-error approach in which the model is used to test and evaluate various decision alternatives. In the production model, this procedure would mean testing and evaluating the model using various production quantities or values of x. As noted in Figure 1.5, we could input trial values for x and check the corresponding output for projected profit and satisfaction of the production capacity constraint. If a particular decision alternative does not satisfy one or more of the model constraints, the decision alternative is rejected as being **infeasible**, regardless of the objective function value. If all constraints are satisfied, the decision alternative is **feasible** and a candidate for the "best" solution or recommended decision. Through this trial-and-error process of evaluating selected decision alternatives, a decision maker can identify a good—and possibly the best—feasible solution to the problem. This solution would then be the recommended decision for the problem.

Table 1.2 shows the results of a trial-and-error approach to solving the production model of Figure 1.5. The recommended decision is a production quantity of 8 because the feasible solution with the highest projected profit occurs at $x = 8$.

TABLE 1.2   TRIAL-AND-ERROR SOLUTION FOR THE PRODUCTION MODEL
OF FIGURE 1.5

Decision Alternative (Production Quantity) x	Projected Profit	Total Hours of Production	Feasible Solution? (Hours Used $\leq$ 40)
0	0	0	Yes
2	20	10	Yes
4	40	20	Yes
6	60	30	Yes
8	80	40	Yes
10	100	50	No
12	120	60	No

Although the trial-and-error solution process is often acceptable and can provide valuable information for the manager, it has the drawbacks of not necessarily providing the best solution and of being inefficient in terms of requiring numerous calculations if many decision alternatives are tried. Thus, quantitative analysts developed special solution procedures for many models that are much more efficient than the trial-and-error approach. Throughout this text, you will be introduced to solution procedures that are applicable to the specific mathematical models. Some relatively small models or problems can be solved by hand computations, but most practical applications require the use of a computer.

The model development and model solution steps are not completely separable. An analyst will want both to develop an accurate model or representation of the actual problem situation and to be able to find a solution to the model. If we approach the model development step by attempting to find the most accurate and realistic mathematical model, we may find the model so large and complex that it is impossible to obtain a solution. In this case, a simpler and perhaps more easily understood model with a readily available solution procedure is preferred even if the recommended solution is only a rough approximation of the best decision. As you learn more about quantitative solution procedures, you will form a better understanding of the types of mathematical models that can be developed and solved.

Try Problem 8 to test your understanding of the concept of a mathematical model and what is referred to as the optimal solution to the model.

After obtaining a model solution, both the quantitative analyst and the manager will be interested in determining how good the solution really is. Even though the analyst has undoubtedly taken many precautions to develop a realistic model, often the goodness or accuracy of the model cannot be assessed until model solutions are generated. Model testing and validation are frequently conducted with relatively small "test" problems with known or at least expected solutions. If the model generates the expected solutions, and if other output information appears correct, the go-ahead may be given to use the model on the full-scale problem. However, if the model test and validation identify potential problems or inaccuracies inherent in the model, corrective action, such as model modification or collection of more accurate input data, may be taken. Whatever the corrective action, the model solution will not be used in practice until the model satisfactorily passes testing and validation.

Report Generation

An important part of the quantitative analysis process is the preparation of managerial reports based on the model's solution. As indicated in Figure 1.3, the solution based on the quantitative analysis of a problem is one of the inputs the manager considers before making a final decision. Thus, the results of the model must appear in a managerial report that can be easily understood by the decision maker. The report includes the recommended decision and other pertinent information about the results that may be helpful to the decision maker.

A Note Regarding Implementation

As discussed in Section 1.2, the manager is responsible for integrating the quantitative solution with qualitative considerations in order to make the best possible decision. After completing the decision-making process, the manager must oversee the implementation and follow-up evaluation of the decision. During the implementation and follow-up, the manager should continue to monitor the contribution of the model. At times, this process may lead to requests for model expansion or refinement that will cause the quantitative analyst to return to an earlier step of the process.

Successful implementation of results is critical to the quantitative analyst as well as the manager. If the results of the quantitative analysis process are not correctly implemented, the entire effort may be of no value. It doesn't take many unsuccessful implementations before the quantitative analyst is out of work. Because implementation often requires people to do things differently, it often meets with resistance. People want to know, "What's wrong with the way we've been doing it?" and so on. One of the most effective ways to ensure successful implementation is to include users throughout the modeling process. A user who feels a part of identifying the problem and developing the solution is much more likely to enthusiastically implement the results. The success rate for implementing the results of a quantitative analysis project is much greater for those projects characterized by extensive user involvement. The Q.M. in Action, Quantitative Analysis at Merrill Lynch, discusses some of the reasons for the success of quantitative analysis at Merrill Lynch.

Q.M. *in* ACTION

QUANTITATIVE ANALYSIS AT MERRILL LYNCH*

The management science group at Merrill Lynch has successfully implemented models and developed systems for asset allocation, financial planning, marketing information technology, database marketing, and portfolio performance measurement. Although technical expertise and objectivity are clearly important factors in any analytical group, the management science group attributes much of its success to communications skills, teamwork, and consulting skills.

Each project begins with face-to-face meetings with the client. A proposal is then prepared to outline the background of the problem, the objectives of the project, the approach, the required resources, the time schedule, and the implementation issues. At this stage, analysts focus on developing solutions that provide significant value and are easily implemented.

As the work progresses, frequent meetings keep the clients up to date. Because people with different skills, perspectives, and motivations must work together for a common goal, teamwork is essential. The group's members take classes in team approaches, facilitation, and conflict resolution. They possess a broad range of multifunctional and multidisciplinary capabilities, and are motivated to provide solutions that focus on the goals of the firm. This approach to problem solving and the implementation of quantitative analysis has been a hallmark of the management science group. The impact and success of the group translates into hard dollars and repeat business. The group received the annual Edelman award given by the Institute for Operations Research and the Management Sciences for effective use of management science for organizational success.

*Based on Russ Labe, Raj Nigam, and Steve Spence, "Management Science at Merrill Lynch Private Client Group," *Interfaces* 29, no. 2 (March/April 1999): 1–14.

NOTES AND COMMENTS

1. Developments in computer technology have increased the availability of quantitative methods to decision makers. A variety of software packages are now available for personal computers. Versions of The Management Scientist, Microsoft Excel, and LINGO are widely used in quantitative methods courses.

2. The Management Scientist is a software package developed by the authors of this text. Version 6.0 is now available for Windows 95 through Windows XP operating systems, as well as Vista. This software can be used to solve problems in the text as well as small-scale problems encountered in practice. Appendix 1.1 provides an overview of the features and use of The Management Scientist.

3. Various chapter appendixes provide step-by-step instructions for using The Management Scientist, Excel, and LINGO to solve problems in the text.

1.4   Models of Cost, Revenue, and Profit

Some of the most basic quantitative models arising in business and economic applications involve the relationship between a volume variable—such as production volume or sales volume—and cost, revenue, and profit. Through the use of these models, a manager can determine the projected cost, revenue, or profit associated with an established production quantity or a forecasted sales volume. Financial planning, production planning, sales quotas, and other areas of decision making can benefit from such cost, revenue, and profit models.

Cost and Volume Models

The cost of manufacturing or producing a product is a function of the volume produced. This cost can usually be defined as a sum of two costs: fixed cost and variable cost. **Fixed cost** is the portion of the total cost that does not depend on the production volume; this cost remains the same no matter how much is produced. **Variable cost**, on the other hand, is the portion of the total cost that depends on and varies with the production volume. To illustrate how cost and volume models can be developed, we will consider a manufacturing problem faced by Nowlin Plastics.

Nowlin Plastics produces a variety of compact disc (CD) storage cases. Nowlin's best-selling product is the CD-50, a slim, plastic CD holder with specially designed linings that protect the optical surface of each CD. Several products are produced on the same manufacturing line, and a setup cost is incurred each time a changeover is made for a new product. Suppose that the setup cost for the CD-50 is $3000. This setup cost is a fixed cost that is incurred regardless of the number of units eventually produced. In addition, suppose that variable labor and material costs are $2 for each unit produced. The cost-volume model for producing x units of the CD-50 can be written as

$$C(x) = 3000 + 2x \qquad \textbf{(1.3)}$$

where

$$x = \text{production volume in units}$$
$$C(x) = \text{total cost of producing } x \text{ units}$$

Once a production volume is established, the model in equation (1.3) can be used to compute the total production cost. For example, the decision to produce $x = 1200$ units would result in a total cost of $C(1200) = 3000 + 2(1200) = \$5400$.

Marginal cost is defined as the rate of change of the total cost with respect to production volume, that is, the cost increase associated with a one-unit increase in the production volume. In the cost model of equation (1.3), we see that the total cost $C(x)$ will increase by $2 for each unit increase in the production volume. Thus, the marginal cost is $2. With more complex total cost models, marginal cost may depend on the production volume. In such cases, we could have marginal cost increasing or decreasing with the production volume x.

Revenue and Volume Models

Management of Nowlin Plastics will also want information about projected revenue associated with selling a specified number of units. Thus, a model of the relationship between revenue and volume is also needed. Suppose that each CD-50 storage unit sells for $5. The model for total revenue can be written as

$$R(x) = 5x \qquad \textbf{(1.4)}$$

where

x = sales volume in units

$R(x)$ = total revenue associated with selling x units

Marginal revenue is defined as the rate of change of total revenue with respect to sales volume, that is, the increase in total revenue resulting from a one-unit increase in sales volume. In the model of equation (1.4), we see that the marginal revenue is $5. In this case, marginal revenue is constant and does not vary with the sales volume. With more complex models, we may find that marginal revenue increases or decreases as the sales volume x increases.

Profit and Volume Models

One of the most important criteria for management decision making is profit. Managers need to know the profit implications of their decisions. If we assume that we will only produce what can be sold, the production volume and sales volume will be equal. We can combine equations (1.3) and (1.4) to develop a profit-volume model that determines profit associated with a specified production-sales volume. Total profit is total revenue minus total cost; therefore, the following model provides the profit associated with producing and selling x units:

$$P(x) = R(x) - C(x)$$
$$= 5x - (3000 + 2x) = -3000 + 3x \qquad (1.5)$$

Thus, the model for profit $P(x)$ can be derived from the models of the revenue-volume and cost-volume relationships.

Breakeven Analysis

Using equation (1.5), we can now determine the profit associated with any production volume x. For example, suppose that a demand forecast indicates that 500 units of the product can be sold. The decision to produce and sell the 500 units results in a projected profit of

$$P(500) = -3000 + 3(500) = -1500$$

In other words, a loss of $1500 is predicted. If sales are expected to be 500 units, the manager may decide against producing the product. However, a demand forecast of 1800 units would show a projected profit of

$$P(1800) = -3000 + 3(1800) = 2400$$

This profit may be enough to justify proceeding with the production and sale of the product.

We see that a volume of 500 units will yield a loss, whereas a volume of 1800 provides a profit. The volume that results in total revenue equaling total cost (providing $0 profit) is called the **breakeven point**. If the breakeven point is known, a manager can quickly infer that a volume above the breakeven point will result in a profit, whereas a volume below the breakeven point will result in a loss. Thus, the breakeven point for a product provides valuable information for a manager who must make a yes/no decision concerning production of the product.

FIGURE 1.6   GRAPH OF THE BREAKEVEN ANALYSIS FOR NOWLIN PLASTICS

Let us now return to the Nowlin Plastics example and show how the profit model in equation (1.5) can be used to compute the breakeven point. The breakeven point can be found by setting the profit expression equal to zero and solving for the production volume. Using equation (1.5), we have

$$P(x) = -3000 + 3x = 0$$
$$3x = 3000$$
$$x = 1000$$

Try Problem 12 to test your ability to determine the breakeven point for a quantitative model.

With this information, we know that production and sales of the product must be at least 1000 units before a profit can be expected. The graphs of the total cost model, the total revenue model, and the location of the breakeven point are shown in Figure 1.6. In Appendix 1.2 we also show how Excel can be used to perform a breakeven analysis for the Nowlin Plastics production example.

1.5   Quantitative Methods in Practice

In this section we present a brief overview of the quantitative methods covered in this text. Over the years, practitioners found numerous applications for the following:

Linear Programming   Linear programming is a problem-solving approach developed for situations involving maximizing or minimizing a linear function subject to linear constraints that limit the degree to which the objective can be pursued. The production model developed in Section 1.3 (see Figure 1.5) is an example of a simple linear programming model.

Integer Linear Programming Integer linear programming is an approach used for problems that can be set up as linear programs with the additional requirement that some or all of the decision recommendations be integer values.

Project Scheduling: PERT/CPM In many situations, managers are responsible for planning, scheduling, and controlling projects that consist of numerous separate jobs or tasks performed by a variety of departments, individuals, and so forth. PERT (Program Evaluation and Review Technique) and CPM (Critical Path Method) help managers carry out their project scheduling responsibilities.

Inventory Models Inventory models are used by managers faced with the dual problems of maintaining sufficient inventories to meet demand for goods and, at the same time, incurring the lowest possible inventory holding costs.

Waiting Line or Queueing Models Waiting line or queueing models help managers understand and make better decisions concerning the operation of systems involving waiting lines.

Simulation Simulation is a technique used to model the operation of a system. This technique employs a computer program to model the operation and perform simulation computations.

Decision Analysis Decision analysis can be used to determine optimal strategies in situations involving several decision alternatives and an uncertain or risk-filled pattern of future events.

Forecasting Forecasting methods are techniques that can be used to predict future aspects of a business operation.

Markov-Process Models Markov-process models are useful in studying the evolution of certain systems over repeated trials. For example, Markov processes have been used to describe the probability that a machine, functioning in one period, will function or break down in another period.

Methods Used Most Frequently

In our experience as both practitioners and educators, the most frequently used quantitative methods are linear programming, integer programming, and simulation. Depending upon the industry, the other methods in the preceding list are used more or less frequently.

Helping to bridge the gap between the manager and the quantitative analyst is a major focus of the text. We believe that the barriers to the use of quantitative methods can best be removed by increasing the manager's understanding of how quantitative analysis can be applied. The text will help you develop an understanding of which quantitative methods are most useful, how they are used, and, most importantly, how they can assist managers in making better decisions.

The Q.M. in Action, Impact of Operations Research on Everyday Living, describes some of the many ways quantitative analysis affects our everyday lives.

IMPACT OF OPERATIONS RESEARCH ON EVERYDAY LIVING*

Mark Eisner, associate director of the School of Operations Research and Industrial Engineering at Cornell University, once said that operations research "is probably the most important field nobody's ever heard of." The impact of operations research on everyday living over the past 20 years is substantial.

Suppose you schedule a vacation to Florida and use Orbitz to book your flights. An algorithm developed by operations researchers will search among millions of options to find the cheapest fare. Another algorithm will schedule the flight crews and aircraft used by the airline. If you rent a car in Florida, the price you pay for the car is determined by a mathematical model that seeks to maximize revenue for the car rental firm. If you do some shopping on your trip

*Based on Virginia Postrel, "Operations Everything," *The Boston Globe,* June 27, 2004.

and decide to ship your purchases home using UPS, another algorithm tells UPS which truck to put the packages on, the route the truck should follow, and where the packages should be placed on the truck to minimize loading and unloading time.

If you enjoy watching college basketball, operations research plays a role in what games you see. Michael Trick, a professor at the Tepper School of Business at Carnegie-Mellon, designed a system for scheduling each year's Atlantic Coast Conference men's and women's basketball games. Even though it might initially appear that scheduling 16 games among the nine men's teams would be easy, it requires sorting through hundreds of millions of possible combinations of possible schedules. Each of those possibilities entails some desirable and some undesirable characteristics. For example, you do not want to schedule too many consecutive home games, and you want to ensure that each team plays the same number of weekend games.

NOTES AND COMMENTS

The Institute for Operations Research and the Management Sciences (INFORMS) and the Decision Sciences Institute (DSI) are two professional societies that publish journals and newsletters dealing with current research and applications of operations research and management science techniques.

Summary

This text is about how quantitative methods may be used to help managers make better decisions. The text focuses on the decision-making process and on the role of quantitative analysis in that process. The discussion in this chapter centered on the problem orientation of this process and an overview of how mathematical models can be used in this type of analysis.

The difference between the model and the situation or managerial problem it represents is an important point. Mathematical models are abstractions of real-world situations and, as such, cannot capture all the aspects of the real situation. However, if a model can capture the major relevant aspects of the problem and can then provide a solution recommendation, it can be a valuable aid to decision making.

One of the characteristics of quantitative analysis that will become increasingly apparent as we proceed through the text is the search for a best solution to the problem. In carrying out the quantitative analysis, we attempt to develop procedures for finding the "best" or optimal solution.

Glossary

Problem solving The process of identifying a difference between the actual and the desired state of affairs and then taking action to resolve the difference.

Decision making The process of defining the problem, identifying the alternatives, determining the criteria, evaluating the alternatives, and choosing an alternative.

Single-criterion decision problem A problem in which the objective is to find the "best" solution with respect to just one criterion.

Multicriteria decision problem A problem that involves more than one criterion; the objective is to find the "best" solution, taking into account all the criteria.

Decision The alternative selected.

Model A representation of a real object or situation.

Iconic model A physical replica, or representation, of a real object.

Analog model Although physical in form, an analog model does not have a physical appearance similar to the real object or situation it represents.

Mathematical model Mathematical symbols and expressions used to represent a real situation.

Constraint A restriction or limitation imposed on a problem.

Objective function The mathematical expression that defines the quantity to be maximized or minimized.

Uncontrollable input The environmental factors or inputs that cannot be controlled by the decision maker.

Controllable input The decision alternatives or inputs that can be specified by the decision maker.

Decision variable Another term for controllable input.

Deterministic model A model in which all uncontrollable inputs are known and cannot vary.

Stochastic model A model in which at least one uncontrollable input is uncertain and subject to variation; stochastic models are also referred to as probabilistic models.

Optimal solution The specific decision variable value or values that provide the "best" output for the model.

Infeasible solution A decision alternative or solution that violates one or more constraints.

Feasible solution A decision alternative or solution that satisfies all constraints.

Fixed cost The portion of the total cost that does not depend on the volume; this cost remains the same no matter how much is produced.

Variable cost The portion of the total cost that is dependent on and varies with the volume.

Marginal cost The rate of change of the total cost with respect to volume.

Marginal revenue The rate of change of total revenue with respect to volume.

Breakeven point The volume at which total revenue equals total cost.

Problems

1. Define the terms *management science* and *operations research*.

2. List and discuss the steps of the decision-making process.

3. Discuss the different roles played by the qualitative and quantitative approaches to managerial decision making. Why is it important for a manager or decision maker to have a good understanding of both of these approaches to decision making?

4. A firm just completed a new plant that will produce more than 500 different products, using more than 50 different production lines and machines. The production scheduling decisions are critical in that sales will be lost if customer demand is not met on time. If no individual in the firm has had experience with this production operation, and if new production schedules must be generated each week, why should the firm consider a quantitative approach to the production scheduling problem?

5. What are the advantages of analyzing and experimenting with a model as opposed to a real object or situation?

6. Suppose that a manager must choose between the following two mathematical models of a given situation: (a) a relatively simple model that is a reasonable approximation of the real situation and (b) a thorough and complex model that is the most accurate mathematical representation of the real situation possible. Why might the model described in part (a) be preferred by the manager?

7. Suppose you are going on a weekend trip to a city that is d miles away. Develop a model that determines your round-trip gasoline costs. What assumptions or approximations are necessary to treat this model as a deterministic model? Are these assumptions or approximations acceptable to you?

8. Recall the production model from Section 1.3:

$$\text{Max} \quad 10x$$
$$\text{s.t.}$$
$$5x \leq 40$$
$$x \geq 0$$

Suppose the firm in this example considers a second product that has a unit profit of $5 and requires 2 hours for each unit produced. Assume total production capacity remains 40. Use y as the number of units of product 2 produced.
a. Show the mathematical model when both products are considered simultaneously.
b. Identify the controllable and uncontrollable inputs for this model.
c. Draw the flowchart of the input-output process for this model (see Figure 1.5).
d. What are the optimal solution values of x and y?
e. Is the model developed a deterministic or a stochastic model? Explain.

9. Suppose we modify the production model from Section 1.3 to obtain the following mathematical model:

$$\text{Max} \quad 10x$$
$$\text{s.t.}$$
$$ax \leq 40$$
$$x \geq 0$$

where a is the number of hours required for each unit produced. With $a = 5$, the optimal solution is $x = 8$. If we have a stochastic model with $a = 3$, $a = 4$, $a = 5$, or $a = 6$ as the possible values for the number of hours required per unit, what is the optimal value for x? What problems does this stochastic model cause?

10. A retail store in Des Moines, Iowa, receives shipments of a particular product from Kansas City and Minneapolis. Let

$$x = \text{units of product received from Kansas City}$$
$$y = \text{units of product received from Minneapolis}$$

a. Write an expression for the total units of product received by the retail store in Des Moines.

b. Shipments from Kansas City cost $0.20 per unit, and shipments from Minneapolis cost $0.25 per unit. Develop an objective function representing the total cost of shipments to Des Moines.

c. Assuming the monthly demand at the retail store is 5000 units, develop a constraint that requires 5000 units to be shipped to Des Moines.

d. No more than 4000 units can be shipped from Kansas City, and no more than 3000 units can be shipped from Minneapolis in a month. Develop constraints to model this situation.

e. Of course, negative amounts cannot be shipped. Combine the objective function and constraints developed to state a mathematical model for satisfying the demand at the Des Moines retail store at minimum cost.

11. For most products, higher prices result in a decreased demand, whereas lower prices result in an increased demand. Let

$$d = \text{annual demand for a product in units}$$

$$p = \text{price per unit}$$

Assume that a firm accepts the following price-demand relationship as being realistic:

$$d = 800 - 10p$$

where p must be between $20 and $70.

a. How many units can the firm sell at the $20 per-unit price? At the $70 per-unit price?

b. Show the mathematical model for the total revenue (TR), which is the annual demand multiplied by the unit price.

c. Based on other considerations, the firm's management will only consider price alternatives of $30, $40, and $50. Use your model from part (b) to determine the price alternative that will maximize the total revenue.

d. What are the expected annual demand and the total revenue according to your recommended price?

12. The O'Neill Shoe Manufacturing Company will produce a special-style shoe if the order size is large enough to provide a reasonable profit. For each special-style order, the company incurs a fixed cost of $1000 for the production setup. The variable cost is $30 per pair, and each pair sells for $40.

a. Let x indicate the number of pairs of shoes produced. Develop a mathematical model for the total cost of producing x pairs of shoes.

b. Let P indicate the total profit. Develop a mathematical model for the total profit realized from an order for x pairs of shoes.

c. What is the breakeven point?

13. Micromedia offers computer training seminars on a variety of topics. In the seminars each student works at a personal computer, practicing the particular activity that the instructor is presenting. Micromedia is currently planning a two-day seminar on the use of Microsoft Excel in statistical analysis. The projected fee for the seminar is $300 per student. The cost for the conference room, instructor compensation, lab assistants, and promotion is $4800. Micromedia rents computers for its seminars at a cost of $30 per computer per day.

a. Develop a model for the total cost to put on the seminar. Let x represent the number of students who enroll in the seminar.

b. Develop a model for the total profit if x students enroll in the seminar.

c. Micromedia has forecasted an enrollment of 30 students for the seminar. How much profit will be earned if their forecast is accurate?

d. Compute the breakeven point.

14. Eastman Publishing Company is considering publishing a paperback textbook on spreadsheet applications for business. The fixed cost of manuscript preparation, textbook design, and production setup is estimated to be $80,000. Variable production and material costs are estimated to be $3 per book. Demand over the life of the book is estimated to be 4000 copies. The publisher plans to sell the text to college and university bookstores for $20 each.
    a. What is the breakeven point?
    b. What profit or loss can be anticipated with a demand of 4000 copies?
    c. With a demand of 4000 copies, what is the minimum price per copy that the publisher must charge to break even?
    d. If the publisher believes that the price per copy could be increased to $25.95 and not affect the anticipated demand of 4000 copies, what action would you recommend? What profit or loss can be anticipated?

15. Preliminary plans are underway for the construction of a new stadium for a major league baseball team. City officials question the number and profitability of the luxury corporate boxes planned for the upper deck of the stadium. Corporations and selected individuals may buy the boxes for $100,000 each. The fixed construction cost for the upper-deck area is estimated to be $1,500,000, with a variable cost of $50,000 for each box constructed.
    a. What is the breakeven point for the number of luxury boxes in the new stadium?
    b. Preliminary drawings for the stadium show that space is available for the construction of up to 50 luxury boxes. Promoters indicate that buyers are available and that all 50 could be sold if constructed. What is your recommendation concerning the construction of luxury boxes? What profit is anticipated?

16. Financial Analysts, Inc., is an investment firm that manages stock portfolios for a number of clients. A new client requested that the firm handle an $80,000 portfolio. As an initial investment strategy, the client would like to restrict the portfolio to a mix of the following two stocks:

Stock	Price/ Share	Estimated Annual Return/Share	Maximum Possible Investment
Oil Alaska	$50	$6	$50,000
Southwest Petroleum	$30	$4	$45,000

    Let

$$x = \text{number of shares of Oil Alaska}$$

$$y = \text{number of shares of Southwest Petroleum}$$

    a. Develop the objective function, assuming that the client desires to maximize the total annual return.
    b. Show the mathematical expression for each of the following three constraints:
        (1) Total investment funds available are $80,000.
        (2) Maximum Oil Alaska investment is $50,000.
        (3) Maximum Southwest Petroleum investment is $45,000.

    Note: Adding the $x \geq 0$ and $y \geq 0$ constraints provides a linear programming model for the investment problem. A solution procedure for this model will be discussed in Chapter 7.

17. Models of inventory systems frequently consider the relationships among a beginning inventory, a production quantity, a demand or sales, and an ending inventory. For a given production period j, let

$$s_{j-1} = \text{ending inventory from the previous period (beginning inventory for period } j)$$
$$x_j = \text{production quantity in period } j$$
$$d_j = \text{demand in period } j$$
$$s_j = \text{ending inventory for period } j$$

a. Write the mathematical relationship or model that shows ending inventory as a function of beginning inventory, production, and demand.
b. What constraint should be added if production capacity for period j is given by C_j?
c. What constraint should be added if inventory requirements for period j mandate an ending inventory of at least I_j?

Case Problem   Scheduling a Golf League

Chris Lane, the head professional at Royal Oak Country Club, must develop a schedule of matches for the couples' golf league that begins its season at 4:00 P.M. tomorrow. Eighteen couples signed up for the league, and each couple must play every other couple over the course of the 17-week season. Chris thought it would be fairly easy to develop a schedule, but after working on it for a couple of hours, he has been unable to come up with a schedule. Because Chris must have a schedule ready by tomorrow afternoon, he asked you to help him. A possible complication is that one of the couples told Chris that they may have to cancel for the season. They told Chris they would let him know by 1:00 P.M. tomorrow whether they will be able to play this season.

Managerial Report

Prepare a report for Chris Lane. Your report should include, at a minimum, the following items:

1. A schedule that will enable each of the 18 couples to play every other couple over the 17-week season.
2. A contingency schedule that can be used if the couple that contacted Chris decides to cancel for the season.

Appendix 1.1   The Management Scientist Software

Developments in computer technology have been a major factor in making quantitative methods available to decision makers. Version 6.0 of the software package called The Management Scientist, prepared by the authors to accompany this text, is now available for Windows 95 through Windows XP operating systems, as well as Vista.[1] This software can be used to solve problems in the text as well as small-scale problems encountered in practice. Using The Management Scientist will give you an understanding and appreciation of the role of the computer in applying quantitative methods to decision problems.

The Management Scientist contains 12 modules, or programs, that will enable you to solve problems in many areas including the following:

- Chapter 4   Decision analysis
- Chapter 6   Forecasting
- Chapters 7–9   Linear programming
- Chapter 10   Distribution and network models
- Chapter 11   Integer linear programming
- Chapter 13   PERT/CPM

---

[1]Version 6.0 is designed to run optimally on computers with screen resolutions of 1024 × 768 or higher. Computers with lower screen resolutions can still run Version 6.0. Scroll bars appear when necessary for working with large problems.

- Chapter 14   Inventory models
- Chapter 15   Waiting line models
- Chapter 17   Markov processes

Use of The Management Scientist with the text is optional. Occasionally, we insert a figure in the text that shows the output The Management Scientist provides for a problem. However, familiarity with the use of the software is not necessary to understand the figure and the text material. The remainder of this appendix provides an overview of the features and the use of the software.

Selecting a Module

After starting The Management Scientist, you will encounter the module selection screen, as shown in Figure 1.7. The choices provide access to the 12 modules. Simply select the desired module and click OK to load the requested module into the computer's memory.

The File Menu

After a module is loaded, you will need to click the File menu to begin working with a problem. The File menu provides the following options.

New Select this option to begin a new problem. Dialog boxes and input templates will guide you through the data input process.

Open Select this option to retrieve a problem previously saved. When the problem is selected, it will be displayed on the screen so that you can verify the problem is the one you want to solve.

FIGURE 1.7 MODULE SELECTION SCREEN FOR THE MANAGEMENT SCIENTIST

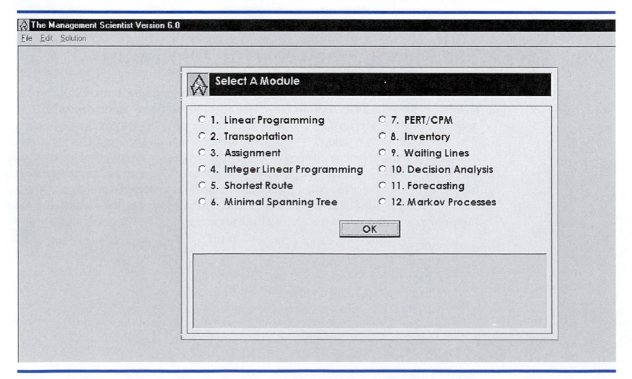

Save Once a new problem has been entered, you may want to save it for future use or modification. The Save option will guide you through the naming and saving process.

Change Modules This option returns the user to the screen in Figure 1.7 and another module may be selected.

Exit This option will exit The Management Scientist.

The Edit Menu

After a new problem has been solved, you may want to make one or more modifications to the problem before resolving. The Edit menu provides the option to display the problem and then make revisions in the problem before solving or saving. In the linear and integer programming modules, the Edit menu also includes options to change the problem size by adding or deleting variables and adding or deleting constraints. Similar options to change the problem size are provided in the Edit menu of the transportation and assignment modules.

The Solution Menu

The Solution menu provides three options:

Solve This option solves the current problem and displays the solution on the screen.

Print Once the solution is on the screen, the Print option sends the solution to a printer.

Save As Text File Once the solution is on the screen, the Save As Text File option enables the solution to be saved as a text file. The text file can be accessed later by a word processor so that the solution output may be displayed as part of a solution report.

Advice About Data Input

Any time a new problem is selected, the appropriate module will provide dialog boxes and forms for describing the features of the problem and for entering data. When using The Management Scientist, you may find the following data input suggestions helpful.

1. Do not enter commas (,) with your input data. For example, the value 104,000 should be entered with the six digits: 104000.
2. Do not enter the dollar sign ($) for profit or cost data. For example, a cost of $20.00 should be entered as 20.
3. Do not enter the percent sign (%) if percentage is requested. For example, 25% should be entered as 25, not 25% or .25.
4. Occasionally, a model may be formulated with fractional values such as $1/4$, $2/3$, $5/6$, and so on. The data input for The Management Scientist must be in decimal form. The fraction $1/4$ can be entered as .25. However, fractions such as $2/3$ and $5/6$ have repeating decimal forms. In these cases, we recommend the convention of rounding to five places such as .66667 and .83333.
5. Finally, we recommend that in general you attempt to scale extremely large input data so that smaller numbers may be input and processed by the computer. For example, costs such as $2,500,000 may be scaled to 2.5 with the understanding that the data used in the problem reflect millions of dollars.

Appendix 1.2   Using Excel for Breakeven Analysis

In Section 1.4 we introduced the Nowlin Plastics production example to illustrate how quantitative models can be used to help a manager determine the projected cost, revenue, and profit associated with an established production quantity or a forecasted sales volume. In this appendix we introduce spreadsheet applications by showing how to use Excel to perform a quantitative analysis of the Nowlin Plastics example.

Refer to the worksheet shown in Figure 1.8. We begin by entering the problem data into the top portion of the worksheet. The value of 3000 in cell B3 is the setup cost, the value of 2 in cell B5 is the variable labor and material costs per unit, and the value of 5 in cell B7 is the selling price per unit. In general, whenever we perform a quantitative analysis using Excel, we will enter the problem data in the top portion of the worksheet and reserve the bottom portion for model development. The label "Models" in cell B10 helps to provide a visual reminder of this convention.

Cell B12 in the models portion of the worksheet contains the proposed production volume in units. Because the values for total cost, total revenue, and total profit depend upon the value of this decision variable, we placed a border around cell B12 and screened the cell for emphasis. Based upon the value in cell B12, the cell formulas in cells B14, B16, and B18 are used to compute values for total cost, total revenue, and total profit (loss), respectively. First, recall that the value of total cost is the sum of the fixed cost (cell B3) and the total variable cost. Because the total variable cost is the product of the variable cost per unit (cell B5) and the production volume (cell B12), it is given by B5*B12. Thus, to compute total cost we entered the formula =B3+B5*B12 into cell B14. Next, total revenue is the product of the selling price per unit (cell B7) and the number of units produced (cell B12); therefore in cell B16 we have entered the formula =B7*B12. Finally, the total profit (or loss) is the difference between the total revenue (cell B16) and the total cost (cell B14). Thus, in

FIGURE 1.8   FORMULA WORKSHEET FOR THE NOWLIN PLASTICS PRODUCTION EXAMPLE

	A	B
1	**Nowlin Plastics**	
2		
3	**Fixed Cost**	3000
4		
5	**Variable Cost Per Unit**	2
6		
7	**Selling Price Per Unit**	5
8		
9		
10	**Models**	
11		
12	**Production Volume**	800
13		
14	**Total Cost**	=B3+B5*B12
15		
16	**Total Revenue**	=B7*B12
17		
18	**Total Profit (Loss)**	=B16-B14

FIGURE 1.9   SOLUTION FOR THE NOWLIN PLASTICS PRODUCTION EXAMPLE USING
A PRODUCTION VOLUME OF 800 UNITS

Nowlin

	A	B
1	**Nowlin Plastics**	
2		
3	**Fixed Cost**	$3,000
4		
5	**Variable Cost Per Unit**	$2
6		
7	**Selling Price Per Unit**	$5
8		
9		
10	**Models**	
11		
12	**Production Volume**	800
13		
14	**Total Cost**	$4,600
15		
16	**Total Revenue**	$4,000
17		
18	**Total Profit (Loss)**	−$600

cell B18 we have entered the formula =B16−B14. The worksheet in Figure 1.8 shows the formulas used to make these computations; we refer to it as a formula worksheet.

To examine the effect of selecting a particular value for the production volume, we have entered a value of 800 in cell B12. The worksheet shown in Figure 1.9 shows the values obtained by the formulas; a production volume of 800 units results in a total cost of $4600, a total revenue of $4000, and a loss of $600. To examine the effect of other production volumes, we only need to enter the other values into cell B12. To examine the effect of different costs and selling prices, we simply enter the appropriate values in the data portion of the worksheet; the results will be displayed in the model section of the worksheet.

In Section 1.4 we illustrated breakeven analysis. Let us now see how a spreadsheet can be used to compute the breakeven point for the Nowlin Plastics production example.

Determining the Breakeven Point Using Excel's Goal Seek Tool

The breakeven point is the production volume that results in total revenue equal to total cost and hence a profit of $0. One way to determine the breakeven point is to use a trial-and-error approach. For example, in Figure 1.9 we saw that a trial production volume of 800 units resulted in a loss of $600. Because this trial solution resulted in a loss, a production volume of 800 units cannot be the breakeven point. We could continue to experiment with other production volumes by simply entering different values into cell B12 and observing the resulting profit or loss in cell B18. A better approach is to use Excel's Goal Seek tool to determine the breakeven point.

Excel's Goal Seek tool allows the user to determine the value for an input cell that will cause the value of a related output cell to equal some specified value (called the *goal*). In the case of breakeven analysis, the "goal" is to set Total Profit to zero by "seeking" an appropriate value for Production Volume. Goal Seek will allow us to find the value of

FIGURE 1.10   GOAL SEEK DIALOG BOX FOR THE NOWLIN PLASTICS
PRODUCTION EXAMPLE

production volume that will set Nowlin Plastics' total profit to zero. The following steps describe how to use Goal Seek to find the breakeven point for Nowlin Plastics:

Step 1. Select the **Data** tab at the top of the Ribbon
Step 2. Select **What-If Analysis** in the **Data Tools** group
Step 3. Select **Goal Seek** in **What-If-Analysis**
Step 4. When the **Goal Seek** dialog box appears (see Figure 1.10):
  Enter B18 in the **Set cell** box
  Enter 0 in the **To value** box
  Enter B12 in the **By changing cell** box
  Click **OK**

The completed Goal Seek dialog box is shown in Figure 1.10, and the worksheet obtained is shown in Figure 1.11. The Total Profit in cell B18 is zero, and the Production Volume in cell B12 has been set to the breakeven point of 1000.

FIGURE 1.11   BREAKEVEN POINT FOUND USING GOAL SEEK TOOL
FOR THE NOWLIN PLASTICS PRODUCTION EXAMPLE

	A	B
1	**Nowlin Plastics**	
2		
3	**Fixed Cost**	$3,000
4		
5	**Variable Cost Per Unit**	$2
6		
7	**Selling Price Per Unit**	$5
8		
9		
10	**Models**	
11		
12	**Production Volume**	1000
13		
14	**Total Cost**	5000
15		
16	**Total Revenue**	5000
17		
18	**Total Profit (Loss)**	0

CHAPTER 2

Introduction to Probability

CONTENTS

Business decisions are often based on an analysis of uncertainties such as the following:

1. What are the "chances" that sales will decrease if we increase prices?
2. What is the "likelihood" that a new assembly method will increase productivity?
3. How "likely" is it that the project will be completed on time?
4. What are the "odds" in favor of a new investment being profitable?

Probability provides a better description of uncertainty than expressions such as chances are "pretty good," chances are "fair," and so on.

Probability is a numerical measure of the likelihood that an event will occur. Thus, probabilities could be used as measures of the degree of uncertainty associated with the four events previously listed. If probabilities were available, we could determine the likelihood of each event occurring.

Probability values are always assigned on a scale from 0 to 1. A probability near 0 indicates that an event is unlikely to occur; a probability near 1 indicates that an event is almost certain to occur. Other probabilities between 0 and 1 represent varying degrees of likelihood that an event will occur. Figure 2.1 depicts this view of probability.

Probability is important in decision making because it provides a way to measure, express, and analyze the uncertainties associated with future events. The Q.M. in Action, Overbooking at American Airlines, describes the role that probability plays in overbooking decisions.

FIGURE 2.1   PROBABILITY AS A NUMERICAL MEASURE OF THE LIKELIHOOD OF AN EVENT OCCURRING

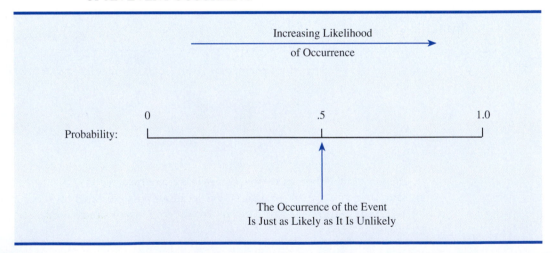

Q.M. *in* ACTION

*OVERBOOKING AT AMERICAN AIRLINES**

Overbooking in the airline industry is the practice of selling more seats for a flight than the airplane's capacity. American Airlines estimates that, without overbooking, about 15% of seats would be unused at departure. As part

of its yield management program, American uses quantitative decision tools to determine the optimal level of overbooking. Management attempts to maximize overbooking profitability by explicitly taking into account various probabilities and the revenue and cost implications of the decision.

*Based on B. C. Smith, J. F. Leimkuhler, and R. M. Darrow, "Yield Management at American Airlines," *Interfaces* 22, no. 3 (1992): 8–31.

(continued)

Perhaps the primary consideration in determining the optimal level of overbooking is in assessing the relevant probabilities. Three probabilities are needed:

1. The probability that a passenger will cancel
2. The probability that a passenger with an active reservation will not show up on the departure day
3. The probability that a passenger who is turned away will choose another American flight (recapture probability)

These probabilities together with the costs of overbooking and underbooking are the key determinants of American Airlines' overbooking policy. Thus, considerable effort is spent in obtaining good estimates of the probabilities. American Airlines expects an annual revenue contribution of more than $500 million from this and other aspects of its yield management program.

2.1 Experiments and the Sample Space

In discussing probability, we define an **experiment** to be any process that generates well-defined outcomes. On any single repetition of an experiment *one and only one* of the possible experimental outcomes will occur. Several examples of experiments and their associated outcomes follow.

Experiment	Experimental Outcomes
Toss a coin	Head, tail
Select a part for inspection	Defective, nondefective
Conduct a sales call	Purchase, no purchase
Roll a die	1, 2, 3, 4, 5, 6
Play a football game	Win, lose, tie

The first step in analyzing a particular experiment is to define carefully the experimental outcomes. When we define *all* possible experimental outcomes, we identify the **sample space** for the experiment, that is, the set of all possible experimental outcomes. Any one particular experimental outcome is also referred to as a **sample point** and is an element of the sample space.

Consider the experiment of tossing a coin. The experimental outcomes are defined by the upward face of the coin—a head or a tail. If we let S denote the sample space, we can use the following notation to describe the sample space and sample points for the coin tossing experiment:

$$S = \{\text{Head, Tail}\}$$

Using this notation for the second experiment in the preceding table, selecting a part for inspection, provides a sample space with sample points as follows:

$$S = \{\text{Defective, Nondefective}\}$$

Finally, suppose that we consider the fourth experiment in the table, rolling a die. The experimental outcomes are defined as the number of dots appearing on the upward face of the

Try Problem 1, parts (a) and (b), for practice in listing the experimental outcomes (sample points) for an experiment.

die. In this experiment, the numerical values 1, 2, 3, 4, 5, and 6 represent the possible experimental outcomes or sample points. Thus the sample space is denoted

$$S = \{1, 2, 3, 4, 5, 6\}$$

NOTES AND COMMENTS

In probability, the notion of an experiment is somewhat different from the laboratory sciences. In the laboratory sciences, the researcher assumes that each time an experiment is repeated in exactly the same way, the same outcome will occur. For the type of experiment we study in probabil-ity, the outcome is determined by chance. Even though the experiment might be repeated in exactly the same way, a different outcome may occur. Because of this difference, the experiments we study in probability are sometimes called random experiments.

2.2 Assigning Probabilities to Experimental Outcomes

With an understanding of an experiment and the sample space, let us now see how probabilities for the experimental outcomes can be determined. The probability of an experimental outcome is a numerical measure of the likelihood that the experimental outcome will occur. In assigning probabilities to experimental outcomes, two **basic requirements of probability** must be satisfied.

1. The probability values assigned to each experimental outcome (sample point) must be between 0 and 1. If we let E_i indicate the ith experimental outcome and $P(E_i)$ indicate the probability of this experimental outcome, we must have

$$0 \leq P(E_1) \leq 1 \text{ (for all } i\text{)} \tag{2.1}$$

2. The sum of *all* of the experimental outcome probabilities must be 1. For example, if a sample space has k experimental outcomes, we must have

$$P(E_1) + P(E_2) + \cdots + P(E_k) = 1 \tag{2.2}$$

Any method of assigning probability values to the experimental outcomes that satisfies these two requirements and results in reasonable numerical measures of the likelihood of the outcomes is acceptable. In practice, the classical method, the relative frequency method, or the subjective method is often used.

Classical Method

To illustrate the classical method of assigning probabilities, let us again consider the experiment of flipping a coin. On any one flip, we will observe one of two experimental outcomes: head or tail. A reasonable assumption is that the two possible outcomes are equally likely. Therefore, as one of the two equally likely outcomes is a head, we logically should conclude that the probability of observing a head is $1/2$, or 0.50. Similarly, the probability of observing a tail is 0.50. When the assumption of equally likely outcomes is used as a basis for assigning probabilities, the approach is referred to as the **classical method**. If an experiment has n possible outcomes, the classical method would assign a probability of $1/n$ to each experimental outcome.

As another illustration of the classical method, consider again the experiment of rolling a die. In Section 2.1 we described the sample space and sample points for this experiment with the notation

$$S = \{1, 2, 3, 4, 5, 6\}$$

A die is designed so that the six experimental outcomes are equally likely, and hence each outcome is assigned a probability of $^1/_6$. Thus, if $P(1)$ denotes the probability that one dot appears on the upward face of the die, then $P(1) = ^1/_6$. Similarly, $P(2) = ^1/_6$, $P(3) = ^1/_6$, $P(4) = ^1/_6$, $P(5) = ^1/_6$, and $P(6) = ^1/_6$. Note that this probability assignment satisfies the two basic requirements for assigning probabilities. In fact, requirements (2.1) and (2.2) are automatically satisfied when the classical method is used, because each of the n sample points is assigned a probability of $1/n$.

Try Problem 2, part (b) for practice with the classical method.

The classical method was developed originally to analyze gambling probabilities, where the assumption of equally likely outcomes often is reasonable. In many business problems, however, this assumption is not valid. Hence, alternative methods of assigning probabilities are required.

Relative Frequency Method

Consider a firm that is preparing to market a new product. In order to estimate the probability that a customer will purchase the product, a test market evaluation has been set up wherein salespeople call on potential customers. Each sales call conducted has two possible outcomes: The customer purchases the product, or the customer does not purchase the product. With no reason to assume that the two experimental outcomes are equally likely, the classical method of assigning probabilities is inappropriate.

Try Problem 2 for practice in assigning probabilities to experimental outcomes using the relative frequency approach.

Suppose that, in the test market evaluation of the product, 400 potential customers were contacted; 100 purchased the product, but 300 did not. In effect, we have repeated the experiment of contacting a customer 400 times and have found that the product was purchased 100 times. Thus, we might decide to use the relative frequency of the number of customers that purchased the product as an estimate of the probability of a customer making a purchase. We could assign a probability of $100/400 = 0.25$ to the experimental outcome of purchasing the product. Similarly, $300/400 = 0.75$ could be assigned to the experimental outcome of not purchasing the product. This approach to assigning probabilities is referred to as the **relative frequency method**.

Subjective Method

The **subjective method** of assigning probabilities is most appropriate when one cannot realistically assume that the experimental outcomes are equally likely and when little relevant data are available. When the subjective method is used to assign probabilities to the experimental outcomes, we may use any information available, such as our experience or intuition. After considering all available information, a probability value that expresses our *degree of belief* (on a scale from 0 to 1) that the experimental outcome will occur is specified. Because subjective probability expresses a person's degree of belief, it is personal. Using the subjective method, different people can be expected to assign different probabilities to the same experimental outcome.

The subjective method requires extra care to ensure that the two basic requirements of equations (2.1) and (2.2) are satisfied. Regardless of a person's degree of belief, the probability value assigned to each experimental outcome must be between 0 and 1, inclusive, and the sum of all the probabilities for the experimental outcomes must equal one.

Consider the case in which Tom and Judy Elsbernd just made an offer to purchase a house. Two outcomes are possible:

$$E_1 = \text{their offer is accepted}$$
$$E_2 = \text{their offer is rejected}$$

Judy believes that the probability their offer will be accepted is 0.8; thus, Judy would set $P(E_1) = 0.8$ and $P(E_2) = 0.2$. Tom, however, believes that the probability that their offer will be accepted is 0.6; hence, Tom would set $P(E_1) = 0.6$ and $P(E_2) = 0.4$. Note that Tom's probability estimate for E_1 reflects a greater pessimism that their offer will be accepted.

Both Judy and Tom assigned probabilities that satisfy the two basic requirements. The fact that their probability estimates differ emphasizes the personal nature of the subjective method.

Even in business situations where either the classical or the relative frequency approach can be applied, managers may want to provide subjective probability estimates. In such cases, the best probability estimates often are obtained by combining the estimates from the classical or relative frequency approach with subjective probability estimates.

Bayes' theorem (see Section 2.5) provides a means for combining subjectively determined prior probabilities with probabilities obtained by other means to obtain revised, or posterior, probabilities.

2.3 Events and Their Probabilities

An **event** is a collection of sample points (experimental outcomes). For example, in the experiment of rolling a die, the sample space has six sample points and is denoted $S = \{1, 2, 3, 4, 5, 6\}$. Now consider the event that the number of dots shown on the upward face of the die is an even number. The three sample points in this event are 2, 4, and 6. Using the letter A to denote this event, we write A as a collection of sample points:

$$A = \{2, 4, 6\}$$

Thus, if the experimental outcome or sample point were 2, 4, or 6, we would say that the event A has occurred.

Much of the focus of probability analysis is involved with computing probabilities for various events that are of interest to a decision maker. If the probabilities of the sample points are defined, the *probability of an event* is equal to the sum of the probabilities of the sample points in the event.

Returning to the experiment of rolling a die, we used the classical method to conclude that the probability associated with each sample point is $1/6$. Thus, the probability of rolling a 2 is $1/6$, the probability of rolling a 4 is $1/6$, and the probability of rolling a 6 is $1/6$. The probability of event A—an even number of dots on the upward face of the die—is

$$P(A) = P(2) + P(4) + P(6)$$
$$= \frac{1}{6} + \frac{1}{6} + \frac{1}{6} = \frac{3}{6} = \frac{1}{2}$$

Any time that we can identify all the sample points of an experiment and assign the corresponding sample point probabilities, we can use the preceding approach to compute the probability of an event. However, in many experiments the number of sample points is large, and the identification of the sample points, as well as determining their associated probabilities, becomes extremely cumbersome if not impossible. In the remainder of this chapter we present some basic probability relationships that can be used to compute the probability of an event without knowing all the individual sample point probabilities. These probability relationships require a knowledge of the probabilities for some events in the experiment. Probabilities of other events are then computed from these known probabilities using one or more of the probability relationships.

Try Problem 6 for practice in assigning probabilities to events.

NOTES AND COMMENTS

1. The sample space, S, is itself an event. It contains all the experimental outcomes, so it has a probability of 1; that is, $P(S) = 1$.
2. When the classical method is used to assign probabilities, the assumption is that the experimental outcomes are equally likely. In such cases, the probability of an event can be computed by counting the number of experimental outcomes in the event and dividing the result by the total number of experimental outcomes.

2.4   Some Basic Relationships of Probability

In this section we present several relationships that will be helpful in computing probabilities. The relationships are the complement of an event, the addition law, conditional probability, and the multiplication law.

Complement of an Event

For an event A, the **complement of event A** is the event consisting of all sample points that are *not* in A. The complement of A is denoted by A^c. Figure 2.2 provides a diagram, known as a **Venn diagram**, that illustrates the concept of a complement. The rectangular area represents the sample space for the experiment and as such contains all possible sample points. The circle represents event A and contains only the sample points that belong to A.

FIGURE 2.2   COMPLEMENT OF EVENT A

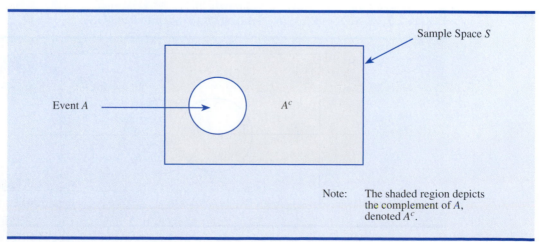

Sample Space S

Event A

A^c

Note: The shaded region depicts the complement of A, denoted A^c.

The remainder of the rectangle contains all sample points not in event A, which by definition is the complement of A.

In any probability application, event A and its complement A^c must satisfy the condition

$$P(A) + P(A^c) = 1$$

Solving for $P(A)$, we have

$$P(A) = 1 - P(A^c) \qquad\qquad \textbf{(2.3)}$$

Equation (2.3) shows that the probability of an event A can be computed by subtraction if the probability of its complement, $P(A^c)$, is known.

Consider the case of a sales manager who, after reviewing sales reports, states that 80% of new customer contacts result in no sale. By letting A denote the event of a sale and A^c denote the event of no sale, the manager is stating that $P(A^c) = 0.80$. Using equation (2.3), we see that

$$P(A) = 1 - P(A^c) = 1 - 0.80 = 0.20$$

which shows that there is a 0.20 probability that a sale will be made on a new customer contact.

In another case, a purchasing agent states a 0.90 probability that a supplier will send a shipment that is free of defective parts. Using the complement, we can conclude a $1 - 0.90 = 0.10$ probability that the shipment will contain some defective parts.

Addition Law

The addition law is a useful relationship when we have two events and are interested in knowing the probability that at least one of the events occurs. That is, with events A and B, we are interested in knowing the probability that event A or event B or both will occur. Before we present the addition law, we need to discuss two concepts concerning the combination of events: the *union* of events and the *intersection* of events.

For two events A and B, the **union of events A and B** is the event containing all sample points belonging to A *or* B *or both*. The union is denoted $A \cup B$. The Venn diagram shown in Figure 2.3 depicts the union of events A and B; the shaded region contains all the

FIGURE 2.3   UNION OF EVENTS A AND B (SHADED REGION)

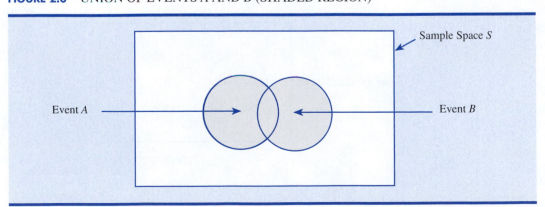

FIGURE 2.4   INTERSECTION OF EVENTS *A* AND *B* (SHADED REGION)

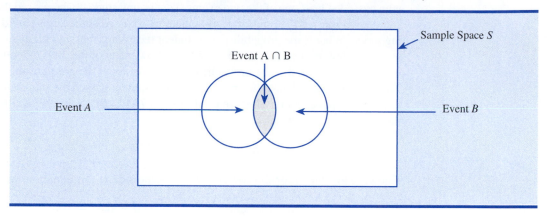

sample points in event *A*, as well as all the sample points in event *B*. The fact that the circles overlap indicates that some sample points are contained in both *A* and *B*.

Key words for the union of events (A ∪ B) are "either A or B occurs" or "at least one of the two events occurs."

For two events *A* and *B*, the **intersection of events *A* and *B*** is the event containing the sample points belonging to *both A and B*. The intersection is denoted by *A* ∩ *B*. The Venn diagram depicting the intersection of the two events is shown in Figure 2.4. The area where the two circles overlap is the intersection; it contains the sample points that are in both *A* and *B*.

The addition law provides a way to compute the probability of event *A* or *B* or both occurring. In other words, the addition law is used to compute the probability of the union of two events, *A* ∪ *B*. The **addition law** is formally stated as follows:

Key words for the intersection of events (A ∩ B) are "both A and B occur."

$$P(A \cup B) = P(A) + P(B) - P(A \cap B) \qquad \text{(2.4)}$$

To obtain an intuitive understanding of the addition law, note that the first two terms in the addition law, $P(A) + P(B)$, account for all the sample points in $A \cup B$. However, as the sample points in the intersection $A \cap B$ are in both *A* and *B*, when we compute $P(A) + P(B)$, we in effect are counting each of the sample points in $A \cap B$ twice. We correct for this double counting by subtracting $P(A \cap B)$.

To apply the addition law, let us consider the following situations in a college course in quantitative methods for decision making. Of 200 students taking the course, 160 passed the midterm examination and 140 passed the final examination; 124 students passed both exams. Let

A = event of passing the midterm exam

B = event of passing the final exam

This relative frequency information leads to the following probabilities:

$$P(A) = \frac{160}{200} = 0.80$$

$$P(B) = \frac{140}{200} = 0.70$$

$$P(A \cap B) = \frac{124}{200} = 0.62$$

After reviewing the grades, the instructor decided to give a passing grade to any student who passed at least one of the two exams. That is, any student who passed the midterm, any student who passed the final, and any student who passed both exams would receive a passing grade. What is the probability of a student receiving a passing grade in this course?

Your first reaction may be to try to count how many of the 200 students passed at least one exam, but note that the probability question is about the union of the events A and B. That is, we want to know the probability that a student passed the midterm (A), passed the final (B), or passed both. Thus we want to know $P(A \cup B)$. Using the addition law (2.4) for the events A and B, we have

$$P(A \cup B) = P(A) + P(B) - P(A \cap B)$$

Knowing the three probabilities on the right-hand side of this equation, we obtain

$$P(A \cup B) = 0.80 + 0.70 - 0.62 = 0.88$$

This result indicates an 88% chance of a student passing the course because of the 0.88 probability of passing at least one of the exams.

Now consider a study involving the television-viewing habits of married couples. It was reported that 30% of the husbands and 20% of the wives were regular viewers of a particular Friday evening program. For 12% of the couples in the study, both husband and wife were regular viewers of the program. What is the probability that at least one member of a married couple is a regular viewer of the program?

Let

$$H = \text{husband is a regular viewer}$$
$$W = \text{wife is a regular viewer}$$

We have $P(H) = 0.30$, $P(W) = 0.20$, and $P(H \cap W) = 0.12$; thus, the addition law yields

$$P(H \cup W) = P(H) + P(W) - P(H \cap W) = 0.30 + 0.20 - 0.12 = 0.38$$

This result shows a 0.38 probability that at least one member of a married couple is a regular viewer of the program.

An event and its complement are mutually exclusive and their union is the entire sample space.

Before going on, let us see how the addition law is applied to **mutually exclusive events**. Two or more events are said to be mutually exclusive if the events do not have any sample points in common—that is, there are no sample points in the intersection of the events. For two events A and B to be mutually exclusive, $P(A \cap B) = 0$. Figure 2.5 provides a Venn diagram depicting two mutually exclusive events. Because $P(A \cap B) = 0$ for the *special case of mutually exclusive events,* the addition law becomes

$$P(A \cup B) = P(A) + P(B) \qquad \textbf{(2.5)}$$

For practice, try solving Problem 7.

To compute the probability of the union of two mutually exclusive events, we simply add the corresponding probabilities.

Conditional Probability

In many probability situations, being able to determine the probability of one event when another related event is known to have occurred is important. Suppose that we have an event

FIGURE 2.5   MUTUALLY EXCLUSIVE EVENTS

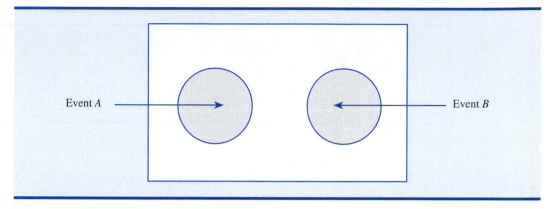

A with probability $P(A)$ and that we obtain new information or learn that another event, denoted B, has occurred. If A is related to B, we will want to take advantage of this information in computing a new or revised probability for event A.

This new probability of event A is written $P(A \mid B)$. The "|" denotes the fact that we are considering the probability of event A *given the condition that event B has occurred*. Thus, the notation $P(A \mid B)$ is read "the probability of A given B."

With two events A and B, the general definitions of **conditional probability** for A given B and for B given A are as follows:

In conditional probability such as $P(A \mid B) = 0.25$, the probability value of 0.25 refers only to the probability of event A. No information is provided about the probability of event B.

$$P(A \mid B) = \frac{P(A \cap B)}{P(B)} \qquad \text{(2.6)}$$

$$P(B \mid A) = \frac{P(A \cap B)}{P(A)} \qquad \text{(2.7)}$$

Note that for these expressions to have meaning, $P(B)$ cannot equal 0 in equation (2.6) and $P(A)$ cannot equal 0 in equation (2.7).

To obtain an intuitive understanding of the use of equation (2.6), consider the Venn diagram in Figure 2.6. The shaded region (both light gray and dark gray) denotes that event B

FIGURE 2.6   CONDITIONAL PROBABILITY $P(A \mid B) = P(A \cap B)/P(B)$

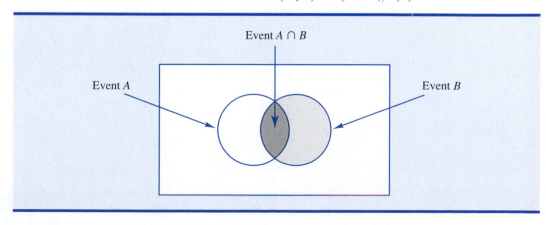

TABLE 2.1   CONTINGENCY TABLE FOR PROMOTIONAL STATUS OF POLICE OFFICERS DURING THE PAST TWO YEARS

	Promoted	Not Promoted	Total
Men	288	672	960
Women	36	204	240
Total	324	876	1200

has occurred; the dark gray shaded region denotes the event $(A \cap B)$. We know that once B has occurred, the only way that we can also observe event A is for event $(A \cap B)$ to occur. Thus, the ratio $P(A \cap B)/P(B)$ provides the probability that we will observe event A when event B has already occurred.

Try Problem 12 for practice computing conditional probabilities.

We can apply conditional probability to the promotional status of male and female officers of a major metropolitan police force. It consists of 1200 officers: 960 men and 240 women. Over the past two years, 324 officers have been promoted. Table 2.1 shows the specific breakdown of promotions for male and female officers. Such a table is often called a *contingency table* or a *crosstabulation*.

After reviewing the promotional record, a committee of female officers filed a discrimination case on the basis that only 36 female officers had received promotions during the past two years. The police administration argued that the relatively low number of promotions for female officers is due not to discrimination but to the fact that few female officers are on the force. We use conditional probability to evaluate the discrimination charge.

Let

$$M = \text{event an officer is a man}$$

$$W = \text{event an officer is a woman}$$

$$B = \text{event an officer is promoted}$$

Dividing the data values in Table 2.1 by the total of 1200 officers permits us to summarize the available information as follows:

$$P(M \cap B) = \frac{288}{1200} = 0.24 \qquad \text{probability that an officer is a man } \textit{and} \text{ is promoted}$$

$$P(M \cap B^c) = \frac{672}{1200} = 0.56 \qquad \text{probability that an officer is a man } \textit{and} \text{ is not promoted}$$

$$P(W \cap B) = \frac{36}{1200} = 0.03 \qquad \text{probability that an officer is a woman } \textit{and} \text{ is promoted}$$

$$P(W \cap B^c) = \frac{204}{1200} = 0.17 \qquad \text{probability that an officer is a woman } \textit{and} \text{ is not promoted}$$

Because each of these values gives the probability of the intersection of two events, these probabilities are called **joint probabilities**. Table 2.2, which provides a summary of the

TABLE 2.2   JOINT PROBABILITY TABLE FOR POLICE OFFICER PROMOTIONS

	Promoted	Not Promoted	Total
Men	0.24	0.56	0.80
Women	0.03	0.17	0.20
Total	0.27	0.73	1.00

Joint probabilities appear in the body of the table.

Marginal probabilities appear in the margins of the table.

probability information for the police officer promotion situation, is referred to as a **joint probability table**.

The values in the margins of the joint probability table provide the probabilities of each event separately: $P(M) = 0.80$, $P(W) = 0.20$, $P(B) = 0.27$, and $P(B^c) = 0.73$, which indicate that 80% of the force is male, 20% of the force is female, 27% of all officers received promotions, and 73% were not promoted. These probabilities are referred to as **marginal probabilities** because of their location in the margins of the joint probability table. Returning to the issue of discrimination against the female officers, we see that the probability of promotion of an officer is $P(B) = 0.27$ (regardless of whether that officer is male or female). However, the critical issue in the discrimination case involves the two conditional probabilities $P(B \mid M)$ and $P(B \mid W)$; that is, what is the probability of a promotion *given* that the officer is a man and what is the probability of a promotion *given* that the officer is a woman? If these two probabilities are equal, the discrimination case has no basis because the chances of a promotion are the same for male and female officers. However, different conditional probabilities will support the position that male and female officers are treated differently in terms of promotion.

Using equation (2.7), the conditional probability relationship, we obtain

$$P(B \mid M) = \frac{P(M \cap B)}{P(M)} = \frac{0.24}{0.80} = 0.30$$

$$P(B \mid W) = \frac{P(W \cap B)}{P(W)} = \frac{0.03}{0.20} = 0.15$$

What conclusions do you draw? The probability of a promotion for a male officer is 0.30, which is twice the 0.15 probability of a promotion for a female officer. Although the use of conditional probability does not in itself prove that discrimination exists in this case, the conditional probability values strongly support the argument presented by the female officers.

In this illustration $P(B) = 0.27$, $P(B \mid M) = 0.30$, and $P(B \mid W) = 0.15$. These probabilities show clearly that promotion (event B) is influenced by whether the officer is male or female. In particular, as $P(B \mid M) \neq P(B)$, events B and M are **dependent events**. The probability of event B (promotion) is altered or affected by knowing whether M (the officer is male) occurs. Similarly, with $P(B \mid W) \neq P(B)$, events B and W are dependent events. But, if the probability of event B was not changed by the existence of event M, that is, $P(B \mid M) = P(B)$, events B and M would be **independent events**. Two events A and B are *independent* if

$$P(B \mid A) = P(B)$$

or

$$P(A \mid B) = P(A)$$

For practice, try solving Problem 13.

Otherwise, the events are *dependent*.

The Q.M. in Action, Product Testing for Quality Control, describes how a subsidiary of Morton International used conditional probability to help decide to implement a quality control test.

Q.M. *in* ACTION

PRODUCT TESTING FOR QUALITY CONTROL AT MORTON INTERNATIONAL*

Morton International is a company with businesses in salt, household products, rocket motors, and specialty chemicals. Carstab Corporation, a subsidiary of Morton, produces a variety of specialty chemical products designed to meet the unique specifications of its customers. For one particular customer, Carstab produced an expensive catalyst used in chemical processing. Some, but not all, of the product produced by Carstab met the customer's specifications.

Carstab's customer agreed to test each lot after receiving it to determine whether the catalyst would perform the desired function. Lots that did not pass the customer's test would be returned to Carstab. Over time, Carstab found that the customer was accepting 60% of the lots and returning 40%. In probability terms, each Carstab shipment to the customer had a 0.60 probability of being accepted and a 0.40 probability of being returned.

Neither Carstab nor its customer was pleased with these results. In an effort to improve service, Carstab explored the possibility of duplicating the customer's test prior to shipment. However, the high cost of the special testing equipment made that alternative infeasible. Carstab's chemists then proposed a new, relatively low-cost test designed to indicate whether a lot would pass the customer's test. The probability question of interest was: What is the probability that a lot will pass the customer's test given that it passed the new Carstab test?

A sample of lots was tested under both the customer's procedure and Carstab's proposed procedure. Results were that 55% of the lots passed Carstab's test, and 50% of the lots passed both the customer's and Carstab's test. In probability notation, we have

A = the event the lot passes the customer's test
B = the event the lot passes Carstab's test

where

$$P(B) = 0.55 \text{ and } P(A \cap B) = 0.50$$

The probability information sought was the conditional probability $P(A \mid B)$ given by

$$P(A \mid B) = \frac{P(A \cap B)}{P(B)} = \frac{0.50}{0.55} = 0.909$$

Prior to Carstab's new test the probability a lot would pass the customer's test was 0.60. However, the new results showed that given a lot passed Carstab's new test, it had a 0.909 probability of passing the customer's test. This result was good supporting evidence for the use of the test prior to shipment. Based on this probability analysis, the preshipment testing procedure was implemented at the company. Immediate results showed an improved level of customer service. A few lots were still being returned; however, the percentage was greatly reduced. The customer was more satisfied and return shipping costs were reduced.

*Based on information provided by Michael Haskell of Morton International.

Multiplication Law

The **multiplication law** can be used to find the probability of an intersection of two events. The multiplication law is derived from the definition of conditional probability. Using equations (2.6) and (2.7) and solving for $P(A \cap B)$, we obtain the multiplication law:

$$P(A \cap B) = P(A \mid B)P(B) \tag{2.8}$$

$$P(A \cap B) = P(B \mid A)P(A) \tag{2.9}$$

The multiplication law is useful in situations where probabilities such as $P(A)$, $P(B)$, $P(A \mid B)$, and/or $P(B \mid A)$ are known but where $P(A \cap B)$ is not. For example, suppose that a newspaper circulation department knows that 84% of its customers subscribe to the daily edition of the paper. Let D denote the event that a customer subscribes to the daily edition; hence, $P(D) = 0.84$. In addition, the department knows that the conditional probability that a customer who already holds a daily subscription also subscribes to the Sunday edition (event S) is 0.75; that is, $P(S \mid D) = 0.75$. What is the probability that a customer subscribes to both the daily and Sunday editions of the newspaper? Using equation (2.9), we compute $P(D \cap S)$:

$$P(D \cap S) = P(S \mid D)P(D) = 0.75(0.84) = 0.63$$

This result tells us that 63% of the newspaper's customers take both the daily and Sunday editions.

Before concluding this section, let us consider the special case of the multiplication law when the events involved are independent. Recall that independent events exist whenever $P(B \mid A) = P(B)$ or $P(A \mid B) = P(A)$. Returning to the multiplication law, equations (2.8) and (2.9), we can substitute $P(A)$ for $P(A \mid B)$ and $P(B)$ for $P(B \mid A)$. Hence, for the *special case of independent events*, the multiplication law becomes

$$P(A \cap B) = P(A)P(B) \tag{2.10}$$

Thus, to compute the probability of the intersection of two independent events, we simply multiply the corresponding probabilities. For example, a service station manager knows from past experience that 40% of her customers use a credit card when purchasing gasoline. What is the probability that the next two customers purchasing gasoline will both use a credit card? If we let

A = the event that the first customer uses a credit card

B = the event that the second customer uses a credit card

the event of interest is $A \cap B$. With no other information, a reasonable assumption is that A and B are independent events. Thus,

$$P(A \cap B) = P(A)P(B) = (.40)(.40) = 0.16$$

NOTES AND COMMENTS

Do not confuse mutually exclusive events with independent events. Two events with nonzero probabilities cannot be both mutually exclusive and independent. If one mutually exclusive event is known to occur, the probability of the other occurring is reduced to zero. Thus, they cannot be independent.

2.5 Bayes' Theorem

In the discussion of conditional probability, we indicated that revising probabilities when new information is obtained is an important phase of probability analysis. Often, we begin an analysis with initial or **prior probability** estimates for specific events of interest. Then, from sources such as a sample, a special report, or a product test, we obtain some additional information about the events. With this new information, we update the prior probability values by calculating revised probabilities, referred to as **posterior probabilities**. **Bayes' theorem** provides a means for making these probability revisions. The steps in this probability revision process are shown in Figure 2.7.

We can apply Bayes' theorem to a manufacturing firm that receives shipments of parts from two different suppliers. Let A_1 denote the event that a part is from supplier 1 and A_2 denote the event that a part is from supplier 2. Currently, 65% of the parts purchased by the company are from supplier 1, and the remaining 35% are from supplier 2. Thus, if a part is selected at random, we would assign the prior probabilities $P(A_1) = 0.65$ and $P(A_2) = 0.35$.

The quality of the purchased parts varies with the source of supply. Based on historical data, the conditional probabilities of receiving good and bad parts from the two suppliers are shown in Table 2.3. Thus, if we let G denote the event that a part is good and B denote the event that a part is bad, the information in Table 2.3 provides the following conditional probability values:

$$P(G \mid A_1) = 0.98 \; P(B \mid A_1) = 0.02$$
$$P(G \mid A_2) = 0.95 \; P(B \mid A_2) = 0.05$$

The tree diagram shown in Figure 2.8 depicts the process of the firm receiving a part from one of the two suppliers and then discovering that the part is good or bad as a two-step experiment. Of the four possible experimental outcomes, two correspond to the part being good, and two correspond to the part being bad.

Each of the experimental outcomes is the intersection of two events, so we can use the multiplication rule to compute the probabilities. For instance,

$$P(A_1 \cap G) = P(A_1)P(G \mid A_1)$$

FIGURE 2.7   PROBABILITY REVISION USING BAYES' THEOREM

Prior Probabilities	New Information	Application of Bayes' Theorem	Posterior Probabilities

TABLE 2.3   CONDITIONAL PROBABILITIES OF RECEIVING GOOD AND BAD PARTS FROM TWO SUPPLIERS

	Good Parts	Bad Parts	
Supplier 1	0.98	0.02	← $P(B \mid A_1)$
Supplier 2	0.95	0.05	

FIGURE 2.8   TWO-STEP TREE DIAGRAM

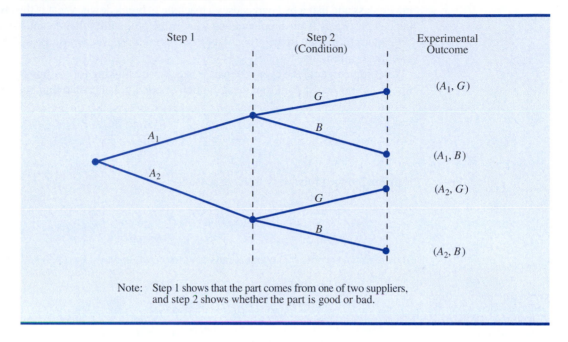

Note: Step 1 shows that the part comes from one of two suppliers, and step 2 shows whether the part is good or bad.

The process of computing these joint probabilities can be depicted in what is sometimes called a *probability tree,* as shown in Figure 2.9. From left to right in the tree, the probabilities for each of the branches at step 1 are the prior probabilities, and the probabilities for each branch at step 2 are conditional probabilities. To find the probabilities of each experimental outcome, we simply multiply the probabilities on the branches leading to the outcome. Each of these joint probabilities is shown in Figure 2.9, along with the known probabilities for each branch. Note that the probabilities of the four experimental outcomes sum to 1.

FIGURE 2.9   PROBABILITY TREE FOR TWO-SUPPLIER EXAMPLE

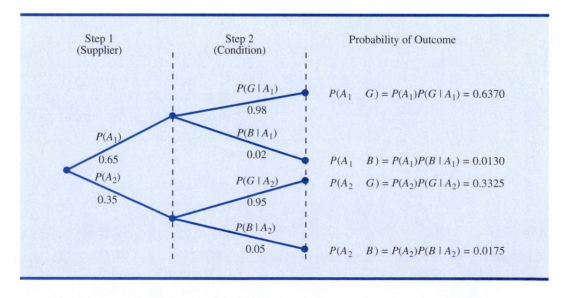

Now suppose that the parts from the two suppliers are used in the firm's manufacturing process and that a bad part causes a machine to break down. What is the probability that the bad part came from supplier 1 and what is the probability that it came from supplier 2? With the information in the probability tree (Figure 2.9), we can use Bayes' theorem to answer these questions.

Letting B denote the event the part is bad, we are looking for the posterior probabilities $P(A_1 \mid B)$ and $P(A_2 \mid B)$. From the definition of conditional probability, we know that

$$P(A_1 \mid B) = \frac{P(A_1 \cap B)}{P(B)} \tag{2.11}$$

Referring to the probability tree, we see that

$$P(A_1 \cap B) = P(A_1)P(B \mid A_1) \tag{2.12}$$

The Reverend Thomas Bayes (1702–1761), a Presbyterian minister, is credited with the original work leading to the version of Bayes' theorem in use today.

To find $P(B)$, we note that event B can occur in only two ways: $(A_1 \cap B)$ and $(A_2 \cap B)$. Therefore, we have

$$\begin{aligned} P(B) &= P(A_1 \cap B) + P(A_2 \cap B) \\ &= P(A_1)P(B \mid A_1) + P(A_2)P(B \mid A_2) \end{aligned} \tag{2.13}$$

Substituting from equations (2.12) and (2.13) into equation (2.11) and writing a similar result for $P(A_2 \mid B)$, we obtain Bayes' theorem for the case of two events.

$$P(A_1 \mid B) = \frac{P(A_1)P(B \mid A_1)}{P(A_1)P(B \mid A_1) + P(A_2)P(B \mid A_2)} \tag{2.14}$$

$$P(A_2 \mid B) = \frac{P(A_2)P(B \mid A_2)}{P(A_1)P(B \mid A_1) + P(A_2)P(B \mid A_2)} \tag{2.15}$$

Using equation (2.14) and the probability values provided in our example, we have

$$\begin{aligned} P(A_1 \mid B) &= \frac{P(A_1)P(B \mid A_1)}{P(A_1)P(B \mid A_1) + P(A_2)P(B \mid A_2)} \\ &= \frac{(0.65)(0.02)}{(0.65)(0.02) + (0.35)(0.05)} = \frac{0.0130}{0.0130 + 0.0175} \\ &= \frac{0.0130}{0.0305} = 0.4262 \end{aligned}$$

In addition, using equation (2.15), we obtain $P(A_2 \mid B)$:

$$\begin{aligned} P(A_2 \mid B) &= \frac{(0.35)(0.05)}{(0.65)(0.02) + (0.35)(0.05)} \\ &= \frac{0.0175}{0.0130 + 0.0175} = \frac{0.0175}{0.0305} = 0.5738 \end{aligned}$$

TABLE 2.4 SUMMARY OF BAYES' THEOREM CALCULATIONS
FOR THE TWO-SUPPLIER PROBLEM

(1) Events A_i	(2) Prior Probabilities $P(A_i)$	(3) Conditional Probabilities $P(B \mid A_i)$	(4) Joint Probabilities $P(A_i \cap B)$	(5) Posterior Probabilities $P(A_i \mid B)$
A_1	0.65	0.02	0.0130	0.0130/0.0305 = 0.4262
A_2	0.35	0.05	0.0175	0.0175/0.0305 = 0.5738
	1.00		$P(B) = 0.0305$	1.0000

Note that in this application we initially started with a probability of 0.65 that a part selected at random was from supplier 1. However, given information that the part is bad, we determine the probability that the part is from supplier 1 drops to 0.4262. In fact, if the part is bad, there is a better than 50/50 chance that the part came from supplier 2; that is, $P(A_2 \mid B) = 0.5738$.

Bayes' theorem is applicable when the events for which we want to compute posterior probabilities are mutually exclusive and their union is the entire sample space.* Bayes' theorem can be extended to the case of n mutually exclusive events $A_1, A_2, \ldots, A_n$, whose union is the entire sample space. In such a case Bayes' theorem for the computation of any posterior probability $P(A_i \mid B)$ becomes

$$P(A_i \mid B) = \frac{P(A_i)P(B \mid A_i)}{P(A_1)P(B \mid A_1) + P(A_2)P(B \mid A_2) + \cdots + P(A_n)P(B \mid A_n)} \quad \textbf{(2.16)}$$

Try Problem 20 for practice using Bayes' theorem to compute posterior probabilities.

With prior probabilities $P(A_1), P(A_2), \ldots, P(A_n)$ and the appropriate conditional probabilities $P(B \mid A_1), P(B \mid A_2), \ldots, P(B \mid A_n)$, equation (2.16) can be used to compute the posterior probability of the events $A_1, A_2, \ldots, A_n$.

The Tabular Approach

The tabular approach is helpful in conducting the Bayes' theorem calculations simultaneously for all events A_i. Such an approach is shown in Table 2.4. The computations shown there involve the following steps.

Step 1. Prepare three columns:
Column 1—The mutually exclusive events for which posterior probabilities are desired
Column 2—The prior probabilities for the events
Column 3—The conditional probabilities of the new information given each event

Step 2. In column 4, compute the joint probabilities for each event and the new information B by using the multiplication law. To get these joint probabilities, multiply the prior probabilities in column 2 by the corresponding conditional probabilities in column 3—that is, $P(A_i \cap B) = P(A_i)P(B \mid A_i)$.

Step 3. Sum the joint probabilities in column 4 to obtain the probability of the new information, $P(B)$. In the example there is a 0.0130 probability that a part is from supplier 1 and is bad and a 0.0175 probability that a part is from supplier 2 and

*If the union of events is the entire sample space, the events are often called *collectively exhausted*.

is bad. These are the only two ways by which a bad part can be obtained, so the sum 0.0130 + 0.0175 shows an overall probability of 0.0305 of finding a bad part from the combined shipments of both suppliers.

Step 4. In column 5, compute the posterior probabilities by using the basic relationship of conditional probability:

$$P(A_i \mid B) = \frac{P(A_i \cap B)}{P(B)}$$

Try Problem 25 for an application of Bayes' theorem involving the tabular approach.

Note that the joint probabilities $P(A_i \cap B)$ appear in column 4, whereas $P(B)$ is the sum of the column 4 values.

NOTES AND COMMENTS

1. Bayes' theorem can be used in Internet marketing to profile visitors to a Web site. The Q.M. in Action, Internet Marketing, explains how clickstream data can be used for this purpose.
2. Bayes' theorem is used in decision analysis (see Chapter 4). The prior probabilities often are subjective estimates provided by a decision maker. Sample information is obtained and posterior probabilities are computed for use in developing a decision strategy.
3. An event and its complement are mutually exclusive, and their union is the entire sample space. Thus, Bayes' theorem is always applicable for computing posterior probabilities of an event and its complement.

Q.M. *in* ACTION

INTERNET MARKETING*

Alan Montgomery explained how quantitative methods can be applied to Internet marketing: He described the use of conjoint analysis to predict the probability of purchase, the use of statistical models to predict the rapid growth in the use of Hotmail, and other approaches involving probability and Bayesian analysis.

The Internet makes interactive marketing possible. Once a potential consumer accesses a Web site, the owner of the Web site can contact that consumer with special offers, direct marketing promotions, and other marketing efforts. A key to successful marketing is identifying the consumers most likely to benefit from an offer so that they can be targeted by e-mail or direct mail campaigns.

The sequence of URLs (Web site addresses) a person visits, along with other information about the visit, is called clickstream data. Clickstream data can be merged with demographic data and past purchase history to profile visitors

to a Web site. For example, Media Metrix reported that 66% of the visitors to *ivillage.com* are female; 73% of the visitors to *netradio.net* are male, and so on. Suppose we want to predict whether a Web site visitor is female. For starters, it is known that 45% of Web users are female. Now, suppose we know from the clickstream that the person also visited *ivillage.com*. Using Bayes' theorem we can compute the revised probability the visitor is female; it is 0.62. With more clickstream information this probability can be revised even further. Montgomery tested this Bayesian methodology using a sample of 19,000 Web users and was able to correctly classify the gender of 60% of the users.

This same approach can be used to predict other demographic variables, such as age and income. For instance, *The Wall Street Journal* conducts surveys to learn about income levels and a variety of other characteristics of its subscribers. So, if clickstream data show a person visited *wsj.com*, we can infer something about that person's income level. Of course, questions about privacy are a major issue in using these techniques.

---

*Based on Alan Montgomery, "Applying Quantitative Marketing Techniques to the Internet," *Interfaces* (March/April 2001): 90–108.

Summary

In this chapter we introduced basic probability concepts and illustrated how probability analysis can provide helpful decision-making information. We described how probability can be interpreted as a numerical measure of the likelihood that an event will occur. In addition, we showed that the probability of an event can be computed either by summing the probabilities of the experimental outcomes (sample points) comprising the event or by using the basic relationships of probability. When additional information becomes available, we showed how conditional probability and Bayes' theorem can be used to obtain revised or posterior probabilities.

The probability concepts covered will be helpful in future chapters when we describe quantitative methods based on the use of probability information. Specific chapters and quantitative methods that make use of probability are

- Chapter 3   Probability distributions
- Chapter 4   Decision analysis
- Chapter 5   Utility and game theory
- Chapter 13   Project scheduling: PERT/CPM
- Chapter 14   Inventory models
- Chapter 15   Waiting line models
- Chapter 16   Simulation
- Chapter 17   Markov processes

Glossary

Probability A numerical measure of the likelihood that an event will occur.

Experiment Any process that generates well-defined outcomes.

Sample space The set of all sample points (experimental outcomes).

Sample point An experimental outcome and an element of the sample space.

Basic requirements of probability Two requirements that restrict the manner in which probability assignments can be made:

1. For each experimental outcome E_i, $0 \leq P(E_i) \leq 1$.
2. $P(E_1) + P(E_2) + \cdots + P(E_k) = 1$.

Classical method A method of assigning probabilities that is based on the assumption that the experimental outcomes are equally likely.

Relative frequency method A method of assigning probabilities based on experimentation or historical data.

Subjective method A method of assigning probabilities based on judgment.

Event A collection of sample points or experimental outcomes.

Complement of event A The event containing all sample points that are not in A.

Venn diagram A graphical device for representing the sample space and operations involving events.

Union of events A and B The event containing all sample points that are in A, in B, or in both.

Intersection of events A and B The event containing all sample points that are in both A and B.

Addition law A probability law used to compute the probability of a union: $P(A \cup B) = P(A) + P(B) - P(A \cap B)$. For mutually exclusive events, $P(A \cap B) = 0$, and the addition law reduces to $P(A \cup B) = P(A) + P(B)$.

Mutually exclusive events Events that have no sample points in common; that is, $A \cap B$ is empty and $P(A \cap B) = 0$.

Conditional probability The probability of an event given another event has occurred. The conditional probability of A given B is $P(A \mid B) = P(A \cap B)/P(B)$.

Joint probability The probability of the intersection of two events.

Joint probability table A table used to display joint and marginal probabilities.

Marginal probabilities The values in the margins of the joint probability table, which provide the probability of each event separately.

Dependent events Two events A and B, where $P(A \mid B) \neq P(A)$ or $P(B \mid A) \neq P(B)$; that is, the probability of one event is altered or affected by knowing whether the other event occurs.

Independent events Two events A and B, where $P(A \mid B) = P(A)$ and $P(B \mid A) = P(B)$; that is, the events have no influence on each other.

Multiplication law A probability law used to compute the probability of an intersection: $P(A \cap B) = P(A \mid B)P(B)$ or $P(A \cap B) = P(B \mid A)P(A)$. For independent events, it reduces to $P(A \cap B) = P(A)P(B)$.

Prior probabilities Initial probabilities of events.

Posterior probabilities Revised probabilities of events based on additional information.

Bayes' theorem A method used to compute posterior probabilities.

Problems

1. A study examined waiting times in the X-ray department for a hospital in Jacksonville, Florida. A clerk recorded the number of patients waiting for service at 9:00 A.M. on 20 consecutive days and obtained the following results.

Number Waiting	Number of Days Outcome Occurred
0	2
1	5
2	6
3	4
4	3
	Total 20

   a.   Define the experiment the clerk conducted.
   b.   List the experimental outcomes.
   c.   Assign probabilities to the experimental outcomes.
   d.   What method did you use?

2. A company that franchises coffee houses conducted taste tests for a new coffee product. The company prepared four blends and randomly chose individuals to do a taste test and state which of the four blends they liked best. Results of the taste test for 100 individuals are given.

Blend	Taste-Testers' Preference
1	20
2	30
3	35
4	15

a. Define the experiment being conducted. How many times was it repeated?
b. Prior to conducting the experiment, it is reasonable to assume preferences for the four blends are equal. What probabilities would you assign to the experimental outcomes prior to conducting the taste test? What method did you use?
c. After conducting the taste test, what probabilities would you assign to the experimental outcomes? What method did you use?

3. A company that manufactures toothpaste is studying five different package designs. Assuming that one design is just as likely to be selected by a consumer as any other design, what selection probability would you assign to each of the package designs? In an actual experiment, 100 consumers were asked to pick the design they preferred. The following data were obtained. Do the data confirm the belief that one design is just as likely to be selected as another? Explain.

Design	Number of Times Preferred
1	5
2	15
3	30
4	40
5	10

4. The availability of venture capital provided a big boost in funds available to companies in recent years. According to Venture Economics (*Investor's Business Daily,* April 28, 2000), 2374 venture capital disbursements were made in 1999. Of these, 1434 were to companies in California, 390 were to companies in Massachusetts, 217 were to companies in New York, and 112 were to companies in Colorado. Twenty-two percent of the companies receiving funds were in the early stages of development and 55% of the companies were in an expansion stage. Suppose you want to randomly choose one of these companies to learn about how they used the funds.
a. What is the probability the company chosen will be from California?
b. What is the probability the company chosen will not be from one of the four states mentioned?
c. What is the probability the company will not be in the early stages of development?
d. Assuming the companies in the early stages of development were evenly distributed across the country, how many Massachusetts companies receiving venture capital funds were in their early stages of development?
e. The total amount of funds invested was $32.4 billion. Estimate the amount that went to Colorado.

5. Strom Construction made a bid on two contracts. The owner identified the possible outcomes and subjectively assigned the following probabilities.

Experimental Outcome	Obtain Contract 1	Obtain Contract 2	Probability
1	Yes	Yes	0.15
2	Yes	No	0.15
3	No	Yes	0.30
4	No	No	0.25

a.   Are these valid probability assignments? Why or why not?

b.   If not, what would have to be done to make the probability assignments valid?

6.   A sample of 100 customers of Montana Gas and Electric resulted in the following frequency distribution of monthly charges.

Amount ($)	Number
0–49	13
50–99	22
100–149	34
150–199	26
200–249	5

a.   Let A be the event that monthly charges are $150 or more. Find $P(A)$.

b.   Let B be the event that monthly charges are less than $150. Find $P(B)$.

7.   Suppose that a sample space has five equally likely experimental outcomes: E_1, E_2, E_3, E_4, E_5. Let

$$A = \{E_1, E_2\}$$
$$B = \{E_3, E_4\}$$
$$C = \{E_2, E_3, E_5\}$$

a.   Find $P(A)$, $P(B)$, and $P(C)$.

b.   Find $P(A \cup B)$. Are A and B mutually exclusive?

c.   Find A^c, C^c, $P(A^c)$, and $P(C^c)$.

d.   Find $A \cup B^c$ and $P(A \cup B^c)$.

e.   Find $P(B \cup C)$.

8.   Data on the 30 largest bond funds provided one-year and five-year percentage returns for the period ending March 31, 2000 (*The Wall Street Journal,* April 10, 2000). Suppose we consider a one-year return in excess of 2% to be high and a five-year return in excess of 44% to be high. One-half of the funds had a one-year return in excess of 2%, 12 of the funds had a five-year return in excess of 44%, and six of the funds had both a one-year return in excess of 2% and a five-year return in excess of 44%.

a.   Find the probability of a fund having a high one-year return, the probability of a fund having a high five-year return, and the probability of a fund having both a high one-year return and a high five-year return.

b.   What is the probability that a fund had a high one-year return or a high five-year return or both?

c.   What is the probability that a fund had neither a high one-year return nor a high five-year return?

9.   A pharmaceutical company conducted a study to evaluate the effect of an allergy relief medicine; 250 patients with symptoms that included itchy eyes and a skin rash received the new drug. The results of the study are as follows: 90 of the patients treated experienced eye relief, 135 had their skin rash clear up, and 45 experienced relief of both itchy eyes and the skin rash. What is the probability that a patient who takes the drug will experience relief of at least one of the two symptoms?

10.   A quality control specialist has sampled 25 widgets from the production line. A widget can have minor or major defects. Of the 25 sampled widgets, 4 have minor defects and 2 have major defects. What is the probability that a widget has a major defect, given that it has a defect?

11. Let *A* be an event that a person's primary method of transportation to and from work is an automobile and *B* be an event that a person's primary method of transportation to and from work is a bus. Suppose that in a large city $P(A) = 0.45$ and $P(B) = 0.35$.
    a. Are events *A* and *B* mutually exclusive? What is the probability that a person uses an automobile or a bus in going to and from work?
    b. Find the probability that a person's primary method of transportation is some means other than a bus.

12. For two events *A* and *B*, $P(A) = 0.5$, $P(B) = 0.60$, and $P(A \cap B) = 0.40$.
    a. Find $P(A \mid B)$.
    b. Find $P(B \mid A)$.
    c. Are *A* and *B* independent? Why or why not?

13. A survey of MBA students obtained the following data on "Students' first reason for application to the school in which they matriculated."

		Reason for Application			
		School Quality	School Cost or Convenience	Other	Totals
Enrollment Status	Full Time	421	393	76	890
	Part Time	400	593	46	1039
	Totals	821	986	122	1929

    a. Develop a joint probability table using these data.
    b. Use the marginal probabilities of school quality, school cost or convenience, and other to comment on the most important reason for choosing a school.
    c. If a student goes full time, what is the probability that school quality will be the first reason for choosing a school?
    d. If a student goes part time, what is the probability that school quality will be the first reason for choosing a school?
    e. Let *A* be the event that a student is full time and let *B* be the event that the student lists school quality as the first reason for applying. Are events *A* and *B* independent? Justify your answer.

14. The checking accounts of Sun Bank are categorized by the age of account and the account balance. Auditors will select accounts at random from the following 1000 accounts (numbers in the table are the number of accounts in each category):

	Account Balance		
Age of the Account	0–$499	$500–$999	$1000 or More
Less than 2 years	120	240	90
2 years or more	75	275	200

    a. What is the probability that an account is less than 2 years old?
    b. What is the probability that an account has a balance of $1000 or more?
    c. What is the probability that two accounts will both have a balance of $1000 or more?
    d. What is the probability has a balance of $500–$999 given that its age is 2 years or more?

e. What is the probability that an account is less than 2 years old and has a balance of $1000 or more?

f. What is the probability that an account is at least 2 years old given that the balance is $500–$999?

15. Due to rising health insurance costs, 43 million people in the United States go without health insurance (*Time,* December 1, 2003). Sample data representative of the national health insurance coverage for individuals 18 years of age and older are shown here.

		Health Insurance	
		Yes	**No**
Age	18 to 34	750	170
	35 and over	950	130

a. Develop a joint probability table for these data and use the table to answer the remaining questions.

b. What do the marginal probabilities tell you about the age of the U.S. population?

c. What is the probability that a randomly selected individual does not have health insurance coverage?

d. If the individual is between the ages of 18 and 34, what is the probability that the individual does not have health insurance coverage?

e. If the individual is age 35 or over, what is the probability that the individual does not have health insurance coverage?

f. If the individual does not have health insurance, what is the probability that the individual is in the 18–34 age group?

g. What does the probability information tell you about health insurance coverage in the United States?

16. A purchasing agent placed a rush order for a particular raw material with two different suppliers, *A* and *B.* If neither order arrives in four days the production process must be shut down until at least one of the orders arrives. The probability that supplier *A* can deliver the material in four days is 0.55. The probability that supplier *B* can deliver the material in four days is 0.35.

a. What is the probability that both suppliers deliver the material in four days? Because two separate suppliers are involved, assume independence.

b. What is the probability that at least one supplier delivers the material in four days?

c. What is the probability the production process is shut down in four days because of a shortage in raw material (that is, both orders are late)?

17. A study of job satisfaction was conducted for four occupations: cabinetmaker, lawyer, physical therapist, and systems analyst. Job satisfaction was measured on a scale of 0–100. The data obtained are summarized in the following crosstabulation.

	Satisfaction Score				
Occupation	**Under 50**	**50–59**	**60–69**	**70–79**	**80–89**
Cabinetmaker	0	2	4	3	1
Lawyer	6	2	1	1	0
Physical Therapist	0	5	2	1	2
Systems Analyst	2	1	4	3	0

    a.   Develop a joint probability table.

    b.   What is the probability a randomly chosen participant has a satisfaction score in the 80s?

    c.   What is the probability of a satisfaction score in the 80s given the study participant was a physical therapist?

    d.   What is the probability a randomly chosen participant is a lawyer?

    e.   What is the probability a randomly chosen participant is a lawyer and received a score under 50?

    f.   What is the probability of a satisfaction score under 50 given a person is a lawyer?

    g.   What is the probability of a satisfaction score of 70 or higher?

18. In the evaluation of a sales training program, a firm discovered that of 50 salespeople receiving a bonus last year, 20 had attended a special sales training program. The firm employs 200 salespeople. Let B = the event that a salesperson makes a bonus and S = the event that a salesperson attends the sales training program.

    a.   Find $P(B)$, $P(S \mid B)$, and $P(S \cap B)$.

    b.   Assume that 40% of the salespeople attended the training program. What is the probability that a salesperson makes a bonus given that the salesperson attended the sales training program, $P(B \mid S)$?

    c.   If the firm evaluates the training program in terms of its effect on the probability of a salesperson's receiving a bonus, what is your evaluation of the training program? Comment on whether B and S are dependent or independent events.

19. A company studied the number of lost-time accidents occurring at its Brownsville, Texas, plant. Historical records show that 6% of the employees had lost-time accidents last year. Management believes that a special safety program will reduce the accidents to 5% during the current year. In addition, it estimates that 15% of those employees having had lost-time accidents last year will have a lost-time accident during the current year.

    a.   What percentage of the employees will have lost-time accidents in both years?

    b.   What percentage of the employees will have at least one lost-time accident over the two-year period?

20. The prior probabilities for events A_1, A_2, and A_3 are $P(A_1) = 0.20$, $P(A_2) = 0.50$, and $P(A_3) = 0.30$. The conditional probabilities of event B given A_1, A_2, and A_3 are $P(B \mid A_1) = 0.50$, $P(B \mid A_2) = 0.40$, and $P(B \mid A_3) = 0.30$.

    a.   Compute $P(B \cap A_1)$, $P(B \cap A_2)$, and $P(B \cap A_3)$.

    b.   Apply Bayes' theorem, equation (2.16), to compute the posterior probability $P(A_2 \mid B)$.

    c.   Use the tabular approach to applying Bayes' theorem to compute $P(A_1 \mid B)$, $P(A_2 \mid B)$, and $P(A_3 \mid B)$.

21. A consulting firm submitted a bid for a large research project. The firm's management initially felt there was a 50/50 chance of getting the bid. However, the agency to which the bid was submitted subsequently requested additional information on the bid. Experience indicates that on 75% of the successful bids and 40% of the unsuccessful bids the agency requested additional information.

    a.   What is the prior probability the bid will be successful (i.e., prior to receiving the request for additional information)?

    b.   What is the conditional probability of a request for additional information given that the bid will ultimately be successful?

    c.   Compute a posterior probability that the bid will be successful given that a request for additional information has been received.

22. Companies that do business over the Internet can often obtain probability information about Web site visitors from previous Web sites visited. For instance, the Q.M. in Action, Internet Marketing, described how clickstream data on Web sites visited could be used in

conjunction with a Bayesian updating scheme to determine the probability that a Web site visitor was female. Par Fore created a Web site to market golf equipment and apparel. Management would like a certain offer to appear for female visitors and a different offer to appear for male visitors. A sample of past Web site visits indicates that 60% of the visitors to *ParFore.com* are male and 40% are female.

a. What is your prior probability that the next visitor to the Web site will be female?
b. Suppose you know that the current visitor previously visited the Dillards Web site and that women are three times as likely to visit this Web site as men. What is your revised probability that the visitor is female? Should you display the offer that has more appeal to female visitors or the one that has more appeal to male visitors?

23. An oil company purchased an option on land in Alaska. Preliminary geologic studies assigned the following prior probabilities.

$$P(\text{high-quality oil}) = 0.50$$
$$P(\text{medium-quality oil}) = 0.20$$
$$P(\text{no oil}) = 0.30$$

a. What is the probability of finding oil?
b. After 200 feet of drilling on the first well, a soil test is made. The probabilities of finding the particular type of soil identified by the test are

$$P(\text{soil} \mid \text{high-quality oil}) = 0.20$$
$$P(\text{soil} \mid \text{medium-quality oil}) = 0.80$$
$$P(\text{soil} \mid \text{no oil}) = 0.30$$

How should the firm interpret the soil test? What are the revised probabilities, and what is the new probability of finding oil?

24. Small cars get better gas mileage, but they are not as safe as bigger cars. Small cars accounted for 18% of the vehicles on the road, but accidents involving small cars led to 11,898 fatalities during a recent year (*Reader's Digest,* May 2000). Assume the probability a small car is involved in an accident is 0.18. The probability of an accident involving a small car leading to a fatality is 0.128 and the probability of an accident not involving a small car leading to a fatality is 0.05. Suppose you learn of an accident involving a fatality. What is the probability a small car was involved?

25. The Wayne Manufacturing Company purchases a certain part from suppliers A, B, and C. Supplier A supplies 60% of the parts, B 30%, and C 10%. The quality of parts varies among the suppliers, with A, B, and C parts having 0.25%, 1%, and 2% defective rates, respectively. The parts are used in one of the company's major products.

a. What is the probability that the company's major product is assembled with a defective part? Use the tabular approach to Bayes' theorem to solve.
b. When a defective part is found, which supplier is the likely source?

26. Bayes' theorem and conditional probability can be used in medical diagnosis. Prior probabilities of diseases are based on the physician's assessment of factors such as geographic location, seasonal influence, and occurrence of epidemics. Assume that a patient is believed to have one of two diseases, denoted D_1 and D_2, with $P(D_1) = 0.60$ and $P(D_2) = 0.40$ and that medical research shows a probability associated with each symptom that may accompany the diseases. Suppose that, given diseases D_1 and D_2, the probabilities a patient will have symptoms S_1, S_2, or S_3 are as follows:

		Symptoms		
		S_1	S_2	S_3
Disease	D_1	0.15	0.10	0.15
	D_2	0.80	0.15	0.03

$P(S_3 \mid D_1)$

After finding that a certain symptom is present, the medical diagnosis may be aided by finding the revised probabilities the patient has each particular disease. Compute the posterior probabilities of each disease for the following medical findings.

a. The patient has symptom S_1.
b. The patient has symptom S_2.
c. The patient has symptom S_3.
d. For the patient with symptom S_1 in part (a), suppose that symptom S_2 also is present. What are the revised probabilities of D_1 and D_2?

Case Problem   Hamilton County Judges

Hamilton County judges try thousands of cases per year. In an overwhelming majority of the cases disposed, the verdict stands as rendered. However, some cases are appealed, and of those appealed, some of the cases are reversed. Kristen DelGuzzi of the *Cincinnati Enquirer* conducted a study of cases handled by Hamilton County judges over a three-year period (*Cincinnati Enquirer*, January 11, 1998). Shown in Table 2.5 are the results for 182,908 cases handled (disposed) by 38 judges in Common Pleas Court, Domestic Relations Court, and Municipal Court. Two of the judges (Dinkelacker and Hogan) did not serve in the same court for the entire three-year period.

The purpose of the newspaper's study was to evaluate the performance of the judges. Appeals are often the result of mistakes made by judges, and the newspaper wanted to know which judges were doing a good job and which were making too many mistakes. You have been called in to assist in the data analysis. Use your knowledge of probability and conditional probability to help with the ranking of the judges. You also may be able to analyze the likelihood of cases handled by the different courts being appealed and reversed.

Managerial Report

Prepare a report with your rankings of the judges. Also include an analysis of the likelihood of appeal and case reversal in the three courts. At a minimum, your report should include the following:

1. The probability of cases being appealed and reversed in the three different courts
2. The probability of a case being appealed for each judge
3. The probability of a case being reversed for each judge
4. The probability of reversal given an appeal for each judge
5. Rank the judges within each court. State the criteria you used and provide a rationale for your choice.

TABLE 2.5   CASES DISPOSED, APPEALED, AND REVERSED IN HAMILTON COUNTY COURTS

Common Pleas Court

Judge	Total Cases Disposed	Appealed Cases	Reversed Cases
Fred Cartolano	3037	137	12
Thomas Crush	3372	119	10
Patrick Dinkelacker	1258	44	8
Timothy Hogan	1954	60	7
Robert Kraft	3138	127	7
William Mathews	2264	91	18
William Morrissey	3032	121	22
Norbert Nadel	2959	131	20
Arthur Ney, Jr.	3219	125	14
Richard Niehaus	3353	137	16
Thomas Nurre	3000	121	6
John O'Connor	2969	129	12
Robert Ruehlman	3205	145	18
J. Howard Sundermann	955	60	10
Ann Marie Tracey	3141	127	13
Ralph Winkler	3089	88	6
Total	43,945	1762	199

Domestic Relations Court

Judge	Total Cases Disposed	Appealed Cases	Reversed Cases
Penelope Cunningham	2729	7	1
Patrick Dinkelacker	6001	19	4
Deborah Gaines	8799	48	9
Ronald Panioto	12,970	32	3
Total	30,499	106	17

Municipal Court

Judge	Total Cases Disposed	Appealed Cases	Reversed Cases
Mike Allen	6149	43	4
Nadine Allen	7812	34	6
Timothy Black	7954	41	6
David Davis	7736	43	5
Leslie Isaiah Gaines	5282	35	13
Karla Grady	5253	6	0
Deidra Hair	2532	5	0
Dennis Helmick	7900	29	5
Timothy Hogan	2308	13	2
James Patrick Kenney	2798	6	1
Joseph Luebbers	4698	25	8
William Mallory	8277	38	9
Melba Marsh	8219	34	7
Beth Mattingly	2971	13	1
Albert Mestemaker	4975	28	9
Mark Painter	2239	7	3
Jack Rosen	7790	41	13
Mark Schweikert	5403	33	6
David Stockdale	5371	22	4
John A. West	2797	4	2
Total	108,464	500	104

CHAPTER 3

Probability Distributions

CONTENTS

In this chapter we continue the study of probability by introducing the concepts of random variables and probability distributions. We consider the probability distributions of both discrete and continuous random variables. Of particular interest are five special probability distributions: the binomial, the Poisson, the uniform, the normal, and the exponential. These probability distributions are important because they are used extensively in practice. The Q.M. in Action, Probability Distributions and a Treasure Hunt, describes how the development and use of a probability distribution helped find a sunken ship.

Q.M. *in* ACTION

PROBABILITY DISTRIBUTIONS AND A TREASURE HUNT*

The use of probability distributions played a key role in the location of a sunken ship. In 1857, while carrying passengers and gold from California to New York, the SS *Central America* sank in a hurricane, taking gold bars and coins worth an estimated $400 million to the ocean bottom. Central to the creation of the search plan was the development of a probability distribution for the position of the sunken ship.

Work began on developing the probability distribution in the summer of 1985. It involved combining information from various sources: Captain Herndon's last

reported position, sightings by other ships, the drift of survivors, estimates of wind speed and ocean currents, and the like. Based on the information available, three separate probability distributions were developed and then merged into one, with subjective weights being assigned by the analysts. A search plan was based on these probabilities, and the actual search began during the summer of 1986.

Not until the summer of 1988 was the wreck finally discovered. In the summer of 1989, one ton of gold bars and gold coins was recovered from the wreck. The search team concluded that the sunken ship probably would not have been found without the use of the probability distribution for its location.

---
*Based on Lawrence D. Stone, "Search for the SS *Central America*: Mathematical Treasure Hunting," *Interfaces* 22, no. 3 (1992): 32–54.

Random Variables

Recall that in Chapter 2 we defined an experiment as any process that generates well-defined outcomes. We now want to concentrate on the process of assigning *numerical values* to experimental outcomes. To do so we introduce the notion of a random variable.

For any particular experiment a random variable can be defined so that each possible experimental outcome generates exactly one numerical value for the random variable. For example, if we consider the experiment of selling automobiles for one day at a particular dealership, we could describe the experimental outcomes in terms of the *number* of cars sold. In this case, if x = number of cars sold, x is called a random variable. The particular numerical value that the random variable assumes depends on the outcome of the experiment; that is, we will not know the specific value of the random variable until we have observed the experimental outcome. For example, if on a given day three cars are sold, the value of the random variable is 3; if on another day (a repeat of the experiment) four cars are sold, the value is 4. We define a random variable as follows:

Random variables must assume numerical values.

A **random variable** is a numerical description of the outcome of an experiment.

Some additional examples of experiments and their associated random variables are given in Table 3.1. Although many experiments have experimental outcomes that lend themselves quite naturally to numerical values, others do not. For example, for the experiment of

TABLE 3.1   EXAMPLES OF RANDOM VARIABLES

Experiment	Random Variable (x)	Possible Values for the Random Variable
Make 100 sales calls	Total number of sales	0, 1, 2, . . . , 100
Inspect a shipment of 70 radios	Number of defective radios	0, 1, 2, . . . , 70
Build a new library	Percentage of project completed after 6 months	$0 \leq x \leq 100$
Operate a restaurant	Number of customers entering in one day	0, 1, 2, . . .

tossing a coin one time, the experimental outcome will be either a head or a tail, neither of which has a natural numerical value. However, we still may want to express the outcomes in terms of a random variable. Thus, we need a rule that can be used to assign a numerical value to each of the experimental outcomes. One possibility is to let the random variable $x = 1$ if the experimental outcome is a head and $x = 0$ if the experimental outcome is a tail. Although the numerical values for x are arbitrary, x is a random variable because it describes the experimental outcomes numerically.

A random variable may be classified as either discrete or continuous, depending on the numerical values it may assume. A random variable that may assume only a finite or an infinite sequence (e.g., 1, 2, 3, . . .) of values is a **discrete random variable**. The number of units sold, the number of defects observed, the number of customers that enter a bank during one day of operation, and so on, are examples of discrete random variables. The first two and the last random variables in Table 3.1 are discrete. Random variables such as weight, time, and temperature that may assume any value in a certain interval or collection of intervals are **continuous random variables**. For instance, the third random variable in Table 3.1 is a continuous random variable because it may assume any value in the interval from 0 to 100 (for example, 56.33 or 64.223).

Try Problem 1 for practice in identifying discrete and continuous random variables.

NOTES AND COMMENTS

One way to determine whether a random variable is discrete or continuous is to think of the values of the random variable as points on a line. Choose two points representing values the random variable might assume. If the entire line segment between the two points also represents possible values for the random variable, the random variable is continuous.

3.2 Discrete Random Variables

We can demonstrate the use of a discrete random variable by considering the sales of automobiles at DiCarlo Motors, Inc., in Saratoga, New York. The owner of DiCarlo Motors is interested in the daily sales volume for automobiles. Suppose that we let x be a random variable denoting the number of cars sold on a given day. Sales records show that 5 is the maximum number of cars that DiCarlo has ever sold during one day. The owner believes that the previous history of sales adequately represents what will occur in the future, so we would expect the random variable x to assume one of the numerical values 0, 1, 2, 3, 4, or 5. The possible values of the random variable are finite; thus we would classify x as a discrete random variable.

TABLE 3.2　CARS SOLD PER DAY AT DICARLO MOTORS

Sales Volume	Number of Days
No sales	54
One car	117
Two cars	72
Three cars	42
Four cars	12
Five cars	3
Total	300

Probability Distribution of a Discrete Random Variable

Suppose that in checking DiCarlo's sales records we find that over the past year the firm was open for business 300 days. The sales volumes generated and the frequency of their occurrence are summarized in Table 3.2. With these historical data available, the owner of DiCarlo Motors believes that the relative frequency method will provide a reasonable means of assessing the probabilities for the random variable x. The **probability function,** denoted $f(x)$, provides the probability that the random variable x takes on a specific value. Because on 54 of the 300 days of historical data DiCarlo Motors did not sell any cars and because no sales corresponds to $x = 0$, we assign to $f(0)$ the value $^{54}/_{300} = 0.18$. Similarly, $f(1)$ denotes the probability that x takes on the value 1, so we assign to $f(1)$ the value $^{117}/_{300} = 0.39$. After computing the relative frequencies for the other possible values of x, we can develop a table of x and $f(x)$ values. Table 3.3 shows a tabular presentation of the probability distribution of the random variable x.

We can also represent the probability distribution of x graphically. In Figure 3.1 the values of the random variable x are shown on the horizontal axis. The probability that x takes on these values is shown on the vertical axis. For many discrete random variables the probability distribution also can be represented as a formula that provides $f(x)$ for every possible value of x. We illustrate this approach in the next section.

In Section 2.2 we defined the two basic requirements of all probability assignments as $0 \leq P(E_i) \leq 1$ and $\Sigma P(E_i) = 1$. Equations (3.1) and (3.2) are the analogs of these basic requirements.

In the development of a **discrete probability distribution,** two requirements must always be satisfied:

$$f(x) \geq 0 \tag{3.1}$$

$$\Sigma f(x) = 1 \tag{3.2}$$

TABLE 3.3　PROBABILITY DISTRIBUTION FOR THE NUMBER OF CARS SOLD PER DAY

x	$f(x)$
0	0.18
1	0.39
2	0.24
3	0.14
4	0.04
5	0.01
Total	1.00

FIGURE 3.1 PROBABILITY DISTRIBUTION FOR THE NUMBER OF CARS SOLD PER DAY

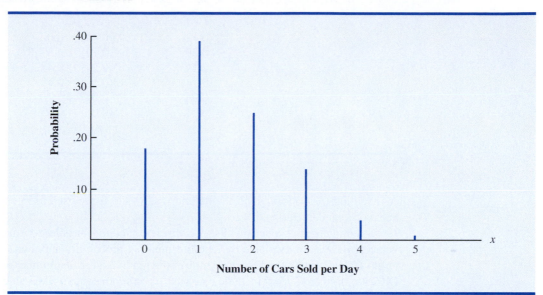

Requirement (3.1) specifies that the probabilities associated with each value of x must be greater than or equal to zero, whereas requirement (3.2) indicates that the sum of the probabilities for all values of the random variable x must be equal to 1. Table 3.3 shows that requirements (3.1) and (3.2) are satisfied. Thus, the probability distribution developed for DiCarlo Motors is a valid discrete probability distribution.

After establishing a random variable and its probability distribution, we can develop a variety of additional probability information, depending on the needs and interests of the decision maker. For example, in the DiCarlo Motors problem the probability distribution shown in Table 3.3 can be used to provide the following information:

1. There is a 0.18 probability that no cars will be sold during a day.
2. The most probable sales volume is 1, with $f(1) = 0.39$.
3. There is a 0.05 probability of an outstanding sales day with four or five cars being sold.

Try Problem 3 for practice in constructing a discrete probability distribution.

Using probability information such as that just given, DiCarlo's management can understand better the uncertainties associated with the car sales operation. Perhaps this improved understanding can serve as the basis for a new policy or decision that will increase the effectiveness of the firm.

Expected Value

After constructing the probability distribution for a random variable, we often want to compute the mean or expected value of the random variable. The **expected value** of a discrete random variable is a weighted average of all possible values of the random variable, where the weights are the probabilities associated with the values. The mathematical formula for computing the expected value of a discrete random variable x is

$$E(x) = \mu = \Sigma x f(x) \qquad \text{(3.3)}$$

TABLE 3.4   EXPECTED VALUE CALCULATION

x	$f(x)$	$xf(x)$
0	0.18	$0(0.18) = 0.00$
1	0.39	$1(0.39) = 0.39$
2	0.24	$2(0.24) = 0.48$
3	0.14	$3(0.14) = 0.42$
4	0.04	$4(0.04) = 0.16$
5	0.01	$5(0.01) = \underline{0.05}$
		$E(x) = 1.50$

As equation (3.3) shows, both the notations $E(x)$ and μ are used to refer to the expected value of a random variable.

To compute the expected value of a discrete random variable, we must multiply each value of the random variable by its corresponding probability and then add the resulting terms. Calculation of the expected value of the random variable (number of daily sales) for DiCarlo Motors is shown in Table 3.4. The first column contains the values of the random variable x, and the second column contains their associated probabilities $f(x)$. Multiplying each value of x by its probability $f(x)$ provides the $xf(x)$ values in the third column. Following equation (3.3), we sum this column, $\sum xf(x)$, to find the expected value of 1.50 cars sold per day.

The expected value of a random variable is the mean, or average, value. For experiments that can be repeated numerous times, the expected value can be interpreted as the "long-run" average value for the random variable. However, the expected value is not necessarily the number that we think the random variable will assume the next time the experiment is conducted. In fact, it is impossible for DiCarlo to sell exactly 1.50 cars on any day. However, if we envision selling cars at DiCarlo Motors for many days into the future, the expected value of 1.50 cars provides the mean, or average, daily sales volume.

The expected value can be important to a manager from both the planning and decision-making points of view. For example, suppose that DiCarlo Motors will be open 60 days during the next three months. How many cars will be sold during this time? Although we can't specify the exact sales for any given day, the expected value of 1.50 cars per day provides an expected or average sales estimate of $60(1.50) = 90$ cars for the next three-month period. In terms of setting sales quotas and/or planning orders, the expected value may provide helpful decision-making information.

Variance

The expected value gives us an idea of the average or central value for the random variable, but we often want a measure of the dispersion, or variability, of the possible values of the random variable. For example, if the values of the random variable range from quite large to quite small, we would expect a large value for the measure of variability. If the values of the random variable show only modest variation, we would expect a relatively small value. The variance is a measure commonly used to summarize the variability in the values of a random variable. The mathematical expression for the *variance* of a discrete random variable is

An alternative formula for the variance of a discrete random variable is Var(x) = $\sum x^2 f(x) - \mu^2$.

$$\text{Var}(x) = \sigma^2 = \sum (x - \mu)^2 f(x) \qquad \textbf{(3.4)}$$

TABLE 3.5 VARIANCE CALCULATION

x	$x - \mu$	$(x - \mu)^2$	$f(x)$	$(x - \mu)^2 f(x)$
0	$0 - 1.50 = -1.50$	2.25	0.18	$2.25(0.18) = 0.4050$
1	$1 - 1.50 = -0.50$	0.25	0.39	$0.25(0.39) = 0.0975$
2	$2 - 1.50 = 0.50$	0.25	0.24	$0.25(0.24) = 0.0600$
3	$3 - 1.50 = 1.50$	2.25	0.14	$2.25(0.14) = 0.3150$
4	$4 - 1.50 = 2.50$	6.25	0.04	$6.25(0.04) = 0.2500$
5	$5 - 1.50 = 3.50$	12.25	0.01	$12.25(0.01) = \underline{0.1225}$
				$\sigma^2 = 1.2500$

As equation (3.4) shows, an essential part of the variance formula is a *deviation, $x - \mu$,* which measures how far a particular value of the random variable is from the expected value or mean, μ. In computing the variance of a discrete random variable, we square the deviations and then weight them by the corresponding probability. The sum of these weighted squared deviations for all values of the random variable is the **variance**. In other words, the variance is a weighted average of the squared deviations.

The calculation of the variance for the number of daily sales in the DiCarlo Motors problem is summarized in Table 3.5. We see that the variance for the number of cars sold per day is 1.25. A related measure of variability is the **standard deviation**, σ, which is defined as the positive square root of the variance. For DiCarlo Motors, the standard deviation of the number of cars sold per day is

$$\sigma = \sqrt{1.25} = 1.118$$

For the purpose of easier managerial interpretation, the standard deviation may be preferred over the variance because it is measured in the same units as the random variable ($\sigma = 1.118$ cars sold per day). The variance (σ^2) is measured in squared units and is thus more difficult for a manager to interpret.

Try Problem 4 to be sure you can compute the expected value, variance, and standard deviation.

At this point our interpretation of the variance and the standard deviation is limited to comparisons of the variability of different random variables. For example, if the daily sales data from a second DiCarlo dealership in Albany, New York, provided $\sigma^2 = 2.56$ and $\sigma = 1.6$, we can conclude that the number of cars sold per day at this dealership exhibits more variability than at the first DiCarlo dealership, where $\sigma^2 = 1.25$ and $\sigma = 1.118$. Later in this chapter we discuss the normal distribution. For that probability distribution, we show that the variance and the standard deviation of the random variable are essential for making probability calculations.

3.3 Binomial Probability Distribution

In this section we consider a class of experiments that meet the following conditions:

1. The experiment consists of a sequence of n identical *trials*.
2. Two outcomes are possible on each trial. We refer to one outcome as a *success* and the other as a *failure*.
3. The probabilities of the two outcomes do not change from one trial to the next.
4. The trials are independent (i.e., the outcome of one trial does not affect the outcome of any other trial).

Experiments that satisfy conditions 2, 3, and 4 are said to be generated by a *Bernoulli process*. In addition, if condition 1 is satisfied (there are *n* identical trials), we have a *binomial experiment*. An important discrete random variable associated with the binomial experiment is the number of outcomes labeled success in the *n* trials. If we let *x* denote the value of this random variable, then *x* can have a value of 0, 1, 2, 3, . . . , *n*, depending on the number of successes observed in the *n* trials. The probability distribution associated with this random variable is called the **binomial probability distribution**.

Try Problem 9, parts (a–d), for practice computing binomial probabilities.

In cases where the binomial distribution is applicable, the mathematical formula for computing the probability of any value for the random variable is the binomial probability function

$$f(x) = \frac{n!}{x!(n-x)!} p^x (1-p)^{n-x} \qquad x = 0, 1, \ldots, n \qquad \text{(3.5)}$$

where

$$n = \text{number of trials}$$
$$p = \text{probability of success on one trial}$$
$$x = \text{number of successes in } n \text{ trials}$$
$$f(x) = \text{probability of } x \text{ successes in } n \text{ trials}$$

The term *n*! in the preceding expression is referred to as *n factorial* and is defined as

$$n! = n(n-1)(n-2) \cdots (2)(1)$$

For example, 4! = (4)(3)(2)(1) = 24. Also, by definition, the special case of zero factorial is 0! = 1.

Nastke Clothing Store Problem

To illustrate the binomial probability distribution, let us consider the experiment of customers entering the Nastke Clothing Store. To keep the problem relatively small, we restrict the experiment to the next three customers. If, based on experience, the store manager estimates that the probability of a customer making a purchase is 0.30, what is the probability that exactly two of the next three customers make a purchase?

We first want to demonstrate that three customers entering the clothing store and deciding whether to make a purchase can be viewed as a binomial experiment. Checking the four requirements for a binomial experiment, we note the following:

1. The experiment can be described as a sequence of three identical trials, one trial for each of the three customers who will enter the store.
2. Two outcomes—the customer makes a purchase (success) or the customer does not make a purchase (failure)—are possible for each trial.
3. The probabilities of the purchase (0.30) and no purchase (0.70) outcomes are assumed to be the same for all customers.
4. The purchase decision of each customer is independent of the purchase decision of the other customers.

Thus, if we define the random variable *x* as the number of customers making a purchase (i.e., the number of successes in the three trials), we satisfy the requirements of the binomial probability distribution.

With $n = 3$ trials and the probability of a purchase $p = 0.30$ for each customer, we use equation (3.5) to compute the probability of two customers making a purchase. This probability, denoted $f(2)$, is

$$f(2) = \frac{3!}{2!1!}(0.30)^2(0.70)^1$$

$$= \frac{3 \times 2 \times 1}{2 \times 1 \times 1}(0.30)^2(0.70)^1 = 0.189$$

Try Problem 12 for an application of the binomial distribution.

Similarly, the probability of no customers making a purchase, denoted $f(0)$, is

$$f(0) = \frac{3!}{0!3!}(0.30)^0(0.70)^3$$

$$= \frac{3 \times 2 \times 1}{1 \times 3 \times 2 \times 1}(0.30)^0(0.70)^3 = 0.343$$

Similarly, equation (3.5) can be used to show that the probabilities of one and three purchases are $f(1) = 0.441$ and $f(3) = 0.027$. Table 3.6 and Figure 3.2 summarize the binomial probability distribution for the Nastke Clothing Store problem.

If we consider any variation of the Nastke problem, such as 10 customers rather than 3 customers entering the store, the binomial probability function given by equation (3.5) still applies. For example, the probability that 4 of the 10 customers make a purchase is

$$f(4) = \frac{10!}{4!6!}(0.30)^4(0.70)^6 = 0.2001$$

In this binomial experiment, $n = 10$, $x = 4$, and $p = 0.30$.

With the use of equation (3.5), tables have been developed that provide the probability of x successes in n trials for a binomial experiment. Such a table of binomial probability values is provided in Appendix B. We include a partial binomial table in Table 3.7. In order to use this table, specify the values of n, p, and x for the binomial experiment of interest. Check the use of this table by employing it to verify the probability of four successes in 10 trials for the Nastke Clothing Store problem. Note that the value of $f(4) = 0.2001$ can be read directly from the table of binomial probabilities, making it unnecessary to perform the calculations required by equation (3.5).

With modern calculators, these tables are almost unnecessary. It is easy to evaluate equation (3.5) directly.

TABLE 3.6   PROBABILITY DISTRIBUTION FOR THE NUMBER OF CUSTOMERS MAKING A PURCHASE

x	$f(x)$
0	0.343
1	0.441
2	0.189
3	0.027
Total	1.000

FIGURE 3.2   PROBABILITY DISTRIBUTION FOR THE NASTKE CLOTHING STORE
PROBLEM

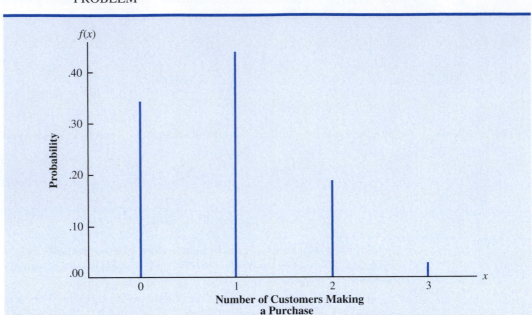

Expected Value and Variance for the Binomial Distribution

From the probability distribution in Table 3.6, we can use equation (3.3) to compute the expected value or expected number of customers making a purchase:

$$\mu = \Sigma x f(x) = 0(0.343) + 1(0.441) + 2(0.189) + 3(0.027) = 0.9$$

Note that we could have obtained this same expected value simply by multiplying n (the number of trials) by p (the probability of success on any one trial):

$$np = 3(0.30) = 0.9$$

For the special case of a binomial probability distribution, the expected value of the random variable is given by

$$\mu = np \tag{3.6}$$

Thus, if you know that the probability distribution is binomial, you do not have to make the detailed calculations required by equation (3.3) to compute the expected value.

Suppose that during the next month Nastke's Clothing Store expects 1000 customers to enter the store. What is the expected number of customers who will make a purchase? Using equation (3.6), the answer is $\mu = np = (1000)(0.3) = 300$. To increase the expected number of sales, Nastke's must induce more customers to enter the store and/or somehow increase the probability that any individual customer will make a purchase after entering.

TABLE 3.7 SELECTED VALUES FROM THE BINOMIAL PROBABILITY TABLE. EXAMPLE: $n = 10, x = 4$, $p = 0.30; f(4) = 0.2001$

n	x					p					
		0.05	0.10	0.15	0.20	0.25	0.30	0.35	0.40	0.45	0.50
9	0	0.6302	0.3874	0.2316	0.1342	0.0751	0.0404	0.0207	0.0101	0.0046	0.0020
	1	0.2985	0.3874	0.3679	0.3020	0.2253	0.1556	0.1004	0.0605	0.0339	0.0176
	2	0.0629	0.1722	0.2597	0.3020	0.3003	0.2668	0.2162	0.1612	0.1110	0.0703
	3	0.0077	0.0446	0.1069	0.1762	0.2336	0.2668	0.2716	0.2508	0.2119	0.1641
	4	0.0006	0.0074	0.0283	0.0661	0.1168	0.1715	0.2194	0.2508	0.2600	0.2461
	5	0.0000	0.0008	0.0050	0.0165	0.0389	0.0735	0.1181	0.1672	0.2128	0.2461
	6	0.0000	0.0001	0.0006	0.0028	0.0087	0.0210	0.0424	0.0743	0.1160	0.1641
	7	0.0000	0.0000	0.0000	0.0003	0.0012	0.0039	0.0098	0.0212	0.0407	0.0703
	8	0.0000	0.0000	0.0000	0.0000	0.0001	0.0004	0.0013	0.0035	0.0083	0.0176
	9	0.0000	0.0000	0.0000	0.0000	0.0000	0.0000	0.0001	0.0003	0.0008	0.0020
10	0	0.5987	0.3487	0.1969	0.1074	0.0563	0.0282	0.0135	0.0060	0.0025	0.0010
	1	0.3151	0.3874	0.3474	0.2684	0.1877	0.1211	0.0725	0.0403	0.0207	0.0098
	2	0.0746	0.1937	0.2759	0.3020	0.2816	0.2335	0.1757	0.1209	0.0763	0.0439
	3	0.0105	0.0574	0.1298	0.2013	0.2503	0.2668	0.2522	0.2150	0.1665	0.1172
	4	0.0010	0.0112	0.0401	0.0881	0.1460	**0.2001**	0.2377	0.2508	0.2384	0.2051
	5	0.0001	0.0015	0.0085	0.0264	0.0584	0.1029	0.1536	0.2007	0.2340	0.2461
	6	0.0000	0.0001	0.0012	0.0055	0.0162	0.0368	0.0689	0.1115	0.1596	0.2051
	7	0.0000	0.0000	0.0001	0.0008	0.0031	0.0090	0.0212	0.0425	0.0746	0.1172
	8	0.0000	0.0000	0.0000	0.0001	0.0004	0.0014	0.0043	0.0106	0.0229	0.0439
	9	0.0000	0.0000	0.0000	0.0000	0.0000	0.0001	0.0005	0.0016	0.0042	0.0098
	10	0.0000	0.0000	0.0000	0.0000	0.0000	0.0000	0.0000	0.0001	0.0003	0.0010
11	0	0.5688	0.3138	0.1673	0.0859	0.0422	0.0198	0.0088	0.0036	0.0014	0.0005
	1	0.3293	0.3835	0.3248	0.2362	0.1549	0.0932	0.0518	0.0266	0.0125	0.0054
	2	0.0867	0.2131	0.2866	0.2953	0.2581	0.1998	0.1395	0.0887	0.0531	0.0269
	3	0.0137	0.0710	0.1517	0.2215	0.2581	0.2568	0.2254	0.1774	0.1259	0.0806
	4	0.0014	0.0158	0.0536	0.1107	0.1721	0.2201	0.2428	0.2365	0.2060	0.1611
	5	0.0001	0.0025	0.0132	0.0388	0.0803	0.1321	0.1830	0.2207	0.2360	0.2256
	6	0.0000	0.0003	0.0023	0.0097	0.0268	0.0566	0.0985	0.1471	0.1931	0.2256
	7	0.0000	0.0000	0.0003	0.0017	0.0064	0.0173	0.0379	0.0701	0.1128	0.1611
	8	0.0000	0.0000	0.0000	0.0002	0.0011	0.0037	0.0102	0.0234	0.0462	0.0806
	9	0.0000	0.0000	0.0000	0.0000	0.0001	0.0005	0.0018	0.0052	0.0126	0.0269
	10	0.0000	0.0000	0.0000	0.0000	0.0000	0.0000	0.0002	0.0007	0.0021	0.0054
	11	0.0000	0.0000	0.0000	0.0000	0.0000	0.0000	0.0000	0.0000	0.0002	0.0005

For the special case of a binomial distribution, the variance of the random variable is

Try Problem 9, part (e), for practice computing the expected value, variance, and standard deviation.

$$\sigma^2 = np(1 - p) \tag{3.7}$$

For the Nastke Clothing Store problem with three customers, the variance and standard deviation for the number of customers making a purchase are

$$\sigma^2 = np(1 - p) = 3(0.3)(0.7) = 0.63$$
$$\sigma = \sqrt{0.63} = 0.79$$

3.4 Poisson Probability Distribution

In this section we will consider a discrete random variable that often is useful when we are dealing with the number of occurrences of an event over a specified interval of time or space. For example, the random variable of interest might be the number of arrivals at a car wash in 1 hour, the number of repairs needed in 10 miles of highway, or the number of leaks in 100 miles of pipeline. If the following two assumptions are satisfied, the **Poisson probability distribution** is applicable:

1. The probability of an occurrence of the event is the same for any two intervals of equal length.
2. The occurrence or nonoccurrence of the event in any interval is independent of the occurrence or nonoccurrence in any other interval.

The probability function of the Poisson random variable is given by equation (3.8):

$$f(x) = \frac{\lambda^x e^{-\lambda}}{x!} \qquad \text{for } x = 0, 1, 2, \ldots \qquad \textbf{(3.8)}$$

where

$$\lambda = \text{mean or average number of occurrences in an interval}$$
$$e = 2.71828$$
$$x = \text{number of occurrences in the interval}$$
$$f(x) = \text{probability of } x \text{ occurrences in the interval}$$

Note that equation (3.8) shows no upper limit to the number of possible values that a Poisson random variable can take on. That is, x is a discrete random variable with an infinite sequence of values ($x = 0, 1, 2, \ldots$); the Poisson random variable has no set upper limit.

An Example Involving Time Intervals

Suppose that we are interested in the number of arrivals at the drive-in teller window of a bank during a 15-minute period on weekday mornings. If we assume that the probability of a car arriving is the same for any two time periods of equal length and that the arrival or nonarrival of a car in any time period is independent of the arrival or nonarrival in any other time period, the Poisson probability function is applicable. Then if we assume that an analysis of historical data shows that the average number of cars arriving during a 15-minute interval of time is 10, the Poisson probability function with $\lambda = 10$ applies,

$$f(x) = \frac{\lambda^x e^{-\lambda}}{x!} = \frac{10^x e^{-10}}{x!} \qquad \text{for } x = 0, 1, 2, \ldots$$

Bell Labs used the Poisson distribution in modeling the arrival of phone calls.

If we wanted to know the probability of five arrivals in 15 minutes, we would set $x = 5$ and obtain[1]

$$f(5) = \frac{10^5 e^{-10}}{5!} = 0.0378$$

---

[1]Values of $e^{-\lambda}$ are available in Appendix E and can be easily computed with most modern calculators.

TABLE 3.8 SELECTED VALUES FROM THE POISSON PROBABILITY TABLE. EXAMPLE: $\lambda = 10$, $x = 5$; $f(5) = 0.0378$

					λ					
x	9.1	9.2	9.3	9.4	9.5	9.6	9.7	9.8	9.9	10
0	0.0001	0.0001	0.0001	0.0001	0.0001	0.0001	0.0001	0.0001	0.0001	0.0000
1	0.0010	0.0009	0.0009	0.0008	0.0007	0.0007	0.0006	0.0005	0.0005	0.0005
2	0.0046	0.0043	0.0040	0.0037	0.0034	0.0031	0.0029	0.0027	0.0025	0.0023
3	0.0140	0.0131	0.0123	0.0115	0.0107	0.0100	0.0093	0.0087	0.0081	0.0076
4	0.0319	0.0302	0.0285	0.0269	0.0254	0.0240	0.0226	0.0213	0.0201	0.0189
5	0.0581	0.0555	0.0530	0.0506	0.0483	0.0460	0.0439	0.0418	0.0398	**0.0378**
6	0.0881	0.0851	0.0822	0.0793	0.0764	0.0736	0.0709	0.0682	0.0656	0.0631
7	0.1145	0.1118	0.1091	0.1064	0.1037	0.1010	0.0982	0.0955	0.0928	0.0901
8	0.1302	0.1286	0.1269	0.1251	0.1232	0.1212	0.1191	0.1170	0.1148	0.1126
9	0.1317	0.1315	0.1311	0.1306	0.1300	0.1293	0.1284	0.1274	0.1263	0.1251
10	0.1198	0.1210	0.1219	0.1228	0.1235	0.1241	0.1245	0.1249	0.1250	0.1251
11	0.0991	0.1012	0.1031	0.1049	0.1067	0.1083	0.1098	0.1112	0.1125	0.1137
12	0.0752	0.0776	0.0799	0.0822	0.0844	0.0866	0.0888	0.0908	0.0928	0.0948
13	0.0526	0.0549	0.0572	0.0594	0.0617	0.0640	0.0662	0.0685	0.0707	0.0729
14	0.0342	0.0361	0.0380	0.0399	0.0419	0.0439	0.0459	0.0479	0.0500	0.0521
15	0.0208	0.0221	0.0235	0.0250	0.0265	0.0281	0.0297	0.0313	0.0330	0.0347
16	0.0118	0.0127	0.0137	0.0147	0.0157	0.0168	0.0180	0.0192	0.0204	0.0217
17	0.0063	0.0069	0.0075	0.0081	0.0088	0.0095	0.0103	0.0111	0.0119	0.0128
18	0.0032	0.0035	0.0039	0.0042	0.0046	0.0051	0.0055	0.0060	0.0065	0.0071
19	0.0015	0.0017	0.0019	0.0021	0.0023	0.0026	0.0028	0.0031	0.0034	0.0037
20	0.0007	0.0008	0.0009	0.0010	0.0011	0.0012	0.0014	0.0015	0.0017	0.0019
21	0.0003	0.0003	0.0004	0.0004	0.0005	0.0006	0.0006	0.0007	0.0008	0.0009
22	0.0001	0.0001	0.0002	0.0002	0.0002	0.0002	0.0003	0.0003	0.0004	0.0004
23	0.0000	0.0001	0.0001	0.0001	0.0001	0.0001	0.0001	0.0001	0.0002	0.0002
24	0.0000	0.0000	0.0000	0.0000	0.0000	0.0000	0.0000	0.0001	0.0001	0.0001

Try Problem 14 for practice computing Poisson probabilities.

Although we determined this probability by evaluating the probability function with $\lambda = 10$ and $x = 5$, the use of Poisson probability distribution tables often is easier. These tables provide probabilities for specific values of x and λ. We included such a table as Appendix C. For convenience we reproduce a portion of it as Table 3.8. To use the table of Poisson probabilities, you need know only the values of x and λ. Thus, from Table 3.8, the probability of five arrivals in a 15-minute period is the value in the row corresponding to $x = 5$ and the column corresponding to $\lambda = 10$. Hence, $f(5) = 0.0378$.

An Example Involving Length or Distance Intervals

Suppose that we are concerned with the occurrence of major defects in a section of highway one month after resurfacing. We assume that the probability of a defect is the same for any two intervals of equal length and that the occurrence or nonoccurrence of a defect in any one interval is independent of the occurrence or nonoccurrence in any other interval. Thus, the Poisson probability distribution applies.

Suppose that major defects occur at the average rate of two per mile. We want to find the probability that no major defects will occur in a particular 3-mile section of the highway. The interval length is 3 miles, so $\lambda = $ (2 defects/mile)(3 miles) $= 6$ represents the expected number of major defects over the 3-mile section of highway. Thus, by using equation (3.8) or Appendix C with $\lambda = 6$ and $x = 0$, we obtain the probability of no major defects of 0.0025. Thus, finding no major defects in the 3-mile section is very unlikely. In fact, there is a $1 - 0.0025 = 0.9975$ probability of at least one major defect in that section of highway.

NOTES AND COMMENTS

When working with the Poisson probability distribution, you need to be sure that λ is the mean number of occurrences for the desired interval. For instance, suppose that you know that 30 calls come into a switchboard every 15 minutes. To compute Poisson probabilities for the number of calls coming in over a 5-minute period, you would use $\lambda = 10$; to compute probabilities for the number of calls coming in over a 1-minute period, you would use $\lambda = 2$.

 ## 3.5   Continuous Random Variables

In this section we introduce probability distributions for continuous random variables. Recall from Section 3.1 that random variables that may assume any value in a certain interval or collection of intervals are said to be *continuous*. Examples of continuous random variables include the following:

1. The *number of ounces* of soup placed in a can labeled "8 ounces"
2. The *flight time* of an airplane traveling from Chicago to New York
3. The *lifetime* of the picture tube in a new television set
4. The *drilling depth* required to reach oil in an offshore drilling operation

To understand the nature of continuous random variables more fully, suppose that, in the first example, one can of soup has 8.2 ounces and another 8.3 ounces. Other cans could weigh 8.25 ounces, 8.225 ounces, and so on. In fact, the actual weight can be any numerical value from 0 ounces for an empty can to, say, 8.5 ounces for a can filled to capacity. Because this interval contains infinitely many values, we can no longer list each value of the random variable and then identify its associated probability. In fact, for continuous random variables we need a new method for computing the probabilities associated with the values of the random variable.

Applying the Uniform Distribution

Let x denote the flight time of an airplane traveling from Chicago to New York. Assume that the minimum time is 2 hours and that the maximum time is 2 hours 20 minutes. Thus, in terms of minutes, the flight time can be any value in the interval from 120 minutes to 140 minutes (e.g., 124 minutes, 125.48 minutes, etc.). As the random variable x can take on any value from 120 to 140 minutes, x is a continuous rather than a discrete random variable. Assume that sufficient actual flight data are available to conclude that the probability of a flight time between 120 and 121 minutes is the same as the probability of a flight time within any other 1-minute interval up to and including 140 minutes. With every 1-minute interval being equally likely, the random variable x has a **uniform probability distribution**.

FIGURE 3.3   UNIFORM PROBABILITY DENSITY FUNCTION FOR FLIGHT TIME

The following **probability density function** describes the uniform probability distribution for the flight time random variable:

$$f(x) = \begin{cases} \dfrac{1}{20} & \text{for } 120 \le x \le 140 \\ 0 & \text{elsewhere} \end{cases} \tag{3.9}$$

Figure 3.3 shows a graph of this probability density function. In general, the uniform probability density function for a random variable x is

$$f(x) = \begin{cases} \dfrac{1}{b - a} & \text{for } a \le x \le b \\ 0 & \text{elsewhere} \end{cases} \tag{3.10}$$

In the flight time example, $a = 120$ and $b = 140$.

In the graph of a probability density function, $f(x)$ shows the height or value of the function at any particular value of x. Because the probability density function for flight time is *uniform,* the height or value of the function is the same for each value of x between 120 and 140. That is, $f(x) = {}^{1}\!/_{20}$ for all values of x between 120 and 140. The probability density function $f(x)$, unlike the probability function for a discrete random variable, represents the height of the function at any particular value of x and *not* probability. Recall that, for each value of a discrete random variable (say, $x = 2$), the probability function yielded the probability of x having *exactly* that value [that is, $f(2)$]. However, a continuous random variable has infinitely many values, so we can no longer identify the probability for each specific value of x. Rather, we must consider probability in terms of the likelihood that a random variable takes on a value within a *specified interval.* For instance, in the flight time example an acceptable probability question is: What is the probability that the flight time is between 120 and 130 minutes? That is, what is $P(120 \le x \le 130)$? As the flight time must be between 120 and 140 minutes and as the probability is uniformly distributed over this interval, we feel comfortable saying that $P(120 \le x \le 130) = 0.50$. Indeed, as we will show, this is correct.

FIGURE 3.4 AREA PROVIDES PROBABILITY OF FLIGHT TIME

Area as a Measure of Probability

Refer to Figure 3.4 and consider the *area under the graph of* $f(x)$ over the interval from 120 to 130. Note that the region is rectangular in shape and that the area of a rectangle is simply the width times the height. With the width of the interval equal to $130 - 120 = 10$ and the height of the graph $f(x) = 1/20$, the area = width 3 height = $10(1/20) = 10/20 = 0.50$.

What observation can you make about the area under the graph of $f(x)$ and probability? They are identical! Indeed, that is true for all continuous random variables. In other words, once you have identified a probability density function $f(x)$ for a continuous random variable, you can obtain the probability that x takes on a value between some lower value a and some higher value b by computing the *area* under the graph of $f(x)$ over the interval a to b.

Whenever the probability is proportional to the length of the interval, the random variable is uniformly distributed.

With the appropriate probability distribution and the interpretation of area as probability, we can answer any number of probability questions. For example, what is the probability of a flight time between 128 and 136 minutes? The width of the interval is $136 - 128 = 8$. With the uniform height of $1/20$, $P(128 \leq x \leq 136) = 8/20 = 0.40$.

Note that $P(120 \leq x \leq 140) = 20(1/20) = 1$; the total area under the $f(x)$ graph is equal to 1. This property holds for all continuous probability distributions and is the analog of the requirement that the sum of the probabilities must equal 1 for a discrete probability distribution. A continuous probability distribution also requires that $f(x) \geq 0$ for all values of x. It is the analog of the requirement that $f(x) \geq 0$ for discrete probability distributions.

Two principal differences between continuous random variables and probability distributions and their discrete counterparts stand out.

1. We no longer talk about the probability of the random variable taking on a particular value. Instead we talk about the probability of the random variable taking on a value within some given interval.

2. The probability of the random variable taking on a value within some given interval is defined to be the area under the graph of the probability density function over the interval. This definition implies that the probability that a continuous random variable takes on any particular value is zero because the area under the graph of $f(x)$ at a single point is zero.

Try Problem 18 to practice computing probabilities using the uniform probability distribution.

NOTES AND COMMENTS

1. For any continuous random variable the probability of any particular value is zero, so $P(a \leq x \leq b) = P(a < x < b)$. Thus, the probability of a random variable assuming a value in any interval is the same whether the endpoints are included or not.

2. To see more clearly why the height of a probability density function is not a probability, think about a random variable with a uniform probability distribution of

$$f(x) = \begin{cases} 2 & \text{for } 0 \leq x \leq 0.5 \\ 0 & \text{elsewhere} \end{cases}$$

The height of the probability density function is 2 for values of x between 0 and 0.5. But, we know that probabilities can never be greater than 1.

 3.6   Normal Probability Distribution

Perhaps the most important probability distribution used to describe a continuous random variable is the **normal probability distribution**. It is applicable in a great many practical problem situations, and its probability density function has the form of the bell-shaped curve shown in Figure 3.5. The mathematical function that provides the bell-shaped curve of the normal probability density function follows:

The normal distribution was first observed by Abraham de Moivre, a French mathematician, in the early 1700s. De Moivre's work was motivated by the study of probability associated with gambling and games of chance.

$$f(x) = \frac{1}{\sigma\sqrt{2\pi}} e^{-(x-\mu)^2/2\sigma^2} \qquad \text{for } -\infty < x < \infty \qquad \textbf{(3.11)}$$

where

μ = mean or expected value of the random variable x

σ^2 = variance of the random variable x

σ = standard deviation of the random variable x

π = 3.14159

e = 2.71828

FIGURE 3.5   NORMAL PROBABILITY DISTRIBUTION

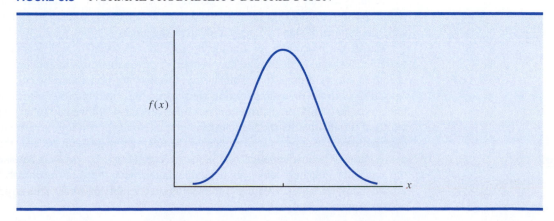

FIGURE 3.6   TWO NORMAL DISTRIBUTIONS WITH $\mu = 50$

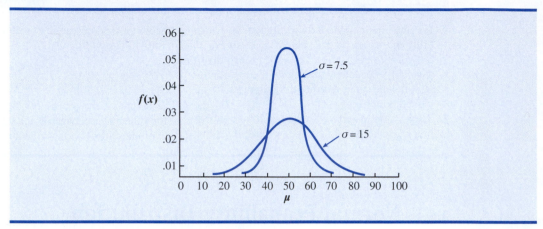

Recall from the previous discussion of continuous random variables that $f(x)$ is the height of the curve at a particular value of x. Thus, once we specify the mean (μ) and either the standard deviation (σ) or variance (σ^2), we can use equation (3.11) to determine the graph for the corresponding normal distribution. Figure 3.6 shows two normal distributions, one with $\mu = 50$ and $\sigma = 15$ and another with $\mu = 50$ and $\sigma = 7.5$. Note in particular the effect that the standard deviation σ has on the general shape of the normal curve. A larger standard deviation tends to flatten and broaden the curve because larger values of σ indicate greater variability in the values of the random variable.

Fortunately, whenever we use the normal distribution to answer probability questions, we do not have to use the probability density function of equation (3.11). In fact, when we use the normal distribution, we will have tables of probability values [areas under the $f(x)$ curve] that can provide the desired probability information. To show how to use the tables of areas or probabilities for the normal distribution, we must first introduce the standard normal distribution.

Standard Normal Distribution

A random variable that has a normal distribution with a mean of 0 and a standard deviation of 1 is said to have a **standard normal distribution**. We use the letter z to designate this particular normal random variable. Figure 3.7 shows the graph of the standard normal distribution. Note that it has the same general appearance as other normal distributions, but with the special properties of $\mu = 0$ and $\sigma = 1$. The units on the horizontal axis (z) measure the number of standard deviations from the mean.

Recall the procedure for finding probabilities associated with a continuous random variable. We want to determine the probability of the random variable having a value in a specified interval from a to b. Thus we have to find the area under the curve in the interval from a to b. In the preceding section we showed that finding probabilities, or areas under the curve, for a uniform distribution was relatively easy. All we had to do was multiply the width of the interval by the height of the graph. However, finding areas under the normal distribution curve appears at first glance to be much more difficult because the height of the curve varies. The mathematical technique for obtaining these areas is beyond the scope of the text, but fortunately tables are available that provide the areas or probability values for the standard normal distribution. Table 3.9 is such a table of areas. This table is also available as Appendix D.

FIGURE 3.7 STANDARD NORMAL DISTRIBUTION

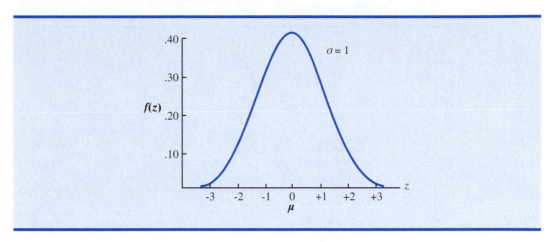

The graphs at the top of Table 3.9 show that the area in the table is the probability of a standard normal random variable being less than or equal to a specific value of z. Such probabilities are referred to as cumulative probabilities. In using Table 3.9 to determine a cumulative probability, note that the value of z with one decimal appears in the left-hand column of the table, with the second decimal appearing in the top row. Negative values of z are provided on the first page of the table, whereas positive values of z are provided on the second page. For example, for $z = -0.85$, we find -0.8 in the left-hand column and the second decimal 0.05 in the top row. Then, by looking in the body of the table, we find an area or probability of 0.1977. This is the cumulative probability that the standard normal random variable is less than or equal to $z = -0.85$. This area is shown graphically at the top of Table 3.9. As another example, we can use the second page of the table to determine that the cumulative probability that the standard normal random variable is less than or equal to $z = 1.25$. We find 1.2 in the left-hand column and the second decimal 0.05 in the top row. In the body of the table we find an area or probability of 0.8944. This is the cumulative probability that the standard normal random variable is less than or equal to $z = 1.25$. This area is also shown graphically at the top of Table 3.9.

Suppose that we wanted to use the cumulative standard normal distribution table to determine the probability the standard normal random variable z will be between -1.00 and $+1.00$. Table 3.9 shows the cumulative probability that z is less than or equal to $+1.00$ is 0.8413 and the cumulative probability that z is less than or equal to -1.00 is 0.1587. Thus, the probability that z will be between -1.00 and $+1.00$ must be the difference between these two cumulative probabilities: $0.8413 - 0.1587 = 0.6826$. This is shown graphically in Figure 3.8.

Similarly, we can find the probability the standard normal random variable z will be between -2.00 and $+2.00$. Using the cumulative probabilities at $z = +2.00$ and $z = -2.00$, the probability that z will be between -2.00 and $+2.00$ is $0.9772 - 0.0228 = 0.9544$. In addition, we can use the cumulative probabilities at $z = +3.00$ and $z = -3.00$ to conclude that the probability z will be between -3.00 and $+3.00$ is $0.9986 - 0.0013 = 0.9973$. With the total probability or total area under the curve equal to 1.0000, the probability of 0.9973 tells us that z will almost always fall between -3.00 and $+3.00$.

The probability that a standard normal random variable z is between a and b is always the difference between two cumulative probabilities: one for $z = b$ and one for $z = a$.

As a final example, what is the probability that the normal random variable z is greater than 2.00. From Table 3.9, we find the cumulative probability that z is less than or equal

TABLE 3.9   CUMULATIVE PROBABILITIES FOR THE STANDARD NORMAL
DISTRIBUTION

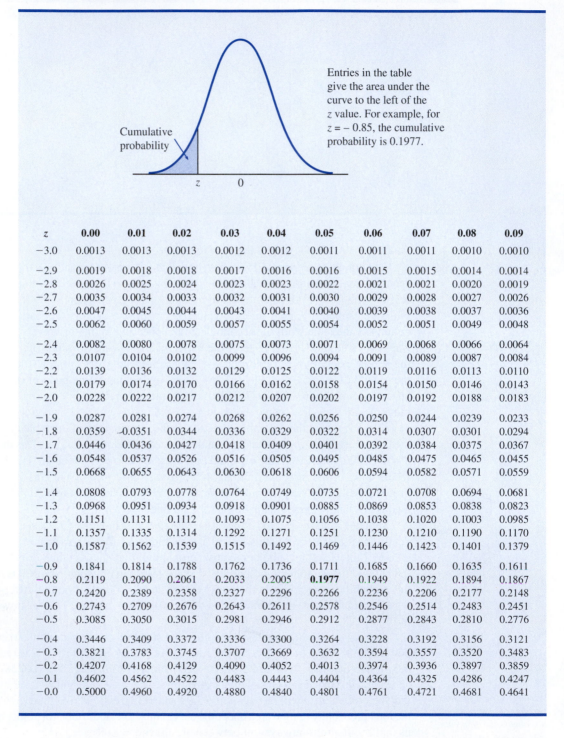

Cumulative probability

Entries in the table give the area under the curve to the left of the z value. For example, for $z = -0.85$, the cumulative probability is 0.1977.

z	0.00	0.01	0.02	0.03	0.04	0.05	0.06	0.07	0.08	0.09
−3.0	0.0013	0.0013	0.0013	0.0012	0.0012	0.0011	0.0011	0.0011	0.0010	0.0010
−2.9	0.0019	0.0018	0.0018	0.0017	0.0016	0.0016	0.0015	0.0015	0.0014	0.0014
−2.8	0.0026	0.0025	0.0024	0.0023	0.0023	0.0022	0.0021	0.0021	0.0020	0.0019
−2.7	0.0035	0.0034	0.0033	0.0032	0.0031	0.0030	0.0029	0.0028	0.0027	0.0026
−2.6	0.0047	0.0045	0.0044	0.0043	0.0041	0.0040	0.0039	0.0038	0.0037	0.0036
−2.5	0.0062	0.0060	0.0059	0.0057	0.0055	0.0054	0.0052	0.0051	0.0049	0.0048
−2.4	0.0082	0.0080	0.0078	0.0075	0.0073	0.0071	0.0069	0.0068	0.0066	0.0064
−2.3	0.0107	0.0104	0.0102	0.0099	0.0096	0.0094	0.0091	0.0089	0.0087	0.0084
−2.2	0.0139	0.0136	0.0132	0.0129	0.0125	0.0122	0.0119	0.0116	0.0113	0.0110
−2.1	0.0179	0.0174	0.0170	0.0166	0.0162	0.0158	0.0154	0.0150	0.0146	0.0143
−2.0	0.0228	0.0222	0.0217	0.0212	0.0207	0.0202	0.0197	0.0192	0.0188	0.0183
−1.9	0.0287	0.0281	0.0274	0.0268	0.0262	0.0256	0.0250	0.0244	0.0239	0.0233
−1.8	0.0359	0.0351	0.0344	0.0336	0.0329	0.0322	0.0314	0.0307	0.0301	0.0294
−1.7	0.0446	0.0436	0.0427	0.0418	0.0409	0.0401	0.0392	0.0384	0.0375	0.0367
−1.6	0.0548	0.0537	0.0526	0.0516	0.0505	0.0495	0.0485	0.0475	0.0465	0.0455
−1.5	0.0668	0.0655	0.0643	0.0630	0.0618	0.0606	0.0594	0.0582	0.0571	0.0559
−1.4	0.0808	0.0793	0.0778	0.0764	0.0749	0.0735	0.0721	0.0708	0.0694	0.0681
−1.3	0.0968	0.0951	0.0934	0.0918	0.0901	0.0885	0.0869	0.0853	0.0838	0.0823
−1.2	0.1151	0.1131	0.1112	0.1093	0.1075	0.1056	0.1038	0.1020	0.1003	0.0985
−1.1	0.1357	0.1335	0.1314	0.1292	0.1271	0.1251	0.1230	0.1210	0.1190	0.1170
−1.0	0.1587	0.1562	0.1539	0.1515	0.1492	0.1469	0.1446	0.1423	0.1401	0.1379
−0.9	0.1841	0.1814	0.1788	0.1762	0.1736	0.1711	0.1685	0.1660	0.1635	0.1611
−0.8	0.2119	0.2090	0.2061	0.2033	0.2005	**0.1977**	0.1949	0.1922	0.1894	0.1867
−0.7	0.2420	0.2389	0.2358	0.2327	0.2296	0.2266	0.2236	0.2206	0.2177	0.2148
−0.6	0.2743	0.2709	0.2676	0.2643	0.2611	0.2578	0.2546	0.2514	0.2483	0.2451
−0.5	0.3085	0.3050	0.3015	0.2981	0.2946	0.2912	0.2877	0.2843	0.2810	0.2776
−0.4	0.3446	0.3409	0.3372	0.3336	0.3300	0.3264	0.3228	0.3192	0.3156	0.3121
−0.3	0.3821	0.3783	0.3745	0.3707	0.3669	0.3632	0.3594	0.3557	0.3520	0.3483
−0.2	0.4207	0.4168	0.4129	0.4090	0.4052	0.4013	0.3974	0.3936	0.3897	0.3859
−0.1	0.4602	0.4562	0.4522	0.4483	0.4443	0.4404	0.4364	0.4325	0.4286	0.4247
−0.0	0.5000	0.4960	0.4920	0.4880	0.4840	0.4801	0.4761	0.4721	0.4681	0.4641

TABLE 3.9 CUMULATIVE PROBABILITIES FOR THE STANDARD NORMAL DISTRIBUTION (*Continued*)

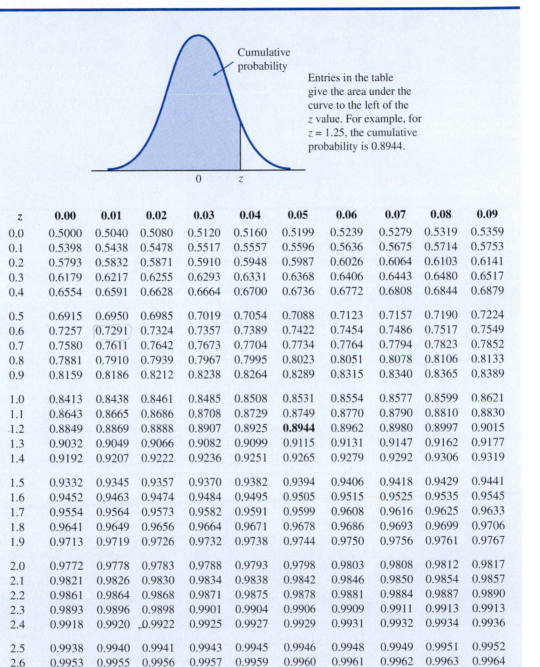

Cumulative probability

Entries in the table give the area under the curve to the left of the z value. For example, for z = 1.25, the cumulative probability is 0.8944.

z	0.00	0.01	0.02	0.03	0.04	0.05	0.06	0.07	0.08	0.09
0.0	0.5000	0.5040	0.5080	0.5120	0.5160	0.5199	0.5239	0.5279	0.5319	0.5359
0.1	0.5398	0.5438	0.5478	0.5517	0.5557	0.5596	0.5636	0.5675	0.5714	0.5753
0.2	0.5793	0.5832	0.5871	0.5910	0.5948	0.5987	0.6026	0.6064	0.6103	0.6141
0.3	0.6179	0.6217	0.6255	0.6293	0.6331	0.6368	0.6406	0.6443	0.6480	0.6517
0.4	0.6554	0.6591	0.6628	0.6664	0.6700	0.6736	0.6772	0.6808	0.6844	0.6879
0.5	0.6915	0.6950	0.6985	0.7019	0.7054	0.7088	0.7123	0.7157	0.7190	0.7224
0.6	0.7257	0.7291	0.7324	0.7357	0.7389	0.7422	0.7454	0.7486	0.7517	0.7549
0.7	0.7580	0.7611	0.7642	0.7673	0.7704	0.7734	0.7764	0.7794	0.7823	0.7852
0.8	0.7881	0.7910	0.7939	0.7967	0.7995	0.8023	0.8051	0.8078	0.8106	0.8133
0.9	0.8159	0.8186	0.8212	0.8238	0.8264	0.8289	0.8315	0.8340	0.8365	0.8389
1.0	0.8413	0.8438	0.8461	0.8485	0.8508	0.8531	0.8554	0.8577	0.8599	0.8621
1.1	0.8643	0.8665	0.8686	0.8708	0.8729	0.8749	0.8770	0.8790	0.8810	0.8830
1.2	0.8849	0.8869	0.8888	0.8907	0.8925	**0.8944**	0.8962	0.8980	0.8997	0.9015
1.3	0.9032	0.9049	0.9066	0.9082	0.9099	0.9115	0.9131	0.9147	0.9162	0.9177
1.4	0.9192	0.9207	0.9222	0.9236	0.9251	0.9265	0.9279	0.9292	0.9306	0.9319
1.5	0.9332	0.9345	0.9357	0.9370	0.9382	0.9394	0.9406	0.9418	0.9429	0.9441
1.6	0.9452	0.9463	0.9474	0.9484	0.9495	0.9505	0.9515	0.9525	0.9535	0.9545
1.7	0.9554	0.9564	0.9573	0.9582	0.9591	0.9599	0.9608	0.9616	0.9625	0.9633
1.8	0.9641	0.9649	0.9656	0.9664	0.9671	0.9678	0.9686	0.9693	0.9699	0.9706
1.9	0.9713	0.9719	0.9726	0.9732	0.9738	0.9744	0.9750	0.9756	0.9761	0.9767
2.0	0.9772	0.9778	0.9783	0.9788	0.9793	0.9798	0.9803	0.9808	0.9812	0.9817
2.1	0.9821	0.9826	0.9830	0.9834	0.9838	0.9842	0.9846	0.9850	0.9854	0.9857
2.2	0.9861	0.9864	0.9868	0.9871	0.9875	0.9878	0.9881	0.9884	0.9887	0.9890
2.3	0.9893	0.9896	0.9898	0.9901	0.9904	0.9906	0.9909	0.9911	0.9913	0.9913
2.4	0.9918	0.9920	0.9922	0.9925	0.9927	0.9929	0.9931	0.9932	0.9934	0.9936
2.5	0.9938	0.9940	0.9941	0.9943	0.9945	0.9946	0.9948	0.9949	0.9951	0.9952
2.6	0.9953	0.9955	0.9956	0.9957	0.9959	0.9960	0.9961	0.9962	0.9963	0.9964
2.7	0.9965	0.9966	0.9967	0.9968	0.9969	0.9970	0.9971	0.9972	0.9973	0.9974
2.8	0.9974	0.9975	0.9976	0.9977	0.9977	0.9978	0.9979	0.9979	0.9980	0.9981
2.9	0.9981	0.9982	0.9982	0.9983	0.9984	0.9984	0.9985	0.9985	0.9986	0.9986
3.0	0.9986	0.9987	0.9987	0.9988	0.9988	0.9989	0.9989	0.9989	0.9990	0.9990

FIGURE 3.8   PROBABILITY OF z BETWEEN -1.00 AND $+1.00$

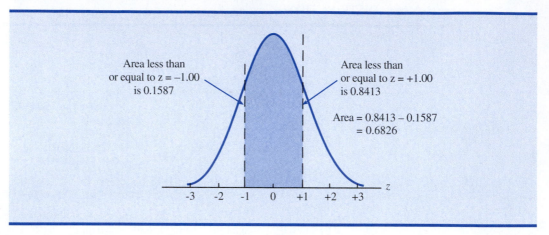

FIGURE 3.9   PROBABILITY OF z GREATER THAN 2.00

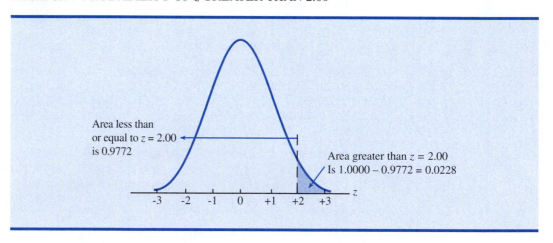

to 2.00 is 0.9772. With the total area under the curve equal to 1.0000, the probability that z will be greater than 2.00 must be $1.0000 - 0.9772 = 0.0228$. This is shown graphically in Figure 3.9. As the examples in this section have shown, you should be able to use the cumulative probabilities in Table 3.9 to answer a variety of probability questions about the standard normal random variable z.

Computing Probabilities for Any Normal Distribution

The reason we discuss the standard normal distribution so extensively is that we can compute probabilities for any normal distribution by first converting to the standard normal distribution. Thus, when we have a normal distribution with any mean μ and any standard deviation σ, we can answer probability questions about this distribution by converting to the standard normal distribution. We then use Table 3.9 and the appropriate z values to find the probability. The formula used to convert any normal random variable x with mean μ and standard deviation σ to the standard normal distribution is

$$z = \frac{x - \mu}{\sigma}$$

(3.12)

FIGURE 3.10   NORMAL DISTRIBUTION WITH $\mu = 10$ AND $\sigma = 2$

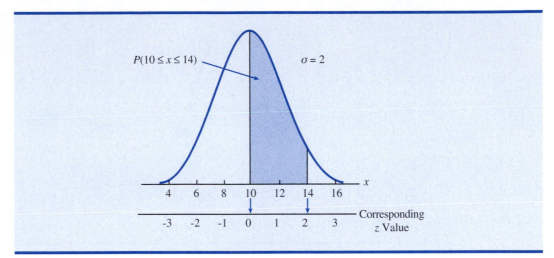

When used in this way, z is a measure of the number of standard deviations that x is from μ.

We can most easily show how the conversion to the z value allows us to use the standard normal distribution to compute probabilities for any normal distribution with an example. Suppose that we have a normal distribution with $\mu = 10$ and $\sigma = 2$, as shown graphically in Figure 3.10. Note that, in addition to the values of the random variable shown on the x axis, we have included a second axis (the z axis) to show that for each value of x there is a corresponding value of z. For example, when $x = 10$ the corresponding z value (the number of standard deviations away from the mean) is $z = (x - \mu)/\sigma = (10 - 10)/2 = 0$. Similarly, for $x = 14$ we have $z = (x - \mu)/\sigma = (14 - 10)/2 = 2$.

Now suppose that we want to know the probability that the random variable x is between 10 and 14, that is, $P(10 \leq x \leq 14)$. We do not have tables that provide this probability directly. However, note that in Figure 3.10 the area under the curve (probability) for x between 10 and 14 is the same as the area under the curve for z between 0 and 2. Using $z = 2.00$ and Table 3.9, we find the cumulative probability of z being less than or equal to 2.00 is 0.9772. Similarly, Table 3.9 shows that the cumulative probability of z being less than or equal to 0.00 is 0.5000. Thus, the probability the standard normal random variable z is between 0.00 and 2.00 is $0.9772 - 0.5000 = 0.4772$. Thus, we conclude that the probability of x being between 10 and 14 is also 0.4772.

This procedure applies to any normal distribution problem. That is, for any x value a corresponding z value is given by equation (3.12). To find the probability that x is in a specified interval, simply convert the x interval to its corresponding z interval. Then use the table for the standard normal distribution to answer the probability question.

Grear Tire Company Problem

Suppose that Grear Tire Company just developed a new steel-belted radial tire that will be sold through a national chain of discount stores. Because the tire is a new product, Grear's management believes that the mileage guarantee offered with the tire will be an important factor in consumer acceptance of the product. Before finalizing the tire mileage guarantee policy, Grear's management wants some probability information concerning the number of miles the tires will last.

FIGURE 3.11   GREAR TIRE COMPANY TIRE MILEAGE

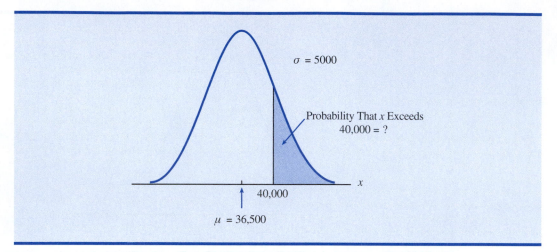

From actual road tests with the tires, Grear's engineering group estimates the mean tire mileage at $\mu = 36{,}500$ miles and the standard deviation at $\sigma = 5000$ miles. In addition, the data collected indicate that a normal distribution is a reasonable assumption.

What percentage of the tires, then, can be expected to last more than 40,000 miles? In other words, what is the probability that the tire mileage will exceed 40,000? To compute this probability, we need to find the area of the shaded region in Figure 3.11.

At $x = 40{,}000$ we have

$$z = \frac{x - \mu}{\sigma} = \frac{40{,}000 - 36{,}500}{5000} = \frac{3500}{5000} = 0.70$$

Thus the probability that the normal distribution for tire mileage will have an x value greater than 40,000 is the same as the probability that the standard normal distribution will have a z value greater than 0.70. Using Table 3.9, we find that the cumulative probability that z is less than or equal to 0.70 is 0.7580. Thus, the probability that z will be greater than 0.70 must be $1.0000 - 0.7580 = 0.2420$. In terms of the tire mileage x, we can conclude that these is a 0.2420 probability that x will be greater than 40,000 miles. Thus, we can anticipate about 24.2% of the tires manufactured by Grear will last more than 40,000 miles.

Let us now assume that Grear is considering a guarantee that will provide a discount on a new set of tires if the mileage on the original tires doesn't exceed the mileage stated on the guarantee. What should the guarantee mileage be if Grear wants no more than 10% of the tires to be eligible for the discount? This question is interpreted graphically in Figure 3.12. Note that 10% of the area is below the unknown guarantee mileage. Because this 10% is the lower tail of the normal probability distribution, 0.1000 is the cumulative probability that the tire mileage will be less than or equal to the unknown guarantee mileage. The question is now, how many standard deviations (z value) do we have to be below the mean to a 0.1000 cumulative probability. This time we will look into the body of Table 3.9 and try to find the cumulative probability 0.1000. We cannot find 0.1000 exactly, but a cumulative probability 0.1003 is close. Here we find the corresponding $z = -1.28$. This tells us that we must be 1.28 below the mean to find the desired tire guarantee mileage. This mileage is

$$\text{Guarantee mileage} = \mu - 1.28\sigma$$
$$= 36{,}500 - 1.28(5000) = 30{,}100$$

FIGURE 3.12 GREAR'S DISCOUNT GUARANTEE

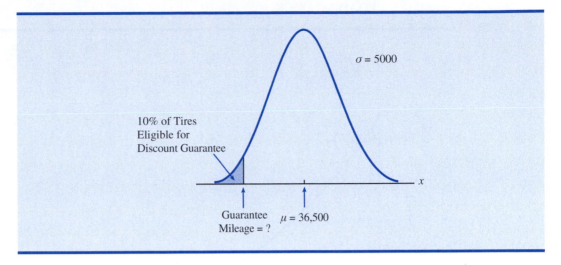

Therefore, a guarantee of 30,100 miles will meet the requirement that approximately 10% of the tires will be eligible for the discount. With this information the firm might confidently set its tire mileage guarantee at 30,000 miles.

Try Problem 23 for practice finding a z value that cuts off a particular probability.

Again we see the important role that probability distributions play in providing decision-making information. Once a probability distribution is established for a particular problem, it can be used rather quickly and easily to provide probability information about the problem. Although this information does not make a decision recommendation directly, it does provide information that helps the decision maker understand the problem better. Ultimately, this information may assist the decision maker in reaching a good decision.

3.7 Exponential Probability Distribution

A continuous probability distribution that is often useful in describing the time needed to complete a task is the exponential probability distribution. The exponential random variable can be used to describe the time between arrivals at a car wash, the time required to load a truck, the distance between major defects in a highway, and so on. The exponential probability density function is

$$f(x) = \frac{1}{\mu} e^{-x/\mu} \qquad \text{for } x \geq 0, \mu > 0 \qquad \textbf{(3.13)}$$

To provide an example of the exponential probability distribution, suppose that the loading time for a truck at the Schips loading dock follows an exponential probability distribution. If the mean, or average, loading time is 15 minutes ($\mu = 15$), the appropriate probability density function is

$$f(x) = \frac{1}{15} e^{-x/15}$$

Figure 3.13 shows the graph of this density function.

FIGURE 3.13   EXPONENTIAL DISTRIBUTION FOR LOADING TIME AT THE SCHIPS
LOADING DOCK

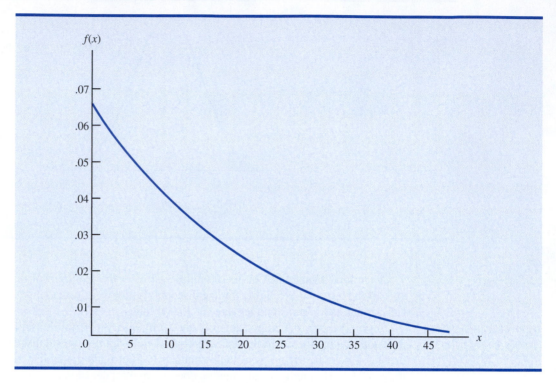

Computing Probabilities for the Exponential Distribution

As with any continuous probability distribution, the area under the curve corresponding to some interval provides the probability that the random variable takes on a value in that interval. For instance, for the Schips loading dock example the probability that 6 minutes or less ($x \leq 6$) are needed to load a truck is defined to be the area under the curve from $x = 0$ to $x = 6$. Similarly, the probability that a loading time is 18 minutes or less ($x \leq 18$) is the area under the curve from $x = 0$ to $x = 18$. Note also that the probability of loading a truck in between 6 and 18 minutes ($6 \leq x \leq 18$) is the area under the curve from $x = 6$ to $x = 18$.

To compute exponential probabilities such as those previously described, the following formula provides the probability of obtaining a value for the exponential random variable of less than or equal to some specific value of x, denoted by x_0:

$$P(x \leq x_0) = 1 - e^{-x_0/\mu} \tag{3.14}$$

Thus, for the Schips loading dock example, equation (3.14) becomes

$$P(\text{loading time} \leq x_0) = 1 - e^{-x_0/15}$$

Hence, the probability that 6 minutes or less ($x \leq 6$) are needed to load a truck is

$$P(\text{loading time} \leq 6) = 1 - e^{-6/15} = 0.3297$$

Try Problem 29 for practice finding probabilities with the exponential probability distribution.

Note also the probability that 18 minutes or less ($x \leq 18$) are needed to load a truck is

$$P(\text{loading time} \leq 18) = 1 - e^{-18/15} = 0.6988$$

Thus, the probability that 6 to 18 minutes are required to load a truck is $0.6988 - 0.3297 = 0.3691$. Probabilities for any other interval can be computed in a similar manner.

Relationship Between the Poisson and Exponential Distributions

In Section 3.4 we introduced the Poisson distribution as a discrete probability distribution that often is useful when we are dealing with the number of occurrences over a specified interval of time or space. Recall that the Poisson probability function is

$$f(x) = \frac{\lambda^x e^{-\lambda}}{x!}$$

where

$$\lambda = \text{expected value or mean number of occurrences in an interval}$$

The Poisson and exponential probability distributions are used in the chapter on waiting line models (Chapter 15). In these models the Poisson distribution is used as the probability distribution for the number of arrivals, while the exponential probability distribution is used as the probability distribution for the service time.

The continuous exponential probability distribution is related to the discrete Poisson distribution. The Poisson distribution provides an appropriate description of the number of occurrences per interval, and the exponential distribution provides a description of the length of the interval between occurrences.

To illustrate this relationship, let us suppose that the number of cars that arrive at a car wash during 1 hour is described by a Poisson probability distribution with a mean of 10 cars per hour. Thus the Poisson probability function that provides the probability of x arrivals per hour is

$$f(x) = \frac{10^x e^{-10}}{x!}$$

The average number of arrivals is 10 cars per hour, so the average time between cars arriving is

$$\frac{1 \text{ hour}}{10 \text{ cars}} = 0.1 \text{ hour/car}$$

Try Problems 30 and 31 for applications of the exponential probability distribution.

Thus, the corresponding exponential distribution that describes the time between the arrival of cars has a mean of $\mu = 0.1$ hours per car. The appropriate exponential probability density function is

$$f(x) = \frac{1}{0.1} e^{-x/0.1} = 10 e^{-10x}$$

Summary

In this chapter we continued the discussion of probability by introducing the important concepts of random variables and probability distributions. Random variables provide numerical descriptions of the outcomes of experiments. When random variables are used, computations of the expected value, variance, and standard deviation can help the decision maker understand characteristics of the problem under study. We discussed the probability distributions for both discrete and continuous random variables.

Of particular interest are special probability distributions such as the binomial, Poisson, uniform, normal, and exponential distributions. These distributions provide wide applicability, and special formulas and/or tables make the probability information easily available.

Through a variety of problems and applications we illustrated the role that probability distributions play in providing decision-making information. Although the probability values generated by the techniques and methods of this chapter do not by themselves make decision recommendations, they do provide assistance to the decision maker in terms of understanding the uncertainties inherent in the problem. Ultimately, this better understanding may lead to new and better decisions.

Glossary

Random variable   A numerical description of the outcome of an experiment.

Discrete random variable   A random variable that may assume only a finite or infinite sequence of values.

Continuous random variable   A random variable that may assume any value in an interval or collection of intervals.

Probability function   A function, denoted $f(x)$, that provides the probability that a discrete random variable x takes on some specific value.

Discrete probability distribution   A table, graph, or equation describing the values of the random variable and the associated probabilities.

Expected value   A weighted average of the values of the random variable, for which the probability function provides the weights. If an experiment can be repeated a large number of times, the expected value can be interpreted as the "long-run average."

Variance   A measure of the dispersion or variability in the random variable. It is a weighted average of the squared deviations from the mean, μ.

Standard deviation   The positive square root of the variance.

Binomial probability distribution   The probability distribution for a discrete random variable, used to compute the probability of x successes in n trials.

Poisson probability distribution   The probability distribution for a discrete random variable, used to compute the probability of x occurrences over a specified interval.

Uniform probability distribution   A continuous probability distribution in which the probability that the random variable will assume a value in any interval of equal length is the same for each interval.

Probability density function   The function that describes the probability distribution of a continuous random variable.

Normal probability distribution   A continuous probability distribution whose probability density function is bell-shaped and determined by the mean, μ, and standard deviation, σ.

Standard normal distribution   A normal distribution with a mean of 0 and a standard deviation of 1.

Cumulative Probability   The probability that a random variable takes on a value less than or equal to stated value.

Exponential probability distribution   A continuous probability distribution that is useful in describing the time to complete a task or the time between occurrences of an event.

Problems

1. The following examples are experiments and their associated random variables. In each case identify the values the random variable can assume and state whether the random variable is discrete or continuous:

Experiment	Random Variable (x)
a. Take a 20-question examination	Number of questions answered correctly
b. Observe cars arriving at a tollbooth	Number of cars arriving at the tollbooth for 1 hour
c. Audit 50 tax returns	Number of returns containing errors
d. Observe an employee's work for 8 hours	Number of nonproductive hours
e. Weigh a shipment of goods	Number of pounds

2. The following table shows a partial probability distribution for the MRA Company's projected profits (in thousands of dollars) for the first year of operation (the negative value denotes a loss):

x	f(x)
−100	0.10
0	0.20
50	0.30
100	0.25
150	0.10
200	

a. Find the missing value of $f(200)$. What is your interpretation of this value?
b. What is the probability that MRA will be profitable?
c. What is the probability that MRA will make at least $100,000?

3. Data were collected on the number of operating rooms in use at Tampa General Hospital over a 20-day period. On 3 of the days only one operating room was used; on 5 days, two were used; on 8 days, three were used; and on 4 days all four rooms were used.
    a. Use the relative frequency approach to construct a probability distribution for the number of operating rooms in use on any given day.
    b. Draw a graph of the probability distribution.
    c. Show that your probability distribution satisfies the requirements for a valid discrete probability distribution.

4. Shown is a probability distribution for the random variable x.

x	f(x)
3	0.25
6	0.50
9	0.25
Total	1.00

  a.   Compute $E(x)$, the expected value of x.
  b.   Compute σ^2, the variance of x.
  c.   Compute σ, the standard deviation of x.

5. Shown are the percent frequency distributions of job satisfaction scores for a sample of in-
    formation systems (IS) senior executives and IS middle managers. The scores range from
    a low of 1 (very dissatisfied) to a high of 5 (very satisfied).

Job Satisfaction Score	IS Senior Executives (%)	IS Middle Managers (%)
1	5	4
2	9	10
3	3	12
4	42	46
5	41	28
Total	100	100

  a.   Develop a probability distribution for the job satisfaction score of a senior executive.
  b.   Develop a probability distribution for the job satisfaction score of a middle manager.
  c.   What is the probability a senior executive will report a job satisfaction score of
       4 or 5?
  d.   What is the probability a middle manager is very satisfied?
  e.   Compare the overall job satisfaction of senior executives and middle managers.

6. The American Housing Survey reported the following data on the number of bedrooms in
    owner-occupied and renter-occupied houses in central cities (*http://www.census.gov*,
    March 31, 2003):

	Number of Houses (1000s)	
Bedrooms	**Renter-Occupied**	**Owner-Occupied**
0	547	23
1	5012	541
2	6100	3832
3	2644	8690
4 or more	557	3783

  a.   Define a random variable x = number of bedrooms in renter-occupied houses and de-
       velop a probability distribution for the random variable. (Let $x = 4$ represent 4 or more
       bedrooms.)
  b.   Compute the expected value and variance for the number of bedrooms in renter-
       occupied houses.
  c.   Define a random variable y = number of bedrooms in owner-occupied houses and de-
       velop a probability distribution for the random variable. (Let $y = 4$ represent 4 or more
       bedrooms.)
  d.   Compute the expected value and variance for the number of bedrooms in owner-
       occupied houses.
  e.   What observations can you make from a comparison of the number of bedrooms in
       renter-occupied versus owner-occupied homes?

7. The demand for a product of Carolina Industries varies greatly from month to month. Based on the past two years of data, the following probability distribution shows the company's monthly demand:

Unit Demand	Probability
300	0.20
400	0.30
500	0.35
600	0.15

a. If the company places monthly orders equal to the expected value of the monthly demand, what should Carolina's monthly order quantity be for this product?
b. Assume that each unit demanded generates $70 in revenue and that each unit ordered costs $50. How much will the company gain or lose in a month if it places an order based on your answer to part a and the actual demand for the item is 300 units?
c. What are the variance and the standard deviation for the number of units demanded?

8. The J. R. Ryland Computer Company is considering a plant expansion that will enable the company to begin production of a new computer product. The company's president must determine whether to make the expansion a medium- or large-scale project. The demand for the new product involves an uncertainty, which for planning purposes may be low demand, medium demand, or high demand. The probability estimates for the demands are 0.20, 0.50, and 0.30, respectively. Letting x indicate the annual profit in $1000s, the firm's planners developed profit forecasts for the medium- and large-scale expansion projects.

		Medium-Scale Expansion Profits		Large-Scale Expansion Profits	
		x	$f(x)$	y	$f(y)$
Demand	**Low**	50	0.20	0	0.20
	Medium	150	0.50	100	0.50
	High	200	0.30	300	0.30

a. Compute the expected value for the profit associated with the two expansion alternatives. Which decision is preferred for the objective of maximizing the expected profit?
b. Compute the variance for the profit associated with the two expansion alternatives. Which decision is preferred for the objective of minimizing the risk or uncertainty?

9. Consider a binomial experiment with 2 trials and $p = 0.4$.
a. Compute the probability of 1 success, $f(1)$.
b. Compute $f(0)$.
c. Compute $f(2)$.
d. Find the probability of at least 1 success.
e. Find the expected value, variance, and standard deviation.

10. Consider a binomial experiment with $n = 10$ and $p = 0.10$. Use the binomial tables (Appendix B) to answer parts (a) through (d).
a. Find $f(0)$.
b. Find $f(2)$.
c. Find $P(x \leq 2)$.

    d.   Find $P(x \geq 1)$.

    e.   Find $E(x)$.

    f.   Find $\text{Var}(x)$ and σ.

11. A Harris Interactive survey for InterContinental Hotels & Resorts asked respondents, "When traveling internationally, do you generally venture out on your own to experience culture or stick with your tour group and itineraries?" The survey found that 23% of the respondents stick with their tour group (*USA Today,* January 21, 2004).

    a.   In a sample of six international travelers, what is the probability that two will stick with their tour group?

    b.   In a sample of six international travelers, what is the probability that at least two will stick with their tour group?

    c.   In a sample of 10 international travelers, what is the probability that none will stick with the tour group?

12. When a new machine is functioning properly, only 3% of the items produced are defective. Assume that we will randomly select two parts produced on the machine and that we are interested in the number of defective parts found.

    a.   Describe the conditions under which this situation would be a binomial experiment.

    b.   How many experimental outcomes yield 1 defect?

    c.   Compute the probabilities associated with finding no defects, 1 defect, and 2 defects.

13. Military radar and missile detection systems are designed to warn a country of enemy attacks. A reliability question deals with the ability of the detection system to identify an attack and issue the warning. Assume that a particular detection system has a 0.90 probability of detecting a missile attack. Answer the following questions using the binomial probability distribution:

    a.   What is the probability that 1 detection system will detect an attack?

    b.   If 2 detection systems are installed in the same area and operate independently, what is the probability that at least 1 of the systems will detect the attack?

    c.   If 3 systems are installed, what is the probability that at least 1 of the systems will detect the attack?

    d.   Would you recommend that multiple detection systems be operated? Explain.

14. Consider a Poisson probability distribution with 2 as the average number of occurrences per time period.

    a.   Write the appropriate Poisson probability function.

    b.   What is the average number of occurrences in three time periods?

    c.   Write the appropriate Poisson probability function to determine the probability of x occurrences in three time periods.

    d.   Find the probability of 2 occurrences in one time period.

    e.   Find the probability of 6 occurrences in three time periods.

    f.   Find the probability of 5 occurrences in two time periods.

15. Telephone calls arrive at the rate of 48 per hour at the reservation desk for Regional Airways.

    a.   Find the probability of receiving 3 calls in a 5-minute interval.

    b.   Find the probability of receiving 10 calls in 15 minutes.

    c.   Suppose that no calls are currently on hold. If the agent takes 5 minutes to complete processing the current call, how many callers do you expect to be waiting by that time? What is the probability that no one will be waiting?

    d.   If no calls are currently being processed, what is the probability the agent can take 3 minutes for personal time without being interrupted?

16. More than 50 million guests stayed at bed and breakfasts (B&Bs) last year. The Web site for the Bed and Breakfast Inns of North America (*http://www.bestinns.com*), which

averages approximately seven visitors per minute, enables many B&Bs to attract guests without waiting years to be mentioned in guidebooks (*Time,* September 2001).
a. What is the probability of no Web site visitors in a 1-minute period?
b. What is the probability of two or more Web site visitors in a 1-minute period?
c. What is the probability of one or more Web site visitors in a 30-second period?
d. What is the probability of five or more Web site visitors in a 1-minute period?

17. Airline passengers arrive randomly and independently at the passenger screening facility at a major international airport. The mean arrival rate is 10 passengers per minute.
a. What is the probability of no arrivals in a 1-minute period?
b. What is the probability of 3 or fewer arrivals in a 1-minute period?
c. What is the probability of no arrivals in a 15-second period?
d. What is the probability of at least 1 arrival in a 15-second period?

18. A random variable x is uniformly distributed between 1.0 and 1.5.
a. Show the graph of the probability density function.
b. Find $P(x = 1.25)$.
c. Find $P(1.0 \leq x \leq 1.25)$.
d. Find $P(1.20 < x < 1.5)$.

19. Delta Airlines quotes a flight time of 2 hours, 5 minutes for its flights from Cincinnati to Tampa. Suppose we believe that actual flight times are uniformly distributed between 2 hours and 2 hours, 20 minutes.
a. Show the graph of the probability density function for flight times.
b. What is the probability that the flight will be no more than 5 minutes late?
c. What is the probability that the flight will be more than 10 minutes late?
d. What is the expected flight time?

20. Most computer languages have a function that can be used to generate random numbers. In Microsoft's Excel, the RAND function can be used to generate random numbers between 0 and 1. If we let x denote the random number generated, then x is a continuous random variable with the probability density function:

$$f(x) = \begin{cases} 1 & \text{for } 0 \leq x \leq 1 \\ 0 & \text{elsewhere} \end{cases}$$

a. Graph the probability density function.
b. What is the probability of generating a random number between 0.25 and 0.75?
c. What is the probability of generating a random number with a value less than or equal to 0.30?
d. What is the probability of generating a random number with a value greater than 0.60?

21. For the standard normal random variable z, compute the following probabilities:
a. $P(0 \leq z \leq 0.83)$
b. $P(-1.57 \leq z \leq 0)$
c. $P(z > 0.44)$
d. $P(z \geq 20.23)$
e. $P(z < 1.20)$
f. $P(z \leq 20.71)$

22. For the standard normal random variable z, find z for each situation.
a. The area to the left of z is 0.9750.
b. The area between 0 and z is 0.4750.
c. The area to the left of z is 0.7291.
d. The area to the right of z is 0.1314.
e. The area to the left of z is 0.6700.
f. The area to the right of z is 0.3300.

23. For the standard normal random variable z, find z for each situation.
     a. The area to the left of z is 0.2119.
     b. The area between $-z$ and z is 0.9030.
     c. The area between $-z$ and z is 0.2052.
     d. The area to the left of z is 0.9948.
     e. The area to the right of z is 0.6915.

24. The demand for a new product is estimated to be normally distributed with $\mu = 200$ and $\sigma = 40$. Let x be the number of units demanded and find the following probabilities:
     a. $P(180 \le x \le 220)$
     b. $P(x \ge 250)$
     c. $P(x \le 100)$
     d. $P(225 \le x \le 250)$

25. The average stock price for companies making up the S&P 500 is $30, and the standard deviation is $8.20 (*BusinessWeek,* Special Annual Issue, Spring 2003). Assume the stock prices are normally distributed.
     a. What is the probability a company will have a stock price of at least $40?
     b. What is the probability a company will have a stock price no higher than $20?
     c. How high does a stock price have to be to put a company in the top 10%?

26. General Hospital's patient account division has compiled data on the age of accounts receivable. The data collected indicate that the age of the accounts follows a normal distribution with $\mu = 28$ days and $\sigma = 8$ days.
     a. What portion of the accounts is between 20 and 40 days old—that is, $P(20 \le x \le 40)$?
     b. The hospital administrator is interested in sending reminder letters to the oldest 15% of accounts. How many days old should an account be before a reminder letter is sent?
     c. The hospital administrator wants to give a discount to those accounts that pay their balance by the 21st day. What percentage of the accounts will receive the discount?

27. The Webster National Bank is reviewing its service charges and interest-paying policies on checking accounts. The average daily balance on personal checking accounts is $550, with a standard deviation of $150. In addition, the average daily balances are normally distributed.
     a. What percentage of personal checking account customers carry average daily balances in excess of $800?
     b. What percentage carry average daily balances below $200?
     c. What percentage carry average daily balances between $300 and $700?
     d. The bank is considering paying interest to customers carrying average daily balances in excess of a certain amount. If the bank does not want to pay interest to more than 5% of its customers, what is the minimum average daily balance it should be willing to pay interest on?

28. A machine fills containers with a particular product. The standard deviation of filling weights computed from past data is 0.6 ounces. If only 2% of the containers hold less than 18 ounces, what is the mean filling weight for the machine? That is, what must μ equal? Assume that the filling weights have a normal distribution.

29. Consider the exponential probability density function:

$$f(x) = \frac{1}{3}e^{-x/3} \qquad \text{for } x \ge 0$$

     a. Write the formula for $P(x \le x_0)$.
     b. Find $P(x \le 2)$.
     c. Find $P(x \ge 3)$.
     d. Find $P(x \le 5)$.
     e. Find $P(2 \le x \le 5)$.

30. *Internet Magazine* monitors Internet service providers (ISPs) and provides statistics on their performance. The average time to download a Web page for free ISPs is approximately 20 seconds for European Web pages (*Internet Magazine,* January 2000). Assume the time to download a Web page follows an exponential distribution.
   a. What is the probability it will take less than 10 seconds to download a Web page?
   b. What is the probability it will take more than 30 seconds to download a Web page?
   c. What is the probability it will take between 10 and 30 seconds to download a Web page?

31. The time between arrivals of vehicles at a particular intersection follows an exponential probability distribution with a mean of 12 seconds.
   a. Sketch this exponential probability distribution.
   b. What is the probability the time between vehicle arrivals is 12 seconds or less?
   c. What is the probability the time between vehicle arrivals is 6 seconds or less?
   d. What is the probability there will be 30 or more seconds between arriving vehicles?

32. The lifetime (hours) of an electronic device is a random variable with the exponential probability density function:

$$f(x) = \frac{1}{50}\, e^{-x/50} \qquad \text{for } x \geq 0$$

   a. What is the mean lifetime of the device?
   b. What is the probability the device fails in the first 25 hours of operation?
   c. What is the probability the device operates 100 or more hours before failure?

33. The time (in minutes) between telephone calls at an insurance claims office has the exponential probability distribution:

$$f(x) = 0.50e^{-0.50x} \qquad \text{for } x \geq 0$$

   a. What is the mean time between telephone calls?
   b. What is the probability of 30 seconds or less between telephone calls?
   c. What is the probability of 1 minute or less between telephone calls?
   d. What is the probability of 5 or more minutes without a telephone call?

34. Sparagowski & Associates conducted a study of service times at the drive-up window of fast-food restaurants. The average time between placing an order and receiving the order at McDonald's restaurants was 2.78 minutes (*The Cincinnati Enquirer,* July 9, 2000). Waiting times, such as these, frequently follow an exponential distribution.
   a. What is the probability that a customer's service time is less than 2 minutes?
   b. What is the probability that a customer's service time is more than 5 minutes?
   c. What is the probability that a customer's service time is more than 2.78 minutes?

Case Problem   # Specialty Toys

Specialty Toys, Inc., sells a variety of new and innovative children's toys and believes that the preholiday season is the best time to introduce a new toy. Many families use this time to look for new ideas for December holiday gifts. When Specialty has a new toy with good market potential, it chooses an October market entry date.

   In order to get toys in its stores by October, Specialty places one-time orders with its manufacturers in June or July of each year. Demand for children's toys can be highly volatile. If a new toy catches on, a sense of shortage in the marketplace often increases the demand to very high levels and large profits can be realized. On the other hand, new toys can also flop, leaving Specialty stuck with high levels of inventory that must be sold at reduced prices. The most important question the company faces is deciding how many units of a new toy should be purchased to meet expected sales demand. If too few are purchased, sales will be lost; if too many are purchased, profits will be reduced because of low prices realized in clearance sales.

For the coming season, Specialty plans to introduce a new product called Weather Teddy. This variation of a talking teddy bear is made by a company in Taiwan. When a child presses Teddy's hand, the bear begins to talk. With the aid of a built-in barometer, Teddy says one of five responses that predict the weather conditions. The responses range from "It looks to be a very nice day! Have fun" to "I think it may rain today. Don't forget your umbrella." Tests with the product show that even though it is not a perfect weather predictor, its predictions are surprisingly good. Several of Specialty's managers claimed Teddy gave predictions of the weather that were as good as the local television weather forecasters.

Specialty faces the decision of how many Weather Teddy units to order for the coming holiday season. Members of the management team recommended order quantities of 15,000, 18,000, 24,000, and 28,000. Considerable disagreement concerning the market potential is evidenced by the different order quantities suggested. The product management team has asked you for an analysis of the stock-out probabilities for various order quantities an estimate of the profit potential, and to help make an order quantity recommendation. Specialty expects to sell Weather Teddy for $24, and the cost is $16 per unit. If inventory remains after the holiday season, Specialty will sell all surplus inventory for $5 per unit. After reviewing the sales history of similar products, Specialty's senior sales forecaster predicted an expected demand of 20,000 units with a 0.95 probability that demand would be between 10,000 units and 30,000 units.

Managerial Report

Prepare a managerial report that addresses the following issues and recommends an order quantity for the Weather Teddy product:

1. Use the sales forecaster's prediction to describe a normal probability distribution that can be used to approximate the demand distribution. Sketch the distribution and show its mean and standard deviation.
2. Compute the probability of a stock-out for the order quantities suggested by members of the management team.
3. Compute the projected profit for the order quantities suggested by the management team under three scenarios. Worst case: sales = 10,000 units; most likely case: sales = 20,000 units; and best case: sales = 30,000 units.
4. One of Specialty's managers felt that the profit potential was so great that the order quantity should have a 70% chance of meeting demand and only a 30% chance of any stock-outs. What quantity would be ordered under this policy and what is the projected profit under the three scenarios in part 3?
5. Provide your own recommendation for an order quantity and note the associated profit projections. Provide a rationale for your recommendation.

Appendix 3.1   Computing Discrete Probabilities with Excel

Excel has the capability of computing probabilities for several discrete probability distributions including the binomial and Poisson. In this appendix, we describe how Excel can be used to compute the probabilities for any binomial probability distribution. The procedures for the Poisson probability distributions are similar to the one we describe for the binomial probability distribution.

Let us return to the Nastke Clothing Store problem, where the binomial probabilities of interest are based on a binomial experiment with $n = 10$ and $p = 0.30$. We assume that the user is interested in the probability of $x = 4$ successes in the 10 trials. The following steps describe how to use Excel to produce the desired binomial probability:

Step 1. Select a cell in the worksheet where you want the binomial probability to appear

Step 2. Select the **Formulas tab** (See Appendix A)

Step 3. Choose the **Insert Function** option

Step 4. When the **Insert Function** dialog box appears:
    Choose **Statistical** from the **Or select a category** box
    Choose **BINOMDIST** from the **Select a function** box
    Click **OK**

Step 5. When the **Function Arguments** dialog box appears:
    Enter 4 in the **Number_s** box (the value of x)
    Enter 10 in the **Trials** box (the value of n)
    Enter .30 in the **Probability_s** box (the value of p)
    Enter false in the **Cumulative** box[2]
        Note: At this point the desired binomial probability of 0.2001 is automatically computed and appears near the bottom of the dialog box.
    Click **OK** and the binomial probability will appear in the worksheet cell requested in Step 1.

A user who wants other binomial probabilities may obtain the information without repeating the steps for each probability desired. Perhaps the easiest alternative is to stay in step 5. After the four entries have been made and the first probability appears, simply return to the **Number_s** box and insert a new value of x. The new probability will appear. Repeated changes can be made in the dialog box, including changes to the trials, probability, and/or cumulative boxes. For each change, the desired probability will appear. When **OK** is selected, only the last binomial probability will be placed in the worksheet.

If the user wants to insert multiple binomial probabilities into the worksheet, the desired values of x are entered into the worksheet first. Then, in step 5, the user enters the cell location of one of the values of x in the numbers box. After completing the steps for one binomial probability, individuals experienced with Excel can use Excel's Copy command to copy the binomial function into the cells where the other binomial probabilities are to appear.

The Excel procedure for generating Poisson probabilities is similar to the procedure just described. Step 4 can be used to select the **POISSON** function name. The dialog box in step 5 will guide the user through the input values required to compute the desired probabilities.

Appendix 3.2   Computing Probabilities for Continuous Distributions with Excel

Excel has the capability of computing probabilities for several continuous probability distributions, including the normal and exponential probability distributions. In this appendix, we describe how Excel can be used to compute probabilities for any normal probability distribution. The procedures for the exponential and other continuous probability distributions are similar to the one we describe for the normal probability distribution.

---

[2]Placing false in the cumulative box provides the probability of exactly four successes. Placing true in this box provides the cumulative probability of four or fewer successes.

Let us return to the Grear Tire Company problem, where the tire mileage was described by a normal probability distribution with $\mu = 36{,}500$ and $\sigma = 5000$. Assume we are interested in the probability that tire mileage will exceed 40,000 miles. The following steps describe how to use Excel to compute the desired normal probability:

Step 1. Select a cell in the worksheet where you want the normal probability to appear
Step 2. Select the **Formulas Tab** (See Appendix A)
Step 3. Choose the **Insert Function** option
Step 4. When the **Insert Function** dialog box appears:
Choose **Statistical** from the **Or select a category** box
Choose **NORMDIST** from the **Select a function** box
Click **OK**
Step 5. When the **Function Arguments** dialog box appears:
Enter 40000 in the **x** box
Enter 36500 in the **mean** box
Enter 5000 in the **standard deviation** box
Enter true in the **cumulative** box
Click **OK**

At this point, 0.7580 will appear in the cell selected in step 1, indicating that the cumulative probability that the tire mileage is less than or equal to 40,000 miles is 0.7580. Therefore, the probability that tire mileage will exceed 40,000 miles is $1 - 0.7580 = 0.2420$.

Excel uses an inverse computation to convert a given cumulative normal probability into a value for the random variable. For example, what mileage guarantee should Grear offer if the company wants no more than 10% of the tires to be eligible for the guarantee? To compute the mileage guarantee by using Excel, follow the procedure just described. However, two changes are necessary: In step 4, choose **NORMINV** from the **Select a function** box; in step 5, enter the cumulative probability of 0.10 in the **probability** box and then enter the mean and the standard deviation. When **OK** is selected in step 5, the tire mileage guarantee of 30,092, or approximately 30,100, miles appears in the worksheet.

The Excel procedure for generating exponential probabilities is similar to the procedure just described. Step 4 can be used to choose the **EXPONDIST** function name. The dialog box in step 5 will guide the user through the input values required to compute the desired probability. Note that the value entered in the lambda box is $1/\mu$. When **OK** is selected in step 5, the cumulative exponential probability appears in the worksheet.

CHAPTER 4

Decision Analysis

CONTENTS

Decision analysis can be used to develop an optimal strategy when a decision maker is faced with several decision alternatives and an uncertain or risk-filled pattern of future events. For example, Ohio Edison used decision analysis to choose the best type of particulate control equipment for coal-fired generating units when it faced future uncertainties concerning sulfur content requirements, construction costs, and so on. The State of North Carolina used decision analysis in evaluating whether to implement a medical screening test to detect metabolic disorders in newborns. Thus, decision analysis repeatedly proves its value in decision making. The Q.M. in Action, Decision Analysis at Eastman Kodak, describes how the use of decision analysis added approximately $1 billion in value.

Even when a careful decision analysis has been conducted, the uncertain future events make the final consequence uncertain. In some cases, the selected decision alternative may provide good or excellent results. In other cases, a relatively unlikely future event may occur, causing the selected decision alternative to provide only fair or even poor results. The risk associated with any decision alternative is a direct result of the uncertainty associated with the final consequence. A good decision analysis includes risk analysis. Through risk analysis the decision maker is provided with probability information about the favorable as well as the unfavorable consequences that may occur.

Q.M. *in* ACTION

DECISION ANALYSIS AT EASTMAN KODAK*

Clemen and Kwit conducted a study to determine the value of decision analysis at the Eastman Kodak Company. The study involved an analysis of 178 decision analysis projects over a 10-year period. The projects involved a variety of applications including strategy development, vendor selection, process analysis, new-product brainstorming, product-portfolio selection, and emission-reduction analysis. These projects required 14,372 hours of analyst time and the involvement of many other individuals at Kodak over the 10-year period. The shortest projects took less than 20 hours, and the longest projects took almost a year to complete.

Most decision analysis projects are one-time activities, which makes it difficult to measure the value added to the corporation. Clemen and Kwit used detailed records that were available and some innovative approaches to develop estimates of the incremental dollar value generated by the decision analysis projects. Their conservative estimate of the average value per project was $6.65 million and their optimistic estimate of the average

value per project was $16.35 million. Their analysis led to the conclusion that all projects taken together added more than $1 billion in value to Eastman Kodak. Using these estimates, Clemen and Kwit concluded that decision analysis returned substantial value to the company. Indeed, they concluded that the value added by the projects was at least 185 times the cost of the analysts' time.

In addition to the monetary benefits, the authors point out that decision analysis adds value by facilitating discussion among stakeholders, promoting careful thinking about strategies, providing a common language for discussing the elements of a decision problem, and speeding implementation by helping to build consensus among decision makers. In commenting on the value of decision analysis at Eastman Kodak, Nancy L. S. Sousa said, "As General Manager, New Businesses, VP Health Imaging, Eastman Kodak, I encourage all of the business planners to use the decision and risk principles and processes as part of evaluating new business opportunities. The processes have clearly led to better decisions about entry and exit of businesses."

Although measuring the value of a particular decision analysis project can be difficult, it would be difficult to dispute the success that decision analysis had at Kodak.

*Based on Robert T. Clemen and Robert C. Kwit, "The Value of Decision Analysis at Eastman Kodak Company," *Interfaces* (September/October 2001): 74–92.

We begin the study of decision analysis by considering problems that involve reasonably few decision alternatives and reasonably few possible future events. Influence diagrams and payoff tables are introduced to provide a structure for the decision problem and to illustrate the fundamentals of decision analysis. We then introduce decision trees to show the sequential nature of decision problems. Decision trees are used to analyze more complex problems and to identify an optimal sequence of decisions, referred to as an optimal decision strategy. Sensitivity analysis shows how changes in various aspects of the problem affect the recommended decision alternative.

4.1   Problem Formulation

The first step in the decision analysis process is problem formulation. We begin with a verbal statement of the problem. We then identify the **decision alternatives**, the uncertain future events, referred to as **chance events**, and the **consequences** associated with each decision alternative and each chance event outcome. Let us begin by considering a construction project of the Pittsburgh Development Corporation.

Pittsburgh Development Corporation (PDC) purchased land that will be the site of a new luxury condominium complex. The location provides a spectacular view of downtown Pittsburgh and the Golden Triangle, where the Allegheny and Monongahela Rivers meet to form the Ohio River. PDC plans to price the individual condominium units between $300,000 and $1,400,000.

PDC commissioned preliminary architectural drawings for three different projects: one with 30 condominiums, one with 60 condominiums, and one with 90 condominiums. The financial success of the project depends upon the size of the condominium complex and the chance event concerning the demand for the condominiums. The statement of the PDC decision problem is to select the size of the new luxury condominium project that will lead to the largest profit given the uncertainty concerning the demand for the condominiums.

Given the statement of the problem, it is clear that the decision is to select the best size for the condominium complex. PDC has the following three decision alternatives:

$$d_1 = \text{a small complex with 30 condominiums}$$
$$d_2 = \text{a medium complex with 60 condominiums}$$
$$d_3 = \text{a large complex with 90 condominiums}$$

A factor in selecting the best decision alternative is the uncertainty associated with the chance event concerning the demand for the condominiums. When asked about the possible demand for the condominiums, PDC's president acknowledged a wide range of possibilities but decided that it would be adequate to consider two possible chance event outcomes: a strong demand and a weak demand.

In decision analysis, the possible outcomes for a chance event are referred to as the **states of nature**. The states of nature are defined so that one and only one of the possible states of nature will occur. For the PDC problem, the chance event concerning the demand for the condominiums has two states of nature:

$$s_1 = \text{strong demand for the condominiums}$$
$$s_2 = \text{weak demand for the condominiums}$$

Management must first select a decision alternative (complex size); then a state of nature follows (demand for the condominiums), and finally a consequence will occur. In this case, the consequence is PDC's profit.

Influence Diagrams

An **influence diagram** is a graphical device that shows the relationships among the decisions, the chance events, and the consequences for a decision problem. The **nodes** in an influence diagram represent the decisions, chance events, and consequences. Rectangles or squares depict **decision nodes**, circles or ovals depict **chance nodes**, and diamonds depict **consequence nodes**. The lines connecting the nodes, referred to as *arcs,* show the direction of influence that the nodes have on one another. Figure 4.1 shows the influence diagram for the PDC problem. The complex size is the decision node, demand is the chance node, and profit is the consequence node. The arcs connecting the nodes show that both the complex size and the demand influence PDC's profit.

Payoff Tables

Given the three decision alternatives and the two states of nature, which complex size should PDC choose? To answer this question, PDC will need to know the consequence associated with each decision alternative and each state of nature. In decision analysis, we refer to the consequence resulting from a specific combination of a decision alternative and a state of nature as a **payoff**. A table showing payoffs for all combinations of decision alternatives and states of nature is a **payoff table**.

Payoffs can be expressed in terms of profit, cost, time, distance, or any other measure appropriate for the decision problem being analyzed.

Because PDC wants to select the complex size that provides the largest profit, profit is used as the consequence. The payoff table with profits expressed in millions of dollars is shown in Table 4.1. Note, for example, that if a medium complex is built and demand turns out to be strong, a profit of $14 million will be realized. We will use the notation V_{ij} to denote the payoff associated with decision alternative i and state of nature j. Using Table 4.1, $V_{31} = 20$ indicates a payoff of $20 million occurs if the decision is to build a large complex (d_3) and the strong demand state of nature (s_1) occurs. Similarly, $V_{32} = -9$ indicates a loss of $9 million if the decision is to build a large complex (d_3) and the weak demand state of nature (s_2) occurs.

FIGURE 4.1   INFLUENCE DIAGRAM FOR THE PDC PROJECT

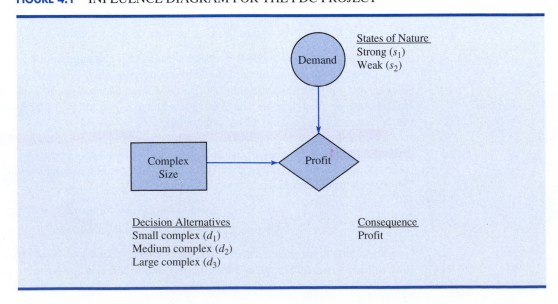

TABLE 4.1   PAYOFF TABLE FOR THE PDC CONDOMINIUM PROJECT
(PAYOFFS IN $ MILLIONS)

	State of Nature	
Decision Alternative	**Strong Demand s_1**	**Weak Demand s_2**
Small complex, d_1	8	7
Medium complex, d_2	14	5
Large complex, d_3	20	−9

Decision Trees

A **decision tree** provides a graphical representation of the decision-making process. Figure 4.2 presents a decision tree for the PDC problem. Note that the decision tree shows the natural or logical progression that will occur over time. First, PDC must make a decision regarding the size of the condominium complex (d_1, d_2, or d_3). Then, after the decision is implemented, either state of nature s_1 or s_2 will occur. The number at each end point of the tree indicates the payoff associated with a particular sequence. For example, the topmost payoff of 8 indicates that an $8 million profit is anticipated if PDC constructs a small condominium complex (d_1) and demand turns out to be strong (s_1). The next payoff of 7 indicates an anticipated profit of $7 million if PDC constructs a small condominium complex (d_1) and demand turns out to be weak (s_2). Thus, the decision tree shows graphically the sequences of decision alternatives and states of nature that provide the six possible payoffs for PDC.

If you have a payoff table, you can develop a decision tree. Try Problem 1, part (a).

The decision tree in Figure 4.2 shows four nodes, numbered 1–4. Squares are used to depict decision nodes and circles are used to depict chance nodes. Thus, node 1 is a decision node, and nodes 2, 3, and 4 are chance nodes. The **branches** connect the nodes; those

FIGURE 4.2   DECISION TREE FOR THE PDC CONDOMINIUM PROJECT
(PAYOFFS IN $ MILLIONS)

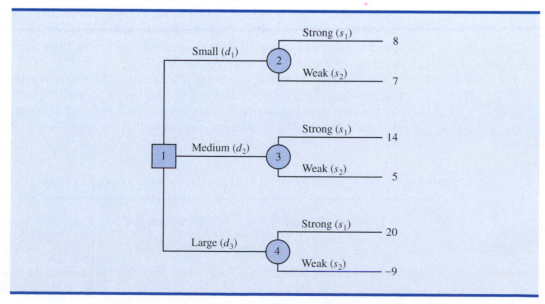

leaving the decision node correspond to the decision alternatives. The branches leaving each chance node correspond to the states of nature. The payoffs are shown at the end of the states-of-nature branches. We now turn to the question: How can the decision maker use the information in the payoff table or the decision tree to select the best decision alternative? Several approaches may be used.

NOTES AND COMMENTS

1. Experts in problem solving agree that the first step in solving a complex problem is to decompose it into a series of smaller subproblems. Decision trees provide a useful way to show how a problem can be decomposed and the sequential nature of the decision process.

2. People often view the same problem from different perspectives. Thus, the discussion regarding the development of a decision tree may provide additional insight about the problem.

 ## 4.2 Decision Making without Probabilities

In this section we consider approaches to decision making that do not require knowledge of the probabilities of the states of nature. These approaches are appropriate in situations in which the decision maker has little confidence in his or her ability to assess the probabilities, or in which a simple best-case and worst-case analysis is desirable. Because different approaches sometimes lead to different decision recommendations, the decision maker must understand the approaches available and then select the specific approach that, according to the judgment of the decision maker, is the most appropriate.

Many people think of a good decision as one in which the consequence is good. However, in some instances, a good, well-thought-out decision may still lead to a bad or undesirable consequence.

Optimistic Approach

The **optimistic approach** evaluates each decision alternative in terms of the *best* payoff that can occur. The decision alternative that is recommended is the one that provides the best possible payoff. For a problem in which maximum profit is desired, as in the PDC problem, the optimistic approach would lead the decision maker to choose the alternative corresponding to the largest profit. For problems involving minimization, this approach leads to choosing the alternative with the smallest payoff.

For a maximization problem, the optimistic approach often is referred to as the maximax approach; for a minimization problem, the corresponding terminology is minimin.

To illustrate the optimistic approach, we use it to develop a recommendation for the PDC problem. First, we determine the maximum payoff for each decision alternative; then we select the decision alternative that provides the overall maximum payoff. These steps systematically identify the decision alternative that provides the largest possible profit. Table 4.2 illustrates these steps.

TABLE 4.2   MAXIMUM PAYOFF FOR EACH PDC DECISION ALTERNATIVE

Decision Alternative	Maximum Payoff	
Small complex, d_1	8	
Medium complex, d_2	14	
Large complex, d_3	20	← Maximum of the maximum payoff values

Because 20, corresponding to d_3, is the largest payoff, the decision to construct the large condominium complex is the recommended decision alternative using the optimistic approach.

Conservative Approach

The **conservative approach** evaluates each decision alternative in terms of the *worst* payoff that can occur. The decision alternative recommended is the one that provides the best of the worst possible payoffs. For a problem in which the output measure is profit, as in the PDC problem, the conservative approach would lead the decision maker to choose the alternative that maximizes the minimum possible profit that could be obtained. For problems involving minimization, this approach identifies the alternative that will minimize the maximum payoff.

For a maximization problem, the conservative approach is often referred to as the maximin approach; for a minimization problem, the corresponding terminology is minimax.

To illustrate the conservative approach, we use it to develop a recommendation for the PDC problem. First, we identify the minimum payoff for each of the decision alternatives; then we select the decision alternative that maximizes the minimum payoff. Table 4.3 illustrates these steps for the PDC problem.

Because 7, corresponding to d_1, yields the maximum of the minimum payoffs, the decision alternative of a small condominium complex is recommended. This decision approach is considered conservative because it identifies the worst possible payoffs and then recommends the decision alternative that avoids the possibility of extremely "bad" payoffs. In the conservative approach, PDC is guaranteed a profit of at least $7 million. Although PDC may make more, it *cannot* make less than $7 million.

Minimax Regret Approach

The **minimax regret approach** to decision making is neither purely optimistic nor purely conservative. Let us illustrate the minimax regret approach by showing how it can be used to select a decision alternative for the PDC problem.

Suppose that PDC constructs a small condominium complex (d_1) and demand turns out to be strong (s_1). Table 4.1 showed that the resulting profit for PDC would be $8 million. However, given that the strong demand state of nature (s_1) has occurred, we realize that the decision to construct a large condominium complex (d_3), yielding a profit of $20 million, would have been the best decision. The difference between the payoff for the best decision alternative ($20 million) and the payoff for the decision to construct a small condominium complex ($8 million) is the **opportunity loss**, or **regret**, associated with decision alternative d_1 when state of nature s_1 occurs; thus, for this case, the opportunity loss or regret is $20 million − $8 million = $12 million. Similarly, if PDC makes the decision to construct a medium condominium complex (d_2) and the strong demand state of nature (s_1) occurs, the opportunity loss, or regret, associated with d_2 would be $20 million − $14 million = $6 million.

TABLE 4.3   MINIMUM PAYOFF FOR EACH PDC DECISION ALTERNATIVE

Decision Alternative	Minimum Payoff	
Small complex, d_1	7	← Maximum of the minimum payoff values
Medium complex, d_2	5	
Large complex, d_3	−9	

TABLE 4.4   OPPORTUNITY LOSS, OR REGRET, TABLE FOR THE PDC CONDOMINIUM
PROJECT ($ MILLIONS)

	State of Nature	
Decision Alternative	**Strong Demand s_1**	**Weak Demand s_2**
Small complex, d_1	12	0
Medium complex, d_2	6	2
Large complex, d_3	0	16

In general, the following expression represents the opportunity loss, or regret:

$$R_{ij} = |V_j^* - V_{ij}| \qquad \text{(4.1)}$$

where

> R_{ij} = the regret associated with decision alternative d_i and state of nature s_j
> V_j^* = the payoff value[1] corresponding to the best decision for the state of nature s_j
> V_{ij} = the payoff corresponding to decision alternative d_i and state of nature s_j

Note the role of the absolute value in equation (4.1). For minimization problems, the best payoff, V_j^*, is the smallest entry in column j. Because this value always is less than or equal to V_{ij}, the absolute value of the difference between V_j^* and V_{ij} ensures that the regret is always the magnitude of the difference.

Using equation (4.1) and the payoffs in Table 4.1, we can compute the regret associated with each combination of decision alternative d_i and state of nature s_j. Because the PDC problem is a maximization problem, V_j^* will be the largest entry in column j of the payoff table. Thus, to compute the regret, we simply subtract each entry in a column from the largest entry in the column. Table 4.4 shows the opportunity loss, or regret, table for the PDC problem.

The next step in applying the minimax regret approach is to list the maximum regret for each decision alternative; Table 4.5 shows the results for the PDC problem. Selecting the decision alternative with the *minimum* of the *maximum* regret values—hence, the name *minimax regret*—yields the minimax regret decision. For the PDC problem, the alternative to construct the medium condominium complex, with a corresponding maximum regret of $6 million, is the recommended minimax regret decision.

TABLE 4.5   MAXIMUM REGRET FOR EACH PDC DECISION ALTERNATIVE

Decision Alternative	**Maximum Regret**	
Small complex, d_1	12	
Medium complex, d_2	6	← Minimum of the maximum regret
Large complex, d_3	16	

---

[1] In maximization problems, V_j^* will be the largest entry in column j of the payoff table. In minimization problems, V_j^* will be the smallest entry in column j of the payoff table.

For practice in developing a decision recommendation using the optimistic, conservative, and minimax regret approaches, try Problem 1, part (b).

Note that the three approaches discussed in this section provide different recommendations, which in itself isn't bad. It simply reflects the difference in decision-making philosophies that underlie the various approaches. Ultimately, the decision maker will have to choose the most appropriate approach and then make the final decision accordingly. The main criticism of the approaches discussed in this section is that they do not consider any information about the probabilities of the various states of nature. In the next section we discuss an approach that utilizes probability information in selecting a decision alternative.

4.3   Decision Making with Probabilities

In many decision-making situations, we can obtain probability assessments for the states of nature. When such probabilities are available, we can use the **expected value approach** to identify the best decision alternative. Let us first define the expected value of a decision alternative and then apply it to the PDC problem.

Let

$$N = \text{the number of states of nature}$$

$$P(s_j) = \text{the probability of state of nature } s_j$$

Because one and only one of the N states of nature can occur, the probabilities must satisfy two conditions:

$$P(s_j) \geq 0 \qquad \text{for all states of nature} \tag{4.2}$$

$$\sum_{j=1}^{N} P(s_j) = P(s_1) + P(s_2) + \cdots + P(s_N) = 1 \tag{4.3}$$

The **expected value (EV)** of decision alternative d_i is defined as follows:

$$EV(d_i) = \sum_{j=1}^{N} P(s_j)V_{ij} \tag{4.4}$$

In words, the expected value of a decision alternative is the sum of weighted payoffs for the decision alternative. The weight for a payoff is the probability of the associated state of nature and therefore the probability that the payoff will occur. Let us return to the PDC problem to see how the expected value approach can be applied.

PDC is optimistic about the potential for the luxury high-rise condominium complex. Suppose that this optimism leads to an initial subjective probability assessment of 0.8 that demand will be strong (s_1) and a corresponding probability of 0.2 that demand will be weak (s_2). Thus, $P(s_1) = 0.8$ and $P(s_2) = 0.2$. Using the payoff values in Table 4.1 and equation (4.4), we compute the expected value for each of the three decision alternatives as follows:

$$EV(d_1) = 0.8(8) + 0.2(7) \quad = 7.8$$
$$EV(d_2) = 0.8(14) + 0.2(5) \quad = 12.2$$
$$EV(d_3) = 0.8(20) + 0.2(-9) = 14.2$$

Can you now use the expected value approach to develop a decision recommendation? Try Problem 5.

Thus, using the expected value approach, we find that the large condominium complex, with an expected value of \$14.2 million, is the recommended decision.

FIGURE 4.3   PDC DECISION TREE WITH STATE-OF-NATURE BRANCH PROBABILITIES

The calculations required to identify the decision alternative with the best expected value can be conveniently carried out on a decision tree. Figure 4.3 shows the decision tree for the PDC problem with state-of-nature branch probabilities. Working backward through the decision tree, we first compute the expected value at each chance node. That is, at each chance node, we weight each possible payoff by its probability of occurrence. By doing so, we obtain the expected values for nodes 2, 3, and 4, as shown in Figure 4.4.

Computer software packages are available to help in constructing more complex decision trees. See Appendix 4.1.

Because the decision maker controls the branch leaving decision node 1 and because we are trying to maximize the expected profit, the best decision alternative at node 1 is d_3.

FIGURE 4.4   APPLYING THE EXPECTED VALUE APPROACH USING A DECISION TREE

Small (d_1)   2   EV(d_1) = 0.8(8) + 0.2(7) = \$7.8

Medium (d_2)   3   EV(d_2) = 0.8(14) + 0.2(5) = \$12.2

Large (d_3)   4   EV(d_3) = 0.8(20) + 0.2(-9) = \$14.2

Thus, the decision tree analysis leads to a recommendation of d_3, with an expected value of $14.2 million. Note that this recommendation is also obtained with the expected value approach in conjunction with the payoff table.

Other decision problems may be substantially more complex than the PDC problem, but if a reasonable number of decision alternatives and states of nature are present, you can use the decision tree approach outlined here. First, draw a decision tree consisting of decision nodes, chance nodes, and branches that describe the sequential nature of the problem. If you use the expected value approach, the next step is to determine the probabilities for each of the states of nature and compute the expected value at each chance node. Then select the decision branch leading to the chance node with the best expected value. The decision alternative associated with this branch is the recommended decision.

The Q.M. in Action, Early Detection of High-Risk Worker Disability Claims, describes how the Workers' Compensation Board of British Columbia used a decision tree and expected cost to help determine whether a short-term disability claim should be considered a high-risk or a low-risk claim.

Q.M. *in* ACTION

EARLY DETECTION OF HIGH-RISK WORKER DISABILITY CLAIMS*

The Workers' Compensation Board of British Columbia (WCB) helps workers and employers maintain safe workplaces and helps injured workers obtain disability income and return to work safely. The funds used to make the disability compensation payments are obtained from assessments levied on employers. In return, employers receive protection from lawsuits arising from work-related injuries. In recent years, the WCB spent more than $1 billion on worker compensation and rehabilitation.

A short-term disability claim occurs when a worker suffers an injury or illness that results in temporary absence from work. Whenever a worker fails to recover completely from a short-term disability, the claim is reclassified as a long-term disability claim, and more expensive long-term benefits are paid.

The WCB wanted a systematic way to identify short-term disability claims that posed a high financial risk of being converted to the more expensive long-term disability claims. If a short-term disability claim could be classified as high risk early in the process, a WCB management team could intervene and monitor the claim and

the recovery process more closely. As a result, WCB could improve the management of the high-risk claims and reduce the cost of any subsequent long-term disability claims.

The WCB used a decision analysis approach to classify each new short-term disability claim as being either a high-risk claim or a low-risk claim. A decision tree consisting of two decision nodes and two states-of-nature nodes was developed. The two decision alternatives were: (1) Classify the new short-term claim as high-risk and intervene; (2) Classify the new short-term claim as low-risk and do not intervene. The two states of nature were: (1) The short-term claim converts to a long-term claim; (2) The short-term claim does not convert to a long-term claim. The characteristics of each new short-term claim were used to determine the probabilities for the states of nature. The payoffs were the disability claim costs associated with each decision alternative and each state-of-nature outcome. The objective of minimizing the expected cost determined whether a new short-term claim should be classified as high-risk.

Implementation of the decision analysis model improved the practice of claim management for the Workers' Compensation Board. Early intervention on the high-risk claims saved an estimated $4.7 million per year.

*Based on E. Urbanovich, E. Young, M. Puterman, and S. Fattedad, "Early Detection of High-Risk Claims at the Workers' Compensation Board of British Columbia," *Interfaces* (July/August 2003): 15–26.

Expected Value of Perfect Information

Suppose that PDC has the opportunity to conduct a market research study that would help evaluate buyer interest in the condominium project and provide information that management could use to improve the probability assessments for the states of nature. To determine the potential value of this information, we begin by supposing that the study could provide *perfect information* regarding the states of nature; that is, we assume for the moment that PDC could determine with certainty, prior to making a decision, which state of nature is going to occur. To make use of this perfect information, we will develop a decision strategy that PDC should follow once it knows which state of nature will occur. A decision strategy is simply a decision rule that specifies the decision alternative to be selected after new information becomes available.

To help determine the decision strategy for PDC, we reproduced PDC's payoff table as Table 4.6. Note that, if PDC knew for sure that state of nature s_1 would occur, the best decision alternative would be d_3, with a payoff of $20 million. Similarly, if PDC knew for sure that state of nature s_2 would occur, the best decision alternative would be d_1, with a payoff of $7 million. Thus, we can state PDC's optimal decision strategy when the perfect information becomes available as follows:

If s_1, select d_3 and receive a payoff of $20 million.

If s_2, select d_1 and receive a payoff of $7 million.

What is the expected value for this decision strategy? To compute the expected value with perfect information, we return to the original probabilities for the states of nature: $P(s_1) = 0.8$ and $P(s_2) = 0.2$. Thus, there is a 0.8 probability that the perfect information will indicate state of nature s_1, and the resulting decision alternative d_3 will provide a $20 million profit. Similarly, with a 0.2 probability for state of nature s_2, the optimal decision alternative d_1 will provide a $7 million profit. Thus, from equation (4.4) the expected value of the decision strategy that uses perfect information is $0.8(20) + 0.2(7) = 17.4$. We refer to the expected value of $17.4 million as the *expected value with perfect information* (EVwPI).

Earlier in this section we showed that the recommended decision using the expected value approach is decision alternative d_3, with an expected value of $14.2 million. Because this decision recommendation and expected value computation were made without the benefit of perfect information, $14.2 million is referred to as the *expected value without perfect information* (EVwoPI).

The expected value with perfect information is $17.4 million, and the expected value without perfect information is $14.2; therefore, the expected value of the perfect information (EVPI) is $17.4 - $14.2 = $3.2 million. In other words, $3.2 million represents the additional expected value that can be obtained if perfect information were available about the states of nature.

TABLE 4.6   PAYOFF TABLE FOR THE PDC CONDOMINIUM PROJECT ($ MILLIONS)

	State of Nature	
Decision Alternative	**Strong Demand s_1**	**Weak Demand s_2**
Small complex, d_1	8	7
Medium complex, d_2	14	5
Large complex, d_3	20	−9

It would be worth $3.2 million for PDC to learn the level of market acceptance before selecting a decision alternative.

Generally speaking, a market research study will not provide "perfect" information; however, if the market research study is a good one, the information gathered might be worth a sizable portion of the $3.2 million. Given the EVPI of $3.2 million, PDC might seriously consider a market survey as a way to obtain more information about the states of nature.

In general, the **expected value of perfect information (EVPI)** is computed as follows:

$$EVPI = |EVwPI - EVwoPI| \qquad \textbf{(4.5)}$$

where

$$EVPI = \text{expected value of perfect information}$$
$$EVwPI = \text{expected value } with \text{ perfect information about the states of nature}$$
$$EVwoPI = \text{expected value } without \text{ perfect information about the states of nature}$$

For practice in determining the expected value of perfect information, try Problem 14.

Note the role of the absolute value in equation (4.5). For minimization problems the expected value with perfect information is always less than or equal to the expected value without perfect information. In this case, EVPI is the magnitude of the difference between EVwPI and EVwoPI, or the absolute value of the difference as shown in equation (4.5).

NOTES AND COMMENTS

We restate the *opportunity loss,* or *regret,* table for the PDC problem (see Table 4.4) as follows:

| | State of Nature | |
| | Strong Demand | Weak Demand |
Decision	s_1	s_2
Small complex, d_1	12	0
Medium complex, d_2	6	2
Large complex, d_3	0	16

Using $P(s_1)$, $P(s_2)$, and the opportunity loss values, we can compute the *expected opportunity loss* (EOL) for each decision alternative. With $P(s_1) = 0.8$

and $P(s_2) = 0.2$, the expected opportunity loss for each of the three decision alternatives is

$$EOL(d_1) = 0.8(12) + 0.2(0) = 9.6$$
$$EOL(d_2) = 0.8(6) + 0.2(2) = 5.2$$
$$EOL(d_3) = 0.8(0) + 0.2(16) = 3.2$$

Regardless of whether the decision analysis involves maximization or minimization, the *minimum* expected opportunity loss always provides the best decision alternative. Thus, with $EOL(d_3) = 3.2$, d_3 is the recommended decision. In addition, the minimum expected opportunity loss always is *equal to the expected value of perfect information.* That is, EOL(best decision) = EVPI; for the PDC problem, this value is $3.2 million.

4.4   Risk Analysis and Sensitivity Analysis

Risk analysis helps the decision maker recognize the difference between the expected value of a decision alternative and the payoff that may actually occur. **Sensitivity analysis** also helps the decision maker by describing how changes in the state-of-nature probabilities and/or changes in the payoffs affect the recommended decision alternative.

Risk Analysis

A decision alternative and a state of nature combine to generate the payoff associated with a decision. The **risk profile** for a decision alternative shows the possible payoffs along with their associated probabilities.

FIGURE 4.5   RISK PROFILE FOR THE LARGE COMPLEX DECISION ALTERNATIVE FOR
THE PDC CONDOMINIUM PROJECT

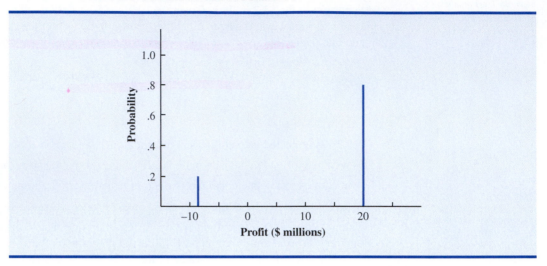

Let us demonstrate risk analysis and the construction of a risk profile by returning to the PDC condominium construction project. Using the expected value approach, we identified the large condominium complex (d_3) as the best decision alternative. The expected value of $14.2 million for d_3 is based on a 0.8 probability of obtaining a $20 million profit and a 0.2 probability of obtaining a $9 million loss. The 0.8 probability for the $20 million payoff and the 0.2 probability for the $-$9 million payoff provide the risk profile for the large complex decision alternative. This risk profile is shown graphically in Figure 4.5.

Sometimes a review of the risk profile associated with an optimal decision alternative may cause the decision maker to choose another decision alternative even though the expected value of the other decision alternative is not as good. For example, the risk profile for the medium complex decision alternative (d_2) shows a 0.8 probability for a $14 million payoff and a 0.2 probability for a $5 million payoff. Because no probability of a loss is associated with decision alternative d_2, the medium complex decision alternative would be judged less risky than the large complex decision alternative. As a result, a decision maker might prefer the less risky medium complex decision alternative even though it has an expected value of $2 million less than the large complex decision alternative.

Sensitivity Analysis

Sensitivity analysis can be used to determine how changes in the probabilities for the states of nature or changes in the payoffs affect the recommended decision alternative. In many cases, the probabilities for the states of nature and the payoffs are based on subjective assessments. Sensitivity analysis helps the decision maker understand which of these inputs are critical to the choice of the best decision alternative. If a small change in the value of one of the inputs causes a change in the recommended decision alternative, the solution to the decision analysis problem is sensitive to that particular input. Extra effort and care should be taken to make sure the input value is as accurate as possible. On the other hand, if a modest-to-large change in the value of one of the inputs does not cause a change in the recommended decision alternative, the solution to the decision analysis problem is not sensitive to that particular input. No extra time or effort would be needed to refine the estimated input value.

One approach to sensitivity analysis is to select different values for the probabilities of the states of nature and the payoffs and then resolve the decision analysis problem. If the recommended decision alternative changes, we know that the solution is sensitive to the changes made. For example, suppose that in the PDC problem the probability for a strong demand is revised to 0.2 and the probability for a weak demand is revised to 0.8. Would the recommended decision alternative change? Using $P(s_1) = 0.2$, $P(s_2) = 0.8$, and equation (4.4), the revised expected values for the three decision alternatives are

$$EV(d_1) = 0.2(8)\ \ + 0.8(7)\ \ = \ \ 7.2$$
$$EV(d_2) = 0.2(14) + 0.8(5)\ \ = \ \ 6.8$$
$$EV(d_3) = 0.2(20) + 0.8(-9) = -3.2$$

With these probability assessments the recommended decision alternative is to construct a small condominium complex (d_1), with an expected value of \$7.2 million. The probability of strong demand is only 0.2, so constructing the large condominium complex (d_3) is the least preferred alternative, with an expected value of $-$\$3.2 million (a loss).

Thus, when the probability of strong demand is large, PDC should build the large complex; when the probability of strong demand is small, PDC should build the small complex. Obviously, we could continue to modify the probabilities of the states of nature and learn even more about how changes in the probabilities affect the recommended decision alternative. The drawback to this approach is the numerous calculations required to evaluate the effect of several possible changes in the state-of-nature probabilities.

Computer software packages for decision analysis make it easy to calculate these revised scenarios.

For the special case of two states of nature, a graphical procedure can be used to determine how changes for the probabilities of the states of nature affect the recommended decision alternative. To demonstrate this procedure, we let p denote the probability of state of nature s_1; that is, $P(s_1) = p$. With only two states of nature in the PDC problem, the probability of state of nature s_2 is

$$P(s_2) = 1 - P(s_1) = 1 - p$$

Using equation (4.4) and the payoff values in Table 4.1, we determine the expected value for decision alternative d_1 as follows:

$$\begin{aligned} EV(d_1) &= P(s_1)(8) + P(s_2)(7) \\ &= p(8) + (1 - p)(7) \\ &= 8p + 7 - 7p = p + 7 \end{aligned} \qquad \textbf{(4.6)}$$

Repeating the expected value computations for decision alternatives d_2 and d_3, we obtain expressions for the expected value of each decision alternative as a function of p:

$$EV(d_2) = 9p + 5 \qquad \textbf{(4.7)}$$

$$EV(d_3) = 29p - 9 \qquad \textbf{(4.8)}$$

Thus, we have developed three equations that show the expected value of the three decision alternatives as a function of the probability of state of nature s_1.

We continue by developing a graph with values of p on the horizontal axis and the associated EVs on the vertical axis. Because equations (4.6), (4.7), and (4.8) are linear equations, the graph of each equation is a straight line. For each equation, we can obtain the line

FIGURE 4.6   EXPECTED VALUE FOR THE PDC DECISION ALTERNATIVES
AS A FUNCTION OF p

by identifying two points that satisfy the equation and drawing a line through the points. For instance, if we let $p = 0$ in equation (4.6), $EV(d_1) = 7$. Then, letting $p = 1$, $EV(d_1) = 8$. Connecting these two points, $(0,7)$ and $(1,8)$, provides the line labeled $EV(d_1)$ in Figure 4.6. Similarly, we obtain the lines labeled $EV(d_2)$ and $EV(d_3)$; these lines are the graphs of equations (4.7) and (4.8), respectively.

Figure 4.6 shows how the recommended decision changes as p, the probability of the strong demand state of nature (s_1), changes. Note that for small values of p, decision alternative d_1 (small complex) provides the largest expected value and is thus the recommended decision. When the value of p increases to a certain point, decision alternative d_2 (medium complex) provides the largest expected value and is the recommended decision. Finally, for large values of p, decision alternative d_3 (large complex) becomes the recommended decision.

The value of p for which the expected values of d_1 and d_2 are equal is the value of p corresponding to the intersection of the $EV(d_1)$ and the $EV(d_2)$ lines. To determine this value, we set $EV(d_1) = EV(d_2)$ and solve for the value of p:

$$p + 7 = 9p + 5$$
$$8p = 2$$
$$p = \frac{2}{8} = 0.25$$

Hence, when $p = 0.25$, decision alternatives d_1 and d_2 provide the same expected value. Repeating this calculation for the value of p corresponding to the intersection of the EV(d_2) and EV(d_3) lines, we obtain $p = 0.70$.

Graphical sensitivity analysis shows how changes in the probabilities for the states of nature affect the recommended decision alternative. Try Problem 8.

Using Figure 4.6, we can conclude that decision alternative d_1 provides the largest expected value for $p \leq 0.25$, decision alternative d_2 provides the largest expected value for $0.25 \leq p \leq 0.70$, and decision alternative d_3 provides the largest expected value for $p \geq 0.70$. Because p is the probability of state of nature s_1 and $(1 - p)$ is the probability of state of nature s_2, we now have the sensitivity analysis information that tells us how changes in the state-of-nature probabilities affect the recommended decision alternative.

Sensitivity analysis calculations can also be made for the values of the payoffs. In the original PDC problem, the expected values for the three decision alternatives were as follows: EV(d_1) = 7.8, EV(d_2) = 12.2, and EV(d_3) = 14.2. Decision alternative d_3 (large complex) was recommended. Note that decision alternative d_2 with EV(d_2) = 12.2 was the second best decision alternative. Decision alternative d_3 will remain the optimal decision alternative as long as EV(d_3) is greater than or equal to the expected value of the second best decision alternative. Thus, decision alternative d_3 will remain the optimal decision alternative as long as

$$\text{EV}(d_3) \geq 12.2 \qquad \textbf{(4.9)}$$

Let

$$S = \text{the payoff of decision alternative } d_3 \text{ when demand is strong}$$

$$W = \text{the payoff of decision alternative } d_3 \text{ when demand is weak}$$

Using $P(s_1) = 0.8$ and $P(s_2) = 0.2$, the general expression for EV(d_3) is

$$\text{EV}(d_3) = 0.8S + 0.2W \qquad \textbf{(4.10)}$$

Assuming that the payoff for d_3 stays at its original value of $-\$9$ million when demand is weak, the large complex decision alternative will remain optimal as long as

$$\text{EV}(d_3) = 0.8S + 0.2(-9) \geq 12.2 \qquad \textbf{(4.11)}$$

Solving for S, we have

$$0.8S - 1.8 \geq 12.2$$
$$0.8S \geq 14$$
$$S \geq 17.5$$

Recall that when demand is strong, decision alternative d_3 has an estimated payoff of $20 million. The preceding calculation shows that decision alternative d_3 will remain optimal as long as the payoff for d_3 when demand is strong is at least $17.5 million.

Assuming that the payoff for d_3 when demand is strong stays at its original value of $20 million, we can make a similar calculation to learn how sensitive the optimal solution is with regard to the payoff for d_3 when demand is weak. Returning to the expected value calculation of equation (4.10), we know that the large complex decision alternative will remain optimal as long as

$$\text{EV}(d_3) = 0.8(20) + 0.2W \geq 12.2 \qquad \textbf{(4.12)}$$

Solving for W, we have

$$16 + 0.2 \geq 12.2$$
$$0.2W \geq -3.8$$
$$W \geq -19$$

Recall that when demand is weak, decision alternative d_3 has an estimated payoff of $-\$9$ million. The preceding calculation shows that decision alternative d_3 will remain optimal as long as the payoff for d_3 when demand is weak is at least $-\$19$ million.

Based on this sensitivity analysis, we conclude that the payoffs for the large complex decision alternative (d_3) could vary considerably, and d_3 would remain the recommended decision alternative. Thus, we conclude that the optimal solution for the PDC decision problem is not particularly sensitive to the payoffs for the large complex decision alternative. We note, however, that this sensitivity analysis has been conducted based on only one change at a time. That is, only one payoff was changed and the probabilities for the states of nature remained $P(s_1) = 0.8$ and $P(s_2) = 0.2$. Note that similar sensitivity analysis calculations can be made for the payoffs associated with the small complex decision alternative d_1 and the medium complex decision alternative d_2. However, in these cases, decision alternative d_3 remains optimal only if the changes in the payoffs for decision alternatives d_1 and d_2 meet the requirements that $EV(d_1) \leq 14.2$ and $EV(d_2) \leq 14.2$.

Sensitivity analysis can assist management in deciding whether more time and effort should be spent obtaining better estimates of payoffs and probabilities.

NOTES AND COMMENTS

1. Some decision analysis software automatically provide the risk profiles for the optimal decision alternative. These packages also allow the user to obtain the risk profiles for other decision alternatives. After comparing the risk profiles, a decision maker may decide to select a decision alternative with a good risk profile even though the expected value of the decision alternative is not as good as the optimal decision alternative.

2. A *tornado diagram,* a graphical display, is particularly helpful when several inputs combine to determine the value of the optimal solution. By varying each input over its range of values, we obtain information about how each input affects the value of the optimal solution. To display this information, a bar is constructed for the input, with the width of the bar showing how the input affects the value of the optimal solution. The widest bar corresponds to the input that is most sensitive. The bars are arranged in a graph with the widest bar at the top, resulting in a graph that has the appearance of a tornado.

4.5 Decision Analysis with Sample Information

In applying the expected value approach, we showed how probability information about the states of nature affects the expected value calculations and thus the decision recommendation. Frequently, decision makers have preliminary or **prior probability** assessments for the states of nature that are the best probability values available at that time. However, to make the best possible decision, the decision maker may want to seek additional information about the states of nature. This new information can be used to revise or update the prior probabilities so that the final decision is based on more accurate probabilities for the states of nature. Most often, additional information is obtained through experiments designed to provide **sample information** about the states of nature. Raw material sampling, product testing, and market research studies are examples of experiments (or studies) that may enable management to revise or update the state-of-nature probabilities. These revised probabilities are called **posterior probabilities**.

Let us return to the PDC problem and assume that management is considering a 6-month market research study designed to learn more about potential market acceptance of the PDC condominium project. Management anticipates that the market research study will provide one of the following two results:

1. Favorable report: A significant number of the individuals contacted express interest in purchasing a PDC condominium.
2. Unfavorable report: Very few of the individuals contacted express interest in purchasing a PDC condominium.

Influence Diagram

By introducing the possibility of conducting a market research study, the PDC problem becomes more complex. The influence diagram for the expanded PDC problem is shown in Figure 4.7. Note that the two decision nodes correspond to the research study and the complex-size decisions. The two chance nodes correspond to the research study results and demand for the condominiums. Finally, the consequence node is the profit. From the arcs of the influence diagram, we see that demand influences both the research study results and profit. Although demand is currently unknown to PDC, some level of demand for the condominiums already exists in the Pittsburgh area. If existing demand is strong, the research study is likely to find a significant number of individuals who express an interest in purchasing a condominium. However, if the existing demand is weak, the research study is more likely to find a significant number of individuals who express little interest in purchasing a condominium. In this sense, existing demand for the condominiums will influence the research study results, and clearly, demand will have an influence upon PDC's profit.

The arc from the research study decision node to the complex-size decision node indicates that the research study decision precedes the complex-size decision. No arc spans from the research study decision node to the research study results node because the decision to conduct the research study does not actually influence the research study results. The decision to conduct the research study makes the research study results available, but it does not influence the results of the research study. Finally, the complex-size node and

FIGURE 4.7   INFLUENCE DIAGRAM FOR THE PDC PROBLEM WITH SAMPLE
INFORMATION

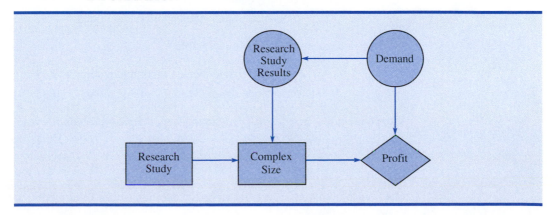

the demand node both influence profit. Note that if a stated cost to conduct the research study were given, the decision to conduct the research study would also influence profit. In such a case, we would need to add an arc from the research study decision node to the profit node to show the influence that the research study cost would have on profit.

Decision Tree

The decision tree for the PDC problem with sample information shows the logical sequence for the decisions and the chance events in Figure 4.8.

First, PDC's management must decide whether the market research should be conducted. If it is conducted, PDC's management must be prepared to make a decision about the size of the condominium project if the market research report is favorable and, possibly, a different decision about the size of the condominium project if the market research report is unfavorable. In Figure 4.8, the squares are decision nodes and the circles are chance nodes. At each decision node, the branch of the tree that is taken is based on the decision made. At each chance node, the branch of the tree that is taken is based on probability or chance. For example, decision node 1 shows that PDC must first make the decision of whether to conduct the market research study. If the market research study is undertaken, chance node 2 indicates that both the favorable report branch and the unfavorable report branch are not under PDC's control and will be determined by chance. Node 3 is a decision node, indicating that PDC must make the decision to construct the small, medium, or large complex if the market research report is favorable. Node 4 is a decision node showing that PDC must make the decision to construct the small, medium, or large complex if the market research report is unfavorable. Node 5 is a decision node indicating that PDC must make the decision to construct the small, medium, or large complex if the market research is not undertaken. Nodes 6 to 14 are chance nodes indicating that the strong demand or weak demand state-of-nature branches will be determined by chance.

We explain in Section 4.6 how these probabilities can be developed.

Analysis of the decision tree and the choice of an optimal strategy require that we know the branch probabilities corresponding to all chance nodes. PDC has developed the following branch probabilities:

If the market research study is undertaken

$$P(\text{Favorable report}) = 0.77$$
$$P(\text{Unfavorable report}) = 0.23$$

If the market research report is favorable

$$P(\text{Strong demand given a favorable report}) = 0.94$$
$$P(\text{Weak demand given a favorable report}) = 0.06$$

If the market research report is unfavorable

$$P(\text{Strong demand given a favorable report}) = 0.35$$
$$P(\text{Weak demand given a favorable report}) = 0.65$$

If the market research report is not undertaken, the prior probabilities are applicable.

$$P(\text{Strong demand}) = 0.80$$
$$P(\text{Weak demand}) = 0.20$$

The branch probabilities are shown on the decision tree in Figure 4.9.

FIGURE 4.8   THE PDC DECISION TREE INCLUDING THE MARKET RESEARCH STUDY

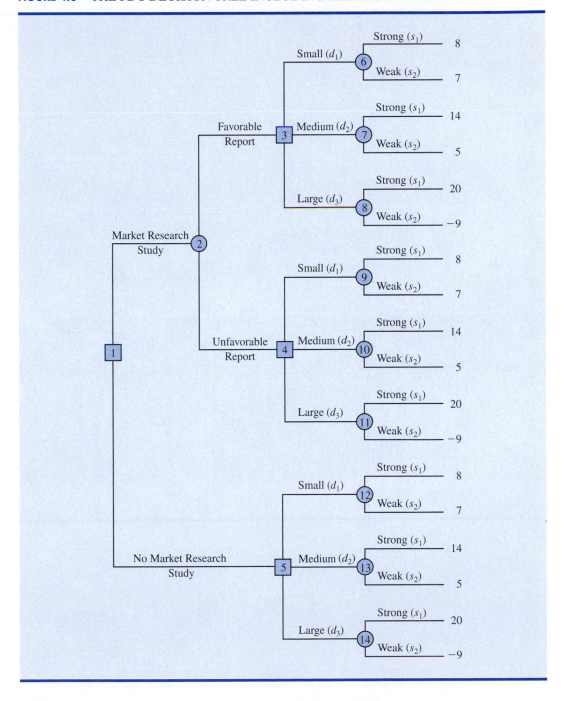

FIGURE 4.9   THE PDC DECISION TREE WITH BRANCH PROBABILITIES

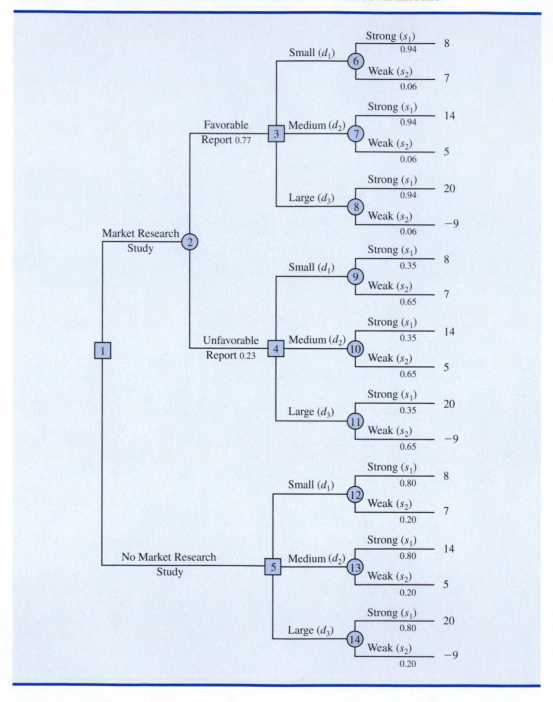

Decision Strategy

A **decision strategy** is a sequence of decisions and chance outcomes where the decisions chosen depend on the yet-to-be-determined outcomes of chance events.

The approach used to determine the optimal decision strategy is based on a backward pass through the decision tree using the following steps:

1. At chance nodes, compute the expected value by multiplying the payoff at the end of each branch by the corresponding branch probabilities.
2. At decision nodes, select the decision branch that leads to the best expected value. This expected value becomes the expected value at the decision node.

Starting the backward pass calculations by computing the expected values at chance nodes 6 to 14 provides the following results:

$$
\begin{aligned}
\text{EV(Node 6)} &= 0.94(8) + 0.06(7)   &&= 7.94 \\
\text{EV(Node 7)} &= 0.94(14) + 0.06(5) &&= 13.46 \\
\text{EV(Node 8)} &= 0.94(20) + 0.06(-9) &&= 18.26 \\
\text{EV(Node 9)} &= 0.35(8) + 0.65(7)   &&= 7.35 \\
\text{EV(Node 10)} &= 0.35(14) + 0.65(5) &&= 8.15 \\
\text{EV(Node 11)} &= 0.35(20) + 0.65(-9) &&= 1.15 \\
\text{EV(Node 12)} &= 0.80(8) + 0.20(7)   &&= 7.80 \\
\text{EV(Node 13)} &= 0.80(14) + 0.20(5) &&= 12.20 \\
\text{EV(Node 14)} &= 0.80(20) + 0.20(-9) &&= 14.20
\end{aligned}
$$

Figure 4.10 shows the reduced decision tree after computing expected values at these chance nodes.

Next, move to decision nodes 3, 4, and 5. For each of these nodes, we select the decision alternative branch that leads to the best expected value. For example, at node 3 we have the choice of the small complex branch with EV(Node 6) = 7.94, the medium complex branch with EV(Node 7) = 13.46, and the large complex branch with EV(Node 8) = 18.26. Thus, we select the large complex decision alternative branch and the expected value at node 3 becomes EV(Node 3) = 18.26.

For node 4, we select the best expected value from nodes 9, 10, and 11. The best decision alternative is the medium complex branch that provides EV(Node 4) = 8.15. For node 5, we select the best expected value from nodes 12, 13, and 14. The best decision alternative is the large complex branch that provides EV(Node 5) = 14.20. Figure 4.11 shows the reduced decision tree after choosing the best decisions at nodes 3, 4, and 5.

The expected value at chance node 2 can now be computed as follows:

$$
\begin{aligned}
\text{EV(Node 2)} &= 0.77\text{EV(Node 3)} + 0.23\text{EV(Node 4)} \\
&= 0.77(18.26) + 0.23(8.15) = 15.93
\end{aligned}
$$

This calculation reduces the decision tree to one involving only the two decision branches from node 1 (see Figure 4.12).

Finally, the decision can be made at decision node 1 by selecting the best expected values from nodes 2 and 5. This action leads to the decision alternative to conduct the market research study, which provides an overall expected value of 15.93.

FIGURE 4.10   PDC DECISION TREE AFTER COMPUTING EXPECTED VALUES AT CHANCE NODES 6 TO 14

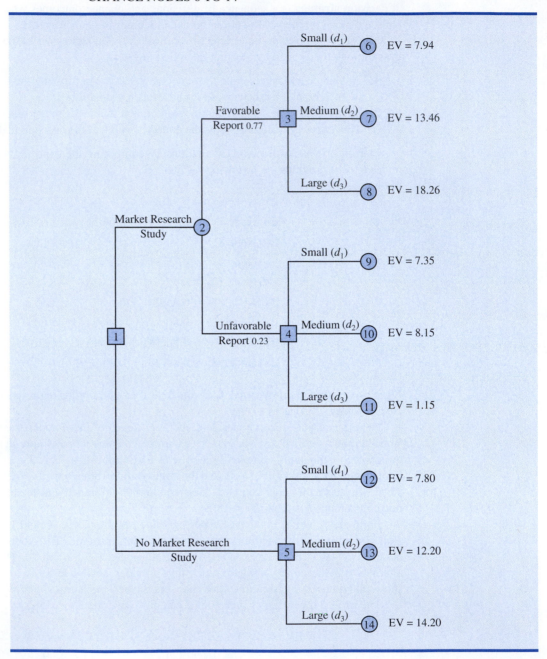

The optimal decision for PDC is to conduct the market research study and then carry out the following decision strategy:

Problem 16 will test your ability to develop an optimal decision strategy.

If the market research is favorable, construct the large condominium complex.

If the market research is unfavorable, construct the medium condominium complex.

FIGURE 4.11 PDC DECISION TREE AFTER CHOOSING BEST DECISIONS AT NODES 3, 4, AND 5

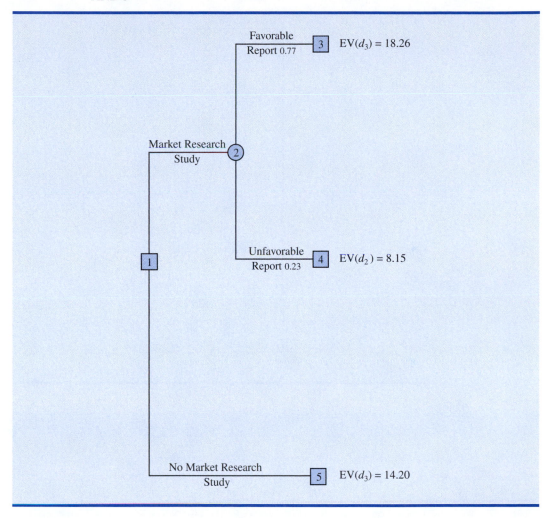

The analysis of the PDC decision tree describes the methods that can be used to analyze more complex sequential decision problems. First, draw a decision tree consisting of decision and chance nodes and branches that describe the sequential nature of the problem. Determine the probabilities for all chance outcomes. Then, by working backward through the tree, compute expected values at all chance nodes and select the best decision branch at all decision nodes. The sequence of optimal decision branches determines the optimal decision strategy for the problem.

The Q.M. in Action, New Drug Decision Analysis at Bayer Pharmaceuticals, describes how an extension of the decision analysis principles presented in this section enabled Bayer to make decisions about the development and marketing of a new drug.

Risk Profile

Figure 4.13 provides a reduced decision tree showing only the sequence of decision alternatives and chance events for the PDC optimal decision strategy. By implementing the

FIGURE 4.12   PDC DECISION TREE REDUCED TO TWO DECISION BRANCHES

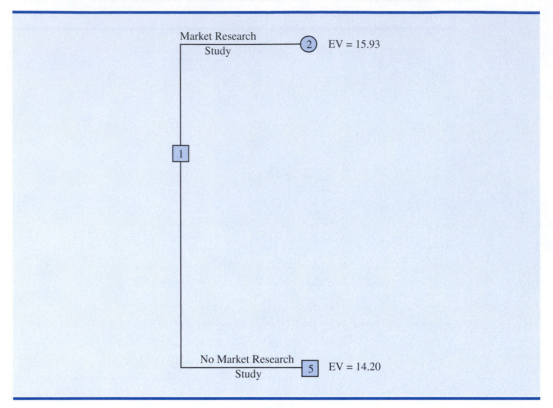

NEW DRUG DECISION ANALYSIS AT BAYER PHARMACEUTICALS*

Drug development in the United States requires substantial investment and is very risky. It takes nearly 15 years to research and develop a new drug. The Bayer Biological Products (BP) group used decision analysis to evaluate the potential for a new blood-clot–busting drug. An influence diagram was used to describe the complex structure of the decision analysis process. Six key yes-or-no decision nodes were identified: (1) begin preclinical development; (2) begin testing in humans; (3) continue development into phase 3; (4) continue development into phase 4; (5) file a license application with the FDA; and (6) launch the new drug into the marketplace. More than 50 chance nodes appeared in the influence diagram. The

chance nodes showed how uncertainties—related to factors such as direct labor costs, process development costs, market share, tax rate, and pricing—affected the outcome. Net present value provided the consequence and the decision-making criterion.

Probability assessments were made concerning both the technical risk and market risk at each stage of the process. The resulting sequential decision tree had 1955 possible paths that led to different net present value outcomes. Cost inputs, judgments of potential outcomes, and the assignment of probabilities helped evaluate the project's potential contribution. Sensitivity analysis was used to identify key variables that would require special attention by the project team and management during the drug development process. Application of decision analysis principles allowed Bayer to make good decisions about how to develop and market the new drug.

*Based on Jeffrey S. Stonebraker, "How Bayer Makes Decisions to Develop New Drugs," *Interfaces*, no. 6 (November/December 2002): 77–90.

FIGURE 4.13   PDC DECISION TREE SHOWING ONLY BRANCHES ASSOCIATED WITH OPTIMAL DECISION STRATEGY

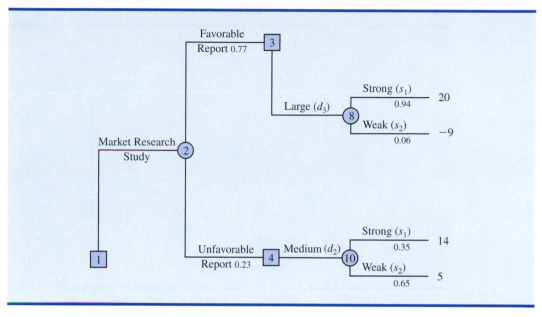

optimal decision strategy, PDC will obtain one of the four payoffs shown at the terminal branches of the decision tree. Recall that a risk profile shows the possible payoffs with their associated probabilities. Thus, in order to construct a risk profile for the optimal decision strategy, we will need to compute the probability for each of the four payoffs.

Note that each payoff results from a sequence of branches leading from node 1 to the payoff. For instance, the payoff of $20 million is obtained by following the upper branch from node 1, the upper branch from node 2, the lower branch from node 3, and the upper branch from node 8. The probability of following that sequence of branches can be found by multiplying the probabilities for the branches from the chance nodes in the sequence. Thus, the probability of the $20 million payoff is $(0.77)(0.94) = 0.72$. Similarly, the probabilities for each of the other payoffs are obtained by multiplying the probabilities for the branches from the chance nodes leading to the payoffs. Doing so, we find the probability of the –$9 million payoff is $(0.77)(0.06) = 0.05$; the probability of the $14 million payoff is $(0.23)(0.35) = 0.08$; and the probability of the $5 million payoff is $(0.23)(0.65) = 0.15$. The following table showing the probability distribution for the payoffs for the PDC optimal decision strategy is the tabular representation of the risk profile for the optimal decision strategy.

Payoff ($ millions)	Probability
−9	0.05
5	0.15
14	0.08
20	0.72
	1.00

Figure 4.14 provides a graphical representation of the risk profile. Comparing Figures 4.5 and 4.14, we see that the PDC risk profile is changed by the strategy to conduct the market

FIGURE 4.14   RISK PROFILE FOR PDC CONDOMINIUM PROJECT WITH SAMPLE INFORMATION SHOWING PAYOFFS ASSOCIATED WITH OPTIMAL DECISION STRATEGY

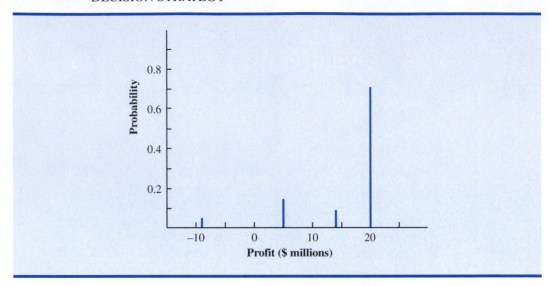

research study. In fact, the use of the market research study lowered the probability of the $9 million loss from 0.20 to 0.05. PDC's management would most likely view that change as a significant reduction in the risk associated with the condominium project.

Expected Value of Sample Information

In the PDC problem, the market research study is the sample information used to determine the optimal decision strategy. The expected value associated with the market research study is $15.93. In Section 4.3 we showed that the best expected value if the market research study is *not* undertaken is $14.20. Thus, we can conclude that the difference, $15.93 − $14.20 = $1.73, is the **expected value of sample information (EVSI)**. In other words, conducting the market research study adds $1.73 million to the PDC expected value. In general, the expected value of sample information is as follows:

$$\text{EVSI} = |\text{EVwSI} - \text{EVwoSI}| \qquad \textbf{(4.13)}$$

where

> EVSI = expected value of sample information
>
> EVwSI = expected value *with* sample information about the states of nature
>
> EVwoSI = expected value *without* sample information about the states of nature

The EVSI = $1.73 million suggests PDC should be willing to pay up to $1.73 million to conduct the market research study.

Note the role of the absolute value in equation (4.13). For minimization problems the expected value with sample information is always less than or equal to the expected value without sample information. In this case, EVSI is the magnitude of the difference between EVwSI and EVwoSI; thus, by taking the absolute value of the difference as shown in equation (4.13), we can handle both the maximization and minimization cases with one equation.

Efficiency of Sample Information

In Section 4.3 we showed that the expected value of perfect information (EVPI) for the PDC problem is $3.2 million. We never anticipated that the market research report would obtain perfect information, but we can use an **efficiency** measure to express the value of the market research information. With perfect information having an efficiency rating of 100%, the efficiency rating E for sample information is computed as follows:

$$E = \frac{EVSI}{EVPI} \times 100 \qquad \textbf{(4.14)}$$

For the PDC problem,

$$E = \frac{1.73}{3.2} \times 100 = 54.1\%$$

In other words, the information from the market research study is 54.1% as efficient as perfect information.

Low efficiency ratings for sample information might lead the decision maker to look for other types of information. However, high efficiency ratings indicate that the sample information is almost as good as perfect information and that additional sources of information would not yield significantly better results.

Computing Branch Probabilities

In Section 4.5 the branch probabilities for the PDC decision tree chance nodes were specified in the problem description. No computations were required to determine these probabilities. In this section we show how **Bayes' theorem** can be used to compute branch probabilities for decision trees.

The PDC decision tree is shown again in Figure 4.15. Let

$$F = \text{Favorable market research report}$$
$$U = \text{Unfavorable market research report}$$
$$s_1 = \text{Strong demand (state of nature 1)}$$
$$s_2 = \text{Weak demand (state of nature 2)}$$

At chance node 2, we need to know the branch probabilities $P(F)$ and $P(U)$. At chance nodes 6, 7, and 8, we need to know the branch probabilities $P(s_1 \mid F)$, the probability of state of nature 1 given a favorable market research report, and $P(s_2 \mid F)$, the probability of state of nature 2 given a favorable market research report. $P(s_1 \mid F)$ and $P(s_2 \mid F)$ are referred to as *posterior probabilities* because they are conditional probabilities based on the outcome of the sample information. At chance nodes 9, 10, and 11, we need to know the branch probabilities $P(s_1 \mid U)$ and $P(s_2 \mid U)$; note that these are also posterior probabilities, denoting the probabilities of the two states of nature *given* that the market research report is unfavorable. Finally, at chance nodes 12, 13, and 14, we need the probabilities for the states of nature, $P(s_1)$ and $P(s_2)$, if the market research study is not undertaken.

In making the probability computations, we need to know PDC's assessment of the probabilities for the two states of nature, $P(s_1)$ and $P(s_2)$, which are the prior probabilities as discussed earlier. In addition, we must know the **conditional probability** of the market

FIGURE 4.15   THE PDC DECISION TREE

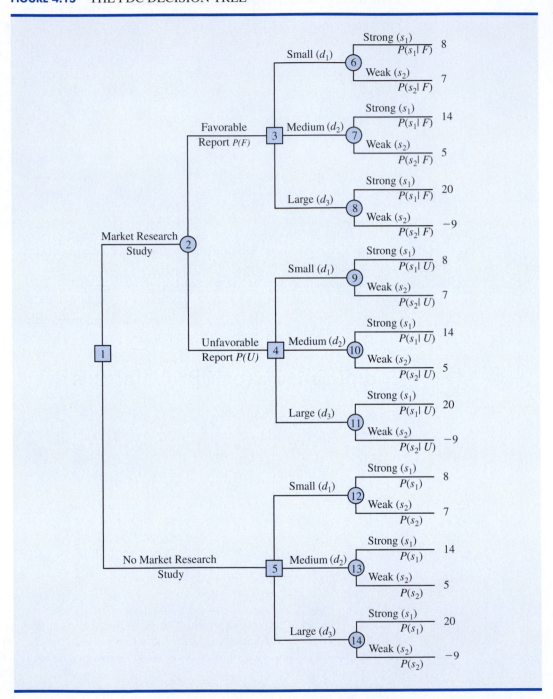

research outcomes (the sample information) *given* each state of nature. For example, we need to know the conditional probability of a favorable market research report given that the state of nature is strong demand for the PDC project; note that this conditional probability of F given state of nature s_1 is written $P(F \mid s_1)$. To carry out the probability calculations, we will need conditional probabilities for all sample outcomes given all states of nature, that is, $P(F \mid s_1)$, $P(F \mid s_2)$, $P(U \mid s_1)$, and $P(U \mid s_2)$. In the PDC problem we assume that the following assessments are available for these conditional probabilities:

	Market Research	
State of Nature	**Favorable, F**	**Unfavorable, U**
Strong demand, s_1	$P(F \mid s_1) = 0.90$	$P(U \mid s_1) = 0.10$
Weak demand, s_2	$P(F \mid s_2) = 0.25$	$P(U \mid s_2) = 0.75$

Note that the preceding probability assessments provide a reasonable degree of confidence in the market research study. If the true state of nature is s_1, the probability of a favorable market research report is 0.90, and the probability of an unfavorable market research report is 0.10. If the true state of nature is s_2, the probability of a favorable market research report is 0.25, and the probability of an unfavorable market research report is 0.75. The reason for a 0.25 probability of a potentially misleading favorable market research report for state of nature s_2 is that when some potential buyers first hear about the new condominium project, their enthusiasm may lead them to overstate their real interest in it. A potential buyer's initial favorable response can change quickly to a "no thank you" when later faced with the reality of signing a purchase contract and making a down payment.

In the following discussion we present a tabular approach as a convenient method for carrying out the probability computations. The computations for the PDC problem based on a favorable market research report (F) are summarized in Table 4.7. The steps used to develop this table are as follows:

Step 1. In column 1 enter the states of nature. In column 2 enter the *prior probabilities* for the states of nature. In column 3 enter the *conditional probabilities* of a favorable market research report (F) given each state of nature.

Step 2. In column 4 compute the **joint probabilities** by multiplying the prior probability values in column 2 by the corresponding conditional probability values in column 3.

Step 3. Sum the joint probabilities in column 4 to obtain the probability of a favorable market research report, $P(F)$.

Step 4. Divide each joint probability in column 4 by $P(F) = 0.77$ to obtain the revised or *posterior probabilities,* $P(s_1 \mid F)$ and $P(s_2 \mid F)$.

Table 4.7 shows that the probability of obtaining a favorable market research report is $P(F) = 0.77$. In addition, $P(s_1 \mid F) = 0.94$ and $P(s_2 \mid F) = 0.06$. In particular, note that a

TABLE 4.7   BRANCH PROBABILITIES FOR THE PDC CONDOMINIUM PROJECT BASED ON A FAVORABLE MARKET RESEARCH REPORT

States of Nature s_j	Prior Probabilities $P(s_j)$	Conditional Probabilities $P(F \mid s_j)$	Joint Probabilities $P(F \cap s_j)$	Posterior Probabilities $P(s_j \mid F)$
s_1	0.8	0.90	0.72	0.94
s_2	0.2	0.25	0.05	0.06
	1.0		$P(F) = 0.77$	1.00

TABLE 4.8   BRANCH PROBABILITIES FOR THE PDC CONDOMINIUM PROJECT BASED ON AN UNFAVORABLE MARKET RESEARCH REPORT

States of Nature s_j	Prior Probabilities $P(s_j)$	Conditional Probabilities $P(U \mid s_j)$	Joint Probabilities $P(U \cap s_j)$	Posterior Probabilities $P(s_j \mid U)$
s_1	0.8	0.10	0.08	0.35
s_2	0.2	0.75	0.15	0.65
	1.0		$P(U) = 0.23$	1.00

favorable market research report will prompt a revised or posterior probability of 0.94 that the market demand of the condominium will be strong, s_1.

The tabular probability computation procedure must be repeated for each possible sample information outcome. Thus, Table 4.8 shows the computations of the branch probabilities of the PDC problem based on an unfavorable market research report. Note that the probability of obtaining an unfavorable market research report is $P(U) = 0.23$. If an unfavorable report is obtained, the posterior probability of a strong market demand, s_1, is 0.35 and of a weak market demand, s_2, is 0.65. The branch probabilities from Tables 4.7 and 4.8 were shown on the PDC decision tree in Figure 4.9.

Problem 23 asks you to compute the posterior probabilities.

The discussion in this section shows an underlying relationship between the probabilities on the various branches in a decision tree. To assume different prior probabilities, $P(s_1)$ and $P(s_2)$, without determining how these changes would alter $P(F)$ and $P(U)$, as well as the posterior probabilities $P(s_1 \mid F)$, $P(s_2 \mid F)$, $P(s_1 \mid U)$, and $P(s_2 \mid U)$, would be inappropriate.

The Q.M. in Action, Medical Screening Test at Duke University Medical Center, shows how posterior probability information and decision analysis helped management understand the risks and costs associated with a new screening procedure.

Q.M. *in* ACTION

MEDICAL SCREENING TEST AT DUKE UNIVERSITY MEDICAL CENTER*

A medical screening test developed at the Duke University Medical Center involved using blood samples from newborns to screen for metabolic disorders. A positive test result indicated that a deficiency was present, while a negative test result indicated that a deficiency was not present. However, it was understood that the screening test was not a perfect predictor; that is, false-positive test results as well as false-negative test results were possible. A false-positive test result meant that the test detected a deficiency when in fact no deficiency was present. This case resulted in unnecessary further testing as well as unnecessary worry for the parents of the newborn. A false-negative test result meant that the test did not detect the presence of an existing deficiency. Using probability and decision analysis, a research team analyzed the role and value of the screening test.

A decision tree with six nodes, 13 branches, and eight outcomes was used to model the screening test procedure. A decision node with the decision branches Test and No Test was placed at the start of the decision tree. Chance nodes and branches were used to describe the

*Based on James E. Smith and Robert L. Winkler, "Casey's Problem: Interpreting and Evaluating a New Test," Interfaces 29, no. 3 (May/June 1999): 63–76.

(continued)

possible sequences of a positive test result, a negative test result, a deficiency present, and a deficiency not present.

The particular deficiency in question was rare, occurring at a rate of one case for every 250,000 newborns. Thus, the prior probability of a deficiency was $1/250,000 = 0.000004$. Based on judgments about the probabilities of false-positive and false-negative test results, Bayes' theorem was used to calculate the posterior probability that a newborn with a positive test result actually had a deficiency. This posterior probability was 0.074. Thus, while a positive test result increased the probability the newborn had a deficiency from 0.000004 to 0.074, the probability that the newborn had a deficiency was still relatively low (0.074).

The probability information was helpful to doctors in reassuring worried parents that even though further testing was recommended, the chances were greater than 90% that a deficiency was not present. After the assignment of costs to the eight possible outcomes, decision analysis showed that the decision alternative to conduct the test provided the optimal decision strategy. The expected cost criterion established the expected cost to be approximately $6 per test. Decision analysis helped provide a realistic understanding of the risks and costs associated with the screening test.

Summary

Decision analysis can be used to determine a recommended decision alternative or an optimal decision strategy when a decision maker is faced with an uncertain and risk-filled pattern of future events. The goal of decision analysis is to identify the best decision alternative or the optimal decision strategy given information about the uncertain events and the possible consequences or payoffs. The uncertain future events are called chance events, and the outcomes of the chance events are called states of nature.

We showed how influence diagrams, payoff tables, and decision trees could be used to structure a decision problem and describe the relationships among the decisions, the chance events, and the consequences. We presented three approaches to decision making without probabilities: the optimistic approach, the conservative approach, and the minimax regret approach. When probability assessments are provided for the states of nature, the expected value approach can be used to identify the recommended decision alternative or decision strategy.

In cases where sample information about the chance events is available, a sequence of decisions has to be made. First we must decide whether to obtain the sample information. If the answer to this decision is yes, an optimal decision strategy based on the specific sample information must be developed. In this situation, decision trees and the expected value approach can be used to determine the optimal decision strategy.

Even though the expected value approach can be used to obtain a recommended decision alternative or optimal decision strategy, the payoff that actually occurs will usually have a value different from the expected value. A risk profile provides a probability distribution for the possible payoffs and can assist the decision maker in assessing the risks associated with different decision alternatives. Finally, sensitivity analysis can be conducted to determine the effect changes in the probabilities for the states of nature and changes in the values of the payoffs have on the recommended decision alternative.

Decision analysis has been widely used in practice. The Q.M. in Action, Investing in a Transmission System at Oglethorpe Power, describes the use of decision analysis to decide whether to invest in a major transmission system between Georgia and Florida.

Q.M. *in* ACTION

INVESTING IN A TRANSMISSION SYSTEM AT OGLETHORPE POWER*

Oglethorpe Power Corporation (OPC) provides wholesale electrical power to consumer-owned cooperatives in the state of Georgia. Florida Power Corporation proposed that OPC join in the building of a major transmission line from Georgia to Florida. Deciding whether to become involved in the building of the transmission line was a major decision for OPC because it would involve the commitment of substantial OPC resources. OPC worked with Applied Decision Analysis, Inc., to conduct a comprehensive decision analysis of the problem.

In the problem formulation step, three decisions were identified: (1) build a transmission line from Georgia to Florida; (2) upgrade existing transmission facilities; and (3) who would control the new facilities. Oglethorpe was faced with five chance events: (1) construction costs, (2) competition, (3) demand in Florida, (4) OPC's share of the operation, and (5) pricing. The

*Based on Adam Borison, "Oglethorpe Power Corporation Decides About Investing in a Major Transmission System," Interfaces (March/April 1995): 25–36.

consequence or payoff was measured in terms of dollars saved. The influence diagram for the problem had three decision nodes, five chance nodes, a consequence node, and several intermediate nodes that described intermediate calculations. The decision tree for the problem had more than 8000 paths from the starting node to the terminal branches.

An expected value analysis of the decision tree provided an optimal decision strategy for OPC. However, the risk profile for the optimal decision strategy showed that the recommended strategy was very risky and had a significant probability of increasing OPC's cost rather than providing a savings. The risk analysis led to the conclusion that more information about the competition was needed in order to reduce OPC's risk. Sensitivity analysis involving various probabilities and payoffs showed that the value of the optimal decision strategy was stable over a reasonable range of input values. The final recommendation from the decision analysis was that OPC should begin negotiations with Florida Power Corporation concerning the building of the new transmission line.

Glossary

Decision alternatives Options available to the decision maker.

Chance event An uncertain future event affecting the consequence, or payoff, associated with a decision.

Consequence The result obtained when a decision alternative is chosen and a chance event occurs. A measure of the consequence is often called a payoff.

States of nature The possible outcomes for chance events that affect the payoff associated with a decision alternative.

Influence diagram A graphical device that shows the relationship among decisions, chance events, and consequences for a decision problem.

Node An intersection or junction point of an influence diagram or a decision tree.

Decision nodes Nodes indicating points where a decision is made.

Chance nodes Nodes indicating points where an uncertain event will occur.

Consequence nodes Nodes of an influence diagram indicating points where a payoff will occur.

Payoff A measure of the consequence of a decision such as profit, cost, or time. Each combination of a decision alternative and a state of nature has an associated payoff (consequence).

Payoff table A tabular representation of the payoffs for a decision problem.

Decision tree A graphical representation of the decision problem that shows the sequential nature of the decision-making process.

Branch Lines showing the alternatives from decision nodes and the outcomes from chance nodes.

Optimistic approach An approach to choosing a decision alternative without using probabilities. For a maximization problem, it leads to choosing the decision alternative corresponding to the largest payoff; for a minimization problem, it leads to choosing the decision alternative corresponding to the smallest payoff.

Conservative approach An approach to choosing a decision alternative without using probabilities. For a maximization problem, it leads to choosing the decision alternative that maximizes the minimum payoff; for a minimization problem, it leads to choosing the decision alternative that minimizes the maximum payoff.

Minimax regret approach An approach to choosing a decision alternative without using probabilities. For each alternative, the maximum regret is computed, which leads to choosing the decision alternative that minimizes the maximum regret.

Opportunity loss, or regret The amount of loss (lower profit or higher cost) from not making the best decision for each state of nature.

Expected value approach An approach to choosing a decision alternative based on the expected value of each decision alternative. The recommended decision alternative is the one that provides the best expected value.

Expected value (EV) For a chance node, it is the weighted average of the payoffs. The weights are the state-of-nature probabilities.

Expected value of perfect information (EVPI) The expected value of information that would tell the decision maker exactly which state of nature is going to occur (i.e., perfect information).

Risk analysis The study of the possible payoffs and probabilities associated with a decision alternative or a decision strategy.

Sensitivity analysis The study of how changes in the probability assessments for the states of nature or changes in the payoffs affect the recommended decision alternative.

Risk profile The probability distribution of the possible payoffs associated with a decision alternative or decision strategy.

Prior probabilities The probabilities of the states of nature prior to obtaining sample information.

Sample information New information obtained through research or experimentation that enables an updating or revision of the state-of-nature probabilities.

Posterior (revised) probabilities The probabilities of the states of nature after revising the prior probabilities based on sample information.

Decision strategy A strategy involving a sequence of decisions and chance outcomes to provide the optimal solution to a decision problem.

Expected value of sample information (EVSI) The difference between the expected value of an optimal strategy based on sample information and the "best" expected value without any sample information.

Efficiency The ratio of EVSI to EVPI as a percentage; perfect information is 100% efficient.

Bayes' theorem A theorem that enables the use of sample information to revise prior probabilities.

Conditional probabilities The probability of one event given the known outcome of a (possibly) related event.

Joint probabilities The probabilities of both sample information and a particular state of nature occurring simultaneously.

Problems

1. The following payoff table shows profit for a decision analysis problem with two decision alternatives and three states of nature:

	State of Nature		
Decision Alternative	s_1	s_2	s_3
d_1	250	100	25
d_2	100	100	75

   a. Construct a decision tree for this problem.
   b. If the decision maker knows nothing about the probabilities of the three states of nature, what is the recommended decision using the optimistic, conservative, and minimax regret approaches?

2. Suppose that a decision maker faced with four decision alternatives and four states of nature develops the following profit payoff table:

	State of Nature			
Decision Alternative	s_1	s_2	s_3	s_4
d_1	14	9	10	5
d_2	11	10	8	7
d_3	9	10	10	11
d_4	8	10	11	13

   a. If the decision maker knows nothing about the probabilities of the four states of nature, what is the recommended decision using the optimistic, conservative, and minimax regret approaches?
   b. Which approach do you prefer? Explain. Is establishing the most appropriate approach before analyzing the problem important for the decision maker? Explain.
   c. Assume that the payoff table provides *cost* rather than profit payoffs. What is the recommended decision using the optimistic, conservative, and minimax regret approaches?

3. Southland Corporation's decision to produce a new line of recreational products resulted in the need to construct either a small plant or a large plant. The best selection of plant size depends on how the marketplace reacts to the new product line. To conduct an analysis, marketing management has decided to view the possible long-run demand as low, medium, or high. The following payoff table shows the projected profit in millions of dollars:

	Long-Run Demand		
Plant Size	**Low**	**Medium**	**High**
Small	150	200	200
Large	50	200	500

   a. What is the decision to be made, and what is the chance event for Southland's problem?
   b. Construct an influence diagram.

   c. Construct a decision tree.

   d. Recommend a decision based on the use of the optimistic, conservative, and minimax regret approaches.

4. Amy Lloyd is interested in leasing a new Saab and has contacted three automobile dealers for pricing information. Each dealer offered Amy a closed-end 36-month lease with no down payment due at the time of signing. Each lease includes a monthly charge and a mileage allowance. Additional miles receive a surcharge on a per-mile basis. The monthly lease cost, the mileage allowance, and the cost for additional miles follow:

Dealer	Monthly Cost	Mileage Allowance	Cost per Additional Mile
Forno Saab	$299	36,000	$0.15
Midtown Motors	$310	45,000	$0.20
Hopkins Automotive	$325	54,000	$0.15

Amy decided to choose the lease option that will minimize her total 36-month cost. The difficulty is that Amy is not sure how many miles she will drive over the next three years. For purposes of this decision she believes it is reasonable to assume that she will drive 12,000 miles per year, 15,000 miles per year, or 18,000 miles per year. With this assumption Amy estimated her total costs for the three lease options. For example, she figures that the Forno Saab lease will cost her $10,764 if she drives 12,000 miles per year, $12,114 if she drives 15,000 miles per year, or $13,464 if she drives 18,000 miles per year.

   a. What is the decision, and what is the chance event?

   b. Construct a payoff table for Amy's problem.

   c. If Amy has no idea which of the three mileage assumptions is most appropriate, what is the recommended decision (leasing option) using the optimistic, conservative, and minimax regret approaches?

   d. Suppose that the probabilities that Amy drives 12,000, 15,000, and 18,000 miles per year are 0.5, 0.4, and 0.1, respectively. What option should Amy choose using the expected value approach?

   e. Develop a risk profile for the decision selected in part (d). What is the most likely cost, and what is its probability?

   f. Suppose that after further consideration Amy concludes that the probabilities that she will drive 12,000, 15,000, and 18,000 miles per year are 0.3, 0.4, and 0.3, respectively. What decision should Amy make using the expected value approach?

5. The following profit payoff table was presented in Problem 1. Suppose that the decision maker obtained the probability assessments $P(s_1) = 0.65$, $P(s_2) = 0.15$, and $P(s_3) = 0.20$. Use the expected value approach to determine the optimal decision.

	State of Nature		
Decision Alternative	s_1	s_2	s_3
d_1	250	100	25
d_2	100	100	75

6. Investment advisors estimated the stock market returns for four market segments: computers, financial, manufacturing, and pharmaceuticals. Annual return projections vary depending on whether the general economic conditions are improving, stable, or declining.

The anticipated annual return percentages for each market segment under each economic condition are as follows:

Market Segment	Economic Condition		
	Improving	Stable	Declining
Computers	10	2	−4
Financial	8	5	−3
Manufacturing	6	4	−2
Pharmaceuticals	6	5	−1

a. Assume that an individual investor wants to select one market segment for a new investment. A forecast shows stable to declining economic conditions with the following probabilities: improving (0.2), stable (0.5), and declining (0.3). What is the preferred market segment for the investor, and what is the expected return percentage?

b. At a later date, a revised forecast shows a potential for an improvement in economic conditions. New probabilities are as follows: improving (0.4), stable (0.4), and declining (0.2). What is the preferred market segment for the investor based on these new probabilities? What is the expected return percentage?

7. Hudson Corporation is considering three options for managing its data processing operation: continuing with its own staff, hiring an outside vendor to do the managing (referred to as *outsourcing*), or using a combination of its own staff and an outside vendor. The cost of the operation depends on future demand. The annual cost of each option (in thousands of dollars) depends on demand as follows:

Staffing Options	Demand		
	High	Medium	Low
Own staff	650	650	600
Outside vendor	900	600	300
Combination	800	650	500

a. If the demand probabilities are 0.2, 0.5, and 0.3, which decision alternative will minimize the expected cost of the data processing operation? What is the expected annual cost associated with that recommendation?

b. Construct a risk profile for the optimal decision in part (a). What is the probability of the cost exceeding $700,000?

8. The following payoff table shows the profit for a decision problem with two states of nature and two decision alternatives:

Decision Alternative	State of Nature	
	s_1	s_2
d_1	10	1
d_2	4	3

a. Use graphical sensitivity analysis to determine the range of probabilities of state of nature s_1 for which each of the decision alternatives has the largest expected value.

b. Suppose $P(s_1) = 0.2$ and $P(s_2) = 0.8$. What is the best decision using the expected value approach?

c. Perform sensitivity analysis on the payoffs for decision alternative d_1. Assume the probabilities are as given in part (b) and find the range of payoffs under states of nature s_1 and s_2 that will keep the solution found in part (b) optimal. Is the solution more sensitive to the payoff under state of nature s_1 or s_2?

9. Myrtle Air Express decided to offer direct service from Cleveland to Myrtle Beach. Management must decide between a full-price service using the company's new fleet of jet aircraft and a discount service using smaller capacity commuter planes. It is clear that the best choice depends on the market reaction to the service Myrtle Air offers. Management developed estimates of the contribution to profit for each type of service based upon two possible levels of demand for service to Myrtle Beach: strong and weak. The following table shows the estimated quarterly profits (in thousands of dollars):

	Demand for Service	
Service	**Strong**	**Weak**
Full price	$960	-$490
Discount	$670	$320

a. What is the decision to be made, what is the chance event, and what is the consequence for this problem? How many decision alternatives are there? How many outcomes are there for the chance event?

b. If nothing is known about the probabilities of the chance outcomes, what is the recommended decision using the optimistic, conservative, and minimax regret approaches?

c. Suppose that management of Myrtle Air Express believes that the probability of strong demand is 0.7 and the probability of weak demand is 0.3. Use the expected value approach to determine an optimal decision.

d. Suppose that the probability of strong demand is 0.8 and the probability of weak demand is 0.2. What is the optimal decision using the expected value approach?

e. Use graphical sensitivity analysis to determine the range of demand probabilities for which each of the decision alternatives has the largest expected value.

10. Video Tech is considering marketing one of two new video games for the coming holiday season: Battle Pacific or Space Pirates. Battle Pacific is a unique game and appears to have no competition. Estimated profits (in thousands of dollars) under high, medium, and low demand are as follows:

	Demand		
Battle Pacific	**High**	**Medium**	**Low**
Profit	$1000	$700	$300
Probability	0.2	0.5	0.3

Video Tech is optimistic about its Space Pirates game. However, the concern is that profitability will be affected by a competitor's introduction of a video game viewed as similar to Space Pirates. Estimated profits (in thousands of dollars) with and without competition are as follows:

Space Pirates With Competition	Demand		
	High	**Medium**	**Low**
Profit	$800	$400	$200
Probability	0.3	0.4	0.3

Space Pirates Without Competition	Demand		
	High	**Medium**	**Low**
Profit	$1600	$800	$400
Probability	0.5	0.3	0.2

a. Develop a decision tree for the Video Tech problem.
b. For planning purposes, Video Tech believes there is a 0.6 probability that its competitor will produce a new game similar to Space Pirates. Given this probability of competition, the director of planning recommends marketing the Battle Pacific video game. Using expected value, what is your recommended decision?
c. Show a risk profile for your recommended decision.
d. Use sensitivity analysis to determine what the probability of competition for Space Pirates would have to be for you to change your recommended decision alternative.

11. For the Pittsburgh Development Corporation problem in Section 4.3, the decision alternative to build the large condominium complex was found to be optimal using the expected value approach. In Section 4.4 we conducted a sensitivity analysis for the payoffs associated with this decision alternative. We found that the large complex remained optimal as long as the payoff for the strong demand was greater than or equal to $17.5 million and as long as the payoff for the weak demand was greater than or equal to −$19 million.
   a. Consider the medium complex decision. How much could the payoff under strong demand increase and still keep decision alternative d_3 the optimal solution?
   b. Consider the small complex decision. How much could the payoff under strong demand increase and still keep decision alternative d_3 the optimal solution?

12. The distance from Potsdam to larger markets and limited air service have hindered the town in attracting new industry. Air Express, a major overnight delivery service, is considering establishing a regional distribution center in Potsdam. However, Air Express will not establish the center unless the length of the runway at the local airport is increased. Another candidate for new development is Diagnostic Research, Inc. (DRI), a leading producer of medical testing equipment. DRI is considering building a new manufacturing plant. Increasing the length of the runway is not a requirement for DRI, but the planning commission feels that doing so will help convince DRI to locate their new plant in Potsdam. Assuming that the town lengthens the runway, the Potsdam planning commission believes that the probabilities shown in the following table are applicable.

	DRI Plant	**No DRI Plant**
Air Express Center	0.30	0.10
No Air Express Center	0.40	0.20

For instance, the probability that Air Express will establish a distribution center and DRI will build a plant is 0.30.

The estimated annual revenue to the town, after deducting the cost of lengthening the runway, is as follows:

	DRI Plant	**No DRI Plant**
Air Express Center	$600,000	$150,000
No Air Express Center	$250,000	−$200,000

If the runway expansion project is not conducted, the planning commission assesses the probability DRI will locate their new plant in Potsdam at 0.6; in this case, the estimated annual revenue to the town will be $450,000. If the runway expansion project is not conducted and DRI does not locate in Potsdam, the annual revenue will be $0 because no cost will have been incurred and no revenues will be forthcoming.

a. What is the decision to be made, what is the chance event, and what is the consequence?

b. Compute the expected annual revenue associated with the decision alternative to lengthen the runway.

c. Compute the expected annual revenue associated with the decision alternative not to lengthen the runway.

d. Should the town elect to lengthen the runway? Explain.

e. Suppose that the probabilities associated with lengthening the runway were as follows:

	DRI Plant	**No DRI Plant**
Air Express Center	0.40	0.10
No Air Express Center	0.30	0.20

What effect, if any, would this change in the probabilities have on the recommended decision?

13. Seneca Hill Winery recently purchased land for the purpose of establishing a new vineyard. Management is considering two varieties of white grapes for the new vineyard: Chardonnay and Riesling. The Chardonnay grapes would be used to produce a dry Chardonnay wine, and the Riesling grapes would be used to produce a semidry Riesling wine. It takes approximately four years from the time of planting before new grapes can be harvested. This length of time creates a great deal of uncertainty concerning future demand and makes the decision about the type of grapes to plant difficult. Three possibilities are being considered: Chardonnay grapes only; Riesling grapes only; and both Chardonnay and Riesling grapes. Seneca management decided that for planning purposes it would be adequate to consider only two demand possibilities for each type of wine: strong or weak. With two possibilities for each type of wine it was necessary to assess four probabilities. With the help of some forecasts in industry publications, management made the following probability assessments:

	Riesling Demand	
Chardonnay Demand	**Weak**	**Strong**
Weak	0.05	0.50
Strong	0.25	0.20

Revenue projections show an annual contribution to profit of $20,000 if Seneca Hill only plants Chardonnay grapes and demand is weak for Chardonnay wine, and $70,000 if they only plant Chardonnay grapes and demand is strong for Chardonnay wine. If they only plant Riesling grapes, the annual profit projection is $25,000 if demand is weak for Riesling grapes and $45,000 if demand is strong for Riesling grapes. If Seneca plants both types of grapes, the annual profit projections are shown in the following table:

	Riesling Demand	
Chardonnay Demand	**Weak**	**Strong**
Weak	$22,000	$40,000
Strong	$26,000	$60,000

a. What is the decision to be made, what is the chance event, and what is the consequence? Identify the alternatives for the decisions and the possible outcomes for the chance events.

b. Develop a decision tree.

c. Use the expected value approach to recommend which alternative Seneca Hill Winery should follow in order to maximize expected annual profit.

d. Suppose management is concerned about the probability assessments when demand for Chardonnay wine is strong. Some believe it is likely for Riesling demand to also be strong in this case. Suppose the probability of strong demand for Chardonnay and weak demand for Riesling is 0.05 and that the probability of strong demand for Chardonnay and strong demand for Riesling is 0.40. How does this change the recommended decision? Assume that the probabilities when Chardonnay demand is weak are still 0.05 and 0.50.

e. Other members of the management team expect the Chardonnay market to become saturated at some point in the future, causing a fall in prices. Suppose that the annual profit projections fall to $50,000 when demand for Chardonnay is strong and Chardonnay grapes only are planted. Using the original probability assessments, determine how this change would affect the optimal decision.

14. The following profit payoff table was presented in Problem 1:

	State of Nature		
Decision Alternative	s_1	s_2	s_3
d_1	250	100	25
d_2	100	100	75

The probabilities for the states of nature are $P(s_1) = 0.65$, $P(s_2) = 0.15$, and $P(s_3) = 0.20$.

a. What is the optimal decision strategy if perfect information were available?

b. What is the expected value for the decision strategy developed in part (a)?

c. Using the expected value approach, what is the recommended decision without perfect information? What is its expected value?

d. What is the expected value of perfect information?

15. The Lake Placid Town Council decided to build a new community center to be used for conventions, concerts, and other public events, but considerable controversy surrounds the appropriate size. Many influential citizens want a large center that would be a showcase for the area. But the mayor feels that if demand does not support such a center, the community

will lose a large amount of money. To provide structure for the decision process, the council narrowed the building alternatives to three sizes: small, medium, and large. Everybody agreed that the critical factor in choosing the best size is the number of people who will want to use the new facility. A regional planning consultant provided demand estimates under three scenarios: worst case, base case, and best case. The worst-case scenario corresponds to a situation in which tourism drops significantly; the base-case scenario corresponds to a situation in which Lake Placid continues to attract visitors at current levels; and the best-case scenario corresponds to a significant increase in tourism. The consultant has provided probability assessments of 0.10, 0.60, and 0.30 for the worst-case, base-case, and best-case scenarios, respectively.

The town council suggested using net cash flow over a 5-year planning horizon as the criterion for deciding on the best size. The following projections of net cash flow (in thousands of dollars) for a 5-year planning horizon have been developed. All costs, including the consultant's fee, have been included.

	Demand Scenario		
Center Size	**Worst Case**	**Base Case**	**Best Case**
Small	400	500	660
Medium	−250	650	800
Large	−400	580	990

a. What decision should Lake Placid make using the expected value approach?
b. Construct risk profiles for the medium and large alternatives. Given the mayor's concern over the possibility of losing money and the result of part (a), which alternative would you recommend?
c. Compute the expected value of perfect information. Do you think it would be worth trying to obtain additional information concerning which scenario is likely to occur?
d. Suppose the probability of the worst-case scenario increases to 0.2, the probability of the base-case scenario decreases to 0.5, and the probability of the best-case scenario remains at 0.3. What effect, if any, would these changes have on the decision recommendation?
e. The consultant has suggested that an expenditure of $150,000 on a promotional campaign over the planning horizon will effectively reduce the probability of the worst-case scenario to zero. If the campaign can be expected to also increase the probability of the best-case scenario to 0.4, is it a good investment?

16. Consider a variation of the PDC decision tree shown in Figure 4.9. The company must first decide whether to undertake the market research study. If the market research study is conducted, the outcome will either be favorable (F) or unfavorable (U). Assume there are only two decision alternatives, d_1 and d_2, and two states of nature, s_1 and s_2. The payoff table showing profit is as follows:

	State of Nature	
Decision Alternative	s_1	s_2
d_1	100	300
d_2	400	200

a. Show the decision tree.
b. Using the following probabilities, what is the optimal decision strategy?

$$P(F) = 0.56 \qquad P(s_1 \mid F) = 0.57 \qquad P(s_1 \mid U) = 0.18 \qquad P(s_1) = 0.40$$
$$P(U) = 0.44 \qquad P(s_2 \mid F) = 0.43 \qquad P(s_2 \mid U) = 0.82 \qquad P(s_2) = 0.60$$

17. Hemmingway, Inc., is considering a $5 million research and development (R&D) project. Profit projections appear promising, but Hemmingway's president is concerned because the probability that the R&D project will be successful is only 0.50. Secondly, the president knows that even if the project is successful, it will require that the company build a new production facility at a cost of $20 million in order to manufacture the product. If the facility is built, uncertainty remains about the demand and thus uncertainty about the profit that will be realized. Another option is that if the R&D project is successful, the company could sell the rights to the product for an estimated $25 million. Under this option, the company would not build the $20 million production facility.

The decision tree is shown in Figure 4.16. The profit projection for each outcome is shown at the end of the branches. For example, the revenue projection for the high demand outcome is $59 million. However, the cost of the R&D project ($5 million) and the cost of the production facility ($20 million) show the profit of this outcome to be $59 − $5 − $20 = $34 million. Branch probabilities are also shown for the chance events.

a. Analyze the decision tree to determine whether the company should undertake the R&D project. If it does, and if the R&D project is successful, what should the company do? What is the expected value of your strategy?
b. What must the selling price be for the company to consider selling the rights to the product?
c. Develop a risk profile for the optimal strategy.

FIGURE 4.16   DECISION TREE FOR HEMMINGWAY, INC.

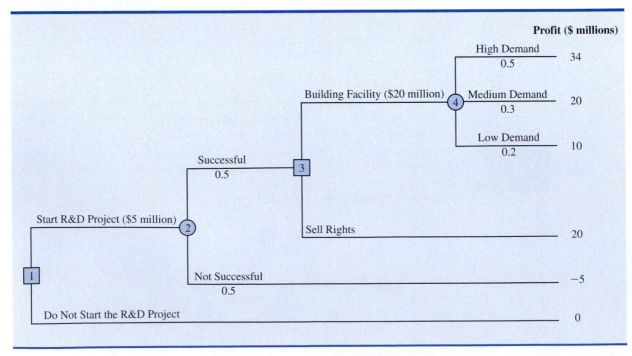

18. Dante Development Corporation is considering bidding on a contract for a new office building complex. Figure 4.17 shows the decision tree prepared by one of Dante's analysts. At node 1, the company must decide whether to bid on the contract. The cost of preparing the bid is $200,000. The upper branch from node 2 shows that the company has a 0.8 probability of winning the contract if it submits a bid. If the company wins the bid, it will have to pay $2,000,000 to become a partner in the project. Node 3 shows that the company will then consider doing a market research study to forecast demand for the office units prior to beginning construction. The cost of this study is $150,000. Node 4 is a chance node showing the possible outcomes of the market research study.

    Nodes 5, 6, and 7 are similar in that they are the decision nodes for Dante to either build the office complex or sell the rights in the project to another developer. The decision to build the complex will result in an income of $5,000,000 if demand is high and $3,000,000 if demand is moderate. If Dante chooses to sell its rights in the project to another developer, income from the sale is estimated to be $3,500,000. The probabilities shown at nodes 4, 8, and 9 are based on the projected outcomes of the market research study.

    a. Verify Dante's profit projections shown at the ending branches of the decision tree by calculating the payoffs of $2,650,000 and $650,000 for first two outcomes.
    b. What is the optimal decision strategy for Dante, and what is the expected profit for this project?
    c. What would the cost of the market research study have to be before Dante would change its decision about the market research study?
    d. Develop a risk profile for Dante.

FIGURE 4.17   DECISION TREE FOR THE DANTE DEVELOPMENT CORPORATION

19. Hale's TV Productions is considering producing a pilot for a comedy series in the hope of selling it to a major television network. The network may decide to reject the series, but it may also decide to purchase the rights to the series for either one or two years. At this point in time, Hale may either produce the pilot and wait for the network's decision or transfer the rights for the pilot and series to a competitor for $100,000. Hale's decision alternatives and profits (in thousands of dollars) are as follows:

	State of Nature		
Decision Alternative	Reject, s_1	1 Year, s_2	2 Years, s_3
Produce pilot, d_1	−100	50	150
Sell to competitor, d_2	100	100	100

The probabilities for the states of nature are $P(s_1) = 0.20$, $P(s_2) = 0.30$, and $P(s_3) = 0.50$. For a consulting fee of $5000, an agency will review the plans for the comedy series and indicate the overall chances of a favorable network reaction to the series. Assume that the agency review will result in a favorable (F) or an unfavorable (U) review and that the following probabilities are relevant:

$$P(F) = 0.69 \qquad P(s_1 \mid F) = 0.09 \qquad P(s_1 \mid U) = 0.45$$
$$P(U) = 0.31 \qquad P(s_2 \mid F) = 0.26 \qquad P(s_2 \mid U) = 0.39$$
$$P(s_3 \mid F) = 0.65 \qquad P(s_3 \mid U) = 0.16$$

a. Construct a decision tree for this problem.
b. What is the recommended decision if the agency opinion is not used? What is the expected value?
c. What is the expected value of perfect information?
d. What is Hale's optimal decision strategy assuming the agency's information is used?
e. What is the expected value of the agency's information?
f. Is the agency's information worth the $5000 fee? What is the maximum that Hale should be willing to pay for the information?
g. What is the recommended decision?

20. Embassy Publishing Company received a six-chapter manuscript for a new college textbook. The editor of the college division is familiar with the manuscript and estimated a 0.65 probability that the textbook will be successful. If successful, a profit of $750,000 will be realized. If the company decides to publish the textbook and it is unsuccessful, a loss of $250,000 will occur.

Before making the decision to accept or reject the manuscript, the editor is considering sending the manuscript out for review. A review process provides either a favorable (F) or unfavorable (U) evaluation of the manuscript. Past experience with the review process suggests probabilities $P(F) = 0.7$ and $P(U) = 0.3$ apply. Let s_1 = the textbook is successful, and s_2 = the textbook is unsuccessful. The editor's initial probabilities of s_1 and s_2 will be revised based on whether the review is favorable or unfavorable. The revised probabilities are as follows:

$$P(s_1 \mid F) = 0.75 \qquad P(s_1 \mid U) = 0.417$$
$$P(s_2 \mid F) = 0.25 \qquad P(s_2 \mid U) = 0.583$$

a. Construct a decision tree assuming that the company will first make the decision of whether to send the manuscript out for review and then make the decision to accept or reject the manuscript.

b. Analyze the decision tree to determine the optimal decision strategy for the publishing company.

c. If the manuscript review costs $5000, what is your recommendation?

d. What is the expected value of perfect information? What does this EVPI suggest for the company?

21. A real estate investor has the opportunity to purchase land currently zoned residential. If the county board approves a request to rezone the property as commercial within the next year, the investor will be able to lease the land to a large discount firm that wants to open a new store on the property. However, if the zoning change is not approved, the investor will have to sell the property at a loss. Profits (in thousands of dollars) are shown in the following payoff table:

	State of Nature	
	Rezoning Approved	Rezoning Not Approved
Decision Alternative	s_1	s_2
Purchase, d_1	600	-200
Do not purchase, d_2	0	0

a. If the probability that the rezoning will be approved is 0.5, what decision is recommended? What is the expected profit?

b. The investor can purchase an option to buy the land. Under the option, the investor maintains the rights to purchase the land anytime during the next three months while learning more about possible resistance to the rezoning proposal from area residents. Probabilities are as follows:

Let H = High resistance to rezoning

L − Low resistance to rezoning

$$P(H) = 0.55 \qquad P(s_1 \mid H) = 0.18 \qquad P(s_2 \mid H) = 0.82$$
$$P(L) = 0.45 \qquad P(s_1 \mid L) = 0.89 \qquad P(s_2 \mid L) = 0.11$$

What is the optimal decision strategy if the investor uses the option period to learn more about the resistance from area residents before making the purchase decision?

c. If the option will cost the investor an additional $10,000, should the investor purchase the option? Why or why not? What is the maximum that the investor should be willing to pay for the option?

22. Lawson's Department Store faces a buying decision for a seasonal product for which demand can be high, medium, or low. The purchaser for Lawson's can order 1, 2, or 3 lots of the product before the season begins but cannot reorder later. Profit projections (in thousands of dollars) are shown.

	State of Nature		
	High Demand	Medium Demand	Low Demand
Decision Alternative	s_1	s_2	s_3
Order 1 lot, d_1	60	60	50
Order 2 lots, d_2	80	80	30
Order 3 lots, d_3	100	70	10

a. If the prior probabilities for the three states of nature are 0.3, 0.3, and 0.4, respectively, what is the recommended order quantity?

b. At each preseason sales meeting, the vice president of sales provides a personal opinion regarding potential demand for this product. Because of the vice president's enthusiasm and optimistic nature, the predictions of market conditions have always been either "excellent" (E) or "very good" (V). Probabilities are as follows:

$$P(E) = 0.70 \qquad P(s_1 \mid E) = 0.34 \qquad P(s_1 \mid V) = 0.20$$
$$P(V) = 0.30 \qquad P(s_2 \mid E) = 0.32 \qquad P(s_2 \mid V) = 0.26$$
$$\qquad\qquad\qquad\; P(s_3 \mid E) = 0.34 \qquad P(s_3 \mid V) = 0.54$$

What is the optimal decision strategy?

c. Use the efficiency of sample information and discuss whether the firm should consider a consulting expert who could provide independent forecasts of market conditions for the product.

23. Suppose that you are given a decision situation with three possible states of nature: s_1, s_2, and s_3. The prior probabilities are $P(s_1) = 0.2$, $P(s_2) = 0.5$, and $P(s_3) = 0.3$. With sample information I, $P(I \mid s_1) = 0.1$, $P(I \mid s_2) = 0.05$, and $P(I \mid s_3) = 0.2$. Compute the revised or posterior probabilities: $P(s_1 \mid I)$, $P(s_2 \mid I)$, and $P(s_3 \mid I)$.

24. To save on expenses, Rona and Jerry agreed to form a carpool for traveling to and from work. Rona preferred to use the somewhat longer but more consistent Queen City Avenue. Although Jerry preferred the quicker expressway, he agreed with Rona that they should take Queen City Avenue if the expressway had a traffic jam. The following payoff table provides the one-way time estimate in minutes for traveling to or from work:

	State of Nature	
Decision Alternative	Expressway Open s_1	Expressway Jammed s_2
Queen City Avenue, d_1	30	30
Expressway, d_2	25	45

Based on their experience with traffic problems, Rona and Jerry agreed on a 0.15 probability that the expressway would be jammed.

In addition, they agreed that weather seemed to affect the traffic conditions on the expressway. Let

$$C = \text{clear}$$
$$O = \text{overcast}$$
$$R = \text{rain}$$

The following conditional probabilities apply:

$$P(C \mid s_1) = 0.8 \qquad P(O \mid s_1) = 0.2 \qquad P(R \mid s_1) = 0.0$$
$$P(C \mid s_2) = 0.1 \qquad P(O \mid s_2) = 0.3 \qquad P(R \mid s_2) = 0.6$$

a. Use Bayes' theorem for probability revision to compute the probability of each weather condition and the conditional probability of the expressway open, s_1, or jammed, s_2, given each weather condition.

b.   Show the decision tree for this problem.

c.   What is the optimal decision strategy, and what is the expected travel time?

25. The Gorman Manufacturing Company must decide whether to manufacture a component part at its Milan, Michigan, plant or purchase the component part from a supplier. The resulting profit is dependent upon the demand for the product. The following payoff table shows the projected profit (in thousands of dollars):

	State of Nature		
	Low Demand	Medium Demand	High Demand
Decision Alternative	s_1	s_2	s_3
Manufacture, d_1	−20	40	100
Purchase, d_2	10	45	70

The state-of-nature probabilities are $P(s_1) = 0.35$, $P(s_2) = 0.35$, and $P(s_3) = 0.30$.

a.   Use a decision tree to recommend a decision.

b.   Use EVPI to determine whether Gorman should attempt to obtain a better estimate of demand.

c.   A test market study of the potential demand for the product is expected to report either a favorable (F) or unfavorable (U) condition. The relevant conditional probabilities are as follows:

$$P(F \mid s_1) = 0.10 \qquad P(U \mid s_1) = 0.90$$
$$P(F \mid s_2) = 0.40 \qquad P(U \mid s_2) = 0.60$$
$$P(F \mid s_3) = 0.60 \qquad P(U \mid s_3) = 0.40$$

What is the probability that the market research report will be favorable?

d.   What is Gorman's optimal decision strategy?

e.   What is the expected value of the market research information?

f.   What is the efficiency of the information?

Case Problem 1   Property Purchase Strategy

Glenn Foreman, president of Oceanview Development Corporation, is considering submitting a bid to purchase property that will be sold by sealed bid at a county tax foreclosure. Glenn's initial judgment is to submit a bid of $5 million. Based on his experience, Glenn estimates that a bid of $5 million will have a 0.2 probability of being the highest bid and securing the property for Oceanview. The current date is June 1. Sealed bids for the property must be submitted by August 15. The winning bid will be announced on September 1.

If Oceanview submits the highest bid and obtains the property, the firm plans to build and sell a complex of luxury condominiums. However, a complicating factor is that the property is currently zoned for single-family residences only. Glenn believes that a referendum could be placed on the voting ballot in time for the November election. Passage of the referendum would change the zoning of the property and permit construction of the condominiums.

The sealed-bid procedure requires the bid to be submitted with a certified check for 10% of the amount bid. If the bid is rejected, the deposit is refunded. If the bid is accepted, the deposit is the down payment for the property. However, if the bid is accepted and the bidder does not follow through with the purchase and meet the remainder of the financial obligation within six months, the deposit will be forfeited. In this case, the county will offer the property to the next highest bidder.

To determine whether Oceanview should submit the $5 million bid, Glenn conducted some preliminary analysis. This preliminary work provided an assessment of 0.3 for the probability that the referendum for a zoning change will be approved and resulted in the following estimates of the costs and revenues that will be incurred if the condominiums are built:

Cost and Revenue Estimates	
Revenue from condominium sales	$15,000,000
Cost	
Property	$5,000,000
Construction expenses	$8,000,000

If Oceanview obtains the property and the zoning change is rejected in November, Glenn believes that the best option would be for the firm not to complete the purchase of the property. In this case, Oceanview would forfeit the 10% deposit that accompanied the bid.

Because the likelihood that the zoning referendum will be approved is such an important factor in the decision process, Glenn suggested that the firm hire a market research service to conduct a survey of voters. The survey would provide a better estimate of the likelihood that the referendum for a zoning change would be approved. The market research firm that Oceanview Development has worked with in the past has agreed to do the study for $15,000. The results of the study will be available August 1, so that Oceanview will have this information before the August 15 bid deadline. The results of the survey will be either a prediction that the zoning change will be approved or a prediction that the zoning change will be rejected. After considering the record of the market research service in previous studies conducted for Oceanview, Glenn developed the following probability estimates concerning the accuracy of the market research information:

$$P(A \mid s_1) = 0.9 \qquad P(N \mid s_1) = 0.1$$
$$P(A \mid s_2) = 0.2 \qquad P(N \mid s_2) = 0.8$$

where

A = prediction of zoning change approval
N = prediction that zoning change will not be approved
s_1 = the zoning change is approved by the voters
s_2 = the zoning change is rejected by the voters

Managerial Report

Perform an analysis of the problem facing the Oceanview Development Corporation, and prepare a report that summarizes your findings and recommendations. Include the following items in your report:

1. A decision tree that shows the logical sequence of the decision problem
2. A recommendation regarding what Oceanview should do if the market research information is not available

3. A decision strategy that Oceanview should follow if the market research is conducted
4. A recommendation as to whether Oceanview should employ the market research firm, along with the value of the information provided by the market research firm

Include the details of your analysis as an appendix to your report.

Case Problem 2   Lawsuit Defense Strategy

John Campbell, an employee of Manhattan Construction Company, claims to have injured his back as a result of a fall while repairing the roof at one of the Eastview apartment buildings. He filed a lawsuit against Doug Reynolds, the owner of Eastview Apartments, asking for damages of $1,500,000. John claims that the roof had rotten sections and that his fall could have been prevented if Mr. Reynolds had told Manhattan Construction about the problem. Mr. Reynolds notified his insurance company, Allied Insurance, of the lawsuit. Allied must defend Mr. Reynolds and decide what action to take regarding the lawsuit.

Some depositions and a series of discussions took place between both sides. As a result, John Campbell offered to accept a settlement of $750,000. Thus, one option is for Allied to pay John $750,000 to settle the claim. Allied is also considering making John a counteroffer of $400,000 in the hope that he will accept a lesser amount to avoid the time and cost of going to trial. Allied's preliminary investigation shows that John's case is strong; Allied is concerned that John may reject their counteroffer and request a jury trial. Allied's lawyers spent some time exploring John's likely reaction if they make a counteroffer of $400,000.

The lawyers concluded that it is adequate to consider three possible outcomes to represent John's possible reaction to a counteroffer of $400,000: (1) John will accept the counteroffer and the case will be closed; (2) John will reject the counteroffer and elect to have a jury decide the settlement amount; or (3) John will make a counteroffer to Allied of $600,000. If John does make a counteroffer, Allied decided that they will not make additional counteroffers. They will either accept John's counteroffer of $600,000 or go to trial.

If the case goes to a jury trial, Allied considers three outcomes possible: (1) the jury may reject John's claim and Allied will not be required to pay any damages; (2) the jury will find in favor of John and award him $750,000 in damages; or (3) the jury will conclude that John has a strong case and award him the full amount of $1,500,000.

Key considerations as Allied develops its strategy for disposing of the case are the probabilities associated with John's response to an Allied counteroffer of $400,000 and the probabilities associated with the three possible trial outcomes. Allied's lawyers believe the probability that John will accept a counteroffer of $400,000 is 0.10, the probability that John will reject a counteroffer of $400,000 is 0.40, and the probability that John will, himself, make a counteroffer to Allied of $600,000 is 0.50. If the case goes to court, they believe that the probability the jury will award John damages of $1,500,000 is 0.30, the probability that the jury will award John damages of $750,000 is 0.50, and the probability that the jury will award John nothing is 0.20.

Managerial Report

Perform an analysis of the problem facing Allied Insurance and prepare a report that summarizes your findings and recommendations. Be sure to include the following items:

1. A decision tree
2. A recommendation regarding whether Allied should accept John's initial offer to settle the claim for $750,000

3. A decision strategy that Allied should follow if they decide to make John a counteroffer of $400,000
4. A risk profile for your recommended strategy

Appendix 4.1   Decision Analysis with TreePlan

TreePlan[2] is an Excel add-in that can be used to develop decision trees for decision analysis problems. The software package is provided at the Web site that accompanies this text. Instructions for installation and a manual containing additional information are also available at the Web site. In this appendix we show how to use TreePlan to build a decision tree and solve the PDC problem presented in Section 4.3. The decision tree for the PDC problem is shown in Figure 4.18.

Getting Started: An Initial Decision Tree

We begin by assuming that TreePlan has been installed and an Excel workbook is open. To build a TreePlan version of the PDC decision tree, proceed as follows:

Step 1. Select cell A1
Step 2. Select the **Add-Ins tab** and choose **Decision Tree** from the **Menu Commands** group
Step 3. When the **TreePlan New** dialog box appears:
Click **New Tree**

FIGURE 4.18 PDC DECISION TREE

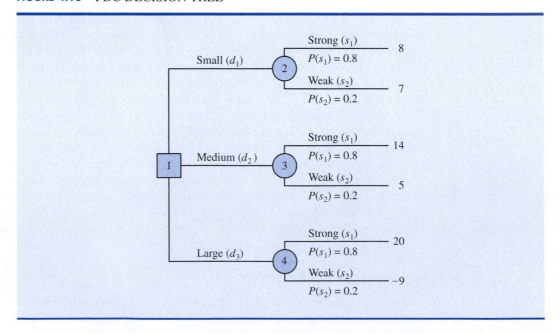

---

[2]TreePlan was developed by Professor Michael R. Middleton at the University of San Francisco and modified for use by Professor James E. Smith at Duke University. The TreePlan Web site is *http://www.treeplan.com*.

A decision tree with one decision node and two branches appears as follows:

	A	B	C	D	E	F	G
1							
2				Decision 1			
3							0
4				0	0		
5		1					
6		0					
7				Decision 2			
8							0
9				0	0		

Adding a Branch

The PDC problem has three decision alternatives (small, medium, and large condominium complexes), so we must add another decision branch to the tree.

Step 1. Select cell B5
Step 2. Select **Decision Tree** from the **Menu Commands** group
Step 3. When the **TreePlan Decision** dialog box appears:
Select **Add branch**
Click **OK**

A revised tree with three decision branches now appears in the Excel worksheet.

Naming the Decision Alternatives

The decision alternatives can be named by selecting the cells containing the labels Decision 1, Decision 2, and Decision 3, and then entering the corresponding PDC names Small, Medium, and Large. After naming the alternatives, the PDC tree with three decision branches appears as follows:

	A	B	C	D	E	F	G
1							
2				Small			
3							0
4				0	0		
5							
6							
7				Medium			
8		1					0
9		0		0	0		
10							
11							
12				Large			
13							0
14				0	0		

Adding Chance Nodes

The chance event for the PDC problem is the demand for the condominiums, which may be either strong or weak. Thus, a chance node with two branches must be added at the end of each decision alternative branch.

Step 1. Select cell F3
Step 2. Select **Decision Tree** from the **Menu Commands** group
Step 3. When the **TreePlan Terminal** dialog box appears:
Select **Change to event node**
Select **Two** in the **Branches** section
Click **OK**

The tree now appears as follows:

	A	B	C	D	E	F	G	H	I	J	K
1								0.5			
2								Event 4			
3											0
4				Small				0	0		
5											
6					0	0		0.5			
7								Event 5			
8											0
9								0	0		
10											
11			1								
12		0		Medium							
13											0
14					0	0					
15											
16											
17				Large							
18											0
19					0	0					

We next select the cells containing Event 4 and Event 5 and rename them Strong and Weak to provide the proper names for the PDC states of nature. After doing so we can copy the subtree for the chance node in cell F5 to the other two decision branches to complete the structure of the PDC decision tree as follows:

Step 1. Select cell F5
Step 2. Select **Decision Tree** from the **Menu Commands** group
Step 3. When the **TreePlan Event** dialog box appears:
Select **Copy subtree**
Click **OK**
Step 4. Select cell F13
Step 5. Select **Decision Tree** from the **Menu Commands** group
Step 6. When the **TreePlan Terminal** dialog box appears:
Select **Paste subtree**
Click **OK**

This copy/paste procedure places a chance node at the end of the Medium decision branch. Repeating the same copy/paste procedure for the Large decision branch completes the structure of the PDC decision tree as shown in Figure 4.19.

Inserting Probabilities and Payoffs

TreePlan provides the capability of inserting probabilities and payoffs into the decision tree. In Figure 4.19 we see that TreePlan automatically assigned an equal probability 0.5 to each of the chance outcomes. For PDC, the probability of strong demand is 0.8 and the probability of weak demand is 0.2. We can select cells H1, H6, H11, H16, H21, and H26 and insert the appropriate probabilities. The payoffs for the chance outcomes are inserted in cells H4, H9, H14, H19, H24, and H29. After inserting the PDC probabilities and payoffs, the PDC decision tree appears as shown in Figure 4.20.

Note that the payoffs also appear in the right-hand margin of the decision tree. The payoffs in the right margin are computed by a formula that adds the payoffs on all of the branches leading to the associated terminal node. For the PDC problem, no payoffs are associated with the decision alternatives branches so we leave the default values of zero in cells D6, D16, and D24. The PDC decision tree is now complete.

FIGURE 4.19   THE PDC DECISION TREE DEVELOPED BY TREEPLAN

FIGURE 4.20   THE PDC DECISION TREE WITH BRANCH PROBABILITIES AND PAYOFFS

	A	B	C	D	E	F	G	H	I	J	K
1								0.8			
2								Strong			
3											8
4				Small				8	8		
5											
6					0	7.8		0.2			
7								Weak			
8											7
9								7	7		
10											
11								0.8			
12								Strong			
13											14
14				Medium				14	14		
15		3									
16	14.2				0	12.2		0.2			
17								Weak			
18											5
19								5	5		
20											
21								0.8			
22								Strong			
23											20
24				Large				20	20		
25											
26					0	14.2		0.2			
27								Weak			
28											-9
29								-9	-9		

Interpreting the Result

When probabilities and payoffs are inserted, TreePlan automatically makes the backward pass computations necessary to determine the optimal solution. Optimal decisions are identified by the number in the corresponding decision node. In the PDC decision tree in Figure 4.20, cell B15 contains the decision node. Note that a 3 appears in this node, which tells us that decision alternative branch 3 provides the optimal decision. Thus, decision analysis recommends PDC construct the Large condominium complex. The expected value of this decision appears at the beginning of the tree in cell A16. Thus, we see the optimal expected value is $14.2 million. The expected values of the other decision alternatives are displayed at the end of the corresponding decision branch. Thus, referring to cells E6 and E16, we see that the expected value of the Small complex is $7.8 million and the expected value of the Medium complex is $12.2 million.

Other Options

TreePlan defaults to a maximization objective. If you would like a minimization objective, follow these steps:

Step 1. Select **Decision Tree** from the **Menu Commands** group
Step 2. Select **Options**
Step 3. Choose **Minimize (costs)**
             Click **OK**

In using a TreePlan decision tree, we can modify probabilities and payoffs and quickly observe the impact of the changes on the optimal solution. Using this "what if" type of sensitivity analysis, we can identify changes in probabilities and payoffs that would change the optimal decision. Also, because TreePlan is an Excel add-in, most of Excel's capabilities are available. For instance, we could use boldface to highlight the name of the optimal decision alternative on the final decision tree solution. A variety of other options TreePlan provides is contained in the TreePlan manual on the Web site that accompanies this text. Computer software packages such as TreePlan make it easier to do a thorough analysis of a decision problem.

CHAPTER 5

Utility and Game Theory

CONTENTS

The decision analysis situations presented in Chapter 4 often expressed consequences or payoffs in terms of monetary values. With probability information available about the outcomes of the chance events, we defined the optimal decision alternative as the one that provided the best expected monetary value. However, in some situations the decision alternative with the best expected monetary value may not be the preferred alternative. A decision maker may also wish to consider intangible factors such as risk, image, or other nonmonetary criteria in order to evaluate the decision alternatives. When monetary value does not necessarily lead to the most preferred decision, expressing the value (or worth) of a consequence in terms of its utility will permit the use of expected utility to identify the most desirable decision alternative. The discussion of utility and its application in decision analysis is presented in the first part of this chapter.

In the last part of this chapter we introduce the topic of game theory. Game theory is the study of developing optimal strategies where two or more decision makers, usually called players, compete as adversaries. Game theory can be viewed as a relative of decision analysis. A key difference, however, is that each player selects a decision strategy not by considering the possible outcomes of a chance event, but by considering the possible strategies selected by one or more competing players.

We note here that utility and game theory are separable topics. Either or both may be studied, and it is not required that you cover one topic before the other.

The Meaning of Utility

Utility is a measure of the total worth of a particular outcome; it reflects the decision maker's attitude toward a collection of factors such as profit, loss, and risk. Researchers have found that as long as the monetary value of payoffs stays within a range that the decision maker considers reasonable, selecting the decision alternative with the best expected monetary value usually leads to selection of the most preferred decision. However, when the payoffs become extreme, most decision makers are not satisfied with the decision that simply provides the best expected monetary value.

As an example of a situation in which utility can help in selecting the best decision alternative, let us consider the problem faced by Swofford, Inc., a relatively small real estate investment firm located in Atlanta, Georgia. Swofford currently has two investment opportunities that require approximately the same cash outlay. The cash requirements necessary prohibit Swofford from making more than one investment at this time. Consequently, three possible decision alternatives may be considered.

The three decision alternatives, denoted d_1, d_2, and d_3, are

$$d_1 = \text{make investment A}$$
$$d_2 = \text{make investment B}$$
$$d_3 = \text{do not invest}$$

The monetary payoffs associated with the investment opportunities depend on the investment decision and on the direction of the real estate market during the next six months (the chance event). Real estate prices will go up, remain stable, or go down. Thus the Swofford states of nature, denoted s_1, s_2, and s_3, are

$$s_1 = \text{real estate prices go up}$$
$$s_2 = \text{real estate prices remain stable}$$
$$s_3 = \text{real estate prices go down}$$

TABLE 5.1 PAYOFF TABLE FOR SWOFFORD, INC.

Decision Alternative	State of Nature		
	Prices Up s_1	Prices Stable s_2	Prices Down s_3
Investment A, d_1	$30,000	$20,000	−$50,000
Investment B, d_2	$50,000	−$20,000	−$30,000
Do not invest, d_3	0	0	0

Using the best information available, Swofford has estimated the profits, or payoffs, associated with each decision alternative and state-of-nature combination. The resulting payoff table is shown in Table 5.1.

The best estimate of the probability that real estate prices will go up is 0.3; the best estimate of the probability that prices will remain stable is 0.5; and the best estimate of the probability that prices will go down is 0.2. Thus the expected values for the three decision alternatives are

$$EV(d_1) = 0.3(30,000) + 0.5(20,000) \quad + 0.2(-50,000) = \quad 9000$$
$$EV(d_2) = 0.3(50,000) + 0.5(-20,000) + 0.2(-30,000) = -1000$$
$$EV(d_3) = 0.3(0) \qquad + 0.5(0) \qquad + 0.2(0) \qquad = \qquad 0$$

Using the expected value approach, the optimal decision is to select investment A with an expected monetary value of $9000. Is it really the best decision alternative? Let us consider some other relevant factors that relate to Swofford's capability for absorbing the loss of $50,000 if investment A is made and prices actually go down.

Actually, Swofford's current financial position is weak. This condition is partly reflected in Swofford's ability to make only one investment. More important, however, the firm's president believes that, if the next investment results in a substantial loss, Swofford's future will be in jeopardy. Although the expected value approach leads to a recommendation for d_1, do you think the firm's president would prefer this decision? We suspect that the president would select d_2 or d_3 to avoid the possibility of incurring a $50,000 loss. In fact, a reasonable conclusion is that, if a loss of even $30,000 could drive Swofford out of business, the president would select d_3, believing that both investments A and B are too risky for Swofford's current financial position.

The way we resolve Swofford's dilemma is first to determine Swofford's utility for the various monetary outcomes. Recall that the utility of any outcome is the total worth of that outcome, taking into account all risks and consequences involved. If the utilities for the various consequences are assessed correctly, the decision alternative with the highest expected utility is the most preferred, or best, alternative. In the next section we show how to determine the utility of the monetary outcomes so that the alternative with the highest expected utility can be identified.

5.2 Utility and Decision Making

The procedure we use to establish utility values for the payoffs in Swofford's situation requires that we first assign a utility value to the best and worst possible payoffs. Any values will work as long as the utility assigned to the best payoff is greater than the utility assigned to the worst payoff. In this case, $50,000 is the best payoff and $-$50,000 is the worst. Suppose, then, that we arbitrarily make assignments to these two payoffs as follows:

Utility values of 0 and 1 could have been selected here; we selected 0 and 10 in order to avoid any possible confusion between the utility value for a payoff and the probability p.

$$\text{Utility of } -\$50,000 = U(-50,000) = \ 0$$
$$\text{Utility of } \ \ \$50,000 = U(50,000) \ \ \ = 10$$

Let us now determine the utility associated with every other payoff.

Consider the process of establishing the utility of a payoff of $30,000. First we ask Swofford's president to state a preference between a guaranteed $30,000 payoff and an opportunity to engage in the following **lottery**, or bet:

Lottery: Swofford obtains a payoff of $50,000 with probability p
and a payoff of $-$50,000 with probability $(1 - p)$.

p is often referred to as the indifference probability.

Obviously, if p is very close to 1, Swofford's president would prefer the lottery to the guaranteed payoff of $30,000 because the firm would virtually ensure itself a payoff of $50,000. If p is very close to 0, Swofford's president would clearly prefer the guarantee of $30,000. In any event, as p changes continuously from 0 to 1, the preference for the guaranteed payoff of $30,000 will change at some point into a preference for the lottery. At this value of p, Swofford's president would have no greater preference for the guaranteed payoff of $30,000 than for the lottery. For example, let us assume that when $p = 0.95$, Swofford's president is indifferent between the guaranteed payoff of $30,000 and the lottery. For this value of p, we can compute the utility of a $30,000 payoff as follows:

$$U(30,000) = pU(50,000) + (1 - p)U(-50,000)$$
$$= 0.95(10) + (0.05)(0)$$
$$= 9.5$$

Obviously, if we had started with a different assignment of utilities for a payoff of $50,000 and $-$50,000, the result would have been a different utility for $30,000. For example, if we had started with an assignment of 100 for $50,000 and 10 for $-$50,000, the utility of a $30,000 payoff would be

$$U(30,000) = 0.95(100) + 0.05(10)$$
$$= 0.95 + 0.05$$
$$= 95.5$$

Hence, we must conclude that the utility assigned to each payoff is not unique but merely depends on the initial choice of utilities for the best and worst payoffs. We will discuss utility choice further at the end of the section. For now, however, we will continue to use a value of 10 for the utility of $50,000 and a value of 0 for the utility of $-$50,000.

Before computing the utility for the other payoffs, let us consider the significance of Swofford's president assigning a utility of 9.5 to a payoff of $30,000. Clearly, when $p = 0.95$, the expected value of the lottery is

$$\text{EV(lottery)} = 0.95(\$50,000) + 0.05(-\$50,000)$$
$$= \$47,500 - \$2,500$$
$$= \$45,000$$

Although the expected value of the lottery when $p = 0.95$ is $45,000, Swofford's president would just as soon take a guaranteed payoff of $30,000. Thus, Swofford's president is taking a conservative, or risk-avoiding, viewpoint. A decision maker who would choose a guaranteed payoff over a lottery with a better expected payoff is a risk avoider. The president would rather have $30,000 for certain than risk anything greater than a 5% chance of incurring a loss of $50,000. In other words, the difference between the EV of $45,000 and the guaranteed payoff of $30,000 is the risk premium that Swofford's president would be willing to pay to avoid the 5% chance of losing $50,000.

The difference between the expected value of the lottery and the guaranteed payoff can be viewed as the risk premium the decision maker is willing to pay.

To compute the utility associated with a payoff of $-$20,000, we must ask Swofford's president to state a preference between a guaranteed $-$20,000 payoff and an opportunity to engage again in the following lottery:

Lottery: Swofford obtains a payoff of $50,000 with probability p
and a payoff of $-$50,000 with probability $(1 - p)$

Note that this lottery is exactly the same as the one we used to establish the utility of a payoff of $30,000. In fact, we use this lottery to establish the utility for any monetary value in the Swofford payoff table. We need to determine the value of p that would make the president indifferent between a guaranteed payoff of $-$20,000 and the lottery. For example, we might begin by asking the president to choose between a certain loss of $20,000 and the lottery with a payoff of $-$50,000 with probability $p = 0.90$ and a payoff of $-$50,000 with probability $(1 - p) = 0.10$. What answer do you think we would get? Surely, with this high probability of obtaining a payoff of $50,000, the president would elect the lottery. Next, we might ask whether $p = 0.85$ would result in indifference between the loss of $20,000 for certain and the lottery. Again the president might prefer the lottery. Suppose that we continue until we get to $p = 0.55$, at which point the president is indifferent between the payoff of $-$20,000 and the lottery. That is, for any value of p less than 0.55, the president would take a loss of $20,000 for certain rather than risk the potential loss of $50,000 with the lottery; and for any value of p above 0.55, the president would choose the lottery. Thus, the utility assigned to a payoff of $-$20,000 is

$$U(-\$20,000) = pU(50,000) + (1 - p)U(-\$50,000)$$
$$= 0.55(10) + 0.45(0)$$
$$= 5.5$$

Again let us compare the significance of this assignment to the expected value approach. When $p = 0.55$, the expected value of the lottery is

$$EV(\text{lottery}) = 0.55(\$50,000) + 0.45(-\$50,000)$$
$$= \$27,500 - \$22,500$$
$$= \$5000$$

Thus, Swofford's president would just as soon absorb a loss of $20,000 for certain as take the lottery, even though the expected value of the lottery is $5000. Once again this preference demonstrates the conservative, or risk-avoiding, point of view of Swofford's president.

In these two examples we computed the utility for the monetary payoffs of $30,000 and $-$20,000. We can determine the utility for any monetary payoff M in a similar fashion. First, we must find the probability p for which the decision maker is indifferent

TABLE 5.2 UTILITY OF MONETARY PAYOFFS FOR SWOFFORD, INC.

Monetary Value	Indifference Value of p	Utility Value
$ 50,000	Does not apply	10.0
30,000	0.95	9.5
20,000	0.90	9.0
0	0.75	7.5
−20,000	0.55	5.5
−30,000	0.40	4.0
−50,000	Does not apply	0

between a guaranteed payoff of M and a lottery with a payoff of $50,000 with probability p and −$50,000 with probability $(1 − p)$. The utility of M is then computed as follows:

$$U(M) = pU(\$50,000) + (1 − p)U(−\$50,000)$$
$$= p(10) + (1 − p)0$$
$$= 10p$$

Using this procedure we developed utility values for the rest of the payoffs in Swofford's problem. The results are presented in Table 5.2.

Now that we have determined the utility value of each of the possible monetary values, we can write the original payoff table in terms of utility values. Table 5.3 shows the utility for the various outcomes in the Swofford problem. The notation we use for the entries in the utility table is U_{ij}, which denotes the utility associated with decision alternative d_i and state of nature s_j. Using this notation, we see that $U_{23} = 4.0$.

The Expected Utility Approach

We can now apply the expected value computations introduced in Chapter 4 to the utilities in Table 5.3 in order to select an optimal decision alternative for Swofford, Inc. However, because utility values represent such a special case of expected value, we will refer to the expected value when applied to utility values as the **expected utility (EU)**. Thus, the expected utility approach requires the analyst to compute the expected utility for each decision alternative and then select the alternative yielding the highest expected utility. With N possible states of nature, the expected utility of a decision alternative d_i is given by

$$EU(d_i) = \sum_{j=1}^{N} P(s_j)U_{ij} \qquad (5.1)$$

TABLE 5.3 UTILITY TABLE FOR SWOFFORD, INC.

Decision Alternative	State of Nature		
	Prices Up s_1	Prices Stable s_2	Prices Down s_3
Investment A, d_1	9.5	9.0	0
Investment B, d_2	10.0	5.5	4.0
Do not invest, d_3	7.5	7.5	7.5

The expected utility for each of the decision alternatives in the Swofford problem is

$$EU(d_1) = 0.3(9.5) + 0.5(9.0) + 0.2(0) \quad = 7.35$$
$$EU(d_2) = 0.3(10) \quad + 0.5(5.5) + 0.2(4.0) = 6.55$$
$$EU(d_3) = 0.3(7.5) + 0.5(7.5) + 0.2(7.5) = 7.50$$

Can you use the expected utility approach to determine the optimal decision? Try Problem 1.

Note that the optimal decision using the expected utility approach is d_3, do not invest. The ranking of alternatives according to the president's utility assignments and the associated monetary values are as follows:

Ranking of Decision Alternatives	Expected Utility	Expected Monetary Value
Do not invest	7.50	0
Investment A	7.35	9000
Investment B	6.55	−1000

Note that although investment A had the highest expected monetary value of $9000, the analysis indicates that Swofford should decline this investment. The rationale behind not selecting investment A is that the 0.20 probability of a $50,000 loss was considered to involve a serious risk by Swofford's president. The seriousness of this risk and its associated impact on the company were not adequately reflected by the expected monetary value of investment A. We assessed the utility for each payoff to assess this risk adequately.

NOTES AND COMMENTS

In the Swofford problem we have been using a utility of 10 for the best payoff and 0 for the worst. The choice of values could have been anything, and we might have chosen 1 for the utility of the best payoff and 0 for the utility of the worst. Had we made this choice, the utility for any monetary value M would have been the value of p at which the decision maker was indifferent between a guaranteed payoff of M and a lottery in which the best payoff is obtained with probability p and the worst payoff is obtained with probability $(1 - p)$. Thus, the utility for any monetary value would have been equal to the probability of earning the best payoff. Often this choice is made because of the ease in computation. We chose not to do so to emphasize the distinction between the utility values and the indifference probabilities for the lottery.

Summary of Steps for Determining the Utility of Money

Before considering other aspects of utility, let us summarize the steps involved in determining the utility for a monetary value and using it within the decision analysis framework. The following steps state in general terms the procedure used to solve the Swofford, Inc., investment problem:

Step 1. Develop a payoff table using monetary values.
Step 2. Identify the best and worst payoff values in the table and assign each a utility value, with $U(\text{best payoff}) > U(\text{worst payoff})$.

Step 3. For every other monetary value M in the original payoff table, do the following to determine its utility value:

   a. Define the lottery: The best payoff is obtained with probability p and the worst payoff is obtained with probability $(1 - p)$.

   b. Determine the value of p such that the decision maker is indifferent between a guaranteed payoff of M and the lottery defined in step 3(a).

   c. Calculate the utility of M as follows:

$$U(M) = pU(\text{best payoff}) + (1 - p)U(\text{worst payoff})$$

Step 4. Convert the payoff table from monetary values to utility values.

Step 5. Apply the expected utility approach to the utility table developed in step 4 and select the decision alternative with the highest expected utility.

NOTES AND COMMENTS

The procedure we described for determining the utility of monetary consequences can also be used to develop a utility measure for nonmonetary consequences. Assign the best consequence a utility of 10 and the worst a utility of 0. Then create a lottery with a probability of p for the best consequence and $(1 - p)$ for the worst consequence. For each of the other consequences, find the value of p that makes the decision maker indifferent between the lottery and the consequence. Then calculate the utility of the consequence in question as follows:

$$U(\text{consequence}) = pU(\text{best consequence})$$
$$+ (1 - p)U(\text{worst consequence})$$

Utility: Other Considerations

In this section we describe how a risk-avoiding decision maker and a risk-taking decision maker differ in their assessment of utility. Expected utility is then used to show how a risk-avoiding decision maker and a risk-taking decision maker may prefer different decision alternatives for the same decision problem. We close this section by comparing expected monetary value and expected utility as criteria for decision making.

Risk Avoiders Versus Risk Takers

The financial position of Swofford, Inc., was such that the firm's president evaluated investment opportunities from a conservative, or risk-avoiding, point of view. However, if the firm had a surplus of cash and a stable future, Swofford's president might have been looking for investment alternatives that, although perhaps risky, contained a potential for substantial profit. That type of behavior would have made the president a risk taker.

A **risk taker** is a decision maker who would choose a lottery over a better guaranteed payoff. In this section we analyze the decision problem faced by Swofford from the point of view of a decision maker who would be classified as a risk taker. We then compare the conservative, or risk-avoiding, point of view of Swofford's president with the behavior of a decision maker who is a risk taker.

For the decision problem facing Swofford, Inc., using the general procedure for developing utilities as discussed in Section 5.2, a risk taker might express the utility for the various payoffs shown in Table 5.4. As before, $U(50,000) = 10$ and $U(-50,000) = 0$. Note the difference in behavior reflected in Table 5.4 and Table 5.2. That is, in determining the value

TABLE 5.4   REVISED UTILITY VALUES FOR SWOFFORD, INC., ASSUMING A RISK TAKER

Monetary Value	Indifference Value of p	Utility Value
$ 50,000	Does not apply	10.0
30,000	0.50	5.0
20,000	0.40	4.0
0	0.25	2.5
−20,000	0.15	1.5
−30,000	0.10	1.0
−50,000	Does not apply	0

TABLE 5.5   PAYOFF TABLE FOR SWOFFORD, INC.

	State of Nature		
Decision Alternative	Prices Up s_1	Prices Stable s_2	Prices Down s_3
Investment A, d_1	$30,000	$20,000	−$50,000
Investment B, d_2	$50,000	−$20,000	−$30,000
Do not invest, d_3	0	0	0

of p at which the decision maker is indifferent between a guaranteed payoff of M and a lottery in which $50,000 is obtained with probability p and −$50,000 with probability $(1 − p)$, the risk taker is willing to accept a greater risk of incurring a loss of $50,000 in order to gain the opportunity to realize a profit of $50,000.

To help develop the utility table for the risk taker, we have reproduced the Swofford, Inc., payoff table in Table 5.5. Using these payoffs and the risk taker's utility values given in Table 5.4, we can write the risk taker's utility table as shown in Table 5.6. Using the state-of-nature probabilities $P(s_1) = 0.3$, $P(s_2) = 0.5$, and $P(s_3) = 0.2$, the expected utility for each decision alternative is

$$EU(d_1) = 0.3(5.0) + 0.5(4.0) + 0.2(0) \quad = 3.50$$
$$EU(d_2) = 0.3(10) \ + 0.5(1.5) + 0.2(1.0) = 3.95$$
$$EU(d_3) = 0.3(2.5) + 0.5(2.5) + 0.2(2.5) = 2.50$$

What is the recommended decision? Perhaps somewhat to your surprise, the analysis recommends investment B, with the highest expected utility of 3.95. Recall that this investment has a −$1000 expected monetary value. Why is it now the recommended decision? Remember that the decision maker in this revised problem is a risk taker. Thus, although

TABLE 5.6   UTILITY TABLE OF A RISK TAKER FOR SWOFFORD, INC.

	State of Nature		
Decision Alternative	Prices Up s_1	Prices Stable s_2	Prices Down s_3
Investment A, d_1	5.0	4.0	0
Investment B, d_2	10.0	1.5	1.0
Do not invest, d_3	2.5	2.5	2.5

the expected value of investment B is negative, utility analysis has shown that this decision maker is enough of a risk taker to prefer investment B and its potential for the $50,000 profit.

The expected utility values give the following order of preference of the decision alternatives for the risk taker and the associated expected monetary values:

Ranking of Decision Alternatives	Expected Utility	Expected Monetary Value
Investment B	3.95	−$1000
Investment A	3.50	$9000
Do not invest	2.50	0

Comparing the utility analysis for a risk taker with the more conservative preferences of the president of Swofford, Inc., who is a risk avoider, we see that, even with the same decision problem, different attitudes toward risk can lead to different recommended decisions. The utility values established by Swofford's president indicated that the firm should not invest at this time, whereas the utilities established by the risk taker showed a preference for investment B. Note that both of these decisions differ from the best expected monetary value decision, which was investment A.

We can obtain another perspective of the difference between behaviors of a risk avoider and a risk taker by developing a graph that depicts the relationship between monetary value and utility. We use the horizontal axis of the graph to represent monetary values and the vertical axis to represent the utility associated with each monetary value. Now, consider the data in Table 5.2, with a utility value corresponding to each monetary value for the original Swofford, Inc., problem. These values can be plotted on a graph such as that in Figure 5.1, and a curve can be drawn through the observed points. The resulting curve is the **utility**

FIGURE 5.1   UTILITY FUNCTION FOR MONEY FOR THE RISK AVOIDER

FIGURE 5.2   UTILITY FUNCTION FOR MONEY FOR THE RISK TAKER

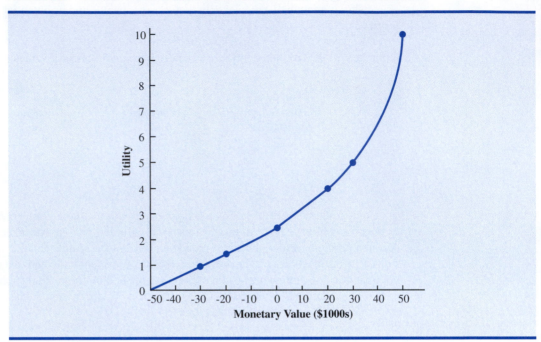

function for money for Swofford's president. Recall that these points reflected the conservative, or risk-avoiding, nature of Swofford's president. Hence, we refer to the curve in Figure 5.1 as a utility function for a risk avoider. Using the data in Table 5.4 developed for a risk taker, we can plot these points on a graph such as that in Figure 5.2. The resulting curve depicts the utility function for a risk taker.

By looking at the utility functions of Figures 5.1 and 5.2, we can begin to generalize about the utility functions for risk avoiders and risk takers. Although the exact shape of the utility function will vary from one decision maker to another, we can see the general shape of these two types of utility functions. The utility function for a risk avoider shows a diminishing marginal return for money. For example, the increase in utility going from a monetary value of −$30,000 to $0 is 7.5 − 4.0 = 3.5, whereas the increase in utility in going from $0 to $30,000 is only 9.5 − 7.5 = 2.0.

However, the utility function for a risk taker shows an increasing marginal return for money. For example, in Figure 5.2, the increase in utility in going from −$30,000 to $0 is 2.5 − 1.0 = 1.5, whereas the increase in utility in going from $0 to $30,000 is 5.0 − 2.5 = 2.5. Note also that in either case the utility function is always increasing; that is, more money leads to more utility. All utility functions possess this property.

We concluded that the utility function for a risk avoider shows a diminishing marginal return for money and that the utility function for a risk taker shows an increasing marginal return. When the marginal return for money is neither decreasing nor increasing but remains constant, the corresponding utility function describes the behavior of a decision maker who is neutral to risk. The following characteristics are associated with a **risk-neutral decision maker**:

Try Problem 5 for practice in plotting the utility function for risk-avoider, risk-taker, and risk-neutral decision makers.

1. The utility function can be drawn as a straight line connecting the "best" and the "worst" points.
2. The expected utility approach and the expected value approach applied to monetary payoffs result in the same action.

FIGURE 5.3   UTILITY FUNCTION FOR RISK-AVOIDER, RISK-TAKER, AND RISK-
NEUTRAL DECISION MAKERS

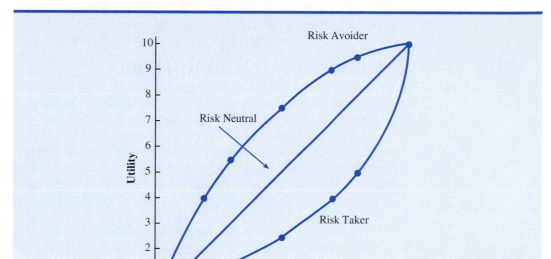

Figure 5.3 depicts the utility function of a risk-neutral decision maker using the Swofford,
Inc., problem data. For comparison purposes, we also show the utility functions for the
cases where the decision maker is either a risk taker or a risk avoider.

Expected Monetary Value Versus Expected Utility

In many decision-making problems, expected monetary value and expected utility will lead
to identical recommendations. In fact, this result will always be true if the decision maker
is risk neutral. In general, if the decision maker is almost risk neutral over the range of payoffs (from lowest to highest) for a particular decision problem, the decision alternative with
the best expected monetary value leads to selection of the most preferred decision alternative. The trick lies in recognizing the range of monetary values over which a decision
maker's utility function is risk neutral.

Generally, when the payoffs for a particular decision-making problem fall into a reasonable range—the best is not too good and the worst is not too bad—decision makers tend
to express preferences in agreement with the expected monetary value approach. Thus, we
suggest asking the decision maker to consider the best and worst possible payoffs for a
problem and assess their reasonableness. If the decision maker believes that they are in the
reasonable range, the decision alternative with the best expected monetary value can be
used. However, if the payoffs appear unreasonably large or unreasonably small (for example, a huge loss) and if the decision maker believes that monetary values do not adequately
reflect her or his true preferences for the payoffs, a utility analysis of the problem should
be considered.

Unfortunately, determination of the appropriate utilities is not a trivial task. As we have
shown, measuring utility requires a degree of subjectivity on the part of the decision maker,
and different decision makers will have different utility functions. This aspect of utility often

causes decision makers to feel uncomfortable about using the expected utility approach. However, if you encounter a decision situation in which you are convinced that monetary value is not the sole measure of performance, and if you agree that a quantitative analysis of the decision problem is desirable, you should recommend that utility analysis be considered.

 ## 5.4   Introduction to Game Theory

In decision analysis, a single decision maker seeks to select an optimal decision alternative after considering the possible outcomes of one or more chance events. In **game theory**, two or more decision makers are called players, and they compete as adversaries against each other. Each player selects a strategy independently without knowing in advance the strategy of the other player or players. The combination of the competing strategies provides the value of the game to the players. Game theory applications have been developed for situations in which the competing players are teams, companies, political candidates, armies, and contract bidders.

Until 1944, when Von Neumann and Morgenstern published the book Theory of Games and Economic Behavior, *the literature on decisions involving risk consisted primarily of applications involving the use of probability in gambling.*

In this section we describe **two-person, zero-sum games**. *Two-person* means that two competing players take part in the game. *Zero-sum* means that the gain (or loss) for one player is equal to the corresponding loss (gain) for the other player. As a result, the gain and loss balance out so that the game results in the sum of zero. What one player wins, the other player loses. Let us demonstrate a two-person, zero-sum game and its solution by considering two companies competing for market share.

Competing for Market Share

Suppose that two companies are the only manufacturers of a particular product; they compete against each other for market share. In planning a marketing strategy for the coming year, each company is considering three strategies designed to take market share from the other company. The three strategies, assumed to be the same for both companies, are as follows:

Strategy 1   Increase advertising
Strategy 2   Provide quantity discounts
Strategy 3   Extend product warranty

A payoff table showing the percentage gain in the market share for Company A expected for each combination of strategies follows. The notations a_1, a_2, and a_3 identify the three strategies for Company A; the notations b_1, b_2, and b_3 identify the three strategies for Company B. It is a zero-sum game because any gain in market share for Company A is a loss in market share for Company B.

		Company B		
		Increase Advertising b_1	Quantity Discounts b_2	Extend Warranty b_3
Company A	Increase Advertising, a_1	4	3	2
	Quantity Discount a_2	−1	4	1
	Extend Warrant, a_3	5	−2	0

In interpreting the entries in the table we see that if Company A increases advertising (a_1) and Company B increases advertising (b_1), Company A will come out ahead with an increase in market share of 4%. On the other hand, if Company A provides quantity discounts (a_2) and Company B increases advertising (b_1), Company A is projected to lose 1% of market share to Company B. Company A is seeking payoff values that show relatively large increases in its market share. Company B is seeking payoff values that show decreases or small increases in Company A's market share, and thus better results for Company B.

This game involving market share meets the requirements of a two-person, zero-sum game. The two companies are the two players and the zero-sum occurs because the gain in market share for Company A is the same as the loss in market share for Company B. Due to the planning horizon, each company must select a strategy before knowing the other company's strategy. What are the optimal strategies for the two companies?

The logic of game theory assumes that each company or player has the same information and will select a strategy that provides the best possible outcome from its point of view. Suppose Company A selects strategy a_1. Market share increases of 4%, 3%, or 2% are possible depending upon Company B's strategy. If Company B believes that Company A will use strategy a_1, then Company B will employ strategy b_3. Under the assumption that Company B will select the strategy that is best for it, Company A analyzes the game by protecting itself against the actions of Company B. In doing so, Company A identifies the minimum possible payoff for each of its actions. This payoff is the minimum value in each row of the payoff matrix. These row minimums are computed in the payoff table as follows:

| | Company B | | | |
	Increase Advertising b_1	Quantity Discounts b_2	Extend Warranty b_3	Minimum
Increase Advertising, a_1	4	3	2	②
Quantity Discounts, a_2	−1	4	1	−1
Extend Warranty, a_3	5	−2	0	−2

Company A

Maximum of
row minimums

Considering the entries in the Minimum column, we see that Company A can be guaranteed an increase in market share of at least 2% by selecting the strategy that provides the *maximum of the row minimums* (strategy a_1). Thus, Company A follows a *maximin* procedure and selects strategy a_1 as its best strategy.

Let us now look at the payoff table from the point of view of the other player, Company B. The entries in the payoff table represent losses in market share. Consider what happens to Company B if strategy b_1 is selected. Market share decreases of 4%, −1%, and 5% are possible. Under the assumption that Company A will select the strategy that is best for it, Company B knows that if it selects strategy b_1, a loss in market share of as much as 5% could be incurred. Thus, Company B analyzes the game by considering the maximum value in each column, which provides the maximum decrease in its market share for each Company A strategy. These column maximums are computed as follows:

| | Company B | | | |
	Increase Advertising b_1	Quantity Discounts b_2	Extend Warranty b_3	Minimum
Increase Advertising, a_1	4	3	2	②
Quantity Discounts a_2	−1	4	1	−1
Extend Warranty, a_3	5	−2	0	−2
Maximum	5	4	②	

Company A

Minimum of column maximums

Maximum of row minimums

By considering the entries in the Maximum row, Company B can be guaranteed a decrease in market share of no more than 2% by selecting the strategy that provides the *minimum of the column maximums* (strategy b_3). Thus, Company B follows a *minimax* procedure and selects strategy b_3 as its best strategy. Under strategy b_3 Company B knows that Company A cannot gain more than 2% in market share.

Identifying a Pure Strategy

Whenever the maximum of the row minimums *equals* the minimum of the column maximums, the players cannot improve their outcomes by changing strategies. The game is said to have a **saddle point**. With a saddle point, the optimal strategies and the value of the game cannot be improved by either player changing strategies. Thus, a **pure strategy** has been identified as being optimal for both players. The requirement for a pure strategy is as follows:

$$\text{Maximum(Row minimums)} = \text{Minimum(Column maximums)}$$

That is, the maximin value for Player A equals the minimax value for Player B. In this example, the solution to the game is for Company A to increase its advertising (strategy a_1) and Company B to extend its product warranty (strategy b_3). The value of the game shows that this optimal solution will increase Company A's market share by 2% and decrease Company B's market share by 2%.

With a pure strategy, neither player can improve its position by changing to a different strategy. In our marketing example, the pure strategy for Company A is a_1. When Company B selects its pure strategy b_3, the value of the game shows an increase in Company A's market share of 2%. Note that if Company B tries to change its pure strategy from b_3, Company A's market share will increase 4% if b_1 is selected or will increase 3% if b_2 is selected. Company B must stay with its pure strategy b_3 to obtain its best result. Similarly, note that if Company A tries to change its pure strategy from a_1, Company A's market share will increase only 1% if a_2 is selected or will not increase at all if a_3 is selected. Company A must stay with its pure strategy a_1 in order to keep its 2% increase in market share. Thus, even if one of the players discovered in advance the opponent's strategy, no advantage could be gained by switching to a different strategy.

If a pure strategy exists, it is the optimal solution for the game.

When a pure strategy is optimal for a two-person, zero-sum game, the following steps will find the optimal strategy for each player:

Step 1. Compute the minimum payoff for each row (Player A).

Step 2. For Player A, select the strategy that provides the *maximum* of the row minimums.

Step 3. Compute the maximum payoff for each column (Player B).

Step 4. For Player B, select the strategy that provides the *minimum* of the column maximums.

Step 5. If the maximin value (step 2) equals the minimax value (step 4), an optimal pure strategy exists for both players. The optimal strategy for Player A is identified in step 2, and the optimal strategy for Player B is identified in step 4. The value of the game is given by the value at the saddle point where the optimal strategies for both players intersect.

If in step 5 the maximin value for Player A does not equal the minimax value for Player B, a pure strategy is not optimal for the two-person, zero-sum game. In this case, a *mixed strategy* is best. We show when it is necessary to employ a mixed strategy in the next section.

Mixed Strategy Games

Consider the two-person, zero-sum game that occurs in a football game. The two competing players are the two football teams. On each play, the game is zero-sum because the yardage gained by one team is equal to the yardage lost by the other team. As usual in game theory, each team must select its strategy before knowing the strategy selected by the other team. In this example, let Team A be the team on offense trying to gain yardage and Team B be the team on defense trying to keep the yardage gained by Team A to a minimum. We define the offensive strategies for Team A as follows:

$$a_1 = \text{running play}$$
$$a_2 = \text{passing play}$$

The defensive strategies for Team B are as follows:

$$b_1 = \text{run defense}$$
$$b_2 = \text{pass defense}$$

The payoff table shows the yardage gained by Team A depending upon the strategies selected by the two teams.

		Team B	
		Run Defense b_1	Pass Defense b_2
Team A	Run, a_1	1	6
	Pass, a_2,	15	0

Applying the five-step procedure used to identify a pure strategy, the row minimums and the column maximums are as follows:

		Team B		
		Run Defense b_1	Pass Defense b_2	Minimum
Team A	Run, a_1	1	6	①
	Pass, a_2	15	0	0
	Maximum	15	⑥	

The maximum of the row minimums is 1 and the minimum of the column maximums is 6. Because these values are not equal, the two-person, zero-sum game does not have an optimal pure strategy. In this case, a **mixed strategy** solution is best. With a mixed strategy the optimal solution for each player is to randomly select among the alternative strategies. In the football example, then, the offensive Team A will mix up or vary its selection of running (a_1) and passing (a_2) plays, while the defensive Team B will mix up or vary its selection of a run defense (b_1) and a pass defense (b_2).

When you think about a football game, it becomes clear that a pure strategy such as Team A always selecting a running play would not work. Team B would recognize Team A's pure strategy and would always be prepared with a run defense. Thus, a Team A mixed strategy of sometimes running and sometimes passing would make sense. When a mixed strategy solution is needed, game theory will determine the optimal probabilities for each strategy for each player. That is, the game theory solution of the football example will tell the offensive team the optimal probabilities for a running play and a passing play. At the same time, the solution will tell the defensive team the optimal probabilities for a run defense and a pass defense. The following discussion shows how to calculate these mixed strategy probabilities.

Let

$$p = \text{the probability Team A selects a running play}$$
$$(1 - p) = \text{the probability Team A selects a passing play}$$

When a mixed strategy solution exists, we seek to determine the probability p for Team A such that Team B cannot improve its result by changing its defensive strategy. First assume that Team B selects a run defense as shown in column b_1. If Team A selects a running play with probability p and a passing play with probability $(1 - p)$, the expected value of the yardage gain for Team A is computed as follows:

If Team B selects b_1:

$$\text{EV(Yardage)} = 1p + 15(1 - p)$$

If Team B selects its pass defense as shown in column b_2, the expected value of the yardage gain for Team A will be as follows:

If Team B selects b_2:

$$\text{EV(Yardage)} = 6p + 0(1 - p) = 6p$$

To guarantee that Team B cannot change its strategy and decrease the expected value of the yardage gained by Team A, we set the two expected values equal and solve for the value of p.

$$1p + 15(1 - p) = 6p$$
$$1p + 15 - 15p = 6p$$
$$20p = 15$$
$$p = 15/20 = 0.75$$

With $p = 0.75$, $(1 - p) = 1 - 0.75 = 0.25$. This result tells Team A it should select a running play with a 0.75 probability and a passing play with a 0.25 probability. The expected value of the yardage gained, which is the *value of the game,* is

$$\text{EV(Yardage)} = 1p + 15(1 - p) = 1(0.75) + 15(0.25) = 4.5 \text{ yards per play}$$

Now let us consider the optimal probabilities for Team B. Let

$$q = \text{the probability Team B selects a run defense}$$
$$(1 - q) = \text{the probability Team B selects a pass defense}$$

Using the same logic we used for computing Team A's optimal probabilities, we want to determine the value of q such that Team A cannot increase the expected value of the yardage gained by changing its offensive strategy. We first compute the expected value of the yardage for Team B for the following two cases:

If Team A selects a_1:

$$\text{EV(Yardage)} = 1q + 6(1 - q)$$

If Team A selects a_2:

$$\text{EV(Yardage)} = 15q + 0(1 - q) = 15q$$

To guarantee that Team A cannot change its strategy and affect the expected value of the yardage for Team B, we set the two expected values equal and solve for the value of q as follows:

$$1q + 6(1 - q) = 15q$$
$$1q + 6 - 6q = 15q$$
$$20q = 6$$
$$q = 6/20 = 0.30$$

With $q = 0.30$, $(1 - q) = 1 - 0.30 = 0.70$. This result tells Team B that it should select a run defense with a 0.30 probability and a pass defense with a 0.70 probability. The expected yardage gained, which is the value of the game, will remain 4.5 yards per play.

Thus, we have the optimal mixed strategy solution for the football game example. Any 2×2 two-person, zero-sum mixed strategy game can be solved algebraically as shown in this example. If a larger two-person, zero-sum game involves a mixed strategy, solving it is a bit more complicated.

A Larger Mixed Strategy Game

Consider the following two-person, zero-sum game:

		Player B		
		b_1	b_2	b_3
	a_1	0	−1	2
Player A	a_2	5	4	−3
	a_3	2	3	−4

Following the usual procedure for identifying a pure strategy, we compute the row minimums and the column maximums:

		Player B			
		b_1	b_2	b_3	**Minimum**
	a_1	0	−1	2	−1
Player A	a_2	5	4	−3	−3
	a_3	2	3	−4	−4
Maximum		5	4	2	

The maximum of the row minimums is −1 and the minimum of the column maximums is 2. Because the maximin and minimax values are not equal, the two-person, zero-sum game does not have an optimal pure strategy. However, with a problem larger than 2×2, we cannot use the algebraic solution for the mixed strategy probabilities as we did in the previous example.

If a game larger than 2×2 requires a mixed strategy, we first look for dominated strategies in order to reduce the size of the game. A **dominated strategy** exists if another strategy *is at least as good* regardless of what the opponent does. For example, consider strategies a_2 and a_3. The payoff table shows that in column b_1, $5 > 2$; in column b_2, $4 > 3$; and in column b_3, $−3 > −4$. Thus, regardless of what Player B does, Player A will always prefer the higher values of strategy a_2 compared to strategy a_3. Thus, strategy a_3 is dominated by strategy a_2 and can be dropped from consideration by Player A. Eliminating dominated strategies from the game reduces its size. After eliminating a_3, the reduced game becomes

		Player B		
		b_1	b_2	b_3
Player A	a_1	0	−1	2
	a_2	5	4	−3

Next, we look for more dominated strategies. Player A finds no other dominated strategies. However, consider strategies b_1 and b_2 for Player B. Remember that Player B is interested in smaller values. The payoff table shows that in row a_1, $−1 < 0$ and in row a_2, $4 < 5$.

Thus, regardless of what Player A does, Player B would always prefer the smaller values of strategy b_2 compared to strategy b_1. Thus, strategy b_1 is dominated by strategy b_2 and can be eliminated from the game. With this dominated strategy eliminated, the reduced game becomes

		Player B	
		b_1	b_3
Player A	a_1	−1	2
	a_2	4	−3

Problem 14 at the end of the chapter will ask you to find the optimal probabilities for this example.

By successively eliminating dominated strategies, we reduce the game to a 2×2 game. The algebraic solution procedure described earlier in this section can now be used to identify the optimal probabilities for the mixed strategy solution.

Finally, it is important to realize that no hard-and-fast rule identifies dominated strategies. Basically, the analyst must make pairwise comparisons of the decision strategies in an attempt to identify dominated strategies. The goal is to identify and eliminate dominated strategies sequentially in order to reduce the game to a 2×2 game so that an algebraic solution procedure can be used to solve for the mixed strategy probabilities.

Identifying and eliminating dominated strategies may reduce the game to a 2×2 game. If so, an algebraic procedure may be used to determine the mixed strategy solution.

Summary of Steps for Solving Two-Person, Zero-Sum Games

The following summary shows the steps used to solve two-person, zero-sum games:

1. Use the maximin procedure for Player A and the minimax procedure for Player B to determine whether a pure strategy solution exists. (See previous steps for identifying a pure strategy.) If a pure strategy exists, it is the optimal solution.
2. If a pure strategy does not exist and the game is larger than 2×2, identify a dominated strategy to eliminate a row or column. Develop the reduced payoff table and continue to use dominance to eliminate as many additional rows and columns as possible.
3. If the reduced game is 2×2, solve for the optimal mixed strategy probabilities algebraically.

If the game cannot be reduced to a 2×2 game, a linear programming model can be used to solve for the optimal mixed strategy probabilities. The formulation of a linear programming model to solve these larger game theory problems is beyond the scope of this text.

Extensions

In 1994, John Harsanui. John Nash, and Reinhard Selten received the Nobel Prize in Economics for their work on noncooperative game theory.

We presented the basic model for two-person, zero-sum games. However, game theory models extend beyond two-person, zero-sum games. One extension is a two-person, constant-sum game that occurs when the payoffs for the strategies chosen sum to a constant other than zero. In addition, game theory can be extended to include more general n-person games. Cooperative games where players are allowed preplay communications are another variation. Finally, some game theory models allow an infinite number of strategies to be available for the players.

Summary

In this chapter we showed how utility could be used in decision-making situations in which monetary value did not provide an adequate measure of the payoffs. Utility is a measure of the total worth of a consequence. As such, utility takes into account the decision maker's assessment of all aspects of a consequence, including profit, loss, risk, and perhaps additional nonmonetary factors. The examples showed how the use of expected utility can lead to decision recommendations that differ from those based on expected monetary value.

A decision maker's judgment must be used to establish the utility for each consequence. We presented a step-by-step procedure to determine a decision maker's utility for monetary payoffs. We also discussed how conservative, risk-avoiding decision makers assess utility differently from more aggressive, risk-taking decision makers. If the decision maker is risk neutral, we showed that the solution using expected utility is identical to the solution using expected monetary value.

We presented an introduction to game theory by describing how to solve two-person, zero-sum games. In these games, the two players end up with the sum of the gain (loss) to one player and the loss (gain) to the other player always equal to zero. We described the steps that can be used to determine whether a two-person, zero-sum game results in an optimal pure strategy. If a pure strategy is optimal, a saddle point determines the value of the game. If an optimal pure strategy does not exist for a two-person, zero-sum 2×2 game, we showed how to identify an optimal mixed strategy. With a mixed strategy, each player uses probability to select a strategy for each play of the game. We showed how dominance could be used to reduce the size of mixed strategy games. If the elimination of dominated strategies can reduce a larger game to a 2×2 game, an algebraic solution procedure can be used to find a solution. If the game cannot be reduced to a 2×2 game, a linear programming model is needed to determine the optimal mixed strategy solution.

Glossary

Utility A measure of the total worth of a consequence reflecting a decision maker's attitude toward considerations such as profit, loss, and risk.

Lottery A hypothetical investment alternative with a probability p of obtaining the best payoff and a probability of $(1 - p)$ of obtaining the worst payoff.

Risk avoider A decision maker who would choose a guaranteed payoff over a lottery with a better expected payoff.

Expected utility (EU) The weighted average of the utilities associated with a decision alternative. The weights are the state-of-nature probabilities.

Risk taker A decision maker who would choose a lottery over a better guaranteed payoff.

Utility function for money A curve that depicts the relationship between monetary value and utility.

Risk-neutral decision maker A decision maker who is neutral to risk. For this decision maker the decision alternative with the best expected monetary value is identical to the alternative with the highest expected utility.

Game theory The study of decision situations in which two or more players compete as adversaries. The combination of strategies chosen by the players determines the value of the game to each player.

Two-person, zero-sum game A game with two players in which the gain to one player is equal to the loss to the other player.

Saddle point A condition that exists when pure strategies are optimal for both players in a two-person, zero-sum game. The saddle point occurs at the intersection of the optimal strategies for the players, and the value of the saddle point is the value of the game.

Pure strategy A game solution that provides a single best strategy for each player.

Mixed strategy A game solution in which the player randomly selects the strategy to play from among several strategies with positive probabilities. The solution to the mixed strategy game identifies the probabilities that each player should use to randomly select the strategy to play.

Dominated strategy A strategy is dominated if another strategy is at least as good for every strategy that the opposing player may employ. A dominated strategy will never be selected by the player and as such can be eliminated in order to reduce the size of the game.

Problems

1. A firm has three investment alternatives. Payoffs are in thousands of dollars.

		Economic Conditions	
Decision Alternative	**Up s_1**	**Stable s_2**	**Down s_3**
Investment A, d_1	100	25	0
Investment B, d_2	75	50	25
Investment C, d_3	50	50	50
Probabilities	0.40	0.30	0.30

a. Using the expected value approach, which decision is preferred?

b. For the lottery having a payoff of $100,000 with probability p and $0 with probability $(1 - p)$, two decision makers expressed the following indifference probabilities. Find the most preferred decision for each decision maker using the expected utility approach.

	Indifference Probability (p)	
Profit	**Decision Maker A**	**Decision Maker B**
$75,000	0.80	0.60
$50,000	0.60	0.30
$25,000	0.30	0.15

c. Why don't decision makers A and B select the same decision alternative?

2. Alexander Industries is considering purchasing an insurance policy for its new office building in St. Louis, Missouri. The policy has an annual cost of $10,000. If Alexander Industries doesn't purchase the insurance and minor fire damage occurs, a cost of $100,000 is anticipated; the cost if major or total destruction occurs is $200,000. The costs, including the state-of-nature probabilities, are as follows:

		Damage	
Decision Alternative	**None s_1**	**Minor s_2**	**Major s_3**
Purchase insurance, d_1	10,000	10,000	10,000
Do not purchase insurance, d_2	0	100,000	200,000
Probabilities	0.96	0.03	0.01

a. Using the expected value approach, what decision do you recommend?
b. What lottery would you use to assess utilities? (*Note:* Because the data are costs, the best payoff is $0.)
c. Assume that you found the following indifference probabilities for the lottery defined in part (b). What decision would you recommend?

Cost	Indifference Probability
10,000	$p = 0.99$
100,000	$p = 0.60$

d. Do you favor using expected value or expected utility for this decision problem? Why?

3. In a certain state lottery, a lottery ticket costs $2. In terms of the decision to purchase or not to purchase a lottery ticket, suppose that the following payoff table applies:

	State of Nature	
Decision Alternatives	**Win s_1**	**Loses s_2**
Purchase lottery ticket, d_1	300,000	-2
Do not purchase lottery ticket, d_2	0	0

a. A realistic estimate of the chances of winning is 1 in 250,000. Use the expected value approach to recommend a decision.
b. If a particular decision maker assigns an indifference probability of 0.000001 to the $0 payoff, would this individual purchase a lottery ticket? Use expected utility to justify your answer.

4. Two different routes accommodate travel between two cities. Route A normally takes 60 minutes and route B normally takes 45 minutes. If traffic problems are encountered on route A, the travel time increases to 70 minutes; traffic problems on route B increase travel time to 90 minutes. The probability of a delay is 0.20 for route A and 0.30 for route B.
a. Using the expected value approach, what is the recommended route?
b. If utilities are to be assigned to the travel times, what is the appropriate lottery? (*Note:* The smaller times should reflect higher utilities.)
c. Use the lottery of part (b) and assume that the decision maker expresses indifference probabilities of

$$p = 0.80 \quad \text{for 60 minutes}$$
$$p = 0.60 \quad \text{for 70 minutes}$$

What route should this decision maker select? Is the decision maker a risk taker or a risk avoider?

5. Three decision makers have assessed utilities for the following decision problem (payoff in dollars):

	State of Nature		
Decision Alternative	s_1	s_2	s_3
d_1	20	50	-20
d_2	80	100	-100

The indifference probabilities are as follows:

	Indifference Probability (p)		
Payoff	**Decision Maker A**	**Decision Maker B**	**Decision Maker C**
100	1.00	1.00	1.00
80	0.95	0.70	0.90
50	0.90	0.60	0.75
20	0.70	0.45	0.60
-20	0.50	0.25	0.40
-100	0.00	0.00	0.00

    a.   Plot the utility function for money for each decision maker.

    b.   Classify each decision maker as a risk avoider, a risk taker, or risk neutral.

    c.   For the payoff of 20, what is the premium that the risk avoider will pay to avoid risk? What is the premium that the risk taker will pay to have the opportunity of the high payoff?

6.   In Problem 5, if $P(s_1) = 0.25$, $P(s_2) = 0.50$, and $P(s_3) = 0.25$, find a recommended decision for each of the three decision makers. (*Note:* For the same decision problem, different utilities can lead to different decisions.)

7.   Suppose that the point spread for a particular sporting event is 10 points and that with this spread you are convinced you would have a 0.60 probability of winning a bet on your team. However, the local bookie will accept only a $1000 bet. Assuming that such bets are legal, would you bet on your team? (Disregard any commission charged by the bookie.) Remember that *you* must pay losses out of your own pocket. Your payoff table is as follows:

	State of Nature	
Decision Alternatives	**You Win**	**You Lose**
Bet	1000	-1000
Don't bet	0	0

    a.   What decision does the expected value approach recommend?

    b.   What is *your* indifference probability for the $0 payoff? (Although this choice isn't easy, be as realistic as possible. It is required for an analysis that reflects your attitude toward risk.)

    c.   What decision would you make based on the expected utility approach? In this case are you a risk taker or a risk avoider?

    d.   Would other individuals assess the same utility values you do? Explain.

    e.   If your decision in part (c) was to place the bet, repeat the analysis assuming a minimum bet of $10,000.

8.   A Las Vegas roulette wheel has 38 different numerical values. If an individual bets on one number and wins, the payoff is 35 to 1.

    a.   Show a payoff table for a $10 bet on one number for decision alternatives of bet and do not bet.

    b.   What is the recommended decision using the expected value approach?

    c.   Do the Las Vegas casinos want risk-taking or risk-avoiding customers? Explain.

    d.   What range of utility values would a decision maker have to assign to the $0 payoff in order to have expected utility justify a decision to place the $10 bet?

9. A new product has the following profit projections and associated probabilities:

Profit	Probability
$150,000	0.10
$100,000	0.25
$ 50,000	0.20
0	0.15
−$ 50,000	0.20
−$100,000	0.10

a. Use the expected value approach to decide whether to market the new product.
b. Because of the high dollar values involved, especially the possibility of a $100,000 loss, the marketing vice president has expressed some concern about the use of the expected value approach. As a consequence, if a utility analysis is performed, what is the appropriate lottery?
c. Assume that the following indifference probabilities are assigned. Do the utilities reflect the behavior of a risk taker or a risk avoider?

Profit	Indifference Probability(p)
$100,000	0.95
$ 50,000	0.70
0	0.50
−$ 50,000	0.25

d. Use expected utility to make a recommended decision.
e. Should the decision maker feel comfortable with the final decision recommended by the analysis?

10. A television network has been receiving low ratings for its programs. Currently, management is considering two alternatives for the Monday night 8:00 P.M.–9:00 P.M. time slot: a western with a well-known star or a musical variety with a relatively unknown husband-and-wife team. The percentages of viewing audience estimates depend on the degree of program acceptance. The relevant data are as follows:

Program Acceptance	Percentage of Viewing Audience	
	Western	Musical Variety
High	30%	40%
Moderate	25%	20%
Poor	20%	15%

The probabilities associated with program acceptance levels are as follows:

Program Acceptance	Probability	
	Western	Musical Variety
High	0.30	0.30
Moderate	0.60	0.40
Poor	0.10	0.30

a.   Using the expected value approach, which program should the network choose?
b.   For a utility analysis, what is the appropriate lottery?
c.   Based on the lottery in part (b), assume that the network's program manager has assigned the following indifference probabilities. Based on the use of utility measures, which program would you recommend? Is the manager a risk taker or a risk avoider?

Percentage of Audience	Indifference Probability (p)
30%	0.40
25%	0.30
20%	0.10

11.   Consider the following two-person, zero-sum game. Identify the pure strategy. What is the value of the game?

		Player B		
		b_1	b_2	b_3
Player A	a_1	8	5	7
	a_2	2	4	10

12.   Two television stations in a market compete with each other for viewing audience. Local programming options for the 5:00 P.M. weekday time slot include a sitcom rerun, an early news program, or a home improvement show. Assume that each station has the same three programming options and must make its preseason program selection before knowing what the other television station will do. The viewing audience changes in thousands of viewers for Station A are as follows:

		Station B		
		Sitcom b_1	News b_2	Home Improvement b_3
Station A	Sitcom, a_1	10	−5	3
	News, a_2	8	8	6
	Home Improvement, a_3	4	7	3

Determine the optimal programming strategy for each station. What is the value of the game?

13.   Two Indiana state senate candidates must decide which city to visit the day before the November election. The same four cities—Indianapolis, Evansville, Fort Wayne, and South Bend—are available for both candidates. These cities are listed as strategies 1 to 4 for each candidate. Travel plans must be made in advance, so the candidates must decide which city to visit prior to knowing the other candidate's plans. Values in the following table show thousands of voters for the Republican candidate based on the strategies selected by the two candidates. Which city should each candidate visit, and what is the value of the game?

	Democrat Candidate			
	Indianapolis b_1	Evansville b_2	Fort Wayne b_3	South Bend b_4
Indianapolis, a_1	0	-15	-8	20
Evansville, a_2	30	-5	5	-10
Fort Wayne, a_3	10	-25	0	20
South Bend, a_4	20	20	10	15

Republican Candidate (label for rows)

14. In Section 5.5, we showed the following two-person, zero-sum game had a mixed strategy:

	Player B		
	b_1	b_2	b_3
a_1	0	-1	2
a_2	5	4	-3
a_3	2	3	-4

Player A (label for rows)

a. Use dominance to reduce the game to a 2 × 2 game. Which strategies are dominated?
b. Determine the optimal mixed strategy solution.
c. What is the value of the game?

15. In a gambling game, Player A and Player B both have a $1 and a $5 bill. Each player selects one of the bills without the other player knowing the bill selected. Simultaneously they both reveal the bills selected. If the bills do not match, Player A wins Player B's bill. If the bills match, Player B wins Player A's bill.
a. Develop the game theory table for this game. The values should be expressed as the gains (or losses) for Player A.
b. Is there a pure strategy? Why or why not?
c. Determine the optimal strategies and the value of this game. Does the game favor one player over the other?
d. Suppose Player B decides to deviate from the optimal strategy and begins playing each bill 50% of the time. What should Player A do to improve Player A's winnings? Comment on why it is important to follow an optimal game theory strategy.

16. Two companies compete for a share of the soft drink market. Each worked with an advertising agency in order to develop alternative advertising strategies for the coming year. A variety of television advertisements, product promotions, in-store displays, and so on provides four different strategies for each company. The following table summarizes the projected change in market share for Company A once the two companies select their advertising strategy for the coming year. What is the optimal solution to this game for each of the players? What is the value of the game?

	Company B			
	b_1	b_2	b_3	b_4
a_1	3	0	2	4
a_2	2	-2	1	0
a_3	4	2	5	6
a_4	-2	6	-1	0

Company A (label for rows)

CHAPTER 6

Forecasting

CONTENTS

An essential aspect of managing any organization is planning for the future. Indeed, the long-run success of an organization depends on how well management is able to anticipate the future and develop appropriate strategies. Good judgment, intuition, and an awareness of the state of the economy may give a manager a rough idea or "feeling" of what is likely to happen in the future. However, converting this feeling into a number that can be used as next quarter's sales volume or next year's raw material cost per unit often is difficult. This chapter introduces several forecasting methods for that purpose.

Suppose that we have been asked to provide quarterly forecasts of the sales volume for a particular product during the coming year. Production schedules, raw material purchasing plans, inventory policies, and sales quotas will be affected by the quarterly forecasts that we provide. Consequently, poor forecasts may result in increased costs for the firm. How should we go about providing the quarterly sales volume forecasts?

We will certainly want to review the actual sales data for the product in previous periods. Using these historical data, we can identify the general level of sales and any trend such as an increase or decrease in sales volume over time. A further review of the data might reveal a seasonal pattern such as peak sales occurring in the third quarter of each year and sales volume bottoming out during the first quarter. By reviewing historical data, we can often develop a better understanding of the pattern of past sales, leading to better predictions of future sales for the product.

Most companies can forecast total demand for all products, as a group, with errors of less than 5%. However, forecasting demand for individual products may result in significantly higher errors.

The historical sales data form a time series. A **time series** is a set of observations of a variable measured at successive points in time or over successive periods of time. In this chapter we introduce several procedures for analyzing time series. The objective of such analyses is to provide good **forecasts** or predictions of future values of the time series.

Forecasting methods can be classified as quantitative or qualitative. Quantitative forecasting methods can be used when (1) past information about the variable being forecast is available, (2) the information can be quantified, and (3) a reasonable assumption is that the pattern of the past will continue into the future. In such cases, a forecast can be developed using a time series method or a causal method.

A forecast is simply a prediction of what will happen in the future. Managers must learn to accept the fact that, regardless of the technique used, they will not be able to develop perfect forecasts.

If the historical data are restricted to past values of the variable that we are trying to forecast, the forecasting procedure is called a **time series method**. The objective of time series methods is to discover a pattern in the historical data and then extrapolate this pattern into the future; the forecast is based solely on past values of the variable that we are trying to forecast and/or on past forecast errors. In this chapter we discuss three time series methods: smoothing (moving averages, weighted moving averages, and exponential smoothing), trend projection, and trend projection adjusted for seasonal influence.

Causal forecasting methods are based on the assumption that the variable we are trying to forecast exhibits a cause–effect relationship with one or more other variables. In this chapter we discuss the use of regression analysis as a causal forecasting method. For instance, the sales volume for many products is influenced by advertising expenditures, so regression analysis may be used to develop an equation showing how these two variables are related. Then, once the advertising budget has been set for the next period, we could substitute this value into the equation to develop a prediction or forecast of the sales volume for that period. Note that if a time series method had been used to develop the forecast, advertising expenditures would not even have been considered; that is, a time series method would have based the forecast solely on past sales.

Qualitative methods generally involve the use of expert judgment to develop forecasts. For instance, a panel of experts might develop a consensus forecast of the prime rate for a year from now. An advantage of qualitative procedures is that they can be applied when the information on the variable being forecast cannot be quantified and when historical data

FIGURE 6.1   AN OVERVIEW OF FORECASTING METHODS

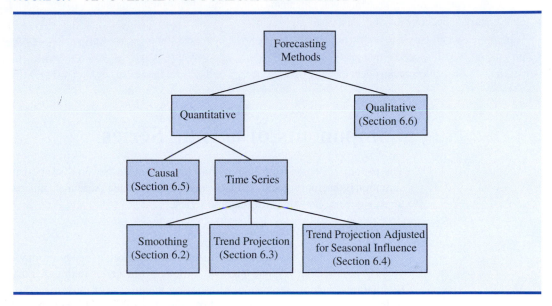

are either not applicable or not available. Figure 6.1 provides an overview of the types of forecasting methods.

Because all companies need to develop forecasts, forecasting is used in a wide variety of applications.

Q.M. *in* ACTION

WHATIFSPORTS.COM*

WhatIfSports.com, a subsidiary of FOXSports.com and News Corp, bills itself as the Internet's foremost authority on sports simulation. The site's technology allows anyone to "play" hypothetical games between historical professional baseball, basketball, football and hockey teams as well as college football and basketball. For example, one can simulate a game between the Cincinnati Reds and the Atlanta Braves in the 1974 season. The simulations are all based on the player and team's actual statistics from the 1974 season.

After being acquired by FOXSports.com, WhatIfSports.com faced a problem when it took over fantasy football content. Fantasy sports require the ability to project how current players will perform next season. Simulating games when a player's comprehensive stats are known is one thing, but the fantasy football content

called for future projections for every player in every game of the upcoming season. How does one account for rookies who have no previous professional experience as well as other players who develop or regress over time? To come up with the statistical inputs it needed for players with so many unknowns, WhatIfSports.com applied a quantitative forecasting model that factors collegiate performance, utilization throughout college, strength of collegiate competition, "measurables" (i.e. height, weight, 40-yard dash time, vertical leap, etc.), likely role, previous performance of a similar player in that role for the coaching staff, and previous performance of similar players with similar level of experience.

The forecasting approach aided the site with many other endeavors as well. A company previously devoted to the "What Ifs" in sports, through the use of forecasting models, can now also focus on the "what wills." So, when

*The authors are indebted to Paul Bessire, Quantitative Analyst and Content Manager, WhatIfSports.com for providing this Q.M. in Action.

(continued)

it wanted to expand into games that involve being in complete control of upcoming college basketball, college football, professional baseball, stockcar racing, or soccer programs, WhatIfSports.com already had a means to determine how players should develop over time. Hence, models for predicting the performance and development of every current athlete over time have allowed the site to complete comprehensive projections and assist many fantasy football players, sports enthusiasts, player personnel, and general fans alike.

6.1   Components of a Time Series

The pattern or behavior of the data in a time series has several components. The usual assumption is that four separate components—trend, cyclical, seasonal, and irregular—combine to provide specific values for the time series.

Trend Component

In time series analysis, the measurements may be taken every hour, day, week, month, or year, or at any other regular interval. Although time series data generally exhibit random fluctuations, the time series may still show gradual shifts or movements to relatively higher or lower values over a longer period of time. The gradual shifting of the time series is referred to as the **trend** in the time series. This shifting or trend is usually the result of long-term factors such as changes in the population, demographic characteristics of the population, technology, and consumer preferences.

For example, a manufacturer of photographic equipment may observe substantial month-to-month variability in the number of cameras sold. However, in reviewing sales over the past 10 to 15 years, this manufacturer may note a gradual increase in the annual sales volume. Suppose that the sales volume was approximately 1700 cameras per month in 1996, 2300 cameras per month in 2001, and 2500 cameras per month in 2006. Although actual month-to-month sales volumes may vary substantially, this gradual growth in sales shows an upward trend for the time series. Figure 6.2 shows a straight line that may be a

FIGURE 6.2   LINEAR TREND OF CAMERA SALES

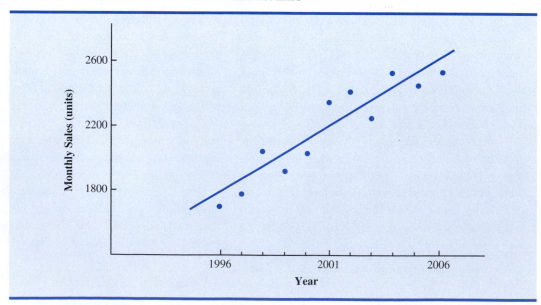

FIGURE 6.3 EXAMPLES OF SOME POSSIBLE TIME SERIES TREND PATTERNS

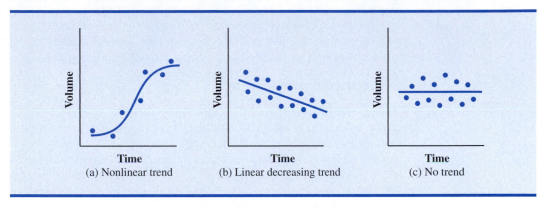

good approximation of the trend in camera sales. Although the trend for camera sales appears to be linear and increasing over time, sometimes the trend in a time series can be described better by some other pattern.

Figure 6.3 shows some other possible time series trend patterns. Part (a) shows a nonlinear trend; in this case, the time series shows little growth initially, then a period of rapid growth, and finally a leveling off. This trend pattern might be a good approximation of sales for a product from introduction through a growth period and into a period of market saturation. The linear decreasing trend in part (b) is useful for time series displaying a steady decline over time. The horizontal line in part (c) represents a time series that has no consistent increase or decrease over time and thus no trend.

Cyclical Component

Although a time series may exhibit a trend over long periods of time, all future values of the time series will not fall exactly on the trend line. In fact, time series often show alternating sequences of points below and above the trend line. Any recurring sequence of points above and below the trend line lasting more than one year can be attributed to the **cyclical component** of the time series. Figure 6.4 shows the graph of a time series with an obvious cyclical component. The observations are taken at intervals of one year.

FIGURE 6.4 TREND AND CYCLICAL COMPONENTS OF A TIME SERIES (DATA POINTS ARE ONE YEAR APART)

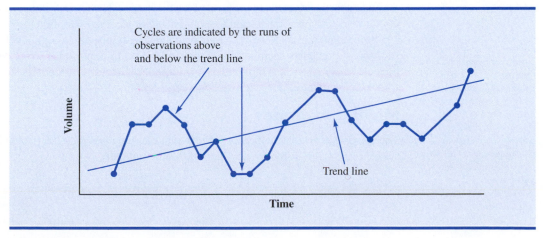

Many time series exhibit cyclical behavior with regular runs of observations below and above the trend line. Generally, this component of the time series results from multiyear cyclical movements in the economy. For example, periods of modest inflation followed by periods of rapid inflation can lead to many time series that alternate below and above a generally increasing trend line (e.g., a time series for housing costs).

Seasonal Component

Whereas the trend and cyclical components of a time series are identified by analyzing multiyear movements in historical data, many time series show a regular pattern over one-year periods. For example, a manufacturer of swimming pools expects low sales activity in the fall and winter months, with peak sales occurring in the spring and summer months. Manufacturers of snow removal equipment and heavy clothing, however, expect just the opposite yearly pattern. Not surprisingly, the component of the time series that represents the variability in the data due to seasonal influences is called the **seasonal component**. Although we generally think of seasonal movement in a time series as occurring within one year, the seasonal component also may be used to represent any regularly repeating pattern that is less than one year in duration. For example, daily traffic volume data show within-the-day "seasonal" behavior, with peak levels during rush hours, moderate flow during the rest of the day, and light flow from midnight to early morning.

Irregular Component

The **irregular component** of the time series is the residual or "catchall" factor that includes deviations of actual time series values from those expected given the effects of the trend, cyclical, and seasonal components. It accounts for the random variability in the time series. The irregular component is caused by the short-term, unanticipated, and nonrecurring factors that affect the time series. Because this component accounts for the random variability in the time series, it is unpredictable. We cannot attempt to predict its impact on the time series.

6.2 Smoothing Methods

In this section we discuss three forecasting methods: moving averages, weighted moving averages, and exponential smoothing. The objective of each of these methods is to "smooth out" the random fluctuations caused by the irregular component of the time series. Therefore, they are referred to as *smoothing methods*. Smoothing methods are appropriate for a stable time series—that is, one that exhibits no significant trend, cyclical, or seasonal effects—because they adapt well to changes in the level of the time series. However, without modification, they do not work as well when a significant trend and/or seasonal variation are present.

Smoothing methods are easy to use and generally provide a high level of accuracy for short-range forecasts such as a forecast for the next time period. One of the methods, exponential smoothing, has minimal data requirements and thus is a good method to use when forecasts are required for large numbers of items.

Many manufacturing environments require forecasts for thousands of items weekly or monthly. Thus, in choosing a forecasting technique, simplicity and ease of use are important criteria. The data requirements for the techniques in this section are minimal, and the techniques are easy to use and understand.

Moving Averages

The **moving averages** method uses the average of the *most recent n* data values in the time series as the forecast for the next period. Mathematically,

$$\text{Moving average} = \frac{\sum (\text{most recent } n \text{ data points})}{n} \tag{6.1}$$

TABLE 6.1 GASOLINE SALES TIMES SERIES

Week	Sales (1000s of gallons)
1	17
2	21
3	19
4	23
5	18
6	16
7	20
8	18
9	22
10	20
11	15
12	22

The term *moving* indicates that, as a new observation becomes available for the time series, it replaces the oldest observation in equation (6.1), and a new average is computed. As a result, the average will change, or move, as new observations become available.

To illustrate the moving averages method, consider the 12 weeks of data presented in Table 6.1 and Figure 6.5. These data show the number of gallons of gasoline sold by a gasoline distributor in Bennington, Vermont, over the past 12 weeks. Figure 6.5 indicates that, although random variability is present, the time series appears to be stable over time. Thus, the smoothing methods of this section are applicable.

FIGURE 6.5 GRAPH OF GASOLINE SALES TIME SERIES

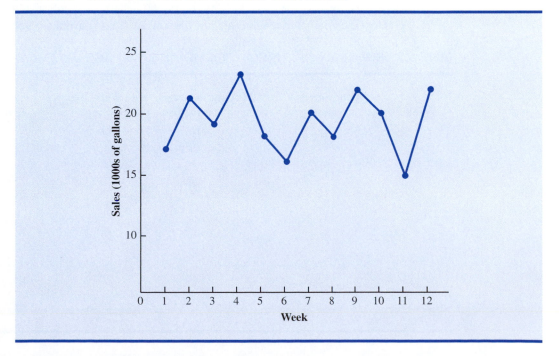

To use moving averages to forecast gasoline sales, we must first select the number of data values to be included in the moving average. For example, let us compute forecasts using a three-week moving average. The moving average calculation for the first three weeks of the gasoline sales time series is

$$\text{Moving average (weeks 1–3)} = \frac{17 + 21 + 19}{3} = 19$$

We then use this moving average value as the forecast for week 4. The actual value observed in week 4 is 23, so the forecast error in week 4 is $23 - 19 = 4$. In general, the error associated with a forecast is the difference between the observed value of the time series and the forecast.

The calculation for the second three-week moving average is

$$\text{Moving average (weeks 2–4)} = \frac{21 + 19 + 23}{3} = 21$$

Try Problem 1 for practice in using moving averages to compute a forecast.

Hence, the forecast for week 5 is 21, and the error associated with this forecast is $18 - 21 = -3$. Thus, the forecast error may be positive or negative, depending on whether the forecast is too low or too high. A complete summary of the three-week moving average calculations for the gasoline sales time series is shown in Table 6.2.

To forecast gasoline sales for week 13 using a three-week moving average, we need to compute the average of sales for weeks 10, 11, and 12. The calculation for this moving average is

$$\text{Moving average (weeks 10–12)} = \frac{20 + 15 + 22}{3} = 19$$

Hence, the forecast for week 13 is 19, or 19,000 gallons of gasoline. Figure 6.6 shows a graph of the original time series and the three-week moving average forecasts.

TABLE 6.2   SUMMARY OF THREE-WEEK MOVING AVERAGE CALCULATIONS

Week	Time Series Value	Moving Average Forecast	Forecast Error	Squared Forecast Error
1	17			
2	21			
3	19			
4	23	19	4	16
5	18	21	−3	9
6	16	20	−4	16
7	20	19	1	1
8	18	18	0	0
9	22	18	4	16
10	20	20	0	0
11	15	20	−5	25
12	22	19	3	9
		Totals	0	92

FIGURE 6.6   GRAPH OF GASOLINE SALES TIME SERIES AND THREE-WEEK MOVING
AVERAGE FORECASTS

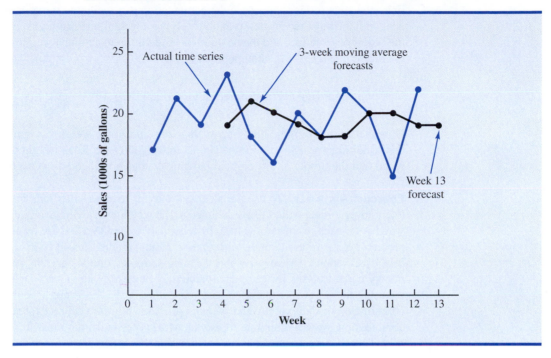

Forecast Accuracy.

An important consideration in selecting a forecasting method is the accuracy of the forecast. Clearly, we want forecast errors to be small. The last two columns of Table 6.2, which contain the forecast errors and the forecast errors squared, can be used to develop measures of forecast accuracy.

For the gasoline sales time series, we can use the last column of Table 6.2 to compute the average of the sum of the squared errors. Doing so, we obtain

$$\text{Average of the sum of squared errors} = \frac{92}{9} = 10.22$$

This average of the sum of squared errors is commonly referred to as the **mean squared error (MSE)**. The MSE is an often-used measure of the accuracy of a forecasting method and is the one we use in this chapter.

As we indicated previously, to use the moving averages method, we must first select the number of data values to be included in the moving average. Not surprisingly, for a particular time series, different lengths of moving averages will affect the accuracy of the forecast. One possible approach to choosing the number of values to be included is to use trial and error to identify the length that minimizes the MSE. Then, if we assume that the length that is best for the past will also be best for the future, we would forecast the next value in the time series using the number of data values that minimized the MSE for the historical time series.

*Problem 2 will test your
ability to use MSE as a
measure of forecast
accuracy.*

Weighted Moving Averages

In the moving averages method, each observation in the calculation receives the same weight. One variation, known as **weighted moving averages**, involves selecting different weights for each data value and then computing a weighted average of the most recent *n* data values as the forecast. In most cases, the most recent observation receives the most weight, and the weight decreases for older data values. For example, we can use the gasoline sales time series to illustrate the computation of a weighted three-week moving average, with the most recent observation receiving a weight three times as great as that given the oldest observation, and the next oldest observation receiving a weight twice as great as the oldest. For week 4 the computation is

$$\text{Weighted moving averages forecast for week 4} = \frac{3}{6}(19) + \frac{2}{6}(21) + \frac{1}{6}(17) = 19.33$$

Note that for the weighted moving average the sum of the weights is equal to 1. Actually, this condition was also true for the simple moving average: Each weight was $1/3$. However, recall that the simple or unweighted moving average provided a forecast of 19.

Forecast Accuracy. To use the weighted moving averages method, we must first select the number of data values to be included in the weighted moving average and then choose weights for each of the data values. In general, if we believe that the recent past is a better predictor of the future than the distant past, larger weights should be given to the more recent observations. However, when the time series is highly variable, selecting approximately equal weights for each data value may be best. Note that the only requirement in selecting the weights is that their sum must equal 1. To determine whether one particular combination of data values and weights provides a more accurate forecast than another combination, we will continue to use the MSE criterion as the measure of forecast accuracy. That is, if we assume that the combination that is best for the past will also be best for the future, we would use the combination of data values and weights that minimized MSE for the historical time series to forecast the next value in the time series.

Exponential Smoothing

Exponential smoothing uses a weighted average of past time series values as the forecast; it is a special case of the weighted moving averages method in which we select only one weight—the weight for the most recent observation. The weights for the other data values are automatically computed and get smaller and smaller as the observations move farther into the past. The basic exponential smoothing model is

$$F_{t+1} = \alpha Y_t + (1 - \alpha)F_t \tag{6.2}$$

Exponential smoothing is simple and has few data requirements. Thus, it is an inexpensive, useful approach for firms that make many forecasts each period.

where

$$F_{t+1} = \text{forecast of the time series for period } t + 1$$
$$Y_t = \text{actual value of the time series in period } t$$
$$F_t = \text{forecast of the time series for period } t$$
$$\alpha = \text{smoothing constant } (0 \le \alpha \le 1)$$

Equation (6.2) shows that the forecast for period $t + 1$ is a weighted average of the actual value in period t and the forecast for period t; note in particular that the weight given to the actual value in period t is α and that the weight given to the forecast in period t is $1 - \alpha$. We can demonstrate that the exponential smoothing forecast for any period also is a weighted average of *all the previous actual values* for the time series with a time series consisting of three periods of data: Y_1, Y_2, and Y_3. To start the calculations, we let F_1

equal the actual value of the time series in period 1; that is, $F_1 = Y_1$. Hence, the forecast for period 2 is

$$F_2 = \alpha Y_1 + (1 - \alpha)F_1$$
$$= \alpha Y_1 + (1 - \alpha)Y_1$$
$$= Y_1$$

Thus, the exponential smoothing forecast for period 2 is equal to the actual value of the time series in period 1.

The forecast for period 3 is

$$F_3 = \alpha Y_2 + (1 - \alpha)F_2 = \alpha Y_2 + (1 - \alpha)Y_1$$

Finally, substituting this expression for F_3 in the expression for F_4, we obtain

$$F_4 = \alpha Y_3 + (1 - \alpha)F_3$$
$$= \alpha Y_3 + (1 - \alpha)[\alpha Y_2 + (1 - \alpha)Y_1]$$
$$= \alpha Y_3 + \alpha(1 - \alpha)Y_2 + (1 - \alpha)^2 Y_1$$

Hence, F_4 is a weighted average of the first three time series values. The sum of the coefficients, or weights, for Y_1, Y_2, and Y_3 equals 1. A similar argument can be made to show that, in general, any forecast F_{t+1} is a weighted average of all the previous time series values.

Despite the fact that exponential smoothing provides a forecast that is a weighted average of all past observations, all the past data do not need to be saved in order to compute the forecast for the next period. In fact, once the **smoothing constant** α has been selected, only two pieces of information are required to compute the forecast. Equation (6.2) shows that with a given α we can compute the forecast for period $t + 1$ simply by knowing the actual and forecast time series values for period t—that is, Y_t and F_t.

To illustrate the exponential smoothing approach to forecasting, consider the gasoline sales time series presented previously in Table 6.1 and Figure 6.5. As indicated, the exponential smoothing forecast for period 2 is equal to the actual value of the time series in period 1. Thus, with $Y_1 = 17$, we set $F_2 = 17$ to get the exponential smoothing computations started. From the time series data in Table 6.1, we find an actual time series value in period 2 of $Y_2 = 21$. Thus, period 2 has a forecast error of $21 - 17 = 4$.

Continuing with the exponential smoothing computations, using a smoothing constant of $\alpha = 0.2$, provides the forecast for period 3:

$$F_3 = 0.2Y_2 + 0.8F_2 = 0.2(21) + 0.8(17) = 17.8$$

Once the actual time series value in period 3, $Y_3 = 19$, is known, we can generate a forecast for period 4:

$$F_4 = 0.2Y_3 + 0.8F_3 = 0.2(19) + 0.8(17.8) = 18.04$$

By continuing the exponential smoothing calculations, we can determine the weekly forecast values and the corresponding weekly forecast errors, as shown in Table 6.3. Note that we have not shown an exponential smoothing forecast or the forecast error for period 1 because no forecast was made. For week 12, we have $Y_{12} = 22$ and $F_{12} = 18.48$. Can we

TABLE 6.3   SUMMARY OF THE EXPONENTIAL SMOOTHING FORECASTS AND
FORECAST ERRORS FOR GASOLINE SALES WITH SMOOTHING
CONSTANT $\alpha = 0.2$

Week (t)	Time Series Value (Y_t)	Exponential Smoothing Forecast (F_t)	Forecast Error ($Y_t - F_t$)
1	17		
2	21	17.00	4.00
3	19	17.80	1.20
4	23	18.04	4.96
5	18	19.03	−1.03
6	16	18.83	−2.83
7	20	18.26	1.74
8	18	18.61	−0.61
9	22	18.49	3.51
10	20	19.19	0.81
11	15	19.35	−4.35
12	22	18.48	3.52

use this information to generate a forecast for week 13 before the actual value of week 13 becomes known? Using the exponential smoothing model, we have

$$F_{13} = 0.2Y_{12} + 0.8F_{12} = 0.2(22) + 0.8(18.48) = 19.18$$

Thus, the exponential smoothing forecast of the amount sold in week 13 is 19.18, or 19,180 gallons of gasoline. With this forecast, the firm can make plans and decisions accordingly. The accuracy of the forecast will not be known until the end of week 13.

Can you now use exponential smoothing to develop forecasts? Try Problem 4.

Figure 6.7 shows the plot of the actual and the forecast values from Table 6.3. Note in particular how the forecasts "smooth out" the irregular fluctuations in the time series.

Forecast Accuracy. In the preceding exponential smoothing calculations, we used a smoothing constant of $\alpha = 0.2$. Although any value of α between 0 and 1 is acceptable, some values will yield better forecasts than others. Insight into choosing a good value for α can be obtained by rewriting the basic exponential smoothing model as follows:

$$F_{t+1} = \alpha Y_t + (1 - \alpha)F_t$$
$$= \alpha Y_t + F_t - \alpha F_t$$
$$= F_t + \alpha(Y_t - F_t) \qquad (6.3)$$

Forecast in period t Forecast error in period t

Thus, the new forecast F_{t+1} is equal to the previous forecast F_t plus an adjustment, which is α times the most recent forecast error, $Y_t - F_t$. That is, the forecast in period $t + 1$ is obtained by adjusting the forecast in period t by a fraction of the forecast error. If the time series contains substantial random variability, a small value of the smoothing constant is preferred. The reason for this choice is that, because much of the forecast error is due to random variability, we do not want to overreact and adjust the forecasts too quickly. For a time series with relatively little random variability, larger values of the smoothing constant have the advantage of quickly adjusting the forecasts when forecasting errors occur and therefore allowing the forecast to react faster to changing conditions.

FIGURE 6.7   GRAPH OF ACTUAL AND FORECAST GASOLINE SALES TIME SERIES WITH SMOOTHING CONSTANT $\alpha = 0.2$

Problem 5 asks you to determine whether moving averages or exponential smoothing provides the best forecasts for a given set of data.

The criterion we use to determine a desirable value for the smoothing constant α is the same as the criterion we proposed earlier for determining the number of periods of data to include in the moving averages calculation. That is, we choose the value of α that minimizes the mean squared error. A summary of the MSE calculations for the exponential smoothing forecast of gasoline sales with $\alpha = 0.2$ is shown in Table 6.4. Note that there is one less squared error term than the number of periods of data because we had no past values with

TABLE 6.4   MEAN SQUARED ERROR COMPUTATIONS FOR FORECASTING GASOLINE SALES WITH $\alpha = 0.2$

Week (t)	Time Series Value (Y_t)	Forecast (F_t)	Forecast Error ($Y_t - F_t$)	Squared Forecast Error ($Y_t - F_t)^2$
1	17			
2	21	17.00	4.00	16.00
3	19	17.80	1.20	1.44
4	23	18.04	4.96	24.60
5	18	19.03	−1.03	1.06
6	16	18.83	−2.83	8.01
7	20	18.26	1.74	3.03
8	18	18.61	−0.61	0.37
9	22	18.49	3.51	12.32
10	20	19.19	0.81	0.66
11	15	19.35	−4.35	18.92
12	22	18.48	3.52	12.39
			Total	98.80

$$\text{MSE} = 98.80/11 = 8.98$$

TABLE 6.5   MEAN SQUARED ERROR COMPUTATIONS FOR FORECASTING GASOLINE
SALES WITH $\alpha = 0.3$

Week (t)	Time Series Value (Y_t)	Forecast (F_t)	Forecast Error ($Y_t - F_t$)	Squared Forecast Error ($Y_t - F_t)^2$
1	17			
2	21	17.00	4.00	16.00
3	19	18.20	0.80	0.64
4	23	18.44	4.56	20.79
5	18	19.81	−1.81	3.28
6	16	19.27	−3.27	10.69
7	20	18.29	1.71	2.92
8	18	18.80	−0.80	0.64
9	22	18.56	3.44	11.83
10	20	19.59	0.41	0.17
11	15	19.71	−4.71	22.18
12	22	18.30	3.70	13.69
			Total	102.83

$$\text{MSE} = 102.83/11 = 9.35$$

which to make a forecast for period 1. Would a different value of α have provided better results in terms of a lower MSE value? Perhaps the most straightforward way to answer this question is simply to try another value for α. We then compare its mean squared error with the MSE value of 8.98, obtained using a smoothing constant of $\alpha = 0.2$.

The exponential smoothing results with $\alpha = 0.3$ are shown in Table 6.5. With MSE = 9.35, a smoothing constant of $\alpha = 0.3$ results in less forecast accuracy than a smoothing constant of $\alpha = 0.2$. Thus, we would be inclined to use the original smoothing constant of 0.2. Using a trial-and-error calculation with other values of α, we can find a "good" value for the smoothing constant. This value can be used in the exponential smoothing model to provide forecasts for the future. At a later date, after new time series observations have been obtained, we analyze the newly collected time series data to determine whether the smoothing constant should be revised to provide better forecasting results.

NOTES AND COMMENTS

1. Another commonly used measure of forecast accuracy is the mean absolute deviation (MAD). This measure is simply the average of the absolute values of all the forecast errors. Using the errors given in Table 6.2, we obtain

$$\text{MAD} = \frac{4 + 3 + 4 + 1 + 0 + 4 + 0 + 5 + 3}{9}$$

$$= 2.67$$

One major difference between the MSE and the MAD is that the MSE measure is influenced much more by large forecast errors than by small errors (for the MSE measure the errors are squared). The selection of the best measure of forecasting accuracy is not a simple matter. Indeed, forecasting experts often disagree as to which measure should be used. We use the MSE measure in this chapter.

2. Spreadsheet packages are an effective aid in choosing a good value of α for exponential smoothing and selecting weights for the weighted moving averages method. With the time series data and the forecasting formulas in a spreadsheet, you can experiment with different values of α (or moving average weights) and choose the value(s) providing the smallest MSE or MAD. In Appendix 6.1 we show how this process can be done.

6.3 Trend Projection

In this section we show how to forecast the values of a time series that exhibits a long-term linear trend. The type of time series for which the trend projection method is applicable shows a consistent increase or decrease over time. Because this type of time series is not stable, the smoothing methods described in the preceding section are not applicable.

Consider the time series for bicycle sales of a particular manufacturer over the past 10 years, as shown in Table 6.6 and Figure 6.8. Note that 21,600 bicycles were sold in year 1; 22,900 were sold in year 2; and so on. In year 10, the most recent year, 31,400 bicycles were

TABLE 6.6   BICYCLE SALES TIME SERIES

Year (t)	Sales (1000s) (Y_t)
1	21.6
2	22.9
3	25.5
4	21.9
5	23.9
6	27.5
7	31.5
8	29.7
9	28.6
10	31.4

FIGURE 6.8   GRAPH OF BICYCLE SALES TIME SERIES

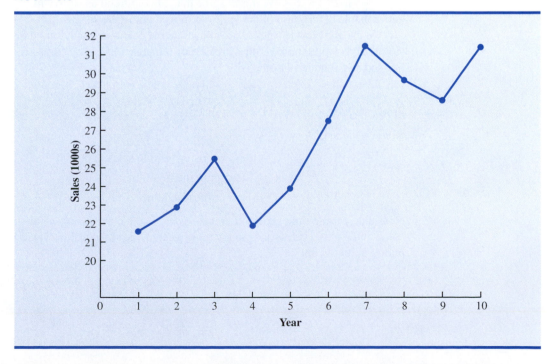

FIGURE 6.9   TREND REPRESENTED BY A LINEAR FUNCTION FOR BICYCLE SALES

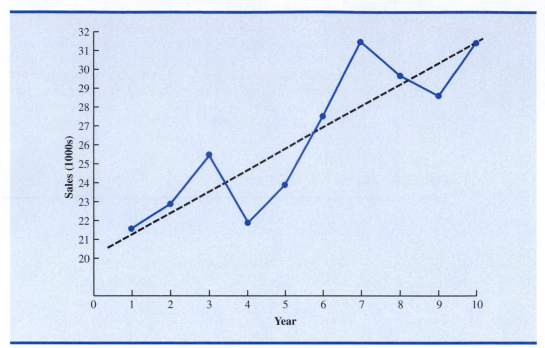

sold. Although Figure 6.8 shows some up-and-down movement over the past 10 years, the time series for the number of bicycles sold seems to have an overall increasing or upward trend.

We do not want the trend component of a time series to follow each and every "up" and "down" movement. Rather, the trend component should reflect the gradual shifting—in this case, growth—of the time series values. After we view the time series data in Table 6.6 and the graph in Figure 6.8, we might agree that a linear trend as shown in Figure 6.9 provides a reasonable description of the long-run movement in the series.

We use the bicycle sales data to illustrate the calculations involved in applying regression analysis to identify a linear trend. For a linear trend, the estimated sales volume expressed as a function of time is

$$T_t = b_0 + b_1 t \qquad (6.4)$$

where

$$T_t = \text{trend value for bicycle sales in period } t$$
$$b_0 = \text{intercept of the trend line}$$
$$b_1 = \text{slope of the trend line}$$

Note that, for the time series on bicycle sales, $t = 1$ corresponds to the oldest time series value and $t = 10$ corresponds to the most recent time series value. The equations for computing b_1 and b_0 are

$$b_1 = \frac{\sum t Y_t - (\sum t \sum Y_t)/n}{\sum t^2 - (\sum t)^2/n} \qquad (6.5)$$

$$b_0 = \overline{Y} - b_1 \overline{t} \qquad (6.6)$$

where

Y_t = actual value of the time series in period t

n = number of period

$\overline{Y}$ = average value of the time series; that is, $\overline{Y} = \sum Y_t / n$

$\overline{t}$ = average value of t; that is, $\overline{t} = \sum t / n$

t	Y_t	tY_t	t^2
1	21.6	21.6	1
2	22.9	45.8	4
3	25.5	76.5	9
4	21.9	87.6	16
5	23.9	119.5	25
6	27.5	165.0	36
7	31.5	220.5	49
8	29.7	237.6	64
9	28.6	257.4	81
10	31.4	314.0	100
Totals 55	264.5	1545.5	385

Using these relationships for b_0 and b_1 and the bicycle sales data of Table 6.6, we obtain the following calculations:

$$\overline{t} = \frac{55}{10} = 5.5$$

$$\overline{Y} = \frac{264.5}{10} = 26.45$$

$$b_1 = \frac{1545.5 - (55)(264.5)/10}{385 - (55)^2/10} = 1.10$$

$$b_0 = 26.45 - 1.10(5.5) = 20.4$$

Therefore,

$$T_t = 20.4 + 1.1t \tag{6.7}$$

is the equation for the linear trend component for the bicycle sales time series.

Try Problem 14 for practice in developing the equation for the linear trend component of a time series.

The slope of 1.1 in the trend equation indicates that over the past 10 years the firm has experienced an average growth in sales of about 1100 units per year. If we assume that the past 10-year trend in sales is a good indicator for the future, we can use equation (6.7) to project the trend component of the time series. For example, substituting $t = 11$ into equation (6.7) yields next year's trend projection, T_{11}:

$$T_{11} = 20.4 + 1.1(11) = 32.5$$

Thus, the trend component yields a sales forecast of 32,500 bicycles for next year.

FIGURE 6.10   SOME POSSIBLE FORMS OF NONLINEAR TREND PATTERNS

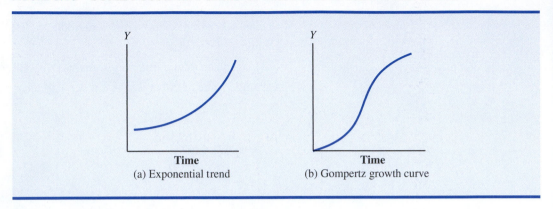

We can also use the trend line to forecast sales farther into the future. For instance, using equation (6.7), we develop forecasts for an additional two and three years into the future as follows:

$$T_{12} = 20.4 + 1.1(12) = 33.6$$
$$T_{13} = 20.4 + 1.1(13) = 34.7$$

The use of a linear function to model the trend is common. However, as we discussed earlier, sometimes time series exhibit a curvilinear (nonlinear) trend similar to those shown in Figure 6.10. More advanced texts discuss how to develop models for these more complex relationships.

6.4   Trend and Seasonal Components

We showed how to forecast the values of a time series that has a trend component. In this section we extend the discussion by showing how to forecast the values of a time series that has both trend and seasonal components.

Many situations in business and economics involve period-to-period comparisons. For instance, we might be interested to learn that unemployment is up 2% compared to last month, steel production is up 5% over last month, or that the production of electric power is down 3% from the previous month. Care must be exercised in using such information, however, because whenever a seasonal influence is present, such comparisons usually are not especially meaningful. For instance, the fact that electric power consumption is down by 3% from August to September might be only the seasonal effect associated with a decrease in the use of air conditioning and not because of a long-term decline in the use of electric power. Indeed, after adjusting for the seasonal effect, we might even find that the use of electric power has increased.

Removing the seasonal effect from a time series is known as *deseasonalizing the time series.* After we do so, period-to-period comparisons are more meaningful and can help identify whether a trend exists. The approach we take in this section is appropriate in situations when only seasonal effects are present or in situations when both seasonal and trend components are present. The first step is to compute seasonal indexes and use them to deseasonalize the data. Then, if a trend is apparent in the deseasonalized data, we use regression analysis on the deseasonalized data to estimate the trend.

Multiplicative Model

In addition to a trend component T and a seasonal component S, we assume that the time series also has an irregular component I. The irregular component accounts for the random effects in the time series that cannot be explained by the trend and seasonal components. Using T_t, S_t, and I_t to identify the trend, seasonal, and irregular components at time t, we assume that the actual time series value, denoted by Y_t, can be described by the **multiplicative time series model**.

$$Y_t = T_t \times S_t \times I_t \qquad (6.8)$$

In this model, T_t is the trend measured in units of the item being forecast. However, the S_t and I_t components are measured in relative terms, with values above 1.00 indicating effects above the trend, and values below 1.00 indicating effects below the trend.

We illustrate the use of the multiplicative model with trend, seasonal, and irregular components by working with the quarterly data presented in Table 6.7 and Figure 6.11. These data show television set sales (in thousands of units) for a particular manufacturer over the past four years. We begin by showing how to identify the seasonal component of the time series.

Calculating the Seasonal Indexes

Figure 6.11 indicates that sales are lowest in the second quarter of each year, followed by higher sales levels in quarters 3 and 4. Thus, we conclude that a seasonal pattern exists for television set sales. We begin the computational procedure used to identify each quarter's seasonal influence by computing a moving average to isolate the combined seasonal and irregular components, S_t and I_t.

To do so, we use one year of data in each calculation. Because we are working with a quarterly series, we use four data values in each moving average. The moving average calculation for the first four quarters of the television set sales data is

$$\text{First moving average} = \frac{4.8 + 4.1 + 6.0 + 6.5}{4} = \frac{21.4}{4} = 5.35$$

TABLE 6.7   QUARTERLY DATA FOR TELEVISION SET SALES

Year	Quarter	Sales (1000s)
1	1	4.8
	2	4.1
	3	6.0
	4	6.5
2	1	5.8
	2	5.2
	3	6.8
	4	7.4
3	1	6.0
	2	5.6
	3	7.5
	4	7.8
4	1	6.3
	2	5.9
	3	8.0
	4	8.4

FIGURE 6.11   GRAPH OF QUARTERLY TELEVISION SET SALES TIME SERIES

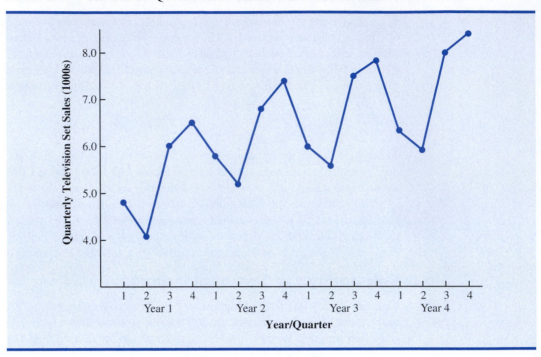

Note that the moving average calculation for the first four quarters yields the average quarterly sales over year 1 of the time series. Continuing the moving average calculation, we next add the 5.8 value for the first quarter of year 2 and drop the 4.8 for the first quarter of year 1. Thus, the second moving average is

$$\text{Second moving average} = \frac{4.1 + 6.0 + 6.5 + 5.8}{4} = \frac{22.4}{4} = 5.6$$

Similarly, the third moving average calculation is $(6.0 + 6.5 + 5.8 + 5.2)/4 = 5.875$.

Before we proceed with the moving average calculations for the entire time series, we return to the first moving average calculation, which resulted in a value of 5.35. The 5.35 value represents an average quarterly sales volume (across all seasons) for year 1. As we look back at the calculation of the 5.35 value, associating 5.35 with the "middle" quarter of the moving average group makes sense. Note, however, that we encounter some difficulty in identifying the middle quarter; four quarters in the moving average allow for no middle quarter. The 5.35 value corresponds to the last half of quarter 2 and the first half of quarter 3. Similarly, if we go to the next moving average value of 5.60, the middle corresponds to the last half of quarter 3 and the first half of quarter 4.

Recall that the reason for computing moving averages is to isolate the combined seasonal and irregular components. However, the moving average values we computed do not correspond directly to the original quarters of the time series. We can resolve this difficulty by using the midpoints between successive moving average values. For example, because 5.35 corresponds to the first half of quarter 3 and 5.60 corresponds to the last half of quarter 3, we can use $(5.35 + 5.60)/2 = 5.475$ as the moving average value for quarter 3. Similarly, we associate a moving average value of $(5.60 + 5.875)/2 = 5.738$ with quarter 4. The result is a *centered moving average.* Table 6.8 shows a complete summary of the moving average and centered moving average calculations for the television set sales data.

TABLE 6.8   CENTERED MOVING AVERAGE CALCULATIONS FOR THE TELEVISION
SET SALES TIME SERIES

Year	Quarter	Sales (1000s)	Four-Quarter Moving Average	Centered Moving Average
1	1	4.8		
	2	4.1		
			5.350	
	3	6.0		5.475
			5.600	
	4	6.5		5.738
			5.875	
2	1	5.8		5.975
			6.075	
	2	5.2		6.188
			6.300	
	3	6.8		6.325
			6.350	
	4	7.4		6.400
			6.450	
3	1	6.0		6.538
			6.625	
	2	5.6		6.675
			6.725	
	3	7.5		6.763
			6.800	
	4	7.8		6.838
			6.875	
4	1	6.3		6.938
			7.000	
	2	5.9		7.075
			7.150	
	3	8.0		
	4	8.4		

If the number of data points in a moving average calculation is an odd number, the middle point will correspond to one of the periods in the time series. In such cases, we would not have to center the moving average values to correspond to a particular time period, as we did in the calculations in Table 6.8.

What do the centered moving averages in Table 6.8 tell us about this time series? Figure 6.12 shows plots of the actual time series values and the corresponding centered moving average. Note particularly how the centered moving average values tend to "smooth out" both the seasonal and irregular fluctuations in the time series. The moving average values computed for four quarters of data do not include the fluctuations due to seasonal influences because the seasonal effect has been averaged out. Each point in the centered moving average represents what the value of the time series would be without seasonal or irregular influences.

By dividing each time series observation by the corresponding centered moving average value, we can identify the seasonal-irregular effect in the time series. For example, the third quarter of year 1 shows $6.0/5.475 = 1.096$ as the combined seasonal-irregular component. Table 6.9 summarizes the resulting seasonal-irregular values for the entire time series.

Consider the third quarter. The results from years 1, 2, and 3 show third-quarter values of 1.096, 1.075, and 1.109, respectively. Thus, in all cases the seasonal-irregular component appears to have an above average influence in the third quarter. The fluctuations over the three years can be attributed to the irregular component, so we can average the computed values to eliminate the irregular influence and obtain an estimate of the third-quarter seasonal influence:

$$\text{Seasonal effect of third quarter} = \frac{1.096 + 1.075 + 1.109}{3} = 1.09$$

FIGURE 6.12   GRAPH OF QUARTERLY TELEVISION SET SALES TIME SERIES AND
CENTERED MOVING AVERAGE

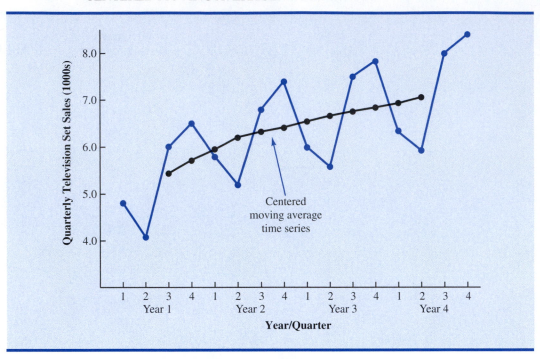

TABLE 6.9   SEASONAL-IRREGULAR VALUES FOR THE TELEVISION SET SALES
TIME SERIES

Year	Quarter	Sales (1000s)	Centered Moving Average	Seasonal-Irregular Value
1	1	4.8		
	2	4.1		
	3	6.0	5.475	1.096
	4	6.5	5.738	1.133
2	1	5.8	5.975	0.971
	2	5.2	6.188	0.840
	3	6.8	6.325	1.075
	4	7.4	6.400	1.156
3	1	6.0	6.538	0.918
	2	5.6	6.675	0.839
	3	7.5	6.763	1.109
	4	7.8	6.838	1.141
4	1	6.3	6.938	0.908
	2	5.9	7.075	0.834
	3	8.0		
	4	8.4		

TABLE 6.10   SEASONAL INDEX CALCULATIONS FOR THE TELEVISION SET SALES TIME SERIES

Quarter	Seasonal-Irregular Component Values $(S_t I_t)$	Seasonal Index (S_t)
1	0.971, 0.918, 0.908	0.93
2	0.840, 0.839, 0.834	0.84
3	1.096, 1.075, 1.109	1.09
4	1.133, 1.156, 1.141	1.14

We refer to 1.09 as the **seasonal index** for the third quarter. In Table 6.10 we summarize the calculations involved in computing the seasonal indexes for the television set sales time series. Thus, the seasonal indexes for all four quarters are: quarter 1, 0.93; quarter 2, 0.84; quarter 3, 1.09; and quarter 4, 1.14.

Interpretation of the values in Table 6.10 provides some observations about the "seasonal" component in television set sales. The best sales quarter is the fourth quarter, with sales averaging 14% above the average quarterly value. The worst, or slowest, sales quarter is the second quarter, with its seasonal index at 0.84, showing the sales average 16% below the average quarterly sales. The seasonal component corresponds to the intuitive expectation that television viewing interest and thus television purchase patterns tend to peak in the fourth quarter, with its coming winter season and fewer outdoor activities. The low second-quarter sales reflect the reduced television interest resulting from the spring and presummer activities of the potential customers.

Can you now compute and interpret seasonal indexes for a time series? Try Problem 25.

One final adjustment may be necessary in obtaining the seasonal indexes. The multiplicative model requires that the average seasonal index equal 1.00, so the sum of the four seasonal indexes in Table 6.10 must equal 4.00. In other words, the seasonal effects must even out over the year. The average of the seasonal indexes in our example is equal to 1.00, and hence this type of adjustment is not necessary. In other cases, a slight adjustment may be necessary. To make the adjustment, multiply each seasonal index by the number of seasons divided by the sum of the unadjusted seasonal indexes. For instance, for quarterly data, multiply each seasonal index by 4/(sum of the unadjusted seasonal indexes). Some of the problems at the end of the chapter require this adjustment.

Deseasonalizing the Time Series

With deseasonalized data, comparing sales in successive periods makes sense. With data that have not been deseasonalized, relevant comparisons can often be made between sales in the current period and sales in the same period one year ago.

The purpose of finding seasonal indexes is to remove the seasonal effects from a time series. This process is referred to as *deseasonalizing* the time series. Economic time series adjusted for seasonal variations (**deseasonalized time series**) are reported in the *Survey of Current Business, The Wall Street Journal,* and *BusinessWeek.* Using the notation of the multiplicative model, we have

$$Y_t = T_t \times S_t \times I_t$$

By dividing each time series observation by the corresponding seasonal index, we remove the effect of season from the time series. The deseasonalized time series for television set sales is summarized in Table 6.11. A graph of the deseasonalized television set sales time series is shown in Figure 6.13.

TABLE 6.11   DESEASONALIZED VALUES FOR THE TELEVISION SET SALES TIMES SERIES

Year	Quarter	Sales (1000s) (Y_t)	Seasonal Index (S_t)	Deseasonalized Sales $(Y_t/S_t = T_t I_t)$
1	1	4.8	0.93	5.16
	2	4.1	0.84	4.88
	3	6.0	1.09	5.50
	4	6.5	1.14	5.70
2	1	5.8	0.93	6.24
	2	5.2	0.84	6.19
	3	6.8	1.09	6.24
	4	7.4	1.14	6.49
3	1	6.0	0.93	6.45
	2	5.6	0.84	6.67
	3	7.5	1.09	6.88
	4	7.8	1.14	6.84
4	1	6.3	0.93	6.77
	2	5.9	0.84	7.02
	3	8.0	1.09	7.34
	4	8.4	1.14	7.37

FIGURE 6.13   DESEASONALIZED TELEVISION SET SALES TIME SERIES

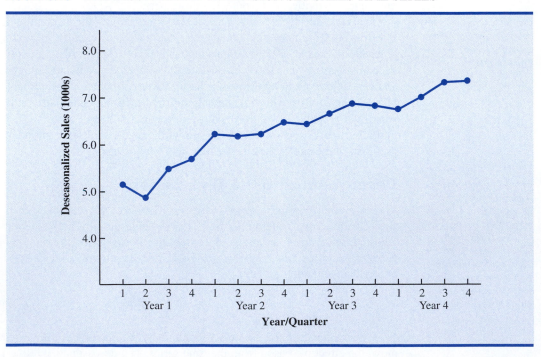

Using Deseasonalized Time Series to Identify Trend

Although the graph in Figure 6.13 shows some up-and-down movement over the past 16 quarters, the time series seems to have an upward linear trend. To identify this trend, we use the same procedure as in the preceding section; in this case, the data used are quarterly deseasonalized sales values. Thus, for a linear trend, the estimated sales volume expressed as a function of time is

$$T_t = b_0 + b_1 t$$

where

T_t = trend value for television set sales in period t

b_0 = intercept of the trend line

b_1 = slope of the trend time

As before, $t = 1$ corresponds to the time of the first observation for the time series, $t = 2$ corresponds to the time of the second observation, and so on. Thus, for the deseasonalized television set sales time series, $t = 1$ corresponds to the first deseasonalized quarterly sales value and $t = 16$ corresponds to the most recent deseasonalized quarterly sales value. The equations for computing the values of b_0 and b_1 are

$$b_1 = \frac{\sum t Y_t - (\sum t \sum Y_t)/n}{\sum t^2 - (\sum t)^2/n} \quad \text{and} \quad b_0 = \bar{Y} - b_1 \bar{t}$$

Note, however, that Y_t now refers to the deseasonalized time series value at time t and not to the actual value of the time series. Using the given relationships for b_0 and b_1 and the deseasonalized sales data of Table 6.11, we make the following calculations:

t	Y_t (deseasonalized)	tY_t	t^2
1	5.16	5.16	1
2	4.88	9.76	4
3	5.50	16.50	9
4	5.70	22.80	16
5	6.24	31.20	25
6	6.19	37.14	36
7	6.24	43.68	49
8	6.49	51.92	64
9	6.45	58.05	81
10	6.67	66.70	100
11	6.88	75.68	121
12	6.84	82.08	144
13	6.77	88.01	169
14	7.02	98.28	196
15	7.34	110.10	225
16	7.37	117.92	256
Totals 136	101.74	914.98	1496

$$\bar{t} = \frac{136}{16} = 8.5$$

$$\bar{Y} = \frac{101.74}{16} = 6.359$$

$$b_1 = \frac{914.98 - (136)(101.74)/16}{1496 - (136)^2/16} = 0.148$$

$$b_0 = 6.359 - 0.148(8.5) = 5.101$$

Therefore,

$$T_t = 5.101 + 0.148t$$

is the equation for the linear trend component of the time series.

The slope of 0.148 indicates that over the past 16 quarters the firm has experienced an average deseasonalized growth in sales of about 148 sets per quarter. If we assume that the past 16-quarter trend in sales data is a reasonably good indicator of the future, we can use this equation to project the trend component of the time series for future quarters. For example, substituting $t = 17$ into the equation yields next quarter's trend projection, T_{17}:

$$T_{17} = 5.101 + 0.148(17) = 7.617$$

Thus, the trend component yields a sales forecast of 7617 television sets for the next quarter. Similarly, the trend component produces sales forecasts of 7765, 7913, and 8061 television sets in quarters 18, 19, and 20, respectively.

Seasonal Adjustments

The final step in developing the forecast when both trend and seasonal components are present is to use the seasonal index to adjust the trend projection. Returning to the television set sales example, we have a trend projection for the next four quarters. Now we must adjust the forecast for the seasonal effect. The seasonal index for the first quarter of year 5 ($t = 17$) is 0.93, so we obtain the quarterly forecast by multiplying the forecast based on trend ($T_{17} = 7617$) times the seasonal index (0.93). Thus, the forecast for the next quarter is 7617(0.93) = 7084. Table 6.12 shows the quarterly forecast for quarters 17–20. The forecasts show the high-volume fourth quarter with a 9190-unit forecast and the low-volume second quarter with a 6523-unit forecast.

Applications that involve seasonal effects are commonplace. When dealing with data that have seasonal effects, firms must estimate the seasonal effects in order to obtain

TABLE 6.12   QUARTERLY FORECASTS FOR THE TELEVISION SET SALES TIME SERIES

Year	Quarter	Trend Forecast	Seasonal Index (see Table 16.10)	Quarterly Forecast
5	1	7617	0.93	(7617)(0.93) = 7084
	2	7765	0.84	(7765)(0.84) = 6523
	3	7913	1.09	(7913)(1.09) = 8625
	4	8061	1.14	(8061)(1.14) = 9190

accurate forecasts. The Q.M. in Action, Measuring and Reporting Radioactive Exposure, describes how one of the world's largest providers of dosimetry services was able to forecast demand for badges that measure radioactive exposure by using seasonal decomposition to capture the seasonality effect.

Q.M. *in* ACTION

MEASURING AND REPORTING RADIOACTIVE EXPOSURE*

U.S. federal law requires X-ray laboratories and nuclear plants to measure and report radioactive exposure for employees. Many organizations satisfy federal requirements by outsourcing the monitoring and reporting to firms that use thermoluminescent badges that record radioactive exposure for specified recording cycles of one month, three months, or six months.

The recording cycle for one of the world's largest providers of radiation dosimetry services begins with the shipment of customized badges to customers. When the customer receives the replenishment badges, the old badges are collected and returned to the firm, which then measures the amount of radioactive exposure recorded on each badge. The variability in the time it takes customers to return badges, the fluctuating demand for badges from cycle to cycle, and the possible mishandling and wear of

badges often affect the number of reusable badges for subsequent cycles. As a result it is difficult for the company to match the demand for customized badges with the supply of reusable badges. The company purchases new badges in order to supplement any shortfall of reusable badges.

One of the key factors in determining an effective new-badge purchasing system is the ability to forecast customer demand at the beginning of each recording cycle. Customers were classified into three groups based upon the length of their recording cycle: one, three, or six months. Historical data were used to create demand forecasts for each customer group using seasonal decomposition to capture the seasonality effect. The sum of the three customer group forecasts provided a forecast of total demand. Actual demand data for an 18-month period were used to estimate the seasonality effect. Tests with the forecasting model showed that it was able to capture the underlying seasonal factors and provide forecasts that were within 5% to 7% of the actual demand for the badges.

*Based on M. Bayiz and C. Tang, "An Integrated Planning System for Managing the Refurbishment of Thermoluminescent Badges," *Interfaces* (September/October 2004): 383–393.

Models Based on Monthly Data

In the preceding television set sales example we used quarterly data to illustrate the computation of seasonal indexes. However, many businesses use monthly rather than quarterly forecasts. In such cases, the procedures introduced in this section can be applied with minor modifications. First, a 12-month moving average replaces the four-quarter moving average; second, 12 monthly seasonal indexes, rather than the four quarterly indexes, must be computed. Other than these changes, the computational and forecasting procedures are identical.

Cyclical Component

Mathematically, the multiplicative model of equation (6.8) can be expanded to include a cyclical component as follows:

$$Y_t = T_t \times C_t \times S_t \times I_t \tag{6.9}$$

The cyclical component is attributable to multiyear cycles in the time series. It is analogous to the seasonal component, but over a longer period of time. However, because of the length of time involved, obtaining enough relevant data to estimate the cyclical component often is difficult. Another difficulty is that the length of cycles usually varies. We leave further discussion of the cyclical component to texts on forecasting methods.

 ## 6.5 Regression Analysis

Regression analysis is a statistical technique that can be used to develop a mathematical equation showing how variables are related. In regression terminology, the variable that is being predicted is called the *dependent* or *response* variable. The variable or variables being used to predict the value of the dependent variable are called the *independent* or *predictor* variables. Regression analysis involving one independent variable and one dependent variable for which the relationship between the variables is approximated by a straight line is called *simple linear regression.* Regression analysis involving two or more independent variables is called *multiple regression analysis.* In Section 6.3 we utilized simple linear regression to fit a linear trend to the bicycle sales time series. Recall that we developed a linear equation relating bicycle sales to the time period. The number of bicycles sold isn't actually causally related to time; instead, time is a surrogate for variables to which the number of bicycles sold is actually related but which are either unknown or too difficult or costly to measure. Thus, the use of regression analysis for trend projection is not a causal forecasting method because only past values of sales, the variable being forecast, were used. When we use regression analysis to relate the variable that we want to forecast to other variables that are supposed to influence or explain that variable, it becomes a causal forecasting method.

Using Regression Analysis as a Causal Forecasting Method

To illustrate how regression analysis is used as a causal forecasting method, we consider the sales forecasting problem faced by Armand's Pizza Parlors, a chain of Italian restaurants doing business in a five-state area. The most successful locations have been near college campuses. The managers believe that quarterly sales for these restaurants (denoted by y) are related positively to the size of the student population (denoted by x); that is, restaurants near campuses with a large population tend to generate more sales than those located near campuses with a small population. Using regression analysis we can develop an equation showing how the dependent variable y is related to the independent variable x. This equation can then be used to forecast quarterly sales for restaurants located near college campuses given the size of the student population.

In situations where time series data are not available, regression analysis can still be used to develop a forecast. For instance, suppose that management wanted to forecast sales for a new restaurant they were considering opening near a college campus. Because no historical data are available on sales for a new restaurant, Armand's cannot use time series data to develop the forecast. But, as we will now illustrate, regression analysis can still be used to forecast quarterly sales.

To develop the equation relating quarterly sales and the size of the student population, Armand's collected data from a sample of 10 of its restaurants located near college campuses. These data are summarized in Table 6.13. For example, restaurant 1, with $y = 58$ and $x = 2$, had \$58,000 in quarterly sales and is located near a campus with 2000 students. Figure 6.14 shows graphically the data presented in Table 6.13. The size of the student population is shown on the horizontal axis, with quarterly sales shown on the vertical axis. This

TABLE 6.13 DATA ON QUARTERLY SALES AND STUDENT POPULATION FOR 10 RESTAURANTS

Restaurant	y = Quarterly Sales ($1000s)	x = Student Population (1000s)
1	58	2
2	105	6
3	88	8
4	118	8
5	117	12
6	137	16
7	157	20
8	169	20
9	149	22
10	202	26

FIGURE 6.14 SCATTER DIAGRAM OF QUARTERLY SALES VERSUS STUDENT POPULATION

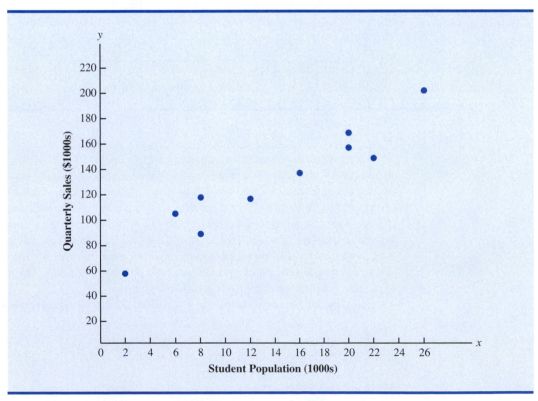

type of graph is called a *scatter diagram.* Usually the independent variable is plotted on the horizontal axis, and the dependent variable is plotted on the vertical axis. The advantage of a scatter diagram is that it provides an overview of the data and enables us to draw preliminary conclusions about a possible relationship between the variables.

FIGURE 6.15   STRAIGHT-LINE APPROXIMATION FOR DATA ON QUARTERLY SALES
AND STUDENT POPULATION

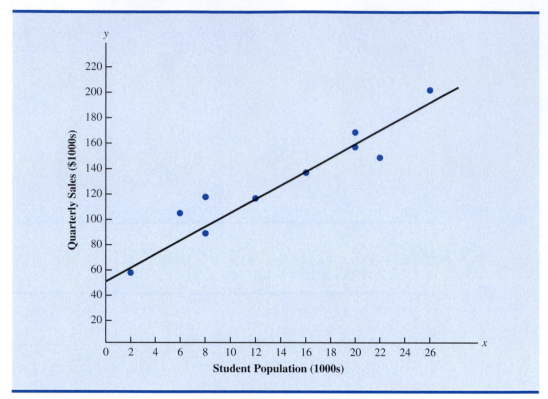

What preliminary conclusions can we draw from Figure 6.14? Sales appear to be higher at campuses with larger student populations. Also, it appears that the relationship between the two variables can be approximated by a straight line; indeed, x and y appear to be positively related. In Figure 6.15 we can draw a straight line through the data that appears to provide a good linear approximation of the relationship between the variables. Observe that the relationship isn't perfect. Indeed, few, if any, of the data fall exactly on the line. However, if we can develop the mathematical expression for this line, we may be able to use it to forecast the value of y corresponding to each possible value of x. The resulting equation of the line is called the *estimated regression equation*.

Using the least-squares method of estimation, the estimated regression equation is

$$\hat{y} = b_0 + b_1 x \tag{6.10}$$

where

$$\hat{y} = \text{estimated value of the dependent variable (quarterly sales)}$$
$$b_0 = \text{intercept of the estimated regression equation}$$
$$b_1 = \text{slope of the estimated regression equation}$$
$$x = \text{value of the independent variable (student population)}$$

We use the sample data and the following equations to compute the intercept b_0 and slope b_1:

$$b_1 = \frac{\sum x_i y_i - (\sum x_i \sum y_i)/n}{\sum x_i^2 - (\sum x_i)^2/n} \qquad \textbf{(6.11)}$$

$$b_0 = \bar{y} - b_1 \bar{x} \qquad \textbf{(6.12)}$$

where

x_i = value of the independent variable for the ith observation

y_i = value of the dependent variable for the ith observation

$\bar{x}$ = mean value for the independent variable

$\bar{y}$ = mean value for the dependent variable

n = total number of observations

Some of the calculations necessary to develop the least-squares estimated regression equation for the data on student population and quarterly sales are shown in Table 6.14. Our example contains 10 restaurants or observations; hence, $n = 10$. Using equations (6.11) and (6.12), we can now compute the slope and intercept of the estimated regression equation. We calculate the slope b_1 as follows:

$$
\begin{aligned}
b_1 &= \frac{\sum x_i y_i - (\sum x_i \sum y_i)/n}{\sum x_i^2 - (\sum x_i)^2/n} \\
&= \frac{21{,}040 - (140)(1300)/10}{2528 - (140)^2/10} \\
&= \frac{2840}{568} \\
&= 5
\end{aligned}
$$

TABLE 6.14   CALCULATIONS FOR THE LEAST-SQUARES ESTIMATED REGRESSION EQUATION FOR ARMAND'S PIZZA PARLORS

Restaurant (i)	y_i	x_i	$x_i y_i$	x_i^2
1	58	2	116	4
2	105	6	630	36
3	88	8	704	64
4	118	8	944	64
5	117	12	1,404	144
6	137	16	2,192	256
7	157	20	3,140	400
8	169	20	3,380	400
9	149	22	3,278	484
10	202	26	5,252	676
Totals	1300	140	21,040	2528

We then calculate the intercept b_0 as follows:

$$\bar{x} = \frac{\sum x_i}{n} = \frac{140}{10} = 14$$

$$\bar{y} = \frac{\sum y_i}{n} = \frac{1300}{10} = 130$$

$$b_0 = \bar{y} - b_1\bar{x}$$

$$= 130 - 5(14)$$

$$= 60$$

Thus, the estimated regression equation found by using the method of least squares is

$$\hat{y} = 60 + 5x$$

We show the graph of this equation in Figure 6.16.

The slope of the estimated regression equation ($b_1 = 5$) is positive, implying that as student population increases, quarterly sales increase. In fact, we can conclude (because sales are measured in thousands of dollars and student population in thousands) that an increase in the student population of 1000 is associated with an increase of $5000 in expected quarterly sales; that is, quarterly sales are expected to increase by $5 per student.

If we believe that the least-squares estimated regression equation adequately describes the relationship between x and y, using the estimated regression equation to forecast the value of y for a given value of x seems reasonable. For example, if we wanted to forecast

FIGURE 6.16 ESTIMATED REGRESSION EQUATION FOR ARMAND'S PIZZA PARLORS

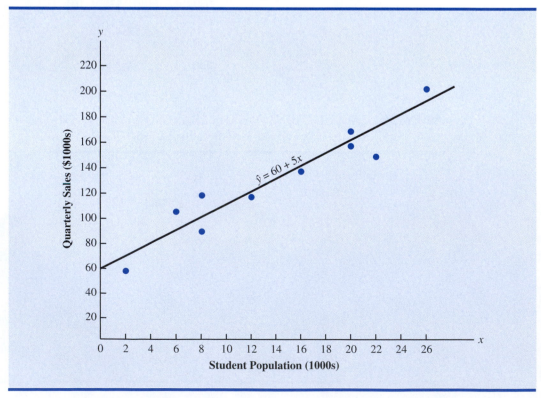

quarterly sales for a new restaurant to be located near a campus with 16,000 students, we would compute

$$\hat{y} = 60 + 5(16)$$
$$= 140$$

Practice using regression analysis to develop a forecast by working Problem 33.

Hence, we would forecast quarterly sales of $140,000.

The sales forecasting problem facing Armand's Pizza Parlors illustrates how simple linear regression analysis can be used to develop forecasts when time series data are not available. Multiple regression analysis also can be applied in these situations if additional data for other independent variables are available. For example, suppose that the management of Armand's Pizza Parlors also believes that the number of competitors near the college campus is related to quarterly sales. Intuitively, management believes that restaurants located near campuses with fewer competitors generate more sales revenue than those located near campuses with more competitors. With additional data, multiple regression analysis could be used to develop an equation relating quarterly sales to the size of the student population and the number of competitors.

Using Regression Analysis with Time Series Data

In Section 6.3 we fit a linear trend to the bicycle sales time series to show how simple linear regression analysis can be used to forecast future values of a time series when past values of the time series are available. Recall that for this problem the annual sales in year t was treated as the dependent variable, and the year t was treated as the independent variable. The inherent complexity of most real-world problems necessitates the consideration of more than one independent variable to predict the dependent variable. We now consider how multiple regression analysis is used to develop forecasts when time series data are available.

To use multiple regression analysis, we need a sample of observations for the dependent variable and all the independent variables. In time series analysis, the n periods of time series data provide a sample of n observations for each variable. To describe the wide variety of regression-based models that can be developed, we use the following notation:

$$Y_t = \text{actual value of the time series in period } t$$
$$x_{1t} = \text{value of independent variable 1 in period } t$$
$$x_{2t} = \text{value of independent variable 2 in period } t$$
$$\cdot$$
$$\cdot$$
$$\cdot$$
$$x_{kt} = \text{value of independent variable } k \text{ in period } t$$

The n periods of data necessary to develop the estimated regression equation would appear as follows:

Period	Dependent Variable Y_t	Independent Variables x_{1t}	x_{2t}	x_{3t}	$\cdot$ $\cdot$ $\cdot$	x_{kt}
1	Y_1	x_{11}	x_{21}	x_{31}	$\cdot$ $\cdot$ $\cdot$	x_{k1}
2	Y_2	x_{12}	x_{22}	x_{32}	$\cdot$ $\cdot$ $\cdot$	x_{k2}
$\cdot$	$\cdot$	$\cdot$	$\cdot$	$\cdot$	$\cdot$ $\cdot$ $\cdot$	$\cdot$
$\cdot$					$\cdot$ $\cdot$ $\cdot$	
$\cdot$					$\cdot$ $\cdot$ $\cdot$	
n	Y_n	x_{1n}	x_{2n}	x_{3n}	$\cdot$ $\cdot$ $\cdot$	x_{kn}

As you might imagine, a number of choices can be made when selecting the independent variables in a forecasting model. One possible choice is simply time. We made this choice in Section 6.3 when we estimated the trend of the time series using a linear function of the independent variable time. Letting

$$x_{1t} = t$$

we obtain an estimated regression equation of the form

$$\hat{Y}_t = b_0 + b_1 t$$

where $\hat{Y}_t$ is the estimate of the time series value Y_t and where b_0 and b_1 are the estimated regression coefficients. In a more complex model, additional terms could be added corresponding to time raised to other powers. For example, if

$$x_{2t} = t^2 \text{ and } x_{3t} = t^3$$

the estimated regression equation would become

$$\hat{Y}_t = b_0 + b_1 x_{1t} + b_2 x_{2t} + b_3 x_{3t}$$
$$= b_0 + b_1 t + b_2 t^2 + b_3 t^3$$

Note that this model provides a forecast of a time series with curvilinear characteristics over time.

Other regression-based forecasting models involve the use of a mixture of economic and demographic independent variables. For example, in forecasting the sale of refrigerators, we might select independent variables such as

x_{1t} = price in period t

x_{2t} = total industry sales in period $t - 1$

x_{3t} = number of building permits for new houses in period $t - 1$

x_{4t} = population forecast for period t

x_{5t} = advertising budget for period t

According to the usual multiple regression procedure, an estimated regression equation with five independent variables would be used to develop forecasts in this case.

Whether a regression approach provides a good forecast depends largely on how well we are able to identify and obtain data for independent variables that are closely related to the time series. Generally, during the development of an estimated regression equation, we will want to consider many possible sets of independent variables. Thus, part of the regression analysis procedure should focus on the selection of the set of independent variables that provides the best forecasting model.

In the chapter introduction we stated that causal forecasting methods are based on the assumption that the variable we are trying to forecast exhibits a cause–effect relationship with one or more other variables. Regression analysis is the tool most often used in developing causal models. The related time series become the independent variables, and the time series being forecast is the dependent variable.

Another type of regression-based forecasting model occurs whenever all the independent variables are previous values of the same time series. For example, if the time series

Spyros Makridakis, a noted forecasting expert, conducted research showing that simple techniques usually outperform more complex procedures for short-term forecasting. Using a more sophisticated and expensive procedure will not guarantee better forecasts.

values are denoted $Y_1, Y_2, \ldots, Y_n$, we might try to find an estimated regression equation relating Y_t to the most recent time series values, Y_{t-1}, Y_{t-2}, and so on. For instance, if we use the actual values of the time series for the three most recent periods as independent variables, the estimated regression equation would be

$$\hat{Y}_t = b_0 + b_1 Y_{t-1} + b_2 Y_{t-2} + b_3 Y_{t-3}$$

Regression models such as this one in which the independent variables are previous values of the time series are referred to as **autoregressive models**.

Finally, another regression-based forecasting approach is one that incorporates a mixture of the independent variables previously discussed. For example, we might select a combination of time variables, some economic/demographic variables, and some previous values of the time series variable itself.

Qualitative Approaches

In the preceding sections we discussed several types of quantitative forecasting methods. Most of these techniques require historical data on the variable of interest, so they cannot be applied when no historical data are available. Furthermore, even when such data are available, a significant change in environmental conditions affecting the time series may make the use of past data questionable in predicting future values of the time series. For example, a government-imposed gasoline rationing program would raise questions about the validity of a gasoline sales forecast based on historical data. Qualitative forecasting techniques offer an alternative in these and other cases.

If historical data are not available, managers may use a qualitative technique to develop forecasts. But the cost of using qualitative techniques can be high because of the time commitment required from the people involved.

Delphi Method

One of the most commonly used qualitative forecasting techniques is the **Delphi method**. This technique, originally developed by a research group at the Rand Corporation, attempts to develop forecasts through "group consensus." In its usual application, the members of a panel of experts—all of whom are physically separated from and unknown to each other— are asked to respond to a series of questionnaires. The responses from the first questionnaire are tabulated and used to prepare a second questionnaire that contains information and opinions of the entire group. Each respondent is then asked to reconsider and possibly revise his or her previous response in light of the group information provided. This process continues until the coordinator feels that some degree of consensus has been reached. The goal of the Delphi method is not to produce a single answer as output, but instead to produce a relatively narrow spread of opinions within which the majority of experts concurs.

Expert Judgment

Qualitative forecasts often are based on the judgment of a single expert or represent the consensus of a group of experts. For example, each year a group of experts at Merrill Lynch gather to forecast the level of the Dow Jones Industrial Average and the prime rate for the next year. In doing so, the experts individually consider information that they believe will influence the stock market and interest rates; then they combine their conclusions into a forecast. No formal model is used, and no two experts are likely to consider the same information in the same way.

Empirical evidence and theoretical arguments suggest that between 5 and 20 experts should be used in judgmental forecasting.

Expert judgment is a forecasting method that is often recommended when conditions in the past are not likely to hold in the future. Even though no formal quantitative model is used, expert judgment provides good forecasts in many situations.

Scenario Writing

The qualitative procedure referred to as **scenario writing** consists of developing a conceptual scenario of the future based on a well-defined set of assumptions. Different sets of assumptions lead to different scenarios. The job of the decision maker is to decide how likely each scenario is and then to make decisions accordingly.

Intuitive Approaches

Subjective, or *intuitive qualitative approaches,* are based on the ability of the human mind to process information that, in most cases, is difficult to quantify. These techniques are often used in group work, wherein a committee or panel seeks to develop new ideas or solve complex problems through a series of "brainstorming sessions." In such sessions, individuals are freed from the usual group restrictions of peer pressure and criticism because they can present any idea or opinion without regard to its relevancy and, even more importantly, without fear of criticism.

Summary

In this chapter we discussed how forecasts can be developed to help managers develop appropriate strategies for the future. We began by defining a time series as a set of observations on a variable measured at successive points in time or over successive periods of time. A time series may involve four separate components: trend, seasonal, irregular, and cyclical. By isolating these components and measuring their apparent effects, future values of the time series can be forecast.

Quantitative forecasting methods include time series methods and causal methods. A time series method is appropriate when the historical data are restricted to past values of the variable being forecast. The three time series methods discussed in the chapter are smoothing (moving averages, weighted moving averages, and exponential smoothing), trend projection, and trend projection adjusted for seasonal influence.

Smoothing methods are appropriate for a stable time series; that is, one that exhibits no significant trend, cyclical, or seasonal effects. The moving averages approach consists of computing an average of past values and then using this average as the forecast for the next period. The weighted moving averages method allows for the possibility of unequal weights for the data; thus, the moving averages method is a special case of the weighted moving averages method in which all the weights are equal. Exponential smoothing also is a special case of the weighted moving averages method involving only one parameter: the weight for the most recent observation.

When a time series consists of random fluctuations around a long-term trend line, a linear equation may be used to estimate the trend. When seasonal effects are present, seasonal indexes can be computed and used to deseasonalize the data and to develop forecasts. When both seasonal and long-term trend effects are present, a trend line is fitted to the deseasonalized data; the seasonal indexes are then used to adjust the trend projections.

Causal forecasting methods are based on the assumption that the variable being forecast exhibits a cause–effect relationship with one or more other variables. A causal forecasting method is one that relates the variable being forecast to other variables that are thought to influence or explain it. Regression analysis is a causal forecasting method that can be used to develop forecasts when time series data are not available.

Qualitative forecasting methods may be used when little or no historical data are available. Qualitative forecasting methods also are considered most appropriate when the historical pattern of the time series is not expected to continue into the future.

Glossary

Time series A set of observations of a variable measured at successive points in time or over successive periods of time.

Forecast A projection or prediction of future values of a time series.

Time series method Forecasting method that is based on the use of historical data that are restricted to past values of the variable we are trying to forecast.

Causal forecasting methods Forecasting methods that are based on the assumption that the variable we are trying to forecast exhibits a cause–effect relationship with one or more other variables.

Trend The gradual shift or movement of the time series to relatively higher or lower values over a longer period of time.

Cyclical component The component of the time series that accounts for the periodic above-trend and below-trend behavior of the time series lasting more than one year.

Seasonal component The component of the time series that represents the variability in the data due to seasonal influences.

Irregular component The component of the time series that accounts for the random variability in the time series.

Moving averages A smoothing method that uses the average of the most recent n data values in the time series as the forecast for the next period.

Mean squared error (MSE) An approach to measuring the accuracy of a forecasting method. This measure is the average of the sum of the squared differences between the actual time series values and the forecasted values.

Weighted moving averages A smoothing method that uses a weighted average of the most recent n data values as the forecast.

Exponential smoothing A smoothing method that uses a weighted average of past time series values as the forecast; it is a special case of the weighted moving averages method in which we select only one weight—the weight for the most recent observation.

Smoothing constant In the exponential smoothing model, the smoothing constant is the weight given to the actual value of the time series in period t.

Mean absolute deviation (MAD) A measure of forecast accuracy. The average of the absolute values of the forecast errors.

Multiplicative time series model A model that assumes that the separate components of the time series can be multiplied together to identify the actual time series value. When the four components of trend, cyclical, seasonal, and irregular are assumed present, we obtain $Y_t = T_t \times C_t \times S_t \times I_t$. When cyclical effects are not modeled, we obtain $Y_t = T_t \times S_t \times I_t$.

Seasonal index A measure of the seasonal effect on a time series. A seasonal index above 1 indicates a positive effect, a seasonal index of 1 indicates no seasonal effect, and a seasonal index less than 1 indicates a negative effect.

Deseasonalized time series A time series that has had the effect of season removed by dividing each original time series observation by the corresponding seasonal index.

Regression analysis A statistical technique used to develop a mathematical equation showing how variables are related.

Autoregressive model A regression model in which the independent variables are previous values of the time series.

Delphi method A qualitative forecasting method that obtains forecasts through group consensus.

Scenario writing A qualitative forecasting method that consists of developing a conceptual scenario of the future based on a well-defined set of assumptions.

Problems

1. Corporate Triple A Bond interest rates for 12 consecutive months are 9.5, 9.3, 9.4, 9.6, 9.8, 9.7, 9.8, 10.5, 9.9, 9.7, 9.6, and 9.6.
    a. Develop three- and four-month moving averages for this time series. Which moving average provides the better forecasts? Explain.
    b. What is the moving average forecast for the next month?

2. Refer to the gasoline sales time series data in Table 6.1.
    a. Compute four- and five-week moving averages for the time series.
    b. Compute the MSE for the four- and five-week moving average forecasts.
    c. What appears to be the best number of weeks of past data to use in the moving average computation? Remember that the MSE for the three-week moving average is 10.22.

3. Refer again to the gasoline sales time series data in Table 6.1.
    a. Use a weight of $1/2$ for the most recent observation, $1/3$ for the second most recent, and $1/6$ for the third most recent to compute a three-week weighted moving average for the time series.
    b. Compute the MSE for the weighted moving average in part (a). Do you prefer this weighted moving average to the unweighted moving average? Remember that the MSE for the unweighted moving average is 10.22.
    c. Suppose that you are allowed to choose any weights as long as they sum to 1. Could you always find a set of weights that would make the MSE smaller for a weighted moving average than for an unweighted moving average? Why or why not?

4. Use the gasoline sales time series data from Table 6.1 to show the exponential smoothing forecasts using $\alpha = 0.1$. Using the mean squared error criterion, would you prefer a smoothing constant of $\alpha = 0.1$ or $\alpha = 0.2$?

5. For the Hawkins Company, the monthly percentages of all shipments that were received on time over the past 12 months are 80, 82, 84, 83, 83, 84, 85, 84, 82, 83, 84, and 83.
    a. Compare a three-month moving average forecast with an exponential smoothing forecast for $\alpha = 0.2$. Which provides the better forecasts?
    b. What is the forecast for next month?

6. With a smoothing constant of $\alpha = 0.2$, equation (6.2) shows that the forecast for the 13th week of the gasoline sales data from Table 6.1 is given by $F_{13} = 0.2Y_{12} + 0.8F_{12}$. However, the forecast for week 12 is given by $F_{12} = 0.2Y_{11} + 0.8F_{11}$. Thus, we could combine these two results to write the forecast for the 13th week as

$$F_{13} = 0.2Y_{12} + 0.8(0.2Y_{11} + 0.8F_{11}) = 0.2Y_{12} + 0.16Y_{11} + 0.64F_{11}$$

    a. Make use of the fact that $F_{11} = 0.2Y_{10} + 0.8F_{10}$ (and similarly for F_{10} and F_9) and continue to expand the expression for F_{13} until you have written it in terms of the past data values Y_{12}, Y_{11}, Y_{10}, Y_9, and Y_8, and the forecast for period 8.
    b. Refer to the coefficients or weights for the past data values Y_{12}, Y_{11}, Y_{10}, Y_9, and Y_8; what observation can you make about how exponential smoothing weights past data values in arriving at new forecasts? Compare this weighting pattern with the weighting pattern of the moving averages method.

7. Alabama building contracts for a 12-month period (in millions of dollars) are 240, 350, 230, 260, 280, 320, 220, 310, 240, 310, 240, and 230.
    a. Compare a 3-month moving average forecast with an exponential smoothing forecast using $\alpha = 0.2$. Which provides the better forecasts?
    b. What is the forecast for the next month?

8. Moving averages often are used to identify movements in stock prices. Daily closing prices (in dollars per share) for SanDisk for August 16, 2002, through September 3, 2002, follow (*http://finance.yahoo.com*):

Day	Price ($)	Day	Price ($)
August 16	14.45	August 26	16.45
August 19	15.75	August 27	15.60
August 20	16.45	August 28	15.09
August 21	17.40	August 29	16.42
August 22	17.32	August 30	16.21
August 23	15.96	September 3	15.22

a. Use a five-day moving average to smooth the time series. Forecast the closing price for September 4, 2002.
b. Use a four-day weighted moving average to smooth the time series. Use a weight of 0.4 for the most recent period, 0.3 for the next period back, 0.2 for the third period back, and 0.1 for the fourth period back. Forecast the closing price for September 4, 2002.
c. Use exponential smoothing with a smoothing constant of $\alpha = 0.7$ to smooth the time series. Forecast the closing price for September 4, 2002.
d. Which of the three methods do you prefer? Why?

9. The following data represent 15 quarters of manufacturing capacity utilization (in percentages):

Quarter/Year	Utilization	Quarter/Year	Utilization
1/2000	82.5	1/2002	78.8
2/2000	81.3	2/2002	78.7
3/2000	81.3	3/2002	78.4
4/2000	79.0	4/2002	80.0
1/2001	76.6	1/2003	80.7
2/2001	78.0	2/2003	80.7
3/2001	78.4	3/2003	80.8
4/2001	78.0		

a. Compute three- and four-quarter moving averages for this time series. Which moving average provides the better forecast for the fourth quarter of 2003?
b. Use smoothing constants of $\alpha = 0.4$ and $\alpha = 0.5$ to develop forecasts for the fourth quarter of 2003. Which smoothing constant provides the better forecast?
c. Based on the analyses in parts (a) and (b), which method—moving averages or exponential smoothing—provides the better forecast? Explain.

10. For the 2001–2002 National Basketball Association season, Philadelphia 76ers Allen Iverson was the scoring leader with an average of 31.4 points per game. The following data show the average number of points per game for the scoring leader from the 1991–1992 season to the 2001–2002 season (*The World Almanac 2002* and *http://www.nba.com*):

Season	Average	Season	Average
1991–1992	30.1	1997–1998	28.7
1992–1993	32.6	1998–1999	26.8
1993–1994	29.8	1999–2000	29.7
1994–1995	29.3	2000–2001	31.1
1995–1996	30.4	2001–2002	31.4
1996–1997	29.6		

a. Use exponential smoothing to forecast this time series. Consider smoothing constants of $\alpha = 0.1$ and 0.2. What value of the smoothing constant provides the best forecast?

b. What is the forecast of the leading scoring average for the 2002–2003 season?

11. The percentage of individual investors' portfolios committed to stock depends on the state of the economy. The following table reports the percentage of stocks in a portfolio for nine quarters:

Quarter	Stock %	Quarter	Stock %
1	29.8	6	31.5
2	31.0	7	32.0
3	29.9	8	31.9
4	30.1	9	30.0
5	32.2		

a. Use exponential smoothing to forecast this time series. Consider smoothing constants of $\alpha = 0.2$, 0.3, and 0.4. What value of the smoothing constant provides the best forecast?

b. What is the forecast of the percentage of assets committed to stocks for the next quarter?

12. United Dairies, Inc., supplies milk to several independent grocers throughout Dade County, Florida. Management wants to develop a forecast of the number of half-gallons of milk sold per week. Sales data (in units) for the past 12 weeks are as follows:

Week	Sales	Week	Sales
1	2750	7	3300
2	3100	8	3100
3	3250	9	2950
4	2800	10	3000
5	2900	11	3200
6	3050	12	3150

Use exponential smoothing, with $\alpha = 0.4$, to develop a forecast of demand for week 13.

13. Ten weeks of data on the Commodity Futures Index are 7.35, 7.40, 7.55, 7.56, 7.60, 7.52, 7.52, 7.70, 7.62, and 7.55.

a. Compute the exponential smoothing values for $\alpha = 0.2$.

b. Compute the exponential smoothing values for $\alpha = 0.3$.

c. Which exponential smoothing model provides the better forecasts? Forecast week 11.

14. The enrollment data (figures in thousands) for a state college for the past six years are shown.

Year	1	2	3	4	5	6
Enrollment	20.5	20.2	19.5	19.0	19.1	18.8

Develop the equation for the linear trend component for this time series. Comment on what is happening to enrollment at this institution.

15. Automobile sales at B. J. Scott Motors, Inc., provided the following 10-year time series:

Year	Sales	Year	Sales
1	400	6	260
2	390	7	300
3	320	8	320
4	340	9	340
5	270	10	370

Plot the time series, and comment on the appropriateness of a linear trend. What type of functional form would be best for the trend pattern of this time series?

16. The president of a small manufacturing firm has been concerned about the continual growth in manufacturing costs over the past several years. The following is a time series of the cost per unit (in dollars) for the firm's leading product over the past eight years:

Year	Cost per Unit ($)	Year	Cost per Unit ($)
1	20.00	5	26.60
2	24.50	6	30.00
3	28.20	7	31.00
4	27.50	8	36.00

a. Graph this time series. Does a linear trend appear?
b. Develop the equation for the linear trend component for the time series. What is the average cost increase per year?

17. TV ratings provided by Nielsen Media Research show the percentage of TV-owning households tuned in to a particular program. The following data show the rating for the top-rated TV show of each season, from 1987–1988 to 2000–2001 (*The New York Times Almanac 2002*):

Season	Rating	Season	Rating
1987–1988	27.8	1994–1995	20.5
1988–1989	25.5	1995–1996	22.0
1989–1990	23.4	1996–1997	21.2
1990–1991	21.6	1997–1998	22.0
1991–1992	21.7	1998–1999	17.8
1992–1993	21.6	1999–2000	16.6
1993–1994	21.9	2000–2001	17.4

a. Graph this time series. Does a linear trend appear?
b. Develop a linear trend equation for this time series.
c. Use the trend equation to estimate the rating for the 2001–2002 season.

18. The Federal Election Commission maintains data showing the voting age population, the number of registered voters, and the turnout for federal elections. The following table

shows the national voter turnout in presidential elections as a percentage of the voting age population from 1964 to 2000 (*http://www.fec.gov*).

Year	Percentage Voting	Year	Percentage Voting
1964	61.92	1984	53.11
1968	60.84	1988	50.11
1972	55.21	1992	55.09
1976	53.55	1996	49.08
1980	52.56	2000	51.30

a. Graph this time series. Does a linear trend appear?
b. Develop the equation for the linear trend component for the time series. What is the average decrease in the percentage voting per presidential election?
c. Use the trend equation to forecast the percentage voting in 2004.

19. The following data show the time series of the most recent quarterly capital expenditures (in billions of dollars) for the 1000 largest manufacturing firms: 24, 25, 23, 24, 22, 26, 28, 31, 29, 32, 37, and 42.
a. Develop a linear trend equation for the time series.
b. Graph the time series and the linear trend equation.
c. What appears to be happening to capital expenditures? What is the forecast one year, or four quarters, into the future?

20. The Costello Music Company has been in business for five years. During that time, the sales of electric organs have grown from 12 units in the first year to 76 units in the most recent year. Fred Costello, the firm's owner, wants to develop a forecast of organ sales for the coming year based on the historical data shown.

Year	1	2	3	4	5
Sales	12	28	34	50	76

a. Graph this time series. Does a linear trend appear?
b. Develop the equation for the linear trend component for the time series. What is the average increase in sales per year for the firm?

21. Hudson Marine has been an authorized dealer for C&D marine radios for the past seven years. The number of radios sold each year is shown.

Year	1	2	3	4	5	6	7
Number Sold	35	50	75	90	105	110	130

a. Graph this time series. Does a linear trend appear?
b. Develop the equation for the linear trend component for the time series.
c. Use the linear trend developed in part (b) to prepare a forecast for sales in year 8.

22. The League of American Theatres and Producers, Inc., collects a variety of statistics for Broadway plays, such as gross revenue, playing time, and number of new productions. The

following data show the season attendance (in millions) for Broadway shows from 1990 to 2001 (*The World Almanac 2002*):

Season	Attendance (in millions)	Season	Attendance (in millions)
1990–1991	7.3	1996–1997	10.6
1991–1992	7.4	1997–1998	11.5
1992–1993	7.9	1998–1999	11.7
1993–1994	8.1	1999–2000	11.4
1994–1995	9.0	2000–2001	11.9
1995–1996	9.5		

a. Plot the time series and comment on the appropriateness of a linear trend.
b. Develop the equation for the linear trend component for this time series.
c. What is the average increase in attendance per season?
d. Use the trend equation to forecast attendance for the 2001–2002 season.

23. The Garden Avenue Seven sells tapes of its musical performances. The following data show sales for the past 18 months. The group's manager wants an accurate method for forecasting future sales.

Month	Sales	Month	Sales	Month	Sales
1	293	7	381	13	549
2	283	8	431	14	544
3	322	9	424	15	601
4	355	10	433	16	587
5	346	11	470	17	644
6	379	12	481	18	660

a. Use exponential smoothing, with $\alpha = 0.3, 0.4$, and 0.5. Which value of α provides the best forecasts?
b. Use trend projection to provide a forecast. What is the value of MSE?
c. Which method of forecasting would you recommend to the manager? Why?

24. The Mayfair Department Store in Davenport, Iowa, is trying to determine the amount of sales lost while it was shut down because of summer floods. Sales data for January through June are shown.

Month	Sales ($1000s)
January	185.72
February	167.84
March	205.11
April	210.36
May	255.57
June	261.19

a.   Use exponential smoothing, with $\alpha = 0.4$, to develop a forecast for July and August. (*Hint:* Use the forecast for July as the actual sales in July in developing the August forecast.) Comment on the use of exponential smoothing for forecasts more than one period into the future.

b.   Use trend projection to forecast sales for July and August.

c.   Mayfair's insurance company proposed a settlement based on lost sales of $240,000 in July and August. Is this amount fair? If not, what amount would you counter with?

25.   The quarterly sales data (number of copies sold) for a college textbook over the past three years are as follows:

Quarter	Year 1	Year 2	Year 3
1	1690	1800	1850
2	940	900	1100
3	2625	2900	2930
4	2500	2360	2615

a.   Show the four-quarter moving average values for this time series. Plot both the original time series and the moving averages on the same graph.

b.   Compute seasonal indexes for the four quarters.

c.   When does the textbook publisher experience the largest seasonal index? Does this result appear to be reasonable? Explain.

26.   Identify the monthly seasonal indexes for the following three years of expenses for a six-unit apartment house in southern Florida. Use a 12-month moving average calculation.

Month	Year 1	Year 2	Year 3
January	170	180	195
February	180	205	210
March	205	215	230
April	230	245	280
May	240	265	290
June	315	330	390
July	360	400	420
August	290	335	330
September	240	260	290
October	240	270	295
November	230	255	280
December	195	220	250

27.   Air pollution control specialists in southern California monitor the amount of ozone, carbon dioxide, and nitrogen dioxide in the air on an hourly basis. The hourly time series data exhibit seasonality, with the levels of pollutants showing similar patterns over the hours in the day. On July 15, 16, and 17, the observed levels of nitrogen dioxide in a city's downtown area for the 12 hours from 6:00 A.M. to 6:00 P.M. were as follows:

July 15   25   28   35   50   60   60   40   35   30   25   25   20
July 16   28   30   35   48   60   65   50   40   35   25   20   20
July 17   35   42   45   70   72   75   60   45   40   25   25   25

a. Identify the hourly seasonal indexes for the 12 hourly daily readings.
b. Based on the seasonal indexes in part (a), the trend equation developed for the deseasonalized data is $T_t = 32.983 + 0.3922t$. Using only the trend equation, develop forecasts for the 12 hours for July 18.
c. Use the seasonal indexes from part (a) to adjust the trend forecasts in part (b).

28. Refer to Problem 21. Suppose that the following are the quarterly sales data for the past seven years:

Year	Quarter 1	Quarter 2	Quarter 3	Quarter 4	Total Sales
1	6	15	10	4	35
2	10	18	15	7	50
3	14	26	23	12	75
4	19	28	25	18	90
5	22	34	28	21	105
6	24	36	30	20	110
7	28	40	35	27	130

a. Show the four-quarter moving average values for this time series. Plot both the original time series and the moving averages on the same graph.
b. Compute the seasonal indexes for the four quarters.
c. When does Hudson Marine experience the largest seasonal effect? Does this result seem reasonable? Explain.

29. Consider the Costello Music Company scenario presented in Problem 20 and the following quarterly sales data:

Year	Quarter 1	Quarter 2	Quarter 3	Quarter 4	Total Yearly Sales
1	4	2	1	5	12
2	6	4	4	14	28
3	10	3	5	16	34
4	12	9	7	22	50
5	18	10	13	35	76

a. Compute the seasonal indexes for the four quarters.
b. When does Costello Music experience the largest seasonal effect? Does this result appear to be reasonable? Explain.

30. Refer to the Hudson Marine data in Problem 28.
a. Deseasonalize the data, and use the deseasonalized time series to identify the trend.
b. Use the results of part (a) to develop a quarterly forecast for next year based on trend.
c. Use the seasonal indexes developed in Problem 28 to adjust the forecasts developed in part (b) to account for the effect of season.

31. Consider the Costello Music Company time series in Problem 29.
a. Deseasonalize the data, and use the deseasonalized time series to identify the trend.
b. Use the results of part (a) to develop a quarterly forecast for next year based on trend.
c. Use the seasonal indexes developed in Problem 29 to adjust the forecasts developed in part (b) to account for seasonal effects.

32. Electric power consumption is measured in kilowatt-hours (kWh). The local utility company has an interrupt program, whereby commercial customers who participate receive favorable rates but must agree to cut back consumption if the utility requests them to do so. Timko Products cut back consumption at 12:00 noon Thursday. To assess the savings, the utility must estimate Timko's usage without the interrupt. The period of interrupted service was from noon to 8:00 P.M. Data on electric consumption for the past 72 hours is available.

Time Period	Monday	Tuesday	Wednesday	Thursday
12–4 A.M.	—	19,281	31,209	27,330
4–8 A.M.	—	33,195	37,014	32,715
8–12 noon	—	99,516	119,968	152,465
12–4 P.M.	124,299	123,666	156,033	
4–8 P.M.	113,545	111,717	128,889	
8–12 midnight	41,300	48,112	73,923	

    a. Is there a seasonal effect over the 24-hour period? Compute seasonal indexes for the six 4-hour periods.

    b. Use trend adjusted for seasonal factors to estimate Timko's normal usage over the period of interrupted service.

33. Eddie's Restaurants collected the following data on the relationship between advertising and sales at a sample of five restaurants:

Advertising Expenditures ($1000s)	1.0	4.0	6.0	10.0	14.0
Sales ($1000s)	19.0	44.0	40.0	52.0	53.0

    a. Let x represent advertising expenditures and y represent sales. Use the method of least squares to develop a straight-line approximation of the relationship between the two variables.

    b. Use the equation developed in part (a) to forecast sales for an advertising expenditure of $8000.

34. The management of a chain of fast-food restaurants wants to investigate the relationship between the daily sales volume (in dollars) of a company restaurant and the number of competitor restaurants within a 1-mile radius. The following data have been collected:

Number of Competitors Within 1 Mile	Sales ($)
1	3600
1	3300
2	3100
3	2900
3	2700
4	2500
5	2300
5	2000

    a. Develop the least-squares estimated regression equation that relates daily sales volume to the number of competitor restaurants within a 1-mile radius.

    b. Use the estimated regression equation developed in part (a) to forecast the daily sales volume for a particular company restaurant that has four competitors within a 1-mile radius.

35. The supervisor of a manufacturing process believed that assembly-line speed (in feet/minute) affected the number of defective parts found during on-line inspection. To test this theory, management had the same batch of parts inspected visually at a variety of line speeds. The following data were collected:

Line Speed	Number of Defective Parts Found
20	21
20	19
40	15
30	16
60	14
40	17

   a. Develop the estimated regression equation that relates line speed to the number of defective parts found.
   b. Use the equation developed in part (a) to forecast the number of defective parts found for a line speed of 50 feet per minute.

Case Problem 1   Forecasting Sales

The Vintage Restaurant is located on Captiva Island, a resort community near Fort Myers, Florida. The restaurant, which is owned and operated by Karen Payne, just completed its third year of operation. During this time, Karen sought to establish a reputation for the restaurant as a high-quality dining establishment that specializes in fresh seafood. The efforts made by Karen and her staff proved successful, and her restaurant is currently one of the best and fastest-growing restaurants on the island.

Karen concluded that to plan better for the growth of the restaurant in the future, she needs to develop a system that will enable her to forecast food and beverage sales by month for up to one year in advance. Karen compiled the following data on total food and beverage sales for the three years of operation:

	Food and Beverage Sales for the Vintage Restaurant ($1000s)		
Month	**First Year**	**Second Year**	**Third Year**
January	242	263	282
February	235	238	255
March	232	247	265
April	178	193	205
May	184	193	210
June	140	149	160
July	145	157	166
August	152	161	174
September	110	122	126
October	130	130	148
November	152	167	173
December	206	230	235

Managerial Report

Perform an analysis of the sales data for the Vintage Restaurant. Prepare a report for Karen that summarizes your findings, forecasts, and recommendations. Include the following:

1. A graph of the time series.
2. An analysis of the seasonality of the data. Indicate the seasonal indexes for each month, and comment on the high seasonal and low seasonal sales months. Do the seasonal indexes make intuitive sense? Discuss.
3. Forecast sales for January through December of the fourth year.
4. Assume that January sales for the fourth year turned out to be $295,000. What was your forecast error? If this error is large, Karen may be puzzled about the difference between your forecast and the actual sales value. What can you do to resolve her uncertainty in the forecasting procedure?
5. Recommendations as to when the system that you developed should be updated to account for new sales data that will occur.
6. Detailed calculations of your analysis in an appendix to your report.

Case Problem 2   Forecasting Lost Sales

The Carlson Department Store suffered heavy damage when a hurricane struck on August 31, 2003. The store was closed for four months (September 2003 through December 2003), and Carlson is now involved in a dispute with its insurance company concerning the amount of lost sales during the time the store was closed. Two key issues must be resolved: (1) the amount of sales Carlson would have made if the hurricane had not struck; and (2) whether Carlson is entitled to any compensation for excess sales from increased business activity after the storm. More than $8 billion in federal disaster relief and insurance money came into the county, resulting in increased sales at department stores and numerous other businesses.

Table 6.15 shows the sales data for the 48 months preceding the storm. Table 6.16 reports total sales for the 48 months preceding the storm for all department stores in the county, as well as the total sales in the county for the four months the Carlson Department

TABLE 6.15   SALES FOR CARLSON DEPARTMENT STORE, SEPTEMBER 1999 THROUGH AUGUST 2003

Month	1999	2000	2001	2002	2003
January		1.45	2.31	2.31	2.56
February		1.80	1.89	1.99	2.28
March		2.03	2.02	2.42	2.69
April		1.99	2.23	2.45	2.48
May		2.32	2.39	2.57	2.73
June		2.20	2.14	2.42	2.37
July		2.13	2.27	2.40	2.31
August		2.43	2.21	2.50	2.23
September	1.71	1.90	1.89	2.09	
October	1.90	2.13	2.29	2.54	
November	2.74	2.56	2.83	2.97	
December	4.20	4.16	4.04	4.35	

TABLE 6.16   DEPARTMENT STORE SALES FOR THE COUNTY, SEPTEMBER 1999
                 THROUGH DECEMBER 2003

Month	1999	2000	2001	2002	2003
January		46.8	46.8	43.8	48.0
February		48.0	48.6	45.6	51.6
March		60.0	59.4	57.6	57.6
April		57.6	58.2	53.4	58.2
May		61.8	60.6	56.4	60.0
June		58.2	55.2	52.8	57.0
July		56.4	51.0	54.0	57.6
August		63.0	58.8	60.6	61.8
September	55.8	57.6	49.8	47.4	69.0
October	56.4	53.4	54.6	54.6	75.0
November	71.4	71.4	65.4	67.8	85.2
December	117.6	114.0	102.0	100.2	121.8

Store was closed. Management asks you to analyze these data and develop estimates of the lost sales at the Carlson Department Store for the months of September through December 2003. Management also wants to determine whether a case can be made for excess storm-related sales during the same period. If such a case can be made, Carlson is entitled to compensation for excess sales it would have earned in addition to ordinary sales.

Managerial Report

Prepare a report for the management of the Carlson Department store that summarizes your findings, forecasts, and recommendations. Include the following:

1. An estimate of sales had there been no hurricane
2. An estimate of countywide department store sales had there been no hurricane
3. An estimate of lost sales for the Carlson Department Store for September through December 2003

Appendix 6.1   Using Excel for Forecasting

In this appendix we show how Excel can be used to develop forecasts using three forecasting methods: moving averages, exponential smoothing, and trend projection.

Moving Averages

To show how Excel can be used to develop forecasts using the moving averages method, we will develop a forecast for the gasoline sales time series in Table 6.1 and Figure 6.5. We assume that the user has entered the sales data for the 12 weeks into worksheet rows 1 through 12 of column A. The following steps can be used to produce a three-week moving average:

Step 1. Select the **Data** tab
Step 2. From the **Analysis** group select the **Data Analysis** option
Step 3. When the **Data Analysis Tools** dialog box appears, choose **Moving Average**

Step 4. When the **Moving Average** dialog box appears:
Enter A1:A12 in the **Input Range** box
Enter 3 in the **Interval** box
Enter B1 in the **Output Range** box
Click **OK**

The three-week moving average forecasts will appear in column B of the worksheet. Note that forecasts for periods of other lengths can be computed easily by entering a different value in the **Interval** box.

Exponential Smoothing

To show how Excel can be used for exponential smoothing, we again develop a forecast for the gasoline sales time series in Table 6.1 and Figure 6.5. We assume that the user has entered the sales data for the 12 weeks into worksheet rows 1 through 12 of column A and that the smoothing constant is $\alpha = 0.2$. The following steps can be used to produce a forecast:

Step 1. Select the **Data** tab
Step 2. From the **Analysis** group select the **Data Analysis** option
Step 3. When the **Data Analysis Tools** dialog box appears, choose **Exponential Smoothing**
Step 4. When the **Exponential Smoothing** dialog box appears:
Enter A1:A12 in the **Input Range** box
Enter 0.8 in the **Damping factor** box
Enter B1 in the **Output Range** box
Click **OK**

The exponential smoothing forecasts will appear in column B of the worksheet. Note that the value we entered in the **Damping factor** box is $1 - \alpha$; forecasts for other smoothing constants can be computed easily by entering a different value for $1 - \alpha$ in the **Damping factor** box.

Trend Projection

To show how Excel can be used for trend projection, we develop a forecast for the bicycle sales time series in Table 6.6 and Figure 6.8. We assume that the user has entered the year (1–10) for each observation into worksheet rows 1 through 10 of column A and the sales values into worksheet rows 1 through 10 of column B. The following steps can be used to produce a forecast for year 11 by trend projection:

Step 1. Select the **Data** tab.
Step 2. From the **Analysis** group select the **Data Analysis** option
Step 3. Choose the **Function** option
Step 4. When the **Insert Function** dialog box appears:
Choose **Statistical** in the **Select a category** box
Choose **Forecast** in the **Select a function** box
Click **OK**
Step 5. When the **Function Arguments** dialog box appears:
Enter 11 in the **x** box
Enter B1:B10 in the **Known y's** box
Enter A1:A10 in the **Known x's** box
Click **OK**

The forecast for year 11, in this case 32.5, will appear in the cell selected in step 1.

Appendix 6.2   Using CB Predictor for Forecasting

CB Predictor is an easy-to-use, graphically oriented forecasting add-in package. It is included as part of the Crystal Ball risk analysis package that accompanies the text. In this appendix we show how CB Predictor can be used to develop forecasts using two forecasting methods: moving averages and exponential smoothing. We also briefly discuss some of the other forecasting techniques available using CB Predictor. Instructions for installing and starting CB Predictor are included with the Crystal Ball software.

Moving Averages

To show how CB Predictor can be used to develop forecasts using the moving averages method, we will develop a forecast for the gasoline sales time series in Table 6.1 and Figure 6.5. The labels Week and Sales are entered into cells A1:B1 of an Excel worksheet. To identify each of the 12 observations, we enter the numbers 1 through 12 into cells A2:A13. The corresponding sales data are entered in cells B2:B13. The following steps can be used to produce a three-week moving average:

Step 1. Click the **Crystal Ball** tab on the Ribbon
Step 2. In the **Run Group,** click **Tools**
Step 3. When the list of **Professional Tools** appears, click **CB Predictor**
Step 4. When the **Input Data** tab of the CB Predictor dialog box appears:
Enter B1:B13 in the **Range** box
Select **First row has headers**
Select **Data in columns**
Click **Next**
Step 5. When the **Data Attributes** tab of the CB Predictor dialog box appears:
Select **weeks** from the **Data is in** list
Select **with no seasonality (all seasonal methods skipped)**
Click **Next**
Step 6. When the **Method Gallery** tab of the CB Predictor dialog box appears:
Select **Single Moving Average**
Double-click over the **Single Moving Average** method area
Step 7. When the **Single Moving Average** dialog box appears:
Select **User defined**
Enter 3 in the **Periods** box
Click **OK**
Step 8. When the **Method Gallery** tab of the CB Predictor dialog box appears:
Click **Next**
Step 9. When the **Results** tab of the CB Predictor dialog box appears:
Enter 1 in the **Enter the number of periods to forecast** box
Enter B14 in the **Paste forecasts at cell** box
Click **Report**
Click **Charts**
Click **Results Table**
Click **Methods Table**
Click **Run**

The three-week moving average forecast of 19 for week 13 will appear in cell B14. Note that four new worksheets, labeled Report, Chart, Results Table, and Methods Table, appear as part of the CB Predictor output. Each of these worksheets provides details regarding the forecast results. For example, in the worksheet labeled Chart, CB Predictor provides a graph of the gasoline sales time series and the three-week moving average forecast similar to Figure 6.6 and a table of the time series data and the moving average forecast similar to Table 6.2. In the worksheet labeled Report, measures of forecast accuracy are also reported. One of these measures, RMSE = 3.1972, is just the square root of the MSE value that we used throughout the chapter.

Exponential Smoothing

To show how CB Predictor can be used for exponential smoothing, we again develop a forecast for the gasoline sales time series in Table 6.1 and Figure 6.5. The same worksheet that we used to develop a moving average forecast for gasoline sales applies: The labels Week and Sales are entered into cells A1:B1 of the worksheet; the numbers 1 through 12 are entered into cells A2:A13 to identify each of the 12 observations; and the sales data are entered in cells B2:B13. The following steps can be used to produce a forecast:

Step 1. Click the **Crystal Ball** tab on the Ribbon

Step 2. In the **Run Group,** click **Tools**

Step 3. When the list of **Professional Tools** appears, click **CB Predictor**

Step 4. When the **Input Data** tab of the CB Predictor dialog box appears:
Enter B1:B13 in the **Range** box
Select **First row has headers**
Select **Data in columns**
Click **Next**

Step 5. When the **Data Attributes** tab of the CB Predictor dialog box appears:
Select **weeks** from the **Data is in** list
Select **with no seasonality (all seasonal methods skipped)**
Click **Next**

Step 6. When the **Method Gallery** tab of the CB Predictor dialog box appears:
Select **Single Exp. Smoothing**
Double-click over the **Single Exp. Smoothing** method area

Step 7. When the **Single Exponential Smoothing** dialog box appears:
Select **User defined**
Enter .2 in the **Alpha** box
Click **OK**

Step 8. When the **Method Gallery** tab of the CB Predictor dialog box appears:
Click **Next**

Step 9. When the **Results** tab of the CB Predictor dialog box appears:
Enter 1 in the **Enter the number of periods to forecast** box
Enter B14 in the **Paste forecasts at cell** box
Click **Report**
Click **Charts**
Click **Results Table**
Click **Methods Table**
Click **Run**

The exponential smoothing forecast will appear in cell B14.

Other Forecasting Methods

In addition to moving averages and exponential smoothing, CB Predictor offers a variety of other forecasting methods that can be used for nonseasonal data with no trend, for non-seasonal data with trend, for seasonal data with no trend, and for seasonal data with trend. The "basic" models available in CB Predictor are the following:

	Nonseasonal		**Seasonal**	
No Trend	Single Moving Average	Single Exponential Smoothing	Seasonal Additive	Seasonal Multiplicative
Trend	Double Moving Average	Double Exponential Smoothing	Holt-Winters Additive	Holt-Winters Multiplicative

Thus, if the time series data contain both seasonal and trend components, the CB Predictor methods that are best designed to work for these situations are the Holt-Winters Additive method or the Holt-Winters Multiplicative method. Although a discussion of all the forecasting methods available using CB Predictor is beyond the scope of this text, more advanced books on forecasting discuss each of these techniques in detail.

In addition to the eight different forecasting methods already listed, CB Predictor also provides a regression capability that can be incorporated with any or all of the techniques. For instance, suppose you wanted to forecast gas usage for the coming year for a utility company and that you have time series data available on gas usage as well as three independent variables: occupancy permits, average temperature, and the cost of natural gas. In other words, you have time series data with one dependent variable, gas usage, and three independent variables. Using CB Predictor you can develop a regression equation that relates gas usage to the three independent variables. CB Predictor will forecast each of the independent variables using time series forecasting methods. Then, the forecasted values of the independent variables are substituted into the regression equation created initially to create the forecast for the dependent variable. CB Predictor refers to this forecasting technique as "Hypercasting."

CHAPTER 7

Introduction to Linear Programming

CONTENTS

Linear programming is a problem-solving approach developed to help managers make decisions. Numerous applications of linear programming can be found in today's competitive business environment. For instance, Eastman Kodak uses linear programming to determine where to manufacture products throughout their worldwide facilities, and GE Capital uses linear programming to help determine optimal lease structuring. Marathon Oil Company uses linear programming for gasoline blending and to evaluate the economics of a new terminal or pipeline. The Q.M. in Action, Timber Harvesting Model at MeadWestvaco Corporation, provides another example of the use of linear programming. Later in the chapter another Q.M. in Action illustrates how the Hanshin Expressway Public Corporation uses linear programming for traffic control on an urban toll expressway in Osaka, Japan.

To illustrate some of the properties that all linear programming problems have in common, consider the following typical applications:

1. A manufacturer wants to develop a production schedule and an inventory policy that will satisfy sales demand in future periods. Ideally, the schedule and policy will enable the company to satisfy demand and at the same time *minimize* the total production and inventory costs.
2. A financial analyst must select an investment portfolio from a variety of stock and bond investment alternatives. The analyst would like to establish the portfolio that *maximizes* the return on investment.
3. A marketing manager wants to determine how best to allocate a fixed advertising budget among alternative advertising media such as radio, television, newspaper, and magazine. The manager would like to determine the media mix that *maximizes* advertising effectiveness.
4. A company has warehouses in a number of locations. Given specific customer demands, the company would like to determine how much each warehouse should ship to each customer so that total transportation costs are *minimized*.

These examples are only a few of the situations in which linear programming has been used successfully, but they illustrate the diversity of linear programming applications. A close scrutiny reveals one basic property they all have in common. In each example, we were concerned with *maximizing* or *minimizing* some quantity. In example 1, the manufacturer wanted to minimize costs; in example 2, the financial analyst wanted to maximize return on investment; in example 3, the marketing manager wanted to maximize advertising effectiveness; and in example 4, the company wanted to minimize total transportation costs. In all linear programming problems, the maximization or minimization of some quantity is the objective.

Q.M. *in* ACTION

TIMBER HARVESTING MODEL AT MEADWESTVACO CORPORATION*

MeadWestvaco Corporation is a major producer of premium papers for periodicals, books, commercial printing, and business forms. The company also produces pulp and lumber, designs and manufactures packaging systems for beverage and other consumables markets, and is a world leader in the production of coated board and shipping containers. Quantitative analyses at MeadWestvaco are developed and implemented by the company's Decision Analysis Department. The department assists decision makers by providing them with analytical tools of quantitative methods as well as personal analysis and recommendations.

*Based on information provided by Dr. Edward P. Winkofsky of MeadWestvaco Corporation.

(*continued*)

MeadWestvaco uses quantitative models to assist with the long-range management of the company's timberland. Through the use of large-scale linear programs, timber harvesting plans are developed to cover a substantial time horizon. These models consider wood market conditions, mill pulpwood requirements, harvesting capacities, and general forest management principles. Within these constraints, the model arrives at an optimal harvesting and purchasing schedule based on discounted cash flow. Alternative schedules reflect changes in the various assumptions concerning forest growth, wood availability, and general economic conditions.

Quantitative methods are also used in the development of the inputs for the linear programming models. Timber prices and supplies as well as mill requirements must be forecast over the time horizon, and advanced sampling techniques are used to evaluate land holdings and to project forest growth. The harvest schedule is then developed using quantitative methods.

Linear programming was initially referred to as "programming in a linear structure." In 1948 Tjalling Koopmans suggested to George Dantzig that the name was much too long: Koopman's suggestion was to shorten it to linear programming. George Dantzig agreed and the field we now know as linear programming was named.

All linear programming problems also have a second property: restrictions or constraints that limit the degree to which the objective can be pursued. In example 1, the manufacturer is restricted by constraints requiring product demand to be satisfied and by the constraints limiting production capacity. The financial analyst's portfolio problem is constrained by the total amount of investment funds available and the maximum amounts that can be invested in each stock or bond. The marketing manager's media selection decision is constrained by a fixed advertising budget and the availability of the various media. In the transportation problem, the minimum-cost shipping schedule is constrained by the supply of product available at each warehouse. Thus, constraints are another general feature of every linear programming problem.

7.1 A Simple Maximization Problem

RMC, Inc., is a small firm that produces a variety of chemical-based products. In a particular production process, three raw materials are used to produce two products: a fuel additive and a solvent base. The fuel additive is sold to oil companies and is used in the production of gasoline and related fuels. The solvent base is sold to a variety of chemical firms and is used in both home and industrial cleaning products. The three raw materials are blended to form the fuel additive and solvent base as indicated in Table 7.1. It shows that a ton of fuel additive is a mixture of 0.4 ton of material 1 and 0.6 ton of material 3. A ton of solvent base is a mixture of 0.5 ton of material 1, 0.2 ton of material 2, and 0.3 ton of material 3.

TABLE 7.1   MATERIAL REQUIREMENTS PER TON FOR THE RMC PROBLEM

	Product	
	Fuel Additive	**Solvent Base**
Material 1	0.4	0.5
Material 2		0.2
Material 3	0.6	0.3

0.6 ton of material 3 is used in each ton of fuel additive

RMC's production is constrained by a limited availability of the three raw materials. For the current production period, RMC has available the following quantities of each raw material:

Material	Amount Available for Production
Material 1	20 tons
Material 2	5 tons
Material 3	21 tons

Because of spoilage and the nature of the production process, any materials not used for current production are useless and must be discarded.

It is important to understand that we are maximizing profit contribution, not profit. Overhead and other shared costs must be deducted before arriving at a profit figure.

The accounting department analyzed the production figures, assigned all relevant costs, and arrived at prices for both products that will result in a profit contribution[1] of $40 for every ton of fuel additive produced and $30 for every ton of solvent base produced. Let us now use linear programming to determine the number of tons of fuel additive and the number of tons of solvent base to produce in order to maximize total profit contribution.

Problem Formulation

Problem formulation is the process of translating a verbal statement of a problem into a mathematical statement. The mathematical statement of the problem is referred to as a **mathematical model**. Developing an appropriate mathematical model is an art that can only be mastered with practice and experience. Even though every problem has at least some unique features, most problems also have many common or similar features. As a result, some general guidelines for developing a mathematical model can be helpful. We will illustrate these guidelines by developing a mathematical model for the RMC problem.

Understand the Problem Thoroughly The RMC problem is relatively easy to understand. RMC wants to determine how much of each product to produce in order to maximize the total contribution to profit. The number of tons available for the three materials that are required to produce the two products will limit the number of tons of each product that can be produced. More complex problems will require more work in order to understand the problem. However, understanding the problem thoroughly is the first step in developing any mathematical model.

Describe the Objective RMC's objective is to maximize the total contribution to profit.

Describe Each Constraint Three constraints limit the number of tons of fuel additive and the number of tons of solvent base that can be produced.

Constraint 1: The number of tons of material 1 used must be less than or equal to the 20 tons available.

Constraint 2: The number of tons of material 2 used must be less than or equal to the 5 tons available.

Constraint 3: The number of tons of material 3 used must be less than or equal to the 21 tons available.

---

[1]From an accounting perspective, profit contribution is more correctly described as the contribution margin per ton; overhead and other shared costs have not been allocated to the fuel additive and solvent base costs.

Define the Decision Variables The **decision variables** are the controllable inputs in the problem. For the RMC problem the two decision variables are (1) the number of tons of fuel additive produced, and (2) the number of tons of solvent base produced. In developing the mathematical model for the RMC problem, we will use the following notation for the decision variables:

$$F = \text{number of tons of fuel additive}$$
$$S = \text{number of tons of solvent base}$$

Write the Objective in Terms of the Decision Variables RMC's profit contribution comes from the production of F tons of fuel additive and S tons of solvent base. Because RMC makes \$40 for every ton of fuel additive produced and \$30 for every ton of solvent base produced, the company will make \$40F from the production of the fuel additive and \$30S from the production of the solvent base. Thus,

$$\text{Total profit contribution} = 40F + 30S$$

Because the objective—maximize total profit contribution—is a function of the decision variables F and S, we refer to $40F + 30S$ as the **objective function**. Using "Max" as an abbreviation for maximize, we can write RMC's objective as follows:

$$\text{Max } 40F + 30S \qquad\qquad \textbf{(7.1)}$$

Write the Constraints in Terms of the Decision Variables

Constraint 1:

$$\text{Tons of material 1 used} \leq \text{Tons of material 1 available}$$

Every ton of fuel additive that RMC produces will use 0.4 ton of material 1. Thus, 0.4F tons of material 1 is used to produce F tons of fuel additive. Similarly, every ton of solvent base that RMC produces will use 0.5 ton of material 1. Thus, 0.5S tons of material 1 is used to produce S tons of solvent base. Therefore, the number of tons of material 1 used to produce F tons of fuel additive and S tons of solvent base is

$$\text{Tons of material 1 used} = 0.4F + 0.5S$$

Because 20 tons of material 1 are available for use in production, the mathematical statement of constraint 1 is

$$0.4F + 0.5S \leq 20 \qquad\qquad \textbf{(7.2)}$$

Constraint 2:

$$\text{Tons of material 2 used} \leq \text{Tons of material 2 available}$$

Fuel additive does not use material 2. However, every ton of solvent base that RMC produces will use 0.2 ton of material 2. Thus, 0.2S tons of material 2 is used to produce S tons of solvent base. Therefore, the number of tons of material 2 used to produce F tons of fuel additive and S tons of solvent base is

$$\text{Tons of material 2 used} = 0.2S$$

Because 5 tons of material 2 are available for production, the mathematical statement of constraint 2 is

$$0.2S \leq 5 \qquad \textbf{(7.3)}$$

Constraint 3:

Tons of material 3 used $\leq$ Tons of material 3 available

Every ton of fuel additive RMC produces will use 0.6 ton of material 3. Thus, $0.6F$ tons of material 1 is used to produce F tons of fuel additive. Similarly, every ton of solvent base RMC produces will use 0.3 ton of material 3. Thus, $0.3S$ tons of material 1 is used to produce S tons of solvent base. Therefore, the number of tons of material 3 used to produce F tons of fuel additive and S tons of solvent base is

Tons of material 3 used $= 0.6F + 0.3S$

Because 21 tons of material 3 are available for production, the mathematical statement of constraint 3 is

$$0.6F + 0.3S \leq 21 \qquad \textbf{(7.4)}$$

Add the Nonnegativity Constraints   RMC cannot produce a negative number of tons of fuel additive or a negative number of tons of solvent base. Therefore, **nonnegativity constraints** must be added to prevent the decision variables F and S from having negative values. These nonnegativity constraints are

$$F \geq 0 \text{ and } S \geq 0$$

Nonnegativity constraints are a general feature of all linear programming problems and may be written in the abbreviated form:

$$F, S \geq 0 \qquad \textbf{(7.5)}$$

Mathematical Model for the RMC Problem

Problem formulation is now complete. We have succeeded in translating the verbal statement of the RMC problem into the following mathematical model:

$$\text{Max } 40F + 30S$$
$$\text{Subject to (s.t.)}$$
$$0.4F + 0.5S \leq 20 \quad \text{Material 1}$$
$$0.2S \leq 5 \quad \text{Material 2}$$
$$0.6F + 0.3S \leq 21 \quad \text{Material 3}$$
$$F, S \geq 0$$

Our job now is to find the product mix (i.e., the combination of F and S) that satisfies all the constraints and, at the same time, yields a maximum value for the objective function. Once these values of F and S are calculated, we will have found the optimal solution to the problem.

This mathematical model of the RMC problem is a **linear program**. The RMC problem has an objective and constraints that, as we said earlier, are common properties of all *linear* programs. But what is the special feature of this mathematical model that makes it a linear program? The special feature that makes it a linear program is that the objective function and all constraint functions (the left-hand sides of the constraint inequalities) are linear functions of the decision variables.

Mathematical functions in which each variable appears in a separate term and is raised to the first power are called **linear functions**. The objective function $(40F + 30S)$ is linear because each decision variable appears in a separate term and has an exponent of 1. The amount of material 1 used $(0.4F + 0.5S)$ is also a linear function of the decision variables for the same reason. Similarly, the functions on the left-hand side of the material 2 and material 3 constraint inequalities (the constraint functions) are also linear functions. Thus, the mathematical formulation is referred to as a linear program.

Try Problem 1 to test your ability to recognize the types of mathematical relationships that can be found in a linear program.

Linear *programming* has nothing to do with computer programming. The use of the word *programming* here means "choosing a course of action." Linear programming involves choosing a course of action when the mathematical model of the problem contains only linear functions.

NOTES AND COMMENTS

1. The three assumptions necessary for a linear programming model to be appropriate are proportionality, additivity, and divisibility. *Proportionality* means that the contribution to the objective function and the amount of resources used in each constraint are proportional to the value of each decision variable. *Additivity* means that the value of the objective function and the total resources used can be found by summing the objective function contribution and the resources used for all decision variables. *Divisibility* means that the decision variables are continuous. The divisibility assumption plus the nonnegativity constraints mean that decision variables can take on any value greater than or equal to zero.

2. Quantitative analysts formulate and solve a variety of mathematical models that contain an objective function and a set of constraints. Models of this type are referred to as *mathematical programming models*. Linear programming models are a special type of mathematical programming model in that the objective function and all constraint functions are linear.

7.2 Graphical Solution Procedure

A linear programming problem involving only two decision variables can be solved using a graphical solution procedure. Let us begin the graphical solution procedure by developing a graph that displays the possible solutions (F and S values) for the RMC problem. The graph in Figure 7.1 has values of F on the horizontal axis and values of S on the vertical axis. Any point on the graph can be identified by its F and S values, which indicate the position of the point along the horizontal and vertical axes, respectively. Thus, every point on the graph corresponds to a possible solution. The solution of $F = 0$ and $S = 0$ is referred to as the origin. Because both F and S must be nonnegative, the graph in Figure 7.1 only displays solutions where $F \geq 0$ and $S \geq 0$.

Earlier we determined that the inequality representing the material 1 constraint was

$$0.4F + 0.5S \leq 20$$

To show all solutions that satisfy this relationship, we start by graphing the line corresponding to the equation

$$0.4F + 0.5S = 20$$

FIGURE 7.1 GRAPH SHOWING TWO SOLUTIONS FOR THE TWO-VARIABLE RMC PROBLEM

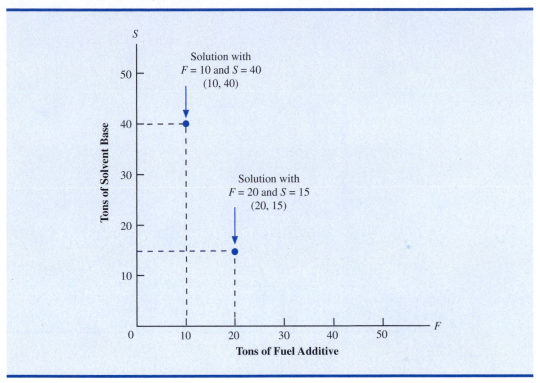

We graph this equation by identifying two points that satisfy this equation and then drawing a line through the points. Setting $F = 0$ and solving for S gives $0.5S = 20$, or $S = 40$; hence the solution ($F = 0$, $S = 40$) satisfies the preceding equation. To find a second solution satisfying this equation, we set $S = 0$ and solve for F. Doing so, we obtain $0.4F = 20$, or $F = 50$. Thus, a second solution satisfying the equation is ($F = 50$, $S = 0$). With these two points, we can now graph the line. This line, called the *material 1 constraint line,* is shown in Figure 7.2.

Recall that the inequality representing the material 1 constraint is

$$0.4F + 0.5S \leq 20$$

Can you identify all the solutions that satisfy this constraint? First, note that any point on the line $0.4F + 0.5S = 20$ must satisfy the constraint. But where are the solutions satisfying $0.4F + 0.5S < 20$? Consider two solutions ($F = 10$, $S = 10$) and ($F = 40$, $S = 30$). Figure 7.2 shows that the first solution is below the constraint line and the second solution is above the constraint line. Which of these solutions satisfies the material 1 constraint? For ($F = 10$, $S = 10$) we have

$$0.4F + 0.5S = 0.4(10) + 0.5(10) = 9$$

Because 9 tons is less than the 20 tons of material 1 available, the $F = 10$, $S = 10$ solution satisfies the constraint. For $F = 40$ and $S = 30$ we have

$$0.4F + 0.5S = 0.4(40) + 0.5(30) = 31$$

FIGURE 7.2   MATERIAL 1 CONSTRAINT LINE

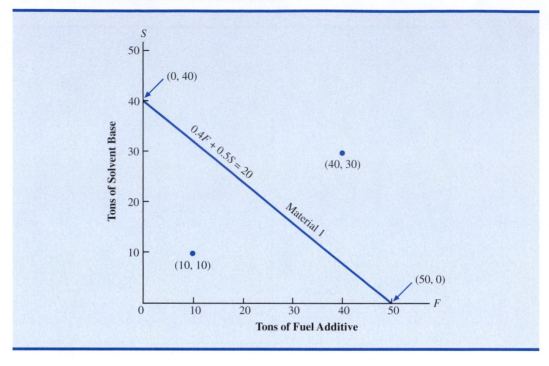

The 31 tons is greater than the 20 tons available, so the $F = 40$, $S = 30$ solution does not satisfy the constraint.

You should now be able to graph a constraint line and find the solution points that satisfy the constraint. Try Problem 2.

If a particular solution satisfies the constraint, all other solutions on the same side of the constraint line will also satisfy the constraint. If a particular solution does not satisfy the constraint, all other solutions on the same side of the constraint line will not satisfy the constraint. Thus, you need to evaluate only one solution to determine which side of a constraint line provides solutions that will satisfy the constraint. The shaded area in Figure 7.3 shows all the solutions that satisfy the material 1 constraint.

Next let us identify all solutions that satisfy the material 2 constraint:

$$0.2S \leq 5$$

We start by drawing the constraint line corresponding to the equation $0.2S = 5$. Because this equation is equivalent to the equation $S = 25$, we simply draw a line whose S value is 25 for every value of F; this line is parallel to and 25 units above the horizontal axis. Figure 7.4 shows the line corresponding to the material 2 constraint. Following the approach we used for the material 1 constraint, we realize that only solutions on or below the line will satisfy the material 2 constraint. Thus, in Figure 7.4 the shaded area corresponds to the solutions that satisfy the material 2 constraint.

Similarly, we can determine the solutions that satisfy the material 3 constraint. Figure 7.5 shows the result. For practice, try to graph the feasible solutions that satisfy the material 3 constraint and determine whether your result agrees with that shown in Figure 7.5.

We now have three separate graphs showing the solutions that satisfy each of the three constraints. In a linear programming problem, we need to identify the solutions that satisfy

FIGURE 7.3   SOLUTIONS THAT SATISFY THE MATERIAL 1 CONSTRAINT

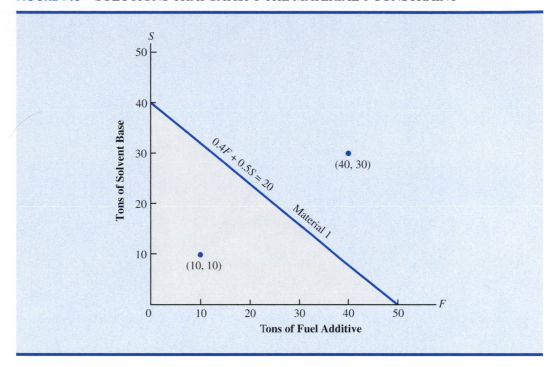

FIGURE 7.4   SOLUTIONS THAT SATISFY THE MATERIAL 2 CONSTRAINT

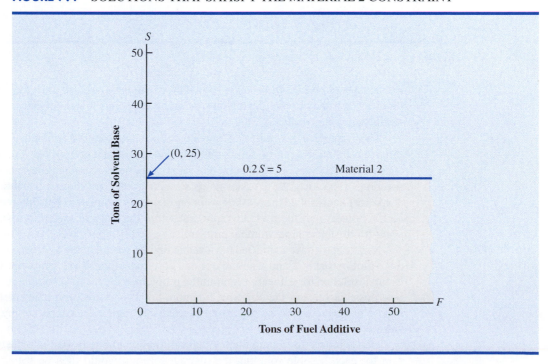

FIGURE 7.5   SOLUTIONS THAT SATISFY THE MATERIAL 3 CONSTRAINT

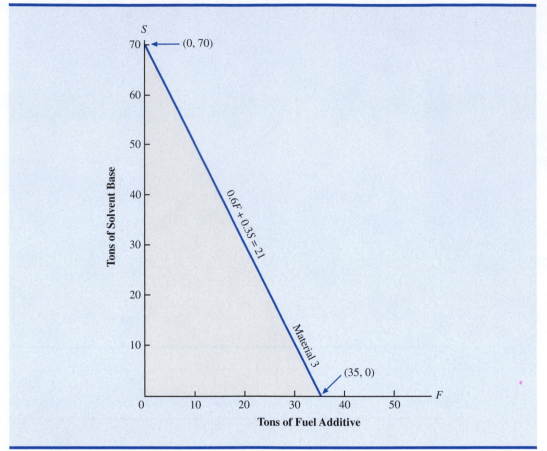

all the constraints *simultaneously.* To find these solutions, we can draw the three constraints on one graph and observe the region containing the points that do in fact satisfy all the constraints simultaneously.

The graphs in Figures 7.3, 7.4, and 7.5 can be superimposed to obtain one graph with all three constraints. Figure 7.6 shows this combined constraint graph. The shaded region in this figure includes every solution point that satisfies all the constraints simultaneously. Because solutions that satisfy all the constraints simultaneously are termed **feasible solutions**, the shaded region is called the *feasible solution region,* or simply the **feasible region**. Any point on the boundary of the feasible region, or within the feasible region, is a *feasible solution point* for the linear programming problem.

Can you now find the feasible region given several constraints? Try Problem 7.

Now that we have identified the feasible region, we are ready to proceed with the graphical solution method and find the optimal solution to the RMC problem. Recall that the optimal solution for a linear programming problem is the feasible solution that provides the best possible value of the objective function. Let us start the optimizing step of the graphical solution procedure by redrawing the feasible region on a separate graph. Figure 7.7 shows the graph.

One approach to finding the optimal solution would be to evaluate the objective function for each feasible solution; the optimal solution would then be the one yielding the

FIGURE 7.6 FEASIBLE REGION FOR THE RMC PROBLEM

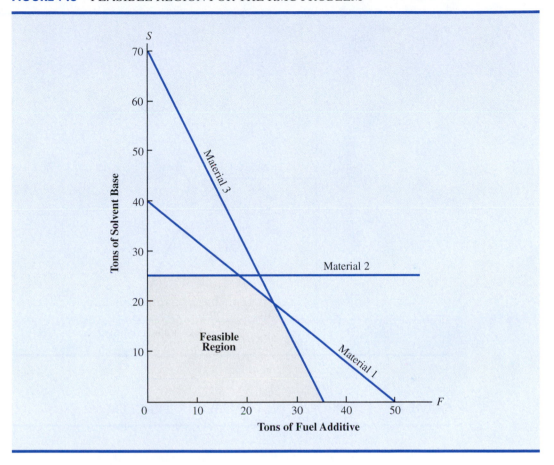

largest value. The difficulty with this approach is that the infinite number of feasible solutions makes evaluating all feasible solutions impossible. Hence, this trial-and-error procedure cannot be used to identify the optimal solution.

Rather than trying to compute the profit contribution for each feasible solution, we select an arbitrary value for profit contribution and identify all the feasible solutions that yield the selected value. For example, what feasible solutions provide a profit contribution of $240? These solutions are given by the values of F and S in the feasible region that will make the objective function

$$40F + 30S = 240$$

This expression is simply the equation of a line. Thus all feasible solutions (F, S) yielding a profit contribution of $240 must be on the line. We learned earlier in this section how to graph a constraint line. The procedure for graphing the profit or objective function line is the same. Letting $F = 0$, we see that S must be 8; thus the solution point $(F = 0, S = 8)$ is on the line. Similarly, by letting $S = 0$ we see that the solution point $(F = 6, S = 0)$ is also on the line. Drawing the line through these two points identifies all the solutions that have a profit contribution of $240. A graph of this profit line is presented in Figure 7.8. It shows that an infinite number of feasible production combinations will provide a $240 profit contribution.

FIGURE 7.7   FEASIBLE REGION FOR THE RMC PROBLEM

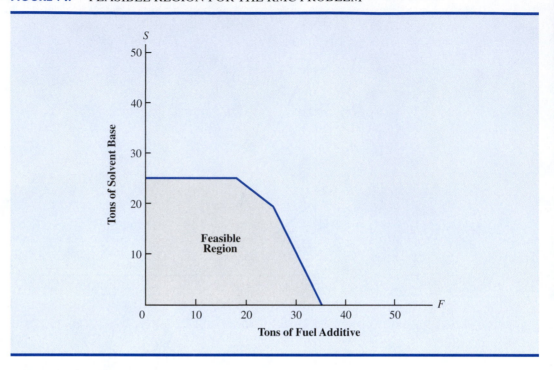

FIGURE 7.8 $240 PROFIT LINE FOR THE RMC PROBLEM

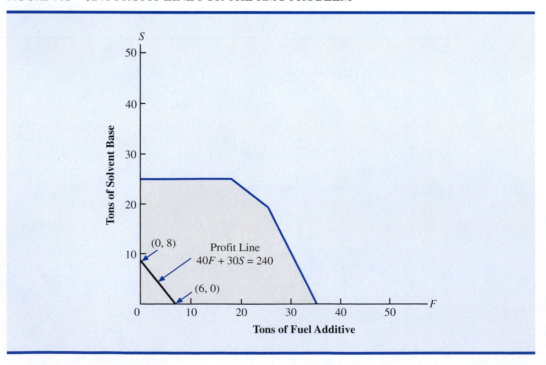

The objective is to find the feasible solution yielding the highest profit contribution, so we proceed by selecting higher profit contributions and finding the solutions that yield the stated values. For example, what solutions provide a profit contribution of $720? What solutions provide a profit contribution of $1200? To answer these questions, we must find the F and S values that are on the profit lines:

$$40F + 30S = 720 \text{ and } 40F + 30S = 1200$$

Using the previous procedure for graphing profit and constraint lines, we graphed the $720 and $1200 profit lines presented in Figure 7.9. Not all solution points on the $1200 profit line are in the feasible region, but at least some points on the line are; thus, we can obtain a feasible solution that provides a $1200 profit contribution.

Can we find a feasible solution yielding an even higher profit contribution? Look at Figure 7.9 and make some general observations about the profit lines. You should be able to identify the following properties: (1) the profit lines are *parallel* to each other, and (2) profit lines with higher profit contributions are farther from the origin.

Because the profit lines are parallel and higher profit lines are farther from the origin, we can obtain solutions that yield increasingly higher values for the objective function by continuing to move the profit line farther from the origin but keeping it parallel to the other profit lines. However, at some point any further outward movement will place the profit line entirely outside the feasible region. Because points outside the feasible region are unacceptable, the point in the feasible region that lies on the highest profit line is an optimal solution to the linear program.

You should now be able to identify the optimal solution point for the RMC problem. Use a ruler and move the profit line as far from the origin as you can. What is the last point in the feasible region? This point, which is the optimal solution, is shown graphically in Figure 7.10. The optimal values for the decision variables are the F and S values at this point.

FIGURE 7.9 SELECTED PROFIT LINES FOR THE RMC PROBLEM

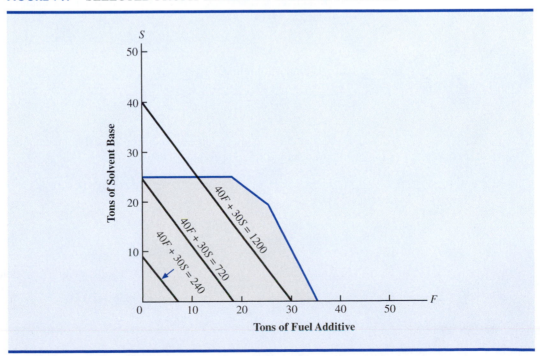

FIGURE 7.10   OPTIMAL SOLUTION FOR THE RMC PROBLEM

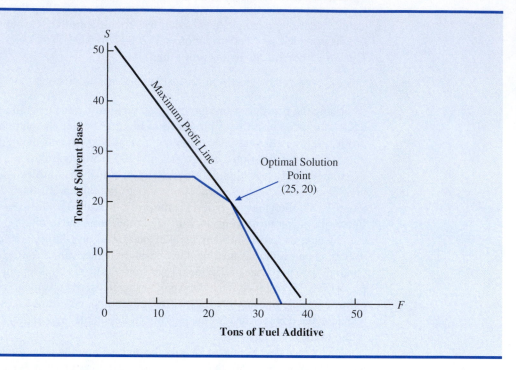

Depending on the accuracy of your graph, you may or may not be able to determine the exact optimal values of F and S directly from the graph. However, refer to Figure 7.6 and note that the optimal solution point for the RMC example is at the *intersection* of the material 1 and material 3 constraint lines. That is, the optimal solution is on both the material 1 constraint line,

$$0.4F + 0.5S = 20 \qquad \text{(7.6)}$$

and the material 3 constraint line,

$$0.6F + 0.3S = 21 \qquad \text{(7.7)}$$

Thus, the values of the decision variables F and S must satisfy both equations (7.6) and (7.7) simultaneously. Using (7.6) and solving for F gives

$$0.4F = 20 - 0.5S$$

or

$$F = 50 - 1.25S \qquad \text{(7.8)}$$

Substituting this expression for F into equation (7.7) and solving for S yields

$$0.6(50 - 1.25S) + 0.3S = 21$$
$$30 - 0.75S + 0.3S = 21$$
$$-0.45S = -9$$
$$S = 20$$

Substituting $S = 20$ in equation (7.8) and solving for F provides

$$F = 50 - 1.25(20)$$
$$= 50 - 25 = 25$$

Although the optimal solution to the RMC problem consists of integer values for the decision variables, this result will not always be the case.

Thus, the exact location of the optimal solution point is $F = 25$ and $S = 20$. This solution point provides the optimal production quantities for RMC at 25 tons of fuel additive and 20 tons of solvent base and yields a profit contribution of $40(25) + 30(20) = \$1600$.

For a linear programming problem with two decision variables, you can determine the exact values of the decision variables at the optimal solution by first using the graphical procedure to identify the optimal solution point and then solving the two simultaneous equations associated with this point.

A Note on Graphing Lines

An important aspect of the graphical method is the ability to graph lines showing the constraints and the objective function of the linear program. The procedure we used for graphing the equation of a line is to find any two points satisfying the equation and then draw the line through the two points. For the RMC constraints, the two points were easily found by setting $F = 0$ and solving the constraint equation for S. Then we set $S = 0$ and solved for F. For the material 1 constraint line

$$0.4F + 0.5S = 20$$

Try Problem 10 to test your ability to use the graphical solution procedure to identify the optimal solution and find the exact values of the decision variables at the optimal solution.

this procedure identified the two points $(F = 0, S = 40)$ and $(F = 50, S = 0)$. The material 1 constraint line was then graphed by drawing a line through these two points.

All constraints and objective function lines in two-variable linear programs can be graphed if two points on the line can be identified. However, finding the two points on the line is not always as easy as shown in the RMC problem. For example, suppose a company manufactures two models of a small hand-held computer: the Professional (P) and the Assistant (A). Management needs 50 units of the Professional model for its own salesforce, and expects sales of the remaining Professionals to be less than or equal to 50% of the sales of the Assistant. A constraint enforcing this requirement is

$$P - 50 \leq 0.5A$$

or

$$P - 0.5A \leq 50$$

Using the equality form of the constraint and setting $P = 0$, we find the point ($P = 0, A = -100$) is on the constraint line. Setting $A = 0$, we find a second point ($P = 50, A = 0$) on the constraint line. If we have drawn only the nonnegative ($P \geq 0, A \geq 0$) portion of the graph, the first point ($P = 0, A = -100$) cannot be plotted because $A = -100$ is not on the graph. Whenever we have two points on the line, but one or both of the points cannot be plotted in the nonnegative portion of the graph, the simplest approach is to enlarge the graph. In this example, the point ($P = 0, A = -100$) can be plotted by extending the graph to include the negative A axis. Once both points satisfying the constraint equation have been located, the line can be drawn. The constraint line and the solutions that satisfy the constraint $P - 0.5A \leq 50$ are shown in Figure 7.11.

FIGURE 7.11 SOLUTIONS THAT SATISFY THE CONSTRAINT $P - 0.5A \leq 50$

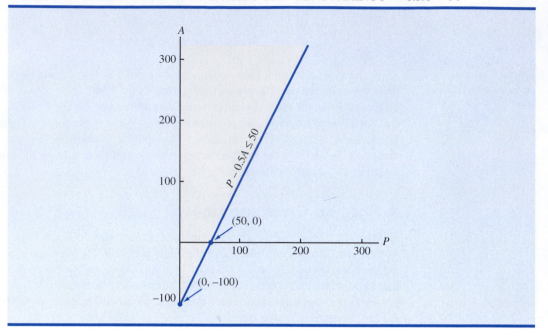

As another example, consider a problem involving two decision variables, R and T. Suppose that the number of units of R produced has to be at least equal to the number of units of T produced. A constraint enforcing this requirement is

$$R \geq T$$

or

$$R - T \geq 0$$

Can you graph a constraint line when the origin is on the constraint line? Try Problem 5.

To find all solutions satisfying the constraint as an equality, we first set $R = 0$ and solve for T. This result shows that the origin ($T = 0, R = 0$) is on the constraint line. Setting $T = 0$ and solving for R provides the same point. However, we can obtain a second point on the line by setting T equal to any value other than zero and then solving for R. For instance, setting $T = 100$ and solving for R, we find that the point ($T = 100, R = 100$) is on the line. With the two points ($R = 0, T = 0$) and ($R = 100, T = 100$), the constraint line $R - T = 0$ and the solutions that satisfy the constraint $R - T \geq 0$ can be plotted as shown in Figure 7.12.

Summary of the Graphical Solution Procedure for Maximization Problems

For additional practice in using the graphical solution procedure, try Problem 24.

As we have seen, the graphical solution procedure is a method for solving two-variable linear programming problems such as the RMC problem. The steps of the graphical solution procedure for a maximization problem are summarized here:

1. Prepare a graph for each constraint that shows the solutions that satisfy the constraint.
2. Determine the feasible region by identifying the solutions that satisfy all the constraints simultaneously.

FIGURE 7.12 FEASIBLE SOLUTIONS FOR THE CONSTRAINT $R - T \geq 0$

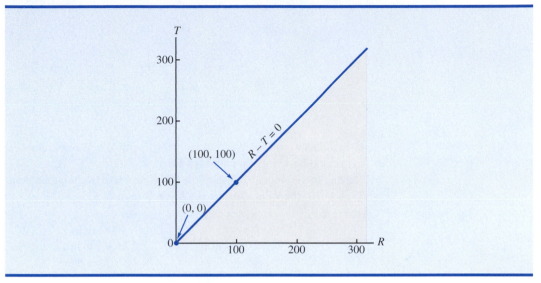

3. Draw an objective function line showing the values of the decision variables that yield a specified value of the objective function.
4. Move parallel objective function lines toward larger objective function values until further movement would take the line completely outside the feasible region.
5. Any feasible solution on the objective function line with the largest value is an optimal solution.

Slack Variables

In addition to the optimal solution and its associated profit contribution, the RMC managers will want information about the production requirements for the three materials. We can determine this information by substituting the optimal solution values ($F = 25$, $S = 20$) into the constraints of the linear program.

Constraint	Tons Required for $F = 25$, $S = 20$ Tons	Tons Available	Unused Tons
Material 1	$0.4(25) + 0.5(20) = 20$	20	0
Material 2	$0.2(20) = 4$	5	1
Material 3	$0.6(25) + 0.3(20) = 21$	21	0

Thus, the optimal solution tells management that the production of 25 tons of fuel additive and 20 tons of solvent base will require all available material 1 and material 3 but only 4 of the 5 tons of material 2. The 1 ton of unused material 2 is referred to as *slack*. In linear programming terminology, any unused or idle capacity for a $\leq$ constraint is referred to as the *slack associated with the constraint.* Thus, the material 2 constraint has a slack of 1 ton.

Can you identify the slack associated with a constraint? Try Problem 24, part (e).

Often variables, called **slack variables**, are added to the formulation of a linear programming problem to represent the slack, or unused capacity, associated with a constraint. Unused capacity makes no contribution to profit, so slack variables have coefficients of zero in the objective function. More generally, slack variables represent the difference between the right-hand side and the left-hand side of a $\leq$ constraint. After the addition of three slack variables, denoted S_1, S_2, and S_3, the mathematical model of the RMC problem becomes

$$\text{Max} \quad 40F + 30S + 0S_1 + 0S_2 + 0S_3$$
$$\text{s.t.}$$
$$0.4F + 0.5S + 1S_1 \qquad\qquad = 20$$
$$0.2S \qquad + 1S_2 \qquad = 5$$
$$0.6F + 0.3S \qquad\qquad + 1S_3 = 21$$
$$F, S, S_1, S_2, S_3 \geq 0$$

Can you write a linear program in standard form? Try Problem 18.

Whenever a linear program is written in a form with all the constraints expressed as equalities, it is said to be written in **standard form**.

Referring to the standard form of the RMC problem, we see that at the optimal solution ($F = 25$, $S = 20$) the values for the slack variables are

Constraint	Value of Slack Variable
Material 1	$S_1 = 0$
Material 2	$S_2 = 1$
Material 3	$S_3 = 0$

Could we have used the graphical analysis to provide some of the previous information? The answer is yes. By finding the optimal solution in Figure 7.6, we see that the material 1 constraint and the material 3 constraint restrict, or *bind,* the feasible region at this point. Thus, the optimal solution requires the use of all of these two resources. In other words, the graph shows that at the optimal solution material 1 and material 3 will have zero slack. But, because the material 2 constraint is not binding the feasible region at the optimal solution, we can expect some slack for this resource.

Recognizing redundant constraints is easy with the graphical solution method. In problems with more than two decision variables, however, redundant constraints usually will not be apparent.

Finally, some linear programs may have one or more constraints that do not affect the feasible region; that is, the feasible region remains the same whether or not the constraint is included in the problem. Because such a constraint does not affect the feasible region and thus cannot affect the optimal solution, it is called a **redundant constraint**. Redundant constraints can be dropped from the problem without having any effect on the optimal solution. However, in most linear programming problems redundant constraints are not discarded because they are not immediately recognizable as being redundant. The RMC problem had no redundant constraints because each constraint had an effect on the feasible region.

NOTES AND COMMENTS

1. In the standard form representation of a linear program, the objective function coefficients for the slack variables are zero. This condition implies that slack variables, which represent unused resources, do not affect the value of the objective function. However, in some applications, some or all of the unused resources can be sold and contribute to profit. In such cases the corresponding slack variables become decision variables representing the amount of resources to be sold. For each of these variables, a nonzero coefficient in the objective function would reflect the profit associated with selling a unit of the corresponding resource.

2. Redundant constraints do not affect the feasible region; as a result they can be removed from a linear programming model without affecting the optimal solution. However, if the linear programming model is to be resolved later, changes in some of the data might change a previously redundant constraint into a binding constraint. Thus, we recommend keeping all constraints in the linear programming model even though one or more of the constraints may be redundant.

7.3 Extreme Points and the Optimal Solution

Suppose that the profit contribution for 1 ton of solvent base increases from \$30 to \$60 while the profit contribution for 1 ton of fuel additive and all the constraints remain unchanged. The complete linear programming model of this new problem is identical to the mathematical model in Section 7.2, except for the revised objective function:

$$\text{Max } 40F + 60S$$

How does this change in the objective function affect the optimal solution to the RMC problem? Figure 7.13 shows the graphical solution of the RMC problem with the revised objective function. Note that because the constraints do not change, the feasible region remains unchanged. However, the profit lines must be altered to reflect the new objective function.

By moving the profit line in a parallel manner away from the origin, we find the optimal solution as shown in Figure 7.13. The values of the decision variables at this point are $F = 18.75$ and $S = 25$. The increased profit for the solvent base caused a change in the optimal solution. In fact, as you might suspect, we cut back the production of the lower profit fuel additive and increase the production of the higher profit solvent base.

What do you notice about the location of the optimal solutions in the linear programming problems that we solved thus far? Look closely at the graphical solutions in Figures 7.10 and 7.13. An important observation that you should be able to make is that the optimal solutions occur at one of the vertices, or "corners," of the feasible region. In linear programming terminology these vertices are referred to as the **extreme points** of the feasible

FIGURE 7.13   OPTIMAL SOLUTION FOR THE RMC PROBLEM WITH AN OBJECTIVE FUNCTION OF $40F + 60S$

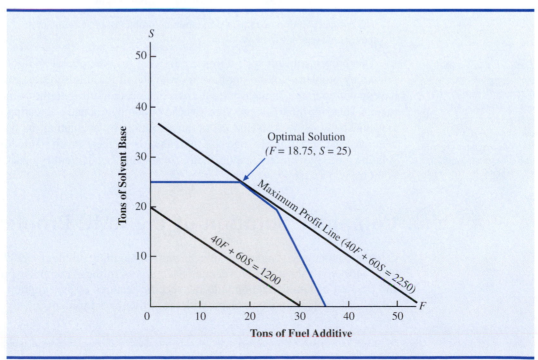

FIGURE 7.14   THE FIVE EXTREME POINTS OF THE FEASIBLE REGION FOR THE RMC PROBLEM

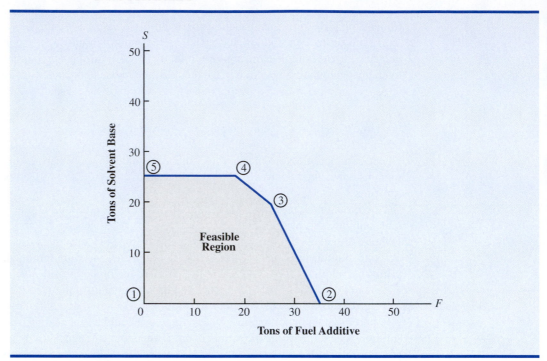

region. Thus, the RMC has five vertices or five extreme points (Figure 7.14). We can now state our observation about the location of optimal solutions:[2]

> The optimal solution to a linear programming problem can be found at an extreme point of the feasible region for the problem.

For additional practice in identifying the extreme points of the feasible region and determining the optimal solution by computing and comparing the objective function value at each extreme point, try Problem 13.

This property means that, if you are looking for the optimal solution to a linear programming problem, you do not have to evaluate all feasible solution points. In fact, you have to consider *only* the feasible solutions that occur at the extreme points of the feasible region. Thus, for the RMC problem, instead of computing and comparing the profit for all feasible solutions, we can find the optimal solution by evaluating the five extreme-point solutions and selecting the one that provides the highest profit. Actually, the graphical solution procedure is nothing more than a convenient way of identifying an optimal extreme point for two-variable problems.

 7.4   # Computer Solution of the RMC Problem

Computer programs designed to solve linear programming problems are now widely available. Most companies and universities have access to these computer programs. After a short period of familiarization with the specific features of the program, most users can solve linear programming problems with few difficulties. Problems involving thousands of

---

[2]In Section 7.6 we show that two special cases (infeasibility and unboundedness) in linear programming have no optimal solution. The observation stated does not apply to these cases.

In January 1952 the first successful computer solution of a linear programming problem was performed on the SEAC (Standards Eastern Automatic Computer). The SEAC, the first digital computer built by the National Bureau of Standards under U.S. Air Force sponsorship, had a 512-word memory and magnetic tape for external storage.

Instructions on how to solve linear programs using The Management Scientist, LINGO, and Excel are provided in appendixes at the end of the chapter.

variables and thousands of constraints are now routinely solved with computer packages. Some of the leading commercial packages include CPLEX, LINGO, MOSEK, Premium Solver for Excel, and Xpress-MP. Packages are also available for free download. A good example is Clp (COIN-OR linear programming) available from the COIN-OR organization at *http://www.coin-or.org*.

As a result of the recent explosion of software for personal computers, a large number of user-friendly computer programs that can solve linear programs are now available. These programs, developed by academicians and small software companies, are almost all easy to use. Most of these programs are designed to solve smaller linear programs (a few hundred variables), but some can be used to solve problems involving thousands of variables and constraints. Linear programming solvers are now part of many spreadsheet packages. In Appendix 7.3 we show how to use the solver available with Excel.

The Management Scientist, a software package developed by the authors of this text, contains a linear programming module. Let us demonstrate its use by solving the RMC problem. The linear program is as follows:

$$\text{Max} \quad 40F + 30S$$
$$\text{s.t.}$$
$$0.4F + 0.5S \leq 20 \quad \text{Material 1}$$
$$0.2S \leq 5 \quad \text{Material 2}$$
$$0.6F + 0.3S \leq 21 \quad \text{Material 3}$$
$$F, S \geq 0$$

The solution[3] generated by The Management Scientist is shown in Figure 7.15.

Interpretation of Computer Output

Let us look more closely at The Management Scientist output in Figure 7.15 and interpret the computer solution provided for the RMC problem. First, note that the number 1600.000, which appears to the right of objective function value, indicates that the optimal solution to this problem will provide a profit of $1600. Directly below the objective function value are the values of the decision variables at the optimal solution. Thus, we have $F = 25$ tons of fuel additive and $S = 20$ tons of solvent base as the optimal production quantities.

The information in the Reduced Costs column indicates how much the objective function coefficient of each decision variable would have to improve[4] before it would be possible for that variable to assume a positive value in the optimal solution. If a decision variable is already positive in the optimal solution, its reduced cost is zero. For the RMC problem, the optimal solution is $F = 25$ and $S = 20$. Both decision variables already have positive values, so their corresponding reduced costs are zero. In Chapter 8 we interpret the reduced cost for a decision variable that does not have a positive value in the optimal solution.

Immediately following the optimal F and S values and the reduced cost information, the computer output provides information about the status of the constraints. Recall that the RMC problem had three less-than-or-equal-to constraints corresponding to the tons available for each of the three raw materials. The information shown in the Slack/Surplus

---

[3]The steps required to generate this solution are described in Appendix 7.1.
[4]For a maximization problem, *improve* means get bigger; for a minimization problem, *improve* means get smaller.

FIGURE 7.15   THE MANAGEMENT SCIENTIST SOLUTION FOR THE RMC PROBLEM

RMC

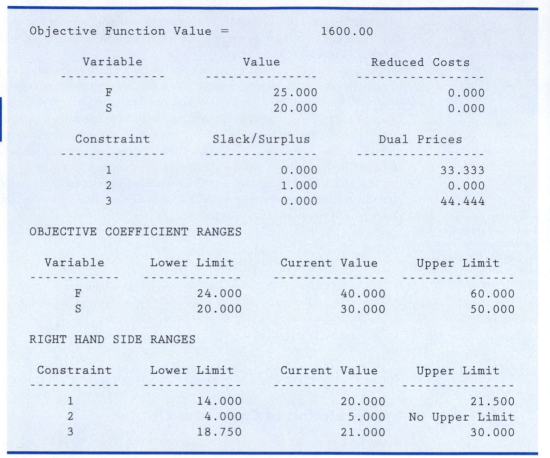

```
Objective Function Value =                  1600.00

            Variable              Value             Reduced Costs
          -------------      ---------------      -----------------
               F                 25.000                 0.000
               S                 20.000                 0.000

           Constraint        Slack/Surplus           Dual Prices
          -------------      ---------------      -----------------
               1                  0.000                33.333
               2                  1.000                 0.000
               3                  0.000                44.444

OBJECTIVE COEFFICIENT RANGES

       Variable      Lower Limit      Current Value      Upper Limit
     ------------    -------------    ---------------    -------------
         F             24.000            40.000             60.000
         S             20.000            30.000             50.000

RIGHT HAND SIDE RANGES

      Constraint      Lower Limit      Current Value      Upper Limit
     ------------    -------------    ---------------    ---------------
          1            14.000            20.000              21.500
          2             4.000             5.000         No Upper Limit
          3            18.750            21.000              30.000
```

column provides the value of the slack variable for each of the three constraints. This information is summarized as follows:

Constraint Number	Constraint Name	Value of Slack Variable
1	Material 1	0
2	Material 2	1
3	Material 3	0

Thus, we see that the binding constraints (the material 1 and material 3 constraints) have zero slack at the optimal solution. The material 2 constraint has 1 ton of slack, or unused capacity.

The rest of the output in Figure 7.15 can be used to determine how a change in a coefficient of the objective function or a change in the right-hand-side value of a constraint will affect the optimal solution. We will discuss the use of this information in Chapter 8 when we study the topic of sensitivity analysis.

NOTES AND COMMENTS

Linear programming solvers are now a standard feature of most spreadsheet packages. Excel, Lotus 1-2-3, and Quattro Pro all come with built-in solvers capable of solving optimization problems, including linear programs. The solver in each of these spreadsheet packages was developed by Frontline Systems and provides a similar user interface. In Appendix 7.3 we show how spreadsheets can be used to solve linear programs by solving the RMC problem using Excel.

 7.5 # A Simple Minimization Problem

M&D Chemicals produces two products that are sold as raw materials to companies manufacturing bath soaps and laundry detergents. Based on an analysis of current inventory levels and potential demand for the coming month, M&D's management has specified that the combined production for products A and B must total at least 350 gallons. Separately, a major customer's order for 125 gallons of product A must also be satisfied. Product A requires 2 hours of processing time per gallon while product B requires 1 hour of processing time per gallon, and for the coming month, 600 hours of processing time are available. M&D's objective is to satisfy these requirements at a minimum total production cost. Production costs are $2 per gallon for product A and $3 per gallon for product B.

To find the minimum-cost production schedule, we will formulate the M&D Chemicals problem as a linear program. Following a procedure similar to the one used for the RMC problem, we first define the decision variables and the objective function for the problem. Let

$$A = \text{number of gallons of product A}$$
$$B = \text{number of gallons of product B}$$

Because the production costs are $2 per gallon for product A and $3 per gallon for product B, the objective function that corresponds to the minimization of the total production cost can be written as

$$\text{Min } 2A + 3B$$

Next, consider the constraints placed on the M&D Chemicals problem. To satisfy the major customer's demand for 125 gallons of product A, we know A must be at least 125. Thus, we write the constraint

$$1A \geq 125$$

Because the combined production for both products must total at least 350 gallons, we can write the constraint

$$1A + 1B \geq 350$$

Finally, the limitation on available processing time of 600 hours means that we need to add the constraint

$$2A + 1B \leq 600$$

After adding the nonnegativity constraints $(A, B \geq 0)$, we have the following linear program for the M&D Chemicals problem:

$$\text{Max} \quad 2A + 3B$$

$$\text{s.t.}$$

$$
\begin{array}{llll}
1A & & \geq 125 & \text{Demand for product A} \\
1A & + 1B & \geq 350 & \text{Total production} \\
2A & + 1B & \leq 600 & \text{Processing time} \\
& A, B & \geq 0 &
\end{array}
$$

Because the linear programming model has only two decision variables, the graphical solution procedure can be used to find the optimal production quantities. The graphical method for this problem, just as in the RMC problem, requires us to first graph the constraint lines to find the feasible region. By graphing each constraint line separately and then checking points on either side of the constraint line, the solutions that satisfy each constraint can be identified. By combining the solutions that satisfy each constraint on the same graph, we obtain the feasible region shown in Figure 7.16.

To find the minimum-cost solution, we now draw the objective function line corresponding to a particular total cost value. For example, we might start by drawing the line $2A + 3B = 1200$. This line is shown in Figure 7.17. Clearly some points in the feasible region would provide a total cost of \$1200. To find the values of A and B that provide smaller

FIGURE 7.16   FEASIBLE REGION FOR THE M&D CHEMICALS PROBLEM

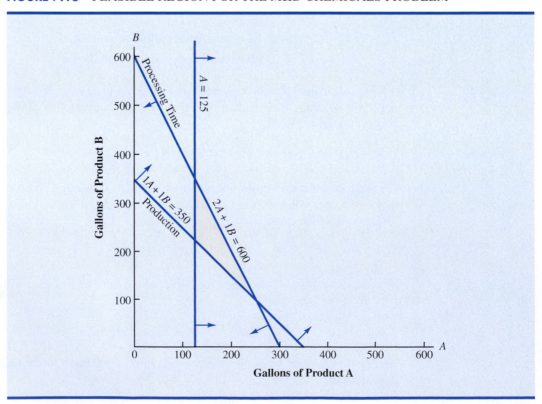

FIGURE 7.17   GRAPHICAL SOLUTION FOR THE M&D CHEMICALS PROBLEM

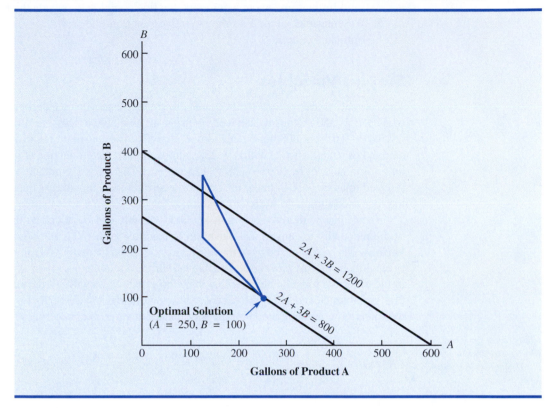

total cost values, we move the objective function line in a lower left direction until, if we moved it any farther, it would be entirely outside the feasible region. Note that the objective function line $2A + 3B = 800$ intersects the feasible region at the extreme point $A = 250$ and $B = 100$. This extreme point provides the minimum-cost solution with an objective function value of 800. From Figures 7.16 and 7.17, we can see that the total production constraint and the processing time constraint are binding. Just as in every linear programming problem, the optimal solution occurs at an extreme point of the feasible region.

Summary of the Graphical Solution Procedure for Minimization Problems

Can you use the graphical solution procedure to determine the optimal solution for a minimization problem? Try Problem 31.

The steps of the graphical solution procedure for a minimization problem are summarized here:

1. Prepare a graph for each constraint that shows the solutions that satisfy the constraint.
2. Determine the feasible region by identifying the solutions that satisfy all the constraints simultaneously.
3. Draw an objective function line showing the values of the decision variables that yield a specified value of the objective function.

4. Move parallel objective function lines toward smaller objective function values until further movement would take the line completely outside the feasible region.
5. Any feasible solution on the objective function line with the smallest value is an optimal solution.

Surplus Variables

The optimal solution to the M&D Chemicals problem shows that the desired total production of $A + B = 350$ gallons is achieved by using all available processing time of $2A + 1B = 2(250) + 1(100) = 600$ hours. In addition, note that the constraint requiring that product A demand be met is satisfied with $A = 250$ gallons. In fact, the production of product A exceeds its minimum level by $250 - 125 = 125$ gallons. This excess production for product A is referred to as *surplus*. In linear programming terminology, any excess quantity corresponding to a $\geq$ constraint is referred to as surplus.

Recall that with a $\leq$ constraint, a slack variable can be added to the left-hand side of the inequality to convert the constraint to equality form. With a $\geq$ constraint, a **surplus variable** can be subtracted from the left-hand side of the inequality to convert the constraint to equality form. Just as with slack variables, surplus variables are given a coefficient of zero in the objective function because they have no effect on its value. After including two surplus variables, S_1 and S_2, for the $\geq$ constraints and one slack variable, S_3, for the $\leq$ constraint, the linear programming model of the M&D Chemicals problem becomes

Try Problem 35 to test your ability to use slack and surplus variables to write a linear program in standard form.

$$
\begin{aligned}
\text{Min} \quad & 2A + 3B + 0S_1 + 0S_2 + 0S_3 \\
\text{s.t.} \quad & \\
& 1A \qquad\quad - 1S_1 \qquad\qquad = 125 \\
& 1A + 1B \qquad - 1S_2 \qquad = 350 \\
& 2A + 1B \qquad\qquad + 1S_3 = 600 \\
& A, B, S_1, S_2, S_3 \geq 0
\end{aligned}
$$

All the constraints are now equalities. Hence, the preceding formulation is the standard form representation of the M&D Chemicals problem. At the optimal solution of $A = 250$ and $B = 100$, the values of the surplus and slack variables are as follows:

Constraint	Value of Surplus or Slack Variable
Demand for product A	$S_1 = 125$
Total production	$S_2 = 0$
Processing time	$S_3 = 0$

Refer to Figures 7.16 and 7.17. Note that the zero surplus and slack variables are associated with the constraints that are binding at the optimal solution—that is, the total production and processing time constraints. The surplus of 125 units is associated with the nonbinding constraint on the demand for product A.

In the RMC problem all the constraints were of the $\leq$ type, and in the M&D Chemicals problem the constraints were a mixture of $\geq$ and $\leq$ types. The number and types of constraints encountered in a particular linear programming problem depend on the specific

Try Problem 34 to practice solving a linear program with all three constraint forms.

conditions existing in the problem. Linear programming problems may have some $\leq$ constraints, some $\geq$ constraints, and some $=$ constraints. For an equality constraint, feasible solutions must lie directly on the constraint line.

An example of a linear program with two decision variables, G and H, and all three constraint forms is given here:

$$\text{Min} \quad 2G + 2H$$
$$\text{s.t.}$$
$$1G + 3H \leq 12$$
$$3G + 1H \geq 13$$
$$1G - 1H = 3$$
$$G, H \geq 0$$

The standard-form representation of this problem is

$$\text{Min} \quad 2G + 2H + 0S_1 + 0S_2$$
$$\text{s.t.}$$
$$1G + 3H + 1S_1 \qquad\quad = 12$$
$$3G + 1H \qquad\quad - 1S_2 = 13$$
$$1G - 1H \qquad\qquad\qquad = 3$$
$$G, H, S_1, S_2 \geq 0$$

The standard form requires a slack variable for the $\leq$ constraint and a surplus variable for the $\geq$ constraint. However, neither a slack nor a surplus variable is required for the third constraint because it is already in equality form.

When solving linear programs graphically, it is not necessary to write the problem in its standard form. Nevertheless, it is helpful to be able to compute the values of the slack and surplus variables and understand what they mean. A final point: The standard form of the linear programming problem is equivalent to the original formulation of the problem. That is, the optimal solution to any linear programming problem is the same as the optimal solution to the standard form of the problem. The standard form does not change the basic problem; it only changes how we write the constraints for the problem.

Computer Solution of the M&D Chemicals Problem

The solution obtained using The Management Scientist is presented in Figure 7.18. The computer output shows that the minimum-cost solution yields an objective function value of $800. The values of the decision variables show that 250 gallons of product A and 100 gallons of product B provide the minimum-cost solution.

The Slack/Surplus column shows that the $\geq$ constraint corresponding to the demand for product A (see constraint 1) has a surplus of 125 units. This column tells us that production of product A in the optimal solution exceeds demand by 125 gallons. The Slack/Surplus values are zero for the total production requirement (constraint 2) and the processing time limitation (constraint 3), which indicates that these constraints are binding at the optimal solution. We will discuss the rest of the computer output in Figure 7.18 in Chapter 8 when we study the topic of sensitivity analysis.

FIGURE 7.18   THE MANAGEMENT SCIENTIST SOLUTION FOR THE M&D
CHEMICALS PROBLEM

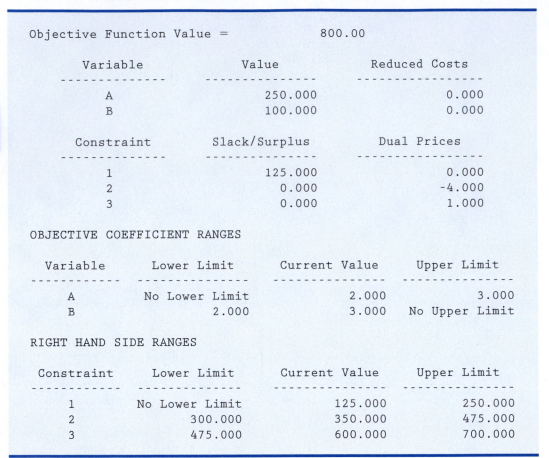

```
Objective Function Value =              800.00

        Variable              Value              Reduced Costs
     -------------      ---------------        -----------------
           A                 250.000                  0.000
           B                 100.000                  0.000

       Constraint         Slack/Surplus          Dual Prices
     -------------      ---------------        -----------------
           1                 125.000                  0.000
           2                   0.000                 -4.000
           3                   0.000                  1.000


OBJECTIVE COEFFICIENT RANGES

    Variable        Lower Limit       Current Value      Upper Limit
  ------------    ---------------    ---------------    ---------------
       A          No Lower Limit          2.000              3.000
       B               2.000              3.000         No Upper Limit


RIGHT HAND SIDE RANGES

  Constraint       Lower Limit       Current Value      Upper Limit
  ------------    ---------------    ---------------    ---------------
       1          No Lower Limit         125.000            250.000
       2               300.000           350.000            475.000
       3               475.000           600.000            700.000
```

7.6   Special Cases

In this section we discuss three special situations that can arise when we attempt to solve linear programming problems.

Alternative Optimal Solutions

From our discussion of the graphical solution procedure, we know that optimal solutions can be found at the extreme points of the feasible region. Now let us consider the special case where the optimal objective function line coincides with one of the binding constraint lines. It can lead to **alternative optimal solutions**, whereby more than one solution provides the optimal value for the objective function.

    To illustrate the case of alternative optimal solutions, we return to the RMC problem. However, let us assume that the profit contribution for the solvent base (S) has increased to $50. The revised objective function is $40F + 50S$. Figure 7.19 shows the graphical solution to this problem. Note that the optimal solution still occurs at an extreme point. In fact, it occurs at two extreme points: extreme point ③ ($F = 25, S = 20$) and extreme point ④ ($F = 18.75, S = 25$).

FIGURE 7.19   OPTIMAL SOLUTIONS FOR THE RMC PROBLEM WITH AN OBJECTIVE
FUNCTION OF $40F + 50S$

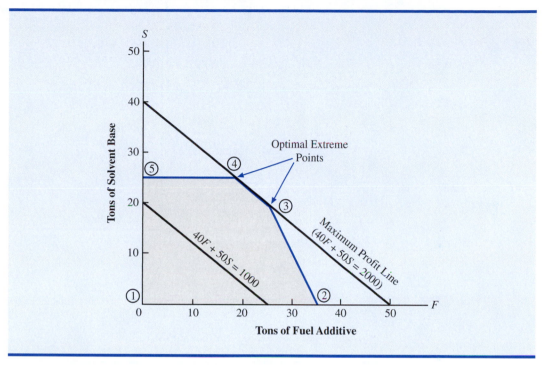

The objective function values at these two extreme points are identical; that is,

$$40F + 50S = 40(25) + 50(20) = 2000$$

and

$$40F + 50S = 40(18.75) + 50(25) = 2000$$

Furthermore, any point on the line connecting the two optimal extreme points also provides an optimal solution. For example, the solution point ($F = 21.875$, $S = 22.5$), which is halfway between the two extreme points, also provides the optimal objective function value of

$$40F + 50S = 40(21.875) + 50(22.5) = 2000$$

A linear programming problem with alternative optimal solutions is generally a good situation for the manager or decision maker. It means that several combinations of the decision variables are optimal and that the manager can select the most desirable optimal solution. Unfortunately, determining whether a problem has alternative optimal solutions is not a simple matter.

Infeasibility

Infeasibility means that no solution to the linear programming problem satisfies all constraints, including the nonnegativity constraints. Graphically, infeasibility means that a feasible region does not exist; that is, no points satisfy all constraint equations and

FIGURE 7.20   NO FEASIBLE REGION FOR THE RMC PROBLEM WITH MINIMUM
PRODUCTION REQUIREMENTS

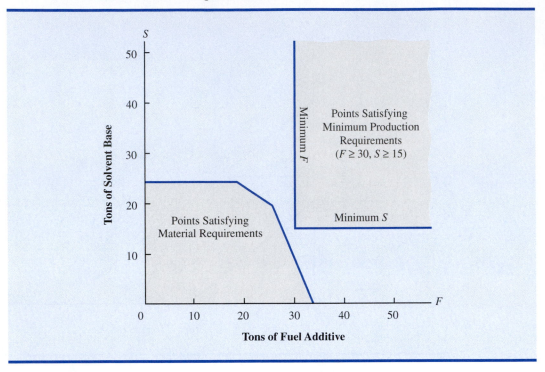

nonnegativity conditions simultaneously. To illustrate this situation, let us return to the
problem facing RMC.

Problems with no feasible solution do arise in practice, most often because management's expectations are too high or because too many restrictions have been placed on the problem.

Suppose that management specified that at least 30 tons of fuel additive and at least
15 tons of solvent base must be produced. Figure 7.20 shows the graph of the solution region that reflects these requirements. The shaded area in the lower left-hand portion of the
graph depicts those points satisfying the less-than-or-equal-to constraints on the amount of
materials available. The shaded area in the upper right-hand portion depicts those points
satisfying the minimum production requirements of 30 tons of fuel additive and 15 tons of
solvent base. But none of the points satisfy both sets of constraints. Thus, if management
imposes these minimum production requirements, no feasible solution to the linear programming problem is possible.

How should we interpret this infeasibility in terms of the current problem? First, we
should tell management that, for the available amounts of the three materials, producing
30 tons of fuel additive and 15 tons of solvent base isn't possible. Moreover, we can tell
management exactly how much more of each material is needed.

Material	Minimum Tons Required for $F = 30, S = 15$	Tons Available	Additional Tons Required
Material 1	$0.4(30) + 0.5(15) = 19.5$	20	—
Material 2	$0.2(15) = 3$	5	—
Material 3	$0.6(30) + 0.3(15) = 22.5$	21	1.5

Thus, RMC has a sufficient supply of materials 1 and 2 but will need 1.5 additional tons of material 3 to meet management's production requirements of 30 tons of fuel additive and 15 tons of solvent base. If, after reviewing the preceding analysis, management still wants this level of production for the two products, RMC will have to obtain the additional 1.5 tons of material 3.

Often, many possibilities are available for corrective management action, once we discover the lack of a feasible solution. The important thing to realize is that linear programming analysis can help determine whether management's plans are feasible. By analyzing the problem using linear programming, we are often able to point out infeasible conditions and initiate corrective action.

Whenever you attempt to solve a problem that is infeasible using The Management Scientist, you will obtain a message that says "No Feasible Solution." In this case, you know that no solution to the linear programming problem will satisfy all constraints. Careful inspection of your formulation is necessary to identify why the problem is infeasible. In some situations the only reasonable approach is to drop one or more constraints and resolve the problem. If you are able to find an optimal solution for this revised problem, you will know that the constraint(s) that were omitted are causing the problem to be infeasible.

Unbounded

The solution to a maximization linear programming problem is **unbounded** if the value of the solution may be made infinitely large without violating any of the constraints; for a minimization problem, the solution is unbounded if the value may be made infinitely small. This condition might be termed *managerial utopia;* for example, if this condition were to occur in a profit maximization problem, the manager could achieve an unlimited profit.

However, in linear programming models of real problems, the occurrence of an unbounded solution means that the problem has been improperly formulated. We know it is not possible to increase profits indefinitely. Therefore, we must conclude that if a profit maximization problem results in an unbounded solution, the mathematical model doesn't represent the real-world problem sufficiently. Usually, an unbounded problem results from the inadvertent omission of a constraint during problem formulation.

As an illustration, consider the following linear program with two decision variables, X and Y:

$$\text{Max} \quad 20X + 10Y$$
$$\text{s.t.}$$
$$1X \qquad\quad \geq 2$$
$$1Y \leq 5$$
$$X, Y \geq 0$$

In Figure 7.21 we graphed the feasible region associated with this problem. Note that we can only indicate part of the feasible region because the feasible region extends indefinitely in the direction of the X axis. Looking at the objective function lines in Figure 7.21, we see that the solution to this problem may be made as large as we desire. No matter what solution we pick, we will always be able to reach some feasible solution with a larger value. Thus, we say that the solution to this linear program is *unbounded.*

Can you recognize whether a linear program involves alternative optimal solutions, infeasibility, or is unbounded? Try Problems 42 and 43.

Whenever you attempt to solve a problem that is unbounded using The Management Scientist, you will obtain a message that says, "Problem is Unbounded." Because unbounded solutions cannot occur in real problems, the first thing you should do is to review your model to determine whether you have incorrectly formulated the problem.

FIGURE 7.21   EXAMPLE OF AN UNBOUNDED PROBLEM

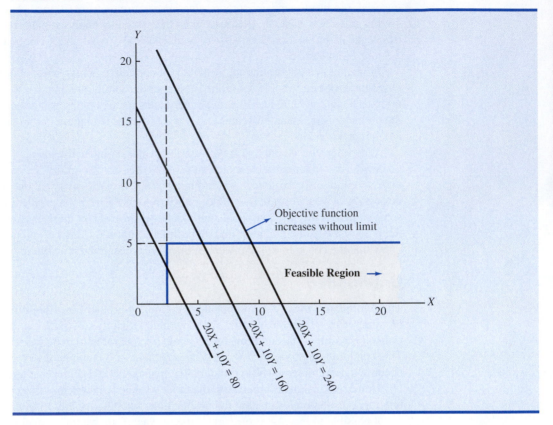

NOTES AND COMMENTS

1. Infeasibility is independent of the objective function. It exists because the constraints are so restrictive that they allow no feasible region for the linear programming model. Thus, when you encounter infeasibility, making changes in the coefficients of the objective function will not help; the problem will remain infeasible.

2. The occurrence of an unbounded solution is often the result of a missing constraint. However,

a change in the objective function may cause a previously unbounded problem to become bounded with an optimal solution. For example, the graph in Figure 7.21 shows an unbounded solution for the objective function Max $20X + 10Y$. However, changing the objective function to Max $-20X - 10Y$ will provide the optimal solution $X = 2$ and $Y = 0$ even though no changes have been made in the constraints.

 7.7   # General Linear Programming Notation

In this chapter we showed how to formulate mathematical models for the RMC and M&D Chemicals linear programming problems. To formulate a mathematical model of the RMC problem we began by defining two decision variables: F = number of tons of fuel additive, and S = number of tons of solvent base. In the M&D Chemicals problem, the two decision variables were defined as A = number of gallons of product A, and B = number of gallons of product B. We selected decision variable names of F and S in the RMC problem and

A and B in the M&D Chemicals problem to make it easier to recall what these decision variables represented in the problem. Although this approach works well for linear programs involving a small number of decision variables, it can become difficult when dealing with problems involving a large number of decision variables.

A more general notation that is often used for linear programs uses the letter x with a subscript. For instance, in the RMC problem, we could have defined the decision variables as follows:

$$x_1 = \text{number of tons of fuel additive}$$
$$x_2 = \text{number of tons of solvent base}$$

In the M&D Chemicals problem, the same variable names would be used, but their definitions would change:

$$x_1 = \text{number of gallons of product A}$$
$$x_2 = \text{number of gallons of product B}$$

A disadvantage of using general notation for decision variables is that we are no longer able to easily identify what the decision variables actually represent in the mathematical model. However, the advantage of general notation is that formulating a mathematical model for a problem that involves a large number of decision variables is much easier. For instance, for a linear programming problem with three decision variables, we would use variable names of x_1, x_2, and x_3; for a problem with four decision variables, we would use variable names of x_1, x_2, x_3, and x_4, and so on. Clearly, if a problem involved 1000 decision variables, trying to identify 1000 unique names would be difficult. However, using the general linear programming notation, the decision variables would be defined as $x_1, x_2, x_3, \ldots, x_{1000}$.

To illustrate the graphical solution procedure for a linear program written using general linear programming notation, consider the following mathematical model for a maximization problem involving two decision variables:

$$\text{Max} \quad 3x_1 + 2x_2$$
$$\text{s.t.}$$
$$2x_1 + 2x_2 \leq 8$$
$$1x_1 + 0.5x_2 \leq 3$$
$$x_1, x_2 \geq 0$$

We must first develop a graph that displays the possible solutions (x_1 and x_2 values) for the problem. The usual convention is to plot values of x_1 along the horizontal axis and values of x_2 along the vertical axis. Figure 7.22 shows the graphical solution for this two-variable problem. Note that for this problem the optimal solution is $x_1 = 2$ and $x_2 = 2$, with an objective function value of 10.

Using general linear programming notation we can write the standard form of the preceding problem as follows:

$$\text{Max} \quad 3x_1 + 2x_2 + 0s_1 + 0s_2$$
$$\text{s.t.}$$
$$2x_1 + 2x_2 + 1s_1 \quad\quad\; = 8$$
$$1x_1 + 0.5x_2 + \quad\quad 1s_2 = 3$$
$$x_1, x_2, s_1, s_2 \geq 0$$

Thus, at the optimal solution $x_1 = 2$ and $x_2 = 2$, the values of the slack variables are $s_1 = s_2 = 0$.

FIGURE 7.22   GRAPHICAL SOLUTION OF A TWO-VARIABLE LINEAR PROGRAM WITH GENERAL NOTATION

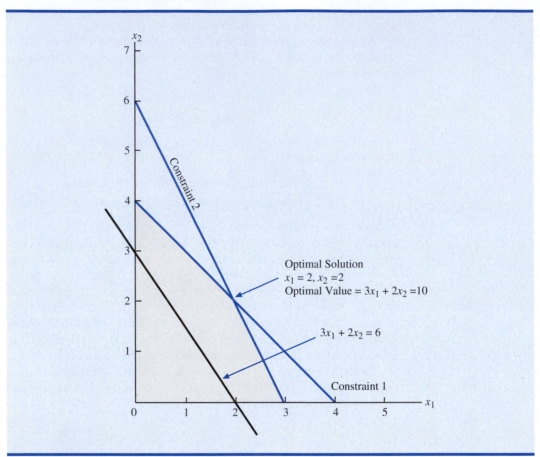

Summary

We formulated linear programming models for the RMC maximization problem and the M&D Chemicals minimization problem. For both problems we showed how a graphical solution procedure and The Management Scientist software package can be used to identify an optimal solution. In formulating a linear programming model of these problems, we developed a general definition of a linear program.

A linear program is a mathematical model with the following qualities:

1. A linear objective function that is to be maximized or minimized
2. A set of linear constraints
3. Variables restricted to nonnegative values

Slack variables may be used to write less-than-or-equal-to constraints in equality form and surplus variables may be used to write greater-than-or-equal-to constraints in equality form. The value of a slack variable can usually be interpreted as the amount of unused resource, whereas the value of a surplus variable indicates the amount over and above some stated minimum requirement. When all constraints have been written as equalities, the linear program has been written in its standard form.

If the solution to a linear program is infeasible or unbounded, no optimal solution to the problem can be found. In the case of infeasibility, no feasible solutions are possible. In the case of an unbounded solution, the objective function can be made infinitely large for a maximization problem and infinitely small for a minimization problem. In the case of alternative optimal solutions, two or more optimal extreme points exist, and all the points on the line segment connecting them are also optimal.

The chapter concluded with a section showing how to write a mathematical model using general linear programming notation. The Q.M. in Action, Linear Programming for Traffic Control at Hanshin Expressway, provides just one of many examples of the widespread use of linear programming. In the next two chapters we will see many more applications of linear programming.

Q.M. *in* ACTION

LINEAR PROGRAMMING FOR TRAFFIC CONTROL AT HANSHIN EXPRESSWAY*

The Hanshin Expressway was the first urban toll expressway in Osaka, Japan. Although in 1964 its length was only 2.3 kilometers, today it is a large-scale urban expressway network of 200 kilometers. The Hanshin Expressway provides service for the Hanshin (Osaka-Kobe) area, the second-most populated area in Japan. An average of 828,000 vehicles use the expressway each day, with daily traffic sometimes exceeding 1 million vehicles. In 1990 the Hanshin Expressway Public Corporation started using an automated traffic control system in order to maximize the number of vehicles flowing into the expressway network.

The automated traffic control system relies on two control methods: (1) limiting the number of cars that enter the expressway at each entrance ramp; and (2) providing drivers with up-to-date and accurate traffic information, including expected travel times and information about

*Based on T. Yoshino, T. Sasaki, and T. Hasegawa, "The Traffic-Control System on the Hanshin Expressway," *Interfaces* (January/February 1995): 94–108.

accidents. The approach used to limit the number of vehicles depends upon whether the expressway is in a normal or steady state of operation, or whether some type of unusual event, such as an accident or a breakdown, has occurred.

In the first phase of the steady-state case, the Hanshin system uses a linear programming model to maximize the total number of vehicles entering the system, while preventing traffic congestion and adverse effects on surrounding road networks. The data that drive the linear programming model are collected from detectors installed every 500 meters along the expressway and at all entrance and exit ramps. Every five minutes the real-time data collected from the detectors are used to update the model coefficients, and a new linear program computes the maximum number of vehicles the expressway can accommodate.

The automated traffic control system proved successful. According to surveys, traffic control decreased the length of congested portions of the expressway by 30% and the duration by 20%. In addition to its extreme cost-effectiveness, drivers consider it an indispensable service.

Glossary

Constraint An equation or inequality that rules out certain combinations of decision variables as feasible solutions.

Problem formulation The process of translating a verbal statement of a problem into a mathematical statement called the *mathematical model*.

Mathematical model A representation of a problem where the objective and all constraint conditions are described by mathematical expressions.

Decision variable A controllable input for a linear programming model.

Objective function The expression that defines the quantity to be maximized or minimized in a linear programming model.

Nonnegativity constraints A set of constraints that requires all variables to be nonnegative.

Linear program A mathematical model with a linear objective function, a set of linear constraints, and nonnegative variables.

Linear functions Mathematical expressions in which the variables appear in separate terms and are raised to the first power.

Feasible solution A solution that satisfies all the constraints simultaneously.

Feasible region The set of all feasible solutions.

Slack variable A variable added to the left-hand side of a less-than-or-equal-to constraint to convert the constraint into an equality. The value of this variable can usually be interpreted as the amount of unused resource.

Standard form A linear program in which all the constraints are written as equalities. The optimal solution of the standard form of a linear program is the same as the optimal solution of the original formulation of the linear program.

Redundant constraint A constraint that does not affect the feasible region. If a constraint is redundant, it can be removed from the problem without affecting the feasible region.

Extreme point Graphically speaking, extreme points are the feasible solution points occurring at the vertices, or "corners," of the feasible region. With two-variable problems, extreme points are determined by the intersection of the constraint lines.

Surplus variable A variable subtracted from the left-hand side of a greater-than-or-equal-to constraint to convert the constraint into an equality. The value of this variable can usually be interpreted as the amount over and above some required minimum level.

Alternative optimal solutions The case in which more than one solution provides the optimal value for the objective function.

Infeasibility The situation in which no solution to the linear programming problem satisfies all the constraints.

Unbounded The situation in which the value of the solution may be made infinitely large in a maximization linear programming problem or infinitely small in a minimization problem without violating any of the constraints.

Problems

1. Which of the following mathematical relationships could be found in a linear programming model, and which could not? For the relationships that are unacceptable for linear programs, state why.
   a. $-1A + 2B \leq 70$
   b. $2A - 2B = 50$
   c. $1A - 2B^2 \leq 10$
   d. $3^2\ A + 2B \geq 15$
   e. $1A + 1B = 6$
   f. $2A + 5B + 1AB \leq 25$

2. Find the solutions that satisfy the following constraints:
   a. $4A + 2B \leq 16$
   b. $4A + 2B \geq 16$
   c. $4A + 2B = 16$

3. Show a separate graph of the constraint lines and the solutions that satisfy each of the following constraints:
   a. $3A + 2B \leq 18$
   b. $12A + 8B \geq 480$
   c. $5A + 10B = 200$

4. Show a separate graph of the constraint lines and the solutions that satisfy each of the following constraints:
   a. $3A - 4B \geq 60$
   b. $-6A + 5B \leq 60$
   c. $5A - 2B \leq 0$

5. Show a separate graph of the constraint lines and the solutions that satisfy each of the following constraints:
   a. $A \geq 0.25 \, (A + B)$
   b. $B \leq 0.10 \, (A + B)$
   c. $A \leq 0.50 \, (A + B)$

6. Three objective functions for linear programming problems are $7A + 10B$, $6A + 4B$, and $-4A + 7B$. Show the graph of each for objective function values equal to 420.

7. Identify the feasible region for the following set of constraints:

$$0.5A + 0.25B \geq 30$$
$$1A + 5B \geq 250$$
$$0.25A + 0.5B \leq 50$$
$$A, B \geq 0$$

8. Identify the feasible region for the following set of constraints:

$$2A - 1B \leq 0$$
$$-1A + 1.5B \leq 200$$
$$A, B \geq 0$$

9. Identify the feasible region for the following set of constraints:

$$3A - 2B \geq 0$$
$$2A - 1B \leq 200$$
$$1A \leq 150$$
$$A, B \geq 0$$

10. For the linear program

$$\text{Max} \quad 2A + 3B$$
$$\text{s.t.}$$
$$1A + 3B \leq 6$$
$$5A + 3B \leq 15$$
$$A, B \geq 0$$

find the optimal solution using the graphical solution procedure. What is the value of the objective function at the optimal solution?

11. Solve the following linear program using the graphical solution procedure:

$$\text{Max} \quad 5A + 5B$$
$$\text{s.t.}$$
$$1A \leq 100$$
$$1B \leq 80$$
$$2A + 4B \leq 400$$
$$A, B \geq 0$$

12. Consider the following linear programming problem:

$$\text{Max} \quad 3A + 3B$$
$$\text{s.t.}$$
$$2A + 4B \le 12$$
$$6A + 4B \le 24$$
$$A, B \ge 0$$

a. Find the optimal solution using the graphical solution procedure.
b. If the objective function is changed to $2A + 6B$, what will the optimal solution be?
c. How many extreme points are there? What are the values of A and B at each extreme point?

13. Consider the following linear program:

$$\text{Max} \quad 1A + 2B$$
$$\text{s.t.}$$
$$1A \quad\quad\; \le \; 5$$
$$\quad\quad 1B \le \; 4$$
$$2A + 2B = 12$$
$$A, B \ge 0$$

a. Show the feasible region.
b. What are the extreme points of the feasible region?
c. Find the optimal solution using the graphical procedure.

14. Par, Inc., is a small manufacturer of golf equipment and supplies. Par's distributor believes a market exists for both a medium-priced golf bag, referred to as a standard model, and a high-priced golf bag, referred to as a deluxe model. The distributor is so confident of the market that, if Par can make the bags at a competitive price, the distributor will purchase all the bags that Par can manufacture over the next three months. A careful analysis of the manufacturing requirements resulted in the following table, which shows the production time requirements for the four required manufacturing operations and the accounting department's estimate of the profit contribution per bag:

| | **Production Time (hours)** | | | | |
Product	Cutting and Dyeing	Sewing	Finishing	Inspection and Packaging	Profit per Bag
Standard	$7/10$	$1/2$	1	$1/10$	$10
Deluxe	1	$5/6$	$2/3$	$1/4$	$ 9

The director of manufacturing estimates that 630 hours of cutting and dyeing time, 600 hours of sewing time, 708 hours of finishing time, and 135 hours of inspection and packaging time will be available for the production of golf bags during the next three months.

a. If the company wants to maximize total profit contribution, how many bags of each model should it manufacture?
b. What profit contribution can Par earn on those production quantities?
c. How many hours of production time will be scheduled for each operation?
d. What is the slack time in each operation?

15. Suppose that Par's management (Problem 14) encounters the following situations:
    a. The accounting department revises its estimate of the profit contribution for the deluxe bag to $18 per bag.
    b. A new low-cost material is available for the standard bag, and the profit contribution per standard bag can be increased to $20 per bag. (Assume that the profit contribution of the deluxe bag is the original $9 value.)
    c. New sewing equipment is available that would increase the sewing operation capacity to 750 hours. (Assume that $10A + 9B$ is the appropriate objective function.)

    If each of these situations is encountered separately, what is the optimal solution and the total profit contribution?

16. Refer to the feasible region for Par, Inc., in Problem 14.
    a. Develop an objective function that will make extreme point (0, 540) the optimal extreme point.
    b. What is the optimal solution for the objective function you selected in part (a)?
    c. What are the values of the slack variables associated with this solution?

17. Write the following linear program in standard form:

$$\text{Max} \quad 5A + 2B$$

$$\text{s.t.}$$

$$1A - 2B \leq 420$$
$$2A + 3B \leq 610$$
$$6A - 1B \leq 125$$
$$A, B \geq 0$$

18. For the linear program

$$\text{Max} \quad 4A + 1B$$

$$\text{s.t.}$$

$$10A + 2B \leq 30$$
$$3A + 2B \leq 12$$
$$2A + 2B \leq 10$$
$$A, B \geq 0$$

    a. Write this problem in standard form.
    b. Solve the problem using the graphical solution procedure.
    c. What are the values of the three slack variables at the optimal solution?

19. Given the linear program

$$\text{Max} \quad 3A + 4B$$

$$\text{s.t.}$$

$$-1A + 2B \leq 8$$
$$1A + 2B \leq 12$$
$$2A + 1B \leq 16$$
$$A, B \geq 0$$

    a. Write the problem in standard form.
    b. Solve the problem using the graphical solution procedure.
    c. What are the values of the three slack variables at the optimal solution?

20. For the linear program

$$\text{Max}\quad 3A + 2B$$

s.t.

$$
\begin{aligned}
A + B &\geq 4 \\
3A + 4B &\leq 24 \\
A &\geq 2 \\
A - B &\leq 0 \\
A, B &\geq 0
\end{aligned}
$$

a.   Write the problem in standard form.
b.   Solve the problem.
c.   What are the values of the slack and surplus variables at the optimal solution?

21. Consider the following linear program:

$$\text{Max}\quad 2A + 3B$$

s.t.

$$
\begin{aligned}
5A + 5B &\leq 400 \quad \text{Constraint 1} \\
-1A + 1B &\leq 10 \quad \text{Constraint 2} \\
1A + 3B &\geq 90 \quad \text{Constraint 3} \\
A, B &\geq 0
\end{aligned}
$$

Figure 7.23 shows a graph of the constraint lines.
a.   Place a number (1, 2, or 3) next to each constraint line to identify which constraint it represents.
b.   Shade in the feasible region on the graph.

FIGURE 7.23   GRAPH OF THE CONSTRAINT LINES FOR EXERCISE 21

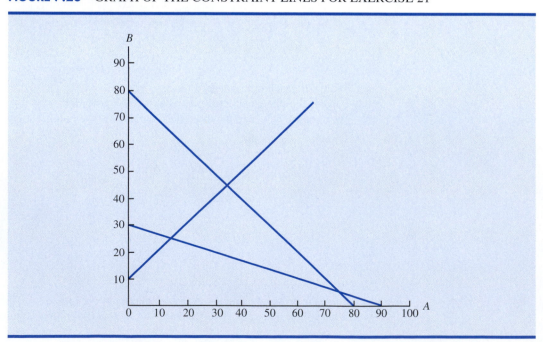

    c.   Identify the optimal extreme point. What is the optimal solution?
    d.   Which constraints are binding? Explain.
    e.   How much slack or surplus is associated with the nonbinding constraint?

22.   Reiser Sports Products wants to determine the number of All-Pro (A) and College (C) footballs to produce in order to maximize profit over the next four-week planning horizon. Constraints affecting the production quantities are the production capacities in three departments: cutting and dyeing; sewing; and inspection and packaging. For the four-week planning period, 340 hours of cutting and dyeing time, 420 hours of sewing time, and 200 hours of inspection and packaging time are available. All-Pro footballs provide a profit of \$5 per unit and College footballs provide a profit of \$4 per unit. The linear programming model with production times expressed in minutes is as follows:

$$\text{Max} \quad 5A + 4C$$
$$\text{s.t.}$$
$$
\begin{aligned}
12A + 6C &\le 20{,}400 \quad \text{Cutting and dyeing} \\
9A + 15C &\le 25{,}200 \quad \text{Sewing} \\
6A + 6C &\le 12{,}000 \quad \text{Inspection and packaging} \\
A, C &\ge 0
\end{aligned}
$$

A portion of the graphical solution to the Reiser problem is shown in Figure 7.24.

FIGURE 7.24   PORTION OF THE GRAPHICAL SOLUTION FOR EXERCISE 22

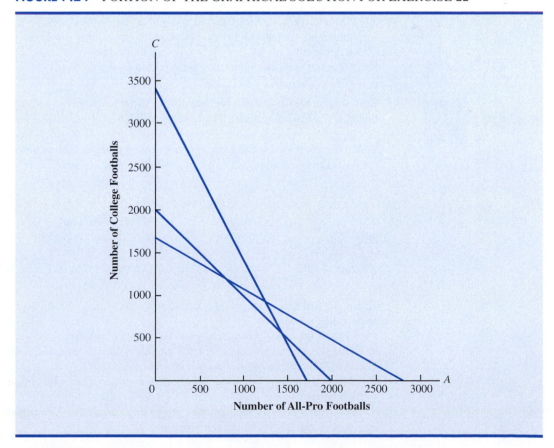

a.   Shade the feasible region for this problem.
b.   Determine the coordinates of each extreme point and the corresponding profit. Which extreme point generates the highest profit?
c.   Draw the profit line corresponding to a profit of $4000. Move the profit line as far from the origin as you can in order to determine which extreme point will provide the optimal solution. Compare your answer with the approach you used in part (b).
d.   Which constraints are binding? Explain.
e.   Suppose that the values of the objective function coefficients are $4 for each All-Pro model produced and $5 for each College model. Use the graphical solution procedure to determine the new optimal solution and the corresponding value of profit.

23.   Embassy Motorcycles (EM) manufacturers two lightweight motorcycles designed for easy handling and safety. The EZ-Rider model has a new engine and a low profile that make it easy to balance. The Lady-Sport model is slightly larger, uses a more traditional engine, and is specifically designed to appeal to women riders. Embassy produces the engines for both models at its Des Moines, Iowa, plant. Each EZ-Rider engine requires 6 hours of manufacturing time and each Lady-Sport engine requires 3 hours of manufacturing time. The Des Moines plant has 2100 hours of engine manufacturing time available for the next production period. Embassy's motorcycle frame supplier can supply as many EZ-Rider frames as needed. However, the Lady-Sport frame is more complex and the supplier can only provide up to 280 Lady-Sport frames for the next production period. Final assembly and testing requires 2 hours for each EZ-Rider model and 2.5 hours for each Lady-Sport model. A maximum of 1000 hours of assembly and testing time are available for the next production period. The company's accounting department projects a profit contribution of $2400 for each EZ-Rider produced and $1800 for each Lady-Sport produced.
a.   Formulate a linear programming model that can be used to determine the number of units of each model that should be produced in order to maximize the total contribution to profit.
b.   Solve the problem graphically. What is the optimal solution?
c.   Which constraints are binding?

24.   Kelson Sporting Equipment, Inc., makes two different types of baseball gloves: a regular model and a catcher's model. The firm has 900 hours of production time available in its cutting and sewing department, 300 hours available in its finishing department, and 100 hours available in its packaging and shipping department. The production time requirements and the profit contribution per glove are given in the following table:

	Production Time (hours)			
Model	**Cutting and Sewing**	**Finishing**	**Packaging and Shipping**	**Profit/Glove**
Regular model	1	$1/2$	$1/8$	$5
Catcher's model	$3/2$	$1/3$	$1/4$	$8

Assuming that the company is interested in maximizing the total profit contribution, answer the following:
a.   What is the linear programming model for this problem?
b.   Find the optimal solution using the graphical solution procedure. How many gloves of each model should Kelson manufacture?
c.   What is the total profit contribution Kelson can earn with the given production quantities?
d.   How many hours of production time will be scheduled in each department?
e.   What is the slack time in each department?

25. George Johnson recently inherited a large sum of money; he wants to use a portion of this money to set up a trust fund for his two children. The trust fund has two investment options: (1) a bond fund and (2) a stock fund. The projected returns over the life of the investments are 6% for the bond fund and 10% for the stock fund. Whatever portion of the inheritance he finally decides to commit to the trust fund, he wants to invest at least 30% of that amount in the bond fund. In addition, he wants to select a mix that will enable him to obtain a total return of at least 7.5%.
    a. Formulate a linear programming model that can be used to determine the percentage that should be allocated to each of the possible investment alternatives.
    b. Solve the problem using the graphical solution procedure.

26. The Sea Wharf Restaurant would like to determine the best way to allocate a monthly advertising budget of $1000 between newspaper advertising and radio advertising. Management decided that at least 25% of the budget must be spent on each type of media, and that the amount of money spent on local newspaper advertising must be at least twice the amount spent on radio advertising. A marketing consultant developed an index that measures audience exposure per dollar of advertising on a scale from 0 to 100, with higher values implying greater audience exposure. If the value of the index for local newspaper advertising is 50 and the value of the index for spot radio advertising is 80, how should the restaurant allocate its advertising budget in order to maximize the value of total audience exposure?
    a. Formulate a linear programming model that can be used to determine how the restaurant should allocate its advertising budget in order to maximize the value of total audience exposure.
    b. Solve the problem using the graphical solution procedure.

27. Blair & Rosen, Inc. (B&R) is a brokerage firm that specializes in investment portfolios designed to meet the specific risk tolerances of its clients. A client who contacted B&R this past week has a maximum of $50,000 to invest. B&R's investment advisor decides to recommend a portfolio consisting of two investment funds: an Internet fund and a Blue Chip fund. The Internet fund has a projected annual return of 12%, while the Blue Chip fund has a projected annual return of 9%. The investment advisor requires that at most $35,000 of the client's funds should be invested in the Internet fund. B&R services include a risk rating for each investment alternative. The Internet fund, which is the more risky of the two investment alternatives, has a risk rating of 6 per thousand dollars invested. The Blue Chip fund has a risk rating of 4 per thousand dollars invested. For example, if $10,000 is invested in each of the two investment funds, B&R's risk rating for the portfolio would be 6(10) + 4(10) = 100. Finally, B&R developed a questionnaire to measure each client's risk tolerance. Based on the responses, each client is classified as a conservative, moderate, or aggressive investor. Suppose that the questionnaire results classified the current client as a moderate investor. B&R recommends that a client who is a moderate investor limit his or her portfolio to a maximum risk rating of 240.
    a. What is the recommended investment portfolio for this client? What is the annual return for the portfolio?
    b. Suppose that a second client with $50,000 to invest has been classified as an aggressive investor. B&R recommends that the maximum portfolio risk rating for an aggressive investor is 320. What is the recommended investment portfolio for this aggressive investor? Discuss what happens to the portfolio under the aggressive investor strategy.
    c. Suppose that a third client with $50,000 to invest has been classified as a conservative investor. B&R recommends that the maximum portfolio risk rating for a conservative investor is 160. Develop the recommended investment portfolio for the conservative investor. Discuss the interpretation of the slack variable for the total investment fund constraint.

28. Tom's, Inc., produces various Mexican food products and sells them to Western Foods, a chain of grocery stores located in Texas and New Mexico. Tom's, Inc., makes two salsa products: Western Foods Salsa and Mexico City Salsa. Essentially, the two products have different blends of whole tomatoes, tomato sauce, and tomato paste. The Western Foods Salsa is a blend of 50% whole tomatoes, 30% tomato sauce, and 20% tomato paste. The Mexico City Salsa, which has a thicker and chunkier consistency, consists of 70% whole tomatoes, 10% tomato sauce, and 20% tomato paste. Each jar of salsa produced weighs 10 ounces. For the current production period, Tom's, Inc., can purchase up to 280 pounds of whole tomatoes, 130 pounds of tomato sauce, and 100 pounds of tomato paste; the price per pound for these ingredients is $0.96, $0.64, and $0.56, respectively. The cost of the spices and the other ingredients is approximately $0.10 per jar. Tom's, Inc., buys empty glass jars for $0.02 each, and labeling and filling costs are estimated to be $0.03 for each jar of salsa produced. Tom's contract with Western Foods results in sales revenue of $1.64 for each jar of Western Foods Salsa and $1.93 for each jar of Mexico City Salsa.

a. Develop a linear programming model that will enable Tom's to determine the mix of salsa products that will maximize the total profit contribution.

b. Find the optimal solution.

29. AutoIgnite produces electronic ignition systems for automobiles at a plant in Cleveland, Ohio. Each ignition system is assembled from two components produced at AutoIgnite's plants in Buffalo, New York, and Dayton, Ohio. The Buffalo plant can produce 2000 units of component 1, 1000 units of component 2, or any combination of the two components each day. For instance, 60% of Buffalo's production time could be used to produce component 1 and 40% of Buffalo's production time could be used to produce component 2; in this case, the Buffalo plant would be able to produce 0.6(2000) = 1200 units of component 1 each day and 0.4(1000) = 400 units of component 2 each day. The Dayton plant can produce 600 units of component 1, 1400 units of component 2, or any combination of the two components each day. At the end of each day, the component production at Buffalo and Dayton is sent to Cleveland for assembly of the ignition systems on the following workday.

a. Formulate a linear programming model that can be used to develop a daily production schedule for the Buffalo and Dayton plants that will maximize daily production of ignition systems at Cleveland.

b. Find the optimal solution.

30. A financial advisor at Diehl Investments identified two companies that are likely candidates for a takeover in the near future. Eastern Cable is a leading manufacturer of flexible cable systems used in the construction industry, and ComSwitch is a new firm specializing in digital switching systems. Eastern Cable is currently trading for $40 per share, and ComSwitch is currently trading for $25 per share. If the takeovers occur, the financial advisor estimates that the price of Eastern Cable will go to $55 per share and ComSwitch will go to $43 per share. At this point in time, the financial advisor has identified ComSwitch as the higher risk alternative. Assume that a client indicated a willingness to invest a maximum of $50,000 in the two companies. The client wants to invest at least $15,000 in Eastern Cable and at least $10,000 in ComSwitch. Because of the higher risk associated with ComSwitch, the financial advisor has recommended that at most $25,000 should be invested in ComSwitch.

a. Formulate a linear programming model that can be used to determine the number of shares of Eastern Cable and the number of shares of ComSwitch that will meet the investment constraints and maximize the total return for the investment.

b. Graph the feasible region.

c. Determine the coordinates of each extreme point.

d. Find the optimal solution.

31. Consider the following linear program:

$$\text{Min} \quad 3A + 4B$$

s.t.

$$1A + 3B \geq 6$$
$$1A + 1B \geq 4$$
$$A, B \geq 0$$

Identify the feasible region and find the optimal solution using the graphical solution procedure. What is the value of the objective function?

32. Identify the three extreme-point solutions for the M&D Chemicals problem (see Section 7.5). Identify the value of the objective function and the values of the slack and surplus variables at each extreme point.

33. Consider the following linear programming problem:

$$\text{Min} \quad A + 2B$$

s.t.

$$A + 4B \leq 21$$
$$2A + B \geq 7$$
$$3A + 1.5B \leq 21$$
$$-2A + 6B \geq 0$$
$$A, B \geq 0$$

a. Find the optimal solution using the graphical solution procedure and the value of the objective function.
b. Determine the amount of slack or surplus for each constraint.
c. Suppose the objective function is changed to max $5A + 2B$. Find the optimal solution and the value of the objective function.

34. Consider the following linear program:

$$\text{Min} \quad 2A + 2B$$

s.t.

$$1A + 3B \leq 12$$
$$3A + 1B \geq 13$$
$$1A - 1B = 3$$
$$A, B \geq 0$$

a. Show the feasible region.
b. What are the extreme points of the feasible region?
c. Find the optimal solution using the graphical solution procedure.

35. For the linear program

$$\text{Min} \quad 6A + 4B$$

s.t.

$$2A + 1B \geq 12$$
$$1A + 1B \geq 10$$
$$1B \leq 4$$
$$A, B \geq 0$$

    a.   Write the problem in standard form.

    b.   Solve the problem using the graphical solution procedure.

    c.   What are the values of the slack and surplus variables?

36. As part of a quality improvement initiative, Consolidated Electronics employees complete a three-day training program on teaming and a two-day training program on problem solving. The manager of quality improvement has requested that at least 8 training programs on teaming and at least 10 training programs on problem solving be offered during the next six months. In addition, senior-level management has specified that at least 25 training programs must be offered during this period. Consolidated Electronics uses a consultant to teach the training programs. During the next quarter, the consultant has 84 days of training time available. Each training program on teaming costs $10,000 and each training program on problem solving costs $8000.

    a.   Formulate a linear programming model that can be used to determine the number of training programs on teaming and the number of training programs on problem solving that should be offered in order to minimize total cost.

    b.   Graph the feasible region.

    c.   Determine the coordinates of each extreme point.

    d.   Solve for the minimum cost solution.

37. The New England Cheese Company produces two cheese spreads by blending mild cheddar cheese with extra sharp cheddar cheese. The cheese spreads are packaged in 12-ounce containers, which are then sold to distributors throughout the Northeast. The Regular blend contains 80% mild cheddar and 20% extra sharp, and the Zesty blend contains 60% mild cheddar and 40% extra sharp. This year, a local dairy cooperative offered to provide up to 8100 pounds of mild cheddar cheese for $1.20 per pound and up to 3000 pounds of extra sharp cheddar cheese for $1.40 per pound. The cost to blend and package the cheese spreads, excluding the cost of the cheese, is $0.20 per container. If each container of Regular is sold for $1.95 and each container of Zesty is sold for $2.20, how many containers of Regular and Zesty should New England Cheese produce?

38. Applied Technology, Inc. (ATI) produces bicycle frames using two fiberglass materials that improve the strength-to-weight ratio of the frames. The cost of the standard grade material is $7.50 per yard and the cost of the professional grade material is $9.00 per yard. The standard and professional grade materials contain different amounts of fiberglass, carbon fiber, and Kevlar, as shown in the following table:

	Standard Grade	**Professional Grade**
Fiberglass	84%	58%
Carbon fiber	10%	30%
Kevlar	6%	12%

ATI signed a contract with a bicycle manufacturer to produce a new frame with a carbon fiber content of at least 20% and a Kevlar content of not greater than 10%. To meet the required weight specification, a total of 30 yards of material must be used for each frame.

    a.   Formulate a linear program to determine the number of yards of each grade of fiberglass material that ATI should use in each frame in order to minimize total cost. Define the decision variables and indicate the purpose of each constraint.

    b.   Use the graphical solution procedure to determine the feasible region. What are the coordinates of the extreme points?

    c.   Compute the total cost at each extreme point. What is the optimal solution?

d.   The distributor of the fiberglass material is currently overstocked with the professional grade material. To reduce inventory, the distributor offered ATI the opportunity to purchase the professional grade for $8 per yard. Will the optimal solution change?

e.   Suppose that the distributor further lowers the price of the professional grade material to $7.40 per yard. Will the optimal solution change? What effect would an even lower price for the professional grade material have on the optimal solution? Explain.

39.   Innis Investments manages funds for a number of companies and wealthy clients. The investment strategy is tailored to each client's needs. For a new client, Innis has been authorized to invest up to $1.2 million in two investment funds: a stock fund and a money market fund. Each unit of the stock fund costs $50 and provides an annual rate of return of 10%; each unit of the money market fund costs $100 and provides an annual rate of return of 4%.

The client wants to minimize risk subject to the requirement that the annual income from the investment be at least $60,000. According to Innis's risk measurement system, each unit invested in the stock fund has a risk index of 8, and each unit invested in the money market fund has a risk index of 3; the higher risk index associated with the stock fund simply indicates that it is the riskier investment. Innis's client also specified that at least $300,000 be invested in the money market fund.

a.   Determine how many units of each fund Innis should purchase for the client to minimize the total risk index for the portfolio.

b.   How much annual income will this investment strategy generate?

c.   Suppose the client desires to maximize annual return. How should the funds be invested?

40.   Photo Chemicals produces two types of photographic developing fluids. Both products cost Photo Chemicals $1 per gallon to produce. Based on an analysis of current inventory levels and outstanding orders for the next month, Photo Chemicals' management specified that at least 30 gallons of product 1 and at least 20 gallons of product 2 must be produced during the next two weeks. Management also stated that an existing inventory of highly perishable raw material required in the production of both fluids must be used within the next two weeks. The current inventory of the perishable raw material is 80 pounds. Although more of this raw material can be ordered if necessary, any of the current inventory that is not used within the next two weeks will spoil—hence, the management requirement that at least 80 pounds be used in the next two weeks. Furthermore, it is known that product 1 requires 1 pound of this perishable raw material per gallon and product 2 requires 2 pounds of the raw material per gallon. Because Photo Chemicals' objective is to keep its production costs at the minimum possible level, the firm's management is looking for a minimum cost production plan that uses all the 80 pounds of perishable raw material and provides at least 30 gallons of product 1 and at least 20 gallons of product 2. What is the minimum cost solution?

41.   Southern Oil Company produces two grades of gasoline: regular and premium. The profit contributions are $0.30 per gallon for regular gasoline and $0.50 per gallon for premium gasoline. Each gallon of regular gasoline contains 0.3 gallons of grade A crude oil and each gallon of premium gasoline contains 0.6 gallons of grade A crude oil. For the next production period, Southern has 18,000 gallons of grade A crude oil available. The refinery used to produce the gasolines has a production capacity of 50,000 gallons for the next production period. Southern Oil's distributors have indicated that demand for the premium gasoline for the next production period will be at most 20,000 gallons.

a.   Formulate a linear programming model that can be used to determine the number of gallons of regular gasoline and the number of gallons of premium gasoline that should be produced in order to maximize total profit contribution.

b.   What is the optimal solution?

c.   What are the values and interpretations of the slack variables?

d.   What are the binding constraints?

42. Does the following linear program involve infeasibility, unbounded, and/or alternative optimal solutions? Explain.

$$\text{Max} \quad 4A + 8B$$
$$\text{s.t.}$$
$$2A + 2B \le 10$$
$$-1A + 1B \ge 8$$
$$A, B \ge 0$$

43. Does the following linear program involve infeasibility, unbounded, and/or alternative optimal solutions? Explain.

$$\text{Max} \quad 1A + 1B$$
$$\text{s.t.}$$
$$8A + 6B \ge 24$$
$$2B \ge 4$$
$$A, B \ge 0$$

44. Consider the following linear program:

$$\text{Max} \quad 1A + 1B$$
$$\text{s.t.}$$
$$5A + 3B \le 15$$
$$3A + 5B \le 15$$
$$A, B \ge 0$$

a. What is the optimal solution for this problem?
b. Suppose that the objective function is changed to $1A + 2B$. Find the new optimal solution.

45. Consider the following linear program:

$$\text{Max} \quad 1A - 2B$$
$$\text{s.t.}$$
$$-4A + 3B \le 3$$
$$1A - 1B \le 3$$
$$A, B \ge 0$$

a. Graph the feasible region for the problem.
b. Is the feasible region unbounded? Explain.
c. Find the optimal solution.
d. Does an unbounded feasible region imply that the optimal solution to the linear program will be unbounded?

46. The manager of a small independent grocery store is trying to determine the best use of her shelf space for soft drinks. The store carries national and generic brands and currently has 200 square feet of shelf space available. The manager wants to allocate at least 60% of the space to the national brands and, regardless of the profitability, allocate at least 10% of the space to the generic brands. How many square feet of space should the manager allocate to the national brands and the generic brands under the following circumstances?

a.   The national brands are more profitable than the generic brands.

b.   Both brands are equally profitable.

c.   The generic brand is more profitable than the national brand.

47.   Discuss what happens to the M&D Chemicals problem (see Section 7.5) if the cost per gallon for product A is increased to $3.00 per gallon. What would you recommend? Explain.

48.   For the M&D Chemicals problem in Section 7.5, discuss the effect of management's requiring total production of 500 gallons for the two products. List two or three actions M&D should consider to correct the situation you encounter.

49.   PharmaPlus operates a chain of 30 pharmacies. The pharmacies are staffed by licensed pharmacists and pharmacy technicians. The company currently employs 85 full-time equivalent pharmacists (combination of full time and part time) and 175 full-time equivalent technicians. Each spring management reviews current staffing levels and makes hiring plans for the year. A recent forecast of the prescription load for the next year shows that at least 250 full-time equivalent employees (pharmacists and technicians) will be required to staff the pharmacies. The personnel department expects 10 pharmacists and 30 technicians to leave over the next year. To accommodate the expected attrition and prepare for future growth, management stated that at least 15 new pharmacists must be hired. In addition, PharmaPlus's new service quality guidelines specify no more than two technicians per licensed pharmacist. The average salary for licensed pharmacists is $40 per hour and the average salary for technicians is $10 per hour.

a.   Determine a minimum-cost staffing plan for PharmaPlus. How many pharmacists and technicians are needed?

b.   Given current staffing levels and expected attrition, how many new hires (if any) must be made to reach the level recommended in part (a)? What will be the impact on the payroll?

50.   Expedition Outfitters manufactures a variety of specialty clothing for hiking, skiing, and mountain climbing. They have decided to begin production on two new parkas designed for use in extremely cold weather: the Mount Everest Parka and the Rocky Mountain Parka. Their manufacturing plant has 120 hours of cutting time and 120 hours of sewing time available for producing these two parkas. Each Mount Everest Parka requires 30 minutes of cutting time and 45 minutes of sewing time, and each Rocky Mountain Parka requires 20 minutes of cutting time and 15 minutes of sewing time. The labor and material cost is $150 for each Mount Everest Parka and $50 for each Rocky Mountain Parka, and the retail prices through the firm's mail order catalog are $250 for the Mount Everest Parka and $200 for the Rocky Mountain Parka. Because management believes that the Mount Everest Parka is a unique coat that will enhance the image of the firm, they specified that at least 20% of the total production must consist of this model. Assuming that Expedition Outfitters can sell as many coats of each type as they can produce, how many units of each model should they manufacture to maximize the total profit contribution?

51.   English Motors, Ltd. (EML), developed a new all-wheel-drive sports utility vehicle. As part of the marketing campaign, EML produced a video tape sales presentation to send to both owners of current EML four-wheel-drive vehicles as well as to owners of four-wheel-drive sports utility vehicles offered by competitors; EML refers to these two target markets as the current customer market and the new customer market. Individuals who receive the new promotion video will also receive a coupon for a test drive of the new EML model for one weekend. A key factor in the success of the new promotion is the response rate, the percentage of individuals who receive the new promotion and test drive the new model. EML estimates that the response rate for the current customer market is 25% and the response rate for the new customer market is 20%. For the customers who test drive the new model, the sales rate is the percentage of individuals that makes a purchase. Marketing

research studies indicate that the sales rate is 12% for the current customer market and 20% for the new customer market. The cost for each promotion, excluding the test drive costs, is $4 for each promotion sent to the current customer market and $6 for each promotion sent to the new customer market. Management also specified that a minimum of 30,000 current customers should test drive the new model and a minimum of 10,000 new customers should test drive the new model. In addition, the number of current customers who test drive the new vehicle must be at least twice the number of new customers who test drive the new vehicle. If the marketing budget, excluding test drive costs, is $1.2 million, how many promotions should be sent to each group of customers in order to maximize total sales?

52. Creative Sports Design (CSD) manufactures a standard-size racket and an oversize racket. The firm's rackets are extremely light due to the use of a magnesium-graphite alloy that was invented by the firm's founder. Each standard-size racket uses 0.125 kilograms of the alloy and each oversize racket uses 0.4 kilograms; over the next two-week production period only 80 kilograms of the alloy are available. Each standard-size racket uses 10 minutes of manufacturing time and each oversize racket uses 12 minutes. The profit contributions are $10 for each standard-size racket and $15 for each oversize racket, and 40 hours of manufacturing time are available each week. Management specified that at least 20% of the total production must be the standard-size racket. How many rackets of each type should CSD manufacture over the next two weeks to maximize the total profit contribution? Assume that because of the unique nature of their products, CSD can sell as many rackets as they can produce.

53. Management of High Tech Services (HTS) would like to develop a model that will help allocate their technicians' time between service calls to regular contract customers and new customers. A maximum of 80 hours of technician time is available over the two-week planning period. To satisfy cash flow requirements, at least $800 in revenue (per technician) must be generated during the two-week period. Technician time for regular customers generates $25 per hour. However, technician time for new customers only generates an average of $8 per hour because in many cases a new customer contact does not provide billable services. To ensure that new customer contacts are being maintained, the technician time spent on new customer contacts must be at least 60% of the time spent on regular customer contacts. Given these revenue and policy requirements, HTS would like to determine how to allocate technician time between regular customers and new customers so that the total number of customers contacted during the two-week period will be maximized. Technicians require an average of 50 minutes for each regular customer contact and 1 hour for each new customer contact.

   a. Develop a linear programming model that will enable HTS to allocate technician time between regular customers and new customers.

   b. Find the optimal solution.

54. Jackson Hole Manufacturing is a small manufacturer of plastic products used in the automotive and computer industries. One of its major contracts is with a large computer company and involves the production of plastic printer cases for the computer company's portable printers. The printer cases are produced on two injection molding machines. The M-100 machine has a production capacity of 25 printer cases per hour, and the M-200 machine has a production capacity of 40 cases per hour. Both machines use the same chemical material to produce the printer cases; the M-100 uses 40 pounds of the raw material per hour and the M-200 uses 50 pounds per hour. The computer company asked Jackson Hole to produce as many of the cases during the upcoming week as possible; it will pay $18 for each case Jackson Hole can deliver. However, next week is a regularly scheduled vacation period for most of Jackson Hole's production employees; during this time, annual maintenance is performed for all equipment in the plant. Because of the downtime for

maintenance, the M-100 will be available for no more than 15 hours, and the M-200 will be available for no more than 10 hours. However, because of the high setup cost involved with both machines, management requires that, if production is scheduled on either machine, the machine must be operated for at least 5 hours. The supplier of the chemical material used in the production process informed Jackson Hole that a maximum of 1000 pounds of the chemical material will be available for next week's production; the cost for this raw material is $6 per pound. In addition to the raw material cost, Jackson Hole estimates that the hourly cost of operating the M-100 and the M-200 are $50 and $75, respectively.

a. Formulate a linear programming model that can be used to maximize the contribution to profit.

b. Find the optimal solution.

Case Problem 1   Workload Balancing

Digital Imaging (DI) produces photo printers for both the professional and consumer markets. The DI consumer division recently introduced two photo printers that provide color prints rivaling those produced by a professional processing lab. The DI-910 model can produce a 4″ × 6″ borderless print in approximately 37 seconds. The more sophisticated and faster DI-950 can even produce a 13″ × 19″ borderless print. Financial projections show profit contributions of $42 for each DI-910 and $87 for each DI-950.

The printers are assembled, tested, and packaged at DI's plant located in New Bern, North Carolina. This plant is highly automated and uses two manufacturing lines to produce the printers. Line 1 performs the assembly operation with times of 3 minutes per DI-910 printer and 6 minutes per DI-950 printer. Line 2 performs both the testing and packaging operations. Times are 4 minutes per DI-910 printer and 2 minutes per DI-950 printer. The shorter time for the DI-950 printer is a result of its faster print speed. Both manufacturing lines are in operation one 8-hour shift per day.

Managerial Report

Perform an analysis for Digital Imaging in order to determine how many units of each printer to produce. Prepare a report to DI's president presenting your findings and recommendations. Include (but do not limit your discussion to) a consideration of the following:

1. The recommended number of units of each printer to produce to maximize the total contribution to profit for an 8-hour shift. What reasons might management have for not implementing your recommendation?

2. Suppose that management also states that the number of DI-910 printers produced must be at least as great as the number of DI-950 units produced. Assuming that the objective is to maximize the total contribution to profit for an 8-hour shift, how many units of each printer should be produced?

3. Does the solution you developed in part (2) balance the total time spent on line 1 and the total time spent on line 2? Why might this balance or lack of it be a concern to management?

4. Management requested an expansion of the model in part (2) that would provide a better balance between the total time on line 1 and the total time on line 2. Management wants to limit the difference between the total time on line 1 and the total time on line 2 to 30 minutes or less. If the objective is still to maximize the total contribution to profit, how many units of each printer should be produced? What effect does this workload balancing have on total profit in part (2)?

5. Suppose that in part (1) management specified the objective of maximizing the total number of printers produced each shift rather than total profit contribution. With this objective, how many units of each printer should be produced per shift? What effect does this objective have on total profit and workload balancing?

For each solution that you develop, include a copy of your linear programming model and graphical solution in the appendix to your report.

Case Problem 2   Production Strategy

Better Fitness, Inc. (BFI) manufactures exercise equipment at its plant in Freeport, Long Island. It recently designed two universal weight machines for the home exercise market. Both machines use BFI-patented technology that provides the user with an extremely wide range of motion capability for each type of exercise performed. Until now, such capabilities have been available only on expensive weight machines used primarily by physical therapists.

At a recent trade show, demonstrations of the machines resulted in significant dealer interest. In fact, the number of orders that BFI received at the trade show far exceeded its manufacturing capabilities for the current production period. As a result, management decided to begin production of the two machines. The two machines, which BFI named the Body-Plus 100 and the BodyPlus 200, require different amounts of resources to produce.

The BodyPlus 100 consists of a frame unit, a press station, and a pec-dec station. Each frame produced uses 4 hours of machining and welding time and 2 hours of painting and finishing time. Each press station requires 2 hours of machining and welding time and 1 hour of painting and finishing time, and each pec-dec station uses 2 hours of machining and welding time and 2 hours of painting and finishing time. In addition, 2 hours are spent assembling, testing, and packaging each BodyPlus 100. The raw material costs are $450 for each frame, $300 for each press station, and $250 for each pec-dec station; packaging costs are estimated to be $50 per unit.

The BodyPlus 200 consists of a frame unit, a press station, a pec-dec station, and a leg-press station. Each frame produced uses 5 hours of machining and welding time and 4 hours of painting and finishing time. Each press station requires 3 hours machining and welding time and 2 hours of painting and finishing time, each pec-dec station uses 2 hours of machining and welding time and 2 hours of painting and finishing time, and each leg-press station requires 2 hours of machining and welding time and 2 hours of painting and finishing time. In addition, 2 hours are spent assembling, testing, and packaging each BodyPlus 200. The raw material costs are $650 for each frame, $400 for each press station, $250 for each pec-dec station, and $200 for each leg-press station; packaging costs are estimated to be $75 per unit.

For the next production period, management estimates that 600 hours of machining and welding time; 450 hours of painting and finishing time; and 140 hours of assembly, testing, and packaging time will be available. Current labor costs are $20 per hour for machining and welding time; $15 per hour for painting and finishing time; and $12 per hour for assembly, testing, and packaging time. The market in which the two machines must compete suggests a retail price of $2400 for the BodyPlus 100 and $3500 for the BodyPlus 200, although some flexibility may be available to BFI because of the unique capabilities of the new machines. Authorized BFI dealers can purchase machines for 70% of the suggested retail price.

BFI's president believes that the unique capabilities of the BodyPlus 200 can help position BFI as one of the leaders in high-end exercise equipment. Consequently, he stated that the number of units of the BodyPlus 200 produced must be at least 25% of the total production.

Managerial Report

Analyze the production problem at Better Fitness, Inc., and prepare a report for BFI's president presenting your findings and recommendations. Include (but do not limit your discussion to) a consideration of the following items:

1. The recommended number of BodyPlus 100 and BodyPlus 200 machines to produce
2. The effect on profits of the requirement that the number of units of the BodyPlus 200 produced must be at least 25% of the total production
3. Where efforts should be expended in order to increase contribution to profits

Include a copy of your linear programming model and graphical solution in an appendix to your report.

Case Problem 3   Hart Venture Capital

Hart Venture Capital (HVC) specializes in providing venture capital for software development and Internet applications. Currently HVC has two investment opportunities: (1) Security Systems, a firm that needs additional capital to develop an Internet security software package, and (2) Market Analysis, a market research company that needs additional capital to develop a software package for conducting customer satisfaction surveys. In exchange for Security Systems stock, the firm asked HVC to provide $600,000 in year 1, $600,000 in year 2, and $250,000 in year 3 over the coming three-year period. In exchange for their stock, Market Analysis asked HVC to provide $500,000 in year 1, $350,000 in year 2, and $400,000 in year 3 over the same three-year period. HVC believes that both investment opportunities are worth pursuing. However, because of other investments, they are willing to commit at most $800,000 for both projects in the first year, at most $700,000 in the second year, and $500,000 in the third year.

HVC's financial analysis team reviewed both projects and recommended that the company's objective should be to maximize the net present value of the total investment in Security Systems and Market Analysis. The net present value takes into account the estimated value of the stock at the end of the three-year period as well as the capital outflows that are necessary during each of the three years. Using an 8% rate of return, HVC's financial analysis team estimates that 100% funding of the Security Systems project has a net present value of $1,800,000, and 100% funding of the Market Analysis project has a net present value of $1,600,000.

HVC has the option to fund any percentage of the Security Systems and Market Analysis projects. For example, if HVC decides to fund 40% of the Security Systems project, investments of 0.40($600,000) = $240,000 would be required in year 1, 0.40($600,000) = $240,000 would be required in year 2, and 0.40($250,000) = $100,000 would be required in year 3. In this case, the net present value of the Security Systems project would be 0.40($1,800,000) = $720,000. The investment amounts and the net present value for partial funding of the Market Analysis project would be computed in the same manner.

Managerial Report

Perform an analysis of HVC's investment problem and prepare a report that presents your findings and recommendations. Be sure to include information on the following:

1. The recommended percentage of each project that HVC should fund and the net present value of the total investment
2. A capital allocation plan for Security Systems and Market Analysis for the coming three-year period and the total HVC investment each year

3. The effect, if any, on the recommended percentage of each project that HVC should fund if HVC is willing to commit an additional $100,000 during the first year
4. A capital allocation plan if an additional $100,000 is made available
5. Your recommendation as to whether HVC should commit the additional $100,000 in the first year

Provide model details and relevant computer output in a report appendix.

Appendix 7.1   Solving Linear Programs with The Management Scientist

In this appendix we describe how The Management Scientist software package can be used to solve the RMC linear programming problem. After starting The Management Scientist, execute the following steps:

Step 1. Select the **Linear Programming** module
Step 2. Select the **File** menu
Select **New**
Step 3. When the **Problem Features** dialog box appears:
Enter 2 in the **Number of Decision Variables** box
Enter 3 in the **Number of Constraints** box
Select **Maximize** in the **Optimization Type** box
Click **OK**
Step 4. When the data input worksheet appears (see Figure 7.25):
Change **Variable Names** from X1 and X2 to F and S, respectively
Enter the **Objective Function Coefficients**
For each constraint:
Enter the **Coefficients**
Enter the **Relation** ($<$, $=$, $>$)
Enter the **Right-Hand-Side** value

The Management Scientist interprets the $<$ symbol as $\leq$ and the $>$ symbol as $\geq$.

Step 5. Select the **Solution** menu
Select **Solve**

The user entries for the data input sheet are shown in Figure 7.25. The output from The Management Scientist is shown in Figure 7.15. The original problem can be edited or

FIGURE 7.25   DATA INPUT WORKSHEET FOR THE RMC PROBLEM USING THE MANAGEMENT SCIENTIST

Optimization Type: Max

	Objective Function			
Variable Names:	F	S		
Coefficients:	40	30		

	Constraints			
Subject To:	F	S	Relation[<,=,>]	Right-Hand-Side
Constraint 1	0.4	0.5	<	20
Constraint 2		0.2	<	5
Constraint 3	0.6	0.3	<	21

changed by selecting the Edit menu. Finally, printed output can be obtained by selecting the **Solution** menu and then selecting the **Print** option.

Appendix 7.2   Solving Linear Programs with LINGO

In this appendix we describe how to use LINGO to solve the RMC problem. When you start LINGO, two windows are immediately displayed. The outer, or main frame, window contains all the command menus and the command toolbar. The smaller window is the model window; this window is used to enter and edit the linear programming model you want to solve.

As with any model, it is good to document your LINGO model with comments. A comment in a LINGO model begins with an exclamation point and ends with a semicolon. If desired, a comment can span multiple lines.

The first item we enter is a comment describing the objective function. Recall that the objective function for the RMC problem is to maximize profit. Hence we enter the following comment:

```
! MAXIMIZE PROFIT;
```

For the latest information on LINGO software see http://www.lindo.com.

Next we press the Enter key and then type the objective function. The objective function for the RMC problem is Max $40F + 30S$. Thus, in the second line of the LINGO model window, we enter the following expression:

```
MAX = 40*F + 30*S;
```

Note that in LINGO the symbol * is used to denote multiplication and that the objective function, like a comment, ends with a semicolon. In general, each mathematical expression (objective function and constraints) in LINGO is terminated with a semicolon.

Next, we press the Enter key to move to a new line. The first constraint in the RMC problem is $0.4F + 0.5S \leq 20$, for material 1. Thus, in the third and fourth lines of the LINGO model window we enter the following expressions:

```
!MATERIAL 1 CONSTRAINT;
0.4*F + .5*S <= 20;
```

Note that LINGO interprets the $<=$ symbol as $\leq$. Alternatively, we could enter $<$ instead of $<=$. As was the case when entering the objective function, a semicolon is required at the end of the first constraint. Pressing the Enter key moves us to a new line as we continue the process by entering the remaining comments and constraints as shown here:

```
!MATERIAL 2 CONSTRAINT;
.2*S <= 5;
!MATERIAL 3 CONSTRAINT;
0.6*F + .3*S <= 21;
```

The model window will now appear as follows:

```
! MAXIMIZE PROFIT;
MAX = 40*F + 30*S;
!MATERIAL 1 CONSTRAINT;
0.4*F + .5*S <= 20;
!MATERIAL 2 CONSTRAINT;
.2*S <= 5;
!MATERIAL 3 CONSTRAINT;
0.6*F + .3*S <= 21;
```

FIGURE 7.26   SOLUTION TO THE RMC PROBLEM USING LINGO

```
Global optimal solution found.
Objective value:                              1600.000
Total solver iterations:                             2

                   Variable           Value        Reduced Cost
                          F        25.00000            0.000000
                          S        20.00000            0.000000

                        Row  Slack or Surplus        Dual Price
                          1         1600.000            1.000000
                          2         0.000000           33.33333
                          3         1.000000            0.000000
                          4         0.000000           44.44444
```

If you make an error in entering the model, you can correct it at any time by simply positioning the cursor where you made the error and entering the necessary correction.

To solve the model, select the Solve command from the LINGO menu or press the Solve button on the toolbar at the top of the main frame window. LINGO will begin the solution process by determining whether the model conforms to all syntax requirements. If the LINGO model doesn't pass these tests, you will be informed by an error message. If LINGO does not find any errors in the model input, it will begin to solve the model. As part of the solution process, LINGO displays a Solver Status window that allows you to monitor the progress of the solver. LINGO displays the solution in a new window titled "Solution Report." The output that appears in the Solution Report window for the RMC problem is shown in Figure 7.26.

The first part of the output shown in Figure 7.26 indicates that an optimal solution has been found and that the value of the objective function is 1600. We see that the optimal solution is $F = 25$ and $S = 20$, and that the slack variables for the three constraints (rows 2–4) are 0, 1, and 0. We will discuss the use of the information in the Reduced Cost column and the Dual Price column in Chapter 8.

Appendix 7.3   Solving Linear Programs with Excel

In this appendix we will use an Excel worksheet to solve the RMC linear programming problem. We will enter the problem data for the RMC problem in the top part of the worksheet and develop the linear programming model in the bottom part of the worksheet.

Formulation

Whenever we formulate a worksheet model of a linear program, we perform the following steps:

Step 1. Enter the problem data in the top part of the worksheet
Step 2. Specify cell locations for the decision variables
Step 3. Select a cell and enter a formula for computing the value of the objective function
Step 4. Select a cell and enter a formula for computing the left-hand side of each constraint
Step 5. Select a cell and enter a formula for computing the right-hand side of each constraint

FIGURE 7.27   FORMULA WORKSHEET FOR THE RMC PROBLEM

RMC

	A	B	C	D
1	**RMC**			
2				
3		**Material Requirements**		
4	**Material**	**Fuel Additive**	**Solvent Base**	**Amount Available**
5	Material 1	0.4	0.5	20
6	Material 2	0	0.2	5
7	Material 3	0.6	0.3	21
8	**Profit Per Ton**	40	30	
9				
10				
11	**Model**			
12				
13		**Decision Variables**		
14		**Fuel Additive**	**Solvent Base**	
15	**Tons Produced**	25	20	
16				
17	**Maximize Total Profit**	=B8*B15+C8*C15		
18				
19	**Constraints**	**Amount Used (LHS)**		**Amount Available (RHS)**
20	Material 1	=B5*B15+C5*C15	<=	=D5
21	Material 2	=B6*B15+C6*C15	<=	=D6
22	Material 3	=B7*B15+C7*C15	<=	=D7

The formula worksheet that we developed for the RMC problem using these five steps is shown in Figure 7.27. Let us review each of the preceding steps as they apply to the RMC problem.

Step 1. Enter the problem data in the top part of the worksheet

Cells B5 to C7 show the material requirements per ton of each product.

Cells B8 and C8 show the profit contribution per ton for the two products.

Cells D5 to D7 show the maximum amounts available for each of the three materials.

Step 2. Specify cell locations for the decision variables

Cell B15 will contain the number of tons of fuel additive produced, and Cell C15 will contain the number of tons of solvent base produced.

Step 3. Select a cell and enter a formula for computing the value of the objective function

Cell B17: =B8*B15+C8*C15

Step 4. Select a cell and enter a formula for computing the left-hand side of each constraint

With three constraints, we have

Cell B20: =B5*B15+C5*C15

Cell B21: =C6*C15

Cell B22: =B7*B15+C7*C15

Step 5. Select a cell and enter a formula for computing the right-hand side of each constraint

With three constraints, we have

Cell D20: =D5

Cell D21: =D6

Cell D22: =D7

Note that descriptive labels make the model section of the worksheet easier to read and understand. For example, we added "Fuel Additive," "Solvent Base," and "Tons Produced" in rows 14 and 15 so that the values of the decision variables appearing in Cells B15 and C15 can be easily interpreted. In addition, we entered "Maximize Total Profit" in Cell A17 to indicate that the value of the objective function appearing in Cell B17 is the maximum profit contribution. In the constraint section of the worksheet we added the constraint names as well as the "<=" symbols to show the relationship that exists between the left-hand side and the right-hand side of each constraint. Although these descriptive labels are not necessary to use Excel Solver to find a solution to the RMC problem, the labels make it easier for the user to understand and interpret the optimal solution.

Excel Solution

The standard Excel Solver developed by Frontline Systems can be used to solve all of the linear programming problems presented in this text. However, Premium Solver, available on the Web site that accompanies this text includes a more powerful version referred to as Premium Solver for Education. When first started, Premium Solver looks and behaves exactly like the standard Excel Solver, but when the Premium button in the main Solver Parameters dialog box is selected, this version provides a variety of new features, including an online user's guide. The Premium Solver for Education has the same problem size limits as the standard Excel Solver: 200 decision variables and 100 constraints. We recommend that you install the new version and use the Premium mode option when developing and solving spreadsheet models of linear programs.

The following steps describe how Frontline Systems' Premium Solver for Education can be used to obtain the optimal solution to the RMC problem:

Step 1. Select the **Add-ins** tab on the Ribbon
Step 2. Select **Premium Solver** in the **Menu Commands** group
Step 3. When the **Solver Parameters** dialog box appears (see Figure 7.28):
  Enter B17 into the **Set Target Cell** box
  Select the **Equal To: Max** option

FIGURE 7.28   SOLVER PARAMETERS DIALOG BOX FOR THE RMC PROBLEM

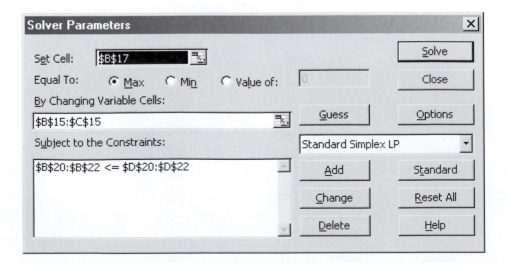

Enter B15:C15 into the **By Changing Cells** box
Select **Add**

Step 4. When the **Add Constraint** dialog box appears:
Enter B20:B22 in the **Cell Reference** box
Select $<=$
Enter D20:D22 in the **Constraint** box
Click **OK**

Step 5. When the **Solver Parameters** dialog box appears:
Choose **Options**

Step 6. When the **Solver Options** dialog box appears:
Select **Assume Non-Negative**
Click **OK**

Step 7. When the **Solver Parameters** dialog box appears:
Choose **Solve**

Step 8. When the **Solver Results** dialog box appears:
Select **Keep Solver Solution**
Click **OK**

If the Standard button and Standard Simplex LP option do not appear, click the Premium button and select the Standard Simplex LP option.

Figure 7.28 shows the completed Solver Parameters dialog box, and Figure 7.29 shows the optimal solution in the worksheet. The optimal solution of 25 tons of fuel additive and 20 tons of solvent base is the same as we obtained using the graphical solution procedure.

FIGURE 7.29   EXCEL SOLUTION FOR THE RMC PROBLEM

	A	B	C	D
1	**RMC**			
2				
3		**Material Requirements**		
4	**Material**	**Fuel Additive**	**Solvent Base**	**Amount Available**
5	Material 1	0.4	0.5	20
6	Material 2	0	0.2	5
7	Material 3	0.6	0.3	21
8	**Profit Per Ton**	40	30	
9				
10				
11	**Model**			
12				
13		**Decision Variables**		
14		**Fuel Additive**	**Solvent Base**	
15	**Tons Produced**	25	20	
16				
17	**Maximize Total Profit**	1600		
18				
19	**Constraints**	**Amount Used (LHS)**		**Amount Available (RHS)**
20	Material 1	20	$<=$	20
21	Material 2	4	$<=$	5
22	Material 3	21	$<=$	21

In addition to the output information shown in Figure 7.29, Solver has an option to provide sensitivity analysis information. We discuss sensitivity analysis in Chapter 8.

In step 6 we selected the **Assume Non-Negative** option in the **Solver Options** dialog box to avoid having to enter nonnegativity constraints for the decision variables. In general, whenever we want to solve a linear programming model in which the decision variables are all restricted to be nonnegative, we will select this option. In addition, in step 4 we entered all three less-than-or-equal-to constraints simultaneously by entering B20:B22 into the **Cell Reference** box, selecting $\leq$, and entering D20:D22 into the **Constraint** box. Alternatively, we could have entered the four constraints one at a time.

CHAPTER 8

Linear Programming: Sensitivity Analysis and Interpretation of Solution

CONTENTS

Sensitivity analysis is the study of how changes in the coefficients of a linear programming problem affect the optimal solution. Using sensitivity analysis, we can answer questions such as the following:

1. How will a change in an *objective function coefficient* affect the optimal solution?
2. How will a change in a *right-hand-side value* for a constraint affect the optimal solution?

Because sensitivity analysis is concerned with how these changes affect the optimal solution, sensitivity analysis does not begin until the optimal solution to the original linear programming problem has been obtained. For this reason, sensitivity analysis is often referred to as *postoptimality analysis.*

Our approach to sensitivity analysis parallels the approach used to introduce linear programming in Chapter 7. We introduce sensitivity analysis by using the graphical method for a linear programming problem with two decision variables. Then, we show how The Management Scientist software package can be used to provide more complete sensitivity analysis information.

Finally, we extend the discussion of problem formulation started in Chapter 7 by formulating and solving three larger linear programming problems. In discussing the solution for each of these problems, we focus on managerial interpretation of the optimal solution and sensitivity analysis information.

Sensitivity analysis and the interpretation of the optimal solution are important aspects of applying linear programming. The Q.M. in Action, Assigning Products to Worldwide Facilities at Eastman Kodak, shows some of the sensitivity analysis and interpretation issues encountered at Kodak in determining the optimal product assignments. Later in the chapter other Q.M. in Action features illustrate how Performance Analysis Corporation uses sensitivity analysis as part of an evaluation model for a chain of fast-food outlets, how General Electric Plastics uses a linear programming model involving thousands of variables and constraints to determine optimal production quantities, how the Nutrition Coordinating Center of the University of Minnesota uses a linear programming model to estimate the nutrient amounts in new food products, and how Duncan Industries Limited's linear programming model for tea distribution convinced management of the benefits of using quantitative analysis techniques to support the decision-making process.

Q.M. *in* ACTION

ASSIGNING PRODUCTS TO WORLDWIDE FACILITIES AT EASTMAN KODAK*

One of the major planning issues at Eastman Kodak involves the determination of which products should be manufactured at Kodak's facilities located throughout the world. The assignment of products to facilities is called the "world load." In determining the world load, Kodak faces a number of interesting trade-offs. For instance, not all manufacturing facilities are equally efficient for all products, and the margins by which some facilities are better varies from product to product. In

addition to manufacturing costs, the transportation costs and the effects of duty and duty drawbacks can significantly affect the allocation decision.

To assist in determining the world load, Kodak developed a linear programming model that accounts for the physical nature of the distribution problem and the various costs (manufacturing, transportation, and duties) involved. The model's objective is to minimize the total cost subject to constraints such as satisfying demand and capacity constraints for each facility.

*Based on information provided by Greg Sampson of Eastman Kodak.

(continued)

The linear programming model is a static representation of the problem situation, and the real world is always changing. Thus, the linear programming model must be used in a dynamic way. For instance, when demand expectations change, the model can be used to determine the effect the change will have on the world load. Suppose that the currency of country A rises compared to the currency of country B. How should the world load be modified? In addition to using the linear programming model in a "how-to-react" mode, the model is useful in a more active mode by considering questions such as the following: Is it worthwhile for facility F to spend d dollars to lower the unit manufacturing cost of product P from x to y? The linear programming model helps Kodak evaluate the overall effect of possible changes at any facility.

In the final analysis, managers recognize that they cannot use the model by simply turning it on, reading the results, and executing the solution. The model's recommendation combined with managerial judgment provides the final decision.

8.1 Introduction to Sensitivity Analysis

Sensitivity analysis is important to decision makers because real-world problems exist in a changing environment. Prices of raw materials change, product demands change, production capacities change, stock prices change, and so on. If a linear programming model has been used in such an environment, we can expect some of the coefficients in the model to change over time. As a result, we will want to determine how these changes affect the optimal solution. Sensitivity analysis provides information needed to respond to such changes without requiring a complete solution of a revised linear program.

Recall the RMC problem introduced in Chapter 7. RMC wanted to determine the number of tons of fuel additive (F) and the number of tons of solvent base (S) to produce in order to maximize the total profit contribution for the two products. Three raw material constraints limit the amounts of the two products that can be produced. The RMC linear programming model is restated here:

$$
\begin{aligned}
\text{Max} \quad & 40F + 30S \\
\text{s.t.} \quad & \\
& 0.4F + 0.5 \le 20 \quad \text{Material 1} \\
& 0.2S \le 5 \quad \text{Material 2} \\
& 0.6F + 0.3S \le 21 \quad \text{Material 3} \\
& F, S \ge 0
\end{aligned}
$$

The optimal solution, $F = 25$ tons and $S = 20$ tons, provided a maximum profit contribution of $1600.

The optimal solution was based on profit contributions of $40 per ton for the fuel additive and $30 per ton for the solvent base. However, suppose that we later learn that a price reduction causes the profit contribution for the fuel additive to fall from $40 to $30 per ton. Sensitivity analysis can be used to determine whether producing 25 tons of fuel additive and 20 tons of solvent base is still best. If it is, solving a modified linear programming problem with $30F + 30S$ as the new objective function is not necessary.

Sensitivity analysis can also be used to determine which coefficients in a linear programming model are crucial. For example, suppose that management believes that the $30 per ton profit contribution for the solvent base is only a rough estimate of the profit contribution that will actually be obtained. If sensitivity analysis shows that 25 tons of fuel additive and 20 tons of solvent base will be the optimal solution as long as the profit contribution for the solvent base is between $20 and $50, management should feel comfortable with the $30 per ton estimate and the recommended production quantities. However, if sensitivity analysis shows that 25 tons of fuel additive and 20 tons of solvent base will be the optimal solution only if the profit contribution for the solvent base is between $29.90 and $30.20 per ton, management may want to review the accuracy of the $30 per ton estimate.

Another aspect of sensitivity analysis concerns changes in the right-hand-side values of the constraints. Recall that in the RMC problem the optimal solution used all available material 1 and material 3. What would happen to the optimal solution and total profit contribution if RMC could obtain additional quantities of either of these resources? Sensitivity analysis can help determine how much each added ton of material is worth and how many tons can be added before diminishing returns set in.

Objective Function Coefficients

Let us begin sensitivity analysis by using the graphical solution procedure to demonstrate how a change in an objective function coefficient can affect the optimal solution to a linear programming problem. We begin with the graphical solution to the original RMC problem shown in Figure 8.1. The feasible region is shaded. The objective function $40F + 30S$ takes on its maximum value at the extreme point $F = 25$ and $S = 20$. Thus, $F = 25$ and $S = 20$ is the optimal solution and $40(25) + 30(20) = 1600$ is the value of the optimal solution.

Now suppose RMC learns that a price reduction in the fuel additive has reduced its profit contribution to $30 per ton. With this reduction, RMC's management may question

FIGURE 8.1   OPTIMAL SOLUTION TO THE ORIGINAL RMC PROBLEM

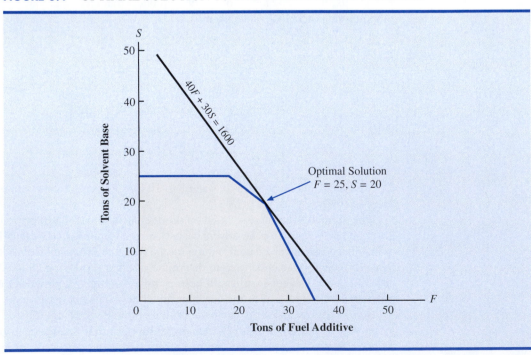

the desirability of maintaining the original optimal solution of $F = 25$ tons and $S = 20$ tons. Perhaps a different solution is now optimal. The RMC linear program with the revised objective function is as follows:

$$\text{Max} \quad 30F + 30S$$

s.t.

$$0.4F + 0.5S \leq 20 \quad \text{Material 1}$$
$$0.2S \leq 5 \quad \text{Material 2}$$
$$0.6F + 0.3S \leq 21 \quad \text{Material 3}$$
$$F, S \geq 0$$

Note that only the objective function has changed. Because the constraints have not changed, the feasible region for the revised RMC problem remains the same as the original problem. The graphical solution to the RMC problem with the objective function $30F + 30S$ is shown in Figure 8.2. Note that the extreme point providing the optimal solution is still $F = 25$ and $S = 20$. Thus, although the total profit contribution decreased to $30(25) + 30(20) = 1350$, the decrease in the profit contribution for the fuel additive from $40 per ton to $30 per ton does not change the optimal solution $F = 25$ and $S = 20$.

Now let us suppose that a further price reduction causes the profit contribution for the fuel additive to be reduced to $20 per ton. Is $F = 25$ and $S = 20$ still the optimal solution? Figure 8.3 shows the graphical solution to the RMC problem with the objective function revised to $20F + 30S$. The extreme point providing the optimal solution is now $F = 18.75$ and $S = 25$. The total profit contribution decreased to $20(18.75) + 30(25) = 1125$. However, in this case, we see that decreasing the profit contribution for the fuel additive to $20 per ton

FIGURE 8.2   REVISED OPTIMAL SOLUTION WITH THE RMC OBJECTIVE FUNCTION $30F + 30S$

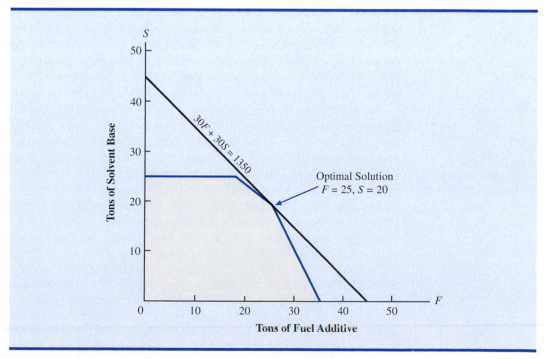

FIGURE 8.3   REVISED OPTIMAL SOLUTION WITH THE RMC OBJECTIVE FUNCTION
$20F + 30S$

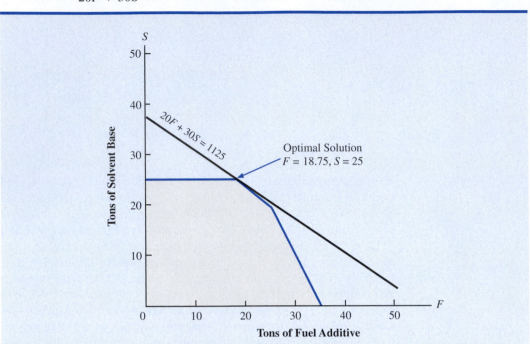

changes the optimal solution. The solution $F = 25$ tons and $S = 20$ is no longer optimal. The solution $F = 18.75$ and $S = 25$ now provides the optimal production quantities for RMC.

The graphical solution is used here to help the reader visualize how changes to an objective function coefficient may or may not change the optimal solution.

What do we learn from the graphical solutions in Figures 8.1, 8.2, and 8.3? Changing one objective function coefficient changes the slope of the objective function line but leaves the feasible region unchanged. If the change in the objective function coefficient is small, the extreme point that provided the optimal solution to the original problem may still provide the optimal solution. However, if the change in the objective function coefficient is large enough, a different extreme point will provide a new optimal solution.

Computer solutions typically provide sensitivity analysis information. The user does not have to solve several revised linear programming problems to obtain sensitivity analysis information.

Fortunately, the linear programming computer solution to the original RMC linear programming problem provides the sensitivity analysis information about the objective function coefficients. *You do not have to reformulate and resolve the linear programming problem to obtain the sensitivity analysis information.* The computer solution to the original RMC linear programming problem is shown in Figure 8.4. Refer to the shaded section labeled OBJECTIVE COEFFICIENT RANGES. Consider the row for the fuel additive F. The Lower Limit is $24, the Current Value is $40, and the Upper Limit is $60. The range $24 to $60 provides the objective coefficient range for the fuel additive. Thus, assuming that all other aspects of the original RMC problem do not change, the profit contribution for the fuel additive can be from $24 per ton to $60 per ton and the solution $F = 25$ tons and $S = 20$ tons will remain the optimal solution. Indeed, this result is what we observed with the graphical solution in Figures 8.2 and 8.3. When the profit contribution of the fuel additive was reduced to $30 per ton (within the $24 to $60 objective coefficient range), the solution $F = 25$ and tons and $S = 20$ tons remained optimal. However, when the profit contribution of the fuel additive was reduced to $20 per ton (outside the $24 to $60 objective coefficient range), the solution $F = 25$ tons and $S = 20$ tons was no longer optimal. In summary, if the objective

FIGURE 8.4 THE MANAGEMENT SCIENTIST SOLUTION FOR THE RMC PROBLEM

```
Objective Function Value =              1600.00

        Variable              Value              Reduced Costs
     --------------      ----------------      ------------------
           F                  25.000                 0.000
           S                  20.000                 0.000

       Constraint          Slack/Surplus           Dual Prices
     --------------      ----------------      ------------------
           1                   0.000                33.333
           2                   1.000                 0.000
           3                   0.000                44.444


OBJECTIVE COEFFICIENT RANGES

     Variable      Lower Limit      Current Value      Upper Limit
   ------------  ----------------  ----------------  ----------------
        F            24.000            40.000            60.000
        S            20.000            30.000            50.000


RIGHT HAND SIDE RANGES

   Constraint      Lower Limit      Current Value      Upper Limit
   ------------  ----------------  ----------------  ----------------
        1            14.000            20.000            21.500
        2             4.000             5.000         No Upper Limit
        3            18.750            21.000            30.000
```

The objective coefficient range is often referred to as the range of optimality.

function coefficient for the fuel additive is within its objective coefficient range, $24 to $60, and all other aspects of the original RMC problem remain unchanged, the optimal solution to the RMC problem will still be $F = 25$ tons and $S = 20$ tons.

Now let us use the sensitivity analysis information in Figure 8.4 to interpret what it tells us about changes in the objective function coefficient for the solvent base. Assuming that the profit contribution for the fuel additive is $40 per ton and that all other aspects of the original RMC problem remain unchanged, the objective coefficient range for the solvent base is $20 to $50. Thus, we conclude that as long as the profit contribution for the solvent base is within the $20 to $50 range, the solution $F = 25$ and $S = 20$ will remain optimal. If the profit contribution for the solvent base is outside this range, a different extreme point and a different solution will become optimal.

Simultaneous Changes

The sensitivity analysis information provided for the objective function coefficients is based on the assumption that only one objective function coefficient changes at a time and that all other aspects of the original problem remain unchanged. Thus, an objective coefficient range is only applicable for changes to a single objective coefficient. However, in some cases, we may be interested in what happens if two or more objective function

TABLE 8.1 OBJECTIVE COEFFICIENT RANGES, ALLOWABLE DECREASES, AND ALLOWABLE INCREASES FOR THE RMC PROBLEM

Decision Variable	Objective Coefficient Range			Allowable Decrease	Allowable Increase
	Lower Limit	Current Value	Upper Limit		
F	24	40	60	16	20
S	20	30	50	10	20

Sensitivity analysis information assumes that only one objective function coefficient changes at a time. Other coefficients in the problem are assumed to be as stated in the original problem.

coefficients change simultaneously. As we will demonstrate, some analysis of simultaneous changes is possible with the help of the **100 percent rule**.

Referring to the computer solution in Figure 8.4, we restate the objective coefficient ranges for the RMC problem in Table 8.1. The Allowable Decrease and Allowable Increase columns indicate how much the current value of the objective function coefficient can decrease or increase without changing the optimal solution. The Allowable Decrease and Allowable Increase values are computed as follows:

$$\text{Allowable Decrease} = \text{Current Value} - \text{Lower Limit}$$
$$\text{Allowable Increase} = \text{Upper Limit} - \text{Current Value}$$

Suppose RMC's accounting department reviews both the price and cost data for the two products. As a result, the profit contribution for the fuel additive is increased to $48 per ton and the profit contribution for the solvent base is decreased to $27 per ton. Thus, the fuel additive has a $48 − $40 = $8 per ton increase. From Table 8.1 we see that the allowable increase for the fuel additive coefficient is $60 − $40 = $20. Thus, the $8 increase in the fuel additive objective function coefficient is 8/20 = 0.40, or 40%, of its allowable increase. Similarly, the solvent base has a $30 − $27 = $3 per ton decrease. With an allowable decrease of $30 − $20 = $10, the $3 decrease in the solvent base objective function coefficient is 3/10 = 0.30, or 30%, of its allowable decrease. The sum of the percentage increase for the fuel additive and the percentage decrease for the solvent base is 40% + 30% = 70%.

Let us now state the 100 percent rule as it applies to simultaneous changes in the objective function coefficients.

100 PERCENT RULE FOR OBJECTIVE FUNCTION COEFFICIENTS

For all objective function coefficients that are changed, sum the percentages of the allowable increases and the allowable decreases. If the sum of the percentages is less than or equal to 100%, the optimal solution will not change.

Applying the 100 percent rule to the RMC problem, we see that the sum of the percentages of the allowable increases and the allowable decreases is 70%. Thus, the 100% rule indicates that if the profit contribution for the fuel additive increases to $48 per ton and the profit contribution for the solvent base decreases to $27 per ton, the solution of $F = 25$ tons and $S = 20$ tons will remain optimal. Thus, with the revised objective function coefficients and the same optimal solution, the total profit contribution becomes 48(25) + 27(20) = $1740.

Finally, note that the 100 percent rule *does not* say that the optimal solution will change if the sum of the percentages of the allowable increases and the allowable decreases is greater than 100%. All we can say is that if the sum of the percentages is greater than 100%, a different optimal solution *may exist*. Thus, whenever the sum of the percentage changes is greater than 100%, the revised problem must be solved in order to determine the new optimal solution.

NOTES AND COMMENTS

If two objective function coefficients change simultaneously, both may move outside their respective objective coefficient ranges and not affect the optimal solution. For instance, in a two-variable linear program, the slope of the objective function will not change at all if both coefficients are changed by the same percentage.

8.3 Right-Hand Sides

Let us expand the discussion of sensitivity analysis by considering how a change in the right-hand side of a constraint affects the feasible region and the optimal solution to a linear programming problem. As with sensitivity analysis for the objective function coefficients, we consider what happens when we make *one change at a time*. For example, suppose that in the RMC problem an additional 4.5 tons of material 3 becomes available. In this case, the right-hand side of the third constraint increases from 21 tons to 25.5 tons. The revised RMC linear programming model is as follows:

$$\text{Max} \quad 40F + 30S$$

s.t.

$$
\begin{array}{llll}
0.4F + 0.5S & \leq 20 & \quad & \text{Material 1} \\
 0.2S & \leq 5 & \quad & \text{Material 2} \\
0.6F + 0.3S & \leq 25.5 & \quad & \text{Material 3} \\
F, S & \geq 0 &
\end{array}
$$

Sensitivity analysis for right-hand sides is based on the assumption that only one right-hand side changes at a time. All other aspects of the problem are assumed to be as stated in the original problem.

The graphical solution to this problem is shown in Figure 8.5. Note how the feasible region expands because of the additional 4.5 tons of material 3. Application of the graphical solution procedure shows that the extreme point $F = 37.5$ tons and $S = 10$ tons is the new optimal solution. The value of the optimal solution is $40(37.5) + 30(10) = \$1800$. Recall that the optimal solution to the original RMC problem was $F = 25$ tons and $S = 20$ tons and the value of the optimal solution was $1600. Thus, the additional 4.5 tons of material 3 in the revised problem provides a new optimal solution and increases the value of the optimal solution by $1800 − \$1600 = \$200$. On a per ton basis, the additional 4.5 tons of material 3 increases the value of the optimal solution at the rate of $\$200/4.5 = \$44.44$ per ton.

Dual prices often provide the economic information that helps make decisions about acquiring additional resources.

The **dual price** is the *improvement* in the value of the optimal solution per unit increase in the right-hand side of a constraint. Hence, the dual price for the material 3 constraint is $44.44 per ton. In other words, if we increase the right-hand side of the material 3 constraint by 1 ton, the value of the optimal solution will improve $44.44. Conversely, if we decrease the right-hand side of the material 3 constraint by 1 ton, the value of the optimal solution will worsen $44.44. In general, the dual price tells us what will happen to the value of the optimal solution if we make a one-unit change in the right-hand side of a constraint.

FIGURE 8.5   GRAPHICAL SOLUTION TO THE RMC PROBLEM WITH MATERIAL 3
CONSTRAINT $0.6F + 0.5S \leq 24.5$

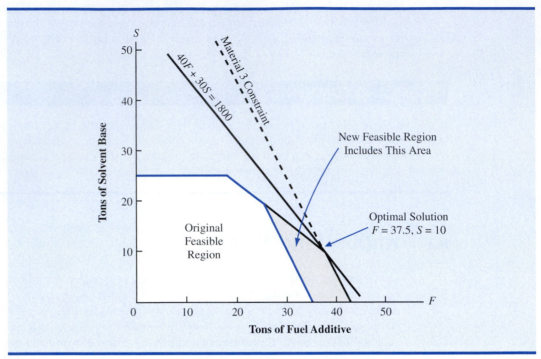

Fortunately, the linear programming computer solution to the original linear programming problem provides the dual prices for all the constraints. *You do not have to reformulate and resolve the linear programming problem to obtain the dual price information.* The computer solution to the original RMC linear programming problem is shown in Figure 8.6. The column labeled Dual Prices provides the following information:

Computer solutions typically provide the dual price and right-hand-side range information for each constraint.

Constraint	Dual Price
Material 1	$33.33
Material 2	$ 0.00
Material 3	$44.44

Note that the dual price for material 3, $44.44 per ton, agrees with the calculations we made using the graphical solution procedure. We also observe that the dual price for the material 1 constraint indicates that the value of the optimal solution will improve at the rate of $33.33 per ton of material 1. Finally, note that the dual price for the material 2 constraint is $0.00. Referring to Figure 8.6, we see that the optimal solution to the RMC problem shows that material 2 has a slack of one ton. Thus, at the optimal solution, one ton of material 2 is unused. The dual price of $0.00 tells us that additional tons of material 2 will simply add to the amount of slack for constraint 2 and will not change the value of the optimal solution.

We caution here that the value of a dual price may be applicable only for small increases in the right-hand side. As more and more resources are obtained and as the right-hand side continues to increase, other constraints will become binding and limit the change in the

FIGURE 8.6 THE MANAGEMENT SCIENTIST SOLUTION FOR THE RMC PROBLEM

```
Objective Function Value =              1600.00

          Variable              Value            Reduced Costs
        --------------      ---------------      ----------------
             F                 25.000                 0.000
             S                 20.000                 0.000

        Constraint         Slack/Surplus           Dual Prices
        --------------     ---------------      ----------------
             1                  0.000                33.333
             2                  1.000                 0.000
             3                  0.000                44.444


OBJECTIVE COEFFICIENT RANGES

     Variable      Lower Limit      Current Value      Upper Limit
    -----------   ---------------   ---------------   ---------------
        F            24.000            40.000            60.000
        S            20.000            30.000            50.000


RIGHT HAND SIDE RANGES

     Constraint    Lower Limit      Current Value      Upper Limit
    -----------   ---------------   ---------------   ---------------
        1            14.000            20.000            21.500
        2             4.000             5.000         No Upper Limit
        3            18.750            21.000            30.000
```

value of the optimal solution. At some point, the dual price can no longer be used to determine the improvement in the value of the optimal solution. To determine the range where the dual price is applicable, refer to Figure 8.6 and the section labeled RIGHT HAND SIDE RANGES. As long as the right-hand side for a constraint stays within its corresponding right-hand-side range, the dual price is applicable. For example, referring to constraint 3, we see that the dual price of $44.44 per ton for material 3 applies as long as the right-hand side of constraint 3 is between 18.75 tons and 30 tons. This range tells us that for each additional ton of material 3 that RMC could obtain, up to a total of 30 tons, the value of the optimal solution would improve by $44.44 for each ton added. However, if more than 30 tons were made available, RMC cannot expect the dual price of $44.44 per ton to be applicable. Similarly, the dual price for constraint 1 is $33.33 per ton as long as the amount of material 1 available is between 14 and 21.5 tons. Note also that the dual price of $0.00 for constraint 2 is applicable as long as the amount of material 2 available is at least 4 tons.

The right-hand-side range is often referred to as the range of feasibility.

The Q.M. in Action, Evaluating Efficiency at Performance Analysis Corporation, illustrates the use of dual prices as part of an evaluation model for a chain of fast-food outlets. This type of model will be studied in more detail in the next chapter when we discuss an application referred to as *data envelopment analysis*.

Q.M. *in* ACTION

EVALUATING EFFICIENCY AT PERFORMANCE ANALYSIS CORPORATION*

Performance Analysis Corporation specializes in the use of management science to design more efficient and effective operations for a wide variety of chain stores. One such application uses linear programming methodology to provide an evaluation model for a chain of fast-food outlets.

According to the concept of Pareto optimality, a restaurant in a given chain is relatively inefficient if other restaurants in the same chain exhibit the following characteristics:

1. Operates in the same or worse environment.
2. Produces at least the same level of *all* outputs.
3. Utilizes no more of *any* resource and *less* of at least one of the resources.

To determine which of the restaurants are Pareto inefficient, Performance Analysis Corporation developed and solved a linear programming model. Model constraints involve requirements concerning the minimum acceptable levels of output and conditions imposed by uncontrollable elements in the environment, and the objective function calls for the minimization of the resources

---

*Based on information provided by Richard C. Morey of Performance Analysis Corporation.

necessary to produce the output. Solving the model produces the following output for each restaurant:

1. A score that assesses the level of so-called relative technical efficiency achieved by the particular restaurant over the time period in question.
2. The reduction in controllable resources or the increase of outputs over the time period in question needed for an inefficient restaurant to be rated as efficient.
3. A peer group of other restaurants with which each restaurant can be compared in the future.

Sensitivity analysis provides important managerial information. For example, for each constraint concerning a minimum acceptable output level, the dual price tells the manager how much one more unit of output would increase the efficiency measure.

The analysis typically identifies 40% to 50% of the restaurants as underperforming, given the previously stated conditions concerning the inputs available and outputs produced. Performance Analysis Corporation finds that if all the relative inefficiencies identified are eliminated simultaneously, corporate profits typically increase approximately 5% to 10%. This increase is truly substantial given the large scale of operations involved.

NOTES AND COMMENTS

Some texts associate the term *shadow price* with each constraint. The concept of a shadow price is closely related to the concept of a dual price. The shadow price associated with a constraint is the *change* in the value of the optimal solution per-unit increase in the right-hand side of the constraint. In general, the dual price and the shadow price are the *same* for all *maximization* linear programs. In *minimization* linear programs, the shadow price is the *negative* of the corresponding dual price.

Simultaneous Changes

Keep in mind that the right-hand-side sensitivity analysis information is based on the assumption that only one right-hand side changes at a time. However, in some cases, we may be interested in what happens if two or more right-hand sides change simultaneously. Some analysis of simultaneous changes is possible with the help of the 100 percent rule.

Referring to the computer solution in Figure 8.6, we restate the right-hand-side range information for the RMC problem in Table 8.2. The Allowable Decrease and Allowable

TABLE 8.2 RIGHT-HAND-SIDE RANGES, ALLOWABLE DECREASES, AND ALLOWABLE INCREASES FOR THE RMC PROBLEM

| | **Right-Hand-Side Ranges** | | | | |
Constraint	**Lower Limit**	**Current Value**	**Upper Limit**	**Allowable Decrease**	**Allowable Increase**
Material 1	14	20	21.5	6	1.5
Material 2	4	5	No Upper Limit	1	No Upper Limit
Material 3	18.75	21	30	2.25	9

Increase columns indicate how much the current value of the right-hand side can decrease or increase without changing the dual price. The Allowable Decrease and Allowable Increase values are computed as follows:

$$\text{Allowable Decrease} = \text{Current Value} - \text{Lower Limit}$$
$$\text{Allowable Increase} = \text{Upper Limit} - \text{Current Value}$$

Now suppose that RMC's management decides to purchase an additional 0.5 tons of material 1 and an additional 4.5 tons of material 3. As Table 8.2 shows, material 1 has an allowable increase of 1.5 tons; therefore, the material 1 right-hand-side increase is $0.5/1.5 = 0.333$, or 33.3%, of its allowable increase. Similarly, because material 3 has an allowable increase of 9 tons, the material 3 right-hand-side increase is $4.5/9 = 0.50$, or 50%, of its allowable increase. The sum of the percentages for the two right-hand sides is $33.3\% + 50\% = 83.3\%$.

Let us now state the 100 percent rule as it applies to simultaneous changes in the right-hand sides of a linear programming problem.

> 100 PERCENT RULE FOR RIGHT-HAND SIDES
>
> For all right-hand sides that are changed, sum the percentages of the allowable increases and the allowable decreases. If the sum of the percentages is less than or equal to 100%, the dual prices do not change.

Applying the 100 percent rule to the RMC problem, we see that the sum of the percentages of the allowable increases and the allowable decreases is 83.3%. Thus, the 100 percent rule indicates that the dual price for the material 1 constraint remains $33.33 per ton, and the dual price for the material 3 constraint remains $44.44 per ton. Thus, the 0.5 additional tons of material 1 and 4.5 additional tons of material 3 will improve the value of the objective function $0.5(33.33) + 4.5(44.44) = \$216.65$. Note, however, that the revised linear program will have to be solved to determine the production quantities F and S that provide the new optimal solution.

The 100 percent rule *does not* say that the dual prices will change if the sum of the percentages of the allowable increases and the allowable decreases is greater than 100%. All we can say is that if the sum of the percentages is greater than 100%, different dual prices *may exist*. Thus, whenever the sum of the percentage changes is greater than 100%, a revised problem must be solved in order to determine the new optimal solution and the new dual prices.

A Second Example

As another example, let us consider the M&D Chemicals minimization problem introduced in Section 7.5. The decision variables are A = number of gallons of product A, and B = number of gallons of product B. The linear programming model is as follows:

$$\text{Min} \quad 2A + 3B$$

s.t.

$$
\begin{array}{rll}
1A & \geq 125 & \text{Demand for product } A \\
1A + 1B & \geq 350 & \text{Total production} \\
2A + 1B & \leq 600 & \text{Processing time} \\
A, B & \geq 0
\end{array}
$$

The solution obtained using The Management Scientist is presented in Figure 8.7. The computer output shows that the value of the optimal solution is $800. The values of the decision variables show that 250 gallons of product A and 100 gallons of product B provide the minimum cost solution.

FIGURE 8.7   THE MANAGEMENT SCIENTIST SOLUTION FOR THE M&D CHEMICALS PROBLEM

WEB file

M&D

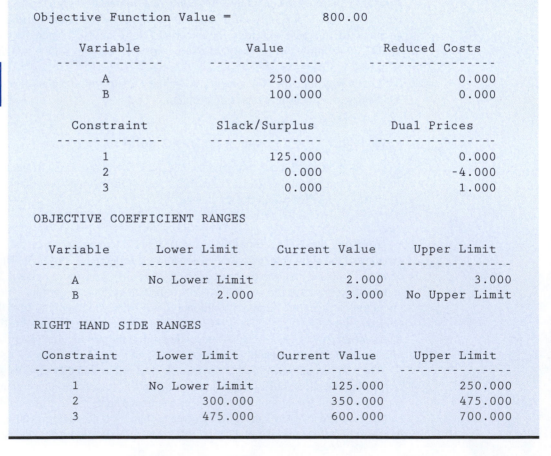

```
Objective Function Value =            800.00

        Variable              Value              Reduced Costs
     --------------      --------------       ------------------
           A                 250.000                   0.000
           B                 100.000                   0.000

       Constraint          Slack/Surplus            Dual Prices
     --------------      --------------       ------------------
           1                 125.000                   0.000
           2                   0.000                  -4.000
           3                   0.000                   1.000


OBJECTIVE COEFFICIENT RANGES

    Variable        Lower Limit      Current Value      Upper Limit
  ------------    --------------    --------------    --------------
       A          No Lower Limit         2.000             3.000
       B               2.000             3.000        No Upper Limit


RIGHT HAND SIDE RANGES

   Constraint       Lower Limit      Current Value      Upper Limit
  ------------    --------------    --------------    --------------
       1          No Lower Limit        125.000           250.000
       2               300.000          350.000           475.000
       3               475.000          600.000           700.000
```

The Slack/Surplus column shows that the $\geq$ constraint corresponding to the demand for product A (constraint 1) has a surplus of 125 units. In other words, the production of product A in the optimal solution exceeds demand by 125 gallons. The Slack/Surplus values are zero for the constraints corresponding to the total production (constraint 2) and the processing time (constraint 3); thus, these constraints are binding at the optimal solution.

The dual price shows the *improvement* in the value of the optimal solution per unit increase in the right-hand side of the constraint. Focusing first on the dual price of 1.00 for the processing time constraint (constraint 3), we see that if we can increase the processing time from 600 to 601 hours, the value of the optimal solution will *improve* by $1. Because the objective is to minimize costs, improvement in this case means a lowering of costs. Thus, if 601 hours of processing time are available, the value of the optimal solution will improve to $800 − $1 = $799. The RIGHT HAND SIDE RANGES section of the output shows that the upper limit for processing time (constraint 3) is 700 hours. Thus, the dual price of $1 per unit would be applicable for every additional hour of processing time up to a total of 700 hours.

Let us again return to the Dual Prices section of the output and consider the dual price for total production (constraint 2). The *negative dual price* tells us that the value of the optimal solution *will not improve* if the right-hand side is increased by one unit. In fact, the dual price of 24.00 tells us that if the right-hand side of the total production constraint is increased from 350 to 351 units, the value of the optimal solution will worsen by the amount of $4. Because worsening means an increase in cost, the value of the optimal solution will become $800 + $4 = $804 if the one-unit increase in the total production requirement is made.

Because the dual price refers to improvement in the value of the optimal solution per unit increase in the right-hand side, a constraint with a negative dual price should not have its right-hand side increased. In fact, if the dual price is negative, efforts should be made to reduce the right-hand side of the constraint. If the right-hand side of the total production constraint were decreased from 350 to 349 units, the dual price indicates that the total cost could be lowered by $4 to $800 − $4 = $796.

Even though the dual price is the improvement in the value of the optimal solution per unit increase in the right-hand side of a constraint, the interpretation of an *improvement* in the value of an objective function depends on whether we are solving a maximization or a minimization problem. The dual price for a $\leq$ constraint will always be greater than or equal to zero because increasing the right-hand side cannot make the value of the objective function worse. Similarly, the dual price for a $\geq$ constraint will always be less than or equal to zero because increasing the right-hand side cannot improve the value of the optimal solution.

Finally, consider the right-hand-side ranges provided in Figure 8.7. The ranges for the M&D Chemicals problem are summarized here:

Constraint	Min RHS	Max RHS
Product A demand	No lower limit	250
Total production	300	475
Processing time	475	700

Try Problem 10 to test your ability to interpret the computer output for a minimization problem.

As long as the right-hand sides are within these ranges, the dual prices shown on the computer printout are applicable.

Cautionary Note on the Interpretation of Dual Prices

As stated previously, the dual price is the improvement in the value of the optimal solution per unit increase in the right-hand side of a constraint. When the right-hand side of the constraint represents the amount of a resource available, the associated dual price is often interpreted as the maximum amount one should be willing to pay for one additional unit of the resource. However, such an interpretation is not always correct. To see why, we need to understand the difference between sunk and relevant costs. A **sunk cost** is one that is not affected by the decision made. It will be incurred no matter what values the decision variables assume. A **relevant cost** is one that depends on the decision made. The amount of a relevant cost will vary depending on the values of the decision variables.

Let us reconsider the RMC problem. The amount of material 1 available is 20 tons. The cost of material 1 is a sunk cost if it must be paid regardless of the number of tons of fuel additive and solvent base produced. It would be a relevant cost if RMC only had to pay for the number of tons of material 1 actually used to produce fuel additive and solvent base. All relevant costs should be included in the objective function of a linear program. Sunk costs should not be included in the objective function. For RMC we have been assuming that the company has already paid for materials 1, 2, and 3. Therefore, the cost of the raw materials for RMC is a sunk cost and has not been included in the objective function.

Only relevant costs should be included in the objective function.

When the cost of a resource is *sunk,* the dual price can be interpreted as the maximum amount the company should be willing to pay for one additional unit of the resource. When the cost of a resource used is relevant, the dual price can be interpreted as the amount by which the value of the resource exceeds its cost. Thus, when the resource cost is relevant, the dual price can be interpreted as the maximum premium over the normal cost that the company should be willing to pay for one unit of the resource.

NOTES AND COMMENTS

1. Computer software packages for solving linear programs are readily available. Most of these provide the optimal solution, dual or shadow price information, the objective coefficient ranges, and the right-hand-side ranges. The labels used for these ranges may vary, but the meaning is the same as what we have described here.

2. Whenever one of the right-hand sides is at an end point of its range, the dual and shadow prices only provide one-sided information. In this case, they only predict the change in the optimal value of the objective function for changes toward the interior of the range.

3. A condition called *degeneracy* can cause a subtle difference in how we interpret changes in the objective function coefficients beyond the end points of the objective coefficient range. Degeneracy occurs when the dual price equals zero for one of the binding constraints. Degeneracy does not affect the interpretation of changes toward the interior of the objective coefficient range. However, when degeneracy is present,

changes beyond the end points of the range do not necessarily mean a different solution will be optimal. From a practical point of view, changes beyond the end points of the range necessitate resolving the problem.

4. The 100 percent rule permits an analysis of multiple changes in the right-hand sides or multiple changes in the objective function coefficients. But the 100 percent rule cannot be applied to changes in both objective function coefficients *and* right-hand sides at the same time. In order to consider simultaneous changes for *both* right-hand-side values and objective function coefficients, the problem must be resolved.

5. Managers are frequently called on to provide an economic justification for new technology. Often the new technology is developed, or purchased, in order to conserve resources. The dual price can be helpful in such cases because it can be used to determine the savings attributable to the new technology by showing the savings per unit of resource conserved.

8.4   More Than Two Decision Variables

The graphical solution procedure is useful only for linear programs involving two decision variables. In practice, the problems solved using linear programming usually involve large numbers of variables and constraints. For instance, the Q.M. in Action, Determining Optimal Production Quantities at GE Plastics, describes how a linear programming model with 3100 variables and 1100 constraints was solved in less than 10 seconds to determine the optimal production quantities at GE Plastics. In this section we discuss the formulation and computer solution for two linear programs with three decision variables. In doing so, we will show how to interpret the reduced-cost portion of the computer output and will also illustrate the interpretation of dual prices for constraints that involve percentages.

Modified RMC Problem

The RMC linear programming problem was introduced in Section 7.1. The original problem formulation is restated here:

$$\text{Max} \quad 40F + 30S$$

$$\text{s.t.}$$

$$0.4F + 0.5S \leq 20 \quad \text{Material 1}$$
$$0.2S \leq 5 \quad \text{Material 2}$$
$$0.6F + 0.3S \leq 21 \quad \text{Material 3}$$
$$F, S \geq 0$$

Recall that F is the number of tons of fuel additive produced and that S is the number of tons of solvent base produced. Suppose that management also is considering producing a carpet cleaning fluid. Estimates are that each ton of carpet cleaning fluid will require 0.6 ton of material 1, 0.1 ton of material 2, and 0.3 ton of material 3. Because of the unique capabilities of the new product, RMC's management believes that the company will realize a profit contribution of $50 for each ton of carpet cleaning fluid produced during the current production period.

Q.M. *in* ACTION

DETERMINING OPTIMAL PRODUCTION QUANTITIES AT GE PLASTICS*

General Electric Plastics (GEP) is a $5 billion global materials supplier of plastics and raw materials to many industries (e.g., automotive, computer, and medical equipment). GEP has plants all over the globe. In the past, GEP followed a pole-centric manufacturing approach wherein each product was manufactured in the geographic area (Americas, Europe, or Pacific) where it

was to be delivered. When many of GEP's customers started shifting their manufacturing operations to the Pacific, a geographic imbalance was created between GEP's capacity and demand in the form of overcapacity in the Americas and undercapacity in the Pacific.

Recognizing that a pole-centric approach was no longer effective, GEP adopted a global approach to its manufacturing operations. Initial work focused on the high-performance polymers (HPP) division. Using a linear programming model, GEP was able to determine the

*Based on R. Tyagi, P. Kalish, and K. Akbay, "GE Plastics Optimizes the Two-Echelon Global Fulfillment Network at Its High-Performance Polymers Division," *Interfaces* (September/October 2004): 359–366.

(continued)

optimal production quantities at each HPP plant to max-imize the total contribution margin for the division. The model included demand constraints, manufacturing ca-pacity constraints, and constraints that modeled the flow of materials produced at resin plants to the finishing plants and on to warehouses in three geographical regions (Americas, Europe, and Pacific). The mathemat-ical model for a one-year problem has 3100 variables and 1100 constraints, and can be solved in less than 10 seconds. The new system proved successful at the HPP division, and other GE Plastics divisions are adapt-ing it for their supply chain planning.

Let us consider the modifications in the original linear programming model that are needed to incorporate the effect of this additional decision variable. We let C denote the number of tons of carpet cleaning fluid produced. After adding C to the objective function and to each of the three constraints, we obtain the linear program for the modified problem:

$$\text{Max} \quad 40F + 30S + 50C$$

s.t.

$$
\begin{array}{rll}
0.4F + 0.5S + 0.6C & \leq 20 & \text{Material 1} \\
0.2S + 0.1C & \leq 5 & \text{Material 2} \\
0.6F + 0.3S + 0.3C & \leq 21 & \text{Material 3} \\
F, S, C & \geq 0
\end{array}
$$

Figure 8.8 shows The Management Scientist solution to the modified RMC problem. The optimal solution calls for the production of 27.5 tons of fuel additive, 0 tons of solvent base, and 15 tons of carpet cleaning fluid. The value of the optimal solution is $1850.

Note the information contained in the Reduced Costs column. The **reduced cost** indi-cates how much the objective function coefficient for a particular variable would have to improve before that decision variable could assume a positive value in the optimal solu-tion. As the computer output shows, the reduced costs for decision variables F and C are zero because these decision variables already have positive values in the optimal solution. The reduced cost of 12.50 for decision variable S tells us that the profit contribution for the solvent base would have to increase to at least $30 + $12.50 = $42.50 before S *could* assume a positive value in the optimal solution.[1] In other words, unless the profit contri-bution for S increases by at least $12.50, the value of S will remain at zero in the optimal solution.

Suppose that we increase the coefficient of S by $12.501 and then re-solve the problem using The Management Scientist. Figure 8.9 shows the new solution. Although S assumes a positive value in the new solution ($S = 20.000$), the value of the optimal solution ($1850.020) has only increased by two cents. Note that the difference of two cents is just 20, the number of units of S produced in the new solution, multiplied by 0.001, the amount we increased the coefficient of S beyond 12.50. In some computer software packages, in-creasing the objective function coefficient of S by *exactly* $12.50 will result in a solution in which S assumes a positive value and the value of the objective function remains at

---

[1]In the case of degeneracy, a decision variable may not assume a positive value in the optimal solution even when the improvement in the profit contribution exceeds the value of the reduced costs. Our definition of reduced costs, stated as ". . . *could* assume a positive value . . . ," provides for such special cases. More advanced texts on mathematical pro-gramming discuss these special types of situations.

FIGURE 8.8   THE MANAGEMENT SCIENTIST SOLUTION FOR THE MODIFIED RMC PROBLEM

```
Objective Function Value =               1850.00

        Variable                 Value              Reduced Costs
      --------------         ---------------       -----------------
           F                     27.500                  0.000
           S                      0.000                 12.500
           C                     15.000                  0.000

       Constraint             Slack/Surplus            Dual Prices
      --------------         ---------------       -----------------
           1                      0.000                 75.000
           2                      3.500                  0.000
           3                      0.000                 16.667

OBJECTIVE COEFFICIENT RANGES

   Variable         Lower Limit        Current Value        Upper Limit
  -----------      ---------------     ---------------      ---------------
      F                 33.333             40.000              100.000
      S            No Lower Limit          30.000               42.500
      C                 33.333             50.000               60.000

RIGHT HAND SIDE RANGES

   Constraint       Lower Limit        Current Value        Upper Limit
  -----------      ---------------     ---------------      ---------------
      1                 14.000             20.000               34.000
      2                  1.500              5.000         No Upper Limit
      3                 10.000             21.000               30.000
```

1850. In other words, increasing the profit contribution of S by exactly the amount of the reduced cost will result in alternative optimal solutions. However, whenever the profit contribution of S is increased by *more than* $12.50, S will not remain at zero in the optimal solution.

Figure 8.8 also shows that the dual prices for constraints 1 and 3 are 75.000 and 16.667, respectively, indicating that these two constraints are binding in the optimal solution. Thus, each additional ton of material 1 would increase the value of the optimal solution by $75 and each additional ton of material 3 would increase the value of the optimal solution by $16.667.

Suppose that after reviewing the solution shown in Figure 8.8, management decides to add the requirement that the number of tons of solvent base produced must be at least 25% of the number of tons of fuel additive produced. Writing this requirement using the decision variables F and S, we obtain

$$S \geq 0.25F \quad \text{or} \quad -0.25F + S \geq 0$$

FIGURE 8.9 THE MANAGEMENT SCIENTIST SOLUTION FOR THE MODIFIED RMC PROBLEM WITH THE COEFFICIENT OF S INCREASED BY $12.501

```
Objective Function Value =               1850.020

      Variable              Value              Reduced Costs
   --------------      ---------------        ------------------
         F                 25.000                   0.000
         S                 20.000                   0.000
         C                  0.000                   0.001

     Constraint         Slack/Surplus              Dual Prices
   --------------      ---------------        ------------------
         1                  0.000                  75.003
         2                  1.000                   0.000
         3                  0.000                  16.664

OBJECTIVE COEFFICIENT RANGES

    Variable         Lower Limit        Current Value        Upper Limit
   ------------    ---------------     ---------------      ---------------
        F               34.001             40.000              40.008
        S               42.500             42.501              50.000
        C          No Lower Limit          50.000              50.001

RIGHT HAND SIDE RANGES

   Constraint        Lower Limit        Current Value        Upper Limit
   ------------    ---------------     ---------------      ---------------
        1               14.000             20.000              21.500
        2                4.000              5.000          No Upper Limit
        3               18.750             21.000              30.000
```

Adding this new constraint to the modified RMC linear program and resolving the problem using The Management Scientist, we obtain the optimal solution shown in Figure 8.10.

Let us interpret the dual price for constraint 4, the requirement that the number of tons of solvent base produced must be at least 25% of the number of tons of fuel additive produced. The dual price of -12.121 indicates that a one-unit increase in the right side of the constraint will lower profits by $12.121. Thus, what the dual price of -12.121 is actually telling us is what will happen to the value of the optimal solution if the constraint is changed to

$$S \geq 0.25F + 1$$

The correct interpretation of the dual price of -12.121 can now be stated as follows: If we produce 1 ton of solvent base over and above the minimum 25% requirement, total profit will decrease by $12.121. Conversely, if we relax the minimum 25% requirement by 1 ton ($S \geq 0.25F - 1$), total profit will increase by $12.121.

The dual price for a percentage (or ratio) constraint such as this will not directly provide answers to questions concerning a percentage increase or decrease in the right-hand

FIGURE 8.10 THE MANAGEMENT SCIENTIST SOLUTION FOR THE MODIFIED RMC PROBLEM WITH THE 25% SOLVENT BASE REQUIREMENT

```
Objective Function Value =              1766.667

          Variable              Value            Reduced Costs
       --------------      ----------------      -----------------
             F                  26.667                 0.000
             S                   6.667                 0.000
             C                  10.000                 0.00

         Constraint         Slack/Surplus          Dual Prices
       --------------      ----------------      -----------------
             1                   0.000                78.788
             2                   2.667                 0.000
             3                   0.000                 9.091
             4                   0.000               -12.121

OBJECTIVE COEFFICIENT RANGES

     Variable        Lower Limit       Current Value      Upper Limit
    ------------    ----------------   ----------------   ----------------
         F              36.250             40.000            105.000
         S              15.000             30.000             42.500
         C              33.333             50.000             54.286

RIGHT HAND SIDE RANGES

    Constraint       Lower Limit       Current Value      Upper Limit
    ------------    ----------------   ----------------   ----------------
         1              16.333             20.000             32.571
         2               2.333              5.000        No Upper Limit
         3              10.000             21.000             25.714
         4              -6.875              0.000             13.750
```

side of the constraint. For example, what would happen to the value of the optimal solution if the number of tons of solvent base produced has to be at least 26% of the total number of tons of fuel additive? To answer such a question, we would resolve the problem using the constraint $-0.26S + F \geq 0$.

Because percentage (or ratio) constraints frequently occur in linear programming models, we need to consider another example. For instance, suppose that RMC's management states that the number of tons of carpet cleaning fluid produced may not exceed 20% of total production. Because total production is $F + S + C$, we can write this constraint as

$$C \leq 0.2(F + S + C)$$
$$C \leq 0.2F + 0.2S + 0.2C$$
$$-0.2F - 0.2S + 0.8C \leq 0$$

FIGURE 8.11   THE MANAGEMENT SCIENTIST SOLUTION FOR THE MODIFIED RMC PROBLEM WITH 25% SOLVENT BASE AND 20% CARPET CLEANING FLUID REQUIREMENTS

```
Objective Function Value =              1745.161

        Variable            Value             Reduced Costs
    --------------      ---------------      -----------------

          F                 26.452                0.000
          S                  8.387                0.000
          C                  8.710                0.000


       Constraint        Slack/Surplus          Dual Prices
    --------------      ---------------      -----------------

          1                  0.000               38.710
          2                  2.452                0.000
          3                  0.000               46.237
          4                  1.774                0.000
          5                  0.000               16.129

OBJECTIVE COEFFICIENT RANGES

     Variable       Lower Limit      Current Value      Upper Limit
    -----------    -------------    ---------------    ---------------

          F             23.462           40.000             64.000
          S             16.667           30.000             42.500
          C             33.333           50.000         No Upper Limit

RIGHT HAND SIDE RANGES

     Constraint     Lower Limit      Current Value      Upper Limit
    -----------    -------------    ---------------    ---------------

          1             19.463           20.000             24.000
          2              2.548            5.000         No Upper Limit
          3             15.698           21.000             21.579
          4         No Lower Limit        0.000              1.774
          5             -9.000            0.000              1.333
```

The solution obtained using The Management Scientist for the model that incorporates both the effects of this new percentage requirement and the previous requirement ($-0.25F + S \geq 0$) is shown in Figure 8.11. After rounding, the dual price corresponding to the new constraint (constraint 5) is 16.13. Thus, every additional ton of carpet cleaning fluid that we are allowed to produce over the current 20% limit will increase the value of the objective function by $16.13; moreover, the right-hand-side range for this constraint shows that this interpretation is valid for increases of up to 1.333 tons.

Bluegrass Farms Problem

To provide additional practice in formulating and interpreting the computer solution for linear programs involving more than two decision variables, we consider a minimization problem involving three decision variables. Bluegrass Farms, located in Lexington, Kentucky, has been experimenting with a special diet for its racehorses. The feed components available for the diet are a standard horse feed product, an enriched oat product, and a new vitamin and mineral feed additive. The nutritional values in units per pound and the costs for the three feed components are summarized in Table 8.3; for example, each pound of the standard feed component contains 0.8 unit of ingredient A, 1 unit of ingredient B, and 0.1 unit of ingredient C. The minimum daily diet requirements for each horse are three units of ingredient A, six units of ingredient B, and four units of ingredient C. In addition, to control the weight of the horses, the total daily feed for a horse should not exceed 6 pounds. Bluegrass Farms would like to determine the minimum-cost mix that will satisfy the daily diet requirements.

To formulate a linear programming model for the Bluegrass Farms problem, we introduce three decision variables:

$$S = \text{number of pounds of the standard horse feed product}$$
$$E = \text{number of pounds of the enriched oat product}$$
$$A = \text{number of pounds of the vitamin and mineral feed additive}$$

Using the data in Table 8.3, the objective function that will minimize the total cost associated with the daily feed can be written as follows:

$$\text{Min } 0.25S + 0.5E + 3A$$

Because the minimum daily requirement for ingredient A is three units, we obtain the constraint

$$0.8S + 0.2E \geq 3$$

The constraint for ingredient B is

$$1.0S + 1.5E + 3.0A \geq 6$$

and the constraint for ingredient C is

$$0.1S + 0.6E + 2.0A \geq 4$$

Finally, the constraint that restricts the mix to at most 6 pounds is

$$S + E + A \leq 6$$

TABLE 8.3   NUTRITIONAL VALUE AND COST DATA FOR THE BLUEGRASS FARMS PROBLEM

Feed Component	Standard	Enriched Oat	Additive
Ingredient A	0.8	0.2	0.0
Ingredient B	1.0	1.5	3.0
Ingredient C	0.1	0.6	2.0
Cost per pound	$0.25	$0.50	$3.00

Combining all the constraints with the nonnegativity requirements enables us to write the complete linear programming model for the Bluegrass Farms problem as follows:

$$\text{Min} \quad 0.25S + 0.50E + 3A$$

s.t.

$$
\begin{array}{llll}
0.8S + 0.2E & \geq 3 & \text{Ingredient A} \\
1.0S + 1.5E + 3.0A & \geq 6 & \text{Ingredient B} \\
0.1S + 0.6E + 2.0A & \geq 4 & \text{Ingredient C} \\
S + E + A & \leq 6 & \text{Weight} \\
S, E, A \geq 0
\end{array}
$$

The output obtained using The Management Scientist to solve the Bluegrass Farms problem is shown in Figure 8.12. After rounding, we see that the optimal solution calls for a daily diet consisting of 3.51 pounds of the standard horse feed product, 0.95 pound of the enriched oat product, and 1.54 pounds of the vitamin and mineral feed additive. Thus, with feed component costs of $0.25, $0.50, and $3.00, the total cost of the optimal diet is

$$
\begin{array}{ll}
3.51 \text{ pounds @ } \$0.25 \text{ per pound} = & \$0.88 \\
0.95 \text{ pound @ } \$0.50 \text{ per pound} = & 0.47 \\
1.54 \text{ pounds @ } \$3.00 \text{ per pound} = & \underline{4.62} \\
\text{Total cost} = & \$5.97
\end{array}
$$

Looking at the Slack/Surplus section of the computer output, we find a value of 3.554 for constraint 2. Because constraint 2 is a greater-than-or-equal-to constraint, 3.554 is the surplus; the optimal solution exceeds the minimum daily diet requirement for ingredient B (6 units) by 3.554 units. Because the surplus values for constraints 1 and 3 are both zero, we see that the optimal diet just meets the minimum requirements for ingredients A and C; moreover, a slack value of zero for constraint 4 shows that the optimal solution provides a total daily feed weight of 6 pounds.

The dual price (after rounding) for constraint 1 (ingredient A) is −1.22. To interpret this value properly, we first look at the sign; it is negative. Thus increasing the right-hand side of constraint 1 will cause the solution value to worsen. In this minimization problem, "worsen" means that the total daily cost will increase. Thus a one-unit increase in the right-hand side of constraint 1 will increase the total cost of the daily diet by $1.22. Conversely, it is also correct to conclude that a decrease of one unit in the right-hand side will decrease the total cost by $1.22. Looking at the RIGHT HAND SIDE RANGES section of the computer output, we see that these interpretations are correct as long as the right-hand side of constraint 1 is between 1.143 and 3.368.

Suppose that the Bluegrass management is willing to reconsider their position regarding the maximum weight of the daily diet. The dual price of 0.92 (after rounding) for constraint 4 shows that a one-unit increase in the right-hand side of constraint 4 will reduce total cost by $0.92. The RIGHT HAND SIDE RANGES section of the output shows that this interpretation is correct for increases in the right-hand side up to a maximum of 8.478 pounds. Thus, the effect of increasing the right-hand side of constraint 4 from 6 to 8 pounds is a decrease in the total daily cost of 2 × $0.92, or $1.84. Keep in mind that if this change were made, the feasible region would change, and we would obtain a new optimal solution.

The OBJECTIVE COEFFICIENT RANGES section of the computer output shows a lower limit of −0.393 for S. Clearly, in a real problem, the objective function coefficient of

FIGURE 8.12 THE MANAGEMENT SCIENTIST SOLUTION FOR THE BLUEGRASS FARMS PROBLEM

WEB file

Bluegrass

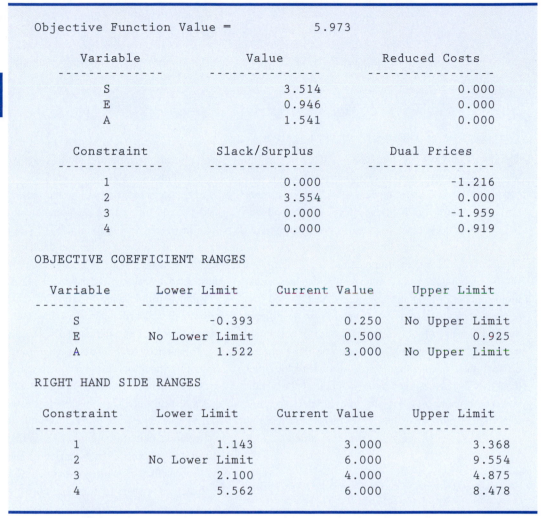

```
Objective Function Value =            5.973

          Variable              Value            Reduced Costs
      - - - - - - - - - - -   - - - - - - - - -   - - - - - - - - - - -
             S                  3.514                 0.000
             E                  0.946                 0.000
             A                  1.541                 0.000

          Constraint          Slack/Surplus         Dual Prices
      - - - - - - - - - - -   - - - - - - - - -   - - - - - - - - - - -
             1                  0.000                -1.216
             2                  3.554                 0.000
             3                  0.000                -1.959
             4                  0.000                 0.919

OBJECTIVE COEFFICIENT RANGES

     Variable      Lower Limit     Current Value     Upper Limit
   - - - - - - - -  - - - - - - - -  - - - - - - - - -  - - - - - - - - -
        S             -0.393            0.250       No Upper Limit
        E        No Lower Limit         0.500            0.925
        A              1.522            3.000       No Upper Limit

RIGHT HAND SIDE RANGES

    Constraint     Lower Limit     Current Value     Upper Limit
   - - - - - - - -  - - - - - - - -  - - - - - - - - -  - - - - - - - - -
        1              1.143            3.000            3.368
        2        No Lower Limit         6.000            9.554
        3              2.100            4.000            4.875
        4              5.562            6.000            8.478
```

S (the cost of the standard horse feed product) cannot take on a negative value. So, from a practical point of view, we can think of the lower limit for the objective function coefficient of *S* as being zero. We can thus conclude that no matter how much the cost of the standard mix were to decrease, the optimal solution would not change. Even if Bluegrass Farms could obtain the standard horse feed product for free, the optimal solution would still specify a daily diet of 3.51 pounds of the standard horse feed product, 0.95 pound of the enriched oat product, and 1.54 pounds of the vitamin and mineral feed additive. However, any decrease in the per-unit cost of the standard feed would result in a decrease in the total cost for the optimal daily diet.

Note that the objective coefficient ranges for *S* and *A* have no upper limit. Even if the cost of *A* were to increase, for example, from $3.00 to $13.00 per pound, the optimal solution would not change; the total cost of the solution, however, would increase by $10 (the amount of the increase) × 1.541, or $15.41. You must always keep in mind that the interpretations we make using the sensitivity analysis information in the computer output are only appropriate if all other coefficients in the problem do not change. To consider simultaneous changes, we must use the 100 percent rule or resolve the problem after making the changes.

Linear programming has been successfully applied to a variety of applications involving food products and nutrition. The Q.M. in Action, Estimation of Food Nutrient Values, discusses how the Nutrition Coordinating Center of the University of Minnesota uses linear programming to help estimate the nutrient amounts in new food products.

Q.M. *in* ACTION

ESTIMATION OF FOOD NUTRIENT VALUES*

The Nutrition Coordinating Center (NCC) of the University of Minnesota maintains a food-composition database that is used by nutritionists and researchers throughout the world. Nutrient information provided by NCC is used to estimate the nutrient intake of individuals, plan menus, research links between diet and disease, and meet regulatory requirements.

Nutrient intake calculations require data on an enormous number of food nutrient values. NCC's food composition database contains information on 93 different nutrients for each food product. With many new brand-name products introduced each year, NCC has the significant task of maintaining an accurate and timely database. The task is made more difficult by the fact that new brand-name products only provide data on a relatively small number of nutrients. Because of the high cost of chemically analyzing the new products, NCC

uses a linear programming model to help estimate thousands of nutrient values per year.

The decision variables in the linear programming model are the amounts of each ingredient in a food product. The objective is to minimize the difference between the estimated nutrient values and the known nutrient values for the food product. Constraints are that ingredients must be in descending order by weight, ingredients must be within nutritionist-specified bounds, and the differences between the calculated nutrient values and the known nutrient values must be within specified tolerances.

In practice, an NCC nutritionist uses the linear programming model to derive estimates of the amounts of each ingredient in a new food product. Given these estimates, the nutritionist refines the estimates based on his or her knowledge of the product formulation and the food composition. Once the amounts of each ingredient are obtained, the amounts of each nutrient in the food product can be calculated. With approximately 1000 products evaluated each year, the time and cost savings provided by using linear programming to help estimate the nutrient values are significant.

*Based on Brian J. Westrich, Michael A. Altmann, and Sandra J. Potthoff, "Minnesota's Nutrition Coordinating Center Uses Mathematical Optimization to Estimate Food Nutrient Values," *Interfaces* (September/October 1998): 86–99.

8.5 Electronic Communications Problem

The Electronic Communications problem is a maximization problem involving four decision variables, two less-than-or-equal-to constraints, one equality constraint, and one greater-than-or-equal-to constraint. We will use this problem to provide a summary of the process of formulating a mathematical model, using The Management Scientist to obtain an optimal solution, and interpreting the solution and sensitivity report information. In the next chapter we will continue to illustrate how linear programming can be applied by showing additional examples from the areas of marketing, finance, and production management.

Electronic Communications manufactures portable radio systems that can be used for two-way communications. The company's new product, which has a range of up to 25 miles, is suitable for use in a variety of business and personal applications. The distribution channels for the new radio are as follows:

1. Marine equipment distributors
2. Business equipment distributors
3. National chain of retail stores
4. Direct mail

Because of differing distribution and promotional costs, the profitability of the product will vary with the distribution channel. In addition, the advertising cost and the personal sales effort required will vary with the distribution channels. Table 8.4 summarizes the contribution to profit, advertising cost, and personal sales effort data for the Electronic Communications problem. The firm set the advertising budget at $5000. A maximum of 1800 hours of sales force time is available for allocation to the sales effort. Management also decided to produce exactly 600 units for the current production period. Finally, an ongoing contract with a national chain of retail stores requires that at least 150 units be distributed through this distribution channel.

Electronic Communications is now faced with the problem of determining the number of units that should be produced for each of the distribution channels in order to maximize the total contribution to profit. In addition to determining how many units should be allocated to each of the four distribution channels, Electronic Communications must also determine how to allocate the advertising budget and sales force effort to each of the four distribution channels.

Problem Formulation

We will now write the objective function and the constraints for the Electronic Communications problem. We begin with the objective function.

Objective function: Maximize profit

Four constraints are needed to account for the following restrictions: (1) a limited advertising budget, (2) limited sales force availability, (3) a production requirement, and (4) a retail stores distribution requirement.

Constraint 1 Advertising expenditure ≤ Budget

Constraint 2 Sales time used ≤ Time available

Constraint 3 Radios produced = Management requirement

Constraint 4 Retail distribution ≥ Contract requirement

TABLE 8.4 PROFIT, ADVERTISING COST, AND PERSONAL SALES TIME DATA FOR THE ELECTRONIC COMMUNICATIONS PROBLEM

Distribution Channel	Profit per Unit Sold	Advertising Cost per Unit Sold	Personal Sales Effort per Unit Sold
Marine distributors	$90	$10	2 hours
Business distributors	$84	$ 8	3 hours
National retail stores	$70	$ 9	3 hours
Direct mail	$60	$15	None

These expressions provide descriptions of the objective function and the constraints. We are now ready to define the decision variables that will represent the decisions the manager must make. For the Electronic Communications problem, we introduce the following four decision variables:

M = the number of units produced for the marine equipment distribution channel

B = the number of units produced for the business equipment distribution channel

R = the number of units produced for the national retail chain distribution channel

D = the number of units produced for the direct mail distribution channel

Using the data in Table 8.4, we can write the objective function for maximizing the total contribution to profit associated with the radios as follows:

$$\text{Max } 90M + 84B + 70R + 60D$$

Let us now develop a mathematical statement of the constraints for the problem. For the advertising budget of $5000, the constraint that limits the amount of advertising expenditure can be written as follows:

$$10M + 8B + 9R + 15D \leq 5000$$

Similarly, with sales time limited to 1800 hours, we obtain the constraint

$$2M + 3B + 3R \leq 1800$$

Management's decision to produce exactly 600 units during the current production period is expressed as

$$M + B + R + D = 600$$

Finally, to account for the fact that the number of units distributed by the national chain of retail stores must be at least 150, we add the constraint

$$R \geq 150$$

Combining all of the constraints with the nonnegativity requirements enables us to write the complete linear programming model for the Electronic Communications problem as follows:

$$
\begin{aligned}
\text{Max} \quad & 90M + 84B + 70R + 60D \\
\text{s.t.} \quad & \\
& 10M + 8B + 9R + 15D \leq 5000 \quad \text{Advertising budget} \\
& 2M + 3B + 3R \leq 1800 \quad \text{Sales force availability} \\
& M + B + R + D = 600 \quad \text{Production level} \\
& R \geq 150 \quad \text{Retail stores requirement} \\
& M, B, R, D \geq 0
\end{aligned}
$$

Computer Solution and Interpretation

A portion of the output obtained using The Management Scientist to solve the Electronic Communications problem is shown in Figure 8.13. The Objective Function Value section shows that the optimal solution to the problem will provide a profit of $48,450. The optimal values of the decision variables are $M = 25$, $B = 425$, $R = 150$, and $D = 0$. Thus, the

FIGURE 8.13 A PORTION OF THE MANAGEMENT SCIENTIST SOLUTION FOR THE ELECTRONIC COMMUNICATIONS PROBLEM

WEB file

Electronic

```
Objective Function Value =            48450.000

      Variable                Value              Reduced Costs
   ---------------      ---------------      ------------------
         M                    25.000                   0.000
         B                   425.000                   0.000
         R                   150.000                   0.000
         D                     0.000                  45.000


     Constraint           Slack/Surplus            Dual Prices
   ---------------      ---------------      ------------------
         1                     0.000                   3.000
         2                    25.000                   0.000
         3                     0.000                  60.000
         4                     0.000                 -17.000
```

optimal strategy for Electronic Communications is to concentrate on the business equipment distribution channel with $B = 425$ units. In addition, the firm should allocate 25 units to the marine distribution channel ($M = 25$) and meet its 150-unit commitment to the national retail chain store distribution channel ($R = 150$). With $D = 0$, the optimal solution indicates that the firm should not use the direct mail distribution channel.

Now consider the information contained in the Reduced Costs column. Recall that the reduced costs indicate how much each objective function coefficient would have to improve before the corresponding decision variable could assume a positive value in the optimal solution. As the computer output shows, the first three reduced costs are zero because the corresponding decision variables already have positive values in the optimal solution. However, the reduced cost of 45 for decision variable D tells us that the profit for the new radios distributed via the direct mail channel would have to increase from its current value of $60 per unit to at least $60 + $45 = $105 per unit before it would be profitable to use the direct mail distribution channel.

The computer output information for the slack/surplus variables and the dual prices is restated here:

Constraint Number	Constraint Name	Type of Constraint	Slack or Surplus	Dual Price
1	Advertising budget	$\leq$	0	3
2	Sales force availability	$\leq$	25	0
3	Production level	$=$	0	60
4	Retail stores requirement	$\geq$	0	-17

The advertising budget constraint has a slack of zero, indicating that the entire budget of $5000 has been used. The corresponding dual price of 3 tells us that an additional dollar added to the advertising budget will improve the objective function (increase the profit) by $3. Thus, the possibility of increasing the advertising budget should be seriously considered by the firm. The slack of 25 hours for the sales force availability constraint shows that

FIGURE 8.14 OBJECTIVE COEFFICIENT AND RIGHT-HAND-SIDE RANGES PROVIDED BY THE
MANAGEMENT SCIENTIST FOR THE ELECTRONIC COMMUNICATIONS PROBLEM

```
OBJECTIVE COEFFICIENT RANGES

    Variable        Lower Limit        Current Value        Upper Limit
  ------------    ---------------    ---------------      ---------------
       M                  84.000             90.000       No Upper Limit
       B                  50.000             84.000              90.000
       R           No Lower Limit            70.000              87.000
       D           No Lower Limit            60.000             105.000


RIGHT HAND SIDE RANGES

    Constraint      Lower Limit        Current Value        Upper Limit
  ------------    ---------------    ---------------      ---------------
       1                4950.000           5000.000            5850.000
       2                1775.000           1800.000       No Upper Limit
       3                 515.000            600.000             603.571
       4                   0.000            150.000             200.000
```

the allocated 1800 hours of sales time are adequate to distribute the radios produced and
that 25 hours of sales time will remain unused. Because the production level constraint is
an equality constraint, the zero slack/surplus shown on the output is expected. However, the
dual price of 60 associated with this constraint shows that if the firm were to consider increasing the production level for the radios, the value of the objective function, or profit,
would improve at the rate of $60 per radio produced. Finally, the surplus of zero associated
with the retail store distribution channel commitment is a result of this constraint being
binding. The negative dual price indicates that increasing the commitment from 150 to 151
units will actually decrease the profit by $17. Thus, Electronic Communications may want
to consider reducing its commitment to the retail store distribution channel. A *decrease* in
the commitment will actually improve profit at the rate of $17 per unit.

We now consider the additional sensitivity analysis information provided by the computer output shown in Figure 8.14. Using C with a subscript of M, B, R, and D to denote the
objective function coefficients, the objective coefficient ranges are

$$84 \leq C_M < \text{No upper limit}$$
$$50 \leq C_B \leq 90$$
$$\text{No lower limit} < C_R \leq 87$$
$$\text{No lower limit} < C_D \leq 105$$

The current solution, or strategy, remains optimal, provided that the objective function coefficients remain in the given ranges. Note in particular the range associated with the direct
mail distribution channel coefficient, C_D. This information is consistent with the earlier observation for the Reduced Costs portion of the output. In both instances, we see that the per-
unit profit would have to increase to $105 before the direct mail distribution channel could
be in the optimal solution with a positive value.

Finally, the sensitivity analysis information on RIGHT HAND SIDE RANGES, as shown in Figure 8.14, provides the following ranges:

Constraint	Min RHS	Current Value	Max RHS
Advertising budget	4950	5000	5850
Sales force	1775	1800	No upper limit
Production level	515	600	603.57
Retail stores requirement	0	150	200

Several interpretations of these right-hand-side ranges are possible. In particular, recall that the dual price for the advertising budget enabled us to conclude that each $1 increase in the budget would improve the profit by $3. The range for the advertising budget shows that this statement about the value of increasing the budget is appropriate up to an advertising budget of $5850. Increases above this level would not necessarily be beneficial. Also note that the dual price of -17 for the retail stores requirement suggested the desirability of reducing this commitment. The right-hand-side range for this constraint shows that the commitment could be reduced to zero and the value of the reduction would be at the rate of $17 per unit.

Again, the *sensitivity analysis* or *postoptimality analysis* provided by computer software packages for linear programming problems considers only *one change at a time,* with all other coefficients of the problem remaining as originally specified. As mentioned earlier, simultaneous changes can sometimes be analyzed without resolving the problem, provided that the cumulative changes are not large enough to violate the 100 percent rule.

Finally, recall that the complete solution to the Electronic Communications problem requested information not only on the number of units to be distributed over each channel, but also on the allocation of the advertising budget and the sales force effort to each distribution channel. Because the optimal solution is $M = 25$, $B = 425$, $R = 150$, and $D = 0$, we can simply evaluate each term in a given constraint to determine how much of the constraint resource is allocated to each distribution channel. For example, the advertising budget constraint of

$$10M + 8B + 9R + 15D \leq 5000$$

shows that $10M = 10(25) = \$250$, $8B = 8(425) = \$3400$, $9R = 9(150) = \$1350$, and $15D = 15(0) = \$0$. Thus, the advertising budget allocations are, respectively, $250, $3400, $1350, and $0 for each of the four distribution channels. Making similar calculations for the sales force constraint results in the managerial summary of the Electronic Communications optimal solution, as shown in Table 8.5.

TABLE 8.5   PROFIT-MAXIMIZING STRATEGY FOR THE ELECTRONIC COMMUNICATIONS PROBLEM

Distribution Channel	Volume	Advertising Allocation	Sales Force Allocation (hours)
Marine distributors	25	$ 250	50
Business distributors	425	3400	1275
National retail stores	150	1350	450
Direct mail	0	0	0
Totals	600	$5000	1775

Projected total profit = $48,450

Summary

We began the chapter with a discussion of sensitivity analysis, the study of how changes in the coefficients of a linear program affect the optimal solution. Specifically, we showed how a change in one of the objective function coefficients or a change in the right-hand-side value for a constraint will affect the optimal solution to the problem.

We continued our discussion of problem formulation, sensitivity analysis, and the interpretation of the solution by introducing modifications of the RMC problem. These modifications involved an additional decision variable and percentage, or ratio, constraints. Then, in order to provide additional practice in formulating and interpreting the solution for linear programs involving more than two decision variables, we introduced the Bluegrass Farms problem, a minimization problem involving three decision variables. In the last section we summarized all the work to date using the Electronic Communications problem, a maximization problem with four decision variables: two less-than-or-equal-to constraints, one equality constraint, and one greater-than-or-equal-to constraint.

The Q.M. in Action, Tea Production and Distribution at Duncan Industries Limited, illustrates the diversity of problem situations in which linear programming can be applied and the importance of sensitivity analysis. In the next chapter we will see many more applications of linear programming.

Q.M. in ACTION

TEA PRODUCTION AND DISTRIBUTION AT DUNCAN INDUSTRIES LIMITED*

In India, one of the largest tea producers in the world, approximately $1 billion of tea packets and loose tea are sold. Duncan Industries Limited (DIL), the third largest producer of tea in the Indian tea market, sells about $37.5 million of tea, almost all of which is sold in packets.

DIL has 16 tea gardens, three blending units, six packing units, and 22 depots. Tea from the gardens is sent to blending units, which then mix various grades of tea to produce blends such as Sargam, Double Diamond, and Runglee Rungliot. The blended tea is transported to packing units, where it is placed in packets of different sizes and shapes to produce about 120 different product lines. For example, one line is Sargam tea packed in 500-gram cartons, another line is Double Diamond packed in 100-gram polythene pouches, and so on. The tea is then shipped to the depots that supply 11,500 distributors through whom the needs of approximately 325,000 retailers are satisfied.

For the coming month, sales managers provide estimates of the demand for each line of tea at each depot. Using these estimates, a team of senior managers would determine the amounts of loose tea of each blend to ship to each packing unit, the quantity of each line of tea to be packed at each packing unit, and the amounts of packed tea of each line to be transported from each packing unit to the various depots. This process requires two to three days each month and often results in stock-outs of lines in demand at specific depots.

Consequently, a linear programming model involving approximately 7000 decision variables and 1500 constraints was developed to minimize the company's freight cost while satisfying demand, supply, and all operational constraints. The model was tested on past data and showed that stock-outs could be prevented at little or no additional cost. Moreover, the model was able to provide management with the ability to perform various what-if types of exercises, convincing them of the potential benefits of using management science techniques to support the decision-making process.

*Based on Nilotpal Chakravarti, "Tea Company Steeped in OR," *OR/MS Today* (April 2000).

Glossary

Sensitivity analysis The study of how changes in the coefficients of a linear programming problem affect the optimal solution.

100 percent rule A rule indicating when simultaneous changes in two or more objective function coefficients will not cause a change in the optimal values for the decision variables. It can also be applied to indicate when two or more right-hand-side changes will not cause a change in any of the dual prices.

Dual price The improvement in the value of the optimal solution per unit increase in the right-hand side of a constraint.

Sunk cost A cost that is not affected by the decision made. It will be incurred no matter what values the decision variables assume.

Relevant cost A cost that depends upon the decision made. The amount of a relevant cost will vary depending on the values of the decision variables.

Reduced cost The amount by which an objective function coefficient would have to improve (increase for a maximization problem, decrease for a minimization problem) before it would be possible for the corresponding variable to assume a positive value in the optimal solution.

Problems

1. Consider the following linear program:

$$\text{Max} \quad 3A + 2B$$
$$\text{s.t.}$$
$$1A + 1B \leq 10$$
$$3A + 1B \leq 24$$
$$1A + 2B \leq 16$$
$$A, B \geq 0$$

   a. Use the graphical solution procedure to find the optimal solution.
   b. Assume that the objective function coefficient for A changes from 3 to 5. Does the optimal solution change? Use the graphical solution procedure to find the new optimal solution.
   c. Assume that the objective function coefficient for A remains 3, but the objective function coefficient for B changes from 2 to 4. Does the optimal solution change? Use the graphical solution procedure to find the new optimal solution.
   d. The Management Scientist computer solution for the linear program in part (a) provides the following objective coefficient range information:

Variable	Lower Limit	Current Value	Upper Limit
A	2	3	6
B	1	2	3

   Use this objective coefficient range information to answer parts (b) and (c).

2. Consider the linear program in Problem 1. The value of the optimal solution is 27. Suppose that the right-hand side for constraint 1 is increased from 10 to 11.
   a. Use the graphical solution procedure to find the new optimal solution.
   b. Use the solution to part (a) to determine the dual price for constraint 1.
   c. The Management Scientist computer solution for the linear program in Problem 1 provides the following right-hand-side range information:

Constraint	Lower Limit	Current Value	Upper Limit
1	8	10	11.2
2	18	24	30
3	13	16	No Upper Limit

   What does the right-hand-side range information for constraint 1 tell you about the dual price for constraint 1?
   d. The dual price for constraint 2 is 0.5. Using this dual price and the right-hand-side range information in part (c), what conclusion can be drawn about the effect of changes to the right-hand side of constraint 2?

3. Consider the following linear program:

$$\text{Min} \quad 8X + 12Y$$
$$\text{s.t.}$$
$$1X + 3Y \geq 9$$
$$2X + 2Y \geq 10$$
$$6X + 2Y \geq 18$$
$$X, Y \geq 0$$

   a. Use the graphical solution procedure to find the optimal solution.
   b. Assume that the objective function coefficient for X changes from 8 to 6. Does the optimal solution change? Use the graphical solution procedure to find the new optimal solution.
   c. Assume that the objective function coefficient for X remains 8, but the objective function coefficient for Y changes from 12 to 6. Does the optimal solution change? Use the graphical solution procedure to find the new optimal solution.
   d. The Management Scientist computer solution for the linear program in part (a) provides the following objective coefficient range information:

Variable	Lower Limit	Current Value	Upper Limit
X	4	8	12
Y	8	12	24

   How would this objective coefficient range information help you answer parts (b) and (c) prior to resolving the problem?

4. Consider the linear program in Problem 3. The value of the optimal solution is 48. Suppose that the right-hand side for constraint 1 is increased from 9 to 10.
   a. Use the graphical solution procedure to find the new optimal solution.
   b. Use the solution to part (a) to determine the dual price for constraint 1.

c.   The Management Scientist computer solution for the linear program in Problem 3 provides the following right-hand-side range information:

Constraint	Lower Limit	Current Value	Upper Limit
1	5	9	11
2	9	10	18
3	No Lower Limit	18	22

What does the right-hand-side range information for constraint 1 tell you about the dual price for constraint 1?

d.   The dual price for constraint 2 is −3. Using this dual price and the right-hand-side range information in part (c), what conclusion can be drawn about the effect of changes to the right-hand side of constraint 2?

5.   Refer to the Kelson Sporting Equipment problem (Chapter 7, Problem 24). Letting

$$R = \text{number of regular gloves}$$
$$C = \text{number of catcher's mitts}$$

leads to the following formulation:

$$
\begin{aligned}
\text{Max} \quad & 5R + 8C \\
\text{s.t.} \quad & \\
& R + \tfrac{3}{2}C \leq 900 \quad \text{Cutting and sewing} \\
& \tfrac{1}{2}R + \tfrac{1}{3}C \leq 300 \quad \text{Finishing} \\
& \tfrac{1}{8}R + \tfrac{1}{4}C \leq 100 \quad \text{Packaging and shipping} \\
& R, C \geq 0
\end{aligned}
$$

The computer solution obtained using The Management Scientist is shown in Figure 8.15.
a.   What is the optimal solution, and what is the value of the total profit contribution?
b.   Which constraints are binding?
c.   What are the dual prices for the resources? Interpret each.
d.   If overtime can be scheduled in one of the departments, where would you recommend doing so?

6.   Refer to the computer solution of the Kelson Sporting Equipment problem in Figure 8.15 (see Problem 5).
a.   Determine the objective coefficient ranges.
b.   Interpret the ranges in part (a).
c.   Interpret the right-hand-side ranges.
d.   How much will the value of the optimal solution improve if 20 extra hours of packaging and shipping time are made available?

7.   Investment Advisors, Inc., is a brokerage firm that manages stock portfolios for a number of clients. A particular portfolio consists of U shares of U.S. Oil and H shares of Huber Steel. The annual return for U.S. Oil is $3 per share and the annual return for Huber Steel is $5 per share. U.S. Oil sells for $25 per share and Huber Steel sells for $50 per share. The portfolio has $80,000 to be invested. The portfolio risk index (0.50 per share of U.S. Oil and 0.25 per share for Huber Steel) has a maximum of 700. In addition, the portfolio is

FIGURE 8.15   THE MANAGEMENT SCIENTIST SOLUTION FOR THE KELSON SPORTING
EQUIPMENT PROBLEM

```
Objective Function Value =        3700.00146

        Variable              Value              Reduced Costs
    ---------------      ---------------        ------------------
           R                500.00153                0.00000
           C                149.99924                0.00000

       Constraint         Slack/Surplus           Dual Prices
    ---------------      ---------------        ------------------
           1                174.99962                0.00000
           2                  0.00000                2.99999
           3                  0.00000               28.00006


OBJECTIVE COEFFICIENT RANGES

    Variable      Lower Limit      Current Value      Upper Limit
  ------------  ---------------   ---------------   ---------------
       R            4.00000           5.00000          12.00012
       C            3.33330           8.00000          10.00000


RIGHT HAND SIDE RANGES

   Constraint     Lower Limit      Current Value      Upper Limit
  ------------  ---------------   ---------------   ---------------
       1          725.00037         900.00000      No Upper Limit
       2          133.33199         300.00000         400.00000
       3           75.00000         100.00000         134.99982
```

limited to a maximum of 1000 shares of U.S. Oil. The linear programming formulation that will maximize the total annual return of the portfolio is as follows:

$$\text{Max} \quad 3U + 5H \qquad \text{Maximize total annual return}$$

s.t.

$$25U + 50H \leq 80{,}000 \quad \text{Funds available}$$
$$0.50U + 0.25H \leq 700 \quad \text{Risk maximum}$$
$$1U \qquad\qquad \leq 1000 \quad \text{U.S. Oil maximum}$$
$$U, H \geq 0$$

The computer solution of this problem is shown in Figure 8.16.

a. What is the optimal solution, and what is the value of the total annual return?
b. Which constraints are binding? What is your interpretation of these constraints in terms of the problem?
c. What are the dual prices for the constraints? Interpret each.
d. Would it be beneficial to increase the maximum amount invested in U.S. Oil? Why or why not?

FIGURE 8.16 THE MANAGEMENT SCIENTIST SOLUTION FOR THE INVESTMENT
ADVISORS PROBLEM

```
Objective Function Value =              8400.000

        Variable              Value              Reduced Costs
     --------------       ---------------       ------------------
           U                800.000                  0.000
           H               1200.000                  0.000


        Constraint        Slack/Surplus            Dual Prices
     --------------       ---------------       ------------------
           1                  0.000                  0.093
           2                  0.000                  1.333
           3                200.000                  0.000


OBJECTIVE COEFFICIENT RANGES

     Variable         Lower Limit       Current Value       Upper Limit
   ------------     ---------------    ---------------     ---------------
        U               2.500              3.000             10.000
        H               1.500              5.000              6.000


RIGHT HAND SIDE RANGES

   Constraint        Lower Limit       Current Value       Upper Limit
  ------------     ---------------    ---------------     ---------------
       1             65000.000          80000.000          140000.000
       2               400.000            700.000             775.000
       3               800.000           1000.000        No Upper Limit
```

8. Refer to Figure 8.16, which shows the computer solution of Problem 7.
    a. How much would the return for U.S. Oil have to increase before it would be beneficial to increase the investment in this stock?
    b. How much would the return for Huber Steel have to decrease before it would be beneficial to reduce the investment in this stock?
    c. How much would the total annual return be reduced if the U.S. Oil maximum were reduced to 900 shares?

9. Recall the Tom's, Inc., problem (Chapter 7, Problem 28). Letting

$$W = \text{jars of Western Foods Salsa}$$
$$M = \text{jars of Mexico City Salsa}$$

leads to the formulation:

$$\text{Max} \quad 1W + 1.25M$$
s.t.
$$5W + 7M \le 4480 \quad \text{Whole tomatoes}$$
$$3W + 1M \le 2080 \quad \text{Tomato sauce}$$
$$2W + 2M \le 1600 \quad \text{Tomato paste}$$
$$W, M \ge 0$$

FIGURE 8.17   THE MANAGEMENT SCIENTIST SOLUTION FOR THE TOM'S, INC., PROBLEM

```
OPTIMAL SOLUTION

Objective Function Value =            860.000

       Variable              Value            Reduced Costs
    -------------       ----------------     ----------------
         W                  560.000               0.000
         M                  240.000               0.000


      Constraint         Slack/Surplus          Dual Prices
    -------------       ----------------     ----------------
         1                   0.000                0.125
         2                 160.000                0.000
         3                   0.000                0.187


OBJECTIVE COEFFICIENT RANGES

   Variable      Lower Limit      Current Value      Upper Limit
 ------------   -------------    ----------------    ------------
      M             0.893             1.000             1.250
      W             1.000             1.250             1.400


RIGHT HAND SIDE RANGES

  Constraint     Lower Limit      Current Value      Upper Limit
 ------------   -------------    ----------------    ------------
      1           4320.000          4480.000          5600.000
      2           1920.000          2080.000        No Upper Limit
      3           1280.000          1600.000          1640.000
```

The Management Scientist solution is shown in Figure 8.17.

a.   What is the optimal solution, and what are the optimal production quantities?
b.   Specify the objective function ranges.
c.   What are the dual prices for each constraint? Interpret each.
d.   Identify each of the right-hand-side ranges.

10.   Recall the Innis Investments problem (Chapter 7, Problem 39). Letting

$$S = \text{units purchased in the stock fund}$$
$$M = \text{units purchased in the money market fund}$$

leads to the following formulation:

$$\text{Min} \quad 8S + 3M$$

s.t.

$50S + 100M \leq 1{,}200{,}000$	Funds available
$5S + 4M \geq 60{,}000$	Annual income
$M \geq 3{,}000$	Units in money market

$$S, M \geq 0$$

FIGURE 8.18 THE MANAGEMENT SCIENTIST SOLUTION FOR THE INNIS INVESTMENTS PROBLEM

```
Objective Function Value =              62000.000

     Variable              Value              Reduced Costs
   --------------      ---------------      -----------------
        S                4000.000                0.000
        M               10000.000                0.000


     Constraint        Slack/Surplus           Dual Prices
   --------------      ---------------      -----------------
        1                   0.000                0.057
        2                   0.000               -2.167
        3                7000.000                0.000


OBJECTIVE COEFFICIENT RANGES

   Variable       Lower Limit       Current Value       Upper Limit
   -----------    ---------------   ---------------    ---------------
      S                 3.750            8.000         No Upper Limit
      M           No Lower Limit         3.000               6.400


RIGHT HAND SIDE RANGES

   Constraint     Lower Limit       Current Value       Upper Limit
   -----------    ---------------   ---------------    ---------------
      1              780000.000       1200000.000       1500000.000
      2               48000.000         60000.000        102000.000
      3           No Lower Limit         3000.000         10000.000
```

The computer solution is shown in Figure 8.18.
a. What is the optimal solution, and what is the minimum total risk?
b. Specify the objective coefficient ranges.
c. How much annual income will be earned by the portfolio?
d. What is the rate of return for the portfolio?
e. What is the dual price for the funds available constraint?
f. What is the marginal rate of return on extra funds added to the portfolio?

11. Refer to Problem 10 and the computer solution shown in Figure 8.18.
 a. Suppose the risk index for the stock fund (the value of C_S) increases from its current value of 8 to 12. How does the optimal solution change, if at all?
 b. Suppose the risk index for the money market fund (the value of C_M) increases from its current value of 3 to 3.5. How does the optimal solution change, if at all?
 c. Suppose C_S increases to 12 and C_M increases to 3.5. How does the optimal solution change, if at all?

12. Quality Air Conditioning manufactures three home air conditioners: an economy model, a standard model, and a deluxe model. The profits per unit are $63, $95, and $135, respectively. The production requirements per unit are as follows:

	Number of Fans	Number of Cooling Coils	Manufacturing Time (hours)
Economy	1	1	8
Standard	1	2	12
Deluxe	1	4	14

For the coming production period, the company has 200 fan motors, 320 cooling coils, and 2400 hours of manufacturing time available. How many economy models (E), standard models (S), and deluxe models (D) should the company produce in order to maximize profit? The linear programming model for the problem is as follows.

$$\text{Max} \quad 63E + 95S + 135D$$

s.t.

$$
\begin{aligned}
1E + 1S + 1D &\le 200 \quad \text{Fan motors} \\
1E + 2S + 4D &\le 320 \quad \text{Cooling coils} \\
8E + 12S + 14D &\le 2400 \quad \text{Manufacturing time} \\
E, S, D &\ge 0
\end{aligned}
$$

The computer solution using The Management Scientist is shown in Figure 8.19.
a. What is the optimal solution, and what is the value of the objective function?
b. Which constraints are binding?
c. Which constraint shows extra capacity? How much?
d. If the profit for the deluxe model were increased to $150 per unit, would the optimal solution change? Use the information in Figure 8.19 to answer this question.

13. Refer to the computer solution of Problem 12 in Figure 8.19.
a. Identify the range of optimality for each objective function coefficient.
b. Suppose the profit for the economy model is increased by $6 per unit, the profit for the standard model is decreased by $2 per unit, and the profit for the deluxe model is increased by $4 per unit. What will the new optimal solution be?
c. Identify the range of feasibility for the right-hand-side values.
d. If the number of fan motors available for production is increased by 100, will the dual price for that constraint change? Explain.

14. Digital Controls, Inc. (DCI) manufactures two models of a radar gun used by police to monitor the speed of automobiles. Model A has an accuracy of plus or minus 1 mile per hour, whereas the smaller model B has an accuracy of plus or minus 3 miles per hour. For the next week, the company has orders for 100 units of model A and 150 units of model B. Although DCI purchases all the electronic components used in both models, the plastic cases for both models are manufactured at a DCI plant in Newark, New Jersey. Each model A case requires 4 minutes of injection-molding time and 6 minutes of assembly time. Each model B case requires 3 minutes of injection-molding time and 8 minutes of assembly time. For next week the Newark plant has 600 minutes of injection-molding time available and 1080 minutes of assembly time available. The manufacturing cost is $10 per case for model A and $6 per case for model B. Depending upon demand and the time available at the Newark plant, DCI occasionally purchases cases for one or both models from an outside supplier in order to fill customer orders that could not be filled otherwise. The purchase cost is $14 for each model A case and $9 for each model B case. Management wants to develop a minimum cost plan that will determine how many cases of each model should be produced at the Newark plant and how many cases of each model should be purchased.

FIGURE 8.19   THE MANAGEMENT SCIENTIST SOLUTION FOR THE QUALITY AIR
CONDITIONING PROBLEM

```
Objective Function Value =              16440.000

        Variable                Value              Reduced Costs
     --------------        ---------------        -----------------
            E                   80.000                  0.000
            S                  120.000                  0.000
            D                    0.000                 24.000

        Constraint          Slack/Surplus            Dual Prices
     --------------        ---------------        -----------------
            1                    0.000                 31.000
            2                    0.000                 32.000
            3                  320.000                  0.000

OBJECTIVE COEFFICIENT RANGES

     Variable       Lower Limit       Current Value       Upper Limit
   ------------   ---------------   ---------------   ---------------
        E              47.500            63.000            75.000
        S              87.000            95.000           126.000
        D          No Lower Limit       135.000           159.000

RIGHT HAND SIDE RANGES

    Constraint       Lower Limit       Current Value       Upper Limit
  ------------   ---------------   ---------------   ---------------
        1             160.000           200.000           280.000
        2             200.000           320.000           400.000
        3            2080.000          2400.000       No Upper Limit
```

The following decision variables were used to formulate a linear programming model for
this problem:

$$AM = \text{number of cases of model A manufactured}$$
$$BM = \text{number of cases of model B manufactured}$$
$$AP = \text{number of cases of model A purchased}$$
$$BP = \text{number of cases of model B purchased}$$

The linear programming model that can be used to solve this problem is as follows:

$$\text{Min} \quad 10AM + 6BM + 14AP + 9BP$$

s.t.

$$
\begin{array}{llll}
1AM + & + 1AP + & = 100 & \text{Demand for model A} \\
& 1BM + & 1BP = 150 & \text{Demand for model B} \\
4AM + 3BM & & \leq 600 & \text{Injection molding time} \\
6AM + 8BM & & \leq 1080 & \text{Assembly time} \\
AM, BM, AP, BP \geq 0
\end{array}
$$

FIGURE 8.20 THE MANAGEMENT SCIENTIST SOLUTION FOR THE DIGITAL CONTROLS, INC., PROBLEM

```
Objective Function Value =              2170.000

        Variable              Value           Reduced Costs
      -------------       ---------------    ----------------
           AM                 100.000                 0.000
           BM                  60.000                 0.000
           AP                   0.000                 1.750
           BP                  90.000                 0.000


        Constraint        Slack/Surplus          Dual Prices
      -------------       ---------------    ----------------
            1                   0.000               -12.250
            2                   0.000                -9.000
            3                  20.000                 0.000
            4                   0.000                 0.375

OBJECTIVE COEFFICIENT RANGES

   Variable      Lower Limit       Current Value      Upper Limit
  -----------  ---------------    ---------------   ---------------
      AM       No Lower Limit          10.000            11.750
      BM             3.667              6.000             9.000
      AP            12.250             14.000        No Upper Limit
      BP             6.000              9.000            11.333

RIGHT HAND SIDE RANGES

  Constraint     Lower Limit       Current Value      Upper Limit
  -----------  ---------------    ---------------   ---------------
      1              0.000            100.000           111.429
      2             60.000            150.000        No Upper Limit
      3            580.000            600.000        No Upper Limit
      4            600.000           1080.000          1133.333
```

The computer solution developed using The Management Scientist is shown in Figure 8.20.

a. What is the optimal solution and what is the optimal value of the objective function?
b. Which constraints are binding?
c. What are the dual prices? Interpret each.
d. If you could change the right-hand side of one constraint by one unit, which one would you choose? Why?

15. Refer to the computer solution to Problem 14 in Figure 8.20.
a. Interpret the ranges of optimality for the objective function coefficients.
b. Suppose that the manufacturing cost increases to $11.20 per case for model A. What is the new optimal solution?

c. Suppose that the manufacturing cost increases to $11.20 per case for model A and the manufacturing cost for model B decreases to $5 per unit. Would the optimal solution change? Use the 100 percent rule and discuss.

16. Tucker Inc. produces high-quality suits and sport coats for men. Each suit requires 1.2 hours of cutting time and 0.7 hours of sewing time, uses 6 yards of material, and provides a profit contribution of $190. Each sport coat requires 0.8 hours of cutting time and 0.6 hours of sewing time, uses 4 yards of material, and provides a profit contribution of $150. For the coming week, 200 hours of cutting time, 180 hours of sewing time, and 1200 yards of fabric are available. Additional cutting and sewing time can be obtained by scheduling overtime for these operations. Each hour of overtime for the cutting operation increases the hourly cost by $15, and each hour of overtime for the sewing operation increases the hourly cost by $10. A maximum of 100 hours of overtime can be scheduled. Marketing requirements specify a minimum production of 100 suits and 75 sport coats. Let

$$S = \text{number of suits produced}$$
$$SC = \text{number of sport coats produced}$$
$$D1 = \text{hours of overtime for the cutting operation}$$
$$D2 = \text{hours of overtime for the sewing operation}$$

The computer solution developed using The Management Scientist is shown in Figure 8.21.

a. What is the optimal solution, and what is the total profit? What is the plan for the use of overtime?
b. A price increase for suits is being considered that would result in a profit contribution of $210 per suit. If this price increase is undertaken, how will the optimal solution change?
c. Discuss the need for additional material during the coming week. If a rush order for material can be placed at the usual price plus an extra $8 per yard for handling, would you recommend the company consider placing a rush order for material? What is the maximum price Tucker would be willing to pay for an additional yard of material? How many additional yards of material should Tucker consider ordering?
d. Suppose the minimum production requirement for suits is lowered to 75. Would this change help or hurt profit? Explain.

17. The Porsche Club of America sponsors driver education events that provide high-performance driving instruction on actual racetracks. Because safety is a primary consideration at such events, many owners elect to install roll bars in their cars. Deegan Industries manufactures two types of roll bars for Porsches. Model DRB is bolted to the car using existing holes in the car's frame. Model DRW is a heavier roll bar that must be welded to the car's frame. Model DRB requires 20 pounds of a special high-alloy steel, 40 minutes of manufacturing time, and 60 minutes of assembly time. Model DRW requires 25 pounds of the special high-alloy steel, 100 minutes of manufacturing time, and 40 minutes of assembly time. Deegan's steel supplier indicated that at most 40,000 pounds of the high-alloy steel will be available next quarter. In addition, Deegan estimates that 2000 hours of manufacturing time and 1600 hours of assembly time will be available next quarter. The profit contributions are $200 per unit for model DRB and $280 per unit for model DRW. The linear programming model for this problem is as follows:

$$\text{Max} \quad 200DRB + 280DRW$$
s.t.
$$
\begin{array}{llll}
20DRB + & 25DRW \le & 40,000 & \text{Steel available} \\
40DRB + & 100DRW \le & 120,000 & \text{Manufacturing minutes} \\
60DRB + & 40DRW \le & 96,000 & \text{Assembly minutes} \\
& DRB, DRW \ge 0 &
\end{array}
$$

FIGURE 8.21   THE MANAGEMENT SCIENTIST SOLUTION FOR THE TUCKER INC. PROBLEM

```
Objective Function Value =              40900.000

        Variable                Value              Reduced Costs
      --------------        --------------       ------------------
             S                100.000                  0.000
             SC               150.000                  0.000
             D1                40.000                  0.000
             D2                 0.000                 10.000


        Constraint          Slack/Surplus           Dual Prices
      --------------        --------------       ------------------
             1                  0.000                 15.000
             2                 20.000                  0.000
             3                  0.000                 34.500
             4                 60.000                  0.000
             5                  0.000                -35.000
             6                 75.000                  0.000


OBJECTIVE COEFFICIENT RANGES

        Variable         Lower Limit      Current Value       Upper Limit
      ------------     ----------------   --------------    ----------------
             S         No Lower Limit        190.000           225.000
             SC            126.667           150.000        No Upper Limit
             D1           -187.500           -15.000             0.000
             D2         No Lower Limit       -10.000             0.000


RIGHT HAND SIDE RANGES

        Constraint       Lower Limit      Current Value       Upper Limit
      ------------     ----------------   --------------    ----------------
             1             140.000           200.000           240.000
             2             160.000           180.000        No Upper Limit
             3            1000.000          1200.000          1333.333
             4              40.000           100.000        No Upper Limit
             5               0.000           100.000           150.000
             6         No Lower Limit         75.000           150.000
```

The Management Scientist solution is shown in Figure 8.22.

a. What are the optimal solution and the total profit contribution?

b. Another supplier offered to provide Deegan Industries with an additional 500 pounds of the steel alloy at $2 per pound. Should Deegan purchase the additional pounds of the steel alloy? Explain.

c. Deegan is considering using overtime to increase the available assembly time. What would you advise Deegan to do regarding this option? Explain.

d. Because of increased competition, Deegan is considering reducing the price of model DRB such that the new contribution to profit is $175 per unit. How would this change in price affect the optimal solution? Explain.

FIGURE 8.22 THE MANAGEMENT SCIENTIST SOLUTION FOR THE DEEGAN INDUSTRIES PROBLEM

```
OPTIMAL SOLUTION

Objective Function Value =          424000.000

        Variable              Value              Reduced Costs
    --------------      ----------------      ------------------
         DRB               1000.000                  0.000
         DRW                800.000                  0.000

        Constraint       Slack/Surplus            Dual Prices
    --------------      ----------------      ------------------
            1                 0.000                  8.800
            2                 0.000                  0.600
            3              4000.000                  0.000

OBJECTIVE COEFFICIENT RANGES

     Variable       Lower Limit       Current Value      Upper Limit
   -----------     -------------      -------------      -------------
        DRB           112.000            200.000            224.000
        DRW           250.000            280.000            500.000

RIGHT HAND SIDE RANGES

     Constraint     Lower Limit       Current Value      Upper Limit
   -----------     -------------      -------------      -------------
         1            30000.000         40000.000          40909.091
         2           114285.714        120000.000         160000.000
         3            92000.000         96000.000       No Upper Limit
```

e. If the available manufacturing time is increased by 500 hours, will the dual price for the manufacturing time constraint change? Explain.

18. Davison Electronics manufactures two LCD television monitors, identified as model A and model B. Each model has its lowest possible production cost when produced on Davison's new production line. However, the new production line does not have the capacity to handle the total production of both models. As a result, at least some of the production must be routed to a higher-cost, old production line. The following table shows the minimum production requirements for next month, the production line capacities in units per month, and the production cost per unit for each production line:

Model	Production Cost per Unit		Minimum Production Requirements
	New Line	Old Line	
A	$30	$50	50,000
B	$25	$40	70,000
Production Line Capacity	80,000	60,000	

Let

$$AN = \text{Units of model A produced on the new production line}$$
$$AO = \text{Units of model A produced on the old production line}$$
$$BN = \text{Units of model B produced on the new production line}$$
$$BO = \text{Units of model B produced on the old production line}$$

Davison's objective is to determine the minimum cost production plan. The computer solution obtained using The Management Scientist is shown in Figure 8.23.

a. Formulate the linear programming model for this problem using the following four constraints:

Constraint 1: Minimum production for model A
Constraint 2: Minimum production for model B
Constraint 3: Capacity of the new production line
Constraint 4: Capacity of the old production line

b. Using The Management Scientist solution in Figure 8.23, what is the optimal solution and what is the total production cost associated with this solution?

c. Which constraints are binding? Explain.

d. The production manager noted that the only constraint with a positive dual price is the constraint on the capacity of the new production line. The manager's interpretation of the dual price was that a one-unit increase in the right-hand side of this constraint would actually increase the total production cost by $15 per unit. Do you agree with this interpretation? Would an increase in capacity for the new production line be desirable? Explain.

e. Would you recommend increasing the capacity of the old production line? Explain.

f. The production cost for model A on the old production line is $50 per unit. How much would this cost have to change to make it worthwhile to produce model A on the old production line? Explain.

g. Suppose that the minimum production requirement for model B is reduced from 70,000 units to 60,000 units. What effect would this change have on the total production cost? Explain.

19. Better Products, Inc., manufactures three products on two machines. In a typical week, 40 hours are available on each machine. The profit contribution and production time in hours per unit are as follows:

Category	Product 1	Product 2	Product 3
Profit/unit	$30	$50	$20
Machine 1 time/unit	0.5	2.0	0.75
Machine 2 time/unit	1.0	1.0	0.5

Two operators are required for machine 1; thus, 2 hours of labor must be scheduled for each hour of machine 1 time. Only one operator is required for machine 2. A maximum of 100 labor-hours is available for assignment to the machines during the coming week. Other production requirements are that product 1 cannot account for more than 50% of the units produced and that product 3 must account for at least 20% of the units produced.

a. How many units of each product should be produced to maximize the total profit contribution? What is the projected weekly profit associated with your solution?

b. How many hours of production time will be scheduled on each machine?

c. What is the value of an additional hour of labor?

FIGURE 8.23 THE MANAGEMENT SCIENTIST SOLUTION TO THE DAVISON
ELECTRONICS PROBLEM

```
OPTIMAL SOLUTION

Objective Function Value =        3850000.000

        Variable              Value            Reduced Costs
     -------------      ----------------      ------------------
         AN               50000.000                 0.000
         AO                   0.000                 5.000
         BN               30000.000                 0.000
         BO               40000.000                 0.000

       Constraint       Slack/Surplus            Dual Prices
     -------------      ----------------      ------------------
           1                  0.000                -45.000
           2                  0.000                -40.000
           3                  0.000                 15.000
           4              20000.000                 0.000

OBJECTIVE COEFFICIENT RANGES

       Variable       Lower Limit       Current Value       Upper Limit
     ------------     ------------     ----------------     -------------
         AN             -15.000            30.000               35.000
         AO              45.000            50.000          No Upper Limit
         BN              20.000            25.000               40.000
         BO              25.000            40.000               45.000

RIGHT HAND SIDE RANGES

      Constraint      Lower Limit       Current Value       Upper Limit
     ------------     ------------     ----------------     -------------
          1           10000.000          50000.000           70000.000
          2           30000.000          70000.000           90000.000
          3           60000.000          80000.000          120000.000
          4           40000.000          60000.000        No Upper Limit
```

d. Assume that labor capacity can be increased to 120 hours. Would you be interested in using the additional 20 hours available for this resource? Develop the optimal product mix assuming the extra hours are made available.

20. Adirondack Savings Bank (ASB) has $1 million in new funds that must be allocated to home loans, personal loans, and automobile loans. The annual rates of return for the three types of loans are 7% for home loans, 12% for personal loans, and 9% for automobile loans. The bank's planning committee has decided that at least 40% of the new funds must be allocated to home loans. In addition, the planning committee has specified that the amount allocated to personal loans cannot exceed 60% of the amount allocated to automobile loans.

    a.   Formulate a linear programming model that can be used to determine the amount of funds ASB should allocate to each type of loan in order to maximize the total annual return for the new funds.

    b.   How much should be allocated to each type of loan? What is the total annual return? What is the annual percentage return?

    c.   If the interest rate on home loans increased to 9%, would the amount allocated to each type of loan change? Explain.

    d.   Suppose the total amount of new funds available was increased by $10,000. What effect would this have on the total annual return? Explain.

    e.   Assume that ASB has the original $1 million in new funds available and that the planning committee has agreed to relax the requirement that at least 40% of the new funds must be allocated to home loans by 1%. How much would the annual return change? How much would the annual percentage return change?

21.   Round Tree Manor is a hotel that provides two types of rooms with three rental classes: Super Saver, Deluxe, and Business. The profit per night for each type of room and rental class is as follows:

		Rental Class		
		Super Saver	Deluxe	Business
Room	Type I	$30	$35	—
	Type II	$20	$30	$40

Type I rooms do not have Internet access and are not available for the Business rental class.

    Round Tree's management makes a forecast of the demand by rental class for each night in the future. A linear programming model developed to maximize profit is used to determine how many reservations to accept for each rental class. The demand forecast for a particular night is 130 rentals in the Super Saver class, 60 rentals in the Deluxe class, and 50 rentals in the Business class. Round Tree has 100 Type I rooms and 120 Type II rooms.

    a.   Use linear programming to determine how many reservations to accept in each rental class and how the reservations should be allocated to room types. Is the demand by any rental class not satisfied? Explain.

    b.   How many reservations can be accommodated in each rental class?

    c.   Management is considering offering a free breakfast to anyone upgrading from a Super Saver reservation to Deluxe class. If the cost of the breakfast to Round Tree is $5, should this incentive be offered?

    d.   With a little work, an unused office area could be converted to a rental room. If the conversion cost is the same for both types of rooms, would you recommend converting the office to a Type I or a Type II room? Why?

    e.   Could the linear programming model be modified to plan for the allocation of rental demand for the next night? What information would be needed and how would the model change?

22.   Industrial Designs has been awarded a contract to design a label for a new wine produced by Lake View Winery. The company estimates that 150 hours will be required to complete the project. The firm's three graphics designers available for assignment to this project are Lisa, a senior designer and team leader; David, a senior designer; and Sarah, a junior designer. Because Lisa has worked on several projects for Lake View Winery, management specified that Lisa must be assigned at least 40% of the total number of hours assigned to the two senior designers. To provide label-designing experience for Sarah, Sarah must be

assigned at least 15% of the total project time. However, the number of hours assigned to Sarah must not exceed 25% of the total number of hours assigned to the two senior designers. Due to other project commitments, Lisa has a maximum of 50 hours available to work on this project. Hourly wage rates are $30 for Lisa, $25 for David, and $18 for Sarah.

a. Formulate a linear program that can be used to determine the number of hours each graphic designer should be assigned to the project in order to minimize total cost.

b. How many hours should each graphic designer be assigned to the project? What is the total cost?

c. Suppose Lisa could be assigned more than 50 hours. What effect would this have on the optimal solution? Explain.

d. If Sarah were not required to work a minimum number of hours on this project, would the optimal solution change? Explain.

23. Vollmer Manufacturing makes three components for sale to refrigeration companies. The components are processed on two machines: a shaper and a grinder. The times (in minutes) required on each machine are as follows:

	Machine	
Component	**Shaper**	**Grinder**
1	6	4
2	4	5
3	4	2

The shaper is available for 120 hours, and the grinder is available for 110 hours. No more than 200 units of component 3 can be sold, but up to 1000 units of each of the other components can be sold. In fact, the company already has orders for 600 units of component 1 that must be satisfied. The profit contributions for components 1, 2, and 3 are $8, $6, and $9, respectively.

a. Formulate and solve for the recommended production quantities.

b. What are the objective coefficient ranges for the three components? Interpret these ranges for company management.

c. What are the right-hand-side ranges? Interpret these ranges for company management.

d. If more time could be made available on the grinder, how much would it be worth?

e. If more units of component 3 can be sold by reducing the sales price by $4, should the company reduce the price?

24. National Insurance Associates carries an investment portfolio of stocks, bonds, and other investment alternatives. Currently $200,000 of funds are available and must be considered for new investment opportunities. The four stock options National is considering and the relevant financial data are as follows:

	Stock			
	A	**B**	**C**	**D**
Price per share	$100	$50	$80	$40
Annual rate of return	0.12	0.08	0.06	0.10
Risk measure per dollar invested	0.10	0.07	0.05	0.08

The risk measure indicates the relative uncertainty associated with the stock in terms of its realizing the projected annual return; higher values indicate greater risk. The risk measures are provided by the firm's top financial advisor.

National's top management has stipulated the following investment guidelines: the annual rate of return for the portfolio must be at least 9%, and no one stock can account for more than 50% of the total dollar investment.

a. Use linear programming to develop an investment portfolio that minimizes risk.

b. If the firm ignores risk and uses a maximum return-on-investment strategy, what is the investment portfolio?

c. What is the dollar difference between the portfolios in parts (a) and (b)? Why might the company prefer the solution developed in part (a)?

25. Georgia Cabinets manufactures kitchen cabinets that are sold to local dealers throughout the Southeast. Because of a large backlog of orders for oak and cherry cabinets, the company decided to contract with three smaller cabinetmakers to do the final finishing operation. For the three cabinetmakers, the number of hours required to complete all the oak cabinets, the number of hours required to complete all the cherry cabinets, the number of hours available for the final finishing operation, and the cost per hour to perform the work are shown here:

	Cabinetmaker 1	**Cabinetmaker 2**	**Cabinetmaker 3**
Hours required to complete all the oak cabinets	50	42	30
Hours required to complete all the cherry cabinets	60	48	35
Hours available	40	30	35
Cost per hour	$36	$42	$55

For example, Cabinetmaker 1 estimates they will take 50 hours to complete all the oak cabinets and 60 hours to complete all the cherry cabinets. However, Cabinetmaker 1 only has 40 hours available for the final finishing operation. Thus, Cabinetmaker 1 can only complete $40/50 = 0.80$, or 80%, of the oak cabinets if they worked only on oak cabinets. Similarly, Cabinetmaker 1 can only complete $40/60 = 0.67$, or 67%, of the cherry cabinets if they worked only on cherry cabinets.

a. Formulate a linear programming model that can be used to determine the percentage of the oak cabinets and the percentage of the cherry cabinets that should be given to each of the three cabinetmakers in order to minimize the total cost of completing both projects.

b. Solve the model formulated in part (a). What percentage of the oak cabinets and what percentage of the cherry cabinets should be assigned to each cabinetmaker? What is the total cost of completing both projects?

c. If Cabinetmaker 1 has additional hours available, would the optimal solution change? Explain.

d. If Cabinetmaker 2 has additional hours available, would the optimal solution change? Explain.

e. Suppose Cabinetmaker 2 reduced their cost to $38 per hour. What effect would this change have on the optimal solution? Explain.

26. Benson Electronics manufactures three components used to produce cell telephones and other communication devices. In a given production period, demand for the three components may exceed Benson's manufacturing capacity. In this case, the company meets demand by purchasing the components from another manufacturer at an increased cost per unit. Benson's manufacturing cost per unit and purchasing cost per unit for the three components are as follows:

Source	Component 1	Component 2	Component 3
Manufacture	$4.50	$5.00	$2.75
Purchase	$6.50	$8.80	$7.00

Manufacturing times in minutes per unit for Benson's three departments are as follows:

Department	Component 1	Component 2	Component 3
Production	2	3	4
Assembly	1	1.5	3
Testing & Packaging	1.5	2	5

For instance, each unit of component 1 that Benson manufactures requires 2 minutes of production time, 1 minute of assembly time, and 1.5 minutes of testing and packaging time. For the next production period, Benson has capacities of 360 hours in the production department, 250 hours in the assembly department, and 300 hours in the testing and packaging department.

a. Formulate a linear programming model that can be used to determine how many units of each component to manufacture and how many units of each component to purchase. Assume that component demands that must be satisfied are 6000 units for component 1, 4000 units for component 2, and 3500 units for component 3. The objective is to minimize the total manufacturing and purchasing costs.

b. What is the optimal solution? How many units of each component should be manufactured and how many units of each component should be purchased?

c. Which departments are limiting Benson's manufacturing quantities? Use the dual price to determine the value of an *extra hour* in each of these departments.

d. Suppose that Benson had to obtain one additional unit of component 2. Discuss what the dual price for the component 2 constraint tells us about the cost to obtain the additional unit.

27. Golf Shafts, Inc. (GSI) produces graphite shafts for several manufacturers of golf clubs. Two GSI manufacturing facilities, one located in San Diego and the other in Tampa, have the capability to produce shafts in varying degrees of stiffness, ranging from regular models used primarily by average golfers to extra stiff models used primarily by low-handicap and professional golfers. GSI just received a contract for the production of 200,000 regular shafts and 75,000 stiff shafts. Because both plants are currently producing shafts for previous orders, neither plant has sufficient capacity by itself to fill the new order. The San Diego plant can produce up to a total of 120,000 shafts and the Tampa plant can produce up to a total of 180,000 shafts. Because of equipment differences at each of the plants and differing labor costs, the per-unit production costs vary as shown here:

	San Diego Cost	Tampa Cost
Regular shaft	$5.25	$4.95
Stiff shaft	$5.45	$5.70

a. Formulate a linear programming model to determine how GSI should schedule production for the new order so that the total production cost is minimized.

b. Solve the model that you developed in part (a).

c. Suppose that some of the previous orders at the Tampa plant could be rescheduled so as to free up additional capacity for the new order. Would this option be worthwhile? Explain.

d. Suppose that the cost to produce a stiff shaft in Tampa had been incorrectly computed, and that the correct cost is $5.30 per shaft. What effect, if any, would the correct cost have on the optimal solution developed in part (b)? What effect would it have on total production cost?

28. The Pfeiffer Company manages approximately $15 million for clients. For each client, Pfeiffer chooses a mix of three investment vehicles: a growth stock fund, an income fund, and a money market fund. Each client has different investment objectives and different tolerances for risk. To accommodate these differences, Pfeiffer places limits on the percentage of each portfolio that may be invested in the three funds and assigns a portfolio risk index to each client.

Here's how the system works for Dennis Hartmann, one of Pfeiffer's clients. Based on an evaluation of Hartmann's risk tolerance, Pfeiffer has assigned Hartmann's portfolio a risk index of 0.05. Furthermore, to maintain diversity, the fraction of Hartmann's portfolio invested in the growth and income funds must be at least 10% for each, and at least 20% must be in the money market fund.

The risk ratings for the growth, income, and money market funds are 0.10, 0.05, and 0.01, respectively. A portfolio risk index is computed as a weighted average of the risk ratings for the three funds, where the weights are the fraction of the portfolio invested in each of the funds. Hartmann has given Pfeiffer $300,000 to manage. Pfeiffer is currently forecasting a yield of 20% on the growth fund, 10% on the income fund, and 6% on the money market fund.

a. Develop a linear programming model to select the best mix of investments for Hartmann's portfolio.

b. Solve the model you developed in part (a).

c. How much may the yields on the three funds vary before it will be necessary for Pfeiffer to modify Hartmann's portfolio?

d. If Hartmann were more risk tolerant, how much of a yield increase could he expect? For instance, what if his portfolio risk index is increased to 0.06?

e. If Pfeiffer revised the yield estimate for the growth fund downward to 0.10, how would you recommend modifying Hartmann's portfolio?

f. What information must Pfeiffer maintain on each client in order to use this system to manage client portfolios?

g. On a weekly basis Pfeiffer revises the yield estimates for the three funds. Suppose Pfeiffer has 50 clients. Describe how you would envision Pfeiffer making weekly modifications in each client's portfolio and allocating the total funds managed among the three investment funds.

29. La Jolla Beverage Products is considering producing a wine cooler that would be a blend of a white wine, a rosé wine, and fruit juice. To meet taste specifications, the wine cooler must consist of at least 50% white wine, at least 20% and no more than 30% rosé, and exactly 20% fruit juice. La Jolla purchases the wine from local wineries and the fruit juice from a processing plant in San Francisco. For the current production period, 10,000 gallons of white wine and 8000 gallons of rosé wine can be purchased; an unlimited amount of fruit juice can be ordered. The costs for the wine are $1.00 per gallon for the white and $1.50 per gallon for the rosé; the fruit juice can be purchased for $0.50 per gallon. La Jolla Beverage Products can sell all of the wine cooler they can produce for $2.50 per gallon.

a. Is the cost of the wine and fruit juice a sunk cost or a relevant cost in this situation? Explain.

b. Formulate a linear program to determine the blend of the three ingredients that will maximize the total profit contribution. Solve the linear program to determine the number of gallons of each ingredient La Jolla should purchase and the total profit contribution they will realize from this blend.

c. If La Jolla could obtain additional amounts of the white wine, should they do so? If so, how much should they be willing to pay for each additional gallon, and how many additional gallons would they want to purchase?

d. If La Jolla Beverage Products could obtain additional amounts of the rosé wine, should they do so? If so, how much should they be willing to pay for each additional gallon, and how many additional gallons would they want to purchase?

e. Interpret the dual price for the constraint corresponding to the requirement that the wine cooler must contain at least 50% white wine. What is your advice to management given this dual price?

f. Interpret the dual price for the constraint corresponding to the requirement that the wine cooler must contain exactly 20% fruit juice. What is your advice to management given this dual price?

30. The program manager for Channel 10 would like to determine the best way to allocate the time for the 11:00–11:30 evening news broadcast. Specifically, she would like to determine the number of minutes of broadcast time to devote to local news, national news, weather, and sports. Over the 30-minute broadcast, 10 minutes are set aside for advertising. The station's broadcast policy states that at least 15% of the time available should be devoted to local news coverage; the time devoted to local news or national news must be at least 50% of the total broadcast time; the time devoted to the weather segment must be less than or equal to the time devoted to the sports segment; the time devoted to the sports segment should be no longer than the total time spent on the local and national news; and at least 20% of the time should be devoted to the weather segment. The production costs per minute are $300 for local news, $200 for national news, $100 for weather, and $100 for sports.

a. Formulate and solve a linear program that can determine how the 20 available minutes should be used to minimize the total cost of producing the program.

b. Interpret the dual price for the constraint corresponding to the available time. What advice would you give the station manager given this dual price?

c. Interpret the dual price for the constraint corresponding to the requirement that at least 15% of the available time should be devoted to local coverage. What advice would you give the station manager given this dual price?

d. Interpret the dual price for the constraint corresponding to the requirement that the time devoted to the local and the national news must be at least 50% of the total broadcast time. What advice would you give the station manager given this dual price?

e. Interpret the dual price for the constraint corresponding to the requirement that the time devoted to the weather segment must be less than or equal to the time devoted to the sports segment. What advice would you give the station manager given this dual price?

31. Gulf Coast Electronics is ready to award contracts for printing their annual report. For the past several years, the four-color annual report has been printed by Johnson Printing and Lakeside Litho. A new firm, Benson Printing, inquired into the possibility of doing a portion of the printing. The quality and service level provided by Lakeside Litho has been extremely high; in fact, only 0.5% of their reports have had to be discarded because of quality problems. Johnson Printing has also had a high quality level historically, producing an average of only 1% unacceptable reports. Because Gulf Coast Electronics has had no experience with Benson Printing, they estimated their defective rate to be 10%. Gulf Coast would like to determine how many reports should be printed by each firm to obtain 75,000 acceptable-quality reports. To ensure that Benson Printing will receive some of the contract, management specified that the number of reports awarded to Benson Printing must be at least 10% of the volume given to Johnson Printing. In addition, the total volume

assigned to Benson Printing, Johnson Printing, and Lakeside Litho should not exceed 30,000, 50,000, and 50,000 copies, respectively. Because of the long-term relationship with Lakeside Litho, management also specified that at least 30,000 reports should be awarded to Lakeside Litho. The cost per copy is $2.45 for Benson Printing, $2.50 for Johnson Printing, and $2.75 for Lakeside Litho.

a. Formulate and solve a linear program for determining how many copies should be assigned to each printing firm to minimize the total cost of obtaining 75,000 acceptable-quality reports.

b. Suppose that the quality level for Benson Printing is much better than estimated. What effect, if any, would this quality level have?

c. Suppose that management is willing to reconsider their requirement that Lakeside Litho be awarded at least 30,000 reports. What effect, if any, would this consideration have?

32. PhotoTech, Inc., a manufacturer of rechargeable batteries for digital cameras, signed a contract with a digital photography company to produce three different lithium-ion battery packs for a new line of digital cameras. The contract calls for the following:

Battery Pack	Production Quantity
PT-100	200,000
PT-200	100,000
PT-300	150,000

PhotoTech can manufacture the battery packs at manufacturing plants located in the Philippines and Mexico. The unit cost of the battery packs differs at the two plants because of differences in production equipment and wage rates. The unit costs for each battery pack at each manufacturing plant are as follows:

	Plant	
Product	**Philippines**	**Mexico**
PT-100	$0.95	$0.98
PT-200	$0.98	$1.06
PT-300	$1.34	$1.15

The PT-100 and PT-200 battery packs are produced using similar production equipment available at both plants. However, each plant has a limited capacity for the total number of PT-100 and PT-200 battery packs produced. The combined PT-100 and PT-200 production capacities are 175,000 units at the Philippines plant and 160,000 units at the Mexico plant. The PT-300 production capacities are 75,000 units at the Philippines plant and 100,000 units at the Mexico plant. The cost of shipping from the Philippines plant is $0.18 per unit, and the cost of shipping from the Mexico plant is $0.10 per unit.

a. Develop a linear program that PhotoTech can use to determine how many units of each battery pack to produce at each plant in order to minimize the total production and shipping cost associated with the new contract.

b. Solve the linear program developed in part (a) to determine the optimal production plan.

c. Use sensitivity analysis to determine how much the production and/or shipping cost per unit would have to change in order to produce additional units of the PT-100 in the Philippines plant.

d. Use sensitivity analysis to determine how much the production and/or shipping cost per unit would have to change in order to produce additional units of the PT-200 in the Mexico plant.

Case Problem 1   Product Mix

TJ's, Inc., makes three nut mixes for sale to grocery chains located in the Southeast. The three mixes, referred to as the Regular Mix, the Deluxe Mix, and the Holiday Mix, are made by mixing different percentages of five types of nuts.

In preparation for the fall season, TJ's purchased the following shipments of nuts at the prices shown:

Type of Nut	Shipment Amount (pounds)	Cost per Shipment
Almond	6000	$7500
Brazil	7500	$7125
Filbert	7500	$6750
Pecan	6000	$7200
Walnut	7500	$7875

The Regular Mix consists of 15% almonds, 25% Brazil nuts, 25% filberts, 10% pecans, and 25% walnuts. The Deluxe Mix consists of 20% of each type of nut, and the Holiday Mix consists of 25% almonds, 15% Brazil nuts, 15% filberts, 25% pecans, and 20% walnuts.

TJ's accountant analyzed the cost of packaging materials, sales price per pound, and so forth, and determined that the profit contribution per pound is $1.65 for the Regular Mix, $2.00 for the Deluxe Mix, and $2.25 for the Holiday Mix. These figures do not include the cost of specific types of nuts in the different mixes because that cost can vary greatly in the commodity markets.

Customer orders already received are summarized here:

Type of Mix	Orders (pounds)
Regular	10,000
Deluxe	3,000
Holiday	5,000

Because demand is running high, TJ's expects to receive many more orders than can be satisfied.

TJ's is committed to using the available nuts to maximize profit over the fall season; nuts not used will be given to the Free Store. Even if it is not profitable to do so, TJ's president indicated that the orders already received must be satisfied.

Managerial Report

Perform an analysis of TJ's product mix problem, and prepare a report for TJ's president that summarizes your findings. Be sure to include information and analysis on the following:

1. The cost per pound of the nuts included in the Regular, Deluxe, and Holiday mixes
2. The optimal product mix and the total profit contribution
3. Recommendations regarding how the total profit contribution can be increased if additional quantities of nuts can be purchased
4. A recommendation as to whether TJ's should purchase an additional 1000 pounds of almonds for $1000 from a supplier who overbought
5. Recommendations on how profit contribution could be increased (if at all) if TJ's does not satisfy all existing orders

Case Problem 2 # Investment Strategy

J. D. Williams, Inc., is an investment advisory firm that manages more than $120 million in funds for its numerous clients. The company uses an asset allocation model that recommends the portion of each client's portfolio to be invested in a growth stock fund, an income fund, and a money market fund. To maintain diversity in each client's portfolio, the firm places limits on the percentage of each portfolio that may be invested in each of the three funds. General guidelines indicate that the amount invested in the growth fund must be between 20% and 40% of the total portfolio value. Similar percentages for the other two funds stipulate that between 20% and 50% of the total portfolio value must be in the income fund and at least 30% of the total portfolio value must be in the money market fund.

In addition, the company attempts to assess the risk tolerance of each client and adjust the portfolio to meet the needs of the individual investor. For example, Williams just contracted with a new client who has $800,000 to invest. Based on an evaluation of the client's risk tolerance, Williams assigned a maximum risk index of 0.05 for the client. The firm's risk indicators show the risk of the growth fund at 0.10, the income fund at 0.07, and the money market fund at 0.01. An overall portfolio risk index is computed as a weighted average of the risk rating for the three funds, where the weights are the fraction of the client's portfolio invested in each of the funds.

Additionally, Williams is currently forecasting annual yields of 18% for the growth fund, 12.5% for the income fund, and 7.5% for the money market fund. Based on the information provided, how should the new client be advised to allocate the $800,000 among the growth, income, and money market funds? Develop a linear programming model that will provide the maximum yield for the portfolio. Use your model to develop a managerial report.

Managerial Report

1. Recommend how much of the $800,000 should be invested in each of the three funds. What is the annual yield you anticipate for the investment recommendation?
2. Assume that the client's risk index could be increased to 0.055. How much would the yield increase and how would the investment recommendation change?
3. Refer again to the original situation where the client's risk index was assessed to be 0.05. How would your investment recommendation change if the annual yield for the growth fund were revised downward to 16% or even to 14%?
4. Assume that the client expressed some concern about having too much money in the growth fund. How would the original recommendation change if the amount invested in the growth fund is not allowed to exceed the amount invested in the income fund?
5. The asset allocation model you developed may be useful in modifying the portfolios for all of the firm's clients whenever the anticipated yields for the three funds are periodically revised. What is your recommendation as to whether use of this model is possible?

Case Problem 3 # Truck Leasing Strategy

Reep Construction recently won a contract for the excavation and site preparation of a new rest area on the Pennsylvania Turnpike. In preparing his bid for the job, Bob Reep, founder and president of Reep Construction, estimated that it would take four months to perform the work and that 10, 12, 14, and 8 trucks would be needed in months 1 through 4, respectively.

The firm currently has 20 trucks of the type needed to perform the work on the new project. These trucks were obtained last year when Bob signed a long-term lease with PennState Leasing. Although most of these trucks are currently being used on existing jobs, Bob estimates that one truck will be available for use on the new project in month 1, two trucks will be available in month 2, three trucks will be available in month 3, and one truck will be available in month 4. Thus, to complete the project, Bob will have to lease additional trucks.

The long-term leasing contract with PennState charges a monthly cost of $600 per truck. Reep Construction pays its truck drivers $20 an hour, and daily fuel costs are approximately $100 per truck. All maintenance costs are paid by PennState Leasing. For planning purposes, Bob estimates that each truck used on the new project will be operating eight hours a day, five days a week for approximately four weeks each month.

Bob does not believe that current business conditions justify committing the firm to additional long-term leases. In discussing the short-term leasing possibilities with PennState Leasing, Bob learned that he can obtain short-term leases of one to four months. Short-term leases differ from long-term leases in that the short-term leasing plans include the cost of both a truck and a driver. Maintenance costs for short-term leases also are paid by PennState Leasing. The following costs for each of the four months cover the lease of a truck and driver:

Length of Lease	Cost per Month
1	$4000
2	$3700
3	$3225
4	$3040

Bob Reep would like to acquire a lease that minimizes the cost of meeting the monthly trucking requirements for his new project, but he also takes great pride in the fact that his company has never laid off employees. Bob is committed to maintaining his no-layoff policy; that is, he will use his own drivers even if costs are higher.

Managerial Report

Perform an analysis of Reep Construction's leasing problem and prepare a report for Bob Reep that summarizes your findings. Be sure to include information on and analysis of the following items:

1. The optimal leasing plan
2. The costs associated with the optimal leasing plan
3. The cost for Reep Construction to maintain its current policy of no layoffs

Appendix 8.1   Sensitivity Analysis with Excel

In Appendix 7.3 we showed how Excel Solver can be used to solve a linear program by using it to solve the RMC problem. Let us now see how it can be used to provide sensitivity analysis information.

When Excel Solver has found the optimal solution to a linear program, the **Solver Results** dialog box (see Figure 8.24) will appear on the screen. If only the solution is desired,

FIGURE 8.24   EXCEL SOLVER RESULTS DIALOG BOX

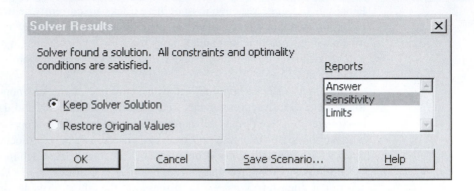

FIGURE 8.25   EXCEL SOLUTION FOR THE RMC PROBLEM

WEB file

RMC

	A	B	C	D
1	**RMC**			
2				
3		**Material Requirements**		
4	**Material**	**Fuel Additive**	**Solvent Base**	**Amount Available**
5	Material 1	0.4	0.5	20
6	Material 2		0.2	5
7	Material 3	0.6	0.3	21
8	**Profit Per Ton**	40	30	
9				
10				
11	**Model**			
12				
13		**Decision Variables**		
14		**Fuel Additive**	**Solvent Base**	
15	**Tons Produced**	25	20	
16				
17	**Maximize Total Profit**	1600		
18				
19	**Constraints**	**Amount Used (LHS)**		**Amount Available (RHS)**
20	Material 1	20	<=	20
21	Material 2	4	<=	5
22	Material 3	21	<=	21

simply click **OK.** To obtain the optimal solution and the sensitivity analysis output, you must select **Sensitivity** in the **Reports** box before clicking **OK;** the sensitivity report is created on another worksheet in the same Excel workbook. Following this procedure for the RMC problem, we obtained the optimal solution shown in Figure 8.25 and the sensitivity report shown in Figure 8.26.

FIGURE 8.26   EXCEL'S SENSITIVITY REPORT FOR THE RMC PROBLEM

Adjustable Cells

Cell	Name	Final Value	Reduced Cost	Objective Coefficient	Allowable Increase	Allowable Decrease
$B$15	Tons Produced Fuel Additive	25	0	40	20	16
$C$15	Tons Produced Solvent Base	20	0	30	20	10

Constraints

Cell	Name	Final Value	Shadow Price	Constraint R.H. Side	Allowable Increase	Allowable Decrease
$B$20	Material 1 Amount Used (LHS)	20	33.333	20	1.5	6
$B$21	Material 2 Amount Used (LHS)	4	0	5	1E+30	1
$B$22	Material 3 Amount Used (LHS)	21	44.444	21	9	2.25

Interpretation of Excel Sensitivity Report

In the Adjustable Cells section of the Sensitivity Report, the column labeled Final Value contains the optimal values of the decision variables. For the RMC problem the optimal solution is 25 tons of fuel additive and 20 tons of solvent base.

Next, let us consider the values in the Reduced Cost column. In Excel, the value of a nonzero reduced cost indicates how much the value of the objective function would change[2] if the corresponding variable was increased by one unit. For the RMC problem, the reduced cost for both decision variables is zero; they are at their optimal values.

To the right of the Reduced Cost column in Figure 8.26, we find three columns labeled Objective Coefficient, Allowable Increase, and Allowable Decrease. The entries in these columns can be used to compute the objective coefficient ranges. For example, the objective function coefficient for the fuel additive is $40. The allowable decrease of $16 per ton provides a lower limit of $40 − $16 = $24, while the allowable increase of $20 provides an upper limit of $40 + $20 = $60. Thus, the objective coefficient range for the fuel additive is $24 to $60. As long as the objective function coefficient is in this range, the optimal solution of 25 tons of fuel additive and 20 tons of solvent base will not change. Similarly, the allowable decrease of $10 and allowable increase of $20 show that the objective coefficient range for the solvent base is $30 − $10 = $20 to $30 + $20 = $50.

Next, consider the information in the Constraints section of the Sensitivity Report. The entries in the Final Value column indicate the number of tons of each material required by the optimal solution. Thus, RMC will need 20 tons of material 1, 4 tons of material 2, and 21 tons of material 3 in order to produce the optimal solution of 25 tons of fuel additive and 20 tons of solvent base.

The values in the Constraint R.H. Side column are the right-hand sides of the constraints for the RMC problem. The differences between the entries in the Constraint R.H. Side column and the Final Value column provide the values of the slack variables for the RMC problem. Thus, there are 20 − 20 = 0 tons of slack for material 1, 5 − 4 = 1 ton of slack for material 2, and 21 − 21 = 0 tons of slack for material 3.

---

[2]This definition of reduced cost is slightly different from (but is equivalent to) the one in the glossary. Excel's solution algorithm permits variables in solution at their upper bound to have a nonzero reduced cost.

The entries in the Shadow Price column provide the *shadow price* for each constraint. The shadow price is the *change* in the value of the solution per unit increase in the right-hand side of the constraint. The Management Scientist uses the term *dual price* to describe the *improvement* in the value of the solution per unit increase in the right-hand side of a constraint. The shadow price and dual price are the same for maximization problems because improvement is an increase in value. For minimization problems, improvement is a decrease in value; thus, for minimization problems the shadow price and dual price have opposite signs.

The sensitivity analysis interpretations provided in this appendix are based on the assumption that only one objective function coefficient or only one right-hand-side change occurs at a time.

The last two columns in the Constraints section of the Sensitivity Report contain the range of feasibility information for the constraint right-hand sides. For example, consider the material 1 constraint with an allowable increase value of 1.5 and an allowable decrease value of 6. The values in the Allowable Increase and Allowable Decrease columns indicate that the shadow price of $33.33 is valid for increases of up to 1.5 tons and decreases down to 6 tons. Thus, the shadow price of $33.33 is applicable for increases up to $20 + 1.5 = 21.5$ tons and decreases down to $20 - 6 = 14$ tons.

In summary, the range of feasibility information provides the limits where the shadow prices are applicable. For changes outside the range, the problem must be resolved to find the new optimal solution and the new shadow price.

Appendix 8.2   Sensitivity Analysis with LINGO

In Appendix 7.2 we showed how LINGO can be used to solve a linear program by using it to solve the RMC problem. A copy of the Solution Report is shown in Figure 8.27. As we discussed previously, the value of the objective function is 1600, the optimal solution is $F = 25$ and $S = 20$, and the values of the slack variables corresponding to the three constraints (rows 2–4) are 0.0, 1.0, and 0.0. Now, let us consider the information in the Reduced Cost column and the Dual Price column.

FIGURE 8.27   LINGO SOLUTION REPORT FOR THE RMC PROBLEM

```
Global optimal solution found.          1600.000
Objective value:                               2
Total solver iterations:


Model Title: RMC CORPORATION


        Variable              Value          Reduced Cost
      -------------      ---------------    ----------------
              F              25.00000             0.00000
              S              20.00000             0.00000


          Row            Slack/Surplus         Dual Price
      -------------      ---------------    ----------------
           1              1600.00000             1.00000
           2                 0.00000            33.33333
           3                 1.00000             0.00000
           4                 0.00000            44.44444
```

In LINGO, the value of a nonzero reduced cost indicates how much the value of the corresponding objective function coefficient would have to improve before that variable could assume a positive value in the optimal solution. For the RMC problem, the reduced costs for both decision variables are zero because both variables are at their optimal values. The nonzero dual prices of 33.3333 for constraint 1 (Material 1 constraint in row 2) and 44.4444 for constraint 3 (Material 3 constraint in row 4) tell us that an additional ton of Material 1 improves (increases) the value of the optimal solution by $33.33 and an additional ton of Material 3 improves (increases) the value of the optimal solution by $44.44.

Next, let us consider how LINGO can be used to compute the range of optimality for each objective function coefficient and the range of feasibility for each of the dual prices. By default, range computations are not enabled in LINGO. To enable range computations, perform the following steps:

Step 1. Choose the **LINGO** menu
Step 2. Select **Options**
Step 3. When the LINGO Options dialog box appears:
Select the **General Solver** tab
Choose **Prices and Ranges** in the Dual Computations box
Click **Apply**
Click **OK**

You will now have to re-solve the RMC problem in order for LINGO to perform the range computations. After re-solving the problem, close or minimize the Solution Report window. To display the range information, select the Range command from the LINGO menu. LINGO displays the range information in a new window titled Range Report. The output that appears in the Range Report window for the RMC problem is shown in Figure 8.28.

We will use the information in the Objective Coefficient Ranges section of the range report to compute the range of optimality for the objective function coefficients. For example, the current objective function coefficient for F (fuel additive) is 40. Note that the

FIGURE 8.28   LINGO RANGE REPORT FOR THE RMC PROBLEM

```
Ranges in which the basis is unchanged:

OBJECTIVE COEFFICIENT RANGES

                    Current        Allowable       Allowable
    Variable      Coefficient       Increase        Decrease
    --------      -----------       ---------       ---------
       F           40.00000        20.00000         16.00000
       S           30.00000        20.00000         10.00000


RIGHTHAND SIDE RANGES

                    Current        Allowable       Allowable
    Row               RHS           Increase        Decrease
    --------      -----------       ---------       ---------
       2           20.00000         1.50000          6.00000
       3            5.00000        INFINITY          1.00000
       4           21.00000         9.00000          2.25000
```

corresponding allowable increase is 20.0 and the corresponding allowable decrease is 16.0. Thus the range of optimality for the contribution to profit for F, the objective function coefficient for F, is 40.0 − 16.0 = 24.0 to 40.0 + 20.0 = 60.0. Using PF to denote the contribution to profit for fuel additive, the range of optimality for PF is $24.0 \leq PF \leq 60.0$. Similarly, with an allowable increase of 20.0 and an allowable decrease of 10.0, the range of optimality for PS, the profit contribution for solvent is $20.0 \leq PS \leq 50.0$.

To compute the range of feasibility for each dual price, we will use the information in the Righthand Side Ranges section of the range report. For example, the current right-hand-side value for Material 1 constraint (row 2) is 20, the allowable increase is 1.5, and the allowable decrease is 6.0. Because the dual price for this constraint is 33.33 (shown in the LINGO solution report), we can conclude that an additional ton will increase the objective function by $33.33 per ton. From the range information given, we see that after rounding, the dual price of $33.33 is valid for increases up to 20.0 + 1.5 = 21.5 and decreases to 20.0 − 6.0 = 14.0. Thus, the range of feasibility for Material 1 is 14.0 to 21.5. The ranges of feasibility for the other constraints can be determined in a similar manner.

CHAPTER 9

Linear Programming Applications in Marketing, Finance, and Operations Management

CONTENTS

Linear programming has proven to be one of the most successful quantitative approaches to decision making. Applications have been reported in almost every industry. These applications include production scheduling, media selection, financial planning, capital budgeting, transportation, distribution system design, product mix, staffing, and blending.

The Q.M. in Action, A Marketing Planning Model at Marathon Oil Company, provides an example of the use of linear programming by showing how Marathon uses a large-scale linear programming model to solve a wide variety of planning problems. Later in the chapter other Q.M. in Action features illustrate how GE Capital uses linear programming for optimal lease structuring; how Jeppesen Sanderson uses linear programming to optimize production of flight manuals; and how the Kellogg Company uses a large-scale linear programming model to integrate production, distribution, and inventory planning.

In this chapter we present a variety of applications from the traditional business areas of marketing, finance, and operations management. Modeling, computer solution, and interpretation of output are emphasized. A mathematical model is developed for each problem studied, and solutions obtained using The Management Scientist are presented for most of the applications. In the chapter appendix we illustrate the use of Excel Solver by solving a financial planning problem.

Q.M. *in* ACTION

A MARKETING PLANNING MODEL AT MARATHON OIL COMPANY*

Marathon Oil Company has four refineries within the United States, operates 50 light products terminals, and has product demand at more than 95 locations. The Supply and Transportation Division faces the problem of determining which refinery should supply which terminal and, at the same time, determining which products should be transported via pipeline, barge, or tanker to minimize cost. Product demand must be satisfied, and the supply capability of each refinery must not be exceeded. To help solve this difficult problem, Marathon Oil developed a marketing planning model.

The marketing planning model is a large-scale linear programming model that takes into account sales not only at Marathon product terminals but also at all exchange locations. An exchange contract is an agreement with other oil product marketers that involves exchanging or trading

Marathon's products for theirs at different locations. All pipelines, barges, and tankers within Marathon's marketing area are also represented in the linear programming model. The objective of the model is to minimize the cost of meeting a given demand structure, taking into account sales price, pipeline tariffs, exchange contract costs, product demand, terminal operating costs, refining costs, and product purchases.

The marketing planning model is used to solve a wide variety of planning problems that vary, from evaluating gasoline blending economics to analyzing the economics of a new terminal or pipeline. With daily sales of about 10 million gallons of refined light product, a savings of even one-thousandth of a cent per gallon can result in significant long-term savings. At the same time, what may appear to be a savings in one area, such as refining or transportation, may actually add to overall costs when the effects are fully realized throughout the system. The marketing planning model allows a simultaneous examination of this total effect.

**Based on information provided by Robert W. Wernert at Marathon Oil Company, Findlay, Ohio.

9.1 Marketing Applications

Applications of linear programming in marketing are numerous. In this section we discuss applications in media selection and marketing research.

Media Selection

Media selection applications of linear programming are designed to help marketing managers allocate a fixed advertising budget to various advertising media. Potential media include newspapers, magazines, radio, television, and direct mail. In these applications, the objective is to maximize reach, frequency, and quality of exposure. Restrictions on the allowable allocation usually arise during consideration of company policy, contract requirements, and media availability. In the application that follows, we illustrate how a media selection problem might be formulated and solved using a linear programming model.

Relax-and-Enjoy Lake Development Corporation is developing a lakeside community at a privately owned lake. The primary market for the lakeside lots and homes includes all middle- and upper-income families within approximately 100 miles of the development. Relax-and-Enjoy employed the advertising firm of Boone, Phillips, and Jackson (BP&J) to design the promotional campaign.

After considering possible advertising media and the market to be covered, BP&J recommended that the first month's advertising be restricted to five media. At the end of the month, BP&J will then reevaluate its strategy based on the month's results. BP&J collected data on the number of potential customers reached, the cost per advertisement, the maximum number of times each medium is available, and the exposure quality rating for each of the five media. The quality rating is measured in terms of an exposure quality unit, a measure of the relative value of one advertisement in each of the media. This measure, based on BP&J's experience in the advertising business, takes into account factors such as audience demographics (age, income, and education of the audience reached), image presented, and quality of the advertisement. The information collected is presented in Table 9.1.

Relax-and-Enjoy provided BP&J with an advertising budget of $30,000 for the first month's campaign. In addition, Relax-and-Enjoy imposed the following restrictions on how BP&J may allocate these funds: At least 10 television commercials must be used, at least 50,000 potential customers must be reached, and no more than $18,000 may be spent on television advertisements. What advertising media selection plan should be recommended?

TABLE 9.1 ADVERTISING MEDIA ALTERNATIVES FOR THE RELAX-AND-ENJOY LAKE DEVELOPMENT CORPORATION

Advertising Media	Number of Potential Customers Reached	Cost ($) per Advertisement	Maximum Times Available per Month*	Exposure Quality Units
1. Daytime TV (1 min), station WKLA	1000	1500	15	65
2. Evening TV (30 sec), station WKLA	2000	3000	10	90
3. Daily newspaper (full page), *The Morning Journal*	1500	400	25	40
4. Sunday newspaper magazine (½ page color), *The Sunday Press*	2500	1000	4	60
5. Radio, 8:00 A.M. or 5:00 P.M. news (30 sec), station KNOP	300	100	30	20

*The maximum number of times the medium is available is either the maximum number of times the advertising medium occurs (e.g., four Sundays per month) or the maximum number of times BP&J recommends that the medium be used.

In Section 7.1 we provided some general guidelines for modeling linear programming problems. You may want to review Section 7.1 before proceeding with the linear programming applications in this chapter.

The decision to be made is how many times to use each medium. We begin by defining the decision variables:

$$DTV = \text{number of times daytime TV is used}$$
$$ETV = \text{number of times evening TV is used}$$
$$DN = \text{number of times daily newspaper is used}$$
$$SN = \text{number of times Sunday newspaper is used}$$
$$R = \text{number of times radio is used}$$

The data on quality of exposure in Table 9.1 show that each daytime TV (DTV) advertisement is rated at 65 exposure quality units. Thus, an advertising plan with DTV advertisements will provide a total of $65DTV$ exposure quality units. Continuing with the data in Table 9.1, we find evening TV (ETV) rated at 90 exposure quality units, daily newspaper (DN) rated at 40 exposure quality units, Sunday newspaper (SN) rated at 60 exposure quality units, and radio (R) rated at 20 exposure quality units. With the objective of maximizing the total exposure quality units for the overall media selection plan, the objective function becomes

$$\text{Max} \quad 65DTV + 90ETV + 40DN + 60SN + 20R \qquad \text{Exposure quality}$$

We now formulate the constraints for the model from the information given:

$$
\begin{array}{rcll}
DTV & \leq & 15 & \left.\begin{array}{l} \\ \\ \\ \\ \\ \end{array}\right\} \\
ETV & \leq & 10 & \\
DN & \leq & 25 & \begin{array}{l}\text{Availability} \\ \text{of media}\end{array} \\
SN & \leq & 4 & \\
R & \leq & 30 & \\
1500DTV + 3000ETV + 400DN + 1000SN + 100R & \leq & 30{,}000 & \text{Budget} \\
DTV + ETV & \geq & 10 & \left.\begin{array}{l} \\ \\ \end{array}\right\}\begin{array}{l}\text{Television}\end{array} \\
1500DTV + 3000ETV & \leq & 18{,}000 & \text{restrictions} \\
1000DTV + 2000ETV + 1500DN + 2500SN + 300R & \geq & 50{,}000 & \text{Customers reached} \\
DTV, ETV, DN, SN, R & \geq & 0 &
\end{array}
$$

Care must be taken to ensure the linear programming model accurately reflects the real problem. Always review your formulation thoroughly before attempting to solve the model.

Problem 1 provides practice at formulating a similar media selection model.

More complex media selection models may include considerations such as the reduced exposure quality value for repeat media usage, cost discounts for repeat media usage, audience overlap by different media, and/or timing recommendations for the advertisements.

The optimal solution to this 5-variable, 9-constraint linear programming model is shown in Figure 9.1; a summary is presented in Table 9.2.

The optimal solution calls for advertisements to be distributed among daytime TV, daily newspaper, Sunday newspaper, and radio. The maximum number of exposure quality units is 2370, and the total number of customers reached is 61,500. The Reduced Costs column in Figure 9.1 indicates that the number of exposure quality units for evening TV would have to increase by at least 65 before this media alternative could appear in the optimal solution. Note that the budget constraint (constraint 6) has a dual price of 0.060. Therefore, a $1.00 increase in the advertising budget will lead to an increase of 0.06 exposure quality units. The dual price of -25.000 for constraint 7 indicates that reducing the number of television commercials by 1 will increase the exposure quality of the advertising plan by 25 units. Thus, Relax-and-Enjoy should consider reducing the requirement of having at least 10 television commercials.

A possible shortcoming of this model is that, even if the exposure quality measure were not subject to error, it offers no guarantee that maximization of total exposure quality will lead to a maximization of profit or of sales (a common surrogate for profit). However, this issue is not a shortcoming of linear programming; rather, it is a shortcoming of the use of exposure quality as a criterion. If we could directly measure the effect of an advertisement on profit, we could use total profit as the objective to be maximized.

FIGURE 9.1 THE MANAGEMENT SCIENTIST SOLUTION FOR THE RELAX-AND-ENJOY LAKE DEVELOPMENT CORPORATION PROBLEM

WEB file

Relax

```
Objective Function Value =      2370.000

    Variable             Value              Reduced Costs
 ---------------     ---------------     ------------------
       DTV               10.000                 0.000
       ETV                0.000                65.000
       DN                25.000                 0.000
       SN                 2.000                 0.000
       R                 30.000                 0.000


   Constraint         Slack/Surplus            Dual Prices
 ---------------     ---------------     ------------------
       1                 5.000                  0.000
       2                10.000                  0.000
       3                 0.000                 16.000
       4                 2.000                  0.000
       5                 0.000                 14.000
       6                 0.000                  0.060
       7                 0.000                -25.000
       8              3000.000                  0.000
       9             11500.003                  0.000
```

Media Availability

Budget

Television Restrictions

Audience Coverage

TABLE 9.2 ADVERTISING PLAN FOR THE RELAX-AND-ENJOY LAKE DEVELOPMENT CORPORATION

Media	Frequency	Budget
Daytime TV	10	$15,000
Daily newspaper	25	10,000
Sunday newspaper	2	2,000
Radio	30	3,000
		$30,000

Exposure quality units = 2370
Total customers reached = 61,500

NOTES AND COMMENTS

1. The media selection model required subjective evaluations of the exposure quality for the media alternatives. Marketing managers may have substantial data concerning exposure quality, but the final coefficients used in the objective function may also include considerations based primarily on managerial judgment. Judgment is an acceptable way of obtaining input for a linear programming model.

2. The media selection model presented in this section uses exposure quality as the objective function and places a constraint on the number of customers reached. An alternative formulation of this problem would be to use the number of customers reached as the objective function and add a constraint indicating the minimum total exposure quality required for the media plan.

Marketing Research

An organization conducts marketing research to learn about consumer characteristics, attitudes, and preferences. Marketing research firms that specialize in providing such information often do the actual research for client organizations. Typical services offered by a marketing research firm include designing the study, conducting market surveys, analyzing the data collected, and providing summary reports and recommendations for the client. In the research design phase, targets or quotas may be established for the number and types of respondents to be surveyed. The marketing research firm's objective is to conduct the survey so as to meet the client's needs at a minimum cost.

Market Survey, Inc. (MSI) specializes in evaluating consumer reaction to new products, services, and advertising campaigns. A client firm requested MSI's assistance in ascertaining consumer reaction to a recently marketed household product. During meetings with the client, MSI agreed to conduct door-to-door personal interviews to obtain responses from households with children and households without children. In addition, MSI agreed to conduct both day and evening interviews. Specifically, the client's contract called for MSI to conduct 1000 interviews under the following quota guidelines:

1. Interview at least 400 households with children.
2. Interview at least 400 households without children.
3. The total number of households interviewed during the evening must be at least as great as the number of households interviewed during the day.
4. At least 40% of the interviews for households with children must be conducted during the evening.
5. At least 60% of the interviews for households without children must be conducted during the evening.

Because the interviews for households with children take additional interviewer time and because evening interviewers are paid more than daytime interviewers, the cost varies with the type of interview. Based on previous research studies, estimates of the interview costs are as follows:

Household	Interview Cost	
	Day	**Evening**
Children	$20	$25
No children	$18	$20

What is the household, time-of-day interview plan that will satisfy the contract requirements at a minimum total interviewing cost?

In formulating the linear programming model for the MSI problem, we utilize the following decision-variable notation:

DC = the number of daytime interviews of households with children

EC = the number of evening interviews of households with children

DNC = the number of daytime interviews of households without children

ENC = the number of evening interviews of households without children

We begin the linear programming model formulation by using the cost-per-interview data to develop the objective function:

$$\text{Min} \quad 20DC + 25EC + 18DNC + 20ENC$$

The constraint requiring a total of 1000 interviews is

$$DC + EC + DNC + ENC = 1000$$

The five specifications concerning the types of interviews are as follows:

- Households with children:

$$DC + EC \geq 400$$

- Households without children:

$$DNC + ENC \geq 400$$

- At least as many evening interviews as day interviews:

$$EC + ENC \geq DC + DNC$$

  The usual format for linear programming model formulation and computer input places all decision variables on the left side of the inequality and a constant (possibly zero) on the right side. Thus, we rewrite this constraint as

$$-DC + EC - DNC + ENC \geq 0$$

- At least 40% of interviews of households with children during the evening:

$$EC \geq 0.4(DC + EC) \quad \text{or} \quad -0.4DC + 0.6EC \geq 0$$

- At least 60% of interviews of households without children during the evening:

$$ENC \geq 0.6(DNC + ENC) \quad \text{or} \quad -0.6DNC + 0.4ENC \geq 0$$

When we add the nonnegativity requirements, the 4-variable and 6-constraint linear programming model becomes

Min $20DC + 25EC + 18DNC + 20ENC$
s.t.

$DC +$	$EC +$	$DNC +$	ENC	$=$	1000	Total interviews
$DC +$	EC			$\geq$	400	Households with children
		$DNC +$	ENC	$\geq$	400	Households without children
$-DC +$	$EC -$	$DNC +$	ENC	$\geq$	0	Evening interviews
$-0.4DC +$	$0.6EC$			$\geq$	0	Evening interviews in households with children
		$-0.6DNC +$	$0.4ENC$	$\geq$	0	Evening interviews in households without children

$$DC, EC, DNC, ENC \geq 0$$

The optimal solution to this linear program is shown in Figure 9.2. The solution reveals that the minimum cost of \$20,320 occurs with the following interview schedule:

	Number of Interviews		
Household	**Day**	**Evening**	**Totals**
Children	240	160	400
No children	240	360	600
Totals	480	520	1000

FIGURE 9.2   THE MANAGEMENT SCIENTIST SOLUTION FOR THE MARKET SURVEY PROBLEM

Market

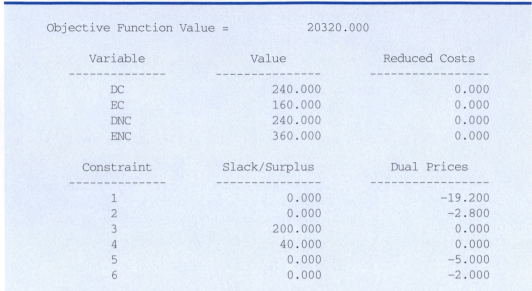

```
Objective Function Value =              20320.000

        Variable              Value            Reduced Costs
      ---------------      ---------------    ------------------
           DC                240.000                0.000
           EC                160.000                0.000
           DNC               240.000                0.000
           ENC               360.000                0.000


       Constraint         Slack/Surplus          Dual Prices
      ---------------      ---------------    ------------------
           1                  0.000                -19.200
           2                  0.000                 -2.800
           3                200.000                  0.000
           4                 40.000                  0.000
           5                  0.000                 -5.000
           6                  0.000                 -2.000
```

Hence, 480 interviews will be scheduled during the day and 520 during the evening. Households with children will be covered by 400 interviews, and households without children will be covered by 600 interviews.

Selected sensitivity analysis information from Figure 9.2 shows a dual price of −19.200 for constraint 1. In other words, the value of the optimal solution will get worse (the total interviewing cost will increase) by $19.20 if the number of interviews is increased from 1000 to 1001. Thus, $19.20 is the incremental cost of obtaining additional interviews. It also is the savings that could be realized by reducing the number of interviews from 1000 to 999.

The surplus variable for constraint 3, with a value of 200.000, shows that 200 more households without children will be interviewed than required. Similarly, the surplus variable for constraint 4, with a value of 40.000, shows that the number of evening interviews exceeds the number of daytime interviews by 40. The zero values for the surplus variables in constraints 5 and 6 indicate that the more expensive evening interviews are being held at a minimum. Indeed, the dual price of −5.000 for constraint 5 indicates that if one more household (with children) than the minimum requirement must be interviewed during the evening, the total interviewing cost will go up by $5.00. Similarly, constraint 6 shows that requiring one more household (without children) to be interviewed during the evening will increase costs by $2.00.

9.2 Financial Applications

In finance, linear programming can be applied in problem situations involving capital budgeting, make-or-buy decisions, asset allocation, portfolio selection, financial planning, and many more. In this section we describe a portfolio selection problem and a problem involving funding of an early retirement program.

Portfolio Selection

Portfolio selection problems involve situations in which a financial manager must select specific investments—for example, stocks and bonds—from a variety of investment alternatives. Managers of mutual funds, credit unions, insurance companies, and banks frequently encounter this type of problem. The objective function for portfolio selection problems usually is maximization of expected return or minimization of risk. The constraints usually take the form of restrictions on the type of permissible investments, state laws, company policy, maximum permissible risk, and so on. Problems of this type have been formulated and solved using a variety of mathematical programming techniques. In this section we formulate and solve a portfolio selection problem as a linear program.

Consider the case of Welte Mutual Funds, Inc., located in New York City. Welte just obtained $100,000 by converting industrial bonds to cash and is now looking for other investment opportunities for these funds. Based on Welte's current investments, the firm's top financial analyst recommends that all new investments be made in the oil industry, steel industry, or in government bonds. Specifically, the analyst identified five investment opportunities and projected their annual rates of return. The investments and rates of return are shown in Table 9.3.

Management of Welte imposed the following investment guidelines:

1. Neither industry (oil or steel) should receive more than $50,000.
2. Government bonds should be at least 25% of the steel industry investments.
3. The investment in Pacific Oil, the high-return but high-risk investment, cannot be more than 60% of the total oil industry investment.

What portfolio recommendations—investments and amounts—should be made for the available $100,000? Given the objective of maximizing projected return subject to the budgetary and managerially imposed constraints, we can answer this question by formulating and solving a linear programming model of the problem. The solution will provide investment recommendations for the management of Welte Mutual Funds.

Let

$$A = \text{dollars invested in Atlantic Oil}$$
$$P = \text{dollars invested in Pacific Oil}$$
$$M = \text{dollars invested in Midwest Steel}$$
$$H = \text{dollars invested in Huber Steel}$$
$$G = \text{dollars invested in government bonds}$$

Using the projected rates of return shown in Table 9.3, we write the objective function for maximizing the total return for the portfolio as

$$\text{Max} \quad 0.073A + 0.103P + 0.064M + 0.075H + 0.045G$$

TABLE 9.3 INVESTMENT OPPORTUNITIES FOR WELTE MUTUAL FUNDS

Investment	Projected Rate of Return (%)
Atlantic Oil	7.3
Pacific Oil	10.3
Midwest Steel	6.4
Huber Steel	7.5
Government bonds	4.5

The constraint specifying investment of the available $100,000 is

$$A + P + M + H + G = 100,000$$

The requirements that neither the oil nor the steel industry should receive more than $50,000 are

$$A + P \leq 50,000$$
$$M + H \leq 50,000$$

The requirement that government bonds be at least 25% of the steel industry investment is expressed as

$$G \geq 0.25(M + H) \quad \text{or} \quad -0.25M - 0.25H + G \geq 0$$

Finally, the constraint that Pacific Oil cannot be more than 60% of the total oil industry investment is

$$P \leq 0.60(A + P) \quad \text{or} \quad -0.60A + 0.40P \leq 0$$

By adding the nonnegativity restrictions, we obtain the complete linear programming model for the Welte Mutual Funds investment problem:

Max $0.073A + 0.103P + 0.064M + 0.075H + 0.045G$

s.t.

$A +$	$P +$	$M +$	$H +$	$G =$	100,000	Available funds
$A +$	P			$\leq$	50,000	Oil industry maximum
		$M +$	H	$\leq$	50,000	Steel industry maximum
		$- \ 0.25M -$	$0.25H +$	$G \geq$	0	Government bonds minimum
$-0.6A +$	$0.4P$			$\leq$	0	Pacific Oil restriction

$$A, P, M, H, G \geq 0$$

The optimal solution to this linear program is shown in Figure 9.3. Table 9.4 shows how the funds are divided among the securities. Note that the optimal solution indicates that the portfolio should be diversified among all the investment opportunities except Midwest Steel. The projected annual return for this portfolio is $8000, which is an over-all return of 8%.

The optimal solution shows the dual price for constraint 3 is zero. The reason is that the steel industry maximum isn't a binding constraint; increases in the steel industry limit of $50,000 will not improve the value of the optimal solution. Indeed, the slack variable for this constraint shows that the current steel industry investment is $10,000 below its limit of $50,000. The dual prices for the other constraints are nonzero, indicating that these constraints are binding.

The dual price of 0.069 for constraint 1 shows that the value of the optimal solution can be increased by 0.069 if one more dollar can be made available for the portfolio investment. If more funds can be obtained at a cost of less than 6.9%, management should consider

FIGURE 9.3 THE MANAGEMENT SCIENTIST SOLUTION FOR THE WELTE MUTUAL FUNDS PROBLEM

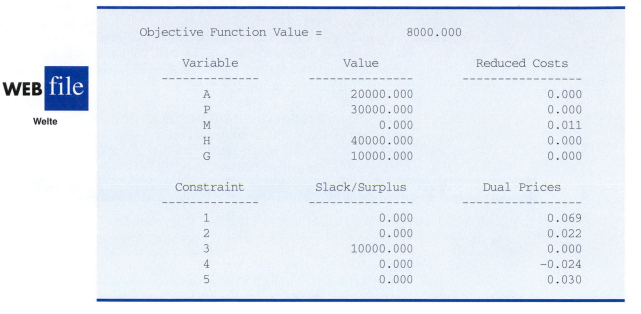

WEB file

Welte

Objective Function Value =   8000.000

Variable	Value	Reduced Costs
A	20000.000	0.000
P	30000.000	0.000
M	0.000	0.011
H	40000.000	0.000
G	10000.000	0.000

Constraint	Slack/Surplus	Dual Prices
1	0.000	0.069
2	0.000	0.022
3	10000.000	0.000
4	0.000	−0.024
5	0.000	0.030

TABLE 9.4 OPTIMAL PORTFOLIO SELECTION FOR WELTE MUTUAL FUNDS

Investment	Amount	Expected Annual Return
Atlantic Oil	$ 20,000	$1460
Pacific Oil	30,000	3090
Huber Steel	40,000	3000
Government bonds	10,000	450
Totals	$100,000	$8000

Expected annual return of $8000
Overall rate of return = 8%

The dual price for the available funds constraint provides information on the rate of return from additional investment funds.

obtaining them. However, if a return in excess of 6.9% can be obtained by investing funds elsewhere (other than in these five securities), management should question the wisdom of investing the entire $100,000 in this portfolio.

Similar interpretations can be given to the other dual prices. Note that the dual price for constraint 4 is negative at 0.024. This result indicates that increasing the value on the right-hand side of the constraint by one unit can be expected to worsen the value of the optimal solution by 0.024. In terms of the optimal portfolio, then, if Welte invests one more dollar in government bonds (beyond the minimum requirement), the total return will decrease by $0.024. To see why this decrease occurs, note again from the dual price for constraint 1 that the marginal return on the funds invested in the portfolio is 6.9% (the average return is 8%). The rate of return on government bonds is 4.5%. Thus, the cost of investing one more dollar in government bonds is the difference between the marginal return on the portfolio and the marginal return on government bonds: 6.9% − 4.5% = 2.4%.

Note that the optimal solution shows that Midwest Steel should not be included in the portfolio ($M = 0$). The associated reduced cost for M of 0.011 tells us that the objective function coefficient for Midwest Steel would have to increase by 0.011 before considering the Midwest Steel investment alternative would be advisable. With such an increase the Midwest Steel return would be $0.064 + 0.011 = 0.075$, making this investment just as desirable as the currently used Huber Steel investment alternative.

Practice formulating a variation of the Welte problem by working Problem 9.

Finally, a simple modification of the Welte linear programming model permits determining the fraction of available funds invested in each security. That is, we divide each of the right-hand-side values by 100,000. Then the optimal values for the variables will give the fraction of funds that should be invested in each security for a portfolio of any size.

NOTES AND COMMENTS

1. The optimal solution to the Welte Mutual Funds problem indicates that $20,000 is to be spent on the Atlantic Oil stock. If Atlantic Oil sells for $75 per share, we would have to purchase exactly $266 \frac{2}{3}$ shares in order to spend exactly $20,000. The difficulty of purchasing fractional shares can be handled by purchasing the largest possible integer number of shares with the allotted funds (e.g., 266 shares of Atlantic Oil). This approach guarantees that the budget constraint will not be violated. This approach, of course, introduces the possibility that the solution will no longer be optimal, but the danger is slight if a large number of securities are involved. In cases where the analyst believes that the decision variables *must* have integer values, the problem must be formulated as an integer linear programming model. Integer linear programming is the topic of Chapter 7.

2. Financial portfolio theory stresses obtaining a proper balance between risk and return. In the Welte problem, we explicitly considered return in the objective function. Risk is controlled by choosing constraints that ensure diversity among oil and steel stocks and a balance between government bonds and the steel industry investment.

Financial Planning

Linear programming has been used for a variety of financial planning applications. The Q.M. in Action, Optimal Lease Structuring at GE Capital, describes how linear programming is used to optimize the structure of a leveraged lease.

Q.M. *in* ACTION

OPTIMAL LEASE STRUCTURING AT GE CAPITAL*

GE Capital is a $70 billion subsidiary of General Electric. As one of the nation's largest and most diverse financial services companies, GE Capital arranges leases in both domestic and international markets, including leases for telecommunications; data processing; construction; and fleets of cars, trucks, and commercial aircraft. To help allocate and schedule the rental and debt payments of a leveraged lease, GE Capital analysts developed an optimization model, which is available as an optional component of the company's lease analysis proprietary software.

Leveraged leases are designed to provide financing for assets with economic lives of at least five years, which require large capital outlays. A leveraged lease represents

*Based on C. J. Litty, "Optimal Lease Structuring at GE Capital," *Interfaces* (May/June 1994): 34–45.

(continued)

an agreement among the lessor (the owner of the asset), the lessee (the user of the asset), and the lender who provides a nonrecourse loan of 50% to 80% of the lessor's purchase price. In a nonrecourse loan, the lenders cannot turn to the lessor for repayment in the event of default. As the lessor in such arrangements, GE Capital is able to claim ownership and realize income tax benefits such as depreciation and interest deductions. These deductions usually produce tax losses during the early years of the lease, which reduces the total tax liability. Approximately 85% of all financial leases in the United States are leveraged leases.

In its simplest form, the leveraged lease structuring problem can be formulated as a linear program. The linear program models the after-tax cash flow for the lessor, taking into consideration rental receipts, borrowing and repaying of the loan, and income taxes. Constraints are formulated to ensure compliance with IRS guidelines and to enable customizing of leases to meet lessee and lessor requirements. The objective function can be entered in a custom fashion or selected from a predefined list. Typically, the objective is to minimize the lessee's cost, expressed as the net present value of rental payments, or to maximize the lessor's after-tax yield.

GE Capital developed an optimization approach that could be applied to single-investor lease structuring. In a study with the department most involved with these transactions, the optimization approach yielded substantial benefits. The approach helped GE Capital win some single-investor transactions ranging in size from $1 million to $20 million.

Hewlitt Corporation established an early retirement program as part of its corporate restructuring. At the close of the voluntary sign-up period, 68 employees had elected early retirement. As a result of these early retirements, the company incurs the following obligations over the next eight years:

Year	1	2	3	4	5	6	7	8
Cash Requirement	430	210	222	231	240	195	225	255

The cash requirements (in thousands of dollars) are due at the beginning of each year.

The corporate treasurer must determine how much money must be set aside today to meet the eight yearly financial obligations as they come due. The financing plan for the retirement program includes investments in government bonds as well as savings. The investments in government bonds are limited to three choices:

Bond	Price	Rate (%)	Years to Maturity
1	$1150	8.875	5
2	1000	5.500	6
3	1350	11.750	7

The government bonds have a par value of $1000, which means that even with different prices each bond pays $1000 at maturity. The rates shown are based on the par value. For purposes of planning, the treasurer assumed that any funds not invested in bonds will be placed in savings and earn interest at an annual rate of 4%.

We define the decision variables as follows:

F = total dollars required to meet the retirement plan's eight-year obligation

B_1 = units of bond 1 purchased at the beginning of year 1

B_2 = units of bond 2 purchased at the beginning of year 1

B_3 = units of bond 3 purchased at the beginning of year 1

S = amount placed in savings at the beginning of year i for $i = 1, \ldots, 8$

The objective function is to minimize the total dollars needed to meet the retirement plan's eight-year obligation, or

$$\text{Min} \quad F$$

A key feature of this type of financial planning problem is that a constraint must be formulated for each year of the planning horizon. In general, each constraint takes the form:

$$\begin{pmatrix} \text{Funds available at} \\ \text{the beginning of the year} \end{pmatrix} - \begin{pmatrix} \text{Funds invested in bonds} \\ \text{and placed in savings} \end{pmatrix} = \begin{pmatrix} \text{Cash obligation for} \\ \text{the current year} \end{pmatrix}$$

The funds available at the beginning of year 1 are given by F. With a current price of $1150 for bond 1 and investments expressed in thousands of dollars, the total investment for B_1 units of bond 1 would be $1.15B_1$. Similarly, the total investment in bonds 2 and 3 would be $1B_2$ and $1.35B_3$, respectively. The investment in savings for year 1 is S_1. Using these results and the first-year obligation of 430, we obtain the constraint for year 1:

$$F - 1.15B_1 - 1B_2 - 1.35B_3 - S_1 = 430 \quad \text{Year 1}$$

Investments in bonds can take place only in this first year, and the bonds will be held until maturity.

The funds available at the beginning of year 2 include the investment returns of 8.875% on the par value of bond 1, 5.5% on the par value of bond 2, 11.75% on the par value of bond 3, and 4% on savings. The new amount to be invested in savings for year 2 is S_2. With an obligation of 210, the constraint for year 2 is

$$0.08875B_1 + 0.055B_2 + 0.1175B_3 + 1.04S_1 - S_2 = 210 \quad \text{Year 2}$$

Similarly, the constraints for years 3 to 8 are

$$0.08875B_1 + 0.055B_2 + 0.1175B_3 + 1.04S_2 - S_3 = 222 \quad \text{Year 3}$$
$$0.08875B_1 + 0.055B_2 + 0.1175B_3 + 1.04S_3 - S_4 = 231 \quad \text{Year 4}$$
$$0.08875B_1 + 0.055B_2 + 0.1175B_3 + 1.04S_4 - S_5 = 240 \quad \text{Year 5}$$
$$1.08875B_1 + 0.055B_2 + 0.1175B_3 + 1.04S_5 - S_6 = 195 \quad \text{Year 6}$$
$$1.055B_2 + 0.1175B_3 + 1.04S_6 - S_7 = 225 \quad \text{Year 7}$$
$$1.1175B_3 + 1.04S_7 - S_8 = 255 \quad \text{Year 8}$$

Note that the constraint for year 6 shows that funds available from bond 1 are $1.08875B_1$. The coefficient of 1.08875 reflects the fact that bond 1 matures at the end of year 5. As a result, the par value plus the interest from bond 1 during year 5 is available at the beginning of year 6. Also, because bond 1 matures in year 5 and becomes available for use at the beginning of year 6, the variable B_1 does not appear in the constraints for years 7 and 8. Note the similar interpretation for bond 2, which matures at the end of year 6 and has the par value plus interest available at the beginning of year 7. In addition, bond 3 matures at the end of year 7 and has the par value plus interest available at the beginning of year 8.

We do not consider future investments in bonds because the future price of bonds depends on interest rates and cannot be known in advance.

Finally, note that a variable S_8 appears in the constraint for year 8. The retirement fund obligation will be completed at the beginning of year 8, so we anticipate that S_8 will be zero and no funds will be put into savings. However, the formulation includes S_8 in the event that the bond income plus interest from the savings in year 7 exceed the 255 cash requirement for year 8. Thus, S_8 is a surplus variable that shows any funds remaining after the eight-year cash requirements have been satisfied.

FIGURE 9.4   THE MANAGEMENT SCIENTIST SOLUTION FOR THE HEWLITT
CORPORATION CASH REQUIREMENTS PROBLEM

```
Objective Function Value =           1728.79385

        Variable              Value            Reduced Costs
      --------------      ---------------     -----------------

          F               1728.79385               0.00000
          B1               144.98815               0.00000
          B2               187.85585               0.00000
          B3               228.18792               0.00000
          S1               636.14794               0.00000
          S2               501.60571               0.00000
          S3               349.68179               0.00000
          S4               182.68091               0.00000
          S5                 0.00000               0.06403
          S6                 0.00000               0.01261
          S7                 0.00000               0.02132
          S8                 0.00000               0.67084


       Constraint       Slack/Surplus          Dual Prices
      --------------    ---------------       -----------------

           1               0.00000               -1.00000
           2               0.00000               -0.96154
           3               0.00000               -0.92456
           4               0.00000               -0.88900
           5               0.00000               -0.85480
           6               0.00000               -0.76036
           7               0.00000               -0.71899
           8               0.00000               -0.67084
```

The optimal solution to this 12-variable, 8-constraint linear program is shown in Figure 9.4. With an objective function value of 1728.79385, the total investment required to meet the retirement plan's eight-year obligation is $1,728,794. Using the current prices of $1150, $1000, and $1350 for each of the bonds, respectively, we can summarize the initial investments in the three bonds as follows:

Bond	Units Purchased	Investment Amount
1	$B_1 = 144.988$	$1150(144.988) = \$166,736$
2	$B_2 = 187.856$	$1000(187.856) = \$187,856$
3	$B_3 = 228.188$	$1350(228.188) = \$308,054$

The solution also shows that $636,148 (see S_1) will be placed in savings at the beginning of the first year. By starting with $1,728,794, the company can make the specified bond and savings investments and have enough left over to meet the retirement program's first-year cash requirement of $430,000.

The optimal solution in Figure 9.4 shows that the decision variables S_1, S_2, S_3, and S_4 all are greater than zero, indicating investments in savings are required in each of the first

In this application, the dual price can be thought of as the negative of the present value of each dollar in the cash requirement. For example, each dollar that must be paid in year 8 has a present value of $0.67084.

four years. However, interest from the bonds plus the bond maturity incomes will be sufficient to cover the retirement program's cash requirements in years 5 through 8.

The dual prices have an interesting interpretation in this application. Each right-hand-side value corresponds to the payment that must be made in that year. Note that the dual prices are negative, indicating that reducing the payment in any year would be beneficial because the total funds required for the retirement program's obligation would be less. Also note that the dual prices show that reductions are more beneficial in the early years, with decreasing benefits in subsequent years. As a result, Hewlitt would benefit by reducing cash requirements in the early years even if it had to make equivalently larger cash payments in later years.

NOTES AND COMMENTS

1. The optimal solution for the Hewlitt Corporation problem shows fractional numbers of government bonds at 144.988, 187.856, and 228.188 units, respectively. However, fractional bond units usually are not available. If we were conservative and rounded up to 145, 188, and 229 units, respectively, the total funds required for the eight-year retirement program obligation would be approximately $1254 more than the total funds indicated by the objective function. Because of the magnitude of the funds involved,

rounding up probably would provide a workable solution. If an optimal integer solution were required, the methods of integer linear programming covered in Chapter 7 would have to be used.

2. We implicitly assumed that interest from the government bonds is paid annually. Investments such as treasury notes actually provide interest payments every six months. In such cases, the model can be reformulated with six-month periods, with interest and/or cash payments occurring every six months.

 ## Operations Management Applications

Linear programming applications developed for production and operations management include scheduling, staffing, inventory control, and capacity planning. In this section we describe examples with make-or-buy decisions, production scheduling, and workforce assignments.

A Make-or-Buy Decision

We illustrate the use of a linear programming model to determine how much of each of several component parts a company should manufacture and how much it should purchase from an outside supplier. Such a decision is referred to as a make-or-buy decision.

The Janders Company markets various business and engineering products. Currently, Janders is preparing to introduce two new calculators: one for the business market, called the Financial Manager, and one for the engineering market, called the Technician. Each calculator has three components: a base, an electronic cartridge, and a faceplate or top. The same base is used for both calculators, but the cartridges and tops are different. All components can be manufactured by the company or purchased from outside suppliers. The manufacturing costs and purchase prices for the components are summarized in Table 9.5.

Company forecasters indicate that 3000 Financial Manager calculators and 2000 Technician calculators will be needed. However, manufacturing capacity is limited. The company has 200 hours of regular manufacturing time and 50 hours of overtime that can be scheduled for the calculators. Overtime involves a premium at the additional cost of $9 per hour. Table 9.6 shows manufacturing times (in minutes) for the components.

TABLE 9.5 MANUFACTURING COSTS AND PURCHASE PRICES FOR JANDERS CALCULATOR COMPONENTS

	Cost per Unit	
Component	**Manufacture (regular time)**	**Purchase**
Base	$0.50	$0.60
Financial cartridge	$3.75	$4.00
Technician cartridge	$3.30	$3.90
Financial top	$0.60	$0.65
Technician top	$0.75	$0.78

TABLE 9.6 MANUFACTURING TIMES IN MINUTES PER UNIT FOR JANDERS CALCULATOR COMPONENTS

Component	**Manufacturing Time**
Base	1.0
Financial cartridge	3.0
Technician cartridge	2.5
Financial top	1.0
Technician top	1.5

The problem for Janders is to determine how many units of each component to manufacture and how many units of each component to purchase. We define the decision variables as follows:

$$BM = \text{number of bases manufactured}$$
$$BP = \text{number of bases purchased}$$
$$FCM = \text{number of Financial cartridges manufactured}$$
$$FCP = \text{number of Financial cartridges purchased}$$
$$TCM = \text{number of Technician cartridges manufactured}$$
$$TCP = \text{number of Technician cartridges purchased}$$
$$FTM = \text{number of Financial tops manufactured}$$
$$FTP = \text{number of Financial tops purchased}$$
$$TTM = \text{number of Technician tops manufactured}$$
$$TTP = \text{number of Technician tops purchased}$$

One additional decision variable is needed to determine the hours of overtime that must be scheduled:

$$OT = \text{number of hours of overtime to be scheduled}$$

The objective function is to minimize the total cost, including manufacturing costs, purchase costs, and overtime costs. Using the cost-per-unit data in Table 9.5 and the overtime premium cost rate of $9 per hour, we write the objective function as

$$\text{Min} \quad 0.5BM + 0.6BP + 3.75FCM + 4FCP + 3.3TCM + 3.9TCP + 0.6FTM$$
$$+ 0.65FTP + 0.75TTM + 0.78TTP + 9OT$$

The first five constraints specify the number of each component needed to satisfy the demand for 3000 Financial Manager calculators and 2000 Technician calculators. A total of 5000 base components are needed, with the number of other components depending on the demand for the particular calculator. The five demand constraints are

$$
\begin{aligned}
BM + BP &= 5000 \quad \text{Bases} \\
FCM + FCP &= 3000 \quad \text{Financial cartridges} \\
TCM + TCP &= 2000 \quad \text{Technician cartridges} \\
FTM + FTP &= 3000 \quad \text{Financial tops} \\
TTM + TTP &= 2000 \quad \text{Technician tops}
\end{aligned}
$$

Two constraints are needed to guarantee that manufacturing capacities for regular time and overtime cannot be exceeded. The first constraint limits overtime capacity to 50 hours, or

$$OT \leq 50$$

The second constraint states that the total manufacturing time required for all components must be less than or equal to the total manufacturing capacity, including regular time plus overtime. The manufacturing times for the components are expressed in minutes, so we state the total manufacturing capacity constraint in minutes, with the 200 hours of regular time capacity becoming $60(200) = 12{,}000$ minutes. The actual overtime required is unknown at this point, so we write the overtime as $60OT$ minutes. Using the manufacturing times from Table 9.6, we have

$$BM + 3FCM + 2.5TCM + FTM + 1.5TTM \leq 12{,}000 + 60OT$$

Moving the decision variable for overtime to the left-hand side of the constraint provides the manufacturing capacity constraint:

$$BM + 3FCM + 2.5TCM + FTM + 1.5TTM - 60OT \leq 12{,}000$$

The complete formulation of the Janders make-or-buy problem with all decision variables greater than or equal to zero is

Min $0.5BM + 0.6BP + 3.75FCM + 4FCP + 3.3TCM + 3.9TCP$
$\quad\quad + 0.6FTM + 0.65FTP + 0.75TTM + 0.78TTP + 9OT$

s.t.

BM					$+$	$BP =$	5000	Bases
	FCM				$+$	$FCP =$	3000	Financial cartridges
		TCM			$+$	$TCP =$	2000	Technician cartridges
			FTM		$+$	$FTP =$	3000	Financial tops
				$TTM +$	$TTP =$	2000	Technician tops
					$OT \leq$	50	Overtime hours
$BM + 3FCM + 2.5TCM + FTM + 1.5TTM - 60OT \leq$						$12{,}000$	Manufacturing capacity

The optimal solution to this 11-variable, 7-constraint linear program is shown in Figure 9.5. The optimal solution indicates that all 5000 bases (BM), 667 Financial Manager cartridges (FCM), and 2000 Technician cartridges (TCM) should be manufactured. The remaining 2333 Financial Manager cartridges (FCP), all the Financial Manager tops (FTP), and all Technician tops (TTP) should be purchased. No overtime manufacturing is necessary, and the total cost associated with the optimal make-or-buy plan is $24,443.33.

```
Objective Function Value =            24443.333

      Variable              Value            Reduced Costs
    --------------      ----------------    ------------------
        BM                5000.000               0.000
        BP                   0.000               0.017
        FCM                666.667               0.000
        FCP               2333.333               0.000
        TCM               2000.000               0.000
        TCP                  0.000               0.392
        FTM                  0.000               0.033
        FTP               3000.000               0.000
        TTM                  0.000               0.095
        TTP               2000.000               0.000
        OT                   0.000               4.000

      Constraint        Slack/Surplus          Dual Prices
    --------------      ----------------    ------------------
         1                   0.000              -0.583
         2                   0.000              -4.000
         3                   0.000              -3.508
         4                   0.000              -0.650
         5                   0.000              -0.780
         6                  50.000               0.000
         7                   0.000               0.083
```

OBJECTIVE COEFFICIENT RANGES

```
      Variable        Lower Limit        Current Value        Upper Limit
    ------------    ----------------    ----------------    ----------------
        BM          No Lower Limit           0.500               0.517
        BP               0.583               0.600          No Upper Limit
        FCM              3.700               3.750               3.850
        FCP              3.900               4.000               4.050
        TCM         No Lower Limit           3.300               3.692
        TCP              3.508               3.900          No Upper Limit
        FTM              0.567               0.600          No Upper Limit
        FTP         No Lower Limit           0.650               0.683
        TTM              0.655               0.750          No Upper Limit
        TTP         No Lower Limit           0.780               0.875
        OT               5.000               9.000          No Upper Limit
```

RIGHT HAND SIDE RANGES

```
      Constraint      Lower Limit        Current Value        Upper Limit
    ------------    ----------------    ----------------    ----------------
         1               0.000             5000.000            7000.000
         2             666.667             3000.000         No Upper Limit
         3               0.000             2000.000            2800.000
         4               0.000             3000.000         No Upper Limit
         5               0.000             2000.000         No Upper Limit
         6               0.000               50.000         No Upper Limit
         7           10000.000            12000.000           19000.000
```

WEB file

Janders

The same units of measure must be used for both the left-hand side and right-hand side of the constraint. In this case, minutes are used.

Sensitivity analysis provides some additional information about the unused overtime capacity. The Reduced Costs column shows that the overtime (*OT*) premium would have to decrease by $4 per hour before overtime production should be considered. That is, if the overtime premium is $9 − $4 = $5 or less, Janders may want to replace some of the purchased components with components manufactured on overtime.

The dual price for the manufacturing capacity constraint 7 is 0.083. This price indicates that an additional hour of manufacturing capacity is worth $0.083 per minute or ($0.083)(60) = $5 per hour. The right-hand-side range for constraint 7 shows that this conclusion is valid until the amount of regular time increases to 19,000 minutes, or 316.7 hours.

Sensitivity analysis also indicates that a change in prices charged by the outside suppliers can affect the optimal solution. For instance, the objective coefficient range for *BP* is 0.583 to no upper limit. If the purchase price for bases remains at $0.583 or more, the number of bases purchased (*BP*) will remain at zero. However, if the purchase price drops below $0.583, Janders should begin to purchase rather than manufacture the base component. Similar sensitivity analysis conclusions about the purchase price ranges can be drawn for the other components.

NOTES AND COMMENTS

The proper interpretation of the dual price for manufacturing capacity (constraint 7) in the Janders problem is that an additional hour of manufacturing capacity is worth ($0.083)(60) = $5 per hour. Thus, the company should be willing to pay a premium of $5 per hour over and above the current regular time cost per hour, which is already included in the manufacturing cost of the product. Thus, if the regular time cost is $18 per hour, Janders should be willing to pay up to $18 + $5 = $23 per hour to obtain additional labor capacity.

Production Scheduling

One of the most important applications of linear programming deals with multiperiod planning such as production scheduling. The solution to a production scheduling problem enables the manager to establish an efficient low-cost production schedule for one or more products over several time periods (weeks or months). Essentially, a production scheduling problem can be viewed as a product-mix problem for each of several periods in the future. The manager must determine the production levels that will allow the company to meet product demand requirements, given limitations on production capacity, labor capacity, and storage space, while minimizing total production costs.

One advantage of using linear programming for production scheduling problems is that they recur. A production schedule must be established for the current month, then again for the next month, for the month after that, and so on. When looking at the problem each month, the production manager will find that, although demand for the products has changed, production times, production capacities, storage space limitations, and so on are roughly the same. Thus, the production manager is basically resolving the same problem handled in previous months, and a general linear programming model of the production scheduling procedure may be frequently applied. Once the model has been formulated, the manager can simply supply the data—demand, capacities, and so on—for the given production period and use the linear programming model repeatedly to develop the production schedule. The Q.M. in Action, Optimizing Production of Flight Manuals at Jeppesen Sanderson, Inc., describes how linear programming is used to minimize the cost of producing weekly revisions to flight manuals.

Q.M. *in* ACTION

OPTIMIZING PRODUCTION OF FLIGHT MANUALS AT JEPPESEN SANDERSON, INC.*

Jeppesen Sanderson, Inc., manufactures and distributes flight manuals that contain safety information to more than 300,000 pilots and 4000 airlines. Every week Jeppesen mails between 5 and 30 million pages of chart revisions to 200,000 customers worldwide, and receives about 1500 new orders each week. In the late 1990s, its customer service deteriorated as its existing production and supporting systems failed to keep up with this level of activity. To meet customer service goals, Jeppesen turned to optimization-based decision support tools for production planning.

Jeppesen developed a large-scale linear program called Scheduler to minimize the cost of producing the weekly revisions. Model constraints included capacity constraints and numerous internal business rules. The model includes 250,000 variables and 40,000–50,000 constraints. Immediately after introducing the model, Jeppesen established a new record for the number of consecutive weeks with 100% on-time revisions. Scheduler decreased tardiness of revisions from approximately 9% to 3% and dramatically improved customer satisfaction. Even more importantly, Scheduler provided a model of the production system for Jeppesen to use in strategic economic analysis. Overall, the use of optimization techniques at Jeppesen resulted in cost reductions of nearly 10% and a 24% increase in profit.

*Based on E. Katok, W. Tarantino, and R. Tiedman, "Improving Performance and Flexibility at Jeppesen: The World's Leading Aviation-Information Company," Interfaces (January/February 2001): 7–29.

Let us consider the case of the Bollinger Electronics Company, which produces two different electronic components for a major airplane engine manufacturer. The airplane engine manufacturer notifies the Bollinger sales office each quarter of its monthly requirements for components for each of the next three months. The monthly requirements for the components may vary considerably depending on the type of engine the airplane engine manufacturer is producing. The order shown in Table 9.7 has just been received for the next three-month period.

After the order is processed, a demand statement is sent to the production control department. The production control department must then develop a three-month production plan for the components. In arriving at the desired schedule, the production manager will want to identify the following:

1. Total production cost
2. Inventory holding cost
3. Change-in-production-level costs

In the remainder of this section, we show how to formulate a linear programming model of the production and inventory process for Bollinger Electronics to minimize the total cost.

TABLE 9.7 THREE-MONTH DEMAND SCHEDULE FOR BOLLINGER ELECTRONICS COMPANY

Component	April	May	June
322A	1000	3000	5000
802B	1000	500	3000

To develop the model, we let x_{im} denote the production volume in units for product i in month m. Here $i = 1, 2,$ and $m = 1, 2, 3$; $i = 1$ refers to component 322A, $i = 2$ refers to component 802B, $m = 1$ refers to April, $m = 2$ refers to May, and $m = 3$ refers to June. The purpose of the double subscript is to provide a more descriptive notation. We could simply use x_6 to represent the number of units of product 2 produced in month 3, but x_{23} is more descriptive, identifying directly the product and month represented by the variable.

If component 322A costs \$20 per unit produced and component 802B costs \$10 per unit produced, the total production cost part of the objective function is

$$\text{Total production cost} = 20x_{11} + 20x_{12} + 20x_{13} + 10x_{21} + 10x_{22} + 10x_{23}$$

Because the production cost per unit is the same each month, we don't need to include the production costs in the objective function; that is, regardless of the production schedule selected, the total production cost will remain the same. In other words, production costs are not relevant costs for the production scheduling decision under consideration. In cases in which the production cost per unit is expected to change each month, the variable production costs per unit per month must be included in the objective function. The solution for the Bollinger Electronics problem will be the same regardless of whether these costs are included; therefore, we included them so that the value of the linear programming objective function will include all the costs associated with the problem.

To incorporate the relevant inventory holding costs into the model, we let s_{im} denote the inventory level for product i at the end of month m. Bollinger determined that on a monthly basis inventory holding costs are 1.5% of the cost of the product; that is, $(0.015)(\$20) = \$0.30$ per unit for component 322A and $(0.015)(\$10) = \$0.15$ per unit for component 802B. A common assumption made in using the linear programming approach to production scheduling is that monthly ending inventories are an acceptable approximation to the average inventory levels throughout the month. Making this assumption, we write the inventory holding cost portion of the objective function as

$$\text{Inventory holding cost} = 0.30s_{11} + 0.30s_{12} + 0.30s_{13} + 0.15s_{21} + 0.15s_{22} + 0.15s_{23}$$

To incorporate the costs of fluctuations in production levels from month to month, we need to define two additional variables:

$$I_m = \text{increase in the total production level necessary during month } m$$
$$D_m = \text{decrease in the total production level necessary during month } m$$

After estimating the effects of employee layoffs, turnovers, reassignment training costs, and other costs associated with fluctuating production levels, Bollinger estimates that the cost associated with increasing the production level for any month is \$0.50 per unit increase. A similar cost associated with decreasing the production level for any month is \$0.20 per unit. Thus, we write the third portion of the objective function as

$$\text{Change-in-production-level costs} = 0.50I_1 + 0.50I_2 + 0.50I_3$$
$$+ 0.20D_1 + 0.20D_2 + 0.20D_3$$

Note that the cost associated with changes in production level is a function of the change in the total number of units produced in month m compared to the total number of units produced in month $m - 1$. In other production scheduling applications, fluctuations in production level might be measured in terms of machine hours or labor-hours required rather than in terms of the total number of units produced.

Combining all three costs, the complete objective function becomes

$$\begin{aligned}
\text{Min} \quad & 20x_{11} + 20x_{12} + 20x_{13} + 10x_{21} + 10x_{22} + 10x_{23} + 0.30s_{11} \\
& + 0.30s_{12} + 0.30s_{13} + 0.15s_{21} + 0.15s_{22} + 0.15s_{23} + 0.50I_1 \\
& + 0.50I_2 + 0.50I_3 + 0.20D_1 + 0.20D_2 + 0.20D_3
\end{aligned}$$

We now consider the constraints. First, we must guarantee that the schedule meets customer demand. Because the units shipped can come from the current month's production or from inventory carried over from previous months, the demand requirement takes the form

$$\begin{pmatrix} \text{Ending} \\ \text{inventory} \\ \text{from previous} \\ \text{month} \end{pmatrix} + \begin{pmatrix} \text{Current} \\ \text{production} \end{pmatrix} - \begin{pmatrix} \text{Ending} \\ \text{inventory} \\ \text{for this} \\ \text{month} \end{pmatrix} = \begin{pmatrix} \text{This month's} \\ \text{demand} \end{pmatrix}$$

Suppose that the inventories at the beginning of the three-month scheduling period were 500 units for component 322A and 200 units for component 802B. The demand for both products in the first month (April) was 1000 units, so the constraints for meeting demand in the first month become

$$500 + x_{11} - s_{11} = 1000$$
$$200 + x_{21} - s_{21} = 1000$$

Moving the constants to the right-hand side, we have

$$x_{11} - s_{11} = 500$$
$$x_{21} - s_{21} = 800$$

Similarly, we need demand constraints for both products in the second and third months. We write them as follows:

Month 2

$$s_{11} + x_{12} - s_{12} = 3000$$
$$s_{21} + x_{22} - s_{22} = 500$$

Month 3

$$s_{12} + x_{13} - s_{13} = 5000$$
$$s_{22} + x_{23} - s_{23} = 3000$$

If the company specifies a minimum inventory level at the end of the three-month period of at least 400 units of component 322A and at least 200 units of component 802B, we can add the constraints

$$s_{13} \geq 400$$
$$s_{23} \geq 200$$

Suppose that we have the additional information on machine, labor, and storage capacity shown in Table 9.8. Machine, labor, and storage space requirements are given in Table 9.9. To reflect these limitations, the following constraints are necessary:

Machine Capacity

$$0.10x_{11} + 0.08x_{21} \leq 400 \quad \text{Month 1}$$
$$0.10x_{12} + 0.08x_{22} \leq 500 \quad \text{Month 2}$$
$$0.10x_{13} + 0.08x_{23} \leq 600 \quad \text{Month 3}$$

TABLE 9.8   MACHINE, LABOR, AND STORAGE CAPACITIES
FOR BOLLINGER ELECTRONICS

Month	Machine Capacity (hours)	Labor Capacity (hours)	Storage Capacity (square feet)
April	400	300	10,000
May	500	300	10,000
June	600	300	10,000

TABLE 9.9   MACHINE, LABOR, AND STORAGE REQUIREMENTS FOR COMPONENTS
322A AND 802B

Component	Machine (hours/unit)	Labor (hours/unit)	Storage (square feet/unit)
322A	0.10	0.05	2
802B	0.08	0.07	3

Labor Capacity

$$0.05x_{11} + 0.07x_{21} \leq 300 \quad \text{Month 1}$$
$$0.05x_{12} + 0.07x_{22} \leq 300 \quad \text{Month 2}$$
$$0.05x_{13} + 0.07x_{23} \leq 300 \quad \text{Month 3}$$

Storage Capacity

$$2s_{11} + 3s_{21} \leq 10{,}000 \quad \text{Month 1}$$
$$2s_{12} + 3s_{22} \leq 10{,}000 \quad \text{Month 2}$$
$$2s_{13} + 3s_{23} \leq 10{,}000 \quad \text{Month 3}$$

One final set of constraints must be added to guarantee that I_m and D_m will reflect the increase or decrease in the total production level for month m. Suppose that the production levels for March, the month before the start of the current production scheduling period, had been 1500 units of component 322A and 1000 units of component 802B for a total production level of $1500 + 1000 = 2500$ units. We can find the amount of the change in production for April from the relationship

$$\text{April production} - \text{March production} = \text{Change}$$

Using the April production variables, x_{11} and x_{21}, and the March production of 2500 units, we have

$$(x_{11} + x_{21}) - 2500 = \text{Change}$$

Note that the change can be positive or negative. A positive change reflects an increase in the total production level, and a negative change reflects a decrease in the total production level. We can use the increase in production for April, I_1, and the decrease in production for April, D_1, to specify the constraint for the change in total production for the month of April:

$$(x_{11} + x_{21}) - 2500 = I_1 - D_1$$

Of course, we cannot have an increase in production and a decrease in production during the same one-month period; thus, either, I_1 or D_1 will be zero. If April requires 3000 units of production, $I_1 = 500$ and $D_1 = 0$. If April requires 2200 units of production, $I_1 = 0$ and $D_1 = 300$. This approach of denoting the change in production level as the difference between two nonnegative variables, I_1 and D_1, permits both positive and negative changes in the total production level. If a single variable (say, c_m) had been used to represent the change in production level, only positive changes would be possible because of the nonnegativity requirement.

Using the same approach in May and June (always subtracting the previous month's total production from the current month's total production), we obtain the constraints for the second and third months of the production scheduling period:

$$(x_{12} + x_{22}) - (x_{11} + x_{21}) = I_2 - D_2$$
$$(x_{13} + x_{23}) - (x_{12} + x_{22}) = I_3 - D_3$$

Placing the variables on the left-hand side and the constants on the right-hand side yields the complete set of what are commonly referred to as production-smoothing constraints:

$$
\begin{aligned}
x_{11} + x_{21} \qquad\qquad\qquad\qquad\qquad - I_1 + D_1 &= 2500 \\
-x_{11} - x_{21} + x_{12} + x_{22} \qquad\qquad\; - I_2 + D_2 &= 0 \\
-x_{12} - x_{22} + x_{13} + x_{23} - I_3 + D_3 &= 0
\end{aligned}
$$

The initially rather small, two-product, three-month scheduling problem has now developed into an 18-variable, 20-constraint linear programming problem. Note that in this problem we were concerned only with one type of machine process, one type of labor, and one type of storage area. Actual production scheduling problems usually involve several machine types, several labor grades, and/or several storage areas, requiring large-scale linear programs. For instance, a problem involving 100 products over a 12-month period could have more than 1000 variables and constraints.

Problem 19 involves a production scheduling application with labor-smoothing constraints.

Figure 9.6 shows the optimal solution to the Bollinger Electronics production scheduling problem. Table 9.10 contains a portion of the managerial report based on the optimal solution.

Consider the monthly variation in the production and inventory schedule shown in Table 9.10. Recall that the inventory cost for component 802B is one-half the inventory cost for component 322A. Therefore, as might be expected, component 802B is produced heavily in the first month (April) and then held in inventory for the demand that will occur in future months. Component 322A tends to be produced when needed, and only small amounts are carried in inventory.

Linear programming models for production scheduling are often very large. Thousands of decision variables and constraints are necessary when the problem involves numerous products, machines, and time periods. Data collection for large-scale models can be more time-consuming than either the formulation of the model or the development of the computer solution.

The costs of increasing and decreasing the total production volume tend to smooth the monthly variations. In fact, the minimum-cost schedule calls for a 500-unit increase in total production in April and a 2200-unit increase in total production in May. The May production level of 5200 units is then maintained during June.

The machine usage section of the report shows ample machine capacity in all three months. However, labor capacity is at full utilization (slack = 0 for constraint 13 in Figure 9.6) in the month of May. The dual price shows that an additional hour of labor capacity in May will improve the value of the optimal solution (lower cost) by approximately $1.11.

FIGURE 9.6   THE MANAGEMENT SCIENTIST SOLUTION FOR THE BOLLINGER
ELECTRONICS PROBLEM

WEB file

Bollinger

```
Objective Function Value =            225295.000

       Variable              Value             Reduced Costs
     --------------      ---------------      -----------------
         X11               500.000                0.000
         X12              3200.000                0.000
         X13              5200.000                0.000
         X21              2500.000                0.000
         X22              2000.000                0.000
         X23                 0.000                0.128
         S11                 0.000                0.172
         S12               200.000                0.000
         S13               400.000                0.000
         S21              1700.000                0.000
         S22              3200.000                0.000
         S23               200.000                0.000
         I1                500.000                0.000
         I2               2200.000                0.000
         I3                  0.000                0.072
         D1                  0.000                0.700
         D2                  0.000                0.700
         D3                  0.000                0.628

       Constraint         Slack/Surplus          Dual Prices
     --------------      ---------------      -----------------
          1                   0.000               -20.000
          2                   0.000               -10.000
          3                   0.000               -20.128
          4                   0.000               -10.150
          5                   0.000               -20.428
          6                   0.000               -10.300
          7                   0.000               -20.728
          8                   0.000               -10.450
          9                 150.000                 0.000
         10                  20.000                 0.000
         11                  80.000                 0.000
         12                 100.000                 0.000
         13                   0.000                 1.111
         14                  40.000                 0.000
         15                4900.000                 0.000
         16                   0.000                 0.000
         17                8600.000                 0.000
         18                   0.000                 0.500
         19                   0.000                 0.500
         20                   0.000                 0.428
```

TABLE 9.10 MINIMUM COST PRODUCTION SCHEDULE INFORMATION
FOR THE BOLLINGER ELECTRONICS PROBLEM

Activity	April	May	June
Production			
Component 322A	500	3200	5200
Component 802B	2500	2000	0
Totals	3000	5200	5200
Ending inventory			
Component 322A	0	200	400
Component 802B	1700	3200	200
Machine usage			
Scheduled hours	250	480	520
Slack capacity hours	150	20	80
Labor usage			
Scheduled hours	200	300	260
Slack capacity hours	100	0	40
Storage usage			
Scheduled storage	5100	10,000	1400
Slack capacity	4900	0	8600
Total production, inventory, and production-smoothing cost = $225,295			

A linear programming model of a two-product, three-month production system can provide valuable information in terms of identifying a minimum-cost production schedule. In
larger production systems, where the number of variables and constraints is too large to
track manually, linear programming models can provide a significant advantage in developing cost-saving production schedules. The Q.M. in Action, Optimizing Production,
Inventory, and Distribution at the Kellogg Company, illustrates the use of a large-scale
multiperiod linear program for production planning and distribution.

Workforce Assignment

Workforce assignment problems frequently occur when production managers must make
decisions involving staffing requirements for a given planning period. Workforce assignments often have some flexibility, and at least some personnel can be assigned to more than
one department or work center. Such is the case when employees have been cross-trained
on two or more jobs or, for instance, when sales personnel can be transferred between stores.
In the following application, we show how linear programming can be used to determine
not only an optimal product mix, but also an optimal workforce assignment.

McCormick Manufacturing Company produces two products with contributions to
profit per unit of $10 and $9, respectively. The labor requirements per unit produced and
the total hours of labor available from personnel assigned to each of four departments are
shown in Table 9.11. Assuming that the number of hours available in each department is
fixed, we can formulate McCormick's problem as a standard product-mix linear program
with the following decision variables:

$$P_1 = \text{units of product 1}$$
$$P_2 = \text{units of product 2}$$

Q.M. *in* ACTION

OPTIMIZING PRODUCTION, INVENTORY, AND DISTRIBUTION AT THE KELLOGG COMPANY*

The Kellogg Company is the largest cereal producer in the world and a leading producer of convenience foods, such as Kellogg's Pop-Tarts and Nutri-Grain cereal bars. Kellogg produces more than 40 different cereals at plants in 19 countries, on six continents. The company markets its products in more than 160 countries and employs more than 15,600 people in its worldwide organization. In the cereal business alone, Kellogg coordinates the production of about 80 products using a total of approximately 90 production lines and 180 packaging lines.

Kellogg has a long history of using linear programming for production planning and distribution. The Kellogg

Planning System (KPS) is a large-scale, multiperiod linear program. The operational version of KPS makes production, packaging, inventory, and distribution decisions on a weekly basis. The primary objective of the system is to minimize the total cost of meeting estimated demand; constraints involve processing line capacities, packaging line capacities, and satisfying safety stock requirements.

A tactical version of KPS helps to establish plant budgets and make capacity-expansion and consolidation decisions on a monthly basis. The tactical version was recently used to guide a consolidation of production capacity that resulted in projected savings of $35 to $40 million per year. Because of the success Kellogg has had using KPS in their North American operations, the company is now introducing KPS into Latin America, and is studying the development of a global KPS model.

*Based on G. Brown, J. Keegan, B. Vigus, and K. Wood, "The Kellogg Company Optimizes Production, Inventory, and Distribution," Interfaces (November/December 2001): 1–15.

The linear program is

$$\text{Max} \quad 10P_1 + 9P_2$$
$$\text{s.t.}$$
$$0.65P_1 + 0.95P_2 \leq 6500$$
$$0.45P_1 + 0.85P_2 \leq 6000$$
$$1.00P_1 + 0.70P_2 \leq 7000$$
$$0.15P_1 + 0.30P_2 \leq 1400$$
$$P_1, P_2 \geq 0$$

The optimal solution to the linear programming model is shown in Figure 9.7. After rounding, it calls for 5744 units of product 1, 1795 units of product 2, and a total profit of $73,590. With this optimal solution, departments 3 and 4 are operating at capacity, and

TABLE 9.11 DEPARTMENTAL LABOR-HOURS PER UNIT AND TOTAL HOURS AVAILABLE FOR THE McCORMICK MANUFACTURING COMPANY

Department	Labor-Hours per Unit		Total Hours Available
	Product 1	**Product 2**	
1	0.65	0.95	6500
2	0.45	0.85	6000
3	1.00	0.70	7000
4	0.15	0.30	1400

FIGURE 9.7 THE MANAGEMENT SCIENTIST SOLUTION FOR THE McCORMICK MANUFACTURING COMPANY PROBLEM WITH NO WORKFORCE TRANSFERS PERMITTED

WEB file

McCormick

```
Objective Function Value =          73589.744

        Variable              Value           Reduced Costs
     --------------      ---------------      ----------------
           P1               5743.590                 0.000
           P2               1794.872                 0.000

      Constraint          Slack/Surplus          Dual Prices
     --------------      ---------------      ----------------
           1                1061.538                 0.000
           2                1889.744                 0.000
           3                   0.000                 8.462
           4                   0.000                10.256
```

departments 1 and 2 have a slack of approximately 1062 and 1890 hours, respectively. We would anticipate that the product mix would change and that the total profit would increase if the workforce assignment could be revised so that the slack, or unused hours, in departments 1 and 2 could be transferred to the departments currently working at capacity. However, the production manager may be uncertain as to how the workforce should be reallocated among the four departments. Let us expand the linear programming model to include decision variables that will help determine the optimal workforce assignment in addition to the profit-maximizing product mix.

Suppose that McCormick has a cross-training program that enables some employees to be transferred between departments. By taking advantage of the cross-training skills, a limited number of employees and labor-hours may be transferred from one department to another. For example, suppose that the cross-training permits transfers as shown in Table 9.12. Row 1 of this table shows that some employees assigned to department 1 have cross-training skills that permit them to be transferred to department 2 or 3. The right-hand column shows that, for the current production planning period, a maximum of 400 hours can be transferred from department 1. Similar cross-training transfer capabilities and capacities are shown for departments 2, 3, and 4.

TABLE 9.12 CROSS-TRAINING ABILITY AND CAPACITY INFORMATION

From Department	Cross-Training Transfers Permitted to Department				Maximum Hours Transferable
	1	**2**	**3**	**4**	
1	—	yes	yes	—	400
2	—	—	yes	yes	800
3	—	—	—	yes	100
4	yes	yes	—	—	200

When workforce assignments are flexible, we do not automatically know how many hours of labor should be assigned to or be transferred from each department. We need to add decision variables to the linear programming model to account for such changes.

b_i = the labor-hours allocated to department i for i = 1, 2, 3, and 4

t_{ij} = the labor-hours transferred from department i to department j

The right-hand sides are now treated as decision variables.

With the addition of decision variables b_1, b_2, b_3, and b_4, we write the capacity restrictions for the four departments as follows:

$$0.65P_1 + 0.95P_2 \leq b_1$$
$$0.45P_1 + 0.85P_2 \leq b_2$$
$$1.00P_1 + 0.70P_2 \leq b_3$$
$$0.15P_1 + 0.30P_2 \leq b_4$$

Because b_1, b_2, b_3, and b_4 are now decision variables, we follow the standard practice of placing these variables on the left side of the inequalities, and the first four constraints of the linear programming model become

$$0.65P_1 + 0.95P_2 - b_1 \qquad\qquad\qquad \leq 0$$
$$0.45P_1 + 0.85P_2 \qquad - b_2 \qquad\qquad \leq 0$$
$$1.00P_1 + 0.70P_2 \qquad\qquad - b_3 \qquad \leq 0$$
$$0.15P_1 + 0.30P_2 \qquad\qquad\qquad - b_4 \leq 0$$

The labor-hours ultimately allocated to each department must be determined by a series of labor balance equations, or constraints, that include the number of hours initially assigned to each department plus the number of hours transferred into the department minus the number of hours transferred out of the department. Using department 1 as an example, we determine the workforce allocation as follows:

$$b_1 = \begin{pmatrix} \text{Hours} \\ \text{initially in} \\ \text{department 1} \end{pmatrix} + \begin{pmatrix} \text{Hours} \\ \text{transferred into} \\ \text{department 1} \end{pmatrix} - \begin{pmatrix} \text{Hours} \\ \text{transferred out of} \\ \text{department 1} \end{pmatrix}$$

Table 9.11 shows 6500 hours initially assigned to department 1. We use the transfer decision variables t_{i1} to denote transfers into department 1 and t_{1j} to denote transfers from department 1. Table 9.12 shows that the cross-training capabilities involving department 1 are restricted to transfers from department 4 (variable t_{41}) and transfers to either department 2 or department 3 (variables t_{12} and t_{13}). Thus, we can express the total workforce allocation for department 1 as

$$b_1 = 6500 + t_{41} - t_{12} - t_{13}$$

Moving the decision variables for the workforce transfers to the left-hand side, we have the labor balance equation or constraint

$$b_1 - t_{41} + t_{12} + t_{13} = 6500$$

This form of constraint will be needed for each of the four departments. Thus, the following labor balance constraints for departments 2, 3, and 4 would be added to the model:

$$b_2 - t_{12} - t_{42} + t_{23} + t_{24} = 6000$$
$$b_3 - t_{13} - t_{23} + t_{34} \qquad\quad = 7000$$
$$b_4 - t_{24} - t_{34} + t_{41} + t_{42} = 1400$$

Finally, Table 9.12 shows the number of hours that may be transferred from each department is limited, indicating that a transfer capacity constraint must be added for each of the four departments. The additional constraints are

$$t_{12} + t_{13} \leq 400$$
$$t_{23} + t_{24} \leq 800$$
$$t_{34} \leq 100$$
$$t_{41} + t_{42} \leq 200$$

Variations in the workforce assignment model could be used in situations such as allocating raw material resources to products, allocating machine time to products, and allocating salesforce time to stores or sales territories.

The complete linear programming model has two product decision variables (P_1 and P_2), four department workforce assignment variables (b_1, b_2, b_3, and b_4), seven transfer variables (t_{12}, t_{13}, t_{23}, t_{24}, t_{34}, t_{41}, and t_{42}), and 12 constraints. Figure 9.8 shows the optimal solution to this linear program.

FIGURE 9.8 THE MANAGEMENT SCIENTIST SOLUTION FOR THE McCORMICK MANUFACTURING COMPANY PROBLEM

WEB file

McCormickMod

```
Objective Function Value =          84011.299

        Variable              Value            Reduced Costs
      --------------       --------------      --------------
           P1                6824.859              0.000
           P2                1751.412              0.000
           B1                6100.000              0.000
           B2                5200.000              0.000
           B3                8050.847              0.000
           B4                1549.153              0.000
          T12                   0.000              8.249
          T13                 400.000              0.000
          T23                 650.847              0.000
          T24                 149.153              0.000
          T34                   0.000              0.000
          T41                   0.000              7.458
          T42                   0.000              8.249


        Constraint         Slack/Surplus          Dual Prices
      --------------       --------------      --------------
            1                   0.000              0.791
            2                 640.113              0.000
            3                   0.000              8.249
            4                   0.000              8.249
            5                   0.000              0.791
            6                   0.000              0.000
            7                   0.000              8.249
            8                   0.000              8.249
            9                   0.000              7.458
           10                   0.000              8.249
           11                 100.000              0.000
           12                 200.000              0.000
```

McCormick's profit can be increased by $84,011 − $73,590 = $10,421 by taking advantage of cross-training and workforce transfers. The optimal product mix of 6825 units of product 1 and 1751 units of product 2 can be achieved if $t_{13} = 400$ hours are transferred from department 1 to department 3; $t_{23} = 651$ hours are transferred from department 2 to department 3; and $t_{24} = 149$ hours are transferred from department 2 to department 4. The resulting workforce assignments for departments 1–4 would provide 6100, 5200, 8051, and 1549 hours, respectively.

If a manager has the flexibility to assign personnel to different departments, reduced workforce idle time, improved workforce utilization, and improved profit should result. The linear programming model in this section automatically assigns employees and labor-hours to the departments in the most profitable manner.

Blending Problems

Blending problems arise whenever a manager must decide how to blend two or more resources to produce one or more products. In these situations, the resources contain one or more essential ingredients that must be blended into final products that will contain specific percentages of each. In most of these applications, then, management must decide how much of each resource to purchase to satisfy product specifications and product demands at minimum cost.

Blending problems occur frequently in the petroleum industry (e.g., blending crude oil to produce different octane gasolines), chemical industry (e.g., blending chemicals to produce fertilizers and weed killers), and food industry (e.g., blending ingredients to produce soft drinks and soups). In this section we illustrate how to apply linear programming to a blending problem in the petroleum industry.

The Grand Strand Oil Company produces regular and premium gasoline for independent service stations in the southeastern United States. The Grand Strand refinery manufactures the gasoline products by blending three petroleum components. The gasolines are sold at different prices, and the petroleum components have different costs. The firm wants to determine how to mix or blend the three components into the two gasoline products and maximize profits.

Data available show that regular gasoline can be sold for $2.90 per gallon and premium gasoline for $3.00 per gallon. For the current production planning period, Grand Strand can obtain the three petroleum components at the cost per gallon and in the quantities shown in Table 9.13.

Product specifications for the regular and premium gasolines restrict the amounts of each component that can be used in each gasoline product. Table 9.14 lists the product specifications. Current commitments to distributors require Grand Strand to produce at least 10,000 gallons of regular gasoline.

TABLE 9.13   PETROLEUM COST AND SUPPLY FOR THE GRAND STRAND
                BLENDING PROBLEM

Petroleum Component	Cost/Gallon	Maximum Available
1	$2.50	5,000 gallons
2	$2.60	10,000 gallons
3	$2.84	10,000 gallons

TABLE 9.14   PRODUCT SPECIFICATIONS FOR THE GRAND STRAND
BLENDING PROBLEM

Product	Specifications
Regular gasoline	At most 30% component 1
	At least 40% component 2
	At most 20% component 3
Premium gasoline	At least 25% component 1
	At most 45% component 2
	At least 30% component 3

The Grand Strand blending problem is to determine how many gallons of each component should be used in the regular gasoline blend and how many should be used in the premium gasoline blend. The optimal blending solution should maximize the firm's profit, subject to the constraints on the available petroleum supplies shown in Table 9.13, the product specifications shown in Table 9.14, and the required 10,000 gallons of regular gasoline.

We define the decision variables as

$$x_{ij} = \text{gallons of component } i \text{ used in gasoline } j,$$
$$\text{where } i = 1, 2, \text{ or } 3 \text{ for components } 1, 2, \text{ or } 3,$$
$$\text{and } j = r \text{ if regular or } j = p \text{ if premium}$$

The six decision variables are

$$x_{1r} = \text{gallons of component 1 in regular gasoline}$$
$$x_{2r} = \text{gallons of component 2 in regular gasoline}$$
$$x_{3r} = \text{gallons of component 3 in regular gasoline}$$
$$x_{1p} = \text{gallons of component 1 in premium gasoline}$$
$$x_{2p} = \text{gallons of component 2 in premium gasoline}$$
$$x_{3p} = \text{gallons of component 3 in premium gasoline}$$

The total number of gallons of each type of gasoline produced is the sum of the number of gallons produced using each of the three petroleum components.

Total Gallons Produced

$$\text{Regular gasoline} = x_{1r} + x_{2r} + x_{3r}$$
$$\text{Premium gasoline} = x_{1p} + x_{2p} + x_{3p}$$

The total gallons of each petroleum component are computed in a similar fashion.

Total Petroleum Component Use

$$\text{Component 1} = x_{1r} + x_{1p}$$
$$\text{Component 2} = x_{2r} + x_{2p}$$
$$\text{Component 3} = x_{3r} + x_{3p}$$

We develop the objective function of maximizing the profit contribution by identifying the difference between the total revenue from both gasolines and the total cost of the three petroleum components. By multiplying the $2.90 per gallon price by the total gallons of regular gasoline, the $3.00 per gallon price by the total gallons of premium gasoline, and the component cost per gallon figures in Table 9.13 by the total gallons of each component used, we obtain the objective function:

$$\text{Max} \quad 2.90(x_{1r} + x_{2r} + x_{3r}) + 3.00(x_{1p} + x_{2p} + x_{3p})$$
$$- 2.50(x_{1r} + x_{1p}) - 2.60(x_{2r} + x_{2p}) - 2.84(x_{3r} + x_{3p})$$

When we combine terms, the objective function becomes

$$\text{Max} \quad 0.40x_{1r} + 0.30x_{2r} + 0.06x_{3r} + 0.50x_{1p} + 0.40x_{2p} + 0.16x_{3p}$$

The limitations on the availability of the three petroleum components are

$$x_{1r} + x_{1p} \leq 5,000 \quad \text{Component 1}$$
$$x_{2r} + x_{2p} \leq 10,000 \quad \text{Component 2}$$
$$x_{3r} + x_{3p} \leq 10,000 \quad \text{Component 3}$$

Six constraints are now required to meet the product specifications stated in Table 9.14. The first specification states that component 1 can account for no more than 30% of the total gallons of regular gasoline produced. That is,

$$x_{1r} \leq 0.30(x_{1r} + x_{2r} + x_{3r})$$

Rewriting this constraint with the variables on the left-hand side and a constant on the right-hand side yields

$$0.70x_{1r} - 0.30x_{2r} - 0.30x_{3r} \leq 0$$

The second product specification listed in Table 9.14 becomes

$$x_{2r} \geq 0.40(x_{1r} + x_{2r} + x_{3r})$$

and thus

$$-0.40x_{1r} + 0.60x_{2r} - 0.40x_{3r} \geq 0$$

Similarly, we write the four remaining blending specifications listed in Table 9.14 as

$$-0.20x_{1r} - 0.20x_{2r} + 0.80x_{3r} \leq 0$$
$$+0.75x_{1p} - 0.25x_{2p} - 0.25x_{3p} \geq 0$$
$$-0.45x_{1p} + 0.55x_{2p} - 0.45x_{3p} \leq 0$$
$$-0.30x_{1p} - 0.30x_{2p} + 0.70x_{3p} \geq 0$$

The constraint for at least 10,000 gallons of regular gasoline is

$$x_{1r} + x_{2r} + x_{3r} \geq 10,000$$

The complete linear programming model with six decision variables and 10 constraints is

$$\text{Max} \quad 0.40x_{1r} + 0.30x_{2r} + 0.06x_{3r} + 0.50x_{1p} + 0.40x_{2p} + 0.16x_{3p}$$

s.t.

$$
\begin{array}{rclclcr}
x_{1r} & & & + & x_{1p} & & \leq & 5{,}000 \\
& x_{2r} & & + & x_{2p} & & \leq & 10{,}000 \\
& & x_{3r} & + & x_{3p} & \leq & 10{,}000 \\
0.70x_{1r} - 0.30x_{2r} - 0.30x_{3r} & & & & & & \leq & 0 \\
-0.40x_{1r} + 0.60x_{2r} - 0.40x_{3r} & & & & & & \geq & 0 \\
-0.20x_{1r} - 0.20x_{2r} + 0.80x_{3r} & & & & & & \leq & 0 \\
& & 0.75x_{1p} - 0.25x_{2p} - 0.25x_{3p} & \geq & 0 \\
& & -0.45x_{1p} + 0.55x_{2p} - 0.45x_{3p} & \leq & 0 \\
& & -0.30x_{1p} - 0.30x_{2p} + 0.70x_{3p} & \geq & 0 \\
x_{1r} + x_{2r} + x_{3r} & & & & & & \geq & 10{,}000 \\
\end{array}
$$

$$x_{1r}, x_{2r}, x_{3r}, x_{1p}, x_{2p}, x_{3p} \geq 0$$

The optimal solution to the Grand Strand blending problem is shown in Figure 9.9. The optimal solution, which provides a profit of $7100, is summarized in Table 9.15. The optimal blending strategy shows that 10,000 gallons of regular gasoline should be produced.

FIGURE 9.9 THE MANAGEMENT SCIENTIST SOLUTION FOR THE GRAND STRAND BLENDING PROBLEM

WEB file

Grand

```
Objective Function Value =            7100.000

        Variable                 Value              Reduced Costs
        --------                 -----              -------------
          X1R                  1250.000                 0.000
          X2R                  6750.000                 0.000
          X3R                  2000.000                 0.000
          X1P                  3750.000                 0.000
          X2P                  3250.000                 0.000
          X3P                  8000.000                 0.000


      Constraint             Slack/Surplus             Dual Prices
      ----------             -------------             -----------
           1                     0.000                    0.500
           2                     0.000                    0.400
           3                     0.000                    0.160
           4                  1750.000                    0.000
           5                  2750.000                    0.000
           6                     0.000                    0.000
           7                     0.000                    0.000
           8                  3500.000                    0.000
           9                  3500.000                    0.000
          10                     0.000                   -0.100
```

TABLE 9.15   GRAND STRAND GASOLINE BLENDING SOLUTION

| Gasoline | Gallons of Component (percentage) | | | Total |
	Component 1	Component 2	Component 3	
Regular	1250 (12.5%)	6750 (67.5%)	2000 (20%)	10,000
Premium	3750 (25%)	3250 (21⅔%)	8000 (53⅓%)	15,000

The regular gasoline will be manufactured as a blend of 1250 gallons of component 1, 6750 gallons of component 2, and 2000 gallons of component 3. The 15,000 gallons of premium gasoline will be manufactured as a blend of 3750 gallons of component 1, 3250 gallons of component 2, and 8000 gallons of component 3.

Try Problem 15 as another example of a blending model.

The interpretation of the slack and surplus variables associated with the product specification constraints (constraints 4–9) in Figure 9.9 needs some clarification. If the constraint is a ≤ constraint, the value of the slack variable can be interpreted as the gallons of component use below the maximum amount of the component use specified by the constraint. For example, the slack of 1750.000 for constraint 4 shows that component 1 use is 1750 gallons below the maximum amount of component 1 that could have been used in the production of 10,000 gallons of regular gasoline. If the product specification constraint is a ≥ constraint, a surplus variable shows the gallons of component use above the minimum amount of component use specified by the blending constraint. For example, the surplus of 2750.000 for constraint 5 shows that component 2 use is 2750 gallons above the minimum amount of component 2 that must be used in the production of 10,000 gallons of regular gasoline.

NOTES AND COMMENTS

A convenient way to define the decision variables in a blending problem is to use a matrix in which the rows correspond to the raw materials and the columns correspond to the final products. For example, in the Grand Strand blending problem, we define the decision variables as follows:

This approach has two advantages: (1) It provides a systematic way to define the decision variables for any blending problem; and (2) it provides a visual image of the decision variables in terms of how they are related to the raw materials, products, and each other.

| | | Final Products | |
		Regular Gasoline	Premium Gasoline
Raw Materials	Component 1	x_{1r}	x_{1p}
	Component 2	x_{2r}	x_{2p}
	Component 3	x_{3r}	x_{3p}

Summary

In this chapter we presented a broad range of applications that demonstrate how to use linear programming to assist in the decision-making process. We formulated and solved problems from marketing, finance, and operations management, and interpreted the computer output.

Many of the illustrations presented in this chapter are scaled-down versions of actual situations in which linear programming has been applied. In real-world applications, the problem may not be so concisely stated, the data for the problem may not be as readily available, and the problem most likely will involve numerous decision variables and/or constraints. However, a thorough study of the applications in this chapter is a good place to begin in applying linear programming to real problems.

Problems

Note: The following problems have been designed to give you an understanding and appreciation of the broad range of problems that can be formulated as linear programs. You should be able to formulate a linear programming model for each of the problems. However, you will need access to a linear programming computer package to develop the solutions and make the requested interpretations.

1. The Westchester Chamber of Commerce periodically sponsors public service seminars and programs. Currently, promotional plans are under way for this year's program. Advertising alternatives include television, radio, and newspaper. Audience estimates, costs, and maximum media usage limitations are as shown:

Constraint	Television	Radio	Newspaper
Audience per advertisement	100,000	18,000	40,000
Cost per advertisement	$2000	$300	$600
Maximum media usage	10	20	10

To ensure a balanced use of advertising media, radio advertisements must not exceed 50% of the total number of advertisements authorized. In addition, television should account for at least 10% of the total number of advertisements authorized.

   a. If the promotional budget is limited to $18,200, how many commercial messages should be run on each medium to maximize total audience contact? What is the allocation of the budget among the three media, and what is the total audience reached?

   b. By how much would audience contact increase if an extra $100 were allocated to the promotional budget?

2. The management of Hartman Company is trying to determine the amount of each of two products to produce over the coming planning period. The following information concerns labor availability, labor utilization, and product profitability:

Department	Product (hours/unit)		Labor-Hours Available
	1	**2**	
A	1.00	0.35	100
B	0.30	0.20	36
C	0.20	0.50	50
Profit contribution/unit	$30.00	$15.00	

   a. Develop a linear programming model of the Hartman Company problem. Solve the model to determine the optimal production quantities of products 1 and 2.

b.   In computing the profit contribution per unit, management doesn't deduct labor costs because they are considered fixed for the upcoming planning period. However, suppose that overtime can be scheduled in some of the departments. Which departments would you recommend scheduling for overtime? How much would you be willing to pay per hour of overtime in each department?

c.   Suppose that 10, 6, and 8 hours of overtime may be scheduled in departments A, B, and C, respectively. The cost per hour of overtime is $18 in department A, $22.50 in department B, and $12 in department C. Formulate a linear programming model that can be used to determine the optimal production quantities if overtime is made available. What are the optimal production quantities, and what is the revised total contribution to profit? How much overtime do you recommend using in each department? What is the increase in the total contribution to profit if overtime is used?

3.   The employee credit union at State University is planning the allocation of funds for the coming year. The credit union makes four types of loans to its members. In addition, the credit union invests in risk-free securities to stabilize income. The various revenue-producing investments together with annual rates of return are as follows:

Type of Loan/Investment	Annual Rate of Return (%)
Automobile loans	8
Furniture loans	10
Other secured loans	11
Signature loans	12
Risk-free securities	9

The credit union will have $2 million available for investment during the coming year. State laws and credit union policies impose the following restrictions on the composition of the loans and investments:

•   Risk-free securities may not exceed 30% of the total funds available for investment.
•   Signature loans may not exceed 10% of the funds invested in all loans (automobile, furniture, other secured, and signature loans).
•   Furniture loans plus other secured loans may not exceed the automobile loans.
•   Other secured loans plus signature loans may not exceed the funds invested in risk-free securities.

How should the $2 million be allocated to each of the loan/investment alternatives to maximize total annual return? What is the projected total annual return?

4.   Hilltop Coffee manufactures a coffee product by blending three types of coffee beans. The cost per pound and the available pounds of each bean are as follows:

Bean	Cost per Pound	Available Pounds
1	$0.50	500
2	$0.70	600
3	$0.45	400

Consumer tests with coffee products were used to provide ratings on a scale of 0–100, with higher ratings indicating higher quality. Product quality standards for the blended coffee require a consumer rating for aroma to be at least 75 and a consumer rating for taste to be at least 80. The individual ratings of the aroma and taste for coffee made from 100% of each bean are as follows:

Bean	Aroma Rating	Taste Rating
1	75	86
2	85	88
3	60	75

Assume that the aroma and taste attributes of the coffee blend will be a weighted average of the attributes of the beans used in the blend.
   a. What is the minimum-cost blend that will meet the quality standards and provide 1000 pounds of the blended coffee product?
   b. What is the cost per pound for the coffee blend?
   c. Determine the aroma and taste ratings for the coffee blend.
   d. If additional coffee were to be produced, what would be the expected cost per pound?

5. Ajax Fuels, Inc., is developing a new additive for airplane fuels. The additive is a mixture of three ingredients: A, B, and C. For proper performance, the total amount of additive (amount of A + amount of B + amount of C) must be at least 10 ounces per gallon of fuel. However, because of safety reasons, the amount of additive must not exceed 15 ounces per gallon of fuel. The mix or blend of the three ingredients is critical. At least 1 ounce of ingredient A must be used for every ounce of ingredient B. The amount of ingredient C must be at least one-half the amount of ingredient A. If the costs per ounce for ingredients A, B, and C are $0.10, $0.03, and $0.09, respectively, find the minimum-cost mixture of A, B, and C for each gallon of airplane fuel.

6. G. Kunz and Sons, Inc., manufactures two products used in the heavy equipment industry. Both products require manufacturing operations in two departments. The following are the production time (in hours) and profit contribution figures for the two products:

		Labor-Hours	
Product	Profit per Unit	Dept. A	Dept. B
1	$25	6	12
2	$20	8	10

For the coming production period, Kunz has available a total of 900 hours of labor that can be allocated to either of the two departments. Find the production plan and labor allocation (hours assigned in each department) that will maximize the total contribution to profit.

7. As part of the settlement for a class action lawsuit, Hoxworth Corporation must provide sufficient cash to make the following annual payments (in thousands of dollars):

Year	1	2	3	4	5	6
Payment	190	215	240	285	315	460

The annual payments must be made at the beginning of each year. The judge will approve an amount that, along with earnings on its investment, will cover the annual payments. Investment of the funds will be limited to savings (at 4% annually) and government securities, at prices and rates currently quoted in *The Wall Street Journal*.

Hoxworth wants to develop a plan for making the annual payments by investing in the following securities (par value = $1000). Funds not invested in these securities will be placed in savings.

Security	Current Price	Rate (%)	Years to Maturity
1	$1055	6.750	3
2	$1000	5.125	4

Assume that interest is paid annually. The plan will be submitted to the judge and, if approved, Hoxworth will be required to pay a trustee the amount that will be required to fund the plan.

   a.   Use linear programming to find the minimum cash settlement necessary to fund the annual payments.

   b.   Use the dual price to determine how much more Hoxworth should be willing to pay now to reduce the payment at the beginning of year 6 to $400,000.

   c.   Use the dual price to determine how much more Hoxworth should be willing to pay to reduce the year 1 payment to $150,000.

   d.   Suppose that the annual payments are to be made at the end of each year. Reformulate the model to accommodate this change. How much would Hoxworth save if this change could be negotiated?

8.   The Clark County Sheriff's Department schedules police officers for 8-hour shifts. The beginning times for the shifts are 8:00 A.M., noon, 4:00 P.M., 8:00 P.M., midnight, and 4:00 A.M. An officer beginning a shift at one of these times works for the next 8 hours. During normal weekday operations, the number of officers needed varies depending on the time of day. The department staffing guidelines require the following minimum number of officers on duty:

Time of Day	Minimum Officers On Duty
8:00 A.M.–Noon	5
Noon–4:00 P.M.	6
4:00 P.M.–8:00 P.M.	10
8:00 P.M.–Midnight	7
Midnight–4:00 A.M.	4
4:00 A.M.–8:00 A.M.	6

Determine the number of police officers that should be scheduled to begin the 8-hour shifts at each of the six times (8:00 A.M., noon, 4:00 P.M., 8:00 P.M., midnight, and 4:00 A.M.) to minimize the total number of officers required. (*Hint:* Let x_1 = the number of officers beginning work at 8:00 A.M., x_2 = the number of officers beginning work at noon, and so on.)

9.   Reconsider the Welte Mutual Funds problem from Section 9.2. Define your decision variables as the fraction of funds invested in each security. Also, modify the constraints limiting investments in the oil and steel industries as follows: No more than 50% of the total funds invested in stock (oil and steel) may be invested in the oil industry, and no more than 50% of the funds invested in stock (oil and steel) may be invested in the steel industry.

   a.   Solve the revised linear programming model. What fraction of the portfolio should be invested in each type of security?

   b.   How much should be invested in each type of security?

c. What are the total earnings for the portfolio?

d. What is the marginal rate of return on the portfolio? That is, how much more could be earned by investing one more dollar in the portfolio?

10. An investment advisor at Shore Financial Services wants to develop a model that can be used to allocate investment funds among four alternatives: stocks, bonds, mutual funds, and cash. For the coming investment period, the company developed estimates of the annual rate of return and the associated risk for each alternative. Risk is measured using an index between 0 and 1, with higher risk values denoting more volatility and thus more uncertainty.

Investment	Annual Rate of Return (%)	Risk
Stocks	10	0.8
Bonds	3	0.2
Mutual funds	4	0.3
Cash	1	0.0

Because cash is held in a money market fund, the annual return is lower, but it carries essentially no risk. The objective is to determine the portion of funds allocated to each investment alternative in order to maximize the total annual return for the portfolio subject to the risk level the client is willing to tolerate.

Total risk is the sum of the risk for all investment alternatives. For instance, if 40% of a client's funds are invested in stocks, 30% in bonds, 20% in mutual funds, and 10% in cash, the total risk for the portfolio would be $0.40(0.8) + 0.30(0.2) + 0.20(0.3) + 0.10(0.0) = 0.44$. An investment advisor will meet with each client to discuss the client's investment objectives and to determine a maximum total risk value for the client. A maximum total risk value of less than 0.3 would be assigned to a conservative investor; a maximum total risk value of between 0.3 and 0.5 would be assigned to a moderate tolerance to risk; and a maximum total risk value greater than 0.5 would be assigned to a more aggressive investor.

Shore Financial Services specified additional guidelines that must be applied to all clients. The guidelines are as follows:

- No more than 75% of the total investment may be in stocks.
- The amount invested in mutual funds must be at least as much as invested in bonds.
- The amount of cash must be at least 10%, but no more than 30% of the total investment funds.

a. Suppose the maximum risk value for a particular client is 0.4. What is the optimal allocation of investment funds among stocks, bonds, mutual funds, and cash? What is the annual rate of return and the total risk for the optimal portfolio?

b. Suppose the maximum risk value for a more conservative client is 0.18. What is the optimal allocation of investment funds for this client? What is the annual rate of return and the total risk for the optimal portfolio?

c. Another more aggressive client has a maximum risk value of 0.7. What is the optimal allocation of investment funds for this client? What is the annual rate of return and the total risk for the optimal portfolio?

d. Refer to the solution for the more aggressive client in part (c). Would this client be interested in having the investment advisor increase the maximum percentage allowed in stocks or decrease the requirement that the amount of cash must be at least 10% of the funds invested? Explain.

e. What is the advantage of defining the decision variables as is done in this model rather than stating the amount to be invested and expressing the decision variables directly in dollar amounts?

11. Edwards Manufacturing Company purchases two component parts from three different suppliers. The suppliers have limited capacity, and no one supplier can meet all the company's needs. In addition, the suppliers charge different prices for the components. Component price data (in price per unit) are as follows:

	Supplier		
Component	**1**	**2**	**3**
1	$12	$13	$14
2	$10	$11	$10

Each supplier has a limited capacity in terms of the total number of components it can supply. However, as long as Edwards provides sufficient advance orders, each supplier can devote its capacity to component 1, component 2, or any combination of the two components, if the total number of units ordered is within its capacity. Supplier capacities are as follows:

Supplier	1	2	3
Capacity	600	1000	800

If the Edwards production plan for the next period includes 1000 units of component 1 and 800 units of component 2, what purchases do you recommend? That is, how many units of each component should be ordered from each supplier? What is the total purchase cost for the components?

12. The Atlantic Seafood Company (ASC) is a buyer and distributor of seafood products that are sold to restaurants and specialty seafood outlets throughout the Northeast. ASC has a frozen storage facility in New York City that serves as the primary distribution point for all products. One of the ASC products is frozen large black tiger shrimp, which are sized at 16–20 pieces per pound. Each Saturday ASC can purchase more tiger shrimp or sell the tiger shrimp at the existing New York City warehouse market price. The ASC goal is to buy tiger shrimp at a low weekly price and sell it later at a higher price. ASC currently has 20,000 pounds of tiger shrimp in storage. Space is available to store a maximum of 100,000 pounds of tiger shrimp each week. In addition, ASC developed the following estimates of tiger shrimp prices for the next four weeks:

Week	**Price/lb.**
1	$6.00
2	$6.20
3	$6.65
4	$5.55

ASC would like to determine the optimal buying/storing/selling strategy for the next four weeks. The cost to store a pound of shrimp for one week is $0.15, and to account for unforeseen changes in supply or demand, management also indicated that 25,000 pounds of tiger shrimp must be in storage at the end of week 4. Determine the optimal buying/storing/selling strategy for ASC. What is the projected four-week profit?

13. Romans Food Market, located in Saratoga, New York, carries a variety of specialty foods from around the world. Two of the store's leading products use the Romans Food Market

name: Romans Regular Coffee and Romans DeCaf Coffee. These coffees are blends of Brazilian Natural and Colombian Mild coffee beans, which are purchased from a distributor located in New York City. Because Romans purchases large quantities, the coffee beans may be purchased on an as-needed basis for a price 10% higher than the market price the distributor pays for the beans. The current market price is $0.47 per pound for Brazilian Natural and $0.62 per pound for Colombian Mild. The compositions of each coffee blend are as follows:

	Blend	
Bean	**Regular**	**DeCaf**
Brazilian Natural	75%	40%
Colombian Mild	25%	60%

Romans sells the Regular blend for $3.60 per pound and the DeCaf blend for $4.40 per pound. Romans would like to place an order for the Brazilian and Colombian coffee beans that will enable the production of 1000 pounds of Romans Regular coffee and 500 pounds of Romans DeCaf coffee. The production cost is $0.80 per pound for the Regular blend. Because of the extra steps required to produce DeCaf, the production cost for the DeCaf blend is $1.05 per pound. Packaging costs for both products are $0.25 per pound. Formulate a linear programming model that can be used to determine the pounds of Brazilian Natural and Colombian Mild that will maximize the total contribution to profit. What is the optimal solution and what is the contribution to profit?

14. The production manager for the Classic Boat Corporation must determine how many units of the Classic 21 model to produce over the next four quarters. The company has a beginning inventory of 100 Classic 21 boats, and demand for the four quarters is 2000 units in quarter 1, 4000 units in quarter 2, 3000 units in quarter 3, and 1500 units in quarter 4. The firm has limited production capacity in each quarter. That is, up to 4000 units can be produced in quarter 1, 3000 units in quarter 2, 2000 units in quarter 3, and 4000 units in quarter 4. Each boat held in inventory in quarters 1 and 2 incurs an inventory holding cost of $250 per unit; the holding cost for quarters 3 and 4 is $300 per unit. The production costs for the first quarter are $10,000 per unit; these costs are expected to increase by 10% each quarter because of increases in labor and material costs. Management specified that the ending inventory for quarter 4 must be at least 500 boats.
    a. Formulate a linear programming model that can be used to determine the production schedule that will minimize the total cost of meeting demand in each quarter subject to the production capacities in each quarter and also to the required ending inventory in quarter 4.
    b. Solve the linear program formulated in part (a). Then develop a table that will show for each quarter the number of units to manufacture, the ending inventory, and the costs incurred.
    c. Interpret each of the dual prices corresponding to the constraints developed to meet demand in each quarter. Based on these dual prices, what advice would you give the production manager?
    d. Interpret each of the dual prices corresponding to the production capacity in each quarter. Based on each of these dual prices, what advice would you give the production manager?

15. Seastrand Oil Company produces two grades of gasoline: regular and high octane. Both gasolines are produced by blending two types of crude oil. Although both types of crude oil contain the two important ingredients required to produce both gasolines, the percentage of

important ingredients in each type of crude oil differs, as does the cost per gallon. The percentage of ingredients A and B in each type of crude oil and the cost per gallon are shown.

Crude Oil	Cost	Ingredient A	Ingredient B
1	$0.10	20%	60%
2	$0.15	50%	30%

Each gallon of regular gasoline must contain at least 40% of ingredient A, whereas each gallon of high octane can contain at most 50% of ingredient B. Daily demand for regular and high-octane gasoline is 800,000 and 500,000 gallons, respectively. How many gallons of each type of crude oil should be used in the two gasolines to satisfy daily demand at a minimum cost?

16. The Ferguson Paper Company produces rolls of paper for use in adding machines, desk calculators, and cash registers. The rolls, which are 200 feet long, are produced in widths of $1\frac{1}{2}$, $2\frac{1}{2}$, and $3\frac{1}{2}$ inches. The production process provides 200-foot rolls in 10-inch widths only. The firm must therefore cut the rolls to the desired final product sizes. The seven cutting alternatives and the amount of waste generated by each are as follows:

Cutting Alternative	Number of Rolls $1\frac{1}{2}$ in.	$2\frac{1}{2}$ in.	$3\frac{1}{2}$ in.	Waste (inches)
1	6	0	0	1
2	0	4	0	0
3	2	0	2	0
4	0	1	2	$\frac{1}{2}$
5	1	3	0	1
6	1	2	1	0
7	4	0	1	$\frac{1}{2}$

The minimum requirements for the three products are

Roll Width (inches)	$1\frac{1}{2}$	$2\frac{1}{2}$	$3\frac{1}{2}$
Units	1000	2000	4000

a.   If the company wants to minimize the number of 10-inch rolls that must be manufactured, how many 10-inch rolls will be processed on each cutting alternative? How many rolls are required, and what is the total waste (inches)?

b.   If the company wants to minimize the waste generated, how many 10-inch rolls will be processed on each cutting alternative? How many rolls are required, and what is the total waste (inches)?

c.   What are the differences in parts (a) and (b) to this problem? In this case, which objective do you prefer? Explain. What types of situations would make the other objective more desirable?

17. Frandec Company manufactures, assembles, and rebuilds material handling equipment used in warehouses and distribution centers. One product, called a Liftmaster, is assembled from four components: a frame, a motor, two supports, and a metal strap. Frandec's production schedule calls for 5000 Liftmasters to be made next month. Frandec purchases

the motors from an outside supplier, but the frames, supports, and straps may be either manufactured by the company or purchased from an outside supplier. Manufacturing and purchase costs per unit are shown.

Component	Manufacturing Cost	Purchase Cost
Frame	$38.00	$51.00
Support	$11.50	$15.00
Strap	$ 6.50	$ 7.50

Three departments are involved in the production of these components. The time (in minutes per unit) required to process each component in each department and the available capacity (in hours) for the three departments are as follows:

	Department		
Component	Cutting	Milling	Shaping
Frame	3.5	2.2	3.1
Support	1.3	1.7	2.6
Strap	0.8	—	1.7
Capacity (hours)	350	420	680

a. Formulate and solve a linear programming model for this make-or-buy application. How many of each component should be manufactured and how many should be purchased?

b. What is the total cost of the manufacturing and purchasing plan?

c. How many hours of production time are used in each department?

d. How much should Frandec be willing to pay for an additional hour of time in the shaping department?

e. Another manufacturer has offered to sell frames to Frandec for $45 each. Could Frandec improve its position by pursuing this opportunity? Why or why not?

18. The Two-Rivers Oil Company near Pittsburgh transports gasoline to its distributors by truck. The company recently contracted to supply gasoline distributors in southern Ohio, and it has $600,000 available to spend on the necessary expansion of its fleet of gasoline tank trucks. Three models of gasoline tank trucks are available.

Truck Model	Capacity (gallons)	Purchase Cost	Monthly Operating Cost, Including Depreciation
Super Tanker	5000	$67,000	$550
Regular Line	2500	$55,000	$425
Econo-Tanker	1000	$46,000	$350

The company estimates that the monthly demand for the region will be 550,000 gallons of gasoline. Because of the size and speed differences of the trucks, the number of deliveries or round trips possible per month for each truck model will vary. Trip capacities are estimated at 15 trips per month for the Super Tanker, 20 trips per month for the Regular Line, and 25 trips per month for the Econo-Tanker. Based on maintenance and driver availability, the firm does not want to add more than 15 new vehicles to its fleet. In addition, the company has decided to purchase at least three of the new Econo-Tankers for use on short-run, low-demand routes. As a final constraint, the company does not want more than half the new models to be Super Tankers.

a. If the company wishes to satisfy the gasoline demand with a minimum monthly operating expense, how many models of each truck should be purchased?

b. If the company did not require at least three Econo-Tankers and did not limit the number of Super Tankers to at most half the new models, how many models of each truck should be purchased?

19. The Silver Star Bicycle Company will be manufacturing both men's and women's models for its Easy-Pedal 10-speed bicycles during the next two months. Management wants to develop a production schedule indicating how many bicycles of each model should be produced in each month. Current demand forecasts call for 150 men's and 125 women's models to be shipped during the first month and 200 men's and 150 women's models to be shipped during the second month. Additional data are shown:

Model	Production Costs	Labor Requirements (hours)		Current Inventory
		Manufacturing	Assembly	
Men's	$120	2.0	1.5	20
Women's	$ 90	1.6	1.0	30

Last month the company used a total of 1000 hours of labor. The company's labor relations policy will not allow the combined total hours of labor (manufacturing plus assembly) to increase or decrease by more than 100 hours from month to month. In addition, the company charges monthly inventory at the rate of 2% of the production cost based on the inventory levels at the end of the month. The company would like to have at least 25 units of each model in inventory at the end of the two months.

a. Establish a production schedule that minimizes production and inventory costs and satisfies the labor-smoothing, demand, and inventory requirements. What inventories will be maintained and what are the monthly labor requirements?

b. If the company changed the constraints so that monthly labor increases and decreases could not exceed 50 hours, what would happen to the production schedule? How much will the cost increase? What would you recommend?

20. Filtron Corporation produces filtration containers used in water treatment systems. Although business has been growing, the demand each month varies considerably. As a result, the company utilizes a mix of part-time and full-time employees to meet production demands. Although this approach provides Filtron with great flexibility, it resulted in increased costs and morale problems among employees. For instance, if Filtron needs to increase production from one month to the next, additional part-time employees have to be hired and trained, and costs go up. If Filtron has to decrease production, the workforce has to be reduced and Filtron incurs additional costs in terms of unemployment benefits and decreased morale. Best estimates are that increasing the number of units produced from one month to the next will increase production costs by $1.25 per unit, and that decreasing the number of units produced will increase production costs by $1.00 per unit. In February Filtron produced 10,000 filtration containers but only sold 7500 units; 2500 units are currently in inventory. The sales forecasts for March, April, and May are for 12,000 units, 8000 units, and 15,000 units, respectively. In addition, Filtron has the capacity to store up to 3000 filtration containers at the end of any month. Management would like to determine the number of units to be produced in March, April, and May that will minimize the total cost of the monthly production increases and decreases.

21. Greenville Cabinets received a contract to produce speaker cabinets for a major speaker manufacturer. The contract calls for the production of 3300 bookshelf speakers and 4100 floor speakers over the next two months, with the following delivery schedule:

Model	Month 1	Month 2
Bookshelf	2100	1200
Floor	1500	2600

Greenville estimates that the production time for each bookshelf model is 0.7 hour and the production time for each floor model is 1 hour. The raw material costs are $10 for each bookshelf model and $12 for each floor model. Labor costs are $22 per hour using regular production time and $33 using overtime. Greenville has up to 2400 hours of regular production time available each month and up to 1000 additional hours of overtime available each month. If production for either cabinet exceeds demand in month 1, the cabinets can be stored at a cost of $5 per cabinet. For each product, determine the number of units that should be manufactured each month on regular time and on overtime to minimize total production and storage costs.

22. TriCity Manufacturing (TCM) makes Styrofoam cups, plates, and sandwich and meal containers. Next week's schedule calls for the production of 80,000 small sandwich containers, 80,000 large sandwich containers, and 65,000 meal containers. To make these containers, Styrofoam sheets are melted and formed into final products using three machines: M1, M2, and M3. Machine M1 can process Styrofoam sheets with a maximum width of 12 inches. The width capacity of machine M2 is 16 inches, and the width capacity of machine M3 is 20 inches. The small sandwich containers require 10-inch-wide Styrofoam sheets; thus, these containers can be produced on each of the three machines. The large sandwich containers require 12-inch-wide sheets; thus, these containers can also be produced on each of the three machines. However, the meal containers require 16-inch-wide Styrofoam sheets, so the meal containers cannot be produced on machine M1. Waste is incurred in the production of all three containers because Styrofoam is lost in the heating and forming process as well as in the final trimming of the product. The amount of waste generated varies depending upon the container produced and the machine used. The following table shows the waste in square inches for each machine and product combination. The waste material is recycled for future use.

Machine	Small Sandwich	Large Sandwich	Meal
M1	20	15	—
M2	24	28	18
M3	32	35	36

Production rates also depend upon the container produced and the machine used. The following table shows the production rates in units per minute for each machine and product combination. Machine capacities are limited for the next week. Time available is 35 hours for machine M1, 35 hours for machine M2, and 40 hours for machine M3.

Machine	Small Sandwich	Large Sandwich	Meal
M1	30	25	—
M2	45	40	30
M3	60	52	44

a.   Costs associated with reprocessing the waste material have been increasing. Thus, TCM would like to minimize the amount of waste generated in meeting next week's production schedule. Formulate a linear programming model that can be used to determine the best production schedule.

b.   Solve the linear program formulated in part (a) to determine the production schedule. How much waste is generated? Which machines, if any, have idle capacity?

23.   EZ-Windows, Inc., manufactures replacement windows for the home remodeling business. In January, the company produced 15,000 windows and ended the month with 9000 windows in inventory. EZ-Windows' management team would like to develop a production schedule for the next three months. A smooth production schedule is obviously desirable because it maintains the current workforce and provides a similar month-to-month operation. However, given the sales forecasts, the production capacities, and the storage capabilities as shown, the management team does not think a smooth production schedule with the same production quantity each month possible.

	February	March	April
Sales forecast	15,000	16,500	20,000
Production capacity	14,000	14,000	18,000
Storage capacity	6,000	6,000	6,000

The company's cost accounting department estimates that increasing production by one window from one month to the next will increase total costs by $1.00 for each unit increase in the production level. In addition, decreasing production by one unit from one month to the next will increase total costs by $0.65 for each unit decrease in the production level. Ignoring production and inventory carrying costs, formulate and solve a linear programming model that will minimize the cost of changing production levels while still satisfying the monthly sales forecasts.

24.   Morton Financial must decide on the percentage of available funds to commit to each of two investments, referred to as A and B, over the next four periods. The following table shows the amount of new funds available for each of the four periods, as well as the cash expenditure required for each investment (negative values) or the cash income from the investment (positive values). The data shown (in thousands of dollars) reflect the amount of expenditure or income if 100% of the funds available in any period are invested in either A or B. For example, if Morton decides to invest 100% of the funds available in any period in investment A, it will incur cash expenditures of $1000 in period 1, $800 in period 2, $200 in period 3, and income of $200 in period 4. Note, however, if Morton made the decision to invest 80% in investment A, the cash expenditures or income would be 80% of the values shown.

	New Investment	Investment	
Period	Funds Available	A	B
1	$1500	−$1000	−$800
2	$ 400	−$ 800	−$500
3	$ 500	−$ 200	−$300
4	$ 100	−$ 200	−$300

The amount of funds available in any period is the sum of the new investment funds for the period, the new loan funds, the savings from the previous period, the cash income from investment A, and the cash income from investment B. The funds available in any period can be used to pay the loan and interest from the previous period, placed in savings, used to pay the cash expenditures for investment A, or used to pay the cash expenditures for investment B.

Assume an interest rate of 10% per period for savings and an interest rate of 18% per period on borrowed funds. Let

$$S(t) = \text{the savings for period } t$$
$$L(t) = \text{the new loan funds for period } t$$

Then, in any period t, the savings income from the previous period is $1.1S(t-1)$ and the loan and interest expenditure from the previous period is $1.18L(t-1)$.

At the end of period 4, investment A is expected to have a cash value of $3200 (assuming a 100% investment in A), and investment B is expected to have a cash value of $2500 (assuming a 100% investment in B). Additional income and expenses at the end of period 4 will be income from savings in period 4 less the repayment of the period 4 loan plus interest.

Suppose that the decision variables are defined as

$$x_1 = \text{the proportion of investment A undertaken}$$
$$x_2 = \text{the proportion of investment B undertaken}$$

For example, if $x_1 = 0.5$, $500 would be invested in investment A during the first period, and all remaining cash flows and ending investment A values would be multiplied by 0.5. The same holds for investment B. The model must include constraints $x_1 \le 1$ and $x_2 \le 1$ to make sure that no more than 100% of the investments can be undertaken.

If no more than $200 can be borrowed in any period, determine the proportions of investments A and B and the amount of savings and borrowing in each period that will maximize the cash value for the firm at the end of the four periods.

25. Western Family Steakhouse offers a variety of low-cost meals and quick service. Other than management, the steakhouse operates with two full-time employees who work 8 hours per day. The rest of the employees are part-time employees who are scheduled for 4-hour shifts during peak meal times. On Saturdays the steakhouse is open from 11:00 A.M. to 10:00 P.M. Management wants to develop a schedule for part-time employees that will minimize labor costs and still provide excellent customer service. The average wage rate for the part-time employees is $7.60 per hour. The total number of full-time and part-time employees needed varies with the time of day as shown.

Time	Total Number of Employees Needed
11:00 A.M.–Noon	9
Noon–1:00 P.M.	9
1:00 P.M.–2:00 P.M.	9
2:00 P.M.–3:00 P.M.	3
3:00 P.M.–4:00 P.M.	3
4:00 P.M.–5:00 P.M.	3
5:00 P.M.–6:00 P.M.	6
6:00 P.M.–7:00 P.M.	12
7:00 P.M.–8:00 P.M.	12
8:00 P.M.–9:00 P.M.	7
9:00 P.M.–10:00 P.M.	7

One full-time employee comes on duty at 11:00 A.M., works 4 hours, takes an hour off, and returns for another 4 hours. The other full-time employee comes to work at 1:00 P.M. and works the same 4-hours-on, 1-hour-off, 4-hours-on pattern.

a. Develop a minimum-cost schedule for part-time employees.

b. What is the total payroll for the part-time employees? How many part-time shifts are needed? Use the surplus variables to comment on the desirability of scheduling at least some of the part-time employees for 3-hour shifts.

c. Assume that part-time employees can be assigned either a 3-hour or a 4-hour shift. Develop a minimum-cost schedule for the part-time employees. How many part-time shifts are needed, and what is the cost savings compared to the previous schedule?

Case Problem 1   Planning an Advertising Campaign

The Flamingo Grill is an upscale restaurant located in St. Petersburg, Florida. To help plan an advertising campaign for the coming season, Flamingo's management team hired the advertising firm of Haskell & Johnson (HJ). The management team requested HJ's recommendation concerning how the advertising budget should be distributed across television, radio, and newspaper advertisements. The budget has been set at $279,000.

In a meeting with Flamingo's management team, HJ consultants provided the following information about the industry exposure effectiveness rating per ad, their estimate of the number of potential new customers reached per ad, and the cost for each ad:

Advertising Media	Exposure Rating per Ad	New Customers per Ad	Cost per Ad
Television	90	4000	$10,000
Radio	25	2000	$ 3000
Newspaper	10	1000	$ 1000

The exposure rating is viewed as a measure of the value of the ad to both existing customers and potential new customers. It is a function of such things as image, message recall, visual and audio appeal, and so on. As expected, the more expensive television advertisement has the highest exposure effectiveness rating along with the greatest potential for reaching new customers.

At this point, the HJ consultants pointed out that the data concerning exposure and reach were only applicable to the first few ads in each medium. For television, HJ stated that the exposure rating of 90 and the 4000 new customers reached per ad were reliable for the first 10 television ads. After 10 ads, the benefit is expected to decline. For planning purposes, HJ recommended reducing the exposure rating to 55 and the estimate of the potential new customers reached to 1500 for any television ads beyond 10. For radio ads, the preceding data are reliable up to a maximum of 15 ads. Beyond 15 ads, the exposure rating declines to 20 and the number of new customers reached declines to 1200 per ad. Similarly, for newspaper ads, the preceding data are reliable up to a maximum of 20; the exposure rating declines to 5 and the potential number of new customers reached declines to 800 for additional ads.

Flamingo's management team accepted maximizing the total exposure rating across all media as the objective of the advertising campaign. Because of management's concern with attracting new customers, management stated that the advertising campaign must reach at least 100,000 new customers. To balance the advertising campaign and make use of all advertising media, Flamingo's management team also adopted the following guidelines:

- Use at least twice as many radio advertisements as television advertisements.
- Use no more than 20 television advertisements.
- The television budget should be at least $140,000.
- The radio advertising budget is restricted to a maximum of $99,000.
- The newspaper budget is to be at least $30,000.

HJ agreed to work with these guidelines and provide a recommendation as to how the $279,000 advertising budget should be allocated among television, radio, and newspaper advertising.

Managerial Report

Develop a model that can be used to determine the advertising budget allocation for the Flamingo Grill. Include a discussion of the following items in your report:

1. A schedule showing the recommended number of television, radio, and newspaper advertisements and the budget allocation for each medium. Show the total exposure and indicate the total number of potential new customers reached.
2. How would the total exposure change if an additional $10,000 were added to the advertising budget?
3. A discussion of the ranges for the objective function coefficients. What do the ranges indicate about how sensitive the recommended solution is to HJ's exposure rating coefficients?
4. After reviewing HJ's recommendation, the Flamingo's management team asked how the recommendation would change if the objective of the advertising campaign was to maximize the number of potential new customers reached. Develop the media schedule under this objective.
5. Compare the recommendations from parts 1 and 4. What is your recommendation for the Flamingo Grill's advertising campaign?

Case Problem 2   Phoenix Computer

Phoenix Computer manufactures and sells personal computers directly to customers. Orders are accepted by phone and through the company's Web site. Phoenix will be introducing several new laptop models over the next few months, and management recognizes a need to develop technical support personnel to specialize in the new laptop systems. One option being considered is to hire new employees and put them through a three-month training program. Another option is to put current customer service specialists through a two-month training program on the new laptop models. Phoenix estimates that the need for laptop specialists will grow from 0 to 100 during the months of May through September as follows: May—20; June—30; July—85; August—85; and September—100. After September, Phoenix expects that maintaining a staff of 100 laptop specialists will be sufficient.

The annual salary for a new employee is estimated to be $27,000 whether the person is hired to enter the training program or to replace a current employee who is entering the training program. The annual salary for the current Phoenix employees who are being considered for the training program is approximately $36,000. The cost of the three-month training program is $1500 per person, and the cost of the two-month training program is $1000 per person. Note that the length of the training program means that a lag will occur between the time when a new person is hired and the time a new laptop specialist is available. The number of current employees who will be available for training is limited. Phoenix estimates that the following numbers can be made available in the coming months: March—15; April—20; May—0; June—5; and July—10. The training center has the capacity to start new three-month and two-month training classes each month; however, the total number of students (new and current employees) that begin training each month cannot exceed 25.

Phoenix needs to determine the number of new hires that should begin the three-month training program each month and the number of current employees that should begin the two-month training program each month. The objective is to satisfy staffing needs during May through September at the lowest possible total cost; that is, minimize the incremental salary cost and the total training cost.

It is currently January, and Phoenix Computer would like to develop a plan for hiring new employees and determining the mix of new hires and current employees to place in the training program.

Managerial Report

Perform an analysis of the Phoenix Computer problem and prepare a report that summarizes your findings. Be sure to include information on and analysis of the following items:

1. The incremental salary and training cost associated with hiring a new employee and training him/her to be a laptop specialist.
2. The incremental salary and training cost associated with putting a current employee through the training program. (Don't forget that a replacement must be hired when the current employee enters the program.)
3. Recommendations regarding the hiring and training plan that will minimize the salary and training costs over the February through August period as well as answers to these questions: What is the total cost of providing technical support for the new laptop models? How much higher will monthly payroll costs be in September than in January?

Case Problem 3   Textile Mill Scheduling

The Scottsville Textile Mill[1] produces five different fabrics. Each fabric can be woven on one or more of the mill's 38 looms. The sales department's forecast of demand for the next month is shown in Table 9.16, along with data on the selling price per yard, variable cost per yard, and purchase price per yard. The mill operates 24 hours a day and is scheduled for 30 days during the coming month.

The mill has two types of looms: dobbie and regular. The dobbie looms are more versatile and can be used for all five fabrics. The regular looms can produce only three of the fabrics. The mill has a total of 38 looms: 8 are dobbie and 30 are regular. The rate of production for each fabric on each type of loom is given in Table 9.17. The time required to change over from producing one fabric to another is negligible and does not have to be considered.

The Scottsville Textile Mill satisfies all demand with either its own fabric or fabric purchased from another mill. Fabrics that cannot be woven at the Scottsville Mill because of limited loom capacity will be purchased from another mill. The purchase price of each fabric is also shown in Table 9.16.

---

[1]This case is based on the Calhoun Textile Mill Case by Jeffrey D. Camm, P. M. Dearing, and Suresh K. Tadisnia, 1987.

TABLE 9.16 MONTHLY DEMAND, SELLING PRICE, VARIABLE COST, AND PURCHASE PRICE DATA FOR SCOTTSVILLE TEXTILE MILL FABRICS

Fabric	Demand (yards)	Selling Price ($/yard)	Variable Cost ($/yard)	Purchase Price ($/yard)
1	16,500	0.99	0.66	0.80
2	22,000	0.86	0.55	0.70
3	62,000	1.10	0.49	0.60
4	7,500	1.24	0.51	0.70
5	62,000	0.70	0.50	0.70

TABLE 9.17 LOOM PRODUCTION RATES FOR THE SCOTTSVILLE TEXTILE MILL

	Loom Rate (yards/hour)	
Fabric	Dobbie	Regular
1	4.63	—
2	4.63	—
3	5.23	5.23
4	5.23	5.23
5	4.17	4.17

Note: Fabrics 1 and 2 can be manufactured only on the dobbie loom.

Managerial Report

Develop a model that can be used to schedule production for the Scottsville Textile Mill, and at the same time, determine how many yards of each fabric must be purchased from another mill. Include a discussion and analysis of the following items in your report:

1. The final production schedule and loom assignments for each fabric.
2. The projected total contribution to profit.
3. A discussion of the value of additional loom time. (The mill is considering purchasing a ninth dobbie loom. What is your estimate of the monthly profit contribution of this additional loom?)
4. A discussion of the objective coefficients' ranges.
5. A discussion of how the objective of minimizing total costs would provide a different model than the objective of maximizing total profit contribution. (How would the interpretation of the objective coefficients' ranges differ for these two models?)

Case Problem 4   Workforce Scheduling

Davis Instruments has two manufacturing plants located in Atlanta, Georgia. Product demand varies considerably from month to month, causing Davis extreme difficulty in workforce scheduling. Recently Davis started hiring temporary workers supplied by WorkForce Unlimited, a company that specializes in providing temporary employees for firms in the greater Atlanta area. WorkForce Unlimited offered to provide temporary employees under three contract options that differ in terms of the length of employment and the cost. The three options are summarized:

Option	Length of Employment	Cost
1	One month	$2000
2	Two months	$4800
3	Three months	$7500

The longer contract periods are more expensive because WorkForce Unlimited experiences greater difficulty finding temporary workers who are willing to commit to longer work assignments.

Over the next six months, Davis projects the following needs for additional employees:

Month	January	February	March	April	May	June
Employees Needed	10	23	19	26	20	14

Each month, Davis can hire as many temporary employees as needed under each of the three options. For instance, if Davis hires five employees in January under Option 2, WorkForce Unlimited will supply Davis with five temporary workers who will work two months: January and February. For these workers, Davis will have to pay 5($4800) = $24,000. Because of some merger negotiations under way, Davis does not want to commit to any contractual obligations for temporary employees that extend beyond June.

Davis's quality control program requires each temporary employee to receive training at the time of hire. The training program is required even if the person worked for Davis Instruments in the past. Davis estimates that the cost of training is $875 each time a temporary employee is hired. Thus, if a temporary employee is hired for one month, Davis will incur a training cost of $875 but will incur no additional training cost if the employee is on a two- or three-month contract.

Managerial Report

Develop a model that can be used to determine the number of temporary employees Davis should hire each month under each contract plan in order to meet the projected needs at a minimum total cost. Include the following items in your report:

1. A schedule that shows the number of temporary employees that Davis should hire each month for each contract option.
2. A summary table that shows the number of temporary employees that Davis should hire under each contract option, the associated contract cost for each option, and the associated training cost for each option. Provide summary totals showing the total number of temporary employees hired, total contract costs, and total training costs.
3. If the cost to train each temporary employee could be reduced to $700 per month, what effect would this change have on the hiring plan? Explain. Discuss the implications that this effect on the hiring plan has for identifying methods for reducing training costs. How much of a reduction in training costs would be required to change the hiring plan based on a training cost of $875 per temporary employee?
4. Suppose that Davis hired 10 full-time employees at the beginning of January in order to satisfy part of the labor requirements over the next six months. If Davis can hire full-time employees for $16.50 per hour, including fringe benefits, what effect

would it have on total labor and training costs over the six-month period as compared to hiring only temporary employees? Assume that full-time and temporary employees both work approximately 160 hours per month. Provide a recommendation regarding the decision to hire additional full-time employees.

Case Problem 5   Duke Energy Coal Allocation[2]

Duke Energy manufactures and distributes electricity to customers in the United States and Latin America. Duke recently purchased Cinergy Corporation, which has generating facilities and energy customers in Indiana, Kentucky, and Ohio. For these customers Cinergy has been spending $725 to $750 million each year for the fuel needed to operate its coal-fired and gas-fired power plants; 92% to 95% of the fuel used is coal. In this region, Duke Energy uses 10 coal-burning generating plants: 5 located inland and 5 located on the Ohio River. Some plants have more than one generating unit. Duke Energy uses 28–29 million tons of coal per year at a cost of approximately $2 million every day in this region.

The company purchases coal using fixed-tonnage or variable-tonnage contracts from mines in Indiana (49%), West Virginia (20%), Ohio (12%), Kentucky (11%), Illinois (5%), and Pennsylvania (3%). The company must purchase all of the coal contracted for on fixed-tonnage contracts, but on variable-tonnage contracts it can purchase varying amounts up to the limit specified in the contract. The coal is shipped from the mines to Duke Energy's generating facilities in Ohio, Kentucky, and Indiana. The cost of coal varies from $19 to $35 per ton and transportation/delivery charges range from $1.50 to $5.00 per ton.

A model is used to determine the megawatt-hours (mWh) of electricity that each generating unit is expected to produce and to provide a measure of each generating unit's efficiency, referred to as the heat rate. The heat rate is the total BTUs required to produce 1 kilowatt-hour (kWh) of electrical power.

Coal Allocation Model

Duke Energy uses a linear programming model, called the coal allocation model, to allocate coal to its generating facilities. The objective of the coal allocation model is to determine the lowest-cost method for purchasing and distributing coal to the generating units. The supply/availability of the coal is determined by the contracts with the various mines, and the demand for coal at the generating units is determined indirectly by the megawatt-hours of electricity each unit must produce.

The cost to process coal, called the add-on cost, depends upon the characteristics of the coal (moisture content, ash content, BTU content, sulfur content, and grindability) and the efficiency of the generating unit. The add-on cost plus the transportation cost are added to the purchase cost of the coal to determine the total cost to purchase and use the coal.

Current Problem

Duke Energy signed three fixed-tonnage contracts and four variable-tonnage contracts. The company would like to determine the least-cost way to allocate the coal available through

---

[2]The authors are indebted to Thomas Mason and David Bossee of Duke Energy Corporation, formerly Cinergy Corp., for their contribution to this case problem.

these contracts to five generating units. The relevant data for the three fixed-tonnage contracts are as follows:

Supplier	Number of Tons Contracted For	Cost ($/ton)	BTUs/lb
RAG	350,000	22	13,000
Peabody Coal Sales	300,000	26	13,300
American Coal Sales	275,000	22	12,600

For example, the contract signed with RAG requires Duke Energy to purchase 350,000 tons of coal at a price of $22 per ton; each pound of this particular coal provides 13,000 BTUs.

The data for the four variable-tonnage contracts follow:

Supplier	Number of Tons Available	Cost ($/ton)	BTUs/lb
Consol, Inc.	200,000	32	12,250
Cyprus Amax	175,000	35	12,000
Addington Mining	200,000	31	12,000
Waterloo	180,000	33	11,300

For example, the contract with Consol, Inc., enables Duke Energy to purchase up to 200,000 tons of coal at a cost of $32 per ton; each pound of this coal provides 12,250 BTUs.

The number of megawatt-hours of electricity that each generating unit must produce and the heat rate provided are as follows:

Generating Unit	Electricity Produced (mWh)	Heat Rate (BTUs per kWh)
Miami Fort Unit 5	550,000	10,500
Miami Fort Unit 7	500,000	10,200
Beckjord Unit 1	650,000	10,100
East Bend Unit 2	750,000	10,000
Zimmer Unit 1	1,100,000	10,000

For example, Miami Fort Unit 5 must produce 550,000 megawatt-hours of electricity, and 10,500 BTUs are needed to produce each kilowatt-hour.

The transportation cost and the add-on cost in dollars per ton are shown here:

	Transportation Cost ($/ton)				
Supplier	Miami Fort Unit 5	Miami Fort Unit 7	Beckjord Unit 1	East Bend Unit 2	Zimmer Unit 1
RAG	5.00	5.00	4.75	5.00	4.75
Peabody	3.75	3.75	3.50	3.75	3.50
American	3.00	3.00	2.75	3.00	2.75
Consol	3.25	3.25	2.85	3.25	2.85
Cyprus	5.00	5.00	4.75	5.00	4.75
Addington	2.25	2.25	2.00	2.25	2.00
Waterloo	2.00	2.00	1.60	2.00	1.60

Supplier	Add-On Cost ($/ton)				
	Miami Fort Unit 5	Miami Fort Unit 7	Beckjord Unit 1	East Bend Unit 2	Zimmer Unit 1
RAG	10.00	10.00	10.00	5.00	6.00
Peabody	10.00	10.00	11.00	6.00	7.00
American	13.00	13.00	15.00	9.00	9.00
Consol	10.00	10.00	11.00	7.00	7.00
Cyprus	10.00	10.00	10.00	5.00	6.00
Addington	5.00	5.00	6.00	4.00	4.00
Waterloo	11.00	11.00	11.00	7.00	9.00

Managerial Report

Prepare a report that summarizes your recommendations regarding Duke Energy's coal allocation problem. Be sure to include information and analysis for the following issues:

1. Determine how much coal to purchase from each of the mining companies and how it should be allocated to the generating units. What is the cost to purchase, deliver, and process the coal?
2. Compute the average cost of coal in cents per million BTUs for each generating unit (a measure of the cost of fuel for the generating units).
3. Compute the average number of BTUs per pound of coal received at each generating unit (a measure of the energy efficiency of the coal received at each unit).
4. Suppose that Duke Energy can purchase an additional 80,000 tons of coal from American Coal Sales as an "all or nothing deal" for $30 per ton. Should Duke Energy purchase the additional 80,000 tons of coal?
5. Suppose that Duke Energy learns that the energy content of the coal from Cyprus Amax is actually 13,000 BTUs per pound. Should Duke Energy revise its procurement plan?
6. Duke Energy has learned from its trading group that Duke Energy can sell 50,000 megawatt-hours of electricity over the grid (to other electricity suppliers) at a price of $30 per megawatt-hour. Should Duke Energy sell the electricity? If so, which generating units should produce the additional electricity?

Appendix 9.1   Excel Solution of Hewlitt Corporation Financial Planning Problem

In Appendix 7.3 we showed how Excel could be used to solve the RMC linear programming problem. To illustrate the use of Excel in solving a more complex linear programming problem, we show the solution to the Hewlitt Corporation financial planning problem presented in Section 9.2.

The spreadsheet formulation and solution of the Hewlitt Corporation problem are shown in Figure 9.10. As described in Appendix 7.3, our practice is to put the data required for the problem in the top part of the worksheet and build the model in the bottom part of the worksheet. The model consists of a set of cells for the decision variables, a cell for the

FIGURE 9.10   EXCEL SOLUTION FOR THE HEWLITT CORPORATION PROBLEM

WEB file

Hewlitt

	A	B	C	D	E	F	G	H	I	J	K	L
1	**Hewlitt Corporation Cash Requirements**											
2												
3		**Cash**										
4	**Year**	**Rqmt.**				**Bond**						
5	1	430			1	2	3					
6	2	210		**Price ($1000)**	1.15	1	1.35					
7	3	222		**Rate**	0.08875	0.055	0.1175					
8	4	231		**Years to Maturity**	5	6	7					
9	5	240										
10	6	195		**Annual Savings Multiple**		1.04						
11	7	225										
12	8	255										
13												
14	**Model**											
15												
16	F	B1	B2	B3	S1	S2	S3	S4	S5	S6	S7	S8
17	1728.794	144.988	187.856	228.188	636.148	501.606	349.682	182.681	0	0	0	0
18												
19					**Cash Flow**		**Net Cash**		**Cash**			
20	**Min Funds**	1728.7939		**Constraints**	**In**	**Out**	**Flow**		**Rqmt.**			
21				Year 1	1728.794	1298.794	430	=	430			
22				Year 2	711.6057	501.6057	210	=	210			
23				Year 3	571.6818	349.6818	222	=	222			
24				Year 4	413.6809	182.6809	231	=	231			
25				Year 5	240	0	240	=	240			
26				Year 6	195	0	195	=	195			
27				Year 7	225	0	225	=	225			
28				Year 8	255	0	255	=	255			

objective function, a set of cells for the left-hand-side functions, and a set of cells for the right-hand sides of the constraints. The cells for each of these model components are screened; the cells for the decision variables are also enclosed by a boldface line. Descriptive labels are used to make the spreadsheet easy to read.

Formulation

The data and descriptive labels are contained in cells A1:G12. The screened cells in the bottom portion of the spreadsheet contain the key elements of the model required by the Excel Solver.

Decision Variables   Cells A17:L17 are reserved for the decision variables. The optimal values (rounded to three places), are shown to be $F = 1728.794$, $B_1 = 144.988$, $B_2 = 187.856$, $B_3 = 228.188$, $S_1 = 636.148$, $S_2 = 501.606$, $S_3 = 349.682$, $S_4 = 182.681$, and $S_5 = S_6 = S_7 = S_8 = 0$.

Objective Function   The formula $= A17$ has been placed into cell B20 to reflect the total funds required. It is simply the value of the decision variable, F. The total funds required by the optimal solution are shown to be $1,728,794$.

Left-Hand Sides   The left-hand sides for the eight constraints represent the annual net cash flow. They are placed into cells G21:G28.
Cell G21 = E21 − F21 (Copy to G22:G28)

For this problem, some of the left-hand-side cells reference other cells that contain formulas. These referenced cells provide Hewlitt's cash flow in and cash flow out for each of the eight years.[3] The cells and their formulas are as follows:

Cell E21 = A17

Cell E22 = SUMPRODUCT($E$7:$G$7,$B$17:$D$17)+$F$10*E17

Cell E23 = SUMPRODUCT($E$7:$G$7,$B$17:$D$17)+$F$10*F17

Cell E24 = SUMPRODUCT($E$7:$G$7,$B$17:$D$17)+$F$10*G17

Cell E25 = SUMPRODUCT($E$7:$G$7,$B$17:$D$17)+$F$10*H17

Cell E26 = (1+E7)*B17+F7*C17+G7*D17+F10*I17

Cell E27 = (1+F7)*C17+G7*D17+F10*J17

Cell E28 = (1+G7)*D17+F10*K17

Cell F21 = SUMPRODUCT(E6:G6,B17:D17)+E17

Cell F22 = F17

Cell F23 = G17

Cell F24 = H17

Cell F25 = I17

Cell F26 = J17

Cell F27 = K17

Cell F28 = L17

Right-Hand Sides   The right-hand sides for the eight constraints represent the annual cash requirements. They are placed into cells I21:I28.
Cell I21 = B5 (Copy to I22:I28)

Excel Solution

We are now ready to use the information in the worksheet to determine the optimal solution to the Hewlitt Corporation problem. The following steps describe how to use Excel to obtain the optimal solution:

Step 1. Select the **Add-ins** tab on the Ribbon
Step 2. Select **Premium Solver** in the **Menu Commands** group
Step 3. When the **Solver Parameters** dialog box appears (see Figure 9.11):
Make sure **Standard LP Simplex** is displayed
Enter B20 in the **Set Cell** box
Select the **Equal to: Min** option
Enter A17:L17 in the **By Changing Variable Cells** box
Choose **Add**

---

[3]The cash flow in is the sum of the positive terms in each constraint equation in the mathematical model, and the cash flow out is the sum of the negative terms in each constraint equation.

FIGURE 9.11 SOLVER PARAMETERS DIALOG BOX FOR THE HEWLITT CORPORATION PROBLEM

Step 4. When the **Add Constraint** dialog box appears:
Enter G21:G28 in the left-hand box of the **Cell Reference** area
Select =
Enter I21:I28 in the right-hand box
Click **OK**

Step 5. When the **Solver Parameters** dialog box reappears (see Figure 9.11):
Choose **Options**

Step 6. When the **LP Simplex Solver Options** dialog box appears:
Select **Assume Non-Negative**
Click **OK**

Step 7. When the **Solver Parameters** dialog box reappears:
Choose **Solve**

Step 8. When the **Solver Results** dialog box appears:
Select **Keep Solver Solution**
Select **Sensitivity** in the **Reports** box
Click **OK**

The Solver Parameters dialog box is shown in Figure 9.11. The optimal solution is shown in Figure 9.10; the accompanying sensitivity report is shown in Figure 9.12.

Discussion

Figures 9.10 and 9.12 contain essentially the same information as that provided by The Management Scientist solution in Figure 9.4. Recall that the Excel sensitivity report uses the term *shadow price* to describe the *change* in value of the solution per unit increase in the right-hand side of a constraint. The Management Scientist and LINGO use the term *dual price* to describe the *improvement* in value of the solution per unit increase in the right-hand

FIGURE 9.12   EXCEL'S SENSITIVITY REPORT FOR THE HEWLITT
CORPORATION PROBLEM

Adjustable Cells

Cell	Name	Final Value	Reduced Cost	Objective Coefficient	Allowable Increase	Allowable Decrease
$A$17	F	1728.793855	0	1	1E + 30	1
$B$17	B1	144.9881496	0	0	0.067026339	0.013026775
$C$17	B2	187.8558478	0	0	0.012795531	0.020273774
$D$17	B3	228.1879195	0	0	0.022906851	0.749663022
$E$17	S1	636.1479438	0	0	0.109559907	0.05507386
$F$17	S2	501.605712	0	0	0.143307365	0.056948823
$G$17	S3	349.681791	0	0	0.210854199	0.059039182
$H$17	S4	182.680913	0	0	0.413598622	0.061382404
$I$17	S5	0	0.064025159	0	1E + 30	0.064025159
$J$17	S6	0	0.012613604	0	1E + 30	0.012613604
$K$17	S7	0	0.021318233	0	1E + 30	0.021318233
$L$17	S8	0	0.670839393	0	1E + 30	0.670839393

Constraints

Cell	Name	Final Value	Shadow Price	Constraint R.H. Side	Allowable Increase	Allowable Decrease
$G$21	Year 1 Flow	430	1	430	1E + 30	1728.793855
$G$22	Year 2 Flow	210	0.961538462	210	1E + 30	661.5938616
$G$23	Year 3 Flow	222	0.924556213	222	1E + 30	521.6699405
$G$24	Year 4 Flow	231	0.888996359	231	1E + 30	363.6690626
$G$25	Year 5 Flow	240	0.854804191	240	1E + 30	189.9881496
$G$26	Year 6 Flow	195	0.760364454	195	2149.927647	157.8558478
$G$27	Year 7 Flow	225	0.718991202	225	3027.962172	198.1879195
$G$28	Year 8 Flow	255	0.670839393	255	1583.881915	255

side of a constraint. For maximization problems, the shadow price and dual price are the same; for minimization problems, the shadow price and dual price have opposite signs. Because the Hewlitt financial planning problem involves minimization, the shadow prices in the Excel sensitivity report (Figure 9.12) are the negative of the dual prices in The Management Scientist solution (Figure 9.4).

CHAPTER 10

Distribution and Network Models

The models discussed in this chapter belong to a special class of linear programming problems called *network flow* problems. Five different problems are considered:

- Transportation problem
- Assignment problem
- Transshipment problem
- Shortest-route problem
- Maximal flow problem

A separate chapter is devoted to these problems because of the similarity in the problem structure and solution procedure. In each case, we present a graphical representation of the problem in the form of a *network*. We then show how the problem can be formulated and solved as a linear program. In the last section of the chapter we present a production and inventory problem that is an interesting application of the transshipment problem.

 # Transportation Problem

The **transportation problem** arises frequently in planning for the distribution of goods and services from several supply locations to several demand locations. Typically, the quantity of goods available at each supply location (origin) is limited, and the quantity of goods needed at each of several demand locations (destinations) is known. The usual objective in a transportation problem is to minimize the cost of shipping goods from the origins to the destinations.

Let us illustrate by considering a transportation problem faced by Foster Generators. This problem involves the transportation of a product from three plants to four distribution centers. Foster Generators operates plants in Cleveland, Ohio; Bedford, Indiana; and York, Pennsylvania. Production capacities over the next three-month planning period for one particular type of generator are as follows:

Origin	Plant	Three-Month Production Capacity (units)
1	Cleveland	5,000
2	Bedford	6,000
3	York	2,500
	Total	13,500

The firm distributes its generators through four regional distribution centers located in Boston, Chicago, St. Louis, and Lexington; the three-month forecast of demand for the distribution centers is as follows:

Destination	Distribution Center	Three-Month Demand Forecast (units)
1	Boston	6,000
2	Chicago	4,000
3	St. Louis	2,000
4	Lexington	1,500
	Total	13,500

FIGURE 10.1   THE NETWORK REPRESENTATION OF THE FOSTER GENERATORS
TRANSPORTATION PROBLEM

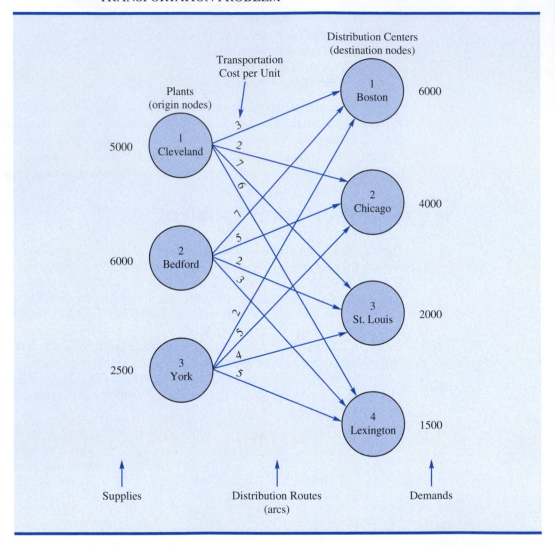

Management would like to determine how much of its production should be shipped
from each plant to each distribution center. Figure 10.1 shows graphically the 12 distribution routes Foster can use. Such a graph is called a **network**; the circles are referred to as
nodes and the lines connecting the nodes as **arcs**. Each origin and destination is represented
by a node, and each possible shipping route is represented by an arc. The amount of the supply is written next to each origin node, and the amount of the demand is written next to each
destination node. The goods shipped from the origins to the destinations represent the flow
in the network. Note that the direction of flow (from origin to destination) is indicated by
the arrows.

*Try Problem 1 for practice
in developing a network
model of a transportation
problem.*

For Foster's transportation problem, the objective is to determine the routes to be used
and the quantity to be shipped via each route that will provide the minimum total transportation cost. The cost for each unit shipped on each route is given in Table 10.1 and is
shown on each arc in Figure 10.1.

TABLE 10.1 TRANSPORTATION COST PER UNIT FOR THE FOSTER GENERATORS TRANSPORTATION PROBLEM

	Destination			
Origin	**Boston**	**Chicago**	**St. Louis**	**Lexington**
Cleveland	3	2	7	6
Bedford	7	5	2	3
York	2	5	4	5

The first subscript identifies the "from" node of the corresponding arc and the second subscript identifies the "to" node of the arc.

A linear programming model can be used to solve this transportation problem. We use double-subscripted decision variables, with x_{11} denoting the number of units shipped from origin 1 (Cleveland) to destination 1 (Boston), x_{12} denoting the number of units shipped from origin 1 (Cleveland) to destination 2 (Chicago), and so on. In general, the decision variables for a transportation problem having m origins and n destinations are written as follows:

$$x_{ij} = \text{number of units shipped from origin } i \text{ to destination } j$$
$$\text{where } i = 1, 2, \ldots, m \text{ and } j = 1, 2, \ldots, n$$

Because the objective of the transportation problem is to minimize the total transportation cost, we can use the cost data in Table 10.1 or on the arcs in Figure 10.1 to develop the following cost expressions:

Transportation costs for
units shipped from Cleveland $= 3x_{11} + 2x_{12} + 7x_{13} + 6x_{14}$

Transportation costs for
units shipped from Bedford $= 7x_{21} + 5x_{22} + 2x_{23} + 3x_{24}$

Transportation costs for
units shipped from York $= 2x_{31} + 5x_{32} + 4x_{33} + 5x_{34}$

The sum of these expressions provides the objective function showing the total transportation cost for Foster Generators.

Transportation problems need constraints because each origin has a limited supply and each destination has a demand requirement. We consider the supply constraints first. The capacity at the Cleveland plant is 5000 units. With the total number of units shipped from the Cleveland plant expressed as $x_{11} + x_{12} + x_{13} + x_{14}$, the supply constraint for the Cleveland plant is

$$x_{11} + x_{12} + x_{13} + x_{14} \leq 5000 \text{ Cleveland supply}$$

With three origins (plants), the Foster transportation problem has three supply constraints. Given the capacity of 6000 units at the Bedford plant and 2500 units at the York plant, the two additional supply constraints are

$$x_{21} + x_{22} + x_{23} + x_{24} \leq 6000 \text{ Bedford supply}$$
$$x_{31} + x_{32} + x_{33} + x_{34} \leq 2500 \text{ York supply}$$

With the four distribution centers as the destinations, four demand constraints are needed to ensure that destination demands will be satisfied:

$$x_{11} + x_{21} + x_{31} = 6000 \quad \text{Boston demand}$$
$$x_{12} + x_{22} + x_{32} = 4000 \quad \text{Chicago demand}$$
$$x_{13} + x_{23} + x_{33} = 2000 \quad \text{St. Louis demand}$$
$$x_{14} + x_{24} + x_{34} = 1500 \quad \text{Lexington demand}$$

To obtain a feasible solution, the total supply must be greater than or equal to the total demand.

Combining the objective function and constraints into one model provides a 12-variable, 7-constraint linear programming formulation of the Foster Generators transportation problem:

$$\text{Min} \quad 3x_{11} + 2x_{12} + 7x_{13} + 6x_{14} + 7x_{21} + 5x_{22} + 2x_{23} + 3x_{24} + 2x_{31} + 5x_{32} + 4x_{33} + 5x_{34}$$

s.t.

$$
\begin{aligned}
x_{11} + x_{12} + x_{13} + x_{14} && &\leq 5000 \\
x_{21} + x_{22} + x_{23} + x_{24} && &\leq 6000 \\
x_{31} + x_{32} + x_{33} + x_{34} && &\leq 2500 \\
x_{11} \qquad\qquad + x_{21} \qquad\qquad + x_{31} \qquad\qquad && &= 6000 \\
x_{12} \qquad\qquad + x_{22} \qquad\qquad + x_{32} \qquad\qquad && &= 4000 \\
x_{13} \qquad\qquad + x_{23} \qquad\qquad + x_{33} \qquad && &= 2000 \\
x_{14} \qquad\qquad + x_{24} \qquad\qquad + x_{34} && &= 1500 \\
\end{aligned}
$$

$$x_{ij} \geq 0 \quad \text{for } i = 1, 2, 3 \text{ and } j = 1, 2, 3, 4$$

Comparing the linear programming formulation to the network in Figure 10.1 leads to several observations. All the information needed for the linear programming formulation is on the network. Each node has one constraint and each arc has one variable. The sum of the variables corresponding to arcs from an origin node must be less than or equal to the origin's supply, and the sum of the variables corresponding to the arcs into a destination node must be equal to the destination's demand.

Can you now use the computer software to solve a linear programming model of a transportation problem? Try Problem 2.

We solved the Foster Generators problem with the linear programming module of The Management Scientist. The computer solution (see Figure 10.2) shows that the minimum total transportation cost is $39,500. The values for the decision variables show the optimal amounts to ship over each route. For example, with $x_{11} = 3500$, 3500 units should be shipped from Cleveland to Boston, and with $x_{12} = 1500$, 1500 units should be shipped from Cleveland to Chicago. Other values of the decision variables indicate the remaining shipping quantities and routes. Table 10.2 shows the minimum cost transportation schedule and Figure 10.3 summarizes the optimal solution on the network.

Problem Variations

The Foster Generators problem illustrates use of the basic transportation model. Variations of the basic transportation model may involve one or more of the following situations:

1. Total supply not equal to total demand
2. Maximization objective function
3. Route capacities or route minimums
4. Unacceptable routes

With slight modifications in the linear programming model, we can easily accommodate these situations.

FIGURE 10.2 THE MANAGEMENT SCIENTIST SOLUTION FOR THE FOSTER
GENERATORS TRANSPORTATION PROBLEM

```
Objective Function Value =              39500.000
         Variable              Value              Reduced Costs
      --------------     ----------------      ------------------
           X11              3500.000                0.000
           X12              1500.000                0.000
           X13                 0.000                8.000
           X14                 0.000                6.000
           X21                 0.000                1.000
           X22              2500.000                0.000
           X23              2000.000                0.000
           X24              1500.000                0.000
           X31              2500.000                0.000
           X32                 0.000                4.000
           X33                 0.000                6.000
           X34                 0.000                6.000
```

WEB file

Foster

TABLE 10.2 OPTIMAL SOLUTION TO THE FOSTER GENERATORS
TRANSPORTATION PROBLEM

Route		Units	Cost	Total
From	To	Shipped	per Unit	Cost
Cleveland	Boston	3500	$3	$10,500
Cleveland	Chicago	1500	$2	3,000
Bedford	Chicago	2500	$5	12,500
Bedford	St. Louis	2000	$2	4,000
Bedford	Lexington	1500	$3	4,500
York	Boston	2500	$2	5,000
				$39,500

Total Supply Not Equal to Total Demand Often *the total supply is not equal to the total demand.* If total supply exceeds total demand, no modification in the linear programming formulation is necessary. Excess supply will appear as slack in the linear programming solution. Slack for any particular origin can be interpreted as the unused supply or amount not shipped from the origin.

Whenever total supply is less than total demand, the model does not determine how the unsatisfied demand is handled (e.g., backorders). The manager must handle this aspect of the problem.

If total supply is less than total demand, the linear programming model of a transportation problem will not have a feasible solution. In this case, we modify the network representation by adding a **dummy origin** with a supply equal to the difference between the total demand and the total supply. With the addition of the dummy origin and an arc from the dummy origin to each destination, the linear programming model will have a feasible solution. A zero cost per unit is assigned to each arc leaving the dummy origin so that the value of the optimal solution for the revised problem will represent the shipping cost for the units actually shipped (no shipments actually will be made from the dummy origin). When the optimal solution is implemented, the destinations showing shipments being

FIGURE 10.3   OPTIMAL SOLUTION TO THE FOSTER GENERATORS
TRANSPORTATION PROBLEM

received from the dummy origin will be the destinations experiencing a shortfall or unsatisfied demand.

Try Problem 6 for practice with a case in which demand is greater than supply with a maximization objective.

Maximization Objective Function   In some transportation problems, the objective is to find a solution that maximizes profit or revenue. Using the values for profit or revenue per unit as coefficients in the objective function, we simply solve a maximization rather than a minimization linear program. This change does not affect the constraints.

Route Capacities or Route Minimums   The linear programming formulation of the transportation problem also can accommodate capacities or minimum quantities for one or more of the routes. For example, suppose that in the Foster Generators problem the York–Boston route (origin 3 to destination 1) had a capacity of 1000 units because of limited space availability on its normal mode of transportation. With x_{31} denoting the amount shipped from York to Boston, the route capacity constraint for the York–Boston route would be

$$x_{31} \leq 1000$$

Similarly, route minimums can be specified. For example,

$$x_{22} \leq 2000$$

would guarantee that a previously committed order for a Bedford–Chicago delivery of at least 2000 units would be maintained in the optimal solution.

Unacceptable Routes Finally, establishing a route from every origin to every destination may not be possible. To handle this situation, we simply drop the corresponding arc from the network and remove the corresponding variable from the linear programming formulation. For example, if the Cleveland–St. Louis route were unacceptable or unusable, the arc from Cleveland to St. Louis could be dropped in Figure 10.1, and x_{13} could be removed from the linear programming formulation. Solving the resulting 11-variable, 7-constraint model would provide the optimal solution while guaranteeing that the Cleveland–St. Louis route is not used.

A General Linear Programming Model

To show the general linear programming model for a transportation problem with m origins and n destinations, we use the notation:

$$x_{ij} = \text{number of units shipped from origin } i \text{ to destination } j$$
$$c_{ij} = \text{cost per unit of shipping from origin } i \text{ to destination } j$$
$$s_i = \text{supply or capacity in units at origin } i$$
$$d_j = \text{demand in units at destination } j$$

The general linear programming model is as follows:

$$\text{Min} \quad \sum_{i=1}^{m} \sum_{j=1}^{n} c_{ij} x_{ij}$$

s.t.

$$\sum_{j=1}^{n} x_{ij} \leq s_i \quad i = 1, 2, \ldots, m \quad \text{Supply}$$

$$\sum_{i=1}^{m} x_{ij} = d_j \quad j = 1, 2, \ldots, n \quad \text{Demand}$$

$$x_{ij} \geq 0 \quad \text{for all } i \text{ and } j$$

As mentioned previously, we can add constraints of the form $x_{ij} \leq L_{ij}$ if the route from origin i to destination j has capacity L_{ij}. A transportation problem that includes constraints of this type is called a **capacitated transportation problem**. Similarly, we can add route minimum constraints of the form $x_{ij} \geq M_{ij}$ if the route from origin i to destination j must handle at least M_{ij} units.

NOTES AND COMMENTS

1. Transportation problems encountered in practice usually lead to large linear programs. Transportation problems with 100 origins and 100 destinations are not unusual. Such a problem would involve $(100)(100) = 10{,}000$ variables.

2. To handle a situation in which some routes may be unacceptable, we stated that you could drop the corresponding arc from the network and remove the corresponding variable from the linear programming formulation. Another approach often used is to assign an extremely large objective function cost coefficient to any unacceptable arc. If the problem has already been formulated, another option is to add a constraint to the formulation that sets the variable you want to remove equal to zero.

3. The optimal solution to a transportation model will consist of integer values for the decision variables as long as all supply and demand values are integers. The reason is the special mathematical structure of the linear programming model. Each variable appears in exactly one supply and one demand constraint, and all coefficients in the constraint equations are 1 or 0.

4. Although many transportation problems involve minimizing the cost of transporting goods between locations, many other applications of the transportation model exist. The Q.M. in Action, Mobilization at the U.S. Marine Corps, illustrates the use of a transportation model to send Marine Corps officers to billets.

Q.M. *in* ACTION

*MOBILIZATION AT THE U.S. MARINE CORPS**

The U.S. Marine Corps developed a network model for mobilizing its officers in the event of a world crisis or war. The problem is to send officers to billets (duty assignments) as quickly as possible. The model developed to solve this problem is a transportation model much like the ones discussed in this section, only much larger. The origins or supply nodes represent the officers available, and the destinations or demand nodes represent the billets. A realistic implementation might involve as many as 40,000 officers and 25,000 billets. If all officer-to-billet arc combinations are permitted, the transportation problem would have 1 billion arcs. To reduce the problem

size, officers with similar qualifications are aggregated into the same supply node, and similar duty assignments are aggregated into the same demand nodes. Using this approach and methods for eliminating infeasible arcs, the Marine Corps has solved problems involving 27,000 officers and 10,000 billets in 10 seconds on a personal computer.

Excellent results in sending officers of appropriate grade and job qualifications to the desired billets have been obtained. In a crisis, the availability and use of this system can make the difference between an appropriate response and disaster. The prior system required two to four days to produce a complete mobilization plan and provided a lower quality match between officer qualifications and billet needs. The Marine Corps is now using the mobilization model to enhance its peacetime capability.

*Based on D. O. Bausch, G. G. Brown, D. R. Hundley, S. H. Rapp, and R. E. Rosenthal, "Mobilizing Marine Corps Officers," *Interfaces* (July/August 1991): 26–38.

10.2 Assignment Problem

The **assignment problem** arises in a variety of decision-making situations; typical assignment problems involve assigning jobs to machines, agents to tasks, sales personnel to sales territories, contracts to bidders, and so on. A distinguishing feature of the assignment problem is that *one* agent is assigned to *one and only one* task. Specifically, we look for the set

TABLE 10.3   ESTIMATED PROJECT COMPLETION TIMES (DAYS) FOR THE FOWLE MARKETING RESEARCH ASSIGNMENT PROBLEM

	Client		
Project Leader	**1**	**2**	**3**
1. Terry	10	15	9
2. Carle	9	18	5
3. McClymonds	6	14	3

of assignments that will optimize a stated objective, such as minimize cost, minimize time, or maximize profits.

To illustrate the assignment problem, let us consider the case of Fowle Marketing Research, which has just received requests for market research studies from three new clients. The company faces the task of assigning a project leader (agent) to each client (task). Currently, three individuals have no other commitments and are available for the project leader assignments. Fowle's management realizes, however, that the time required to complete each study will depend on the experience and ability of the project leader assigned. The three projects have approximately the same priority, and management wants to assign project leaders to minimize the total number of days required to complete all three projects. If a project leader is to be assigned to one client only, what assignments should be made?

To answer the assignment question, Fowle's management must first consider all possible project leader–client assignments and then estimate the corresponding project completion times. With three project leaders and three clients, nine assignment alternatives are possible. The alternatives and the estimated project completion times in days are summarized in Table 10.3.

Figure 10.4 shows the network representation of Fowle's assignment problem. The nodes correspond to the project leaders and clients, and the arcs represent the possible assignments of project leaders to clients. The supply at each origin node and the demand at each destination node are 1; the cost of assigning a project leader to a client is the time it takes that project leader to complete the client's task. Note the similarity between the network models of the assignment problem (Figure 10.4) and the transportation problem (Figure 10.1). The assignment problem is a special case of the transportation problem in which all supply and demand values equal 1, and the amount shipped over each arc is either 0 or 1.

Try Problem 9, part (a), for practice in developing a network model for an assignment problem.

Because the assignment problem is a special case of the transportation problem, a linear programming formulation can be developed. Again, we need a constraint for each node and a variable for each arc. As in the transportation problem, we use double-subscripted decision variables, with x_{11} denoting the assignment of project leader 1 (Terry) to client 1, x_{12} denoting the assignment of project leader 1 (Terry) to client 2, and so on. Thus, we define the decision variables for Fowle's assignment problem as

The assignment problem is a special case of the transportation problem.

$$x_{ij} = \begin{cases} 1 & \text{if project leader } i \text{ is assigned to client } j \\ 0 & \text{otherwise} \end{cases}$$

where $i = 1, 2, 3$, and $j = 1, 2, 3$

Using this notation and the completion time data in Table 10.3, we develop completion time expressions:

Days required for Terry's assignment $\qquad = 10x_{11} + 15x_{12} + 9x_{13}$

Days required for Carle's assignment $\qquad = 9x_{21} + 18x_{22} + 5x_{23}$

Days required for McClymonds's assignment $= 6x_{31} + 14x_{32} + 3x_{33}$

FIGURE 10.4   A NETWORK MODEL OF THE FOWLE MARKETING RESEARCH ASSIGNMENT PROBLEM

The sum of the completion times for the three project leaders will provide the total days required to complete the three assignments. Thus, the objective function is

$$\text{Min } 10x_{11} + 15x_{12} + 9x_{13} + 9x_{21} + 18x_{22} + 5x_{23} + 6x_{31} + 14x_{32} + 3x_{33}$$

Because the number of project leaders equals the number of clients, all the constraints could be written as equalities. But when the number of project leaders exceeds the number of clients, less-than-or-equal-to constraints must be used for the project leader constraints.

The constraints for the assignment problem reflect the conditions that each project leader can be assigned to at most one client and that each client must have one assigned project leader. These constraints are written as follows:

$$x_{11} + x_{12} + x_{13} \leq 1 \text{ Terry's assignment}$$
$$x_{21} + x_{22} + x_{23} \leq 1 \text{ Carle's assignment}$$
$$x_{31} + x_{32} + x_{33} \leq 1 \text{ McClymonds's assignment}$$
$$x_{11} + x_{21} + x_{31} = 1 \text{ Client 1}$$
$$x_{12} + x_{22} + x_{32} = 1 \text{ Client 2}$$
$$x_{13} + x_{23} + x_{33} = 1 \text{ Client 3}$$

Note that each node in Figure 10.4 has one constraint.

Combining the objective function and constraints into one model provides the following 9-variable, 6-constraint linear programming model of the Fowle Marketing Research assignment problem:

Try Problem 9, part (b), for practice in formulating and solving a linear programming model for an assignment problem on the computer.

$$\text{Min} \quad 10x_{11} + 15x_{12} + 9x_{13} + 9x_{21} + 18x_{22} + 5x_{23} + 6x_{31} + 14x_{32} + 3x_{33}$$

s.t.

$$
\begin{array}{llllll}
x_{11} + & x_{12} + & x_{13} & & & \le 1 \\
& x_{21} + & x_{22} + & x_{23} & & \le 1 \\
& & & x_{31} + & x_{32} + x_{33} & \le 1 \\
x_{11} & & + x_{21} & & + x_{31} & = 1 \\
& x_{12} & & + x_{22} & & + x_{32} = 1 \\
& & x_{13} & & + x_{23} & + x_{33} = 1
\end{array}
$$

$$x_{ij} \ge 0 \quad \text{for } i = 1, 2, 3; \, j = 1, 2, 3$$

Figure 10.5 shows the computer solution for this model. Terry is assigned to client 2 ($x_{12} = 1$), Carle is assigned to client 3 ($x_{23} = 1$), and McClymonds is assigned to client 1 ($x_{31} = 1$). The total completion time required is 26 days. This solution is summarized in Table 10.4.

FIGURE 10.5   THE MANAGEMENT SCIENTIST SOLUTION FOR THE FOWLE MARKETING RESEARCH ASSIGNMENT PROBLEM

WEB file

Fowle

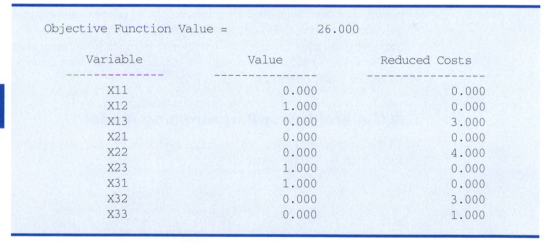

```
Objective Function Value =              26.000

        Variable              Value              Reduced Costs
     ---------------     ---------------      ------------------
          X11               0.000                  0.000
          X12               1.000                  0.000
          X13               0.000                  3.000
          X21               0.000                  0.000
          X22               0.000                  4.000
          X23               1.000                  0.000
          X31               1.000                  0.000
          X32               0.000                  3.000
          X33               0.000                  1.000
```

TABLE 10.4   OPTIMAL PROJECT LEADER ASSIGNMENTS FOR THE FOWLE MARKETING RESEARCH ASSIGNMENT PROBLEM

Project Leader	Assigned Client	Days
Terry	2	15
Carle	3	5
McClymonds	1	6
Total		26

Problem Variations

Because the assignment problem can be viewed as a special case of the transportation problem, the problem variations that may arise in an assignment problem parallel those for the transportation problem. Specifically, we can handle

1. Total number of agents (supply) not equal to the total number of tasks (demand)
2. A maximization objective function
3. Unacceptable assignments

The situation in which the number of agents does not equal the number of tasks is analogous to total supply not equaling total demand in a transportation problem. If the number of agents exceeds the number of tasks, the extra agents simply remain unassigned in the linear programming solution. If the number of tasks exceeds the number of agents, the linear programming model will not have a feasible solution. In this situation, a simple modification is to add enough dummy agents to equalize the number of agents and the number of tasks. For instance, in the Fowle problem we might have had five clients (tasks) and only three project leaders (agents). By adding two dummy project leaders, we can create a new assignment problem with the number of project leaders equal to the number of clients. The objective function coefficients for the assignment of dummy project leaders would be zero so that the value of the optimal solution would represent the total number of days required by the assignments actually made (no assignments will actually be made to the clients receiving dummy project leaders).

If the assignment alternatives are evaluated in terms of revenue or profit rather than time or cost, the linear programming formulation can be solved as a maximization rather than a minimization problem. In addition, if one or more assignments are unacceptable, the corresponding decision variable can be removed from the linear programming formulation. This situation could happen, for example, if an agent did not have the experience necessary for one or more of the tasks.

A General Linear Programming Model

To show the general linear programming model for an assignment problem with m agents and n tasks, we use the notation:

$$x_{ij} = \begin{cases} 1 & \text{if agent } i \text{ is assigned to task } j \\ 0 & \text{otherwise} \end{cases}$$

$$c_{ij} = \text{the cost of assigning agent } i \text{ to task } j$$

The general linear programming model is as follows:

$$\text{Min} \quad \sum_{i=1}^{m} \sum_{j=1}^{n} c_{ij} x_{ij}$$

s.t.

$$\sum_{j=1}^{n} x_{ij} \leq 1 \quad i = 1, 2, \ldots, m \quad \text{Agents}$$

$$\sum_{i=1}^{m} x_{ij} = 1 \quad j = 1, 2, \ldots, n \quad \text{Tasks}$$

$$x_{ij} \geq 0 \quad \text{for all } i \text{ and } j$$

At the beginning of this section, we indicated that a distinguishing feature of the assignment problem is that *one* agent is assigned to *one and only one* task. In generalizations of the assignment problem where one agent can be assigned to two or more tasks, the linear programming formulation of the problem can be easily modified. For example, let us assume that in the Fowle Marketing Research problem Terry could be assigned up to two clients; in this case, the constraint representing Terry's assignment would be $x_{11} + x_{12} + x_{13} \leq 2$. In general, if a_i denotes the upper limit for the number of tasks to which agent i can be assigned, we write the agent constraints as

$$\sum_{j=1}^{n} x_{ij} \leq a_i \qquad i = 1, 2, \ldots, m$$

If some tasks require more than one agent, the linear programming formulation can also accommodate the situation. Use the number of agents required as the right-hand side of the appropriate task constraint.

NOTES AND COMMENTS

1. As noted, the assignment model is a special case of the transportation model. We stated in the notes and comments at the end of the preceding section that the optimal solution to the transportation problem will consist of integer values for the decision variables as long as the supplies and demands are integers. For the assignment problem, all supplies and demands equal 1; thus, the optimal solution must be integer valued and the integer values must be 0 or 1.

2. Combining the method for handling multiple assignments with the notion of a dummy agent provides another means of dealing with situations when the number of tasks exceeds the number of agents. That is, we add one dummy agent but provide the dummy agent with the capability to handle multiple tasks. The number of tasks the dummy agent can handle is equal to the difference between the number of tasks and the number of agents.

3. The Q.M. in Action, Assigning Project Managers at Heery International, describes how managers are assigned to construction projects. The application involves multiple assignments.

Q.M. *in* ACTION

ASSIGNING PROJECT MANAGERS AT HEERY INTERNATIONAL*

Heery International contracts with the State of Tennessee and others for a variety of construction projects including higher education facilities, hotels, and park facilities. At any particular time, Heery typically has more than 100 ongoing projects. Each of these projects must be assigned a single manager. With seven managers available, it means that more than 700 = 7(100) assignments are possible. Assisted by an outside consultant, Heery International developed a mathematical model for assigning construction managers to projects.

The assignment problem developed by Heery uses 0–1 decision variables for each manager/project pair, just as in the assignment problem discussed previously. The goal in assigning managers is to balance the workload among managers and, at the same time, to minimize travel cost from the manager's home to the construction site. Thus, an objective function coefficient for each possible assignment was developed that combined project intensity (a function of the size of the project budget) with the

*Based on Larry J. LeBlanc, Dale Randels, Jr., and T. K. Swann, "Heery International's Spreadsheet Optimization Model for Assigning Managers to Construction Projects," *Interfaces* (November/December 2000): 95–106.

(continued)

travel distance from the manager's home to the construction site. The objective function calls for minimizing the sum over all possible assignments of the product of these coefficients with the assignment variables.

With more construction projects than managers, it was necessary to consider a variation of the standard assignment problem involving multiple assignments. Of the two sets of constraints, one set enforces the requirement that each project receive one and only one manager. The other set of constraints limits the number of assignments each

manager can accept by placing an upper bound on the total intensity that is acceptable over all projects assigned.

Heery International implemented this assignment model with considerable success. According to Emory F. Redden, a Heery vice president, "The optimization model . . . has been very helpful for assigning managers to projects. . . . We have been satisfied with the assignments chosen at the Nashville office. . . . We look forward to using the model in our Atlanta office and elsewhere in the Heery organization."

 ## 10.3 Transshipment Problem

The **transshipment problem** is an extension of the transportation problem in which intermediate nodes, referred to as *transshipment nodes,* are added to account for locations such as warehouses. In this more general type of distribution problem, shipments may be made between any pair of the three general types of nodes: origin nodes, transshipment nodes, and destination nodes. For example, the transshipment problem permits shipments of goods from origins to intermediate nodes and on to destinations, from one origin to another origin, from one intermediate location to another, from one destination location to another, and directly from origins to destinations.

As was true for the transportation problem, the supply available at each origin is limited, and the demand at each destination is specified. The objective in the transshipment problem is to determine how many units should be shipped over each arc in the network so that all destination demands are satisfied with the minimum possible transportation cost.

Try Problem 17, part (a), for practice in developing a network representation of a transshipment problem.

Let us consider the transshipment problem faced by Ryan Electronics. Ryan is an electronics company with production facilities in Denver and Atlanta. Components produced at either facility may be shipped to either of the firm's regional warehouses, which are located in Kansas City and Louisville. From the regional warehouses, the firm supplies retail outlets in Detroit, Miami, Dallas, and New Orleans. The key features of the problem are shown in the network model depicted in Figure 10.6. Note that the supply at each origin and demand at each destination are shown in the left and right margins, respectively. Nodes 1 and 2 are the origin nodes; nodes 3 and 4 are the transshipment nodes; and nodes 5, 6, 7, and 8 are the destination nodes. The transportation cost per unit for each distribution route is shown in Table 10.5 and on the arcs of the network model in Figure 10.6.

As with the transportation and assignment problems, we can formulate a linear programming model of the transshipment problem from a network representation. Again, we need a constraint for each node and a variable for each arc. Let x_{ij} denote the number of units shipped from node i to node j. For example, x_{13} denotes the number of units shipped from the Denver plant to the Kansas City warehouse, x_{14} denotes the number of units shipped from the Denver plant to the Louisville warehouse, and so on. Because the supply at the Denver plant is 600 units, the amount shipped from the Denver plant must be less than or equal to 600. Mathematically, we write this supply constraint as

$$x_{13} + x_{14} \leq 600$$

FIGURE 10.6   NETWORK REPRESENTATION OF THE RYAN ELECTRONICS TRANSSHIPMENT PROBLEM

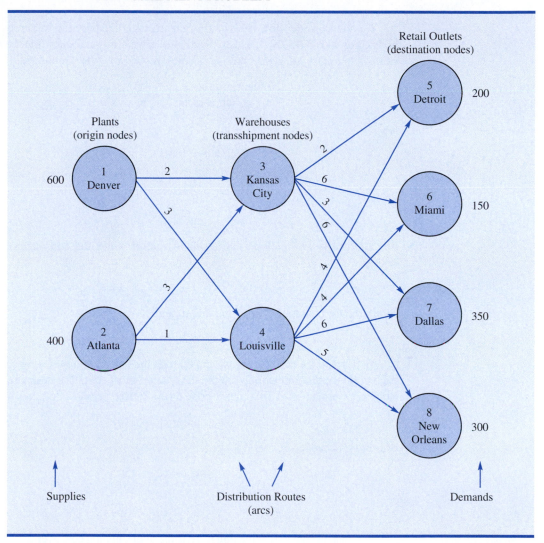

TABLE 10.5   TRANSPORTATION COST PER UNIT FOR THE RYAN ELECTRONICS TRANSSHIPMENT PROBLEM

	Warehouse	
Plant	**Kansas City**	**Louisville**
Denver	2	3
Atlanta	3	1

	Retail Outlet			
Warehouse	**Detroit**	**Miami**	**Dallas**	**New Orleans**
Kansas City	2	6	3	6
Louisville	4	4	6	5

Similarly, for the Atlanta plant we have

$$x_{23} + x_{24} \leq 400$$

We now consider how to write the constraints corresponding to the two transshipment nodes. For node 3 (the Kansas City warehouse), we must guarantee that the number of units shipped out must equal the number of units shipped into the warehouse. If

$$\text{Number of units} \\ \text{shipped out of node 3} = x_{35} + x_{36} + x_{37} + x_{38}$$

and

$$\text{Number of units} \\ \text{shipped into node 3} = x_{13} + x_{23}$$

we obtain

$$x_{35} + x_{36} + x_{37} + x_{38} = x_{13} + x_{23}$$

Placing all the variables on the left-hand side provides the constraint corresponding to node 3 as

$$- x_{13} - x_{23} + x_{35} + x_{36} + x_{37} + x_{38} = 0$$

Similarly, the constraint corresponding to node 4 is

$$- x_{14} - x_{24} + x_{45} + x_{46} + x_{47} + x_{48} = 0$$

To develop the constraints associated with the destination nodes, we recognize that for each node the amount shipped to the destination must equal the demand. For example, to satisfy the demand for 200 units at node 5 (the Detroit retail outlet), we write

$$x_{35} + x_{45} = 200$$

Similarly, for nodes 6, 7, and 8, we have

$$x_{36} + x_{46} = 150$$
$$x_{37} + x_{47} = 350$$
$$x_{38} + x_{48} = 300$$

Try Problem 17, parts (b) and (c), for practice in developing the linear programming model and in solving a transshipment problem on the computer.

As usual, the objective function reflects the total shipping cost over the 12 shipping routes. Combining the objective function and constraints leads to a 12-variable, 8-constraint linear programming model of the Ryan Electronics transshipment problem (see Figure 10.7). We used the linear programming module of The Management Scientist to obtain the optimal solution. Figure 10.8 shows the computer output, and Table 10.6 summarizes the optimal solution.

As mentioned at the beginning of this section, in the transshipment problem, arcs may connect any pair of nodes. All such shipping patterns are possible in a transshipment problem. We still require only one constraint per node, but the constraint must include a variable for every arc entering or leaving the node. For origin nodes, the sum of the shipments out minus the sum of the shipments in must be less than or equal to the origin supply. For destination nodes, the sum of the shipments in minus the sum of the shipments out must equal demand. For transshipment nodes, the sum of the shipments out must equal the sum of the shipments in, as before.

For an illustration of this more general type of transshipment problem, let us modify the Ryan Electronics problem. Suppose that it is possible to ship directly from Atlanta to

FIGURE 10.7 LINEAR PROGRAMMING FORMULATION OF THE RYAN ELECTRONICS TRANSSHIPMENT PROBLEM

$$\text{Min } 2x_{13} + 3x_{14} + 3x_{23} + 1x_{24} + 2x_{35} + 6x_{36} + 3x_{37} + 6x_{38} + 4x_{45} + 4x_{46} + 6x_{47} + 5x_{48}$$

s.t.

$$
\begin{array}{llll}
x_{13} + x_{14} & & \leq 600 & \left.\rule{0pt}{16pt}\right\} \text{Origin node} \\
\quad x_{23} + x_{24} & & \leq 400 & \text{constraints} \\
-x_{13} \quad - x_{23} \quad + x_{35} + x_{36} + x_{37} + x_{38} & = 0 & \left.\rule{0pt}{16pt}\right\} \text{Transshipment node} \\
\quad - x_{14} \quad - x_{24} \quad + x_{45} + x_{46} + x_{47} + x_{48} & = 0 & \text{constraints} \\
x_{35} \quad + x_{45} & = 200 & \left.\rule{0pt}{26pt}\right\} \\
x_{36} \quad + x_{46} & = 150 & \text{Destination node} \\
x_{37} \quad + x_{47} & = 350 & \text{constraints} \\
x_{38} \quad + x_{48} & = 300 &
\end{array}
$$

$x_{ij} \geq 0$ for all i and j

FIGURE 10.8 THE MANAGEMENT SCIENTIST SOLUTION FOR THE RYAN ELECTRONICS TRANSSHIPMENT PROBLEM

WEB file

Ryan

```
Objective Function Value =            5200.000

       Variable              Value              Reduced Costs
     ------------         ------------         --------------
        X13                 550.000                0.000
        X14                  50.000                0.000
        X23                   0.000                3.000
        X24                 400.000                0.000
        X35                 200.000                0.000
        X36                   0.000                1.000
        X37                 350.000                0.000
        X38                   0.000                0.000
        X45                   0.000                3.000
        X46                 150.000                0.000
        X47                   0.000                4.000
        X48                 300.000                0.000
```

Try Problem 18 for practice working with transshipment problems with this more general structure.

New Orleans at $4 per unit and from Dallas to New Orleans at $1 per unit. The network model corresponding to this modified Ryan Electronics problem is shown in Figure 10.9, the linear programming formulation is shown in Figure 10.10, and the computer solution is shown in Figure 10.11.

In Figure 10.9 we added two new arcs to the network model. Thus, two new variables are necessary in the linear programming formulation. Figure 10.10 shows that the new variables x_{28} and x_{78} appear in the objective function and in the constraints corresponding to the nodes to which the new arcs are connected. Figure 10.11 shows that the value of the optimal solution has been reduced $600 by adding the two new shipping routes; $x_{28} = 250$ units

TABLE 10.6   OPTIMAL SOLUTION TO THE RYAN ELECTRONICS
TRANSSHIPMENT PROBLEM

| Route | | | | |
From	To	Units Shipped	Cost per Unit	Total Cost
Denver	Kansas City	550	$2	$1100
Denver	Louisville	50	$3	150
Atlanta	Louisville	400	$1	400
Kansas City	Detroit	200	$2	400
Kansas City	Dallas	350	$3	1050
Louisville	Miami	150	$4	600
Louisville	New Orleans	300	$5	1500
				$5200

FIGURE 10.9   NETWORK REPRESENTATION OF THE MODIFIED RYAN ELECTRONICS
TRANSSHIPMENT PROBLEM

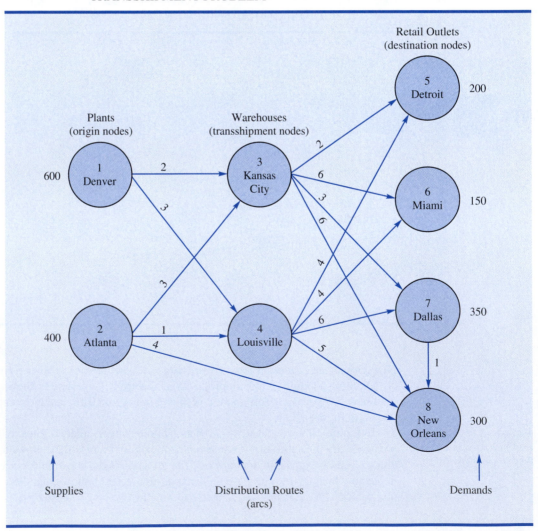

FIGURE 10.10 LINEAR PROGRAMMING FORMULATION OF THE MODIFIED RYAN ELECTRONICS TRANSSHIPMENT PROBLEM

$$\text{Min} \quad 2x_{13} + 3x_{14} + 3x_{23} + 1x_{24} + 2x_{35} + 6x_{36} + 3x_{37} + 6x_{38} + 4x_{45} + 4x_{46} + 6x_{47} + 5x_{48} + 4x_{28} + 1x_{78}$$

s.t.

$$
\begin{array}{llll}
x_{13} + x_{14} & & \leq 600 & \left.\begin{array}{l}\\ \\\end{array}\right\} \text{Origin node constraints} \\
\quad x_{23} + x_{24} & + x_{28} & \leq 400 & \\
-x_{13} \quad - x_{23} + x_{35} + x_{36} + x_{37} + x_{38} & & = 0 & \left.\begin{array}{l}\\ \\\end{array}\right\} \text{Transshipment node constraints} \\
\quad - x_{14} \quad - x_{24} & + x_{45} + x_{46} + x_{47} + x_{48} & = 0 & \\
\quad x_{35} & + x_{45} & = 200 & \left.\begin{array}{l}\\ \\\\ \\\end{array}\right\} \text{Destination node constraints} \\
\quad x_{36} & + x_{46} & = 150 & \\
\quad x_{37} & + x_{47} \quad - x_{78} & = 350 & \\
\quad x_{38} & + x_{48} + x_{28} + x_{78} & = 300 & \\
\end{array}
$$

$$x_{ij} \geq 0 \text{ for all } i \text{ and } j$$

FIGURE 10.11 THE MANAGEMENT SCIENTIST SOLUTION FOR THE MODIFIED RYAN ELECTRONICS TRANSSHIPMENT PROBLEM

```
Objective Function Value =          4600.000

        Variable              Value           Reduced Costs
    ----------------     ----------------    --------------------
           X13              600.000                0.000
           X14                0.000                0.000
           X23                0.000                3.000
           X24              150.000                0.000
           X35              200.000                0.000
           X36                0.000                1.000
           X37              400.000                0.000
           X38                0.000                2.000
           X45                0.000                3.000
           X46              150.000                0.000
           X47                0.000                4.000
           X48                0.000                2.000
           X28              250.000                0.000
           X78               50.000                0.000
```

are being shipped directly from Atlanta to New Orleans, and $x_{78} = 50$ units are being shipped from Dallas to New Orleans.

Problem Variations

As with transportation and assignment problems, transshipment problems may be formulated with several variations, including

1. Total supply not equal to total demand
2. Maximization objective function

3. Route capacities or route minimums
4. Unacceptable routes

The linear programming model modifications required to accommodate these variations are identical to the modifications required for the transportation problem described in Section 10.1. When we add one or more constraints of the form $x_{ij} \leq L_{ij}$ to show that the route from node i to node j has capacity L_{ij}, we refer to the transshipment problem as a **capacitated transshipment problem**.

A General Linear Programming Model

To show the general linear programming model for the transshipment problem, we use the notation:

$$x_{ij} = \text{number of units shipped from the node } i \text{ to node } j$$
$$c_{ij} = \text{cost per unit of shipping from node } i \text{ to node } j$$
$$s_i = \text{supply at origin node } i$$
$$d_j = \text{demand at destination node } j$$

The general linear programming model for the transshipment problem is as follows:

$$\text{Min} \quad \sum_{\text{all arcs}} c_{ij} x_{ij}$$

s.t.

$$\sum_{\text{arcs out}} x_{ij} - \sum_{\text{arcs in}} x_{ij} \leq s_i \quad \text{Origin nodes } i$$

$$\sum_{\text{arcs out}} x_{ij} - \sum_{\text{arcs in}} x_{ij} = 0 \quad \text{Transshipment nodes}$$

$$\sum_{\text{arcs in}} x_{ij} - \sum_{\text{arcs out}} x_{ij} = d_j \quad \text{Destination nodes } j$$

$$x_{ij} \geq 0 \text{ for all } i \text{ and } j$$

NOTES AND COMMENTS

1. The Q.M. in Action, Product Sourcing Heuristic at Procter & Gamble, describes how Procter & Gamble used a transshipment model to redesign its North American distribution system.
2. In more advanced treatments of linear programming and network flow problems, the capacitated transshipment problem is called the *pure network flow problem*. Efficient special-purpose solution procedures are available for network flow problems and their special cases.

3. In the general linear programming formulation of the transshipment problem, the constraints for the destination nodes are often written as

$$\sum_{\text{arcs out}} x_{ij} - \sum_{\text{arcs in}} x_{ij} = -d_j$$

The advantage of writing the constraints this way is that the left-hand side of each constraint then represents the flow out of the node minus the flow in.

PRODUCT SOURCING HEURISTIC AT PROCTER & GAMBLE*

A few years ago Procter & Gamble (P&G) embarked on a major strategic planning initiative called the North American Product Sourcing Study. P&G wanted to consolidate its product sources and optimize its distribution system design throughout North America. A decision support system used to aid in this project was called the Product Sourcing Heuristic (PSH) and was based on a transshipment model much like the ones described in this chapter.

In a preprocessing phase, the many P&G products were aggregated into groups that shared the same technology and could be made at the same plant. The PSH employing the transshipment model was then used by product strategy teams responsible for developing product sourcing options for these product groups. The various plants that could produce the product group were the source nodes, the company's regional distribution centers were the transshipment nodes, and P&G's customer zones

were the destinations. Direct shipments to customer zones as well as shipments through distribution centers were employed.

The product strategy teams used the heuristic interactively to explore a variety of questions concerning product sourcing and distribution. For instance, the team might be interested in the impact of closing two of five plants and consolidating production in the three remaining plants. The product sourcing heuristic would then delete the source nodes corresponding to the two closed plants, make any capacity modifications necessary to the sources corresponding to the remaining three plants, and re-solve the transshipment problem. The product strategy team could then examine the new solution, make some more modifications, solve again, and so on.

The Product Sourcing Heuristic was viewed as a valuable decision support system by all who used it. When P&G implemented the results of the study, it realized annual savings in the $200 million range. The PSH proved so successful in North America that P&G used it in other markets around the world.

*Based on information provided by Franz Dill and Tom Chorman of Procter & Gamble.

 10.4 ## Shortest–Route Problem

In this section we consider a problem in which the objective is to determine the **shortest route**, or *path,* between two nodes in a network. We will demonstrate the shortest-route problem by considering the situation facing the Gorman Construction Company. Gorman has several construction sites located throughout a three-county area. With multiple daily trips carrying personnel, equipment, and supplies from Gorman's office to the construction sites, the costs associated with transportation activities are substantial. The travel alternatives between Gorman's office and each construction site can be described by the road network shown in Figure 10.12. The road distances in miles between the nodes are shown above the corresponding arcs. In this application, Gorman would like to determine the route that will minimize the total travel distance between Gorman's office (located at node 1) and the construction site located at node 6.

A key to developing a model for the shortest-route problem is to understand that the problem is a special case of the transshipment problem. Specifically, the Gorman shortest-route problem can be viewed as a transshipment problem with one origin node (node 1), one destination node (node 6), and four transshipment nodes (nodes 2, 3, 4 and 5). The transshipment network for the Gorman shortest-route problem is shown in Figure 10.13. Arrows added to the arcs show the direction of flow, which is always *out* of the origin node

FIGURE 10.12 ROAD NETWORK FOR THE GORMAN COMPANY
SHORTEST-ROUTE PROBLEM

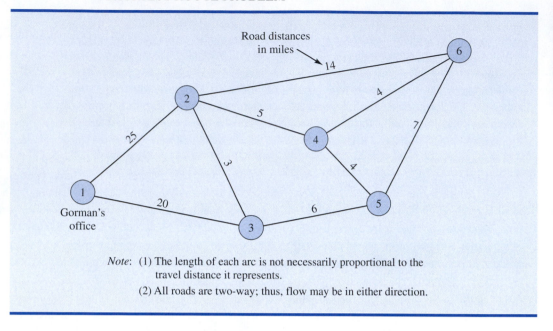

Road distances
in miles

Note: (1) The length of each arc is not necessarily proportional to the
travel distance it represents.
(2) All roads are two-way; thus, flow may be in either direction.

FIGURE 10.13 TRANSSHIPMENT NETWORK FOR THE GORMAN
SHORTEST-ROUTE PROBLEM

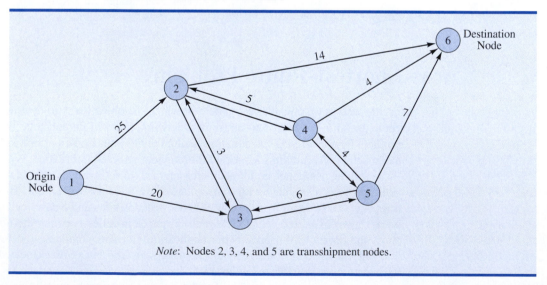

Note: Nodes 2, 3, 4, and 5 are transshipment nodes.

and *into* the destination node. Note also that two directed arcs are shown between the pairs
of transshipment nodes. For example, one arc going from node 2 to node 3 indicates that
the shortest route may go from node 2 to node 3, and one arc going from node 3 to node
2 indicates that the shortest route may go from node 3 to node 2. The distance between two
transshipment nodes is the same in either direction.

To find the shortest route between node 1 and node 6, think of node 1 as having a supply of 1 unit and node 6 as having a demand of 1 unit. Let x_{ij} denote the number of units that

flow or are shipped from node i to node j. Because only 1 unit will be shipped from node 1 to node 6, the value of x_{ij} will be either 1 or 0. Thus, if $x_{ij} = 1$, the arc from node i to node j is on the shortest route from node 1 to node 6; if $x_{ij} = 0$, the arc from node i to node j is not on the shortest route. Because we are looking for the shortest route between node 1 and node 6, the objective function for the Gorman problem is

$$\text{Min} \quad 25x_{12} + 20x_{13} + 3x_{23} + 3x_{32} + 5x_{24} + 5x_{42} + 14x_{26} + 6x_{35} + 6x_{53} \\ + 4x_{45} + 4x_{54} + 4x_{46} + 7x_{56}$$

To develop the constraints for the model, we begin with node 1. Because the supply at node 1 is 1 unit, the flow out of node 1 must equal 1. Thus, the constraint for node 1 is written

$$x_{12} + x_{13} = 1$$

For transshipment nodes 2, 3, 4, and 5, the flow out of each node must equal the flow into each node; thus, the flow out minus the flow in must be 0. The constraints for the four transshipment nodes are as follows:

	Flow Out	**Flow In**
Node 2	$x_{23} + x_{24} + x_{26}$	$-x_{12} - x_{32} - x_{42} = 0$
Node 3	$x_{32} + x_{35}$	$-x_{13} - x_{23} - x_{53} = 0$
Node 4	$x_{42} + x_{45} + x_{46}$	$-x_{24} - x_{54} \quad\quad = 0$
Node 5	$x_{53} + x_{54} + x_{56}$	$-x_{35} - x_{45} \quad\quad = 0$

Because node 6 is the destination node with a demand of one unit, the flow into node 6 must equal 1. Thus, the constraint for node 6 is written as

$$x_{26} + x_{46} + x_{56} = 1$$

Including the negative constraints $x_{ij} \geq 0$ for all i and j, the linear programming model for the Gorman shortest-route problem is shown in Figure 10.14.

The Management Scientist solution to the Gorman shortest-route problem is shown in Figure 10.15. The objective function value of 32 indicates that the shortest route between Gorman's office located at node 1 to the construction site located at node 6 is 32 miles. With $x_{13} = 1$, $x_{32} = 1$, $x_{24} = 1$, and $x_{46} = 1$, the shortest-route from node 1 to node 6 is 1–3–2–4–6; in other words, the shortest route takes us from node 1 to node 3; then from node 3 to node 2; then from node 2 to node 4; and finally from node 4 to node 6.

Try Problem 22 to practice solving a shortest-route problem.

FIGURE 10.14 LINEAR PROGRAMMING FORMULATION OF THE GORMAN SHORTEST-ROUTE PROBLEM

EB file

Gorman

$\text{Min } 25x_{12} + 20x_{13} + 3x_{23} + 3x_{32} + 5x_{24} + 5x_{42} + 14x_{26} + 6x_{35} + 6x_{53} + 4x_{45} + 4x_{54} + 4x_{46} + 7x_{56}$
s.t.

$x_{12} + x_{13}$	$= 1$	Origin node
$-x_{12} \quad + x_{23} - x_{32} + x_{24} - x_{42} + x_{26}$	$= 0$	
$- x_{13} - x_{23} + x_{32} \quad\quad + x_{35} - x_{53}$	$= 0$	Transshipment nodes
$- x_{24} + x_{42} \quad\quad + x_{45} - x_{54} + x_{46}$	$= 0$	
$- x_{35} + x_{53} - x_{45} + x_{54} \quad + x_{56} = 0$		
$x_{26} \quad\quad + x_{46} + x_{56} = 1$		Destination node

$x_{ij} \geq 0$ for all i and j

FIGURE 10.15   THE MANAGEMENT SCIENTIST SOLUTION OF THE GORMAN SHORTEST-ROUTE PROBLEM

```
OPTIMAL SOLUTION
Objective Function Value =              32.000

      Variable                 Value             Reduced Costs
    ------------            ---------------      ---------------
       X12                       0.000                2.000
       X13                       1.000                0.000
       X23                       0.000                6.000
       X32                       1.000                0.000
       X24                       1.000                0.000
       X42                       0.000               10.000
       X26                       0.000                5.000
       X35                       0.000                1.000
       X53                       0.000               11.000
       X45                       0.000                7.000
       X54                       0.000                1.000
       X46                       1.000                0.000
       X56                       0.000                0.000
```

A General Linear Programming Model

To show the general linear programming model for the shortest-route problem, we use the notation:

$$x_{ij} = \begin{cases} 1 & \text{if the arc from node } i \text{ to node } j \text{ is on the shortest route} \\ 0 & \text{otherwise} \end{cases}$$

$c_{ij} =$ the distance, time, or cost associated with the arc from node i to node j

The general linear programming model for the shortest-route problem is as follows:

$$\text{Min} \quad \sum_{\text{all arcs}} c_{ij} x_{ij}$$

s.t.

$$\sum_{\text{arcs out}} x_{ij} = 1 \quad \text{Origin node } i$$

$$\sum_{\text{arcs out}} x_{ij} - \sum_{\text{arcs in}} x_{ij} = 0 \quad \text{Transshipment nodes}$$

$$\sum_{\text{arcs in}} x_{ij} = 1 \quad \text{Destination node } j$$

NOTES AND COMMENTS

In the Gorman problem we assumed that all roads in the network are two-way. As a result, the road connecting nodes 2 and 3 in the road network resulted in the creation of two corresponding arcs in the transshipment network. Two decision variables, x_{23} and x_{32}, were required to show that the shortest route might go from node 2 to node 3 or from node 3 to node 2. If the road connecting nodes 2 and 3 had been a one-way road allowing flow only from node 2 to node 3, decision variable x_{32} would not have been included in the model.

10.5 Maximal Flow Problem

The objective in a **maximal flow** problem is to determine the maximum amount of flow (vehicles, messages, fluid, etc.) that can enter and exit a network system in a given period of time. In this problem, we attempt to transmit flow through all arcs of the network as efficiently as possible. The amount of flow is limited due to capacity restrictions on the various arcs of the network. For example, highway types limit vehicle flow in a transportation system, while pipe sizes limit oil flow in an oil distribution system. The maximum or upper limit on the flow in an arc is referred to as the **flow capacity** of the arc. Even though we do not specify capacities for the nodes, we do assume that the flow out of a node is equal to the flow into the node.

As an example of the maximal flow problem, consider the north–south interstate highway system passing through Cincinnati, Ohio. The north–south vehicle flow reaches a level of 15,000 vehicles per hour at peak times. Due to a summer highway maintenance program, which calls for the temporary closing of lanes and lower speed limits, a network of alternate routes through Cincinnati has been proposed by a transportation planning committee. The alternate routes include other highways as well as city streets. Because of differences in speed limits and traffic patterns, flow capacities vary depending on the particular streets and roads used. The proposed network with arc flow capacities is shown in Figure 10.16.

The direction of flow for each arc is indicated, and the arc capacity is shown next to each arc. Note that most of the streets are one-way. However, a two-way street can be found between nodes 2 and 3 and between nodes 5 and 6. In both cases, the capacity is the same in each direction.

We will show how to develop a capacitated transshipment model for the maximal flow problem. First, we will add an arc from node 7 back to node 1 to represent the total flow through the highway system. Figure 10.17 shows the modified network. The newly added arc shows no capacity; indeed, we will want to maximize the flow over that arc. Maximizing the flow over the arc from node 7 to node 1 is equivalent to maximizing the number of cars that can get through the north–south highway system passing through Cincinnati.

FIGURE 10.16 NETWORK OF HIGHWAY SYSTEM AND FLOW CAPACITIES (1000s/HOUR) FOR CINCINNATI

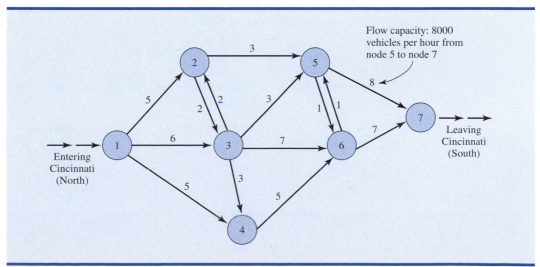

FIGURE 10.17   FLOW OVER ARC FROM NODE 7 TO NODE 1 TO REPRESENT TOTAL
FLOW THROUGH THE CINCINNATI HIGHWAY SYSTEM

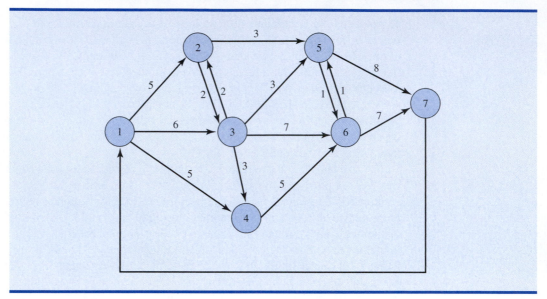

The decision variables are as follows:

$$x_{ij} = \text{amount of traffic flow from node } i \text{ to node } j$$

The objective function that maximizes the flow over the highway system is

$$\text{Max} \quad x_{71}$$

As with all transshipment problems, each arc generates a variable and each node generates a constraint. For each node, a conservation of flow constraint represents the requirement that the flow out must equal the flow in. Or, stated another way, the flow out minus the flow in must equal zero. For node 1, the flow out is $x_{12} + x_{13} + x_{14}$, and the flow in is x_{71}. Therefore, the constraint for node 1 is

$$x_{12} + x_{13} + x_{14} - x_{71} = 0$$

The conservation of flow constraints for the other six nodes are developed in a similar fashion.

	Flow Out	**Flow In**
Node 2	$x_{23} + x_{25}$	$-x_{12} - x_{32}$ $= 0$
Node 3	$x_{32} + x_{34} + x_{35} + x_{36}$	$-x_{13} - x_{23}$ $= 0$
Node 4	x_{46}	$-x_{14} - x_{34}$ $= 0$
Node 5	$x_{56} + x_{57}$	$-x_{25} - x_{35} - x_{65} = 0$
Node 6	$x_{65} + x_{67}$	$-x_{36} - x_{46} - x_{56} = 0$
Node 7	x_{71}	$-x_{57} - x_{67}$ $= 0$

Additional constraints are needed to enforce the capacities on the arcs. These 14 simple upper-bound constraints are given.

$$x_{12} \leq 5 \quad x_{13} \leq 6 \quad x_{14} \leq 5$$
$$x_{23} \leq 2 \quad x_{25} \leq 3$$
$$x_{32} \leq 2 \quad x_{34} \leq 3 \quad x_{35} \leq 3 \quad x_{36} \leq 7$$
$$x_{46} \leq 5$$
$$x_{56} \leq 1 \quad x_{57} \leq 8$$
$$x_{65} \leq 1 \quad x_{67} \leq 7$$

Note that the only arc without a capacity is the one we added from node 7 to node 1.

The Management Scientist solution to this 15-variable, 21-constraint linear programming problem is shown in Figure 10.18. We note that the value of the optimal solution is 14. This result implies that the maximal flow over the highway system is 14,000 vehicles. Figure 10.19 shows how the vehicle flow is routed through the original highway network. We note, for instance, that 5000 vehicles per hour are routed between nodes 1 and 2, 2000 vehicles per hour are routed between nodes 2 and 3, and so on.

Try Problem 29 for practice in solving a maximal flow problem.

The results of the maximal flow analysis indicate that the planned highway network system will not handle the peak flow of 15,000 vehicles per hour. The transportation planners will have to expand the highway network, increase current arc flow capacities, or be prepared for serious traffic problems. If the network is extended or modified, another maximal flow analysis will determine the extent of any improved flow. The Q.M. in Action, Optimizing Restoration Capacity at AT&T, notes that AT&T solved shortest-route and maximal flow problems in designing a transmission network.

FIGURE 10.18   THE MANAGEMENT SCIENTIST SOLUTION TO THE CINCINNATI HIGHWAY SYSTEM MAXIMAL FLOW PROBLEM

WEB file

Cincinnati

```
OPTIMAL SOLUTION

Objective Function Value = 14.000

         Variable              Value
       -------------        ---------------
          X12                    5.000
          X13                    6.000
          X14                    3.000
          X23                    2.000
          X25                    3.000
          X34                    0.000
          X35                    3.000
          X36                    5.000
          X32                    0.000
          X46                    3.000
          X56                    0.000
          X57                    7.000
          X65                    1.000
          X67                    7.000
          X71                   14.000
```

FIGURE 10.19   MAXIMAL FLOW PATTERN FOR THE CINCINNATI HIGHWAY
SYSTEM NETWORK

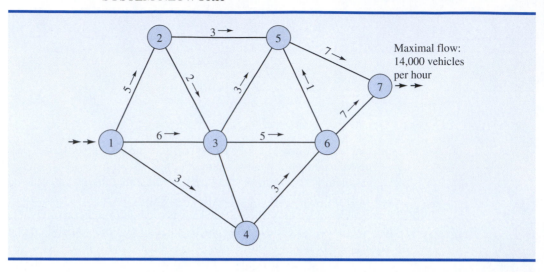

NOTES AND COMMENTS

1. The maximal flow problem of this section can also be solved with a slightly different formulation if the extra arc between nodes 7 and 1 is not used. The alternate approach is to maximize the flow into node 7 ($x_{57} + x_{67}$) and drop the conservation of flow constraints for nodes 1 and 7. However, the formulation used in this section is most common in practice.

2. Network models can be used to describe a variety of management science problems. Unfortunately, no one network solution algorithm can be used to solve every network problem. It is important to recognize the specific type of problem being modeled in order to select the correct specialized solution algorithm.

Q.M. in ACTION

OPTIMIZING RESTORATION CAPACITY AT AT&T*

AT&T is a global telecommunications company that provides long-distance voice and data, video, wireless, satellite, and Internet services. The company uses state-of-the-art switching and transmission equipment to provide service to more than 80 million customers. In the continental United States, AT&T's transmission network consists of more than 40,000 miles of fiber-optic cable. On peak days AT&T handles as many as 290 million calls of various types.

Power outages, natural disasters, cable cuts, and other events can disable a portion of the transmission network.

*Based on Ken Ambs, Sebastian Cwilich, Mei Deng, David J. Houck, David F. Lynch, and Dicky Yan, "Optimizing Restoration Capacity in the AT&T Network," *Interfaces* (January/February 2000): 26–44.

When such events occur, spare capacity comprising the restoration network must be immediately employed so that service is not disrupted. Critical issues with respect to the restoration network are: How much capacity is necessary? and Where should it be located? In 1997, AT&T assembled a RestNet team to address these issues.

To optimize restoration capacity, the RestNet team developed a large-scale linear programming model. One subproblem in their model involves determining the shortest route connecting an origin and destination whenever a failure occurs in a span of the transmission network. Another subproblem solves a maximal flow

(*continued*)

A Production and Inventory Application

The introduction to the transportation and transshipment problems in Sections 10.1 and 10.3 involved applications for the shipment of goods from several supply locations or origins to several demand sites or destinations. Although the shipment of goods is the subject of many transportation and transshipment problems, transportation or transshipment models can be developed for applications that have nothing to do with the physical shipment of goods from origins to destinations. In this section we show how to use a transshipment model to solve a production and inventory problem.

Contois Carpets is a small manufacturer of carpeting for home and office installations. Production capacity, demand, production cost per square yard, and inventory holding cost per square yard for the next four quarters are shown in Table 10.7. Note that production capacity, demand, and production costs vary by quarter, whereas the cost of carrying inventory from one quarter to the next is constant at $0.25 per yard. Contois wants to determine how many yards of carpeting to manufacture each quarter to minimize the total production and inventory cost for the four-quarter period.

The network flows into and out of demand nodes are what make the model a transshipment model.

We begin by developing a network representation of the problem. First, we create four nodes corresponding to the production in each quarter and four nodes corresponding to the demand in each quarter. Each production node is connected by an outgoing arc to the demand node for the same period. The flow on the arc represents the number of square yards of carpet manufactured for the period. For each demand node, an outgoing arc represents the amount of inventory (square yards of carpet) carried over to the demand node for the next period. Figure 10.20 shows the network model. Note that nodes 1–4 represent the production for each quarter and that nodes 5–8 represent the demand for each quarter. The quarterly production capacities are shown in the left margin, and the quarterly demands are shown in the right margin.

The objective is to determine a production scheduling and inventory policy that will minimize the total production and inventory cost for the four quarters. Constraints involve production capacity and demand in each quarter. As usual, a linear programming model can be developed from the network by establishing a constraint for each node and a variable for each arc.

TABLE 10.7   PRODUCTION, DEMAND, AND COST ESTIMATES FOR CONTOIS CARPETS

Quarter	Production Capacity (square yards)	Demand (square yards)	Production Cost ($/square yard)	Inventory Cost ($/square yard)
1	600	400	2	0.25
2	300	500	5	0.25
3	500	400	3	0.25
4	400	400	3	0.25

FIGURE 10.20   NETWORK REPRESENTATION OF THE CONTOIS CARPETS PROBLEM

Let x_{15} denote the number of square yards of carpet manufactured in quarter 1. The capacity of the facility is 600 square yards in quarter 1, so the production capacity constraint is

$$x_{15} \leq 300$$

Using similar decision variables, we obtain the production capacities for quarters 2–4:

$$x_{26} \leq 300$$
$$x_{37} \leq 500$$
$$x_{48} \leq 400$$

We now consider the development of the constraints for each of the demand nodes. For node 5, one arc enters the node, which represents the number of square yards of carpet produced in quarter 1, and one arc leaves the node, which represents the number of square yards of carpet that will not be sold in quarter 1 and will be carried over for possible sale in quarter 2. In general, for each quarter the beginning inventory plus the production minus the ending inventory must equal demand. However, because quarter 1 has no beginning inventory, the constraint for node 5 is

$$x_{15} - x_{56} = 400$$

The constraints associated with the demand nodes in quarters 2, 3, and 4 are

$$x_{56} + x_{26} - x_{67} = 500$$
$$x_{67} + x_{37} - x_{78} = 400$$
$$x_{78} + x_{48} = 400$$

Note that the constraint for node 8 (fourth-quarter demand) involves only two variables because no provision is made for holding inventory for a fifth quarter.

The objective is to minimize total production and inventory cost, so we write the objective function as

$$\text{Min} \quad 2x_{15} + 5x_{26} + 3x_{37} + 3x_{48} + 0.25x_{56} + 0.25x_{67} + 0.25x_{78}$$

The complete linear programming formulation of the Contois Carpets problem is

$$\text{Min} \quad 2x_{15} + 5x_{26} + 3x_{37} + 3x_{48} + 0.25x_{56} + 0.25x_{67} + 0.25x_{78}$$

$$\text{s.t.}$$

$$
\begin{array}{llllll}
x_{15} & & & & & \leq 600 \\
& x_{26} & & & & \leq 300 \\
& & x_{37} & & & \leq 500 \\
& & & x_{48} & & \leq 400 \\
x_{15} & & & & -\; x_{56} & = 400 \\
& x_{26} & & & +\; x_{56} - x_{67} & = 500 \\
& & x_{37} & & +\; x_{67} - x_{78} & = 400 \\
& & & x_{48} & +\; x_{78} & = 400 \\
\end{array}
$$

$$x_{ij} \geq 0 \quad \text{for all } i \text{ and } j$$

We used the linear programming module of The Management Scientist to solve the Contois Carpets problem. Figure 10.21 shows the results: Contois Carpets should manufacture 600 square yards of carpet in quarter 1, 300 square yards in quarter 2, 400 square yards in quarter 3, and 400 square yards in quarter 4. Note also that 200 square yards will be carried over from quarter 1 to quarter 2. The total production and inventory cost is $5150.

NOTES AND COMMENTS

For the network models presented in this chapter, the amount leaving the starting node for an arc is always equal to the amount entering the ending node for that arc. An extension of such a network model is the case where a gain or a loss occurs as an arc is traversed. The amount entering the destination node may be greater or smaller than the amount leaving the origin node. For instance, if cash is the commodity flowing across an arc, the cash earns interest from one period to the next. Thus, the amount of cash entering the next period is greater than the amount leaving the previous period by the amount of interest earned. Networks with gains or losses are treated in more advanced texts on network flow programming.

FIGURE 10.21   THE MANAGEMENT SCIENTIST SOLUTION FOR THE CONTOIS
CARPETS PROBLEM

WEB file

Contois

```
Objective Function Value =            5150.000

       Variable              Value            Reduced Costs
    ---------------      ---------------      -----------------
         X15               600.000               0.000
         X26               300.000               0.000
         X37               400.000               0.000
         X48               400.000               0.000
         X56               200.000               0.000
         X67                 0.000               2.250
         X78                 0.000               0.000
```

Summary

In this chapter we introduced transportation, assignment, transshipment, shortest-route, and maximal flow problems. All five types of problems belong to the special category of linear programs called *network flow problems*. In general, the network model for these problems consists of nodes representing origins, destinations, and if necessary, transshipment points in the network system. Arcs are used to represent the routes for shipment, travel, or flow between the various nodes.

The general transportation problem has *m* origins and *n* destinations. Given the supply at each origin, the demand at each destination, and unit shipping cost between each origin and each destination, the transportation model determines the optimal amounts to ship from each origin to each destination.

The assignment problem is a special case of the transportation problem in which all supply and all demand values are 1. We represent each agent as an origin node and each task as a destination node. The assignment model determines the minimum cost or maximum profit assignment of agents to tasks.

The transshipment problem is an extension of the transportation problem involving transfer points referred to as transshipment nodes. In this more general model, we allow arcs between any pair of nodes in the network. If desired, capacities can be specified for arcs, which makes it a capacitated transshipment problem.

The shortest-route problem finds the shortest route or path between two nodes of a network. Distance, time, and cost are often the criteria used for this model. The shortest-route problem can be expressed as a transshipment problem with one origin and one destination. By shipping one unit from the origin to the destination, the solution will determine the shortest route through the network.

The maximal flow problem can be used to allocate flow to the arcs of the network so that flow through the network system is maximized. Arc capacities determine the maximum amount of flow for each arc. With these flow capacity constraints, the maximal flow problem is expressed as a capacitated transshipment problem.

In the last section of the chapter, we showed how a variation of the transshipment problem could be used to solve a production and inventory problem. In the chapter appendix we show how to use Excel to solve three of the distribution and network problems presented in the chapter.

Glossary

Transportation problem A network flow problem that often involves minimizing the cost of shipping goods from a set of origins to a set of destinations; it can be formulated and solved as a linear program by including a variable for each arc and a constraint for each node.

Network A graphical representation of a problem consisting of numbered circles (nodes) interconnected by a series of lines (arcs); arrowheads on the arcs show the direction of flow. Transportation, assignment, and transshipment problems are network flow problems.

Nodes The intersection or junction points of a network.

Arcs The lines connecting the nodes in a network.

Dummy origin An origin added to a transportation problem to make the total supply equal to the total demand. The supply assigned to the dummy origin is the difference between the total demand and the total supply.

Capacitated transportation problem A variation of the basic transportation problem in which some or all of the arcs are subject to capacity restrictions.

Assignment problem A network flow problem that often involves the assignment of agents to tasks; it can be formulated as a linear program and is a special case of the transportation problem.

Transshipment problem An extension of the transportation problem to distribution problems involving transfer points and possible shipments between any pair of nodes.

Capacitated transshipment problem A variation of the transshipment problem in which some or all of the arcs are subject to capacity restrictions.

Shortest route Shortest path between two nodes in a network.

Maximal flow The maximum amount of flow that can enter and exit a network system during a given period of time.

Flow capacity The maximum flow for an arc of the network. The flow capacity in one direction may not equal the flow capacity in the reverse direction.

Problems

1. A company imports goods at two ports: Philadelphia and New Orleans. Shipments of one product are made to customers in Atlanta, Dallas, Columbus, and Boston. For the next planning period, the supplies at each port, customer demands, and shipping costs per case from each port to each customer are as follows:

Port	Atlanta	Dallas	Columbus	Boston	Port Supply
Philadelphia	2	6	6	2	5000
New Orleans	1	2	5	7	3000
Demand	1400	3200	2000	1400	

Note: Columns Atlanta–Boston are grouped under the heading **Customers**.

Develop a network representation of the distribution system (transportation problem).

2. Consider the following network representation of a transportation problem:

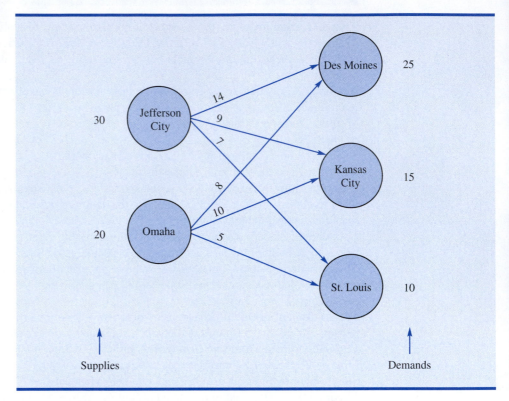

The supplies, demands, and transportation costs per unit are shown on the network.
a. Develop a linear programming model for this problem; be sure to define the variables in your model.
b. Solve the linear program to determine the optimal solution.

3. Tri-County Utilities, Inc., supplies natural gas to customers in a three-county area. The company purchases natural gas from two companies: Southern Gas and Northwest Gas.

Demand forecasts for the coming winter season are Hamilton County, 400 units; Butler County, 200 units; and Clermont County, 300 units. Contracts to provide the following quantities have been written: Southern Gas, 500 units; and Northwest Gas, 400 units. Distribution costs for the counties vary, depending upon the location of the suppliers. The distribution costs per unit (in thousands of dollars) are as follows:

		To	
From	**Hamilton**	**Butler**	**Clermont**
Southern Gas	10	20	15
Northwest Gas	12	15	18

a. Develop a network representation of this problem.
b. Develop a linear programming model that can be used to determine the plan that will minimize total distribution costs.
c. Describe the distribution plan and show the total distribution cost.

d. Recent residential and industrial growth in Butler County has the potential for increasing demand by as much as 100 units. Which supplier should Tri-County contract with to supply the additional capacity?

4. Arnoff Enterprises manufactures the central processing unit (CPU) for a line of personal computers. The CPUs are manufactured in Seattle, Columbus, and New York and shipped to warehouses in Pittsburgh, Mobile, Denver, Los Angeles, and Washington, D.C., for further distribution. The following table shows the number of CPUs available at each plant, the number of CPUs required by each warehouse, and the shipping costs (dollars per unit):

	Warehouse					
Plant	**Pittsburgh**	**Mobile**	**Denver**	**Los Angeles**	**Washington**	**CPUs Available**
Seattle	10	20	5	9	10	9000
Columbus	2	10	8	30	6	4000
New York	1	20	7	10	4	8000
CPUs Required	3000	5000	4000	6000	3000	21,000

a. Develop a network representation of this problem.
b. Determine the amount that should be shipped from each plant to each warehouse to minimize the total shipping cost.
c. The Pittsburgh warehouse just increased its order by 1000 units, and Arnoff authorized the Columbus plant to increase its production by 1000 units. Will this production increase lead to an increase or decrease in total shipping costs? Solve for the new optimal solution.

5. Premier Consulting's two consultants, Avery and Baker, can be scheduled to work for clients up to a maximum of 160 hours each over the next four weeks. A third consultant, Campbell, has some administrative assignments already planned and is available for clients up to a maximum of 140 hours over the next four weeks. The company has four clients with projects in process. The estimated hourly requirements for each of the clients over the four-week period are

Client	Hours
A	180
B	75
C	100
D	85

Hourly rates vary for the consultant–client combination and are based on several factors, including project type and the consultant's experience. The rates (dollars per hour) for each consultant–client combination are

	Client			
Consultant	**A**	**B**	**C**	**D**
Avery	100	125	115	100
Baker	120	135	115	120
Campbell	155	150	140	130

a. Develop a network representation of the problem.
b. Formulate the problem as a linear program, with the optimal solution providing the hours each consultant should be scheduled for each client to maximize the consulting firm's billings. What is the schedule and what is the total billing?
c. New information shows that Avery doesn't have the experience to be scheduled for client B. If this consulting assignment is not permitted, what impact does it have on total billings? What is the revised schedule?

6. Klein Chemicals, Inc., produces a special oil-based material that is currently in short supply. Four of Klein's customers have already placed orders that together exceed the combined capacity of Klein's two plants. Klein's management faces the problem of deciding how many units it should supply to each customer. Because the four customers are in different industries, different prices can be charged because of the various industry pricing structures. However, slightly different production costs at the two plants and varying transportation costs between the plants and customers make a "sell to the highest bidder" strategy unacceptable. After considering price, production costs, and transportation costs, Klein established the following profit per unit for each plant-customer alternative:

	Customer			
Plant	D_1	D_2	D_3	D_4
Clifton Springs	$32	$34	$32	$40
Danville	$34	$30	$28	$38

The plant capacities and customer orders are as follows:

Plant	Capacity (units)	Distributor Orders (units)
Clifton Springs	5000	D_1 2000
		D_2 5000
Danville	3000	D_3 3000
		D_4 2000

How many units should each plant produce for each customer to maximize profits? Which customer demands will not be met? Show your network model and linear programming formulation.

7. Forbelt Corporation has a one-year contract to supply motors for all refrigerators produced by the Ice Age Corporation. Ice Age manufactures the refrigerators at four locations around the country: Boston, Dallas, Los Angeles, and St. Paul. Plans call for the following number (in thousands) of refrigerators to be produced at each location:

Boston	50
Dallas	70
Los Angeles	60
St. Paul	80

Forbelt's three plants are capable of producing the motors. The plants and production capacities (in thousands) are

Denver	100
Atlanta	100
Chicago	150

Because of varying production and transportation costs, the profit that Forbelt earns on each lot of 1000 units depends on which plant produced the lot and which destination it was shipped to. The following table gives the accounting department estimates of the profit per unit (shipments will be made in lots of 1000 units):

	Shipped To			
Produced At	**Boston**	**Dallas**	**Los Angeles**	**St. Paul**
Denver	7	11	8	13
Atlanta	20	17	12	10
Chicago	8	18	13	16

With profit maximization as a criterion, Forbelt's management wants to determine how many motors should be produced at each plant and how many motors should be shipped from each plant to each destination.
a. Develop a network representation of this problem.
b. Find the optimal solution.

8. The Ace Manufacturing Company has orders for three similar products:

Product	Orders (units)
A	2000
B	500
C	1200

Three machines are available for the manufacturing operations. All three machines can produce all the products at the same production rate. However, due to varying defect percentages of each product on each machine, the unit costs of the products vary depending on the machine used. Machine capacities for the next week and the unit costs are as follows:

Machine	Capacity (units)
1	1500
2	1500
3	1000

	Product		
Machine	**A**	**B**	**C**
1	$1.00	$1.20	$0.90
2	$1.30	$1.40	$1.20
3	$1.10	$1.00	$1.20

Use the transportation model to develop the minimum cost production schedule for the products and machines. Show the linear programming formulation.

9. Scott and Associates, Inc., is an accounting firm that has three new clients. Project leaders will be assigned to the three clients. Based on the different backgrounds and experiences of the leaders, the various leader–client assignments differ in terms of projected completion times. The possible assignments and the estimated completion times in days are as follows:

	Client		
Project Leader	**1**	**2**	**3**
Jackson	10	16	32
Ellis	14	22	40
Smith	22	24	34

a. Develop a network representation of this problem.
b. Formulate the problem as a linear program, and solve. What is the total time required?

10. CarpetPlus sells and installs floor covering for commercial buildings. Brad Sweeney, a CarpetPlus account executive, was just awarded the contract for five jobs. Brad must now assign a CarpetPlus installation crew to each of the five jobs. Because the commission Brad will earn depends on the profit CarpetPlus makes, Brad would like to determine an assignment that will minimize total installation costs. Currently, five installation crews are available for assignment. Each crew is identified by a color code, which aids in tracking of job progress on a large white board. The following table shows the costs (in hundreds of dollars) for each crew to complete each of the five jobs:

		Job				
		1	**2**	**3**	**4**	**5**
	Red	30	44	38	47	31
	White	25	32	45	44	25
Crew	Blue	23	40	37	39	29
	Green	26	38	37	45	28
	Brown	26	34	44	43	28

a. Develop a network representation of the problem.
b. Formulate and solve a linear programming model to determine the minimum cost assignment.

11. A local television station plans to drop four Friday evening programs at the end of the season. Steve Botuchis, the station manager, developed a list of six potential replacement programs. Estimates of the advertising revenue ($) that can be expected for each of the new programs in the four vacated time slots are as follows. Mr. Botuchis asked you to find the assignment of programs to time slots that will maximize total advertising revenue.

	5:00–5:30 P.M.	5:30–6:00 P.M.	7:00–7:30 P.M.	8:00–8:30 P.M.
Home Improvement	5000	3000	6000	4000
World News	7500	8000	7000	5500
NASCAR Live	8500	5000	6500	8000
Wall Street Today	7000	6000	6500	5000
Hollywood Briefings	7000	8000	3000	6000
Ramundo & Son	6000	4000	4500	7000

12. The U.S. Cable Company uses a distribution system with five distribution centers and eight customer zones. Each customer zone is assigned a sole source supplier; each customer zone receives all of its cable products from the same distribution center. In an effort to balance demand and workload at the distribution centers, the company's vice president of logistics specified that distribution centers may not be assigned more than three customer zones. The following table shows the five distribution centers and cost of supplying each customer zone (in thousands of dollars):

Distribution Centers	Los Angeles	Chicago	Columbus	Atlanta	Newark	Kansas City	Denver	Dallas
						Customer Zones		
Plano	70	47	22	53	98	21	27	13
Nashville	75	38	19	58	90	34	40	26
Flagstaff	15	78	37	82	111	40	29	32
Springfield	60	23	8	39	82	36	32	45
Boulder	45	40	29	75	86	25	11	37

a. Determine the assignment of customer zones to distribution centers that will minimize cost.

b. Which distribution centers, if any, are not used?

c. Suppose that each distribution center is limited to a maximum of two customer zones. How does this constraint change the assignment and the cost of supplying customer zones?

13. United Express Service (UES) uses large quantities of packaging materials at its four distribution hubs. After screening potential suppliers, UES identified six vendors that can provide packaging materials that will satisfy its quality standards. UES asked each of the six vendors to submit bids to satisfy annual demand at each of its four distribution hubs over the next year. The following table lists the bids received (in thousands of dollars). UES wants to ensure that each of the distribution hubs is serviced by a different vendor. Which bids should UES accept, and which vendors should UES select to supply each distribution hub?

Bidder	Distribution Hub			
	1	**2**	**3**	**4**
Martin Products	190	175	125	230
Schmidt Materials	150	235	155	220
Miller Containers	210	225	135	260
D&J Burns	170	185	190	280
Larbes Furnishings	220	190	140	240
Lawler Depot	270	200	130	260

14. The quantitative methods department head at a major midwestern university will be scheduling faculty to teach courses during the coming autumn term. Four core courses need to be covered. The four courses are at the UG, MBA, MS, and Ph.D. levels. Four professors will be assigned to the courses, with each professor receiving one of the courses. Student evaluations of professors are available from previous terms. Based on a rating scale of 4 (excellent), 3 (very good), 2 (average), 1 (fair), and 0 (poor), the average student evaluations for each professor are shown. Professor D does not have a Ph.D. and cannot be assigned to teach the Ph.D. level course. If the department head makes teaching assignments based on maximizing the student evaluation ratings over all four courses, what staffing assignments should be made?

Professor	Course			
	UG	**MBA**	**MS**	**Ph.D.**
A	2.8	2.2	3.3	3.0
B	3.2	3.0	3.6	3.6
C	3.3	3.2	3.5	3.5
D	3.2	2.8	2.5	—

15. A market research firm's three clients each requested that the firm conduct a sample survey. Four available statisticians can be assigned to these three projects; however, all four statisticians are busy, and therefore each can handle only one client. The following data show the number of hours required for each statistician to complete each job; the differences in time are based on experience and ability of the statisticians.

		Client	
Statistician	**A**	**B**	**C**
1	150	210	270
2	170	230	220
3	180	230	225
4	160	240	230

  a. Formulate and solve a linear programming model for this problem.
  b. Suppose that the time statistician 4 needs to complete the job for client A is increased from 160 to 165 hours. What effect will this change have on the solution?
  c. Suppose that the time statistician 4 needs to complete the job for client A is decreased to 140 hours. What effect will this change have on the solution?
  d. Suppose that the time statistician 3 needs to complete the job for client B increases to 250 hours. What effect will this change have on the solution?

16. Hatcher Enterprises uses a chemical called Rbase in production operations at five divisions. Only six suppliers of Rbase meet Hatcher's quality control standards. All six suppliers can produce Rbase in sufficient quantities to accommodate the needs of each division. The quantity of Rbase needed by each Hatcher division and the price per gallon charged by each supplier are as follows:

Division	Demand (1000s of gallons)
1	40
2	45
3	50
4	35
5	45

Supplier	Price per gallon ($)
1	12.60
2	14.00
3	10.20
4	14.20
5	12.00
6	13.00

The cost per gallon ($) for shipping from each supplier to each division is provided in the following table:

	Supplier					
Division	**1**	**2**	**3**	**4**	**5**	**6**
1	2.75	2.50	3.15	2.80	2.75	2.75
2	0.80	0.20	5.40	1.20	3.40	1.00
3	4.70	2.60	5.30	2.80	6.00	5.60
4	2.60	1.80	4.40	2.40	5.00	2.80
5	3.40	0.40	5.00	1.20	2.60	3.60

Hatcher believes in spreading its business among suppliers so that the company will be less affected by supplier problems (e.g., labor strikes or resource availability). Company policy requires that each division have a separate supplier.

a. For each supplier–division combination, compute the total cost of supplying the division's demand.

b. Determine the optimal assignment of suppliers to divisions.

17. The distribution system for the Herman Company consists of three plants, two warehouses, and four customers. Plant capacities and shipping costs per unit (in $) from each plant to each warehouse are as follows:

	Warehouse		
Plant	1	2	Capacity
1	4	7	450
2	8	5	600
3	5	6	380

Customer demand and shipping costs per unit (in $) from each warehouse to each customer are

	Customer			
Warehouse	1	2	3	4
1	6	4	8	4
2	3	6	7	7
Demand	300	300	300	400

a. Develop a network representation of this problem.
b. Formulate a linear programming model of the problem.
c. Solve the linear program to determine the optimal shipping plan.

18. Refer to Problem 17. Suppose that shipments between the two warehouses are permitted at $2 per unit and that direct shipments can be made from plant 3 to customer 4 at a cost of $7 per unit.
a. Develop a network representation of this problem.
b. Formulate a linear programming model of this problem.
c. Solve the linear program to determine the optimal shipping plan.

19. Adirondack Paper Mills, Inc., operates paper plants in Augusta, Maine, and Tupper Lake, New York. Warehouse facilities are located in Albany, New York, and Portsmouth, New Hampshire. Distributors are located in Boston, New York, and Philadelphia. The plant capacities and distributor demands for the next month are as follows:

Plant	Capacity (units)	Distributor	Demand (units)
Augusta	300	Boston	150
Tupper Lake	100	New York	100
		Philadelphia	150

The unit transportation costs (in $) for shipments from the two plants to the two warehouses and from the two warehouses to the three distributors are as follows:

	Warehouse	
Plant	Albany	Portsmouth
Augusta	7	5
Tupper Lake	3	4

		Distributor	
Warehouse	**Boston**	**New York**	**Philadelphia**
Albany	8	5	7
Portsmouth	5	6	10

a. Draw the network representation of the Adirondack Paper Mills problem.
b. Formulate the Adirondack Paper Mills problem as a linear programming problem.
c. Solve the linear program to determine the minimum cost shipping schedule for the problem.

20. The Moore & Harman Company is in the business of buying and selling grain. An important aspect of the company's business is arranging for the purchased grain to be shipped to customers. If the company can keep freight costs low, profitability will improve.

The company recently purchased three rail cars of grain at Muncie, Indiana; six rail cars at Brazil, Indiana; and five rail cars at Xenia, Ohio. Twelve carloads of grain have been sold. The locations and the amount sold at each location are as follows:

Location	Number of Rail Car Loads
Macon, GA	2
Greenwood, SC	4
Concord, SC	3
Chatham, NC	3

All shipments must be routed through either Louisville or Cincinnati. Shown are the shipping costs per bushel (in cents) from the origins to Louisville and Cincinnati and the costs per bushel to ship from Louisville and Cincinnati to the destinations.

	To	
From	**Louisville**	**Cincinnati**
Muncie	8	6 ← Cost per bushel
Brazil	3	8 from Muncie to
Xenia	9	3 Cincinnati is 6¢

		To		
From	**Macon**	**Greenwood**	**Concord**	**Chatham**
Louisville	44	34	34	32
Cincinnati	57	35	28	24

Cost per bushel from
Cincinnati to Greenwood is 35¢

Determine a shipping schedule that will minimize the freight costs necessary to satisfy demand. Which (if any) rail cars of grain must be held at the origin until buyers can be found?

21. The following linear programming formulation is for a transshipment problem:

$$\text{Min} \quad 11x_{13} + 12x_{14} + 10x_{21} + 8x_{34} + 10x_{35} + 11x_{42} + 9x_{45} + 12x_{52}$$

s.t.

$$
\begin{aligned}
x_{13} + x_{14} - x_{21} &\le 5 \\
x_{21} \qquad\qquad\quad - x_{42} \qquad\quad - x_{52} &\le 3 \\
x_{13} \qquad\quad - x_{34} - x_{35} &= 6 \\
- x_{14} \qquad - x_{34} \qquad + x_{42} + x_{45} &\le 2 \\
x_{35} \qquad\qquad + x_{45} - x_{52} &= 4
\end{aligned}
$$

$$x_{ij} \ge 0 \quad \text{for all } i, j$$

Show the network representation of this problem.

22. A rental car company has an imbalance of cars at seven of its locations. The following network shows the locations of concern (the nodes) and the cost to move a car between locations. A positive number by a node indicates an excess supply at the node, and a negative number indicates an excess demand.

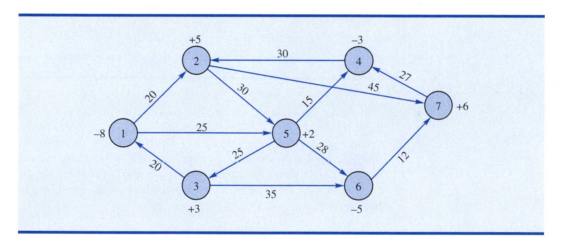

a. Develop a linear programming model of this problem.
b. Solve the model formulated in part (a) to determine how the cars should be redistributed among the locations.

23. Find the shortest route from node 1 to node 7 in the network shown.

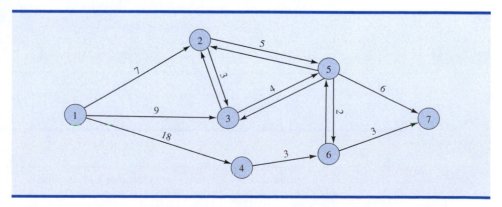

24. In the original Gorman Construction Company problem, we found the shortest distance from the office (node 1) to the construction site located at node 6. Because some of the roads are highways and others are city streets, the shortest-distance routes between the office and the construction site may not necessarily provide the quickest or shortest-time route. Shown here is the Gorman road network with travel time rather than distance. Find the shortest route from Gorman's office to the construction site at node 6 if the objective is to minimize travel time rather than distance.

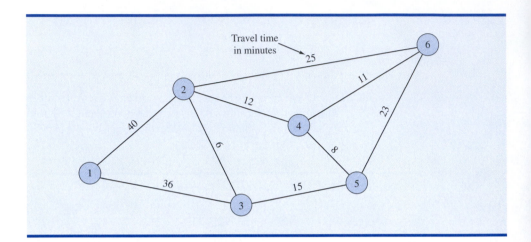

25. Cleveland Area Rapid Delivery (CARD) operates a delivery service in the Cleveland metropolitan area. Most of CARD's business involves rapid delivery of documents and parcels between offices during the business day. CARD promotes its ability to make fast and on-time deliveries anywhere in the metropolitan area. When a customer calls with a delivery request, CARD quotes a guaranteed delivery time. The following network shows the street routes available. The numbers above each arc indicate the travel time in minutes between the two locations.

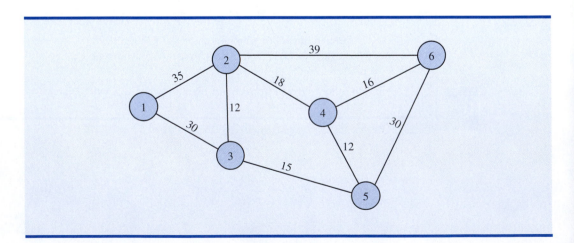

a. Develop a linear programming model that can be used to find the minimum time required to make a delivery from location 1 to location 6.
b. How long does it take to make a delivery from location 1 to location 6?

c. Assume that it is now 1:00 P.M. CARD just received a request for a pickup at location 1, and the closest CARD courier is 8 minutes away from location 1. If CARD provides a 20% safety margin in guaranteeing a delivery time, what is the guaranteed delivery time if the package picked up at location 1 is to be delivered to location 6?

26. Morgan Trucking Company operates a special pickup and delivery service between Chicago and six other cities located in a four-state area. When Morgan receives a request for service, it dispatches a truck from Chicago to the city requesting service as soon as possible. With both fast service and minimum travel costs as objectives for Morgan, it is important that the dispatched truck take the shortest route from Chicago to the specified city. Assume that the following network (not drawn to scale) with distances given in miles represents the high-way network for this problem. Find the shortest-route distances from Chicago to node 6.

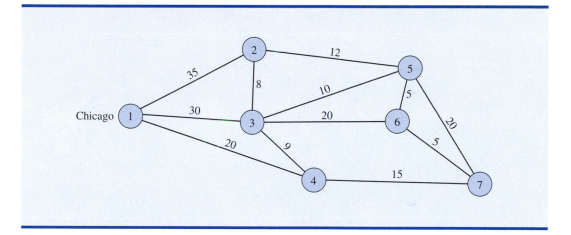

27. City Cab Company identified 10 primary pickup and drop locations for cab riders in New York City. In an effort to minimize travel time and improve customer service and the utilization of the company's fleet of cabs, management would like the cab drivers to take the shortest route between locations whenever possible. Using the following network of roads and streets, what is the route a driver beginning at location 1 should take to reach location 10? The travel times in minutes are shown on the arcs of the network. Note that there are two one-way streets with the direction shown by the arrows.

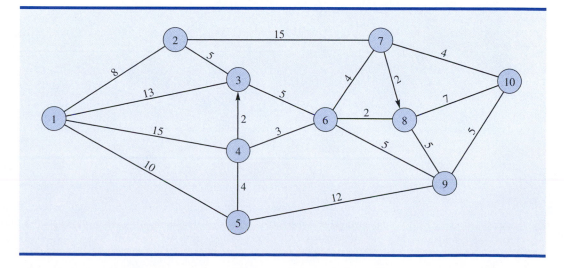

28.   The five nodes in the following network represent points one year apart over a four-year period. Each node indicates a time when a decision is made to keep or replace a firm's computer equipment. If a decision is made to replace the equipment, a decision must also be made as to how long the new equipment will be used. The arc from node 0 to node 1 represents the decision to keep the current equipment one year and replace it at the end of the year. The arc from node 0 to node 2 represents the decision to keep the current equipment two years and replace it at the end of year 2. The numbers above the arcs indicate the total cost associated with the equipment replacement decisions. These costs include discounted purchase price, trade-in value, operating costs, and maintenance costs. Use a shortest-route model to determine the minimum cost equipment replacement policy for the four-year period.

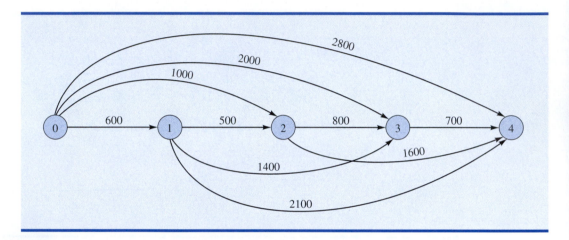

SELF test

29.   The north–south highway system passing through Albany, New York, can accommodate the capacities shown.

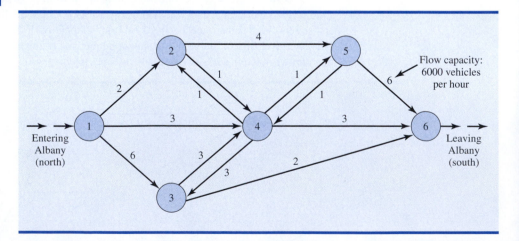

Can the highway system accommodate a north–south flow of 10,000 vehicles per hour?

30.   If the Albany highway system described in Problem 29 has revised flow capacities as shown in the following network, what is the maximal flow in vehicles per hour through the

system? How many vehicles per hour must travel over each road (arc) to obtain this maximal flow?

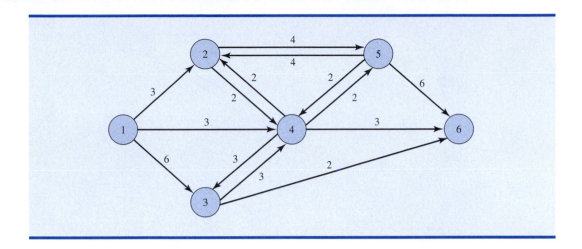

31. A long-distance telephone company uses a fiber-optic network to transmit phone calls and other information between locations. Calls are carried through cable lines and switching nodes. A portion of the company's transmission network is shown here. The numbers above each arc show the capacity in thousands of messages that can be transmitted over that branch of the network.

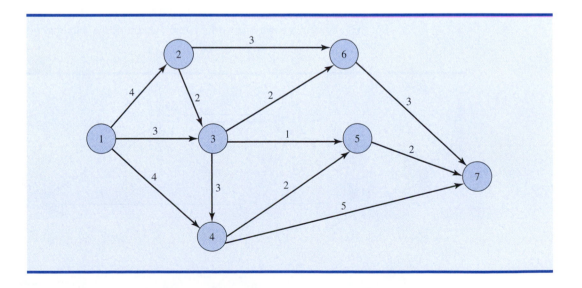

To keep up with the volume of information transmitted between origin and destination points, use the network to determine the maximum number of messages that may be sent from a city located at node 1 to a city located at node 7.

32. The High-Price Oil Company owns a pipeline network that is used to convey oil from its source to several storage locations. A portion of the network is as follows:

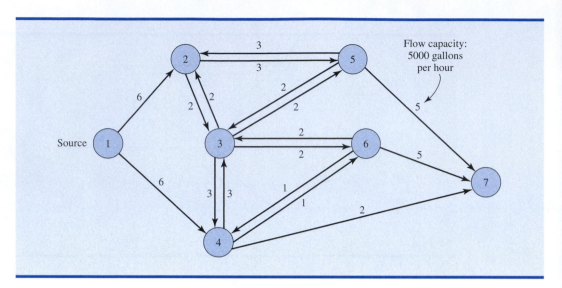

Due to the varying pipe sizes, the flow capacities vary. By selectively opening and closing sections of the pipeline network, the firm can supply any of the storage locations.

a. If the firm wants to fully utilize the system capacity to supply storage location 7, how long will it take to satisfy a location 7 demand of 100,000 gallons? What is the maximal flow for this pipeline system?

b. If a break occurs on line 2–3 and it is closed down, what is the maximal flow for the system? How long will it take to transmit 100,000 gallons to location 7?

33. For the following highway network system, determine the maximal flow in vehicles per hour:

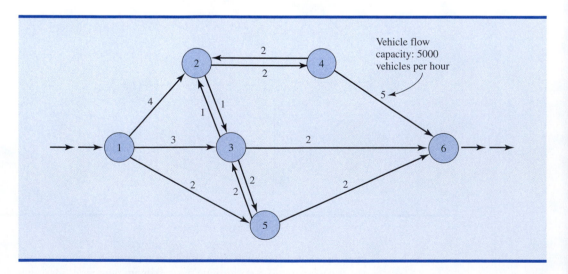

The highway commission is considering adding highway section 3–4 to permit a flow of 2000 vehicles per hour or, at an additional cost, a flow of 3000 vehicles per hour. What is your recommendation for the 3–4 arc of the network?

34. A chemical processing plant has a network of pipes that are used to transfer liquid chemical products from one part of the plant to another. The following pipe network has pipe flow capacities in gallons per minute as shown. What is the maximum flow capacity for the system if the company wishes to transfer as much liquid chemical as possible from location 1 to location 9? How much of the chemical will flow through the section of pipe from node 3 to node 5?

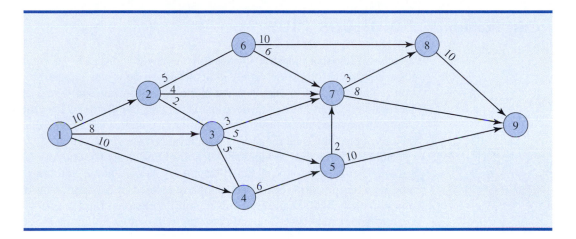

35. Refer to the Contois Carpets problem, for which the network representation is shown in Figure 10.20. Suppose that Contois has a beginning inventory of 50 yards of carpet and requires an inventory of 100 yards at the end of quarter 4.
    a. Develop a network representation of this modified problem.
    b. Develop a linear programming model and solve for the optimal solution.

36. Sanders Fishing Supply of Naples, Florida, manufactures a variety of fishing equipment that it sells throughout the United States. For the next three months, Sanders estimates demand for a particular product at 150, 250, and 300 units, respectively. Sanders can supply this demand by producing on regular time or overtime. Because of other commitments and anticipated cost increases in month 3, the production capacities in units and the production costs per unit are as follows:

Production	Capacity (units)	Cost per Unit
Month 1—Regular	275	$ 50
Month 1—Overtime	100	80
Month 2—Regular	200	50
Month 2—Overtime	50	80
Month 3—Regular	100	60
Month 3—Overtime	50	100

Inventory may be carried from one month to the next, but the cost is $20 per unit per month. For example, regular production from month 1 used to meet demand in month 2 would cost Sanders $50 + $20 = $70 per unit. This same month 1 production used to meet demand in month 3 would cost Sanders $50 + 2($20) = $90 per unit.
    a. Develop a network representation of this production scheduling problem as a transportation problem. (*Hint:* Use six origin nodes; the supply for origin node 1 is the maximum that can be produced in month 1 on regular time, and so on.)

b. Develop a linear programming model that can be used to schedule regular and overtime production for each of the three months.

c. What is the production schedule, how many units are carried in inventory each month, and what is the total cost?

d. Is there any unused production capacity? If so, where?

Case Problem 1   Solutions Plus

Solutions Plus is an industrial chemicals company that produces specialized cleaning fluids and solvents for a wide variety of applications. Solutions Plus just received an invitation to submit a bid to supply Great North American railroad with a cleaning fluid for locomotives. Great North American needs the cleaning fluid at 11 locations (railway stations); it provided the following information to Solutions Plus regarding the number of gallons of cleaning fluid required at each location (see Table 10.8).

Solutions Plus can produce the cleaning fluid at its Cincinnati plant for $1.20 per gallon. Even though the Cincinnati location is its only plant, Solutions Plus has negotiated with an industrial chemicals company located in Oakland, California, to produce and ship up to 50,000 gallons of the locomotive cleaning fluid to selected Solutions Plus customer locations. The Oakland company will charge Solutions Plus $1.65 per gallon to produce the cleaning fluid, but Solutions Plus thinks that the lower shipping costs from Oakland to some customer locations may offset the added cost to produce the product.

The president of Solutions Plus, Charlie Weaver, contacted several trucking companies to negotiate shipping rates between the two production facilities (Cincinnati and Oakland) and the locations where the railroad locomotives are cleaned. Table 10.9 shows the quotes received in terms of dollars per gallon. The "—" entries in Table 10.9 identify shipping routes that will not be considered because of the large distances involved. These quotes for shipping rates are guaranteed for one year.

To submit a bid to the railroad company, Solutions Plus must determine the price per gallon they will charge. Solutions Plus usually sells its cleaning fluids for 15% more than its cost to produce and deliver the product. For this big contract, however, Fred Roedel, the director of marketing, suggested that maybe the company should consider a smaller profit margin. In addition, to ensure that if Solutions Plus wins the bid, they will have adequate capacity to satisfy existing orders as well as accept orders for other new business, the management team decided to limit the number of gallons of the locomotive cleaning fluid produced in the Cincinnati plant to 500,000 gallons at most.

TABLE 10.8   GALLONS OF CLEANING FLUID REQUIRED AT EACH LOCATION

Location	Gallons Required	Location	Gallons Required
Santa Ana	22,418	Glendale	33,689
El Paso	6,800	Jacksonville	68,486
Pendleton	80,290	Little Rock	148,586
Houston	100,447	Bridgeport	111,475
Kansas City	241,570	Sacramento	112,000
Los Angeles	64,761		

TABLE 10.9   FREIGHT COST ($ PER GALLON)

	Cincinnati	Oakland
Santa Ana	—	0.22
El Paso	0.84	0.74
Pendleton	0.83	0.49
Houston	0.45	—
Kansas City	0.36	—
Los Angeles	—	0.22
Glendale	—	0.22
Jacksonville	0.34	—
Little Rock	0.34	—
Bridgeport	0.34	—
Sacramento	—	0.15

Managerial Report

You are asked to make recommendations that will help Solutions Plus prepare a bid. Your report should address, but not be limited to, the following issues:

1. If Solutions Plus wins the bid, which production facility (Cincinnati or Oakland) should supply the cleaning fluid to the locations where the railroad locomotives are cleaned? How much should be shipped from each facility to each location?
2. What is the breakeven point for Solutions Plus? That is, how low can the company go on its bid without losing money?
3. If Solutions Plus wants to use its standard 15% markup, how much should it bid?
4. Freight costs are significantly affected by the price of oil. The contract on which Solutions Plus is bidding is for two years. Discuss how fluctuation in freight costs might affect the bid Solutions Plus submits.

Case Problem 2   Distribution System Design

The Darby Company manufactures and distributes meters used to measure electric power consumption. The company started with a small production plant in El Paso and gradually built a customer base throughout Texas. A distribution center was established in Fort Worth, Texas, and later, as business expanded, a second distribution center was established in Santa Fe, New Mexico.

The El Paso plant was expanded when the company began marketing its meters in Arizona, California, Nevada, and Utah. With the growth of the West Coast business, the Darby Company opened a third distribution center in Las Vegas and just two years ago opened a second production plant in San Bernardino, California.

Manufacturing costs differ between the company's production plants. The cost of each meter produced at the El Paso plant is $10.50. The San Bernardino plant utilizes newer and more efficient equipment; as a result, manufacturing costs are $0.50 per meter less than at the El Paso plant.

Due to the company's rapid growth, not much attention had been paid to the efficiency of the distribution system, but Darby's management decided that it is time to address this

TABLE 10.10 SHIPPING COST PER UNIT FROM PRODUCTION PLANTS TO DISTRIBUTION CENTERS (IN $)

	Distribution Center		
Plant	**Fort Worth**	**Santa Fe**	**Las Vegas**
El Paso	3.20	2.20	4.20
San Bernardino	—	3.90	1.20

issue. The cost of shipping a meter from each of the two plants to each of the three distribution centers is shown in Table 10.10.

The quarterly production capacity is 30,000 meters at the older El Paso plant and 20,000 meters at the San Bernardino plant. Note that no shipments are allowed from the San Bernardino plant to the Fort Worth distribution center.

The company serves nine customer zones from the three distribution centers. The forecast of the number of meters needed in each customer zone for the next quarter is shown in Table 10.11.

The cost per unit of shipping from each distribution center to each customer zone is given in Table 10.12; note that some distribution centers cannot serve certain customer zones.

In the current distribution system, demand at the Dallas, San Antonio, Wichita, and Kansas City customer zones is satisfied by shipments from the Fort Worth distribution center. In a similar manner, the Denver, Salt Lake City, and Phoenix customer zones are

TABLE 10.11 QUARTERLY DEMAND FORECAST

Customer Zone	Demand (meters)
Dallas	6300
San Antonio	4880
Wichita	2130
Kansas City	1210
Denver	6120
Salt Lake City	4830
Phoenix	2750
Los Angeles	8580
San Diego	4460

TABLE 10.12 SHIPPING COST FROM THE DISTRIBUTION CENTERS TO THE CUSTOMER ZONES

Distribution Center	Customer Zone								
	Dallas	**San Antonio**	**Wichita**	**Kansas City**	**Denver**	**Salt Lake City**	**Phoenix**	**Los Angeles**	**San Diego**
Fort Worth	0.3	2.1	3.1	4.4	6.0	—	—	—	—
Santa Fe	5.2	5.4	4.5	6.0	2.7	4.7	3.4	3.3	2.7
Las Vegas	—	—	—	—	5.4	3.3	2.4	2.1	2.5

served by the Santa Fe distribution center, and the Los Angeles and San Diego customer zones are served by the Las Vegas distribution center. To determine how many units to ship from each plant, the quarterly customer demand forecasts are aggregated at the distribution centers, and a transportation model is used to minimize the cost of shipping from the production plants to the distribution centers.

Managerial Report

You are asked to make recommendations for improving the distribution system. Your report should address, but not be limited to, the following issues:

1. If the company does not change its current distribution strategy, what will its distribution costs be for the following quarter?
2. Suppose that the company is willing to consider dropping the distribution center limitations; that is, customers could be served by any of the distribution centers for which costs are available. Can costs be reduced? By how much?
3. The company wants to explore the possibility of satisfying some of the customer demand directly from the production plants. In particular, the shipping cost is $0.30 per unit from San Bernardino to Los Angeles and $0.70 from San Bernardino to San Diego. The cost for direct shipments from El Paso to San Antonio is $3.50 per unit. Can distribution costs be further reduced by considering these direct plant-to-customer shipments?
4. Over the next five years, Darby is anticipating moderate growth (5000 meters) to the North and West. Would you recommend that they consider plant expansion at this time?

Appendix 10.1   Excel Solution of Transportation, Assignment, and Transshipment Problems

In this appendix we will use an Excel Worksheet to solve transportation, assignment, and transshipment problems. We start with the Foster Generators transportation problem (see Section 10.1).

Transportation Problem

The first step is to enter the data for the transportation costs, the origin supplies, and the destination demands in the top portion of the worksheet. Then the linear programming model is developed in the bottom portion of the worksheet. As with all linear programs, the worksheet model has four key elements: the decision variables, the objective function, the constraint left-hand sides, and the constraint right-hand sides. For a transportation problem, the decision variables are the amounts shipped from each origin to each destination; the objective function is the total transportation cost; the left-hand sides are the number of units shipped from each origin and the number of units shipped into each destination; and the right-hand sides are the origin supplies and the destination demands.

The formulation and solution of the Foster Generators problem are shown in Figure 10.22. The data are in the top portion of the worksheet. The model appears in the bottom portion of the worksheet; the key elements are screened.

Formulation

The data and descriptive labels are contained in cells A1:F8. The transportation costs are in cells B5:E7. The origin supplies are in cells F5:F7, and the destination demands are in cells

FIGURE 10.22   EXCEL SOLUTION OF THE FOSTER GENERATORS PROBLEM

WEB **file**

Foster

	A	B	C	D	E	F	G	H
1	**Foster Generators**							
2								
3			**Destination**					
4	**Origin**	Boston	Chicago	St. Louis	Lexington	**Supply**		
5	Cleveland	3	2	7	6	5000		
6	Bedford	7	5	2	3	6000		
7	York	2	5	4	5	2500		
8	**Demand**	6000	4000	2000	1500			
9								
10								
11	**Model**							
12								
13		**Min Cost**	39500					
14								
15			**Destination**					
16	**Origin**	Boston	Chicago	St. Louis	Lexington	**Total**		
17	Cleveland	3500	1500	0	0	5000	<=	5000
18	Bedford	0	2500	2000	1500	6000	<=	6000
19	York	2500	0	0	0	2500	<=	2500
20	**Total**	6000	4000	2000	1500			
21		=	=	=	=			
22		6000	4000	2000	1500			

B8:E8. The key elements of the model required by the Excel Solver are the decision variables, the objective function, the constraint left-hand sides, and the constraint right-hand sides. These cells are screened in the bottom portion of the worksheet.

Decision Variables   Cells B17:E19 are reserved for the decision variables. The optimal values are shown to be $x_{11} = 3500$, $x_{12} = 1500$, $x_{22} = 2500$, $x_{23} = 2000$, $x_{24} = 1500$, and $x_{41} = 2500$. All other decision variables equal zero, indicating nothing will be shipped over the corresponding routes.

Objective Function   The formula =SUMPRODUCT(B5:E7,B17:E19) has been placed into cell C13 to compute the cost of the solution. The minimum cost solution is shown to have a value of $39,500.

Left-Hand Sides   Cells F17:F19 contain the left-hand sides for the supply constraints, and cells B20:E20 contain the left-hand sides for the demand constraints.
Cell F17 =SUM(B17:E17) (Copy to F18:F19)
Cell B20 =SUM(B17:B19) (Copy to C20:E20)

Right-Hand Sides   Cells H17:H19 contain the right-hand sides for the supply constraints and Cells B22:E22 contain the right-hand sides for the demand constraints.
Cell H17 =F5 (Copy to H18:H19)
Cell B22 =B8 (Copy to C22:E22)

Excel Solution

The solution shown in Figure 10.22 can be obtained by selecting **Premium Solver** from the **Add-ins** tab, entering the proper values into the **Solver Parameters** dialog box, selecting

FIGURE 10.23   SOLVER PARAMETERS DIALOG BOX FOR THE FOSTER
GENERATORS PROBLEM

Standard LP Simplex, and specifying the option **Assume Non-Negative.** Then click **Solve.**
The information entered into the **Solver Parameters** dialog box is shown in Figure 10.23.

Assignment Problem

The first step is to enter the data for the assignment costs in the top portion of the worksheet. Even though the assignment model is a special case of the transportation model, it is
not necessary to enter values for origin supplies and destination demands because they are
always equal to one.

The linear programming model is developed in the bottom portion of the worksheet. As
with all linear programs, the model has four key elements: the decision variables, the objective function, the constraint left-hand sides, and the constraint right-hand sides. For an
assignment problem the decision variables indicate whether an agent is assigned to a task
(with a 1 for yes or 0 for no); the objective function is the total cost of all assignments; the
constraint left-hand sides are the number of tasks that are assigned to each agent and the
number of agents that are assigned to each task; and the right-hand sides are the number of
tasks each agent can handle (1) and the number of agents each task requires (1). The worksheet formulation and solution for the Fowle Marketing Research Problem are shown in
Figure 10.24.

Formulation

The data and descriptive labels are contained in cells A1:D7. Note that we have not inserted
supply and demand values because they are always equal to 1 in an assignment problem.
The model appears in the bottom portion of the worksheet with the key elements screened.

Decision Variables   Cells B16:D18 are reserved for the decision variables. The optimal values are shown to be $x_{12} = 1$, $x_{23} = 1$, and $x_{31} = 1$, with all
other variables = 0.

FIGURE 10.24   EXCEL SOLUTION OF THE FOWLE MARKETING RESEARCH PROBLEM

WEB **file**

Fowle

	A	B	C	D	E	F	G
1	**Fowle Marketing Research**						
2							
3			**Client**				
4	**Project Leader**	1	2	3			
5	Terry	10	15	9			
6	Carle	9	18	5			
7	McClymonds	6	14	3			
8							
9							
10	**Model**						
11							
12		**Min Time**	26				
13							
14			**Client**				
15	**Project Leader**	1	2	3	**Total**		
16	Terry	0	1	0	1	<=	1
17	Carle	0	0	1	1	<=	1
18	McClymonds	1	0	0	1	<=	1
19	**Total**	1	1	1			
20		=	=	=			
21		1	1	1			

Objective Function	The formula =SUMPRODUCT(B5:D7, B16:D18) has been placed into cell C12 to compute the number of days required to complete all the jobs. The minimum time solution has a value of 26 days.

Left-Hand Sides	Cells E16:E18 contain the left-hand sides of the constraints for the number of clients each project leader can handle. Cells B19:D19 contain the left-hand sides of the constraints requiring that each client must be assigned a project leader.
	   Cell E16 =SUM(B16:D16) (Copy to E17:E18)
	   Cell B19 =SUM(B16:B18) (Copy to C19:D19)

Right-Hand Sides	Cells G16:G18 contain the right-hand sides for the project leader constraints, and cells B21:D21 contain the right-hand sides for the client constraints. All right-hand side cell values are 1.

Excel Solution

The solution shown in Figure 10.24 can be obtained by selecting **Premium Solver** from the **Add-ins** tab menu, entering the proper values into the **Solver Parameters** dialog box, selecting **Standard LP Simplex,** and specifying the option **Assume Non-Negative.** Then click **Solve.** The information entered into the **Solver Parameters** dialog box is shown in Figure 10.25.

FIGURE 10.25   SOLVER PARAMETERS DIALOG BOX FOR THE FOWLE MARKETING
RESEARCH PROBLEM

Transshipment Problem

The worksheet model we present for the transshipment problem can be used for all the network flow problems (transportation, assignment, and transshipment) in this chapter. We organize the worksheet into two sections: an arc section and a node section. Let us illustrate by showing the worksheet formulation and solution of the Ryan Electronics transshipment problem. Refer to Figure 10.26 as we describe the steps involved. The key elements are screened.

FIGURE 10.26   EXCEL SOLUTION FOR THE RYAN ELECTRONICS PROBLEM

WEB file

Ryan

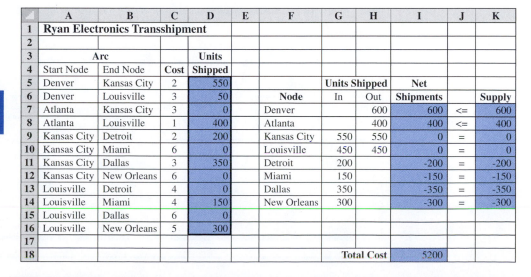

	A	B	C	D	E	F	G	H	I	J	K
1	**Ryan Electronics Transshipment**										
2											
3		**Arc**		**Units**							
4	Start Node	End Node	**Cost**	**Shipped**							
5	Denver	Kansas City	2	550			**Units Shipped**		**Net**		
6	Denver	Louisville	3	50		**Node**	In	Out	**Shipments**		**Supply**
7	Atlanta	Kansas City	3	0		Denver		600	600	<=	600
8	Atlanta	Louisville	1	400		Atlanta		400	400	<=	400
9	Kansas City	Detroit	2	200		Kansas City	550	550	0	=	0
10	Kansas City	Miami	6	0		Louisville	450	450	0	=	0
11	Kansas City	Dallas	3	350		Detroit	200		-200	=	-200
12	Kansas City	New Orleans	6	0		Miami	150		-150	=	-150
13	Louisville	Detroit	4	0		Dallas	350		-350	=	-350
14	Louisville	Miami	4	150		New Orleans	300		-300	=	-300
15	Louisville	Dallas	6	0							
16	Louisville	New Orleans	5	300							
17											
18								**Total Cost**	5200		

Formulation

The arc section uses cells A3:D16. For each arc, the start node and end node are identified in cells A5:B16. The arc costs are identified in cells C5:C16, and cells D5:D16 are reserved for the values of the decision variables (the amount shipped over the arcs).

The node section uses cells F5:K14. Each of the nodes is identified in cells F7:F14. The following formulas are entered into cells G7:H14 to represent the flow out and the flow in for each node:

Units shipped in: Cell G9   =D5 + D7
                     Cell G10 =D6 + D8
                     Cell G11 =D9 + D13
                     Cell G12 =D10 + D14
                     Cell G13 =D11 + D15
                     Cell G14 =D12 + D16

Units shipped out: Cell H7 =SUM(D5:D6)
                     Cell H8 =SUM(D7:D8)
                     Cell H9 =SUM(D9:D12)
                     Cell H10 =SUM(D13:D16)

The net shipments in cells I7:I14 are the flows out minus the flows in for each node. For supply nodes, the flow out will exceed the flow in, resulting in positive net shipments. For demand nodes, the flow out will be less than the flow in, resulting in negative net shipments. The "net" supply appears in cells K7:K14. Note that the net supply is negative for demand nodes.

FIGURE 10.27   SOLVER PARAMETERS DIALOG BOX FOR THE RYAN
                    ELECTRONICS PROBLEM

As in previous worksheet formulations, we screened the key elements required by the Excel Solver.

Decision Variables	Cells D5:D16 are reserved for the decision variables. The optimal number of units to ship over each arc is shown.
Objective Function	The formula =SUMPRODUCT(C5:C16,D5:D16) is placed into cell I18 to show the total cost associated with the solution. As shown, the minimum total cost is $5200.
Left-Hand Sides	The left-hand sides of the constraints represent the net shipments for each node. Cells I7:I14 are reserved for these constraints. Cell I7 =H7-G7 (Copy to I8:I14)
Right-Hand Sides	The right-hand sides of the constraints represent the supply at each node. Cells K7:K14 are reserved for these values. (Note the negative supply at the four demand nodes.)

Excel Solution

The solution can be obtained by selecting **Premium Solver** from the **Add-ins** tab menu, entering the proper values into the **Solver Parameters** dialog box, selecting **Standard LP Simplex,** and specifying the option **Assume Non-Negative.** Then click **Solve.** The information entered into the **Solver Parameters** dialog box is shown in Figure 10.27.

CHAPTER 11

Integer Linear Programming

CONTENTS

In this chapter we discuss a class of problems that are modeled as linear programs with the additional requirement that one or more variables must be integer. Such problems are called **integer linear programs**. If all variables must be integer, we have an all-integer linear program. If some, but not all, variables must be integer, we have a mixed-integer linear program. In many applications of integer linear programming, one or more integer variables are required to equal either 0 or 1. Such variables are called 0-1 or *binary variables*. If all variables are 0-1 variables, we have a 0-1 integer linear program.

Integer variables—especially 0-1 variables—provide substantial modeling flexibility. As a result, the number of applications that can be addressed with linear programming methodology is expanded. For instance, the Q.M. in Action, Crew Scheduling at Air New Zealand, describes how that airline company employs 0-1 integer programming models to schedule its pilots and flight attendants. Later Q.M. in Actions describe how Valley Metal Containers uses a mixed integer program for scheduling aluminum can production for Coors beer, and how a series of three integer programming models was used to schedule volunteers for the 2003 Edmonton Folk Festival. Many other applications of integer programming are described throughout the chapter.

The objective of this chapter is to provide an applications-oriented introduction to integer linear programming. First, we discuss the different types of integer linear programming models. Then we show the formulation, graphical solution, and computer solution of an all-integer linear program. In Section 11.3 we discuss five applications of integer linear programming that make use of 0-1 variables: capital budgeting, fixed cost, distribution system design, bank location, and market share optimization problems. In Section 11.4 we provide additional illustrations of the modeling flexibility provided by 0-1 variables. Appendix 11.1 and Appendix 11.2 illustrate the use of Excel and LINGO for solving integer programs.

The cost of the added modeling flexibility provided by integer programming is that problems involving integer variables are often much more difficult to solve. A linear programming problem with several thousand continuous variables can be solved with any of several commercial linear programming solvers. However, an all-integer linear programming problem with less than 100 variables can be extremely difficult to solve. Experienced management scientists can help identify the types of integer linear programs that are easy, or at least reasonable, to solve. Commercial computer software packages, such as LINGO, CPLEX, Xpress-MP, and the commercial version of Premium Solver have extensive integer programming capability, and very robust open-source software packages for integer programming are also available. The Management Scientist and spreadsheet packages, such as Excel, have the capability for solving smaller integer linear programs.

Information about open-source software can be found at http:www.coin-or.org.

Q.M. *in* ACTION

CREW SCHEDULING AT AIR NEW ZEALAND*

As noted in Chapter 1, airlines make extensive use of quantitative methods (see Q.M. in Action, Revenue Management at American Airlines). Air New Zealand is the largest national and international airline based in New

Zealand. Over the past 15 years, Air New Zealand developed integer programming models for crew scheduling.

Air New Zealand finalizes flight schedules at least 12 weeks in advance of when the flights are to take place. At that point the process of assigning crews to

*Based on E. Rod Butchers et al., "Optimized Crew Scheduling at Air New Zealand," *Interfaces* (January/February 2001): 30–56.

(*continued*)

implement the flight schedule begins. The crew scheduling problem involves staffing the flight schedule with pilots and flight attendants. It is solved in two phases. In the first phase, tours of duty (ToD) are generated that will permit constructing sequences of flights for pilots and flight attendants that will allow the airline's flight schedule to be implemented. A tour of duty is a one-day or multiday alternating sequence of duty periods (flight legs, training, etc.) and rest periods (layovers). In the ToD problem, no consideration is given to which individual crew members will perform the tours of duty. In the second phase, individual crew members are assigned to the tours of duty, which is called the rostering problem.

Air New Zealand employs integer programming models to solve both the ToD problem and the rostering problem. In the integer programming model of the ToD problem, each variable is a 0-1 variable that corresponds to a possible tour of duty that could be flown by a crew member (e.g., pilot or flight attendant). Each constraint corresponds to a particular flight and ensures that the flight is included in exactly one tour of duty. The cost of variable j reflects the cost of operating the jth tour of duty, and the objective is to minimize total cost. Air New Zealand solves a separate ToD problem for each crew type (pilot type or flight attendant type).

In the rostering problem, the tours of duty from the solution to the ToD problem are used to construct lines of work (LoW) for each crew member. In the integer programming model of the rostering problem, a 0-1 variable represents the possible LoWs for each crew member. A separate constraint for each crew member guarantees that each will be assigned a single LoW. Other constraints correspond to the ToDs that must be covered by any feasible solution to the rostering problem.

The crew scheduling optimizers developed by Air New Zealand showed a significant impact on profitability. Over the 15 years it took to develop these systems, the estimated development costs were approximately NZ\$2 million. The estimated savings are NZ\$15.6 million per year. In 1999 the savings from employing these integer programming models represented 11% of Air New Zealand's net operating profit. In addition to the direct dollar savings, the optimization systems provided many intangible benefits such as higher-quality solutions in less time, less dependence on a small number of highly skilled schedulers, flexibility to accommodate small changes in the schedule, and a guarantee that the airline satisfies legislative and contractual rules.

NOTES AND COMMENTS

1. Because integer linear programs are harder to solve than linear programs, one should not try to solve a problem as an integer program if simply rounding the linear programming solution is adequate. In many linear programming problems, such as those in previous chapters, rounding has little economic consequence on the objective function, and feasibility is not an issue. But, in problems such as determining how many jet engines to manufacture, the consequences of rounding can be substantial, and integer programming methodology should be employed.

2. Some linear programming problems have a special structure, which guarantees that the variables will have integer values. The assignment, transportation, and transshipment problems of Chapter 10 have such structures. If the supply and the demand for transportation and transshipment problems are integer, the optimal linear programming solution will provide integer amounts shipped. For the assignment problem, the optimal linear programming solution will consist of 0s and 1s. So, for these specially structured problems, linear programming methodology can be used to find optimal integer solutions. Integer linear programming algorithms are not necessary.

11.1 Types of Integer Linear Programming Models

The only difference between the problems studied in this chapter and the ones studied in earlier chapters on linear programming is that one or more variables are required to be integer. If all variables are required to be integer, we have an **all-integer linear program**. The following is a two-variable, all-integer linear programming model:

$$\text{Max} \quad 2x_1 + 3x_2$$
$$\text{s.t.}$$
$$3x_1 + 3x_2 \le 12$$
$$\tfrac{2}{3}x_1 + 1x_2 \le 4$$
$$1x_1 + 2x_2 \le 6$$
$$x_1, x_2 \ge 0 \text{ and integer}$$

If we drop the phrase "and integer" from the last line of this model, we have the familiar two-variable linear program. The linear program that results from dropping the integer requirements is called the **LP Relaxation** of the integer linear program.

If some, but not necessarily all, variables are required to be integer, we have a **mixed-integer linear program**. The following is a two-variable, mixed-integer linear program:

$$\text{Max} \quad 3x_1 + 4x_2$$
$$\text{s.t.}$$
$$-1x_1 + 2x_2 \le 8$$
$$1x_1 + 2x_2 \le 12$$
$$2x_1 + 1x_2 \le 16$$
$$x_1, x_2 \ge 0 \text{ and } x_2 \text{ integer}$$

We obtain the LP Relaxation of this mixed-integer linear program by dropping the requirement that x_2 be integer.

In some applications, the integer variables may only take on the values 0 or 1. Then we have a **0-1 linear integer program**. As we see later in the chapter, 0-1 variables provide additional modeling capability. The Q.M. in Action, Aluminum Can Production at Valley Metal Container, describes how a mixed-integer linear program involving 0-1 integer variables is used to schedule production of aluminum beer cans for Coors Breweries. The 0-1 variables are used to model production line changeovers; the continuous variables model production quantities.

Q.M. *in* ACTION

ALUMINUM CAN PRODUCTION AT VALLEY METAL CONTAINER*

Valley Metal Container (VMC) produces cans for the seven brands of beer produced by the Coors' breweries: Coors Extra Gold, Coors Light, Coors Original, Keystone

Ale, Keystone Ice, Keystone Light, and Keystone Premium. VMC produces these cans on six production lines and stores them in three separate inventory storage areas from which they are shipped on to the Coors breweries in Golden, Colorado; Memphis, Tennessee; and Shenandoah, Virginia.

---

*Based on Elena Katok and Dennis Ott, "Using Mixed-Integer Programming to Reduce Label Changes in the Coors Aluminum Can Plant," *Interfaces* (March/April 2000): 1–12.

(*continued*)

Two important issues face production scheduling at the VMC facility. First, each time a production line must be changed over from producing one type of can to another (label change), it takes time to get the color just right for the new label. As a result, downtime is incurred and scrap is generated. Second, proper scheduling can reduce the amount of inventory that must be transferred from long-term to short-term storage. Thus, two costs are critical in determining the best production schedule at the VMC facility: the label-change cost and the cost of transferring inventory from one type of storage to another. To determine a production schedule that will minimize these two costs, VMC developed a mixed-integer linear programming model of its production process.

The model's objective function calls for minimizing the sum of the weekly cost of changing labels and the cost of transferring inventory from long-term to short-term storage. Binary (0-1) variables are used to represent a label change in the production process. Continuous variables are used to represent the size of the production run for each type of label on each line during each shift; analogous variables are used to represent inventories for each type of can produced. Additional continuous variables are used to represent the amount of inventory transferred to short-term storage during the week.

The VMC production scheduling problem is solved weekly using a personal computer. Excel worksheets are used for input data preparation and for storing the output report. The GAMS mathematical programming system is used to solve the mixed-integer linear program. Susan Schultz, manager of Logistics for Coors Container Operations, reports that using the system resulted in documented annual savings of $169,230.

 11.2 # Graphical and Computer Solutions for an All-Integer Linear Program

Eastborne Realty has $2 million available for the purchase of new rental property. After an initial screening, Eastborne reduced the investment alternatives to townhouses and apartment buildings. Each townhouse can be purchased for $282,000, and five are available. Each apartment building can be purchased for $400,000, and the developer will construct as many buildings as Eastborne wants to purchase.

Eastborne's property manager can devote up to 140 hours per month to these new properties; each townhouse is expected to require 4 hours per month, and each apartment building is expected to require 40 hours per month. The annual cash flow, after deducting mortgage payments and operating expenses, is estimated to be $10,000 per townhouse and $15,000 per apartment building. Eastborne's owner would like to determine the number of townhouses and the number of apartment buildings to purchase to maximize annual cash flow.

We begin by defining the decision variables as follows:

$$T = \text{number of townhouse}$$
$$A = \text{number of apartment buildings}$$

The objective function for cash flow (in thousands of dollars) is

$$\text{Max } 10T + 15A$$

Three constraints must be satisfied:

$$282T + 400A \leq 2000 \qquad \text{Funds available (\$1000s)}$$
$$4T + 40A \leq 140 \qquad \text{Manager's time (hours)}$$
$$T \qquad \leq 5 \qquad \text{Townhouses available}$$

The variables T and A must be nonnegative. In addition, the purchase of a fractional number of townhouses and/or a fractional number of apartment buildings is unacceptable. Thus, T and A must be integer. The model for the Eastborne Realty problem is the following all-integer linear program:

$$\begin{aligned}
\text{Max} \quad & 10T + 15A \\
\text{s.t.} \quad & \\
& 282T + 400A \le 2000 \\
& 4T + 40A \le 140 \\
& T \le 5 \\
& T, A \ge 0 \text{ and integer}
\end{aligned}$$

Graphical Solution of the LP Relaxation

Suppose that we drop the integer requirements for T and A and solve the LP Relaxation of the Eastborne Realty problem. Using the graphical solution procedure, as presented in Chapter 7, the optimal linear programming solution is shown in Figure 11.1. It is $T = 2.479$ townhouses and $A = 3.252$ apartment buildings. The optimal value of the objective function is 73.574, which indicates an annual cash flow of $73,574. Unfortunately, Eastborne

FIGURE 11.1   GRAPHICAL SOLUTION TO THE LP RELAXATION OF THE EASTBORNE REALTY PROBLEM

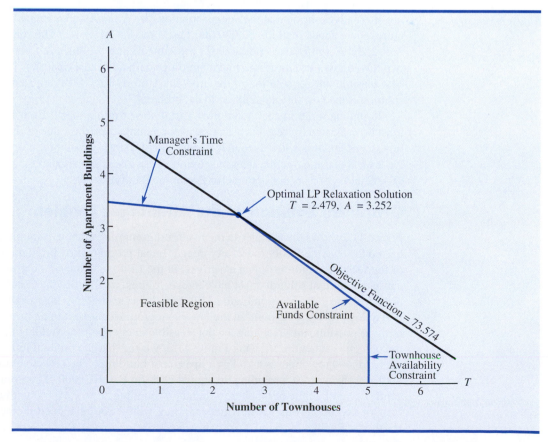

cannot purchase fractional numbers of townhouses and apartment buildings; further analysis is necessary.

Rounding to Obtain an Integer Solution

In many cases, a noninteger solution can be rounded to obtain an acceptable integer solution. For instance, a linear programming solution to a production scheduling problem might call for the production of 15,132.4 cases of breakfast cereal. The rounded integer solution of 15,132 cases would probably have minimal impact on the value of the objective function and the feasibility of the solution. Rounding would be a sensible approach. Indeed, whenever rounding has a minimal impact on the objective function and constraints, most managers find it acceptable. A near-optimal solution is fine.

However, rounding may not always be a good strategy. When the decision variables take on small values that have a major impact on the value of the objective function or feasibility, an optimal integer solution is needed. Let us return to the Eastborne Realty problem and examine the impact of rounding. The optimal solution to the LP Relaxation for Eastborne Realty resulted in $T = 2.479$ townhouses and $A = 3.252$ apartment buildings. Because each townhouse costs \$282,000 and each apartment building costs \$400,000, rounding to an integer solution can be expected to have a significant economic impact on the problem.

If a problem has only less-than-or-equal-to constraints with positive coefficients for the variables, rounding down will always provide a feasible integer solution.

Suppose that we round the solution to the LP Relaxation to obtain the integer solution $T = 2$ and $A = 3$, with an objective function value of $10(2) + 15(3) = 65$. The annual cash flow of \$65,000 is substantially less than the annual cash flow of \$73,574 provided by the solution to the LP Relaxation. Do other rounding possibilities exist? Exploring other rounding alternatives shows that the integer solution $T = 3$ and $A = 3$ is infeasible because it requires more funds than the \$2,000,000 Eastborne has available. The rounded solution of $T = 2$ and $A = 4$ is also infeasible for the same reason. At this point, rounding has led to two townhouses and three apartment buildings with an annual cash flow of \$65,000 as the best feasible integer solution to the problem. Unfortunately, we don't know whether this solution is the best integer solution to the problem.

Rounding to an integer solution is a trial-and-error approach. Each rounded solution must be evaluated for feasibility as well as for its impact on the value of the objective function. Even in cases where a rounded solution is feasible, we do not have a guarantee that we have found the optimal integer solution. We will see shortly that the rounded solution ($T = 2$ and $A = 3$) is not optimal for Eastborne Realty.

Graphical Solution of the All-Integer Problem

Figure 11.2 shows the changes in the linear programming graphical solution procedure required to solve the Eastborne Realty integer linear programming problem. First, the graph of the feasible region is drawn exactly as in the LP Relaxation of the problem. Then, because the optimal solution must have integer values, we identify the feasible integer solutions with the dots shown in Figure 11.2. Finally, instead of moving the objective function line to the best extreme point in the feasible region, we move it in an improving direction as far as possible until reaching the dot (feasible integer point) providing the best value for the objective function. Viewing Figure 11.2, we see that the optimal integer solution occurs at $T = 4$ townhouses and $A = 2$ apartment buildings. The objective function value is $10(4) + 15(2) = 70$, providing an annual cash flow of \$70,000. This solution is significantly better than the best solution found by rounding: $T = 2$, $A = 3$ with an annual cash flow of \$65,000. Thus, we see that rounding would not have been the best strategy for Eastborne Realty.

Try Problem 2 for practice with the graphical solution of an integer program.

FIGURE 11.2   GRAPHICAL SOLUTION OF THE EASTBORNE REALTY INTEGER PROBLEM

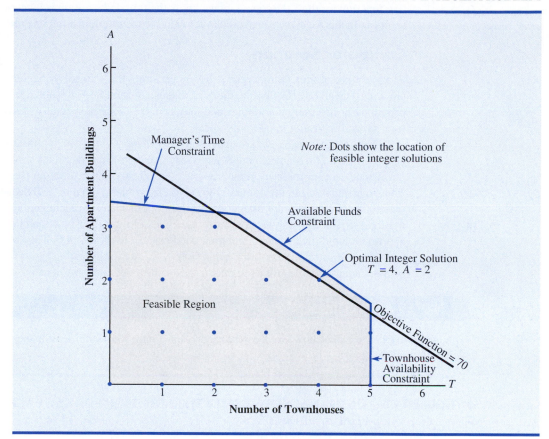

Using the LP Relaxation to Establish Bounds

An important observation can be made from the analysis of the Eastborne Realty problem. It has to do with the relationship between the value of the optimal integer solution and the value of the optimal solution to the LP Relaxation.

> For integer linear programs involving maximization, the value of the optimal solution to the LP Relaxation provides an upper bound on the value of the optimal integer solution. For integer linear programs involving minimization, the value of the optimal solution to the LP Relaxation provides a lower bound on the value of the optimal integer solution.

This observation is valid for the Eastborne Realty problem. The value of the optimal integer solution is $70,000, and the value of the optimal solution to the LP Relaxation is $73,574. Thus, we know from the LP Relaxation solution that the upper bound for the value of the objective function is $73,574.

The bounding property of the LP Relaxation allows us to conclude that if, by chance, the solution to an LP Relaxation turns out to be an integer solution, it is also optimal for the integer linear program. This bounding property can also be helpful in determining whether a rounded solution is "good enough." If a rounded LP Relaxation solution is feasible and

Try Problem 5 for the graphical solution of a mixed-integer program.

provides a value of the objective function that is "almost as good as" the value of the objective function for the LP Relaxation, we know the rounded solution is a near-optimal integer solution. In this case, we can avoid having to solve the problem as an integer linear program.

Computer Solution

As mentioned earlier, commercial software packages that can solve integer linear programs are widely available. Generally, these packages are reliable for problems having up to approximately 100 integer variables and may be used to solve specially structured problems with several thousand integer variables.

The Management Scientist can be used to solve most of the integer linear programs in this chapter. To use The Management Scientist to solve the Eastborne Realty problem, the data input worksheet is completed in the same way as for any linear program (see Appendix 7.1). Then, after instructing the computer to solve the problem, the user will be asked to indicate which of the variables are integers. Specifying both T and A as integers provides the optimal integer solution shown in Figure 11.3. The solution of $T = 4$ townhouses and $A = 2$ apartment buildings has a maximum annual cash flow of $70,000. The values of the slack variables tell us that the optimal solution has $72,000 of available funds unused, 44 hours of the manager's time still available, and 1 of the available townhouses not purchased.

NOTES AND COMMENTS

In Appendix 11.1 we show how Excel can be used to solve integer linear programs such as the Eastborne Realty problem.

FIGURE 11.3 THE MANAGEMENT SCIENTIST SOLUTION FOR THE EASTBORNE REALTY PROBLEM

```
        Objective Function Value = 70.000

              Variable                    Value
           --------------            ----------------

                  T                          4.000
                  A                          2.000


              Constraint               Slack/Surplus
           --------------            ----------------

                  1                         72.000
                  2                         44.000
                  3                          1.000
```

Eastborne

11.3 Applications Involving 0–1 Variables

Much of the modeling flexibility provided by integer linear programming is due to the use of 0-1 variables. In many applications, 0-1 variables provide selections or choices with the value of the variable equal to 1 if a corresponding activity is undertaken and equal to 0 if the corresponding activity is not undertaken. The capital budgeting, fixed cost, distribution system design, bank location, and product design/market share applications presented in this section make use of 0-1 variables.

Capital Budgeting

The Ice-Cold Refrigerator Company is considering investing in several projects that have varying capital requirements over the next four years. Faced with limited capital each year, management would like to select the most profitable projects. The estimated net present value for each project,[1] the capital requirements, and the available capital over the four-year period are shown in Table 11.1.

The four 0-1 decision variables are as follows:

$P = 1$ if the plant expansion project is accepted; 0 if rejected

$W = 1$ if the warehouse expansion project is accepted; 0 if rejected

$M = 1$ if the new machinery project is accepted; 0 if rejected

$R = 1$ if the new product research project is accepted; 0 if rejected

In a **capital budgeting problem**, the company's objective function is to maximize the net present value of the capital budgeting projects. This problem has four constraints: one for the funds available in each of the next four years.

A 0-1 integer linear programming model with dollars in thousands is as follows:

$$\text{Max} \quad 90P + 40W + 10M + 37R$$

$$\text{s.t.}$$

$$
\begin{array}{ll}
15P + 10W + 10M + 15R \le 40 & \text{(Year 1 capital available)} \\
20P + 15W + 10R \le 50 & \text{(Year 2 capital available)} \\
20P + 20W + 10R \le 40 & \text{(Year 3 capital available)} \\
15P + 5W + 4M + 10R \le 35 & \text{(Year 4 capital available)} \\
\end{array}
$$

$$P, W, M, R = 0, 1$$

The integer programming solution from The Management Scientist is shown in Figure 11.4. The optimal solution is $P = 1$, $W = 1$, $M = 1$, $R = 0$, with a total estimated

---

[1]The estimated net present value is the net cash flow discounted back to the beginning of year 1.

TABLE 11.1   PROJECT NET PRESENT VALUE, CAPITAL REQUIREMENTS, AND AVAILABLE CAPITAL FOR THE ICE-COLD REFRIGERATOR COMPANY

	Project				
	Plant Expansion	**Warehouse Expansion**	**New Machinery**	**New Product Research**	**Total Capital Available**
Present Value	$90,000	$40,000	$10,000	$37,000	
Year 1 Cap Rqmt	$15,000	$10,000	$10,000	$15,000	$40,000
Year 2 Cap Rqmt	$20,000	$15,000		$10,000	$50,000
Year 3 Cap Rqmt	$20,000	$20,000		$10,000	$40,000
Year 4 Cap Rqmt	$15,000	$ 5,000	$ 4,000	$10,000	$35,000

FIGURE 11.4   THE MANAGEMENT SCIENTIST SOLUTION FOR THE ICE-COLD
REFRIGERATOR COMPANY PROBLEM

WEB file

Ice-Cold

```
            Objective Function Value = 140.000

              Variable                    Value
            -------------             ---------------
                 P                          1.000
                 W                          1.000
                 M                          1.000
                 R                          0.000


             Constraint               Slack/Surplus
            -------------             ---------------
                 1                          5.000
                 2                         15.000
                 3                          0.000
                 4                         11.000
```

net present value of $140,000. Thus, the company should fund the plant expansion, the warehouse expansion, and the new machinery projects. The new product research project should be put on hold unless additional capital funds become available. The values of the slack variables (see Figure 11.4) show that the company will have $5,000 remaining in year 1, $15,000 remaining in year 2, and $11,000 remaining in year 4. Checking the capital requirements for the new product research project, we see that enough funds are available for this project in year 2 and year 4. However, the company would have to find additional capital funds of $10,000 in year 1 and $10,000 in year 3 to fund the new product research project.

Fixed Cost

In many applications, the cost of production has two components: a setup cost, which is a fixed cost, and a variable cost, which is directly related to the production quantity. The use of 0-1 variables makes including the setup cost possible in a model for a production application.

As an example of a **fixed cost problem**, consider the RMC problem. Three raw materials are used to produce 3 products: a fuel additive, a solvent base, and a carpet cleaning fluid. The following decision variables are used:

$$F = \text{tons of fuel additive produced}$$
$$S = \text{tons of solvent base produced}$$
$$C = \text{tons of carpet cleaning fluid produced}$$

The profit contributions are $40 per ton for the fuel additive, $30 per ton for the solvent base, and $50 per ton for the carpet cleaning fluid. Each ton of fuel additive is a blend of 0.4 tons of material 1 and 0.6 tons of material 3. Each ton of solvent base requires 0.5 tons of material 1, 0.2 tons of material 2, and 0.3 tons of material 3. Each ton of carpet cleaning fluid is a blend of 0.6 tons of material 1, 0.1 tons of material 2, and 0.3 tons of material 3.

RMC has 20 tons of material 1, 5 tons of material 2, and 21 tons of material 3, and is interested in determining the optimal production quantities for the upcoming planning period.
A linear programming model of the RMC problem is shown:

$$\text{Max} \quad 40F + 30S + 50C$$

s.t.

$$0.4F + 0.5S + 0.6C \le 20 \quad \text{Material 1}$$
$$0.2S + 0.1C \le 5 \quad \text{Material 2}$$
$$0.6F + 0.3S + 0.3C \le 21 \quad \text{Material 3}$$
$$F, S, C \ge 0$$

Using the linear programming module of The Management Scientist, we obtained an optimal solution consisting of 27.5 tons of fuel additive, 0 tons of solvent base, and 15 tons of carpet cleaning fluid, with a value of $1850, as shown in Figure 11.5.

This linear programming formulation of the RMC problem does not include a fixed cost for production setup of the products. Suppose that the following data are available concerning the setup cost and the maximum production quantity for each of the three products:

Product	Setup Cost	Maximum Production
Fuel additive	$200	50 tons
Solvent base	$ 50	25 tons
Carpet cleaning fluid	$400	40 tons

The modeling flexibility provided by 0-1 variables can now be used to incorporate the fixed setup costs into the production model. The 0-1 variables are defined as follows:

$$SF = 1 \text{ if the fuel additive is produced; 0 if not}$$
$$SS = 1 \text{ if the solvent base is produced; 0 if not}$$
$$SC = 1 \text{ if the carpet cleaning fluid is produced; 0 if not}$$

Using these setup variables, the total setup cost is

$$200SF + 50SS + 400SC$$

We can now rewrite the objective function to include the setup cost. Thus, the net profit objective function becomes

$$\text{Max } 40F + 30S + 50C - 200SF - 50SS - 400SC$$

FIGURE 11.5   THE MANAGEMENT SCIENTIST SOLUTION TO THE RMC PROBLEM

```
Objective Function Value = 1850.00

        Variable              Value              Reduced Costs
     --------------      ---------------      ------------------
              F                 27.500                    0.000
              S                  0.000                   12.500
              C                 15.000                    0.000
```

Next, we must write production capacity constraints so that if a setup variable equals 0, production of the corresponding product is not permitted and, if a setup variable equals 1, production is permitted up to the maximum quantity. For the fuel additive, we do so by adding the following constraint:

$$F \leq 50SF$$

Note that, with this constraint present, production of the fuel additive is not permitted when $SF = 0$. When $SF = 1$, production of up to 50 tons of fuel additive is permitted. We can think of the setup variable as a switch. When it is off ($SF = 0$), production is not permitted; when it is on ($SF = 1$), production is permitted.

Similar production capacity constraints, using 0-1 variables, are added for the solvent base and carpet cleaning products:

$$S \leq 25SS$$

$$C \leq 40SC$$

Moving all the variables to the left-hand side of the constraints provides the following fixed cost model for the RMC problem:

Max $40F + 30S + 50C - 200SF - 50SS - 400SC$

s.t.

$0.4F + 0.5S + 0.6C$		≤ 20	Material 1
$0.2S + 0.1C$		≤ 5	Material 2
$0.6F + 0.3S + 0.3C$		≤ 21	Material 3
$F - 50SF$		≤ 0	Maximum F
$S - 25SS$		≤ 0	Maximum S
$C - 40SC$		≤ 0	Maximum C

$$F, S, C \geq 0; SF, SS, SC = 0, 1$$

We solved the RMC problem with setup costs using The Management Scientist. As shown in Figure 11.6, the optimal solution shows 25 tons of fuel additive and 20 tons of solvent base. The value of the objective function after deducting the setup cost is $1350. The setup cost for the fuel additive and the solvent base is $200 + $50 = $250. The optimal

FIGURE 11.6   THE MANAGEMENT SCIENTIST SOLUTION TO THE RMC PROBLEM WITH SETUP COSTS

WEB file

RMC-Setup

```
          Objective Function Value = 1350.000

              Variable                  Value
          --------------          --------------
                 F                        25.000
                 S                        20.000
                 C                         0.000
                SF                         1.000
                SS                         1.000
                SC                         0.000
```

solution shows $SC = 0$, which indicates that the more expensive \$400 setup cost for the carpet cleaning fluid should be avoided. Thus, the carpet cleaning fluid is not produced.

The Q.M. in Action, Aluminum Can Production at Valley Metal Containers, (see Section 11.1) employs 0-1 fixed cost variables for production line changeovers.

The key to developing a fixed-cost model is the introduction of a 0-1 variable for each fixed cost and the specification of an upper bound for the corresponding production variable. For a production quantity x, a constraint of the form $x \le My$ can then be used to allow production when the setup variable $y = 1$ and not to allow production when the setup variable $y = 0$. The value of the maximum production quantity M should be large enough to allow for all reasonable levels of production. But research has shown that choosing values of M excessively large will slow the solution procedure.

Distribution System Design

The Martin-Beck Company operates a plant in St. Louis with an annual capacity of 30,000 units. Product is shipped to regional distribution centers located in Boston, Atlanta, and Houston. Because of an anticipated increase in demand, Martin-Beck plans to increase capacity by constructing a new plant in one or more of the following cities: Detroit, Toledo, Denver, or Kansas City. The estimated annual fixed cost and the annual capacity for the four proposed plants are as follows:

Proposed Plant	Annual Fixed Cost	Annual Capacity
Detroit	\$175,000	10,000
Toledo	\$300,000	20,000
Denver	\$375,000	30,000
Kansas City	\$500,000	40,000

The company's long-range planning group developed forecasts of the anticipated annual demand at the distribution centers as follows:

Distribution Center	Annual Demand
Boston	30,000
Atlanta	20,000
Houston	20,000

The shipping cost per unit from each plant to each distribution center is shown in Table 11.2. A network representation of the potential Martin-Beck distribution system is shown in Figure 11.7. Each potential plant location is shown; capacities and demands are shown in thousands of units. This network representation is for a transportation problem

TABLE 11.2   SHIPPING COST PER UNIT FOR THE MARTIN-BECK DISTRIBUTION SYSTEM

	Distribution Centers		
Plant Site	**Boston**	**Atlanta**	**Houston**
Detroit	5	2	3
Toledo	4	3	4
Denver	9	7	5
Kansas City	10	4	2
St. Louis	8	4	3

FIGURE 11.7   THE NETWORK REPRESENTATION OF THE MARTIN-BECK COMPANY
DISTRIBUTION SYSTEM PROBLEM

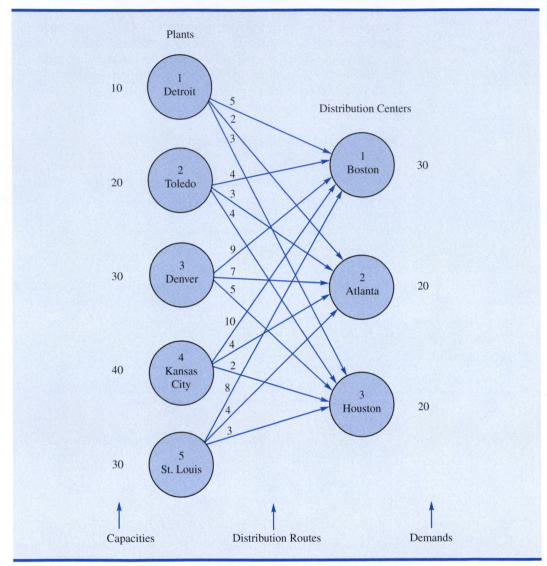

with a plant at St. Louis and at all four proposed sites. However, the decision has not yet
been made as to which new plant or plants will be constructed.

Let us now show how 0-1 variables can be used in this **distribution system design
problem** to develop a model for choosing the best plant locations and for determining how
much to ship from each plant to each distribution center. We can use the following 0-1
variables to represent the plant construction decision:

$$y_1 = 1 \text{ if a plant is constructed in Detroit; 0 if not}$$
$$y_2 = 1 \text{ if a plant is constructed in Toledo; 0 if not}$$
$$y_3 = 1 \text{ if a plant is constructed in Denver; 0 if not}$$
$$y_4 = 1 \text{ if a plant is constructed in Kansas City; 0 if not}$$

The variables representing the amount shipped from each plant site to each distribution center are defined just as for a transportation problem.

$$x_{ij} = \text{the units shipped in thousands from plant } i \text{ to distribution center } j$$
$$i = 1, 2, 3, 4, 5 \text{ and } j = 1, 2, 3$$

Using the shipping cost data in Table 11.2, the annual transportation cost in thousands of dollars is written

$$5x_{11} + 2x_{12} + 3x_{13} + 4x_{21} + 3x_{22} + 4x_{23} + 9x_{31} + 7x_{32} + 5x_{33}$$
$$+ 10x_{41} + 4x_{42} + 2x_{43} + 8x_{51} + 4x_{52} + 3x_{53}$$

The annual fixed cost of operating the new plant or plants in thousands of dollars is written as

$$175y_1 + 300y_2 + 375y_3 + 500y_4$$

Note that the 0-1 variables are defined so that the annual fixed cost of operating the new plants is only calculated for the plant or plants that are actually constructed (i.e., $y_i = 1$). If a plant is not constructed, $y_i = 0$ and the corresponding annual fixed cost is \$0.

The Martin-Beck objective function is the sum of the annual transportation cost plus the annual fixed cost of operating the newly constructed plants.

Now let us consider the capacity constraints at the four proposed plants. Using Detroit as an example, we write the following constraint:

$$x_{11} + x_{12} + x_{13} \leq 10y_1$$

If the Detroit plant is constructed, $y_1 = 1$ and the total amount shipped from Detroit to the three distribution centers must be less than or equal to Detroit's 10,000-unit capacity. If the Detroit plant is not constructed, $y_1 = 0$ will result in a 0 capacity at Detroit. In this case, the variables corresponding to the shipments from Detroit must all equal zero: $x_{11} = 0$, $x_{12} = 0$, and $x_{13} = 0$. By placing all variables on the left-hand side of the constraints, we have the following Detroit capacity constraint:

$$x_{11} + x_{12} + x_{13} - 10y_1 \leq 0 \quad \text{Detroit capacity}$$

In a similar fashion, the capacity constraint for the proposed plant in Toledo can be written

$$x_{21} + x_{22} + x_{23} - 20y_2 \leq 0 \quad \text{Toledo capacity}$$

Similar constraints can be written for the proposed plants in Denver and Kansas City. Note that since the plant already exists in St. Louis, we do not define a 0-1 variable for this plant. Its capacity constraint can be written as follows:

$$x_{51} + x_{52} + x_{53} \leq 30 \quad \text{St. Louis capacity}$$

Three demand constraints will be needed, one for each of the three distribution centers. The demand constraint for the Boston distribution center with units in thousands is written as

$$x_{11} + x_{21} + x_{31} + x_{41} + x_{51} = 30 \quad \text{Boston demand}$$

Similar constraints appear for the Atlanta and Houston distribution centers.

The complete model for the Martin-Beck distribution system design problem is as follows:

$$\text{Min} \quad 5x_{11} + 2x_{12} + 3x_{13} + 4x_{21} + 3x_{22} + 4x_{23} + 9x_{31} + 7x_{32} + 5x_{33} + 10x_{41} + 4x_{42}$$
$$+ 2x_{43} + 8x_{51} + 4x_{52} + 3x_{53} + 175y_1 + 300y_2 + 375y_3 + 500y_4$$

s.t.

$x_{11} + x_{12} + x_{13} \qquad - 10y_1$	≤ 0	Detroit capacity
$x_{21} + x_{22} + x_{23} \qquad - 20y_2$	≤ 0	Toledo capacity
$x_{31} + x_{32} + x_{33} \qquad - 30y_3$	≤ 0	Denver capacity
$x_{41} + x_{42} + x_{43} \qquad - 40y_4$	≤ 0	Kansas City capacity
$x_{51} + x_{52} + x_{53}$	≤ 30	St. Louis capacity
$x_{11} + x_{21} + x_{31} + x_{41} + x_{51}$	$= 30$	Boston demand
$x_{12} + x_{22} + x_{32} + x_{42} + x_{52}$	$= 20$	Atlanta demand
$x_{13} + x_{23} + x_{33} + x_{43} + x_{53}$	$= 20$	Houston demand

$x_{ij} \geq$ for all i and j; $y_1, y_2, y_3, y_4 = 0, 1$

Using the integer linear programming module of The Management Scientist, we obtained the solution shown in Figure 11.8. The optimal solution calls for the construction of a plant in Kansas City ($y_4 = 1$); 20,000 units will be shipped from Kansas City to Atlanta ($x_{42} = 20$), 20,000 units will be shipped from Kansas City to Houston ($x_{43} = 20$), and 30,000 units will be shipped from St. Louis to Boston ($x_{51} = 30$). Note that the total cost of this solution including the fixed cost of $500,000 for the plant in Kansas City is $860,000.

This basic model can be expanded to accommodate distribution systems involving direct shipments from plants to warehouses, from plants to retail outlets, and multiple products.[2] Using the special properties of 0-1 variables, the model can also be expanded to accommodate a variety of configuration constraints on the plant locations. For example, suppose in another problem site 1 was in Dallas and site 2 was in Fort Worth. A company might not want to locate plants in both Dallas and Fort Worth because the cities are so close together. To prevent this from happening, the following constraint can be added to the model:

$$y_1 + y_2 \leq 1$$

Problem 13, which is based on the Martin-Beck distribution system problem, provides additional practice involving 0-1 variables.

This constraint allows either y_1 or y_2 to equal 1, but not both. If we had written the constraints as an equality, it would require that a plant be located in either Dallas or Fort Worth.

Bank Location

The long-range planning department for the Ohio Trust Company is considering expanding its operation into a 20-county region in northeastern Ohio (see Figure 11.9). Currently, Ohio Trust does not have a principal place of business in any of the 20 counties. According to the banking laws in Ohio, if a bank establishes a principal place of business (PPB) in any county, branch banks can be established in that county and in any adjacent county. However, to establish a new principal place of business, Ohio Trust must either obtain approval for a new bank from the state's superintendent of banks or purchase an existing bank.

Table 11.3 lists the 20 counties in the region and adjacent counties. For example, Ashtabula County is adjacent to Lake, Geauga, and Trumbull counties; Lake County is adjacent to Ashtabula, Cuyahoga, and Geauga counties; and so on.

---

[2]For computational reasons, it is usually preferable to replace the m plant capacity constraints with mn shipping route capacity constraints of the form $x_{ij} \leq \text{Min}\{s_i, d_j\} y_i$ for $i = 1, \ldots, m$, and $j = 1, \ldots, n$. The coefficient for y_i in each of these constraints is the smaller of the origin capacity (s_i) or the destination demand (d_j). These additional constraints often cause the solution of the LP Relaxation to be integer.

FIGURE 11.8   THE MANAGEMENT SCIENTIST SOLUTION FOR THE MARTIN-BECK
COMPANY DISTRIBUTION SYSTEM PROBLEM

```
              OPTIMAL SOLUTION

              Objective Function Value = 860.000

                   Variable              Value
                  ------------          ------------
                     X11                  0.000
                     X12                  0.000
                     X13                  0.000
                     X21                  0.000
                     X22                  0.000
                     X23                  0.000
                     X31                  0.000
                     X32                  0.000
                     X33                  0.000
                     X41                  0.000
                     X42                 20.000
                     X43                 20.000
                     X51                 30.000
                     X52                  0.000
                     X53                  0.000
                     Y1                   0.000
                     Y2                   0.000
                     Y3                   0.000
                     Y4                   1.000

                  Constraint          Slack/Surplus
                  ------------          ------------
                      1                   0.000
                      2                   0.000
                      3                   0.000
                      4                   0.000
                      5                   0.000
                      6                   0.000
                      7                   0.000
                      8                   0.000
```

As an initial step in its planning, Ohio Trust would like to determine the minimum number of PPBs necessary to do business throughout the 20-county region. A 0-1 integer programming model can be used to solve this **location problem** for Ohio Trust. We define the variables as

$$x_i = 1 \text{ if a PBB is established in county } i; 0 \text{ otherwise}$$

To minimize the number of PPBs needed, we write the objective function as

$$\text{Min } x_1 + x_2 + \cdots + x_{20}$$

FIGURE 11.9   THE 20-COUNTY REGION IN NORTHEASTERN OHIO

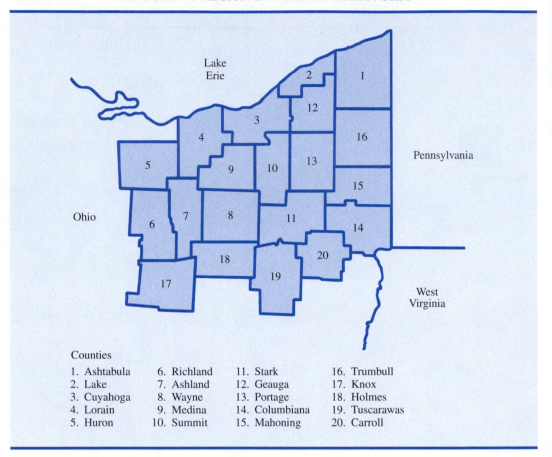

Counties

1. Ashtabula	6. Richland	11. Stark	16. Trumbull
2. Lake	7. Ashland	12. Geauga	17. Knox
3. Cuyahoga	8. Wayne	13. Portage	18. Holmes
4. Lorain	9. Medina	14. Columbiana	19. Tuscarawas
5. Huron	10. Summit	15. Mahoning	20. Carroll

The bank may locate branches in a county if the county contains a PPB or is adjacent to another county with a PPB. Thus, the linear program will need one constraint for each county. For example, the constraint for Ashtabula County is

$$x_1 + x_2 + x_{12} + x_{16} \geq 1 \text{ Ashtabula}$$

Note that satisfaction of this constraint ensures that a PPB will be placed in Ashtabula County *or* in one or more of the adjacent counties. This constraint thus guarantees that Ohio Trust will be able to place branch banks in Ashtabula County.

The complete statement of the bank location problem is

$$
\begin{array}{llll}
\text{Min} & x_1 + x_2 + \quad\cdots\quad + x_{20} \\
\text{s.t.} \\
& x_1 + x_2 + x_{12} + x_{16} & \geq 1 & \text{Ashtabula} \\
& x_1 + x_2 + x_3 + x_{12} & \geq 1 & \text{Lake} \\
& \quad\vdots & \quad\vdots \\
& x_{11} + x_{14} + x_{19} + x_{20} \geq 1 & & \text{Carroll} \\
& x_i = 0, 1 \quad i = 1, 2, \dots, 20
\end{array}
$$

TABLE 11.3   COUNTIES IN THE OHIO TRUST EXPANSION REGION

Counties Under Consideration	Adjacent Counties (by Number)
1. Ashtabula	2, 12, 16
2. Lake	1, 3, 12
3. Cuyahoga	2, 4, 9, 10, 12, 13
4. Lorain	3, 5, 7, 9
5. Huron	4, 6, 7
6. Richland	5, 7, 17
7. Ashland	4, 5, 6, 8, 9, 17, 18
8. Wayne	7, 9, 10, 11, 18
9. Medina	3, 4, 7, 8, 10
10. Summit	3, 8, 9, 11, 12, 13
11. Stark	8, 10, 13, 14, 15, 18, 19, 20
12. Geauga	1, 2, 3, 10, 13, 16
13. Portage	3, 10, 11, 12, 15, 16
14. Columbiana	11, 15, 20
15. Mahoning	11, 13, 14, 16
16. Trumbull	1, 12, 13, 15
17. Knox	6, 7, 18
18. Holmes	7, 8, 11, 17, 19
19. Tuscarawas	11, 18, 20
20. Carroll	11, 14, 19

We used The Management Scientist to solve this 20-variable, 20-constraint problem formulation. In Figure 11.10 we show a portion of the computer output. Note that the variable names correspond to the first four letters in the name of each county. Using the output, we see that the optimal solution calls for principal places of business in Ashland, Stark, and Geauga counties. With PPBs in these three counties, Ohio Trust can place branch banks in all 20 counties (see Figure 11.11). All other decision variables have an optimal value of zero, indicating that a PPB should not be placed in these counties. Clearly the integer programming model could be enlarged to allow for expansion into a larger area or throughout the entire state.

Product Design and Market Share Optimization

Conjoint analysis is a market research technique that can be used to learn how prospective buyers of a product value the product's attributes. In this section we will show how the results of conjoint analysis can be used in an integer programming model of a **product design and market share optimization problem**. We illustrate the approach by considering a problem facing Salem Foods, a major producer of frozen foods.

Salem Foods is planning to enter the frozen pizza market. Currently, two existing brands, Antonio's and King's, have the major share of the market. In trying to develop a sausage pizza that will capture a significant share of the market, Salem determined that the four most important attributes when consumers purchase a frozen sausage pizza are crust, cheese, sauce, and sausage flavor. The crust attribute has two levels (thin and thick); the cheese attribute has two levels (mozzarella and blend); the sauce attribute has two levels (smooth and chunky); and the sausage flavor attribute has three levels (mild, medium, and hot).

FIGURE 11.10   THE MANAGEMENT SCIENTIST SOLUTION FOR THE OHIO TRUST PPB
LOCATION PROBLEM

Ohio-Trust

```
            OPTIMAL SOLUTION

            Objective Function Value = 3.000

                    Variable                Value
                 --------------          ---------------
                      ASHT                   0.000
                      LAKE                   0.000
                      CUYA                   0.000
                      LORA                   0.000
                      HURO                   0.000
                      RICH                   0.000
                      ASHL                   1.000
                      WAYN                   0.000
                      MEDI                   0.000
                      SUMM                   0.000
                      STAR                   1.000
                      GEAU                   1.000
                      PORT                   0.000
                      COLU                   0.000
                      MAHO                   0.000
                      TRUM                   0.000
                      KNOX                   0.000
                      HOLM                   0.000
                      TUSC                   0.000
                      CARR                   0.000
```

In a typical conjoint analysis, a sample of consumers is asked to express their preference for specially prepared pizzas with chosen levels for the attributes. Then regression analysis is used to determine the part-worth for each of the attribute levels. In essence, the part-worth is the utility value that a consumer attaches to each level of each attribute. A discussion of how to use regression analysis to compute the part-worths is beyond the scope of this text, but we will show how the part-worths can be used to determine the overall value a consumer attaches to a particular pizza.

Table 11.4 shows the part-worths for each level of each attribute provided by a sample of eight potential Salem customers who are currently buying either King's or Antonio's pizza. For consumer 1 the part-worths for the crust attribute are 11 for thin crust and 2 for thick crust, indicating a preference for thin crust. For the cheese attribute, the part-worths are 6 for the mozzarella cheese and 7 for the cheese blend; thus, consumer 1 has a slight preference for the cheese blend. From the other part-worths, we see that consumer 1 shows a strong preference for the chunky sauce over the smooth sauce (17 to 3), and has a slight preference for the medium-flavored sausage. Note that consumer 2 shows a preference for the thin crust, the cheese blend, the chunky sauce, and mild-flavored sausage. The part-worths for the others consumers are interpreted in a similar manner.

FIGURE 11.11 PRINCIPAL PLACE OF BUSINESS COUNTIES FOR OHIO TRUST

Counties

1. Ashtabula	6. Richland	11. Stark	16. Trumbull	★ A principal place
2. Lake	7. Ashland	12. Geauga	17. Knox	of business
3. Cuyahoga	8. Wayne	13. Portage	18. Holmes	should be located
4. Lorain	9. Medina	14. Columbiana	19. Tuscarawas	in these counties.
5. Huron	10. Summit	15. Mahoning	20. Carroll	

The part-worths can be used to determine the overall value (utility) each consumer attaches to a particular type of pizza. For instance, consumer 1's current favorite pizza is the Antonio's brand, which has a thick crust, mozzarella cheese, chunky sauce, and medium-flavored sausage. We can determine consumer 1's utility for this particular type of pizza using the part-worths in Table 11.4. For consumer 1 the part-worths are 2 for thick crust, 6 for

TABLE 11.4 PART-WORTHS FOR THE SALEM FOODS PROBLEM

| | Crust | | Cheese | | Sauce | | Sausage Flavor | | |
Consumer	Thin	Thick	Mozzarella	Blend	Smooth	Chunky	Mild	Medium	Hot
1	11	2	6	7	3	17	26	27	8
2	11	7	15	17	16	26	14	1	10
3	7	5	8	14	16	7	29	16	19
4	13	20	20	17	17	14	25	29	10
5	2	8	6	11	30	20	15	5	12
6	12	17	11	9	2	30	22	12	20
7	9	19	12	16	16	25	30	23	19
8	5	9	4	14	23	16	16	30	3

mozzarella cheese, 17 for chunky sauce, and 27 for medium-flavored sausage. Thus, consumer 1's utility for the Antonio's brand pizza is $2 + 6 + 17 + 27 = 52$. We can compute consumer 1's utility for a King's brand pizza in a similar manner. The King's brand pizza has a thin crust, a cheese blend, smooth sauce, and mild-flavored sausage. Because the part-worths for consumer 1 are 11 for thin crust, 7 for cheese blend, 3 for smooth sauce, and 26 for mild-flavored sausage, consumer 1's utility for the King's brand pizza is $11 + 7 + 3 + 26 = 47$. In general, each consumer's utility for a particular type of pizza is just the sum of the appropriate part-worths.

In order to be successful with its brand, Salem Foods realizes that it must entice consumers in the marketplace to switch from their current favorite brand of pizza to the Salem product. That is, Salem must design a pizza (choose the type of crust, cheese, sauce, and sausage flavor) that will have the highest utility for enough people to ensure sufficient sales to justify making the product. Assuming the sample of eight consumers in the current study is representative of the marketplace for frozen sausage pizza, we can formulate and solve an integer programming model that can help Salem come up with such a design. In marketing literature, the problem being solved is called the *share of choice* problem.

The decision variables are defined as follows:

$$l_{ij} = 1 \text{ if Salem chooses level } i \text{ for attribute } j; 0 \text{ otherwise}$$
$$y_k = 1 \text{ if consumer } k \text{ chooses the Salem brand}; 0 \text{ otherwise}$$

The objective is to choose the levels of each attribute that will maximize the number of consumers preferring the Salem brand pizza. Because the number of customers preferring the Salem brand pizza is just the sum of the y_k variables, the objective function is

$$\text{Max } y_1 + y_2 + \cdots + y_8$$

One constraint is needed for each consumer in the sample. To illustrate how the constraints are formulated, let us consider the constraint corresponding to consumer 1. For consumer 1, the utility of a particular type of pizza can be expressed as the sum of the part-worths:

$$\text{Utility for Customer } 1 = 11l_{11} + 2l_{21} + 6l_{12} + 7l_{22} + 3l_{13} + 17l_{23} + 26l_{14} + 27l_{24} + 8l_{34}$$

In order for consumer 1 to prefer the Salem pizza, the utility for the Salem pizza must be greater than the utility for consumer 1's current favorite. Recall that consumer 1's current favorite brand of pizza is Antonio's, with a utility of 52. Thus, consumer 1 will only purchase the Salem brand if the levels of the attributes for the Salem brand are chosen such that

$$11l_{11} + 2l_{21} + 6l_{12} + 7l_{22} + 3l_{13} + 17l_{23} + 26l_{14} + 27l_{24} + 8l_{34} > 52$$

Given the definitions of the y_k decision variables, we want $y_1 = 1$ when the consumer prefers the Salem brand and $y_1 = 0$ when the consumer does not prefer the Salem brand. Thus, we write the constraint for consumer 1 as follows:

$$11l_{11} + 2l_{21} + 6l_{12} + 7l_{22} + 3l_{13} + 17l_{23} + 26l_{14} + 27l_{24} + 8l_{34} \geq 1 + 52y_1$$

With this constraint, y_1 cannot equal 1 unless the utility for the Salem design (the left-hand side of the constraint) exceeds the utility for consumer 1's current favorite by at least 1.

Because the objective function is to maximize the sum of the y_k variables, the optimization will seek a product design that will allow as many y_k as possible to equal 1.

Placing all the decision variables on the left-hand side of the constraint enables us to rewrite constraint 1 as follows:

$$11l_{11} + 2l_{21} + 6l_{12} + 7l_{22} + 3l_{13} + 17l_{23} + 26l_{14} + 27l_{24} + 8l_{34} - 52y_1 \geq 1$$

A similar constraint is written for each consumer in the sample. The coefficients for the l_{ij} variables in the utility functions are taken from Table 11.4 and the coefficients for the y_k variables are obtained by computing the overall utility of the consumer's current favorite brand of pizza. The following constraints correspond to the eight consumers in the study:

Antonio's brand is the current favorite pizza for consumers 1, 4, 6, 7, and 8. King's brand is the current favorite pizza for consumers 2, 3, and 5.

$$11l_{11} + \ 2l_{21} + \ \ 6l_{12} + \ \ 7l_{22} + \ \ 3l_{13} + 17l_{23} + 26l_{14} + 27l_{24} + \ \ 8l_{34} - 52y_1 \geq 1$$
$$11l_{11} + \ 7l_{21} + 15l_{12} + 17l_{22} + 16l_{13} + 26l_{23} + 14l_{14} + \ \ 1l_{24} + 10l_{34} - 58y_2 \geq 1$$
$$\ 7l_{11} + \ 5l_{21} + \ \ 8l_{12} + 14l_{22} + 16l_{13} + \ \ 7l_{23} + 29l_{14} + 16l_{24} + 19l_{34} - 66y_3 \geq 1$$
$$13l_{11} + 20l_{21} + 20l_{12} + 17l_{22} + 17l_{13} + 14l_{23} + 25l_{14} + 29l_{24} + 10l_{34} - 83y_4 \geq 1$$
$$\ 2l_{11} + \ 8l_{21} + \ \ 6l_{12} + 11l_{22} + 30l_{13} + 20l_{23} + 15l_{14} + \ \ 5l_{24} + 12l_{34} - 58y_5 \geq 1$$
$$12l_{11} + 17l_{21} + 11l_{12} + \ \ 9l_{22} + \ \ 2l_{13} + 30l_{23} + 22l_{14} + 12l_{24} + 20l_{34} - 70y_6 \geq 1$$
$$\ 9l_{11} + 19l_{21} + 12l_{12} + 16l_{22} + 16l_{13} + 25l_{23} + 30l_{14} + 23l_{24} + 19l_{34} - 79y_7 \geq 1$$
$$\ 5l_{11} + \ 9l_{21} + \ \ 4l_{12} + 14l_{22} + 23l_{13} + 16l_{23} + 16l_{14} + 30l_{24} + \ \ 3l_{34} - 59y_8 \geq 1$$

Four more constraints must be added, one for each attribute. These constraints are necessary to ensure that one and only one level is selected for each attribute. For attribute 1 (crust), we must add the constraint

$$l_{11} + l_{21} = 1$$

Because l_{11} and l_{21} are both 0-1 variables, this constraint requires that one of the two variables equals 1 and the other equals zero. The following three constraints ensure that one and only one level is selected for each of the other three attributes:

$$l_{12} + l_{22} = 1$$
$$l_{13} + l_{23} = 1$$
$$l_{14} + l_{24} + l_{34} = 1$$

WEB file

Salem

The optimal solution (obtained using LINGO[3]) to this 17-variable, 12-constraint integer linear program is $l_{21} = l_{22} = l_{23} = l_{14} = 1$ and $y_2 = y_5 = y_6 = y_7 = 1$. The value of the optimal solution is 4, indicating that if Salem makes this type of pizza, it will be preferable to the current favorite for four of the eight consumers. With $l_{21} = l_{22} = l_{23} = l_{14} = 1$, the pizza design that obtains the largest market share for Salem has a thick crust, a cheese blend, a chunky sauce, and mild-flavored sausage. Note also that with $y_2 = y_5 = y_6 = y_7 = 1$, consumers 2, 5, 6, and 7 will prefer the Salem pizza. With this information Salem may choose to market this type of pizza.

---

[3]We noted at the beginning of this chapter that some fairly small integer programs can be difficult to solve. The combinatorial structure of the share of choices problem in this section makes it too difficult for The Management Scientist. We have solved the Salem Foods problem using LINGO. For the Excel solution to this problem see the Webfiles link on the Web site that accompanies this book.

NOTES AND COMMENTS

1. Most practical applications of integer linear programming involve only 0-1 integer variables. Indeed, some mixed-integer computer codes are designed to handle only integer variables with binary values. However, if a clever mathematical trick is employed, these codes can still be used for problems involving general integer variables. The trick is called *binary expansion* and requires that an upper bound be established for each integer variable. More advanced texts on integer programming show how it can be done.

2. The Q.M. in Action, Volunteer Scheduling for the Edmonton Folk Festival, describes how a series of three integer programming models was used to schedule volunteers. Two of the models employ 0-1 variables.

3. General-purpose mixed-integer linear programming codes and some spreadsheet packages can be used for linear programming problems, all-integer problems, and problems involving some continuous and some integer variables. General-purpose codes are seldom the fastest for solving problems with special structure (such as the transportation, assignment, and transshipment problems); however, unless the problems are very large, speed is usually not a critical issue. Thus, most practitioners prefer to use one general-purpose computer package that can be used on a variety of problems rather than to maintain a variety of computer programs designed for special problems.

Q.M. *in* ACTION

VOLUNTEER SCHEDULING FOR THE EDMONTON FOLK FESTIVAL*

The Edmonton Folk Festival is a four-day outdoor event that is run almost entirely by volunteers. In 2002, 1800 volunteers worked on 35 different crews and contributed more than 50,000 volunteer hours. With this many volunteers, coordination requires a major effort. For instance, in 2002, two volunteer coordinators used a trial-and-error procedure to develop schedules for the volunteers in the two gate crews. However, developing these schedules proved to be time consuming and frustrating; the coordinators spent as much time scheduling as they did supervising volunteers during the festival. To reduce the time spent on gate-crew scheduling, one of the coordinators asked the Centre for Excellence in Operations at the University of Alberta School of Business for help in automating the scheduling process. The Centre agreed to help.

The scheduling system developed consists of three integer programming models. Model 1 is used to determine daily shift schedules. This model determines the length of each shift (number of hours) and how many volunteers are needed for each shift to meet the peaks and valleys in demand. Model 2 is a binary integer program used to assign volunteers to shifts. The objective is to maximize volunteer preferences subject to several constraints, such as number of hours worked, balance between morning and afternoon shifts, a mix of experienced and inexperienced volunteers on each shift, no conflicting shifts, and so on. Model 3 is used to allocate volunteers between the two gates.

The coordinators of the gate crews were pleased with the results provided by the models and learned to use them effectively. Vicki Fannon, the manager of volunteers for the festival, now has plans to expand the use of the integer programming models to the scheduling of other crews in the future.

*Based on L. Gordon and E. Erkut, "Improving Volunteer Scheduling for the Edmonton Folk Festival," *Interfaces* (September/October 2004): 367–376.

11.4 Modeling Flexibility Provided by 0–1 Integer Variables

In Section 11.3 we presented four applications involving 0-1 integer variables. In this section we continue the discussion of the use of 0-1 integer variables in modeling. First, we show how 0-1 integer variables can be used to model multiple-choice and mutually exclusive constraints. Then, we show how 0-1 integer variables can be used to model situations in which k projects out of a set of n projects must be selected, as well as situations in which the acceptance of one project is conditional on the acceptance of another. We close the section with a cautionary note on the role of sensitivity analysis in integer linear programming.

Multiple-Choice and Mutually Exclusive Constraints

Recall the Ice-Cold Refrigerator capital budgeting problem introduced in Section 11.3. The decision variables were defined as

$P = 1$ if the plant expansion project is accepted; 0 if rejected

$W = 1$ if the warehouse expansion project is accepted; 0 if reject

$M = 1$ if the new machinery project is accepted; 0 if rejected

$R = 1$ if the new product research project is accepted; 0 if rejected

Suppose that, instead of one warehouse expansion project, the Ice-Cold Refrigerator Company actually has three warehouse expansion projects under consideration. One of the warehouses *must* be expanded because of increasing product demand, but new demand isn't sufficient to make expansion of more than one warehouse necessary. The following variable definitions and **multiple-choice constraint** could be incorporated into the previous 0-1 integer linear programming model to reflect this situation. Let

$W_1 = 1$ if the original warehouse expansion project is accepted; 0 if rejected

$W_2 = 1$ if the second warehouse expansion project is accepted; 0 if rejected

$W_3 = 1$ if the third warehouse expansion project is accepted; 0 if rejected

The multiple-choice constraint reflecting the requirement that exactly one of these projects must be selected is

$$W_1 + W_2 + W_3 = 1$$

If W_1, W_2, and W_3 are allowed to assume only the values 0 or 1, then one and only one of these projects will be selected from among the three choices.

   If the requirement that one warehouse must be expanded did not exist, the multiple-choice constraint could be modified as follows:

$$W_1 + W_2 + W_3 \leq 1$$

This modification allows for the case of no warehouse expansion ($W_1 = W_2 = W_3 = 0$) but does not permit more than one warehouse to be expanded. This type of constraint is often called a **mutually exclusive constraint**.

k out of n Alternatives Constraint

An extension of the notion of a multiple-choice constraint can be used to model situations in which k *out of a set of n* projects must be selected—a **k out of n alternatives constraint**. Suppose that W_1, W_2, W_3, W_4, and W_5 represent five potential warehouse expansion projects and that two of the five projects must be accepted. The constraint that satisfies this new requirement is

$$W_1 + W_2 + W_3 + W_4 + W_5 = 2$$

If no more than two of the projects are to be selected, we would use the following less-than-or-equal-to constraint:

$$W_1 + W_2 + W_3 + W_4 + W_5 \leq 2$$

Again, each of these variables must be restricted to 0-1 values.

Conditional and Corequisite Constraints

Sometimes the acceptance of one project is conditional on the acceptance of another. For example, suppose for the Ice-Cold Refrigerator Company that the warehouse expansion project was conditional on the plant expansion project. That is, management will not consider expanding the warehouse unless the plant is expanded. With P representing plant expansion and W representing warehouse expansion, a **conditional constraint** could be introduced to enforce this requirement:

$$W \leq P$$

Both P and W must be 0 or 1; whenever P is 0, W will be forced to 0. When P is 1, W is also allowed to be 1; thus, both the plant and the warehouse can be expanded. However, we note that the preceding constraint does not force the warehouse expansion project (W) to be accepted if the plant expansion project (P) is accepted.

If the warehouse expansion project had to be accepted whenever the plant expansion project was, and vice versa, we would say that P and W represented **corequisite constraint** projects. To model such a situation, we simply write the preceding constraint as an equality:

$$W = P$$

Try Problem 7 for practice with the modeling flexibility provided by 0-1 variables.

The constraint forces P and W to take on the same value.

The Q.M. in Action, Customer Order Allocation Model at Ketron, describes how the modeling flexibility provided by 0-1 variables helped Ketron build a customer order allocation model for a sporting goods company.

Q.M. *in* ACTION

CUSTOMER ORDER ALLOCATION MODEL AT KETRON*

Ketron Management Science provides consulting services for the design and implementation of mathematical programming applications. One such application involved the development of a mixed-integer programming model of the customer order allocation problem for a major sporting goods company. The sporting goods company markets approximately 300 products and has about 30 sources of supply (factory and warehouse locations). The problem is to determine how best to allocate customer orders to the various sources of supply such that the total manufacturing cost for the products ordered is minimized. Figure 11.12 provides a graphical repre-

sentation of this problem. Note in the figure that each customer can receive shipments from only a few of the various sources of supply. For example, we see that customer 1 may be supplied by source A or B, customer 2 may be supplied only by source A, and so on.

The sporting equipment company classifies each customer order as either a "guaranteed" or "secondary" order. Guaranteed orders are single-source orders in that they must be filled by a single supplier to ensure that the complete order will be delivered to the customer at one time. This single-source requirement necessitates the use of 0-1 integer variables in the model. Approximately 80% of the company's orders are guaranteed orders. Secondary orders can be split among the various sources of supply.

*Based on information provided by J. A. Tomlin of Ketron Management Science.

(*continued*)

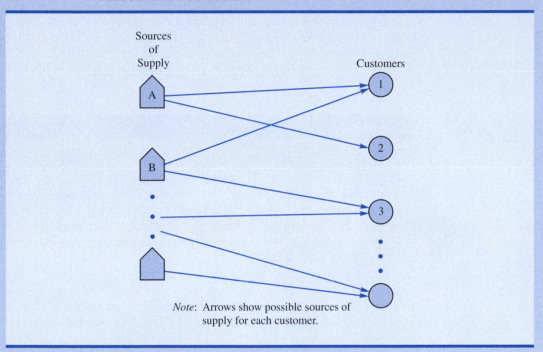

FIGURE 11.12   GRAPHICAL REPRESENTATION OF THE CUSTOMER ORDER ALLOCATION PROBLEM

Sources of Supply

Customers

Note: Arrows show possible sources of supply for each customer.

These orders are made by customers restocking inventory, and receiving partial shipments from different sources at different times is not a problem. The 0-1 variables are used to represent the assignment of a guaranteed order to a supplier and continuous variables are used to represent the secondary orders.

Constraints for the problem involve raw material capacities, manufacturing capacities, and individual product capacities. A fairly typical problem has about 800 constraints, 2000 0-1 assignment variables, and 500 continuous variables associated with the secondary orders. The customer order allocation problem is solved periodically as orders are received. In a typical period, between 20 and 40 customers are to be supplied. Because most customers require several products, usually between 600 and 800 orders must be assigned to the sources of supply.

A Cautionary Note About Sensitivity Analysis

Sensitivity analysis often is more crucial for integer linear programming problems than for linear programming problems. A small change in one of the coefficients in the constraints can cause a relatively large change in the value of the optimal solution. To understand why, consider the following integer programming model of a simple capital budgeting problem involving four projects and a budgetary constraint for a single time period:

$$\text{Max} \quad 40x_1 + 60x_2 + 70x_3 + 160x_4$$
$$\text{s.t.}$$
$$16x_1 + 35x_2 + 45x_3 + 85x_4 \le 100$$
$$x_1, x_2, x_3, x_4 = 0, 1$$

We can obtain the optimal solution to this problem by enumerating the alternatives. It is $x_1 = 1, x_2 = 1, x_3 = 1$, and $x_4 = 0$, with an objective function value of \$170. However, note that if the budget available is increased by \$1 (from \$100 to \$101), the optimal solution changes to $x_1 = 1, x_2 = 0, x_3 = 0$, and $x_4 = 1$, with an objective function value of \$200. That is, one additional dollar in the budget would lead to a \$30 increase in the return. Surely management, when faced with such a situation, would increase the budget by \$1. Because of the extreme sensitivity of the value of the optimal solution to the constraint coefficients, practitioners usually recommend re-solving the integer linear program several times with slight variations in the coefficients before attempting to choose the best solution for implementation.

Summary

In this chapter we introduced the important extension of linear programming referred to as *integer linear programming*. The only difference between the integer linear programming problems discussed in this chapter and the linear programming problems studied in previous chapters is that one or more of the variables must be integer. If all variables must be integer, we have an all-integer linear program. If some, but not necessarily all, variables must be integer, we have a mixed-integer linear program. Most integer programming applications involve 0-1 or binary variables.

Studying integer linear programming is important for two major reasons. First, integer linear programming may be helpful when fractional values for the variables are not permitted. Rounding a linear programming solution may not provide an optimal integer solution; methods for finding optimal integer solutions are needed when the economic consequences of rounding are significant. A second reason for studying integer linear programming is the increased modeling flexibility provided through the use of 0-1 variables. We showed how 0-1 variables could be used to model important managerial considerations in capital budgeting, fixed cost, distribution system design, bank location, and product design/market share applications.

The number of applications of integer linear programming continues to grow rapidly. This growth is due in part to the availability of good integer linear programming software packages. As researchers develop solution procedures capable of solving larger integer linear programs and as computer speed increases, a continuation of the growth of integer programming applications is expected.

Glossary

Integer linear program A linear program with the additional requirement that one or more of the variables must be integer.

All-integer linear program An integer linear program in which all variables are required to be integer.

LP Relaxation The linear program that results from dropping the integer requirements for the variables in an integer linear program.

Mixed-integer linear program An integer linear program in which some, but not necessarily all, variables are required to be integer.

0-1 integer linear program An all-integer or mixed-integer linear program in which the integer variables are only permitted to assume the values 0 or 1. Also called *binary integer program*.

Capital budgeting problem A 0-1 integer programming problem that involves choosing which possible projects or activities provide the best investment return.

Fixed cost problem A 0-1 mixed-integer programming problem in which the binary variables represent whether an activity, such as a production run, is undertaken (variable $= 1$) or not (variable $= 0$).

Distribution system design problem A mixed-integer linear program in which the binary integer variables usually represent sites selected for warehouses or plants and continuous variables represent the amount shipped over arcs in the distribution network.

Location problem A 0-1 integer programming problem in which the objective is to select the best locations to meet a stated objective. Variations of this problem (see the bank location problem in Section 11.3) are known as covering problems.

Product design and market share optimization problem Sometimes called the share of choice problem, it involves choosing a product design that maximizes the number of consumers preferring it.

Multiple-choice constraint A constraint requiring that the sum of two or more 0-1 variables equals 1. Thus, any feasible solution makes a choice of which variable to set equal to 1.

Mutually exclusive constraint A constraint requiring that the sum of two or more 0-1 variables be less than or equal to 1. Thus, if one of the variables equals 1, the others must equal 0. However, all variables could equal 0.

k out of n alternatives constraint An extension of the multiple-choice constraint. This constraint requires that the sum of n 0-1 variables equals k.

Conditional constraint A constraint involving 0-1 variables that does not allow certain variables to equal 1 unless certain other variables are equal to 1.

Corequisite constraint A constraint requiring that two 0-1 variables be equal. Thus, they are both either in or out of solution together.

Problems

1. Indicate which of the following is an all-integer linear program and which is a mixed-integer linear program. Write the LP Relaxation for the problem but do not attempt to solve.

   a. Max $30x_1 + 25x_2$

      s.t.

      $$3x_1 + 1.5x_2 \leq 400$$
      $$1.5x_1 + 2x_2 \leq 250$$
      $$1x_1 + 1x_2 \leq 150$$
      $$x_1, x_2 \geq 0 \text{ and } x_2 \text{ integer}$$

   b. Min $3x_1 + 4x_2$

      s.t.

      $$2x_1 + 4x_2 \geq 8$$
      $$2x_1 + 6x_2 \geq 12$$
      $$x_1, x_2 \geq 0 \text{ and integer}$$

2. Consider the following all-integer linear program:

   $$\text{Max} \quad 5x_1 + 8x_2$$

   s.t.

   $$6x_1 + 5x_2 \leq 30$$
   $$9x_1 + 4x_2 \leq 36$$
   $$1x_1 + 2x_2 \leq 10$$
   $$x_1, x_2 \geq 0 \text{ and integer}$$

    a.   Graph the constraints for this problem. Use dots to indicate all feasible integer solutions.

    b.   Find the optimal solution to the LP Relaxation. Round down to find a feasible integer solution.

    c.   Find the optimal integer solution. Is it the same as the solution obtained in part (b) by rounding down?

3. Consider the following all-integer linear program:

$$\text{Max}\quad 1x_1 + 1x_2$$

$$\text{s.t.}$$

$$4x_1 + 6x_2 \leq 22$$
$$1x_1 + 5x_2 \leq 15$$
$$2x_1 + 1x_2 \leq 9$$
$$x_1, x_2 \geq 0 \text{ and integer}$$

    a.   Graph the constraints for this problem. Use dots to indicate all feasible integer solutions.

    b.   Solve the LP Relaxation of this problem.

    c.   Find the optimal integer solution.

4. Consider the following all-integer linear program:

$$\text{Max}\quad 10x_1 + 3x_2$$

$$\text{s.t.}$$

$$6x_1 + 7x_2 \leq 40$$
$$3x_1 + 1x_2 \leq 11$$
$$x_1, x_2 \geq 0 \text{ and integer}$$

    a.   Formulate and solve the LP Relaxation of the problem. Solve it graphically, and round down to find a feasible solution. Specify an upper bound on the value of the optimal solution.

    b.   Solve the integer linear program graphically. Compare the value of this solution with the solution obtained in part (a).

    c.   Suppose the objective function changes to Max $3x_1 + 6x_2$. Repeat parts (a) and (b).

5. Consider the following mixed-integer linear program:

$$\text{Max}\quad 2x_1 + 3x_2$$

$$\text{s.t.}$$

$$4x_1 + 9x_2 \leq 36$$
$$7x_1 + 5x_2 \leq 35$$
$$x_1, x_2 \geq 0 \text{ and } x_1 \text{ integer}$$

    a.   Graph the constraints for this problem. Indicate on your graph all feasible mixed-integer solutions.

    b.   Find the optimal solution to the LP Relaxation. Round the value of x_1 down to find a feasible mixed-integer solution. Is this solution optimal? Why or why not?

    c.   Find the optimal solution for the mixed-integer linear program.

6. Consider the following mixed-integer linear program:

$$\text{Max}\quad 1x_1 + 1x_2$$

$$\text{s.t.}$$

$$7x_1 + 9x_2 \leq 63$$
$$9x_1 + 5x_2 \leq 45$$
$$3x_1 + 1x_2 \leq 12$$
$$x_1, x_2 \geq 0 \text{ and } x_2 \text{ integer}$$

a. Graph the constraints for this problem. Indicate on your graph all feasible mixed-integer solutions.

b. Find the optimal solution to the LP Relaxation. Round the value of x_2 down to find a feasible mixed-integer solution. Specify upper and lower bounds on the value of the optimal solution to the mixed-integer linear program.

c. Find the optimal solution to the mixed-integer linear program.

7. The following questions refer to a capital budgeting problem with six projects represented by 0-1 variables x_1, x_2, x_3, x_4, x_5, and x_6:

a. Write a constraint modeling a situation in which two of the projects 1, 3, 5, and 6 must be undertaken.

b. Write a constraint modeling a situation in which, if projects 3 and 5 must be undertaken, they must be undertaken simultaneously.

c. Write a constraint modeling a situation in which project 1 or 4 must be undertaken, but not both.

d. Write constraints modeling a situation where project 4 cannot be undertaken unless projects 1 and 3 also are undertaken.

e. Revise the requirement in part (d) to accommodate the case in which, when projects 1 and 3 are undertaken, project 4 also must be undertaken.

8. Spencer Enterprises is attempting to choose among a series of new investment alternatives. The potential investment alternatives, the net present value of the future stream of returns, the capital requirements, and the available capital funds over the next three years are summarized as follows:

Alternative	Net Present Value ($)	Capital Requirements ($)		
		Year 1	Year 2	Year 3
Limited warehouse expansion	4,000	3,000	1,000	4,000
Extensive warehouse expansion	6,000	2,500	3,500	3,500
Test market new product	10,500	6,000	4,000	5,000
Advertising campaign	4,000	2,000	1,500	1,800
Basic research	8,000	5,000	1,000	4,000
Purchase new equipment	3,000	1,000	500	900
Capital funds available		10,500	7,000	8,750

a. Develop and solve an integer programming model for maximizing the net present value.

b. Assume that only one of the warehouse expansion projects can be implemented. Modify your model of part (a).

c. Suppose that, if test marketing of the new product is carried out, the advertising campaign also must be conducted. Modify your formulation of part (b) to reflect this new situation.

9. Hawkins Manufacturing Company produces connecting rods for 4- and 6-cylinder automobile engines using the same production line. The cost required to set up the production line to produce the 4-cylinder connecting rods is $2000, and the cost required to set up the production line for the 6-cylinder connecting rods is $3500. Manufacturing costs are $15 for each 4-cylinder connecting rod and $18 for each 6-cylinder connecting rod. Hawkins makes a decision at the end of each week as to which product will be manufactured the following week. If there is a production changeover from one week to the next, the weekend is used to reconfigure the production line. Once the line has been set up, the

weekly production capacities are 6000 6-cylinder connecting rods and 8000 4-cylinder connecting rods. Let

x_4 = the number of 4-cylinder connecting rods produced next week

x_6 = the number of 6-cylinder connecting rods produced next week

s_4 = 1 if the production line is set up to produce the 4-cylinder connecting rods; 0 if otherwise

s_6 = 1 if the production line is set up to produce the 6-cylinder connecting rods; 0 if otherwise

a. Using the decision variables x_4 and s_4, write a constraint that limits next week's production of the 4-cylinder connecting rods to either 0 or 8000 units.

b. Using the decision variables x_6 and s_6, write a constraint that limits next week's production of the 6-cylinder connecting rods to either 0 or 6000 units.

c. Write three constraints that, taken together, limit the production of connecting rods for next week.

d. Write an objective function for minimizing the cost of production for next week.

10. Grave City is considering the relocation of several police substations to obtain better enforcement in high-crime areas. The locations under consideration together with the areas that can be covered from these locations are given in the following table:

Potential Locations for Substations	Areas Covered
A	1, 5, 7
B	1, 2, 5, 7
C	1, 3, 5
D	2, 4, 5
E	3, 4, 6
F	4, 5, 6
G	1, 5, 6, 7

a. Formulate an integer programming model that could be used to find the minimum number of locations necessary to provide coverage to all areas.

b. Solve the problem in part (a).

11. Hart Manufacturing makes three products. Each product requires manufacturing operations in three departments: A, B, and C. The labor-hour requirements, by department, are as follows:

Department	Product 1	Product 2	Product 3
A	1.50	3.00	2.00
B	2.00	1.00	2.50
C	0.25	0.25	0.25

During the next production period, the labor-hours available are 450 in department A, 350 in department B, and 50 in department C. The profit contributions per unit are $25 for product 1, $28 for product 2, and $30 for product 3.

a. Formulate a linear programming model for maximizing total profit contribution.

b. Solve the linear program formulated in part (a). How much of each product should be produced and what is the projected total profit contribution?

c.   After evaluating the solution obtained in part (b), one of the production supervisors noted that production setup costs had not been taken into account. She noted that setup costs are $400 for product 1, $550 for product 2, and $600 for product 3. If the solution developed in part (b) is to be used, what is the total profit contribution after taking into account the setup costs?

d.   Management realized that the optimal product mix, taking setup costs into account, might be different from the one recommended in part (b). Formulate a mixed-integer linear program that takes setup costs into account. Management also stated that we should not consider making more than 175 units of product 1, 150 units of product 2, or 140 units of product 3.

e.   Solve the mixed-integer linear program formulated in part (d). How much of each product should be produced and what is the projected total profit contribution? Compare this profit contribution to that obtained in part (c).

12.   Yates Company supplies road salt to county highway departments. The company has three trucks, and the dispatcher is trying to schedule tomorrow's deliveries to Polk, Dallas, and Jasper counties. Two trucks have 15-ton capacities, and the third truck has a 30-ton capacity. Based on these truck capacities, two counties will receive 15 tons and the third will receive 30 tons of road salt. The dispatcher wants to determine how much to ship to each county. Let

$$x_1 = \text{amount shipped to Polk County}$$
$$x_2 = \text{amount shipped to Dallas County}$$
$$x_3 = \text{amount shipped to Jasper County}$$

and

$$y_i = \begin{cases} 1 \text{ if the 30-ton truck is assigned to county } i \\ 0 \text{ otherwise} \end{cases}$$

a.   Use these variable definitions and write constraints that appropriately restrict the amount shipped to each county.

b.   The cost of assigning the 30-ton truck to the three counties is $100 to Polk, $85 to Dallas, and $50 to Jasper. Formulate and solve a mixed-integer linear program to determine how much to ship to each county.

13.   Recall the Martin-Beck Company distribution system problem in Section 11.3.

a.   Modify the formulation shown in Section 11.3 to account for the policy restriction that one plant, but not two, must be located either in Detroit or in Toledo.

b.   Modify the formulation shown in Section 11.3 to account for the policy restriction that no more than two plants can be located in Denver, Kansas City, and St. Louis.

14.   An automobile manufacturer has five outdated plants: one each in Michigan, Ohio, and California and two in New York. Management is considering modernizing these plants to manufacture engine blocks and transmissions for a new model car. The cost to modernize each plant and the manufacturing capacity after modernization is as follows:

Plant	Cost ($ millions)	Engine Blocks (1000s)	Transmissions (1000s)
Michigan	25	500	300
New York	35	800	400
New York	35	400	800
Ohio	40	900	600
California	20	200	300

The projected needs are for total capacities of 900,000 engine blocks and 900,000 transmissions. Management wants to determine which plants to modernize to meet projected manufacturing needs and, at the same time, minimize the total cost of modernization.

a. Develop a table that lists every possible option available to management. As part of your table, indicate the total engine block capacity and transmission capacity for each possible option, whether the option is feasible based on the projected needs, and the total modernization cost for each option.

b. Based on your analysis in part (a), what recommendation would you provide management?

c. Formulate a 0-1 integer programming model that could be used to determine the optimal solution to the modernization question facing management.

d. Solve the model formulated in part (c) to provide a recommendation for management.

15. CHB, Inc., is a bank holding company that is evaluating the potential for expanding into a 13-county region in the southwestern part of the state. State law permits establishing branches in any county that is adjacent to a county in which a PPB (principal place of business) is located. The following map shows the 13-county region, with the population of each county indicated:

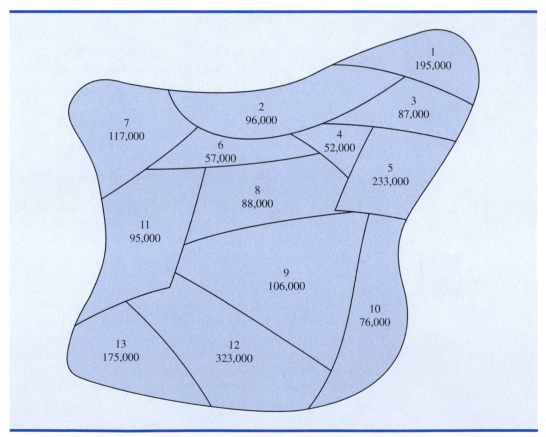

a. Assume that only one PPB can be established in the region. Where should it be located to maximize the population served? (*Hint:* Review the Ohio Trust formulation in Section 11.3. Consider minimizing the population not served, and introduce variable $y_i = 1$ if it is not possible to establish a branch in county i, and $y_i = 0$ otherwise).

b. Suppose that two PPBs can be established in the region. Where should they be located to maximize the population served?

c. Management learned that a bank located in county 5 is considering selling. If CHB purchases this bank, the requisite PPB will be established in county 5, and a base for beginning expansion in the region will also be established. What advice would you give the management of CHB?

16. The Northshore Bank is working to develop an efficient work schedule for full-time and part-time tellers. The schedule must provide for efficient operation of the bank including adequate customer service, employee breaks, and so on. On Fridays the bank is open from 9:00 A.M. to 7:00 P.M. The number of tellers necessary to provide adequate customer service during each hour of operation is summarized here.

Time	Number of Tellers	Time	Number of Tellers
9:00 A.M.–10:00 A.M.	6	2:00 P.M.–3:00 P.M.	6
10:00 A.M.–11:00 A.M.	4	3:00 P.M.–4:00 P.M.	4
11:00 A.M.–Noon	8	4:00 P.M.–5:00 P.M.	7
Noon–1:00 P.M.	10	5:00 P.M.–6:00 P.M.	6
1:00 P.M.–2:00 P.M.	9	6:00 P.M.–7:00 P.M.	6

Each full-time employee starts on the hour and works a 4-hour shift, followed by 1 hour for lunch and then a 3-hour shift. Part-time employees work one 4-hour shift beginning on the hour. Considering salary and fringe benefits, full-time employees cost the bank $15 per hour ($105 a day), and part-time employees cost the bank $8 per hour ($32 per day).

a. Formulate an integer programming model that can be used to develop a schedule that will satisfy customer service needs at a minimum employee cost. (*Hint:* Let x_i = number of full-time employees coming on duty at the beginning of hour i and y_i = number of part-time employees coming on duty at the beginning of hour i.)

b. Solve the LP Relaxation of your model in part (a).

c. Solve for the optimal schedule of tellers. Comment on the solution.

d. After reviewing the solution to part (c), the bank manager realized that some additional requirements must be specified. Specifically, she wants to ensure that one full-time employee is on duty at all times and that there is a staff of at least five full-time employees. Revise your model to incorporate these additional requirements and solve for the optimal solution.

17. Refer to the Ohio Trust bank location problem introduced in Section 11.3. Table 11.3 shows the counties under consideration and the adjacent counties.

a. Write the complete integer programming model for expansion into the following counties only: Lorain, Huron, Richland, Ashland, Wayne, Medina, and Knox.

b. Use trial and error to solve the problem in part (a).

c. Use a computer program for integer programs to solve the problem.

18. Refer to the Salem Foods share of choices problem in Section 11.3 and address the following issues. It is rumored that King's is getting out of the frozen pizza business. If so, the major competitor for Salem Foods will be the Antonio's brand pizza.

a. Compute the overall utility for the Antonio's brand pizza for each of the consumers in Table 11.4.

b. Assume that Salem's only competitor is the Antonio's brand pizza. Formulate and solve the share of choices problem that will maximize market share. What is the best product design and what share of the market can be expected?

19. Burnside Marketing Research conducted a study for Barker Foods on some designs for a new dry cereal. Three attributes were found to be most influential in determining which cereal had the best taste: ratio of wheat to corn in the cereal flake, type of sweetener (sugar,

honey, or artificial), and the presence or absence of flavor bits. Seven children participated in taste tests and provided the following part-worths for the attributes:

	Wheat/Corn			Sweetener		Flavor Bits	
Child	Low	High	Sugar	Honey	Artificial	Present	Absent
1	15	35	30	40	25	15	9
2	30	20	40	35	35	8	11
3	40	25	20	40	10	7	14
4	35	30	25	20	30	15	18
5	25	40	40	20	35	18	14
6	20	25	20	35	30	9	16
7	30	15	25	40	40	20	11

    a.   Suppose the overall utility (sum of part-worths) of the current favorite cereal is 75 for each child. What is the product design that will maximize the share of choices for the seven children in the sample?

    b.   Assume the overall utility of the current favorite cereal for children 1–4 is 70, and the overall utility of the current favorite cereal for children 5–7 is 80. What is the product design that will maximize the share of choice for the seven children in the sample?

20.   Refer to Problem 14. Suppose that management determined that its cost estimates to modernize the New York plants were too low. Specifically, suppose that the actual cost is $40 million to modernize each plant.

    a.   What changes in your previous 0-1 integer linear programming model are needed to incorporate these changes in costs?

    b.   For these cost changes, what recommendations would you now provide management regarding the modernization plan?

    c.   Reconsider the solution obtained using the revised cost figures. Suppose that management decides that closing two plants in the same state is not acceptable. How could this policy restriction be added to your 0-1 integer programming model?

    d.   Based on the cost revision and the policy restriction presented in part (c), what recommendations would you now provide management regarding the modernization plan?

21.   The Bayside Art Gallery is considering installing a video camera security system to reduce its insurance premiums. A diagram of the eight display rooms that Bayside uses for exhibitions is shown in Figure 11.13; the openings between the rooms are numbered 1–13. A security firm proposed that two-way cameras be installed at some room openings. Each camera has the ability to monitor the two rooms between which the camera is located. For example, if a camera were located at opening number 4, rooms 1 and 4 would be covered; if a camera were located at opening 11, rooms 7 and 8 would be covered; and so on. Management decided not to locate a camera system at the entrance to the display rooms. The objective is to provide security coverage for all eight rooms using the minimum number of two-way cameras.

    a.   Formulate a 0-1 integer linear programming model that will enable Bayside's management to determine the locations for the camera systems.

    b.   Solve the model formulated in part (a) to determine how many two-way cameras to purchase and where they should be located.

    c.   Suppose that management wants to provide additional security coverage for room 7. Specifically, management wants room 7 to be covered by two cameras. How would your model formulated in part (a) have to change to accommodate this policy restriction?

    d.   With the policy restriction specified in part (c), determine how many two-way camera systems will need to be purchased and where they will be located.

FIGURE 11.13   DIAGRAM OF DISPLAY ROOMS FOR BAYSIDE ART GALLERY

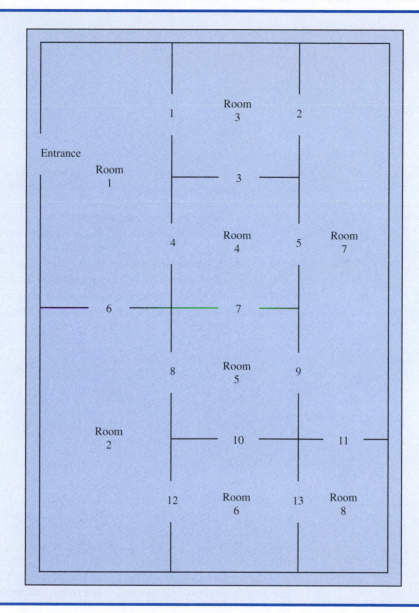

22. The Delta Group is a management consulting firm specializing in the health care industry. A team is being formed to study possible new markets, and a linear programming model has been developed for selecting team members. However, one constraint the president imposed is a team size of three, five, or seven members. The staff cannot figure out how to incorporate this requirement in the model. The current model requires that team members be selected from three departments and uses the following variable definitions:

$$x_1 = \text{the number of employees selected from department 1}$$
$$x_2 = \text{the number of employees selected from department 2}$$
$$x_3 = \text{the number of employees selected from department 3}$$

Show the staff how to write constraints that will ensure that the team will consist of three, five, or seven employees. The following integer variables should be helpful:

$$y_1 = \begin{cases} 1 & \text{if team size is 3} \\ 0 & \text{otherwise} \end{cases}$$

$$y_2 = \begin{cases} 1 & \text{if team size is 5} \\ 0 & \text{otherwise} \end{cases}$$

$$y_3 = \begin{cases} 1 & \text{if team size is 7} \\ 0 & \text{otherwise} \end{cases}$$

23. Roedel Electronics produces a variety of electrical components, including a remote controller for televisions and a remote controller for DVD players. Each controller consists of three subassemblies that are manufactured by Roedel: a base, a cartridge, and a keypad. Both controllers use the same base subassembly, but different cartridge and keypad subassemblies.

    Roedel's sales forecast indicates that 7000 TV controllers and 5000 DVD controllers will be needed to satisfy demand during the upcoming Christmas season. Because only 500 hours of in-house manufacturing time are available, Roedel is considering purchasing some, or all, of the subassemblies from outside suppliers. If Roedel manufactures a subassembly in-house, it incurs a fixed setup cost as well as a variable manufacturing cost. The following table shows the setup cost, the manufacturing time per subassembly, the manufacturing cost per subassembly, and the cost to purchase each of the subassemblies from an outside supplier:

Subassembly	Setup Cost ($)	Manufacturing Time per Unit (min.)	Manufacturing Cost per Unit ($)	Purchase Cost per Unit ($)
Base	1000	0.9	0.40	0.65
TV cartridge	1200	2.2	2.90	3.45
DVD cartridge	1900	3.0	3.15	3.70
TV keypad	1500	0.8	0.30	0.50
DVD keypad	1500	1.0	0.55	0.70

  a. Determine how many units of each subassembly Roedel should manufacture and how many units Roedel should purchase. What is the total manufacturing and purchase cost associated with your recommendation?
  b. Suppose Roedel is considering purchasing new machinery to produce DVD cartridges. For the new machinery, the setup cost is $3000; the manufacturing time is 2.5 minutes per cartridge, and the manufacturing cost is $2.60 per cartridge. Assuming that the new machinery is purchased, determine how many units of each subassembly Roedel should manufacture and how many units of each subassembly Roedel should purchase. What is the total manufacturing and purchase cost associated with your recommendation? Do you think the new machinery should be purchased? Explain.

24. A mathematical programming system named SilverScreener uses a 0-1 integer programming model to help theater managers decide which movies to show on a weekly basis in a multiple-screen theater (*Interfaces,* May/June 2001). Suppose that management of Valley Cinemas would like to investigate the potential of using a similar scheduling system for their chain of multiple-screen theaters. Valley selected a small two-screen movie theater for the pilot testing and would like to develop an integer programming model to help schedule movies for the next four weeks. Six movies are available. The first week each movie is available, the last week each movie can be shown, and the maximum number of weeks that each movie can run are shown here:

Movie	First Week Available	Last Week Available	Max. Run (weeks)
1	1	2	2
2	1	3	2
3	1	1	2
4	2	4	2
5	3	6	3
6	3	5	3

The overall viewing schedule for the theater is composed of the individual schedules for each of the six movies. For each movie a schedule must be developed that specifies the week the movie starts and the number of consecutive weeks it will run. For instance, one possible schedule for movie 2 is for it to start in week 1 and run for two weeks. Theater policy requires that once a movie is started, it must be shown in consecutive weeks. It cannot be stopped and restarted again. To represent the schedule possibilities for each movie, the following decision variables were developed:

$$x_{ijw} = \begin{cases} 1 & \text{if movie } i \text{ is scheduled to start in week } j \text{ and run for } w \text{ weeks} \\ 0 & \text{otherwise} \end{cases}$$

For example, $x_{532} = 1$ means that the schedule selected for movie 5 to begin in week 3 and run for two weeks. For each movie, a separate variable is given for each possible schedule.

a. Three schedules are associated with movie 1. List the variables that represent these schedules.

b. Write a constraint requiring that only one schedule be selected for movie 1.

c. Write a constraint requiring that only one schedule be selected for movie 5.

d. What restricts the number of movies that can be shown in week 1? Write a constraint that restricts the number of movies selected for viewing in week 1.

e. Write a constraint that restricts the number of movies selected for viewing in week 3.

25. East Coast Trucking provides service from Boston to Miami using regional offices located in Boston, New York, Philadelphia, Baltimore, Washington, Richmond, Raleigh, Florence, Savannah, Jacksonville, and Tampa. The number of miles between each of the regional offices is provided in the following table:

	New York	Philadelphia	Baltimore	Washington	Richmond	Raleigh	Florence	Savannah	Jacksonville	Tampa	Miami
Boston	211	320	424	459	565	713	884	1056	1196	1399	1669
New York		109	213	248	354	502	673	845	985	1188	1458
Philadelphia			104	139	245	393	564	736	876	1079	1349
Baltimore				35	141	289	460	632	772	975	1245
Washington					106	254	425	597	737	940	1210
Richmond						148	319	491	631	834	1104
Raleigh							171	343	483	686	956
Florence								172	312	515	785
Savannah									140	343	613
Jacksonville										203	473
Tampa											270

The company's expansion plans involve constructing service facilities in some of the cities where a regional office is located. Each regional office must be within 400 miles of a service facility. For instance, if a service facility is constructed in Richmond, it can provide service to regional offices located in New York, Philadelphia, Baltimore, Washington, Richmond, Raleigh, and Florence. Management would like to determine the minimum number of service facilities needed and where they should be located.

a. Formulate an integer linear program that can be used to determine the minimum number of service facilities needed and their locations.
b. Solve the integer linear program formulated in part (a). How many service facilities are required and where should they be located?
c. Suppose that each service facility can only provide service to regional offices within 300 miles. How many service facilities are required and where should they be located?

Case Problem 1   Textbook Publishing

ASW Publishing, Inc., a small publisher of college textbooks, must make a decision regarding which books to publish next year. The books under consideration are listed in the following table, along with the projected three-year sales expected from each book:

Book Subject	Type of Book	Projected Sales (1000s)
Business calculus	New	20
Finite mathematics	Revision	30
General statistics	New	15
Mathematical statistics	New	10
Business statistics	Revision	25
Finance	New	18
Financial accounting	New	25
Managerial accounting	Revision	50
English literature	New	20
German	New	30

The books listed as revisions are texts that ASW already has under contract; these texts are being considered for publication as new editions. The books that are listed as new have been reviewed by the company, but contracts have not yet been signed.

Three individuals in the company can be assigned to these projects, all of whom have varying amounts of time available; John has 60 days available, and Susan and Monica both have 40 days available. The days required by each person to complete each project are shown in the following table. For instance, if the business calculus book is published, it will require 30 days of John's time and 40 days of Susan's time. An "X" indicates that the person will not be used on the project. Note that at least two staff members will be assigned to each project except the finance book.

Book Subject	John	Susan	Monica
Business calculus	30	40	X
Finite mathematics	16	24	X
General statistics	24	X	30
Mathematical statistics	20	X	24
Business statistics	10	X	16
Finance	X	X	14
Financial accounting	X	24	26
Managerial accounting	X	28	30
English literature	40	34	30
German	X	50	36

ASW will not publish more than two statistics books or more than one accounting text in a single year. In addition, management decided that one of the mathematics books (business calculus or finite math) must be published, but not both.

Managerial Report

Prepare a report for the managing editor of ASW that describes your findings and recommendations regarding the best publication strategy for next year. In carrying out your analysis, assume that the fixed costs and the sales revenues per unit are approximately equal for all books; management is interested primarily in maximizing the total unit sales volume.

The managing editor also asked that you include recommendations regarding the following possible changes:

1. If it would be advantageous to do so, Susan can be moved off another project to allow her to work 12 more days.
2. If it would be advantageous to do so, Monica can also be made available for another 10 days.
3. If one or more of the revisions could be postponed for another year, should they be? Clearly the company will risk losing market share by postponing a revision.

Include details of your analysis in an appendix to your report.

Case Problem 2   Yeager National Bank

Using aggressive mail promotion with low introductory interest rates, Yeager National Bank (YNB) built a large base of credit card customers throughout the continental United States. Currently, all customers send their regular payments to the bank's corporate office located in Charlotte, North Carolina. Daily collections from customers making their regular payments are substantial, with an average of approximately $600,000. YNB estimates that it makes about 15% on its funds and would like to ensure that customer payments are credited to the bank's account as soon as possible. For instance, if it takes five days for a customer's payment to be sent through the mail, processed, and credited to the bank's account, YNB has potentially lost five days' worth of interest income. Although the time needed for this collection process cannot be completely eliminated, reducing it can be beneficial given the large amounts of money involved.

Instead of having all its credit card customers send their payments to Charlotte, YNB is considering having customers send their payments to one or more regional collection centers, referred to in the banking industry as lockboxes. Four lockbox locations have been proposed: Phoenix, Salt Lake City, Atlanta, and Boston. To determine which lockboxes to open and where lockbox customers should send their payments, YNB divided its customer base into five geographical regions: Northwest, Southwest, Central, Northeast, and Southeast. Every customer in the same region will be instructed to send his or her payment to the same lockbox. The following table shows the average number of days it takes before a customer's payment is credited to the bank's account when the payment is sent from each of the regions to each of the potential lockboxes:

Customer Zone	Phoenix	Salt Lake City	Atlanta	Boston	Daily Collection ($1000s)
Northwest	4	2	4	4	80
Southwest	2	3	4	6	90
Central	5	3	3	4	150
Northeast	5	4	3	2	180
Southeast	4	6	2	3	100

Managerial Report

Dave Wolff, the vice president for cash management, asked you to prepare a report containing your recommendations for the number of lockboxes and the best lockbox locations. Mr. Wolff is primarily concerned with minimizing lost interest income, but he wants you to also consider the effect of an annual fee charged for maintaining a lockbox at any location. Although the amount of the fee is unknown at this time, we can assume that the fees will be in the range of $20,000 to $30,000 per location. Once good potential locations have been selected, Mr. Wolff will inquire as to the annual fees.

Case Problem 3

Production Scheduling with Changeover Costs

Buckeye Manufacturing produces heads for engines used in the manufacture of trucks. The production line is highly complex, and it measures 900 feet in length. Two types of engine heads are produced on this line: the P-Head and the H-Head. The P-Head is used in heavy-duty trucks and the H-Head is used in smaller trucks. Because only one type of head can be produced at a time, the line is either set up to manufacture the P-Head or the H-Head, but not both. Changeovers are made over a weekend; costs are $500 in going from a setup for the P-Head to a setup for the H-Head, and vice versa. When set up for the P-Head, the maximum production rate is 100 units per week and when set up for the H-Head, the maximum production rate is 80 units per week.

Buckeye just shut down for the week after using the line to produce the P-Head. The manager wants to plan production and changeovers for the next eight weeks. Currently, Buckeye's inventory consists of 125 P-Heads and 143 H-Heads. Inventory carrying costs are charged at an annual rate of 19.5% of the value of inventory. The production cost for the P-Head is $225, and the production cost for the H-Head is $310. The objective in developing a production schedule is to minimize the sum of production cost, plus inventory carrying cost, plus changeover cost.

Buckeye received the following requirements schedule from its customer (an engine assembly plant) for the next nine weeks:

	Product Demand	
Week	**P-Head**	**H-Head**
1	55	38
2	55	38
3	44	30
4	0	0
5	45	48
6	45	48
7	36	58
8	35	57
9	35	58

Safety stock requirements are such that week-ending inventory must provide for at least 80% of the next week's demand.

Managerial Report

Prepare a report for Buckeye's management with a production and changeover schedule for the next eight weeks. Be sure to note how much of the total cost is due to production, how much is due to inventory, and how much is due to changeover.

Appendix 11.1   Excel Solution of Integer Linear Programs

Worksheet formulation and solution for integer linear programs is similar to that for linear programming problems. Actually the worksheet formulation is exactly the same, but some additional information must be provided when setting up the Solver Parameters and Integer Options dialog boxes. First, constraints must be added in the Solver Parameters dialog box to identify the integer variables. In addition, the value for Tolerance in the Integer Options dialog box may need to be adjusted to obtain a solution.

Let us demonstrate the Excel solution of an integer linear program by showing how Excel can be used to solve the Eastborne Realty problem. The worksheet with the optimal solution is shown in Figure 11.14. We will describe the key elements of the worksheet and how to obtain the solution, and then interpret the solution.

Formulation

The data and descriptive labels appear in cells A1:G7 of the worksheet in Figure 11.14. The screened cells in the lower portion of the worksheet contain the information required by the

FIGURE 11.14   EXCEL SOLUTION FOR THE EASTBORNE REALTY PROBLEM

WEB file

Eastborne

	A	B	C	D	E	F	G	H
1	**Eastborne Realty Problem**							
2								
3		**Townhouse**	**Apt. Bldg.**					
4	**Price($1000s)**	282	400		**Funds Avl.($1000s)**		2000	
5	**Mgr. Time**	4	40		**Mgr. Time Avl.**		140	
6					**Townhouses Avl.**		5	
7	**Ann. Cash Flow ($1000s)**	10	15					
8								
9								
10	**Model**							
11								
12								
13	**Max Cash Flow**	70						
14					**Constraints**	**LHS**		**RHS**
15		**Number of**			Funds	1928	<=	2000
16		Townhouses	Apt. Bldgs.		Time	96	<=	140
17	**Purchase Plan**	4	2		Townhouses	4	<=	5
18								

Excel Solver (decision variables, objective function, constraint left-hand sides, and constraint right-hand sides).

Decision Variables	Cells B17:C17 are reserved for the decision variables. The optimal solution is to purchase four townhouses and two apartment buildings.
Objective Function	The formula =SUMPRODUCT(B7:C7,B17:C17) has been placed into cell B13 to reflect the annual cash flow associated with the solution. The optimal solution provides an annual cash flow of $70,000.
Left-Hand Sides	The left-hand sides for the three constraints are placed into cells F15:F17.

> Cell F15 =SUMPRODUCT(B4:C4, $B$17:$C$17)
> > (Copy to sell F16)
>
> Cell F17 =B17

Right-Hand Sides	The right-hand sides for the three constraints are placed into cells H15:H17.

> Cell H15 =G4 (Copy to cells H16:H17)

Excel Solution

Begin the solution procedure by selecting the **Add-ins** tab on the Ribbon and then **Premium Solver** in the **Menu Commands** group. Enter the proper values into the **Solver Parameters** dialog box as shown in Figure 11.15. The first constraint shown is $B$17:$C$17 = integer. This constraint tells Solver that the decision variables in cell B17 and cell C17 must be integer. The integer requirement is created by using the **Add-Constraint** procedure. $B$17:$C$17 is entered as the **Cell Reference** and "int"

FIGURE 11.15   SOLVER PARAMETERS DIALOG BOX FOR THE EASTBORNE REALTY PROBLEM

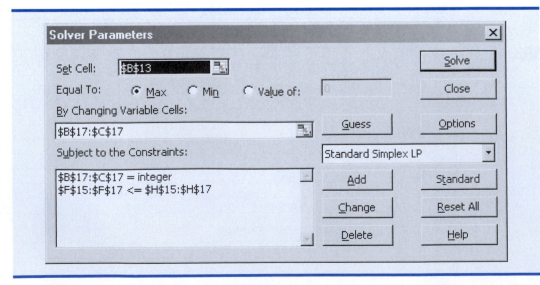

FIGURE 11.16   SOLVER OPTIONS DIALOG BOX FOR THE EASTBORNE REALTY PROBLEM

rather than ≤, =, or ≥ is selected as the form of the constraint. When **"int"** is selected, the term integer automatically appears as the right-hand side of the constraint. Figure 11.15 shows the additional information required to complete the **Solver Parameters** dialog box.

Next the **Options** button must be selected. The option **Assume Non-Negative** must be checked. Figure 11.16 shows the completed **Solver Options** dialog box for the Eastborne Realty problem. Clicking **OK** in the **Solver Options** dialog box and selecting **Solve** in the **Solver Parameters** dialog box will instruct Solver to compute the optimal integer solution. The worksheet in Figure 11.14 shows that the optimal solution is to purchase four townhouses and two apartment buildings. The annual cash flow is $70,000.

0-1 variables are identified with the "bin" designation in the Solver Parameters dialog box.

If binary variables are present in an integer linear programming problem, you must select the designation **"bin"** instead of **"int"** when setting up the constraints in the **Solver Parameters** dialog box.

The time required to obtain an optimal solution can be highly variable for integer linear programs. If an optimal solution cannot be found within a reasonable amount of time, the tolerance can be reset to 5%, or some higher value, so that the search procedure may stop when a near-optimal solution (within the tolerance of being optimal) has been found. To reset the tolerance, click on **Integer Options . . .** in the **Solver Options** dialog box (see Figure 11.16). Then, when the **Integer Options** dialog box appears (see Figure 11.17), enter the desired value in the **Tolerance** box. Figure 11.17 shows a 0 in the **Tolerance** box for the Eastborne Realty problem. In a more difficult problem, .05 could be entered to allow the solution procedure to stop with a solution within 5% of optimal.

FIGURE 11.17 INTEGER OPTIONS DIALOG BOX FOR THE EASTBORNE REALTY PROBLEM

Appendix 11.2 LINGO Solution of Integer Linear Programs

LINGO may be used to solve linear integer programs. An integer linear model is entered into LINGO exactly as described in Appendix 7.2, but with additional statements for declaring variables as either general integer or binary. For example, to declare a variable x integer, you need to include the following statement:

$$@GIN(x) ;$$

Note the use of the semicolon to end the statement. GIN stands for general integer. Likewise to declare a variable y a binary variable, the following statement is required:

$$@BIN(y) ;$$

BIN stands for binary.

To illustrate the use of integer variables, the following statements are used to model the Eastborne Reality problem discussed in this chapter:

First we enter the following:

```
MODEL:
TITLE    EASTBORNE REALTY;
```

This statement gives the LINGO model the title Eastborne Realty.

Next we enter the following two lines to document the definition of our decision variables (recall that ! denotes a comment, and each comment ends with a semicolon).

```
! T = NUMBER OF TOWNHOUSES PURCHASED;
! A = NUMBER OF APARTMENT BUILDINGS PURCHASED;
```

Next we enter the objective function and constraints, each with a descriptive comment.

```
! MAXIMIZE THE CASH FLOW;
MAX = 10*T + 15*A;

! FUNDS AVAILABLE ($1000);
282*T + 400*A <= 2000;

! TIME AVAILABLILITY;
4*T + 40*A <= 140;

! TOWNHOUSES AVAILABLE;
T <= 5;
```

Finally we must declare the variables T and A as general integer variables. Again, to document the model we begin with a descriptive comment and then declare each variable as a general integer variable:

```
! DECLARE THE VARIABLES TO BE GENERAL INTEGER VARIABLES;
@GIN(T);
@GIN(A);
```

The complete LINGO model is available on the Web site that accompanies this book.

CHAPTER 12

Advanced Optimization Applications

This chapter begins with the study of linear programming applications. Two new applications of linear programming are introduced. The first application is revenue management. Revenue management involves managing the short-term demand for a fixed perishable inventory in order to maximize the revenue potential for an organization. For example, revenue management is critically important in the airline industry. After a flight departs, empty seats are worthless (a perishable good), so airlines try to price their seats in such a way as to maximize revenue. We illustrate the concept by determining the optimal full-fare and discount-fare seat allocations for flights among five cities. Management science has also made a major impact in finance. In Section 12.2 we show how linear programming is used to design portfolios that are consistent with a client's risk preferences.

Although linear programming is used to solve a wide variety of important business problems, many business processes are nonlinear. For example, the price of a bond is a nonlinear function of interest rates, and the price of a stock option is a nonlinear function of the price of the underlying stock. The marginal cost of production often decreases with the quantity produced, and the profit function for most products is usually a nonlinear function of the price. These and many other nonlinear relationships are present in many business applications.

In Section 12.3 we allow the optimization model to be nonlinear. A **nonlinear optimization problem** is any optimization problem in which at least one term in the objective function or a constraint is nonlinear. We begin our study of nonlinear applications by considering a production problem in which the objective function is a nonlinear function of the decision variables. In Section 12.4 we develop a nonlinear application that involves designing a portfolio of securities to track a stock market index. As a further illustration of the use of nonlinear optimization in practice, there are two Q.M. in Action inserts that describe applications of nonlinear programming. The first, Scheduling Flights and Crews for Bombardier Flexjet, discusses how Flexjet used nonlinear optimization to assign aircraft and crews to flights. The second, Pricing for Environmental Compliance in the Auto Industry, describes a nonlinear pricing application in the auto industry in order to meet overall federal government requirements on average miles per gallon across all cars in an auto companies fleet. There is also a case based on this Q.M. in Action.

The computer solutions presented in the chapter were developed using LINGO. However, Excel Solver can also be used to solve these problems. Chapter appendixes describe how to solve nonlinear programs using LINGO and Excel Solver. The Management Scientist cannot be used to solve nonlinear optimization problems.

12.1   Revenue Management

Revenue management involves managing the short-term demand for a fixed perishable inventory in order to maximize the revenue potential for an organization. The methodology, originally developed for American Airlines, was first used to determine how many airline flight seats to sell at an early reservation discount fare and how many airline flight seats to sell at a full fare. By making the optimal decision for the number of discount-fare seats and the number of full-fare seats on each flight, the airline is able to increase its average number of passengers per flight and maximize the total revenue generated by the combined sale of discount-fare and full-fare seats. Today, all major airlines use some form of revenue management.

Given the success of revenue management in the airline industry, it was not long before other industries began using this approach. Revenue management systems often include pricing strategies and overbooking policies. Overbooking policies attempt to determine the number of items to sell over and above capacity so as to compensate for no-shows. Application areas now include hotels, apartment rentals, car rentals, cruise lines, and golf courses.

The Q.M. in Action, Revenue Management at National Car Rental, discusses how National implemented revenue management.

The development of a revenue management system can be expensive and time-consuming, but the potential payoffs may be substantial. For instance, the revenue management system used at American Airlines generates nearly $1 billion in annual incremental revenue. To illustrate the fundamentals of revenue management, we will use a linear programming model to develop a revenue management plan for Leisure Air, a regional airline that provides service for Pittsburgh, Newark, Charlotte, Myrtle Beach, and Orlando.

Leisure Air has two Boeing 737-400 airplanes, one based in Pittsburgh and the other in Newark. Both airplanes have a coach section with a 132-seat capacity. Each morning the Pittsburgh-based plane flies to Orlando with a stopover in Charlotte, and the Newark-based plane flies to Myrtle Beach, also with a stopover in Charlotte. At the end of the day, both planes return to their home bases. To keep the size of the problem reasonable, we restrict our attention to the Pittsburgh–Charlotte, Charlotte–Orlando, Newark–Charlotte, and Charlotte–Myrtle Beach flight legs for the morning flights. Figure 12.1 illustrates the logistics of the Leisure Air problem situation.

Leisure Air uses two fare classes: a discount-fare Q class and a full-fare Y class. Reservations using the discount-fare Q class must be made 14 days in advance and must include a Saturday night stay in the destination city. Reservations using the full-fare Y class may be made any time, with no penalty for changing the reservation at a later date. To determine the itinerary and fare alternatives that Leisure Air can offer its customers, we must consider not only the origin and the destination of each flight, but also the fare class. For instance, possible products include Pittsburgh to Charlotte using Q class, Newark to Orlando using Q class, Charlotte to Myrtle Beach using Y class, and so on. Each product is referred to as an origin-destination-itinerary fare (ODIF). For May 5, Leisure Air established fares and developed forecasts of customer demand for each of 16 ODIFs. These data are shown in Table 12.1.

Suppose that on April 4 a customer calls the Leisure Air reservation office and requests a Q class seat on the May 5 flight from Pittsburgh to Myrtle Beach. Should Leisure Air

Q.M. *in* ACTION

REVENUE MANAGEMENT AT NATIONAL CAR RENTAL*

During its recovery from a near liquidation in the mid-1990s, National Car Rental developed a revenue management system that uses linear programming and other analytical models to help manage rental car capacity, pricing, and reservations. The goal of the revenue management system is to develop procedures that identify unrealized revenue opportunities, improve utilization, and ultimately increase revenue for the company.

Management science models play a key role in revenue management at National. For instance, a linear programming model is used for length-of-rent control. An overbooking model identifies optimal overbooking levels subject to service level constraints, and a planned upgrade algorithm allows cars in a higher-priced class to be used to satisfy excess demand for cars in a lower-priced class.

Another model generates length-of-rent categories for each arrival day, which maximizes revenue. Pricing models are used to manage revenue by segmenting the market between business and leisure travel. For example, fares are adjusted to account for the fact that leisure travelers are willing to commit further in advance than business travelers and are willing to stay over a weekend.

The implementation of the revenue management system is credited with returning National Car Rental to profitability. In the first year of use, revenue management resulted in increased revenues of $56 million.

*Based on M. K. Geraghty and Ernest Johnson, "Revenue Management Saves National Car Rental," *Interfaces* 27, no. 1 (January/February 1997): 107–127.

FIGURE 12.1 LOGISTICS OF THE LEISURE AIR PROBLEM

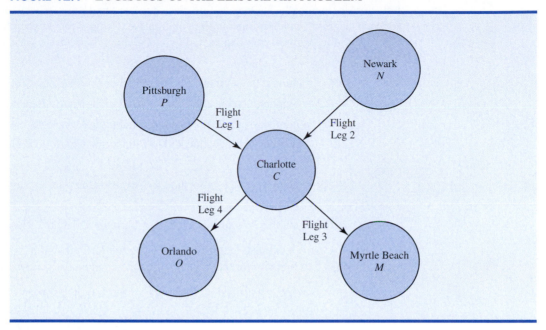

TABLE 12.1 FARE AND DEMAND DATA FOR 16 LEISURE AIR
ORIGIN-DESTINATION-ITINERARY FARES (ODIFs)

ODIF	Origin	Destination	Fare Class	ODIF Code	Fare	Forecasted Demand
1	Pittsburgh	Charlotte	Q	PCQ	$178	33
2	Pittsburgh	Myrtle Beach	Q	PMQ	268	44
3	Pittsburgh	Orlando	Q	POQ	228	45
4	Pittsburgh	Charlotte	Y	PCY	380	16
5	Pittsburgh	Myrtle Beach	Y	PMY	456	6
6	Pittsburgh	Orlando	Y	POY	560	11
7	Newark	Charlotte	Q	NCQ	199	26
8	Newark	Myrtle Beach	Q	NMQ	249	56
9	Newark	Orlando	Q	NOQ	349	39
10	Newark	Charlotte	Y	NCY	385	15
11	Newark	Myrtle Beach	Y	NMY	444	7
12	Newark	Orlando	Y	NOY	580	9
13	Charlotte	Myrtle Beach	Q	CMQ	179	64
14	Charlotte	Myrtle Beach	Y	CMY	380	8
15	Charlotte	Orlando	Q	COQ	224	46
16	Charlotte	Orlando	Y	COY	582	10

accept the reservation? The difficulty in making this decision is that even though Leisure Air may have seats available, the company may not want to accept this reservation at the Q class fare of $268, especially if it is possible to sell the same reservation later at the Y class fare of $456. Thus, determining how many Q and Y class seats to make available are important decisions that Leisure Air must make in order to operate its reservation system.

To develop a linear programming model that can be used to determine how many seats Leisure Air should allocate to each fare class, we need to define 16 decision variables, one for each origin-destination-itinerary fare alternative. Using P for Pittsburgh, N for Newark, C for Charlotte, M for Myrtle Beach, and O for Orlando, the decision variables take the following form:

PCQ = number of seats allocated to Pittsburgh–Charlotte Q class

PMQ = number of seats allocated to Pittsburgh–Myrtle Beach Q class

POQ = number of seats allocated to Pittsburgh–Orlando Q class

PCY = number of seats allocated to Pittsburgh–Charlotte Y class

$\vdots$

NCQ = number of seats allocated to Newark–Charlotte Q class

$\vdots$

COY = number of seats allocated to Charlotte–Orlando Y class

The objective is to maximize total revenue. Using the fares shown in Table 12.1, we can write the objective function for the linear programming model as follows:

$$
\begin{aligned}
\text{Max} \quad & 178PCQ + 268PMQ + 228POQ + 380PCY + 456PMY + 560POY \\
& + 199NCQ + 249NMQ + 349NOQ + 385NCY + 444NMY \\
& + 580NOY + 179CMQ + 380CMY + 224COQ + 582COY
\end{aligned}
$$

Next, we must write the constraints. We need two types of constraints: capacity and demand. We begin with the capacity constraints.

Consider the Pittsburgh–Charlotte flight leg in Figure 12.1. The Boeing 737-400 airplane has a 132-seat capacity. Three possible final destinations for passengers on this flight (Charlotte, Myrtle Beach, or Orlando) and two fare classes (Q and Y) provide six ODIF alternatives: (1) Pittsburgh–Charlotte Q class; (2) Pittsburgh–Myrtle Beach Q class; (3) Pittsburgh–Orlando Q class; (4) Pittsburgh–Charlotte Y class; (5) Pittsburgh–Myrtle Beach Y class; and (6) Pittsburgh–Orlando Y class. Thus, the number of seats allocated to the Pittsburgh–Charlotte flight leg is $PCQ + PMQ + POQ + PCY + PMY + POY$. With the capacity of 132 seats, the capacity constraint is as follows:

$$PCQ + PMQ + POQ + PCY + PMY + POY \leq 132 \quad \text{Pittsburgh–Charlotte}$$

The capacity constraints for the Newark–Charlotte, Charlotte–Myrtle Beach, and Charlotte–Orlando flight legs are developed in a similar manner. These three constraints are as follows:

$$NCQ + NMQ + NOQ + NCY + NMY + NOY \leq 132 \quad \text{Newark–Charlotte}$$
$$PMQ + PMY + NMQ + NMY + CMQ + CMY \leq 132 \quad \text{Charlotte–Myrtle Beach}$$
$$POQ + POY + NOQ + NOY + COQ + COY \leq 132 \quad \text{Charlotte–Orlando}$$

The demand constraints limit the number of seats for each ODIF based on the forecasted demand. Using the demand forecasts in Table 12.1, 16 demand constraints must be added to the model. The first four demand constraints are as follows:

$$PCQ \leq 33 \quad \text{Pittsburgh–Charlotte Q class}$$
$$PMQ \leq 44 \quad \text{Pittsburgh–Myrtle Beach Q class}$$
$$POQ \leq 45 \quad \text{Pittsburgh–Orlando Q class}$$
$$PCY \leq 16 \quad \text{Pittsburgh–Charlotte Y class}$$

The complete linear programming model with 16 decision variables, 4 capacity constraints, and 16 demand constraints is as follows:

Max $178PCQ + 268PMQ + 228POQ + 380PCY + 456PMY + 560POY$
$\quad + 199NCQ + 249NMQ + 349NOQ + 385NCY + 444NMY$
$\quad + 580NOY + 179CMQ + 380CMY + 224COQ + 582COY$

s.t.

$$PCQ + PMQ + POQ + PCY + PMY + POY \le 132 \quad \text{Pittsburgh–Charlotte}$$
$$NCQ + NMQ + NOQ + NCY + NMY + NOY \le 132 \quad \text{Newark–Charlotte}$$
$$PMQ + PMY + NMQ + NMY + CMQ + CMY \le 132 \quad \text{Charlotte–Myrtle Beach}$$
$$POQ + POY + NOQ + NOY + COQ + COY \le 132 \quad \text{Charlotte–Orlando}$$

$$
\left.
\begin{aligned}
PCQ &\le 33 \\
PMQ &\le 44 \\
POQ &\le 45 \\
PCY &\le 16 \\
PMY &\le 6 \\
POY &\le 11 \\
NCQ &\le 26 \\
NMQ &\le 56 \\
NOQ &\le 39 \\
NCY &\le 15 \\
NMY &\le 7 \\
NOY &\le 9 \\
CMQ &\le 64 \\
CMY &\le 8 \\
COQ &\le 46 \\
COY &\le 10
\end{aligned}
\right\} \quad \text{Demand Constraints}
$$

$$PCQ, PMQ, POQ, PCY, \ldots, COY \ge 0$$

The optimal solution to the Leisure Air revenue management problem is shown in Figure 12.2. The value of the optimal solution is $103,103. The optimal solution shows that $PCQ = 33$, $PMQ = 44$, $POQ = 22$, $PCY = 16$, and so on. Thus, to maximize revenue, Leisure Air should allocate 33 Q class seats to Pittsburgh–Charlotte, 44 Q class seats to Pittsburgh–Myrtle Beach, 22 Q class seats to Pittsburgh–Orlando, 16 Y class seats to Pittsburgh–Charlotte, and so on.

Over time, reservations will come into the system and the number of remaining seats available for each ODIF will decrease. For example, the optimal solution allocated 44 Q class seats to Pittsburgh–Myrtle Beach. Suppose that two weeks prior to the departure date of May 5, all 44 seats have been sold. Now, suppose that a new customer calls the Leisure Air reservation office and requests a Q class seat for the Pittsburgh–Myrtle Beach flight. Should Leisure Air accept the new reservation even though it exceeds the original 44-seat allocation? The dual price for the Pittsburgh–Myrtle Beach Q class demand constraint will provide information that will help a Leisure Air reservation agent make this decision.

Constraint 6, $PMQ \le 44$, restricts the number of Q class seats that can be allocated to Pittsburgh–Myrtle Beach to 44 seats. In Figure 12.2 we see that the dual price for constraint 6 is $85. The dual price tells us that if one more Q class seat were available from Pittsburgh to Myrtle Beach, revenue would improve by $85. This increase in revenue is referred to as

FIGURE 12.2   THE MANAGEMENT SCIENTIST SOLUTION FOR THE LEISURE AIR
REVENUE MANAGEMENT PROBLEM

Leisure

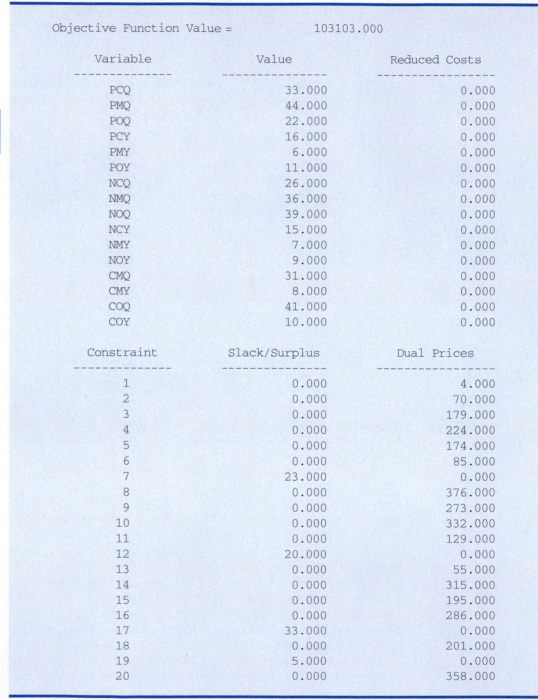

```
Objective Function Value =              103103.000

           Variable              Value           Reduced Costs
       --------------       ---------------     ------------------
             PCQ                 33.000                0.000
             PMQ                 44.000                0.000
             POQ                 22.000                0.000
             PCY                 16.000                0.000
             PMY                  6.000                0.000
             POY                 11.000                0.000
             NCQ                 26.000                0.000
             NMQ                 36.000                0.000
             NOQ                 39.000                0.000
             NCY                 15.000                0.000
             NMY                  7.000                0.000
             NOY                  9.000                0.000
             CMQ                 31.000                0.000
             CMY                  8.000                0.000
             COQ                 41.000                0.000
             COY                 10.000                0.000


           Constraint         Slack/Surplus         Dual Prices
       --------------       ---------------     ------------------
              1                   0.000                4.000
              2                   0.000               70.000
              3                   0.000              179.000
              4                   0.000              224.000
              5                   0.000              174.000
              6                   0.000               85.000
              7                  23.000                0.000
              8                   0.000              376.000
              9                   0.000              273.000
             10                   0.000              332.000
             11                   0.000              129.000
             12                  20.000                0.000
             13                   0.000               55.000
             14                   0.000              315.000
             15                   0.000              195.000
             16                   0.000              286.000
             17                  33.000                0.000
             18                   0.000              201.000
             19                   5.000                0.000
             20                   0.000              358.000
```

the bid price for this origin-destination-itinerary fare. In general, the bid price for an ODIF tells a Leisure Air reservation agent the value of one additional reservation once a particular ODIF has been sold out.

Dual prices tell reservation agents the additional revenue associated with overbooking each ODIF.

By looking at the dual prices for the demand constraints in Figure 12.2, we see that the highest dual price (bid price) is $376 for constraint 8, $PCY \leq 16$. This constraint corresponds to the Pittsburgh–Charlotte Y class itinerary. Thus, if all 16 seats allocated to this itinerary have been sold, accepting another reservation will provide additional revenue of $376. Given this revenue contribution, a reservation agent would most likely accept the additional reservation even if it resulted in an overbooking of the flight. Other dual prices for the demand constraints show a bid price of $358 for constraint 20 ($COY$) and a bid price of $332 for constraint 10 ($POY$). Thus, accepting additional reservations for the Charlotte–Orlando Y class and the Pittsburgh–Orlando Y class itineraries is a good choice for increasing revenue.

A revenue management system like the one at Leisure Air must be flexible and adjust to the ever-changing reservation status. Conceptually, each time a reservation is accepted for an origin-destination-itinerary fare that is at its capacity, the linear programming model should be updated and re-solved to obtain new seat allocations along with the revised bid price information. In practice, updating the allocations on a real-time basis is not practical because of the large number of itineraries involved. However, the bid prices from a current solution and some simple decision rules enable reservation agents to make decisions that improve the revenue for the firm. Then, on a periodic basis such as once a day or once a week, the entire linear programming model can be updated and re-solved to generate new seat allocations and revised bid price information.

12.2 Portfolio Models and Asset Allocation

Asset allocation refers to the process of determining how to allocate investment funds across a variety of asset classes such as stocks, bonds, mutual funds, real estate, and cash. Portfolio models are used to determine the percentage of the investment funds that should be made in each asset class. The goal is to create a portfolio that provides the best balance between risk and return. In this section we show how linear programming models can be developed to determine an optimal portfolio involving a mix of mutual funds. The first model is designed for conservative investors who are strongly averse to risk. The second model is designed for investors with a variety of risk tolerances.

In 1952 Harry Markowitz showed how to develop a portfolio that optimized the trade-off between risk and return. His work earned him a share of the 1990 Nobel Prize in Economics.

A Portfolio of Mutual Funds

Hauck Investment Services designs annuities, IRAs, 401(k) plans, and other investment vehicles for investors with a variety of risk tolerances. Hauck would like to develop a portfolio model that can be used to determine an optimal portfolio involving a mix of six mutual funds. A variety of measures can be used to indicate risk, but for portfolios of financial assets all are related to variability in return. Table 12.2 shows the annual return (%) for five 1-year periods for the six mutual funds. Year 1 represents a year in which the annual returns are good for all the mutual funds. Year 2 is also a good year for most of the mutual funds. But year 3 is a bad year for the small-cap value fund; year 4 is a bad year for the intermediate-term bond fund; and year 5 is a bad year for four of the six mutual funds.

It is not possible to predict exactly the returns for any of the funds over the next 12 months, but the portfolio managers at Hauck Financial Services think that the returns for the five years shown in Table 12.2 are scenarios that can be used to represent the possibilities for the next year. For the purpose of building portfolios for their clients, Hauck's portfolio managers

TABLE 12.2   MUTUAL FUND PERFORMANCE IN FIVE SELECTED YEARS (USED AS PLANNING SCENARIOS FOR THE NEXT 12 MONTHS)

Mutual Fund	Annual Return (%)				
	Year 1	Year 2	Year 3	Year 4	Year 5
Foreign Stock	10.06	13.12	13.47	45.42	−21.93
Intermediate-Term Bond	17.64	3.25	7.51	−1.33	7.36
Large-Cap Growth	32.41	18.71	33.28	41.46	−23.26
Large-Cap Value	32.36	20.61	12.93	7.06	−5.37
Small-Cap Growth	33.44	19.40	3.85	58.68	−9.02
Small-Cap Value	24.56	25.32	−6.70	5.43	17.31

will choose a mix of these six mutual funds and assume that one of the five possible scenarios will describe the return over the next 12 months.

Conservative Portfolio

One of Hauck's portfolio managers has been asked to develop a portfolio for the firm's conservative clients who express a strong aversion to risk. The manager's task is to determine the proportion of the portfolio to invest in each of the six mutual funds so that the portfolio provides the best return possible with a minimum risk. Let us see how linear programming can be used to develop a portfolio for these clients.

In portfolio models, risk is minimized by diversification. To see the value of diversification, suppose we first consider investing the entire portfolio in just one of the six mutual funds. Assuming the data in Table 12.2 represent the possible outcomes over the next 12 months, the clients run the risk of losing 21.93% over the next 12 months if the entire portfolio is invested in the foreign stock mutual fund. Similarly, if the entire portfolio is invested in any one of the other five mutual funds, the clients will also run the risk of losing money; that is, the possible losses are 1.33% for the intermediate-term bond fund, 23.26% for the large-cap growth fund, 5.37% for the large-cap value fund, 9.02% for the small-cap growth fund, and 6.70% for the small-cap value fund. Let us now see how we can construct a diversified portfolio of these mutual funds that minimizes the risk of a loss.

To determine the proportion of the portfolio that will be invested in each of the mutual funds, we use the following decision variables:

FS = proportion of portfolio invested in the foreign stock mutual fund

IB = proportion of portfolio invested in the intermediate-term bond fund

LG = proportion of portfolio invested in the large-cap growth fund

LV = proportion of portfolio invested in the large-cap value fund

SG = proportion of portfolio invested in the small-cap growth fund

SV = proportion of portfolio invested in the small-cap value fund

Because the sum of these proportions must equal 1, we need the following constraint:

$$FS + IB + LG + LV + SG + SV = 1$$

The other constraints are concerned with the return that the portfolio will earn under each of the planning scenarios in Table 12.2.

The portfolio return over the next 12 months depends on which of the possible scenarios (years 1 through 5) in Table 12.2 occurs. Let $R1$ denote the portfolio return if the scenario represented by year 1 occurs, $R2$ denote the portfolio return if the scenario represented by year 2 occurs, and so on. The portfolio returns for the five planning scenarios are as follows:

Scenario 1 return:

$$R1 = \quad 10.06FS + 17.64IB + 32.41LG + 32.36LV + 33.44SG + 24.56SV$$

Scenario 2 return:

$$R2 = \quad 13.12FS + \quad 3.25IB + 18.71LG + 20.61LV + 19.40SG + 25.32SV$$

Scenario 3 return:

$$R3 = \quad 13.47FS + \quad 7.51IB + 33.28LG + 12.93LV + \quad 3.85SG - \quad 6.70SV$$

Scenario 4 return:

$$R4 = \quad 45.42FS - \quad 1.33IB + 41.46LG + \quad 7.06LV + 58.68SG + \quad 5.43SV$$

Scenario 5 return:

$$R5 = -21.93FS + \quad 7.36IB - 23.26LG - \quad 5.37LV - \quad 9.02SG + 17.31SV$$

Let us now introduce a variable M to represent the minimum return for the portfolio. As we have already shown, one of the five possible scenarios in Table 12.2 will determine the portfolio return. Thus, the minimum possible return for the portfolio will be determined by the scenario that provides the worst-case return. But we don't know which of the scenarios will turn out to represent what happens over the next 12 months. To ensure that the return under each scenario is at least as large as the minimum return M, we must add the following minimum-return constraints:

$$R1 \geq M \qquad \text{Scenario 1 minimum return}$$
$$R2 \geq M \qquad \text{Scenario 2 minimum return}$$
$$R3 \geq M \qquad \text{Scenario 3 minimum return}$$
$$R4 \geq M \qquad \text{Scenario 4 minimum return}$$
$$R5 \geq M \qquad \text{Scenario 5 minimum return}$$

Substituting the values shown previously for $R1$, $R2$, and so on, provides the following five minimum-return constraints:

Scenario 1

$$10.06FS + 17.64IB + 32.41LG + 32.36LV + 33.44SG + 24.56SV \geq M$$

Scenario 2

$$13.12FS + \quad 3.25IB + 18.71LG + 20.61LV + 19.40SG + 25.32SV \geq M$$

Scenario 3

$$13.47FS + \quad 7.51IB + 33.28LG + 12.93LV + \quad 3.85SG - \quad 6.70SV \geq M$$

Scenario 4

$$45.42FS - \quad 1.33IB + 41.46LG + \quad 7.06LV + 58.68SG + \quad 5.43SV \geq M$$

Scenario 5

$$- 21.93FS + \quad 7.36IB - 23.26LG - \quad 5.37LV - \quad 9.02SG + 17.31SV \geq M$$

To develop a portfolio that provides the best return possible with a minimum risk, we need to maximize the minimum return for the portfolio. Thus, the objective function is simple:

$$\text{Max } M$$

With the five minimum-return constraints present, the optimal value of M will equal the value of the minimum return scenario. The objective is to maximize the value of the minimum return scenario.

Because the linear programming model was designed to maximize the minimum return over all the scenarios considered, we refer to it as the maximin model. The complete maximin model for the problem of choosing a portfolio of mutual funds for a conservative, risk-averse investor involves seven variables and six constraints. After moving all the variables in the five minimum-return constraints to the left-hand side, the complete maximin model is rewritten as follows:

Max M

s.t.

$$-M + 10.06FS + 17.64IB + 32.41LG + 32.36LV + 33.44SG + 24.56SV \geq 0$$
$$-M + 13.12FS + 3.25IB + 18.71LG + 20.61LV + 19.40SG + 25.32SV \geq 0$$
$$-M + 13.47FS + 7.51IB + 33.28LG + 12.93LV + 3.85SG - 6.70SV \geq 0$$
$$-M + 45.42FS - 1.33IB + 41.46LG + 7.06LV + 58.68SG + 5.43SV \geq 0$$
$$-M - 21.93FS + 7.36IB - 23.26LG - 5.37LV - 9.02SG + 17.31SV \geq 0$$
$$FS + IB + LG + LV + SG + SV = 1$$
$$M, FS, IB, LG, LV, SG, SV \geq 0$$

Note that we have written the constraint that requires the sum of the proportion of the portfolio invested in each mutual fund as the last constraint in the model. In this way, when we interpret the computer solution of the model, constraint 1 will correspond to planning scenario 1 constraint 2 will correspond to planning scenario 2, and so on.

The optimal solution to the Hauck maximin model is shown in Figure 12.3. The optimal value of the objective function is 6.445; thus, the optimal portfolio will earn 6.445% in

FIGURE 12.3   THE MANAGEMENT SCIENTIST SOLUTION FOR THE HAUCK MAXIMIN PORTFOLIO PROBLEM

WEB file

Maximin

```
OPTIMAL SOLUTION
Objective Function Value =              6.445

        Variable              Value              Reduced Costs
     --------------       ---------------       ------------------
          FS                   0.000                 6.768
          IB                   0.554                 0.000
          LG                   0.132                 0.000
          LV                   0.000                 3.156
          SG                   0.000                 2.764
          SV                   0.314                 0.000
          M                    6.445                 0.000


       Constraint          Slack/Surplus            Dual Prices
     --------------       ---------------       ------------------
           1                  15.321                 0.000
           2                   5.785                 0.000
           3                   0.000                -0.397
           4                   0.000                -0.112
           5                   0.000                -0.491
           6                   0.000                 6.445
```

the worst-case scenario. The optimal solution calls for 55.4% of the portfolio to be invested in the intermediate-term bond fund, 13.2% of the portfolio to be invested in the large-cap growth fund, and 31.4% of the portfolio to be invested in the small-cap value fund.

Because we do not know at the time of solving the model which of the five possible scenarios will occur, we cannot say for sure that the portfolio return will be 6.445%. However, using the surplus variables, we can learn what the portfolio return will be under each of the scenarios. Constraints 3, 4, and 5 correspond to scenarios 3, 4, and 5 (years 3, 4, and 5 in Table 12.2). The surplus variables for these constraints are zero to indicate that the portfolio return will be $M = 6.445\%$ if any of these three scenarios occur. The surplus variable for constraint 1 is 15.321, indicating that the portfolio return will exceed $M = 6.445$ by 15.321 if scenario 1 occurs. So, if scenario 1 occurs, the portfolio return will be 6.445% = 15.321% = 21.766%. Referring to the surplus variable for constraint 2, we see that the portfolio return will be 6.445% + 5.785% = 12.230% if scenario 2 occurs.

We must also keep in mind that in order to develop the portfolio model, Hauck made the assumption that over the next 12 months one of the five possible scenarios in Table 12.2 will occur. But we also recognize that the actual scenario that occurs over the next 12 months may be different from the scenarios Hauck considered. Thus, Hauck's experience and judgment in selecting representative scenarios plays a key part in determining how valuable the model recommendations will be for the client.

Moderate Risk Portfolio

Hauck's portfolio manager would like to also construct a portfolio for clients who are willing to accept a moderate amount of risk in order to attempt to achieve better returns. Suppose that clients in this risk category are willing to accept some risk, but do not want the annual return for the portfolio to drop below 2%. By setting $M = 2$ in the minimum-return constraints in the maximin model we can constrain the model to provide a solution with an annual return of at least 2%. The minimum-return constraints needed to provide an annual return of at least 2% are as follows:

$$R1 \geq 2 \qquad \text{Scenario 1 minimum return}$$
$$R2 \geq 2 \qquad \text{Scenario 2 minimum return}$$
$$R3 \geq 2 \qquad \text{Scenario 3 minimum return}$$
$$R4 \geq 2 \qquad \text{Scenario 4 minimum return}$$
$$R5 \geq 2 \qquad \text{Scenario 5 minimum return}$$

Substituting the expressions previously developed for $R1$, $R2$, and so on, provides the following five minimum-return constraints:

Scenario 1
$$10.06FS + 17.64IB + 32.41LG + 32.36LV + 33.44SG + 24.56SV \geq 2$$
Scenario 2
$$13.12FS + 3.25IB + 18.71LG + 20.61LV + 19.40SG + 25.32SV \geq 2$$
Scenario 3
$$13.47FS + 7.51IB + 33.28LG + 12.93LV + 3.85SG - 6.70SV \geq 2$$
Scenario 4
$$45.42FS - 1.33IB + 41.46LG + 7.06LV + 58.68SG + 5.43SV \geq 2$$
Scenario 5
$$-21.93FS + 7.36IB - 23.26LG - 5.37LV - 9.02SG + 17.31SV \geq 2$$

In addition to these five minimum-return constraints, we still need the constraint that requires that the sum of the proportions invested in the separate mutual funds add to 1.

$$FS + IB + LG + LV + SG + SV = 1$$

A different objective is needed for this portfolio optimization problem. A common approach is to maximize the expected value of the return for the portfolio. For instance, if we assume that the planning scenarios are equally likely, we would assign a probability of 0.20 to each scenario. In this case the objective function is

$$\text{Expected value of the return} = 0.2R1 + 0.2R2 + 0.2R3 + 0.2R4 + 0.2R5$$

The coefficient of FS in the objective function is given by $0.2(10.06) + 0.2(13.12) + 0.2(13.47) + 0.2(45.42) + 0.2(-21.93) = 12.03$; the coefficient of IB is $0.2(17.64) + 0.2(3.25) + 0.2(7.51) + 0.2(-1.33) + 0.2(7.36) = 6.89$; and so on. Thus, the objective function is

$$12.03FS + 6.89IB + 20.52LG + 13.52LV + 21.27SG + 13.18SV$$

Because the objective is to maximize the expected value of the return we write Hauck's objective as follows:

$$\text{Max } 12.03FS + 6.89IB + 20.52LG + 13.52LV + 21.27SG + 13.18SV$$

The complete linear programming formulation for this version of the portfolio optimization problem involves six variables and six constraints.

$$\text{Max } 12.03FS + 6.89IB + 20.52LG + 13.52LV + 21.27SG + 13.18SV$$
$$\text{s.t.}$$
$$10.06FS + 17.64IB + 32.41LG + 32.36LV + 33.44SG + 24.56SV \geq 2$$
$$13.12FS + 3.25IB + 18.71LG + 20.61LV + 19.40SG + 25.32SV \geq 2$$
$$13.47FS + 7.51IB + 33.28LG + 12.93LV + 3.85SG - 6.70SV \geq 2$$
$$45.42FS - 1.33IB + 41.46LG + 7.06LV + 58.68SG + 5.43SV \geq 2$$
$$-21.93FS + 7.36IB - 23.26LG - 5.37LV - 9.02SG + 17.31SV \geq 2$$
$$FS + IB + LG + LV + SG + SV = 1$$
$$FS, IB, LG, LV, SG, SV \geq 0$$

The optimal solution is shown in Figure 12.4. The optimal allocation is to invest 10.8% of the portfolio in a large-cap growth mutual fund, 41.5% in a small-cap growth mutual fund, and 47.7% in a small-cap value mutual fund. The objective function value shows that this allocation provides a maximum expected return of 17.33%. From the surplus variables, we see that the portfolio return will only be 2% if scenarios 3 or 5 occur (constraints 3 and 5 are binding). The returns will be excellent if scenarios 1, 2, or 4 occur: The portfolio return will be 29.093% if scenario 1 occurs, 22.149% if scenario 2 occurs, and 31.417% if scenario 4 occurs.

The moderate risk portfolio exposes Hauck's clients to more risk than the maximin portfolio developed for a conservative investor. With the maximin portfolio, the worst-case scenario provided a return of 6.44%. With this moderate risk portfolio, the worst-case

FIGURE 12.4   THE MANAGEMENT SCIENTIST SOLUTION FOR THE MODERATE RISK
PORTFOLIO PROBLEM

```
Objective Function Value =              17.330

        Variable              Value              Reduced Costs
     --------------      ----------------      ------------------
          FS                  0.000                  12.246
          IB                  0.000                   7.139
          LG                  0.108                   0.000
          LV                  0.000                   4.351
          SG                  0.415                   0.000
          SV                  0.477                   0.000


       Constraint         Slack/Surplus          Dual Prices
     --------------      ----------------      ------------------
           1                 27.093                  0.000
           2                 20.149                  0.000
           3                  0.000                 -0.216
           4                 29.417                  0.000
           5                  0.000                 -0.394
           6                  0.000                 18.550


OBJECTIVE COEFFICIENT RANGES

    Variable      Lower Limit      Current Value      Upper Limit
  ------------   ---------------  ----------------   ---------------
       FS        No Lower Limit        12.030             24.276
       IB        No Lower Limit         6.890             14.029
       LG            10.729            20.520             25.645
       LV        No Lower Limit        13.520             17.871
       SG            17.944            21.270             46.224
       SV             4.832            13.180             21.539


RIGHT HAND SIDE RANGES

    Constraint    Lower Limit      Current Value      Upper Limit
  ------------   ---------------  ----------------   ---------------
        1        No Lower Limit         2.000             29.093
        2        No Lower Limit         2.000             22.149
        3            -0.566             2.000              8.387
        4        No Lower Limit         2.000             31.417
        5            -4.403             2.000              8.482
        6             0.383             1.000             11.879
```

scenarios (scenarios 3 and 5) only provide a return of 2%, but it also provides the possibility of higher returns.

The formulation we have developed for a moderate risk portfolio can be modified to account for other risk tolerances. If an investor can tolerate the risk of no return, the right-hand sides of the minimum-return constraints would be set to 0. If an investor can tolerate a loss of 3%, the right-hand side of the minimum-return constraints would be set equal to −3.

NOTES AND COMMENTS

1. The Q.M. in Action, Asset Allocation and Variable Annuities, describes how insurance companies use asset allocation models to choose a portfolio of mutual funds for their clients' variable annuity investments.

2. Other constraints may be added to portfolio models to make them more flexible. For instance, if a client wanted to have at least 10% of the portfolio invested in foreign stocks, we would add the constraint $FS \geq .10$ to either the maximin or moderate risk portfolio models.

3. The portfolio models developed in this section are based on a working paper entitled "Decision Analysis, Diversification, and Financial Services" (December 2005) by George G. Polak and Dennis J. Sweeney. Related models can be found in "A Minimax Portfolio Selection Rule with Linear Programming," by Martin R. Young, *Management Science* (1998).

4. Harry Markowitz pioneered the use of mathematical models for portfolio selection. The primary model he developed is nonlinear and uses the statistical variance of returns for the portfolio as a measure of risk.

Q.M. *in* ACTION

ASSET ALLOCATION AND VARIABLE ANNUITIES*

Insurance companies use portfolio models for asset allocation to structure a portfolio for their clients who purchase variable annuities. A variable annuity is an insurance contract that involves an accumulation phase and a distribution phase. In the accumulation phase the individual either makes a lump sum contribution or contributes to the annuity over a period of time. In the distribution phase the investor receives payments either in a lump sum or over a period of time. The distribution phase usually occurs at retirement, but because a variable annuity is an insurance product, a benefit is paid to a beneficiary should the annuitant die before or during the distribution period.

Most insurance companies selling variable annuities offer their clients the benefit of an asset allocation model to help them decide how to allocate their investment among a family of mutual funds. Usually the client fills out a questionnaire to assess his or her level of risk tolerance. Then, given that risk tolerance, the insurance company's asset allocation model recommends how the client's investment should be allocated over a family of mutual funds. American Skandia, a Prudential Financial Company, markets variable annuities that provide the types of services mentioned. A questionnaire is used to assess the client's risk tolerance, and the Morningstar Asset Allocator is used to develop portfolios for five levels of risk tolerance. Clients with low levels of risk tolerance are guided to portfolios consisting of bond funds and T-bills, and the most risk-tolerant investors are guided to portfolios consisting of a large proportion of growth stock mutual funds. Investors with intermediate, or moderate, risk tolerances are guided to portfolios that may consist of suitable mixtures of value and growth stock funds as well as some bond funds.

*Based on information provided by James R. Martin of the Martin Company, a financial services company.

12.3 Nonlinear Optimization—The RMC Problem Revisited

We introduce constrained and unconstrained nonlinear optimization problems by considering an extension of the RMC linear program introduced in Chapter 7. We first consider the case in which the relationship between price and quantity sold causes the objective function to become nonlinear. The resulting unconstrained nonlinear program is then solved and we observe that the unconstrained optimal solution does not satisfy the production constraints. Adding the production constraints back into the problem allows us to show the formulation and solution of a constrained nonlinear program. The section closes with a discussion of local and global optima.

Q.M. *in* ACTION

PRICING FOR ENVIRONMENTAL COMPLIANCE IN THE AUTO INDUSTRY*

As a result of the 1973 oil embargo Congress put into law the Corporate Average Fuel Economy (CAFE) regulations in 1975. The CAFE standards are designed to promote the sale of fuel efficient automobiles and light trucks thus reducing dependence on oil. The CAFE standards were modified when President Bush signed into law the Clean Energy Act of 2007. This law requires that automakers boost fleet gas mileage average to 35 mpg by the year 2020. Although polls reveal strong support for such regulatory action, actual consumer behavior runs counter to supporting the purchase of fuel-efficient cars. Indeed, car manufactures are faced with the problem of influencing consumers to purchase more fuel-efficient cars in order for the manufacturer to meet the CAFE mandated standard. One way to influence consumer pur-

chase behavior is through price. Lowering the price of fuel-efficient cars is one way to shift demand to this market. Of course, this should be done in a way to keep profits as large as possible subject to the CAFE constraints.

In order to meet the CAFE constraints, while maximizing profits, General Motors (GM) used a mathematical model for coordinated pricing and production called Visual CAFÉ. This was built into an Excel spreadsheet with data input from Microsoft Access. The objective function for this model is much like the objective function for the nonlinear version of RMC that we develop in this section. In both cases the objective is to maximize profit and the profit function is the product of quantity sold times the contribution margin of each product. The quantity sold is based on a linear demand function. A key constraint is the CAFE constraint, which is a constraint on the average miles per gallon for the GM fleet of cars. In addition, there are constraints on assembly, engine, and transmission capacity.

---

*Based on Stephan Biller and Julie Swan, "Pricing for Environmental Compliance in the Auto Industry," *Interfaces* 36, no. 2 (March/April 2006): 118–125.

An Unconstrained Problem

Let us consider a revision of the RMC problem from Chapter 7. Recall that RMC produced a variety of chemical-based products including a fuel additive and a solvent base. In formulating the linear programming model for the RMC problem, we assumed that it could sell all of the fuel additive and solvent base produced. However, depending on the price of the fuel additive and solvent base, this assumption may not hold. An inverse relationship usually exists between price and demand. As price goes up, the quantity demanded goes down. Let P_F denote the price RMC charges for each ton of fuel additive and P_S denote the price for each ton of solvent base. Assume that the demand for tons of fuel additive F and the demand for tons of solvent base S is

$$F = 580 - 2P_F \tag{12.1}$$

$$S = 840 - 2.5P_S \tag{12.2}$$

The revenue generated from selling fuel additive is the price per ton P_F times the number of tons of fuel additive sold, F. If the cost to produce a ton of fuel additive is \$250, the cost to produce F tons of fuel additive is 250F. Thus, the profit contribution for producing and selling F tons of fuel additive (revenue − cost) is

$$P_F F - 250F \tag{12.3}$$

We can solve equation (12.1) for P_F to show how the price of a ton of fuel additive is related to the number of tons of fuel additive sold. It is $P_F = 290 - \frac{1}{2}F$. Substituting $290 - \frac{1}{2}F$ for P_F in equation (12.3), the profit contribution for fuel additive is

$$P_F F - 250F = (290 - F/2)F - 250F = 40F - 0.5F^2 \tag{12.4}$$

Suppose that the cost to produce each ton of solvent base is \$300. Using the same logic we used to develop equation (12.4), the profit contribution for solvent base is

$$P_S S - 300S = (336 - S/2.5)S - 300S = 36S - 0.4S^2$$

(Note we have written $1/2.5 = 0.4$.) Total profit contribution is the sum of the profit contribution from the fuel additive and the profit contribution for the solvent base. Thus, total profit contribution is written as

$$\text{Total profit contribution} = 40F - 0.5F^2 + 36S - 0.4S^2 \tag{12.5}$$

Note that the two linear demand functions, equations (12.1) and (12.2), give a nonlinear total profit contribution function, equation (12.5). This function is an example of a quadratic function because the nonlinear terms have a power of 2.

WEB file

RMCNonlinearUcon

Using LINGO (see Appendix 12.1), we find that the values of F and S that maximize the profit contribution function are $F = 40$ and $S = 45$. The corresponding prices are \$270 for a ton of fuel additive and \$318 for solvent base, and the profit contribution is \$1610. These values provide the optimal solution for RMC if all material limit constraints are also satisfied.

A Constrained Problem

Unfortunately, RMC cannot make the profit contribution associated with the optimal solution to the unconstrained problem because the constraints defining the feasible region are violated. For instance, the Material 1 constraint is $0.4F + 0.5S \leq 20$.

A production quantity of 40 tons of fuel additive and solvent will require $0.4(40) + 0.5(45) = 38.5$ tons, which exceeds the limit of 20 tons by 18.5. The feasible region for the original RMC problem, along with the unconstrained optimal solution point (40, 45), is shown in Figure 12.5. The unconstrained optimum of (40, 45) is obviously outside the feasible region.

Clearly the problem that RMC must solve is to maximize the total profit contribution

$$40F - 0.5F^2 + 36S - 0.4S^2$$

FIGURE 12.5   THE RMC FEASIBLE REGION AND THE OPTIMAL SOLUTION FOR THE
UNCONSTRAINED OPTIMIZATION PROBLEM

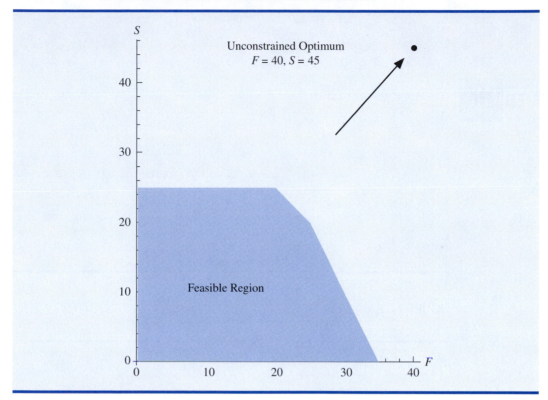

subject to all of the material tonnage constraints that were given in Chapter 7. The complete
mathematical model for the RMC constrained nonlinear maximization problem follows:

$$\text{Max} \quad 40F - 0.5F^2 + 36S - 0.4S^2$$

$$\text{s.t.}$$

$$0.4F + 0.5S \leq 20 \quad \text{Material 1}$$
$$0.2S \leq 5 \quad \text{Material 2}$$
$$0.6F + 0.3S \leq 21 \quad \text{Material 3}$$
$$F, S \geq 0$$

This maximization problem is exactly the same as the RMC problem in Chapter 7 except for the nonlinear objective function. The LINGO solution to this constrained nonlinear
maximization problem is shown in Figure 12.6.

The first line shows that a local optimal solution has been found. This local optimum is
also a global optimum (see the next subsection). The optimal value of the objective function is $1247.83. The Variable section shows that the optimal solution is to produce
24.33862 tons of fuel additive and 20.5291 tons of solvent base. In the Row section, row 1
corresponds to the objective function and rows 2 through 4 correspond to the three material tonnage constraints. In the Slack or Surplus column, the value of 0 in row 2 indicates
that the optimal solution uses all of Material 1 that is available; but the nonzero values in
rows 3 and 4 indicate that there is excess tonnage of Material 2 and 3.

A graphical view of the optimal solution of 24.33862 tons of fuel additive and 20.5291 tons
of solvent base is shown in Figure 12.7.

FIGURE 12.6   LINGO SOLUTION FOR THE NONLINEAR RMC PROBLEM

RMCNonlinear

```
LOCAL OPTIMAL SOLUTION FOUND.
Objective value:              1247.831
Extended solver steps:               5
Total solver iterations:            26

      Variable              Value            Reduced Cost
   ---------------      ---------------      ---------------
           F                24.33862             0.000000
           S                20.52910             0.000000

        Row            Slack/Surplus            Dual Price
   ---------------      ---------------      ---------------
           1               1247.831             1.000000
           2               0.000000            39.15344
           3               0.8941799            0.000000
           4               0.2380952            0.000000
```

FIGURE 12.7   THE RMC FEASIBLE REGION WITH OBJECTIVE FUNCTION
CONTOUR LINES

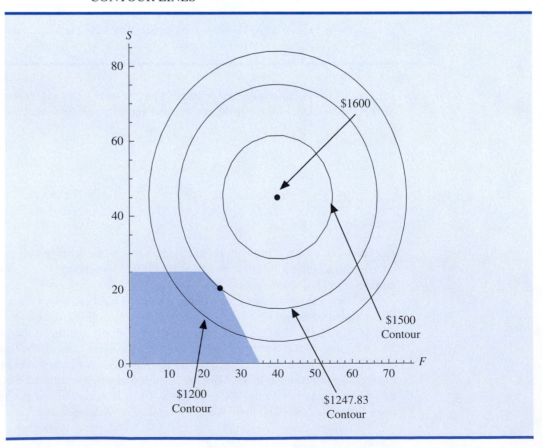

Note that the optimal solution is no longer at an extreme point of the feasible region. The optimal solution lies on the Material 1 constraint line

$$0.4F + 0.5S = 20$$

but not at the extreme point formed by the intersection of the Material 1 constraint and Material 2 constraint, nor the extreme point formed by the intersection of the Material 1 constraint and the Material 3 constraint. To understand why, we look at Figure 12.7.

In Figure 12.7 we see three profit contribution contour lines. Each point on the same contour line is a point of equal profit. Here, the contour lines show profit contributions of $1200, $1247.831, and $1500. In the original RMC problem described in Chapter 7, the objective function is linear and thus the profit contours are straight lines. However, for the RMC problem with a quadratic objective function, the profit contours are ellipses.

Because part of the $1200 profit contour line cuts through the feasible region, we know an infinite number of combinations of fuel additive and solvent base tonnages will yield a profit of $1200. An infinite number of combinations of fuel additive and solvent base tonnages provide a profit of $1500. However, none of the points on the $1500 contour profit line are in the feasible region. As the contour lines move further out from the unconstrained optimum of (40, 45) the profit contribution associated with each contour line decreases. The contour line representing a profit of $1247.831 intersects the feasible region at a single point. This solution provides the maximum possible profit. No contour line that has a profit contribution greater than 1247.831 will intersect the feasible region. Because the contour lines are nonlinear, the contour line with the highest profit can touch the boundary of the feasible region at any point, not just an extreme point. In the RMC case, the optimal solution is on the Material 1 constraint line part way between two extreme points.

It is also possible for the optimal solution to a nonlinear optimization problem to lie in the interior of the feasible region. For instance, if the right-hand sides of the constraints in the RMC problem were all increased by a sufficient amount, the feasible region would expand so that the optimal unconstrained solution point of (40, 45) in Figure 12.7 would be in the interior of the feasible region. Many linear programming algorithms (e.g., the simplex method) optimize by examining only the extreme points and selecting the extreme point that gives the best solution value. As the solution to the constrained RMC nonlinear problem illustrates, such a method will not work in the nonlinear case because the optimal solution is generally not an extreme point solution. Hence, nonlinear programming algorithms are more complex than linear programming algorithms, and the details are beyond the scope of this text. Fortunately, we don't need to know how nonlinear algorithms work, we just need to know how to use them. Computer software such as LINGO and Excel Solver are available to solve nonlinear programming problems and we describe how to use these software packages in the chapter appendices.

Local and Global Optima

The first line of the LINGO solution to the nonlinear RMC problem in Figure 12.6 says, "Local optimal solution found." A feasible solution is a **local optimum** if no other feasible solutions with a better objective function value are found in the immediate neighborhood. For example, for the constrained RMC problem, the local optimum corresponds to a **local maximum**; a point is a local maximum if no other feasible solutions with a larger objective function value are in the immediate neighborhood. Similarly, for a minimization problem, a point is a **local minimum** if no other feasible solutions with a smaller objective function value are in the immediate neighborhood.

Nonlinear optimization problems can have multiple local optimal solutions, which means we are concerned with finding the best of the local optimal solutions. A feasible solution is a **global optimum** if no other feasible points with a better objective function value are found in the feasible region. In the case of a maximization problem, the global optimum corresponds to a global maximum. A point is a **global maximum** if no other points in the feasible region give a strictly larger objective function value. For a minimization problem, a point is a **global minimum** if no other feasible points with a strictly smaller objective function value are in the feasible region. Obviously a global maximum is also a local maximum, and a global minimum is also a local minimum.

Nonlinear problems with multiple local optima are difficult to solve. But in many nonlinear applications, a single local optimal solution is also the global optimal solution. For such problems, we only need to find a local optimal solution. We will now present some of the more common classes of nonlinear problems of this type.

Consider the function $f(X, Y) = -X^2 - Y^2$. The shape of this function is illustrated in Figure 12.8. A function that is bowl-shaped down is called a **concave function**. The maximum value for this particular function is 0, and the point $(0, 0)$ gives the optimal value of 0. The point $(0, 0)$ is a local maximum; but it is also a global maximum because no point gives a larger function value. In other words, no values of X or Y result in an objective function value greater than 0. Functions that are concave, such as $f(X, Y) = -X^2 - Y^2$, have a single local maximum that is also a global maximum. This type of nonlinear problem is relatively easy to maximize.

The objective function for the nonlinear RMC problem is another example of a concave function:

$$40F - 0.5F^2 + 36S - 0.4S^2$$

In general, if all of the squared terms in a quadratic function have a negative coefficient and there are no cross-product terms, such as xy, then the function is a concave quadratic function. Thus, for the RMC problem, we are assured that the local maximum identified by LINGO in Figure 12.6 is the global maximum.

Let us now consider another type of function with a single local optimum that is also a global optimum. Consider the function $f(X, Y) = X^2 + Y^2$. The shape of this function is illustrated in Figure 12.9. It is bowl-shaped up and called a **convex function**. The minimum value for this particular function is 0, and the point $(0, 0)$ gives the minimum value of 0. The point $(0, 0)$ is a local minimum and a global minimum because no values of X or Y give an objective function value less than 0. Functions that are convex, such as $f(X, Y) = X^2 + Y^2$, have a single local minimum and are relatively easy to minimize.

FIGURE 12.8   A CONCAVE FUNCTION $f(X, Y) = -X^2 - Y^2$

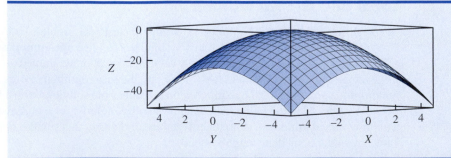

FIGURE 12.9   A CONVEX FUNCTION $f(X, Y) = X^2 + Y^2$

For a concave function, we can be assured that if our computer software finds a local maximum, it is a global maximum. Similarly, for a convex function, we know that if our computer software finds a local minimum, it is a global minimum. Concave and convex functions are well behaved. However, some nonlinear functions have multiple local optima. For example, Figure 12.10 shows the graph of the following function:[1]

$$f(X, Y) = 3(1 - X)^2 e^{-X^2 - (Y+1)^2} - 10(X/5 - X^3 - Y^5)e^{-X^2 - Y^2} - e^{-(X+1)^2 - Y^2}/3$$

The hills and valleys in this graph show that this function has several local maximums and local minimums. These concepts are further illustrated in Figure 12.11, which is the same function as in Figure 12.10 but from a different viewpoint. It indicates two local minimums and three local maximums. One of the local minimums is also the global minimum, and one of the local maximums is also the global maximum.

FIGURE 12.10   A FUNCTION WITH LOCAL MAXIMA AND MINIMA

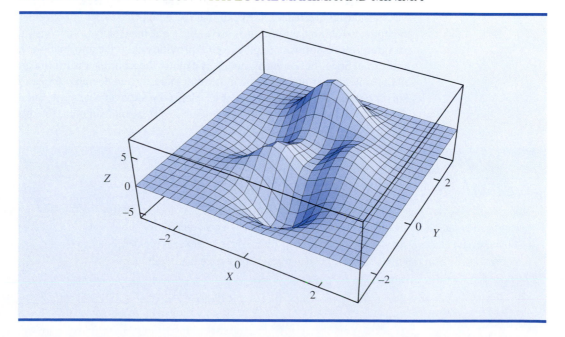

[1]This example is taken from the LINDO API manual available at *http://www.LINDO.com.*

FIGURE 12.11   ANOTHER VIEWPOINT OF A FUNCTION WITH LOCAL MAXIMUMS AND MINIMUMS

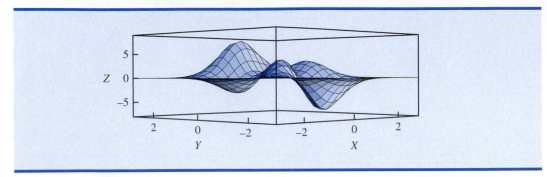

From a technical standpoint, functions with multiple local optima pose a serious challenge for optimization software; most nonlinear optimization software methods can get "stuck" and terminate at a local optimum. Unfortunately, many applications can be nonlinear and there is a severe penalty for finding a local optimum that is not a global optimum. Developing algorithms capable of finding the global optimum is currently an active research area. But the problem of minimizing a convex quadratic function over a linear constraint set is relatively easy, and for problems of this type there is no danger in getting stuck at a local minimum that is not a global minimum. Similarly, the problem of maximizing a concave quadratic function over a linear constraint set is also relatively easy to solve without getting stuck at a local maximum that is not the global maximum.

Dual Prices

We conclude this section with a brief discussion of dual prices. The concept of a dual price was introduced in Chapter 8. Recall that the dual price is the improvement in the value of the optimal solution per unit increase in the right-hand side of the constraint. Most nonlinear optimization software (e.g., LINGO) provide dual price information. The interpretation of the dual price for nonlinear models is exactly the same as it is for linear programs. However, for nonlinear problems the allowable increase and decrease are not usually reported. This is because for typical nonlinear problems the allowable increase and decrease are zero. That is, if you change the right-hand side by even a small amount, the dual price changes.

Q.M. *in* ACTION

SCHEDULING FLIGHTS AND CREWS FOR BOMBARDIER FLEXJET*

Bombardier Flexjet is a leading company in the fast-growing fractional aircraft industry. Flexjet sells shares of business jets in share sizes equal to 50 hours of flying per year. A firm with fractional ownership is guaranteed 24-hour access to an aircraft with as little as a 4-hour lead time. Companies with a fractional share pay monthly management and usage fees. In exchange for the management fee, Flexjet provides hangar facilities, maintenance, and flight crews.

Because of the flexibility provided in the fractional aircraft business, the problem of scheduling crews and flights is even more complicated than in the commercial

*Based on Richard Hicks et al., "Bombardier Flexjet Significantly Improves Its Fractional Aircraft Ownership Operations," *Interfaces* 35, no. 1 (January/February 2005): 49–60.

(*continued*)

airline industry. Initially, Flex-jet attempted to schedule flights by hand. However, this task quickly proved to be infeasible. Indeed, the inadequate manual scheduling resulted in Flexjet maintaining extra business jets and crews. The cost of the extra jets and crews was estimated at several hundred dollars per flight hour. A scheduling system using optimization was clearly required.

The scheduling system developed for Flexjet includes a large nonlinear optimization model that is integrated with a graphical user interface (GUI) used by Flexjet personnel. The model includes "hard" constraints based on Federal Aviation Administration (FAA) regulations, company rules, and aircraft performance characteristics. It also includes "soft constraints" that involve cost tradeoffs. The model is used to assign aircraft and crews to flights.

The resulting model is too large to solve directly with commercial optimization software. Models with too many variables to solve directly are often solved using decomposition methods. Decomposition methods work with a master problem that includes only a small fraction of the total number of variables. Variables that are good candidates to be part of the optimal solution are identified through the solution of a subproblem. In the Flexjet model, the subproblem is a nonlinear integer program. The heart of the nonlinearity is the product of a binary variable that is 1 if a particular pair of flight legs is used and a continuous variable that is used to impose a time window on flight times. The subproblem is optimized using a technique called dynamic programming.

The optimization model was a big success. The model initially saved Flexjet $54 million, with a projected annual savings of $27 million. Much of this cost saving is the result of reducing crew levels by 20% and aircraft inventory by 40%. Aircraft utilization also increased by 10%.

12.4 Constructing an Index Fund

In Section 12.2 we studied portfolio and asset allocation models for Hauck Financial Services. Several linear programs were built to model different client attitudes toward risk. In this section we study an important related application.

Index funds are an extremely popular investment vehicle in the mutual fund industry. Indeed, the Vanguard 500 Index Fund is the single largest mutual fund in the United States, with more than $70 billion in net assets in 2005. An **index fund** is an example of passive asset management. The key idea behind an index fund is to construct a portfolio of stocks, mutual funds, or other securities that matches as closely as possible the performance of a broad market index such as the S&P 500.

Table 12.3 shows the one-year returns for four Vanguard Index Funds[2] and the returns for the corresponding market indexes. Several interesting issues are illustrated in this table. First, Vanguard has index funds for numerous types of investments. For example, the first two index funds are stock funds: the S&P 500 Index Fund and the MSCI Broad Market

TABLE 12.3   ONE-YEAR RETURNS FOR FOUR VANGUARD INDEX FUNDS

Vanguard Fund	Vanguard Fund Return	Market Index	Market Index Return
500 Index Fund	4.77%	S&P 500	4.91%
Total Stock Index	5.98%	MSCI Broad Market	6.08%
REIT Index	11.90%	MSCI REIT	12.13%
Short-Term Bond	1.31%	Lehman 1-5 Index	1.44%

[2]These data were taken from *http://www.vanguard.com* and are the one-year period ending December 31, 2005.

fund. The MSCI REIT fund is an investment in the real estate market, and the Short-Term Bond (Lehman 1-5) fund is an investment in the corporate bond market. Second, notice that even though the returns show considerable variation between the funds, the index funds do a good job of matching the return of the corresponding market index.

Why are index funds so popular? Behind the popularity of index funds is a substantial amount of research in finance that basically says, "You can't beat the market." In fact, the vast majority of mutual fund managers actually underperform leading market indexes such as the S&P 500. Therefore, many investors are satisfied with investments that provide a return that more closely matches the market return.

Now, let's revisit the Hauck Financial Services example. Assume that Hauck has a substantial number of clients who wish to own a mutual fund portfolio with the characteristic that the portfolio, as a whole, closely matches the performance of the S&P 500 stock index. What percentage of the portfolio should be invested in each mutual fund in order to most closely mimic the performance of the entire S&P 500 index?

In Table 12.4 we reproduce Table 12.2 with an additional row that gives the S&P 500 return for each planning scenario. Recall that the columns show the actual percentage return that was earned by each mutual fund in that year. These five columns represent the most likely scenarios for the coming year.

The variables used in the model presented in Section 12.2 represented the proportion of the portfolio invested in each mutual fund.

FS = proportion of portfolio invested in a foreign stock mutual fund

IB = proportion of portfolio invested in an intermediate-term bond fund

LG = proportion of portfolio invested in a large-cap growth fund

LV = proportion of portfolio invested in a large-cap value fund

SG = proportion of portfolio invested in a small-cap growth fund

SV = proportion of portfolio invested in a small-cap value fund

The portfolio models presented in Section 12.2 chose the proportion of the portfolio to invest in each mutual fund in order to maximize return subject to constraints on the portfolio risk. Here we wish to choose the proportion of the portfolio to invest in each mutual fund in order to track as closely as possible the S&P 500 return.

TABLE 12.4   MUTUAL FUND PERFORMANCE IN FIVE SELECTED YEARS USED AS PLANNING SCENARIOS FOR THE NEXT 12 MONTHS

Mutual Fund	Planning Scenarios				
	Year 1	Year 2	Year 3	Year 4	Year 5
Foreign Stock	10.06	13.12	13.47	45.42	−21.93
Intermediate-Term Bond	17.64	3.25	7.51	−1.33	7.36
Large-Cap Growth	32.41	18.71	33.28	41.46	−23.26
Large-Cap Value	32.36	20.61	12.93	7.06	−5.37
Small-Cap Growth	33.44	19.40	3.85	58.68	−9.02
Small-Cap Value	24.56	25.32	−6.70	5.43	17.31
S&P 500 Return	**25.00**	**20.00**	**8.00**	**30.00**	**−10.00**

For clarity of model exposition, we introduce variables $R1$, $R2$, $R3$, $R4$, and $R5$ that measure the portfolio return for each scenario. Consider, for example, variable $R1$. If the scenario represented by year 1 reflects what happens over the next 12 months, the portfolio return under scenario 1 is

$$10.06FS + 17.64IB + 32.41LG + 32.36LV + 33.44SG + 24.56SV = R1$$

Similarly, if scenarios 2–5 reflect the returns obtained over the next 12 months, the portfolio returns under scenarios 2–5 are as follows:

Scenario 2 return:

$$13.12FS + 3.25IB + 18.71LG + 20.61LV + 19.40SG + 25.32SV = R2$$

Scenario 3 return:

$$13.47FS + 7.51IB + 33.28LG + 12.93LV + 3.85SG - 6.70SV = R3$$

Scenario 4 return:

$$45.42FS - 1.33IB + 41.46LG + 7.06LV + 58.68SG + 5.43SV = R4$$

Scenario 5 return:

$$-21.93FS + 7.36IB - 23.26LG - 5.37LV - 9.02SG + 17.31SV = R5$$

Next, for each scenario we compute the deviation between the return for the scenario and the S&P 500 return. Based on the last row of Table 12.4, the deviations are

$$R1 - 25, \quad R2 - 20, \quad R3 - 8, \quad R4 - 30, \quad R5 - (-10) \quad \textbf{(12.6)}$$

The objective is for the portfolio returns to match as closely as possible the S&P 500 returns. To do so, we might try minimizing the sum of the deviations given in equation (12.6) as follows:

$$\text{Min} \quad (R1 - 25) + (R2 - 20) + (R3 - 8) + (R4 - 30) + (R5 - (-10)) \quad \textbf{(12.7)}$$

Unfortunately, if we use equation (12.7), positive and negative deviations will cancel each other out, so a portfolio that has a small value for equation (12.7) might actually behave quite differently than the target index. Also, because we want to get as close to the target returns as possible, it makes sense to assign a higher marginal penalty cost for large deviations than for small deviations. A function that achieves this goal is

$$\text{Min} \ (R1 - 25)^2 + (R2 - 20)^2 + (R3 - 8)^2 + (R4 - 30)^2 + (R5 - (-10))^2$$

When we square each term, positive and negative deviations do not cancel each other out and the marginal penalty cost for deviations increases as the deviation gets larger. The complete mathematical model we have developed involves 11 variables and 6 constraints (excluding the nonnegativity constraints).

Min $(R1 - 25)^2 + (R2 - 20)^2 + (R3 - 8)^2 + (R4 - 30)^2 + (R5 - (-10))^2$
s.t.

$$10.06FS + 17.64IB + 32.41LG + 32.36LV + 33.44SG + 24.56SV = R1$$
$$13.12FS + 3.25IB + 18.71LG + 20.61LV + 19.40SG + 25.32SV = R2$$
$$13.47FS + 7.51IB + 33.28LG + 12.93LV + 3.85SG - 6.70SV = R3$$
$$45.42FS - 1.33IB + 41.46LG + 7.06LV + 58.68SG + 5.43SV = R4$$
$$-21.93FS + 7.36IB - 23.26LG - 5.37LV - 9.02SG + 17.31SV = R5$$
$$FS + IB + LG + LV + SG + SV = 1$$
$$FS, IB, LG, LV, SG, SV \geq 0$$

WEB file

HauckIndex

This minimization problem is nonlinear because of the quadratic terms that appear in the objective function. For example, in the term $(R1 - 25)^2$ the variable $R1$ is raised to a power of 2 and is therefore nonlinear. However, because the coefficient of each squared term is positive, and there are no cross-product terms, the objective function is a convex function. Therefore, we are guaranteed that any local minimum is also a global minimum.

The LINGO solution is given in Figure 12.12. The optimal value of the objective function is 4.426893, the sum of the squares of the return deviations. The portfolio calls for approximately 30% of the funds to be invested in the foreign stock fund ($FS = 0.3033377$),

FIGURE 12.12   LINGO SOLUTION FOR THE HAUCK FINANCIAL SERVICES PROBLEM

```
Local optimal solution found.
   Objective Value:                    4.426893
   Total solver iterations:                  13


      Variable              Value          Reduced Cost
   --------------     --------------     ------------------
            R1            25.02024              0.000000
            R2            18.55903              0.000000
            R3            8.973028              0.000000
            R4            30.21927              0.000000
            R5           -8.835857              0.000000
            FS            0.3033377             0.000000
            IB            0.000000             64.84669
            LG            0.000000             18.51276
            LV            0.3649815             0.000000
            SG            0.2265517             0.000000
            SV            0.1051291             0.000000


       Row          Slack or Surplus         Dual Price
   --------------     --------------      ------------------
            1             4.426893            -1.000000
            2             0.000000             0.4047736E-01
            3             0.000000            -2.881937
            4             0.000000             1.946056
            5             0.000000             0.4385427
            6             0.000000             2.328287
            7             0.000000            42.33116
```

TABLE 12.5 PORTFOLIO RETURN VERSUS S&P 500 RETURN

Scenario	Portfolio Return	S&P 500 Return
1	25.02	25
2	18.56	20
3	8.97	8
4	30.22	30
5	−8.84	−10

36% of the funds to be invested in the large-cap value fund ($LV = 0.3649815$), 23% of the funds to be invested in the small-cap growth fund ($SG = 0.2265517$), and 11% of the funds to be invested in the small-cap value fund ($SV = 0.1051291$).

Table 12.5 shows a comparison of the portfolio return (see $R1$, $R2$, $R3$, $R4$, $R5$ in Figure 12.12) to the S&P 500 return for each scenario. Notice how closely the portfolio returns match the S&P 500 returns. Based on historical data, a portfolio with this mix of Hauck mutual funds will indeed closely match the returns for the S&P 500 stock index.

NOTES AND COMMENTS

1. The returns for the planning scenarios in Table 12.4 are the actual returns for five years in the past. They were chosen as the past data most likely to represent what could happen over the next year. By using actual past data, the correlation among the mutual funds is automatically incorporated into the model.

2. It would not be practical for an individual investor who desires to receive the same return as the S&P 500 to purchase all the S&P 500 stocks. The index fund we have constructed permits such an investor to approximate the S&P 500 return.

3. In this section we constructed an index fund from among mutual funds. The investment alternatives used to develop the index fund could also be individual stocks that are part of the S&P 500.

Summary

In this chapter we presented two advanced linear programming applications. In particular, we applied linear programming to maximizing revenue for airlines and constructing mutual fund portfolios. In practice, most of the modeling effort in these types of linear programming applications involves clearly understanding the problem, stating the problem mathematically, and then finding reliable data in the format required by the model.

In this chapter we introduced nonlinear optimization models. A nonlinear optimization model is a model with at least one nonlinear term in either a constraint or the objective function. Because so many processes in business and nature behave in a nonlinear fashion, allowing nonlinear terms greatly increases the number of important applications that can be modeled as an optimization problem. Numerous problems in portfolio optimization, pricing options, blending, economics, facility location, forecasting, and scheduling lend themselves to nonlinear models.

Unfortunately, nonlinear optimization models are not as easy to solve as linear optimization models, or even linear integer optimization models. As a rule of thumb, if a problem can be modeled realistically as a linear or linear integer problem then it is probably best to do so. Many nonlinear formulations have local optima that are not globally optimal. Because most nonlinear optimization codes will terminate with a local optimum, the solution returned by the code may not be the best solution available. However, as pointed out in this chapter, numerous important classes of optimization problems, such as the Index portfolio model, are convex optimization problems. For a convex optimization problem, a local optimum is also the global optimum. Additionally, the development of nonlinear optimization codes that do find globally optimal solutions is proceeding at a rapid rate.

Glossary

Nonlinear optimization problem An optimization problem that contains at least one non-linear term in the objective function or a constraint.

Local optimum A feasible solution is a local optimum if there are no other feasible solutions with a better objective function value in the immediate neighborhood. A local optimum may be either a local maximum or a local minimum.

Local maximum A feasible solution is a local maximum if there are no other feasible solutions with a larger objective function value in the immediate neighborhood.

Local minimum A feasible solution is a local minimum if there are no other feasible solutions with a smaller objective function value in the immediate neighborhood.

Global optimum A feasible solution is a global optimum if there are no other feasible points with a better objective function value in the entire feasible region. A global optimum may be either a global maximum or a global minimum.

Global maximum A feasible solution is a global maximum if there are no other feasible points with a larger objective function value in the entire feasible region. A global maximum is also a local maximum.

Global minimum A feasible solution is a global minimum if there are no other feasible points with a smaller objective function value in the entire feasible region. A global minimum is also a local minimum.

Concave function A function that is bowl-shaped down: For example, the functions and $f(x) = -5x^2 - 5x$ and $f(x,y) = -x^2 - 11y^2$ are concave functions.

Convex function A function that is bowl-shaped up: For example, the functions and $f(x) = x^2 - 5x$ and $f(x,y) = x^2 + 5y^2$ are convex functions.

Index fund A portfolio of stocks, mutual funds, or other securities that matches as closely as possible the performance of a broad market index such as the S&P 500.

Problems

1. Reconsider the Leisure Airlines problem from Section 12.1. The demand forecasts shown in Table 12.1 represent Leisure Air's best estimates of demand. But because demand cannot be forecasted perfectly, the number of seats actually sold for each origin-destination-itinerary fare (ODIF) may turn out to be smaller or larger than forecasted. Suppose that Leisure Air believes that economic conditions have improved and that their original forecast may be too

low. To account for this possibility, Leisure Air is considering switching the Boeing 737-400 airplanes that are based in Pittsburgh and Newark with Boeing 757-200 airplanes that Leisure Air has available in other markets. The Boeing 757-200 airplane has a seating capacity of 158 in the coach section.

a. Because of scheduling conflicts in other markets, suppose that Leisure Air is only able to obtain one Boeing 757-200. Should the larger plane be based in Pittsburgh or in Newark? Explain.

b. Based upon your answer in part (a), determine a new allocation for the ODIFs. Briefly summarize the major differences between the new allocation using one Boeing 757-200 and the original allocation summarized in Figure 12.2.

c. Suppose that two Boeing 757-200 airplanes are available. Determine a new allocation for the ODIF's using the two larger airplanes. Briefly summarize the major differences between the new allocation using two Boeing 757-200 airplanes and the original allocation shown in Figure 12.2.

d. Consider the new solution obtained in part (b). Which ODIF has the highest bid price? What is the interpretation for this bid price?

2. Reconsider the Leisure Airlines problem from Section 12.1. Suppose that as of May 1 the following number of seats have been sold:

ODIF	1	2	3	4	5	6	7	8	9	10	11	12	13	14	15	16
Seats Sold	25	44	18	12	5	9	20	33	37	11	5	8	27	6	35	7

a. Determine how many seats are still available for sale on each flight leg.

b. Using the original demand forecasted for each ODIF, determine the remaining demand for each ODIF.

c. Revise the linear programming model presented in Section 12.1 to account for the number of seats currently sold and a demand of one additional seat for the Pittsburgh–Myrtle Beach Q class ODIF. Resolve the linear programming model to determine a new allocation schedule for the ODIFs.

3. Hanson Inn is a 96-room hotel located near the airport and convention center in Louisville, Kentucky. When a convention or a special event is in town, Hanson increases its normal room rates and takes reservations based on a revenue management system. The Classic Corvette Owners Association scheduled its annual convention in Louisville for the first weekend in June. Hanson Inn agreed to make at least 50% of its rooms available for convention attendees at a special convention rate in order to be listed as a recommended hotel for the convention. Although the majority of attendees at the annual meeting typically requests a Friday and Saturday two-night package, some attendees may select a Friday night only or a Saturday night only reservation. Customers not attending the convention may also request a Friday and Saturday two-night package, or make a Friday night only or Saturday night only reservation. Thus, six types of reservations are possible: convention customers/two-night package; convention customers/Friday night only; convention customers/Saturday night only; regular customers/two-night package; regular customers/Friday night only; and regular customers/Saturday night only.

The cost for each type of reservation is shown here.

	Two-Night Package	Friday Night Only	Saturday Night Only
Convention	$225	$123	$130
Regular	$295	$146	$152

The anticipated demand for each type of reservation is as follows:

	Two-Night Package	Friday Night Only	Saturday Night Only
Convention	40	20	15
Regular	20	30	25

Hanson Inn would like to determine how many rooms to make available for each type of reservation in order to maximize total revenue.

a. Define the decision variables and state the objective function.

b. Formulate a linear programming model for this revenue management application.

c. What is the optimal allocation and the anticipated total revenue?

d. Suppose that one week before the convention, the number of regular customers/Saturday night only rooms that were made available sell out. If another nonconvention customer calls and requests a Saturday only room, what is the value of accepting this additional reservation?

4. In the latter part of Section 12.2 we developed a moderate risk portfolio model for Hauck Investment Services. Modify the model given so that it can be used to construct a portfolio for more aggressive investors. In particular, do the following:

a. Develop a portfolio model for investors who are willing to risk a portfolio with a return as low as 0%.

b. What is the recommended allocation for this type of investor?

c. How would you modify your recommendation in part (b) for an investor who also wants to have at least 10% of his or her portfolio invested in the foreign stock mutual fund? How does requiring at least 10% of the portfolio be invested in the foreign stock fund affect the expected return?

5. Table 12.6 shows data on the returns over five 1-year periods for six mutual funds. A firm's portfolio managers will assume that one of these scenarios will accurately reflect the investing climate over the next 12 months. The probabilities of each of the scenarios occurring are 0.1, 0.3, 0.1, 0.1, and 0.4 for years 1 to 5, respectively.

a. Develop a portfolio model for investors who are willing to risk a portfolio with a return no lower than 2%.

b. Solve the model in part (a) and recommend a portfolio allocation for the investor with this risk tolerance.

c. Modify the portfolio model in part (a) and solve it to develop a portfolio for an investor with a risk tolerance of 0%.

TABLE 12.6   RETURNS OVER FIVE 1-YEAR PERIODS FOR SIX MUTUAL FUNDS

	Planning Scenarios for Next 12 Months				
Mutual Funds	**Year 1**	**Year 2**	**Year 3**	**Year 4**	**Year 5**
Large-Cap Stock	35.3	20.0	28.3	10.4	−9.3
Mid-Cap Stock	32.3	23.2	−0.9	49.3	−22.8
Small-Cap Stock	20.8	22.5	6.0	33.3	6.1
Energy/Resources Sector	25.3	33.9	−20.5	20.9	−2.5
Health Sector	49.1	5.5	29.7	77.7	−24.9
Technology Sector	46.2	21.7	45.7	93.1	−20.1
Real Estate Sector	20.5	44.0	−21.1	2.6	5.1

d.   Is the expected return higher for investors following the portfolio recommendations in part (c) as compared to the returns for the portfolio in part (b)? If so, do you believe the returns are enough higher to justify investing in that portfolio?

6.   The purpose of this exercise is to provide practice using the LINGO or Excel solvers. Find the values of X and Y that minimize the function

$$\text{Min } X^2 - 4X + Y^2 + 8Y + 20$$

Do not assume nonnegativity of the X and Y variables. Recall that by default LINGO assumes nonnegative variables. In order to allow the variables to take on negative values, you can add

$$@FREE(X); \ @FREE(Y);$$

Alternatively, if you want LINGO to allow for negative values by default, in the LINGO menu select **Options** and then click **General Solver,** and then uncheck the **Variables assumed nonnegative** tab.

7.   Consider the problem

$$\text{Min} \quad 2X^2 - 20X + 2XY + Y^2 - 14Y + 58$$
$$\text{s.t.} \qquad X + 4Y \le 8$$

a.   Find the minimum solution to this problem.
b.   If the right-hand side of the constraint is increased from 8 to 9, how much do you expect the objective function to change?
c.   Resolve the problem with a new right-hand side of 9. How does the actual change compare with your estimate?

8.   GreenLawns provides a lawn fertilizer and weed control service. The company is adding a special aeration treatment as a low-cost extra service option, which it hopes will help attract new customers. Management is planning to promote this new service in two media: radio and direct-mail advertising. A media budget of $3000 is available for this promotional campaign. Based on past experience in promoting its other services, GreenLawns obtained the following estimate of the relationship between sales and the amount spent on promotion in these two media:

$$S = -2R^2 - 10M^2 - 8RM + 18R + 34M$$

where

$$S = \text{total sales in thousands of dollars}$$
$$R = \text{thousands of dollars spent on radio advertising}$$
$$M = \text{thousands of dollars spent on direct-mail advertising}$$

GreenLawns would like to develop a promotional strategy that will lead to maximum sales subject to the restriction provided by the media budget.
a.   What is the value of sales if $2000 is spent on radio advertising and $1000 is spent on direct-mail advertising?
b.   Formulate an optimization problem that can be solved to maximize sales subject to the media budget.
c.   Determine the optimal amount to spend on radio and direct-mail advertising. How much in sales will be generated?

LINGO must be used to get the global optimal solution for Problem 9.

9.   The function

$$f(X, Y) = 3(1 - X)^2 e^{(-X^2 - (Y+1)^2)} - 10(X/5 - X^3 - Y^5)e^{(-X^2 - Y^2)} - e^{(-(X+1)^2 - Y^2)}/3$$

was used to generate Figures 12.10 and 12.11 in order to illustrate the concept of local optima versus global optima.

a. Minimize this function using LINGO. (*Warning:* Make sure you use the unary minus sign correctly. In other words, rewrite a term such as $-X^2$ as $-(X)^2$. (See Appendix 12.1.)

b. Now minimize this function using LINGO with the Global Solver option turned on.

10. The Cobb-Douglas production function is a classic model from economics used to model output as a function of capital and labor. It has the form

$$f(L, C) = c_0 L^{c_1} C^{c_2}$$

where c_0, c_1, and c_2 are constants. The variable L represents the units of input of labor and the variable C represents the units of input of capital.

a. In this example, assume $c_0 = 5$, $c_1 = 0.25$, and $c_2 = 0.75$. Assume each unit of labor costs \$25 and each unit of capital costs \$75. With \$75,000 available in the budget, develop an optimization model for determining how the budgeted amount should be allocated between capital and labor in order to maximize output.

b. Find the optimal solution to the model you formulated in part (a). *Hint:* When using Excel Solver, start with an initial $L > 0$ and $C > 0$.

11. Let S represent the amount of steel produced (in tons). Steel production is related to the amount of labor used (L) and the amount of capital used (C) by the following function:

$$S = 20L^{0.30}C^{0.70}$$

In this formula L represents the units of labor input and C the units of capital input. Each unit of labor costs \$50, and each unit of capital costs \$100.

a. Formulate an optimization problem that will determine how much labor and capital are needed in order to produce 50,000 tons of steel at minimum cost.

b. Solve the optimization problem you formulated in part (a). *Hint:* When using Excel Solver, start with an initial $L > 0$ and $C > 0$.

12. The profit function for two products is

$$\text{Profit} = -3x_1^2 + 42x_1 - 3x_2^2 + 48x_2 + 700$$

where x_1 represents units of production of product 1 and x_2 represents units of production of product 2. Producing one unit of product 1 requires 4 labor-hours and producing one unit of product 2 requires 6 labor-hours. Currently, 24 labor-hours are available. The cost of labor-hours is already factored into the profit function. However, it is possible to schedule overtime at a premium of \$5 per hour.

a. Formulate an optimization problem that can be used to find the optimal production quantity of products 1 and the optimal number of overtime hours to schedule.

b. Solve the optimization model you formulated in part (a). How much should be produced and how many overtime hours should be scheduled?

13. Heller Manufacturing has two production facilities that manufacture baseball gloves. Production costs at the two facilities differ because of varying labor rates, local property taxes, type of equipment, capacity, and so on. The Dayton plant has weekly costs that can be expressed as a function of the number of gloves produced:

$$TCD(X) = X^2 - X + 5$$

where X is the weekly production volume in thousands of units and $TCD(X)$ is the cost in thousands of dollars. The Hamilton plant's weekly production costs are given by

$$TCH(Y) = Y^2 + 2Y + 3$$

where Y is the weekly production volume in thousands of units and $TCH(Y)$ is the cost in thousands of dollars. Heller Manufacturing would like to produce 8000 gloves per week at the lowest possible cost.

a. Formulate a mathematical model that can be used to determine the optimal number of gloves to produce each week at each facility.

b. Use LINGO or Excel Solver to find the solution to your mathematical model to determine the optimal number of gloves to produce at each facility.

14. Harry Markowitz received the 1990 Nobel Prize for his path-breaking work in portfolio optimization. One version of the Markowitz model is based on minimizing the variance of the portfolio subject to a constraint on return. We use the data and notation developed for the Hauck Index Fund in Section 12.4 to develop an example of the Markowitz mean-variance model. If each of the scenarios is equally likely and occurs with probability 1/5, then the mean return or expected return of the portfolio is

$$\overline{R} = \tfrac{1}{5}\sum_{S=1}^{5} R_s$$

The variance of the portfolio return is

$$\text{Var} = \tfrac{1}{5}\sum_{S=1}^{5} (R_s - \overline{R})^2$$

See Section 2 in Chapter 3 for a review of the mean and variance concept. Using the scenario return data given in Table 12.2, formulate the Markowitz mean-variance model. The objective function is the variance of the portfolio and should be minimized. Assume that the required return on the portfolio is 10%. There is also a unity constraint that all of the money must be invested in mutual funds. Solve this mean-variance model using either LINGO or Excel solver.

15. Many forecasting models use parameters that are estimated using nonlinear optimization. This is true of many of the models developed in Chapter 6. Consider the exponential smoothing forecasting model from Section 6.2. For instance, the basic exponential smoothing model for forecasting sales is

$$F_{t+1} = \alpha Y_t + (1 - \alpha)F_t$$

where

$$
\begin{aligned}
F_{t+1} &= \text{forecast of sales for period } t + 1 \\
Y_t &= \text{actual value of sales for period } t \\
F_t &= \text{forecast of sales for period } t \\
\alpha &= \text{smoothing constant } 0 \le \alpha \le 1
\end{aligned}
$$

This model is used recursively; the forecast for time period $t + 1$ is based on the forecast for period t, F_t, the observed value of sales in period t, Y_t, and the smoothing parameter α. The use of this model to forecast sales for 12 months is illustrated in Table 12.7 with the smoothing constant $\alpha = 0.3$. The forecast errors, $Y_t - F_t$, are calculated in the fourth column. The value of α is often chosen by minimizing the sum of squared forecast errors, commonly referred to as the mean squared error (MSE). The last column of Table 12.7 shows the square of the forecast error and the sum of squared forecast errors.

In using exponential smoothing models one tries to choose the value of α that provides the best forecasts. Build an Excel Solver or LINGO optimization model that will find the smoothing parameter, α, that minimizes the sum of forecast errors squared. You may find it easiest to put Table 12.7 into an Excel spreadsheet and then use Solver to find the optimal value of α.

16. The purpose of this exercise is to learn how to calculate stock returns for portfolio models using actual stock price data. First, it is necessary to obtain stock price data. One source

TABLE 12.7 EXPONENTIAL SMOOTHING MODEL FOR $\alpha = 0.3$

Week (t)	Observed Value (Y_t)	Forecast (F_t)	Forecast Error ($Y_t - F_t$)	Squared Forecast Error ($Y_t - F_t$)^2
1	17	17.00	0.00	0.00
2	21	17.00	4.00	16.00
3	19	18.20	0.80	0.64
4	23	18.44	4.56	20.79
5	18	19.81	−1.81	3.27
6	16	19.27	−3.27	10.66
7	20	18.29	1.71	2.94
8	18	18.80	−0.80	0.64
9	22	18.56	3.44	11.83
10	20	19.59	0.41	0.17
11	15	19.71	−4.71	22.23
12	22	18.30	3.70	13.69
				SUM = 102.86

(of many) is Yahoo! Go to the link *http://finance.yahoo.com* and type in a ticker symbol such as AAPL (for Apple Computer). Then, on the left-hand side of the page, select Historical Data.

These data are easily downloaded to a spreadsheet by clicking on the link "Download to Spreadsheet" at the bottom of the page. For Apple Computer (AAPL), Advanced Micro Devices (AMD), and Oracle Corporation (ORCL), download the monthly price data for January 1997 through January 2006. These data contain closing prices that are adjusted for stock dividends and splits.

You now have stock prices for 10 years, and the objective is to calculate the annual returns for each stock for the years 1997 through 2005. Returns are often calculated using continuous compounding. If the stock prices are adjusted for splits and stock dividends, then the price of stock i in period $t + 1$, $P_{i,t+1}$, is given by

$$p_{i,t+1} = p_t \, e^{r_{it}}$$

where $p_{i,t}$ is the price of stock i in period t and r_{it} is the return on stock i in period t. This calculation assumes no cash dividends were paid, which is true of Apple Computer, Advanced Micro Devices, and Oracle Corporation. Solving the equation $p_{i,t+1} = p_t \, e^{r_{it}}$ for the return on stock i in period t gives

$$r_{it} = \ln\left(\frac{p_{i,t+1}}{p_t}\right)$$

For example, the Apple Computer adjusted closing price in January 2005 was 38.45. The closing price in January 2006 was 75.51. Thus, the continuously compounded return for Apple Computer from January 2005 to January 2006 is

$$\ln(75.51/38.45) = 0.6749064$$

We use this calculation as our estimate of the annual return for Apple Computer for the year 2005.

Take the closing stock prices that you have downloaded and calculate the annual returns for 1997 through 2005 for AAPL, AMD, and ORCL using $r_{it} = \ln(p_{i,t+1}/p_t)$. If you calculate the returns properly, your results should appear as in Figure 12.13.

FIGURE 12.13 YEARLY RETURNS FOR AAPL, AMD, AND ORCL

Date	AAPL Adj. Close	AMD Adj. Close	ORCL Adj. Close	AAPL Return	AMD Return	ORCL Return
2-Jan-97	4.16	17.57	4.32	0.0962	−0.5537	−0.1074
2-Jan-98	4.58	10.1	3.88	0.8104	0.1272	0.8666
4-Jan-99	10.3	11.47	9.23	0.9236	0.4506	0.9956
3-Jan-00	25.94	18	24.98	−0.8753	0.3124	0.1533
2-Jan-01	10.81	24.6	29.12	0.1340	−0.4270	−0.5230
2-Jan-02	12.36	16.05	17.26	−0.5432	−1.1194	−0.3610
2-Jan-03	7.18	5.24	12.03	0.4517	1.0424	0.1416
2-Jan-04	11.28	14.86	13.86	1.2263	0.0613	−0.0065
3-Jan-05	38.45	15.8	13.77	0.6749	0.9729	−0.0912
3-Jan-06	75.51	41.8	12.57			

Data Source: CSI
Web site: *http://www.csidata.com*

WEB file

StockReturns

17. Formulate and solve the Markowitz portfolio optimization model that was introduced in Problem 14 using the data from Problem 16. In this case, nine scenarios correspond to the yearly returns from 1997 through 2005, inclusive. Treat each scenario as being equally likely and use the scenario returns that were calculated in Problem 16.

18. Using the data obtained in Problem 16, construct a portfolio from Apple, AMD, and Oracle that matches the Information Technology S&P index as closely as possible. Use the return data for the Information Technology S&P index given in the following table. The model for constructing the portfolio should be similar to the one developed for Hauck Financial Services in Section 12.4.

Year	Return
1997	28.54%
1998	78.14
1999	78.74
2000	−40.90
2001	−25.87
2002	−37.41
2003	48.40
2004	2.56
2005	0.99

19. Most investors are happy when their returns are "above average," but not so happy when they are "below average." In the Markowitz portfolio optimization model in Problem 14, the objective function is to minimize variance which is given by

$$\text{Min } \frac{1}{5}\sum_{s=1}^{5}(R_s - \overline{R})^2$$

where R_s is the portfolio return under scenario s and $\overline{R}$ is the expected or average return of the portfolio.

With this objective function, we are choosing a portfolio that minimizes deviations both above and below the average, $\overline{R}$. However, most investors are happy when $R_s > \overline{R}$, but unhappy when $R_s < \overline{R}$. With this preference in mind, an alternative to the variance measure in the objective function for the Markowitz model is the semivariance. The semivariance is calculated by only considering deviations below $\overline{R}$.

Let $D_{sp} - D_{sn} = R_s - \overline{R}$ and restrict D_{sp} and D_{sn} to be nonnegative. Then D_{sp} measures the positive deviation from the mean return in scenario s (i.e., $D_{sp} = R_s - \overline{R}$ when $R_s > \overline{R}$). In the case where the scenario return is below the average return, $R_s < \overline{R}$, we have $-D_{sn} = R_s - \overline{R}$. Using these new variables we can reformulate the Markowitz model to only minimize the square of negative deviations below the average return. By doing so, we will use the semivariance rather than the variance in the objective function.

Reformulate the Markowitz portfolio optimization model given in Problem 14 to use semivariance in the objective function. Solve the model using either Excel Solver or LINGO. *Hint:* When using Excel Solver assume $^1/_6$ of the portfolio is allocated to each mutual fund for a starting solution.

20. This problem requires a basic understanding of the normal probability distribution. Investors are often interested in knowing the probabilities of poor returns. For example, for what cutoff return will the probability of the actual return falling below this cutoff value be at most 1%?

Consider the solution to the Markowitz portfolio model from Problem 14. The mean return of the portfolio is 10% and the standard deviation (calculated by taking the square root of the variance, which is the objective function value) is

$$\sigma = \sqrt{27.13615} = 5.209237$$

Assume that the portfolio scenario returns are normally distributed about the mean return. From the normal probability table, we see that less than 1% of the returns fall more than 2.33 standard deviations below the mean. This result implies a probability of 1% or less that a portfolio return will fall below

$$10 - (2.33)(5.209237) = -2.1375$$

Stated another way, if the initial value of the portfolio is $1, then the investor faces a probability of 1% of incurring a loss of 2.1375 cents or more. The value at risk is 2.1375 cents at 1%. This measure of risk is called the *value at risk*, or VaR. It was popularized by JPMorgan Chase & Co. in the early 1990s (then, just JP Morgan).

A table of normal probabilities appears in Appendix D, but they are also easily calculated in LINGO and Excel. In LINGO, the function @PSN(Z) and the equivalent function NORMDIST in Excel provide the probability that a standard normal random variables is less than Z.

a. Consider the Markowitz portfolio problem given in Problem 14. Delete the required return constraint and reformulate this problem to minimize the VaR at 1%.

b. Is minimizing the VaR the same as minimizing the variance of the portfolio? Answer Yes or No, and justify.

c. For a fixed return, is minimizing the VaR the same as minimizing the variance of the portfolio? Answer Yes or No, and justify.

21. Options are popular instruments in the world of finance. A call option on a stock gives the owner the right to buy the stock at a predetermined price before the expiration date of the option. For example, on Friday, August 25, 2006, call options were selling for Procter & Gamble stock that gave the owner of the option the right to buy a share of stock for $60 on or before September 15, 2006. The asking price on the option was $1.45 at the market close. How are options priced? A pricing formula for options was developed by Fischer Black and Myron Scholes and published in 1973. Scholes was later (Black was dead) awarded the

Nobel Prize for this work in 1997. The Black-Scholes pricing model is widely used today by hedge funds and traders. The Black-Scholes formula for the price of a call option is

$$C = S[PSN(Z)] - Xe^{-rT}[PSN(Z - \sigma\sqrt{T})]$$

where

$$C = \text{market price of the call option}$$
$$X = \text{strike or exercise price of the stock}$$
$$S = \text{current price of the stock}$$
$$r = \text{annual risk-free interest rate}$$
$$T = \text{time to maturity of the option}$$
$$\sigma = \text{yearly standard deviation}$$

In the Black-Scholes formula, $Z = [(r + \sigma^2/2)T + \ln(S/X)]/(\sigma\sqrt{T})$ and $PSN(Z)$ is the probability of an observation of Z or less for a normal distribution with mean 0 and variance 1.

   The purpose of this exercise is to price a Procter & Gamble call option offered on August 25, 2006. The option expires September 15, 2006, which includes 21 days between the market close on August 25, 2006, and the expiration of the option on September 15, 2006. Use the yield on three-month Treasury bills as the risk-free interest rate. As of August 25, 2006, this yield was 0.0494. The strike price on the option is $60, and at the market close on August 25, 2006, the stock was trading at $60.87. In order to use the Black-Scholes formula, the yearly standard deviation, is required. One way to obtain this number is to estimate the weekly variance of Procter & Gamble, multiply the weekly variance by 52, and then take the square root to get the annual standard deviation. For this problem, use a weekly variance of 0.000479376. Use these data to calculate the option price using the Black-Scholes formula. For Friday, August 25, 2006, the actual bid on this option was $1.35 and actual ask was $1.45.

22. The port of Lajitas has three loading docks. The distance (in meters) between the loading docks is given in the table below:

	1	2	3
1	0	100	150
2	100	0	50
3	150	50	0

LINGO must be used to get the global optimal solution for Problem 22.

Three tankers currently at sea are coming into Lajitas. It is necessary to assign a dock for each tanker. Also, only one tanker can anchor in a given dock. Currently, ships 2 and 3 are empty and have no cargo. However, ship 1 has cargo that must be loaded onto the other two ships. The number of tons that must be transferred are as follows:

To From		1	2	3
	1	0	60	80

Formulate and solve with Excel Solver or LINGO an optimization problem that will assign ships to docks so that the product of tonnage moved times distance is minimized. (*Hints:* This problem is an extension of the assignment problem introduced in Chapter 10. Also, be careful with the objective function. Only include the nonzero terms. Each of the 12 nonzero terms in the objective function is a quadratic term, or the product of two variables.) There are 12 nonzero terms in the objective function.

   This problem formulation is an example of a quadratic assignment problem. The quadratic assignment problem is a powerful model. It is used in a number of facility location problems and components on circuit boards. It is also used to assign jets to gates at airports to minimize product of passengers and distance walked.

23. Andalus Furniture Company has two manufacturing plants, one at Aynor and another at Spartanburg. The cost in dollars of producing a kitchen chair at each of the two plants is given here.

$$\text{Aynor: Cost} = 75Q_1 + 5Q_1^2 + 100$$
$$\text{Spartanburg: Cost} = 25Q_2 + 2.5Q_2^2 + 150$$

where

Q_1 = number of chairs produced at Aynor
Q_2 = number of chairs produced at Spartanburg

Andalus needs to manufacture a total of 40 kitchen chairs to meet an order just received. How many chairs should be made at Aynor and how many should be made at Spartanburg in order to minimize total production cost?

Case Problem # CAFE Compliance in the Auto Industry

This case is based on the Q.M. in Action, Pricing for Environmental Compliance in the Auto Industry. In this case we build a model similar to the one built for General Motors. The CAFE requirement on fleet miles per gallon is based on an average. The **harmonic average** is used to calculate the CAFE requirement on average miles per gallon.

In order to understand the harmonic average, assume that there is a passenger car and a light truck. The passenger car gets 30 miles per gallon (MPG) and the light truck gets 20 miles per gallon (MPG). Assume each vehicle is driven exactly one mile. Then the passenger car consumes $1/30$ gallon of gasoline in driving one mile and the light truck consumes $1/20$ gallon of gasoline in driving one mile. The amount of gasoline consumed in total is

$$\text{Gas consumption} = (1/30) + (1/20) = (5/60) = (1/12) \text{ gallon}$$

The average MPG of the two vehicles calculated the "normal way" is $(30 + 20)/2 = 25$ MPG. If both vehicles are "average," and each vehicle is driven exactly one mile, then the total gasoline consumption is

$$\text{Gas consumption} = (1/25) + (1/25) = (2/25) \text{ gallon}$$

Because $(2/25)$ is not equal to $(5/60)$ the total gas consumption of two "average vehicles" driving exactly one mile is not equal to the total gas consumption of each of the original vehicles driving exactly one mile. This is unfortunate. In order to make it easy for the government to impose and enforce MPG constraints on the auto companies, it would be nice to have a single target value MPG that every company in the auto industry must meet. As just illustrated, there is a problem with requiring an average MPG on the industry because it will incorrectly estimate the gas mileage consumption of the fleet. Fortunately, there is a statistic called the **harmonic average** so that total gas consumption by harmonic average vehicles is equal to gas consumption of the actual vehicles.

For simplicity, first assume that there are two types of vehicles in the fleet, passenger cars and light trucks. If there is one passenger car getting 30 miles per gallon and there is one light truck getting 20 miles per gallon, the harmonic average of these two vehicles is

$$\frac{2}{\dfrac{1}{30} + \dfrac{1}{20}} = \frac{2}{\dfrac{5}{60}} = \frac{120}{5} = 24$$

If each vehicle were to drive exactly one mile each vehicle would consume $1/24$ gallon of gasoline for a total of $2/24 = 1/12$ gallon of gasoline. In this case each "average" vehicle driving exactly one mile results in total gas consumption equal to the total gas consumption of each vehicle with a different MPG rating driving exactly one mile.

If there are three passenger vehicles and two light trucks, the harmonic average is given by

$$\frac{5}{\dfrac{3}{30} + \dfrac{2}{20}} = \frac{5}{0.1 + 0.1} = \frac{5}{0.2} = 25$$

In general, when calculating the harmonic average the numerator is the total number of vehicles. The denominator is sum of two terms. Each term is the ratio of the number of vehicles in that class to the MPG of cars in that class. For example, the first ratio in the denominator is $3/30$ because there are 3 cars (the numerator) each getting 30 MPG (the denominator). These calculations are illustrated in Figure 12.14.

Based on Figure 12.14, if each of the 5 cars is average and drives exactly one mile, $(5/25) = (1/5)$ gallon of gas is consumed. If three cars getting 30 MPG drive exactly one mile each and two cars getting 20 MPG drive exactly one mile, then $(3/30) + (2/20) = (2/10) = (1/5)$ gallon is consumed. Thus the average cars exactly duplicate the gas consumption of the fleet with varying MPG.

Now assume that the demand function for passenger cars is

$$\text{Demand} = 750 - P_C \tag{12.8}$$

where P_C is the price of a passenger car. Similarly, the demand function for light trucks is

$$\text{Demand} = 830 - P_T \tag{12.9}$$

where P_T is the price of a light truck.

FIGURE 12.14   AN EXCEL SPREADSHEET WITH A CAFÉ CALCULATION

	A	B	C	D
1			Number	
2		MPG	of Vehicles	CAFE Weight
3	Passenger Cars	30	3	0.1000
4	Light Trucks	20	2	0.1000
5			5	0.2000
6				
7	CAFE Average	25		

Managerial Report

1. Using the formulas given in (12.8) and (12.9), develop an expression for the total profit contribution as a function of the price of cars and the price of light trucks. Assume the marginal cost for passenger cars is 15 and the marginal cost for light trucks is 17.
2. Using Excel Solver or LINGO, find the price for each car so that the total profit contribution is maximized.
3. Given the prices determined in Question 2, calculate the number of passenger cars sold and the number of light trucks sold.
4. Duplicate the spreadsheet in Figure 12.14. Your spreadsheet should have formulas in cells D3:D5 and B7 and be able to calculate the harmonic (CAFE) average for any MPG rating and any number of vehicles in each category.
5. Again, assume that passenger cars get 30 MPG and light trucks get 20 MPG calculate the CAFE average for the fleet size from Question 3.
6. If you do the calculation in Question 5 correctly, the CAFE average of the fleet is 23.57. Add a constraint that the fleet average must be 25 MPG and resolve the model to get the maximum total profit contribution subject to meeting the CAFE constraint.

Appendix 12.1   Solving Nonlinear Problems with LINGO

Solving a nonlinear optimization problem in LINGO is no different from solving a linear optimization problem in LINGO. Simply type in the formulation, select the **LINGO** menu and choose the **Solve** option. Just remember that LINGO uses the ^ sign for exponentiation and the / sign for division. Also note that an asterisk (*) must be used to indicate multiplication.

We show how the unconstrained RMC problem from Section 12.3 is solved using LINGO. After starting LINGO, we type in the problem formulation in the model window as follows:

```
MAX = F*(290 − F/2) − 250*F + S*(336 − S/2.5) − 300*S;
```

Appendix 7.2 shows how to use LINGO to solve linear programs.

To solve the problem, select the **Solve** command from the **LINGO** menu, or press the **Solve** button on the toolbar. Note that the value of the objective function is 1610.00, $F = 40$, and $S = 45$.

Now solve the constrained RMC problem from Section 12.3 using LINGO. The only difference from the unconstrained problem is that three lines must be added to the formulation to account for the constraints. After starting LINGO, we type in the problem formulation in the model window as follows:

```
! MAXIMIZE PROFIT;
MAX =  F*(290 − F/2) − 250*F + S*(336 − S/2.5) − 300*S;
!MATERIAL 1 CONSTRAINT;
0.4*F + .5*S < 20;
!MATERIAL 2 CONSTRAINT;
 .2*S < 5;
!MATERIAL 3 CONSTRAINT;
0.6*F + .3*S < 21;
```

Note that at the end of the objective function and each constraint a semicolon is used. After selecting the **Solve** command from the **LINGO** menu, the solution shown in Figure 12.6 is obtained.

In the RMC problem, all the variables are constrained to be nonnegative. If some of the variables may assume negative values, extra lines must be added to the LINGO formulation and the @FREE command must be used. For instance, the Hauck index fund model shown in Section 12.4 does not have nonnegativity constraints for variables $R1, R2, R3, R4$, and $R5$ because these variables are allowed to assume negative values. Thus, after entering the objective function and constraints, the following five lines must be added to the LINGO model to produce the solution shown in Figure 12.12:

$$@FREE(R1);$$
$$@FREE(R2);$$
$$@FREE(R3);$$
$$@FREE(R4);$$
$$@FREE(R5);$$

LINGO also provides the user with a wide variety of nonlinear functions that are useful in finance, inventory management, statistics, and other applications. To get a list of these functions, use the online LINGO User's Manual that is available under the Help menu. In the User's Manual you will find a chapter entitled LINGO's Operators and Functions. This chapter contains a list of the available functions. When using a LINGO function you must precede the function name with the @ sign. For example, if you wanted to take the natural logarithm of X you would write @LOG(X).

We have discussed the concept of global versus local optimum. By default, LINGO finds a local optimum and the global solver is turned off. In order to turn on the global solver, select **Options** from the **LINGO** menu. When the Options dialog box appears, select the **Global Solver** tab and check the **Use Global Solver** box.

The demo at the LINGO link on the Web site accompanying this text allows only five variables for problems that use the global solver.

When using LINGO one must exercise care in how the minus sign is used. When used in an expression such as $y - x^2$, the minus sign is a binary operator because it connects two terms, y and x^2. By convention, exponentiation has higher "precedence" than the minus; so if $y = 2$ and $x = -1$ the expression $y - x^2$ evaluates to

$$y - x^2 = 2 - (-1)^2 = 2 - 1 = 1$$

However, in the expression $-x^2 + y$, the minus sign is a unary operator because it does not combine terms. LINGO, by default, assigns the unary minus sign higher precedence than exponentiation. Thus, if $y = 2$ and $x = -1$ the expression $-x^2 + y$ evaluates to

$$-x^2 + y = (-x)^2 + y = 1^2 + 2 = 3$$

This is a potential source of confusion. In this text we, like many authors, expect $-x^2$ to be interpreted as $-(x^2)$, not $(-x)^2$. Excel also treats the unary minus sign in this fashion.

Appendix 12.2   Solving Nonlinear Problems with Excel Solver

Excel's Premium Solver for Education can be used for nonlinear optimization. The Excel formulation of the nonlinear version of the RMC problem developed in Section 12.3 is shown in Figure 12.15. A worksheet model is constructed just as in the linear case. The

FIGURE 12.15   EXCEL SPREADSHEET MODEL FOR MODIFIED RMC PROBLEM

	A	B	C	D
1	**RMC**			
2				
3		**Material Requirements**		
4	**Material**	**Fuel Additive**	**Solvent Base**	**Amount Available**
5	Material 1	0.4	0.5	20
6	Material 2	0	0.2	5
7	Material 3	0.6	0.3	21
8	**Profit Per Ton**	40	30	
9				
10				
11	**Model**			
12				
13		**Decision Variables**		
14		**Fuel Additive**	**Solvent Base**	
15	**Tons Produced**	24.3386243386243	20.5291005291005	
16				
17	**Maximize Total Profit**	=40*-0.5*F*F+36S-0.4*S*S		
18				
19	**Constraints**	**Amount Used (LHS)**		**Amount Available (RHS)**
20	Material 1	=B5*F+C5*S	<=	=D5
21	Material 2	=B6*F+C6*S	<=	=D6
22	Material 3	=B7*F+C7*S	<=	=D7

formula in cell B17 is the objective function. The formulas in cells B20:B22 are the left-hand sides of constraint inequalities. And the formulas in cells D20:D22 provide the right-hand sides for the constraint inequalities.

Note how the nonlinearity comes into the model. The formula in cell B17, the objective function cell, is

$$=40\text{*}F\text{-}0.5\text{*}F\text{*}F\text{+}36\text{*}S\text{-}0.4\text{*}S\text{*}S$$

In the formula above, F is the name of the range, in this case cell B15, that holds the value for the number of tons of fuel additive. Similarly, S is the name of the range, in this case cell C15, that holds the value for the number of tons of solvent base. Thus, the objective function cell is a nonlinear function of the decision variables, and Excel cannot solve the model using the standard LP Simplex Solver engine.

However, this is not a problem. Three possible "solver engines" are available with the version of Premium Solver for Education included at the Premium Solverlink on the Web site accompanying this book. One engine is Standard LP Simplex and is the option we have used so far in the book for solving linear and linear integer programming problems. If you use this engine on the nonlinear version of the RMC problem, you will get the error message: "The linearity conditions required by this LP Solver are not satisfied." This message is not surprising because the objective function is a nonlinear function of the variable cells.

Another solver engine is Standard GRG Nonlinear. For this version of the RMC problem, you should select the Standard GRG Nonlinear solver in the Solver Dialog Box. The Standard GRG Nonlinear solver engine is based on the (Generalized Reduced Gradient)

GRG Nonlinear algorithm, which uses a calculus tool called the gradient. The gradient essentially calculates a direction of improvement for the objective function based on the contour lines.

The last solver engine is the Standard Evolutionary engine, and it is based on a class of solution techniques called genetic algorithms. These algorithms are designed for nonlinear problems that are nonsmooth. In Section 12.3 we pointed out that some classes of nonlinear problems are more difficult to solve than others. In general, smooth problems are easier to solve than nonsmooth problems. By nonsmooth, we mean the graph of the function may have discontinuities (holes) or may have sharp edges or angles (such as the absolute value function). Standard Excel functions such as ABS, IF, MAX, and MIN are examples of nonsmooth but useful functions.

If you solve a nonsmooth problem using the Evolutionary Solver, you may not find the optimal solution. This outcome often happens with genetic solution algorithms. So the bottom line is this: It is often convenient and easy to develop models using functions such as IF, but you may pay a price and not find the optimal solution.

When using Excel, one must exercise care in how the minus sign is used. When used in a cell formula such as =A1-B1^2, the minus sign is a binary operator because it connects two terms, A1 and B1^2. By convention, exponentiation has higher "precedence" than the minus, so if cell A1 contains 2 and cell B1 contains -1, the expression =A1-B1^2 evaluates to

$$=A1\text{-}B1\text{^}2=2\text{-}(-1)^2=2\text{-}1=1$$

However, in the expression -B1^2+A1, the minus sign is a unary operator because it does not combine terms. Excel, by default, assigns the unary minus sign higher precedence than exponentiation. Thus, if cell A1 contains 2 and cell B1 contains -1, the expression -B1^2-A1 evaluates to

$$\text{-}B1\text{^}2+A1=(-B1)\text{^}2+A1=1^2+2=3$$

LINGO also treats the unary minus sign in this fashion. This is a potential source of confusion. In this text we, like many authors, expect $-x^2$ to be interpreted as $-(x^2)$, not $(-x)^2$.

Project Scheduling: PERT/CPM

CONTENTS

In many situations, managers are responsible for planning, scheduling, and controlling projects that consist of numerous separate jobs or tasks performed by a variety of departments and individuals. Often these projects are so large or complex that the manager cannot possibly remember all the information pertaining to the plan, schedule, and progress of the project. In these situations the **program evaluation and review technique (PERT)** and the **critical path method (CPM)** have proven to be extremely valuable.

PERT and CPM can be used to plan, schedule, and control a wide variety of projects:

1. Research and development of new products and processes
2. Construction of plants, buildings, and highways
3. Maintenance of large and complex equipment
4. Design and installation of new systems

Henry L. Gantt developed the Gantt Chart as a graphical aid to scheduling jobs on machines in 1918. This application was the first of what has become known as project scheduling techniques.

In these types of projects, project managers must schedule and coordinate the various jobs or **activities** so that the entire project is completed on time. A complicating factor in carrying out this task is the interdependence of the activities; for example, some activities depend on the completion of other activities before they can be started. Because projects may have as many as several thousand activities, project managers look for procedures that will help them answer questions such as the following:

1. What is the total time to complete the project?
2. What are the scheduled start and finish dates for each specific activity?
3. Which activities are "critical" and must be completed *exactly* as scheduled to keep the project on schedule?
4. How long can "noncritical" activities be delayed before they cause an increase in the total project completion time?

PERT (Navy) and CPM (DuPont and Remington Rand) differ because they were developed by different people working on different projects. Today, the best aspects of each have been combined to provide a valuable project scheduling technique.

PERT and CPM can help answer these questions.

Although PERT and CPM have the same general purpose and utilize much of the same terminology, the techniques were developed independently. PERT was developed in the late 1950s specifically for the Polaris missile project. Many activities associated with this project had never been attempted previously, so PERT was developed to handle uncertain activity times. CPM was developed primarily for industrial projects for which activity times were known. CPM offered the option of reducing activity times by adding more workers and/or resources, usually at an increased cost. Thus, a distinguishing feature of CPM was that it identified trade-offs between time and cost for various project activities.

Today's computerized versions of PERT and CPM combine the best features of both approaches. Thus, the distinction between the two techniques is no longer necessary. As a result, we refer to the project scheduling procedures covered in this chapter as PERT/CPM. We begin the discussion of PERT/CPM by considering a project for the expansion of the Western Hills Shopping Center. At the end of the section, we describe how the investment securities firm of Seasongood & Mayer used PERT/CPM to schedule a $31 million hospital revenue bond project.

13.1 Project Scheduling with Known Activity Times

The owner of the Western Hills Shopping Center is planning to modernize and expand the current 32-business shopping center complex. The project is expected to provide room for 8 to 10 new businesses. Financing has been arranged through a private investor. All that

TABLE 13.1   LIST OF ACTIVITIES FOR THE WESTERN HILLS SHOPPING CENTER PROJECT

Activity	Activity Description	Immediate Predecessor	Activity Time
A	Prepare architectural drawings	—	5
B	Identify potential new tenants	—	6
C	Develop prospectus for tenants	A	4
D	Select contractor	A	3
E	Prepare building permits	A	1
F	Obtain approval for building permits	E	4
G	Perform construction	D, F	14
H	Finalize contracts with tenants	B, C	12
I	Tenants move in	G, H	2
		Total	51

The effort that goes into identifying activities, determining interrelationships among activities, and estimating activity times is crucial to the success of PERT/CPM. A significant amount of time may be needed to complete this initial phase of the project scheduling process.

Immediate predecessor information determines whether activities can be completed in parallel (worked on simultaneously) or in series (one completed before another begins). Generally, the more series relationships present in a project, the more time will be required to complete the project.

A project network is extremely helpful in visualizing the interrelationships among the activities. No rules guide the conversion of a list of activities and immediate predecessor information into a project network. The process of constructing a project network generally improves with practice and experience.

remains is for the owner of the shopping center to plan, schedule, and complete the expansion project. Let us show how PERT/CPM can help.

The first step in the PERT/CPM scheduling process is to develop a list of the activities that make up the project. Table 13.1 shows the list of activities for the Western Hills Shopping Center expansion project. Nine activities are described and denoted A through I for later reference. Table 13.1 also shows the immediate predecessor(s) and the activity time (in weeks) for each activity. For a given activity, the **immediate predecessor** column identifies the activities that must be completed *immediately prior* to the start of that activity. Activities A and B do not have immediate predecessors and can be started as soon as the project begins; thus, a dash is written in the immediate predecessor column for these activities. The other entries in the immediate predecessor column show that activities C, D, and E cannot be started until activity A has been completed; activity F cannot be started until activity E has been completed; activity G cannot be started until both activities D and F have been completed; activity H cannot be started until both activities B and C have been completed; and, finally, activity I cannot be started until both activities G and H have been completed. The project is finished when activity I is completed.

The last column in Table 13.1 shows the number of weeks required to complete each activity. For example, activity A takes 5 weeks, activity B takes 6 weeks, and so on. The sum of activity times is 51. As a result, you may think that the total time required to complete the project is 51 weeks. However, as we show, two or more activities often may be scheduled concurrently, thus shortening the completion time for the project. Ultimately, PERT/CPM will provide a detailed activity schedule for completing the project in the shortest time possible.

Using the immediate predecessor information in Table 13.1, we can construct a graphical representation of the project, or the **project network**. Figure 13.1 depicts the project network for Western Hills Shopping Center. The activities correspond to the *nodes* of the network (drawn as rectangles), and the *arcs* (the lines with arrows) show the precedence relationships among the activities. In addition, nodes have been added to the network to denote the start and the finish of the project. A project network will help a manager visualize the activity relationships and provide a basis for carrying out the PERT/CPM computations.

The Concept of a Critical Path

To facilitate the PERT/CPM computations, we modified the project network as shown in Figure 13.2. Note that the upper left-hand corner of each node contains the corresponding activity letter. The activity time appears immediately below the letter.

FIGURE 13.1 PROJECT NETWORK FOR THE WESTERN HILLS SHOPPING CENTER

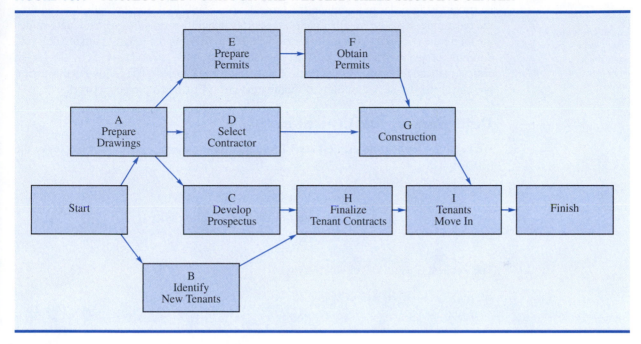

FIGURE 13.2 WESTERN HILLS SHOPPING CENTER PROJECT NETWORK WITH ACTIVITY TIMES

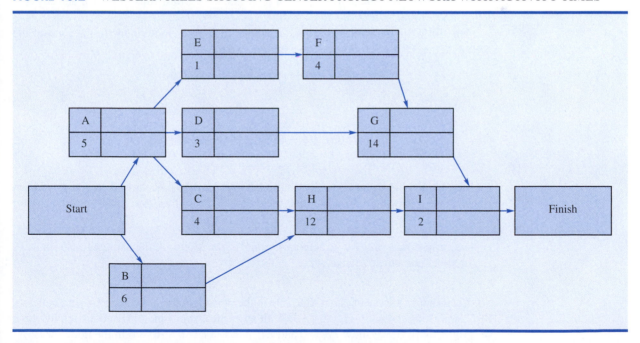

Problem 3 provides the immediate predecessor information for a project with seven activities and asks you to develop the project network.

To determine the project completion time, we have to analyze the network and identify what is called the **critical path** for the network. However, before doing so, we need to define the concept of a path through the network. A **path** is a sequence of connected nodes that leads from the Start node to the Finish node. For instance, one path for the network in Figure 13.2 is defined by the sequence of nodes A-E-F-G-I. By inspection, we see that other

For convenience, we use the convention of referencing activities with letters. Generally, we assign the letters in approximate order as we move from left to right through the project network.

paths are possible, such as A-D-G-I, A-C-H-I, and B-H-I. All paths in the network must be traversed in order to complete the project, so we will look for the path that requires the most time. Because all other paths are shorter in duration, this *longest* path determines the total time required to complete the project. If activities on the longest path are delayed, the entire project will be delayed. Thus, the longest path is the *critical path.* Activities on the critical path are referred to as the **critical activities** for the project. The following discussion presents a step-by-step algorithm for finding the critical path in a project network.

Determining the Critical Path

We begin by finding the **earliest start time** and a **latest start time** for all activities in the network. Let

$$ES = \text{earliest start time for an activity}$$
$$EF = \text{earliest finish time for an activity}$$
$$t = \text{activity time}$$

The **earliest finish time** for any activity is

$$EF = ES + t \tag{13.1}$$

Activity A can start as soon as the project starts, so we set the earliest start time for activity A equal to 0. With an activity time of 5 weeks, the earliest finish time for activity A is $EF = ES + t = 0 + 5 = 5$.

We will write the earliest start and earliest finish times in the node to the right of the activity letter. Using activity A as an example, we have

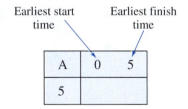

Because an activity cannot be started until *all* immediately preceding activities have been finished, the following rule can be used to determine the earliest start time for each activity:

The earliest start time for an activity is equal to the *largest* of the earliest finish times for all its immediate predecessors.

Let us apply the earliest start time rule to the portion of the network involving nodes A, B, C, and H, as shown in Figure 13.3. With an earliest start time of 0 and an activity time of 6 for activity B, we show $ES = 0$ and $EF = ES + t = 0 + 6 = 6$ in the node for activity B. Looking at node C, we note that activity A is the only immediate predecessor for activity C. The earliest finish time for activity A is 5, so the earliest start time for activity C must be $ES = 5$. Thus, with an activity time of 4, the earliest finish time for activity C is $EF = ES + t = 5 + 4 = 9$. Both the earliest start time and the earliest finish time can be shown in the node for activity C (see Figure 13.4).

FIGURE 13.3   A PORTION OF THE WESTERN HILLS SHOPPING CENTER PROJECT
NETWORK, SHOWING ACTIVITIES A, B, C, AND H

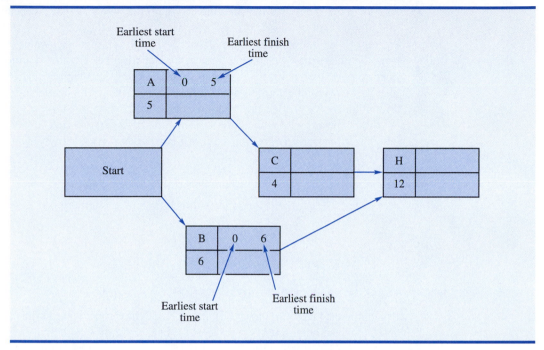

FIGURE 13.4   DETERMINING THE EARLIEST START TIME FOR ACTIVITY H

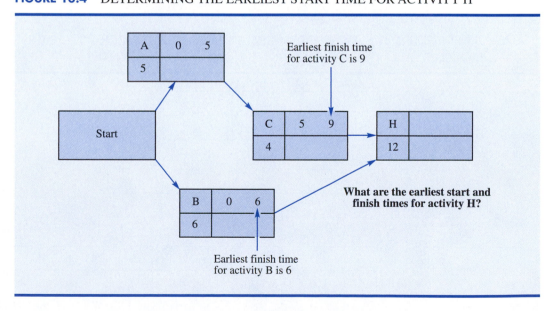

Continuing with Figure 13.4, we move on to activity H and apply the earliest start time
rule for this activity. With both activities B and C as immediate predecessors, the earliest
start time for activity H must be equal to the largest of the earliest finish times for activities
B and C. Thus, with $EF = 6$ for activity B and $EF = 9$ for activity C, we select the largest
value, 9, as the earliest start time for activity H ($ES = 9$). With an activity time of 12 as

shown in the node for activity H, the earliest finish time is $EF = ES + t = 9 + 12 = 21$. The $ES = 9$ and $EF = 21$ values can now be entered in the node for activity H in Figure 13.4.

Continuing with this **forward pass** through the network, we can establish the earliest start times and the earliest finish times for all activities in the network. Figure 13.5 shows the Western Hills Shopping Center project network with the *ES* and *EF* values for each activity. Note that the earliest finish time for activity I, the last activity in the project, is 26 weeks. Therefore, we now know that the total completion time for the project is 26 weeks.

We now continue the algorithm for finding the critical path by making a **backward pass** through the network. Because the total completion time for the project is 26 weeks, we begin the backward pass with a **latest finish time** of 26 for activity I. Once the latest finish time for an activity is known, the *latest start time* for an activity can be computed as follows. Let

$$LS = \text{latest start time for an activity}$$

$$LF = \text{latest finish time for an activity}$$

then

$$LS = LF - t \qquad (13.2)$$

Beginning the backward pass with activity I, we know that the latest finish time is $LF = 26$ and that the activity time is $t = 2$. Thus, the latest start time for activity I is $LS = LF - t = 26 - 2 = 24$. We will write the *LS* and *LF* values in the node directly below the earliest start (*ES*) and earliest finish (*EF*) times. Thus, for node I, we have

FIGURE 13.5   WESTERN HILLS SHOPPING CENTER PROJECT NETWORK WITH EARLIEST START AND EARLIEST FINISH TIMES SHOWN FOR ALL ACTIVITIES

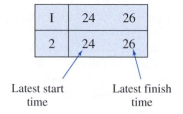

Latest start   Latest finish
time   time

The following rule can be used to determine the latest finish time for each activity in the network:

> The latest finish time for an activity is the smallest of the latest start times for all activities that immediately follow the activity.

Logically, this rule states that the latest time an activity can be finished equals the earliest (smallest) value for the latest start time of following activities. Figure 13.6 shows the complete project network with the *LS* and *LF* backward pass results. We can use the latest finish time rule to verify the *LS* and *LF* values shown for activity H. The latest finish time for activity H must be the latest start time for activity I. Thus, we set *LF* = 24 for activity H. Using equation (13.2), we find that $LS = LF - t = 24 - 12 = 12$ as the latest start time for activity H. These values are shown in the node for activity H in Figure 13.6.

Activity A requires a more involved application of the latest start time rule. First, note that three activities (C, D, and E) immediately follow activity A. Figure 13.6 shows that the

FIGURE 13.6   WESTERN HILLS SHOPPING CENTER PROJECT NETWORK WITH LATEST START AND LATEST FINISH TIMES SHOWN IN EACH NODE

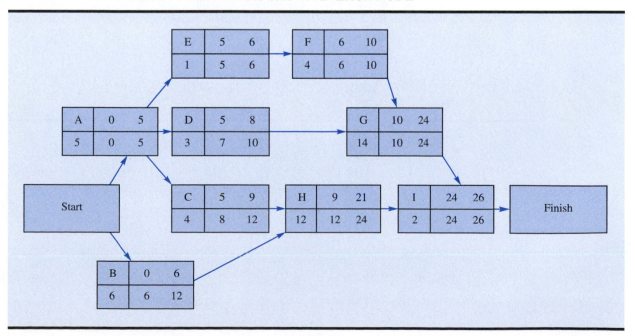

latest start times for activities C, D, and E are $LS = 8$, $LS = 7$, and $LS = 5$, respectively. The latest finish time rule for activity A states that the LF for activity A is the smallest of the latest start times for activities C, D, and E. With the smallest value being 5 for activity E, we set the latest finish time for activity A to $LF = 5$. Verify this result and the other latest start times and latest finish times shown in the nodes in Figure 13.6.

The slack for each activity indicates the length of time the activity can be delayed without increasing the project completion time.

After we complete the forward and backward passes, we can determine the amount of slack associated with each activity. **Slack** is the length of time an activity can be delayed without increasing the project completion time. The amount of slack for an activity is computed as follows:

$$\text{Slack} = LS - ES = LF - EF \qquad \textbf{(13.3)}$$

One of the primary contributions of PERT/CPM is the identification of the critical activities. The project manager will want to monitor critical activities closely because a delay in any one of these activities will lengthen the project completion time.

For example, the slack associated with activity C is $LS - ES = 8 - 5 = 3$ weeks. Hence, activity C can be delayed up to 3 weeks, and the entire project can still be completed in 26 weeks. In this sense, activity C is not critical to the completion of the entire project in 26 weeks. Next, we consider activity E. Using the information in Figure 13.6, we find that the slack is $LS - ES = 5 - 5 = 0$. Thus, activity E has zero, or no, slack. Thus, this activity cannot be delayed without increasing the completion time for the entire project. In other words, completing activity E exactly as scheduled is critical in terms of keeping the project on schedule. Thus, activity E is a critical activity. In general, the *critical activities* are the activities with zero slack.

The critical path algorithm is essentially a longest path algorithm. From the start node to the finish node, the critical path identifies the path that requires the most time.

The start and finish times shown in Figure 13.6 can be used to develop a detailed start time and finish time schedule for all activities. Putting this information in tabular form provides the activity schedule shown in Table 13.2. Note that the slack column shows that activities A, E, F, G, and I have zero slack. Hence, these activities are the critical activities for the project. The path formed by nodes A-E-F-G-I is the *critical path* in the Western Hills Shopping Center project network. The detailed schedule shown in Table 13.2 indicates the slack or delay that can be tolerated for the noncritical activities before these activities will increase project completion time.

TABLE 13.2 ACTIVITY SCHEDULE FOR THE WESTERN HILLS SHOPPING CENTER PROJECT

Activity	Earliest Start (ES)	Latest Start (LS)	Earliest Finish (EF)	Latest Finish (LF)	Slack (LS − ES)	Critical Path?
A	0	0	5	5	0	Yes
B	0	6	6	12	6	
C	5	8	9	12	3	
D	5	7	8	10	2	
E	5	5	6	6	0	Yes
F	6	6	10	10	0	Yes
G	10	10	24	24	0	Yes
H	9	12	21	24	3	
I	24	24	26	26	0	Yes

Contributions of PERT/CPM

Previously, we stated that project managers look for procedures that will help answer important questions regarding the planning, scheduling, and controlling of projects. Let us reconsider these questions in light of the information that the critical path calculations have given us.

If the total time required to complete the project is too long, judgment about where and how to shorten the time of critical activities must be exercised. If any activity times are altered, the critical path calculations should be repeated to determine the impact on the activity schedule and the impact on total project completion time. In Section 13.3 we show how to use linear programming to find the least-cost way to shorten the project completion time.

1. How long will the project take to complete?
   Answer: The project can be completed in 26 weeks if each activity is completed on schedule.
2. What are the scheduled start and completion times for each activity?
   Answer: The activity schedule (see Table 13.2) shows the earliest start, latest start, earliest finish, and latest finish times for each activity.
3. Which activities are critical and must be completed *exactly* as scheduled to keep the project on schedule?
   Answer: A, E, F, G, and I are the critical activities.
4. How long can noncritical activities be delayed before they cause an increase in the completion time for the project?
   Answer: The activity schedule (see Table 13.2) shows the slack associated with each activity.

Such information is valuable in managing any project. Although larger projects usually increase the effort required to develop the immediate predecessor relationships and the activity time estimates, the procedure and contribution of PERT/CPM to larger projects are identical to those shown for the shopping center expansion project. The Q.M. in Action, Hospital Revenue Bond at Seasongood & Mayer, describes a 23-activity project that introduced a $31 million hospital revenue bond. PERT/CPM identified the critical activities, the expected project completion time of 29 weeks, and the activity start times and finish times necessary to keep the entire project on schedule.

Software packages such as The Management Scientist perform the critical path calculations quickly and efficiently. The project manager can modify any aspect of the project and quickly determine how the modification affects the activity schedule and the total time required to complete the project.

Finally, computer packages may be used to carry out the steps of the PERT/CPM procedure. Figure 13.7 shows the activity schedule for the shopping center expansion project developed by The Management Scientist software package. Input to the program included the activities, their immediate predecessors, and the expected activity times. Only a few minutes were required to input the information and generate the critical path and activity schedule.

Summary of the PERT/CPM Critical Path Procedure

Before leaving this section, let us summarize the PERT/CPM critical path procedure.

Step 1. Develop a list of the activities that make up the project.
Step 2. Determine the immediate predecessor(s) for each activity in the project.
Step 3. Estimate the completion time for each activity.
Step 4. Draw a project network depicting the activities and immediate predecessors listed in steps 1 and 2.
Step 5. Use the project network and the activity time estimates to determine the earliest start and the earliest finish time for each activity by making a forward pass through the network. The earliest finish time for the last activity in the project identifies the total time required to complete the project.
Step 6. Use the project completion time identified in step 5 as the latest finish time for the last activity and make a backward pass through the network to identify the latest start and latest finish time for each activity.

FIGURE 13.7 THE MANAGEMENT SCIENTIST ACTIVITY SCHEDULE FOR THE WESTERN HILLS SHOPPING CENTER PROJECT

```
            ***     ACTIVITY SCHEDULE     ***

          EARLIEST  LATEST  EARLIEST  LATEST          CRITICAL
ACTIVITY   START    START    FINISH   FINISH  SLACK   ACTIVITY
-----------------------------------------------------------------
   A         0        0        5        5       0      YES
   B         0        6        6       12       6
   C         5        8        9       12       3
   D         5        7        8       10       2
   E         5        5        6        6       0      YES
   F         6        6       10       10       0      YES
   G        10       10       24       24       0      YES
   H         9       12       21       24       3
   I        24       24       26       26       0      YES
-----------------------------------------------------------------

     CRITICAL PATH:  A-E-F-G-I

     PROJECT COMPLETION TIME = 26
```

Step 7. Use the difference between the latest start time and the earliest start time for each activity to determine the slack for each activity.

Step 8. Find the activities with zero slack; these are the critical activities.

Step 9. Use the information from steps 5 and 6 to develop the activity schedule for the project.

Q.M. *in* ACTION

HOSPITAL REVENUE BOND AT SEASONGOOD & MAYER

Seasongood & Mayer is an investment securities firm located in Cincinnati, Ohio. The firm engages in municipal financing including the underwriting of new issues of municipal bonds, acting as a market maker for previously issued bonds, and performing other investment banking services.

Seasongood & Mayer provided the underwriting for a $31 million issue of hospital facilities revenue bonds for Providence Hospital in Hamilton County, Ohio. The project of underwriting this municipal bond issue began with activities such as drafting the legal documents, drafting a description of the existing hospital facilities, and completing a feasibility study. A total of 23 activities defined the project that would be completed when the hospital signed the construction contract and then made the bond proceeds available. The immediate predecessor relationships for the activities and the activity times were developed by a project management team.

PERT/CPM analysis of the project network identified the 10 critical path activities. The analysis also provided the expected completion time of 29 weeks, or approximately seven months. The activity schedule showed the start time and finish time for each activity and provided the information necessary to monitor the project and keep it on schedule. PERT/ CPM was instrumental in helping Seasongood & Mayer obtain the financing for the project within the time specified in the construction bid.

NOTES AND COMMENTS

Suppose that, after analyzing a PERT/CPM network, the project manager finds that the project completion time is unacceptable (i.e., the project is going to take too long). In this case, the manager must take one or both of the following steps. First, review the original PERT/CPM network to see whether any immediate predecessor relationships can be modified so that at least some of the critical path activities can be done simultaneously. Second, consider adding resources to critical path activities in an attempt to shorten the critical path; we discuss this alternative, referred to as *crashing*, in Section 13.3.

Project Scheduling with Uncertain Activity Times

In this section we consider the details of project scheduling for a problem involving new-product research and development. Because many of the activities in this project have never been attempted, the project manager wants to account for uncertainties in the activity times. Let us show how project scheduling can be conducted with uncertain activity times.

The Daugherty Porta-Vac Project

The H. S. Daugherty Company has manufactured industrial vacuum cleaning systems for many years. Recently, a member of the company's new-product research team submitted a report suggesting that the company consider manufacturing a cordless vacuum cleaner. The new product, referred to as Porta-Vac, could contribute to Daugherty's expansion into the household market. Management hopes that it can be manufactured at a reasonable cost and that its portability and no-cord convenience will make it extremely attractive.

Daugherty's management wants to study the feasibility of manufacturing the Porta-Vac product. The feasibility study will recommend the action to be taken. To complete this study, information must be obtained from the firm's research and development (R&D), product testing, manufacturing, cost estimating, and market research groups. How long will this feasibility study take? In the following discussion, we show how to answer this question and provide an activity schedule for the project.

Again, the first step in the project scheduling process is to identify all activities that make up the project and then determine the immediate predecessor(s) for each activity. Table 13.3 shows these data for the Porta-Vac project.

The Porta-Vac project network is shown in Figure 13.8. Verify that the network does in fact maintain the immediate predecessor relationships shown in Table 13.3.

Accurate activity time estimates are important in the development of an activity schedule. When activity times are uncertain, the three time estimates— optimistic, most probable, and pessimistic—allow the project manager to take uncertainty into consideration in determining the critical path and the activity schedule. This approach was developed by the designers of PERT.

Uncertain Activity Times

Once we develop the project network, we will need information on the time required to complete each activity. This information is used in the calculation of the total time required to complete the project and in the scheduling of specific activities. For repeat projects, such as construction and maintenance projects, managers may have the experience and historical data necessary to provide accurate activity time estimates. However, for new or unique projects, estimating the time for each activity may be quite difficult. In fact, in many cases, activity times are uncertain and are best described by a range of possible values rather than by one specific time estimate. In these instances, the uncertain activity times are treated as

TABLE 13.3 ACTIVITY LIST FOR THE PORTA-VAC PROJECT

Activity	Description	Immediate Predecessor
A	Develop product design	—
B	Plan market research	—
C	Prepare routing (manufacturing engineering)	A
D	Build prototype model	A
E	Prepare marketing brochure	A
F	Prepare cost estimates (industrial engineering)	C
G	Do preliminary product testing	D
H	Complete market survey	B, E
I	Prepare pricing and forecast report	H
J	Prepare final report	F, G, I

FIGURE 13.8 PORTA-VAC CORDLESS VACUUM CLEANER PROJECT NETWORK

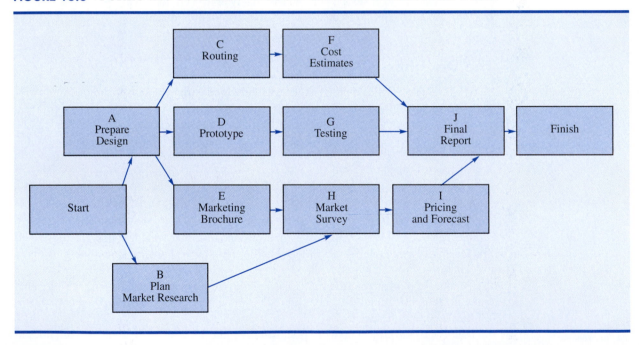

random variables with associated probability distributions. As a result, probability statements will be provided about the ability to meet a specific project completion date.

To incorporate uncertain activity times into the analysis, we need to obtain three time estimates for each activity:

Optimistic time a = the minimum activity time if everything progresses ideally

Most probable time m = the most probable activity time under normal conditions

Pessimistic time b = the maximum activity time if significant delays are encountered

To illustrate the PERT/CPM procedure with uncertain activity times, let us consider the optimistic, most probable, and pessimistic time estimates for the Porta-Vac activities as

TABLE 13.4   OPTIMISTIC, MOST PROBABLE, AND PESSIMISTIC ACTIVITY TIME
ESTIMATES (IN WEEKS) FOR THE PORTA-VAC PROJECT

Activity	Optimistic (a)	Most Probable (m)	Pessimistic (b)
A	4	5	12
B	1	1.5	5
C	2	3	4
D	3	4	11
E	2	3	4
F	1.5	2	2.5
G	1.5	3	4.5
H	2.5	3.5	7.5
I	1.5	2	2.5
J	1	2	3

presented in Table 13.4. Using activity A as an example, we see that the most probable time
is 5 weeks with a range from 4 weeks (optimistic) to 12 weeks (pessimistic). If the activity
could be repeated a large number of times, what is the average time for the activity? This
average or **expected time** (t) is as follows:

$$t = \frac{a + 4m + b}{6} \tag{13.4}$$

For activity A we have an average or expected time of

$$t_A = \frac{4 + 4(5) + 12}{6} = \frac{36}{6} = 6 \text{ weeks}$$

With uncertain activity times, we can use the *variance* to describe the dispersion or variation in the activity time values. The variance of the activity time is given by the formula[1]

$$\sigma^2 = \left(\frac{b - a}{6}\right)^2 \tag{13.5}$$

The difference between the pessimistic (b) and optimistic (a) time estimates greatly affects
the value of the variance. Large differences in these two values reflect a high degree of uncertainty in the activity time. Using equation (13.5), we obtain the measure of uncertainty—
that is, the variance—of activity A, denoted σ_A^2:

$$\sigma_A^2 = \left(\frac{12 - 4}{6}\right)^2 = \left(\frac{8}{6}\right)^2 = 1.78$$

---

[1]The variance equation is based on the notion that a standard deviation is approximately $\frac{1}{6}$ of the difference between the
extreme values of the distribution: $(b - a)/6$. The variance is the square of the standard deviation.

FIGURE 13.9   ACTIVITY TIME DISTRIBUTION FOR PRODUCT DESIGN (ACTIVITY A)
FOR THE PORTA-VAC PROJECT

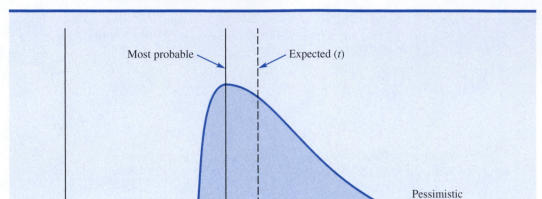

Equations (13.4) and (13.5) are based on the assumption that the activity time distribution can be described by a **beta probability distribution**.[2] With this assumption, the probability distribution for the time to complete activity A is as shown in Figure 13.9. Using equations (13.4) and (13.5) and the data in Table 13.4, we calculated the expected times and variances for all Porta-Vac activities; the results are summarized in Table 13.5. The Porta-Vac project network with expected activity times is shown in Figure 13.10.

TABLE 13.5   EXPECTED TIMES AND VARIANCES FOR THE PORTA-VAC
PROJECT ACTIVITIES

Activity	Expected Time (weeks)	Variance
A	6	1.78
B	2	0.44
C	3	0.11
D	5	1.78
E	3	0.11
F	2	0.03
G	3	0.25
H	4	0.69
I	2	0.03
J	2	0.11
Total	32	

---

[2]The equations for t and σ^2 require additional assumptions about the parameters of the beta probability distribution. However, even when these additional assumptions are not made, the equations still provide good approximations of t and σ^2.

FIGURE 13.10 PORTA-VAC PROJECT NETWORK WITH EXPECTED ACTIVITY TIMES

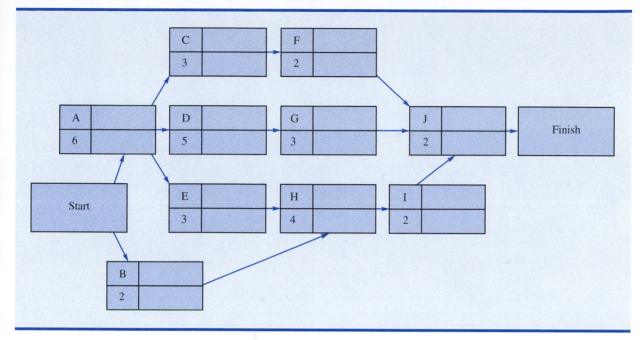

The Critical Path

When we have the project network and the expected activity times, we are ready to proceed with the critical path calculations necessary to determine the expected time required to complete the project and determine the activity schedule. In these calculations, we treat the expected activity times (Table 13.5) as the fixed length or known duration of each activity. As a result, we can use the critical path procedure introduced in Section 13.1 to find the critical path for the Porta-Vac project. After the critical activities and the expected time to complete the project have been determined, we analyze the effect of the activity time variability.

When uncertain activity times are used, the critical path calculations will determine only the expected or average time to complete the project. The actual time required to complete the project may differ. However, for planning purposes, the expected time should be valuable information for the project manager.

Proceeding with a forward pass through the network shown in Figure 13.10, we can establish the earliest start (*ES*) and earliest finish (*EF*) times for each activity. Figure 13.11 shows the project network with the *ES* and *EF* values. Note that the earliest finish time for activity J, the last activity, is 17 weeks. Thus, the expected completion time for the project is 17 weeks. Next, we make a backward pass through the network. The backward pass provides the latest start (*LS*) and latest finish (*LF*) times shown in Figure 13.12.

The activity schedule for the Porta-Vac project is shown in Table 13.6. Note that the slack time (*LS − ES*) is also shown for each activity. The activities with zero slack (A, E, H, I, and J) form the critical path for the Porta-Vac project network.

Variability in Project Completion Time

Activities that have larger variances show a greater degree of uncertainty. The project manager should monitor the progress of any activity with a large variance even if the expected time does not identify the activity as a critical activity.

We know that for the Porta-Vac project the critical path of A-E-H-I-J resulted in an expected total project completion time of 17 weeks. However, variation in critical activities can cause variation in the project completion time. Variation in noncritical activities ordinarily has no effect on the project completion time because of the slack time associated with these activities. However, if a noncritical activity is delayed long enough to expend its slack time, it becomes part of a new critical path and may affect the project completion time. Variability

FIGURE 13.11   PORTA-VAC PROJECT NETWORK WITH EARLIEST START AND EARLIEST FINISH TIMES

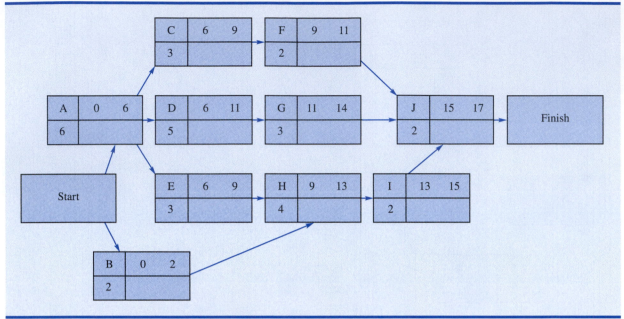

FIGURE 13.12   PORTA-VAC PROJECT NETWORK WITH LATEST START AND LATEST FINISH TIMES

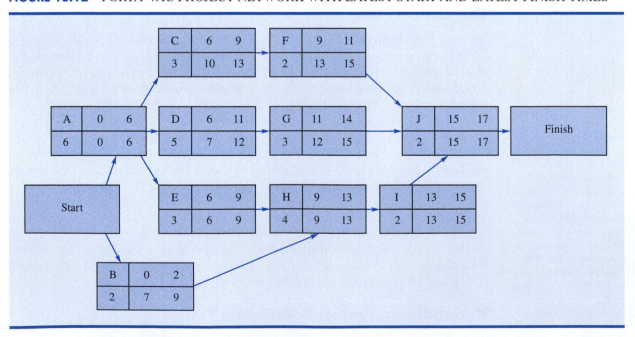

leading to a longer-than-expected total time for the critical activities will always extend the project completion time, and conversely, variability that results in a shorter-than-expected total time for the critical activities will reduce the project completion time, unless other activities become critical. Let us now use the variance in the critical activities to determine the variance in the project completion time.

TABLE 13.6   ACTIVITY SCHEDULE FOR THE PORTA-VAC PROJECT

Activity	Earliest Start (ES)	Latest Start (LS)	Earliest Finish (EF)	Latest Finish (LF)	Slack (LS − ES)	Critical Path?
A	0	0	6	6	0	Yes
B	0	7	2	9	7	
C	6	10	9	13	4	
D	6	7	11	12	1	
E	6	6	9	9	0	Yes
F	9	13	11	15	4	
G	11	12	14	15	1	
H	9	9	13	13	0	Yes
I	13	13	15	15	0	Yes
J	15	15	17	17	0	Yes

Let T denote the total time required to complete the project. The expected value of T, which is the sum of the expected times for the critical activities, is

$$E(T) = t_A + t_E + t_H + t_I + t_J$$
$$= 6 + 3 + 4 + 2 + 2 = 17 \text{ weeks}$$

The variance in the project completion time is the sum of the variances of the critical path activities. Thus, the variance for the Porta-Vac project completion time is

Problem 10 involves a project with uncertain activity times and asks you to compute the expected completion time and the variance for the project.

$$\sigma^2 = \sigma_A^2 + \sigma_E^2 + \sigma_H^2 + \sigma_I^2 + \sigma_J^2$$
$$= 1.78 + 0.11 + 0.69 + 0.03 + 0.11 = 2.72$$

where σ_A^2, σ_E^2, σ_H^2, σ_I^2, and σ_J^2 are the variances of the critical activities.

The formula for σ^2 is based on the assumption that the activity times are independent. If two or more activities are dependent, the formula provides only an approximation of the variance of the project completion time. The closer the activities are to being independent, the better the approximation.

Knowing that the standard deviation is the square root of the variance, we compute the standard deviation σ for the Porta-Vac project completion time as

$$\sigma = \sqrt{\sigma^2} = \sqrt{2.72} = 1.65$$

The normal distribution tends to be a better approximation of the distribution of total time for larger projects where the critical path has many activities.

Assuming that the distribution of the project completion time T follows a normal or bell-shaped distribution[3] allows us to draw the distribution shown in Figure 13.13. With this distribution, we can compute the probability of meeting a specified project completion date. For example, suppose that management allotted 20 weeks for the Porta-Vac project. What is the probability that we will meet the 20-week deadline? Using the normal probability

---

[3]Use of the normal distribution as an approximation is based on the central limit theorem, which indicates that the sum of independent random variables (activity times) follows a normal distribution as the number of random variables becomes large.

FIGURE 13.13   NORMAL DISTRIBUTION OF THE PROJECT COMPLETION TIME
FOR THE PORTA-VAC PROJECT

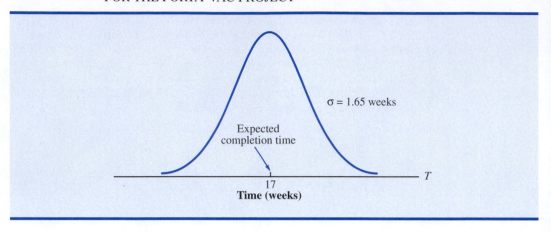

FIGURE 13.14   PROBABILITY THE PORTA-VAC PROJECT WILL MEET
THE 20-WEEK DEADLINE

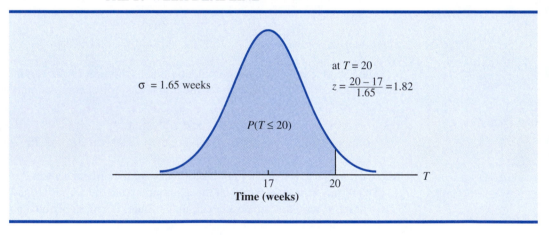

distribution shown in Figure 13.14, we are asking for the probability that $T \leq 20$; this probability is shown graphically as the shaded area in the figure. The z value for the normal probability distribution at $T = 20$ is

$$z = \frac{20 - 17}{1.65} = 1.82$$

Using $z = 1.82$ and the table for the normal distribution (see Appendix D), we find that the probability of the project meeting the 20-week deadline is 0.9656. Thus, even though activity time variability may cause the completion time to exceed 17 weeks, calculations indicate an excellent chance that the project will be completed before the 20-week deadline. Similar probability calculations can be made for other project deadline alternatives.

NOTES AND COMMENTS

For projects involving uncertain activity times, the probability that the project can be completed within a specified amount of time is helpful managerial information. However, remember that this probability estimate is based *only* on the critical activities. When uncertain activity times exist, longer-than-expected completion times for one or more noncritical activities may cause an original noncritical activity to become critical and hence increase the time required to complete the project. By frequently monitoring the progress of the project to make sure all activities are on schedule, the project manager will be better prepared to take corrective action if a noncritical activity begins to lengthen the duration of the project.

13.3   Considering Time-Cost Trade-Offs

The original developers of CPM provided the project manager with the option of adding resources to selected activities to reduce project completion time. Added resources (such as more workers, overtime, and so on) generally increase project costs, so the decision to reduce activity times must take into consideration the additional cost involved. In effect, the project manager must make a decision that involves trading reduced activity time for additional project cost.

Using more resources to reduce activity times was proposed by the developers of CPM. The shortening of activity times is referred to as crashing.

Table 13.7 defines a two-machine maintenance project consisting of five activities. Because management has had substantial experience with similar projects, the times for maintenance activities are considered to be known; hence, a single time estimate is given for each activity. The project network is shown in Figure 13.15.

The procedure for making critical path calculations for the maintenance project network is the same one used to find the critical path in the networks for both the Western Hills Shopping Center expansion project and the Porta-Vac project. Making the forward pass and backward pass calculations for the network in Figure 13.15, we obtained the activity schedule shown in Table 13.8. The zero slack times, and thus the critical path, are associated with activities A-B-E. The length of the critical path, and thus the total time required to complete the project, is 12 days.

Crashing Activity Times

Now suppose that current production levels make completing the maintenance project within 10 days imperative. By looking at the length of the critical path of the network (12 days), we realize that meeting the desired project completion time is impossible unless we can shorten

TABLE 13.7   ACTIVITY LIST FOR THE TWO-MACHINE MAINTENANCE PROJECT

Activity	Description	Immediate Predecessor	Expected Time (days)
A	Overhaul machine I	—	7
B	Adjust machine I	A	3
C	Overhaul machine II	—	6
D	Adjust machine II	C	3
E	Test system	B, D	2

FIGURE 13.15   TWO-MACHINE MAINTENANCE PROJECT NETWORK

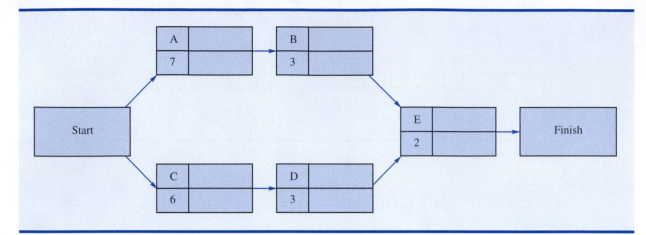

TABLE 13.8   ACTIVITY SCHEDULE FOR THE TWO-MACHINE MAINTENANCE PROJECT

Activity	Earliest Start (ES)	Latest Start (LS)	Earliest Finish (EF)	Latest Finish (LF)	Slack (LS − ES)	Critical Path?
A	0	0	7	7	0	Yes
B	7	7	10	10	0	Yes
C	0	1	6	7	1	
D	6	7	9	10	1	
E	10	10	12	12	0	Yes

selected activity times. This shortening of activity times, which usually can be achieved by adding resources, is referred to as **crashing**. However, the added resources associated with crashing activity times usually result in added project costs, so we will want to identify the activities that cost the least to crash and then crash those activities only the amount necessary to meet the desired project completion time.

To determine just where and how much to crash activity times, we need information on how much each activity can be crashed and how much the crashing process costs. Hence, we must ask for the following information:

1. Activity cost under the normal or expected activity time
2. Time to complete the activity under maximum crashing (i.e., the shortest possible activity time)
3. Activity cost under maximum crashing

Let

$$\tau_i = \text{expected time for activity } i$$
$$\tau_i' = \text{time for activity } i \text{ under maximum crashing}$$
$$M_i = \text{maximum possible reduction in time for activity } i \text{ due to crashing}$$

Given τ_i and τ_i', we can compute M_i:

$$M_i = \tau_i - \tau_i' \qquad\qquad \textbf{(13.6)}$$

Next, let C_i denote the cost for activity i under the normal or expected activity time and denote the cost for activity i under maximum crashing. Thus, per unit of time (e.g., per day), the crashing cost K_i for each activity is given by

$$K_i = \frac{C_i' - C_i}{M_i} \qquad\qquad \textbf{(13.7)}$$

For example, if the normal or expected time for activity A is 7 days at a cost of $C_A = \$500$ and the time under maximum crashing is 4 days at a cost of $C_A' = \$800$, equations (13.6) and (13.7) show that the maximum possible reduction in time for activity A is

$$M_A = 7 - 4 = 3 \text{ days}$$

with a crashing cost of

$$K_A = \frac{C_A' - C_A}{M_A} = \frac{800 - 500}{3} = \frac{300}{3} = \$100 \text{ per day}$$

We make the assumption that any portion or fraction of the activity crash time can be achieved for a corresponding portion of the activity crashing cost. For example, if we decided to crash activity A by only $1\frac{1}{2}$ days, the added cost would be $1\frac{1}{2}(\$100) = \$150$, which results in a total activity cost of $\$500 + \$150 = \$650$. Figure 13.16 shows the graph of the time-cost relationship for activity A. The complete normal and crash activity data for the two-machine maintenance project are given in Table 13.9.

FIGURE 13.16   TIME-COST RELATIONSHIP FOR ACTIVITY A

TABLE 13.9   NORMAL AND CRASH ACTIVITY DATA FOR THE TWO-MACHINE MAINTENANCE PROJECT

Activity	Time (days) Normal	Time (days) Crash	Total Cost Normal (C_i)	Total Cost Crash (C_i')	Maximum Reduction in Time (M_i)	Crash Cost per Day $\left(K_i = \dfrac{C_i' - C_i}{M_i} \right)$
A	7	4	$ 500	$ 800	3	$100
B	3	2	200	350	1	150
C	6	4	500	900	2	200
D	3	1	200	500	2	150
E	2	1	300	550	1	250
			$1700	$3100		

Which activities should be crashed—and by how much—to meet the 10-day project completion deadline at minimum cost? Your first reaction to this question may be to consider crashing the critical activities—A, B, or E. Activity A has the lowest crashing cost per day of the three, and crashing this activity by 2 days will reduce the A-B-E path to the desired 10 days. Keep in mind, however, that as you crash the current critical activities, other paths may become critical. Thus, you will need to check the critical path in the revised network and perhaps either identify additional activities to crash or modify your initial crashing decision. For a small network, this trial-and-error approach can be used to make crashing decisions; in larger networks, however, a mathematical procedure is required to determine the optimal crashing decisions.

Linear Programming Model for Crashing

Let us describe how linear programming can be used to solve the network crashing problem. With PERT/CPM, we know that when an activity starts at its earliest start time, then

$$\text{Finish time} = \text{Earliest start time} + \text{Activity time}$$

However, if slack time is associated with an activity, then the activity need not start at its earliest start time. In this case, we may have

$$\text{Finish time} > \text{Earliest start time} + \text{Activity time}$$

Because we do not know ahead of time whether an activity will start at its earliest start time, we use the following inequality to show the general relationship among finish time, earliest start time, and activity time for each activity:

$$\text{Finish time} \geq \text{Earliest start time} + \text{Activity time}$$

Consider activity A, which has an expected time of 7 days. Let x_A = finish time for activity A, and y_A = amount of time activity A is crashed. If we assume that the project begins at time 0, the earliest start time for activity A is 0. Because the time for activity A is reduced by the amount of time that activity A is crashed, the finish time for activity A must satisfy the relationship

$$x_A \geq 0 + (7 - y_A)$$

Moving y_A to the left side,

$$x_A + y_A \geq 7$$

In general, let

$$x_i = \text{the finish time for activity } i \qquad i = \text{A, B, C, D, E}$$
$$y_i = \text{the amount of time activity } i \text{ is crashed} \quad i = \text{A, B, C, D, E}$$

If we follow the same approach that we used for activity A, the constraint corresponding to the finish time for activity C (expected time = 6 days) is

$$x_C \geq 0 + (6 - y_C) \quad \text{or} \quad x_C + y_C \geq 6$$

Continuing with the forward pass of the PERT/CPM procedure, we see that the earliest start time for activity B is x_A, the finish time for activity A. Thus, the constraint corresponding to the finish time for activity B is

$$x_B \geq x_A + (3 - y_B) \quad \text{or} \quad x_B + y_B - x_A \geq 3$$

Similarly, we obtain the constraint for the finish time for activity D:

$$x_D \geq x_C + (3 - y_D) \quad \text{or} \quad x_D + y_D - x_C \geq 3$$

Finally, we consider activity E. The earliest start time for activity E equals the *largest* of the finish times for activities B and D. Because the finish times for both activities B and D will be determined by the crashing procedure, we must write two constraints for activity E, one based on the finish time for activity B and one based upon the finish time for activity D:

$$x_E + y_E - x_B \geq 2 \quad \text{and} \quad x_E + y_E - x_D \geq 2$$

Recall that current production levels made completing the maintenance project within 10 days imperative. Thus, the constraint for the finish time for activity E is

$$x_E \leq 10$$

In addition, we must add the following five constraints corresponding to the maximum allowable crashing time for each activity:

$$y_A \leq 3, \quad y_B \leq 1, \quad y_C \leq 2, \quad y_D \leq 2, \quad \text{and} \quad y_E \leq 1$$

As with all linear programs, we add the usual nonnegativity requirements for the decision variables.

All that remains is to develop an objective function for the model. Because the total project cost for a normal completion time is fixed at $1700 (see Table 13.9), we can minimize the total project cost (normal cost plus crashing cost) by minimizing the total crashing costs. Thus, the linear programming objective function becomes

$$\text{Min } 100y_A + 150y_B + 200y_C + 150y_D + 250y_E$$

Thus, to determine the optimal crashing for each of the activities, we must solve a 10-variable, 12-constraint linear programming model. The linear programming module of The Management Scientist provides the optimal solution of crashing activity A by 1 day and activity E by 1 day, with a total crashing cost of $100 + $250 = $350. With the minimum cost crashing solution, the activity times are as follows:

Activity	Time in Days
A	6 (Crash 1 day)
B	3
C	6
D	3
E	1 (Crash 1 day)

The linear programming solution provided the revised activity times, but not the revised earliest start time, latest start time, and slack information. The revised activity times and the usual PERT/CPM procedure must be used to develop the activity schedule for the project.

NOTES AND COMMENTS

Note that the two-machine maintenance project network for the crashing illustration (see Figure 13.15) has only one activity, activity E, leading directly to the Finish node. As a result, the project completion time is equal to the completion time for activity E. Thus, the linear programming constraint requiring the project completion in 10 days or less could be written $x_E \leq 10$.

If two or more activities lead directly to the Finish node of a project network, a slight modification is required in the linear programming model for crashing. Consider the portion of the project network shown here. In this case, we suggest creating an additional variable, x_{FIN}, which indicates the finish or completion time for the entire project. The fact that the project cannot be finished until both activities E and G are completed can be modeled by the two constraints

$$x_{FIN} \geq x_E \quad \text{or} \quad x_{FIN} - x_E \geq 0$$
$$x_{FIN} \geq x_G \quad \text{or} \quad x_{FIN} - x_G \geq 0$$

The constraint that the project must be finished by time T can be added as $x_{FIN} \leq T$. Problem 22 gives you practice with this type of project network.

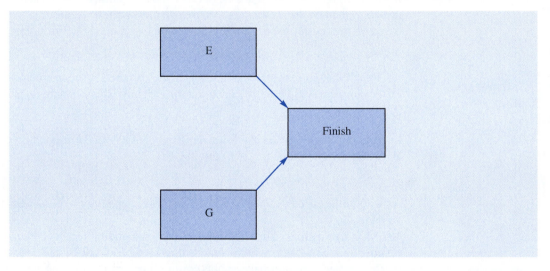

Summary

In this chapter we showed how PERT/CPM can be used to plan, schedule, and control a wide variety of projects. The key to this approach to project scheduling is the development of a PERT/CPM project network that depicts the activities and their precedence relationships. From this project network and activity time estimates, the critical path for the network and the associated critical activities can be identified. In the process, an activity schedule showing the earliest start and earliest finish times, the latest start and latest finish times, and the slack for each activity can be identified.

We showed how we can include capabilities for handling variable or uncertain activity times and how to use this information to provide a probability statement about the chances the project can be completed in a specified period of time. We introduced crashing as a procedure for reducing activity times to meet project completion deadlines, and showed how a linear programming model can be used to determine the crashing decisions that will minimize the cost of reducing the project completion time.

Glossary

Program evaluation and review technique (PERT) A network-based project scheduling procedure.

Critical path method (CPM) A network-based project scheduling procedure.

Activities Specific jobs or tasks that are components of a project. Activities are represented by nodes in a project network.

Immediate predecessors The activities that must be completed immediately prior to the start of a given activity.

Project network A graphical representation of a project that depicts the activities and shows the predecessor relationships among the activities.

Critical path The longest path in a project network.

Path A sequence of connected nodes that leads from the Start node to the Finish node.

Critical activities The activities on the critical path.

Earliest start time The earliest time an activity may begin.

Latest start time The latest time an activity may begin without increasing the project completion time.

Earliest finish time The earliest time an activity may be completed.

Forward pass Part of the PERT/CPM procedure that involves moving forward through the project network to determine the earliest start and earliest finish times for each activity.

Backward pass Part of the PERT/CPM procedure that involves moving backward through the network to determine the latest start and latest finish times for each activity.

Latest finish time The latest time an activity may be completed without increasing the project completion time.

Slack The length of time an activity can be delayed without affecting the project completion time.

Optimistic time The minimum activity time if everything progresses ideally.

Most probable time The most probable activity time under normal conditions.

Pessimistic time The maximum activity time if significant delays are encountered.

Expected time The average activity time.

Beta probability distribution A probability distribution used to describe activity times.

Crashing The shortening of activity times by adding resources and hence usually increasing cost.

Problems

1. The Mohawk Discount Store is designing a management training program for individuals at its corporate headquarters. The company wants to design the program so that trainees can complete it as quickly as possible. Important precedence relationships must be maintained between assignments or activities in the program. For example, a trainee cannot serve as an assistant to the store manager until the trainee has obtained experience in the credit department and at least one sales department. The following activities are the assignments that must be completed by each trainee in the program. Construct a project network for this problem. Do not perform any further analysis.

Activity	A	B	C	D	E	F	G	H
Immediate Predecessor	—	—	A	A, B	A, B	C	D, F	E, G

2. Bridge City Developers is coordinating the construction of an office complex. As part of the planning process, the company generated the following activity list. Draw a project network that can be used to assist in the scheduling of the project activities.

Activity	A	B	C	D	E	F	G	H	I	J
Immediate Predecessor	—	—	—	A, B	A, B	D	E	C	C	F, G, H, I

3. Construct a project network for the following project. The project is completed when activities F and G are both complete.

Activity	A	B	C	D	E	F	G
Immediate Predecessor	—	—	A	A	C, B	C, B	D, E

4. Assume that the project in Problem 3 has the following activity times (in months):

Activity	A	B	C	D	E	F	G
Time	4	6	2	6	3	3	5

   a. Find the critical path.
   b. The project must be completed in $1\frac{1}{2}$ years. Do you anticipate difficulty in meeting the deadline? Explain.

5. Management Decision Systems (MDS) is a consulting company that specializes in the development of decision support systems. MDS obtained a contract to develop a computer system to assist the management of a large company in formulating its capital expenditure plan. The project leader developed the following list of activities and immediate predecessors. Construct a project network for this problem.

Activity	A	B	C	D	E	F	G	H	I	J
Immediate Predecessor	—	—	—	B	A	B	C, D	B, E	F, G	H

6. Consider the following project network and activity times (in weeks):

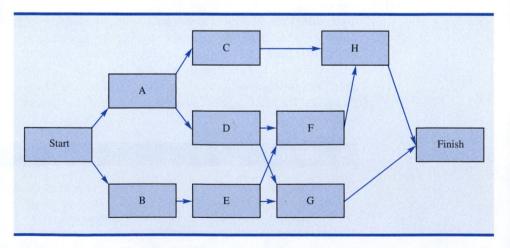

Activity	A	B	C	D	E	F	G	H
Time	5	3	7	6	7	3	10	8

   a. Identify the critical path.
   b. How much time will be needed to complete this project?
   c. Can activity D be delayed without delaying the entire project? If so, by how many weeks?

d. Can activity C be delayed without delaying the entire project? If so, by how many weeks?
e. What is the schedule for activity E?

7. Embassy Club Condominium, located on the west coast of Florida, is undertaking a summer renovation of its main building. The project is scheduled to begin May 1, and a September 1 (17-week) completion date is desired. The condominium manager identified the following renovation activities and their estimated times:

Activity	Immediate Predecessor	Time
A	—	3
B	—	1
C	—	2
D	A, B, C	4
E	C, D	5
F	A	3
G	D, F	6
H	E	4

a. Draw a project network.
b. What are the critical activities?
c. What activity has the most slack time?
d. Will the project be completed by September 1?

8. Colonial State College is considering building a new multipurpose athletic complex on campus. The complex would provide a new gymnasium for intercollegiate basketball games, expanded office space, classrooms, and intramural facilities. The following activities would have to be undertaken before construction can begin:

Activity	Description	Immediate Predecessor	Time (weeks)
A	Survey building site	—	6
B	Develop initial design	—	8
C	Obtain board approval	A, B	12
D	Select architect	C	4
E	Establish budget	C	6
F	Finalize design	D, E	15
G	Obtain financing	E	12
H	Hire contractor	F, G	8

a. Draw a project network.
b. Identify the critical path.
c. Develop the activity schedule for the project.
d. Does it appear reasonable that construction of the athletic complex could begin one year after the decision to begin the project with the site survey and initial design plans? What is the expected completion time for the project?

9. Hamilton County Parks is planning to develop a new park and recreational area on a recently purchased 100-acre tract. Project development activities include clearing playground and picnic areas, constructing roads, constructing a shelter house, purchasing

picnic equipment, and so on. The following network and activity times (in weeks) are being used in the planning, scheduling, and controlling of this project:

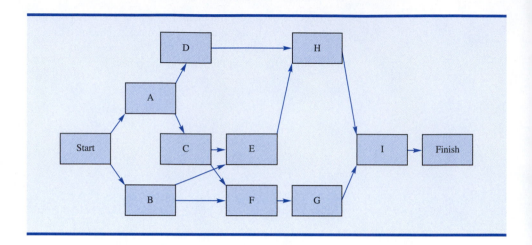

Activity	A	B	C	D	E	F	G	H	I
Time	9	6	6	3	0	3	2	6	3

a.   What is the critical path for this network?
b.   Show the activity schedule for this project.
c.   The park commissioner would like to open the park to the public within six months from the time the work on the project is started. Does this opening date appear to be feasible? Explain.

10.   The following estimates of activity times (in days) are available for a small project:

Activity	Optimistic	Most Probable	Pessimistic
A	4	5.0	6
B	8	9.0	10
C	7	7.5	11
D	7	9.0	10
E	6	7.0	9
F	5	6.0	7

a.   Compute the expected activity completion times and the variance for each activity.
b.   An analyst determined that the critical path consists of activities B-D-F. Compute the expected project completion time and the variance.

11.   Building a backyard swimming pool consists of nine major activities. The activities and their immediate predecessors are shown. Develop the project network.

Activity	A	B	C	D	E	F	G	H	I
Immediate Predecessor	—	—	A, B	A, B	B	C	D	D, F	E, G, H

12.   Assume that the activity time estimates (in days) for the swimming pool construction project in Problem 11 are as follows:

Activity	Optimistic	Most Probable	Pessimistic
A	3	5	6
B	2	4	6
C	5	6	7
D	7	9	10
E	2	4	6
F	1	2	3
G	5	8	10
H	6	8	10
I	3	4	5

a. What are the critical activities?
b. What is the expected time to complete the project?
c. What is the probability that the project can be completed in 25 or fewer days?

13. Suppose that the following estimates of activity times (in weeks) were provided for the network shown in Problem 6:

Activity	Optimistic	Most Probable	Pessimistic
A	4.0	5.0	6.0
B	2.5	3.0	3.5
C	6.0	7.0	8.0
D	5.0	5.5	9.0
E	5.0	7.0	9.0
F	2.0	3.0	4.0
G	8.0	10.0	12.0
H	6.0	7.0	14.0

What is the probability that the project will be completed
a. Within 21 weeks?
b. Within 22 weeks?
c. Within 25 weeks?

14. Davison Construction Company is building a luxury lakefront home in the Finger Lakes region of New York. Coordination of the architect and subcontractors will require a major effort to meet the 44-week (approximately 10-month) completion date requested by the owner. The Davison project manager prepared the following project network:

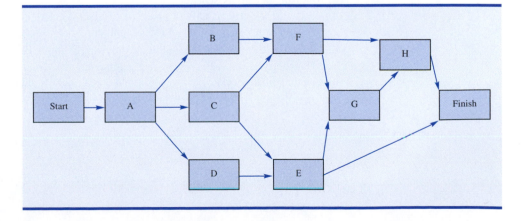

Estimates of the optimistic, most probable, and pessimistic times (in weeks) for the activities are as follows:

Activity	Optimistic	Most Probable	Pessimistic
A	4	8	12
B	6	7	8
C	6	12	18
D	3	5	7
E	6	9	18
F	5	8	17
G	10	15	20
H	5	6	13

a. Find the critical path.
b. What is the expected project completion time?
c. What is the probability the project can be completed in the 44 weeks as requested by the owner?
d. What is the probability the building project could run more than 3 months late? Use 57 weeks for this calculation.
e. What should the construction company tell the owner?

15. Doug Casey is in charge of planning and coordinating next spring's sales management training program for his company. Doug listed the following activity information for this project:

Activity	Description	Immediate Predecessor	Time (weeks)		
			Optimistic	Most Probable	Pessimistic
A	Plan topic	—	1.5	2.0	2.5
B	Obtain speakers	A	2.0	2.5	6.0
C	List meeting locations	—	1.0	2.0	3.0
D	Select location	C	1.5	2.0	2.5
E	Finalize speaker travel plans	B, D	0.5	1.0	1.5
F	Make final check with speakers	E	1.0	2.0	3.0
G	Prepare and mail brochure	B, D	3.0	3.5	7.0
H	Take reservations	G	3.0	4.0	5.0
I	Handle last-minute details	F, H	1.5	2.0	2.5

a. Draw a project network.
b. Prepare an activity schedule.
c. What are the critical activities and what is the expected project completion time?
d. If Doug wants a 0.99 probability of completing the project on time, how far ahead of the scheduled meeting date should he begin working on the project?

16. The Daugherty Porta-Vac project discussed in Section 13.2 has an expected project completion time of 17 weeks. The probability that the project could be completed in 20 weeks or less is 0.9656. The noncritical paths in the Porta-Vac project network are

$$A\text{-}D\text{-}G\text{-}J$$

$$A\text{-}C\text{-}F\text{-}J$$

$$B\text{-}H\text{-}I\text{-}J$$

a. Use the information in Table 13.5 to compute the expected time and variance for each path shown.
b. Compute the probability that each path will be completed in the desired 20-week period.

c. Why is the computation of the probability of completing a project on time based on the analysis of the critical path? In what case, if any, would making the probability computation for a noncritical path be desirable?

17. The Porsche Shop, founded in 1985 by Dale Jensen, specializes in the restoration of vintage Porsche automobiles. One of Jensen's regular customers asked him to prepare an estimate for the restoration of a 1964 model 356SC Porsche. To estimate the time and cost to perform such a restoration, Jensen broke the restoration process into four separate activities: disassembly and initial preparation work (A), body restoration (B), engine restoration (C), and final assembly (D). Once activity A has been completed, activities B and C can be performed independently of each other; however, activity D can be started only if both activities B and C have been completed. Based on his inspection of the car, Jensen believes that the following time estimates (in days) are applicable:

Activity	Optimistic	Most Probable	Pessimistic
A	3	4	8
B	5	8	11
C	2	4	6
D	4	5	12

Jensen estimates that the parts needed to restore the body will cost $3000 and that the parts needed to restore the engine will cost $5000. His current labor costs are $400 a day.
   a. Develop a project network.
   b. What is the expected project completion time?
   c. Jensen's business philosophy is based on making decisions using a best- and worst-case scenario. Develop cost estimates for completing the restoration based on both a best- and worst-case analysis. Assume that the total restoration cost is the sum of the labor cost plus the material cost.
   d. If Jensen obtains the job with a bid that is based on the costs associated with an expected completion time, what is the probability that he will lose money on the job?
   e. If Jensen obtains the job based on a bid of $16,800, what is the probability that he will lose money on the job?

18. The manager of the Oak Hills Swimming Club is planning the club's swimming team program. The first team practice is scheduled for May 1. The activities, their immediate predecessors, and the activity time estimates (in weeks) are as follows:

Activity	Description	Immediate Predecessor	Time (weeks) Optimistic	Most Probable	Pessimistic
A	Meet with board	—	1	1	2
B	Hire coaches	A	4	6	8
C	Reserve pool	A	2	4	6
D	Announce program	B, C	1	2	3
E	Meet with coaches	B	2	3	4
F	Order team suits	A	1	2	3
G	Register swimmers	D	1	2	3
H	Collect fees	G	1	2	3
I	Plan first practice	E, H, F	1	1	1

   a. Draw a project network.
   b. Develop an activity schedule.
   c. What are the critical activities, and what is the expected project completion time?

d. If the club manager plans to start the project on February 1, what is the probability the swimming program will be ready by the scheduled May 1 date (13 weeks)? Should the manager begin planning the swimming program before February 1?

19. The product development group at Landon Corporation has been working on a new computer software product that has the potential to capture a large market share. Through outside sources, Landon's management learned that a competitor is working to introduce a similar product. As a result, Landon's top management increased its pressure on the product development group. The group's leader turned to PERT/CPM as an aid to scheduling the activities remaining before the new product can be brought to the market. The project network is as follows:

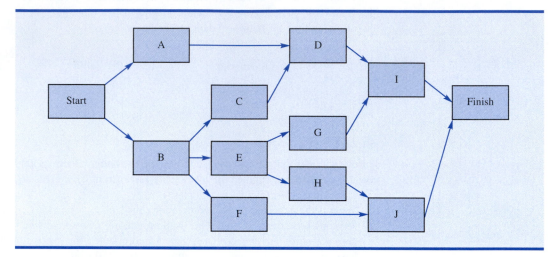

The activity time estimates (in weeks) are as follows:

Activity	Optimistic	Most Probable	Pessimistic
A	3.0	4.0	5.0
B	3.0	3.5	7.0
C	4.0	5.0	6.0
D	2.0	3.0	4.0
E	6.0	10.0	14.0
F	7.5	8.5	12.5
G	4.5	6.0	7.5
H	5.0	6.0	13.0
I	2.0	2.5	6.0
J	4.0	5.0	6.0

a. Develop an activity schedule for this project and identify the critical path activities.
b. What is the probability that the project will be completed so that Landon Corporation may introduce the new product within 25 weeks? Within 30 weeks?

20. Norton Industries is installing a new computer system. The activities, the activity times, and the project network are as follows:

Activity	Time	Activity	Time
A	3	E	4
B	6	F	3
C	2	G	9
D	5	H	3

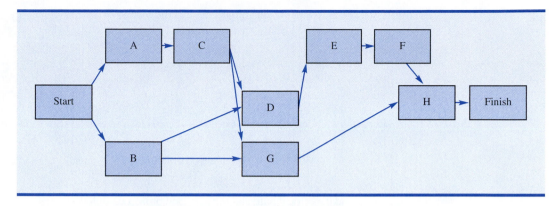

The critical path calculation shows B-D-E-F-H is the critical path, and the expected project completion time is 21 weeks. After viewing this information, management requested overtime be used to complete the project in 16 weeks. Thus, crashing of the project is necessary. The following information is relevant:

	Time (weeks)		Cost ($)	
Activity	**Normal**	**Crash**	**Normal**	**Crash**
A	3	1	900	1700
B	6	3	2000	4000
C	2	1	500	1000
D	5	3	1800	2400
E	4	3	1500	1850
F	3	1	3000	3900
G	9	4	8000	9800
H	3	2	1000	2000

a. Formulate a linear programming model that can be used to make the crashing decisions for this project.
b. Solve the linear programming model and make the minimum cost crashing decisions. What is the added cost of meeting the 16-week completion time?
c. Develop a complete activity schedule based on the crashed activity times.

21. Consider the following project network and activity times (in days):

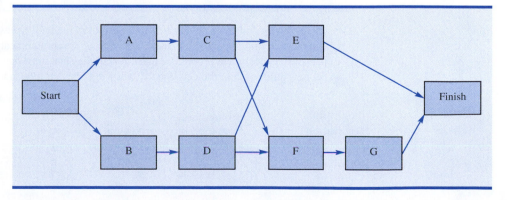

Activity	A	B	C	D	E	F	G
Time	3	2	5	5	6	2	2

The crashing data for this project are as follows:

Activity	Time (days)		Cost ($)	
	Normal	**Crash**	**Normal**	**Crash**
A	3	2	800	1400
B	2	1	1200	1900
C	5	3	2000	2800
D	5	3	1500	2300
E	6	4	1800	2800
F	2	1	600	1000
G	2	1	500	1000

   a.   Find the critical path and the expected project completion time.

   b.   What is the total project cost using the normal times?

22.   Refer to Problem 21. Assume that management desires a 12-day project completion time.

   a.   Formulate a linear programming model that can be used to assist with the crashing decisions.

   b.   What activities should be crashed?

   c.   What is the total project cost for the 12-day completion time?

23.   Consider the following project network. Note that the normal or expected activity times are denoted τ_i, i = A, B, . . . , I. Let x_i = the earliest finish time for activity i. Formulate a linear programming model that can be used to determine the length of the critical path.

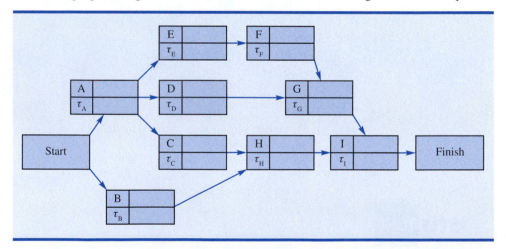

24.   Office Automation, Inc., developed a proposal for introducing a new computerized office system that will improve word processing and interoffice communications for a particular company. Contained in the proposal is a list of activities that must be accomplished to complete the new office system project. Use the following relevant information about the activities:

Activity	Description	Immediate Predecessor	Time (weeks)		Cost ($1000s)	
			Normal	**Crash**	**Normal**	**Crash**
A	Plan needs	—	10	8	30	70
B	Order equipment	A	8	6	120	150
C	Install equipment	B	10	7	100	160
D	Set up training lab	A	7	6	40	50
E	Conduct training course	D	10	8	50	75
F	Test system	C, E	3	3	60	—

   a.   Develop a project network.

   b.   Develop an activity schedule.

   c.   What are the critical activities, and what is the expected project completion time?

   d.   Assume that the company wants to complete the project in six months or 26 weeks. What crashing decisions do you recommend to meet the desired completion time at the least possible cost? Work through the network and attempt to make the crashing decisions by inspection.

   e.   Develop an activity schedule for the crashed project.

   f.   What added project cost is required to meet the six-month completion time?

25. Because Landon Corporation (see Problem 19) is being pressured to complete the product development project at the earliest possible date, the project leader requested that the possibility of crashing the project be evaluated.

   a.   Formulate a linear programming model that could be used in making the crashing decisions.

   b.   What information would have to be provided before the linear programming model could be implemented?

Case Problem   R. C. Coleman

R. C. Coleman distributes a variety of food products that are sold through grocery store and supermarket outlets. The company receives orders directly from the individual outlets, with a typical order requesting the delivery of several cases of anywhere from 20 to 50 different products. Under the company's current warehouse operation, warehouse clerks dispatch order-picking personnel to fill each order and have the goods moved to the warehouse shipping area. Because of the high labor costs and relatively low productivity of hand order-picking, management has decided to automate the warehouse operation by installing a computer-controlled order-picking system, along with a conveyor system for moving goods from storage to the warehouse shipping area.

    R. C. Coleman's director of material management has been named the project manager in charge of the automated warehouse system. After consulting with members of the engineering staff and warehouse management personnel, the director compiled a list of activities associated with the project. The optimistic, most probable, and pessimistic times (in weeks) have also been provided for each activity.

Activity	Description	Immediate Predecessor
A	Determine equipment needs	—
B	Obtain vendor proposals	—
C	Select vendor	A, B
D	Order system	C
E	Design new warehouse layout	C
F	Design warehouse	E
G	Design computer interface	C
H	Interface computer	D, F, G
I	Install system	D, F
J	Train system operators	H
K	Test system	I, J

Activity	Optimistic	Time Most Probable	Pessimistic
A	4	6	8
B	6	8	16
C	2	4	6
D	8	10	24
E	7	10	13
F	4	6	8
G	4	6	20
H	4	6	8
I	4	6	14
J	3	4	5
K	2	4	6

Managerial Report

Develop a report that presents the activity schedule and expected project completion time for the warehouse expansion project. Include a project network in the report. In addition, take into consideration the following issues:

1. R. C. Coleman's top management established a required 40-week completion time for the project. Can this completion time be achieved? Include probability information in your discussion. What recommendations do you have if the 40-week completion time is required?

2. Suppose that management requests that activity times be shortened to provide an 80% chance of meeting the 40-week completion time. If the variance in the project completion time is the same as you found in part (1), how much should the expected project completion time be shortened to achieve the goal of an 80% chance of completion within 40 weeks?

3. Using the expected activity times as the normal times and the following crashing information, determine the activity crashing decisions and revised activity schedule for the warehouse expansion project:

Activity	Crashed Activity Time (weeks)	Cost ($) Normal	Crashed
A	4	1,000	1,900
B	7	1,000	1,800
C	2	1,500	2,700
D	8	2,000	3,200
E	7	5,000	8,000
F	4	3,000	4,100
G	5	8,000	10,250
H	4	5,000	6,400
I	4	10,000	12,400
J	3	4,000	4,400
K	3	5,000	5,500

CHAPTER 14

Inventory Models

CONTENTS

Inventory refers to idle goods or materials held by an organization for use sometime in the future. Items carried in inventory include raw materials, purchased parts, components, sub-assemblies, work-in-process, finished goods, and supplies. Some reasons organizations maintain inventory include the difficulties in precisely predicting sales levels, production times, demand, and usage needs. Thus, inventory serves as a buffer against uncertain and fluctuating usage and keeps a supply of items available in case the items are needed by the organization or its customers. Even though inventory serves an important and essential role, the expense associated with financing and maintaining inventories is a substantial part of the cost of doing business. In large organizations, the cost associated with inventory can run into the millions of dollars.

In applications involving inventory, managers must answer two important questions.

1. *How much* should be ordered when the inventory is replenished?
2. *When* should the inventory be replenished?

Virtually every business uses some sort of inventory management model or system to address the preceding questions. Hewlett-Packard works with its retailers to help determine the retailer's inventory replenishment strategies for the printers and other HP products. IBM developed inventory management policies for a range of microelectronic parts that are used in IBM plants as well as sold to a number of outside customers. The Q.M. in Action, Inventory Management at CVS Corporation, describes an inventory system used to determine order quantities in the drugstore industry.

The inventory procedure described for the drugstore industry is discussed in detail in Section 14.7.

The purpose of this chapter is to show how quantitative models can assist in making the how-much-to-order and when-to-order inventory decisions. We will first consider *deterministic* inventory models in which we assume that the rate of demand for the item is constant or nearly constant. Later we will consider *probabilistic* inventory models in which the demand for the item fluctuates and can be described only in probabilistic terms.

Q.M. *in* ACTION

INVENTORY MANAGEMENT AT CVS CORPORATION*

CVS is one of the largest drugstore chains in the United States. The primary inventory management area in the drugstore involves the numerous basic products that are carried in inventory on an everyday basis. For these items, the most important issue is the replenishment quantity or order size each time an order is placed. In most drugstore chains, basic products are ordered under a periodic review inventory system, with the review period being one week.

*Based on information provided by Bob Carver. (The inventory system described was originally implemented in the CVS stores formerly known as SuperRx.)

The weekly review system uses electronic ordering equipment that scans an order label affixed to the shelf directly below each item. Among other information on the label is the item's replenishment level or order-to-quantity. The store employee placing the order determines the weekly order quantity by counting the number of units of the product on the shelf and subtracting this quantity from the replenishment level. A computer program determines the replenishment quantity for each item in each individual store, based on each store's movement, rather than on the company movement. To minimize stock-outs the replenishment quantity is set equal to the store's three-week demand or movement for the product.

Economic Order Quantity (EOQ) Model

The **economic order quantity (EOQ)** model is applicable when the demand for an item shows a constant, or nearly constant, rate and when the entire quantity ordered arrives in inventory at one point in time. The **constant demand rate** assumption means that the same number of units is taken from inventory each period of time such as 5 units every day, 25 units every week, 100 units every four-week period, and so on.

The cost associated with developing and maintaining inventory is larger than many people think. Models such as the ones presented in this chapter can be used to develop cost-effective inventory management decisions.

To illustrate the EOQ model, let us consider the situation faced by the R&B Beverage Company. R&B Beverage is a distributor of beer, wine, and soft drink products. From a main warehouse located in Columbus, Ohio, R&B supplies nearly 1000 retail stores with beverage products. The beer inventory, which constitutes about 40% of the company's total inventory, averages approximately 50,000 cases. With an average cost per case of approximately $8, R&B estimates the value of its beer inventory to be $400,000.

The warehouse manager decided to conduct a detailed study of the inventory costs associated with Bub Beer, the number-one-selling R&B beer. The purpose of the study is to establish the how-much-to-order and the when-to-order decisions for Bub Beer that will result in the lowest possible total cost. As the first step in the study, the warehouse manager obtained the following demand data for the past 10 weeks:

One of the most criticized assumptions of the EOQ model is the constant demand rate. Obviously, the model would be inappropriate for items with widely fluctuating and variable demand rates. However, as this example shows, the EOQ model can provide a realistic approximation of the optimal order quantity when demand is relatively stable and occurs at a nearly constant rate.

Week	Demand (cases)
1	2000
2	2025
3	1950
4	2000
5	2100
6	2050
7	2000
8	1975
9	1900
10	2000
Total cases	20,000
Average cases per week	2000

Strictly speaking, these weekly demand figures do not show a constant demand rate. However, given the relatively low variability exhibited by the weekly demand, inventory planning with a constant demand rate of 2000 cases per week appears acceptable. In practice, you will find that the actual inventory situation seldom, if ever, satisfies the assumptions of the model exactly. Thus, in any particular application, the manager must determine whether the model assumptions are close enough to reality for the model to be useful. In this situation, because demand varies from a low of 1900 cases to a high of 2100 cases, the assumption of constant demand of 2000 cases per week appears to be a reasonable approximation.

The how-much-to-order decision involves selecting an order quantity that draws a compromise between (1) keeping small inventories and ordering frequently, and (2) keeping large inventories and ordering infrequently. The first alternative can result in undesirably high ordering costs, while the second alternative can result in undesirably high inventory holding costs. To find an optimal compromise between these conflicting alternatives, let us consider a mathematical model that shows the total cost as the sum of the holding cost and the ordering cost.[1]

As with other quantitative models, accurate estimates of cost parameters are critical. In the EOQ model, estimates of both the inventory holding cost and the ordering cost are needed. Also see footnote 1, which refers to relevant costs.

Holding costs are the costs associated with maintaining or carrying a given level of inventory; these costs depend on the size of the inventory. The first holding cost to consider is the cost of financing the inventory investment. When a firm borrows money, it incurs an interest charge. If the firm uses its own money, it experiences an opportunity cost associated with not being able to use the money for other investments. In either case, an interest cost exists for the capital tied up in inventory. This **cost of capital** is usually expressed as a percentage of the amount invested. R&B estimates its cost of capital at an annual rate of 18%.

A number of other holding costs such as insurance, taxes, breakage, pilferage, and warehouse overhead also depend on the value of the inventory. R&B estimates these other costs at an annual rate of approximately 7% of the value of its inventory. Thus, the total holding cost for the R&B beer inventory is 18% + 7% = 25% of the value of the inventory. The cost of one case of Bub Beer is $8. With an annual holding cost rate of 25%, the cost of holding one case of Bub Beer in inventory for 1 year is 0.25($8) = $2.00.

The next step in the inventory analysis is to determine the **ordering cost**. This cost, which is considered fixed regardless of the order quantity, covers the preparation of the voucher, the processing of the order including payment, postage, telephone, transportation, invoice verification, receiving, and so on. For R&B Beverage, the largest portion of the ordering cost involves the salaries of the purchasers. An analysis of the purchasing process showed that a purchaser spends approximately 45 minutes preparing and processing an order for Bub Beer. With a wage rate and fringe benefit cost for purchasers of $20 per hour, the labor portion of the ordering cost is $15. Making allowances for paper, postage, telephone, transportation, and receiving costs at $17 per order, the manager estimates that the ordering cost is $32 per order. That is, R&B is paying $32 per order regardless of the quantity requested in the order.

The holding cost, ordering cost, and demand information are the three data items that must be known prior to the use of the EOQ model. After developing these data for the R&B problem, we can look at how they are used to develop a total cost model. We begin by defining Q as the order quantity. Thus, the how-much-to-order decision involves finding the value of Q that will minimize the sum of holding and ordering costs.

The inventory for Bub Beer will have a maximum value of Q units when an order of size Q is received from the supplier. R&B will then satisfy customer demand from inventory until the inventory is depleted, at which time another shipment of Q units will be received. Thus, assuming a constant demand, the graph of the inventory for Bub Beer is as shown in Figure 14.1. Note that the graph indicates an average inventory of $\frac{1}{2}Q$ for the period in question. This level should appear reasonable because the maximum inventory is Q, the minimum is zero, and the inventory declines at a constant rate over the period.

Figure 14.1 shows the inventory pattern during one order cycle of length T. As time goes on, this pattern will repeat. The complete inventory pattern is shown in Figure 14.2. If the average inventory during each cycle is $\frac{1}{2}Q$, the average inventory over any number of cycles is also $\frac{1}{2}Q$.

Most inventory cost models use an annual cost. Thus, demand should be expressed in units per year, and inventory holding cost should be based on an annual rate.

The holding cost can be calculated using the average inventory. That is, we can calculate the holding cost by multiplying the average inventory by the cost of carrying one unit in inventory for the stated period. The period selected for the model is up to you; it could be one week, one month, one year, or more. However, because the holding cost for many

---

[1]Even though analysts typically refer to "total cost" models for inventory systems, often these models describe only the total variable or total relevant costs for the decision being considered. Costs that are not affected by the how-much-to-order decision are considered fixed or constant and are not included in the model.

FIGURE 14.1   INVENTORY FOR BUB BEER

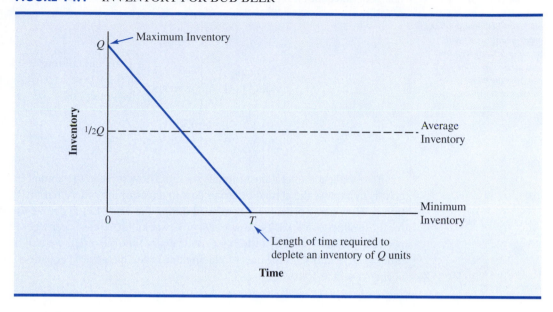

FIGURE 14.2   INVENTORY PATTERN FOR THE EOQ INVENTORY MODEL

industries and businesses is expressed as an *annual* percentage, most inventory models are developed on an *annual* cost basis.

Let

$$I = \text{annual holding cost rate}$$
$$C = \text{unit cost of the inventory item}$$
$$C_h = \text{annual cost of holding one unit in inventory}$$

The annual cost of holding one unit in inventory is

$$C_h = IC \qquad\qquad \textbf{(14.1)}$$

C_h is the cost of holding one unit in inventory for one year. Because smaller order quantities Q will result in lower inventory, total annual holding cost can be reduced by using smaller order quantities.

The general equation for the annual holding cost for the average inventory of $\frac{1}{2}Q$ units is as follows:

$$\begin{array}{c} \text{Annual} \\ \text{holding cost} \end{array} = \left(\begin{array}{c} \text{Average} \\ \text{inventory} \end{array}\right)\left(\begin{array}{c} \text{Annual holding} \\ \text{cost} \\ \text{per unit} \end{array}\right)$$

$$= \frac{1}{2}QC_h \qquad \qquad \textbf{(14.2)}$$

To complete the total cost model, we must now include the annual ordering cost. The goal is to express the annual ordering cost in terms of the order quantity Q. The first question is, How many orders will be placed during the year? Let D denote the annual demand for the product. For R&B Beverage, $D = (52 \text{ weeks})(2000 \text{ cases per week}) = 104,000$ cases per year. We know that by ordering Q units every time we order, we will have to place D/Q orders per year. If C_o is the cost of placing one order, the general equation for the annual ordering cost is as follows:

C_o, the fixed cost per order, is independent of the amount ordered. For a given annual demand of D units, the total annual ordering cost can be reduced by using larger order quantities.

$$\begin{array}{c} \text{Annual} \\ \text{ordering cost} \end{array} = \left(\begin{array}{c} \text{Number of} \\ \text{orders} \\ \text{per year} \end{array}\right)\left(\begin{array}{c} \text{Cost} \\ \text{per} \\ \text{order} \end{array}\right)$$

$$= \left(\frac{D}{Q}\right)C_o \qquad \qquad \textbf{(14.3)}$$

Thus, the total annual cost, denoted TC, can be expressed as follows:

$$\begin{array}{ccc} \text{Total} & \text{Annual} & \text{Annual} \\ \text{annual} = & \text{holding} + & \text{ordering} \\ \text{cost} & \text{cost} & \text{cost} \end{array}$$

$$TC = \frac{1}{2}QC_h + \frac{D}{Q}C_o \qquad \qquad \textbf{(14.4)}$$

Using the Bub Beer data [$C_h = IC = (0.25)(\$8) = \$2$, $C_o = \$32$, and $D = 104,000$], the total annual cost model is

$$TC = \frac{1}{2}Q(\$2) + \frac{104,000}{Q}(\$32) = Q + \frac{3,328,000}{Q}$$

The development of the total cost model goes a long way toward solving the inventory problem. We now are able to express the total annual cost as a function of *how much* should be ordered. The development of a realistic total cost model is perhaps the most important part of the application of quantitative methods to inventory decision making. Equation (14.4) is the general total cost equation for inventory situations in which the assumptions of the economic order quantity model are valid.

The How-Much-to-Order Decision

The next step is to find the order quantity Q that will minimize the total annual cost for Bub Beer. Using a trial-and-error approach, we can compute the total annual cost for several possible order quantities. As a starting point, let us consider $Q = 8000$. The total annual cost for Bub Beer is

$$TC = Q + \frac{3{,}328{,}000}{Q}$$

$$= 8000 + \frac{3{,}328{,}000}{8000} = \$8416$$

A trial order quantity of 5000 gives

$$TC = 5000 + \frac{3{,}328{,}000}{5000} = \$5666$$

The results of several other trial order quantities are shown in Table 14.1. It shows the lowest cost solution to be about 2000 cases. Graphs of the annual holding and ordering costs and total annual costs are shown in Figure 14.3.

The advantage of the trial-and-error approach is that it is rather easy to do and provides the total annual cost for a number of possible order quantity decisions. In this case, the minimum cost order quantity appears to be approximately 2000 cases. The disadvantage of this approach, however, is that it does not provide the exact minimum cost order quantity.

The EOQ formula determines the optimal order quantity by balancing the annual holding cost and the annual ordering cost.

Refer to Figure 14.3. The minimum total cost order quantity is denoted by an order size of Q^*. By using differential calculus, it can be shown (see Appendix 14.1) that the value of Q^* that minimizes the total annual cost is given by the formula

In 1915 F. W. Harris derived the mathematical formula for the economic order quantity. It was the first application of quantitative methods to the area of inventory management.

$$Q^* = \sqrt{\frac{2DC_o}{C_h}} \qquad \textbf{(14.5)}$$

This formula is referred to as the *economic order quantity (EOQ) formula*.

Using equation (14.5), the minimum total annual cost order quantity for Bub Beer is

$$Q^* = \sqrt{\frac{2(104{,}000)32}{2}} = 1824 \text{ cases}$$

TABLE 14.1 ANNUAL HOLDING, ORDERING, AND TOTAL COSTS FOR VARIOUS ORDER QUANTITIES OF BUB BEER

Order Quantity	Annual Cost		
	Holding	Ordering	Total
5000	$5000	$ 666	$5666
4000	$4000	$ 832	$4832
3000	$3000	$1109	$4109
2000	$2000	$1664	$3664
1000	$1000	$3328	$4328

FIGURE 14.3   ANNUAL HOLDING, ORDERING, AND TOTAL COSTS FOR BUB BEER

The use of an order quantity of 1824 in equation (14.4) shows that the minimum cost inventory policy for Bub Beer has a total annual cost of $3649. Note that $Q* = 1824$ balances the holding and ordering costs. Check for yourself to see that these costs are equal.[2]

The When-to-Order Decision

Now that we know how much to order, we want to address the question of *when* to order. To answer this question, we need to introduce the concept of inventory position. The **inventory position** is defined as the amount of inventory on hand plus the amount of inventory on order. The when-to-order decision is expressed in terms of a **reorder point**— the inventory position at which a new order should be placed.

The manufacturer of Bub Beer guarantees a two-day delivery on any order placed by R&B Beverage. Hence, assuming R&B Beverage operates 250 days per year, the annual demand of 104,000 cases implies a daily demand of $104{,}000/250 = 416$ cases. Thus, we expect (2 days)(416 cases per day) = 832 cases of Bub to be sold during the two days it takes a new order to reach the R&B warehouse. In inventory terminology, the two-day delivery period is referred to as the **lead time** for a new order, and the 832-case demand anticipated during this period is referred to as the **lead-time demand**. Thus, R&B should order a new shipment of Bub Beer from the manufacturer when the inventory reaches 832 cases. For inventory systems using the constant demand rate assumption and a fixed lead time, the

---

[2]Actually, $Q*$ from equation (14.5) is 1824.28, but because we cannot order fractional cases of beer, a $Q*$ of 1824 is shown. This value of $Q*$ may cause a few cents deviation between the two costs. If $Q*$ is used at its exact value, the holding and ordering costs will be exactly the same.

reorder point is the same as the lead-time demand. For these systems, the general expression for the reorder point is as follows:

$$r = dm \qquad \textbf{(14.6)}$$

where

$$r = \text{reorder point}$$
$$d = \text{demand per day}$$
$$m = \text{lead time for a new order in days}$$

The question of how frequently the order will be placed can now be answered. The period between orders is referred to as the **cycle time**. Previously in equation (14.2), we defined D/Q as the number of orders that will be placed in a year. Thus, $D/Q^* = 104,000/1824 = 57$ is the number of orders R&B Beverage will place for Bub Beer each year. If R&B places 57 orders over 250 working days, it will order approximately every $250/57 = 4.39$ working days. Thus, the cycle time is 4.39 working days. The general expression for a cycle time[3] of T days is given by

$$T = \frac{250}{D/Q^*} = \frac{250Q^*}{D} \qquad \textbf{(14.7)}$$

Sensitivity Analysis for the EOQ Model

Even though substantial time may have been spent in arriving at the cost per order ($32) and the holding cost rate (25%), we should realize that these figures are at best good estimates. Thus, we may want to consider how much the recommended order quantity would change with different estimated ordering and holding costs. To determine the effects of various cost scenarios, we can calculate the recommended order quantity under several different cost conditions. Table 14.2 shows the minimum total cost order quantity for several cost possibilities. As you can see from the table, the value of Q^* appears relatively stable, even with some variations in the cost estimates. Based on these results, the best order quantity for Bub Beer is in the range of 1700–2000 cases. If operated properly, the total cost for the Bub Beer inventory system should be close to $3400–$3800 per year. We also note that little risk is associated with implementing the calculated order quantity of 1824. For example, if holding cost rate = 24%, $C_o = \$34$, and the true optimal order quantity $Q^* = 1919$, R&B experiences only a $5 increase in the total annual cost; that is, $3690 − $3685 = $5, with $Q = 1824$.

From the preceding analysis, we would say that this EOQ model is insensitive to small variations or errors in the cost estimates. This insensitivity is a property of EOQ models in general, which indicates that if we have at least reasonable estimates of ordering cost and holding cost, we can expect to obtain a good approximation of the true minimum cost order quantity.

---

[3]This general expression for cycle time is based on 250 working days per year. If the firm operated 300 working days per year and wanted to express cycle time in terms of working days, the cycle time would be given by $T = 300Q^*/D$.

TABLE 14.2   OPTIMAL ORDER QUANTITIES FOR SEVERAL COST POSSIBILITIES

Possible Inventory Holding Cost (%)	Possible Cost per Order	Optimal Order Quantity (Q^*)	Projected Total Annual Cost	
			Using Q^*	Using $Q = 1824$
24	$30	1803	$3461	$3462
24	34	1919	3685	3690
26	30	1732	3603	3607
26	34	1844	3835	3836

Excel Solution of the EOQ Model

Inventory models such as the EOQ model are easily implemented with the aid of worksheets. The Excel EOQ worksheet for Bub Beer is shown in Figure 14.4. The formula worksheet is in the background; the value worksheet is in the foreground. Data on annual demand, ordering cost, annual inventory holding cost rate, cost per unit, working days per year, and lead time in days are input in cells B3 to B8. The appropriate EOQ model formulas, which determine the optimal inventory policy, are placed in cells B13 to B21. The

FIGURE 14.4   WORKSHEET FOR THE BUB BEER EOQ INVENTORY MODEL

WEB file

EOQ

	A	B	C
1	**Economic Order Quantity**		
2			
3	Annual Demand	104,000	
4	Ordering Cost	$32.00	
5	Annual Inventory Holding Rate %	25	
6	Cost per Unit	$8.00	
7	Working Days per Year	250	
8	Lead Time (Days)	2	
9			
10			
11	**Optimal Inventory Policy**		
12			
13	Economic Order Quantity	=SQRT(2*B3*B4/(B5/100*B6))	
14	Annual Inventory Holding Cost	=(1/2)*B13*(B5/100*B6)	
15	Annual Ordering Cost	=(B3/B13)*B4	
16	Total Annual Cost	=B14+B15	
17	Maximum Inventory Level	=B13	
18	Average Inventory Level	=B17/2	
19	Reorder Point	=(B3/B7)*B8	
20	Number of Orders per Year	=B3/B13	
21	Cycle Time (Days)	=B7/B20	
22			

	A	B
1	**Economic Order Quantity**	
2		
3	Annual Demand	104,000
4	Ordering Cost	$32.00
5	Annual Inventory Holding Rate %	25
6	Cost per Unit	$8.00
7	Working Days per Year	250
8	Lead Time (Days)	2
9		
10		
11	**Optimal Inventory Policy**	
12		
13	Economic Order Quantity	1824.28
14	Annual Inventory Holding Cost	$1,824.28
15	Annual Ordering Cost	$1,824.28
16	Total Annual Cost	$3,648.56
17	Maximum Inventory Level	1824.28
18	Average Inventory Level	912.14
19	Reorder Point	832.00
20	Number of Orders per Year	57.01
21	Cycle Time (Days)	4.39
22		

TABLE 14.3 THE EOQ MODEL ASSUMPTIONS

1. Demand D is deterministic and occurs at a constant rate.
2. The order quantity Q is the same for each order. The inventory level increases by Q units each time an order is received.
3. The cost per order, C_o, is constant and does not depend on the quantity ordered.
4. The purchase cost per unit, C, is constant and does not depend on the quantity ordered.
5. The inventory holding cost per unit per time period, C_h, is constant. The total inventory holding cost depends on both C_h and the size of the inventory.
6. Shortages such as stock-outs or backorders are not permitted.
7. The lead time for an order is constant.
8. The inventory position is reviewed continuously. As a result, an order is placed as soon as the inventory position reaches the reorder point.

value worksheet in the foreground shows the optimal economic order quantity 1824.28, the total annual cost $3,648.56, and a variety of additional information. If sensitivity analysis is desired, one or more of the input data values can be modified. The impact of any change or changes on the optimal inventory policy will then appear in the worksheet.

The Excel worksheet in Figure 14.4 is a template that can be used for the EOQ model. This worksheet and similar Excel worksheets for the other inventory models presented in this chapter are available on the file named at the WEBfiles link on the Web site that accompanies this text.

Summary of the EOQ Model Assumptions

You should carefully review the assumptions of the inventory model before applying it in an actual situation. Several inventory models discussed later in this chapter alter one or more of the assumptions of the EOQ model.

To use the optimal order quantity and reorder point model described in this section, an analyst must make assumptions about how the inventory system operates. The EOQ model with its economic order quantity formula is based on some specific assumptions about the R&B inventory system. A summary of the assumptions for this model is provided in Table 14.3. Before using the EOQ formula, carefully review these assumptions to ensure that they are applicable to the inventory system being analyzed. If the assumptions are not reasonable, seek a different inventory model.

Various types of inventory systems are used in practice, and the inventory models presented in the following sections alter one or more of the EOQ model assumptions shown in Table 14.3. When the assumptions change, a different inventory model with different optimal operating policies becomes necessary.

NOTES AND COMMENTS

With relatively long lead times, the lead-time demand and the resulting reorder point r, determined by equation (14.6), may exceed $Q*$. If this condition occurs, at least one order will be outstanding when a new order is placed. For example, assume that Bub Beer has a lead time of $m = 6$ days. With a daily demand of $d = 432$ cases, equation (14.6) shows that the reorder point would be $r = dm =$ $6 \times 432 = 2592$ cases. Thus, a new order for Bub Beer should be placed whenever the inventory position (the amount of inventory on hand plus the amount of inventory on order) reaches 2592. With an order quantity of $Q = 2000$ cases, the inventory position of 2592 cases occurs when one order of 2000 cases is outstanding and $2592 - 2000 = 592$ cases are on hand.

14.2 Economic Production Lot Size Model

The inventory model presented in this section is similar to the EOQ model in that we are attempting to determine *how much* we should order and *when* the order should be placed. We again assume a constant demand rate. However, instead of assuming that the order arrives in a shipment of size Q^*, as in the EOQ model, we assume that units are supplied to inventory at a constant rate over several days or several weeks. The **constant supply rate** assumption implies that the same number of units is supplied to inventory each period of time (e.g., 10 units every day or 50 units every week). This model is designed for production situations in which, once an order is placed, production begins and a constant number of units is added to inventory each day until the production run has been completed.

The inventory model in this section alters assumption 2 of the EOQ model (see Table 14.3). The assumption concerning the arrival of Q units each time an order is received is changed to a constant production supply rate.

If we have a production system that produces 50 units per day and we decide to schedule 10 days of production, we have a $50(10) = 500$-unit production lot size. The **lot size** is the number of units in an order. In general, if we let Q indicate the production lot size, the approach to the inventory decisions is similar to the EOQ model; that is, we build a holding and ordering cost model that expresses the total cost as a function of the production lot size. Then we attempt to find the production lot size that minimizes the total cost.

One other condition that should be mentioned at this time is that the model only applies to situations where the production rate is greater than the demand rate; the production system must be able to satisfy demand. For instance, if the constant demand rate is 400 units per day, the production rate must be at least 400 units per day to satisfy demand.

During the production run, demand reduces the inventory while production adds to inventory. Because we assume that the production rate exceeds the demand rate, each day during a production run we produce more units than are demanded. Thus, the excess production causes a gradual inventory buildup during the production period. When the production run is completed, the continuing demand causes the inventory to gradually decline until a new production run is started. The inventory pattern for this system is shown in Figure 14.5.

This model differs from the EOQ model in that a setup cost replaces the ordering cost, and the saw-tooth inventory pattern shown in Figure 14.5 differs from the inventory pattern shown in Figure 14.2.

As in the EOQ model, we are now dealing with two costs, the holding cost and the ordering cost. Here the holding cost is identical to the definition in the EOQ model, but the interpretation of the ordering cost is slightly different. In fact, in a production situation the ordering cost is more correctly referred to as the production **setup cost**. This cost, which includes labor, material, and lost production costs incurred while preparing the production

FIGURE 14.5   INVENTORY PATTERN FOR THE PRODUCTION LOT SIZE
INVENTORY MODEL

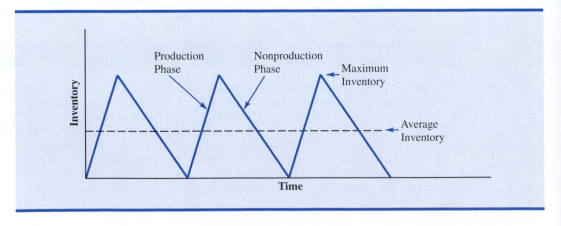

system for operation, is a fixed cost that occurs for every production run regardless of the production lot size.

Total Cost Model

Let us begin building the production lot size model by writing the holding cost in terms of the production lot size Q. Again, the approach is to develop an expression for average inventory and then establish the holding costs associated with the average inventory. We use a one-year time period and an annual cost for the model.

In the EOQ model the average inventory is one-half the maximum inventory, or $\frac{1}{2}Q$. Figure 14.5 shows that for a production lot size model a constant inventory buildup rate occurs during the production run, and a constant inventory depletion rate occurs during the nonproduction period; thus, the average inventory will be one-half the maximum inventory. However, in this inventory system the production lot size Q does not go into inventory at one point in time, and thus the inventory never reaches a level of Q units.

To show how we can compute the maximum inventory, let

$$d = \text{daily demand rate}$$
$$p = \text{daily production rate}$$
$$t = \text{number of days for a production run}$$

Because we are assuming that p will be larger than d, the daily inventory buildup rate during the production phase is $p - d$. If we run production for t days and place $p - d$ units in inventory each day, the inventory at the end of the production run will be $(p - d)t$. From Figure 14.5 we can see that the inventory at the end of the production run is also the maximum inventory. Thus,

At this point, the logic of the production lot size model is easier to follow using a daily demand rate d and a daily production rate p. However, when the total annual cost model is eventually developed, we recommend that inputs to the model be expressed in terms of the annual demand rate D and the annual production rate P.

$$\text{Maximum inventory} = (p - d)t \tag{14.8}$$

If we know we are producing a production lot size of Q units at a daily production rate of p units, then $Q = pt$, and the length of the production run t must be

$$t = \frac{Q}{p} \text{ days} \tag{14.9}$$

Thus,

$$\text{Maximum inventory} = (p - d)t = (p - d)\left(\frac{Q}{p}\right)$$
$$= \left(1 - \frac{d}{p}\right)Q \tag{14.10}$$

The average inventory, which is one-half the maximum inventory, is given by

$$\text{Average inventory} = \frac{1}{2}\left(1 - \frac{d}{p}\right)Q \tag{14.11}$$

With an annual per unit holding cost of C_h, the general equation for annual holding cost is as follows:

$$\begin{pmatrix} \text{Annual} \\ \text{holding cost} \end{pmatrix} = \begin{pmatrix} \text{Average} \\ \text{inventory} \end{pmatrix} \begin{pmatrix} \text{Annual} \\ \text{cost} \\ \text{per unit} \end{pmatrix}$$

$$= \frac{1}{2}\left(1 - \frac{d}{p}\right)QC_h \qquad \text{(14.12)}$$

If D is the annual demand for the product and C_o is the setup cost for a production run, then the annual setup cost, which takes the place of the annual ordering cost in the EOQ model, is as follows:

$$\text{Annual setup cost} = \begin{pmatrix} \text{Number of production} \\ \text{runs per year} \end{pmatrix} \begin{pmatrix} \text{Setup cost} \\ \text{per run} \end{pmatrix}$$

$$= \frac{D}{Q}C_o \qquad \text{(14.13)}$$

Thus, the total annual cost (TC) model is

$$TC = \frac{1}{2}\left(1 - \frac{d}{p}\right)QC_h + \frac{D}{Q}C_o \qquad \text{(14.14)}$$

Suppose that a production facility operates 250 days per year. Then we can write daily demand d in terms of annual demand D as follows:

$$d = \frac{D}{250}$$

Now let P denote the annual production for the product if the product were produced every day. Then

$$P = 250p \qquad \text{and} \qquad p = \frac{P}{250}$$

Thus,[4]

$$\frac{d}{p} = \frac{D/250}{P/250} = \frac{D}{P}$$

Therefore, we can write the total annual cost model as follows:

$$TC = \frac{1}{2}\left(1 - \frac{D}{P}\right)QC_h + \frac{D}{Q}C_o \qquad \text{(14.15)}$$

---

[4]The ratio $d/p = D/P$ holds regardless of the number of days of operation; 250 days is used here merely as an illustration.

Equations (14.14) and (14.15) are equivalent. However, equation (14.15) may be used more frequently because an *annual* cost model tends to make the analyst think in terms of collecting *annual* demand data (D) and *annual* production data (P) rather than daily data.

Economic Production Lot Size

As the production rate P approaches infinity, D/P approaches zero. In this case, equation (14.16) is equivalent to the EOQ model in equation (14.5).

Given estimates of the holding cost (C_h), setup cost (C_o), annual demand rate (D), and annual production rate (P), we could use a trial-and-error approach to compute the total annual cost for various production lot sizes (Q). However, trial and error is not necessary; we can use the minimum cost formula for Q^* that has been developed using differential calculus (see Appendix 14.2). The equation is as follows:

$$Q^* = \sqrt{\frac{2DC_o}{(1 - D/P)C_h}} \qquad (14.16)$$

Lot Size

An Example Beauty Bar Soap is produced on a production line that has an annual capacity of 60,000 cases. The annual demand is estimated at 26,000 cases, with the demand rate essentially constant throughout the year. The cleaning, preparation, and setup of the production line cost approximately $135. The manufacturing cost per case is $4.50, and the annual holding cost is figured at a 24% rate. Thus, $C_h = IC = 0.24(\$4.50) = \$1.08$. What is the recommended production lot size?

Using equation (14.16), we have

$$Q^* = \sqrt{\frac{2(26,000)(135)}{(1 - 26,000/60,000)(1.08)}} = 3387$$

Work Problem 13 as an example of an economic production lot size model.

The total annual cost using equation (14.15) and $Q^* = 3387$ is $2073.

Other relevant data include a five-day lead time to schedule and set up a production run and 250 working days per year. Thus, the lead-time demand of $(26,000/250)(5) = 520$ cases is the reorder point. The cycle time is the time between production runs. Using equation (14.7), the cycle time is $T = 250Q^*/D = [(250)(3387)]/26,000$, or 33 working days. Thus, we should plan a production run of 3387 units every 33 working days.

14.3   Inventory Model with Planned Shortages

A **shortage** or **stock-out** is a demand that cannot be supplied. In many situations, shortages are undesirable and should be avoided if at all possible. However, in other cases it may be desirable—from an economic point of view—to plan for and allow shortages. In practice, these types of situations are most commonly found where the value of the inventory per unit is high and hence the holding cost is high. An example of this type of situation is a new car dealer's inventory. Often a specific car that a customer wants is not in stock. However, if the customer is willing to wait a few weeks, the dealer is usually able to order the car.

The assumptions of the EOQ model in Table 14.3 apply to this inventory model with the exception that shortages, referred to as backorders, are now permitted.

The model developed in this section takes into account a type of shortage known as a **backorder**. In a backorder situation, we assume that when a customer places an order and discovers that the supplier is out of stock, the customer waits until the new shipment arrives, and then the order is filled. Frequently, the waiting period in backorder situations is relatively short. Thus, by promising the customer top priority and immediate delivery when the goods become available, companies may be able to convince the customer to wait until the order arrives. In these cases, the backorder assumption is valid.

The backorder model that we develop is an extension of the EOQ model presented in Section 14.1. We use the EOQ model in which all goods arrive in inventory at one time and are subject to a constant demand rate. If we let S indicate the number of backorders that are accumulated when a new shipment of size Q is received, then the inventory system for the backorder case has the following characteristics:

- If S backorders exist when a new shipment of size Q arrives, then S backorders are shipped to the appropriate customers, and the remaining $Q - S$ units are placed in inventory. Therefore, $Q - S$ is the maximum inventory.
- The inventory cycle of T days is divided into two distinct phases: t_1 days when inventory is on hand and orders are filled as they occur, and t_2 days when stock-outs occur and all new orders are placed on backorder.

The inventory pattern for the inventory model with backorders, where negative inventory represents the number of backorders, is shown in Figure 14.6.

With the inventory pattern now defined, we can proceed with the basic step of all inventory models—namely, the development of a total cost model. For the inventory model with backorders, we encounter the usual holding costs and ordering costs. We also incur a backorder cost in terms of the labor and special delivery costs directly associated with the handling of the backorders. Another portion of the backorder cost accounts for the loss of goodwill because some customers will have to wait for their orders. Because the **goodwill cost** depends on how long a customer has to wait, it is customary to adopt the convention of expressing backorder cost in terms of the cost of having a unit on backorder for a stated period of time. This method of costing backorders on a time basis is similar to the method used to compute the inventory holding cost, and we can use it to compute a total annual cost of backorders once the average backorder level and the backorder cost per unit per period are known.

Let us begin the development of a total cost model by calculating the average inventory for a hypothetical problem. If we have an average inventory of two units for three days and no inventory on the fourth day, what is the average inventory over the four-day period? It is

$$\frac{2 \text{ units } (3 \text{ days}) + 0 \text{ units } (1 \text{ day})}{4 \text{ days}} = \frac{6}{4} = 1.5 \text{ units}$$

FIGURE 14.6 INVENTORY PATTERN FOR AN INVENTORY MODEL WITH BACKORDERS

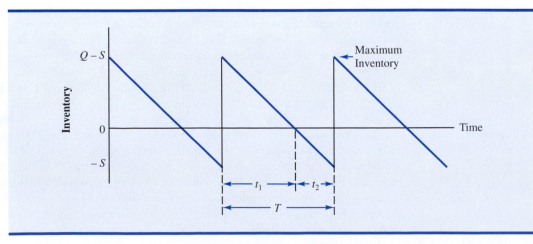

Refer to Figure 14.6. You can see that this situation is what happens in the backorder model. With a maximum inventory of $Q - S$ units, the t_1 days we have inventory on hand will have an average inventory of $(Q - S)/2$. No inventory is carried for the t_2 days in which we experience backorders. Thus, over the total cycle time of $T = t_1 + t_2$ days, we can compute the average inventory as follows:

$$\text{Average inventory} = \frac{\frac{1}{2}(Q - S)t_1 + 0t_2}{t_1 + t_2} = \frac{\frac{1}{2}(Q - S)t_1}{T} \qquad (14.17)$$

Can we find other ways of expressing t_1 and T? Because we know that the maximum inventory is $Q - S$ and that d represents the constant daily demand, we have

$$t_1 = \frac{Q - S}{d} \text{ days} \qquad (14.18)$$

That is, the maximum inventory of $Q - S$ units will be used up in $(Q - S)/d$ days. Because Q units are ordered each cycle, we know the length of a cycle must be

$$T = \frac{Q}{d} \text{ days} \qquad (14.19)$$

Combining equations (14.18) and (14.19) with equation (14.17), we can compute the average inventory as follows:

$$\text{Average inventory} = \frac{\frac{1}{2}(Q - S)[(Q - S)/d]}{Q/d} = \frac{(Q - S)^2}{2Q} \qquad (14.20)$$

Thus, the average inventory is expressed in terms of two inventory decisions: how much we will order (Q) and the maximum number of backorders (S).

The formula for the annual number of orders placed using this model is identical to that for the EOQ model. With D representing the annual demand, we have

$$\text{Annual number of orders} = \frac{D}{Q} \qquad (14.21)$$

The next step is to develop an expression for the average backorder level. Because we know the maximum for backorders is S, we can use the same logic we used to establish average inventory in finding the average number of backorders. We have an average number of backorders during the period t_2 of $\frac{1}{2}$ the maximum number of backorders or $\frac{1}{2}S$. We do not have any backorders during the t_1 days we have inventory; therefore we can calculate the average backorders in a manner similar to equation (14.17). Using this approach, we have

$$\text{Average backorders} = \frac{0 t_1 + (S/2) t_2}{T} = \frac{(S/2) t_2}{T} \tag{14.22}$$

When we let the maximum number of backorders reach an amount S at a daily rate of d, the length of the backorder portion of the inventory cycle is

$$t_2 = \frac{S}{d} \tag{14.23}$$

Using equations (14.23) and (14.19) in equation (14.22), we have

$$\text{Average backorders} = \frac{(S/2)(S/d)}{Q/d} = \frac{S^2}{2Q} \tag{14.24}$$

Let

$$C_h = \text{cost to maintain one unit in inventory for one year}$$
$$C_o = \text{cost per order}$$
$$C_b = \text{cost to maintain one unit on backorder for one year}$$

The total annual cost (TC) for the inventory model with backorders becomes

$$TC = \frac{(Q - S)^2}{2Q} C_h + \frac{D}{Q} C_o + \frac{S^2}{2Q} C_b \tag{14.25}$$

Given C_h, C_o, and C_b and the annual demand D, differential calculus can be used to show that the minimum cost values for the order quantity Q^* and the planned backorders S^* are as follows:

$$Q^* = \sqrt{\frac{2 D C_o}{C_h} \left(\frac{C_h + C_b}{C_b} \right)} \tag{14.26}$$

$$S^* = Q^* \left(\frac{C_h}{C_h + C_b} \right) \tag{14.27}$$

Shortage

An Example Suppose that the Higley Radio Components Company has a product for which the assumptions of the inventory model with backorders are valid. Information obtained by the company is as follows:

$$D = 2000 \text{ units per year}$$
$$I = 20\%$$
$$C = \$50 \text{ per unit}$$
$$C_h = IC = (0.20)(\$50) = \$10 \text{ per unit per year}$$
$$C_o = \$25 = \text{per order}$$

An inventory situation that incorporates backorder costs is considered in Problem 15.

The company is considering the possibility of allowing some backorders to occur for the product. The annual backorder cost is estimated to be $30 per unit per year. Using equations (14.26) and (14.27), we have

$$Q^* = \sqrt{\frac{2(2000)(25)}{10}\left(\frac{10 + 30}{20}\right)} = 115.47$$

The backorder cost C_b is one of the most difficult costs to estimate in inventory models. The reason is that it attempts to measure the cost associated with the loss of goodwill when a customer must wait for an order. Expressing this cost on an annual basis adds to the difficulty.

and

$$S^* = 115\left(\frac{10}{10 + 30}\right) = 28.87$$

If this solution is implemented, the system will operate with the following properties:

$$\text{Maximum inventory} = Q - S = 115.47 - 28.87 = 86.6$$

$$\text{Cycle time} = T = \frac{Q}{D}(250) = \frac{115.47}{2000}(250) = 14.43 \text{ working days}$$

The total annual cost is

If backorders can be tolerated, the total cost including the backorder cost will be less than the total cost of the EOQ model. Some people think the model with backorders will have a greater cost because it includes a backorder cost in addition to the usual inventory holding and ordering costs. You can point out the fallacy in this thinking by noting that the backorder model leads to lower inventory and hence lower inventory holding costs.

$$\text{Holding cost} = \frac{(86.6)^2}{2(115.47)}(10) = \$325$$

$$\text{Ordering cost} = \frac{2000}{115.47}(25) \quad = \$433$$

$$\text{Backorder cost} = \frac{(28.87)^2}{2(115.47)}(30) = \$108$$

$$\text{Total cost} = \$866$$

If the company chooses to prohibit backorders and adopts the regular EOQ model, the recommended inventory decision would be

$$Q^* = \sqrt{\frac{2(2000)(25)}{10}} = \sqrt{10,000} = 100$$

This order quantity would result in a holding cost and an ordering cost of $500 each or a total annual cost of $1000. Thus, in this problem, allowing backorders is projecting a $1000 − $866 = $134, or 13.4%, savings in cost from the no-stock-out EOQ model. The preceding comparison and conclusion are based on the assumption that the backorder model with an annual cost per backordered unit of $30 is a valid model for the actual inventory situation. If the company is concerned that stock-outs might lead to lost sales, then the savings might not be enough to warrant switching to an inventory policy that allowed for planned shortages.

NOTES AND COMMENTS

Equation (14.27) shows that the optimal number of planned backorders S^* is proportional to the ratio $C_h/(C_h + C_b)$, where C_h is the annual holding cost per unit and C_b is the annual backorder cost per unit. Whenever C_h increases, this ratio becomes larger, and the number of planned backorders increases. This relationship explains why items that have a high per-unit cost and a correspondingly high annual holding cost are more economically handled on a backorder basis. On the other hand, whenever the backorder cost C_b increases, the ratio becomes smaller, and the number of planned backorders decreases. Thus, the model provides the intuitive result that items with high backorder costs will be handled with few backorders. In fact, with high backorder costs, the backorder model and the EOQ model with no backordering allowed provide similar inventory policies.

14.4 Quantity Discounts for the EOQ Model

In the quantity discount model, assumption 4 of the EOQ model in Table 14.3 is altered. The cost per unit varies depending on the quantity ordered.

Quantity discounts occur in numerous situations in which suppliers provide an incentive for large order quantities by offering a lower purchase cost when items are ordered in larger quantities. In this section we show how the EOQ model can be used when quantity discounts are available.

Assume that we have a product in which the basic EOQ model (see Table 14.3) is applicable. Instead of a fixed unit cost, the supplier quotes the following discount schedule:

Discount Category	Order Size	Discount (%)	Unit Cost
1	0 to 999	0	$5.00
2	1000 to 2499	3	4.85
3	2500 and over	5	4.75

The 5% discount for the 2500-unit minimum order quantity looks tempting. However, realizing that higher order quantities result in higher inventory holding costs, we should prepare a thorough cost analysis before making a final ordering and inventory policy recommendation.

Suppose that the data and cost analyses show an annual holding cost rate of 20%, an ordering cost of $49 per order, and an annual demand of 5000 units; what order quantity should we select? The following three-step procedure shows the calculations necessary to make this decision. In the preliminary calculations, we use Q_1 to indicate the order quantity for discount category 1, Q_2 for discount category 2, and Q_3 for discount category 3.

Step 1. For each discount category, compute a Q^* using the EOQ formula based on the unit cost associated with the discount category.

Recall that the EOQ model provides $Q^* = \sqrt{2DC_o/C_h}$, where $C_h = IC = (0.20)C$. With three discount categories providing three different unit costs C, we obtain

Discount

$$Q_1^* = \sqrt{\frac{2(5000)49}{(0.20)(5.00)}} = 700$$

$$Q_2^* = \sqrt{\frac{2(5000)49}{(0.20)(4.85)}} = 711$$

$$Q_3^* = \sqrt{\frac{2(5000)49}{(0.20)(4.75)}} = 718$$

Because the only differences in the EOQ formulas come from slight differences in the holding cost, the economic order quantities resulting from this step will be approximately the same. However, these order quantities will usually not all be of the size necessary to qualify for the discount price assumed. In the preceding case, both Q_2^* and Q_3^* are insufficient order quantities to obtain their assumed discounted costs of $4.85 and $4.75, respectively. For those order quantities for which the assumed price cannot be obtained, the following procedure must be used:

Step 2. For the Q^* that is too small to qualify for the assumed discount price, adjust the order quantity upward to the nearest order quantity that will allow the product to be purchased at the assumed price.

TABLE 14.4 TOTAL ANNUAL COST CALCULATIONS FOR THE EOQ MODEL WITH QUANTITY DISCOUNTS

Discount Category	Unit Cost	Order Quantity	Annual Cost Holding	Annual Cost Ordering	Annual Cost Purchase	Total
1	$5.00	700	$ 350	$350	$25,000	$25,700
2	4.85	1000	$ 485	$245	$24,250	$24,980
3	4.75	2500	$1188	$ 98	$23,750	$25,036

In our example, this adjustment causes us to set

$$Q_2^* = 1000$$

and

$$Q_3^* = 2500$$

Problem 23 at the end of the chapter asks you to show that this property is true.

If a calculated Q^* for a given discount price is large enough to qualify for a bigger discount, that value of Q^* cannot lead to an optimal solution. Although the reason may not be obvious, it does turn out to be a property of the EOQ quantity discount model.

In the EOQ model with quantity discounts, the annual purchase cost must be included because purchase cost depends on the order quantity. Thus, it is a relevant cost.

In the previous inventory models considered, the annual purchase cost of the item was not included because it was constant and never affected by the inventory order policy decision. However, in the quantity discount model, the annual purchase cost depends on the order quantity and the associated unit cost. Thus, annual purchase cost (annual demand $D \times$ unit cost C) is included in the equation for total cost as shown here.

$$TC = \frac{Q}{2}C_h + \frac{D}{Q}C_o + DC \qquad (14.28)$$

Using this total cost equation, we can determine the optimal order quantity for the EOQ discount model in step 3.

Step 3. For each order quantity resulting from steps 1 and 2, compute the total annual cost using the unit price from the appropriate discount category and equation (14.28). The order quantity yielding the minimum total annual cost is the optimal order quantity.

Problem 21 will give you practice in applying the EOQ model to situations with quantity discounts.

The step 3 calculations for the example problem are summarized in Table 14.4. As you can see, a decision to order 1000 units at the 3% discount rate yields the minimum cost solution. Even though the 2500-unit order quantity would result in a 5% discount, its excessive holding cost makes it the second-best solution. Figure 14.7 shows the total cost curve for each of the three discount categories. Note that $Q^* = 1000$ provides the minimum cost order quantity.

14.5 Single-Period Inventory Model with Probabilistic Demand

The inventory models discussed thus far were based on the assumption that the demand rate is constant and **deterministic** throughout the year. We developed minimum cost order quantity and reorder point policies based on this assumption. In situations in which the demand rate is not deterministic, other models treat demand as **probabilistic** and best described by

FIGURE 14.7   TOTAL COST CURVES FOR THE THREE DISCOUNT CATEGORIES

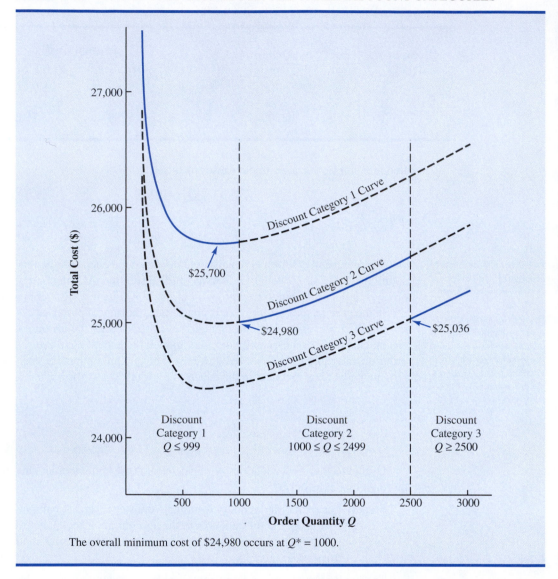

The overall minimum cost of $24,980 occurs at $Q^* = 1000$.

This inventory model is the first in the chapter that explicitly treats probabilistic demand. Unlike the EOQ model, it is for a single period with unused inventory not carried over to future periods.

a probability distribution. In this section we consider a **single-period inventory model** with probabilistic demand.

The single-period inventory model refers to inventory situations in which *one* order is placed for the product; at the end of the period, the product has either sold out, or a surplus of unsold items will be sold for a salvage value. The single-period inventory model is applicable in situations involving seasonal or perishable items that cannot be carried in inventory and sold in future periods. Seasonal clothing (such as bathing suits and winter coats) are typically handled in a single-period manner. In these situations, a buyer places one preseason order for each item and then experiences a stock-out or holds a clearance sale on the surplus stock at the end of the season. No items are carried in inventory and sold the following year. Newspapers are another example of a product that is ordered one time and is either sold or not sold during the single period. Although newspapers are ordered daily, they cannot be carried in inventory and sold in later periods. Thus, newspaper orders may be treated as a sequence of single-period models; that is, each day or period is separate, and a single-period inventory decision must be made each period (day). Because we order only once for the period, the only inventory decision we must make is *how much* of the product to order at the start of the period.

Obviously, if the demand were known for a single-period inventory situation, the solution would be easy; we would simply order the amount we knew would be demanded. However, in most single-period models, the exact demand is not known. In fact, forecasts may show that demand can have a wide variety of values. If we are going to analyze this type of inventory problem in a quantitative manner, we need information about the probabilities associated with the various demand values. Thus, the single-period model presented in this section is based on probabilistic demand.

Johnson Shoe Company

Let us consider a single-period inventory model that could be used to make a how-much-to-order decision for the Johnson Shoe Company. The buyer for the Johnson Shoe Company decided to order a men's shoe shown at a buyers' meeting in New York City. The shoe will be part of the company's spring–summer promotion and will be sold through nine retail stores in the Chicago area. Because the shoe is designed for spring and summer months, it cannot be expected to sell in the fall. Johnson plans to hold a special August clearance sale in an attempt to sell all shoes not sold by July 31. The shoes cost $40 a pair and retail for $60 a pair. At the sale price of $30 a pair, all surplus shoes can be expected to sell during the August sale. If you were the buyer for the Johnson Shoe Company, how many pairs of the shoes would you order?

An obvious question at this time is, What are the possible values of demand for the shoe? We need this information to answer the question of how much to order. Let us suppose that the uniform probability distribution shown in Figure 14.8 can be used to describe the demand for the size 10D shoes. In particular, note that the range of demand is from 350 to 650 pairs of shoes, with an average, or expected, demand of 500 pairs of shoes.

Incremental analysis is a method that can be used to determine the optimal order quantity for a single-period inventory model. Incremental analysis addresses the how-much-to-order question by comparing the cost or loss of *ordering one additional unit* with the cost or loss of *not ordering one additional unit*. The costs involved are defined as follows:

c_o = cost per unit of *overestimating* demand. This cost represents the loss of ordering one additional unit and finding that it cannot be sold.

c_u = cost per unit of *underestimating* demand. This cost represents the opportunity loss of not ordering one additional unit and finding that it could have been sold.

FIGURE 14.8   UNIFORM PROBABILITY DISTRIBUTION OF DEMAND FOR THE JOHNSON SHOE COMPANY PROBLEM

In the Johnson Shoe Company problem, the company will incur the cost of overestimating demand whenever it orders too much and has to sell the extra shoes during the August sale. Thus, the cost per unit of overestimating demand is equal to the purchase cost per unit minus the August sales price per unit; that is, $c_o = \$40 - \$30 = \$10$. Therefore, Johnson will lose \$10 for each pair of shoes that it orders over the quantity demanded. The cost of underestimating demand is the lost profit because a pair of shoes that could have been sold was not available in inventory. Thus, the per-unit cost of underestimating demand is the difference between the regular selling price per unit and the purchase cost per unit; that is, $c_u = \$60 - \$40 = \$20$.

The cost of underestimating demand is usually harder to determine than the cost of overestimating demand. The reason is that the cost of underestimating demand includes a lost profit and may include a customer goodwill cost because the customer is unable to purchase the item when desired.

Because the exact level of demand for the size 10D shoes is unknown, we have to consider the probability of demand and thus the probability of obtaining the associated costs or losses. For example, let us assume that Johnson Shoe Company management wishes to consider an order quantity equal to the average or expected demand for 500 pairs of shoes. In incremental analysis, we consider the possible losses associated with an order quantity of 501 (ordering one additional unit) and an order quantity of 500 (not ordering one additional unit). The order quantity alternatives and the possible losses are summarized here.

The key to incremental analysis is to focus on the costs that are different when comparing an order quantity $Q + 1$ to an order quantity Q.

Order Quantity Alternatives	Loss Occurs If	Possible Loss	Probability Loss Occurs
$Q = 501$	Demand overestimated; the additional unit *cannot* be sold	$c_o = \$10$	$P(\text{demand} \leq 500)$
$Q = 500$	Demand underestimated; an additional unit *could have* been sold	$c_u = \$20$	$P(\text{demand} > 500)$

Using the demand probability distribution in Figure 14.8, we see that $P(\text{demand} \leq 500) = 0.50$ and that $P(\text{demand} > 500) = 0.50$. By multiplying the possible losses, $c_o = \$10$ and $c_u = \$20$, by the probability of obtaining the loss, we can compute the expected value of the loss, or simply the *expected loss* (EL), associated with the order quantity alternatives. Thus,

$$\text{EL}(Q = 501) = c_o P(\text{demand} \leq 500) = \$10(0.50) = \$5$$
$$\text{EL}(Q = 500) = c_u P(\text{demand} > 500) = \$20(0.50) = \$10$$

Based on these expected losses, do you prefer an order quantity of 501 or 500 pairs of shoes? Because the expected loss is greater for $Q = 500$, and because we want to avoid this higher cost or loss, we should make $Q = 501$ the preferred decision. We could now consider incrementing the order quantity one additional unit to $Q = 502$ and repeating the expected loss calculations.

Although we could continue this unit-by-unit analysis, it would be time-consuming and cumbersome. We would have to evaluate $Q = 502$, $Q = 503$, $Q = 504$, and so on, until we found the value of Q where the expected loss of ordering one incremental unit is equal to the expected loss of not ordering one incremental unit; that is, the optimal order quantity Q^* occurs when the incremental analysis shows that

$$\text{EL}(Q^* + 1) = \text{EL}(Q^*) \qquad \textbf{(14.29)}$$

When this relationship holds, increasing the order quantity by one additional unit has no economic advantage. Using the logic with which we computed the expected losses for the order quantities of 501 and 500, the general expressions for $EL(Q^* + 1)$ and $EL(Q^*)$ can be written

$$EL(Q^* + 1) = c_{\text{o}}P(\text{demand} \le Q^*) \tag{14.30}$$

$$EL(Q^*) = c_{\text{u}}P(\text{demand} > Q^*) \tag{14.31}$$

Because we know from basic probability that

$$P(\text{demand} \le Q^*) + P(\text{demand} > Q^*) = 1 \tag{14.32}$$

we can write

$$P(\text{demand} > Q^*) = 1 - P(\text{demand} \le Q^*) \tag{14.33}$$

Using this expression, equation (14.31) can be rewritten as

$$EL(Q^*) = c_{\text{u}}[1 - P(\text{demand} \le Q^*)] \tag{14.34}$$

Equations (14.30) and (14.34) can be used to show that $EL(Q^* + 1) = EL(Q^*)$ whenever

$$c_{\text{o}}P(\text{demand} \le Q^*) = c_{\text{u}}[1 - P(\text{demand} \le Q^*)] \tag{14.35}$$

Solving for $P(\text{demand} \le Q^*)$, we have

$$P(\text{demand} \le Q^*) = \frac{c_{\text{u}}}{c_{\text{u}} + c_{\text{o}}} \tag{14.36}$$

This expression provides the general condition for the optimal order quantity Q^* in the single-period inventory model.

In the Johnson Shoe Company problem $c_{\text{o}} = \$10$ and $c_{\text{u}} = \$20$. Thus, equation (14.36) shows that the optimal order size for Johnson shoes must satisfy the following condition:

$$P(\text{demand} \le Q^*) = \frac{c_{\text{u}}}{c_{\text{u}} + c_{\text{o}}} = \frac{20}{20 + 10} = \frac{20}{30} = \frac{2}{3}$$

We can find the optimal order quantity Q^* by referring to the probability distribution shown in Figure 14.8 and finding the value of Q that will provide $P(\text{demand} \le Q^*) = 2/3$. To find this solution, we note that in the uniform distribution the probability is evenly distributed over the entire range of 350–650 pairs of shoes. Thus, we can satisfy the expression for Q^* by moving two-thirds of the way from 350 to 650. Because this range is $650 - 350 = 300$, we move 200 units from 350 toward 650. Doing so provides the optimal order quantity of 550 pairs of shoes.

In summary, the key to establishing an optimal order quantity for single-period inventory models is to identify the probability distribution that describes the demand for the item and the costs of overestimation and underestimation. Then, using the information for the costs of overestimation and underestimation, equation (14.36) can be used to find the location of Q^* in the probability distribution.

Nationwide Car Rental

As another example of a single-period inventory model with probabilistic demand, consider the situation faced by Nationwide Car Rental. Nationwide must decide how many automobiles to have available at each car rental location at specific points in time throughout the year. Using the Myrtle Beach, South Carolina, location as an example, management would like to know the number of full-sized automobiles to have available for the Labor Day weekend. Based on previous experience, customer demand for full-sized automobiles for the Labor Day weekend has a normal distribution with a mean of 150 automobiles and a standard deviation of 14 automobiles.

The Nationwide Car Rental situation can benefit from use of a single-period inventory model. The company must establish the number of full-sized automobiles to have available prior to the weekend. Customer demand over the weekend will then result in either a stock-out or a surplus. Let us denote the number of full-sized automobiles available by Q. If Q is greater than customer demand, Nationwide will have a surplus of cars. The cost of a surplus is the cost of overestimating demand. This cost is set at $80 per car, which reflects, in part, the opportunity cost of not having the car available for rent elsewhere.

If Q is less than customer demand, Nationwide will rent all available cars and experience a stock-out or shortage. A shortage results in an underestimation cost of $200 per car. This figure reflects the cost due to lost profit and the lost goodwill of not having a car available for a customer. Given this information, how many full-sized automobiles should Nationwide make available for the Labor Day weekend?

Using the cost of underestimation, $c_u = \$200$, and the cost of overestimation, $c_o = \$80$, equation (14.36) indicates that the optimal order quantity must satisfy the following condition:

$$P(\text{demand} \leq Q^*) = \frac{c_u}{(c_u + c_o)} = \frac{200}{200 + 80} = 0.7143$$

We can use the normal probability distribution for demand as shown in Figure 14.9 to find the order quantity that satisfies the condition that $P(\text{demand} \leq Q^*) = 0.7143$. From Appendix D, we see that 0.7143 of the area in the left tail of the normal probability distribution occurs at $z = 0.57$ standard deviations *above* the mean. With a mean demand of $\mu = 150$ automobiles and a standard deviation of $\sigma = 14$ automobiles, we have

$$Q^* = \mu + 0.57\sigma$$
$$= 150 + 0.57(14) = 158$$

WEB file

Single-Period

An example of a single-period inventory model with probabilistic demand described by a normal probability distribution is considered in Problem 25.

Thus, Nationwide Car Rental should plan to have 158 full-sized automobiles available in Myrtle Beach for the Labor Day weekend. Note that in this case the cost of overestimation is less than the cost of underestimation. Thus, Nationwide is willing to risk a higher probability of overestimating demand and hence a higher probability of a surplus. In fact, Nationwide's optimal order quantity has a 0.7143 probability of a surplus and a $1 - 0.7143 = 0.2857$ probability of a stock-out. As a result, the probability is 0.2857 that all 158 full-sized automobiles will be rented during the Labor Day weekend.

FIGURE 14.9   PROBABILITY DISTRIBUTION OF DEMAND FOR THE NATIONWIDE
CAR RENTAL PROBLEM SHOWING THE LOCATION OF Q^*

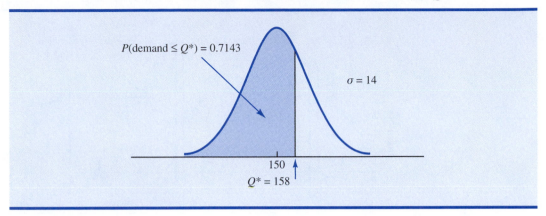

$P(\text{demand} \leq Q^*) = 0.7143$

$\sigma = 14$

150

$Q^* = 158$

NOTES AND COMMENTS

1. In any probabilistic inventory model, the assumption about the probability distribution for demand is critical and can affect the recommended inventory decision. In the problems presented in this section, we used the uniform and the normal probability distributions to describe demand. In some situations, other probability distributions may be more appropriate. In using probabilistic inventory models, we must exercise care in selecting the probability distribution that most realistically describes demand.

2. In the single-period inventory model, the value of $c_u/(c_u + c_o)$ plays a critical role in selecting the order quantity [see equation (14.36)]. Whenever $c_u = c_o$, $c_u/(c_u + c_o)$ equals 0.50; in this case, we should select an order quantity corresponding to the median demand. With this choice, a stock-out is just as likely as a surplus because the two costs are equal. However, whenever $c_u < c_o$, a smaller order quantity will be recommended. In this case, the smaller order quantity will provide a higher probability of a stock-out; however, the more expensive cost of overestimating demand and having a surplus will tend to be avoided. Finally, whenever $c_u > c_o$, a larger order quantity will be recommended. In this case, the larger order quantity provides a lower probability of a stock-out in an attempt to avoid the more expensive cost of underestimating demand and experiencing a stock-out.

 ## 14.6   Order–Quantity, Reorder Point Model with Probabilistic Demand

The inventory model in this section is based on the assumptions of the EOQ model shown in Table 14.3 with the exception that demand is probabilistic rather than deterministic. With probabilistic demand, occasional shortages may occur.

In the previous section we considered a single-period inventory model with probabilistic demand. In this section we extend our discussion to a multiperiod order-quantity, reorder point inventory model with probabilistic demand. In the multiperiod model, the inventory system operates continuously with many repeating periods or cycles; inventory can be carried from one period to the next. Whenever the inventory position reaches the reorder point, an order for Q units is placed. Because demand is probabilistic, the time the reorder point will be reached, the time between orders, and the time the order of Q units will arrive in inventory cannot be determined in advance.

The inventory pattern for the order-quantity, reorder point model with probabilistic demand will have the general appearance shown in Figure 14.10. Note that the increases, or

FIGURE 14.10   INVENTORY PATTERN FOR AN ORDER-QUANTITY, REORDER POINT
MODEL WITH PROBABILISTIC DEMAND

jumps, in the inventory occur whenever an order of Q units arrives. The inventory decreases
at a nonconstant rate based on the probabilistic demand. A new order is placed whenever
the reorder point is reached. At times, the order quantity of Q units will arrive before inventory reaches zero. However, at other times, higher demand will cause a stock-out before
a new order is received. As with other order-quantity, reorder point models, the manager
must determine the order quantity Q and the reorder point r for the inventory system.

The exact mathematical formulation of an order-quantity, reorder point inventory
model with probabilistic demand is beyond the scope of this text. However, we present a
procedure that can be used to obtain good, workable order quantity and reorder point inventory policies. The solution procedure can be expected to provide only an approximation
of the optimal solution, but it can yield good solutions in many practical situations.

Let us consider the inventory problem of Dabco Industrial Lighting Distributors. Dabco
purchases a special high-intensity lightbulb for industrial lighting systems from a well-
known lightbulb manufacturer. Dabco would like a recommendation on how much to order
and when to order so that a low-cost inventory policy can be maintained. Pertinent facts are
that the ordering cost is $12 per order, one bulb costs $6, and Dabco uses a 20% annual
holding cost rate for its inventory ($C_h = IC = 0.20 \times \$6 = \$1.20$). Dabco, which has more
than 1000 customers, experiences a probabilistic demand; in fact, the number of units demanded varies considerably from day to day and from week to week. The lead time for a
new order of lightbulbs is one week. Historical sales data indicate that demand during a one-
week lead time can be described by a normal probability distribution with a mean of 154
lightbulbs and a standard deviation of 25 lightbulbs. The normal distribution of demand during the lead time is shown in Figure 14.11. Because the mean demand during one week is
154 units, Dabco can anticipate a mean or expected annual demand of 154 units per week $\times$
52 weeks per year = 8008 units per year.

The How-Much-to-Order Decision

Although we are in a probabilistic demand situation, we have an estimate of the expected
annual demand of 8008 units. We can apply the EOQ model from Section 14.1 as an

FIGURE 14.11   LEAD-TIME DEMAND PROBABILITY DISTRIBUTION
FOR DABCO LIGHTBULBS

approximation of the best order quantity, with the expected annual demand used for D. In Dabco's case

$$Q^* = \sqrt{\frac{2DC_o}{C_h}} = \sqrt{\frac{2(8008)(12)}{(1.20)}} = 400 \text{ units}$$

When we studied the sensitivity of the EOQ model, we learned that the total cost of operating an inventory system was relatively insensitive to order quantities that were in the neighborhood of Q^*. Using this knowledge, we expect 400 units per order to be a good approximation of the optimal order quantity. Even if annual demand were as low as 7000 units or as high as 9000 units, an order quantity of 400 units should be a relatively good low-cost order size. Thus, given our best estimate of annual demand at 8008 units, we will use $Q^* = 400$.

We have established the 400-unit order quantity by ignoring the fact that demand is probabilistic. Using $Q^* = 400$, Dabco can anticipate placing approximately $D/Q^* = 8008/400 = 20$ orders per year with an average of approximately $250/20 = 12.5$ working days between orders.

The When-to-Order Decision

The probability of a stock-out during any one inventory cycle is easiest to estimate by first determining the number of orders that are expected during the year. The inventory manager can usually state a willingness to allow perhaps one, two, or three stock-outs during the year. The allowable stock-outs per year divided by the number of orders per year will provide the desired probability of a stock-out.

We now want to establish a when-to-order decision rule or reorder point that will trigger the ordering process. With a mean lead-time demand of 154 units, you might first suggest a 154-unit reorder point. However, considering the probability of demand now becomes extremely important. If 154 is the mean lead-time demand, and if demand is symmetrically distributed about 154, then the lead-time demand will be more than 154 units roughly 50% of the time. When the demand during the one-week lead time exceeds 154 units, Dabco will experience a shortage or stock-out. Thus, using a reorder point of 154 units, approximately 50% of the time (10 of the 20 orders a year) Dabco will be short of bulbs before the new supply arrives. This shortage rate would most likely be viewed as unacceptable.

Refer to the **lead-time demand distribution** shown in Figure 14.11. Given this distribution, we can now determine how the reorder point r affects the probability of a stock-out. Because stock-outs occur whenever the demand during the lead time exceeds the reorder point, we can find the probability of a stock-out by using the lead-time demand distribution to compute the probability that demand will exceed r.

We could now approach the when-to-order problem by defining a cost per stock-out and then attempting to include this cost in a total cost equation. Alternatively, we can ask

FIGURE 14.12   REORDER POINT r THAT ALLOWS A 5% CHANCE OF A STOCK-OUT FOR DABCO LIGHTBULBS

management to specify the average number of stock-outs that can be tolerated per year. If demand for a product is probabilistic, a manager who will never tolerate a stock-out is being somewhat unrealistic because attempting to avoid stock-outs completely will require high reorder points, high inventory, and an associated high holding cost.

Suppose in this case that Dabco management is willing to tolerate an average of one stock-out per year. Because Dabco places 20 orders per year, this decision implies that management is willing to allow demand during lead time to exceed the reorder point one time in 20, or 5% of the time. The reorder point r can be found by using the lead-time demand distribution to find the value of r with a 5% chance of having a lead-time demand that will exceed it. This situation is shown graphically in Figure 14.12.

From the standard normal probability distribution table in Appendix D, we see that the r value is 1.645 standard deviations above the mean. Therefore, for the assumed normal distribution for lead-time demand with $\mu = 154$ and $\sigma = 25$, the reorder point r is

$$r = 154 + 1.645(25) = 195$$

If a normal distribution is used for lead-time demand, the general equation for r is

$$r = \mu + z\sigma \qquad\qquad \textbf{(14.37)}$$

where z is the number of standard deviations necessary to obtain the acceptable stock-out probability.

Thus, the recommended inventory decision is to order 400 units whenever the inventory reaches the reorder point of 195. Because the mean or expected demand during the lead time is 154 units, the $195 - 154 = 41$ units serve as a **safety stock**, which absorbs higher-than-usual demand during the lead time. Roughly 95% of the time, the 195 units will be able to satisfy demand during the lead time. The anticipated annual cost for this system is as follows:

Try Problem 29 as an example of an order-quantity, reorder point model with probabilistic demand.

Holding cost, normal inventory $(Q/2)C_h =$	$(400/2)(1.20) =$	$240
Holding cost, safety stock $\quad\quad (41)C_h =$	$41(1.20) =$	$ 49
Ordering cost $\quad\quad\quad\quad (D/Q)C_o =$	$(8008/400)12 =$	$240
	Total	$529

If Dabco could assume that a known, constant demand rate of 8008 units per year existed for the lightbulbs, then $Q^* = 400$, $r = 154$, and a total annual cost of $240 + $240 = $480 would be optimal. When demand is uncertain and can only be expressed in probabilistic terms, a larger total cost can be expected. The larger cost occurs in the form of larger holding costs because more inventory must be maintained to limit the number of stock-outs. For Dabco, this additional inventory or safety stock was 41 units, with an additional annual holding cost of $49. The Q.M. in Action, Lowering Inventory Cost at Dutch Companies, describes how a warehouser in the Netherlands implemented an order-quantity, reorder point system with probabilistic demand.

Q.M. *in* ACTION

LOWERING INVENTORY COST AT DUTCH COMPANIES*

In the Netherlands, companies such as Philips, Rank Xerox, and Fokker have followed the trend of developing closer relations between the firm and its suppliers. As teamwork, coordination, and information sharing improve, opportunities are available for better cost control in the operation of inventory systems.

One Dutch public warehouser has a contract with its supplier under which the supplier routinely provides information regarding the status and schedule of upcoming production runs. The warehouser's inventory system operates as an order-quantity, reorder point system with

*Based on F. A. van der Duyn Schouten, M. J. G. van Eijs, and R. M. J. Heuts, "The Value of Supplier Information to Improve Management of a Retailer's Inventory," Decision Sciences 25, no. 1 (January/February 1994): 1–14.

probabilistic demand. When the order quantity Q has been determined, the warehouser selects the desired reorder point for the product. The distribution of the lead-time demand is essential in determining the reorder point. Usually, the lead-time demand distribution is approximated directly, taking into account both the probabilistic demand and the probabilistic length of the lead-time period.

The supplier's information concerning scheduled production runs provides the warehouser with a better understanding of the lead time involved for a product and the resulting lead-time demand distribution. With this information, the warehouse can modify the reorder point accordingly. Information sharing by the supplier thus enables the order-quantity, reorder point system to operate with a lower inventory holding cost.

NOTES AND COMMENTS

The Dabco reorder point was based on a 5% probability of a stock-out during the lead-time period. Thus, on 95% of all order cycles Dabco will be able to satisfy customer demand without experiencing a stock-out. Defining service level as the percentage of all order cycles that do not experience a stock-out, we would say that Dabco has a 95% service level. However, other definitions of service level may include the percentage of all customer demand that can be satisfied from inventory. Thus, when an inventory manager expresses a desired service level, it is a good idea to clarify exactly what the manager means by the term *service level*.

14.7 Periodic Review Model with Probabilistic Demand

The order-quantity, reorder point inventory models previously discussed require a **continuous review inventory system**. In a continuous review inventory system, the inventory position is monitored continuously so that an order can be placed whenever the reorder point is reached. Computerized inventory systems can easily provide the continuous review required by the order-quantity, reorder point models.

An alternative to the continuous review system is the **periodic review inventory system**. With a periodic review system, the inventory is checked and reordering is done only at specified points in time. For example, inventory may be checked and orders placed on a weekly, biweekly, monthly, or some other periodic basis. When a firm or business handles multiple products, the periodic review system offers the advantage of requiring that orders for several items be placed at the same preset periodic review time. With this type of inventory system, the shipping and receiving of orders for multiple products are easily coordinated. Under the previously discussed order-quantity, reorder point systems, the reorder points for various products can be encountered at substantially different points in time, making the coordination of orders for multiple products more difficult.

To illustrate this system, let us consider Dollar Discounts, a firm with several retail stores that carry a wide variety of products for household use. The company operates its inventory system with a two-week periodic review. Under this system, a retail store manager may order any number of units of any product from the Dollar Discounts central warehouse every two weeks. Orders for all products going to a particular store are combined into one shipment. When making the order quantity decision for each product at a given review period, the store manager knows that a reorder for the product cannot be made until the next review period.

Assuming that the lead time is less than the length of the review period, an order placed at a review period will be received prior to the next review period. In this case, the how-much-to-order decision at any review period is determined using the following:

$$Q = M - H \tag{14.38}$$

where

$$Q = \text{the order quantity}$$
$$M = \text{the replenishment level}$$
$$H = \text{the inventory on hand at the review period}$$

Because the demand is probabilistic, the inventory on hand at the review period, H, will vary. Thus, the order quantity that must be sufficient to bring the inventory position back to its maximum or replenishment level M can be expected to vary each period. For example, if the replenishment level for a particular product is 50 units, and the inventory on hand at the review period is $H = 12$ units, an order of $Q = M - H = 50 - 12 = 38$ units should be made. Thus, under the periodic review model, enough units are ordered each review period to bring the inventory position back up to the replenishment level.

A typical inventory pattern for a periodic review system with probabilistic demand is shown in Figure 14.13. Note that the time between periodic reviews is predetermined and fixed. The order quantity Q at each review period can vary and is shown to be the difference between the replenishment level and the inventory on hand. Finally, as with other probabilistic models, an unusually high demand can result in an occasional stock-out.

The decision variable in the periodic review model is the replenishment level M. To determine M, we could begin by developing a total cost model, including holding, ordering, and stock-out costs. Instead, we describe an approach that is often used in practice. In this approach, the objective is to determine a replenishment level that will meet a desired performance level, such as a reasonably low probability of stock-out or a reasonably low number of stock-outs per year.

In the Dollar Discounts problem, we assume that management's objective is to determine the replenishment level with only a 1% chance of a stock-out. In the periodic review

FIGURE 14.13   INVENTORY PATTERN FOR PERIODIC REVIEW MODEL
WITH PROBABILISTIC DEMAND

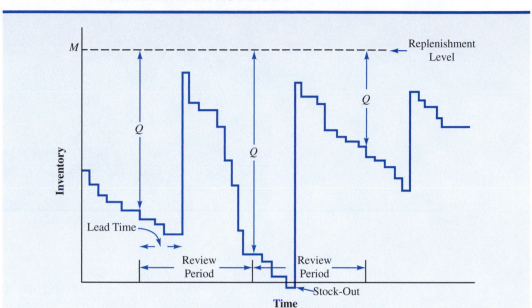

model, the order quantity at each review period must be sufficient to cover demand for the
review period plus the demand for the following lead time. That is, the order quantity that
brings the inventory position up to the replenishment level M must last until the order made
at the next review period is received in inventory. The length of this time is equal to the review period plus the lead time. Figure 14.14 shows the normal probability distribution of
demand during the review period plus the lead-time period for one of the Dollar Discounts
products. The mean demand is 250 units, and the standard deviation of demand is 45 units.
Given this situation, the logic used to establish M is similar to the logic used to establish
the reorder point in Section 14.6. Figure 14.15 shows the replenishment level M with a 1%
chance that demand will exceed that replenishment level. In other words, Figure 14.15

FIGURE 14.14   PROBABILITY DISTRIBUTION OF DEMAND DURING THE REVIEW
PERIOD AND LEAD TIME FOR THE DOLLAR DISCOUNTS PROBLEM

FIGURE 14.15 REPLENISHMENT LEVEL *M* THAT ALLOWS A 1% CHANCE OF A STOCK-OUT FOR THE DOLLAR DISCOUNTS PROBLEM

shows the replenishment level that allows a 1% chance of a stock-out associated with the replenishment decision. Using the normal probability distribution table in Appendix D, we see that a value of *M* that is 2.33 standard deviations above the mean will allow stock-outs with a 1% probability. Therefore, for the assumed normal probability distribution with $\mu = 250$ and $\sigma = 45$, the replenishment level is determined by

$$M = 250 + 2.33(45) = 355$$

Periodic

Problem 33 gives you practice in computing the replenishment level for a periodic review model with probabilistic demand.

Although other probability distributions can be used to express the demand during the review period plus the lead-time period, if the normal probability distribution is used, the general expression for *M* is

$$M = \mu + z\sigma \qquad \text{(14.39)}$$

where *z* is the number of standard deviations necessary to obtain the acceptable stock-out probability.

Periodic review systems provide advantages of coordinated orders for multiple items. However, periodic review systems require larger safety stock levels than corresponding continuous review systems.

If demand had been deterministic rather than probabilistic, the replenishment level would have been the demand during the review period plus the demand during the lead-time period. In this case, the replenishment level would have been 250 units, and no stock-out would have occurred. However, with the probabilistic demand, we have seen that higher inventory is necessary to allow for uncertain demand and to control the probability of a stock-out. In the Dollar Discounts problem, $355 - 250 = 105$ is the safety stock that is necessary to absorb any higher-than-usual demand during the review period plus the demand during the lead-time period. This safety stock limits the probability of a stock-out to 1%.

More Complex Periodic Review Models

The periodic review model just discussed is one approach to determining a replenishment level for the periodic review inventory system with probabilistic demand. More complex versions of the periodic review model incorporate a reorder point as another decision variable; that is, instead of ordering at every periodic review, a reorder point is established. If the inventory on hand at the periodic review is at or below the reorder point, a decision is made to order up to the replenishment level. However, if the inventory on hand at the periodic review is greater than the reorder level, such an order is not placed, and the system continues until the next periodic review. In this case, the cost of ordering is a relevant cost and can be included in a cost model along with holding and stock-out costs. Optimal policies can be reached based on minimizing the expected total cost. Situations with lead times longer than the review period add to the complexity of the model. The mathematical level required to treat these more extensive periodic review models is beyond the scope of this text.

NOTES AND COMMENTS

1. The periodic review model presented in this section is based on the assumption that the lead time for an order is less than the periodic review period. Most periodic review systems operate under this condition. However, the case in which the lead time is longer than the review period can be handled by defining H in equation (14.38) as the inventory position, where H includes the inventory on hand plus the inventory on order. In this case, the order quantity at any review period is the amount needed for the inventory on hand plus all outstanding orders needed to reach the replenishment level.

2. In the order-quantity, reorder point model discussed in Section 14.6, a continuous review was used to initiate an order whenever the reorder point was reached. The safety stock for this model was based on the probabilistic demand during the lead time. The periodic review model presented in this section also determined a recommended safety stock. However, because the inventory review was only periodic, the safety stock was based on the probabilistic demand during the review period plus the lead-time period. This longer period for the safety stock computation means that periodic review systems tend to require a larger safety stock than do continuous review systems.

Summary

In this chapter we presented some of the approaches management scientists use to assist managers in establishing low-cost inventory policies. We first considered cases in which the demand rate for the product is constant. In analyzing these inventory systems, total cost models were developed, which included ordering costs, holding costs, and, in some cases, backorder costs. Then minimum cost formulas for the order quantity Q were presented. A reorder point r can be established by considering the lead-time demand.

In addition, we discussed inventory models in which a deterministic and constant rate could not be assumed, and thus demand was described by a probability distribution. A critical issue with these probabilistic inventory models is obtaining a probability distribution that most realistically approximates the demand distribution. We first described a single-period model where only one order is placed for the product and, at the end of the period, either the product has sold out or a surplus remains of unsold products that will be sold for a salvage value. Solution procedures were then presented for multiperiod models based on either an order-quantity, reorder point, continuous review system or a replenishment-level, periodic review system.

In closing this chapter, we reemphasize that inventory and inventory systems can be an expensive phase of a firm's operation. It is important for managers to be aware of the cost of inventory systems and to make the best possible operating policy decisions for the inventory system. Inventory models, as presented in this chapter, can help managers to develop good inventory policies. The Q.M. in Action, Multistage Inventory Planning at Deere & Company, provides another example of how computer-based inventory models can be used to provide optimal inventory policies and cost reductions.

Q.M. *in* ACTION

MULTISTAGE INVENTORY PLANNING AT DEERE & COMPANY*

Deere & Company's Commercial & Consumer Equipment (C&CE) Division, located in Raleigh, North Carolina, produces seasonal products such as lawn mowers and snow blowers. The seasonal aspect of demand requires the products to be built in advance. Because many of the products involve impulse purchases, the products must be available at dealerships when the customers walk in. Historically, high inventory levels resulted in high inventory costs and an unacceptable return on assets. As a result, management concluded that C&CE needed an inventory planning system that would reduce the average finished goods inventory levels in company warehouses and dealer locations, and at the same time would ensure that stock-outs would not cause a negative impact on sales.

In order to optimize inventory levels, Deere moved from an aggregate inventory planning model to a series of individual product inventory models. This approach enabled Deere to determine optimal inventory levels for each product at each dealer, as well as optimal levels for each product at each plant and warehouse. The computerized system developed, known as SmartOps Multistage Inventory Planning and Optimization (MIPO), manages inventory for four C&CE Division plants, 21 dealers, and 150 products. Easily updated, MIPO provides target inventory levels for each product on a weekly basis. In addition, the system provides information about how optimal inventory levels are affected by lead times, forecast errors, and target service levels.

The inventory optimization system enabled the C&CE Division to meet its inventory reduction goals. C&CE management estimates that the company will continue to achieve annual cost savings from lower inventory carrying costs. Meanwhile, the dealers also benefit from lower warehouse expenses, as well as lower interest and insurance costs.

*Based on "Deere's New Software Achieves Inventory Reduction Goals," *Inventory Management Report* (March 2003): 2.

Glossary

Economic order quantity (EOQ) The order quantity that minimizes the annual holding cost plus the annual ordering cost.

Constant demand rate An assumption of many inventory models that states that the same number of units are taken from inventory each period of time.

Holding cost The cost associated with maintaining an inventory investment, including the cost of the capital investment in the inventory, insurance, taxes, warehouse overhead, and so on. This cost may be stated as a percentage of the inventory investment or as a cost per unit.

Cost of capital The cost a firm incurs to obtain capital for investment. It may be stated as an annual percentage rate, and it is part of the holding cost associated with maintaining inventory.

Ordering cost The fixed cost (salaries, paper, transportation, etc.) associated with placing an order for an item.

Inventory position The inventory on hand plus the inventory on order.

Reorder point The inventory position at which a new order should be placed.

Lead time The time between the placing of an order and its receipt in the inventory system.

Lead-time demand The number of units demanded during the lead-time period.

Cycle time The length of time between the placing of two consecutive orders.

Constant supply rate A situation in which the inventory is built up at a constant rate over a period of time.

Lot size The order quantity in the production inventory model.

Setup cost The fixed cost (labor, materials, lost production) associated with preparing for a new production run.

Shortage or stock-out Demand that cannot be supplied from inventory.

Backorder The receipt of an order for a product when no units are in inventory. These backorders become shortages, which are eventually satisfied when a new supply of the product becomes available.

Goodwill cost A cost associated with a backorder, a lost sale, or any form of stock-out or unsatisfied demand. This cost may be used to reflect the loss of future profits because a customer experienced an unsatisfied demand.

Quantity discounts Discounts or lower unit costs offered by the manufacturer when a customer purchases larger quantities of the product.

Deterministic inventory model A model where demand is considered known and not subject to uncertainty.

Probabilistic inventory model A model where demand is not known exactly; probabilities must be associated with the possible values for demand.

Single-period inventory model An inventory model in which only one order is placed for the product, and at the end of the period either the item has sold out, or a surplus of unsold items will be sold for a salvage value.

Incremental analysis A method used to determine an optimal order quantity by comparing the cost of ordering an additional unit with the cost of not ordering an additional unit.

Lead-time demand distribution The distribution of demand that occurs during the lead-time period.

Safety stock Inventory maintained in order to reduce the number of stock-outs resulting from higher-than-expected demand.

Continuous review inventory system A system in which the inventory position is monitored or reviewed on a continuous basis so that a new order can be placed as soon as the reorder point is reached.

Periodic review inventory system A system in which the inventory position is checked or reviewed at predetermined periodic points in time. Reorders are placed only at periodic review points.

Problems

1. Suppose that the R&B Beverage Company has a soft drink product that shows a constant annual demand rate of 3600 cases. A case of the soft drink costs R&B $3. Ordering costs are $20 per order and holding costs are 25% of the value of the inventory. R&B has 250 working days per year, and the lead time is 5 days. Identify the following aspects of the inventory policy:
   a. Economic order quantity
   b. Reorder point
   c. Cycle time
   d. Total annual cost

2. A general property of the EOQ inventory model is that total inventory holding and total ordering costs are equal at the optimal solution. Use the data in Problem 1 to show that this result is true. Use equations (14.1), (14.2), and (14.3) to show that, in general, total holding costs and total ordering costs are equal whenever Q^* is used.

3. The reorder point [see equation (14.6)] is defined as the lead-time demand for an item. In cases of long lead times, the lead-time demand and thus the reorder point may exceed the

economic order quantity Q^*. In such cases, the inventory position will not equal the inventory on hand when an order is placed, and the reorder point may be expressed in terms of either the inventory position or the inventory on hand. Consider the economic order quantity model with $D = 5000$, $C_o = \$32$, $C_h = \$2$, and 250 working days per year. Identify the reorder point in terms of the inventory position and in terms of the inventory on hand for each of the following lead times:

a.   5 days
b.   15 days
c.   25 days
d.   45 days

4.   Westside Auto purchases a component used in the manufacture of automobile generators directly from the supplier. Westside's generator production operation, which is operated at a constant rate, will require 1000 components per month throughout the year (12,000 units annually). Assume that the ordering costs are $25 per order, the unit cost is $2.50 per component, and annual holding costs are 20% of the value of the inventory. Westside has 250 working days per year and a lead time of 5 days. Answer the following inventory policy questions:

a.   What is the EOQ for this component?
b.   What is the reorder point?
c.   What is the cycle time?
d.   What are the total annual holding and ordering costs associated with your recommended EOQ?

5.   The Metropolitan Bus Company (MBC) purchases diesel fuel from American Petroleum Supply. In addition to the fuel cost, American Petroleum Supply charges MBC $250 per order to cover the expenses of delivering and transferring the fuel to MBC's storage tanks. The lead time for a new shipment from American Petroleum is 10 days; the cost of holding a gallon of fuel in the storage tanks is $0.04 per month, or $0.48 per year; and annual fuel usage is 150,000 gallons. MBC buses operate 300 days a year.

a.   What is the optimal order quantity for MBC?
b.   How frequently should MBC order to replenish the gasoline supply?
c.   The MBC storage tanks have a capacity of 15,000 gallons. Should MBC consider expanding the capacity of its storage tanks?
d.   What is the reorder point?

6.   Tele-Reco is a new specialty store that sells television sets, videotape recorders, video games, and other television-related products. A new Japanese-manufactured videotape recorder costs Tele-Reco $600 per unit. Tele-Reco's annual holding cost rate is 22%. Ordering costs are estimated to be $70 per order.

a.   If demand for the new videotape recorder is expected to be constant with a rate of 20 units per month, what is the recommended order quantity for the videotape recorder?
b.   What are the estimated annual inventory holding and ordering costs associated with this product?
c.   How many orders will be placed per year?
d.   With 250 working days per year, what is the cycle time for this product?

7.   A large distributor of oil-well drilling equipment operated over the past two years with EOQ policies based on an annual holding cost rate of 22%. Under the EOQ policy, a particular product has been ordered with a $Q^* = 80$. A recent evaluation of holding costs shows that because of an increase in the interest rate associated with bank loans, the annual holding cost rate should be 27%.

a.   What is the new economic order quantity for the product?
b.   Develop a general expression showing how the economic order quantity changes when the annual holding cost rate is changed from I to I'.

8. Nation-Wide Bus Lines is proud of its six-week bus driver–training program that it conducts for all new Nation-Wide drivers. As long as the class size remains less than or equal to 35, a six-week training program costs Nation-Wide $22,000 for instructors, equipment, and so on. The Nation-Wide training program must provide the company with approximately five new drivers per month. After completing the training program, new drivers are paid $1600 per month but do not work until a full-time driver position is open. Nation-Wide views the $1600 per month paid to each idle new driver as a holding cost necessary to maintain a supply of newly trained drivers available for immediate service. Viewing new drivers as inventory-type units, how large should the training classes be to minimize Nation-Wide's total annual training and new driver idle-time costs? How many training classes should the company hold each year? What is the total annual cost associated with your recommendation?

9. Cress Electronic Products manufactures components used in the automotive industry. Cress purchases parts for use in its manufacturing operation from a variety of different suppliers. One particular supplier provides a part where the assumptions of the EOQ model are realistic. The annual demand is 5000 units, the ordering cost is $80 per order, and the annual holding cost rate is 25%.
   a. If the cost of the part is $20 per unit, what is the economic order quantity?
   b. Assume 250 days of operation per year. If the lead time for an order is 12 days, what is the reorder point?
   c. If the lead time for the part is seven weeks (35 days), what is the reorder point?
   d. What is the reorder point for part (c) if the reorder point is expressed in terms of the inventory on hand rather than the inventory position?

10. All-Star Bat Manufacturing, Inc., supplies baseball bats to major and minor league baseball teams. After an initial order in January, demand over the six-month baseball season is approximately constant at 1000 bats per month. Assuming that the bat production process can handle up to 4000 bats per month, the bat production setup costs are $150 per setup, the production cost is $10 per bat, and the holding costs have a monthly rate of 2%, what production lot size would you recommend to meet the demand during the baseball season? If All-Star operates 20 days per month, how often will the production process operate, and what is the length of a production run?

11. Assume that a production line operates such that the production lot size model of Section 14.2 is applicable. Given $D = 6400$ units per year, $C_o = \$100$, and $C_h = \$2$ per unit per year, compute the minimum cost production lot size for each of the following production rates:
   a. 8000 units per year
   b. 10,000 units per year
   c. 32,000 units per year
   d. 100,000 units per year
   Compute the EOQ recommended lot size using equation (14.5). What two observations can you make about the relationship between the EOQ model and the production lot size model?

12. EL Computer produces its multimedia notebook computer on a production line that has an annual capacity of 16,000 units. EL Computer estimates the annual demand for this model at 6000 units. The cost to set up the production line is $2345, and the annual holding cost is $20 per unit. Current practice calls for production runs of 500 notebook computers each month.
   a. What is the optimal production lot size?
   b. How many production runs should be made each year? What is the recommended cycle time?
   c. Would you recommend changing the current production lot size policy from the monthly 500 unit production runs? Why or why not? What is the projected savings of your recommendation?

13. Wilson Publishing Company produces books for the retail market. Demand for a current book is expected to occur at a constant annual rate of 7200 copies. The cost of one copy of the book is $14.50. The holding cost is based on an 18% annual rate, and production setup costs are $150 per setup. The equipment on which the book is produced has an annual production volume of 25,000 copies. Wilson has 250 working days per year, and the lead time for a production run is 15 days. Use the production lot size model to compute the following values:
    a. Minimum cost production lot size
    b. Number of production runs per year
    c. Cycle time
    d. Length of a production run
    e. Maximum inventory
    f. Total annual cost
    g. Reorder point

14. A well-known manufacturer of several brands of toothpaste uses the production lot size model to determine production quantities for its various products. The product known as Extra White is currently being produced in production lot sizes of 5000 units. The length of the production run for this quantity is 10 days. Because of a recent shortage of a particular raw material, the supplier of the material announced that a cost increase will be passed along to the manufacturer of Extra White. Current estimates are that the new raw material cost will increase the manufacturing cost of the toothpaste products by 23% per unit. What will be the effect of this price increase on the production lot sizes for Extra White?

15. Suppose that Westside Auto of Problem 4, with $D = 12{,}000$ units per year, $C_h = (2.50)(0.20) = \$0.50$, and $C_o = \$25$, decided to operate with a backorder inventory policy. Backorder costs are estimated to be $5 per unit per year. Identify the following:
    a. Minimum cost order quantity
    b. Maximum number of backorders
    c. Maximum inventory
    d. Cycle time
    e. Total annual cost

16. Assuming 250 days of operation per year and a lead time of five days, what is the reorder point for Westside Auto in Problem 15? Show the general formula for the reorder point for the EOQ model with backorders. In general, is the reorder point when backorders are allowed greater than or less than the reorder point when backorders are not allowed? Explain.

17. A manager of an inventory system believes that inventory models are important decision-making aids. Even though often using an EOQ policy, the manager never considered a backorder model because of the assumption that backorders were "bad" and should be avoided. However, with upper management's continued pressure for cost reduction, you have been asked to analyze the economics of a backorder policy for some products that can possibly be backordered. For a specific product with $D = 800$ units per year, $C_o = \$150$, $C_h = \$3$, and $C_b = \$20$, what is the difference in total annual cost between the EOQ model and the planned shortage or backorder model? If the manager adds constraints that no more than 25% of the units can be backordered and that no customer will have to wait more than 15 days for an order, should the backorder inventory policy be adopted? Assume 250 working days per year.

18. If the lead time for new orders is 20 days for the inventory system discussed in Problem 17, find the reorder point for both the EOQ and the backorder models.

19. The A&M Hobby Shop carries a line of radio-controlled model racing cars. Demand for the cars is assumed to be constant at a rate of 40 cars per month. The cars cost $60 each, and ordering costs are approximately $15 per order, regardless of the order size. The annual holding cost rate is 20%.

a. Determine the economic order quantity and total annual cost under the assumption that no backorders are permitted.
b. Using a $45 per-unit per-year backorder cost, determine the minimum cost inventory policy and total annual cost for the model racing cars.
c. What is the maximum number of days a customer would have to wait for a backorder under the policy in part (b)? Assume that the Hobby Shop is open for business 300 days per year.
d. Would you recommend a no-backorder or a backorder inventory policy for this product? Explain.
e. If the lead time is six days, what is the reorder point for both the no-backorder and backorder inventory policies?

20. Assume that the following quantity discount schedule is appropriate. If annual demand is 120 units, ordering costs are $20 per order, and the annual holding cost rate is 25%, what order quantity would you recommend?

Order Size	Discount (%)	Unit Cost
0 to 49	0	$30.00
50 to 99	5	$28.50
100 or more	10	$27.00

21. Apply the EOQ model to the following quantity discount situation in which $D = 500$ units per year, $C_o = \$40$, and the annual holding cost rate is 20%. What order quantity do you recommend?

Discount Category	Order Size	Discount (%)	Unit Cost
1	0 to 99	0	$10.00
2	100 or more	3	$ 9.70

22. Keith Shoe Stores carries a basic black dress shoe for men that sells at an approximate constant rate of 500 pairs of shoes every three months. Keith's current buying policy is to order 500 pairs each time an order is placed. It costs Keith $30 to place an order. The annual holding cost rate is 20%. With the order quantity of 500, Keith obtains the shoes at the lowest possible unit cost of $28 per pair. Other quantity discounts offered by the manufacturer are as follows. What is the minimum cost order quantity for the shoes? What are the annual savings of your inventory policy over the policy currently being used by Keith?

Order Quantity	Price per Pair
0–99	$36
100–199	$32
200–299	$30
300 or more	$28

23. In the EOQ model with quantity discounts, we stated that if the Q^* for a price category is larger than necessary to qualify for the category price, the category cannot be optimal. Use the two discount categories in Problem 21 to show that this statement is true. That is, plot total cost curves for the two categories and show that if the category 2 minimum cost Q is an acceptable solution, we do not have to consider category 1.

24. The J&B Card Shop sells calendars depicting a different Colonial scene each month. The once-a-year order for each year's calendar arrives in September. From past experience, the September-to-July demand for the calendars can be approximated by a normal probability distribution with $\mu = 500$ and $\sigma = 120$. The calendars cost $1.50 each, and J&B sells them for $3 each.

a. If J&B throws out all unsold calendars at the end of July (i.e., salvage value is zero), how many calendars should be ordered?

b. If J&B reduces the calendar price to $1 at the end of July and can sell all surplus calendars at this price, how many calendars should be ordered?

25. The Gilbert Air-Conditioning Company is considering the purchase of a special shipment of portable air conditioners manufactured in Japan. Each unit will cost Gilbert $80, and it will be sold for $125. Gilbert does not want to carry surplus air conditioners over until the following year. Thus, all surplus air conditioners will be sold to a wholesaler for $50 per unit. Assume that the air conditioner demand follows a normal probability distribution with $\mu = 20$ and $\sigma = 8$.

a. What is the recommended order quantity?

b. What is the probability that Gilbert will sell all units it orders?

26. The Bridgeport city manager and the chief of police agreed on the size of the police force necessary for normal daily operations. However, they need assistance in determining the number of additional police officers needed to cover daily absences due to injuries, sickness, vacations, and personal leave. Records over the past three years show that the daily demand for additional police officers is normally distributed with a mean of 50 officers and a standard deviation of 10 officers. The cost of an additional police officer is based on the average pay rate of $150 per day. If the daily demand for additional police officers exceeds the number of additional officers available, the excess demand will be covered by overtime at the pay rate of $240 per day for each overtime officer.

a. If the number of additional police officers available is greater than demand, the city will have to pay for more additional police officers than needed. What is the cost of overestimating demand?

b. If the number of additional police officers available is less than demand, the city will have to use overtime to meet the demand. What is the cost of underestimating demand?

c. What is the optimal number of additional police officers that should be included in the police force?

d. On a typical day, what is the probability that overtime will be necessary?

27. A perishable dairy product is ordered daily at a particular supermarket. The product, which costs $1.19 per unit, sells for $1.65 per unit. If units are unsold at the end of the day, the supplier takes them back at a rebate of $1 per unit. Assume that daily demand is approximately normally distributed with $\mu = 150$ and $\sigma = 30$.

a. What is your recommended daily order quantity for the supermarket?

b. What is the probability that the supermarket will sell all the units it orders?

c. In problems such as these, why would the supplier offer a rebate as high as $1? For example, why not offer a nominal rebate of, say, 25¢ per unit? What happens to the supermarket order quantity as the rebate is reduced?

28. A retail outlet sells a seasonal product for $10 per unit. The cost of the product is $8 per unit. All units not sold during the regular season are sold for half the retail price in an end-of-season clearance sale. Assume that demand for the product is uniformly distributed between 200 and 800.

a. What is the recommended order quantity?

b. What is the probability that at least some customers will ask to purchase the product after the outlet is sold out? That is, what is the probability of a stock-out using your order quantity in part (a)?

c. To keep customers happy and returning to the store later, the owner feels that stock-outs should be avoided if at all possible. What is your recommended order quantity if the owner is willing to tolerate a 0.15 probability of a stock-out?

d. Using your answer to part (c), what is the goodwill cost you are assigning to a stock-out?

29. Floyd Distributors, Inc., provides a variety of auto parts to small local garages. Floyd purchases parts from manufacturers according to the EOQ model and then ships the parts from a regional warehouse direct to its customers. For a particular type of muffler, Floyd's EOQ analysis recommends orders with $Q^* = 25$ to satisfy an annual demand of 200 mufflers. Floyd's has 250 working days per year, and the lead time averages 15 days.

a. What is the reorder point if Floyd assumes a constant demand rate?

b. Suppose that an analysis of Floyd's muffler demand shows that the lead-time demand follows a normal probability distribution with $\mu = 12$ and $\sigma = 2.5$. If Floyd's management can tolerate one stock-out per year, what is the revised reorder point?

c. What is the safety stock for part (b)? If $C_h = \$5/\text{unit/year}$, what is the extra cost due to the uncertainty of demand?

30. For Floyd Distributors in Problem 29, we were given $Q^* = 25$, $D = 200$, $C_h = \$5$, and a normal lead-time demand distribution with $\mu = 12$ and $\sigma = 2.5$.

a. What is Floyd's reorder point if the firm is willing to tolerate two stock-outs during the year?

b. What is Floyd's reorder point if the firm wants to restrict the probability of a stock-out on any one cycle to at most 1%?

c. What are the safety stock levels and the annual safety stock costs for the reorder points found in parts (a) and (b)?

31. A product with an annual demand of 1000 units has $C_o = \$25.50$ and $C_h = \$8$. The demand exhibits some variability such that the lead-time demand follows a normal probability distribution with $\mu = 25$ and $\sigma = 5$.

a. What is the recommended order quantity?

b. What are the reorder point and safety stock if the firm desires at most a 2% probability of stock-out on any given order cycle?

c. If a manager sets the reorder point at 30, what is the probability of a stock-out on any given order cycle? How many times would you expect a stock-out during the year if this reorder point were used?

32. The B&S Novelty and Craft Shop in Bennington, Vermont, sells a variety of quality handmade items to tourists. B&S will sell 300 hand-carved miniature replicas of a Colonial soldier each year, but the demand pattern during the year is uncertain. The replicas sell for $20 each, and B&S uses a 15% annual inventory holding cost rate. Ordering costs are $5 per order, and demand during the lead time follows a normal probability distribution with $\mu = 15$ and $\sigma = 6$.

a. What is the recommended order quantity?

b. If B&S is willing to accept a stock-out roughly twice a year, what reorder point would you recommend? What is the probability that B&S will have a stock-out in any one order cycle?

c. What are the safety stock and annual safety stock costs for this product?

33. A firm uses a one-week periodic review inventory system. A two-day lead time is needed for any order, and the firm is willing to tolerate an average of one stock-out per year.

a. Using the firm's service guideline, what is the probability of a stock-out associated with each replenishment decision?

b. What is the replenishment level if demand during the review period plus lead-time period is normally distributed with a mean of 60 units and a standard deviation of 12 units?

c. What is the replenishment level if demand during the review period plus lead-time period is uniformly distributed between 35 and 85 units?

34. Foster Drugs, Inc., handles a variety of health and beauty aid products. A particular hair conditioner product costs Foster Drugs $2.95 per unit. The annual holding cost rate is 20%. An order-quantity, reorder point inventory model recommends an order quantity of 300 units per order.
     a. Lead time is one week and the lead-time demand is normally distributed with a mean of 150 units and a standard deviation of 40 units. What is the reorder point if the firm is willing to tolerate a 1% chance of stock-out on any one cycle?
     b. What safety stock and annual safety stock costs are associated with your recommendation in part (a)?
     c. The order-quantity, reorder point model requires a continuous review system. Management is considering making a transition to a periodic review system in an attempt to coordinate ordering for many of its products. The demand during the proposed two-week review period and the one-week lead-time period is normally distributed with a mean of 450 units and a standard deviation of 70 units. What is the recommended replenishment level for this periodic review system if the firm is willing to tolerate the same 1% chance of stock-out associated with any replenishment decision?
     d. What safety stock and annual safety stock costs are associated with your recommendation in part (c)?
     e. Compare your answers to parts (b) and (d). The company is seriously considering the periodic review system. Would you support this decision? Explain.
     f. Would you tend to favor the continuous review system for more expensive items? For example, assume that the product in the preceding example sold for $295 per unit. Explain.

35. Statewide Auto Parts uses a four-week periodic review system to reorder parts for its inventory stock. A one-week lead time is required to fill the order. Demand for one particular part during the five-week replenishment period is normally distributed with a mean of 18 units and a standard deviation of 6 units.
     a. At a particular periodic review, 8 units are in inventory. The parts manager places an order for 16 units. What is the probability that this part will have a stock-out before an order that is placed at the next four-week review period arrives?
     b. Assume that the company is willing to tolerate a 2.5% chance of a stock-out associated with a replenishment decision. How many parts should the manager have ordered in part (a)? What is the replenishment level for the four-week periodic review system?

36. Rose Office Supplies, Inc., which is open six days a week, uses a two-week periodic review for its store inventory. On alternating Monday mornings, the store manager fills out an order sheet requiring a shipment of various items from the company's warehouse. A particular three-ring notebook sells at an average rate of 16 notebooks per week. The standard deviation in sales is 5 notebooks per week. The lead time for a new shipment is three days. The mean lead-time demand is 8 notebooks with a standard deviation of 3.5.
     a. What is the mean or expected demand during the review period plus the lead-time period?
     b. Under the assumption of independent demand from week to week, the variances in demands are additive. Thus, the variance of the demand during the review period plus the lead-time period is equal to the variance of demand during the first week plus the variance of demand during the second week plus the variance of demand during the lead-time period. What is the variance of demand during the review period plus the lead-time period? What is the standard deviation of demand during the review period plus the lead-time period?
     c. Assuming that demand has a normal probability distribution, what is the replenishment level that will provide an expected stock-out rate of one per year?
     d. On Monday, March 22, 18 notebooks remain in inventory at the store. How many notebooks should the store manager order?

Case Problem 1   Wagner Fabricating Company

Managers at Wagner Fabricating Company are reviewing the economic feasibility of manufacturing a part that it currently purchases from a supplier. Forecasted annual demand for the part is 3200 units. Wagner operates 250 days per year.

Wagner's financial analysts established a cost of capital of 14% for the use of funds for investments within the company. In addition, over the past year $600,000 was the average investment in the company's inventory. Accounting information shows that a total of $24,000 was spent on taxes and insurance related to the company's inventory. In addition, an estimated $9000 was lost due to inventory shrinkage, which included damaged goods as well as pilferage. A remaining $15,000 was spent on warehouse overhead, including utility expenses for heating and lighting.

An analysis of the purchasing operation shows that approximately two hours are required to process and coordinate an order for the part regardless of the quantity ordered. Purchasing salaries average $28 per hour, including employee benefits. In addition, a detailed analysis of 125 orders showed that $2375 was spent on telephone, paper, and postage directly related to the ordering process.

A one-week lead time is required to obtain the part from the supplier. An analysis of demand during the lead time shows it is approximately normally distributed with a mean of 64 units and a standard deviation of 10 units. Service level guidelines indicate that one stock-out per year is acceptable.

Currently, the company has a contract to purchase the part from a supplier at a cost of $18 per unit. However, over the past few months, the company's production capacity has been expanded. As a result, excess capacity is now available in certain production departments, and the company is considering the alternative of producing the parts itself.

Forecasted utilization of equipment shows that production capacity will be available for the part being considered. The production capacity is available at the rate of 1000 units per month, with up to five months of production time available. Management believes that with a two-week lead time, schedules can be arranged so that the part can be produced whenever needed. The demand during the two-week lead time is approximately normally distributed, with a mean of 128 units and a standard deviation of 20 units. Production costs are expected to be $17 per part.

A concern of management is that setup costs will be significant. The total cost of labor and lost production time is estimated to be $50 per hour, and a full eight-hour shift will be needed to set up the equipment for producing the part.

Managerial Report

Develop a report for management of Wagner Fabricating that will address the question of whether the company should continue to purchase the part from the supplier or begin to produce the part itself. Include the following factors in your report:

1. An analysis of the holding costs, including the appropriate annual holding cost rate
2. An analysis of ordering costs, including the appropriate cost per order from the supplier
3. An analysis of setup costs for the production operation
4. A development of the inventory policy for the following two alternatives:
   a. Ordering a fixed quantity Q from the supplier
   b. Ordering a fixed quantity Q from in-plant production

5. Include the following in the policies of parts 4(a) and 4(b):
   a. Optimal quantity Q^*
   b. Number of order or production runs per year
   c. Cycle time
   d. Reorder point
   e. Amount of safety stock
   f. Expected maximum inventory
   g. Average inventory
   h. Annual holding cost
   i. Annual ordering cost
   j. Annual cost of the units purchased or manufactured
   k. Total annual cost of the purchase policy and the total annual cost of the production policy
6. Make a recommendation as to whether the company should purchase or manufacture the part. What savings are associated with your recommendation as compared with the other alternative?

Case Problem 2 # River City Fire Department

The River City Fire Department (RCFD) fights fires and provides a variety of rescue operations in the River City metropolitan area. The RCFD staffs 13 ladder companies, 26 pumper companies, and several rescue units and ambulances. Normal staffing requires 186 firefighters to be on duty every day.

RCFD is organized with three firefighting units. Each unit works a full 24-hour day and then has two days (48 hours) off. For example, Unit 1 covers Monday, Unit 2 covers Tuesday, and Unit 3 covers Wednesday. Then Unit 1 returns on Thursday, and so on. Over a three-week (21-day) scheduling period, each unit will be scheduled for seven days. On a rotational basis, firefighters within each unit are given one of the seven regularly scheduled days off. This day off is referred to as a Kelley day. Thus, over a three-week scheduling period, each firefighter in a unit works six of the seven scheduled unit days and gets one Kelley day off.

Determining the number of firefighters to be assigned to each unit includes the 186 firefighters who must be on duty plus the number of firefighters in the unit who are off for a Kelley day. Furthermore, each unit needs additional staffing to cover firefighter absences due to injury, sick leave, vacations, or personal time. This additional staffing involves finding the best mix of adding full-time firefighters to each unit and the selective use of overtime. If the number of absences on a particular day brings the number of available firefighters below the required 186, firefighters who are currently off (e.g., on a Kelley day) must be scheduled to work overtime. Overtime is compensated at 1.55 times the regular pay rate.

Analysis of the records maintained over the last several years concerning the number of daily absences shows a normal probability distribution. A mean of 20 and a standard deviation of 5 provides a good approximation of the probability distribution for the number of daily absences.

Managerial Report

Develop a report that will enable Fire Chief O. E. Smith to determine the necessary numbers for the Fire Department. Include, at a minimum, the following items in your report:

1. Assuming no daily absences and taking into account the need to staff Kelley days, determine the base number of firefighters needed by each unit.

2. Using a minimum cost criterion, how many additional firefighters should be added to each unit in order to cover the daily absences? These extra daily needs will be filled by the additional firefighters and, when necessary, the more expensive use of overtime by off-duty firefighters.

3. On a given day, what is the probability that Kelley-day firefighters will be called in to work overtime?

4. Based on the three-unit organization, how many firefighters should be assigned to each unit? What is the total number of full-time firefighters required for the River City Fire Department?

Appendix 14.1   Development of the Optimal Order Quantity (Q) Formula for the EOQ Model

Given equation (14.4) as the total annual cost for the EOQ model,

$$TC = \frac{1}{2}QC_\text{h} + \frac{D}{Q}C_\text{o} \qquad\qquad \textbf{(14.4)}$$

we can find the order quantity Q that minimizes the total cost by setting the derivative, dTC/dQ, equal to zero and solving for Q^*.

$$\frac{dTC}{dQ} = \frac{1}{2}C_\text{h} - \frac{D}{Q^2}C_\text{o} = 0$$

$$\frac{1}{2}C_\text{h} = \frac{D}{Q^2}C_\text{o}$$

$$C_\text{h}Q^2 = 2DC_\text{o}$$

$$Q^2 = \frac{2DC_\text{o}}{C_\text{h}}$$

Hence,

$$Q^* = \sqrt{\frac{2DC_\text{o}}{C_\text{h}}} \qquad\qquad \textbf{(14.5)}$$

The second derivative is

$$\frac{d^2TC}{dQ^2} = \frac{2D}{Q^3}C_\text{o}$$

Because the value of the second derivative is greater than zero, Q^* from equation (14.5) is the minimum cost solution.

Appendix 14.2 # Development of the Optimal Lot Size (Q^*) Formula for the Production Lot Size Model

Given equation (14.15) as the total annual cost for the production lot size model,

$$TC = \frac{1}{2}\left(1 - \frac{D}{P}\right)QC_h + \frac{D}{Q}C_o \qquad \textbf{(14.15)}$$

we can find the order quantity Q that minimizes the total cost by setting the derivative, dTC/dQ, equal to zero and solving for Q^*.

$$\frac{dTC}{dQ} = \frac{1}{2}\left(1 - \frac{D}{P}\right)C_h - \frac{D}{Q^2}C_o = 0$$

Solving for Q^*, we have

$$\frac{1}{2}\left(1 - \frac{D}{P}\right)C_h = \frac{D}{Q^2}C_o$$

$$\left(1 - \frac{D}{P}\right)C_h Q^2 = 2DC_o$$

$$Q^2 = \frac{2DC_o}{(1 - D/P)C_h}$$

Hence,

$$Q^* = \sqrt{\frac{2DC_o}{(1 - D/P)C_h}} \qquad \textbf{(14.16)}$$

The second derivative is

$$\frac{d^2TC}{dQ^2} = \frac{2DC_o}{Q^3}$$

Because the value of the second derivative is greater than zero, Q^* from equation (14.16) is a minimum cost solution.

CHAPTER 15

Waiting Line Models

CONTENTS

Recall the last time that you had to wait at a supermarket checkout counter, for a teller at your local bank, or to be served at a fast-food restaurant. In these and many other waiting line situations, the time spent waiting is undesirable. Adding more checkout clerks, bank tellers, or servers is not always the most economical strategy for improving service, so businesses need to determine ways to keep waiting times within tolerable limits.

Models have been developed to help managers understand and make better decisions concerning the operation of waiting lines. In management science terminology, a waiting line is also known as a **queue**, and the body of knowledge dealing with waiting lines is known as **queueing theory**. In the early 1900s, A. K. Erlang, a Danish telephone engineer, began a study of the congestion and waiting times occurring in the completion of telephone calls. Since then, queueing theory has grown far more sophisticated, with applications in a wide variety of waiting line situations.

Waiting line models consist of mathematical formulas and relationships that can be used to determine the **operating characteristics** (performance measures) for a waiting line. Operating characteristics of interest include these:

1. The probability that no units are in the system
2. The average number of units in the waiting line
3. The average number of units in the system (the number of units in the waiting line plus the number of units being served)
4. The average time a unit spends in the waiting line
5. The average time a unit spends in the system (the waiting time plus the service time)
6. The probability that an arriving unit has to wait for service

Managers who have such information are better able to make decisions that balance desirable service levels against the cost of providing the service.

The Q.M. in Action, ATM Waiting Times at Citibank, describes how a waiting line model was used to help determine the number of automatic teller machines (ATMs) to place at New York City banking centers. A waiting line model prompted the creation of a new kind of line and a chief line director to implement first-come, first-served queue discipline at Whole Foods Market in the Chelsea neighborhood of New York City. In addition, a waiting line model helped the New Haven, Connecticut, fire department develop policies to improve response time for both fire and medical emergencies.

Q.M. *(in)* ACTION

ATM WAITING TIMES AT CITIBANK*

The waiting line model used at Citibank is discussed in Section 15.3.

The New York City franchise of U.S. Citibanking operates more than 250 banking centers. Each center provides one or more automatic teller machines (ATMs) capable of performing a variety of banking transactions. At each center, a waiting line is formed by randomly arriving customers who seek service at one of the ATMs.

In order to make decisions on the number of ATMs to have at selected banking center locations, management needed information about potential waiting times and general customer service. Waiting line operating characteristics such as average number of customers in the waiting line, average time a customer spends waiting, and the probability that an arriving customer has to wait would help management determine the number of ATMs to recommend at each banking center.

For example, one busy Midtown Manhattan center had a peak arrival rate of 172 customers per hour. A multiple-channel waiting line model

*Based on information provided by Stacey Karter of Citibank.

(*continued*)

with six ATMs showed that 88% of the customers would have to wait, with an average wait time between six and seven minutes. This level of service was judged unacceptable. Expansion to seven ATMs was recommended for this location based on the waiting line model's projection of acceptable waiting times. Use of the waiting line model provided guidelines for making incremental ATM decisions at each banking center location.

15.1   Structure of a Waiting Line System

To illustrate the basic features of a waiting line model, we consider the waiting line at the Burger Dome fast-food restaurant. Burger Dome sells hamburgers, cheeseburgers, french fries, soft drinks, and milk shakes, as well as a limited number of specialty items and dessert selections. Although Burger Dome would like to serve each customer immediately, at times more customers arrive than can be handled by the Burger Dome food service staff. Thus, customers wait in line to place and receive their orders.

Burger Dome is concerned that the methods currently used to serve customers are resulting in excessive waiting times. Management wants to conduct a waiting line study to help determine the best approach to reduce waiting times and improve service.

Single-Channel Waiting Line

In the current Burger Dome operation, a server takes a customer's order, determines the total cost of the order, takes the money from the customer, and then fills the order. Once the first customer's order is filled, the server takes the order of the next customer waiting for service. This operation is an example of a **single-channel waiting line**. Each customer entering the Burger Dome restaurant must pass through the *one* channel—one order-taking and order-filling station—to place an order, pay the bill, and receive the food. When more customers arrive than can be served immediately, they form a waiting line and wait for the order-taking and order-filling station to become available. A diagram of the Burger Dome single-channel waiting line is shown in Figure 15.1.

Distribution of Arrivals

Defining the arrival process for a waiting line involves determining the probability distribution for the number of arrivals in a given period of time. For many waiting line situations,

FIGURE 15.1   THE BURGER DOME SINGLE-CHANNEL WAITING LINE

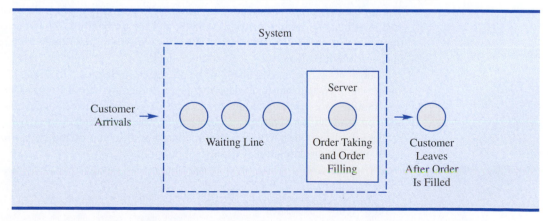

the arrivals occur *randomly and independently* of other arrivals, and we cannot predict when an arrival will occur. In such cases, quantitative analysts have found that the **Poisson probability distribution** provides a good description of the arrival pattern.

The Poisson probability function provides the probability of x arrivals in a specific time period. The probability function is as follows:[1]

$$P(x) = \frac{\lambda^x e^{-\lambda}}{x!} \quad \text{for } x = 0, 1, 2, \ldots \tag{15.1}$$

where

$$x = \text{the number of arrivals in the time period}$$
$$\lambda = \text{the } mean \text{ number of arrivals per time period}$$
$$e = 2.71828$$

The mean number of arrivals per time period, λ, is called the **arrival rate**. Values of $e^{-\lambda}$ can be found using a calculator or by using Appendix E.

Suppose that Burger Dome analyzed data on customer arrivals and concluded that the arrival rate is 45 customers per hour. For a one-minute period, the arrival rate would be $\lambda = 45$ customers/60 minutes $= 0.75$ customers per minute. Thus, we can use the following Poisson probability function to compute the probability of x customer arrivals during a one-minute period:

$$P(x) = \frac{\lambda^x e^{-\lambda}}{x!} = \frac{0.75^x e^{-0.75}}{x!} \tag{15.2}$$

Thus, the probabilities of 0, 1, and 2 customer arrivals during a one-minute period are

$$P(0) = \frac{(0.75)^0 e^{-0.75}}{0!} = e^{-0.75} = 0.4724$$

$$P(1) = \frac{(0.75)^1 e^{-0.75}}{1!} = 0.75 e^{-0.75} = 0.75(0.4724) = 0.3543$$

$$P(2) = \frac{(0.75)^2 e^{-0.75}}{2!} = \frac{(0.75)^2 e^{-0.75}}{2!} = \frac{(0.5625)(0.4724)}{2} = 0.1329$$

The probability of no customers in a one-minute period is 0.4724, the probability of one customer in a one-minute period is 0.3543, and the probability of two customers in a one-minute period is 0.1329. Table 15.1 shows the Poisson probabilities for customer arrivals during a one-minute period.

The waiting line models that will be presented in Sections 15.2 and 15.3 use the Poisson probability distribution to describe the customer arrivals at Burger Dome. In practice, you should record the actual number of arrivals per time period for several days or weeks and compare the frequency distribution of the observed number of arrivals to the Poisson probability distribution to determine whether the Poisson probability distribution provides a reasonable approximation of the arrival distribution.

---

[1]The term $x!$, x *factorial*, is defined as $x! = x(x - 1)(x - 2) \ldots (2)(1)$. For example, $4! = (4)(3)(2)(1) = 24$. For the special case of $x = 0$, $0! = 1$ by definition.

TABLE 15.1   POISSON PROBABILITIES FOR THE NUMBER OF CUSTOMER ARRIVALS
AT A BURGER DOME RESTAURANT DURING A ONE-MINUTE PERIOD
($\lambda = 0.75$)

Number of Arrivals	Probability
0	0.4724
1	0.3543
2	0.1329
3	0.0332
4	0.0062
5 or more	0.0010

Distribution of Service Times

The service time is the time a customer spends at the service facility once the service has
started. At Burger Dome, the service time starts when a customer begins to place the order
with the food server and continues until the customer receives the order. Service times are
rarely constant. At Burger Dome, the number of items ordered and the mix of items ordered
vary considerably from one customer to the next. Small orders can be handled in a matter
of seconds, but large orders may require more than two minutes.

Quantitative analysts have found that if the probability distribution for the service time
can be assumed to follow an **exponential probability distribution**, formulas are available
for providing useful information about the operation of the waiting line. Using an exponential probability distribution, the probability that the service time will be less than or
equal to a time of length t is

$$P(\text{service time} \leq t) = 1 - e^{-\mu t} \qquad \textbf{(15.3)}$$

where

μ = the *mean* number of units that can be served per time period

$e = 2.71828$

*A property of the
exponential probability
distribution is that there is
a 0.6321 probability that
the random variable takes
on a value less than its
mean. In waiting line
applications, the
exponential probability
distribution indicates that
approximately 63% of the
service times are less than
the mean service time and
approximately 37% of the
service times are greater
than the mean service time.*

The mean number of units that can be served per time period, μ, is called the **service rate**.

Suppose that Burger Dome studied the order-taking and order-filling process and found
that the single food server can process an average of 60 customer orders per hour. On a one-
minute basis, the service rate would be $\mu = 60$ customers/60 minutes $= 1$ customer per
minute. For example, with $\mu = 1$, we can use equation (15.3) to compute probabilities such
as the probability an order can be processed in $1/2$ minute or less, 1 minute or less, and 2
minutes or less. These computations are

$$P(\text{service time} \leq 0.5 \text{ min.}) = 1 - e^{-1(0.5)} = 1 - 0.6065 = 0.3935$$
$$P(\text{service time} \leq 1.0 \text{ min.}) = 1 - e^{-1(1.0)} = 1 - 0.3679 = 0.6321$$
$$P(\text{service time} \leq 2.0 \text{ min.}) = 1 - e^{-1(2.0)} = 1 - 0.1353 = 0.8647$$

Thus, we would conclude that there is a 0.3935 probability that an order can be processed
in $1/2$ minute or less, a 0.6321 probability that it can be processed in 1 minute or less, and a
0.8647 probability that it can be processed in 2 minutes or less.

In several waiting line models presented in this chapter, we assume that the probability
distribution for the service time follows an exponential probability distribution. In practice,

you should collect data on actual service times to determine whether the exponential probability distribution is a reasonable approximation of the service times for your application.

Queue Discipline

In describing a waiting line system, we must define the manner in which the waiting units are arranged for service. For the Burger Dome waiting line, and in general for most customer-oriented waiting lines, the units waiting for service are arranged on a **first-come, first-served** basis; this approach is referred to as an **FCFS** queue discipline. However, some situations call for different queue disciplines. For example, when people wait for an elevator, the last one on the elevator is often the first one to complete service (i.e., the first to leave the elevator). Other types of queue disciplines assign priorities to the waiting units and then serve the unit with the highest priority first. In this chapter we consider only waiting lines based on a first-come, first-served queue discipline. The Q.M. in Action, The Serpentine Line and an FCFS Queue Discipline at Whole Foods Market, describes how an FCFS queue discipline is used at a supermarket.

Steady-State Operation

When the Burger Dome restaurant opens in the morning, no customers are in the restaurant. Gradually, activity builds up to a normal or steady state. The beginning or start-up period is referred to as the **transient period**. The transient period ends when the system reaches the normal or **steady-state operation**. Waiting line models describe the steady-state operating characteristics of a waiting line.

Q.M. *in* ACTION

THE SERPENTINE LINE AND AN FCFS QUEUE DISCIPLINE AT WHOLE FOODS MARKET*

The Whole Foods Market in the Chelsea neighborhood of New York City employs a chief line director to implement a first-come, first-served (FCFS) queue discipline. Companies such as Wendy's, American Airlines, and Chemical Bank were among the first to employ serpentine lines to implement an FCFS queue discipline. Such lines are commonplace today. We see them at banks, amusement parks, and fast-food outlets. The line is called *serpentine* because of the way it winds around. When a customer gets to the front of the line, the customer then goes to the first available server. People like serpentine lines because they prevent people who join the line later from being served ahead of an earlier arrival.

As popular as serpentine lines have become, supermarkets have not employed them because of a lack of space. At the typical supermarket, a separate line forms at each checkout counter. When ready to check out, a person picks one of the checkout counters and stays in that line until receiving service. Sometimes a person joining another checkout line later will receive service first, which tends to upset people. Manhattan's Whole Foods Market solved this problem by creating a new kind of line and employing a chief line director to direct the first person in line to the next available checkout counter.

The waiting line at the Whole Foods Market is actually three parallel lines. Customers join the shortest line and follow a rotation when they reach the front of the line. For instance, if the first customer in line 1 is sent to a checkout counter, the next customer sent to a checkout counter is the first person in line 2, then the first person in line 3, and so on. This way an FCFS queue discipline is implemented without a long, winding serpentine line.

The Whole Foods Market's customers seem to really like the system, and the line director, Bill Jones, has become something of a celebrity. Children point to him on the street and customers invite him over for dinner.

*Based on Ian Parker, "Mr. Next," The New Yorker (January 13, 2003).

15.2 Single-Channel Waiting Line Model with Poisson Arrivals and Exponential Service Times

Waiting line models are often based on assumptions such as Poisson arrivals and exponential service times. When applying any waiting line model, data should be collected on the actual system to ensure that the assumptions of the model are reasonable.

In this section we present formulas that can be used to determine the steady-state operating characteristics for a single-channel waiting line. The formulas are applicable if the arrivals follow a Poisson probability distribution and the service times follow an exponential probability distribution. As these assumptions apply to the Burger Dome waiting line problem introduced in Section 15.1, we show how formulas can be used to determine Burger Dome's operating characteristics and thus provide management with helpful decision-making information.

The mathematical methodology used to derive the formulas for the operating characteristics of waiting lines is rather complex. However, our purpose in this chapter is not to provide the theoretical development of waiting line models, but rather to show how the formulas that have been developed can provide information about operating characteristics of the waiting line. Readers interested in the mathematical development of the formulas can consult the specialized texts listed in Appendix F at the end of the text.

Operating Characteristics

The following formulas can be used to compute the steady-state operating characteristics for a single-channel waiting line with Poisson arrivals and exponential service times, where

$$\lambda = \text{the mean number of arrivals per time period (the arrival rate)}$$
$$\mu = \text{the mean number of services per time period (the service rate)}$$

Equations (15.4) through (15.10) do not provide formulas for optimal conditions. Rather, these equations provide information about the steady-state operating characteristics of a waiting line.

1. The probability that no units are in the system:

$$P_0 = 1 - \frac{\lambda}{\mu} \qquad\qquad \textbf{(15.4)}$$

2. The average number of units in the waiting line:

$$L_q = \frac{\lambda^2}{\mu(\mu - \lambda)} \qquad\qquad \textbf{(15.5)}$$

3. The average number of units in the system:

$$L = L_q + \frac{\lambda}{\mu} \qquad\qquad \textbf{(15.6)}$$

4. The average time a unit spends in the waiting line:

$$W_q = \frac{L_q}{\lambda} \qquad\qquad \textbf{(15.7)}$$

5. The average time a unit spends in the system:

$$W = W_q + \frac{1}{\mu}$$

(15.8)

6. The probability that an arriving unit has to wait for service:

$$P_w = \frac{\lambda}{\mu}$$

(15.9)

7. The probability of n units in the system:

$$P_n = \left(\frac{\lambda}{\mu}\right)^n P_0$$

(15.10)

The values of the arrival rate λ and the service rate μ are clearly important components in determining the operating characteristics. Equation (15.9) shows that the ratio of the arrival rate to the service rate, λ/μ, provides the probability that an arriving unit has to wait because the service facility is in use. Hence, λ/μ is referred to as the *utilization factor* for the service facility.

The operating characteristics presented in equations (15.4) through (15.10) are applicable only when the service rate μ is *greater than* the arrival rate λ—in other words, when $\lambda/\mu < 1$. If this condition does not exist, the waiting line will continue to grow without limit because the service facility does not have sufficient capacity to handle the arriving units. Thus, in using equations (15.4) through (15.10), we must have $\mu > \lambda$.

Operating Characteristics for the Burger Dome Problem

Recall that for the Burger Dome problem we had an arrival rate of $\lambda = 0.75$ customers per minute and a service rate of $\mu = 1$ customer per minute. Thus, with $\mu > \lambda$, equations (15.4) through (15.10) can be used to provide operating characteristics for the Burger Dome single-channel waiting line:

$$P_0 = 1 - \frac{\lambda}{\mu} = 1 - \frac{0.75}{1} = 0.25$$

$$L_q = \frac{\lambda^2}{\mu(\mu - \lambda)} = \frac{0.75^2}{1(1 - 0.75)} = 2.25 \text{ customers}$$

$$L = L_q + \frac{\lambda}{\mu} = 2.25 + \frac{0.75}{1} = 3 \text{ customers}$$

$$W_q = \frac{L_q}{\lambda} = \frac{2.25}{0.75} = 3 \text{ minutes}$$

$$W = W_q + \frac{1}{\mu} = 3 + \frac{1}{1} = 4 \text{ minutes}$$

$$P_w = \frac{\lambda}{\mu} = \frac{0.75}{1} = 0.75$$

Problem 5 asks you to compute the operating characteristics for a single-channel waiting line application.

Equation (15.10) can be used to determine the probability of any number of customers in the system. Applying it provides the probability information in Table 15.2.

TABLE 15.2   THE PROBABILITY OF *n* CUSTOMERS IN THE SYSTEM FOR THE BURGER DOME WAITING LINE PROBLEM

Number of Customers	Probability
0	0.2500
1	0.1875
2	0.1406
3	0.1055
4	0.0791
5	0.0593
6	0.0445
7 or more	0.1335

Managers' Use of Waiting Line Models

The results of the single-channel waiting line for Burger Dome show several important things about the operation of the waiting line. In particular, customers wait an average of three minutes before beginning to place an order, which appears somewhat long for a business based on fast service. In addition, the facts that the average number of customers waiting in line is 2.25 and that 75% of the arriving customers have to wait for service are indicators that something should be done to improve the waiting line operation. Table 15.2 shows a 0.1335 probability that seven or more customers are in the Burger Dome system at one time. This condition indicates a fairly high probability that Burger Dome will experience some long waiting lines if it continues to use the single-channel operation.

If the operating characteristics are unsatisfactory in terms of meeting company standards for service, Burger Dome's management should consider alternative designs or plans for improving the waiting line operation.

Improving the Waiting Line Operation

Waiting line models often indicate when improvements in operating characteristics are desirable. However, the decision of how to modify the waiting line configuration to improve the operating characteristics must be based on the insights and creativity of the analyst.

After reviewing the operating characteristics provided by the waiting line model, Burger Dome's management concluded that improvements designed to reduce waiting times are desirable. To make improvements in the waiting line operation, analysts often focus on ways to improve the service rate. Generally, service rate improvements are obtained by making either or both of the following changes:

1. Increase the service rate by making a creative design change or by using new technology.
2. Add one or more service channels so that more customers can be served simultaneously.

Assume that in considering alternative 1, Burger Dome's management decides to employ an order filler who will assist the order taker at the cash register. The customer begins the service process by placing the order with the order taker. As the order is placed, the order taker announces the order over an intercom system, and the order filler begins filling the order. When the order is completed, the order taker handles the money, while the order filler continues to fill the order. With this design, Burger Dome's management estimates the service rate can be increased from the current 60 customers per hour to 75 customers per hour. Thus, the service rate for the revised system is $\mu = 75$ customers/60 minutes = 1.25 customers per minute. For $\lambda = 0.75$ customers per minute and $\mu = 1.25$ customers per minute, equations (15.4) through (15.10) can be used to provide the new operating characteristics for the Burger Dome waiting line. These operating characteristics are summarized in Table 15.3.

The information in Table 15.3 indicates that all operating characteristics have improved because of the increased service rate. In particular, the average time a customer spends in the waiting line has been reduced from 3 to 1.2 minutes, and the average time a customer spends in the system has been reduced from 4 to 2 minutes. Are any other alternatives available that Burger Dome can use to increase the service rate? If so, and if the mean service rate μ can be identified for each alternative, equations (15.4) through (15.10) can be used to determine the revised operating characteristics and any improvements in the waiting line system. The added cost of any proposed change can be compared to the corresponding service improvements to help the manager determine whether the proposed service improvements are worthwhile.

Problem 11 asks you to determine whether a change in the service rate will meet the company's service guideline for its customers.

As mentioned previously, another option often available is to add one or more service channels so that more customers can be served simultaneously. The extension of the single-channel waiting line model to the multiple-channel waiting line model is the topic of the next section.

Excel Solution of Waiting Line Model

Waiting line models are easily implemented with the aid of worksheets. The Excel worksheet for the Burger Dome single-channel waiting line is shown in Figure 15.2. The formula worksheet is in the background; the value worksheet is in the foreground. The arrival rate and the service rate are entered in cells B7 and B8. The formulas for the waiting line's operating characteristics are placed in cells C13 to C18. The worksheet shows the same values for the operating characteristics that we obtained earlier. Modifications in the waiting line design can be evaluated by entering different arrival rates and/or service rates into cells B7 and B8. The new operating characteristics of the waiting line will be shown immediately.

The Management Scientist software also has a waiting line module that can be used to solve the waiting line problems in this chapter.

The Excel worksheet in Figure 15.2 is a template that can be used with any single-channel waiting line model with Poisson arrivals and exponential service times. This worksheet and similar Excel worksheets for the other waiting line models presented in this chapter are available at the Web files link on the Web site that accompanies this text.

TABLE 15.3 OPERATING CHARACTERISTICS FOR THE BURGER DOME SYSTEM WITH THE SERVICE RATE INCREASED TO $\mu = 1.25$ CUSTOMERS PER MINUTE

Probability of no customers in the system	0.400
Average number of customers in the waiting line	0.900
Average number of customers in the system	1.500
Average time in the waiting line	1.200 minutes
Average time in the system	2.000 minutes
Probability that an arriving customer has to wait	0.600
Probability that seven or more customers are in the system	0.028

FIGURE 15.2   WORKSHEET FOR THE BURGER DOME SINGLE-CHANNEL WAITING LINE

	A	B	C	D
1	Single-Channel Waiting Line Model			
2				
3	Assumptions			
4	Poisson Arrivals			
5	Exponential Service Times			
6				
7	Arrival Rate	0.75		
8	Service Rate	1		
9				
10				
11	Operating Characteristics			
12				
13	Probability that no customers are in the system, Po		=1-B7/B8	
14	Average number of customers in the waiting line, Lq		=B7^2/(B8*(B8-B7))	
15	Average number of customers in the system, L		=C14+B7/B8	
16	Average time a customer spends in the waiting line, Wq		=C14/B7	
17	Average time a customer spends in the system, W		=C16+1/B8	
18	Probability an arriving customer has to wait, Pw		=B7/B8	
19				

	A	B	C
1	Single-Channel Waiting Line Model		
2			
3	Assumptions		
4	Poisson Arrivals		
5	Exponential Service Times		
6			
7	Arrival Rate	0.75	
8	Service Rate	1	
9			
10			
11	Operating Characteristics		
12			
13	Probability that no customers are in the system, Po		0.2500
14	Average number of customers in the waiting line, Lq		2.2500
15	Average number of customers in the system, L		3.0000
16	Average time a customer spends in the waiting line, Wq		3.0000
17	Average time a customer spends in the system, W		4.0000
18	Probability an arriving customer has to wait, Pw		0.7500
19			

WEB file

Single

NOTES AND COMMENTS

1. The assumption that arrivals follow a Poisson probability distribution is equivalent to the assumption that the time between arrivals has an exponential probability distribution. For example, if the arrivals for a waiting line follow a Poisson probability distribution with a mean of 20 arrivals per hour, the time between arrivals will follow an exponential probability distribution, with a mean time between arrivals of $1/20$ or 0.05 hour.

2. Many individuals believe that whenever the service rate μ is greater than the arrival rate λ, the system should be able to handle or serve all arrivals. However, as the Burger Dome example shows, the variability of arrival times and service times may result in long waiting times even when the service rate exceeds the arrival rate. A contribution of waiting line models is that they can point out undesirable waiting line operating characteristics even when the $\mu > \lambda$ condition appears satisfactory.

15.3

Multiple-Channel Waiting Line Model with Poisson Arrivals and Exponential Service Times

A **multiple-channel waiting line** consists of two or more service channels that are assumed to be identical in terms of service capability. In the multiple-channel system, arriving units wait in a single waiting line and then move to the first available channel to be served. The single-channel Burger Dome operation can be expanded to a two-channel

FIGURE 15.3   THE BURGER DOME TWO-CHANNEL WAITING LINE

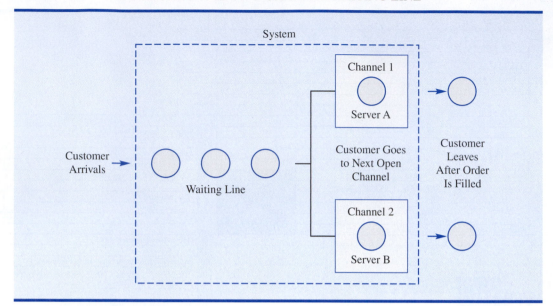

system by opening a second service channel. Figure 15.3 shows a diagram of the Burger Dome two-channel waiting line.

In this section we present formulas that can be used to determine the steady-state operating characteristics for a multiple-channel waiting line. These formulas are applicable if the following conditions exist:

You may be familiar with multiple-channel systems that also have multiple waiting lines. The waiting line model in this section has multiple channels, but only a single waiting line. Operating characteristics for a multiple-channel system are better when a single waiting line, rather than multiple waiting lines, is used.

1. The arrivals follow a Poisson probability distribution.
2. The service time for each channel follows an exponential probability distribution.
3. The service rate μ is the same for each channel.
4. The arrivals wait in a single waiting line and then move to the first open channel for service.

Operating Characteristics

The following formulas can be used to compute the steady-state operating characteristics for multiple-channel waiting lines, where

$$\lambda = \text{the arrival rate for the system}$$
$$\mu = \text{the service rate for } each \text{ channel}$$
$$k = \text{the number of channels}$$

1. The probability that no units are in the system:

$$P_0 = \frac{1}{\displaystyle\sum_{n=0}^{k-1} \frac{(\lambda/\mu)^n}{n!} + \frac{(\lambda/\mu)^k}{k!}\left(\frac{k\mu}{k\mu - \lambda}\right)} \qquad \textbf{(15.11)}$$

2. The average number of units in the waiting line:

$$L_q = \frac{(\lambda/\mu)^k \lambda\mu}{(k-1)!(k\mu - \lambda)^2} P_0 \qquad \textbf{(15.12)}$$

3. The average number of units in the system:

$$L = L_q + \frac{\lambda}{\mu} \qquad \textbf{(15.13)}$$

4. The average time a unit spends in the waiting line:

$$W_q = \frac{L_q}{\lambda} \qquad \textbf{(15.14)}$$

5. The average time a unit spends in the system:

$$W = W_q + \frac{1}{\mu} \qquad \textbf{(15.15)}$$

6. The probability that an arriving unit has to wait for service:

$$P_w = \frac{1}{k!}\left(\frac{\lambda}{\mu}\right)^k \left(\frac{k\mu}{k\mu - \lambda}\right) P_0 \qquad \textbf{(15.16)}$$

7. The probability of n units in the system:

$$P_n = \frac{(\lambda/\mu)^n}{n!} P_0 \qquad \text{for } n \leq k \qquad \textbf{(15.17)}$$

$$P_n = \frac{(\lambda/\mu)^n}{k!k^{(n-k)}} P_0 \qquad \text{for } n > k \qquad \textbf{(15.18)}$$

Because μ is the service rate for each channel, $k\mu$ is the service rate for the multiple-channel system. As was true for the single-channel waiting line model, the formulas for the operating characteristics of multiple-channel waiting lines can be applied only in situations where the service rate for the system is greater than the arrival rate for the system; in other words, the formulas are applicable only if $k\mu$ is greater than λ.

Some expressions for the operating characteristics of multiple-channel waiting lines are more complex than their single-channel counterparts. However, equations (15.11) through (15.18) provide the same information as provided by the single-channel model. To help simplify the use of the multiple-channel equations, Table 15.4 contains values of P_0 for selected values of λ/μ and k. The values provided in the table correspond to cases where $k\mu > \lambda$, and hence the service rate is sufficient to process all arrivals.

TABLE 15.4   VALUES OF P_0 FOR MULTIPLE-CHANNEL WAITING LINES WITH POISSON ARRIVALS AND EXPONENTIAL SERVICE TIMES

Ratio λ/μ	Number of Channels (k)			
	2	**3**	**4**	**5**
0.15	0.8605	0.8607	0.8607	0.8607
0.20	0.8182	0.8187	0.8187	0.8187
0.25	0.7778	0.7788	0.7788	0.7788
0.30	0.7391	0.7407	0.7408	0.7408
0.35	0.7021	0.7046	0.7047	0.7047
0.40	0.6667	0.6701	0.6703	0.6703
0.45	0.6327	0.6373	0.6376	0.6376
0.50	0.6000	0.6061	0.6065	0.6065
0.55	0.5686	0.5763	0.5769	0.5769
0.60	0.5385	0.5479	0.5487	0.5488
0.65	0.5094	0.5209	0.5219	0.5220
0.70	0.4815	0.4952	0.4965	0.4966
0.75	0.4545	0.4706	0.4722	0.4724
0.80	0.4286	0.4472	0.4491	0.4493
0.85	0.4035	0.4248	0.4271	0.4274
0.90	0.3793	0.4035	0.4062	0.4065
0.95	0.3559	0.3831	0.3863	0.3867
1.00	0.3333	0.3636	0.3673	0.3678
1.20	0.2500	0.2941	0.3002	0.3011
1.40	0.1765	0.2360	0.2449	0.2463
1.60	0.1111	0.1872	0.1993	0.2014
1.80	0.0526	0.1460	0.1616	0.1646
2.00		0.1111	0.1304	0.1343
2.20		0.0815	0.1046	0.1094
2.40		0.0562	0.0831	0.0889
2.60		0.0345	0.0651	0.0721
2.80		0.0160	0.0521	0.0581
3.00			0.0377	0.0466
3.20			0.0273	0.0372
3.40			0.0186	0.0293
3.60			0.0113	0.0228
3.80			0.0051	0.0174
4.00				0.0130
4.20				0.0093
4.40				0.0063
4.60				0.0038
4.80				0.0017

Operating Characteristics for the Burger Dome Problem

To illustrate the multiple-channel waiting line model, we return to the Burger Dome fast-food restaurant waiting line problem. Suppose that management wants to evaluate the desirability of opening a second order-processing station so that two customers can be served simultaneously. Assume a single waiting line with the first customer in line moving to the first available server. Let us evaluate the operating characteristics for this two-channel system.

We use equations (15.12) through (15.18) for the $k = 2$-channel system. For an arrival rate of $\lambda = 0.75$ customers per minute and a service rate of $\mu = 1$ customer per minute for each channel, we obtain the operating characteristics:

WEB file

Multiple

$$P_0 = 0.4545 \quad \text{(from Table 15.4 with } \lambda/\mu = 0.75)$$

$$L_q = \frac{(0.75/1)^2(0.75)(1)}{(2-1)![2(1)-0.75]^2}(0.4545) = 0.1227 \text{ customer}$$

$$L = L_q + \frac{\lambda}{\mu} = 0.1227 + \frac{0.75}{1} = 0.8727 \text{ customer}$$

$$W_q = \frac{L_q}{\lambda} = \frac{0.1227}{0.75} = 0.1636 \text{ minute}$$

$$W = W_q + \frac{1}{\mu} = 0.1636 + \frac{1}{1} = 1.1636 \text{ minutes}$$

$$P_w = \frac{1}{2!}\left(\frac{0.75}{1}\right)^2\left[\frac{2(1)}{2(1)-0.75}\right](0.4545) = 0.2045$$

Try Problem 18 for practice in determining the operating characteristics for a two-channel waiting line.

Using equations (15.17) and (15.18), we can compute the probabilities of n customers in the system. The results from these computations are summarized in Table 15.5.

We can now compare the steady-state operating characteristics of the two-channel system to the operating characteristics of the original single-channel system discussed in Section 15.2.

1. The average time a customer spends in the system (waiting time plus service time) is reduced from $W = 4$ minutes to $W = 1.1636$ minutes.
2. The average number of customers in the waiting line is reduced from $L_q = 2.25$ customers to $L_q = 0.1227$ customer.
3. The average time a customer spends in the waiting line is reduced from $W_q = 3$ minutes to $W_q = 0.1636$ minute.
4. The probability that a customer has to wait for service is reduced from $P_w = 0.75$ to $P_w = 0.2045$.

Clearly the two-channel system will significantly improve the operating characteristics of the waiting line. However, adding an order filler at each service station would further increase the service rate and improve the operating characteristics. The final decision regarding the staffing policy at Burger Dome rests with the Burger Dome management. The waiting line study simply provides the operating characteristics that can be anticipated under three configurations: a single-channel system with one employee, a single-channel system with two employees, and a two-channel system with an employee for each channel.

TABLE 15.5   THE PROBABILITY OF n CUSTOMERS IN THE SYSTEM FOR THE BURGER DOME TWO-CHANNEL WAITING LINE

Number of Customers	Probability
0	0.4545
1	0.3409
2	0.1278
3	0.0479
4	0.0180
5 or more	0.0109

After considering these results, what action would you recommend? In this case, Burger Dome adopted the following policy statement: For periods when customer arrivals are expected to average 45 customers per hour, Burger Dome will open two order-processing channels with one employee assigned to each.

By changing the arrival rate λ to reflect arrival rates at different times of the day, and then computing the operating characteristics, Burger Dome's management can establish guidelines and policies that tell the store managers when to schedule service operations with a single channel, two channels, or perhaps even three or more channels.

NOTES AND COMMENTS

The multiple-channel waiting line model is based on a single waiting line. You may have also encountered situations where each of the k channels has its own waiting line. Analysts have shown that the operating characteristics of multiple-channel systems are better if a single waiting line is used.

People like them better also; no one who comes in after you can be served ahead of you. Thus, when possible, banks, airline reservation counters, food-service establishments, and other businesses frequently use a single waiting line for a multiple-channel system.

15.4 Some General Relationships for Waiting Line Models

In Sections 15.2 and 15.3 we presented formulas for computing the operating characteristics for single-channel and multiple-channel waiting lines with Poisson arrivals and exponential service times. The operating characteristics of interest included

$$L_q = \text{the average number of units in the waiting line}$$
$$L = \text{the average number of units in the system}$$
$$W_q = \text{the average time a unit spends in the waiting line}$$
$$W = \text{the average time a unit spends in the system}$$

John D. C. Little showed that several relationships exist among these four characteristics and that these relationships apply to a variety of different waiting line systems. Two of the relationships, referred to as *Little's flow equations,* are

$$L = \lambda W \tag{15.19}$$

$$L_q = \lambda W_q \tag{15.20}$$

Equation (15.19) shows that the average number of units in the system, L, can be found by multiplying the arrival rate, λ, by the average time a unit spends in the system, W. Equation (15.20) shows that the same relationship holds between the average number of units in the waiting line, L_q, and the average time a unit spends in the waiting line, W_q.

Using equation (15.20) and solving for W_q, we obtain

$$W_q = \frac{L_q}{\lambda} \tag{15.21}$$

Equation (15.21) follows directly from Little's second flow equation. We used it for the single-channel waiting line model in Section 15.2 and the multiple-channel waiting line model in Section 15.3 [see equations (15.7) and (15.14)]. Once L_q is computed for either of these models, equation (15.21) can then be used to compute W_q.

Another general expression that applies to waiting line models is that the average time in the system, W, is equal to the average time in the waiting line, W_q, plus the average service time. For a system with a service rate μ, the mean service time is $1/\mu$. Thus, we have the general relationship

$$W = W_q + \frac{1}{\mu} \qquad \textbf{(15.22)}$$

Recall that we used equation (15.22) to provide the average time in the system for both the single- and multiple-channel waiting line models [see equations (15.8) and (15.15)].

The importance of Little's flow equations is that they apply to *any waiting line model* regardless of whether arrivals follow the Poisson probability distribution and regardless of whether service times follow the exponential probability distribution. For example, in a study of the grocery checkout counters at Murphy's Foodliner, an analyst concluded that arrivals follow the Poisson probability distribution with an arrival rate of 24 customers per hour, or $\lambda = 24/60 = 0.40$ customers per minute. However, the analyst found that service times follow a normal probability distribution rather than an exponential probability distribution. The service rate was found to be 30 customers per hour, or $\mu = 30/60 = 0.50$ customers per minute. A time study of actual customer waiting times showed that, on average, a customer spends 4.5 minutes in the system (waiting time plus checkout time); that is, $W = 4.5$. Using the waiting line relationships discussed in this section, we can now compute other operating characteristics for this waiting line.

The advantage of Little's flow equations is that they show how operating characteristics L, L_q, W, and W_q are related in any waiting line system. Arrivals and service times do not have to follow specific probability distributions for the flow equations to be applicable.

First, using equation (15.22) and solving for W_q, we have

$$W_q = W - \frac{1}{\mu} = 4.5 - \frac{1}{0.50} = 2.5 \text{ minutes}$$

With both W and W_q known, we can use Little's flow equations, (15.19) and (15.20), to compute

$$L = \lambda W = 0.40(4.5) = 1.8 \text{ customers}$$
$$L_q = \lambda W_q = 0.40(2.5) = 1 \text{ customer}$$

The application of Little's flow equations is demonstrated in Problem 25.

The manager of Murphy's Foodliner can now review these operating characteristics to see whether action should be taken to improve the service and to reduce the waiting time and the length of the waiting line.

NOTES AND COMMENTS

In waiting line systems where the length of the waiting line is limited (e.g., a small waiting area), some arriving units will be blocked from joining the waiting line and will be lost. In this case, the blocked or lost arrivals will make the mean number of units entering the system something less than the arrival rate. By defining λ as the mean number of units *joining the system,* rather than the arrival rate, the relationships discussed in this section can be used to determine W, L, W_q, and L_q.

15.5   Economic Analysis of Waiting Lines

Frequently, decisions involving the design of waiting lines will be based on a subjective evaluation of the operating characteristics of the waiting line. For example, a manager may decide that an average waiting time of one minute or less and an average of two customers or fewer in the system are reasonable goals. The waiting line models presented in the preceding sections can be used to determine the number of channels that will meet the manager's waiting line performance goals.

On the other hand, a manager may want to identify the cost of operating the waiting line system and then base the decision regarding system design on a minimum hourly or daily operating cost. Before an economic analysis of a waiting line can be conducted, a total cost model, which includes the cost of waiting and the cost of service, must be developed.

To develop a total cost model for a waiting line, we begin by defining the notation to be used:

Waiting cost is based on average number of units in the system. It includes the time spent waiting in line plus the time spent being served.

$$c_w = \text{the waiting cost per time period for each unit}$$
$$L = \text{the average number of units in the system}$$
$$c_s = \text{the service cost per time period for each channel}$$
$$k = \text{the number of channels}$$
$$TC = \text{the total cost per time period}$$

The total cost is the sum of the waiting cost and the service cost; that is,

$$TC = c_w L + c_s k \tag{15.23}$$

Adding more channels always improves the operating characteristics of the waiting line and reduces the waiting cost. However, additional channels increase the service cost. An economic analysis of waiting lines attempts to find the number of channels that will minimize total cost by balancing the waiting cost and the service cost.

To conduct an economic analysis of a waiting line, we must obtain reasonable estimates of the waiting cost and the service cost. Of these two costs, the waiting cost is usually the more difficult to evaluate. In the Burger Dome restaurant problem, the waiting cost would be the cost per minute for a customer waiting for service. This cost is not a direct cost to Burger Dome. However, if Burger Dome ignores this cost and allows long waiting lines, customers ultimately will take their business elsewhere. Thus, Burger Dome will experience lost sales and, in effect, incur a cost.

The service cost is generally easier to determine. This cost is the relevant cost associated with operating each service channel. In the Burger Dome problem, this cost would include the server's wages, benefits, and any other direct costs associated with operating the service channel. At Burger Dome, this cost is estimated to be $7 per hour.

To demonstrate the use of equation (15.23), we assume that Burger Dome is willing to assign a cost of $10 per hour for customer waiting time. We use the average number of units in the system, L, as computed in Sections 15.2 and 15.3 to obtain the total hourly cost for the single-channel and two-channel systems:

Single-channel system ($L = 3$ customers):

$$TC = c_w L + c_s k$$
$$= 10(3) + 7(1) = \$37.00 \text{ per hour}$$

FIGURE 15.4   THE GENERAL SHAPE OF WAITING COST, SERVICE COST, AND TOTAL COST CURVES IN WAITING LINE MODELS

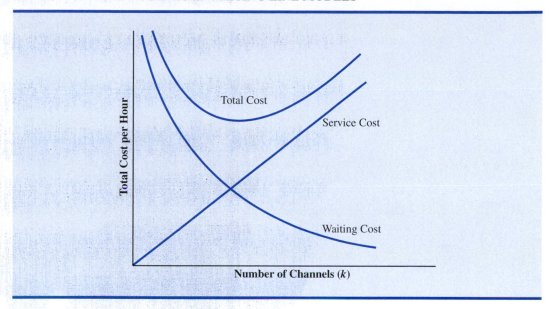

Two-channel system ($L = 0.8727$ customer):

$$TC = c_w L + c_s k$$
$$= 10(0.8727) + 7(2) = \$22.73 \text{ per hour}$$

Problem 21 tests your ability to conduct an economic analysis of proposed single-channel and two-channel waiting line systems.

Thus, based on the cost data provided by Burger Dome, the two-channel system provides the most economical operation.

Figure 15.4 shows the general shape of the cost curves in the economic analysis of waiting lines. The service cost increases as the number of channels is increased. However, with more channels, the service is better. As a result, waiting time and cost decrease as the number of channels is increased. The number of channels that will provide a good approximation of the minimum total cost design can be found by evaluating the total cost for several design alternatives.

NOTES AND COMMENTS

1. In dealing with government agencies and utility companies, customers may not be able to take their business elsewhere. In these situations, no lost business occurs when long waiting times are encountered. This condition is one reason that service in such organizations may be poor and that customers in such situations may experience long waiting times.

2. In some instances, the organization providing the service also employs the units waiting for the service. For example, consider the case of a company that owns and operates the trucks used to deliver goods to and from its manufacturing plant. In addition to the costs associated with the trucks waiting to be loaded or unloaded, the firm also pays the wages of the truck loaders and unloaders who operate the service channel. In this case, the cost of having the trucks wait and the cost of operating the service channel are direct expenses to the firm. An economic analysis of the waiting line system is highly recommended for these types of situations.

Other Waiting Line Models

D. G. Kendall suggested a notation that is helpful in classifying the wide variety of different waiting line models that have been developed. The three-symbol Kendall notation is as follows:

$$A/B/k$$

where

      A denotes the probability distribution for the arrivals

      B denotes the probability distribution for the service time

      k denotes the number of channels

Depending on the letter appearing in the A or B position, a variety of waiting line systems can be described. The letters that are commonly used are as follows:

    M designates a Poisson probability distribution for the arrivals or an exponential probability distribution for service time

    D designates that the arrivals or the service time is deterministic or constant

    G designates that the arrivals or the service time has a general probability distribution with a known mean and variance

Using the Kendall notation, the single-channel waiting line model with Poisson arrivals and exponential service times is classified as an $M/M/1$ model. The two-channel waiting line model with Poisson arrivals and exponential service times presented in Section 15.3 would be classified as an $M/M/2$ model.

NOTES AND COMMENTS

In some cases, the Kendall notation is extended to five symbols. The fourth symbol indicates the largest number of units that can be in the system, and the fifth symbol indicates the size of the population. The fourth symbol is used in situations where the waiting line can hold a finite or maximum number of units, and the fifth symbol is necessary when the population of arriving units or customers is finite. When the fourth and fifth symbols of the Kendall notation are omitted, the waiting line system is assumed to have infinite capacity, and the population is assumed to be infinite.

Single-Channel Waiting Line Model with Poisson Arrivals and Arbitrary Service Times

Let us return to the single-channel waiting line model where arrivals are described by a Poisson probability distribution. However, we now assume that the probability distribution for the service times is not an exponential probability distribution. Thus, using the Kendall notation, the waiting line model that is appropriate is an $M/G/1$ model, where G denotes a general or unspecified probability distribution.

When providing input to the M/G/1 model, be consistent in terms of the time period. For example, if λ and μ are expressed in terms of the number of units per hour, the standard deviation of the service time should be expressed in hours. The example that follows uses minutes as the time period for the arrival and service data.

Operating Characteristics for the $M/G/1$ Model

The notation used to describe the operating characteristics for the $M/G/1$ model is

$$\lambda = \text{the arrival rate}$$
$$\mu = \text{the service rate}$$
$$\sigma = \text{the standard deviation of the service time}$$

Some of the steady-state operating characteristics of the $M/G/1$ waiting line model are as follows:

1. The probability that no units are in the system:

$$P_0 = 1 - \frac{\lambda}{\mu} \qquad \textbf{(15.24)}$$

2. The average number of units in the waiting line:

$$L_q = \frac{\lambda^2\sigma^2 + (\lambda/\mu)^2}{2(1 - \lambda/\mu)} \qquad \textbf{(15.25)}$$

3. The average number of units in the system:

$$L = L_q + \frac{\lambda}{\mu} \qquad \textbf{(15.26)}$$

4. The average time a unit spends in the waiting line:

$$W_q = \frac{L_q}{\lambda} \qquad \textbf{(15.27)}$$

5. The average time a unit spends in the system:

$$W = W_q + \frac{1}{\mu} \qquad \textbf{(15.28)}$$

6. The probability that an arriving unit has to wait for service:

$$P_w = \frac{\lambda}{\mu} \qquad \textbf{(15.29)}$$

Note that the relationships for L, W_q, and W are the same as the relationships used for the waiting line models in Sections 15.2 and 15.3. They are given by Little's flow equations.

Problem 27 provides another application of a single-channel waiting line with Poisson arrivals and arbitrary service times.

An Example   Retail sales at Hartlage's Seafood Supply are handled by one clerk. Customer arrivals are random, and the arrival rate is 21 customers per hour or $\lambda = 21/60 = 0.35$ customers per minute. A study of the service process shows that the service time is

2 minutes per customer, with a standard deviation of $\sigma = 1.2$ minutes. The mean time of 2 minutes per customer shows that the clerk has a service rate of $\mu = 1/2 = 0.50$ customers per minute. The operating characteristics of this $M/G/1$ waiting line system are

WEB file

Single-Arbitrary

$$P_0 = 1 - \frac{\lambda}{\mu} = 1 - \frac{0.35}{0.50} = 0.30$$

$$L_q = \frac{(0.35)^2(1.2)^2 + (0.35/0.50)^2}{2(1 - 0.35/0.50)} = 1.1107 \text{ customers}$$

$$L = L_q + \frac{\lambda}{\mu} = 1.1107 + \frac{0.35}{0.50} = 1.8107 \text{ customers}$$

$$W_q = \frac{L_q}{\lambda} = \frac{1.1107}{0.35} = 3.1733 \text{ minutes}$$

$$W = W_q + \frac{1}{\mu} = 3.1733 + \frac{1}{0.50} = 5.1733 \text{ minutes}$$

$$P_w = \frac{\lambda}{\mu} = \frac{0.35}{0.50} = 0.70$$

Hartlage's manager can review these operating characteristics to determine whether scheduling a second clerk appears to be worthwhile.

Constant Service Times

We want to comment briefly on the single-channel waiting line model that assumes random arrivals but constant service times. Such a waiting line can occur in production and manufacturing environments where machine-controlled service times are constant. This waiting line is described by the $M/D/1$ model, with the D referring to the deterministic service times. With the $M/D/1$ model, the average number of units in the waiting line, L_q, can be found by using equation (15.25) with the condition that the standard deviation of the constant service time is $\sigma = 0$. Thus, the expression for the average number of units in the waiting line for the $M/D/1$ waiting line becomes

$$L_q = \frac{(\lambda/\mu)^2}{2(1 - \lambda/\mu)} \tag{15.30}$$

The other expressions presented earlier in this section can be used to determine additional operating characteristics of the $M/D/1$ system.

NOTES AND COMMENTS

Whenever the operating characteristics of a waiting line are unacceptable, managers often try to improve service by increasing the service rate μ. This approach is good, but equation (15.25) shows that the variation in the service times also affects the operating characteristics of the waiting line. Because the standard deviation of service times, σ, appears in the numerator of equation (15.25), a larger variation in service times results in a larger average number of units in the waiting line. Hence, another alternative for improving the service capabilities of a waiting line is to reduce the variation in the service times. Thus, even when the service rate of the service facility cannot be increased, a reduction in σ will reduce the average number of units in the waiting line and improve the operating characteristics of the system.

15.8 Multiple–Channel Model with Poisson Arrivals, Arbitrary Service Times, and no Waiting Line

An interesting variation of the waiting line models discussed so far involves a system in which no waiting is allowed. Arriving units or customers seek service from one of several service channels. If all channels are busy, arriving units are denied access to the system. In waiting line terminology, arrivals occurring when the system is full are **blocked** and are cleared from the system. Such customers may be lost or may attempt a return to the system later.

The specific model considered in this section is based on the following assumptions:

1. The system has k channels.
2. The arrivals follow a Poisson probability distribution, with arrival rate λ.
3. The service times for each channel may have any probability distribution.
4. The service rate μ is the same for each channel.
5. An arrival enters the system only if at least one channel is available. An arrival occurring when all channels are busy is blocked—that is, denied service and not allowed to enter the system.

With G denoting a general or unspecified probability distribution for service times, the appropriate model for this situation is referred to as an *M/G/k* model with "blocked customers cleared." The question addressed in this type of situation is, How many channels or servers should be used?

A primary application of this model involves the design of telephone and other communication systems where the arrivals are the calls and the channels are the number of telephone or communication lines available. In such a system, the calls are made to one telephone number, with each call automatically switched to an open channel if possible. When all channels are busy, additional calls receive a busy signal and are denied access to the system.

Operating Characteristics for the *M/G/k* Model with Blocked Customers Cleared

With no waiting allowed, operating characteristics L_q and W_q considered in previous waiting line models are automatically zero regardless of the number of service channels. In this situation, the more important design consideration involves determining how the percentage of blocked customers is affected by the number of service channels.

We approach the problem of selecting the best number of channels by computing the steady-state probabilities that j of the k channels will be busy. These probabilities are

$$P_j = \frac{(\lambda/\mu)^j/j!}{\sum_{i=0}^{k}(\lambda/\mu)^i/i!} \qquad (15.31)$$

where

$$\lambda = \text{the arrival rate}$$
$$\mu = \text{the service rate for each channel}$$
$$k = \text{the number of channels}$$
$$P_j = \text{the probability that } j \text{ of the } k \text{ channels are busy}$$
$$\qquad \text{for } j = 0, 1, 2, \ldots, k$$

The most important probability value is P_k, which is the probability that all k channels are busy. On a percentage basis, P_k indicates the percentage of arrivals that are blocked and denied access to the system.

Another operating characteristic of interest is the average number of units in the system; note that this number is equivalent to the average number of channels in use. Letting L denote the average number of units in the system, we have

$$L = \frac{\lambda}{\mu}(1 - P_k) \tag{15.32}$$

An Example Microdata Software, Inc., uses a telephone ordering system for its computer software products. Callers place orders with Microdata by using the company's 800 telephone number. Assume that calls to this telephone number arrive at a rate of $\lambda = 12$ calls per hour. The time required to process a telephone order varies considerably from order to order. However, each Microdata sales representative can be expected to handle $\mu = 6$ calls per hour. Currently, the Microdata 800 telephone number has three internal lines or channels, each operated by a separate sales representative. Calls received on the 800 number are automatically transferred to an open line or channel if available.

Whenever all three lines are busy, callers receive a busy signal. In the past, Microdata's management assumed that callers receiving a busy signal would call back later. However, recent research on telephone ordering showed that a substantial number of callers who are denied access do not call back later. These lost calls represent lost revenues for the firm, so Microdata's management requested an analysis of the telephone ordering system. Specifically, management wanted to know the percentage of callers who get busy signals and are blocked from the system. If management's goal is to provide sufficient capacity to handle 90% of the callers, how many telephone lines and sales representatives should Microdata use?

We can demonstrate the use of equation (15.31) by computing P_3, the probability that all three of the currently available telephone lines will be in use and additional callers will be blocked:

No Waiting

$$P_3 = \frac{(^{12}/_6)^3/3!}{(^{12}/_6)^0/0! + (^{12}/_6)^1/1! + (^{12}/_6)^2/2! + (^{12}/_6)^3/3!} = \frac{1.3333}{6.3333} = 0.2105$$

With $P_3 = 0.2105$, approximately 21% of the calls, or slightly more than one in five calls, are being blocked. Only 79% of the calls are being handled immediately by the three-line system.

Let us assume that Microdata expands to a four-line system. Then, the probability that all four channels will be in use and that callers will be blocked is

$$P_4 = \frac{(^{12}/_6)^4/4!}{(^{12}/_6)^0/0! + (^{12}/_6)^1/1! + (^{12}/_6)^2/2! + (^{12}/_6)^3/3! + (^{12}/_6)^4/4!} = \frac{0.667}{7} = 0.0952$$

Problem 30 provides practice in calculating probabilities for multiple-channel systems with no waiting line.

With only 9.52% of the callers blocked, 90.48% of the callers will reach the Microdata sales representatives. Thus, Microdata should expand its order-processing operation to four lines to meet management's goal of providing sufficient capacity to handle at least 90% of the callers. The average number of calls in the four-line system and thus the average number of lines and sales representatives that will be busy is

$$L = \frac{\lambda}{\mu}(1 - P_4) = \frac{12}{6}(1 - 0.0952) = 1.8095$$

TABLE 15.6   PROBABILITIES OF BUSY LINES FOR THE MICRODATA FOUR-LINE SYSTEM

Number of Busy Lines	Probability
0	0.1429
1	0.2857
2	0.2857
3	0.1905
4	0.0952

Although an average of fewer than two lines will be busy, the four-line system is necessary to provide the capacity to handle at least 90% of the callers. We used equation (15.31) to calculate the probability that 0, 1, 2, 3, or 4 lines will be busy. These probabilities are summarized in Table 15.6.

As we discussed in Section 15.5, an economic analysis of waiting lines can be used to guide system design decisions. In the Microdata system, the cost of the additional line and additional sales representative should be relatively easy to establish. This cost can be balanced against the cost of the blocked calls. With 9.52% of the calls blocked and $\lambda = 12$ calls per hour, an eight-hour day will have an average of $8(12)(0.0952) = 9.1$ blocked calls. If Microdata can estimate the cost of possible lost sales, the cost of these blocked calls can be established. The economic analysis based on the service cost and the blocked-call cost can assist in determining the optimal number of lines for the system.

NOTES AND COMMENTS

Many of the operating characteristics considered in previous sections are not relevant for the $M/G/k$ model with blocked customers cleared. In particular, the average time in the waiting line, W_q, and the average number of units in the waiting line, L_q, are no longer considered because waiting is not permitted in this type of system.

15.9   Waiting Line Models with Finite Calling Populations

In previous waiting line models, the arrival rate was constant and independent of the number of units in the system. With a finite calling population, the arrival rate decreases as the number of units in the system increases because, with more units in the system, fewer units are available for arrivals.

For the waiting line models introduced so far, the population of units or customers arriving for service has been considered to be unlimited. In technical terms, when no limit is placed on how many units may seek service, the model is said to have an **infinite calling population**. Under this assumption, the arrival rate λ remains constant regardless of how many units are in the waiting line system. This assumption of an infinite calling population is made in most waiting line models.

In other cases, the maximum number of units or customers that may seek service is assumed to be finite. In this situation the arrival rate for the system changes, depending on the number of units in the waiting line, and the waiting line model is said to have a **finite calling population**. The formulas for the operating characteristics of the previous waiting line models must be modified to account for the effect of the finite calling population.

The finite calling population model discussed in this section is based on the following assumptions:

1. The arrivals for *each unit* follow a Poisson probability distribution, with arrival rate λ.
2. The service times follow an exponential probability distribution, with service rate μ.
3. The population of units that may seek service is finite.

With a single channel, the waiting line model is referred to as an *M/M/1* model with a finite calling population.

The arrival rate λ is defined differently for the finite calling population model. Specifically, λ is defined in terms of the arrival rate for each unit.

The arrival rate for the *M/M/1* model with a finite calling population is defined in terms of how often each unit arrives or seeks service. This situation differs from that for previous waiting line models in which λ denoted the arrival rate for the system. With a finite calling population, the arrival rate for the system varies, depending on the number of units in the system. Instead of adjusting for the changing system arrival rate, in the finite calling population model λ indicates the arrival rate for each unit.

Operating Characteristics for the *M/M/1* Model with a Finite Calling Population

The following formulas are used to determine the steady-state operating characteristics for an *M/M/1* model with a finite calling population, where

$$\lambda = \text{the arrival rate for each unit}$$
$$\mu = \text{the service rate}$$
$$N = \text{the size of the population}$$

1. The probability that no units are in the system:

$$P_0 = \frac{1}{\displaystyle\sum_{n=0}^{N} \frac{N!}{(N-n)!}\left(\frac{\lambda}{\mu}\right)^n} \tag{15.33}$$

2. The average number of units in the waiting line:

$$L_q = N - \frac{\lambda + \mu}{\lambda}(1 - P_0) \tag{15.34}$$

3. The average number of units in the system:

$$L = L_q + (1 - P_0) \tag{15.35}$$

4. The average time a unit spends in the waiting line:

$$W_q = \frac{L_q}{(N - L)\lambda} \tag{15.36}$$

5. The average time a unit spends in the system:

$$W = W_q + \frac{1}{\mu} \qquad \text{(15.37)}$$

6. The probability an arriving unit has to wait for service:

$$P_w = 1 - P_0 \qquad \text{(15.38)}$$

7. The probability of n units in the system:

$$P_n = \frac{N!}{(N-n)!}\left(\frac{\lambda}{\mu}\right)^n P_0 \quad \text{for } n = 0, 1, \ldots, N \qquad \text{(15.39)}$$

One of the primary applications of the $M/M/1$ model with a finite calling population is referred to as the *machine repair problem*. In this problem, a group of machines is considered to be the finite population of "customers" that may request repair service. Whenever a machine breaks down, an arrival occurs in the sense that a new repair request is initiated. If another machine breaks down before the repair work has been completed on the first machine, the second machine begins to form a "waiting line" for repair service. Additional breakdowns by other machines will add to the length of the waiting line. The assumption of first-come, first-served indicates that machines are repaired in the order they break down. The $M/M/1$ model shows that one person or one channel is available to perform the repair service. To return the machine to operation, each machine with a breakdown must be repaired by the single-channel operation.

An Example The Kolkmeyer Manufacturing Company uses a group of six identical machines; each machine operates an average of 20 hours between breakdowns. Thus, the arrival rate or request for repair service for each machine is $\lambda = \frac{1}{20} = 0.05$ per hour. With randomly occurring breakdowns, the Poisson probability distribution is used to describe the machine breakdown arrival process. One person from the maintenance department provides the single-channel repair service for the six machines. The exponentially distributed service times have a mean of two hours per machine, or a service rate of $\mu = \frac{1}{2} = 0.50$ machines per hour.

With $\lambda = 0.05$ and $\mu = 0.50$, we use equations (15.33) through (15.38) to compute the operating characteristics for this system. Note that the use of equation (15.33) makes the computations involved somewhat cumbersome. Confirm for yourself that equation (15.33) provides the value of $P_0 = 0.4845$. The computations for the other operating characteristics are

$$L_q = 6 - \left(\frac{0.05 + 0.50}{0.05}\right)(1 - 0.4845) = 0.3297 \text{ machine}$$

$$L = 0.3295 + (1 - 0.4845) = 0.8451 \text{ machine}$$

$$W_q = \frac{0.3295}{(6 - 0.845)0.50} = 1.279 \text{ hours}$$

$$W = 1.279 + \frac{1}{0.50} = 3.279 \text{ hours}$$

$$P_w = 1 - P_0 = 1 - 0.4845 = 0.5155$$

Finally, equation (15.39) can be used to compute the probabilities of any number of machines being in the repair system.

Operating characteristics of an M/M/1 waiting line with a finite calling population are considered in Problem 34.

As with other waiting line models, the operating characteristics provide the manager with information about the operation of the waiting line. In this case, the fact that a machine breakdown waits an average of $W_q = 1.279$ hours before maintenance begins and the fact that more than 50% of the machine breakdowns must wait for service, $P_w = 0.5155$, indicates a two-channel system may be needed to improve the machine repair service.

An Excel worksheet template at the Web files link on the Web site that accompanies this text or The Management Scientist software may be used to analyze the multiple-channel finite calling population model.

Computations of the operating characteristics of a multiple-channel finite calling population waiting line are more complex than those for the single-channel model. A computer solution is virtually mandatory in this case. The Excel worksheet for the Kolkmeyer two-channel machine repair system is shown in Figure 15.5. With two repair personnel, the average machine breakdown waiting time is reduced to $W_q = 0.0834$ hours, or 5 minutes, and only 10%, $P_w = 0.1036$, of the machine breakdowns wait for service. Thus, the two-channel system significantly improves the machine repair service operation. Ultimately, by considering the cost of machine downtime and the cost of the repair personnel, management can determine whether the improved service of the two-channel system is cost effective.

FIGURE 15.5   WORKSHEET FOR THE KOLKMEYER TWO-CHANNEL MACHINE REPAIR PROBLEM

WEB file

Finite

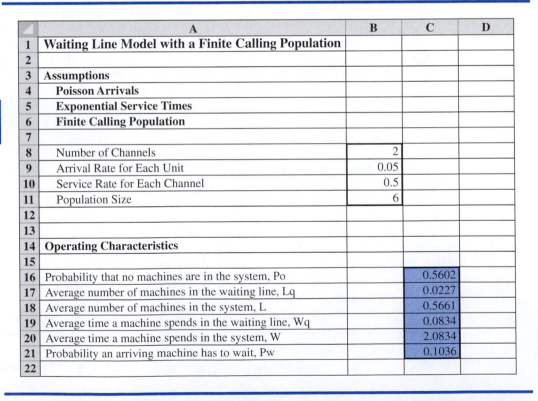

	A	B	C	D
1	**Waiting Line Model with a Finite Calling Population**			
2				
3	**Assumptions**			
4	**Poisson Arrivals**			
5	**Exponential Service Times**			
6	**Finite Calling Population**			
7				
8	Number of Channels	2		
9	Arrival Rate for Each Unit	0.05		
10	Service Rate for Each Channel	0.5		
11	Population Size	6		
12				
13				
14	**Operating Characteristics**			
15				
16	Probability that no machines are in the system, Po		0.5602	
17	Average number of machines in the waiting line, Lq		0.0227	
18	Average number of machines in the system, L		0.5661	
19	Average time a machine spends in the waiting line, Wq		0.0834	
20	Average time a machine spends in the system, W		2.0834	
21	Probability an arriving machine has to wait, Pw		0.1036	
22				

Summary

In this chapter we presented a variety of waiting line models that have been developed to help managers make better decisions concerning the operation of waiting lines. For each model we presented formulas that could be used to develop operating characteristics or performance measures for the system being studied. The operating characteristics presented include the following:

1. Probability that no units are in the system
2. Average number of units in the waiting line
3. Average number of units in the system
4. Average time a unit spends in the waiting line
5. Average time a unit spends in the system
6. Probability that arriving units will have to wait for service

We also showed how an economic analysis of the waiting line could be conducted by developing a total cost model that includes the cost associated with units waiting for service and the cost required to operate the service facility.

As many of the examples in this chapter show, the most obvious applications of waiting line models are situations in which customers arrive for service such as at a grocery checkout counter, bank, or restaurant. However, with a little creativity, waiting line models can be applied to many different situations such as telephone calls waiting for connections, mail orders waiting for processing, machines waiting for repairs, manufacturing jobs waiting to be processed, and money waiting to be spent or invested. The Q.M. in Action, Improving Productivity at the New Haven Fire Department, describes an application in which a waiting line model helped improve emergency medical response time and also provided a significant savings in operating costs.

The complexity and diversity of waiting line systems found in practice often prevent an analyst from finding an existing waiting line model that fits the specific application being studied. Simulation, the topic discussed in Chapter 16, provides an approach to determining the operating characteristics of such waiting line systems.

Q.M. *in* ACTION

IMPROVING PRODUCTIVITY AT THE NEW HAVEN FIRE DEPARTMENT*

The New Haven, Connecticut, Fire Department implemented a reorganization plan with cross-trained fire and medical personnel responding to both fire and medical emergencies. A waiting line model provided the basis for the reorganization by demonstrating that substantial improvements in emergency medical response time could be achieved with only a small reduction in fire protection. Annual savings were reported to be $1.4 million.

The model was based on Poisson arrivals and exponential service times for both fire and medical emergencies. It was used to estimate the average time that a person

placing a call would have to wait for the appropriate emergency unit to arrive at the location. Waiting times were estimated by the model's prediction of the average travel time to reach each of the city's 28 census tracts.

The model was first applied to the original system of 16 fire units and 4 emergency medical units that operated independently. It was then applied to the proposed reorganization plan that involved cross-trained department personnel qualified to respond to both fire and medical emergencies. Results from the model demonstrated that average travel times could be reduced under the reorganization plan. Various facility location alternatives also were evaluated. When implemented, the reorganization plan reduced operating cost and improved public safety services.

*Based on A. J. Swersey, L. Goldring, and E. D. Geyer, "Improving Fire Department Productivity: Merging Fire and Emergency Medical Units in New Haven," *Interfaces* 23, no. 1 (January/February 1993): 109–129.

Glossary

Queue A waiting line.

Queueing theory The body of knowledge dealing with waiting lines.

Operating characteristics The performance measures for a waiting line, including the probability that no units are in the system, the average number of units in the waiting line, the average waiting time, and so on.

Single-channel waiting line A waiting line with only one service facility.

Poisson probability distribution A probability distribution used to describe the arrival pattern for some waiting line models.

Arrival rate The mean number of customers or units arriving in a given period of time.

Exponential probability distribution A probability distribution used to describe the service time for some waiting line models.

Service rate The mean number of customers or units that can be served by one service facility in a given period of time.

First-come, first-served (FCFS) The queue discipline that serves waiting units on a first-come, first-served basis.

Transient period The start-up period for a waiting line, occurring before the waiting line reaches a normal or steady-state operation.

Steady-state operation The normal operation of the waiting line after it has gone through a start-up or transient period. The operating characteristics of waiting lines are computed for steady-state conditions.

Multiple-channel waiting line A waiting line with two or more parallel service facilities.

Blocked When arriving units cannot enter the waiting line because the system is full. Blocked units can occur when waiting lines are not allowed or when waiting lines have a finite capacity.

Infinite calling population The population of customers or units that may seek service has no specified upper limit.

Finite calling population The population of customers or units that may seek service has a fixed and finite value.

Problems

1. Willow Brook National Bank operates a drive-up teller window that allows customers to complete bank transactions without getting out of their cars. On weekday mornings, arrivals to the drive-up teller window occur at random, with an arrival rate of 24 customers per hour or 0.4 customer per minute.
    a.   What is the mean or expected number of customers that will arrive in a five-minute period?
    b.   Assume that the Poisson probability distribution can be used to describe the arrival process. Use the arrival rate in part (a) and compute the probabilities that exactly 0, 1, 2, and 3 customers will arrive during a five-minute period.
    c.   Delays are expected if more than three customers arrive during any five-minute period. What is the probability that delays will occur?

2. In the Willow Brook National Bank waiting line system (see Problem 1), assume that the service times for the drive-up teller follow an exponential probability distribution with a

service rate of 36 customers per hour, or 0.6 customer per minute. Use the exponential probability distribution to answer the following questions:
a. What is the probability the service time is one minute or less?
b. What is the probability the service time is two minutes or less?
c. What is the probability the service time is more than two minutes?

3. Use the single-channel drive-up bank teller operation referred to in Problems 1 and 2 to determine the following operating characteristics for the system:
a. The probability that no customers are in the system
b. The average number of customers waiting
c. The average number of customers in the system
d. The average time a customer spends waiting
e. The average time a customer spends in the system
f. The probability that arriving customers will have to wait for service

4. Use the single-channel drive-up bank teller operation referred to in Problems 1–3 to determine the probabilities of 0, 1, 2, and 3 customers in the system. What is the probability that more than three customers will be in the drive-up teller system at the same time?

5. The reference desk of a university library receives requests for assistance. Assume that a Poisson probability distribution with an arrival rate of 10 requests per hour can be used to describe the arrival pattern and that service times follow an exponential probability distribution with a service rate of 12 requests per hour.
a. What is the probability that no requests for assistance are in the system?
b. What is the average number of requests that will be waiting for service?
c. What is the average waiting time in minutes before service begins?
d. What is the average time at the reference desk in minutes (waiting time plus service time)?
e. What is the probability that a new arrival has to wait for service?

6. Movies Tonight is a typical video and DVD movie rental outlet for home-viewing customers. During the weeknight evenings, customers arrive at Movies Tonight with an arrival rate of 1.25 customers per minute. The checkout clerk has a service rate of 2 customers per minute. Assume Poisson arrivals and exponential service times.
a. What is the probability that no customers are in the system?
b. What is the average number of customers waiting for service?
c. What is the average time a customer waits for service to begin?
d. What is the probability that an arriving customer will have to wait for service?
e. Do the operating characteristics indicate that the one-clerk checkout system provides an acceptable level of service?

7. Speedy Oil provides a single-channel automobile oil change and lubrication service. Customers provide an arrival rate of 2.5 cars per hour. The service rate is 5 cars per hour. Assume that arrivals follow a Poisson probability distribution and that service times follow an exponential probability distribution.
a. What is the average number of cars in the system?
b. What is the average time that a car waits for the oil and lubrication service to begin?
c. What is the average time a car spends in the system?
d. What is the probability that an arrival has to wait for service?

8. For the Burger Dome single-channel waiting line in Section 15.2, assume that the arrival rate is increased to 1 customer per minute and that the service rate is increased to 1.25 customers per minute. Compute the following operating characteristics for the new system: P_0, L_q, L, W_q, W, and P_w. Does this system provide better or poorer service compared to the original system? Discuss any differences and the reason for these differences.

9. Marty's Barber Shop has one barber. Customers have an arrival rate of 2.2 customers per hour, and haircuts are given with a service rate of 5 per hour. Use the Poisson arrivals and exponential service times model to answer the following questions:
   a. What is the probability that no units are in the system?
   b. What is the probability that one customer is receiving a haircut and no one is waiting?
   c. What is the probability that one customer is receiving a haircut and one customer is waiting?
   d. What is the probability that one customer is receiving a haircut and two customers are waiting?
   e. What is the probability that more than two customers are waiting?
   f. What is the average time a customer waits for service?

10. Trosper Tire Company decided to hire a new mechanic to handle all tire changes for customers ordering a new set of tires. Two mechanics applied for the job. One mechanic has limited experience, can be hired for $14 per hour, and can service an average of three customers per hour. The other mechanic has several years of experience, can service an average of four customers per hour, but must be paid $20 per hour. Assume that customers arrive at the Trosper garage at the rate of two customers per hour.
    a. What are the waiting line operating characteristics using each mechanic, assuming Poisson arrivals and exponential service times?
    b. If the company assigns a customer waiting cost of $30 per hour, which mechanic provides the lower operating cost?

11. Agan Interior Design provides home and office decorating assistance to its customers. In normal operation, an average of 2.5 customers arrive each hour. One design consultant is available to answer customer questions and make product recommendations. The consultant averages 10 minutes with each customer.
    a. Compute the operating characteristics of the customer waiting line, assuming Poisson arrivals and exponential service times.
    b. Service goals dictate that an arriving customer should not wait for service more than an average of 5 minutes. Is this goal being met? If not, what action do you recommend?
    c. If the consultant can reduce the average time spent per customer to 8 minutes, what is the mean service rate? Will the service goal be met?

12. Pete's Market is a small local grocery store with only one checkout counter. Assume that shoppers arrive at the checkout lane according to a Poisson probability distribution, with an arrival rate of 15 customers per hour. The checkout service times follow an exponential probability distribution, with a service rate of 20 customers per hour.
    a. Compute the operating characteristics for this waiting line.
    b. If the manager's service goal is to limit the waiting time prior to beginning the checkout process to no more than five minutes, what recommendations would you provide regarding the current checkout system?

13. After reviewing the waiting line analysis of Problem 12, the manager of Pete's Market wants to consider one of the following alternatives for improving service. What alternative would you recommend? Justify your recommendation.
    a. Hire a second person to bag the groceries while the cash register operator is entering the cost data and collecting money from the customer. With this improved single-channel operation, the service rate could be increased to 30 customers per hour.
    b. Hire a second person to operate a second checkout counter. The two-channel operation would have a service rate of 20 customers per hour for each channel.

14. Ocala Software Systems operates a technical support center for its software customers. If customers have installation or use problems with Ocala software products, they may telephone the technical support center and obtain free consultation. Currently, Ocala operates

its support center with one consultant. If the consultant is busy when a new customer call arrives, the customer hears a recorded message stating that all consultants are currently busy with other customers. The customer is then asked to hold and a consultant will provide assistance as soon as possible. The customer calls follow a Poisson probability distribution, with an arrival rate of five calls per hour. On average, it takes 7.5 minutes for a consultant to answer a customer's questions. The service time follows an exponential probability distribution.

a. What is the service rate in terms of customers per hour?
b. What is the probability that no customers are in the system and the consultant is idle?
c. What is the average number of customers waiting for a consultant?
d. What is the average time a customer waits for a consultant?
e. What is the probability that a customer will have to wait for a consultant?
f. Ocala's customer service department recently received several letters from customers complaining about the difficulty in obtaining technical support. If Ocala's customer service guidelines state that no more than 35% of all customers should have to wait for technical support and that the average waiting time should be two minutes or less, does your waiting line analysis indicate that Ocala is or is not meeting its customer service guidelines? What action, if any, would you recommend?

15. To improve customer service, Ocala Software Systems (see Problem 14) wants to investigate the effect of using a second consultant at its technical support center. What effect would the additional consultant have on customer service? Would two technical consultants enable Ocala to meet its service guidelines, with no more than 35% of all customers having to wait for technical support and an average customer waiting time of two minutes or less? Discuss.

16. The new Fore and Aft Marina is to be located on the Ohio River near Madison, Indiana. Assume that Fore and Aft decides to build a docking facility where one boat at a time can stop for gas and servicing. Assume that arrivals follow a Poisson probability distribution, with an arrival rate of 5 boats per hour, and that service times follow an exponential probability distribution, with a service rate of 10 boats per hour. Answer the following questions:

a. What is the probability that no boats are in the system?
b. What is the average number of boats that will be waiting for service?
c. What is the average time a boat will spend waiting for service?
d. What is the average time a boat will spend at the dock?
e. If you were the manager of Fore and Aft Marina, would you be satisfied with the service level your system will be providing? Why or why not?

17. The manager of the Fore and Aft Marina in Problem 16 wants to investigate the possibility of enlarging the docking facility so that two boats can stop for gas and servicing simultaneously. Assume that the arrival rate is 5 boats per hour and that the service rate for each channel is 10 boats per hour.

a. What is the probability that the boat dock will be idle?
b. What is the average number of boats that will be waiting for service?
c. What is the average time a boat will spend waiting for service?
d. What is the average time a boat will spend at the dock?
e. If you were the manager of Fore and Aft Marina, would you be satisfied with the service level your system will be providing? Why or why not?

18. All airplane passengers at the Lake City Regional Airport must pass through a security screening area before proceeding to the boarding area. The airport has three screening stations available, and the facility manager must decide how many to have open at any particular time. The service rate for processing passengers at each screening station is 3 passengers per minute. On Monday morning the arrival rate is 5.4 passengers per minute.

Assume that processing times at each screening station follow an exponential distribution and that arrivals follow a Poisson distribution.

a. Suppose two of the three screening stations are open on Monday morning. Compute the operating characteristics for the screening facility.

b. Because of space considerations, the facility manager's goal is to limit the average number of passengers waiting in line to 10 or fewer. Will the two-screening-station system be able to meet the manager's goal?

c. What is the average time required for a passenger to pass through security screening?

19. Refer again to the Lake City Regional Airport described in Problem 18. When the security level is raised to high, the service rate for processing passengers is reduced to 2 passengers per minute at each screening station. Suppose the security level is raised to high on Monday morning. The arrival rate is 5.4 passengers per minute.

a. The facility manager's goal is to limit the average number of passengers waiting in line to 10 or fewer. How many screening stations must be open in order to satisfy the manager's goal?

b. What is the average time required for a passenger to pass through security screening?

20. A Florida coastal community experiences a population increase during the winter months, with seasonal residents arriving from northern states and Canada. Staffing at a local post office is often in a state of change due to the relatively low volume of customers in the summer months and the relatively high volume of customers in the winter months. The service rate of a postal clerk is 0.75 customer per minute. The post office counter has a maximum of three workstations. The target maximum time a customer waits in the system is five minutes.

a. For a particular Monday morning in November, the anticipated arrival rate is 1.2 customers per minute. What is the recommended staffing for this Monday morning? Show the operating characteristics of the waiting line.

b. A new population growth study suggests that over the next two years the arrival rate at the postal office during the busy winter months can be expected to be 2.1 customers per minute. Use a waiting line analysis to make a recommendation to the post office manager.

21. Refer to the Agan Interior Design situation in Problem 11. Agan's management would like to evaluate two alternatives:

• Use one consultant with an average service time of 8 minutes per customer.
• Expand to two consultants, each of whom has an average service time of 10 minutes per customer.

If the consultants are paid $16 per hour and the customer waiting time is valued at $25 per hour for waiting time prior to service, should Agan expand to the two-consultant system? Explain.

22. A fast-food franchise is considering operating a drive-up window food-service operation. Assume that customer arrivals follow a Poisson probability distribution, with an arrival rate of 24 cars per hour, and that service times follow an exponential probability distribution. Arriving customers place orders at an intercom station at the back of the parking lot and then drive to the service window to pay for and receive their orders. The following three service alternatives are being considered:

• A single-channel operation in which one employee fills the order and takes the money from the customer. The average service time for this alternative is 2 minutes.
• A single-channel operation in which one employee fills the order while a second employee takes the money from the customer. The average service time for this alternative is 1.25 minutes.
• A two-channel operation with two service windows and two employees. The employee stationed at each window fills the order and takes the money for customers arriving at the window. The average service time for this alternative is 2 minutes for each channel.

Answer the following questions and recommend an alternative design for the fast-food franchise:

a. What is the probability that no cars are in the system?
b. What is the average number of cars waiting for service?
c. What is the average number of cars in the system?
d. What is the average time a car waits for service?
e. What is the average time in the system?
f. What is the probability that an arriving car will have to wait for service?

23. The following cost information is available for the fast-food franchise in Problem 22:
   • Customer waiting time is valued at $25 per hour to reflect the fact that waiting time is costly to the fast-food business.
   • The cost of each employee is $6.50 per hour.
   • To account for equipment and space, an additional cost of $20 per hour is attributable to each channel.

   What is the lowest-cost design for the fast-food business?

24. Patients arrive at a dentist's office with an arrival rate of 2.8 patients per hour. The dentist can treat patients at a service rate of 3 patients per hour. A study of patient waiting times shows that a patient waits an average of 30 minutes before seeing the dentist.

a. What are the arrival and service rates in terms of patients per minute?
b. What is the average number of patients in the waiting room?
c. If a patient arrives at 10:10 A.M., at what time is the patient expected to leave the office?

25. A study of the multiple-channel food-service operation at the Red Birds baseball park shows that the average time between the arrival of a customer at the food-service counter and his or her departure with a filled order is 10 minutes. During the game, customers arrive at the rate of four per minute. The food-service operation requires an average of 2 minutes per customer order.

a. What is the service rate per channel in terms of customers per minute?
b. What is the average waiting time in the line prior to placing an order?
c. On average, how many customers are in the food-service system?

26. Manning Autos operates an automotive service counter. While completing the repair work, Manning mechanics arrive at the company's parts department counter, with an arrival rate of four per hour. The parts coordinator spends an average of 6 minutes with each mechanic, discussing the parts the mechanic needs and retrieving the parts from inventory.

a. Currently, Manning has one parts coordinator. On average, each mechanic waits 4 minutes before the parts coordinator is available to answer questions or retrieve parts from inventory. Find L_q, W, and L for this single-channel parts operation.
b. A trial period with a second parts coordinator showed that, on average, each mechanic waited only 1 minute before a parts coordinator was available. Find L_q, W, and L for this two-channel parts operation.
c. If the cost of each mechanic is $20 per hour and the cost of each parts coordinator is $12 per hour, is the one-channel or the two-channel system more economical?

27. Gubser Welding, Inc., operates a welding service for construction and automotive repair jobs. Assume that the arrival of jobs at the company's office can be described by a Poisson probability distribution with an arrival rate of two jobs per 8-hour day. The time required to complete the jobs follows a normal probability distribution, with a mean time of 3.2 hours and a standard deviation of 2 hours. Answer the following questions, assuming that Gubser uses one welder to complete all jobs:

a. What is the mean arrival rate in jobs per hour?
b. What is the mean service rate in jobs per hour?
c. What is the average number of jobs waiting for service?

    d.   What is the average time a job waits before the welder can begin working on it?

    e.   What is the average number of hours between when a job is received and when it is completed?

    f.   What percentage of the time is Gubser's welder busy?

28.   Jobs arrive randomly at a particular assembly plant; assume that the arrival rate is five jobs per hour. Service times (in minutes per job) do not follow the exponential probability distribution. Two proposed designs for the plant's assembly operation are shown.

	Service Time	
Design	**Mean**	**Standard Deviation**
A	6.0	3.0
B	6.25	0.6

    a.   What is the service rate in jobs per hour for each design?

    b.   For the service rates in part (a), what design appears to provide the best or fastest service rate?

    c.   What are the standard deviations of the service times in hours?

    d.   Use the $M/G/1$ model to compute the operating characteristics for each design.

    e.   Which design provides the best operating characteristics? Why?

29.   The Robotics Manufacturing Company operates an equipment repair business where emergency jobs arrive randomly at the rate of three jobs per 8-hour day. The company's repair facility is a single-channel system operated by a repair technician. The service time varies, with a mean repair time of 2 hours and a standard deviation of 1.5 hours. The company's cost of the repair operation is $28 per hour. In the economic analysis of the waiting line system, Robotics uses $35 per hour cost for customers waiting during the repair process.

    a.   What are the arrival rate and service rate in jobs per hour?

    b.   Show the operating characteristics including the total cost per hour.

    c.   The company is considering purchasing a computer-based equipment repair system that would enable a constant repair time of 2 hours. For practical purposes, the standard deviation is 0. Because of the computer-based system, the company's cost of the new operation would be $32 per hour. The firm's director of operations said No to the request for the new system because the hourly cost is $4 higher and the mean repair time is the same. Do you agree? What effect will the new system have on the waiting line characteristics of the repair service?

    d.   Does paying for the computer-based system to reduce the variation in service time make economic sense? How much will the new system save the company during a 40-hour workweek?

30.   A large insurance company maintains a central computing system that contains a variety of information about customer accounts. Insurance agents in a six-state area use telephone lines to access the customer information database. Currently, the company's central computer system allows three users to access the central computer simultaneously. Agents who attempt to use the system when it is full are denied access; no waiting is allowed. Management realizes that with its expanding business, more requests will be made to the central information system. Being denied access to the system is inefficient as well as annoying for agents. Access requests follow a Poisson probability distribution, with a mean of 42 calls per hour. The service rate per line is 20 calls per hour.

    a.   What is the probability that 0, 1, 2, and 3 access lines will be in use?

    b.   What is the probability that an agent will be denied access to the system?

    c.   What is the average number of access lines in use?

d.   In planning for the future, management wants to be able to handle $\lambda = 50$ calls per hour; in addition, the probability that an agent will be denied access to the system should be no greater than the value computed in part (b). How many access lines should this system have?

31.   Mid-West Publishing Company publishes college textbooks. The company operates an 800 telephone number whereby potential adopters can ask questions about forthcoming texts, request examination copies of texts, and place orders. Currently, two extension lines are used, with two representatives handling the telephone inquiries. Calls occurring when both extension lines are being used receive a busy signal; no waiting is allowed. Each representative can accommodate an average of 12 calls per hour. The arrival rate is 20 calls per hour.
a.   How many extension lines should be used if the company wants to handle 90% of the calls immediately?
b.   What is the average number of extension lines that will be busy if your recommendation in part (a) is used?
c.   What percentage of calls receive a busy signal for the current telephone system with two extension lines?

32.   City Cab, Inc., uses two dispatchers to handle requests for service and to dispatch the cabs. The telephone calls that are made to City Cab use a common telephone number. When both dispatchers are busy, the caller hears a busy signal; no waiting is allowed. Callers who receive a busy signal can call back later or call another cab service. Assume that the arrival of calls follows a Poisson probability distribution, with a mean of 40 calls per hour, and that each dispatcher can handle a mean of 30 calls per hour.
a.   What percentage of time are both dispatchers idle?
b.   What percentage of time are both dispatchers busy?
c.   What is the probability that callers will receive a busy signal if two, three, or four dispatchers are used?
d.   If management wants no more than 12% of the callers to receive a busy signal, how many dispatchers should be used?

33.   Kolkmeyer Manufacturing Company (see Section 15.9) is considering adding two machines to its manufacturing operation. This addition will bring the number of machines to eight. The president of Kolkmeyer asked for a study of the need to add a second employee to the repair operation. The arrival rate is 0.05 machine per hour for each machine, and the service rate for each individual assigned to the repair operation is 0.50 machine per hour.
a.   Compute the operating characteristics if the company retains the single-employee repair operation.
b.   Compute the operating characteristics if a second employee is added to the machine repair operation.
c.   Each employee is paid $20 per hour. Machine downtime is valued at $80 per hour. From an economic point of view, should one or two employees handle the machine repair operation? Explain.

34.   Five administrative assistants use an office copier. The average time between arrivals for each assistant is 40 minutes, which is equivalent to an arrival rate of $\frac{1}{40} = 0.025$ arrival per minute. The mean time each assistant spends at the copier is 5 minutes, which is equivalent to a service rate of $\frac{1}{5} = 0.20$ per minute. Use the $M/M/1$ model with a finite calling population to determine the following:
a.   The probability that the copier is idle
b.   The average number of administrative assistants in the waiting line
c.   The average number of administrative assistants at the copier
d.   The average time an assistant spends waiting for the copier
e.   The average time an assistant spends at the copier

    f.   During an 8-hour day, how many minutes does an assistant spend at the copier? How much of this time is waiting time?

    g.   Should management consider purchasing a second copier? Explain.

35.   Schips Department Store operates a fleet of 10 trucks. The trucks arrive at random times throughout the day at the store's truck dock to be loaded with new deliveries or to have incoming shipments from the regional warehouse unloaded. Each truck returns to the truck dock for service two times per 8-hour day. Thus, the arrival rate per truck is 0.25 trucks per hour. The service rate is 4 trucks per hour. Using the Poisson arrivals and exponential service times model with a finite calling population of 10 trucks, determine the following operating characteristics:

    a.   The probability no trucks are at the truck dock

    b.   The average number of trucks waiting for loading/unloading

    c.   The average number of trucks in the truck dock area

    d.   The average waiting time before loading/unloading begins

    e.   The average waiting time in the system

    f.   What is the hourly cost of operation if the cost is $50 per hour for each truck and $30 per hour for the truck dock?

    g.   Consider a two-channel truck dock operation where the second channel could be operated for an additional $30 per hour. How much would the average number of trucks waiting for loading/unloading have to be reduced to make the two-channel truck dock economically feasible?

    h.   Should the company consider expanding to the two-channel truck dock? Explain.

Case Problem 1   Regional Airlines

Regional Airlines is establishing a new telephone system for handling flight reservations. During the 10:00 A.M. to 11:00 A.M. time period, calls to the reservation agent occur randomly at an average of one call every 3.75 minutes. Historical service time data show that a reservation agent spends an average of 3 minutes with each customer. The waiting line model assumptions of Poisson arrivals and exponential service times appear reasonable for the telephone reservation system.

Regional Airlines' management believes that offering an efficient telephone reservation system is an important part of establishing an image as a service-oriented airline. If the system is properly implemented, Regional Airlines will establish good customer relations, which in the long run will increase business. However, if the telephone reservation system is frequently overloaded and customers have difficulty contacting an agent, a negative customer reaction may lead to an eventual loss of business. The cost of a ticket reservation agent is $20 per hour. Thus, management wants to provide good service, but it does not want to incur the cost of overstaffing the telephone reservation operation by using more agents than necessary.

At a planning meeting, Regional's management team agreed that an acceptable customer service goal is to answer at least 85% of the incoming calls immediately. During the planning meeting, Regional's vice president of administration pointed out that the data show that the average service rate for an agent is faster than the average arrival rate of the telephone calls. The vice president's conclusion was that personnel costs could be minimized by using one agent and that the single agent should be able to handle the telephone reservations and still have some idle time. The vice president of marketing restated the importance of customer service and expressed support for at least two reservation agents.

The current telephone reservation system design does not allow callers to wait. Callers who attempt to reach a reservation agent when all agents are occupied receive a busy signal and are blocked from the system. A representative from the telephone company suggested that Regional Airlines consider an expanded system that accommodates waiting. In the expanded system, when a customer calls and all agents are busy, a recorded message tells the customer that the call is being held in the order received and that an agent will be available shortly. The customer can stay on the line and listen to background music while waiting for an agent. Regional's management will need more information before switching to the expanded system.

Managerial Report

Prepare a managerial report for Regional Airlines analyzing the telephone reservation system. Evaluate both the system that does not allow waiting and the expanded system that allows waiting. Include the following information in your report:

1. A detailed analysis of the operating characteristics of the reservation system with one agent as proposed by the vice president of administration. What is your recommendation concerning a single-agent system?

2. A detailed analysis of the operating characteristics of the reservation system based on your recommendation regarding the number of agents Regional should use.

3. What appear to be the advantages or disadvantages of the expanded system? Discuss the number of waiting callers the expanded system would need to accommodate.

4. The telephone arrival data presented are for the 10:00 A.M. to 11:00 A.M. time period; however, the arrival rate of incoming calls is expected to change from hour to hour. Describe how your waiting line analysis could be used to develop a ticket agent staffing plan that would enable the company to provide different levels of staffing for the ticket reservation system at different times during the day. Indicate the information that you would need to develop this staffing plan.

Case Problem 2   Office Equipment, Inc.

Office Equipment, Inc. (OEI), leases automatic mailing machines to business customers in Fort Wayne, Indiana. The company built its success on a reputation of providing timely maintenance and repair service. Each OEI service contract states that a service technician will arrive at a customer's business site within an average of three hours from the time that the customer notifies OEI of an equipment problem.

Currently, OEI has 10 customers with service contracts. One service technician is responsible for handling all service calls. A statistical analysis of historical service records indicates that a customer requests a service call at an average rate of one call per 50 hours of operation. If the service technician is available when a customer calls for service, it takes the technician an average of 1 hour of travel time to reach the customer's office and an average of 1.5 hours to complete the repair service. However, if the service technician is busy with another customer when a new customer calls for service, the technician completes the current service call and any other waiting service calls before responding to the new service call. In such cases, once the technician is free from all existing service commitments, the technician takes an average of 1 hour of travel time to reach the new customer's office and an average of 1.5 hours to complete the repair service. The cost of the service technician is $80 per hour. The downtime cost (wait time and service time) for customers is $100 per hour.

OEI is planning to expand its business. Within one year, OEI projects that it will have 20 customers, and within two years, OEI projects that it will have 30 customers. Although

OEI is satisfied that one service technician can handle the 10 existing customers, management is concerned about the ability of one technician to meet the average three-hour service call guarantee when the OEI customer base expands. In a recent planning meeting, the marketing manager made a proposal to add a second service technician when OEI reaches 20 customers and to add a third service technician when OEI reaches 30 customers. Before making a final decision, management would like an analysis of OEI service capabilities. OEI is particularly interested in meeting the average three-hour waiting time guarantee at the lowest possible total cost.

Managerial Report

Develop a managerial report summarizing your analysis of the OEI service capabilities. Make recommendations regarding the number of technicians to be used when OEI reaches 20 customers and when OEI reaches 30 customers. Include a discussion of the following issues in your report:

1. What is the arrival rate for each customer per hour?
2. What is the service rate in terms of the number of customers per hour? Note that the average travel time of 1 hour becomes part of the service time because the time that the service technician is busy handling a service call includes the travel time plus the time required to complete the repair.
3. Waiting line models generally assume that the arriving customers are in the same location as the service facility. Discuss the OEI situation in light of the fact that a service technician travels an average of 1 hour to reach each customer. How should the travel time and the waiting time predicted by the waiting line model be combined to determine the total customer waiting time?
4. OEI is satisfied that one service technician can handle the 10 existing customers. Use a waiting line model to determine the following information:
   - Probability that no customers are in the system
   - Average number of customers in the waiting line
   - Average number of customers in the system
   - Average time a customer waits until the service technician arrives
   - Average time a customer waits until the machine is back in operation
   - Probability that a customer will have to wait more than one hour for the service technician to arrive
   - The number of hours a week the technician is not making service calls
   - The total cost per hour for the service operation

   Do you agree with OEI management that one technician can meet the average three-hour service call guarantee? Explain.
5. What is your recommendation for the number of service technicians to hire when OEI expands to 20 customers? Use the information that you developed in part (4) to justify your answer.
6. What is your recommendation for the number of service technicians to hire when OEI expands to 30 customers? Use the information that you developed in part (4) to justify your answer.
7. What are the annual savings of your recommendation in part (6) compared to the planning committee's proposal that 30 customers will require three service technicians? Assume 250 days of operation per year.

CHAPTER 16

Simulation

CONTENTS

Simulation is one of the most widely used quantitative approaches to decision making. It is a method for learning about a real system by experimenting with a model that represents the system. The simulation model contains the mathematical expressions and logical relationships that describe how to compute the value of the outputs given the values of the inputs. Any simulation model has two inputs: controllable inputs and probabilistic inputs. Figure 16.1 shows a conceptual diagram of a simulation model.

In conducting a **simulation experiment**, an analyst selects the value, or values, for the **controllable inputs**. Then values for the **probabilistic inputs** are randomly generated. The simulation model uses the values of the controllable inputs and the values of the probabilistic inputs to compute the value, or values, of the output. By conducting a series of experiments using a variety of values for the controllable inputs, the analyst learns how values of the controllable inputs affect or change the output of the simulation model. After reviewing the simulation results, the analyst is often able to make decision recommendations for the controllable inputs that will provide the desired output for the real system.

Simulation has been successfully applied in a variety of applications. The following examples are typical:

1. *New Product Development* The objective of this simulation is to determine the probability that a new product will be profitable. A model is developed relating profit (the output measure) to various probabilistic inputs such as demand, parts cost, and labor cost. The only controllable input is whether to introduce the product. A variety of possible values will be generated for the probabilistic inputs, and the resulting profit will be computed. We develop a simulation model for this type of application in Section 16.1.

2. *Airline Overbooking* The objective of this simulation is to determine the number of reservations an airline should accept for a particular flight. A simulation model is developed relating profit for the flight to a probabilistic input, the number of passengers with a reservation who show up and use their reservation, and a controllable input, the number of reservations accepted for the flight. For each selected value for the controllable input, a variety of possible values will be generated for the number of passengers who show up, and the resulting profit can be computed. Similar simulation models are applicable for hotel and car rental reservation systems.

3. *Inventory Policy* The objective of this simulation is to choose an inventory policy that will provide good customer service at a reasonable cost. A model is developed relating two output measures, total inventory cost and the service level, to probabilistic inputs, such as product demand and delivery lead time from vendors, and controllable inputs, such as the order quantity and the reorder point. For each setting of the controllable inputs, a variety of possible values would be generated for the probabilistic inputs, and the resulting cost and service levels would be computed.

4. *Traffic Flow* The objective of this simulation is to determine the effect of installing a left turn signal on the flow of traffic through a busy intersection. A model is developed

FIGURE 16.1   DIAGRAM OF A SIMULATION MODEL

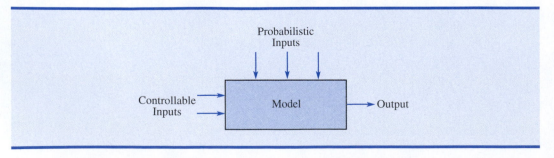

relating waiting time for vehicles to get through the intersection to probabilistic inputs such as the number of vehicle arrivals and the fraction that want to make a left turn, and controllable inputs such as the length of time the left turn signal is on. For each setting of the controllable inputs, values would be generated for the probabilistic inputs, and the resulting vehicle waiting times would be computed.

5. *Waiting Lines* The objective of this simulation is to determine the waiting times for customers at a bank's automated teller machine (ATM). A model is developed relating customer waiting times to probabilistic inputs such as customer arrivals and service times, and a controllable input, the number of ATM machines installed. For each value of the controllable input (the number of ATM machines), a variety of values would be generated for the probabilistic inputs and the customer waiting times would be computed. The Q.M. in Action, Call Center Design, describes how simulation of a waiting line system at a call center helped the company balance the service to its customers with the cost of agents providing the service.

Simulation is not an optimization technique. It is a method that can be used to describe or predict how a system will operate given certain choices for the controllable inputs and randomly generated values for the probabilistic inputs. Quantitative analysts often use simulation to determine values for the controllable inputs that are likely to lead to desirable system outputs. In this sense, simulation can be an effective tool in designing a system to provide good performance.

Q.M. *in* ACTION

CALL CENTER DESIGN*

A call center is a place where large volumes of calls are made to or received from current or potential customers. More than 60,000 call centers operate in the United States. Saltzman and Mehrotra describe how a simulation model helped make a strategic change in the design of the technical support call center for a major software company. The application used a waiting line simulation model to balance the service to customers calling for assistance with the cost of agents providing the service.

Historically, the software company provided free phone-in technical support, but over time service requests grew to the point where 80% of the callers were waiting between 5 and 10 minutes and abandonment rates were too high. On some days 40% of the callers hung up before receiving service. This service level was unacceptable. As a result, management considered instituting a Rapid Program in which customers would pay a fee for service, but would be guaranteed to receive service within one minute, or the service would be free. Nonpaying cus-

tomers would continue receiving service but without a guarantee of short service times.

A simulation model was developed to help understand the impact of this new program on the waiting line characteristics of the call center. Data available were used to develop the arrival distribution, the service time distribution, and the probability distribution for abandonment. The key design variables considered were the number of agents (channels) and the percentage of callers subscribing to the Rapid Program. The model was developed using the Arena simulation package.

The simulation results helped the company decide to go ahead with the Rapid Program. Under most of the scenarios considered, the simulation model showed that 95% of the callers in the Rapid Program would receive service within one minute and that free service to the remaining customers could be maintained within acceptable limits. Within nine months, 10% of the software company's customers subscribed to the Rapid Program, generating $2 million in incremental revenue. The company viewed the simulation model as a vehicle for mitigating risk. The model helped evaluate the likely impact of the Rapid Program without experimenting with actual customers.

*Based on Robert M. Saltzman and Vijay Mehrotra, "A Call Center Uses Simulation to Drive Strategic Change," *Interfaces* (May/June 2001): 87–101.

In this chapter we begin by showing how simulation can be used to study the financial risks associated with the development of a new product. We continue with illustrations showing how simulation can be used to establish an effective inventory policy and how it can be used to design waiting line systems. Other issues, such as verifying the simulation program, validating the model, and selecting a simulation software package, are discussed in Section 16.4.

Risk Analysis

Risk analysis is the process of predicting the outcome of a decision in the face of uncertainty. In this section we describe a problem that involves considerable uncertainty: the development of a new product. We first show how risk analysis can be conducted without using simulation; then we show how a more comprehensive risk analysis can be conducted with the aid of simulation.

PortaCom Project

PortaCom manufactures personal computers and related equipment. PortaCom's product design group developed a prototype for a new high-quality portable printer. The new printer features an innovative design and has the potential to capture a significant share of the portable printer market. Preliminary marketing and financial analyses provided the following selling price, first-year administrative cost, and first-year advertising cost:

$$\text{Selling price} = \$249 \text{ per unit}$$
$$\text{Administrative cost} = \$400{,}000$$
$$\text{Advertising cost} = \$600{,}000$$

In the simulation model for the PortaCom problem, the preceding values are constants and are referred to as **parameters** of the model.

The cost of direct labor, the cost of parts, and the first-year demand for the printer are not known with certainty and are considered probabilistic inputs. At this stage of the planning process, PortaCom's best estimates of these inputs are $45 per unit for the direct labor cost, $90 per unit for the parts cost, and 15,000 units for the first-year demand. PortaCom would like an analysis of the first-year profit potential for the printer. Because of PortaCom's tight cash flow situation, management is particularly concerned about the potential for a loss.

What-If Analysis

One approach to risk analysis is called **what-if analysis**. A what-if analysis involves generating values for the probabilistic inputs (direct labor cost, parts cost, and first-year demand) and computing the resulting value for the output (profit). With a selling price of $249 per unit and administrative plus advertising costs equal to $400,000 + $600,000 = $1,000,000, the PortaCom profit model is

$$\text{Profit} = (\$249 - \text{Direct labor cost per unit} - \text{Parts cost per unit})(\text{Demand}) - \$1{,}000{,}000$$

Letting

$$c_1 = \text{direct labor cost per unit}$$
$$c_2 = \text{parts cost per unit}$$
$$x = \text{first-year demand}$$

FIGURE 16.2   PORTACOM PROFIT MODEL

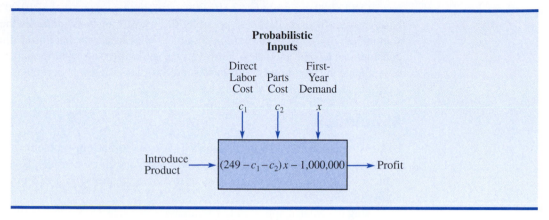

the profit model for the first year can be written as follows:

$$\text{Profit} = (249 - c_1 - c_2)x - 1{,}000{,}000 \qquad \textbf{(16.1)}$$

The PortaCom profit model can be depicted as shown in Figure 16.2.

Recall that PortaCom's best estimates of the direct labor cost per unit, the parts cost per unit, and first-year demand are $45, $90, and 15,000 units, respectively. These values constitute the **base-case scenario** for PortaCom. Substituting these values into equation (16.1) yields the following profit projection:

$$\text{Profit} = (249 - 45 - 90)(15{,}000) - 1{,}000{,}000 = 710{,}000$$

Thus, the base-case scenario leads to an anticipated profit of $710,000.

In risk analysis we are concerned with both the probability of a loss and the magnitude of a loss. Although the base-case scenario looks appealing, PortaCom might be interested in what happens if the estimates of the direct labor cost per unit, parts cost per unit, and first-year demand do not turn out to be as expected under the base-case scenario. For instance, suppose that PortaCom believes that direct labor costs could range from $43 to $47 per unit, parts cost could range from $80 to $100 per unit, and first-year demand could range from 1500 to 28,500 units. Using these ranges, what-if analysis can be used to evaluate a **worst-case scenario** and a **best-case scenario**.

The worst-case value for the direct labor cost is $47 (the highest value), the worst-case value for the parts cost is $100 (the highest value), and the worst-case value for demand is 1500 units (the lowest value). Thus, in the worst-case scenario, $c_1 = 47$, $c_2 = 100$, and $x = 1500$. Substituting these values into equation (16.1) leads to the following profit projection:

$$\text{Profit} = (249 - 47 - 100)(1500) - 1{,}000{,}000 = -847{,}000$$

So the worst-case scenario leads to a projected loss of $847,000.

The best-case value for the direct labor cost is $43 (the lowest value), the best-case value for the parts cost is $80 (the lowest value), and the best-case value for demand is 28,500 units (the highest value). Substituting these values into equation (16.1) leads to the following profit projection:

Problem 2 will give you practice using what-if analysis.

$$\text{Profit} = (249 - 43 - 80)(28{,}500) - 1{,}000{,}000 = 2{,}591{,}000$$

So the best-case scenario leads to a projected profit of $2,591,000.

At this point the what-if analysis provides the conclusion that profits can range from a loss of $847,000 to a profit of $2,591,000 with a base-case profit of $710,000. Although the base-case profit of $710,000 is possible, the what-if analysis indicates that either a substantial loss or a substantial profit is possible. Other scenarios that PortaCom might want to consider can also be evaluated. However, the difficulty with what-if analysis is that it does not indicate the likelihood of the various profit or loss values. In particular, we do not know anything about the *probability* of a loss.

Simulation

Using simulation to perform risk analysis for the PortaCom problem is like playing out many what-if scenarios by randomly generating values for the probabilistic inputs. The advantage of simulation is that it allows us to assess the probability of a profit and the probability of a loss.

Using the what-if approach to risk analysis, we selected values for the probabilistic inputs [direct labor cost per unit (c_1), parts cost per unit (c_2), and first-year demand (x)], and then computed the resulting profit. Applying simulation to the PortaCom problem requires generating values for the probabilistic inputs that are representative of what we might observe in practice. To generate such values, we must know the probability distribution for each probabilistic input. Further analysis by PortaCom led to the following probability distributions for the direct labor cost per unit, the parts cost per unit, and first-year demand:

Direct Labor Cost PortaCom believes that the direct labor cost will range from $43 to $47 per unit and is described by the discrete probability distribution shown in Table 16.1. Thus, we see a 0.1 probability that the direct labor cost will be $43 per unit, a 0.2 probability that the direct labor cost will be $44 per unit, and so on. The highest probability of 0.4 is associated with a direct labor cost of $45 per unit.

One advantage of simulation is the ability to use probability distributions that are unique to the system being studied.

Parts Cost This cost depends upon the general economy, the overall demand for parts, and the pricing policy of PortaCom's parts suppliers. PortaCom believes that the parts cost will range from $80 to $100 per unit and is described by the uniform probability distribution shown in Figure 16.3. Costs per unit between $80 and $100 are equally likely.

First-Year Demand PortaCom believes that first-year demand is described by the normal probability distribution shown in Figure 16.4. The mean or expected value of first-year demand is 15,000 units. The standard deviation of 4500 units describes the variability in the first-year demand.

To simulate the PortaCom problem, we must generate values for the three probabilistic inputs and compute the resulting profit. Then, we generate another set of values for the

TABLE 16.1   PROBABILITY DISTRIBUTION FOR DIRECT LABOR COST PER UNIT

Direct Labor Cost per Unit	Probability
$43	0.1
$44	0.2
$45	0.4
$46	0.2
$47	0.1

FIGURE 16.3   UNIFORM PROBABILITY DISTRIBUTION FOR THE PARTS COST PER UNIT

Parts Cost per Unit

FIGURE 16.4   NORMAL PROBABILITY DISTRIBUTION OF FIRST-YEAR DEMAND

Number of Units Sold

probabilistic inputs, compute a second value for profit, and so on. We continue this process until we are satisfied that enough trials have been conducted to describe the probability distribution for profit. This process of generating probabilistic inputs and computing the value of the output is called *simulation*. The sequence of logical and mathematical operations required to conduct a simulation can be depicted with a flowchart. A flowchart for the Porta-Com simulation is shown in Figure 16.5.

A flowchart provides a graphical representation that helps describe the logic of the simulation model.

Following the logic described by the flowchart we see that the model parameters—selling price, administrative cost, and advertising cost—are $249, $400,000, and $600,000, respectively. These values will remain fixed throughout the simulation.

The next three blocks depict the generation of values for the probabilistic inputs. First, a value for the direct labor cost (c_1) is generated. Then a value for the parts cost (c_2) is generated, followed by a value for the first-year demand (x). These probabilistic input values are combined using the profit model given by equation (16.1).

$$\text{Profit} = (249 - c_1 - c_2)x - 1,000,000$$

The computation of profit completes one trial of the simulation. We then return to the block where we generated the direct labor cost and begin another trial. This process is repeated until a satisfactory number of trials has been generated.

FIGURE 16.5   FLOWCHART FOR THE PORTACOM SIMULATION

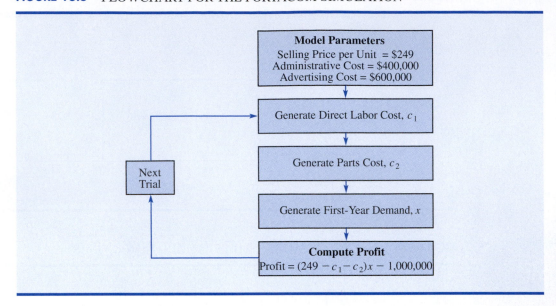

At the end of the simulation, output measures of interest can be developed. For example, we will be interested in computing the average profit and the probability of a loss. For the output measures to be meaningful, the values of the probabilistic inputs must be representative of what is likely to happen when the PortaCom printer is introduced into the market. An essential part of the simulation procedure is the ability to generate representative values for the probabilistic inputs. We now discuss how to generate these values.

Random Numbers and Generating Probabilistic Input Values   In the PortaCom simulation, representative values must be generated for the direct labor cost per unit (c_1), the parts cost per unit (c_2), and the first-year demand (x). Random numbers and the probability distributions associated with each probabilistic input are used to generate representative values. To illustrate how to generate these values, we need to introduce the concept of *computer-generated random numbers*.

Computer-generated random numbers[1] are randomly selected decimal numbers from 0 up to, but not including, 1. The computer-generated random numbers are equally likely and are uniformly distributed over the interval from 0 to 1. Computer-generated random numbers can be obtained using built-in functions available in computer simulation packages and spreadsheets. For instance, placing =RAND() in a cell of an Excel worksheet will result in a random number between 0 and 1 being placed into that cell.

Table 16.2 contains 500 random numbers generated using Excel. These numbers can be viewed as a random sample of 500 values from a uniform probability distribution over the interval from 0 to 1. Let us show how random numbers can be used to generate values for the PortaCom probability distributions. We begin by showing how to generate a value for the direct labor cost per unit. The approach described is applicable for generating values from any discrete probability distribution.

Because random numbers are equally likely, quantitative analysts can assign ranges of random numbers to corresponding values of probabilistic inputs so that the probability of any input value to the simulation model is identical to the probability of its occurrence in the real system.

---

[1]Computer-generated random numbers are called pseudorandom numbers. Because they are generated through the use of mathematical formulas, they are not technically random. The difference between random numbers and pseudorandom numbers is primarily philosophical, and we use the term random numbers regardless of whether they are generated by a computer.

TABLE 16.2   500 COMPUTER-GENERATED RANDOM NUMBERS

0.6953	0.5247	0.1368	0.9850	0.7467	0.3813	0.5827	0.7893	0.7169	0.8166
0.0082	0.9925	0.6874	0.2122	0.6885	0.2159	0.4299	0.3467	0.2186	0.1033
0.6799	0.1241	0.3056	0.5590	0.0423	0.6515	0.2750	0.8156	0.2871	0.4680
0.8898	0.1514	0.1826	0.0004	0.5259	0.2425	0.8421	0.9248	0.9155	0.9518
0.6515	0.5027	0.9290	0.5177	0.3134	0.9177	0.2605	0.6668	0.1167	0.7870
0.3976	0.7790	0.0035	0.0064	0.0441	0.3437	0.1248	0.5442	0.9800	0.1857
0.0642	0.4086	0.6078	0.2044	0.0484	0.4691	0.7058	0.8552	0.5029	0.3288
0.0377	0.5250	0.7774	0.2390	0.9121	0.5345	0.8178	0.8443	0.4154	0.2526
0.5739	0.5181	0.0234	0.7305	0.0376	0.5169	0.5679	0.5495	0.7872	0.5321
0.5827	0.0341	0.7482	0.6351	0.9146	0.4700	0.7869	0.1337	0.0702	0.4219
0.0508	0.7905	0.2932	0.4971	0.0225	0.4466	0.5118	0.1200	0.0200	0.5445
0.4757	0.1399	0.5668	0.9569	0.7255	0.4650	0.4084	0.3701	0.9446	0.8064
0.6805	0.9931	0.4166	0.1091	0.7730	0.0691	0.9411	0.3468	0.0014	0.7379
0.2603	0.7507	0.6414	0.9907	0.2699	0.4571	0.9254	0.2371	0.8664	0.9553
0.8143	0.7625	0.1708	0.1900	0.2781	0.2830	0.6877	0.0488	0.8635	0.3155
0.5681	0.7854	0.5016	0.9403	0.1078	0.5255	0.8727	0.3815	0.5541	0.9833
0.1501	0.9363	0.3858	0.3545	0.5448	0.0643	0.3167	0.6732	0.6283	0.2631
0.8806	0.7989	0.7484	0.8083	0.2701	0.5039	0.9439	0.1027	0.9677	0.4597
0.4582	0.7590	0.4393	0.4704	0.6903	0.3732	0.6587	0.8675	0.2905	0.3058
0.0785	0.1467	0.3880	0.5274	0.8723	0.7517	0.9905	0.8904	0.8177	0.6660
0.1158	0.6635	0.4992	0.9070	0.2975	0.5686	0.8495	0.1652	0.2039	0.2553
0.2762	0.7018	0.6782	0.4013	0.2224	0.4672	0.5753	0.6219	0.6871	0.9255
0.9382	0.6411	0.7984	0.0608	0.5945	0.3977	0.4570	0.9924	0.8398	0.8361
0.5102	0.7021	0.4353	0.3398	0.8038	0.2260	0.1250	0.1884	0.3432	0.1192
0.2354	0.7410	0.7089	0.2579	0.1358	0.8446	0.1648	0.3889	0.5620	0.6555
0.9082	0.7906	0.7589	0.8870	0.1189	0.7125	0.6324	0.1096	0.5155	0.3449
0.6936	0.0702	0.9716	0.0374	0.0683	0.2397	0.7753	0.2029	0.1464	0.8000
0.4042	0.8158	0.3623	0.6614	0.7954	0.7516	0.6518	0.3638	0.3107	0.2718
0.9410	0.2201	0.6348	0.0367	0.0311	0.0688	0.2346	0.3927	0.7327	0.9994
0.0917	0.2504	0.2878	0.1735	0.3872	0.6816	0.2731	0.3846	0.6621	0.8983
0.8532	0.4869	0.2685	0.6349	0.9364	0.3451	0.4998	0.2842	0.0643	0.6656
0.8980	0.0455	0.8314	0.8189	0.6783	0.8086	0.1386	0.4442	0.9941	0.6812
0.8412	0.8792	0.2025	0.9320	0.7656	0.3815	0.5302	0.8744	0.4584	0.3585
0.5688	0.8633	0.5818	0.0692	0.2543	0.5453	0.9955	0.1237	0.7535	0.5993
0.5006	0.1215	0.8102	0.1026	0.9251	0.6851	0.1559	0.1214	0.2628	0.9374
0.5748	0.4164	0.3427	0.2809	0.8064	0.5855	0.2229	0.2805	0.9139	0.9013
0.1100	0.0873	0.9407	0.8747	0.0496	0.4380	0.5847	0.4183	0.5929	0.4863
0.5802	0.7747	0.1285	0.0074	0.6252	0.7747	0.0112	0.3958	0.3285	0.5389
0.1019	0.6628	0.8998	0.1334	0.2798	0.7351	0.7330	0.6723	0.6924	0.3963
0.9909	0.8991	0.2298	0.2603	0.6921	0.5573	0.8191	0.0384	0.2954	0.0636
0.6292	0.4923	0.0276	0.6734	0.6562	0.4231	0.1980	0.6551	0.3716	0.0507
0.9430	0.2579	0.7933	0.0945	0.3192	0.3195	0.7772	0.4672	0.7070	0.5925
0.9938	0.7098	0.7964	0.7952	0.8947	0.1214	0.8454	0.8294	0.5394	0.9413
0.4690	0.1395	0.0930	0.3189	0.6972	0.7291	0.8513	0.9256	0.7478	0.8124
0.2028	0.3774	0.0485	0.7718	0.9656	0.2444	0.0304	0.1395	0.1577	0.8625
0.6141	0.4131	0.2006	0.2329	0.6182	0.5151	0.6300	0.9311	0.3837	0.7828
0.2757	0.8479	0.7880	0.8492	0.6859	0.8947	0.6246	0.1574	0.4936	0.8077
0.0561	0.0126	0.6531	0.0378	0.4975	0.1133	0.3572	0.0071	0.4555	0.7563
0.1419	0.4308	0.8073	0.4681	0.0481	0.2918	0.2975	0.0685	0.6384	0.0812
0.3125	0.0053	0.9209	0.9768	0.3584	0.0390	0.2161	0.6333	0.4391	0.6991

TABLE 16.3 RANDOM NUMBER INTERVALS FOR GENERATING VALUES OF DIRECT LABOR COST PER UNIT

Direct Labor Cost per Unit	Probability	Interval of Random Numbers
$43	0.1	0.0 but less than 0.1
$44	0.2	0.1 but less than 0.3
$45	0.4	0.3 but less than 0.7
$46	0.2	0.7 but less than 0.9
$47	0.1	0.9 but less than 1.0

An interval of random numbers is assigned to each possible value of the direct labor cost in such a fashion that the probability of generating a random number in the interval is equal to the probability of the corresponding direct labor cost. Table 16.3 shows how this process is done. The interval of random numbers 0.0 but less than 0.1 is associated with a direct labor cost of $43, the interval of random numbers 0.1 but less than 0.3 is associated with a direct labor cost of $44, and so on. With this assignment of random number intervals to the possible values of the direct labor cost, the probability of generating a random number in any interval is equal to the probability of obtaining the corresponding value for the direct labor cost. Thus, to select a value for the direct labor cost, we generate a random number between 0 and 1. If the random number is 0.0 but less than 0.1, we set the direct labor cost equal to $43. If the random number is 0.1 but less than 0.3, we set the direct labor cost equal to $44, and so on.

Each trial of the simulation requires a value for the direct labor cost. Suppose that on the first trial the random number is 0.9109. From Table 16.3, the simulated value for the direct labor cost is $47 per unit. Suppose that on the second trial the random number is 0.2841. From Table 16.3, the simulated value for the direct labor cost is $44 per unit. Table 16.4 shows the results obtained for the first 10 simulation trials.

Try Problem 5 for an opportunity to establish intervals of random numbers and simulate demand from a discrete probability distribution.

Each trial in the simulation requires a value of the direct labor cost, parts cost, and first-year demand. Let us now turn to the issue of generating values for the parts cost. The probability distribution for the parts cost per unit is the uniform distribution shown in Figure 16.3. Because this random variable has a different probability distribution than direct labor cost, we use random numbers in a slightly different way to generate values for parts cost. With a

TABLE 16.4 RANDOM GENERATION OF 10 VALUES FOR THE DIRECT LABOR COST PER UNIT

Trial	Random Number	Direct Labor Cost ($)
1	0.9109	47
2	0.2841	44
3	0.6531	45
4	0.0367	43
5	0.3451	45
6	0.2757	44
7	0.6859	45
8	0.6246	45
9	0.4936	45
10	0.8077	46

uniform probability distribution, the following relationship between the random number and the associated value of the parts cost is used:

$$\text{Parts cost} = a + r(b - a) \qquad \textbf{(16.2)}$$

where

$$r = \text{random number between 0 and 1}$$
$$a = \text{smallest value for parts cost}$$
$$b = \text{largest value for parts cost}$$

For PortaCom, the smallest value for the parts cost is $80, and the largest value is $100. Applying equation (16.2) with $a = 80$ and $b = 100$ leads to the following formula for generating the parts cost given a random number, r:

$$\text{Parts cost} = 80 + r(100 - 80) = 80 + r20 \qquad \textbf{(16.3)}$$

Equation (16.3) generates a value for the parts cost. Suppose that a random number of 0.2680 is obtained. The value for the parts cost is

$$\text{Parts cost} = 80 + 0.2680(20) = 85.36 \text{ per unit}$$

Suppose that a random number of 0.5842 is generated on the next trial. The value for the parts cost is

$$\text{Parts cost} = 80 + 0.5842(20) = 91.68 \text{ per unit}$$

Spreadsheet packages such as Excel have built-in functions that make simulations based on probability distributions such as the normal probability distribution relatively easy.

With appropriate choices of a and b, equation (16.2) can be used to generate values for any uniform probability distribution. Table 16.5 shows the generation of 10 values for the parts cost per unit.

Finally, we need a random number procedure for generating the first-year demand. Because first-year demand is normally distributed with a mean of 15,000 units and a standard deviation of 4500 units (see Figure 16.4), we need a procedure for generating random values from this normal probability distribution. Once again we will use a random number between 0 and 1 for this simulation. Suppose that the random number of 0.6026 is obtained. Using 0.6026 as the cumulative normal probability and the standard normal distribution table in Appendix D, this cumulative probability occurs at $z = 0.26$ standard deviations

TABLE 16.5 RANDOM GENERATION OF 10 VALUES FOR THE PARTS COST PER UNIT

Trial	Random Number	Parts Cost ($)
1	0.2680	85.36
2	0.5842	91.68
3	0.6675	93.35
4	0.9280	98.56
5	0.4180	88.36
6	0.7342	94.68
7	0.4325	88.65
8	0.1186	82.37
9	0.6944	93.89
10	0.7869	95.74

above the mean. Because demand is normally distributed with a mean $\mu = 15{,}000$ and a standard deviation $\sigma = 4500$, the simulated first-year demand is $\mu + z\sigma = 15{,}000 + 0.26(4500) = 16{,}170$ units.

In practice, special computer simulation software and software such as Excel provide built-in functions that can be used to generate values from a normal probability distribution quickly and easily. In most cases, the user only needs to provide the mean and standard deviation of the normal distribution to obtain the simulated value. For example, the following Excel function can be placed into a worksheet cell to obtain a simulated value from a normal distribution:

$$=\text{NORMINV(RAND(), Mean, Standard Deviation)}$$

The RAND() function provides the random number between 0 and 1, which is used as the cumulative normal probability. Using the PortaCom normal distribution with mean $\mu = 15{,}000$ and a standard deviation $\sigma = 4500$, the Excel function

$$=\text{NORMINV(RAND(),15000,4500)} \qquad (16.4)$$

will provide a normally distributed value for first-year demand. For example, if Excel's RAND() function generates the random number 0.7005, the Excel function shown in equation (16.4) will provide a first-year demand of 17,366 units. If RAND() generates the random number 0.3204, equation (16.4) will provide a first-year demand of 12,900. Table 16.6 shows the results for the first 10 randomly generated values for demand. Note that random numbers less than 0.5 generate first-year demand values below the mean and that random numbers greater than 0.5 generate first-year demand values greater than the mean.

The computer simulation calculations use more decimal places and are generally more accurate than the simulated values obtained from hand calculations and the cumulative standard normal distribution table in Appendix D.

Running the Simulation Model Running the simulation model means implementing the sequence of logical and mathematical operations described in the flowchart in Figure 16.5. The model parameters are \$249 per unit for the selling price, \$400,000 for the administrative cost, and \$600,000 for the advertising cost. Each trial in the simulation involves randomly generating values for the probabilistic inputs (direct labor cost, parts cost, and first-year demand) and computing profit. The simulation is complete when a satisfactory number of trials have been conducted.

Let us compute the profit for the first trial assuming the following probabilistic inputs:

$$\text{Direct labor cost:} \quad c_1 = 47$$
$$\text{Parts cost:} \quad c_2 = 85.36$$
$$\text{First-year demand:} \quad x = 17{,}366$$

TABLE 16.6   RANDOM GENERATION OF 10 VALUES FOR FIRST-YEAR DEMAND

Trial	Random Number	Demand
1	0.7005	17,366
2	0.3204	12,900
3	0.8968	20,686
4	0.1804	10,888
5	0.4346	14,259
6	0.9605	22,904
7	0.5646	15,732
8	0.7334	17,804
9	0.0216	5,902
10	0.3218	12,918

TABLE 16.7 PORTACOM SIMULATION RESULTS FOR 10 TRIALS

Trial	Direct Labor Cost per Unit ($)	Parts Cost per Unit ($)	Units Sold	Profit ($)
1	47	85.36	17,366	1,025,570
2	44	91.68	12,900	461,828
3	45	93.35	20,686	1,288,906
4	43	98.56	10,888	169,807
5	45	88.36	14,259	648,911
6	44	94.68	22,904	1,526,769
7	45	88.65	15,732	814,686
8	45	82.37	17,804	1,165,501
9	45	93.89	5,902	−350,131
10	46	95.74	12,918	385,585
Total	449	912.64	151,359	7,137,432
Average	$44.90	$91.26	15,136	$713,743

Referring to the flowchart in Figure 16.5, we see that the profit obtained is

$$\text{Profit} = (249 - c_1 - c_2)x - 1,000,000$$
$$= (249 - 47 - 85.36)17,366 - 1,000,000 = 1,025,570$$

The first row of Table 16.7 shows the result of this trial of the PortaCom simulation.

The simulated profit for the PortaCom printer if the direct labor cost is $47 per unit, the parts cost is $85.36 per unit, and first-year demand is 17,366 units is $1,025,570. Of course, one simulation trial does not provide a complete understanding of the possible profit and loss. Because other values are possible for the probabilistic inputs, we can benefit from additional simulation trials.

Suppose that on a second simulation trial, random numbers of 0.2841, 0.5842, and 0.3204 are generated for the direct labor cost, the parts cost, and first-year demand, respectively. These random numbers will provide the probabilistic inputs of $44 for the direct labor cost, $91.68 for the parts cost, and 12,900 for first-year demand. These values provide a simulated profit of $461,828 on the second simulation trial (see the second row of Table 16.7).

Repetition of the simulation process with different values for the probabilistic inputs is an essential part of any simulation. Through the repeated trials, management will begin to understand what might happen when the product is introduced into the real world. We have shown the results of 10 simulation trials in Table 16.7. For these 10 cases, we find a profit as high as $1,526,769 for the 6th trial and a loss of $350,131 for the 9th trial. Thus, we see both the possibility of a profit and a loss. Averages for the 10 trials are presented at the bottom of the table. We see that the average profit for the 10 trials is $713,743. The probability of a loss is 0.10, because one of the 10 trials (the 9th) resulted in a loss. We note also that the average values for labor cost, parts cost, and first-year demand are fairly close to their means of $45, $90, and 15,000, respectively.

Simulation of the PortaCom Problem

Using an Excel worksheet, we simulated the PortaCom project 500 times. The worksheet used to carry out the simulation is shown in Figure 16.6. Note that the simulation results for

FIGURE 16.6   EXCEL WORKSHEET FOR THE PORTACOM PROBLEM

PortaCom

	A	B	C	D	E	F
1	**PortaCom Risk Analysis**					
2						
3	Selling Price per Unit		$249			
4	Administrative Cost		$400,000			
5	Advertising Cost		$600,000			
6						
7	**Direct Labor Cost**			**Parts Cost (Uniform Distribution)**		
8	Lower	Upper		Smallest Value	$80	
9	Random No.	Random No.	Cost per Unit	Largest Value	$100	
10	0.0	0.1	$43			
11	0.1	0.3	$44			
12	0.3	0.7	$45	**Demand (Normal Distribution)**		
13	0.7	0.9	$46	Mean	15000	
14	0.9	1.0	$47	Std Deviation	4500	
15						
16						
17	**Simulation Trials**					
18						
19		Direct Labor	Parts	First-Year		
20	Trial	Cost per Unit	Cost per Unit	Demand	Profit	
21	1	47	$85.36	17,366	$1,025,570	
22	2	44	$91.68	12,900	$461,828	
23	3	45	$93.35	20,686	$1,288,906	
24	4	43	$98.56	10,888	$169,807	
25	5	45	$88.36	14,259	$648,911	
516	496	44	$98.67	8,730	($71,739)	
517	497	45	$94.38	19,257	$1,110,952	
518	498	44	$90.85	14,920	$703,118	
519	499	43	$90.37	13,471	$557,652	
520	500	46	$92.50	18,614	$1,056,847	
521						
522			**Summary Statistics**			
523			Mean Profit		$698,457	
524			Standard Deviation		$520,485	
525			Minimum Profit		($785,234)	
526			Maximum Profit		$2,367,058	
527			Number of Losses		51	
528			Probability of Loss		0.1020	
529						

Excel worksheets for all simulations presented in this chapter are available at the WEBfile linke on the Web site that accompanies this text.

trials 6 through 495 have been hidden so that the results can be shown in a reasonably sized figure. If desired, the rows for these trials can be shown and the simulation results displayed for all 500 trials. The details of the Excel worksheet that provided the PortaCom simulation are described in Appendix 16.1.

The simulation summary statistics in Figure 16.6 provide information about the risk associated with PortaCom's new printer. The worst result obtained in a simulation of 500 trials

FIGURE 16.7   HISTOGRAM OF SIMULATED PROFIT FOR 500 TRIALS
OF THE PORTACOM SIMULATION

is a loss of $785,234, and the best result is a profit of $2,367,058. The mean profit is $698,457. Fifty-one of the trials resulted in a loss; thus, the estimated probability of a loss is $51/500 = 0.1020$.

Simulation studies enable an objective estimate of the probability of a loss, which is an important aspect of risk analysis.

A histogram of simulated profit values is shown in Figure 16.7. We note that the distribution of profit values is fairly symmetric, with a large number of values in the range of $250,000 to $1,250,000. The probability of a large loss or a large gain is small. Only 3 trials resulted in a loss of more than $500,000, and only 3 trials resulted in a profit greater than $2,000,000. However, the probability of a loss is significant. Forty-eight of the 500 trials resulted in a loss in the $0 to $500,000 range—almost 10%. The modal category, the one with the largest number of values, is the range of profits between $750,000 and $1,000,000.

In comparing the simulation approach to risk analysis to the what-if approach, we see that much more information is obtained by using simulation. With the what-if analysis, we learned that the base-case scenario projected a profit of $710,000. The worst-case scenario projected a loss of $847,000, and the best-case scenario projected a profit of $2,591,000. From the 500 trials of the simulation run, we see that the worst- and best-case scenarios, although possible, are unlikely. None of the 500 trials provided a loss as low as the worst case or a profit as high as the best case. Indeed, the advantage of simulation for risk analysis is the information it provides on the likely values of the output. We now know the probability of a loss, how the profit values are distributed over their range, and what profit values are most likely.

For practice working through a simulation problem, try Problems 9 and 14.

The simulation results help PortaCom's management better understand the profit/loss potential of the PortaCom portable printer. The 0.1020 probability of a loss may be acceptable to management given a probability of almost 0.80 (see Figure 16.7) that profit will exceed $250,000. On the other hand, PortaCom might want to conduct further market research before deciding whether to introduce the product. In any case, the simulation results should be helpful in reaching an appropriate decision. The Q.M. in Action, Meeting Demand Levels at Pfizer, describes how a simulation model helped find ways to meet increasing demand for a product.

Q.M. *in* ACTION

MEETING DEMAND LEVELS AT PFIZER*

Pharmacia & Upjohn's merger with Pfizer created one of the world's largest pharmaceutical firms. Demand for one of Pharmacia & Upjohn's long-standing products remained stable for several years at a level easily satisfied by the company's manufacturing facility. However, changes in market conditions caused an increase in demand to a level beyond the current capacity. A simulation model of the production process was developed to explore ways to increase production to meet the new level of demand in a cost-effective manner.

Simulation results were used to help answer the following questions:

- What is the maximum throughput of the existing facility?

*Based on information provided by David B. Magerlein, James M. Magerlein, and Michael J. Goodrich.

- How can the existing production process be modified to increase throughput?
- How much equipment must be added to the existing facility to meet the increased demand?
- What is the desired size and configuration of the new production process?

The simulation model was able to demonstrate that the existing facilities, with some operating policy improvements, were large enough to satisfy the increased demand for the next several years. Expansion to a new production facility was not necessary. The simulation model also helped determine the number of operators required as the production level increased in the future. This result helped ensure that the proper number of operators would be trained by the time they were needed. The simulation model also provided a way reprocessed material could be used to replace fresh raw materials, resulting in a savings of approximately $3 million per year.

NOTES AND COMMENTS

Appendix 16.2 shows how to perform a simulation of the PortaCom problem using Crystal Ball.

1. The PortaCom simulation model is based on independent trials in which the results for one trial do not affect what happens in subsequent trials. Historically, this type of simulation study was referred to as a *Monte Carlo simulation*. The term *Monte Carlo simulation* was used because early practitioners of simulation saw similarities between the models they were developing and the gambling games played in the casinos of Monte Carlo. Today, many individuals interpret the term *Monte Carlo simulation* more broadly to mean any simulation that involves randomly generating values for the probabilistic inputs.

2. The probability distribution used to generate values for probabilistic inputs in a simulation model is often developed using historical data. For instance, suppose that an analysis of daily sales at a new car dealership for the past 50 days showed that on 2 days no cars were sold, on 5 days one car was sold, on 9 days two cars were sold, on 24 days three cars were sold, on 7 days four cars were sold, and on 3 days five cars were

sold. We can estimate the probability distribution of daily demand using the relative frequencies for the observed data. An estimate of the probability that no cars are sold on a given day is $2/50 = 0.04$, an estimate of the probability that one car is sold is $5/50 = 0.10$, and so on. The estimated probability distribution of daily demand is shown in the table below.

3. Spreadsheet add-in packages such as @RISK® and Crystal Ball® have been developed to make spreadsheet simulation easier. For instance, using Crystal Ball we could simulate the PortaCom new product introduction by first entering the formulas showing the relationships between the probabilistic inputs and the output measure, profit. Then, a probability distribution type is selected for each probabilistic input from among a number of available choices. Crystal Ball will generate random values for each probabilistic input, compute the profit, and repeat the simulation for as many trials as specified. Graphical displays and a variety of descriptive statistics can be easily obtained.

Daily Sales	0	1	2	3	4	5
Probability	0.04	0.10	0.18	0.48	0.14	0.06

16.2   Inventory Simulation

In this section we describe how simulation can be used to establish an inventory policy for a product that has an uncertain demand. The product is a home ventilation fan distributed by the Butler Electrical Supply Company. Each fan costs Butler $75 and sells for $125. Thus Butler realizes a gross profit of $125 − $75 = $50 for each fan sold. Monthly demand for the fan is described by a normal probability distribution with a mean of 100 units and a standard deviation of 20 units.

Butler receives monthly deliveries from its supplier and replenishes its inventory to a level of Q at the beginning of each month. This beginning inventory level is referred to as the replenishment level. If monthly demand is less than the replenishment level, an inventory holding cost of $15 is charged for each unit that is not sold. However, if monthly demand is greater than the replenishment level, a stock-out occurs and a shortage cost is incurred. Because Butler assigns a goodwill cost of $30 for each customer turned away, a shortage cost of $30 is charged for each unit of demand that cannot be satisfied. Management would like to use a simulation model to determine the average monthly net profit resulting from using a particular replenishment level. Management would also like information on the percentage of total demand that will be satisfied. This percentage is referred to as the *service level*.

The controllable input to the Butler simulation model is the replenishment level, Q. The probabilistic input is the monthly demand, D. The two output measures are the average monthly net profit and the service level. Computation of the service level requires that we keep track of the number of fans sold each month and the total demand for fans for each month. The service level will be computed at the end of the simulation run as the ratio of total units sold to total demand. A diagram of the relationship between the inputs and the outputs is shown in Figure 16.8.

When demand is less than or equal to the replenishment level ($D \leq Q$), D units are sold, and an inventory holding cost of $15 is incurred for each of the $Q - D$ units that remain in inventory. Net profit for this case is computed as follows:

Case 1: $D \leq Q$

$$
\begin{aligned}
\text{Gross profit} &= \$50D \\
\text{Holding cost} &= \$15(Q - D) \\
\text{Net profit} &= \text{Gross profit} - \text{Holding cost} = \$50D - \$15(Q - D)
\end{aligned}
$$

(16.5)

When demand is greater than the replenishment level ($D > Q$), Q fans are sold, and a shortage cost of $30 is imposed for each of the $D - Q$ units of demand not satisfied. Net profit for this case is computed as follows:

Case 2: $D > Q$

$$
\begin{aligned}
\text{Gross profit} &= \$50Q \\
\text{Holding cost} &= \$30(D - Q) \\
\text{Net profit} &= \text{Gross profit} - \text{Holding cost} = \$50Q - \$30(D - Q)
\end{aligned}
$$

(16.6)

Figure 16.9 shows a flowchart that defines the sequence of logical and mathematical operations required to simulate the Butler inventory system. Each trial in the simulation represents one month of operation. The simulation is run for 300 months using a given

FIGURE 16.8   BUTLER INVENTORY SIMULATION MODEL

FIGURE 16.9   FLOWCHART FOR THE BUTLER INVENTORY SIMULATION

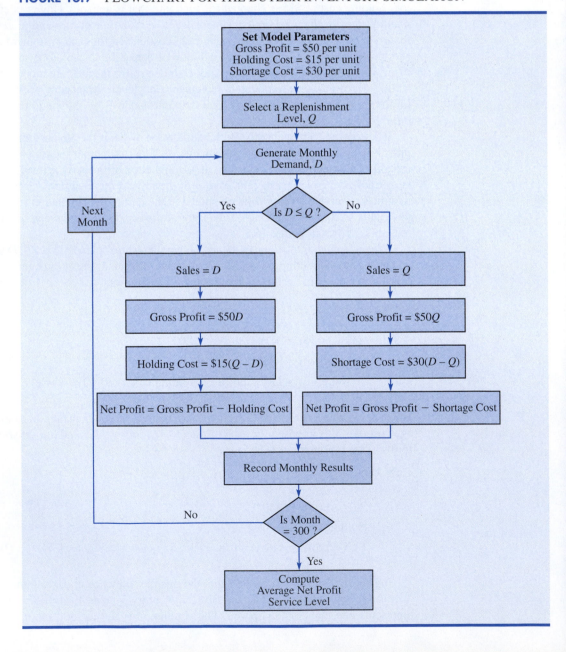

replenishment level, Q. Then, the average profit and service level output measures are computed. Let us describe the steps involved in the simulation by illustrating the results for the first two months of a simulation run using a replenishment level of $Q = 100$.

The first block of the flowchart in Figure 16.9 sets the values of the model parameters: gross profit = $50 per unit, holding cost = $15 per unit, and shortage cost = $30 per unit. The next block shows that a replenishment level of Q is selected; in our illustration, $Q = 100$. Then, a value for monthly demand is generated. Because monthly demand is normally distributed with a mean of 100 units and a standard deviation of 20 units, we can use the Excel function =NORMINV(RAND(),100,20), as described in Section 16.1, to generate a value for monthly demand. Suppose that a value of $D = 79$ is generated on the first trial. This value of demand is then compared with the replenishment level, Q. With the replenishment level set at $Q = 100$, demand is less than the replenishment level, and the left branch of the flowchart is followed. Sales are set equal to demand (79), and gross profit, holding cost, and net profit are computed as follows:

$$\text{Gross profit} = 50D = 50(79) = 3950$$

$$\text{Holding cost} = 15(Q - D) = 15(100 - 79) = 315$$

$$\text{Net profit} = \text{Gross profit} - \text{Holding cost} = 3950 - 315 = 3635$$

The values of demand, sales, gross profit, holding cost, and net profit are recorded for the first month. The first row of Table 16.8 summarizes the information for this first trial.

For the second month, suppose that a value of 111 is generated for monthly demand. Because demand is greater than the replenishment level, the right branch of the flowchart is followed. Sales are set equal to the replenishment level (100), and gross profit, shortage cost, and net profit are computed as follows:

$$\text{Gross profit} = 50Q = 50(100) = 5000$$

$$\text{Shortage cost} = 30(D - Q) = 30(111 - 100) = 330$$

$$\text{Net profit} = \text{Gross profit} - \text{Shortage cost} = 5000 - 330 = 4670$$

The values of demand, sales, gross profit, holding cost, shortage cost, and net profit are recorded for the second month. The second row of Table 16.8 summarizes the information generated in the second trial.

Results for the first five months of the simulation are shown in Table 16.8. The totals show an accumulated total net profit of $22,310, which is an average monthly net profit of $22,310/5 = $4462. Total unit sales are 472, and total demand is 501. Thus, the service level is $472/501 = 0.942$, indicating Butler has been able to satisfy 94.2% of demand during the five-month period.

TABLE 16.8 BUTLER INVENTORY SIMULATION RESULTS FOR FIVE TRIALS WITH $Q = 100$

Month	Demand	Sales	Gross Profit ($)	Holding Cost ($)	Shortage Cost ($)	Net Profit ($)
1	79	79	3,950	315	0	3,635
2	111	100	5,000	0	330	4,670
3	93	93	4,650	105	0	4,545
4	100	100	5,000	0	0	5,000
5	118	100	5,000	0	540	4,460
Totals	501	472	23,600	420	870	22,310
Average	100	94	$4,720	$ 84	$174	$4,462

Simulation of the Butler Inventory Problem

Using Excel, we simulated the Butler inventory operation for 300 months. The worksheet used to carry out the simulation is shown in Figure 16.10. Note that the simulation results for months 6 through 295 have been hidden so that the results can be shown in a reasonably sized figure. If desired, the rows for these months can be shown and the simulation results displayed for all 300 months.

The summary statistics in Figure 16.10 show what can be anticipated over 300 months if Butler operates its inventory system using a replenishment level of 100. The average net profit is $4293 per month. Because 27,917 units of the total demand of 30,181 units were satisfied, the service level is 27,917/30,181 = 92.5%. We are now ready to use the simulation model to consider other replenishment levels that may improve the net profit and the service level.

FIGURE 16.10   EXCEL WORKSHEET FOR THE BUTLER INVENTORY PROBLEM

WEB file

Butler

	A	B	C	D	E	F	G	H
1	**Butler Inventory**							
2								
3	Gross Profit per Unit		$50					
4	Holding Cost per Unit		$15					
5	Shortage Cost per Unit		$30					
6								
7	**Replenishment Level**		100					
8								
9	**Demand (Normal Distribution)**							
10	Mean	100						
11	Std Deviation	20						
12								
13								
14	**Simulation**							
15								
16	Month	Demand	Sales	Gross Profit	Holding Cost	Shortage Cost	Net Profit	
17	1	79	79	$3,950	$315	$0	$3,635	
18	2	111	100	$5,000	$0	$330	$4,670	
19	3	93	93	$4,650	$105	$0	$4,545	
20	4	100	100	$5,000	$0	$0	$5,000	
21	5	118	100	$5,000	$0	$540	$4,460	
312	296	89	89	$4,450	$165	$0	$4,285	
313	297	91	91	$4,550	$135	$0	$4,415	
314	298	122	100	$5,000	$0	$660	$4,340	
315	299	93	93	$4,650	$105	$0	$4,545	
316	300	126	100	$5,000	$0	$780	$4,220	
317								
318	**Totals**	30,181	27,917		**Summary Statistics**			
319					Mean Profit		$4,293	
320					Standard Deviation		$658	
321					Minimum Profit		($206)	
322					Maximum Profit		$5,000	
323					Service Level		92.5%	
324								

TABLE 16.9   BUTLER INVENTORY SIMULATION RESULTS FOR 300 TRIALS

Replenishment Level	Average Net Profit ($)	Service Level (%)
100	4293	92.5
110	4524	96.5
120	4575	98.6
130	4519	99.6
140	4399	99.9

Simulation allows the user to consider different operating policies and changes to model parameters and then to observe the impact of the changes on output measures such as profit or service level.

At this point, we conducted a series of simulation experiments by repeating the Butler inventory simulation with replenishment levels of 110, 120, 130, and 140 units. The average monthly net profits and the service levels are shown in Table 16.9. The highest monthly net profit of $4575 occurs with a replenishment level of $Q = 120$. The associated service level is 98.6%. On the basis of these results, Butler selected a replenishment level of $Q = 120$.

Experimental simulation studies, such as this one for Butler's inventory policy, can help identify good operating policies and decisions. Butler's management used simulation to choose a replenishment level of 120 for its home ventilation fan. With the simulation model in place, management can also explore the sensitivity of this decision to some of the model parameters. For instance, we assigned a shortage cost of $30 for any customer demand not met. With this shortage cost, the replenishment level was $Q = 120$ and the service level was 98.6%. If management felt a more appropriate shortage cost was $10 per unit, running the simulation again using $10 as the shortage cost would be a simple matter.

Problem 18 gives you a chance to develop a different simulation model.

We mentioned earlier that simulation is not an optimization technique. Even though we used simulation to choose a replenishment level, it does not guarantee that this choice is optimal. All possible replenishment levels were not tested. Perhaps a manager would like to consider additional simulation runs with replenishment levels of $Q = 115$ and $Q = 125$ to search for an even better inventory policy. Also, we have no guarantee that with another set of 300 randomly generated demand values the replenishment level with the highest profit would not change. However, with a large number of simulation trials, we should find a good and, at least, near optimal solution. The Q.M. in Action, Petroleum Distribution in the Gulf of Mexico, describes a simulation application for 15 petroleum companies in the state of Florida.

Q.M. *in* ACTION

PETROLEUM DISTRIBUTION IN THE GULF OF MEXICO*

Domestic suppliers who operate oil refineries along the Gulf Coast are helping to satisfy Florida's increasing demand for refined petroleum products. Barge fleets, operated either by independent shipping companies or by the petroleum companies themselves, are used to transport more than 20 different petroleum products to 15 Florida petroleum companies. The petroleum products are loaded at refineries in Texas, Louisiana, and Mississippi and are discharged at tank terminals concentrated in Tampa, Port Everglades, and Jacksonville.

Barges operate under three types of contracts between the fleet operator and the client petroleum company:

- The client assumes total control of a barge and uses it for trips between its own refinery and one or more discharging ports.
- The client is guaranteed a certain volume will be moved during the contract period. Schedules vary

*Based on E. D. Chajakis, "Sophisticated Crude Transportation," *OR/MS Today* (December 1997): 30–34.

(continued)

considerably depending upon the customer's needs and the fleet operator's capabilities.

- The client hires a barge for a single trip.

A simulation model was developed to analyze the complex process of operating barge fleets in the Gulf of Mexico. An appropriate probability distribution was used to simulate requests for shipments by the petroleum companies. Additional probability distributions were used to simulate the travel times depending upon the size and type of barge. Using this information, the simulation model was used to track barge loading times, barge discharge times, barge utilization, and total cost.

Analysts used simulation runs with a variety of what-if scenarios to answer questions about the petroleum dis-

tribution system and to make recommendations for improving the efficiency of the operation. Simulation helped determine the following:

- The optimal trade-off between fleet utilization and on-time delivery
- The recommended fleet size
- The recommended barge capacities
- The best service contract structure to balance the trade-off between customer service and delivery cost

Implementation of the simulation-based recommendations demonstrated a significant improvement in the operation and a significant lowering of petroleum distribution costs.

16.3 Waiting Line Simulation

The simulation models discussed thus far have been based on independent trials in which the results for one trial do not affect what happens in subsequent trials. In this sense, the system being modeled does not change or evolve over time. Simulation models such as these are referred to as **static simulation models**. In this section we develop a simulation model of a waiting line system where the state of the system, including the number of customers in the waiting line and whether the service facility is busy or idle, changes or evolves over time. To incorporate time into the simulation model, we use a simulation clock to record the time that each customer arrives for service as well as the time that each customer completes service. Simulation models that must take into account how the system changes or evolves over time are referred to as **dynamic simulation models**. In situations where the arrivals and departures of customers are **events** that occur at *discrete* points in time, the simulation model is also referred to as a **discrete-event simulation model**.

In Chapter 15 we presented formulas that could be used to compute the steady-state operating characteristics of a waiting line, including the average waiting time, the average number of units in the waiting line, the probability of waiting, and so on. In most cases, the waiting line formulas were based on specific assumptions about the probability distribution for arrivals, the probability distribution for service times, the queue discipline, and so on. Simulation, as an alternative for studying waiting lines, is more flexible. In applications where the assumptions required by the waiting line formulas are not reasonable, simulation may be the only feasible approach to studying the waiting line system. In this section we discuss the simulation of the waiting line for the Hammondsport Savings Bank automated teller machine (ATM).

Hammondsport Savings Bank ATM Waiting Line

Hammondsport Savings Bank will open several new branch banks during the coming year. Each new branch is designed to have one automated teller machine (ATM). A concern is that during busy periods several customers may have to wait to use the ATM. This concern prompted the bank to undertake a study of the ATM waiting line system. The bank's vice president wants to determine whether one ATM will be sufficient. The bank established service guidelines for its ATM system stating that the average customer waiting time for an ATM should be one minute or less. Let us show how a simulation model can be used to study the ATM waiting line at a particular branch.

Customer Arrival Times

One probabilistic input to the ATM simulation model is the arrival times of customers who use the ATM. In waiting line simulations, arrival times are determined by randomly generating the time between two successive arrivals, referred to as the *interarrival time*. For the branch bank being studied, the customer interarrival times are assumed to be uniformly distributed between 0 and 5 minutes as shown in Figure 16.11. With r denoting a random number between 0 and 1, an interarrival time for two successive customers can be simulated by using the formula for generating values from a uniform probability distribution.

$$\text{Interarrival time} = a + r(b - a) \qquad (16.7)$$

where

$$r = \text{random number between 0 and 1}$$
$$a = \text{minimum interarrival time}$$
$$b = \text{maximum interarrival time}$$

A uniform probability distribution of interarrival times is used here to illustrate the simulation computations. Actually, any interarrival time probability distribution can be assumed, and the logic of the waiting line simulation model will not change.

For the Hammondsport ATM system, the minimum interarrival time is $a = 0$ minutes, and the maximum interarrival time is $b = 5$ minutes; therefore, the formula for generating an interarrival time is

$$\text{Interarrival time} = 0 + r(5 - 0) = 5r \qquad (16.8)$$

Assume that the simulation run begins at time $= 0$. A random number of $r = 0.2804$ generates an interarrival time of $5(0.2804) = 1.4$ minutes for customer 1. Thus, customer 1 arrives 1.4 minutes after the simulation run begins. A second random number of $r = 0.2598$ generates an interarrival time of $5(0.2598) = 1.3$ minutes, indicating that customer 2 arrives

FIGURE 16.11   UNIFORM PROBABILITY DISTRIBUTION OF INTERARRIVAL TIMES
FOR THE ATM WAITING LINE SYSTEM

Interarrival Time in Minutes

FIGURE 16.12   NORMAL PROBABILITY DISTRIBUTION OF SERVICE TIMES
FOR THE ATM WAITING LINE SYSTEM

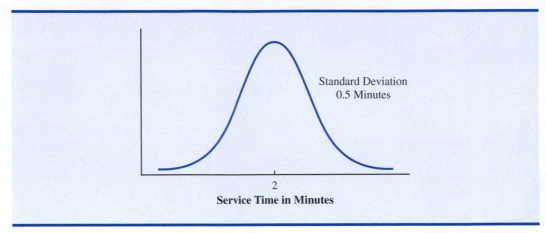

1.3 minutes after customer 1. Thus, customer 2 arrives $1.4 + 1.3 = 2.7$ minutes after the simulation begins. Continuing, a third random number of $r = 0.9802$ indicates that customer 3 arrives 4.9 minutes after customer 2, which is 7.6 minutes after the simulation begins.

Customer Service Times

Another probabilistic input in the ATM simulation model is the service time, which is the time a customer spends using the ATM machine. Past data from similar ATMs indicate that a normal probability distribution with a mean of 2 minutes and a standard deviation of 0.5 minutes, as shown in Figure 16.12, can be used to describe service times. As discussed in Sections 16.1 and 16.2, values from a normal probability distribution with mean 2 and standard deviation 0.5 can be generated using the Excel function =NORMINV(RAND(),2,0.5). For example, the random number of 0.7257 generates a customer service time of 2.3 minutes.

Simulation Model

The probabilistic inputs to the Hammondsport Savings Bank ATM simulation model are the interarrival time and the service time. The controllable input is the number of ATMs used. The output will consist of various operating characteristics such as the probability of waiting, the average waiting time, the maximum waiting time, and so on. We show a diagram of the ATM simulation model in Figure 16.13.

FIGURE 16.13   HAMMONDSPORT SAVINGS BANK ATM SIMULATION MODEL

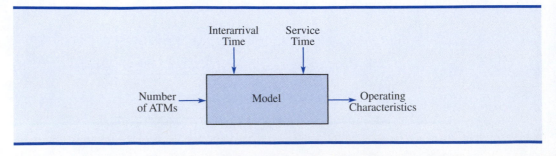

FIGURE 16.14   FLOWCHART OF THE HAMMONDSPORT SAVINGS BANK ATM WAITING
LINE SIMULATION

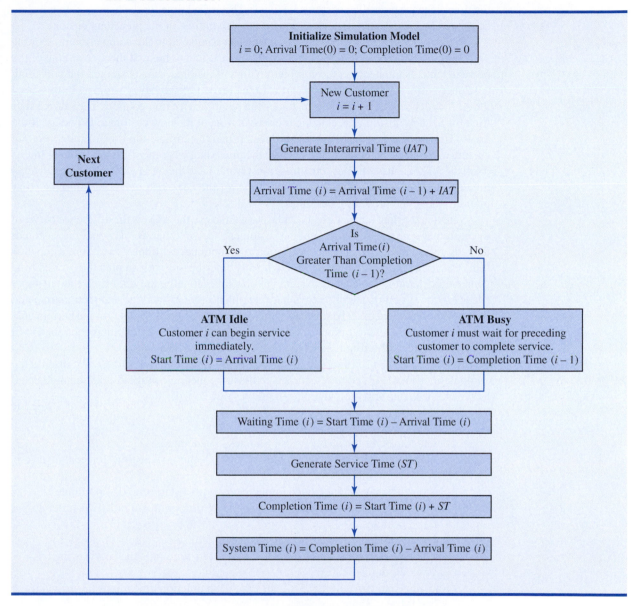

Figure 16.14 shows a flowchart that defines the sequence of logical and mathematical operations required to simulate the Hammondsport ATM system. The flowchart uses the following notation:

$$IAT = \text{Interarrival time generated}$$

Arrival time (i) = Time at which customer i arrives

Start time (i) = Time at which customer i starts service

Wait time (i) = Waiting time for customer i

$$ST = \text{Service time generated}$$

Completion time (i) = Time at which customer i completes service

System time (i) = System time for customer i (completion time $-$ arrival time)

Referring to Figure 16.14, we see that the simulation is initialized in the first block of the flowchart. Then a new customer is created. An interarrival time is generated to determine the time since the preceding customer arrived.[2] The arrival time for the new customer is then computed by adding the interarrival time to the arrival time of the preceding customer.

The decision rule for deciding whether the ATM is idle or busy is the most difficult aspect of the logic in a waiting line simulation model.

The arrival time for the new customer must be compared to the completion time of the preceding customer to determine whether the ATM is idle or busy. If the arrival time of the new customer is greater than the completion time of the preceding customer, the preceding customer will have finished service prior to the arrival of the new customer. In this case, the ATM will be idle, and the new customer can begin service immediately. The service start time for the new customer is equal to the arrival time of the new customer. However, if the arrival time for the new customer is not greater than the completion time of the preceding customer, the new customer arrived before the preceding customer finished service. In this case, the ATM is busy; the new customer must wait to use the ATM until the preceding customer completes service. The service start time for the new customer is equal to the completion time of the preceding customer.

Note that the time the new customer has to wait to use the ATM is the difference between the customer's service start time and the customer's arrival time. At this point, the customer is ready to use the ATM, and the simulation run continues with the generation of the customer's service time. The time at which the customer begins service plus the service time generated determine the customer's completion time. Finally, the total time the customer spends in the system is the difference between the customer's service completion time and the customer's arrival time. At this point, the computations are complete for the current customer, and the simulation continues with the next customer. The simulation is continued until a specified number of customers have been served by the ATM.

Simulation results for the first 10 customers are shown in Table 16.10. We discuss the computations for the first three customers to illustrate the logic of the simulation model and to show how the information in Table 16.10 was developed.

Customer 1

- An interarrival time of $IAT = 1.4$ minutes is generated.
- Because the simulation run begins at time 0, the arrival time for customer 1 is $0 + 1.4 = 1.4$ minutes.
- Customer 1 may begin service immediately with a start time of 1.4 minutes.
- The waiting time for customer 1 is the start time minus the arrival time: $1.4 - 1.4 = 0$ minutes.
- A service time of $ST = 2.3$ minutes is generated for customer 1.
- The completion time for customer 1 is the start time plus the service time: $1.4 + 2.3 = 3.7$ minutes.
- The time in the system for customer 1 is the completion time minus the arrival time: $3.7 - 1.4 = 2.3$ minutes.

Customer 2

- An interarrival time of $IAT = 1.3$ minutes is generated.
- Because the arrival time of customer 1 is 1.4, the arrival time for customer 2 is $1.4 + 1.3 = 2.7$ minutes.
- Because the completion time of customer 1 is 3.7 minutes, the arrival time of customer 2 is not greater than the completion time of customer 1; thus, the ATM is busy when customer 2 arrives.

---

[2]For the first customer, the interarrival time determines the time since the simulation started. Thus, the first interarrival time determines the time the first customer arrives.

TABLE 16.10   SIMULATION RESULTS FOR 10 ATM CUSTOMERS

Customer	Interarrival Time	Arrival Time	Service Start Time	Waiting Time	Service Time	Completion Time	Time in System
1	1.4	1.4	1.4	0.0	2.3	3.7	2.3
2	1.3	2.7	3.7	1.0	1.5	5.2	2.5
3	4.9	7.6	7.6	0.0	2.2	9.8	2.2
4	3.5	11.1	11.1	0.0	2.5	13.6	2.5
5	0.7	11.8	13.6	1.8	1.8	15.4	3.6
6	2.8	14.6	15.4	0.8	2.4	17.8	3.2
7	2.1	16.7	17.8	1.1	2.1	19.9	3.2
8	0.6	17.3	19.9	2.6	1.8	21.7	4.4
9	2.5	19.8	21.7	1.9	2.0	23.7	3.9
10	1.9	21.7	23.7	2.0	2.3	26.0	4.3
Totals	21.7			11.2	20.9		32.1
Averages	2.17			1.12	2.09		3.21

- Customer 2 must wait for customer 1 to complete service before beginning service. Customer 1 completes service at 3.7 minutes, which becomes the start time for customer 2.
- The waiting time for customer 2 is the start time minus the arrival time: $3.7 - 2.7 = 1$ minute.
- A service time of $ST = 1.5$ minutes is generated for customer 2.
- The completion time for customer 2 is the start time plus the service time: $3.7 + 1.5 = 5.2$ minutes.
- The time in the system for customer 2 is the completion time minus the arrival time: $5.2 - 2.7 = 2.5$ minutes.

Customer 3

- An interarrival time of $IAT = 4.9$ minutes is generated.
- Because the arrival time of customer 2 was 2.7 minutes, the arrival time for customer 3 is $2.7 + 4.9 = 7.6$ minutes.
- The completion time of customer 2 is 5.2 minutes, so the arrival time for customer 3 is greater than the completion time of customer 2. Thus, the ATM is idle when customer 3 arrives.
- Customer 3 begins service immediately with a start time of 7.6 minutes.
- The waiting time for customer 3 is the start time minus the arrival time: $7.6 - 7.6 = 0$ minutes.
- A service time of $ST = 2.2$ minutes is generated for customer 3.
- The completion time for customer 3 is the start time plus the service time: $7.6 + 2.2 = 9.8$ minutes.
- The time in the system for customer 3 is the completion time minus the arrival time: $9.8 - 7.6 = 2.2$ minutes.

Using the totals in Table 16.10, we can compute an average waiting time for the 10 customers of $11.2/10 = 1.12$ minutes, and an average time in the system of $32.1/10 = 3.21$ minutes. Table 16.10 shows that 7 of the 10 customers had to wait. The total time for the 10-customer simulation is given by the completion time of the 10th customer: 26.0 minutes. However, at this point, we realize that a simulation for 10 customers is much too short a period to draw any firm conclusions about the operation of the waiting line.

Simulation of the Hammondsport Savings Bank ATM Problem

Using an Excel worksheet, we simulated the operation of the Hammondsport ATM waiting line system for 1000 customers. The worksheet used to carry out the simulation is shown in Figure 16.15. Note that the simulation results for customers 6 through 995 have been hidden so that the results can be shown in a reasonably sized figure. If desired, the rows for these customers can be shown and the simulation results displayed for all 1000 customers.

Ultimately, summary statistics will be collected in order to describe the results of 1000 customers. Before collecting the summary statistics, let us point out that most simulation

FIGURE 16.15   EXCEL WORKSHEET FOR THE HAMMONDSPORT SAVINGS BANK WITH ONE ATM

WEB file

Hammondsport1

	A	B	C	D	E	F	G	H	I
1	**Hammondsport Savings Bank with One ATM**								
2									
3	**Interarrival Times (Uniform Distribution)**								
4	Smallest Value	0							
5	Largest Value	5							
6									
7	**Service Times (Normal Distribution)**								
8	Mean	2							
9	Std Deviation	0.5							
10									
11									
12	**Simulation**								
13									
14		Interarrival	Arrival	Service	Waiting	Service	Completion	Time	
15	Customer	Time	Time	Start Time	Time	Time	Time	in System	
16	1	1.4	1.4	1.4	0.0	2.3	3.7	2.3	
17	2	1.3	2.7	3.7	1.0	1.5	5.2	2.5	
18	3	4.9	7.6	7.6	0.0	2.2	9.8	2.2	
19	4	3.5	11.1	11.1	0.0	2.5	13.6	2.5	
20	5	0.7	11.8	13.6	1.8	1.8	15.4	3.6	
1011	996	0.5	2496.8	2498.1	1.3	0.6	2498.7	1.9	
1012	997	0.2	2497.0	2498.7	1.7	2.0	2500.7	3.7	
1013	998	2.7	2499.7	2500.7	1.0	1.8	2502.5	2.8	
1014	999	3.7	2503.4	2503.4	0.0	2.4	2505.8	2.4	
1015	1000	4.0	2507.4	2507.4	0.0	1.9	2509.3	1.9	
1016									
1017		**Summary Statistics**							
1018		Number Waiting			549				
1019		Probability of Waiting			0.6100				
1020		Average Waiting Time			1.59				
1021		Maximum Waiting Time			13.5				
1022		Utilization of ATM			0.7860				
1023		Number Waiting > 1 Min			393				
1024		Probability of Waiting > 1 Min			0.4367				
1025									

FIGURE 16.16   HISTOGRAM SHOWING THE WAITING TIME FOR 900 ATM CUSTOMERS

studies of dynamic systems focus on the operation of the system during its long-run or steady-state operation. To ensure that the effect of start-up conditions are not included in the steady-state calculations, a dynamic simulation model is usually run for a specified period without collecting any data about the operation of the system. The length of the start-up period can vary depending on the application. For the Hammondsport Savings Bank ATM simulation, we treated the results for the first 100 customers as the start-up period. Thus, the summary statistics shown in Figure 16.15 are for the 900 customers arriving during the steady-state period.

The summary statistics show that 549 of the 900 Hammondsport customers had to wait. This result provides a $549/900 = 0.61$ probability that a customer will have to wait for service. In other words, approximately 61% of the customers will have to wait because the ATM is in use. The average waiting time is 1.59 minutes per customer, with at least one customer waiting the maximum time of 13.5 minutes. The utilization rate of 0.7860 indicates that the ATM is in use 78.6% of the time. Finally, 393 of the 900 customers had to wait more than 1 minute (43.67% of all customers). A histogram of waiting times for the 900 customers is shown in Figure 16.16. This figure shows that 45 customers (5%) had a waiting time greater than 6 minutes.

The simulation supports the conclusion that the branch will have a busy ATM system. With an average customer wait time of 1.59 minutes, the branch does not satisfy the bank's customer service guideline. This branch is a good candidate for installation of a second ATM.

Simulation with Two ATMs

We extended the simulation model to the case of two ATMs. For the second ATM we also assume that the service time is normally distributed with a mean of 2 minutes and a standard deviation of 0.5 minutes. Table 16.11 shows the simulation results for the first 10 customers. In comparing the two-ATM system results in Table 16.11 with the single ATM simulation results shown in Table 16.10, we see that two additional columns are needed. These two columns show when each ATM becomes available for customer service. We assume that, when a new customer arrives, the customer will be served by the ATM that frees up first. When the simulation begins, the first customer is assigned to ATM 1.

Table 16.11 shows that customer 7 is the first customer who has to wait to use an ATM. We describe how customers 6, 7, and 8 are processed to show how the logic of the simulation run for two ATMs differs from that with a single ATM.

TABLE 16.11   SIMULATION RESULTS FOR 10 CUSTOMERS FOR A TWO-ATM SYSTEM

Customer	Interarrival Time	Arrival Time	Service Start Time	Waiting Time	Service Time	Completion Time	Time in System	Time Available ATM 1	ATM 2
1	1.7	1.7	1.7	0.0	2.1	3.8	2.1	3.8	0.0
2	0.7	2.4	2.4	0.0	2.0	4.4	2.0	3.8	4.4
3	2.0	4.4	4.4	0.0	1.4	5.8	1.4	5.8	4.4
4	0.1	4.5	4.5	0.0	0.9	5.4	0.9	5.8	5.4
5	4.6	9.1	9.1	0.0	2.2	11.3	2.2	5.8	11.3
6	1.3	10.4	10.4	0.0	1.6	12.0	1.6	12.0	11.3
7	0.6	11.0	11.3	0.3	1.7	13.0	2.0	12.0	13.0
8	0.3	11.3	12.0	0.7	2.2	14.2	2.9	14.2	13.0
9	3.4	14.7	14.7	0.0	2.9	17.6	2.9	14.2	17.6
10	0.1	14.8	14.8	0.0	2.8	17.6	2.8	17.6	17.6
Totals	14.8			1.0	19.8		20.8		
Averages	1.48			0.1	1.98		2.08		

Customer 6

- An interarrival time of 1.3 minutes is generated, and customer 6 arrives 9.1 + 1.3 = 10.4 minutes into the simulation.
- From the customer 5 row, we see that ATM 1 frees up at 5.8 minutes, and ATM 2 will free up at 11.3 minutes into the simulation. Because ATM 1 is free, customer 6 does not wait and begins service on ATM 1 at the arrival time of 10.4 minutes.
- A service time of 1.6 minutes is generated for customer 6. So customer 6 has a completion time of 10.4 + 1.6 = 12.0 minutes.
- The time ATM 1 will next become available is set at 12.0 minutes; the time available for ATM 2 remains 11.3 minutes.

Customer 7

- An interarrival time of 0.6 minute is generated, and customer 7 arrives 10.4 + 0.6 = 11.0 minutes into the simulation.
- From the previous row, we see that ATM 1 will not be available until 12.0 minutes, and ATM 2 will not be available until 11.3 minutes. So customer 7 must wait to use an ATM. Because ATM 2 will free up first, customer 7 begins service on that machine at a start time of 11.3 minutes. With an arrival time of 11.0 and a service start time of 11.3, customer 7 experiences a waiting time of 11.3 − 11.0 = 0.3 minute.
- A service time of 1.7 minutes is generated leading to a completion time of 11.3 + 1.7 = 13.0 minutes.
- The time available for ATM 2 is updated to 13.0 minutes, and the time available for ATM 1 remains at 12.0 minutes.

Customer 8

- An interarrival time of 0.3 minute is generated, and customer 8 arrives 11.0 + 0.3 = 11.3 minutes into the simulation.
- From the previous row, we see that ATM 1 will be the first available. Thus, customer 8 starts service on ATM 1 at 12.0 minutes, resulting in a waiting time of 12.0 − 11.3 = 0.7 minute.

- A service time of 2.2 minutes is generated, resulting in a completion time of 12.0 + 2.2 = 14.2 minutes and a system time of 0.7 + 2.2 = 2.9 minutes.
- The time available for ATM 1 is updated to 14.2 minutes, and the time available for ATM 2 remains at 13.0 minutes.

From the totals in Table 16.11, we see that the average waiting time for these 10 customers is only 1.0/10 = 0.1 minute. Of course, a much longer simulation will be necessary before any conclusions can be drawn.

Simulation Results with Two ATMs

Worksheets for the Hammondsport one-ATM and two-ATM systems are available at the WEBfile linke on the Web site that accompanies this text.

The Excel worksheet that we used to conduct a simulation for 1000 customers using two ATMs is shown in Figure 16.17. Results for the first 100 customers were discarded to account for the start-up period. With two ATMs, the number of customers who had to wait was reduced from 549 to 78. This reduction provides a 78/900 = 0.0867 probability that a customer will have to wait for service when two ATMs are used. The two-ATM system also

FIGURE 16.17 EXCEL WORKSHEET FOR THE HAMMONDSPORT SAVINGS BANK WITH TWO ATMs

WEB file

Hammondsport2

	A	B	C	D	E	F	G	H	I	J	K
1	Hammondsport Savings Bank with Two ATMs										
2											
3	Interarrival Times (Uniform Distribution)										
4	Smallest Value	0									
5	Largest Value	5									
6											
7	Service Times (Normal Distribution)										
8	Mean	2									
9	Std Deviation	0.5									
10											
11											
12	Simulation										
13											
14		Interarrival	Arrival	Service	Waiting	Service	Completion	Time	Time Available		
15	Customer	Time	Time	Start Time	Time	Time	Time	in System	ATM 1	ATM 2	
16	1	1.7	1.7	1.7	0.0	2.1	3.8	2.1	3.8	0.0	
17	2	0.7	2.4	2.4	0.0	2.0	4.4	2.0	3.8	4.4	
18	3	2.0	4.4	4.4	0.0	1.4	5.8	1.4	5.8	4.4	
19	4	0.1	4.5	4.5	0.0	0.9	5.4	0.9	5.8	5.4	
20	5	4.6	9.1	9.1	0.0	2.2	11.3	2.2	5.8	11.3	
1011	996	3.3	2483.2	2483.2	0.0	2.2	2485.4	2.2	2485.4	2482.1	
1012	997	4.5	2487.7	2487.7	0.0	1.9	2489.6	1.9	2485.4	2489.6	
1013	998	3.8	2491.5	2491.5	0.0	3.2	2494.7	3.2	2494.7	2489.6	
1014	999	0.0	2491.5	2491.5	0.0	2.4	2493.9	2.4	2494.7	2493.9	
1015	1000	2.6	2494.1	2494.1	0.0	2.8	2496.9	2.8	2494.7	2496.9	
1016											
1017		Summary Statistics									
1018		Number Waiting			78						
1019		Probability of Waiting			0.0867						
1020		Average Waiting Time			0.07						
1021		Maximum Waiting Time			2.9						
1022		Utilization of ATMs			0.4084						
1023		Number Waiting > 1 Min			23						
1024		Probability of Waiting > 1 Min			0.0256						
1025											

reduced the average waiting time to 0.07 minute (4.2 seconds) per customer. The maximum waiting time was reduced from 13.5 to 2.9 minutes, and each ATM was in use 40.84% of the time. Finally, only 23 of the 900 customers had to wait more than 1 minute for an ATM to become available. Thus, only 2.56% of customers had to wait more than 1 minute. The simulation results provide evidence that Hammondsport Savings Bank needs to expand to the two-ATM system.

The simulation models that we developed can now be used to study the ATM operation at other branch banks. In each case, assumptions must be made about the appropriate inter-arrival time and service time probability distributions. However, once appropriate assumptions have been made, the same simulation models can be used to determine the operating characteristics of the ATM waiting line system. The Q.M. in Action, Preboard Screening at Vancouver International Airport, describes another use of simulation for a queuing system.

Q.M. *in* ACTION

PREBOARD SCREENING AT VANCOUVER INTERNATIONAL AIRPORT*

Following the September 11, 2001, terrorist attacks in the United States, long lines at airport security check-points became commonplace. In order to reduce passen-ger waiting time, the Vancouver International Airport Authority teamed up with students and faculty at the University of British Columbia's Centre for Operations Excellence (COE) to build a simulation model of the air-port's preboard screening security checkpoints. The goal was to use the simulation model to help achieve accept-able service standards.

Prior to building the simulation model, students from the COE observed the flow of passengers through the screening process and collected data on the service time at each process step. In addition to service time data, passenger demand data provided input to the sim-ulation model. Two triangular probability distributions

were used to simulate passenger arrivals at the pre-boarding facilities. For flights to Canadian destinations a 90-40-20 triangle was used. This distribution assumes that, for each flight, the first passenger will arrive at the screening checkpoint 90 minutes before departure, the last passenger will arrive 20 minutes before departure, and the most likely arrival time is 40 minutes before departure. For international flights a 150-80-20 triangle was used.

Output statistics from the simulation model pro-vided information concerning resource utilization, wait-ing line lengths and the time passengers spend in the system. The simulation model provided information concerning the number of personnel needed to process 90% of the passengers with a waiting time of 10 minutes or less. Ultimately the airport authority was able to design and staff the preboarding checkpoints in such a fashion that waiting times for 90% of the passengers were a maximum of 10 minutes.

*Based on Derek Atkins et al., "Right on Queue," *OR/MS Today* (April 2003): 26–29.

NOTES AND COMMENTS

1. The ATM waiting line model was based on uni-formly distributed interarrival times and nor-mally distributed service times. One advantage of simulation is its flexibility in accommodating a variety of different probability distributions. For instance, if we believe an exponential dis-tribution is more appropriate for interarrival times, the ATM simulation could be repeated by

simply changing the way the interarrival times are generated.

2. At the beginning of this section, we defined discrete-event simulation as involving a dynamic system that evolves over time. The simulation computations focus on the sequence of events as

(continued)

they occur at discrete points in time. In the ATM waiting line example, customer arrivals and the customer service completions were the discrete events. Referring to the arrival times and completion times in Table 16.10, we see that the first five discrete events for the ATM waiting line simulation were as follows:

Event	Time
Customer 1 arrives	1.4
Customer 2 arrives	2.7
Customer 1 finished	3.7
Customer 2 finished	5.2
Customer 3 arrives	7.6

3. We did not keep track of the number of customers in the ATM waiting line as we carried out the ATM simulation computations on a customer-by-customer basis. However, we can determine the average number of customers in the waiting line from other information in the simulation output. The following relationship is valid for any waiting line system:

$$\text{Average number in waiting line} = \frac{\text{Total waiting time}}{\text{Total time of simulation}}$$

For the system with one ATM, the 100th customer completed service at 247.8 minutes into the simulation. Thus, the total time of the simulation for the next 900 customers was $2509.3 - 247.8 = 2261.5$ minutes. The average waiting time was 1.59 minutes. During the simulation, the 900 customers had a total waiting time of $900(1.59) = 1431$ minutes. Therefore, the average number of customers in the waiting line is

$$\begin{aligned}\text{Average number in waiting line} &= 1431/2261.5 \\ &= 0.63 \text{ customer}\end{aligned}$$

Other Simulation Issues

Because simulation is one of the most widely used quantitative analysis techniques, various software tools have been developed to help analysts implement a simulation model on a computer. In this section we comment on the software available and discuss some issues involved in verifying and validating a simulation model. We close the section with a discussion of some of the advantages and disadvantages of using simulation to study a real system.

Computer Implementation

The use of spreadsheets for simulation has grown rapidly in recent years, and third-party software vendors have developed spreadsheet add-ins that make building simulation models on a spreadsheet much easier. These add-in packages provide an easy facility for generating random values from a variety of probability distributions and provide a rich array of statistics describing the simulation output. Two popular spreadsheet add-ins are Crystal Ball® from Decisioneering and @RISK® from Palisade Corporation. Although spreadsheets can be a valuable tool for some simulation studies, they are generally limited to smaller, less complex systems.

With the growth of simulation applications, both users of simulation and software developers began to realize that computer simulations have many common features: model development, generating values from probability distributions, maintaining a record of what happens during the simulation, and recording and summarizing the simulation output. A variety of special-purpose simulation packages are available, including GPSS®, SIMSCRIPT®, SLAM®, and Arena®. These packages have built-in simulation clocks, simplified methods for generating probabilistic inputs, and procedures for collecting and summarizing the simulation output. Special-purpose simulation packages enable quantitative analysts to simplify the process of developing and implementing the simulation model. Indeed, Arena 6.0 was used to develop the simulation model described in the Q.M. in Action, Preboard Screening at Vancouver International Airport.

Simulation models can also be developed using general-purpose computer programming languages such as BASIC, FORTRAN, PASCAL, C, and C++. The disadvantage of using these languages is that special simulation procedures are not built in. One command in a special-purpose simulation package often performs the computations and record-keeping tasks that would require several BASIC, FORTRAN, PASCAL, C, or C++ statements to duplicate. The advantage of using a general-purpose programming language is that they offer greater flexibility in terms of being able to model more complex systems.

To decide which software to use, an analyst will have to consider the relative merits of a spreadsheet, a special-purpose simulation package, and a general-purpose computer programming language. The goal is to select the method that is easy to use while still providing an adequate representation of the system being studied.

The computational and record-keeping aspects of simulation models are assisted by special simulation software packages. The packages ease the tasks of developing a computer simulation model.

Verification and Validation

An important aspect of any simulation study involves confirming that the simulation model accurately describes the real system. Inaccurate simulation models cannot be expected to provide worthwhile information. Thus, before using simulation results to draw conclusions about a real system, one must take steps to verify and validate the simulation model.

Verification is the process of determining that the computer procedure that performs the simulation calculations is logically correct. Verification is largely a debugging task to make sure that no errors are in the computer procedure that implements the simulation. In some cases, an analyst may compare computer results for a limited number of events with independent hand calculations. In other cases, tests may be performed to verify that the probabilistic inputs are being generated correctly and that the output from the simulation model seems reasonable. The verification step is not complete until the user develops a high degree of confidence that the computer procedure is error free.

Validation is the process of ensuring that the simulation model provides an accurate representation of a real system. Validation requires an agreement among analysts and managers that the logic and the assumptions used in the design of the simulation model accurately reflect how the real system operates. The first phase of the validation process is done prior to, or in conjunction with, the development of the computer procedure for the simulation process. Validation continues after the computer program has been developed, with the analyst reviewing the simulation output to see whether the simulation results closely approximate the performance of the real system. If possible, the output of the simulation model is compared to the output of an existing real system to make sure that the simulation output closely approximates the performance of the real system. If this form of validation is not possible, an analyst can experiment with the simulation model and have one or more individuals experienced with the operation of the real system review the simulation output to determine whether it is a reasonable approximation of what would be obtained with the real system under similar conditions.

Verification and validation are not tasks to be taken lightly. They are key steps in any simulation study and are necessary to ensure that decisions and conclusions based on the simulation results are appropriate for the real system.

Advantages and Disadvantages of Using Simulation

The primary advantages of simulation are that it is easy to understand and that the methodology can be used to model and learn about the behavior of complex systems that would be difficult, if not impossible, to deal with analytically. Simulation models are flexible; they can be used to describe systems without requiring the assumptions that are often required by mathematical models. In general, the larger the number of probabilistic inputs a system has, the more likely that a simulation model will provide the best approach for studying the system. Another advantage of simulation is that a simulation model provides a convenient experimental laboratory for the real system. Changing assumptions or operating policies in the simulation model and rerunning it can provide results that help predict how such changes will affect the operation of the real system. Experimenting directly with a real system is often not feasible.

Using simulation, we can ask what-if questions and project how the real system will behave. Although simulation does not guarantee optimality, it will usually provide near-optimal solutions. In addition, simulation models often warn against poor decision strategies by projecting disastrous outcomes such as system failures, large financial losses, and so on.

Simulation is not without some disadvantages. For complex systems, the process of developing, verifying, and validating a simulation model can be time-consuming and expensive. In addition, each simulation run provides only a sample of how the real system will operate. As such, the summary of the simulation data provides only estimates or approximations about the real system. Consequently, simulation does not guarantee an optimal solution. Nonetheless, the danger of obtaining poor solutions is slight if the analyst exercises good judgment in developing the simulation model and if the simulation process is run long enough under a wide variety of conditions so that the analyst has sufficient data to predict how the real system will operate.

Summary

Simulation is a method for learning about a real system by experimenting with a model that represents the system. Some of the reasons simulation is frequently used are

1. It can be used for a wide variety of practical problems.
2. The simulation approach is relatively easy to explain and understand. As a result, management confidence is increased, and acceptance of the results is more easily obtained.
3. Spreadsheet packages now provide another alternative for model implementation, and third-party vendors have developed add-ins that expand the capabilities of the spreadsheet packages.
4. Computer software developers have produced simulation packages that make it easier to develop and implement simulation models for more complex problems.

We first showed how simulation can be used for risk analysis by analyzing a situation involving the development of a new product: the PortaCom printer. We then showed how simulation can be used to select an inventory replenishment level that would provide both a good profit and a good customer service level. Finally, we developed a simulation model for the Hammondsport Savings Bank ATM waiting line system. This model is an example of a dynamic simulation model in which the state of the system changes or evolves over time.

Our approach was to develop a simulation model that contained both controllable inputs and probabilistic inputs. Procedures were developed for randomly generating values for the probabilistic inputs, and a flowchart was developed to show the sequence of logical and mathematical operations that describe the steps of the simulation process. Simulation results were obtained by running the simulation for a suitable number of trials or length of time. Simulation results were obtained and conclusions were drawn about the operation of the real system.

The Q.M. in Action, Netherlands Company Improves Warehouse Order-Picking Efficiency, describes how a simulation model determined the warehouse storage location for 18,000 products and the sequence in which products were retrieved by order-picking personnel.

Q.M. *in* ACTION

NETHERLANDS COMPANY IMPROVES WAREHOUSE ORDER-PICKING EFFICIENCY*

As a wholesaler of tools, hardware, and garden equipment, Ankor, based in The Netherlands, warehouses more than 18,000 different products for customers who are primarily retail store chains, do-it-yourself businesses, and garden centers. Warehouse managers store the fastest-moving products on the ends of the aisles on the ground floor, the medium-moving products in the middle section of the aisles on the ground floor, and the slow-moving products on the mezzanine.

When a new order is received, a warehouse order-picker travels to each product location and selects the requested number of units. An average order includes 25 different products, which requires the order-picker to travel to 25 different locations in the warehouse. In order to minimize damage to the products, heavier products are picked first and breakable products are picked last. Order-picking is typically one of the most time-consuming and expensive aspects of operating the warehouse. The company is under continuous pressure to improve the efficiency of this operation.

To increase efficiency, researchers developed a simulation model of the warehouse order-picking system. Using a sequence of 1098 orders received for 27,790 products over a seven-week period, the researchers used the model to simulate the required order-picking times. The researchers, with the help of the model, varied the assignment of products to storage locations and the sequence in which products were retrieved from the storage locations. The model simulated order-picking times for a variety of product storage location alternatives and four different routing policies that determined the sequence in which products were picked.

Analysis of the simulation results provided a new storage assignment policy for the warehouse as well as new routing rules for the sequence in which to retrieve products from storage. Implementation of the new storage and routing procedures reduced the average route length of the order-picking operation by 31%. Due to the increased efficiency of the operation, the number of order pickers was reduced by more than 25%, saving the company an estimated €140,000 per year.

*Based on R. Dekker, M. B. M. de Koster, K. J. Roodbergen, and H. van Kalleveen, "Improving Order-Picking Response Time at Ankor's Warehouse," *Interfaces* (July/August 2004): 303–313.

Glossary

Simulation A method for learning about a real system by experimenting with a model that represents the system.

Simulation experiment The generation of a sample of values for the probabilistic inputs of a simulation model and computing the resulting values of the model outputs.

Controllable input Input to a simulation model that is selected by the decision maker.

Probabilistic input Input to a simulation model that is subject to uncertainty. A probabilistic input is described by a probability distribution.

Risk analysis The process of predicting the outcome of a decision in the face of uncertainty.

Parameters Numerical values that appear in the mathematical relationships of a model. Parameters are considered known and remain constant over all trials of a simulation.

What-if analysis A trial-and-error approach to learning about the range of possible outputs for a model. Trial values are chosen for the model inputs (these are the what-ifs) and the value of the output(s) is computed.

Base-case scenario Determining the output given the most likely values for the probabilistic inputs of a model.

Worst-case scenario Determining the output given the worst values that can be expected for the probabilistic inputs of a model.

Best-case scenario Determining the output given the best values that can be expected for the probabilistic inputs of a model.

Static simulation model A simulation model used in situations where the state of the system at one point in time does not affect the state of the system at future points in time. Each trial of the simulation is independent.

Dynamic simulation model A simulation model used in situations where the state of the system affects how the system changes or evolves over time.

Event An instantaneous occurrence that changes the state of the system in a simulation model.

Discrete-event simulation model A simulation model that describes how a system evolves over time by using events that occur at discrete points in time.

Verification The process of determining that a computer program implements a simulation model as it is intended.

Validation The process of determining that a simulation model provides an accurate representation of a real system.

Problems

Note: Problems 1–12 are designed to give you practice in setting up a simulation model and demonstrating how random numbers can be used to generate values for the probabilistic inputs. These problems, which ask you to provide a small number of simulation trials, can be done with hand calculations. This approach should give you a good understanding of the simulation process, but the simulation results will not be sufficient for you to draw final conclusions or make decisions about the situation. Problems 13–24 are more realistic in that they ask you to generate simulation output(s) for a large number of trials and use the results to draw conclusions about the behavior of the system being studied. These problems require the use of a computer to carry out the simulation computations. The ability to use Excel will be necessary when you attempt Problems 13–24.

1. Consider the PortaCom project discussed in Section 16.1.
    a. An engineer on the product development team believes that first-year sales for the new printer will be 20,000 units. Using estimates of $45 per unit for the direct labor cost and $90 per unit for the parts cost, what is the first-year profit using the engineer's sales estimate?
    b. The financial analyst on the product development team is more conservative, indicating that parts cost may well be $100 per unit. In addition, the analyst suggests that a sales volume of 10,000 units is more realistic. Using the most likely value of $45 per unit for the direct labor cost, what is the first-year profit using the financial analyst's estimates?
    c. Why is the simulation approach to risk analysis preferable to generating a variety of what-if scenarios such as those suggested by the engineer and the financial analyst?

2. The management of Madeira Manufacturing Company is considering the introduction of a new product. The fixed cost to begin the production of the product is $30,000. The variable cost for the product is expected to be between $16 and $24, with a most likely value of $20 per unit. The product will sell for $50 per unit. Demand for the product is expected to range from 300 to 2100 units, with 1200 units the most likely demand.

a. Develop the profit model for this product.
b. Provide the base-case, worst-case, and best-case analyses.
c. Discuss why simulation would be desirable.

3. a. Use the random numbers 0.3753, 0.9218, 0.0336, 0.5145, and 0.7000 to generate five simulated values for the PortaCom direct labor cost per unit.
    b. Use the random numbers 0.6221, 0.3418, 0.1402, 0.5198, and 0.9375 to generate five simulated values for the PortaCom parts cost.
    c. Use the random numbers 0.8531, 0.1762, 0.5000, 0.6810, and 0.2879 and the table for the cumulative standard normal distribution to generate five simulated values for the PortaCom first-year demand.

4. To generate leads for new business, Gustin Investment Services offers free financial planning seminars at major hotels in Southwest Florida. Attendance is limited to 25 individuals per seminar. Each seminar costs Gustin $3500, and the average first-year commission for each new account opened is $5000. Historical data collected over the past four years show that the number of new accounts opened at a seminar varies from no accounts opened to a maximum of six accounts opened according to the following probability distribution:

Number of New Accounts Opened	Probability
0	0.01
1	0.04
2	0.10
3	0.25
4	0.40
5	0.15
6	0.05

a. Set up intervals of random numbers that can be used to simulate the number of new accounts opened at a seminar.
b. Using the first 10 random numbers in column 9 of Table 16.2, simulate the number of new accounts opened for 10 seminars.
c. Would you recommend that Gustin continue running the seminars?

5. The price of a share of a particular stock listed on the New York Stock Exchange is currently $39. The following probability distribution shows how the price per share is expected to change over a three-month period:

Stock Price Change ($)	Probability
−2	0.05
−1	0.10
0	0.25
+1	0.20
+2	0.20
+3	0.10
+4	0.10

a. Set up intervals of random numbers that can be used to generate the change in stock price over a three-month period.

b. With the current price of $39 per share and the random numbers 0.1091, 0.9407, 0.1941, and 0.8083, simulate the price per share for the next four 3-month periods. What is the ending simulated price per share?

6. The Statewide Auto Insurance Company developed the following probability distribution for automobile collision claims paid during the past year:

Payment($)	Probability
0	0.83
500	0.06
1,000	0.05
2,000	0.02
5,000	0.02
8,000	0.01
10,000	0.01

a. Set up intervals of random numbers that can be used to generate automobile collision claim payments.

b. Using the first 20 random numbers in column 4 of Table 16.2, simulate the payments for 20 policyholders. How many claims are paid and what is the total amount paid to the policyholders?

7. A variety of routine maintenance checks are made on commercial airplanes prior to each takeoff. A particular maintenance check of an airplane's landing gear requires an average of 15 minutes of a maintenance engineer's time. In fact, the exact time required is normally distributed with a mean of 15 minutes and a standard deviation of 3 minutes. As part of a larger simulation model designed to determine total on-ground maintenance time for an airplane, we will need to simulate the actual time required to perform this maintenance check on the airplane's landing gear. Using random numbers of 0.1562, 0.9821, 0.3409, 0.5594, and 0.7758, compute the time required for each of five simulated maintenance checks of the airplane's landing gear.

8. Baseball's World Series is a maximum of seven games, with the winner being the first team to win four games. Assume that the Atlanta Braves are in the World Series and that the first two games are to be played in Atlanta, the next three games at the opponent's ballpark, and the last two games, if necessary, back in Atlanta. Taking into account the projected starting pitchers for each game and the home field advantage, the probabilities of Atlanta winning each game are as follows:

Game	1	2	3	4	5	6	7
Probability of Win	0.60	0.55	0.48	0.45	0.48	0.55	0.50

a. Set up random number intervals that can be used to determine the winner of each game. Let the smaller random numbers indicate that Atlanta wins the game. For example, the random number interval "0.00 but less than 0.60" corresponds to Atlanta winning game 1.

b. Use the random numbers in column 6 of Table 16.2 beginning with 0.3813 to simulate the playing of the World Series. Do the Atlanta Braves win the series? How many games are played?

c. Discuss how repeated simulation trials could be used to estimate the overall probability of Atlanta winning the series as well as the most likely number of games in the series.

9. A project has four activities (A, B, C, and D) that must be performed sequentially. The probability distributions for the time required to complete each of the activities are as follows:

Activity	Activity Time (weeks)	Probability
A	5	0.25
	6	0.35
	7	0.25
	8	0.15
B	3	0.20
	5	0.55
	7	0.25
C	10	0.10
	12	0.25
	14	0.40
	16	0.20
	18	0.05
D	8	0.60
	10	0.40

a. Provide the base-case, worst-case, and best-case calculations for the time to complete the project.
b. Use the random numbers 0.1778, 0.9617, 0.6849, and 0.4503 to simulate the completion time of the project in weeks.
c. Discuss how simulation could be used to estimate the probability the project can be completed in 35 weeks or less.

10. Blackjack, or 21, is a popular casino game that begins with each player and the dealer being dealt two cards. The value of each hand is determined by the point total of the cards in the hand. Face cards and 10s count 10 points, aces can be counted as either 1 or 11 points, and all other cards count at their face value. For instance, the value of a hand consisting of a jack and an 8 is 18; the value of a hand consisting of an ace and a two is either 3 or 13 depending on whether the ace is counted as 1 or 11 points. The goal is to obtain a hand with a value of 21, or as close to it as possible without exceeding 21. After the initial deal, each player and the dealer may draw additional cards (called "taking a hit") in order to improve their hand. If a player or the dealer takes a hit and the value of their hand exceeds 21, that person "goes broke" and loses. The dealer's advantage is that each player must decide whether to take a hit before the dealer. If a player takes a hit and goes over 21, the player loses even if the dealer later takes a hit and goes over 21. For this reason, players will often decide not to take a hit when the value of their hand is 12 or greater.

The dealer's hand is dealt with one card up and one card down. The player then decides whether to take a hit based on knowledge of the dealer's up card. A gambling professional determined that when the dealer's up card is a 6, the following probabilities describe the ending value of the dealer's hand:

Value of Hand	17	18	19	20	21	Broke
Probability	0.1654	0.1063	0.1063	0.1017	0.0972	0.4231

a. Set up intervals of random numbers that can be used to simulate the ending value of the dealer's hand when the dealer has a 6 as the up card.

b. Use the random numbers in column 4 of Table 16.2 to simulate the ending value of the dealer's hand for 20 plays of the game.

c. Suppose you are playing blackjack and your hand has a value of 16 for the two cards initially dealt. If you decide to take a hit, the following cards will improve your hand: ace, 2, 3, 4, and 5. Any card with a point count greater than 5 will result in you going broke. Suppose you have a hand with a value of 16 and decide to take a hit. The following probabilities describe the ending value of your hand:

Value of Hand	17	18	19	20	21	Broke
Probability	0.0769	0.0769	0.0769	0.0769	0.0769	0.6155

Use the random numbers in column 5 of Table 16.2 to simulate the ending value of your hand after taking a hit for 20 plays of the game.

d. Use the results of parts (b) and (c) to simulate the result of 20 blackjack hands when the dealer has a 6 up and the player chooses to take a hit with a hand that has a value of 16. How many hands result in the dealer winning, a push (a tie), and the player winning.

e. If the player has a hand with a value of 16 and doesn't take a hit, the only way the player can win is if the dealer goes broke. How many of the hands in part (b) result in the player winning without taking a hit? On the basis of this result and the results in part (d), would you recommend the player take a hit if the player has a hand with a value of 16 and the dealer has a 6 up?

11. Over a five-year period, the quarterly change in the price per share of common stock for a major oil company ranged from 28% to 112%. A financial analyst wants to learn what can be expected for price appreciation of this stock over the next two years. Using the five-year history as a basis, the analyst is willing to assume the change in price for each quarter is uniformly distributed between 28% and 12%. Use simulation to provide information about the price per share for the stock over the coming two-year period (eight quarters).

a. Use two-digit random numbers from column 2 of Table 16.2, beginning with 0.52, 0.99, and so on, to simulate the quarterly price change for each of the eight quarters.

b. If the current price per share is $80, what is the simulated price per share at the end of the two-year period?

c. Discuss how risk analysis would be helpful in identifying the risk associated with a two-year investment in this stock.

12. The management of Brinkley Corporation is interested in using simulation to estimate the profit per unit for a new product. Probability distributions for the purchase cost, the labor cost, and the transportation cost are as follows:

Purchase Cost ($)	Probability	Labor Cost ($)	Probability	Transportation Cost ($)	Probability
10	0.25	20	0.10	3	0.75
11	0.45	22	0.25	5	0.25
12	0.30	24	0.35		
		25	0.30		

Assume that these are the only costs and that the selling price for the product will be $45 per unit.

a. Provide the base-case, worst-case, and best-case calculations for the profit per unit.

b. Set up intervals of random numbers that can be used to randomly generate the three cost components.

c. Using the random numbers 0.3726, 0.5839, and 0.8275, calculate the profit per unit.

d.   Using the random numbers 0.1862, 0.7466, and 0.6171, calculate the profit per unit.

e.   Management believes the project may not be profitable if the profit per unit is less than $5. Explain how simulation can be used to estimate the probability the profit per unit will be less than $5.

13.   Using the PortaCom Risk Analysis worksheet in Figure 16.6 and available at the WEBfile link on the Web site accompanying the text, develop your own worksheet for the PortaCom simulation model.

a.   Compute the mean profit, the minimum profit, and the maximum profit.

b.   What is your estimate of the probability of a loss?

14.   Develop a worksheet simulation for the following problem. The management of Madeira Manufacturing Company is considering the introduction of a new product. The fixed cost to begin the production of the product is $30,000. The variable cost for the product is uniformly distributed between $16 and $24 per unit. The product will sell for $50 per unit. Demand for the product is best described by a normal probability distribution with a mean of 1200 units and a standard deviation of 300 units. Develop a spreadsheet simulation similar to Figure 16.6. Use 500 simulation trials to answer the following questions:

a.   What is the mean profit for the simulation?

b.   What is the probability the project will result in a loss?

c.   What is your recommendation concerning the introduction of the product?

15.   Use a worksheet to simulate the rolling of dice. Use the VLOOKUP function as described in Appendix 16.1 to select the outcome for each die. Place the number for the first die in column B and the number for the second die in column C. Show the sum in column D. Repeat the simulation for 1000 rolls of the dice. What is your simulation estimate of the probability of rolling a 7?

16.   Strassel Investors buys real estate, develops it, and resells it for a profit. A new property is available, and Bud Strassel, the president and owner of Strassel Investors, believes it can be sold for $160,000. The current property owner asked for bids and stated that the property will be sold for the highest bid in excess of $100,000. Two competitors will be submitting bids for the property. Strassel does not know what the competitors will bid, but he assumes for planning purposes that the amount bid by each competitor will be uniformly distributed between $100,000 and $150,000.

a.   Develop a worksheet that can be used to simulate the bids made by the two competitors. Strassel is considering a bid of $130,000 for the property. Using a simulation of 1000 trials, what is the estimate of the probability Strassel will be able to obtain the property using a bid of $130,000?

b.   How much does Strassel need to bid to be assured of obtaining the property? What is the profit associated with this bid?

c.   Use the simulation model to compute the profit for each trial of the simulation run. With maximization of profit as Strassel's objective, use simulation to evaluate Strassel's bid alternatives of $130,000, $140,000, or $150,000. What is the recommended bid, and what is the expected profit?

17.   Grear Tire Company has produced a new tire with an estimated mean lifetime mileage of 36,500 miles. Management also believes that the standard deviation is 5000 miles and that tire mileage is normally distributed. Use a worksheet to simulate the miles obtained for a sample of 500 tires.

a.   Use the Excel COUNTIF function to determine the number of tires that last longer than 40,000 miles. What is your estimate of the percentage of tires that will exceed 40,000 miles?

b.   Use COUNTIF to find the number of tires that obtain mileage less than 32,000 miles. Then, find the number with less than 30,000 miles and the number with less than 28,000 miles.

c. If management would like to advertise a tire mileage guarantee such that approximately no more than 10% of the tires would obtain mileage low enough to qualify for the guarantee, what tire mileage considered in part (b) would you recommend for the guarantee?

18. A building contractor is preparing a bid on a new construction project. Two other contractors will be submitting bids for the same project. Based on past bidding practices, bids from the other contractors can be described by the following probability distributions:

Contractor	Probability Distribution of Bid
A	Uniform probability distribution between $600,000 and $800,000
B	Normal probability distribution with a mean bid of $700,000 and a standard deviation of $50,000

a. If the building contractor submits a bid of $750,000, what is the probability the building contractor will obtain the bid? Use a worksheet to simulate 1000 trials of the contract bidding process.

b. The building contractor is also considering bids of $775,000 and $785,000. If the building contractor would like to bid such that the probability of winning the bid is about 0.80, what bid would you recommend? Repeat the simulation process with bids of $775,000 and $785,000 to justify your recommendation.

19. Develop your own worksheet for the Butler inventory simulation model shown in Figure 16.10. Suppose that management prefers not to charge for loss of goodwill. Run the Butler inventory simulation model with replenishment levels of 110, 115, 120, and 125. What is your recommendation?

20. In preparing for the upcoming holiday season, Mandrell Toy Company designed a new doll called Freddy. The fixed cost to produce the doll is $100,000. The variable cost, which includes material, labor, and shipping costs, is $34 per doll. During the holiday selling season, Mandrell will sell the dolls for $42 each. If Mandrell overproduces the dolls, the excess dolls will be sold in January through a distributor who has agreed to pay Mandrell $10 per doll. Demand for new toys during the holiday selling season is extremely uncertain. Forecasts are for expected sales of 60,000 dolls with a standard deviation of 15,000. The normal probability distribution is assumed to be a good description of the demand.

a. Create a worksheet similar to the inventory worksheet in Figure 16.10. Include columns showing demand, sales, revenue from sales, amount of surplus, revenue from sales of surplus, total cost, and net profit. Use your worksheet to simulate the sales of the Freddy doll using a production quantity of 60,000 units. Using 500 simulation trials, what is the estimate of the mean profit associated with the production quantity of 60,000 dolls?

b. Before making a final decision on the production quantity, management wants an analysis of a more aggressive 70,000-unit production quantity and a more conservative 50,000-unit production quantity. Run your simulation with these two production quantities. What is the mean profit associated with each? What is your recommendation on the production of the Freddy doll?

c. Assuming that Mandrell's management adopts your recommendation, what is the probability of a stock-out and a shortage of the Freddy dolls during the holiday season?

21. South Central Airlines operates a commuter flight between Atlanta and Charlotte. The plane holds 30 passengers, and the airline makes a $100 profit on each passenger on the flight. When South Central takes 30 reservations for the flight, experience has shown that, on average, two passengers do not show up. As a result, with 30 reservations, South Central is averaging 28 passengers with a profit of $28(100) = \$2800$ per flight. The airline operations office has asked for an evaluation of an overbooking strategy where they would accept 32

reservations even though the airplane holds only 30 passengers. The probability distribution for the number of passengers showing up when 32 reservations are accepted is as follows:

Passengers Showing Up	Probability
28	0.05
29	0.25
30	0.50
31	0.15
32	0.05

The airline will receive a profit of $100 for each passenger on the flight, up to the capacity of 30 passengers. The airline will incur a cost for any passenger denied seating on the flight. This cost covers added expenses of rescheduling the passenger as well as loss of goodwill, estimated to be $150 per passenger. Develop a worksheet model that will simulate the performance of the overbooking system. Simulate the number of passengers showing up for each of 500 flights by using the VLOOKUP function. Use the results to compute the profit for each flight.

a. Does your simulation recommend the overbooking strategy? What is the mean profit per flight if overbooking is implemented?

b. Explain how your simulation model could be used to evaluate other overbooking levels such as 31, 33, and 34 and for recommending a best overbooking strategy.

22. Develop your own waiting line simulation model for the Hammondsport Savings Bank problem (see Figure 16.14). Assume that a new branch is expected to open with interarrival times uniformly distributed between 0 and 4 minutes. The service times at this branch are anticipated to be normal, with a mean of 2 minutes and a standard deviation of 0.5 minute. Simulate the operation of this system for 600 customers using one ATM. What is your assessment of the ability to operate this branch with one ATM? What happens to the average waiting time for customers near the end of the simulation period?

23. The Burger Dome waiting line model in Section 16.1 studies the waiting time of customers at its fast-food restaurant. Burger Dome's single-channel waiting line system has an arrival rate of 0.75 customers per minute and a service rate of 1 customer per minute.

a. Use a worksheet based on Figure 16.15 to simulate the operation of this waiting line. Assuming that customer arrivals follow a Poisson probability distribution, the interarrival times can be simulated with the cell formula $-(1/\lambda)*LN(RAND())$, where $\lambda = 0.75$. Assuming that the service time follows an exponential probability distribution, the service times can be simulated with the cell formula $-\mu*LN(RAND())$, where $\mu = 1$. Run the Burger Dome simulation for 500 customers. The analytical model in Chapter 14 indicates an average waiting time of 3 minutes per customer. What average waiting time does your simulation model show?

b. One advantage of using simulation is that a simulation model can be altered easily to reflect other assumptions about the probabilistic inputs. Assume that the service time is more accurately described by a normal probability distribution with a mean of 1 minute and a standard deviation of 0.2 minute. This distribution has less service time variability than the exponential probability distribution used in part (a). What is the impact of this change on the average waiting time?

24. Telephone calls come into an airline reservations office randomly at the mean rate of 15 calls per hour. The time between calls follows an exponential distribution with a mean of 4 minutes. When the two reservation agents are busy, a telephone message tells the caller that the call is important and to please wait on the line until the next reservation agent becomes available. The service time for each reservation agent is normally distributed with a mean of 4 minutes and a standard deviation of 1 minute. Use a two-channel waiting line simulation model to evaluate this waiting line system. Use the worksheet design shown in

Figure 16.17. The cell formula $=-4*\mathrm{LN}(\mathrm{RAND}())$ can be used to generate the interarrival times. Simulate the operation of the telephone reservation system for 600 customers. Discard the first 100 customers, and collect data over the next 500 customers.

a. Compute the mean interarrival time and the mean service time. If your simulation model is operating correctly, both of these should have means of approximately 4 minutes.

b. What is the mean customer waiting time for this system?

c. Use the =COUNTIF function to determine the number of customers who have to wait for a reservation agent. What percentage of the customers have to wait?

Case Problem 1   Tri-State Corporation

What will your portfolio be worth in 10 years? In 20 years? When you stop working? The Human Resources Department at Tri-State Corporation was asked to develop a financial planning model that would help employees address these questions. Tom Gifford was asked to lead this effort and decided to begin by developing a financial plan for himself. Tom has a degree in business and, at the age of 25, is making $34,000 per year. After two years of contributions to his company's retirement program and the receipt of a small inheritance, Tom has accumulated a portfolio valued at $14,500. Tom plans to work 30 more years and hopes to accumulate a portfolio valued at $1,000,000. Can he do it?

Tom began with a few assumptions about his future salary, his new investment contributions, and his portfolio growth rate. He assumed 5% annual salary growth rate as reasonable and wanted to make new investment contributions at 4% of his salary. After some research on historical stock market performance, Tom decided that a 10% annual portfolio growth rate was reasonable. Using these assumptions, Tom developed the Excel worksheet shown in Figure 16.18. Tom's specific situation and his assumptions are in the top portion of the worksheet (cells D3:D8). The worksheet provides a financial plan for the next five years. In computing the portfolio earnings for a given year, Tom assumed that his new investment contribution would occur evenly throughout the year, and thus half of the new

FIGURE 16.18   FINANCIAL PLANNING WORKSHEET FOR TOM GIFFORD

WEB file

Gifford

	A	B	C	D	E	F	G	H
1	Financial Analysis - Portfolio Projection							
2								
3	Age			25				
4	Current Salary			$34,000				
5	Current Portfolio			$14,500				
6	Annual Salary Growth Rate			5%				
7	Annual Investment Rate			4%				
8	Annual Portfolio Growth Rate			10%				
9								
10			Beginning		New	Portfolio	Ending	
11	Year	Age	Portfolio	Salary	Investment	Earnings	Portfolio	
12	1	25	14,500	34,000	1,360	1,518	17,378	
13	2	26	17,378	35,700	1,428	1,809	20,615	
14	3	27	20,615	37,485	1,499	2,136	24,251	
15	4	28	24,251	39,359	1,574	2,504	28,329	
16	5	29	28,329	41,327	1,653	2,916	32,898	
17								

investment could be included in the computation of the portfolio earnings for the year. Using Figure 16.18, we see that at age 29, Tom is projected to have a portfolio valued at $32,898.

Tom's plan was to use this worksheet as a template to develop financial plans for the company's employees. The assumptions in cells D3:D8 would be different for each employee, and rows would be added to the worksheet to reflect the number of years appropriate for each employee. After adding another 25 rows to the worksheet, Tom found that he could expect to have a portfolio of $627,937 after 30 years. Tom then took his results to show his boss, Kate Riegle.

Although Kate was pleased with Tom's progress, she voiced several criticisms. One of the criticisms was the assumption of a constant annual salary growth rate. She noted that most employees experience some variation in the annual salary growth rate from year to year. In addition, she pointed out that the constant annual portfolio growth rate was unrealistic and that the actual growth rate would vary considerably from year to year. She further suggested that a simulation model for the portfolio projection might allow Tom to account for the random variability in the salary growth rate and the portfolio growth rate.

After some research, Tom and Kate decided to assume that the annual salary growth rate would vary from 0% to 10% and that a uniform probability distribution would provide a realistic approximation. Tri-State's accounting firm suggested that the annual portfolio growth rate could be approximated by a normal probability distribution with a mean of 10% and a standard deviation of 5%. With this information, Tom set off to develop a simulation model that could be used by the company's employees for financial planning.

Managerial Report

Play the role of Tom Gifford and develop a simulation model for financial planning. Write a report for Tom's boss and, at a minimum, include the following:

1. Without considering the random variability in growth rates, extend the worksheet in Figure 16.18 to 30 years. Confirm that by using the constant annual salary growth rate and the constant annual portfolio growth rate, Tom can expect to have a 30-year portfolio of $627,937. What would Tom's annual investment rate have to increase to in order for his portfolio to reach a 30-year, $1,000,000 goal?

2. Incorporate the random variability of the annual salary growth rate and the annual portfolio growth rate into a simulation model. Assume that Tom is willing to use the annual investment rate that predicted a 30-year, $1,000,000 portfolio in part 1. Show how to simulate Tom's 30-year financial plan. Use results from the simulation model to comment on the uncertainty associated with Tom reaching the 30-year, $1,000,000 goal. Discuss the advantages of repeating the simulation numerous times.

3. What recommendations do you have for employees with a current profile similar to Tom's after seeing the impact of the uncertainty in the annual salary growth rate and the annual portfolio growth rate?

4. Assume that Tom is willing to consider working 35 years instead of 30 years. What is your assessment of this strategy if Tom's goal is to have a portfolio worth $1,000,000?

5. Discuss how the financial planning model developed for Tom Gifford can be used as a template to develop a financial plan for any of the company's employees.

Case Problem 2   Harbor Dunes Golf Course

Harbor Dunes Golf Course was recently honored as one of the top public golf courses in South Carolina. The course, situated on land that was once a rice plantation, offers some of the best views of saltwater marshes available in the Carolinas. Harbor Dunes targets the

TABLE 16.12   PROBABILITY DISTRIBUTION OF SALES FOR THE AFTERNOON TEE TIMES

Number of Tee Times Sold	Probability
8	0.01
9	0.04
10	0.06
11	0.08
12	0.10
13	0.11
14	0.12
15	0.15
16	0.10
17	0.09
18	0.07
19	0.05
20	0.02

upper end of the golf market and in the peak spring golfing season, charges green fees of $160 per person and golf cart fees of $20 per person.

Harbor Dunes takes reservations for tee times for groups of four players (foursomes) starting at 7:30 each morning. Foursomes start at the same time on both the front nine and the back nine of the course, with a new group teeing off every nine minutes. The process continues with new foursomes starting play on both the front and back nine at noon. To enable all players to complete 18 holes before darkness, the last two afternoon foursomes start their rounds at 1:21 P.M. Under this plan, Harbor Dunes can sell a maximum of 20 afternoon tee times.

Last year Harbor Dunes was able to sell every morning tee time available for every day of the spring golf season. The same result is anticipated for the coming year. Afternoon tee times, however, are generally more difficult to sell. An analysis of the sales data for last year enabled Harbor Dunes to develop the probability distribution of sales for the afternoon tee times as shown in Table 16.12. For the season, Harbor Dunes averaged selling approximately 14 of the 20 available afternoon tee times. The average income from afternoon green fees and cart fees has been $10,240. However, the average of six unused tee times per day resulted in lost revenue.

In an effort to increase the sale of afternoon tee times, Harbor Dunes is considering an idea popular at other golf courses. These courses offer foursomes that play in the morning the option to play another round of golf in the afternoon by paying a reduced fee for the afternoon round. Harbor Dunes is considering two replay options: (1) a green fee of $25 per player plus a cart fee of $20 per player; (2) a green fee of $50 per player plus a cart fee of $20 per player. For option 1, each foursome will generate additional revenues of $180; for option 2, each foursome will generate additional revenues of $280. The key in making a decision as to what option is best depends upon the number of groups that find the option attractive enough to take the replay offer. Working with a consultant who has expertise in statistics and the golf industry, Harbor Dunes developed probability distributions for the number of foursomes requesting a replay for each of the two options. These probability distributions are shown in Table 16.13.

In offering these replay options, Harbor Dunes' first priority will be to sell full-price afternoon advance reservations. If the demand for replay tee times exceeds the number of afternoon tee times available, Harbor Dunes will post a notice that the course is full. In this case, any excess replay requests will not be accepted.

TABLE 16.13   PROBABILITY DISTRIBUTIONS FOR THE NUMBER OF GROUPS
REQUESTING A REPLAY

Option 1: $25 per person + Cart Fee		Option 2: $50 per person + Cart Fee	
Number of Foursomes Requesting a Replay	Probability	Number of Foursomes Requesting a Replay	Probability
0	0.01	0	0.06
1	0.03	1	0.09
2	0.05	2	0.12
3	0.05	3	0.17
4	0.11	4	0.20
5	0.15	5	0.13
6	0.17	6	0.11
7	0.15	7	0.07
8	0.13	8	0.05
9	0.09		
10	0.06		

Managerial Report

Develop simulation models for both replay options using Crystal Ball. Run each simulation
for 5000 trials. Prepare a report that will help management of Harbor Dunes Golf Course
decide which replay option to implement for the upcoming spring golf season. In preparing your report, be sure to include the following:

1. Statistical summaries of the revenue expected under each replay option
2. Your recommendation as to the best replay option
3. Assuming a 90-day spring golf season, an estimate of the added revenue using your
   recommendation
4. Any other recommendations you have that might improve the income for Harbor Dunes

Case Problem 3   County Beverage Drive-Thru

County Beverage Drive-Thru, Inc., operates a chain of beverage supply stores in Northern
Illinois. Each store has a single service lane; cars enter at one end of the store and exit at
the other end. Customers pick up soft drinks, beer, snacks, and party supplies without getting out of their cars. When a new customer arrives at the store, the customer waits until the
preceding customer's order is complete and then drives into the store for service.

Typically, three employees operate each store during peak periods; two clerks take
and fill orders, and a third clerk serves as cashier and store supervisor. County Beverage is considering a revised store design in which computerized order-taking and payment are integrated with specialized warehousing equipment. Management hopes that
the new design will permit operating each store with one clerk. To determine whether
the new design is beneficial, management decided to build a new store using the revised
design.

County Beverage's new store will be located near a major shopping center. Based on
experience at other locations, management believes that during the peak late afternoon and
evening hours, the time between arrivals follows an exponential probability distribution

with a mean of six minutes. These peak hours are the most critical time period for the company; most of their profit is generated during these peak hours.

An extensive study of times required to fill orders with a single clerk led to the following probability distribution of service times:

Service Time (minutes)	Probability
2	0.24
3	0.20
4	0.15
5	0.14
6	0.12
7	0.08
8	0.05
9	0.02
Total	1.00

In case customer waiting times prove too long with just a single clerk, County Beverage's management is considering two alternatives: add a second clerk to help with bagging, taking orders, and related tasks, or enlarge the drive-through area so that two cars can be served at once (a two-channel system). With either of these options, two clerks will be needed. With the two-channel option, service times are expected to be the same for each channel. With the second clerk helping with a single channel, service times will be reduced. The following probability distribution describes service times given that option.

Service Time (minutes)	Probability
1	0.20
2	0.35
3	0.30
4	0.10
5	0.05
Total	1.00

County Beverage's management would like you to develop a spreadsheet simulation model of the new system and use it to compare the operation of the system using the following three designs:

Design	
A	One channel, one clerk
B	One channel, two clerks
C	Two channels, each with one clerk

Management is especially concerned with how long customers have to wait for service. Research has shown that 30% of the customers will wait no longer than 6 minutes and that 90% will wait no longer than 10 minutes. As a guideline, management requires the average waiting time to be less than 1.5 minutes.

Managerial Report

Prepare a report that discusses the general development of the spreadsheet simulation model, and make any recommendations that you have regarding the best store design and staffing plan for County Beverage. One additional consideration is that the design allowing for a two-channel system will cost an additional $10,000 to build.

1. List the information the spreadsheet simulation model should generate so that a decision can be made on the store design and the desired number of clerks.
2. Run the simulation for 1000 customers for each alternative considered. You may want to consider making more than one run with each alternative. [*Note:* Values from an exponential probability distribution with mean mu (μ) can be generated in Excel using the following function: $= -\mu*LN(RAND())$.]
3. Be sure to note the number of customers County Beverage is likely to lose due to long customer waiting times with each design alternative.

Appendix 16.1   Simulation with Excel

Excel enables small and moderate-sized simulation models to be implemented relatively easily and quickly. In this appendix we show the Excel worksheets for the three simulation models presented in the chapter.

The PortaCom Simulation Model

We simulated the PortaCom problem 500 times. The worksheet used to carry out the simulation is shown again in Figure 16.19. Note that the simulation results for trials 6 through 495 have been hidden so that the results can be shown in a reasonably sized figure. If desired, the rows for these trials can be shown and the simulation results displayed for all 500 trials. Let us describe the details of the Excel worksheet that provided the PortaCom simulation.

First, the PortaCom data are presented in the first 14 rows of the worksheet. The selling price per unit, administrative cost, and advertising cost parameters are entered directly into cells C3, C4, and C5. The discrete probability distribution for the direct labor cost per unit is shown in a tabular format. Note that the random number intervals are entered first, followed by the corresponding cost per unit. For example, 0.0 in cell A10 and 0.1 in cell B10 show that a cost of $43 per unit will be assigned if the random number is in the interval 0.0 but less than 0.1. Thus, approximately 10% of the simulated direct labor costs will be $43 per unit. The uniform probability distribution with a smallest value of $80 in cell E8 and a largest value of $100 in cell E9 describes the parts cost per unit. Finally, a normal probability distribution with a mean of 15,000 units in cell E13 and a standard deviation of 4500 units in cell E14 describes the first-year demand distribution for the product. At this point we are ready to insert the Excel formulas that will carry out each simulation trial.

Simulation information for the first trial appears in row 21 of the worksheet. The cell formulas for row 21 are as follows:

Cell A21   Enter 1 for the first simulation trial

Cell B21   Simulate the direct labor cost per unit[3]
            $=VLOOKUP(RAND(),\$A\$10:\$C\$14,3)$

Cell C21   Simulate the parts cost per unit (uniform distribution)
            $=\$E\$8+(\$E\$9-\$E\$8)*RAND()$

---

[3]See Excel Appendix for an explanation of the VLOOKUP function.

FIGURE 16.19 WORKSHEET FOR THE PORTACOM PROBLEM

WEB file

PortaCom

	A	B	C	D	E	F
1	**PortaCom Risk Analysis**					
2						
3	Selling Price per Unit		$249			
4	Administrative Cost		$400,000			
5	Advertising Cost		$600,000			
6						
7	**Direct Labor Cost**			**Parts Cost (Uniform Distribution)**		
8	Lower	Upper		Smallest Value	$80	
9	Random No.	Random No.	Cost per Unit	Largest Value	$100	
10	0.0	0.1	$43			
11	0.1	0.3	$44			
12	0.3	0.7	$45	**Demand (Normal Distribution)**		
13	0.7	0.9	$46	Mean	15000	
14	0.9	1.0	$47	Std Deviation	4500	
15						
16						
17	**Simulation Trials**					
18						
19		Direct Labor	Parts	First-Year		
20	Trial	Cost per Unit	Cost per Unit	Demand	Profit	
21	1	47	$85.36	17,366	$1,025,570	
22	2	44	$91.68	12,900	$461,828	
23	3	45	$93.35	20,686	$1,288,906	
24	4	43	$98.56	10,888	$169,807	
25	5	45	$88.36	14,259	$648,911	
516	496	44	$98.67	8,730	($71,739)	
517	497	45	$94.38	19,257	$1,110,952	
518	498	44	$90.85	14,920	$703,118	
519	499	43	$90.37	13,471	$557,652	
520	500	46	$92.50	18,614	$1,056,847	
521						
522			**Summary Statistics**			
523			Mean Profit		$698,457	
524			Standard Deviation		$520,485	
525			Minimum Profit		($785,234)	
526			Maximum Profit		$2,367,058	
527			Number of Losses		51	
528			Probability of Loss		0.1020	
529						

Cell D21   Simulate the first-year demand (normal distribution)
=NORMINV(RAND(),$E$13,$E$14)

Cell E21   The profit obtained for the first trial
=($C$3–B21–C21)*D21–$C$4–$C$5

Cells A21:E21 can be copied to A520:E520 in order to provide the 500 simulation trials.

Ultimately, summary statistics will be collected in order to describe the results of the 500 simulated trials. Using the standard Excel functions, the following summary statistics are computed for the 500 simulated profits appearing in cells E21 to E520:

Cell E523   The mean profit per trial =AVERAGE(E21:E520)

Cell E524   The standard deviation of profit =STDEV(E21:E520)

Cell E525   The minimum profit =MIN(E21:E520)

Cell E526   The maximum profit =MAX(E21:E520)

Cell E527   The count of the number of trials where a loss occurred
            (i.e., profit < $0) =COUNTIF(E21:E520,"<0")

Cell E528   The percentage or probability of a loss based on the 500 trials =E527/500

The F9 key can be used to perform another complete simulation of PortaCom. In this case, the entire worksheet will be recalculated and a set of new simulation results will be provided. Any data summaries, measures, or functions that have been built into the worksheet earlier will be updated automatically.

The Butler Inventory Simulation Model

We simulated the Butler inventory operation for 300 months. The worksheet used to carry out the simulation is shown again in Figure 16.20. Note that the simulation results for months 6 through 295 have been hidden so that the results can be shown in a reasonably sized figure. If desired, the rows for these months can be shown and the simulation results displayed for all 300 months. Let us describe the details of the Excel worksheet that provided the Butler inventory simulation.

First, the Butler inventory data are presented in the first 11 rows of the worksheet. The gross profit per unit, holding cost per unit, and shortage cost per unit data are entered directly into cells C3, C4, and C5. The replenishment level is entered into cell C7, and the mean and standard deviation of the normal probability distribution for demand are entered into cells B10 and B11. At this point we are ready to insert Excel formulas that will carry out each simulation month or trial.

Simulation information for the first month or trial appears in row 17 of the worksheet. The cell formulas for row 17 are as follows:

Cell A17   Enter 1 for the first simulation month

Cell B17   Simulate demand (normal distribution)
            =NORMINV(RAND(),$B$10,$B$11)

Next compute the sales, which is equal to demand (cell B17) if demand is less than or equal to the replenishment level, or is equal to the replenishment level (cell C7) if demand is greater than the replenishment level.

Cell C17   Compute sales =IF(B17<=$C$7,B17,$C$7)

Cell D17   Calculate gross profit =$C$3*C17

Cell E17   Calculate the holding cost if demand is less than or equal to the replenishment level
            =IF(B17<= $C$7,$C$4*($C$7–B17),0)

Cell F17   Calculate the shortage cost if demand is greater than the replenishment level
            =IF(B17>$C$7,$C$5*(B17–$C$7),0)

Cell G17   Calculate net profit =D17–E17–F17

Cells A17:G17 can be copied to cells A316:G316 in order to provide the 300 simulation months.

FIGURE 16.20 WORKSHEET FOR THE BUTLER INVENTORY PROBLEM

Butler

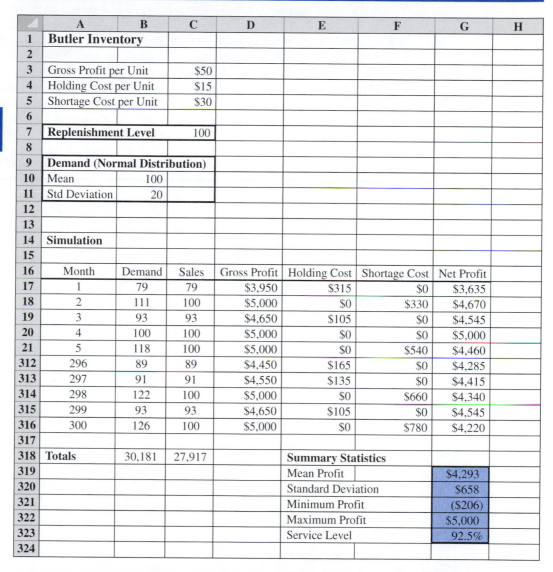

	A	B	C	D	E	F	G	H
1	**Butler Inventory**							
2								
3	Gross Profit per Unit		$50					
4	Holding Cost per Unit		$15					
5	Shortage Cost per Unit		$30					
6								
7	**Replenishment Level**		100					
8								
9	**Demand (Normal Distribution)**							
10	Mean	100						
11	Std Deviation	20						
12								
13								
14	**Simulation**							
15								
16	Month	Demand	Sales	Gross Profit	Holding Cost	Shortage Cost	Net Profit	
17	1	79	79	$3,950	$315	$0	$3,635	
18	2	111	100	$5,000	$0	$330	$4,670	
19	3	93	93	$4,650	$105	$0	$4,545	
20	4	100	100	$5,000	$0	$0	$5,000	
21	5	118	100	$5,000	$0	$540	$4,460	
312	296	89	89	$4,450	$165	$0	$4,285	
313	297	91	91	$4,550	$135	$0	$4,415	
314	298	122	100	$5,000	$0	$660	$4,340	
315	299	93	93	$4,650	$105	$0	$4,545	
316	300	126	100	$5,000	$0	$780	$4,220	
317								
318	**Totals**	30,181	27,917		**Summary Statistics**			
319					Mean Profit		$4,293	
320					Standard Deviation		$658	
321					Minimum Profit		($206)	
322					Maximum Profit		$5,000	
323					Service Level		92.5%	
324								

Finally, summary statistics will be collected in order to describe the results of the 300 simulated trials. Using the standard Excel functions, the following totals and summary statistics are computed for the 300 months:

Cell B318   Total demand =SUM(B17:B316)

Cell C319   Total sales =SUM(C17:C316)

Cell G319   The mean profit per month =AVERAGE(G17:G316)

Cell G320   The standard deviation of net profit =STDEV(G17:G316)

Cell G321   The minimum net profit =MIN(G17:G316)

Cell G322   The maximum net profit =MAX(G17:G316)

Cell G323   The service level =C318/B318

The Hammondsport ATM Simulation Model

We simulated the operation of the Hammondsport ATM waiting line system for 1000 customers. The worksheet used to carry out the simulation is shown again in Figure 16.21. Note that the simulation results for customers 6 through 995 have been hidden so that the results can be shown in a reasonably sized figure. If desired, the rows for these customers can be shown and the simulation results displayed for all 1000 customers. Let us describe the details of the Excel worksheet that provided the Hammondsport ATM simulation.

The data are presented in the first 9 rows of the worksheet. The interarrival times are described by a uniform distribution with a smallest time of 0 minutes (cell B4) and a largest

FIGURE 16.21   WORKSHEET FOR THE HAMMONDSPORT SAVINGS BANK WITH ONE ATM

WEB file

Hammondsport1

	A	B	C	D	E	F	G	H	I
1	Hammondsport Savings Bank with One ATM								
2									
3	Interarrival Times (Uniform Distribution)								
4	Smallest Value	0							
5	Largest Value	5							
6									
7	Service Times (Normal Distribution)								
8	Mean	2							
9	Std Deviation	0.5							
10									
11									
12	Simulation								
13									
14		Interarrival	Arrival	Service	Waiting	Service	Completion	Time	
15	Customer	Time	Time	Start Time	Time	Time	Time	in System	
16	1	1.4	1.4	1.4	0.0	2.3	3.7	2.3	
17	2	1.3	2.7	3.7	1.0	1.5	5.2	2.5	
18	3	4.9	7.6	7.6	0.0	2.2	9.8	2.2	
19	4	3.5	11.1	11.1	0.0	2.5	13.6	2.5	
20	5	0.7	11.8	13.6	1.8	1.8	15.4	3.6	
1011	996	0.5	2496.8	2498.1	1.3	0.6	2498.7	1.9	
1012	997	0.2	2497.0	2498.7	1.7	2.0	2500.7	3.7	
1013	998	2.7	2499.7	2500.7	1.0	1.8	2502.5	2.8	
1014	999	3.7	2503.4	2503.4	0.0	2.4	2505.8	2.4	
1015	1000	4.0	2507.4	2507.4	0.0	1.9	2509.3	1.9	
1016									
1017		Summary Statistics							
1018		Number Waiting			549				
1019		Probability of Waiting			0.6100				
1020		Average Waiting Time			1.59				
1021		Maximum Waiting Time			13.5				
1022		Utilization of ATM			0.7860				
1023		Number Waiting > 1 Min			393				
1024		Probability of Waiting > 1 Min			0.4367				
1025									

time of 5 minutes (cell B5). A normal probability distribution with a mean of 2 minutes (cell B8) and a standard deviation of 0.5 minute (cell B9) describes the service time distribution.

Simulation information for the first customer appears in row 16 of the worksheet. The cell formulas for row 16 are as follows:

Cell A16	Enter 1 for the first customer
Cell B16	Simulate the interarrival time for customer 1 (uniform distribution) =$B$4+RAND()*($B$5–$B$4)
Cell C16	Compute the arrival time for customer 1 =B16
Cell D16	Compute the start time for customer 1 =C16
Cell E16	Compute the waiting time for customer 1 =D1–C16
Cell F16	Simulate the service time for customer 1 (normal distribution) =NORMINV(RAND(),$B$8,$B$9)
Cell G16	Compute the completion time for customer 1 =D16+F16
Cell H16	Compute the time in the system for customer 1 =G16–C16

Simulation information for the second customer appears in row 17 of the worksheet. The cell formulas for row 17 are as follows:

Cell A17	Enter 2 for the second customer
Cell B17	Simulate the interarrival time for customer 2 (uniform distribution) =$B$4+RAND()*($B$5–$B$4)
Cell C17	Compute the arrival time for customer 2 =C16+B17
Cell D17	Compute the start time for customer 2 =IF(C17>G16,C17,G16)
Cell E17	Compute the waiting time for customer 2 =D17–C17
Cell F17	Simulate the service time for customer 2 (normal distribution) =NORMINV(RAND(),$B$8,$B$9)
Cell G17	Compute the completion time for customer 2 =D17+F17
Cell H17	Compute the time in the system for customer 2 =G17–C17

Cells A17:H17 can be copied to cells A1015:H1015 in order to provide the 1000-customer simulation.

Ultimately, summary statistics will be collected in order to describe the results of 1000 customers. Before collecting the summary statistics, let us point out that most simulation studies of dynamic systems focus on the operation of the system during its long-run or steady-state operation. To ensure that the effect of start-up conditions are not included in the steady-state calculations, a dynamic simulation model is usually run for a specified period without collecting any data about the operation of the system. The length of the start-up period can vary depending on the application. For the Hammondsport Savings Bank ATM simulation, we treated the results for the first 100 customers as the start-up period. The simulation information for customer 100 appears in row 115 of the spreadsheet. Cell G115 shows that the completion time for the 100th customer is 247.8. Thus, the length of the start-up period is 247.8 minutes.

Summary statistics are collected for the next 900 customers, corresponding to rows 116 to 1015 of the spreadsheet. The following Excel formulas provided the summary statistics:

Cell E1018	Number of customers who had to wait (i.e., waiting time > 0) =COUNTIF(E116:E1015,">0")

Cell E1019   Probability of waiting =E1018/900

Cell E1020   The average waiting time =AVERAGE(E116:E1015)

Cell E1021   The maximum waiting time =MAX(E116:E1015)

Cell E1022   The utilization of the ATM[4] =SUM(F116:F1015)/(G1015–G115)

Cell E1023   The number of customers who had to wait more than 1 minute
                =COUNTIF(E116:E1015,">1")

Cell E1024   Probability of waiting more than 1 minute =E1023/900

Appendix 16.2   Simulation Using Crystal Ball

In Section 16.1 we used simulation to perform risk analysis for the PortaCom problem, and in Appendix 16.1 we showed how to construct the Excel worksheet that provided the simulation results. Developing the worksheet simulation for the PortaCom problem using the basic Excel package was relatively easy. The use of add-ins enable larger and more complex simulation problems to be easily analyzed using spreadsheets. In this appendix we show how Crystal Ball, an add-in package, can be used to perform the PortaCom simulation. We will run the simulation for 1000 trials here. Instructions for installing and starting Crystal Ball are included with the Crystal Ball software.

Formulating a Crystal Ball Model

We begin by entering the problem data into the top portion of the worksheet. For the Porta-Com problem, we must enter the following data: selling price, administrative cost, advertising cost, probability distribution for the direct labor cost per unit, smallest and largest values for the parts cost per unit (uniform distribution), and the mean and standard deviation for first-year demand (normal distribution). These data with appropriate descriptive labels are shown in cells A1:E13 of Figure 16.22.

For the PortaCom problem, the Crystal Ball model contains the following two components: (1) cells for the probabilistic inputs (direct labor cost, parts cost, first-year demand), and (2) a cell containing a formula for computing the value of the simulation model output (profit). In Crystal Ball the cells that contain the values of the probabilistic inputs are called *assumption cells,* and the cells that contain the formulas for the model outputs are referred to as *forecast cells*. The PortaCom problem requires only one output (profit), and thus the Crystal Ball model only contains one forecast cell. In more complex simulation problems more than one forecast cell may be necessary.

The assumption cells may only contain simple numeric values. In this model-building stage, we entered PortaCom's best estimates of the direct labor cost ($45), the parts cost ($90), and the first-year demand (15,000) into cells C21:C23, respectively. The forecast cells in a Crystal Ball model contain formulas that refer to one or more of the assumption cells. Because only one forecast cell in the PortaCom problem corresponds to profit, we entered the following formula into cell C27:

$$=(C3-C21-C22)*C23-C4-C5$$

The resulting value of $710,000 is the profit corresponding to the base-case scenario discussed in Section 16.1.

---

[4]The proportion of time the ATM is in use is equal to the sum of the 900 customer service times in column F divided by the total elapsed time required for the 900 customers to complete service. This total elapsed time is the difference between the completion time of customer 1000 and the completion time of customer 100.

FIGURE 16.22   CRYSTAL BALL WORKSHEET FOR THE PORTACOM PROBLEM

WEB file

PortaCom Crystal

	A	B	C	D	E	F
1	PortaCom Risk Analysis					
2						
3	Selling Price per Unit		$249			
4	Administrative Cost		$400,000			
5	Advertising Cost		$600,000			
6						
7		Direct Labor		Parts Cost (Uniform Distribution)		
8		Cost per Unit	Probability	Smallest Value	$80	
9		$43	0.1	Largest Value	$100	
10		$44	0.2			
11		$45	0.4	Demand (Normal Distribution)		
12		$46	0.2	Mean	15,000	
13		$47	0.1	Standard Dev	4,500	
14						
15						
16						
17	Crystal Ball Model					
18						
19			Assumption			
20			Cells			
21		Direct Labor Cost	$45			
22		Parts Cost	$90			
23		Demand	15,000			
24						
25			Forecast			
26			Cell			
27		Profit	$710,000			
28						

Defining and Entering Assumptions

We are now ready to define the probability distributions corresponding to each of the assumption cells. We begin by defining the probability distribution for the direct labor cost.

Step 1. Select cell C21

Step 2. Choose **Define Assumption**

Step 3. When the **Distribution Gallery: Cell 21** dialog box appears:

Choose **Custom**[5]

Click **OK**

Step 4. When the **Define Assumption: Cell C21** dialog box appears:

If the ⌄ button is to the right of the **Name** box, proceed to Step 5

---

[5]You may have to click All and use the scroll bar to see all possible distributions.

If the $\boxed{\wedge}$ button is to the right of the **Name** box, click the $\boxed{\wedge}$ button to obtain the $\boxed{\vee}$ button

Step 5. Choose **Load Data**
Enter B9:C13 in the **Location of data** box
Click **Keep Linked to Spreadsheet**
Click **OK** to terminate the data entry process
Click **OK**

The procedure for defining the probability distribution for the parts cost is similar.

Step 1. Select cell C22
Step 2. Choose **Define Assumption**
Step 3. When the **Distribution Gallery: Cell C22** dialog box appears:
Choose **Uniform** (Use the scroll bar to see all possible distributions.)
Click **OK**
Step 4. When the **Define Assumption: Cell C22** dialog box appears:
Enter =E8 in the **Minimum** box
Enter =E9 in the **Maximum** box
Click **Enter**
Click **OK**

Finally, we perform the following steps to define the probability distribution for first-year demand:

Step 1. Select cell C23
Step 2. Choose **Define Assumption**
Step 3. When the **Distribution Gallery: Cell 23** dialog box appears:
Choose **Normal**
Click **OK**
Step 4. When the **Define Assumption: Cell C23** dialog box appears:
Enter =E12 in the **Mean** box
Enter =E13 in the **Std. Dev.** box
Click **Enter**
Click **OK**

Defining Forecasts

After defining the assumption cells, we are ready to define the forecast cells. The following steps show this process for cell C27, which is the profit forecast cell for the PortaCom problem:

Step 1. Select cell C27
Step 2. Choose **Define Forecast**
Step 3. When the **Define Forecast: Cell C27** dialog box appears:
Profit will appear in the **Name** box
Click **OK**

Setting Run Preferences

We must now make the choices that determine how Crystal Ball runs the simulation. For the PortaCom simulation, we only need to specify the number of trials.

Step 1. Choose **Run Preferences**
Step 2. When the **Run Preferences** dialog box appears:
        Make sure the **Trials** tab has been selected
        Enter 1000 in the **Number of trials to run:** box
        Click **OK**

Running the Simulation

Crystal Ball repeats three steps on each of the 1000 trials of the PortaCom simulation.

1. Values are generated for the three assumption cells according to the defined probability distributions.
2. A new simulated profit (forecast cell) is computed based on the new values in the three assumption cells.
3. The new simulated profit is recorded.

To begin the simulation, choose **Start.**

   When the run is complete, Crystal Ball displays a Forecast: Profit window, which shows a frequency distribution of the simulated profit values obtained during the simulation run (see Figure 16.23). Other types of charts and output can be displayed. For instance, the following steps describe how to display the descriptive statistics for the simulation run:

Step 1. Select the **View** menu in the **Forecast: Profit** window
Step 2. Choose **Statistics**

FIGURE 16.23   CRYSTAL BALL FREQUENCY CHART FOR THE PORTACOM
               SIMULATION

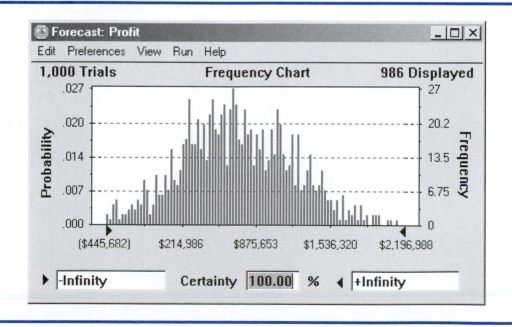

FIGURE 16.24 CRYSTAL BALL STATISTICS FOR THE PORTACOM SIMULATION

Forecast: Profit	
Edit Preferences View Run Help	
Cell C27	**Statistics**

Statistic	Value
Trials	1,000
Mean	$710,984
Median	$689,401
Mode	---
Standard Deviation	$512,211
Variance	$262,360,016,711
Skewness	0.10
Kurtosis	3.11
Coeff. of Variability	0.72
Range Minimum	($970,444)
Range Maximum	$2,855,888
Range Width	$3,826,332
Mean Std. Error	$16,197.53

Figure 16.24 shows the Forecast: Profit window with descriptive statistics. Note that the worst result obtained in this simulation of 1000 trials is a loss of $970,444, and the best result is a profit of $2,855,888. The mean profit is $710,984. These values are similar to the results obtained in Section 16.1. The differences result from the different random numbers used in the two simulations and from the fact that we used 1000 trials with Crystal Ball. If you perform another simulation, your results will differ slightly.

CHAPTER 17

Markov Processes

CONTENTS

Markov process models are useful in studying the evolution of systems over repeated trials. The repeated trials are often successive time periods where the state of the system in any particular period cannot be determined with certainty. Rather, transition probabilities are used to describe the manner in which the system makes transitions from one period to the next. Hence, we are interested in the probability of the system being in a particular state at a given time period.

Markov process models can be used to describe the probability that a machine that is functioning in one period will continue to function or will break down in the next period. Models can also be used to describe the probability that a consumer purchasing brand A in one period will purchase brand B in the next period. The Q.M. in Action, Benefit of Health Care Services, describes how a Markov process model was used to determine the health status probabilities for persons aged 65 and older. Such information was helpful in understanding the future need for health care services and the benefits of expanding current health care programs.

In this chapter we present a marketing application that involves an analysis of the store-switching behavior of supermarket customers. As a second illustration, we consider an accounting application that is concerned with the transitioning of accounts receivable dollars to different account-aging categories. Because an in-depth treatment of Markov processes is beyond the scope of this text, the analysis in both illustrations is restricted to situations consisting of a finite number of states, the transition probabilities remaining constant over time, and the probability of being in a particular state at any one time period depending only on the state in the immediately preceding time period. Such Markov processes are referred to as *Markov chains with stationary transition probabilities.*

Q.M. *in* ACTION

*BENEFIT OF HEALTH CARE SERVICES**

The U.S. Government Accountability Office (GAO) is an independent, nonpolitical audit organization in the legislative branch of the federal government. GAO evaluators obtained data on the health conditions of individuals aged 65 and older. The individuals were identified as being in three possible states:

Best: Able to perform daily activities without assistance

Next Best: Able to perform some daily activities without assistance

Worst: Unable to perform daily activities without assistance

Using a two-year period, the evaluators developed estimates of the transition probabilities among the three states. For example, a transition probability that a person in the Best state is still in the Best state one year later was

*Based on information provided by Bill Ammann, U.S. Government Accountability Office.

0.80, while the transition probability that a person in the Best state moves to the Next Best state one year later is 0.10. The Markov analysis of the full set of transition probabilities determined the steady-state probabilities that individuals would be in each state. Thus, for a given population aged 65 and older, the steady-state probabilities would indicate the percentage of the population that would be in each state in future years.

The GAO study further subdivided individuals into two groups: those receiving appropriate health care and those not receiving appropriate health care. For individuals not receiving appropriate health care, the kind of additional care and the cost of that care were estimated. The revised transition probabilities showed that with appropriate health care, the steady-state probabilities indicated the larger percentage of the population that would be in the Best and Next Best health states in future years. Using these results, the model provided evidence of the future benefits that would be achieved by expanding current health care programs.

17.1 Market Share Analysis

Suppose we are interested in analyzing the market share and customer loyalty for Murphy's Foodliner and Ashley's Supermarket, the only two grocery stores in a small town. We focus on the sequence of shopping trips of one customer and assume that the customer makes one shopping trip each week to either Murphy's Foodliner or Ashley's Supermarket, but not both.

Using the terminology of Markov processes, we refer to the weekly periods or shopping trips as the **trials of the process**. Thus, at each trial, the customer will shop at either Murphy's Foodliner or Ashley's Supermarket. The particular store selected in a given week is referred to as the **state of the system** in that period. Because the customer has two shopping alternatives at each trial, we say the system has two states. With a finite number of states, we identify the states as follows:

State 1. The customer shops at Murphy's Foodliner.
State 2. The customer shops at Ashley's Supermarket.

If we say the system is in state 1 at trial 3, we are simply saying that the customer shops at Murphy's during the third weekly shopping period.

As we continue the shopping trip process into the future, we cannot say for certain where the customer will shop during a given week or trial. In fact, we realize that during any given week, the customer may be either a Murphy's customer or an Ashley's customer. However, using a Markov process model, we will be able to compute the probability that the customer shops at each store during any period. For example, we may find a 0.6 probability that the customer will shop at Murphy's during a particular week and a 0.4 probability that the customer will shop at Ashley's.

To determine the probabilities of the various states occurring at successive trials of the Markov process, we need information on the probability that a customer remains with the same store or switches to the competing store as the process continues from trial to trial or week to week.

Suppose that, as part of a market research study, we collect data from 100 shoppers over a 10-week period. Suppose further that these data show each customer's weekly shopping trip pattern in terms of the sequence of visits to Murphy's and Ashley's. To develop a Markov process model for the sequence of weekly shopping trips, we need to express the probability of selecting each store (state) in a given period solely in terms of the store (state) that was selected during the previous period. In reviewing the data, suppose that we find that of all customers who shopped at Murphy's in a given week, 90% shopped at Murphy's the following week while 10% switched to Ashley's. Suppose that similar data for the customers who shopped at Ashley's in a given week show that 80% shopped at Ashley's the following week while 20% switched to Murphy's. Probabilities based on these data are shown in Table 17.1. Because these probabilities indicate that a customer moves, or makes

TABLE 17.1   TRANSITION PROBABILITIES FOR MURPHY'S AND ASHLEY'S
GROCERY SALES

Current Weekly Shopping Period	Next Weekly Shopping Period	
	Murphy's Foodliner	**Ashley's Supermarket**
Murphy's Foodliner	0.9	0.1
Ashley's Supermarket	0.2	0.8

a transition, from a state in a given period to each state in the following period, these probabilities are called **transition probabilities**.

An important property of the table of transition probabilities is that the sum of the probabilities in each row is 1; each row of the table provides a probability distribution. For example, a customer who shops at Murphy's one week must shop at either Murphy's or Ashley's the next week. The entries in row 1 give the probabilities associated with each of these events. The 0.9 and 0.8 probabilities in Table 17.1 can be interpreted as measures of store loyalty in that they indicate the probability of a repeat visit to the same store. Similarly, the 0.1 and 0.2 probabilities are measures of the store-switching characteristics of the customers. In developing a Markov process model for this problem, we are assuming that the transition probabilities will be the same for any customer and that the transition probabilities will not change over time.

Appendix 17.1 contains a review of matrix notation and operations.

Note that Table 17.1 has one row and one column for each state of the system. We will use the symbol p_{ij} to represent the transition probabilities and the symbol P to represent the matrix of transition probabilities; that is,

$$p_{ij} = \text{probability of making a transition from state } i \text{ in a given period to state } j \text{ in the next period}$$

For the supermarket problem, we have

A quick check for a valid matrix of transition probabilities is to make sure the sum of the probabilities in each row equals 1.

$$P = \begin{bmatrix} p_{11} & p_{12} \\ p_{21} & p_{22} \end{bmatrix} = \begin{bmatrix} 0.9 & 0.1 \\ 0.2 & 0.8 \end{bmatrix}$$

Using the matrix of transition probabilities, we can now determine the probability that a customer will be a Murphy's customer or an Ashley's customer at some period in the future. Let us begin by assuming that we have a customer whose last weekly shopping trip was to Murphy's. What is the probability that this customer will shop at Murphy's on the next weekly shopping trip, period 1? In other words, what is the probability that the system will be in state 1 after the first transition? The matrix of transition probabilities indicates that this probability is $p_{11} = 0.9$.

Now let us consider the state of the system in period 2. A useful way of depicting what can happen on the second weekly shopping trip is to draw a tree diagram of the possible outcomes (see Figure 17.1). Using this tree diagram, we see that the probability that the customer shops at Murphy's during both the first and the second weeks is $(0.9)(0.9) = 0.81$. Also, note that the probability of the customer switching to Ashley's on the first trip and then switching back to Murphy's on the second trip is $(0.1)(0.2) = 0.02$. Because these options are the only two ways that the customer can be in state 1 (shopping at Murphy's) during the second period, the probability of the system being in state 1 during the second period is $0.81 + 0.02 = 0.83$. Similarly, the probability of the system being in state 2 during the second period is $0.09 + 0.08 = 0.17$.

As desirable as the tree diagram approach may be from an intuitive point of view, it becomes cumbersome when we want to extend the analysis to three or more periods. Fortunately, we have an easier way to calculate the probabilities of the system being in state 1 or state 2 for any subsequent period. First, we introduce a notation that will allow us to represent these probabilities for any given period. Let

$$\pi_i(n) = \text{probability that the system is in state } i \text{ in period } n$$

Index denotes the state   Denotes the time period or number of transitions

FIGURE 17.1 TREE DIAGRAM DEPICTING TWO WEEKLY SHOPPING TRIPS OF A CUSTOMER WHO SHOPPED LAST AT MURPHY'S

	Week 1 (first shopping trip)	Week 2 (second shopping trip)	Probability of Each Two-Week Pattern

Customer Shopped Last at Murphy's Week 0

0.9 — Shops at Murphy's

0.9 — Shops at Murphy's — (0.9)(0.9) = 0.81

0.1 — Shops at Ashley's — (0.9)(0.1) = 0.09

0.1 — Shops at Ashley's

0.2 — Shops at Murphy's — (0.1)(0.2) = 0.02

0.8 — Shops at Ashley's — (0.1)(0.8) = 0.08

For example, $\pi_1(1)$ denotes the probability of the system being in state 1 in period 1, while $\pi_2(1)$ denotes the probability of the system being in state 2 in period 1. Because $\pi_i(n)$ is the probability that the system is in state i in period n, this probability is referred to as a **state probability**.

The terms $\pi_1(0)$ and $\pi_2(0)$ will denote the probability of the system being in state 1 or state 2 at some initial or starting period. Week 0 represents the most recent period, when we are beginning the analysis of a Markov process. If we set $\pi_1(0) = 1$ and $\pi_2(0) = 0$, we are saying that as an initial condition the customer shopped last week at Murphy's; alternatively, if we set $\pi_1(0) = 0$ and $\pi_2(0) = 1$, we would be starting the system with a customer who shopped last week at Ashley's. In the tree diagram of Figure 17.1, we consider the situation in which the customer shopped last at Murphy's. Thus,

$$[\pi_1(0) \quad \pi_2(0)] = [1 \quad 0]$$

is a vector that represents the initial state probabilities of the system. In general, we use the notation

$$\Pi(n) = [\pi_1(n) \quad \pi_2(n)]$$

to denote the vector of state probabilities for the system in period n. In the example, $\Pi(1)$ is a vector representing the state probabilities for the first week, $\Pi(2)$ is a vector representing the state probabilities for the second week, and so on.

Using this notation, we can find the state probabilities for period $n + 1$ by simply multiplying the known state probabilities for period n by the transition probability matrix.

Using the vector of state probabilities and the matrix of transition probabilities, the multiplication[1] can be expressed as follows:

$$\Pi(\text{next period}) = \Pi(\text{current period})P$$

or

$$\Pi(n + 1) = \Pi(n)P \qquad (17.1)$$

Beginning with the system in state 1 at period 0, we have $\Pi(0) = [1\ 0]$. We can compute the state probabilities for period 1 as follows:

$$\Pi(1) = \Pi(0)P$$

or

$$[\pi_1(1)\quad \pi_2(1)] = [\pi_1(0)\quad \pi_2(0)]\begin{bmatrix} p_{11} & p_{12} \\ p_{21} & p_{22} \end{bmatrix}$$

$$= [1\quad 0]\begin{bmatrix} 0.9 & 0.1 \\ 0.2 & 0.8 \end{bmatrix}$$

$$= [0.9\quad 0.1]$$

The state probabilities $\pi_1(1) = 0.9$ and $\pi_2(1) = 0.1$ are the probabilities that a customer who shopped at Murphy's during week 0 will shop at Murphy's or at Ashley's during week 1.

Using equation (17.1), we can compute the state probabilities for the second week as follows:

$$\Pi(2) = \Pi(1)P$$

or

$$[\pi_1(2)\quad \pi_2(2)] = [\pi_1(1)\quad \pi_2(1)]\begin{bmatrix} p_{11} & p_{12} \\ p_{21} & p_{22} \end{bmatrix}$$

$$= [0.9\quad 0.1]\begin{bmatrix} 0.9 & 0.1 \\ 0.2 & 0.8 \end{bmatrix}$$

$$= [0.83\quad 0.17]$$

We see that the probability of shopping at Murphy's during the second week is 0.83, while the probability of shopping at Ashley's during the second week is 0.17. These same results were previously obtained using the tree diagram of Figure 17.1. By continuing to apply equation (17.1), we can compute the state probabilities for any future period; that is,

$$\Pi(3) = \Pi(2)P$$
$$\Pi(4) = \Pi(3)P$$
$$\vdots \qquad \vdots$$
$$\Pi(n + 1) = \Pi(n)P$$

Table 17.2 shows the result of carrying out these calculations for 10 periods.

[1]Appendix 17.1 provides the step-by-step procedure for vector and matrix multiplication.

TABLE 17.2   STATE PROBABILITIES FOR FUTURE PERIODS BEGINNING INITIALLY
WITH A MURPHY'S CUSTOMER

State Probability	0	1	2	3	4	5	6	7	8	9	10
$\pi_1(n)$	1	0.9	0.83	0.781	0.747	0.723	0.706	0.694	0.686	0.680	0.676
$\pi_2(n)$	0	0.1	0.17	0.219	0.253	0.277	0.294	0.306	0.314	0.320	0.324

The vectors $\Pi(1)$, $\Pi(2)$, $\Pi(3)$, . . . contain the probabilities that a customer who started out as a Murphy customer will be in state 1 or state 2 in the first period, the second period, the third period, and so on. In Table 17.2 we see that after a few periods these probabilities do not change much from one period to the next.

If we had started with 1000 Murphy customers—that is, 1000 customers who last shopped at Murphy's—our analysis indicates that during the fifth weekly shopping period, 723 would be customers of Murphy's, and 277 would be customers of Ashley's. Moreover, during the tenth weekly shopping period, 676 would be customers of Murphy's, and 324 would be customers of Ashley's.

Now let us repeat the analysis, but this time we will begin the process with a customer who shopped last at Ashley's. Thus,

$$\Pi(0) = [\pi_1(0) \quad \pi_2(0)] = [0 \quad 1]$$

Using equation (17.1), the probability of the system being in state 1 or state 2 in period 1 is given by

$$\Pi(1) = \Pi(0)P$$

or

$$[\pi_1(1) \quad \pi_2(1)] = [\pi_1(0) \quad \pi_2(0)]\begin{bmatrix} p_{11} & p_{12} \\ p_{21} & p_{22} \end{bmatrix}$$
$$= [0 \quad 1]\begin{bmatrix} 0.9 & 0.1 \\ 0.2 & 0.8 \end{bmatrix}$$
$$= [0.2 \quad 0.8]$$

Proceeding as before, we can calculate subsequent state probabilities. Doing so, we obtain the results shown in Table 17.3.

In the fifth shopping period, the probability that the customer will be shopping at Murphy's is 0.555, and the probability that the customer will be shopping at Ashley's is 0.445. In the

TABLE 17.3   STATE PROBABILITIES FOR FUTURE PERIODS BEGINNING INITIALLY
WITH AN ASHLEY'S CUSTOMER

State Probability	0	1	2	3	4	5	6	7	8	9	10
$\pi_1(n)$	0	0.2	0.34	0.438	0.507	0.555	0.589	0.612	0.628	0.640	0.648
$\pi_2(n)$	1	0.8	0.66	0.562	0.493	0.445	0.411	0.388	0.372	0.360	0.352

10th period, the probability that a customer will be shopping at Murphy's is 0.648, and the probability that a customer will be shopping at Ashley's is 0.352.

As we continue the Markov process, we find that the probability of the system being in a particular state after a large number of periods is independent of the beginning state of the system. The probabilities that we approach after a large number of transitions are referred to as the **steady-state probabilities**. We shall denote the steady-state probability for state 1 with the symbol π_1 and the steady-state probability for state 2 with the symbol π_2. In other words, in the steady-state case, we simply omit the period designation from $\pi_i(n)$ because it is no longer necessary.

Analyses of Tables 17.2 and 17.3 indicate that as n gets larger, the difference between the state probabilities for the nth period and the $(n + 1)$th period becomes increasingly smaller. This analysis leads us to the conclusion that as n gets large, the state probabilities at the $(n + 1)$th period are very close to those at the nth period. This observation provides the basis of a simple method for computing the steady-state probabilities without having to actually carry out a large number of calculations.

In general, we know from equation (17.1) that

$$[\pi_1(n + 1) \quad \pi_2(n + 1)] = [\pi_1(n) \quad \pi_2(n)] \begin{bmatrix} p_{11} & p_{12} \\ p_{21} & p_{22} \end{bmatrix}$$

Because for sufficiently large n the difference between $\Pi(n + 1)$ and $\Pi(n)$ is negligible, we see that in the steady state $\pi_1(n + 1) = \pi_1(n) = \pi_1$ and $\pi_2(n + 1) = \pi_2(n) = \pi_2$. Thus, we have

$$[\pi_1 \quad \pi_2] = [\pi_1 \quad \pi_2] \begin{bmatrix} p_{11} & p_{12} \\ p_{21} & p_{22} \end{bmatrix}$$

$$= [\pi_1 \quad \pi_2] \begin{bmatrix} 0.9 & 0.1 \\ 0.2 & 0.8 \end{bmatrix}$$

After carrying out the multiplications, we obtain

$$\pi_1 = 0.9\pi_1 + 0.2\pi_2 \qquad \text{(17.2)}$$

and

$$\pi_2 = 0.1\pi_1 + 0.8\pi_2 \qquad \text{(17.3)}$$

However, we also know the steady-state probabilities must sum to 1 with

$$\pi_1 + \pi_2 = 1 \qquad \text{(17.4)}$$

Using equation (17.4) to solve for π_2 and substituting the result in equation (17.2), we obtain

$$\pi_1 = 0.9\pi_1 + 0.2(1 - \pi_1)$$
$$\pi_1 = 0.9\pi_1 + 0.2 - 0.2\pi_1$$
$$\pi_1 - 0.7\pi_1 = 0.2$$
$$0.3\pi_1 = 0.2$$
$$\pi_1 = \tfrac{2}{3}$$

Can you now compute the steady-state probabilities for Markov processes with two states? Problem 3 provides an application.

Then, using equation (17.4), we can conclude that $\pi_2 = 1 - \pi_1 = \frac{1}{3}$. Thus, using equations (17.2) and (17.4), we can solve for the steady-state probabilities directly. You can check for yourself that we could have obtained the same result using equations (17.3) and (17.4).[2]

Thus, if we have 1000 customers in the system, the Markov process model tells us that in the long run, with steady-state probabilities $\pi_1 = \frac{2}{3}$ and $\pi_2 = \frac{1}{3}$, $\frac{2}{3}(1000) = 667$ customers will be Murphy's and $\frac{1}{3}(1000) = 333$ customers will be Ashley's. The steady-state probabilities can be interpreted as the market shares for the two stores.

Market share information is often quite valuable in decision making. For example, suppose Ashley's Supermarket is contemplating an advertising campaign to attract more of Murphy's customers to its store. Let us suppose further that Ashley's believes this promotional strategy will increase the probability of a Murphy's customer switching to Ashley's from 0.10 to 0.15. The revised transition probabilities are given in Table 17.4.

Given the new transition probabilities, we can modify equations (17.2) and (17.4) to solve for the new steady-state probabilities or market shares. Thus, we obtain

$$\pi_1 = 0.85\pi_1 + 0.20\pi_2$$

With three states, the steady-state probabilities are found by solving three equations for the three unknown steady-state probabilities. Try Problem 7 as a slightly more difficult problem involving three states.

Substituting $\pi_2 = 1 - \pi_1$ from equation (17.4), we have

$$\pi_1 = 0.85\pi_1 + 0.20(1 - \pi_1)$$
$$\pi_1 = 0.85\pi_1 + 0.20 - 0.20\pi_1$$
$$\pi_1 - 0.65\pi_1 = 0.20$$
$$0.35\pi_1 = 0.20$$
$$\pi_1 = 0.57$$

Other examples of Markov processes include the promotion of managers to various positions within an organization, the migration of people into and out of various regions of the country, and the progression of students through the years of college, including eventually dropping out or graduating.

and

$$\pi_2 = 1 - 0.57 = 0.43$$

We see that the proposed promotional strategy will increase Ashley's market share from $\pi_2 = 0.33$ to $\pi_2 = 0.43$. Suppose that the total market consists of 6000 customers per week. The new promotional strategy will increase the number of customers doing their weekly shopping at Ashley's from 2000 to 2580. If the average weekly profit per customer is $10, the proposed promotional strategy can be expected to increase Ashley's profits by $5800 per week. If the cost of the promotional campaign is less than $5800 per week, Ashley should consider implementing the strategy.

TABLE 17.4   REVISED TRANSITION PROBABILITIES FOR MURPHY'S AND ASHLEY'S GROCERY STORES

Current Weekly Shopping Period	Next Weekly Shopping Period	
	Murphy's Foodliner	**Ashley's Supermarket**
Murphy's Foodliner	0.85	0.15
Ashley's Supermarket	0.20	0.80

[2]Even though equations (17.2) and (17.3) provide two equations and two unknowns, we must include equation (17.4) when solving for π_1 and π_2 to ensure that the sum of steady-state probabilities will equal 1.

This example demonstrates how a Markov analysis of a firm's market share can be useful in decision making. Suppose that instead of trying to attract customers from Murphy's Foodliner, Ashley's directed a promotional effort at increasing the loyalty of its own customers. In this case, p_{22} would increase and p_{21} would decrease. Once we knew the amount of the change, we could calculate new steady-state probabilities and compute the impact on profits.

NOTES AND COMMENTS

1. The Markov processes presented in this section have what is called the memoryless property: the current state of the system together with the transition probabilities contain all the information necessary to predict the future behavior of the system. The prior states of the system do not have to be considered. Such Markov processes are considered first-order Markov processes. Higher-order Markov processes are ones in which future states of the system depend on two or more previous states.

2. Analysis of a Markov process model is not intended to optimize any particular aspect of a system. Rather, the analysis predicts or describes the future and steady-state behavior of the system.

For instance, in the grocery store example, the analysis of the steady-state behavior provided a forecast or prediction of the market shares for the two competitors. In other applications, quantitative analysts have extended the study of Markov processes to what are called *Markov decision processes.* In these models, decisions can be made at each period that affect the transition probabilities and hence influence the future behavior of the system. Markov decision processes have been used in analyzing machine breakdown and maintenance operations, planning the movement of patients in hospitals, developing inspection strategies, determining newspaper subscription duration, and analyzing equipment replacement.

 17.2 ## Accounts Receivable Analysis

An accounting application in which Markov processes have produced useful results involves the estimation of the allowance for doubtful accounts receivable. This allowance is an estimate of the amount of accounts receivable that will ultimately prove to be uncollectible (i.e., bad debts).

Let us consider the accounts receivable situation for Heidman's Department Store. Heidman's uses two aging categories for its accounts receivable: (1) accounts that are classified as 0–30 days old, and (2) accounts that are classified as 31–90 days old. If any portion of an account balance exceeds 90 days, that portion is written off as a bad debt. Heidman's follows the procedure of aging the total balance in any customer's account according to the oldest unpaid bill. For example, suppose that one customer's account balance on September 30 is as follows:

Date of Purchase	Amount Charged
August 15	$25
September 18	10
September 28	50
Total	$85

An aging of accounts receivable on September 30 would assign the total balance of $85 to the 31–90-day category because the oldest unpaid bill of August 15 is 46 days old. Let us assume that one week later, October 7, the customer pays the August 15 bill of $25. The remaining total balance of $60 would now be placed in the 0–30-day category since the oldest unpaid amount, corresponding to the September 18 purchase, is less than 31 days old. This method of aging accounts receivable is called the *total balance method* because the total account balance is placed in the age category corresponding to the oldest unpaid amount.

Note that under the total balance method of aging accounts receivable, dollars appearing in a 31–90-day category at one point in time may appear in a 0–30-day category at a later point in time. In the preceding example, this movement between categories was true for $60 of September billings, which shifted from a 31–90-day to a 0–30-day category after the August bill had been paid.

Let us assume that on December 31 Heidman's shows a total of $3000 in its accounts receivable and that the firm's management would like an estimate of how much of the $3000 will eventually be collected and how much will eventually result in bad debts. The estimated amount of bad debts will appear as an allowance for doubtful accounts in the year-end financial statements.

Let us see how we can view the accounts receivable operation as a Markov process. First, concentrate on what happens to *one* dollar currently in accounts receivable. As the firm continues to operate into the future, we can consider each week as a trial of a Markov process with a dollar existing in one of the following states of the system:

State 1. Paid category
State 2. Bad debt category
State 3. 0–30-day category
State 4. 31–90-day category

Thus, we can track the week-by-week status of one dollar by using a Markov analysis to identify the state of the system at a particular week or period.

Using a Markov process model with the preceding states, we define the transition probabilities as follows:

p_{ij} = probability of a dollar in state i in one week moving to state j in the next week

Based on historical transitions of accounts receivable dollars, the following matrix of transition probabilities, P, has been developed for Heidman's Department Store:

$$
P = \begin{bmatrix} p_{11} & p_{12} & p_{13} & p_{14} \\ p_{21} & p_{22} & p_{23} & p_{24} \\ p_{31} & p_{32} & p_{33} & p_{34} \\ p_{41} & p_{42} & p_{43} & p_{44} \end{bmatrix} = \begin{bmatrix} 1.0 & 0.0 & 0.0 & 0.0 \\ 0.0 & 1.0 & 0.0 & 0.0 \\ 0.4 & 0.0 & 0.3 & 0.3 \\ 0.4 & 0.2 & 0.3 & 0.1 \end{bmatrix}
$$

Note that the probability of a dollar in the 0–30-day category (state 3) moving to the paid category (state 1) in the next period is 0.4. Also, this dollar has a 0.3 probability it will remain in the 0–30-day category (state 3) one week later, and a 0.3 probability that it will be in the 31–90-day category (state 4) one week later. Note also that a dollar in a 0–30-day account cannot make the transition to a bad debt (state 2) in one week.

When absorbing states are present, each row of the transition matrix corresponding to an absorbing state will have a single 1 and all other probabilities will be 0.

An important property of the Markov process model for Heidman's accounts receivable situation is the presence of *absorbing states*. For example, once a dollar makes a transition to state 1, the paid state, the probability of making a transition to any other state is zero. Similarly, once a dollar is in state 2, the bad debt state, the probability of a transition to any other state is zero. Thus, once a dollar reaches state 1 or state 2, the system will remain in this state forever. We can conclude that all accounts receivable dollars will eventually be absorbed into either the paid or the bad debt state, and hence the name **absorbing state**.

Fundamental Matrix and Associated Calculations

Whenever a Markov process has absorbing states, we do not compute steady-state probabilities because each unit ultimately ends up in one of the absorbing states. With absorbing states present, we are interested in knowing the probability that a unit will end up in each of the absorbing states. For the Heidman's Department Store problem, we want to know the probability that a dollar currently in the 0–30-day age category will end up paid (absorbing state 1) as well as the probability that a dollar in this age category will end up a bad debt (absorbing state 2). We also want to know these absorbing-state probabilities for a dollar currently in the 31–90-day age category.

The computation of the absorbing-state probabilities requires the determination and use of what is called a **fundamental matrix**. The mathematical logic underlying the fundamental matrix is beyond the scope of this text. However, as we show, the fundamental matrix is derived from the matrix of transition probabilities and is relatively easy to compute for Markov processes with a small number of states. In the following example, we show the computation of the fundamental matrix and the determination of the absorbing-state probabilities for Heidman's Department Store.

We begin the computations by partitioning the matrix of transition probabilities into the following four parts:

$$P = \begin{bmatrix} 1.0 & 0.0 & | & 0.0 & 0.0 \\ 0.0 & 1.0 & | & 0.0 & 0.0 \\ -- & -- & -- & -- & -- \\ 0.4 & 0.0 & | & 0.3 & 0.3 \\ 0.4 & 0.2 & | & 0.3 & 0.1 \end{bmatrix} = \begin{bmatrix} 1.0 & 0.0 & | & 0.0 & 0.0 \\ 0.0 & 1.0 & | & 0.0 & 0.0 \\ -- & -- & -- & -- & -- \\ & R & | & Q & \\ & & | & & \end{bmatrix}$$

where

$$R = \begin{bmatrix} 0.4 & 0.0 \\ 0.4 & 0.2 \end{bmatrix} \quad Q = \begin{bmatrix} 0.3 & 0.3 \\ 0.3 & 0.1 \end{bmatrix}$$

A matrix N, called a *fundamental matrix,* can be calculated using the following formula:

$$N = (I - Q)^{-1} \tag{17.5}$$

where I is an identity matrix with 1s on the main diagonal and 0s elsewhere. The superscript -1 is used to indicate the inverse of the matrix $(I - Q)$. In Appendix 17.1 we present formulas for finding the inverse of a matrix with two rows and two columns. In Appendix 17.2 we show how Excel's MINVERSE function can be used to compute an inverse.

Before proceeding, we note that to use equation (17.5), the identity matrix I must be chosen such that it has the *same size or dimensionality* as the matrix Q. In our example problem, Q has two rows and two columns, so we must choose

$$I = \begin{bmatrix} 1.0 & 0.0 \\ 0.0 & 1.0 \end{bmatrix}$$

Let us now continue with the example problem by computing the fundamental matrix.

$$I - Q = \begin{bmatrix} 1.0 & 0.0 \\ 0.0 & 1.0 \end{bmatrix} - \begin{bmatrix} 0.3 & 0.3 \\ 0.3 & 0.1 \end{bmatrix}$$

$$= \begin{bmatrix} 0.7 & -0.3 \\ -0.3 & 0.9 \end{bmatrix}$$

and (see Appendix 17.1)

$$N = (I - Q)^{-1} = \begin{bmatrix} 1.67 & 0.56 \\ 0.56 & 1.30 \end{bmatrix}$$

If we multiply the fundamental matrix N times the R portion of the P matrix, we obtain the probabilities that accounts receivable dollars initially in states 3 or 4 will eventually reach each of the absorbing states. The multiplication of N times R for the Heidman's Department Store problem provides the following results (again, see Appendix 17.1 for the steps of this matrix multiplication):

$$NR = \begin{bmatrix} 1.67 & 0.56 \\ 0.56 & 1.30 \end{bmatrix} \begin{bmatrix} 0.4 & 0.0 \\ 0.4 & 0.2 \end{bmatrix} = \begin{bmatrix} 0.89 & 0.11 \\ 0.74 & 0.26 \end{bmatrix}$$

The first row of the product NR is the probability that a dollar in the 0–30-day age category will end up in each absorbing state. Thus, we see a 0.89 probability that a dollar in the 0–30-day category will eventually be paid and a 0.11 probability that it will become a bad debt. Similarly, the second row shows the probabilities associated with a dollar in the 31–90-day category; that is, a dollar in the 31–90-day category has a 0.74 probability of eventually being paid and a 0.26 probability of proving to be uncollectible. Using this information, we can predict the amount of money that will be paid and the amount that will be lost as bad debts.

Establishing the Allowance for Doubtful Accounts

Let B represent a two-element vector that contains the current accounts receivable balances in the 0–30-day and the 31–90-day categories; that is,

$$B = \begin{bmatrix} b_1 & b_2 \end{bmatrix}$$

Total dollars in the   Total dollars in the
0–30-day category   31–90-day category

Suppose that the December 31 balance of accounts receivable for Heidman's shows $1000 in the 0–30-day category (state 3) and $2000 in the 31–90-day category (state 4).

$$B = [1000 \quad 2000]$$

We can multiply B times NR to determine how much of the $3000 will be collected and how much will be lost. For example,

$$BNR = [1000 \quad 2000] \begin{bmatrix} 0.89 & 0.11 \\ 0.74 & 0.26 \end{bmatrix}$$

$$= [2370 \quad 630]$$

Thus, we see that $2370 of the accounts receivable balances will be collected and $630 will be written off as a bad debt expense. Based on this analysis, the accounting department would set up an allowance for doubtful accounts of $630.

The matrix multiplication of BNR is simply a convenient way of computing the eventual collections and bad debts of the accounts receivable. Recall that the NR matrix showed a 0.89 probability of collecting dollars in the 0–30-day category and a 0.74 probability of collecting dollars in the 31–90-day category. Thus, as was shown by the BNR calculation, we expect to collect a total of $(1000)0.89 + (2000)0.74 = 890 + 1480 = \$2370$.

Suppose that on the basis of the previous analysis Heidman's would like to investigate the possibility of reducing the amount of bad debts. Recall that the analysis indicated that a 0.11 probability, or 11% of the amount in the 0–30-day age category, and 26% of the amount in the 31–90-day age category will prove to be uncollectible. Let us assume that Heidman's is considering instituting a new credit policy involving a discount for prompt payment.

Management believes that the policy under consideration will increase the probability of a transition from the 0–30-day age category to the paid category and decrease the probability of a transition from the 0–30-day to the 31–90-day age category. Let us assume that a careful study of the effects of this new policy leads management to conclude that the following transition matrix would be applicable:

$$P = \begin{bmatrix} 1.0 & 0.0 & | & 0.0 & 0.0 \\ 0.0 & 1.0 & | & 0.0 & 0.0 \\ - & - & - & - & - \\ 0.6 & 0.0 & | & 0.3 & 0.1 \\ 0.4 & 0.2 & | & 0.3 & 0.1 \end{bmatrix}$$

We see that the probability of a dollar in the 0–30-day age category making a transition to the paid category in the next period has increased to 0.6, and that the probability of a dollar in the 0–30-day age category making a transition to the 31–90-day category has decreased to 0.1. To determine the effect of these changes on bad debt expense, we must calculate N, NR, and BNR. We begin by using equation (17.5) to calculate the fundamental matrix N:

$$N = (I - Q)^{-1} = \left\{ \begin{bmatrix} 1.0 & 0.0 \\ 0.0 & 1.0 \end{bmatrix} - \begin{bmatrix} 0.3 & 0.1 \\ 0.3 & 0.1 \end{bmatrix} \right\}^{-1}$$

$$= \begin{bmatrix} 0.7 & -0.1 \\ -0.3 & 0.9 \end{bmatrix}^{-1}$$

$$= \begin{bmatrix} 1.5 & 0.17 \\ 0.5 & 1.17 \end{bmatrix}$$

By multiplying N times R, we obtain the new probabilities that the dollars in each age category will end up in the two absorbing states:

$$NR = \begin{bmatrix} 1.5 & 0.17 \\ 0.5 & 1.17 \end{bmatrix} \begin{bmatrix} 0.6 & 0.0 \\ 0.4 & 0.2 \end{bmatrix}$$

$$= \begin{bmatrix} 0.97 & 0.03 \\ 0.77 & 0.23 \end{bmatrix}$$

We see that with the new credit policy we would expect only 3% of the funds in the 0–30-day age category and 23% of the funds in the 31–90-day age category to prove to be uncollectible. If, as before, we assume a current balance of $1000 in the 0–30-day age category and $2000 in the 31–90-day age category, we can calculate the total amount of accounts receivable that will end up in the two absorbing states by multiplying B times NR. We obtain

$$BNR = \begin{bmatrix} 1000 & 2000 \end{bmatrix} \begin{bmatrix} 0.97 & 0.03 \\ 0.77 & 0.23 \end{bmatrix}$$

$$= \begin{bmatrix} 2510 & 490 \end{bmatrix}$$

Problem 11, which provides a variation of Heidman's Department Store problem, will give you practice in analyzing Markov processes with absorbing states.

Thus, the new credit policy shows a bad debt expense of $490. Under the previous credit policy, we found the bad debt expense to be $630. Thus, a savings of $630 − $490 = $140 could be expected as a result of the new credit policy. Given the total accounts receivable balance of $3000, this savings represents a 4.7% reduction in bad debt expense. After considering the costs involved, management can evaluate the economics of adopting the new credit policy. If the cost, including discounts, is less than 4.7% of the accounts receivable balance, we would expect the new policy to lead to increased profits for Heidman's Department Store.

Summary

In this chapter we presented Markov process models as well as examples of their application. We saw that a Markov analysis could provide helpful decision-making information about a situation that involves a sequence of repeated trials with a finite number of possible states on each trial. A primary objective is obtaining information about the probability of each state after a large number of transitions or time periods.

A market share application showed the computational procedure for determining the steady-state probabilities that could be interpreted as market shares for two competing supermarkets. In an accounts receivable application, we introduced the notion of absorbing states; for the two absorbing states, referred to as the paid and bad debt categories, we showed how to determine the percentage of an accounts receivable balance that would be absorbed in each of these states.

Markov process models have also been used to analyze strategies in sporting events. The Q.M. in Action, Markov Processes and Canadian Curling, describes the advantage gained in the sport of curling from winning the opening coin toss.

Q.M. *in* ACTION

MARKOV PROCESSES AND CANADIAN CURLING*

Curling is a sport played on a strip of ice 14 feet wide and 146 feet long—about half the length of a football field. At the end of each strip is a "house" composed of four concentric circles etched in the ice, much like the target in a dartboard. The object is to slide a curling stone—called a rock—down the strip of ice and have it finish as close to the center of the house (the bulls-eye) as possible. A game consists of 10 ends. In an end, each team slides eight rocks down the strip and then the score is tallied. The team with the rock closest to the center of the house wins one or more points. A point is scored for every rock inside the closest rock for the other team. No rocks in the house means no score for the end.

The team that goes last has an advantage. For instance, that team has the opportunity to execute a "take out" by knocking the other team's rock(s) out of the house with their last shot. The team that goes last in an end is said to have the hammer. At the beginning of the game a coin toss determines which team starts with the

hammer. As the game progresses, the hammer switches sides after any end in which the team with the hammer scores. If no score is made in an end, the hammer does not switch sides.

A Markov model was developed to determine the expected value of winning the coin toss to start the game with the hammer. Data were obtained for 8421 games played in the Canadian Men's Curling Championship over the 13 years from 1985 to 1997. The transition probabilities were based on the probability distributions for points scored in each of the 10 ends. An interesting finding was that the transition probabilities for the first end and the last end (and any extra ends) differed from those for the middle ends (ends 2 through 9).

Results of the Markov analysis showed that the expected score differential in favor of the team winning the opening coin toss was 1.115 when using three separate sets of transition probabilities. When one set of aggregate transition probabilities was used for all ends, the expected score differential in favor of the team winning the opening toss was 1.006. These results clearly indicate a significant advantage in winning the opening toss.

*Based on Kent J. Kostuk and Keith A. Willoughby, "OR/MS 'Rocks' the 'House,'" *OR/MS Today* (December 1999): 36–39.

Glossary

Trials of the process The events that trigger transitions of the system from one state to another. In many applications, successive time periods represent the trials of the process.

State of the system The condition of the system at any particular trial or time period.

Transition probability Given that the system is in state i during one period, the transition probability p_{ij} is the probability that the system will be in state j during the next period.

State probability The probability that the system will be in any particular state. (That is, $\pi_i(n)$ is the probability of the system being in state i in period n.)

Steady-state probability The probability that the system will be in any particular state after a large number of transitions. Once steady state has been reached, the state probabilities do not change from period to period.

Absorbing state A state is said to be absorbing if the probability of making a transition out of that state is zero. Thus, once the system has made a transition into an absorbing state, it will remain there.

Fundamental matrix A matrix necessary for the computation of probabilities associated with absorbing states of a Markov process.

Problems

1. In the market share analysis of Section 17.1, suppose that we are considering the Markov process associated with the shopping trips of one customer, but we do not know where the customer shopped during the last week. Thus, we might assume a 0.5 probability that the customer shopped at Murphy's and a 0.5 probability that the customer shopped at Ashley's at period 0; that is, $\pi_1(0) = 0.5$ and $\pi_2(0) = 0.5$. Given these initial state probabilities, develop a table similar to Table 17.2, showing the probability of each state in future periods. What do you observe about the long-run probabilities of each state?

2. Management of the New Fangled Softdrink Company believes that the probability of a customer purchasing Red Pop or the company's major competition, Super Cola, is based on the customer's most recent purchase. Suppose that the following transition probabilities are appropriate:

		To	
From	**Red Pop**	**Super Cola**
Red Pop	0.9	0.1
Super Cola	0.1	0.9

  a. Show the two-period tree diagram for a customer who last purchased Red Pop. What is the probability that this customer purchases Red Pop on the second purchase?
  b. What is the long-run market share for each of these two products?
  c. A Red Pop advertising campaign is being planned to increase the probability of attracting Super Cola customers. Management believes that the new campaign will increase to 0.15 the probability of a customer switching from Super Cola to Red Pop. What is the projected effect of the advertising campaign on the market shares?

3. The computer center at Rockbottom University has been experiencing computer downtime. Let us assume that the trials of an associated Markov process are defined as one-hour periods and that the probability of the system being in a running state or a down state is

based on the state of the system in the previous period. Historical data show the following transition probabilities:

From	To Running	Down
Running	0.90	0.10
Down	0.30	0.70

a. If the system is initially running, what is the probability of the system being down in the next hour of operation?
b. What are the steady-state probabilities of the system being in the running state and in the down state?

4. One cause of the downtime in Problem 3 was traced to a specific piece of computer hardware. Management believes that switching to a different hardware component will result in the following transition probabilities:

From	To Running	Down
Running	0.95	0.05
Down	0.60	0.40

a. What are the steady-state probabilities of the system being in the running and down states?
b. If the cost of the system being down for any period is estimated to be $500 (including lost profits for time down and maintenance), what is the breakeven cost for the new hardware component on a time-period basis?

5. A major traffic problem in the Greater Cincinnati area involves traffic attempting to cross the Ohio River from Cincinnati to Kentucky using Interstate 75. Let us assume that the probability of no traffic delay in one period, given no traffic delay in the preceding period, is 0.85 and that the probability of finding a traffic delay in one period, given a delay in the preceding period, is 0.75. Traffic is classified as having either a delay or a no-delay state, and the period considered is 30 minutes.
a. Assume that you are a motorist entering the traffic system and receive a radio report of a traffic delay. What is the probability that for the next 60 minutes (two time periods) the system will be in the delay state? Note that this result is the probability of being in the delay state for two consecutive periods.
b. What is the probability that in the long run the traffic will not be in the delay state?
c. An important assumption of the Markov process models presented in this chapter has been the constant or stationary transition probabilities as the system operates in the future. Do you believe this assumption should be questioned for this traffic problem? Explain.

6. Data collected from selected major metropolitan areas in the eastern United States show that 2% of individuals living within the city limits move to the suburbs during a one-year period while 1% of individuals living in the suburbs move to the city during a one-year period. Answer the following questions assuming that this process is modeled by a Markov process with two states: city and suburbs:
a. Prepare the matrix of transition probabilities.
b. Compute the steady-state probabilities.
c. In a particular metropolitan area, 40% of the population lives in the city, and 60% of the population lives in the suburbs. What population changes do your steady-state probabilities project for this metropolitan area?

7. Assume that a third grocery store, Quick Stop Groceries, enters the market share and cus-
    tomer loyalty situation described in Section 17.1. Quick Stop Groceries is smaller than
    either Murphy's Foodliner or Ashley's Supermarket. However, Quick Stop's convenience
    with faster service and gasoline for automobiles can be expected to attract some customers
    who currently make weekly shopping visits to either Murphy's or Ashley's. Assume that
    the transition probabilities are as follows:

		To	
From	**Murphy's**	**Ashley's**	**Quick Stop**
Murphy's Foodliner	0.85	0.10	0.05
Ashley's Supermarket	0.20	0.75	0.05
Quick Stop Groceries	0.15	0.10	0.75

a. Compute the steady-state probabilities for this three-state Markov process.
b. What market share will Quick Stop obtain?
c. With 1000 customers, the original two-state Markov process in Section 17.1 projected
    667 weekly customer trips to Murphy's Foodliner and 333 weekly customer trips to
    Ashley's Supermarket. What impact will Quick Stop have on the customer visits at
    Murphy's and Ashley's? Explain.

8. The purchase patterns for two brands of toothpaste can be expressed as a Markov process
    with the following transition probabilities:

	To	
From	**Special B**	**MDA**
Special B	0.90	0.10
MDA	0.05	0.95

a. Which brand appears to have the most loyal customers? Explain.
b. What are the projected market shares for the two brands?

9. Suppose that in Problem 8 a new toothpaste brand enters the market such that the following
    transition probabilities exist:

		To	
From	**Special B**	**MDA**	**T-White**
Special B	0.80	0.10	0.10
MDA	0.05	0.75	0.20
T-White	0.40	0.30	0.30

What are the new long-run market shares? Which brand will suffer most from the introduction of the new brand of toothpaste?

10. Given the following transition matrix with states 1 and 2 as absorbing states, what is the
    probability that units in states 3 and 4 end up in each of the absorbing states?

$$
P = \begin{bmatrix}
1.0 & 0.0 & 0.0 & 0.0 \\
0.0 & 1.0 & 0.0 & 0.0 \\
0.2 & 0.1 & 0.4 & 0.3 \\
0.2 & 0.2 & 0.1 & 0.5
\end{bmatrix}
$$

11. In the Heidman's Department Store problem of Section 17.2, suppose that the following transition matrix is appropriate:

$$P = \begin{bmatrix} 1.0 & 0.0 & 0.0 & 0.0 \\ 0.0 & 1.0 & 0.0 & 0.0 \\ 0.5 & 0.0 & 0.25 & 0.25 \\ 0.5 & 0.2 & 0.05 & 0.25 \end{bmatrix}$$

If Heidman's has \$4000 in the 0–30-day category and \$5000 in the 31–90-day category, what is your estimate of the amount of bad debts the company will experience?

12. The KLM Christmas Tree Farm owns a plot of land with 5000 evergreen trees. Each year KLM allows retailers of Christmas trees to select and cut trees for sale to individual customers. KLM protects small trees (usually less than 4 feet tall) so that they will be available for sale in future years. Currently, 1500 trees are classified as protected trees, while the remaining 3500 are available for cutting. However, even though a tree is available for cutting in a given year, it may not be selected for cutting until future years. Most trees not cut in a given year live until the next year, but some diseased trees are lost every year.

   In viewing the KLM Christmas tree operation as a Markov process with yearly periods, we define the following four states:

   State 1. Cut and sold

   State 2. Lost to disease

   State 3. Too small for cutting

   State 4. Available for cutting but not cut and sold

   The following transition matrix is appropriate:

$$P = \begin{bmatrix} 1.0 & 0.0 & 0.0 & 0.0 \\ 0.0 & 1.0 & 0.0 & 0.0 \\ 0.1 & 0.2 & 0.5 & 0.2 \\ 0.4 & 0.1 & 0.0 & 0.5 \end{bmatrix}$$

   How many of the farm's 5000 trees will be sold eventually, and how many will be lost?

13. A large corporation collected data on the reasons both middle managers and senior managers leave the company. Some managers eventually retire, but others leave the company prior to retirement for personal reasons including more attractive positions with other firms. Assume that the following matrix of one-year transition probabilities applies with the four states of the Markov process being retirement, leaves prior to retirement for personal reasons, stays as a middle manager, and stays as a senior manager.

	Retirement	Leaves— Personal	Middle Manager	Senior Manager
Retirement	1.00	0.00	0.00	0.00
Leaves—Personal	0.00	1.00	0.00	0.00
Middle Manager	0.03	0.07	0.80	0.10
Senior Manager	0.08	0.01	0.03	0.88

   a. What states are considered absorbing states? Why?
   b. Interpret the transition probabilities for the middle managers.
   c. Interpret the transition probabilities for the senior managers.
   d. What percentage of the current middle managers will eventually retire from the company? What percentage will leave the company for personal reasons?

e.   The company currently has 920 managers: 640 middle managers and 280 senior managers. How many of these managers will eventually retire from the company? How many will leave the company for personal reasons?

14.   Data for the progression of college students at a particular college are summarized in the following matrix of transition probabilities.

	Graduate	Drop Out	Freshman	Sophomore	Junior	Senior
Graduate	1.00	0.00	0.00	0.00	0.00	0.00
Drop Out	0.00	1.00	0.00	0.00	0.00	0.00
Freshman	0.00	0.20	0.15	0.65	0.00	0.00
Sophomore	0.00	0.15	0.00	0.10	0.75	0.00
Junior	0.00	0.10	0.00	0.00	0.05	0.85
Senior	0.90	0.05	0.00	0.00	0.00	0.05

a.   What states are absorbing states?
b.   Interpret the transition probabilities for a sophomore.
c.   Use The Management Scientist software package to compute the probabilities that a sophomore will graduate and that a sophomore will drop out.
d.   In an address to the incoming class of 600 freshmen, the dean asks the students to look around the auditorium and realize that about 50% of the freshmen present today will not make it to graduation day. Does your Markov process analysis support the dean's statement? Explain.
e.   Currently, the college has 600 freshmen, 520 sophomores, 460 juniors, and 420 seniors. What percentage of the 2000 students attending the college will eventually graduate?

Case Problem # Dealer's Absorbing State Probabilities in Blackjack

The game of blackjack (sometimes called "21") is a popular casino game. The goal is to have a hand with a value of 21 or as close to 21 as possible without exceeding 21. The player and the dealer are each dealt two cards initially. Both the player and dealer may draw additional cards (called "taking a hit") in order to improve their hand. If either the player or dealer takes a hit and the value of the hand exceeds 21, the player or dealer is said to have gone broke and loses. Face cards and tens count 10 points, aces can be counted as 1 or 11, and all other cards count at their face value. The dealer's advantage is that the player must decide on whether to take a hit first. The player who takes a hit and goes over 21 goes broke and loses, even if the dealer later goes broke. For instance, if the player has 16 and draws any card with a value higher than a 5, the player goes broke and loses. For this reason, players will often decide not to take a hit when the value of their hand is 12 or greater.

The dealer's hand is dealt with one card up and one card down. So, the player's decision of whether to take a hit is based on knowledge of the dealer's up card. A gambling professional asks you to help determine the probability of the ending value of the dealer's hand given different up cards. House rules at casinos require that the dealer continue to take a hit until the dealer's hand reaches a value of 17 or higher. Having just studied Markov processes, you suggest that the dealer's process of taking hits can be modeled as a Markov process with absorbing states.

Managerial Report

Prepare a report for the professional gambler that summarizes your findings. Include the following:

1. At some casinos, the dealer is required to stay (stop taking hits) when the dealer hand reaches soft or hard 17. A hand of soft 17 is one including an ace that may be counted as 1 or 11. In all casinos, the dealer is required to stay with soft 18, 19, 20, or 21. For each possible up card, determine the probability that the ending value of the dealer's hand is 17, 18, 19, 20, 21, or broke.
2. At other casinos, the dealer is required to take a hit on soft 17, but must stay on all other hands with a value of 17, 18, 19, 20, or 21. For this situation, determine the probability of the ending value of the dealer's hand.
3. Comment on whether the house rule of staying on soft 17 or hitting on soft 17 appears better for the player.

Appendix 17.1 Matrix Notation and Operations

Matrix Notation

A *matrix* is a rectangular arrangement of numbers. For example, consider the following matrix that we have named D:

$$D = \begin{bmatrix} 1 & 3 & 2 \\ 0 & 4 & 5 \end{bmatrix}$$

The matrix D is said to consist of six elements, where each element of D is a number. To identify a particular element of a matrix, we have to specify its location. Therefore, we introduce the concepts of rows and columns.

All elements across some horizontal line in a matrix are said to be in a row of the matrix. For example, elements 1, 3, and 2 in D are in the first row, and elements 0, 4, and 5 are in the second row. By convention, we refer to the top row as row 1, the second row from the top as row 2, and so on.

All elements along some vertical line are said to be in a column of the matrix. Elements 1 and 0 in D are elements in the first column, elements 3 and 4 are elements of the second column, and elements 2 and 5 are elements of the third column. By convention, we refer to the leftmost column as column 1, the next column to the right as column 2, and so on.

We can identify a particular element in a matrix by specifying its row and column position. For example, the element in row 1 and column 2 of D is the number 3. This position is written as

$$d_{12} = 3$$

In general, we use the following notation to refer to the specific elements of D:

$$d_{ij} = \text{element located in the } i\text{th row and } j\text{th column of } D$$

We always use capital letters for the names of matrixes and the corresponding lowercase letters with two subscripts to denote the elements.

The *size* of a matrix is the number of rows and columns in the matrix and is written as the number of rows $\times$ the number of columns. Thus, the size of D is 2×3.

Frequently we will encounter matrixes that have only one row or one column. For example,

$$G = \begin{bmatrix} 6 \\ 4 \\ 2 \\ 3 \end{bmatrix}$$

is a matrix that has only one column. Whenever a matrix has only one column, we call the matrix a *column vector*. In a similar manner, any matrix that has only one row is called a *row vector*. Using our previous notation for the elements of a matrix, we could refer to specific elements in G by writing g_{ij}. However, since G has only one column, the column position is unimportant, and we need only specify the row the element of interest is in. That is, instead of referring to elements in a vector using g_{ij}, we specify only one subscript, which denotes the position of the element in the vector. For example,

$$g_1 = 6 \qquad g_2 = 4 \qquad g_3 = 2 \qquad g_4 = 3$$

Matrix Operations

Matrix Transpose   The transpose of a matrix is formed by making the rows in the original matrix the columns in the transpose matrix, and by making the columns in the original matrix the rows in the transpose matrix. For example, the transpose of the matrix

$$D = \begin{bmatrix} 1 & 3 & 2 \\ 0 & 4 & 5 \end{bmatrix}$$

is

$$D^t = \begin{bmatrix} 1 & 0 \\ 3 & 4 \\ 2 & 5 \end{bmatrix}$$

Note that we use the superscript t to denote the transpose of a matrix.

Matrix Multiplication   We demonstrate how to perform two types of matrix multiplication: (1) multiplying two vectors, and (2) multiplying a matrix times a matrix.

The product of a row vector of size $1 \times n$ times a column vector of size $n \times 1$ is the number obtained by multiplying the first element in the row vector times the first element in the column vector, the second element in the row vector times the second element in the column vector, and continuing on through the last element in the row vector times the last element in the column vector, and then summing the products. Suppose, for example, that we wanted to multiply the row vector H times the column vector G, where

$$H = \begin{bmatrix} 2 & 1 & 5 & 0 \end{bmatrix} \text{ and } G = \begin{bmatrix} 6 \\ 4 \\ 2 \\ 3 \end{bmatrix}$$

The product HG, referred to as a vector product, is given by

$$HG = 2(6) + 1(4) + 5(2) + 0(3) = 26$$

The product of a matrix of size $p \times n$ and a matrix of size $n \times m$ is a new matrix of size $p \times m$. The element in the ith row and jth column of the new matrix is given by the vector product of the ith row of the $p \times n$ matrix times the jth column of the $n \times m$ matrix. Suppose, for example, that we want to multiply D times A, where

$$D = \begin{bmatrix} 1 & 3 & 2 \\ 0 & 4 & 5 \end{bmatrix} \quad A = \begin{bmatrix} 1 & 3 & 5 \\ 2 & 0 & 4 \\ 1 & 5 & 2 \end{bmatrix}$$

Let $C = DA$ denote the product of D times A. The element in row 1 and column 1 of C is given by the vector product of the first row of D times the first column of A. Thus,

$$c_{11} = \begin{bmatrix} 1 & 3 & 2 \end{bmatrix} \begin{bmatrix} 1 \\ 2 \\ 1 \end{bmatrix} = 1(1) + 3(2) + 2(1) = 9$$

The element in row 2 and column 1 of C is given by the vector product of the second row of D times the first column of A. Thus,

$$c_{21} = \begin{bmatrix} 0 & 4 & 5 \end{bmatrix} \begin{bmatrix} 1 \\ 2 \\ 1 \end{bmatrix} = 0(1) + 4(2) + 5(1) = 13$$

Calculating the remaining elements of C in a similar fashion, we obtain

$$C = \begin{bmatrix} 9 & 13 & 21 \\ 13 & 25 & 26 \end{bmatrix}$$

Clearly, the product of a matrix and a vector is just a special case of multiplying a matrix times a matrix. For example, the product of a matrix of size $m \times n$ and a vector of size $n \times 1$ is a new vector of size $m \times 1$. The element in the ith position of the new vector is given by the vector product of the ith row of the $m \times n$ matrix times the $n \times 1$ column vector. Suppose, for example, that we want to multiply D times K, where

$$D = \begin{bmatrix} 1 & 3 & 2 \\ 0 & 4 & 5 \end{bmatrix} \quad K = \begin{bmatrix} 1 \\ 4 \\ 2 \end{bmatrix}$$

The first element of DK is given by the vector product of the first row of D times K. Thus,

$$\begin{bmatrix} 1 & 3 & 2 \end{bmatrix} \begin{bmatrix} 1 \\ 4 \\ 2 \end{bmatrix} = 1(1) + 3(4) + 2(2) = 17$$

The second element of DK is given by the vector product of the second row of D and K. Thus,

$$\begin{bmatrix} 0 & 4 & 5 \end{bmatrix} \begin{bmatrix} 1 \\ 4 \\ 2 \end{bmatrix} = 0(1) + 4(4) + 5(2) = 26$$

Hence, we see that the product of the matrix D times the vector K is given by

$$DK = \begin{bmatrix} 1 & 3 & 2 \\ 0 & 4 & 5 \end{bmatrix} \begin{bmatrix} 1 \\ 4 \\ 2 \end{bmatrix} = \begin{bmatrix} 17 \\ 26 \end{bmatrix}$$

Can any two matrixes be multiplied? The answer is no. To multiply two matrixes, the number of the columns in the first matrix must equal the number of rows in the second. If this property is satisfied, the matrixes are said to *conform for multiplication*. Thus, in our example, D and K could be multiplied because D had three columns and K had three rows.

Matrix Inverse The inverse of a matrix A is another matrix, denoted A^{-1}, such that $A^{-1}A = I$ and $AA^{-1} = I$. The inverse of any square matrix A consisting of two rows and two columns is computed as follows:

$$A = \begin{bmatrix} a_{11} & a_{12} \\ a_{21} & a_{22} \end{bmatrix}$$

$$A^{-1} = \begin{bmatrix} a_{22}/d & -a_{12}/d \\ -a_{21}/d & a_{11}/d \end{bmatrix}$$

where $d = a_{11}a_{22} - a_{21}a_{12}$ is the determinant of the 2×2 matrix A. For example, if

$$A = \begin{bmatrix} 0.7 & -0.3 \\ -0.3 & 0.9 \end{bmatrix}$$

then

$$d = (0.7)(0.9) - (-0.3)(-0.3) = 0.54$$

and

$$A^{-1} = \begin{bmatrix} 0.9/0.54 & 0.3/0.54 \\ 0.3/0.54 & 0.7/0.54 \end{bmatrix} = \begin{bmatrix} 1.67 & 0.56 \\ 0.56 & 1.30 \end{bmatrix}$$

Appendix 17.2 Matrix Inversion with Excel

Excel provides a function called MINVERSE that can be used to compute the inverse of a matrix. This function is extremely useful when the inverse of a matrix of size 3×3 or larger is desired. To see how it is used, suppose we want to invert the following 3×3 matrix:

$$\begin{bmatrix} 3 & 5 & 0 \\ 0 & 1 & 1 \\ 8 & 5 & 0 \end{bmatrix}$$

Enter the matrix into cells B3:D5 of an Excel worksheet. The following steps will compute the inverse and place it in cells B7:D9:

Step 1. Select cells **B7:D9**
Step 2. Type **=MINVERSE(B3:D5)**
Step 3. Press **Ctrl + Shift + Enter**

Step 3 may appear strange. Excel's MINVERSE function returns an array (matrix) and must be used in what Excel calls an array formula. In step 3, we must press the Ctrl and Shift keys while we press Enter. The inverse matrix will then appear in cells B7:D9. It is

$$\begin{bmatrix} -.20 & 0 & .20 \\ .32 & 1 & -.12 \\ -.32 & 0 & .12 \end{bmatrix}$$

APPENDIXES

The purpose of this appendix is twofold. First, we provide an overview of Excel and discuss the basic operations needed to work with Excel workbooks and worksheets. Second, we provide an introduction to building mathematical models using Excel, including a discussion of how to find and use particular Excel functions, how to design and build good spreadsheet models, and how to ensure that these models are free of errors.

Overview of Microsoft Excel

When using Excel for modeling, the data and the model are displayed in workbooks, each of which contains a series of worksheets. Figure A.1 shows the layout of a blank workbook created each time Excel is opened. The workbook is named Book1 and consists of three worksheets named Sheet1, Sheet2, and Sheet3. Excel highlights the worksheet currently displayed (Sheet1) by setting the name on the worksheet tab in bold. To select a different worksheet, simply click on the corresponding tab. Note that cell A1 is initially selected.

A workbook is a file containing one or more worksheets.

The wide bar located across the top of the workbook is referred to as the Ribbon. Tabs, located at the top of the Ribbon, provide quick access to groups of related commands. There are eight tabs: Home, Insert, Page Layout, Formulas, Data, Review, View, and Add-Ins. Each tab contains several groups of related commands. Note that the Home tab is selected when Excel is opened. Four of the seven groups are displayed in Figure A.2. Under the Home tab there are seven groups of related commands: Clipboard, Font, Alignment, Number, Styles, Cells, and Editing. Commands are arranged within each group. For example, to change selected text to boldface, click the Home tab and click the Bold button in the Font group.

Figure A.3 illustrates the location of the Office Button, the Quick Access Toolbar, and the Formula Bar. When you click the Office Button, Excel provides a list of workbook options such as opening, saving, and printing (worksheets). The Quick Access Toolbar allows you to quickly access these workbook options. For instance, the Quick Access Toolbar shown in Figure A.3 includes an Open button 📂 that can be used to open files without having to first click the Office Button. To add or remove features on the Quick Access Toolbar click the Customize Quick Access Toolbar button ⧩ on the Quick Access Toolbar.

The Formula Bar contains a Name box, the Insert Function button f_x, and a Formula box. In Figure A.3, "A1" appears in the Name box because cell A1 is selected. You can select any other cell in the worksheet by using the mouse to move the cursor to another cell and clicking or by typing the new cell location in the name box and pressing the enter key. The Formula box is used to display the formula in the currently selected cell. For instance, if you had entered $=A1+A2$ into cell A3, whenever you select cell A3, the formula $=A1+A2$ will be shown in the Formula box. This feature makes it very easy to see and edit a formula in a particular cell. The Insert Function button allows you to quickly access all of the functions available in Excel. Later, we show how to find and use a particular function.

FIGURE A.1   BLANK WORKBOOK CREATED WHEN EXCEL IS STARTED

Basic Workbook Operations

Figure A.4 illustrates the worksheet options that can be performed after right clicking on a worksheet tab. For instance, to change the name of the current worksheet from "Sheet1" to "NowlinModel," right click the worksheet tab named "Sheet1" and select the Rename option. The current worksheet name (Sheet1) will be highlighted. Then, simply type the new name (NowlinModel) and press the Enter key to rename the worksheet.

FIGURE A.2   PORTION OF THE HOME TAB

FIGURE A.3   EXCEL OFFICE BUTTON, QUICK ACCESS TOOLBAR, AND
                   FORMULA BAR

FIGURE A.4   WORKSHEET OPTIONS OBTAINED AFTER RIGHT CLICKING ON A
WORKSHEET TAB

Suppose that you wanted to create a copy of "Sheet 1." After right-clicking the tab named "Sheet1," select the Move or Copy option. When the Move or Copy dialog box appears, select Create a Copy and click OK. The name of the copied worksheet will appear as "Sheet1 (2)." You can then rename it, if desired.

To add a worksheet to the workbook, right click any worksheet tab and select the Insert option; when the Insert dialog box appears, select Worksheet and click OK. An additional blank worksheet titled "Sheet 4" will appear in the workbook. You can also insert a new worksheet by clicking the Insert Worksheet tab button that appears to the right of the last worksheet tab displayed. Worksheets can be deleted by right clicking the worksheet tab and choosing Delete. After clicking Delete, a window will appear warning you that any data appearing in the worksheet will be lost. Click Delete to confirm that you do want to delete the worksheet. Worksheets can also be moved to other workbooks or a different position in the current workbook by using the Move or Copy option.

Creating, Saving, and Opening Files

As an illustration of manually entering, saving, and opening a file, we will use the Nowlin Plastics production example from Chapter 1. The objective is to compute the breakeven point for a product that has a fixed cost of $3000, a variable cost per unit of $2, and a selling price per unit of $5. We begin by creating a worksheet containing the problem data.

If you have just opened Excel, a blank workbook containing three worksheets will be displayed. The Nowlin data can now be entered manually by simply typing the fixed cost of $3000, the variable cost of $2, and the selling price of $5 into one of the worksheets. If Excel is currently running and no blank workbook is displayed, you can create a new blank workbook using the following steps:

Step 1. Click the **Office** button
Step 2. Click **New** in the list of options

Step 3. When the New Workbook dialog box appears:
Select **Blank and recent** under Templates
Double click **Blank Workbook**

A new workbook containing three worksheets labeled Sheet1, Sheet2, and Sheet3 will appear.

We will place the data for the Nowlin example in the top portion of Sheet1 of the new workbook. First, we enter the label "Nowlin Plastics" into cell A1. To identify each of the three data values we enter the label "Fixed Cost" into cell A3, the label "Variable Cost Per Unit" into cell A5, and the label "Selling Price Per Unit" into cell A7. Next, we enter the actual cost and price data into the corresponding cells in column B: the value of $3000 in cell B3; the value of $2 in cell B5; and the value of $5 into cell B7. Finally, we will change the name of the worksheet from "Sheet1" to "NowlinModel" using the procedure described previously. Figure A.5 shows a portion of the worksheet we have just developed.

Before we begin the development of the model portion of the worksheet, we recommend that you first save the current file; this will prevent you from having to reenter the data in case something happens that causes Excel to close. To save the workbook using the filename Nowlin we perform the following steps:

Step 1. Click the **Office** button
Step 2. Click **Save** in the list of options
Step 3. When the **Save As** dialog box appears:
In the **Save in** box select the location where you want to save the file
Type the file name Nowlin in the **File name** box
Click **Save**

FIGURE A.5   NOWLIN PLASTICS DATA

	A	B
1	**Nowlin Plastics**	
2		
3	**Fixed Cost**	$3,000
4		
5	**Variable Cost Per Unit**	$2
6		
7	**Selling Price Per Unit**	$5
8		
9		
10		
11		
12		
13		
14		
15		
16		
17		
18		

Excel's Save command is designed to save the file as an Excel workbook. As you work with and build models in Excel, you should follow the practice of periodically saving the file so you will not lose any work. Simply follow the procedure described above using the Save command.

*Keyboard shortcut: To save the file, press **CTRL S**.*

Sometimes you may want to create a copy of an existing file. For instance, suppose you change one or more of the data values and would like to save the modified file using the filename "NowlinMod." The following steps show how to save the modified workbook using filename NowlinMod.

Step 1. Click the **Office** button
Step 2. Position the mouse pointer over **Save As**
Step 3. Click **Excel Workbook** from the list of options
Step 4. When the **Save As** dialog box appears:
  In the **Save in** box select the location where you want to save the file
  Type the filename NowlinMod in the **File name** box
  Click **Save**

Once the NowlinMod workbook has been saved, you can continue to work with the file to perform whatever type of analysis is appropriate. When you are finished working with the file, simply click the close window button located at the top right-hand corner of the Ribbon.

You can easily access a saved file at another point in time. For example, the following steps show how to open the previously saved Nowlin workbook.

Step 1. Click the **Office** button
Step 2. Click **Open** in the list of options
Step 3. When the **Open** dialog box appears:
  In the **Look in** box select the location where you previously saved the file
  Type the filename Nowlin in the **File name** box
  Click **Open**

The procedures we showed for saving or opening a workbook begin by clicking on the Office Button to access the Save and Open commands. Once you have used Excel for a while you will probably find it more convenient to add these commands to the Quick Access Toolbar.

Cells, References, and Formulas in Excel

Assume that the Nowlin workbook is open again and that we would like to develop a model that can be used to compute the profit or loss associated with a given production volume. We will use the bottom portion of the worksheet shown in Figure A.5 to develop the model. The model will contain formulas that *refer to the location of the data cells* in the upper section of the worksheet. By putting the location of the data cells in the formula, we will build a model that can be easily updated with new data. This will be discussed in more detail later in this appendix in the section Principles for Building Good Spreadsheet Models.

We enter the label "Models" into cell A10 to provide a visual reminder that the bottom portion of this worksheet will contain the model. Next, we enter the labels "Production Volume" into cell A12, "Total Cost" into cell A14, "Total Revenue" into cell A16, and "Total

FIGURE A.6   NOWLIN PLASTICS DATA AND MODEL

	A	B
1	**Nowlin Plastics**	
2		
3	**Fixed Cost**	3000
4		
5	**Variable Cost Per Unit**	2
6		
7	**Selling Price Per Unit**	5
8		
9		
10	**Models**	
11		
12	**Production Volume**	
13		
14	**Total Cost**	=B3+B5*B12
15		
16	**Total Revenue**	=B7*B12
17		
18	**Total Profit (Loss)**	=B16-B14

Profit (Loss)" into cell A18. Cell B12 is used to contain a value for the production volume. We will now enter formulas into cells B14, B16, and B18 that use the production volume in cell B12 to compute the values for total cost, total revenue, and total profit or loss.

Total cost is the sum of the fixed cost (cell B3) and the total variable cost. The total variable cost is the product of the variable cost per unit (cell B5) and production volume (cell B12). Thus, the formula for total variable cost is B5*B12 and to compute the value of total cost, we enter the formula =B3+B5*B12 into cell B14. Next, total revenue is the product of the selling price per unit (cell B7) and the number of units produced (cell B12), which we enter in cell B16 as the formula =B7*B12. Finally, the total profit or loss is the difference between the total revenue (cell B16) and the total cost (cell B14). Thus, in cell B18 we enter the formula =B16-B14. Figure A.6 shows a portion of the formula worksheet just described.

We can now compute the total profit or loss for a particular production volume by entering a value for the production volume into cell B12. Figure A.7 shows the results after entering a value of 800 into cell B12. We see that a production volume of 800 units results in a total cost of $4600, a total revenue of $4000, and a loss of $600.

Using Excel Functions

Excel provides a wealth of built-in formulas or functions for developing mathematical models. If we know which function is needed and how to use it, we can simply enter the function into the appropriate worksheet cell. However, if we are not sure which functions are available to accomplish a task or are not sure how to use a particular function, Excel can provide assistance.

FIGURE A.7   NOWLIN PLASTICS RESULTS

	A	B
1	**Nowlin Plastics**	
2		
3	**Fixed Cost**	$3,000
4		
5	**Variable Cost Per Unit**	$2
6		
7	**Selling Price Per Unit**	$5
8		
9		
10	**Models**	
11		
12	**Production Volume**	800
13		
14	**Total Cost**	$4,600
15		
16	**Total Revenue**	$4,000
17		
18	**Total Profit (Loss)**	−$600

Finding the Right Excel Function

To identify the functions available in Excel, click the Formulas tab on the Ribbon and then click the Insert Function button in the Function Library group. Alternatively, click the Insert Function button f_x on the formula bar. Either approach provides the Insert Function dialog box shown in Figure A.8.

The Search for a function box at the top of the Insert Function dialog box enables us to type a brief description for what we want to do. After doing so and clicking Go, Excel will search for and display, in the Select a function box, the functions that may accomplish our task. In many situations, however, we may want to browse through an entire category of functions to see what is available. For this task, the *Or select a category* box is helpful.

It contains a drop-down list of several categories of functions provided by Excel. Figure A.8 shows that we selected the Math & Trig category. As a result, Excel's Math & Trig functions appear in alphabetical order in the Select a function box. We see the ABS function listed first, followed by the ACOS function, and so on.

Colon Notation

Although many functions, such as the ABS function, have a single argument, some Excel functions depend on arrays. Colon notation provides an efficient way to convey arrays and matrices of cells to functions. The colon notation may be described as follows: B3:B5 means cell B1 "through" cell B5, namely the array of values stored in the locations (B1,B2,B3,B4,B5). Consider for example the following function =SUM(B1:B5). The sum function adds up the elements contained in the function's argument. Hence, =SUM(B1:B5) evaluates the following formula:

$$=B1+B2+B3+B4+B5.$$

FIGURE A.8   INSERT FUNCTION DIALOG BOX

Inserting a Function into a Worksheet Cell

Through the use of an example, we will now show how to use the Insert Function and Function Arguments dialog boxes to select a function, develop its arguments, and insert the function into a worksheet cell. We also illustrate the use of a very useful function, the SUMPRODUCT function, and how to use colon notation in the argument of a function.

The SUMPRODUCT function, as shown in Figure A.9, is used in many of the Solver examples in the textbook. Note that SUMPRODUCT is now highlighted, and that immediately below the Select a function box we see SUMPRODUCT(array1,array2,array3, . . .), which indicates that the SUMPRODUCT function contains the array arguments array1, array2, array3, ... In addition, we see that the description of the SUMPRODUCT function is "Returns the sum of the products of corresponding ranges or arrays." For example, the function =SUMPRODUCT(A1:A3, B1:B3) evaluates the formula A1*B1 + A2*B2 + A3*B3. As shown in the following example, this function can be very useful in calculations of cost, profit, and other such functions involving multiple arrays of numbers.

Figure A.10 displays an Excel worksheet for the Foster Generators Problem that appears in Chapter 10. This problem involves the transportation of a product from three plants (Cleveland, Bedford, and York) to four distribution centers (Boston, Chicago, St. Louis, and Lexington). The costs for each unit shipped from each plant to each distribution center are shown in cells B5:E7, and the values in cells B17:E19 are the number of units shipped from

FIGURE A.9   DESCRIPTION OF THE SUMPRODUCT FUNCTION IN THE INSERT
FUNCTION DIALOG BOX

each plant to each distribution center. Cell B13 will contain the total transportation cost corresponding to the transportation cost values in cells B5:E7 and the values of the number of
units shipped in cells B17:E19.

The following steps show how to use the SUMPRODUCT function to compute the total
transportation cost for Foster Generators.

Step 1. Select **cell C13**
Step 2. Click f_x on the formula bar
Step 3. When the **Insert Function** dialog box appears:
  Select **Math&Trig** in the **Or select a category** box
  Select **SUMPRODUCT** in the **Select a function** box (as shown in Figure A.9)
  Click **OK**
Step 4. When the **Function Arguments** box appears (see Figure A.11):
  Enter B5:E7 in the **Array1** box
  Enter B17:E19 in the **Array2** box
  Click **OK**

The worksheet then appears as shown in Figure A.12. The value of the total transportation
cost in cell C13 is 39500, or $39,500.

FIGURE A.10   EXCEL WORKSHEET USED TO CALCULATE TOTAL SHIPPING COSTS
FOR THE FOSTER GENERATORS TRANSPORTATION PROBLEM

Foster Generators

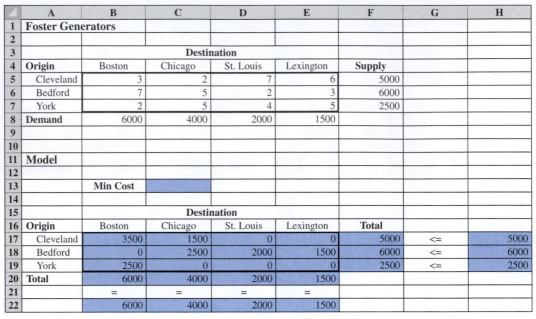

	A	B	C	D	E	F	G	H
1	**Foster Generators**							
2								
3				**Destination**				
4	**Origin**	Boston	Chicago	St. Louis	Lexington	**Supply**		
5	Cleveland	3	2	7	6	5000		
6	Bedford	7	5	2	3	6000		
7	York	2	5	4	5	2500		
8	**Demand**	6000	4000	2000	1500			
9								
10								
11	**Model**							
12								
13		**Min Cost**						
14								
15				**Destination**				
16	**Origin**	Boston	Chicago	St. Louis	Lexington	**Total**		
17	Cleveland	3500	1500	0	0	5000	<=	5000
18	Bedford	0	2500	2000	1500	6000	<=	6000
19	York	2500	0	0	0	2500	<=	2500
20	**Total**	6000	4000	2000	1500			
21		=	=	=	=			
22		6000	4000	2000	1500			

FIGURE A.11   COMPLETED FUNCTION ARGUMENTS DIALOG BOX FOR THE
SUMPRODUCT FUNCTION

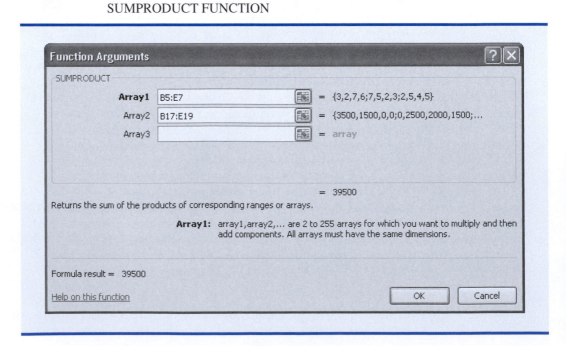

FIGURE A.12   EXCEL WORKSHEET SHOWING THE USE OF EXCEL'S SUMPRODUCT FUNCTION TO CALCULATE TOTAL SHIPPING COSTS

	A	B	C	D	E	F	G	H
1	**Foster Generators**							
2								
3				**Destination**				
4	**Origin**	Boston	Chicago	St. Louis	Lexington	**Supply**		
5	Cleveland	3	2	7	6	5000		
6	Bedford	7	5	2	3	6000		
7	York	2	5	4	5	2500		
8	**Demand**	6000	4000	2000	1500			
9								
10								
11	**Model**							
12								
13		**Min Cost**	39500					
14								
15				**Destination**				
16	**Origin**	Boston	Chicago	St. Louis	Lexington	**Total**		
17	Cleveland	3500	1500	0	0	5000	<=	5000
18	Bedford	0	2500	2000	1500	6000	<=	6000
19	York	2500	0	0	0	2500	<=	2500
20	**Total**	6000	4000	2000	1500			
21		=	=	=	=			
22		6000	4000	2000	1500			

We illustrated the use of Excel's capability to provide assistance in using the SUMPRODUCT function. The procedure is similar for all Excel functions. This capability is especially helpful if you do not know which function to use or forget the proper name and/or syntax for a function.

Additional Excel Functions for Modeling

In this section we introduce some additional Excel functions that have proven useful in modeling decision problems.

IF and COUNTIF Functions

Let us consider the case of Gambrell Manufacturing. Gambrell Manufacturing produces car stereos. Stereos are composed of a variety of components that the company must carry in inventory to keep production running smoothly. However, because inventory can be a costly investment, Gambrell generally likes to keep the amount of inventory of the components it uses in manufacturing to a minimum. To help monitor and control its inventory of components, Gambrell uses an inventory policy known as an "order up to" policy. This type of inventory policy and others are discussed in detail in Chapter 14.

The "order up to policy" is as follows. Whenever the inventory on hand drops below a certain level, enough units are ordered to return the inventory to that predetermined level. If the current number of units in inventory, denoted by H, drops below M units, we order enough to get the inventory level back up to M units. M is called the Order Up to Point. Stated mathematically, if Q is the amount we order, then

$$Q = M - H$$

An inventory model for Gambrell Manufacturing appears in Figure A.13. In this worksheet, labeled "OrderQuantity" in the upper half of the worksheet, the component ID number, inventory on hand (H), order up to point (M), and cost per unit are given for each of four components. Also given in this sheet is the fixed cost per order. The fixed cost is interpreted as follows: Each time a component is ordered, it costs Gambrell $120 to process the order. The fixed cost of $120 is incurred regardless of how many units are ordered.

The model portion of the worksheet calculates the order quantity for each component. For example, for component 570, $M = 100$ and $H = 5$, so $Q = M - H = 100 - 5 = 95$. For component 741, $M = 70$ and $H = 70$ and no units are ordered because the on-hand inventory of 70 units is equal to the order point of 70. The calculations are similar for the other two components.

Depending on the number of units ordered, Gambrell receives a discount on the cost per unit. If 50 or more units are ordered, there is a quantity discount of 10% on every unit purchased. For example, for component 741, the cost per unit is $4.50 and 95 units are ordered. Because 95 exceeds the 50-unit requirement, there is a 10% discount and the cost per unit is reduced to $4.50 - 0.1($4.50) = $4.50 - $0.45 = $4.05. Not including the fixed cost, the cost of goods purchased is then $4.05(95) = $384.75.

The Excel functions used to perform these calculations are shown in Figure A.14. The IF function is used to calculate the purchase cost of goods for each component in row 15. The general form of the IF function is

$$=\text{IF}(condition, result\ if\ condition\ is\ true, result\ if\ condition\ is\ false)$$

FIGURE A.13   THE GAMBRELL MANUFACTURING COMPONENT ORDERING MODEL

WEB file

Gambrell

	A	B	C	D	E	F
4	Component ID	570	578	741	755	
5	Inventory On-Hand	5	30	70	17	
6	Up to Order Point	100	55	70	45	
7	Cost per unit	$4.50	$12.50	$3.26	$4.15	
8						
9	Fixed Cost per Order	$120				
10						
11	**Model**					
12						
13	Component ID	570	578	741	755	
14	Order Quantity	95	25	0	28	
15	Cost of Goods	$384.75	$312.50	$0.00	$116.20	
16						
17	Total Number of Orders	3				
18						
19	Total Fixed costs	$360.00				
20	Total Cost of Goods	$813.45				
21	Total Cost	$1,173.45				
22						

FIGURE A.14   FORMULAS AND FUNCTIONS FOR GAMBRELL MANUFACTURING

	A	B	C	D	E
1					
2	**Gambrell Manufacturing**				
3					
4	Component ID	570	578	741	755
5	Inventory On-Hand	5	30	70	17
6	Up to Order Point	100	55	70	45
7	Cost per unit	4.5	12.5	3.26	4.15
8					
9	Fixed Cost per Order	120			
10					
11	**Model**				
12					
13	Component ID	=B4	=C4	=D4	=E4
14	Order Quantity	=B6-B5	=C6-C5	=D6-D5	=E6-E5
15	Cost of Goods	=IF(B14>=50,0.9*B7,B7)*B14	=IF(C14>=50, 0.9*C7,C7)*C14	=IF(D14>=50, 0.9*D7,D7)*D14	=IF(E14>=50, 0.9*E7,E7)*E14
16					
17	Total Number of Orders	=COUNTIF(B14:E14,">0")			
18					
19	Total Fixed Costs	=B17*B9			
20	Total Cost of Goods	=SUM(B15:E15)			
21	Total Cost	=SUM(B19:B20)			
22					

For example, in cell B15 we have =IF(B14>=50,0.9*B7,B7)*B14. This statement says if the order quantity (cell B14) is greater than or equal to 50, then the cost per unit is 0.9*B7 (there is a 10% discount); otherwise, there is no discount and the cost per unit is the amount given in cell B7. The purchase cost of goods for the other components are computed in a like manner.

The total cost in cell B21 is the sum of the purchase cost of goods ordered in row 15 and the fixed ordering costs. Because we place three orders (one each for components 570, 578 and 755), the fixed cost of the orders is 3*120 = $360.

The COUNTIF function in cell B17 is used to count how many times we order. In particular, it counts the number of components having a positive order quantity. The general form of the COUNTIF function is

$$=COUNTIF(range, condition)$$

The *range* is the range to search for the *condition*. The condition is the test to be counted when satisfied. *Note that quotes are required for the condition with the COUNTIF function.* In the Gambrell model in Figure A.14, cell B17 counts the number of cells that are greater than zero in the range of cells B14:E14. In the model, since only cells B14, C14 and E14 are greater than zero, the COUNTIF function in cell B17 returns 3.

As we have seen, IF and COUNTIF are powerful functions that allow us to make calculations based on a condition holding (or not). There are other such conditional functions available in Excel. In the problems at the end of this appendix, we ask you to investigate one such function, the SUMIF function. Another conditional function that is extremely useful in modeling is the VLOOKUP function. We discuss the VLOOKUP function with an example in the next section.

VLOOKUP Function

Next, consider the workbook named *OM455* shown in Figure A.15. The worksheet named Grades is shown. This worksheet calculates the course grades for the course OM 455. There are 11 students in the course. Each student has a midterm exam score and a final exam score, and these are averaged in column D to get the course average. The scale given in the upper portion of the worksheet is used to determine the course grade for each student. Consider, for example, the performance of student Choi in row 16. This student earned an 82 on the midterm, an 80 on the final, and a course average of 81. From the grading scale, this equates to a course grade of B.

The course average is simply the average of the midterm and final scores, but how do we get Excel to look in the grading scale table and automatically assign the correct course letter grade to each student? The VLOOKUP function allows us to do just that. The formulas and functions used in *OM455* are shown in Figure A.16.

The VLOOKUP function allows the user to pull a subset of data from a larger table of data based on some criterion. The general form of the VLOOKUP function is

$$=\text{VLOOKUP(arg1, arg2, arg3, arg4)}$$

where arg1 is the value to search for in the first column of the table, arg2 is the table location, arg3 is the column location in the table to be returned, and arg4 is TRUE if looking for the first partial match of arg1 and FALSE for looking for an exact match of arg1. We will explain the difference between a partial and exact match in a moment. VLOOKUP assumes that the first column of the table is sorted in ascending order.

FIGURE A.15   OM455 GRADE SPREADSHEET

WEB file

OM455

	A	B	C	D	E	F
1	OM455					
2	Section 001					
3	Course Grading Scale Based on Course Average:					
4		Lower	Upper	Course		
5		Limit	Limit	Grade		
6		0	59	F		
7		60	69	D		
8		70	79	C		
9		80	89	B		
10		90	100	A		
11						
12		Midterm	Final	Course	Course	
13	Lastname	Score	Score	Average	Grade	
14	Benson	70	56	63.0	D	
15	Chin	95	91	93.0	A	
16	Choi	82	80	81.0	B	
17	Cruz	45	78	61.5	D	
18	Doe	68	45	56.5	F	
19	Honda	91	98	94.5	A	
20	Hume	87	74	80.5	B	
21	Jones	60	80	70.0	C	
22	Miranda	80	93	86.5	B	
23	Murigami	97	98	97.5	A	
24	Ruebush	90	91	90.5	A	
25						

FIGURE A.16   THE FORMULAS AND FUNCTIONS USED IN OM 455

	A	B	C	D	E
1	OM 455				
2	Section 001				
3	Course Grading Scale Based on Course Average:				
4		Lower	Upper	Course	
5		Limit	Limit	Grade	
6		0	59	F	
7		60	69	D	
8		70	79	C	
9		80	89	B	
10		90	100	A	
11					
12		Midterm	Final	Course	Course
13	Lastname	Score	Score	Average	Grade
14	Benson	70	56	=AVERAGE(B14:C14)	=VLOOKUP(D14,B6:D10,3,TRUE)
15	Chin	95	91	=AVERAGE(B15:C15)	=VLOOKUP(D15,B6:D10,3,TRUE)
16	Choi	82	80	=AVERAGE(B16:C16)	=VLOOKUP(D16,B6:D10,3,TRUE)
17	Cruz	45	78	=AVERAGE(B17:C17)	=VLOOKUP(D17,B6:D10,3,TRUE)
18	Doe	68	45	=AVERAGE(B18:C18)	=VLOOKUP(D18,B6:D10,3,TRUE)
19	Honda	91	98	=AVERAGE(B19:C19)	=VLOOKUP(D19,B6:D10,3,TRUE)
20	Hume	87	74	=AVERAGE(B20:C20)	=VLOOKUP(D20,B6:D10,3,TRUE)
21	Jones	60	80	=AVERAGE(B21:C21)	=VLOOKUP(D21,B6:D10,3,TRUE)
22	Miranda	80	93	=AVERAGE(B22:C22)	=VLOOKUP(D22,B6:D10,3,TRUE)
23	Murigami	97	98	=AVERAGE(B23:C23)	=VLOOKUP(D23,B6:D10,3,TRUE)
24	Ruebush	90	91	=AVERAGE(B24:C24)	=VLOOKUP(D24,B6:D10,3,TRUE)
25					

The VLOOKUP function for student Choi in cell E16 is as follows:

$$=VLOOKUP(D16,B6:D10,3,TRUE)$$

This function uses the course average from cell D16 and searches the first column of the table defined by B6:D10. In the first column of the table (column B), Excel searches from the top until it finds a number strictly greater than the value of D16 (81). It then backs up one row (to row 9). That is, it finds the last value in the first column less than or equal to 81. Because there is a 3 in the third argument of the VLOOKUP function, it takes the element in row 9 in the third column of the table, which is the letter "B." In summary, the VLOOKUP takes the first argument and searches the first column of the table for the last row that is strictly less than the first argument. It then selects from that row the element in the column number of the third argument.

Note: If the last element of the VLOOKUP function is "False," the only change is that Excel searches for an exact match of the first argument in the first column of the data. VLOOKUP is very useful when you seek subsets of a table based on a condition.

Principles for Building Good Spreadsheet Models

We have covered some of the fundamentals of building spreadsheet models. There are some generally accepted guiding principles for how to build a spreadsheet so that it is more easily used by others and so that the risk of error is mitigated. In this section we discuss some of those principles.

Separate the Data from the Model

One of the first principles of good modeling is to separate the data from the model. This enables the user to update the model parameters without fear of mistakenly typing over a formula or function. For this reason, it is good practice to have a data section at the top of the spreadsheet. A separate model section should contain all calculations and in general should not be updated by a user. For a what-if model or an optimization model, there might also be a separate section for decision cells (values that are not data or calculations, but are the outputs we seek from the model).

The Nowlin model in Figure A.6 is a good example. The data section is in the upper part of the spreadsheet followed by the model section that contains the calculations. The Gambrell model in Figure A.13 does not totally employ the principle of data/model separation. A better model would have the 50-unit hurdle and the 90% cost (10% discount) as data in the upper section. Then the formulas in row 15 would simply refer to the cells in the upper section. This would allow the user to easily change the discount, for example, without having to change all four formulas in row 15.

Document the Model

A good spreadsheet model is well documented. Clear labels and proper formatting and alignment make the spreadsheet easier to navigate and understand. For example, if the values in a worksheet are cost, currency formatting should be used. No cells should be unlabeled. A new user should be able to easily understand the model and its calculations. Figure A.17

FIGURE A.17   A BETTER-DOCUMENTED FOSTER GENERATORS MODEL

WEB file

Foster Rev

	A	B	C	D	E	F	G	H
1	**Foster Generators**							
2								
3	Origin to Destination—Cost per unit to ship							
4			**Destination**					
5	**Origin**	Boston	Chicago	St. Louis	Lexington	**Units Available**		
6	Cleveland	$3.00	$2.00	$7.00	$6.00	5000		
7	Bedford	$7.00	$5.00	$2.00	$3.00	6000		
8	York	$2.00	$5.00	$4.00	$5.00	2500		
9	**Units Demanded**	6000	4000	2000	1500			
10								
11								
12	**Model**							
13								
14		**Min Cost**	$39,500.00					
15								
16	Origin to Destination—Units Shipped							
17			**Destination**					
18	**Origin**	Boston	Chicago	St. Louis	Lexington	**Units Shipped**		
19	Cleveland	3500	1500	0	0	5000	<=	5000
20	Bedford	0	2500	2000	1500	6000	<=	6000
21	York	2500	0	0	0	2500	<=	2500
22	**Units Received**	6000	4000	2000	1500			
23		=	=	=	=			
24		6000	4000	2000	1500			

shows a better-documented version of the Foster Generators model previously discussed (Figure A.10). The tables are more explicitly labeled, and shading focuses the user on the objective and the decision cells (amount to ship). The per-unit shipping cost data and total (Min) cost have been properly formatted as currency.

Use Simple Formulas and Cell Names

Clear formulas can eliminate unnecessary calculations, reduce errors, and make it easier to maintain your spreadsheet. Long and complex calculations should be divided into several cells. This makes the formula easier to understand and easier to edit. Avoid using numbers in a formula. Instead, put the number in a cell in the data section of your worksheet and refer to the cell location of the data in the formula. Building the formula in this manner avoids having to edit the formula for a simple data change.

Using cell names can make a formula much easier to understand. To assign a name to a cell, use the following steps:

Step 1. Select the cell or range of cells you would like to name
Step 2. Select the **Formulas** tab from the Ribbon
Step 3. Choose **Define Name** from the Define Names section
Step 4. The **New Name** dialog box will appear, as shown in Figure A.18
Enter the name you would like to use in the top portion of the dialog box and Click **OK**

Following this procedure and naming all cells in the *Nowlin Plastics* spreadsheet model leads to the model shown in Figure A.19. Compare this to Figure A.6 to easily understand the formulas in the model.

A name is also easily applied to range as follows. First, highlight the range of interest. Then click on the Name Box in the Formula Bar (refer back to Figure A.3) and type in the desired range name.

FIGURE A.18   THE DEFINE NAME DIALOG BOX

WEB file

Nowlin Plastics

FIGURE A.19   THE NOWLIN PLASTIC MODEL FORMULAS WITH NAMED CELLS

	A	B
1	Nowlin Plastics	
2		
3	Fixed Cost	3000
4		
5	Variable Cost Per Unit	2
6		
7	Selling Price Per Unit	5
8		
9		
10	Models	
11		
12	Production Volume	800
13		
14	Total Cost	=Fixed_Cost+Variable_Cost*Production_Volume
15		
16	Total Revenue	=Selling_Price*Production_Volume
17		
18	Total Profit (Loss)	=Total_Revenue-Total_Cost

Use of Relative and Absolute Cell References

There are a number of ways to copy a formula from one cell to another in an Excel worksheet. One way to copy the a formula from one cell to another is presented here:

Step 1. Select the cell you would like to copy
Step 2. Right-click on the mouse
Step 3. Click **Copy**
Step 4. Select the cell where you would like to put the copy
Step 5. Right click on the mouse
Step 6. Click **Paste**

When copying in Excel, one can use a relative or an absolute address. When copied, a relative address adjusts with the move of the copy, whereas an absolute address stays in its original form. Relative addresses are of the form C7. Absolute addresses have $ in front of the column and row, for example, $C$7. How you use relative and absolute addresses can have an impact on the amount of effort it takes to build a model and the opportunity for error in constructing the model.

Let us reconsider the OM455 grading spreadsheet previously discussed in this appendix and shown in Figure A.16. Recall that we used the VLOOKUP function to retrieve the appropriate letter grade for each student. The following formula is in cell E14:

$$=VLOOKUP(D14,B6:D10,3,TRUE)$$

Note that this formula contains only relative addresses. If we copy this to cell E15, we get the following result:

$$=VLOOKUP(D15,B7:D11,3,TRUE)$$

Although the first argument has correctly changed to D15 (we want to calculate the letter grade for the student in row 15), the table in the function has also shifted to B7:D11. What we desired was for this table location to remain the same. A better approach would have been to use the following formula in cell E14:

$$=VLOOKUP(D14,\$B\$6:\$D\$10,3,TRUE)$$

Copying this formula to cell E15 results in the following formula:

$$=VLOOKUP(D15,\$B\$6:\$D\$10,3,TRUE)$$

This correctly changes the first argument to D15 and keeps the data table intact. Using absolute referencing is extremely useful if you have a function that has a reference that should not change when applied to another cell and you are copying the formula to other locations. In the case of the OM455 workbook, instead of typing the VLOOKUP for each student, we can use absolute referencing on the table and then copy from row 14 to rows 15 through 24.

In this section we have discussed guidelines for good spreadsheet model building. In the next section we discuss EXCEL tools available for checking and debugging spreadsheet models.

Auditing Excel Models

EXCEL contains a variety of tools to assist you in the development and debugging of spreadsheet models. These tools are found in the Formula Auditing group of the Formulas Tab as shown in Figure A.20. Let us review each of the tools available in this group.

Trace Precedents and Dependents

The Trace Precedents button [Trace Precedents] creates arrows pointing to the selected cell from cells that are part of the formula in that cell. The Trace Dependents button [Trace Dependents], on the other hand, shows arrows pointing from the selected cell, to cells that depend on the selected cells. Both of the tools are excellent for quickly ascertaining how parts of a model are linked.

An example of Trace Precedents is shown in Figure A.21. Here we have opened the *Foster Rev* worksheet, selected cell C14, and clicked the Trace Precedents button in the Formula Auditing Group. Recall that the cost in cell C14 is calculated as the SUMPRODUCT of the per-unit shipping cost and units shipped. In Figure A.21, to show this relationship, arrows are drawn to these respective areas of the spreadsheet to cell C14. These arrows may be removed by clicking on the Remove Arrows button in the Auditing Tools Group.

FIGURE A.20   THE FORMULA AUDITING GROUP OF THE FORMULAS TAB

FIGURE A.21   TRACE PRECEDENTS FOR CELL C14 (COST) IN THE FOSTER
GENERATORS REV MODEL

	C14	▼	●	f_x	=SUMPRODUCT(B6:E8,B19:E21)			
	A	B	C	D	E	F	G	H
1	**Foster Generators**							
2								
3	Origin to Destination—Cost per unit to ship							
4			**Destination**					
5	**Origin**	Boston	Chicago	St. Louis	Lexington	**Units Available**		
6	Cleveland	$3.00	$2.00	$7.00	$6.00	5000		
7	Bedford	$7.00	$5.00	$2.00	$3.00	6000		
8	York	$2.00	$5.00	$4.00	$5.00	2500		
9	**Units Demanded**	6000	4000	2000	1500			
10								
11								
12	**Model**							
13								
14		**Min Cost**	$39,500.00					
15								
16	Origin to Destination—Units Shipped							
17			**Destination**					
18	**Origin**	Boston	Chicago	St. Louis	Lexington	**Units Shipped**		
19	Cleveland	3500	1500	0	0	5000	<=	5000
20	Bedford	0	2500	2000	1500	6000	<=	6000
21	York	2500	0	0	0	2500	<=	2500
22	**Units Received**	6000	4000	2000	1500			
23		=	=	=	=			
24		6000	4000	2000	1500			

WEB file

Foster Rev

An example of Trace Dependents is shown in Figure A.22. We have selected cell E20, the units shipped from Bedford to Lexington, and clicked on the Trace Dependents button in the Formula Auditing Group. As shown in Figure A.22, units shipped from Bedford to Lexington impacts the cost function in cell C14, the total units shipped from Bedford given in cell F20, and the total units shipped to Lexington in cell E22. These arrows may be removed by clicking on the Remove Arrows button in the Auditing Tools Group.

Trace Precedents and Trace Dependents can highlight errors in copying and formula construction by showing that incorrect sections of the worksheet are referenced.

Show Formulas

The Show Formulas button, 🔲 Show Formulas , does exactly that. To see the formulas in a worksheet, simply click on any cell in the worksheet and then click on Show Formulas. You will see the formulas that exist in that worksheet. To go back to hiding the formulas, click again on the Show Formulas button. Figure A.6 gives an example of the show formulas view. This allows you to inspect each formula in detail in its cell location.

Evaluate Formulas

The Evaluate Formula button, 🔘 Evaluate Formula , allows you to investigate the calculations of particular cell in great detail. To invoke this tool, we simply select a cell containing

FIGURE A.22   TRACE DEPENDENTS FOR CELL C14 (COST) IN THE FOSTER GENERATORS REV MODEL

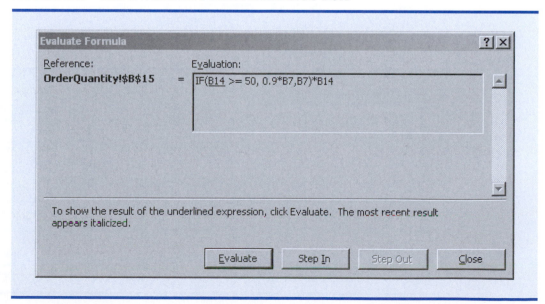

	A	B	C	D	E	F	G	H
12	Model							
13								
14		**Min Cost**	$39,500.00					
15								
16	Origin to Destination—Units Shipped							
17			**Destination**					
18	**Origin**	Boston	Chicago	St. Louis	Lexington	**Units Shipped**		
19	Cleveland	3500	1500	0	0	5000	<=	5000
20	Bedford	0	2500	2000	1500	6000	<=	6000
21	York	2500	0	0	0	2500	<=	2500
22	**Units Received**	6000	4000	2000	1500			
23		=	=	=	=			
24		6000	4000	2000	1500			

Cell reference box: E20 — f_x — 1500

a formula and click on the Evaluate Formula button in the Formula Auditing Group. As an example, we select cell B15 of the Gambrell Manufacturing model (see Figures A.13 and A.14). Recall we are calculating cost of goods based upon whether or not there is a quantity discount. Clicking on the Evaluate button allows you to evaluate this formula explicitly. The Evaluate Formula dialog box appears in Figure A.23. Figure A.24 shows the result of one click of the Evaluate button. The B14 has changed to its value of 95. Further clicks would evaluate in order, from left to right, the remaining components of the formula. We ask the reader to further explore this tool in an exercise at the end of this appendix.

The Evaluate Formula tool provides an excellent means of identifying the exact location of an error in a formula.

FIGURE A.23   THE EVALUATE FORMULA DIALOG BOX

Evaluate Formula   ? X

Reference: Evaluation:
OrderQuantity!$B$15   =   IF(B14 >= 50, 0.9*B7,B7)*B14

To show the result of the underlined expression, click Evaluate. The most recent result appears italicized.

Evaluate   Step In   Step Out   Close

FIGURE A.24   THE EVALUATE FORMULA AFTER ONE CLICK OF THE
EVALUATE BUTTON

Error Checking

The Error Checking Button, ⬧ Error Checking ▾ , provides an automatic means of checking for mathematical errors within formulas of a worksheet. Clicking on the Error Checking button causes Excel to check every formula in the sheet for calculation errors. If an error is found, the Error Checking dialog box appears. An example for a hypothetical division by zero error is shown in Figure A.25. From this box, the formula can be edited or the calculation steps can be observed (as in the previous section on Evaluate Formulas).

FIGURE A.25   THE ERROR CHECKING DIALOG BOX FOR A DIVISION
BY ZERO ERROR

FIGURE A.26   THE WATCH WINDOW FOR THE GAMBRELL MANUFACTURING
MODEL

Watch Window					▼ ✕
⤷ Add Watch... ⤷ Delete Watch					
Book	Sheet	Name	Cell	Value	Formula
Gambr...	Order...		B15	$384.75	=IF(B14 >= 50, 0.9*B7,B7)*B14

Watch Window

The Watch Window, located in the Formula Auditing Group, allows the user to observe the values of cells included in the Watch Window box list. This is useful for large models when not all the model is observable on the screen or when multiple worksheets are used. The user can monitor how the listed cells change with a change in the model without searching through the worksheet or changing from one worksheet to another.

A Watch Window for the Gambrell Manufacturing model is shown in Figure A.26. The following steps were used from the OrderQuantity worksheet to add cell B14 of the OrderQuantity worksheet to the watch list:

Step 1. Select the **Formulas** tab
Step 2. Select **Watch Window** from the Formula Auditing Group
The Watch Window will appear
Step 3. Select **Add Watch**
Step 4. Click on the cell you would like to add to the watch list (in this case B14)

As shown in Figure A.26, the list gives the workbook name, worksheet name, cell name (if used), cell location, cell value, and cell formula. To delete a cell from the watch list, select the entry from the list and then click on the Delete Watch button in the upper part of the Watch Window.

The Watch Window, as shown in Figure A.26, allows us to monitor the value of B15 as we make changes elsewhere in the worksheet. Furthermore, if we had other worksheets in this workbook, we could monitor changes to B15 of the OrderQuantity worksheet even from these other work sheets. The Watch Window is observable regardless of where we are in any worksheet of a workbook.

Summary

In this appendix we have discussed how to build effective spreadsheet models using Excel. We provided an overview on workbooks and worksheets and details on useful Excel functions. We also discussed a set of principles for good modeling and tools for auditing spreadsheet models.

Problems

Nowlin Plastics

1. Open the file *Nowlin Plastics*. Recall that we have modeled total profit for the product CD-50 in this spreadsheet. Suppose we have a second product called a CD-100, with the following characteristics:

    Fixed Cost = $2500

    Variable Cost per Unit = $1.67

    Selling Price per Unit = $4.40

    Extend the model so that the profit is calculated for each product and then totaled to give an overall profit generated for the two products. Use a CD-100 production volume of 1200. Save this file as *Nowlin Plastics2.xls*. *Hint:* Place the data for CD-100 in column C and copy the formulas in rows 14, 16, and 18 to column C.

2. Assume that in an empty Excel worksheet in cell A1 you enter the formula =B1*$F$3. You now copy this formula into cell E6. What is the modified formula that appears in E6?

Foster Rev

3. Open the file *Foster Rev*. Select cells B6:E8 and name these cells Shipping_Cost. Select cells B19:E21 and name these cells Units_Shipped. Use these names in the sumproduct function in cell C14 to compute cost and verify that you obtain the same cost ($39,500).

4. Open the file *Nowlin Plastics*. Recall that we have modeled total profit for the product CD-50 in this spreadsheet. Modify the spreadsheet to take into account production capacity and forecasted demand. If forecasted demand is less than or equal to capacity, Nowlin will produce only the forecasted demand; otherwise, they will produce the full capacity. For this example, use forecasted demand of 1200 and capacity of 1500. *Hint:* Enter demand and capacity into the data section of the model. Then use an IF statement to calculate production volume.

Cox Electric

5. Cox Electric makes electronic components and has estimated the following for a new design of one of its products:

    Fixed Cost = $10,000

    Revenue per unit = $0.65

    Material cost per unit = $0.15

    Labor cost per unit = $0.10

    These data are given in the spreadsheet *Cox Electric*. Also in the spreadsheet in row 14 is a profit model that gives the profit (or loss) for a specified volume (cell C14).
    a. Use the Show Formula button in the Formula Auditing Group of the Formulas tab to see the formulas and cell references used in row 14.
    b. Use the Trace Precedents tool to see how the formulas are dependent on the elements of the data section.
    c. Use trial and error, by trying various values of volume in cell C14, to arrive at a breakeven volume.

6. Return to the Cox Electric spreadsheet. Build a table of profits based on different volume levels by doing the following: In cell C15, enter a volume of 20,000. Look at each formula in row 14 and decide which references should be absolute or relative for purposes of copying the formulas to row 15. Make the necessary changes to row 14 (change any references that should be absolute by putting in $). Copy cells D14:I14 to row 15. Continue this with new rows until a positive profit is found. Save your file as *Cox_Breakeven*.

OM455

7. Open the workbook *OM455*. Save the file under a new name, *OM455COUNTIF.xls*. Suppose we wish to automatically count the number of each letter grade.
   a. Begin by putting the letters A, B, C, D, and F in cells C29:C33. Use the COUNTIF function in cells D29:D33 to count the number of each letter grade. *Hint*: Create the necessary COUNTIF function in cell D29. Use absolute referencing on the range ($E14:$E$24) and then copy the function to cells D30:D33 to count the number of each of the other letter grades.
   b. We are considering a different grading scale as follows:

Lower	Upper	Grade
0	69	F
70	76	D
77	84	C
85	92	B
93	100	A

For the current list of students, use the COUNTIF function to determine the number of A, B, C, D, and F letter grades earned under this new system.

OM455

8. Open the workbook *OM455*. Save the file under a new name, *OM4555Revised.xls*. Suppose we wish to use a more refined grading system, as shown below:

Lower	Upper	Grade
0	59	F
60	69	D
70	72	C−
73	76	C−
77	79	C+
80	82	B−
83	86	B
87	89	B+
90	92	A−
93	100	A

Update the file to use this more refined grading system. How many of each letter grade are awarded under the new system? *Hint:* Build a new grading table and use VLOOKUP and an absolute reference to the table. Then use COUNTIF to count the number of each letter grade.

Newton_data

9. Newton Manufacturing produces scientific calculators. The models are N350, N450, and the N900. Newton has planned its distribution of these products around eight customer zones: Brazil, China, France, Malaysia, U.S. Northeast, U.S. Southeast, U.S. Midwest, and U.S. West. Data for the current quarter (volume to be shipped in thousands of units) for each product and each customer zone are given in the file *Newton_data*.

   Newton would like to know the total number of units going to each customer zone and also the total units of each product shipped. There are several ways to get this information from the data set. One way is to use the SUMIF function.

   The SUMIF function extends the SUM function by allowing the user to add the values of cells meeting a logical condition. This general form of the function is

$$=\text{SUMIF}(\textit{test range, condition, range to be summed})$$

The *test range* is an area to search to test the *condition,* and the *range to be summed* is the position of the data to be summed. So, for example, using the *Newton_data* file, we would use the following function to get the total units sent to Malaysia:

$$=\text{SUMIF(A3:A26,A3,C3:C26)}$$

Here, A3 is Malaysia, A3:A26 is the range of customer zones, and C3:C26 are the volumes for each product for these customer zones. The SUMIF looks for matches of Malaysia in column A and, if a match is found, adds the volume to the total. Use the SUMIF function to get each total volume by zone and each total volume by product.

Williamson

10. Consider the transportation model given in the Excel file *Williamson*. It is a model that is very similar to the Foster Generators model. Williamson produces a single product and has plants in Atlanta, Lexington, Chicago, and Salt Lake City and warehouses in Portland, St. Paul, Las Vegas, Tuscon, and Cleveland. Each plant has a capacity and each warehouse has a demand. Williamson would like to find a low-cost shipping plan. Mr. Williamson has reviewed the results and notices right away that the total cost is way out of line. Use the Formula Auditing Tools under the Formulas tab in Excel to find any errors in this model. Correct the errors. *Hint:* There are two errors in this model. Be sure to check every formula.

Entries in the following table give the probability of x successes in n trials of a binomial experiment, where p is the probability of a success on one trial. For example, with $n = 6$ trials and $p = 0.40$, the probability of $x = 2$ successes is 0.3110.

n	x	p 0.05	0.10	0.15	0.20	0.25	0.30	0.35	0.40	0.45	0.50
1	0	0.9500	0.9000	0.8500	0.8000	0.7500	0.7000	0.6500	0.6000	0.5500	0.5000
	1	0.0500	0.1000	0.1500	0.2000	0.2500	0.3000	0.3500	0.4000	0.4500	0.5000
2	0	0.9025	0.8100	0.7225	0.6400	0.5625	0.4900	0.4225	0.3600	0.3025	0.2500
	1	0.0950	0.1800	0.2550	0.3200	0.3750	0.4200	0.4550	0.4800	0.4950	0.5000
	2	0.0025	0.0100	0.0225	0.0400	0.0625	0.0900	0.1225	0.1600	0.2025	0.2500
3	0	0.8574	0.7290	0.6141	0.5120	0.4219	0.3430	0.2746	0.2160	0.1664	0.1250
	1	0.1354	0.2430	0.3251	0.3840	0.4219	0.4410	0.4436	0.4320	0.4084	0.3750
	2	0.0071	0.0270	0.0574	0.0960	0.1406	0.1890	0.2389	0.2880	0.3341	0.3750
	3	0.0001	0.0010	0.0034	0.0080	0.0156	0.0270	0.0429	0.0640	0.0911	0.1250
4	0	0.8145	0.6561	0.5220	0.4096	0.3164	0.2401	0.1785	0.1296	0.0915	0.0625
	1	0.1715	0.2916	0.3685	0.4096	0.4219	0.4116	0.3845	0.3456	0.2995	0.2500
	2	0.0135	0.0486	0.0975	0.1536	0.2109	0.2646	0.3105	0.3456	0.3675	0.3750
	3	0.0005	0.0036	0.0115	0.0256	0.0469	0.0756	0.1115	0.1536	0.2005	0.2500
	4	0.0000	0.0001	0.0005	0.0016	0.0039	0.0081	0.0150	0.0256	0.0410	0.0625
5	0	0.7738	0.5905	0.4437	0.3277	0.2373	0.1681	0.1160	0.0778	0.0503	0.0312
	1	0.2036	0.3280	0.3915	0.4096	0.3955	0.3602	0.3124	0.2592	0.2059	0.1562
	2	0.0214	0.0729	0.1382	0.2048	0.2637	0.3087	0.3364	0.3456	0.3369	0.3125
	3	0.0011	0.0081	0.0244	0.0512	0.0879	0.1323	0.1811	0.2304	0.2757	0.3125
	4	0.0000	0.0004	0.0022	0.0064	0.0146	0.0284	0.0488	0.0768	0.1128	0.1562
	5	0.0000	0.0000	0.0001	0.0003	0.0010	0.0024	0.0053	0.0102	0.0185	0.0312
6	0	0.7351	0.5314	0.3771	0.2621	0.1780	0.1176	0.0754	0.0467	0.0277	0.0156
	1	0.2321	0.3543	0.3993	0.3932	0.3560	0.3025	0.2437	0.1866	0.1359	0.0938
	2	0.0305	0.0984	0.1762	0.2458	0.2966	0.3241	0.3280	0.3110	0.2780	0.2344
	3	0.0021	0.0146	0.0415	0.0819	0.1318	0.1852	0.2355	0.2765	0.3032	0.3125
	4	0.0001	0.0012	0.0055	0.0154	0.0330	0.0595	0.0951	0.1382	0.1861	0.2344
	5	0.0000	0.0001	0.0004	0.0015	0.0044	0.0102	0.0205	0.0369	0.0609	0.0938
	6	0.0000	0.0000	0.0000	0.0001	0.0002	0.0007	0.0018	0.0041	0.0083	0.0156
7	0	0.6983	0.4783	0.3206	0.2097	0.1335	0.0824	0.0490	0.0280	0.0152	0.0078
	1	0.2573	0.3720	0.3960	0.3670	0.3115	0.2471	0.1848	0.1306	0.0872	0.0547
	2	0.0406	0.1240	0.2097	0.2753	0.3115	0.3177	0.2985	0.2613	0.2140	0.1641
	3	0.0036	0.0230	0.0617	0.1147	0.1730	0.2269	0.2679	0.2903	0.2918	0.2734
	4	0.0002	0.0026	0.0109	0.0287	0.0577	0.0972	0.1442	0.1935	0.2388	0.2734
	5	0.0000	0.0002	0.0012	0.0043	0.0115	0.0250	0.0466	0.0774	0.1172	0.1641
	6	0.0000	0.0000	0.0001	0.0004	0.0013	0.0036	0.0084	0.0172	0.0320	0.0547
	7	0.0000	0.0000	0.0000	0.0000	0.0001	0.0002	0.0006	0.0016	0.0037	0.0078

Binomial Probabilities (*Continued*)

n	x	0.05	0.10	0.15	0.20	0.25	0.30	0.35	0.40	0.45	0.50
8	0	0.6634	0.4305	0.2725	0.1678	0.1001	0.0576	0.0319	0.0168	0.0084	0.0039
	1	0.2793	0.3826	0.3847	0.3355	0.2670	0.1977	0.1373	0.0896	0.0548	0.0312
	2	0.0515	0.1488	0.2376	0.2936	0.3115	0.2965	0.2587	0.2090	0.1569	0.1094
	3	0.0054	0.0331	0.0839	0.1468	0.2076	0.2541	0.2786	0.2787	0.2568	0.2188
	4	0.0004	0.0046	0.0185	0.0459	0.0865	0.1361	0.1875	0.2322	0.2627	0.2734
	5	0.0000	0.0004	0.0026	0.0092	0.0231	0.0467	0.0808	0.1239	0.1719	0.2188
	6	0.0000	0.0000	0.0002	0.0011	0.0038	0.0100	0.0217	0.0413	0.0703	0.1094
	7	0.0000	0.0000	0.0000	0.0001	0.0004	0.0012	0.0033	0.0079	0.0164	0.0312
	8	0.0000	0.0000	0.0000	0.0000	0.0000	0.0001	0.0002	0.0007	0.0017	0.0039
9	0	0.6302	0.3874	0.2316	0.1342	0.0751	0.0404	0.0207	0.0101	0.0046	0.0020
	1	0.2985	0.3874	0.3679	0.3020	0.2253	0.1556	0.1004	0.0605	0.0339	0.0176
	2	0.0629	0.1722	0.2597	0.3020	0.3003	0.2668	0.2162	0.1612	0.1110	0.0703
	3	0.0077	0.0446	0.1069	0.1762	0.2336	0.2668	0.2716	0.2508	0.2119	0.1641
	4	0.0006	0.0074	0.0283	0.0661	0.1168	0.1715	0.2194	0.2508	0.2600	0.2461
	5	0.0000	0.0008	0.0050	0.0165	0.0389	0.0735	0.1181	0.1672	0.2128	0.2461
	6	0.0000	0.0001	0.0006	0.0028	0.0087	0.0210	0.0424	0.0743	0.1160	0.1641
	7	0.0000	0.0000	0.0000	0.0003	0.0012	0.0039	0.0098	0.0212	0.0407	0.0703
	8	0.0000	0.0000	0.0000	0.0000	0.0001	0.0004	0.0013	0.0035	0.0083	0.0176
	9	0.0000	0.0000	0.0000	0.0000	0.0000	0.0000	0.0001	0.0003	0.0008	0.0020
10	0	0.5987	0.3487	0.1969	0.1074	0.0563	0.0282	0.0135	0.0060	0.0025	0.0010
	1	0.3151	0.3874	0.3474	0.2684	0.1877	0.1211	0.0725	0.0403	0.0207	0.0098
	2	0.0746	0.1937	0.2759	0.3020	0.2816	0.2335	0.1757	0.1209	0.0763	0.0439
	3	0.0105	0.0574	0.1298	0.2013	0.2503	0.2668	0.2522	0.2150	0.1665	0.1172
	4	0.0010	0.0112	0.0401	0.0881	0.1460	0.2001	0.2377	0.2508	0.2384	0.2051
	5	0.0001	0.0015	0.0085	0.0264	0.0584	0.1029	0.1536	0.2007	0.2340	0.2461
	6	0.0000	0.0001	0.0012	0.0055	0.0162	0.0368	0.0689	0.1115	0.1596	0.2051
	7	0.0000	0.0000	0.0001	0.0008	0.0031	0.0090	0.0212	0.0425	0.0746	0.1172
	8	0.0000	0.0000	0.0000	0.0001	0.0004	0.0014	0.0043	0.0106	0.0229	0.0439
	9	0.0000	0.0000	0.0000	0.0000	0.0000	0.0001	0.0005	0.0016	0.0042	0.0098
	10	0.0000	0.0000	0.0000	0.0000	0.0000	0.0000	0.0000	0.0001	0.0003	0.0010
12	0	0.5404	0.2824	0.1422	0.0687	0.0317	0.0138	0.0057	0.0022	0.0008	0.0002
	1	0.3413	0.3766	0.3012	0.2062	0.1267	0.0712	0.0368	0.0174	0.0075	0.0029
	2	0.0988	0.2301	0.2924	0.2835	0.2323	0.1678	0.1088	0.0639	0.0339	0.0161
	3	0.0173	0.0853	0.1720	0.2362	0.2581	0.2397	0.1954	0.1419	0.0923	0.0537
	4	0.0021	0.0213	0.0683	0.1329	0.1936	0.2311	0.2367	0.2128	0.1700	0.1208
	5	0.0002	0.0038	0.0193	0.0532	0.1032	0.1585	0.2039	0.2270	0.2225	0.1934
	6	0.0000	0.0005	0.0040	0.0155	0.0401	0.0792	0.1281	0.1766	0.2124	0.2256
	7	0.0000	0.0000	0.0006	0.0033	0.0115	0.0291	0.0591	0.1009	0.1489	0.1934
	8	0.0000	0.0000	0.0001	0.0005	0.0024	0.0078	0.0199	0.0420	0.0762	0.1208
	9	0.0000	0.0000	0.0000	0.0001	0.0004	0.0015	0.0048	0.0125	0.0277	0.0537
	10	0.0000	0.0000	0.0000	0.0000	0.0000	0.0002	0.0008	0.0025	0.0068	0.0161
	11	0.0000	0.0000	0.0000	0.0000	0.0000	0.0000	0.0001	0.0003	0.0010	0.0029
	12	0.0000	0.0000	0.0000	0.0000	0.0000	0.0000	0.0000	0.0000	0.0001	0.0002
15	0	0.4633	0.2059	0.0874	0.0352	0.0134	0.0047	0.0016	0.0005	0.0001	0.0000
	1	0.3658	0.3432	0.2312	0.1319	0.0668	0.0305	0.0126	0.0047	0.0016	0.0005
	2	0.1348	0.2669	0.2856	0.2309	0.1559	0.0916	0.0476	0.0219	0.0090	0.0032

Binomial Probabilities (*Continued*)

						p					
n	*x*	0.05	0.10	0.15	0.20	0.25	0.30	0.35	0.40	0.45	0.50
	3	0.0307	0.1285	0.2184	0.2501	0.2252	0.1700	0.1110	0.0634	0.0318	0.0139
	4	0.0049	0.0428	0.1156	0.1876	0.2252	0.2186	0.1792	0.1268	0.0780	0.0417
	5	0.0006	0.0105	0.0449	0.1032	0.1651	0.2061	0.2123	0.1859	0.1404	0.0916
	6	0.0000	0.0019	0.0132	0.0430	0.0917	0.1472	0.1906	0.2066	0.1914	0.1527
	7	0.0000	0.0003	0.0030	0.0138	0.0393	0.0811	0.1319	0.1771	0.2013	0.1964
	8	0.0000	0.0000	0.0005	0.0035	0.0131	0.0348	0.0710	0.1181	0.1647	0.1964
	9	0.0000	0.0000	0.0001	0.0007	0.0034	0.0116	0.0298	0.0612	0.1048	0.1527
	10	0.0000	0.0000	0.0000	0.0001	0.0007	0.0030	0.0096	0.0245	0.0515	0.0916
	11	0.0000	0.0000	0.0000	0.0000	0.0001	0.0006	0.0024	0.0074	0.0191	0.0417
	12	0.0000	0.0000	0.0000	0.0000	0.0000	0.0001	0.0004	0.0016	0.0052	0.0139
	13	0.0000	0.0000	0.0000	0.0000	0.0000	0.0000	0.0001	0.0003	0.0010	0.0032
	14	0.0000	0.0000	0.0000	0.0000	0.0000	0.0000	0.0000	0.0000	0.0001	0.0005
	15	0.0000	0.0000	0.0000	0.0000	0.0000	0.0000	0.0000	0.0000	0.0000	0.0000
18	0	0.3972	0.1501	0.0536	0.0180	0.0056	0.0016	0.0004	0.0001	0.0000	0.0000
	1	0.3763	0.3002	0.1704	0.0811	0.0338	0.0126	0.0042	0.0012	0.0003	0.0001
	2	0.1683	0.2835	0.2556	0.1723	0.0958	0.0458	0.0190	0.0069	0.0022	0.0006
	3	0.0473	0.1680	0.2406	0.2297	0.1704	0.1046	0.0547	0.0246	0.0095	0.0031
	4	0.0093	0.0700	0.1592	0.2153	0.2130	0.1681	0.1104	0.0614	0.0291	0.0117
	5	0.0014	0.0218	0.0787	0.1507	0.1988	0.2017	0.1664	0.1146	0.0666	0.0327
	6	0.0002	0.0052	0.0301	0.0816	0.1436	0.1873	0.1941	0.1655	0.1181	0.0708
	7	0.0000	0.0010	0.0091	0.0350	0.0820	0.1376	0.1792	0.1892	0.1657	0.1214
	8	0.0000	0.0002	0.0022	0.0120	0.0376	0.0811	0.1327	0.1734	0.1864	0.1669
	9	0.0000	0.0000	0.0004	0.0033	0.0139	0.0386	0.0794	0.1284	0.1694	0.1855
	10	0.0000	0.0000	0.0001	0.0008	0.0042	0.0149	0.0385	0.0771	0.1248	0.1669
	11	0.0000	0.0000	0.0000	0.0001	0.0010	0.0046	0.0151	0.0374	0.0742	0.1214
	12	0.0000	0.0000	0.0000	0.0000	0.0002	0.0012	0.0047	0.0145	0.0354	0.0708
	13	0.0000	0.0000	0.0000	0.0000	0.0000	0.0002	0.0012	0.0045	0.0134	0.0327
	14	0.0000	0.0000	0.0000	0.0000	0.0000	0.0000	0.0002	0.0011	0.0039	0.0117
	15	0.0000	0.0000	0.0000	0.0000	0.0000	0.0000	0.0000	0.0002	0.0009	0.0031
	16	0.0000	0.0000	0.0000	0.0000	0.0000	0.0000	0.0000	0.0000	0.0001	0.0006
	17	0.0000	0.0000	0.0000	0.0000	0.0000	0.0000	0.0000	0.0000	0.0000	0.0001
	18	0.0000	0.0000	0.0000	0.0000	0.0000	0.0000	0.0000	0.0000	0.0000	0.0000
20	0	0.3585	0.1216	0.0388	0.0115	0.0032	0.0008	0.0002	0.0000	0.0000	0.0000
	1	0.3774	0.2702	0.1368	0.0576	0.0211	0.0068	0.0020	0.0005	0.0001	0.0000
	2	0.1887	0.2852	0.2293	0.1369	0.0669	0.0278	0.0100	0.0031	0.0008	0.0002
	3	0.0596	0.1901	0.2428	0.2054	0.1339	0.0716	0.0323	0.0123	0.0040	0.0011
	4	0.0133	0.0898	0.1821	0.2182	0.1897	0.1304	0.0738	0.0350	0.0139	0.0046
	5	0.0022	0.0319	0.1028	0.1746	0.2023	0.1789	0.1272	0.0746	0.0365	0.0148
	6	0.0003	0.0089	0.0454	0.1091	0.1686	0.1916	0.1712	0.1244	0.0746	0.0370
	7	0.0000	0.0020	0.0160	0.0545	0.1124	0.1643	0.1844	0.1659	0.1221	0.0739
	8	0.0000	0.0004	0.0046	0.0222	0.0609	0.1144	0.1614	0.1797	0.1623	0.1201
	9	0.0000	0.0001	0.0011	0.0074	0.0271	0.0654	0.1158	0.1597	0.1771	0.1602
	10	0.0000	0.0000	0.0002	0.0020	0.0099	0.0308	0.0686	0.1171	0.1593	0.1762
	11	0.0000	0.0000	0.0000	0.0005	0.0030	0.0120	0.0336	0.0710	0.1185	0.1602
	12	0.0000	0.0000	0.0000	0.0001	0.0008	0.0039	0.0136	0.0355	0.0727	0.1201
	13	0.0000	0.0000	0.0000	0.0000	0.0002	0.0010	0.0045	0.0146	0.0366	0.0739
	14	0.0000	0.0000	0.0000	0.0000	0.0000	0.0002	0.0012	0.0049	0.0150	0.0370

Binomial Probabilities (*Continued*)

n	x	0.05	0.10	0.15	0.20	0.25	0.30	0.35	0.40	0.45	0.50
	15	0.0000	0.0000	0.0000	0.0000	0.0000	0.0000	0.0003	0.0013	0.0049	0.0148
	16	0.0000	0.0000	0.0000	0.0000	0.0000	0.0000	0.0000	0.0003	0.0013	0.0046
	17	0.0000	0.0000	0.0000	0.0000	0.0000	0.0000	0.0000	0.0000	0.0002	0.0011
	18	0.0000	0.0000	0.0000	0.0000	0.0000	0.0000	0.0000	0.0000	0.0000	0.0002
	19	0.0000	0.0000	0.0000	0.0000	0.0000	0.0000	0.0000	0.0000	0.0000	0.0000
	20	0.0000	0.0000	0.0000	0.0000	0.0000	0.0000	0.0000	0.0000	0.0000	0.0000

The column header *p* spans the probability columns 0.05 through 0.50.

Binomial Probabilities (*Continued*)

n	x	0.55	0.60	0.65	0.70	0.75	0.80	0.85	0.90	0.95
2	0	0.2025	0.1600	0.1225	0.0900	0.0625	0.0400	0.0225	0.0100	0.0025
	1	0.4950	0.4800	0.4550	0.4200	0.3750	0.3200	0.2550	0.1800	0.0950
	2	0.3025	0.3600	0.4225	0.4900	0.5625	0.6400	0.7225	0.8100	0.9025
3	0	0.0911	0.0640	0.0429	0.0270	0.0156	0.0080	0.0034	0.0010	0.0001
	1	0.3341	0.2880	0.2389	0.1890	0.1406	0.0960	0.0574	0.0270	0.0071
	2	0.4084	0.4320	0.4436	0.4410	0.4219	0.3840	0.3251	0.2430	0.1354
	3	0.1664	0.2160	0.2746	0.3430	0.4219	0.5120	0.6141	0.7290	0.8574
4	0	0.0410	0.0256	0.0150	0.0081	0.0039	0.0016	0.0005	0.0001	0.0000
	1	0.2005	0.1536	0.1115	0.0756	0.0469	0.0256	0.0115	0.0036	0.0005
	2	0.3675	0.3456	0.3105	0.2646	0.2109	0.1536	0.0975	0.0486	0.0135
	3	0.2995	0.3456	0.3845	0.4116	0.4219	0.4096	0.3685	0.2916	0.1715
	4	0.0915	0.1296	0.1785	0.2401	0.3164	0.4096	0.5220	0.6561	0.8145
5	0	0.0185	0.0102	0.0053	0.0024	0.0010	0.0003	0.0001	0.0000	0.0000
	1	0.1128	0.0768	0.0488	0.0284	0.0146	0.0064	0.0022	0.0005	0.0000
	2	0.2757	0.2304	0.1811	0.1323	0.0879	0.0512	0.0244	0.0081	0.0011
	3	0.3369	0.3456	0.3364	0.3087	0.2637	0.2048	0.1382	0.0729	0.0214
	4	0.2059	0.2592	0.3124	0.3601	0.3955	0.4096	0.3915	0.3281	0.2036
	5	0.0503	0.0778	0.1160	0.1681	0.2373	0.3277	0.4437	0.5905	0.7738
6	0	0.0083	0.0041	0.0018	0.0007	0.0002	0.0001	0.0000	0.0000	0.0000
	1	0.0609	0.0369	0.0205	0.0102	0.0044	0.0015	0.0004	0.0001	0.0000
	2	0.1861	0.1382	0.0951	0.0595	0.0330	0.0154	0.0055	0.0012	0.0001
	3	0.3032	0.2765	0.2355	0.1852	0.1318	0.0819	0.0415	0.0146	0.0021
	4	0.2780	0.3110	0.3280	0.3241	0.2966	0.2458	0.1762	0.0984	0.0305
	5	0.1359	0.1866	0.2437	0.3025	0.3560	0.3932	0.3993	0.3543	0.2321
	6	0.0277	0.0467	0.0754	0.1176	0.1780	0.2621	0.3771	0.5314	0.7351
7	0	0.0037	0.0016	0.0006	0.0002	0.0001	0.0000	0.0000	0.0000	0.0000
	1	0.0320	0.0172	0.0084	0.0036	0.0013	0.0004	0.0001	0.0000	0.0000
	2	0.1172	0.0774	0.0466	0.0250	0.0115	0.0043	0.0012	0.0002	0.0000
	3	0.2388	0.1935	0.1442	0.0972	0.0577	0.0287	0.0109	0.0026	0.0002
	4	0.2918	0.2903	0.2679	0.2269	0.1730	0.1147	0.0617	0.0230	0.0036
	5	0.2140	0.2613	0.2985	0.3177	0.3115	0.2753	0.2097	0.1240	0.0406
	6	0.0872	0.1306	0.1848	0.2471	0.3115	0.3670	0.3960	0.3720	0.2573
	7	0.0152	0.0280	0.0490	0.0824	0.1335	0.2097	0.3206	0.4783	0.6983
8	0	0.0017	0.0007	0.0002	0.0001	0.0000	0.0000	0.0000	0.0000	0.0000
	1	0.0164	0.0079	0.0033	0.0012	0.0004	0.0001	0.0000	0.0000	0.0000
	2	0.0703	0.0413	0.0217	0.0100	0.0038	0.0011	0.0002	0.0000	0.0000
	3	0.1719	0.1239	0.0808	0.0467	0.0231	0.0092	0.0026	0.0004	0.0000
	4	0.2627	0.2322	0.1875	0.1361	0.0865	0.0459	0.0185	0.0046	0.0004
	5	0.2568	0.2787	0.2786	0.2541	0.2076	0.1468	0.0839	0.0331	0.0054
	6	0.1569	0.2090	0.2587	0.2965	0.3115	0.2936	0.2376	0.1488	0.0515
	7	0.0548	0.0896	0.1373	0.1977	0.2670	0.3355	0.3847	0.3826	0.2793
	8	0.0084	0.0168	0.0319	0.0576	0.1001	0.1678	0.2725	0.4305	0.6634

Binomial Probabilities (*Continued*)

						p				
n	*x*	0.55	0.60	0.65	0.70	0.75	0.80	0.85	0.90	0.95
9	0	0.0008	0.0003	0.0001	0.0000	0.0000	0.0000	0.0000	0.0000	0.0000
	1	0.0083	0.0035	0.0013	0.0004	0.0001	0.0000	0.0000	0.0000	0.0000
	2	0.0407	0.0212	0.0098	0.0039	0.0012	0.0003	0.0000	0.0000	0.0000
	3	0.1160	0.0743	0.0424	0.0210	0.0087	0.0028	0.0006	0.0001	0.0000
	4	0.2128	0.1672	0.1181	0.0735	0.0389	0.0165	0.0050	0.0008	0.0000
	5	0.2600	0.2508	0.2194	0.1715	0.1168	0.0661	0.0283	0.0074	0.0006
	6	0.2119	0.2508	0.2716	0.2668	0.2336	0.1762	0.1069	0.0446	0.0077
	7	0.1110	0.1612	0.2162	0.2668	0.3003	0.3020	0.2597	0.1722	0.0629
	8	0.0339	0.0605	0.1004	0.1556	0.2253	0.3020	0.3679	0.3874	0.2985
	9	0.0046	0.0101	0.0207	0.0404	0.0751	0.1342	0.2316	0.3874	0.6302
10	0	0.0003	0.0001	0.0000	0.0000	0.0000	0.0000	0.0000	0.0000	0.0000
	1	0.0042	0.0016	0.0005	0.0001	0.0000	0.0000	0.0000	0.0000	0.0000
	2	0.0229	0.0106	0.0043	0.0014	0.0004	0.0001	0.0000	0.0000	0.0000
	3	0.0746	0.0425	0.0212	0.0090	0.0031	0.0008	0.0001	0.0000	0.0000
	4	0.1596	0.1115	0.0689	0.0368	0.0162	0.0055	0.0012	0.0001	0.0000
	5	0.2340	0.2007	0.1536	0.1029	0.0584	0.0264	0.0085	0.0015	0.0001
	6	0.2384	0.2508	0.2377	0.2001	0.1460	0.0881	0.0401	0.0112	0.0010
	7	0.1665	0.2150	0.2522	0.2668	0.2503	0.2013	0.1298	0.0574	0.0105
	8	0.0763	0.1209	0.1757	0.2335	0.2816	0.3020	0.2759	0.1937	0.0746
	9	0.0207	0.0403	0.0725	0.1211	0.1877	0.2684	0.3474	0.3874	0.3151
	10	0.0025	0.0060	0.0135	0.0282	0.0563	0.1074	0.1969	0.3487	0.5987
12	0	0.0001	0.0000	0.0000	0.0000	0.0000	0.0000	0.0000	0.0000	0.0000
	1	0.0010	0.0003	0.0001	0.0000	0.0000	0.0000	0.0000	0.0000	0.0000
	2	0.0068	0.0025	0.0008	0.0002	0.0000	0.0000	0.0000	0.0000	0.0000
	3	0.0277	0.0125	0.0048	0.0015	0.0004	0.0001	0.0000	0.0000	0.0000
	4	0.0762	0.0420	0.0199	0.0078	0.0024	0.0005	0.0001	0.0000	0.0000
	5	0.1489	0.1009	0.0591	0.0291	0.0115	0.0033	0.0006	0.0000	0.0000
	6	0.2124	0.1766	0.1281	0.0792	0.0401	0.0155	0.0040	0.0005	0.0000
	7	0.2225	0.2270	0.2039	0.1585	0.1032	0.0532	0.0193	0.0038	0.0002
	8	0.1700	0.2128	0.2367	0.2311	0.1936	0.1329	0.0683	0.0213	0.0021
	9	0.0923	0.1419	0.1954	0.2397	0.2581	0.2362	0.1720	0.0852	0.0173
	10	0.0339	0.0639	0.1088	0.1678	0.2323	0.2835	0.2924	0.2301	0.0988
	11	0.0075	0.0174	0.0368	0.0712	0.1267	0.2062	0.3012	0.3766	0.3413
	12	0.0008	0.0022	0.0057	0.0138	0.0317	0.0687	0.1422	0.2824	0.5404
15	0	0.0000	0.0000	0.0000	0.0000	0.0000	0.0000	0.0000	0.0000	0.0000
	1	0.0001	0.0000	0.0000	0.0000	0.0000	0.0000	0.0000	0.0000	0.0000
	2	0.0010	0.0003	0.0001	0.0000	0.0000	0.0000	0.0000	0.0000	0.0000
	3	0.0052	0.0016	0.0004	0.0001	0.0000	0.0000	0.0000	0.0000	0.0000
	4	0.0191	0.0074	0.0024	0.0006	0.0001	0.0000	0.0000	0.0000	0.0000
	5	0.0515	0.0245	0.0096	0.0030	0.0007	0.0001	0.0000	0.0000	0.0000
	6	0.1048	0.0612	0.0298	0.0116	0.0034	0.0007	0.0001	0.0000	0.0000
	7	0.1647	0.1181	0.0710	0.0348	0.0131	0.0035	0.0005	0.0000	0.0000
	8	0.2013	0.1771	0.1319	0.0811	0.0393	0.0138	0.0030	0.0003	0.0000
	9	0.1914	0.2066	0.1906	0.1472	0.0917	0.0430	0.0132	0.0019	0.0000
	10	0.1404	0.1859	0.2123	0.2061	0.1651	0.1032	0.0449	0.0105	0.0006
	11	0.0780	0.1268	0.1792	0.2186	0.2252	0.1876	0.1156	0.0428	0.0049

Binomial Probabilities (*Continued*)

						p				
n	x	**0.55**	**0.60**	**0.65**	**0.70**	**0.75**	**0.80**	**0.85**	**0.90**	**0.95**
	12	0.0318	0.0634	0.1110	0.1700	0.2252	0.2501	0.2184	0.1285	0.0307
	13	0.0090	0.0219	0.0476	0.0916	0.1559	0.2309	0.2856	0.2669	0.1348
	14	0.0016	0.0047	0.0126	0.0305	0.0668	0.1319	0.2312	0.3432	0.3658
	15	0.0001	0.0005	0.0016	0.0047	0.0134	0.0352	0.0874	0.2059	0.4633
18	0	0.0000	0.0000	0.0000	0.0000	0.0000	0.0000	0.0000	0.0000	0.0000
	1	0.0000	0.0000	0.0000	0.0000	0.0000	0.0000	0.0000	0.0000	0.0000
	2	0.0001	0.0000	0.0000	0.0000	0.0000	0.0000	0.0000	0.0000	0.0000
	3	0.0009	0.0002	0.0000	0.0000	0.0000	0.0000	0.0000	0.0000	0.0000
	4	0.0039	0.0011	0.0002	0.0000	0.0000	0.0000	0.0000	0.0000	0.0000
	5	0.0134	0.0045	0.0012	0.0002	0.0000	0.0000	0.0000	0.0000	0.0000
	6	0.0354	0.0145	0.0047	0.0012	0.0002	0.0000	0.0000	0.0000	0.0000
	7	0.0742	0.0374	0.0151	0.0046	0.0010	0.0001	0.0000	0.0000	0.0000
	8	0.1248	0.0771	0.0385	0.0149	0.0042	0.0008	0.0001	0.0000	0.0000
	9	0.1694	0.1284	0.0794	0.0386	0.0139	0.0033	0.0004	0.0000	0.0000
	10	0.1864	0.1734	0.1327	0.0811	0.0376	0.0120	0.0022	0.0002	0.0000
	11	0.1657	0.1892	0.1792	0.1376	0.0820	0.0350	0.0091	0.0010	0.0000
	12	0.1181	0.1655	0.1941	0.1873	0.1436	0.0816	0.0301	0.0052	0.0002
	13	0.0666	0.1146	0.1664	0.2017	0.1988	0.1507	0.0787	0.0218	0.0014
	14	0.0291	0.0614	0.1104	0.1681	0.2130	0.2153	0.1592	0.0700	0.0093
	15	0.0095	0.0246	0.0547	0.1046	0.1704	0.2297	0.2406	0.1680	0.0473
	16	0.0022	0.0069	0.0190	0.0458	0.0958	0.1723	0.2556	0.2835	0.1683
	17	0.0003	0.0012	0.0042	0.0126	0.0338	0.0811	0.1704	0.3002	0.3763
	18	0.0000	0.0001	0.0004	0.0016	0.0056	0.0180	0.0536	0.1501	0.3972
20	0	0.0000	0.0000	0.0000	0.0000	0.0000	0.0000	0.0000	0.0000	0.0000
	1	0.0000	0.0000	0.0000	0.0000	0.0000	0.0000	0.0000	0.0000	0.0000
	2	0.0000	0.0000	0.0000	0.0000	0.0000	0.0000	0.0000	0.0000	0.0000
	3	0.0002	0.0000	0.0000	0.0000	0.0000	0.0000	0.0000	0.0000	0.0000
	4	0.0013	0.0003	0.0000	0.0000	0.0000	0.0000	0.0000	0.0000	0.0000
	5	0.0049	0.0013	0.0003	0.0000	0.0000	0.0000	0.0000	0.0000	0.0000
	6	0.0150	0.0049	0.0012	0.0002	0.0000	0.0000	0.0000	0.0000	0.0000
	7	0.0366	0.0146	0.0045	0.0010	0.0002	0.0000	0.0000	0.0000	0.0000
	8	0.0727	0.0355	0.0136	0.0039	0.0008	0.0001	0.0000	0.0000	0.0000
	9	0.1185	0.0710	0.0336	0.0120	0.0030	0.0005	0.0000	0.0000	0.0000
	10	0.1593	0.1171	0.0686	0.0308	0.0099	0.0020	0.0002	0.0000	0.0000
	11	0.1771	0.1597	0.1158	0.0654	0.0271	0.0074	0.0011	0.0001	0.0000
	12	0.1623	0.1797	0.1614	0.1144	0.0609	0.0222	0.0046	0.0004	0.0000
	13	0.1221	0.1659	0.1844	0.1643	0.1124	0.0545	0.0160	0.0020	0.0000
	14	0.0746	0.1244	0.1712	0.1916	0.1686	0.1091	0.0454	0.0089	0.0003
	15	0.0365	0.0746	0.1272	0.1789	0.2023	0.1746	0.1028	0.0319	0.0022
	16	0.0139	0.0350	0.0738	0.1304	0.1897	0.2182	0.1821	0.0898	0.0133
	17	0.0040	0.0123	0.0323	0.0716	0.1339	0.2054	0.2428	0.1901	0.0596
	18	0.0008	0.0031	0.0100	0.0278	0.0669	0.1369	0.2293	0.2852	0.1887
	19	0.0001	0.0005	0.0020	0.0068	0.0211	0.0576	0.1368	0.2702	0.3774
	20	0.0000	0.0000	0.0002	0.0008	0.0032	0.0115	0.0388	0.1216	0.3585

Appendix C   Poisson Probabilities

Entries in the following table give the probability of x occurrences for a Poisson process with a mean λ. For example, when $\lambda = 2.5$, the probability of $x = 4$ occurrences is 0.1336.

	λ									
x	0.1	0.2	0.3	0.4	0.5	0.6	0.7	0.8	0.9	1.0
0	0.9048	0.8187	0.7408	0.6703	0.6065	0.5488	0.4966	0.4493	0.4066	0.3679
1	0.0905	0.1637	0.2222	0.2681	0.3033	0.3293	0.3476	0.3595	0.3659	0.3679
2	0.0045	0.0164	0.0333	0.0536	0.0758	0.0988	0.1217	0.1438	0.1647	0.1839
3	0.0002	0.0011	0.0033	0.0072	0.0126	0.0198	0.0284	0.0383	0.0494	0.0613
4	0.0000	0.0001	0.0002	0.0007	0.0016	0.0030	0.0050	0.0077	0.0111	0.0153
5	0.0000	0.0000	0.0000	0.0001	0.0002	0.0004	0.0007	0.0012	0.0020	0.0031
6	0.0000	0.0000	0.0000	0.0000	0.0000	0.0000	0.0001	0.0002	0.0003	0.0005
7	0.0000	0.0000	0.0000	0.0000	0.0000	0.0000	0.0000	0.0000	0.0000	0.0001

	λ									
x	1.1	1.2	1.3	1.4	1.5	1.6	1.7	1.8	1.9	2.0
0	0.3329	0.3012	0.2725	0.2466	0.2231	0.2019	0.1827	0.1653	0.1496	0.1353
1	0.3662	0.3614	0.3543	0.3452	0.3347	0.3230	0.3106	0.2975	0.2842	0.2707
2	0.2014	0.2169	0.2303	0.2417	0.2510	0.2584	0.2640	0.2678	0.2700	0.2707
3	0.0738	0.0867	0.0998	0.1128	0.1255	0.1378	0.1496	0.1607	0.1710	0.1804
4	0.0203	0.0260	0.0324	0.0395	0.0471	0.0551	0.0636	0.0723	0.0812	0.0902
5	0.0045	0.0062	0.0084	0.0111	0.0141	0.0176	0.0216	0.0260	0.0309	0.0361
6	0.0008	0.0012	0.0018	0.0026	0.0035	0.0047	0.0061	0.0078	0.0098	0.0120
7	0.0001	0.0002	0.0003	0.0005	0.0008	0.0011	0.0015	0.0020	0.0027	0.0034
8	0.0000	0.0000	0.0001	0.0001	0.0001	0.0002	0.0003	0.0005	0.0006	0.0009
9	0.0000	0.0000	0.0000	0.0000	0.0000	0.0000	0.0001	0.0001	0.0001	0.0002

	λ									
x	2.1	2.2	2.3	2.4	2.5	2.6	2.7	2.8	2.9	3.0
0	0.1225	0.1108	0.1003	0.0907	0.0821	0.0743	0.0672	0.0608	0.0550	0.0498
1	0.2572	0.2438	0.2306	0.2177	0.2052	0.1931	0.1815	0.1703	0.1596	0.1494
2	0.2700	0.2681	0.2652	0.2613	0.2565	0.2510	0.2450	0.2384	0.2314	0.2240
3	0.1890	0.1966	0.2033	0.2090	0.2138	0.2176	0.2205	0.2225	0.2237	0.2240
4	0.0992	0.1082	0.1169	0.1254	0.1336	0.1414	0.1488	0.1557	0.1622	0.1680
5	0.0417	0.0476	0.0538	0.0602	0.0668	0.0735	0.0804	0.0872	0.0940	0.1008
6	0.0146	0.0174	0.0206	0.0241	0.0278	0.0319	0.0362	0.0407	0.0455	0.0540
7	0.0044	0.0055	0.0068	0.0083	0.0099	0.0118	0.0139	0.0163	0.0188	0.0216

Poisson Probabilities (*Continued*)

					λ					
x	2.1	2.2	2.3	2.4	2.5	2.6	2.7	2.8	2.9	3.0
8	0.0011	0.0015	0.0019	0.0025	0.0031	0.0038	0.0047	0.0057	0.0068	0.0081
9	0.0003	0.0004	0.0005	0.0007	0.0009	0.0011	0.0014	0.0018	0.0022	0.0027
10	0.0001	0.0001	0.0001	0.0002	0.0002	0.0003	0.0004	0.0005	0.0006	0.0008
11	0.0000	0.0000	0.0000	0.0000	0.0000	0.0001	0.0001	0.0001	0.0002	0.0002
12	0.0000	0.0000	0.0000	0.0000	0.0000	0.0000	0.0000	0.0000	0.0000	0.0001

					λ					
x	3.1	3.2	3.3	3.4	3.5	3.6	3.7	3.8	3.9	4.0
0	0.0450	0.0408	0.0369	0.0344	0.0302	0.0273	0.0247	0.0224	0.0202	0.0183
1	0.1397	0.1304	0.1217	0.1135	0.1057	0.0984	0.0915	0.0850	0.0789	0.0733
2	0.2165	0.2087	0.2008	0.1929	0.1850	0.1771	0.1692	0.1615	0.1539	0.1465
3	0.2237	0.2226	0.2209	0.2186	0.2158	0.2125	0.2087	0.2046	0.2001	0.1954
4	0.1734	0.1781	0.1823	0.1858	0.1888	0.1912	0.1931	0.1944	0.1951	0.1954
5	0.1075	0.1140	0.1203	0.1264	0.1322	0.1377	0.1429	0.1477	0.1522	0.1563
6	0.0555	0.0608	0.0662	0.0716	0.0771	0.0826	0.0881	0.0936	0.0989	0.1042
7	0.0246	0.0278	0.0312	0.0348	0.0385	0.0425	0.0466	0.0508	0.0551	0.0595
8	0.0095	0.0111	0.0129	0.0148	0.0169	0.0191	0.0215	0.0241	0.0269	0.0298
9	0.0033	0.0040	0.0047	0.0056	0.0066	0.0076	0.0089	0.0102	0.0116	0.0132
10	0.0010	0.0013	0.0016	0.0019	0.0023	0.0028	0.0033	0.0039	0.0045	0.0053
11	0.0003	0.0004	0.0005	0.0006	0.0007	0.0009	0.0011	0.0013	0.0016	0.0019
12	0.0001	0.0001	0.0001	0.0002	0.0002	0.0003	0.0003	0.0004	0.0005	0.0006
13	0.0000	0.0000	0.0000	0.0000	0.0001	0.0001	0.0001	0.0001	0.0002	0.0002
14	0.0000	0.0000	0.0000	0.0000	0.0000	0.0000	0.0000	0.0000	0.0000	0.0001

					λ					
x	4.1	4.2	4.3	4.4	4.5	4.6	4.7	4.8	4.9	5.0
0	0.0166	0.0150	0.0136	0.0123	0.0111	0.0101	0.0091	0.0082	0.0074	0.0067
1	0.0679	0.0630	0.0583	0.0540	0.0500	0.0462	0.0427	0.0395	0.0365	0.0337
2	0.1393	0.1323	0.1254	0.1188	0.1125	0.1063	0.1005	0.0948	0.0894	0.0842
3	0.1904	0.1852	0.1798	0.1743	0.1687	0.1631	0.1574	0.1517	0.1460	0.1404
4	0.1951	0.1944	0.1933	0.1917	0.1898	0.1875	0.1849	0.1820	0.1789	0.1755
5	0.1600	0.1633	0.1662	0.1687	0.1708	0.1725	0.1738	0.1747	0.1753	0.1755
6	0.1093	0.1143	0.1191	0.1237	0.1281	0.1323	0.1362	0.1398	0.1432	0.1462
7	0.0640	0.0686	0.0732	0.0778	0.0824	0.0869	0.0914	0.0959	0.1002	0.1044
8	0.0328	0.0360	0.0393	0.0428	0.0463	0.0500	0.0537	0.0575	0.0614	0.0653
9	0.0150	0.0168	0.0188	0.0209	0.0232	0.0255	0.0280	0.0307	0.0334	0.0363
10	0.0061	0.0071	0.0081	0.0092	0.0104	0.0118	0.0132	0.0147	0.0164	0.0181
11	0.0023	0.0027	0.0032	0.0037	0.0043	0.0049	0.0056	0.0064	0.0073	0.0082
12	0.0008	0.0009	0.0011	0.0014	0.0016	0.0019	0.0022	0.0026	0.0030	0.0034
13	0.0002	0.0003	0.0004	0.0005	0.0006	0.0007	0.0008	0.0009	0.0011	0.0013
14	0.0001	0.0001	0.0001	0.0001	0.0002	0.0002	0.0003	0.0003	0.0004	0.0005
15	0.0000	0.0000	0.0000	0.0000	0.0001	0.0001	0.0001	0.0001	0.0001	0.0002

Binomial Probabilities (*Continued*)

	λ									
x	5.1	5.2	5.3	5.4	5.5	5.6	5.7	5.8	5.9	6.0
0	0.0061	0.0055	0.0050	0.0045	0.0041	0.0037	0.0033	0.0030	0.0027	0.0025
1	0.0311	0.0287	0.0265	0.0244	0.0225	0.0207	0.0191	0.0176	0.0162	0.0149
2	0.0793	0.0746	0.0701	0.0659	0.0618	0.0580	0.0544	0.0509	0.0477	0.0446
3	0.1348	0.1293	0.1239	0.1185	0.1133	0.1082	0.1033	0.0985	0.0938	0.0892
4	0.1719	0.1681	0.1641	0.1600	0.1558	0.1515	0.1472	0.1428	0.1383	0.1339
5	0.1753	0.1748	0.1740	0.1728	0.1714	0.1697	0.1678	0.1656	0.1632	0.1606
6	0.1490	0.1515	0.1537	0.1555	0.1571	0.1587	0.1594	0.1601	0.1605	0.1606
7	0.1086	0.1125	0.1163	0.1200	0.1234	0.1267	0.1298	0.1326	0.1353	0.1377
8	0.0692	0.0731	0.0771	0.0810	0.0849	0.0887	0.0925	0.0962	0.0998	0.1033
9	0.0392	0.0423	0.0454	0.0486	0.0519	0.0552	0.0586	0.0620	0.0654	0.0688
10	0.0200	0.0220	0.0241	0.0262	0.0285	0.0309	0.0334	0.0359	0.0386	0.0413
11	0.0093	0.0104	0.0116	0.0129	0.0143	0.0157	0.0173	0.0190	0.0207	0.0225
12	0.0039	0.0045	0.0051	0.0058	0.0065	0.0073	0.0082	0.0092	0.0102	0.0113
13	0.0015	0.0018	0.0021	0.0024	0.0028	0.0032	0.0036	0.0041	0.0046	0.0052
14	0.0006	0.0007	0.0008	0.0009	0.0011	0.0013	0.0015	0.0017	0.0019	0.0022
15	0.0002	0.0002	0.0003	0.0003	0.0004	0.0005	0.0006	0.0007	0.0008	0.0009
16	0.0001	0.0001	0.0001	0.0001	0.0001	0.0002	0.0002	0.0002	0.0003	0.0003
17	0.0000	0.0000	0.0000	0.0000	0.0000	0.0001	0.0001	0.0001	0.0001	0.0001

	λ									
x	6.1	6.2	6.3	6.4	6.5	6.6	6.7	6.8	6.9	7.0
0	0.0022	0.0020	0.0018	0.0017	0.0015	0.0014	0.0012	0.0011	0.0010	0.0009
1	0.0137	0.0126	0.0116	0.0106	0.0098	0.0090	0.0082	0.0076	0.0070	0.0064
2	0.0417	0.0390	0.0364	0.0340	0.0318	0.0296	0.0276	0.0258	0.0240	0.0223
3	0.0848	0.0806	0.0765	0.0726	0.0688	0.0652	0.0617	0.0584	0.0552	0.0521
4	0.1294	0.1249	0.1205	0.1162	0.1118	0.1076	0.1034	0.0992	0.0952	0.0912
5	0.1579	0.1549	0.1519	0.1487	0.1454	0.1420	0.1385	0.1349	0.1314	0.1277
6	0.1605	0.1601	0.1595	0.1586	0.1575	0.1562	0.1546	0.1529	0.1511	0.1490
7	0.1399	0.1418	0.1435	0.1450	0.1462	0.1472	0.1480	0.1486	0.1489	0.1490
8	0.1066	0.1099	0.1130	0.1160	0.1188	0.1215	0.1240	0.1263	0.1284	0.1304
9	0.0723	0.0757	0.0791	0.0825	0.0858	0.0891	0.0923	0.0954	0.0985	0.1014
10	0.0441	0.0469	0.0498	0.0528	0.0558	0.0588	0.0618	0.0649	0.0679	0.0710
11	0.0245	0.0265	0.0285	0.0307	0.0330	0.0353	0.0377	0.0401	0.0426	0.0452
12	0.0124	0.0137	0.0150	0.0164	0.0179	0.0194	0.0210	0.0227	0.0245	0.0264
13	0.0058	0.0065	0.0073	0.0081	0.0089	0.0098	0.0108	0.0119	0.0130	0.0142
14	0.0025	0.0029	0.0033	0.0037	0.0041	0.0046	0.0052	0.0058	0.0064	0.0071
15	0.0010	0.0012	0.0014	0.0016	0.0018	0.0020	0.0023	0.0025	0.0029	0.0033
16	0.0004	0.0005	0.0005	0.0006	0.0007	0.0008	0.0010	0.0011	0.0013	0.0014
17	0.0001	0.0002	0.0002	0.0002	0.0003	0.0003	0.0004	0.0004	0.0005	0.0006
18	0.0000	0.0001	0.0001	0.0001	0.0001	0.0001	0.0001	0.0002	0.0002	0.0002
19	0.0000	0.0000	0.0000	0.0000	0.0000	0.0000	0.0000	0.0001	0.0001	0.0001

Poisson Probabilities (*Continued*)

	λ									
x	7.1	7.2	7.3	7.4	7.5	7.6	7.7	7.8	7.9	8.0
0	0.0008	0.0007	0.0007	0.0006	0.0006	0.0005	0.0005	0.0004	0.0004	0.0003
1	0.0059	0.0054	0.0049	0.0045	0.0041	0.0038	0.0035	0.0032	0.0029	0.0027
2	0.0208	0.0194	0.0180	0.0167	0.0156	0.0145	0.0134	0.0125	0.0116	0.0107
3	0.0492	0.0464	0.0438	0.0413	0.0389	0.0366	0.0345	0.0324	0.0305	0.0286
4	0.0874	0.0836	0.0799	0.0764	0.0729	0.0696	0.0663	0.0632	0.0602	0.0573
5	0.1241	0.1204	0.1167	0.1130	0.1094	0.1057	0.1021	0.0986	0.0951	0.0916
6	0.1468	0.1445	0.1420	0.1394	0.1367	0.1339	0.1311	0.1282	0.1252	0.1221
7	0.1489	0.1486	0.1481	0.1474	0.1465	0.1454	0.1442	0.1428	0.1413	0.1396
8	0.1321	0.1337	0.1351	0.1363	0.1373	0.1382	0.1388	0.1392	0.1395	0.1396
9	0.1042	0.1070	0.1096	0.1121	0.1144	0.1167	0.1187	0.1207	0.1224	0.1241
10	0.0740	0.0770	0.0800	0.0829	0.0858	0.0887	0.0914	0.0941	0.0967	0.0993
11	0.0478	0.0504	0.0531	0.0558	0.0585	0.0613	0.0640	0.0667	0.0695	0.0722
12	0.0283	0.0303	0.0323	0.0344	0.0366	0.0388	0.0411	0.0434	0.0457	0.0481
13	0.0154	0.0168	0.0181	0.0196	0.0211	0.0227	0.0243	0.0260	0.0278	0.0296
14	0.0078	0.0086	0.0095	0.0104	0.0113	0.0123	0.0134	0.0145	0.0157	0.0169
15	0.0037	0.0041	0.0046	0.0051	0.0057	0.0062	0.0069	0.0075	0.0083	0.0090
16	0.0016	0.0019	0.0021	0.0024	0.0026	0.0030	0.0033	0.0037	0.0041	0.0045
17	0.0007	0.0008	0.0009	0.0010	0.0012	0.0013	0.0015	0.0017	0.0019	0.0021
18	0.0003	0.0003	0.0004	0.0004	0.0005	0.0006	0.0006	0.0007	0.0008	0.0009
19	0.0001	0.0001	0.0001	0.0002	0.0002	0.0002	0.0003	0.0003	0.0003	0.0004
20	0.0000	0.0000	0.0001	0.0001	0.0001	0.0001	0.0001	0.0001	0.0001	0.0002
21	0.0000	0.0000	0.0000	0.0000	0.0000	0.0000	0.0000	0.0000	0.0001	0.0001

	λ									
x	8.1	8.2	8.3	8.4	8.5	8.6	8.7	8.8	8.9	9.0
0	0.0003	0.0003	0.0002	0.0002	0.0002	0.0002	0.0002	0.0002	0.0001	0.0001
1	0.0025	0.0023	0.0021	0.0019	0.0017	0.0016	0.0014	0.0013	0.0012	0.0011
2	0.0100	0.0092	0.0086	0.0079	0.0074	0.0068	0.0063	0.0058	0.0054	0.0050
3	0.0269	0.0252	0.0237	0.0222	0.0208	0.0195	0.0183	0.0171	0.0160	0.0150
4	0.0544	0.0517	0.0491	0.0466	0.0443	0.0420	0.0398	0.0377	0.0357	0.0337
5	0.0882	0.0849	0.0816	0.0784	0.0752	0.0722	0.0692	0.0663	0.0635	0.0607
6	0.1191	0.1160	0.1128	0.1097	0.1066	0.1034	0.1003	0.0972	0.0941	0.0911
7	0.1378	0.1358	0.1338	0.1317	0.1294	0.1271	0.1247	0.1222	0.1197	0.1171
8	0.1395	0.1392	0.1388	0.1382	0.1375	0.1366	0.1356	0.1344	0.1332	0.1318
9	0.1256	0.1269	0.1280	0.1290	0.1299	0.1306	0.1311	0.1315	0.1317	0.1318
10	0.1017	0.1040	0.1063	0.1084	0.1104	0.1123	0.1140	0.1157	0.1172	0.1186
11	0.0749	0.0776	0.0802	0.0828	0.0853	0.0878	0.0902	0.0925	0.0948	0.0970
12	0.0505	0.0530	0.0555	0.0579	0.0604	0.0629	0.0654	0.0679	0.0703	0.0728
13	0.0315	0.0334	0.0354	0.0374	0.0395	0.0416	0.0438	0.0459	0.0481	0.0504
14	0.0182	0.0196	0.0210	0.0225	0.0240	0.0256	0.0272	0.0289	0.0306	0.0324

Poisson Probabilities (*Continued*)

					λ					
x	**8.1**	**8.2**	**8.3**	**8.4**	**8.5**	**8.6**	**8.7**	**8.8**	**8.9**	**9.0**
15	0.0098	0.0107	0.0116	0.0126	0.0136	0.0147	0.0158	0.0169	0.0182	0.1094
16	0.0050	0.0055	0.0060	0.0066	0.0072	0.0079	0.0086	0.0093	0.0101	0.0109
17	0.0024	0.0026	0.0029	0.0033	0.0036	0.0040	0.0044	0.0048	0.0053	0.0058
18	0.0011	0.0012	0.0014	0.0015	0.0017	0.0019	0.0021	0.0024	0.0026	0.0029
19	0.0005	0.0005	0.0006	0.0007	0.0008	0.0009	0.0010	0.0011	0.0012	0.0014
20	0.0002	0.0002	0.0002	0.0003	0.0003	0.0004	0.0004	0.0005	0.0005	0.0006
21	0.0001	0.0001	0.0001	0.0001	0.0001	0.0002	0.0002	0.0002	0.0002	0.0003
22	0.0000	0.0000	0.0000	0.0000	0.0001	0.0001	0.0001	0.0001	0.0001	0.0001

					λ					
x	**9.1**	**9.2**	**9.3**	**9.4**	**9.5**	**9.6**	**9.7**	**9.8**	**9.9**	**10**
0	0.0001	0.0001	0.0001	0.0001	0.0001	0.0001	0.0001	0.0001	0.0001	0.0000
1	0.0010	0.0009	0.0009	0.0008	0.0007	0.0007	0.0006	0.0005	0.0005	0.0005
2	0.0046	0.0043	0.0040	0.0037	0.0034	0.0031	0.0029	0.0027	0.0025	0.0023
3	0.0140	0.0131	0.0123	0.0115	0.0107	0.0100	0.0093	0.0087	0.0081	0.0076
4	0.0319	0.0302	0.0285	0.0269	0.0254	0.0240	0.0226	0.0213	0.0201	0.0189
5	0.0581	0.0555	0.0530	0.0506	0.0483	0.0460	0.0439	0.0418	0.0398	0.0378
6	0.0881	0.0851	0.0822	0.0793	0.0764	0.0736	0.0709	0.0682	0.0656	0.0631
7	0.1145	0.1118	0.1091	0.1064	0.1037	0.1010	0.0982	0.0955	0.0928	0.0901
8	0.1302	0.1286	0.1269	0.1251	0.1232	0.1212	0.1191	0.1170	0.1148	0.1126
9	0.1317	0.1315	0.1311	0.1306	0.1300	0.1293	0.1284	0.1274	0.1263	0.1251
10	0.1198	0.1210	0.1219	0.1228	0.1235	0.1241	0.1245	0.1249	0.1250	0.1251
11	0.0991	0.1012	0.1031	0.1049	0.1067	0.1083	0.1098	0.1112	0.1125	0.1137
12	0.0752	0.0776	0.0799	0.0822	0.0844	0.0866	0.0888	0.0908	0.0928	0.0948
13	0.0526	0.0549	0.0572	0.0594	0.0617	0.0640	0.0662	0.0685	0.0707	0.0729
14	0.0342	0.0361	0.0380	0.0399	0.0419	0.0439	0.0459	0.0479	0.0500	0.0521
15	0.0208	0.0221	0.0235	0.0250	0.0265	0.0281	0.0297	0.0313	0.0330	0.0347
16	0.0118	0.0127	0.0137	0.0147	0.0157	0.0168	0.0180	0.0192	0.0204	0.0217
17	0.0063	0.0069	0.0075	0.0081	0.0088	0.0095	0.0103	0.0111	0.0119	0.0128
18	0.0032	0.0035	0.0039	0.0042	0.0046	0.0051	0.0055	0.0060	0.0065	0.0071
19	0.0015	0.0017	0.0019	0.0021	0.0023	0.0026	0.0028	0.0031	0.0034	0.0027
20	0.0007	0.0008	0.0009	0.0010	0.0011	0.0012	0.0014	0.0015	0.0017	0.0019
21	0.0003	0.0003	0.0004	0.0004	0.0005	0.0006	0.0006	0.0007	0.0008	0.0009
22	0.0001	0.0001	0.0002	0.0002	0.0002	0.0002	0.0003	0.0003	0.0004	0.0004
23	0.0000	0.0001	0.0001	0.0001	0.0001	0.0001	0.0001	0.0001	0.0002	0.0002
24	0.0000	0.0000	0.0000	0.0000	0.0000	0.0000	0.0000	0.0001	0.0001	0.0001

Poisson Probabilities (*Continued*)

					λ					
x	11	12	13	14	15	16	17	18	19	20
0	0.0000	0.0000	0.0000	0.0000	0.0000	0.0000	0.0000	0.0000	0.0000	0.0000
1	0.0002	0.0001	0.0000	0.0000	0.0000	0.0000	0.0000	0.0000	0.0000	0.0000
2	0.0010	0.0004	0.0002	0.0001	0.0000	0.0000	0.0000	0.0000	0.0000	0.0000
3	0.0037	0.0018	0.0008	0.0004	0.0002	0.0001	0.0000	0.0000	0.0000	0.0000
4	0.0102	0.0053	0.0027	0.0013	0.0006	0.0003	0.0001	0.0001	0.0000	0.0000
5	0.0224	0.0127	0.0070	0.0037	0.0019	0.0010	0.0005	0.0002	0.0001	0.0001
6	0.0411	0.0255	0.0152	0.0087	0.0048	0.0026	0.0014	0.0007	0.0004	0.0002
7	0.0646	0.0437	0.0281	0.0174	0.0104	0.0060	0.0034	0.0018	0.0010	0.0005
8	0.0888	0.0655	0.0457	0.0304	0.0194	0.0120	0.0072	0.0042	0.0024	0.0013
9	0.1085	0.0874	0.0661	0.0473	0.0324	0.0213	0.0135	0.0083	0.0050	0.0029
10	0.1194	0.1048	0.0859	0.0663	0.0486	0.0341	0.0230	0.0150	0.0095	0.0058
11	0.1194	0.1144	0.1015	0.0844	0.0663	0.0496	0.0355	0.0245	0.0164	0.0106
12	0.1094	0.1144	0.1099	0.0984	0.0829	0.0661	0.0504	0.0368	0.0259	0.0176
13	0.0926	0.1056	0.1099	0.1060	0.0956	0.0814	0.0658	0.0509	0.0378	0.0271
14	0.0728	0.0905	0.1021	0.1060	0.1024	0.0930	0.0800	0.0655	0.0514	0.0387
15	0.0534	0.0724	0.0885	0.0989	0.1024	0.0992	0.0906	0.0786	0.0650	0.0516
16	0.0367	0.0543	0.0719	0.0866	0.0960	0.0992	0.0963	0.0884	0.0772	0.0646
17	0.0237	0.0383	0.0550	0.0713	0.0847	0.0934	0.0963	0.0936	0.0863	0.0760
18	0.0145	0.0256	0.0397	0.0554	0.0706	0.0830	0.0909	0.0936	0.0911	0.0844
19	0.0084	0.0161	0.0272	0.0409	0.0557	0.0699	0.0814	0.0887	0.0911	0.0888
20	0.0046	0.0097	0.0177	0.0286	0.0418	0.0559	0.0692	0.0798	0.0866	0.0888
21	0.0024	0.0055	0.0109	0.0191	0.0299	0.0426	0.0560	0.0684	0.0783	0.0846
22	0.0012	0.0030	0.0065	0.0121	0.0204	0.0310	0.0433	0.0560	0.0676	0.0769
23	0.0006	0.0016	0.0037	0.0074	0.0133	0.0216	0.0320	0.0438	0.0559	0.0669
24	0.0003	0.0008	0.0020	0.0043	0.0083	0.0144	0.0226	0.0328	0.0442	0.0557
25	0.0001	0.0004	0.0010	0.0024	0.0050	0.0092	0.0154	0.0237	0.0336	0.0446
26	0.0000	0.0002	0.0005	0.0013	0.0029	0.0057	0.0101	0.0164	0.0246	0.0343
27	0.0000	0.0001	0.0002	0.0007	0.0016	0.0034	0.0063	0.0109	0.0173	0.0254
28	0.0000	0.0000	0.0001	0.0003	0.0009	0.0019	0.0038	0.0070	0.0117	0.0181
29	0.0000	0.0000	0.0001	0.0002	0.0004	0.0011	0.0023	0.0044	0.0077	0.0125
30	0.0000	0.0000	0.0000	0.0001	0.0002	0.0006	0.0013	0.0026	0.0049	0.0083
31	0.0000	0.0000	0.0000	0.0000	0.0001	0.0003	0.0007	0.0015	0.0030	0.0054
32	0.0000	0.0000	0.0000	0.0000	0.0001	0.0001	0.0004	0.0009	0.0018	0.0034
33	0.0000	0.0000	0.0000	0.0000	0.0000	0.0001	0.0002	0.0005	0.0010	0.0020
34	0.0000	0.0000	0.0000	0.0000	0.0000	0.0000	0.0001	0.0002	0.0006	0.0012
35	0.0000	0.0000	0.0000	0.0000	0.0000	0.0000	0.0000	0.0001	0.0003	0.0007
36	0.0000	0.0000	0.0000	0.0000	0.0000	0.0000	0.0000	0.0001	0.0002	0.0004
37	0.0000	0.0000	0.0000	0.0000	0.0000	0.0000	0.0000	0.0000	0.0001	0.0002
38	0.0000	0.0000	0.0000	0.0000	0.0000	0.0000	0.0000	0.0000	0.0000	0.0001
39	0.0000	0.0000	0.0000	0.0000	0.0000	0.0000	0.0000	0.0000	0.0000	0.0001

Appendix D   Areas for the Standard Normal Distribution

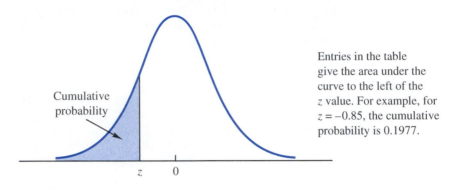

Cumulative probability

Entries in the table give the area under the curve to the left of the z value. For example, for $z = -0.85$, the cumulative probability is 0.1977.

z	0.00	0.01	0.02	0.03	0.04	0.05	0.06	0.07	0.08	0.09
−3.0	0.0013	0.0013	0.0013	0.0012	0.0012	0.0011	0.0011	0.0011	0.0010	0.0010
−2.9	0.0019	0.0018	0.0018	0.0017	0.0016	0.0016	0.0015	0.0015	0.0014	0.0014
−2.8	0.0026	0.0025	0.0024	0.0023	0.0023	0.0022	0.0021	0.0021	0.0020	0.0019
−2.7	0.0035	0.0034	0.0033	0.0032	0.0031	0.0030	0.0029	0.0028	0.0027	0.0026
−2.6	0.0047	0.0045	0.0044	0.0043	0.0041	0.0040	0.0039	0.0038	0.0037	0.0036
−2.5	0.0062	0.0060	0.0059	0.0057	0.0055	0.0054	0.0052	0.0051	0.0049	0.0048
−2.4	0.0082	0.0080	0.0078	0.0075	0.0073	0.0071	0.0069	0.0068	0.0066	0.0064
−2.3	0.0107	0.0104	0.0102	0.0099	0.0096	0.0094	0.0091	0.0089	0.0087	0.0084
−2.2	0.0139	0.0136	0.0132	0.0129	0.0125	0.0122	0.0119	0.0116	0.0113	0.0110
−2.1	0.0179	0.0174	0.0170	0.0166	0.0162	0.0158	0.0154	0.0150	0.0146	0.0143
−2.0	0.0228	0.0222	0.0217	0.0212	0.0207	0.0202	0.0197	0.0192	0.0188	0.0183
−1.9	0.0287	0.0281	0.0274	0.0268	0.0262	0.0256	0.0250	0.0244	0.0239	0.0233
−1.8	0.0359	0.0351	0.0344	0.0336	0.0329	0.0322	0.0314	0.0307	0.0301	0.0294
−1.7	0.0446	0.0436	0.0427	0.0418	0.0409	0.0401	0.0392	0.0384	0.0375	0.0367
−1.6	0.0548	0.0537	0.0526	0.0516	0.0505	0.0495	0.0485	0.0475	0.0465	0.0455
−1.5	0.0668	0.0655	0.0643	0.0630	0.0618	0.0606	0.0594	0.0582	0.0571	0.0559
−1.4	0.0808	0.0793	0.0778	0.0764	0.0749	0.0735	0.0721	0.0708	0.0694	0.0681
−1.3	0.0968	0.0951	0.0934	0.0918	0.0901	0.0885	0.0869	0.0853	0.0838	0.0823
−1.2	0.1151	0.1131	0.1112	0.1093	0.1075	0.1056	0.1038	0.1020	0.1003	0.0985
−1.1	0.1357	0.1335	0.1314	0.1292	0.1271	0.1251	0.1230	0.1210	0.1190	0.1170
−1.0	0.1587	0.1562	0.1539	0.1515	0.1492	0.1469	0.1446	0.1423	0.1401	0.1379
−0.9	0.1841	0.1814	0.1788	0.1762	0.1736	0.1711	0.1685	0.1660	0.1635	0.1611
−0.8	0.2119	0.2090	0.2061	0.2033	0.2005	0.1977	0.1949	0.1922	0.1894	0.1867
−0.7	0.2420	0.2389	0.2358	0.2327	0.2296	0.2266	0.2236	0.2206	0.2177	0.2148
−0.6	0.2743	0.2709	0.2676	0.2643	0.2611	0.2578	0.2546	0.2514	0.2483	0.2451
−0.5	0.3085	0.3050	0.3015	0.2981	0.2946	0.2912	0.2877	0.2843	0.2810	0.2776
−0.4	0.3446	0.3409	0.3372	0.3336	0.3300	0.3264	0.3228	0.3192	0.3156	0.3121
−0.3	0.3821	0.3783	0.3745	0.3707	0.3669	0.3632	0.3594	0.3557	0.3520	0.3483
−0.2	0.4207	0.4168	0.4129	0.4090	0.4052	0.4013	0.3974	0.3936	0.3897	0.3859
−0.1	0.4602	0.4562	0.4522	0.4483	0.4443	0.4404	0.4364	0.4325	0.4286	0.4247
−0.0	0.5000	0.4960	0.4920	0.4880	0.4840	0.4801	0.4761	0.4721	0.4681	0.4641

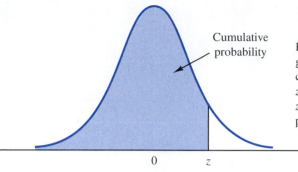

Cumulative probability

Entries in the table give the area under the curve to the left of the z value. For example, for $z = 1.25$, the cumulative probability is 0.8944.

z	0.00	0.01	0.02	0.03	0.04	0.05	0.06	0.07	0.08	0.09
0.0	0.5000	0.5040	0.5080	0.5120	0.5160	0.5199	0.5239	0.5279	0.5319	0.5359
0.1	0.5398	0.5438	0.5478	0.5517	0.5557	0.5596	0.5636	0.5675	0.5714	0.5753
0.2	0.5793	0.5832	0.5871	0.5910	0.5948	0.5987	0.6026	0.6064	0.6103	0.6141
0.3	0.6179	0.6217	0.6255	0.6293	0.6331	0.6368	0.6406	0.6443	0.6480	0.6517
0.4	0.6554	0.6591	0.6628	0.6664	0.6700	0.6736	0.6772	0.6808	0.6844	0.6879
0.5	0.6915	0.6950	0.6985	0.7019	0.7054	0.7088	0.7123	0.7157	0.7190	0.7224
0.6	0.7257	0.7291	0.7324	0.7357	0.7389	0.7422	0.7454	0.7486	0.7517	0.7549
0.7	0.7580	0.7611	0.7642	0.7673	0.7704	0.7734	0.7764	0.7794	0.7823	0.7852
0.8	0.7881	0.7910	0.7939	0.7967	0.7995	0.8023	0.8051	0.8078	0.8106	0.8133
0.9	0.8159	0.8186	0.8212	0.8238	0.8264	0.8289	0.8315	0.8340	0.8365	0.8389
1.0	0.8413	0.8438	0.8461	0.8485	0.8508	0.8531	0.8554	0.8577	0.8599	0.8621
1.1	0.8643	0.8665	0.8686	0.8708	0.8729	0.8749	0.8770	0.8790	0.8810	0.8830
1.2	0.8849	0.8869	0.8888	0.8907	0.8925	0.8944	0.8962	0.8980	0.8997	0.9015
1.3	0.9032	0.9049	0.9066	0.9082	0.9099	0.9115	0.9131	0.9147	0.9162	0.9177
1.4	0.9192	0.9207	0.9222	0.9236	0.9251	0.9265	0.9279	0.9292	0.9306	0.9319
1.5	0.9332	0.9345	0.9357	0.9370	0.9382	0.9394	0.9406	0.9418	0.9429	0.9441
1.6	0.9452	0.9463	0.9474	0.9484	0.9495	0.9505	0.9515	0.9525	0.9535	0.9545
1.7	0.9554	0.9564	0.9573	0.9582	0.9591	0.9599	0.9608	0.9616	0.9625	0.9633
1.8	0.9641	0.9649	0.9656	0.9664	0.9671	0.9678	0.9686	0.9693	0.9699	0.9706
1.9	0.9713	0.9719	0.9726	0.9732	0.9738	0.9744	0.9750	0.9756	0.9761	0.9767
2.0	0.9772	0.9778	0.9783	0.9788	0.9793	0.9798	0.9803	0.9808	0.9812	0.9817
2.1	0.9821	0.9826	0.9830	0.9834	0.9838	0.9842	0.9846	0.9850	0.9854	0.9857
2.2	0.9861	0.9864	0.9868	0.9871	0.9875	0.9878	0.9881	0.9884	0.9887	0.9890
2.3	0.9893	0.9896	0.9898	0.9901	0.9904	0.9906	0.9909	0.9911	0.9913	0.9913
2.4	0.9918	0.9920	0.9922	0.9925	0.9927	0.9929	0.9931	0.9932	0.9934	0.9936
2.5	0.9938	0.9940	0.9941	0.9943	0.9945	0.9946	0.9948	0.9949	0.9951	0.9952
2.6	0.9953	0.9955	0.9956	0.9957	0.9959	0.9960	0.9961	0.9962	0.9963	0.9964
2.7	0.9965	0.9966	0.9967	0.9968	0.9969	0.9970	0.9971	0.9972	0.9973	0.9974
2.8	0.9974	0.9975	0.9976	0.9977	0.9977	0.9978	0.9979	0.9979	0.9980	0.9981
2.9	0.9981	0.9982	0.9982	0.9983	0.9984	0.9984	0.9985	0.9985	0.9986	0.9986
3.0	0.9986	0.9987	0.9987	0.9988	0.9988	0.9989	0.9989	0.9989	0.9990	0.9990

Appendix E   Values of $e^{-\lambda}$

λ	$e^{-\lambda}$	λ	$e^{-\lambda}$	λ	$e^{-\lambda}$
0.05	0.9512	2.05	0.1287	4.05	0.0174
0.10	0.9048	2.10	0.1225	4.10	0.0166
0.15	0.8607	2.15	0.1165	4.15	0.0158
0.20	0.8187	2.20	0.1108	4.20	0.0150
0.25	0.7788	2.25	0.1054	4.25	0.0143
0.30	0.7408	2.30	0.1003	4.30	0.0136
0.35	0.7047	2.35	0.0954	4.35	0.0129
0.40	0.6703	2.40	0.0907	4.40	0.0123
0.45	0.6376	2.45	0.0863	4.45	0.0117
0.50	0.6065	2.50	0.0821	4.50	0.0111
0.55	0.5769	2.55	0.0781	4.55	0.0106
0.60	0.5488	2.60	0.0743	4.60	0.0101
0.65	0.5220	2.65	0.0707	4.65	0.0096
0.70	0.4966	2.70	0.0672	4.70	0.0091
0.75	0.4724	2.75	0.0639	4.75	0.0087
0.80	0.4493	2.80	0.0608	4.80	0.0082
0.85	0.4274	2.85	0.0578	4.85	0.0078
0.90	0.4066	2.90	0.0550	4.90	0.0074
0.95	0.3867	2.95	0.0523	4.95	0.0071
1.00	0.3679	3.00	0.0498	5.00	0.0067
1.05	0.3499	3.05	0.0474	5.05	0.0064
1.10	0.3329	3.10	0.0450	5.10	0.0061
1.15	0.3166	3.15	0.0429	5.15	0.0058
1.20	0.3012	3.20	0.0408	5.20	0.0055
1.25	0.2865	3.25	0.0388	5.25	0.0052
1.30	0.2725	3.30	0.0369	5.30	0.0050
1.35	0.2592	3.35	0.0351	5.35	0.0047
1.40	0.2466	3.40	0.0334	5.40	0.0045
1.45	0.2346	3.45	0.0317	5.45	0.0043
1.50	0.2231	3.50	0.0302	5.50	0.0041
1.55	0.2122	3.55	0.0287	5.55	0.0039
1.60	0.2019	3.60	0.0273	5.60	0.0037
1.65	0.1920	3.65	0.0260	5.65	0.0035
1.70	0.1827	3.70	0.0247	5.70	0.0033
1.75	0.1738	3.75	0.0235	5.75	0.0032
1.80	0.1653	3.80	0.0224	5.80	0.0030
1.85	0.1572	3.85	0.0213	5.85	0.0029
1.90	0.1496	3.90	0.0202	5.90	0.0027
1.95	0.1423	3.95	0.0193	5.95	0.0026
2.00	0.1353	4.00	0.0183	6.00	0.0025
				7.00	0.0009
				8.00	0.000335
				9.00	0.000123
				10.00	0.000045

Chapter 1 Introduction

Churchman, C. W., R. L. Ackoff, and E. L. Arnoff. *Introduction to Operations Research.* Wiley, 1957.

Horner, Peter. "The Sabre Story." *OR/MS Today* (June 2000).

Leon, Linda, Z. Przasnyski, and K. C. Seal. "Spreadsheets and OR/MS Models: An End-User Perspective." *Interfaces* (March/April 1996).

Powell, S. G. "Innovative Approaches to Management Science." *OR/MS Today* (October 1996).

Savage, S. "Weighing the Pros and Cons of Decision Technology and Spreadsheets." *OR/MS Today* (February 1997).

Winston, W. L. "The Teachers' Forum: Management Science with Spreadsheets for MBAs at Indiana University." *Interfaces* (March/April 1996).

Chapters 2 and 3 Probability

Anderson, D. R., D. J. Sweeney, and T. A. Williams. *Statistics for Business and Economics,* 10th ed. South-Western, 2008.

Hogg, R. V., and E. A. Tanis. *Probability and Statistical Inference,* 6th ed. Prentice Hall, 2001.

Ross, S. M. *Introduction to Probability Models,* 7th ed. Academic Press, 1993.

Wackerly, D. D., W. Mendenhall, and R. L. Scheaffer. *Mathematical Statistics with Applications,* 6th ed. Duxbury Press, 2002.

Chapters 4 and 5 Decision Analysis and Game Theory

Clemen, R. T., and T. Reilly. *Making Hard Decisions with Decision Tools.* Duxbury Press, 2001.

Davis, Morton D. *Game Theory: A Nontechnical Introduction.* Dover, 1997.

Goodwin, P., and G. Wright. *Decision Analysis for Management Judgment,* 2d ed. Wiley, 1999.

McMillian, John. *Games, Strategies, and Managers.* Oxford University Press, 1992.

Myerson, Roger B. *Game Theory: Analysis of Conflict.* Harvard University Press, 1997.

Osborne, Martin J. *An Introduction to Game Theory.* Oxford University Press, 2004.

Pratt, J. W., H. Raiffa, and R. Schlaiter. *Introduction to Statistical Decision Theory.* MIT Press, 1995.

Raiffa, H. *Decision Analysis.* McGraw-Hill, 1997.

Schlaiter, R. *Analysis of Decisions Under Uncertainty.* Krieger, 1978.

Chapter 6 Forecasting

Bowerman, B. L., and R. T. O'Connell. *Forecasting and Time Series: An Applied Approach,* 3d ed. Duxbury Press, 1993.

Box, G. E. P., G. M. Jenkins, and G. C. Reinsel. *Time Series Analysis: Forecasting and Control,* 3d ed. Prentice Hall, 1994.

Hanke, J. E., and A. G. Reitsch. *Business Forecasting,* 6th ed. Prentice Hall, 1998.

Makridakis, S. G., S. C. Wheelwright, and R. J. Hyndman. *Forecasting: Methods and Applications,* 3d ed. Wiley, 1997.

Wilson, J. H., and B. Keating. *Business Forecasting,* 3d ed. Irwin, 1998.

Chapters 7 to 11 Linear Programming, Distribution and Network Models, Integer Programming Problems

Ahuja, R. K., T. L. Magnanti, and J. B. Orlin. *Network Flows, Theory, Algorithms, and Applications.* Prentice-Hall 1993.

Bazarra, M. S., J. J. Jarvis, and H. D. Sherali. *Linear Programming and Network Flows,* 2d ed. Wiley, 1990.

Dantzig, G. B. *Linear Programming and Extensions.* Princeton University Press, 1963.

Greenberg, H. J. "How to Analyze the Results of Linear Programs—Part 1: Preliminaries." *Interfaces* 23, no. 4 (July/August 1993): 56–67.

Greenberg, H. J. "How to Analyze the Results of Linear Programs—Part 2: Price Interpretation." *Interfaces* 23, no. 5 (September/October 1993): 97–114.

Greenberg, H. J. "How to Analyze the Results of Linear Programs—Part 3: Infeasibility Diagnosis." *Interfaces* 23, no. 6 (November/December 1993): 120–139.

Lillien, G., and A. Rangaswamy. *Marketing Engineering: Computer-Assisted Marketing Analysis and Planning.* Addison-Wesley, 1998.

Nemhauser, G. L., and L. A. Wolsey. *Integer and Combinatorial Optimization.* Wiley, 1988.

Schrage, L. *Optimization Modeling with LINGO,* 4th ed. LINDO Systems Inc., 2000.

Winston, W. L., and S. C. Albright. *Practical Management Science,* 2d ed. Duxbury Press, 2001.

Chapter 12 Advanced Optimization Applications

Bazarra, M. S., H. D. Sherali, and C. M. Shetty. *Nonlinear Programming Theory and Applications*. Wiley, 1993.

Benninga, Simon. *Financial Modeling*. The MIT Press, 2000.

Luenberger, D. *Linear and Nonlinear Programming*, 2d ed. Addison-Wesley Publishing Company, 1984.

Rardin, R. L. *Optimization in Operations Research*. Prentice-Hall, 1998.

Chapter 13 Project Scheduling: PERT/CPM

Moder, J. J., C. R. Phillips, and E. W. Davis. *Project Management with CPM, PERT and Precedence Diagramming*, 3d ed. Blitz, 1995.

Wiest, J., and F. Levy. *Management Guide to PERT-CPM*, 2d ed. Prentice Hall, 1977.

Chapter 14 Inventory Models

Fogarty, D. W., J. H. Blackstone, and T. R. Hoffman. *Production and Inventory Management*, 2d ed. South-Western, 1990.

Hillier, F., and G. J. Lieberman. *Introduction to Operations Research*, 7th ed. McGraw-Hill, 2000.

Narasimhan, S. L., D. W. McLeavey, and P. B. Lington. *Production Planning and Inventory Control*, 2d ed. Prentice Hall, 1995.

Orlicky, J., and G. W. Plossi. *Orlicky's Material Requirements Planning*. McGraw-Hill, 1994.

Vollmann, T. E., W. L. Berry, and D. C. Whybark. *Manufacturing Planning and Control Systems*, 4th ed. McGraw-Hill, 1997.

Zipkin, P. H. *Foundations of Inventory Management*. McGraw-Hill/Irwin, 2000.

Chapter 15 Waiting Line Models

Bunday, B. D. *An Introduction to Queueing Theory*. Wiley, 1996.

Gross, D., and C. M. Harris. *Fundamentals of Queueing Theory*, 3d ed. Wiley, 1997.

Hall, R. W. *Queueing Methods: For Service and Manufacturing*. Prentice Hall, 1991.

Hillier, F., and G. J. Lieberman. *Introduction to Operations Research*, 7th ed. McGraw-Hill, 2000.

Kao, E. P. C. *An Introduction to Stochastic Processes*. Duxbury Press, 1996.

Chapter 16 Simulation

Banks, J., J. S. Carson, and B. L. Nelson. *Discrete-Event System Simulation*, 2d ed. Prentice Hall, 1995.

Fishwick, P. A. *Simulation Model Design and Execution: Building Digital Worlds*. Prentice Hall, 1995.

Harrell, C. R., and K. Tumau. *Simulation Made Easy: A Manager's Guide*. Institute of Industrial Engineers, 1996.

Kelton, W. D., R. P. Sadowski, and D. T. Sturrock. *Simulation with Arena*, 4th ed. McGraw-Hill, 2007.

Law, A. M., and W. D. Kelton. *Simulation Modeling and Analysis*, 3d ed. McGraw-Hill, 1999.

Pidd, M. *Computer Simulation in Management Science*, 4th ed. Wiley, 1998.

Thesen, A., and L. E. Travis. *Simulation for Decision Making*. Wadsworth, 1992.

Chapter 17 Markov Processes

Bharucha-Reid, A. T. *Elements of the Theory of Markov Processes and Their Applications*. Dover, 1997.

Filar, J. A., and K. Vrieze. *Competitive Markov Decision Processes*. Springer-Verlag, 1996.

Norris, J. *Markov Chains*. Cambridge, 1997.

Chapter 1

2. Define the problem; identify the alternatives; determine the criteria; evaluate the alternatives; choose an alternative.

4. A quantitative approach should be considered because the problem is large, complex, important, new, and repetitive.

6. Quicker to formulate, easier to solve, and/or more easily understood

8. a. Max $10x + 5y$
  s.t.
$$5x + 2y \leq 40$$
$$x \geq 0, y \geq 0$$
  b. Controllable inputs: x and y
  Uncontrollable inputs: profit $(10, 5)$, labor-hours $(5, 2)$, and labor-hour availability (40)
  c. See Figure G1.8c.
  d. $x = 0, y = 20$; Profit $= \$100$ (solution by trial and error)
  e. Deterministic

10. a. Total units received $= x + y$
  b. Total cost $= 0.20x + 0.25y$
  c. $x + y = 5000$
  d. $x \leq 4000$ Kansas City
  $y \leq 3000$ Minneapolis
  e. Min $0.20x + 0.25y$
  s.t.
$$x + \quad y = 5000$$
$$x \quad\quad \leq 4000$$
$$y \leq 3000$$
$$x, y \geq 0$$

FIGURE G1.8c SOLUTION

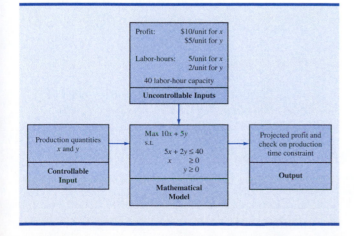

12. a. $TC = 1000 + 30x$
  b. $P = 40x - (1000 + 30x) = 10x - 1000$
  c. Break even when $P = 0$
  Thus, $10x - 1000 = 0$
$$10x = 1000$$
$$x = 100$$

14. a. 4706
  b. Loss of $12,000
  c. $23
  d. $11,800

16. a. Max $6x + 4y$
  b. $50x + 30y \leq 80,000$
$$50x \quad\quad \leq 50,000$$
$$30y \leq 45,000$$

Chapter 2

1. a. Record the number of persons waiting at the X-ray department at 9:00 A.M.
  b. The experimental outcomes (sample points) are the number of people waiting: 0, 1, 2, 3, and 4. (*Note:* Although it is theoretically possible for more than four people to be waiting, we use what has actually been observed to define the experimental outcomes.)
  c.

Number Waiting	Probability
0	0.10
1	0.25
2	0.30
3	0.20
4	0.15
Total	1.00

  d. The relative frequency method

2. a. Choose a person at random, and have him/her taste the four blends of coffee and state a preference.
  b. Assign a probability of $1/4$ to each blend, using the classical method of equally likely outcomes.
  c.

Blend	Probability
1	0.20
2	0.30
3	0.35
4	0.15
Total	1.00

The relative frequency method was used.

4. a. Use the relative frequency approach:
$P(\text{California}) = 1434/2374 = 0.60$

b. Number not from 4 states = $2374 - 1434 - 390 - 217 - 112 = 221$
$P(\text{Not from 4 States}) = 221/2374 = 0.09$

c. $P(\text{Not in Early Stages}) = 1 - 0.22 = 0.78$

d. Estimate of number of Massachusetts companies in early stage of development = $(0.22)390 \approx 86$

e. If we assume the size of the awards did not differ by states, we can multiply the probability an award went to Colorado by the total venture funds disbursed to get an estimate:

Estimate of Colorado funds = $(112/2374)(\$32.4)$
= \$1.53 billion

(*Note:* The actual amount going to Colorado was \$1.74 billion.)

6. a. $P(A) = P(150 - 199) + P(200 \text{ and over})$
$$= \frac{26}{100} + \frac{5}{100}$$
$$= 0.31$$

b. $P(B) = P(\text{less than } 50) + P(50 - 99) + P(100 - 149)$
$= 0.13 + 0.22 + 0.34$
$= 0.69$

7. a. $P(A) = 0.40, P(B) = 0.40, P(C) = 0.60$

b. $P(A < B) = P(E_1, E_2, E_3, E_4) = 0.80.$
Yes, $P(A < B) = P(A) + P(B)$

c. $A^c = \{E_3, E_4, E_5\}; C^c = \{E_1, E_4\}; P(A^c) = 0.60;$
$P(C^c) = 0.40$

d. $A < B^c = \{E_1, E_2, E_5\}; P(A < B^c) = 0.60$

e. $P(B < C) = P(E_2, E_3, E_4, E_5) = 0.80$

8. a. $0.5, 0.4, 0.2$

b. 0.70

c. 0.30

10. $P(\text{Defective and Minor}) = 4/25$
$P(\text{Defective and Major}) = 2/25$
$P(\text{Defective}) = (4/25) + (2/25) = 6/25$
$P(\text{Major Defect} \mid \text{Defective}) = P(\text{Defective and Major})/$
$P(\text{Defective}) = (2/25)/(6/25) = 2/6 = 1/3.$

12. a. $P(A \mid B) = \dfrac{P(A \cap B)}{P(B)} = \dfrac{0.40}{0.60} = 0.6667$

b. $P(B \mid A) = \dfrac{P(A \cap B)}{P(A)} = \dfrac{0.40}{0.50} = 0.80$

c. No, because $P(A \mid B) \neq P(A)$

13. a.

	Reason for Applying			
	Quality	**Cost/ Convenience**	**Other**	**Total**
Full Time	0.218	0.204	0.039	0.461
Part Time	0.208	0.307	0.024	0.539
Total	0.426	0.511	0.063	1.000

b. A student will most likely cite cost or convenience as the first reason: probability = 0.511; school quality is the first reason cited by the second largest number of students: probability = 0.426.

c. $P(\text{Quality} \mid \text{Full Time}) = 0.218/0.461 = 0.473$

d. $P(\text{Quality} \mid \text{Part Time}) = 0.208/0.539 = 0.386$

e. $P(B) = 0.426$ and $P(B \mid A) = 0.473$
Because $P(B) \neq P(B \mid A)$, the events are dependent.

14.

	$0–$499	**$500–$999**	**$\geq $1000**	
<2 yrs	120	240	90	450
≥2 yrs	75	275	200	550
	195	515	290	1000

	$0–$499	**$500–$999**	**$\geq $1000**	
<2 yrs	0.12	0.24	0.09	0.45
≥2 yrs	0.075	0.275	0.2	0.55
	0.195	0.515	0.29	1.00

a. $P(< 2 \text{ yrs}) = 0.45$

b. $P(\geq \$1000) = 0.29$

c. $P(2 \text{ accounts have} \geq \$1000) = (0.29)(0.29) = 0.0841$

d. $P(\$500 - \$999 \mid \geq 2 \text{ yrs}) = P(\$500 - \$999 \text{ and } \geq 2 \text{ yrs})/P(\geq 2\text{yrs}) = 0.275/0.55 = 0.5$

e. $P(< 2 \text{ yrs and} \geq \$1000) = 0.09$

f. $P(\geq 2 \text{ yrs} \mid \$500 - \$999) = 0.275/0.515 = 0.533981$

16. a. 0.19

b. 0.71

c. 0.29

18. a. $0.25, 0.40, 0.10$

b. 0.25

c. Independent; program does not help

20. a. $P(B \cap A_1) = P(A_1)P(B \mid A_1) = (0.20)(0.50) = 0.10$
$P(B \cap A_2) = P(A_2)P(B \mid A_2) = (0.50)(0.40) = 0.20$
$P(B \cap A_3) = P(A_3)P(B \mid A_3) = (0.30)(0.30) = 0.09$

b. $P(A_2 \mid B) = \dfrac{0.20}{0.10 + 0.20 + 0.09} = 0.51$

c.

Events	$P(A_i)$	$P(B \mid A_i)$	$P(A_i \cap B)$	$P(A_i \mid B)$
A_1	0.20	0.50	0.10	0.26
A_2	0.50	0.40	0.20	0.51
A_3	0.30	0.30	0.09	0.23
	1.00		0.39	1.00

22. a. 0.40

b. 0.67

24. Let S = small car
S^c = other type of vehicle
F = accident leads to fatality for vehicle occupant
We have $P(S) = 0.18$, so $P(S^c) = 0.82$; $P(F \mid S) = 0.128$ and $P(F \mid S^c) = 0.05$
Using the tabular form of Bayes' theorem provides:

Events	Prior Proba-bilities	Conditional Proba-bilities	Joint Proba-bilities	Posterior Proba-bilities
S	0.18	0.128	0.023	0.36
S^c	0.82	0.050	0.041	0.64
	1.00		0.064	1.00

From the posterior probability column, we have $P(S \mid F) = 0.36$; so, if an accident leads to a fatality, the probability a small car was involved is 0.36.

25. a. P(defective part) = 0.0065 (see below)

Events	$P(A_i)$	$(PD \mid A_i)$	$P(A_i \cap D)$	$P(A_i \cap D)$
Supplier A	0.60	0.0025	0.0015	0.23
Supplier B	0.30	0.0100	0.0030	0.46
Supplier C	0.10	0.020	0.0020	0.31
	1.00		$P(D) = 0.0065$	1.00

b. Supplier B (prob. = 0.46) is the most likely source.

26. a. $P(D_1 \mid S_1) = 0.2195$, $P(D_2 \mid S_1) = 0.7805$
b. $P(D_1 \mid S_2) = 0.50$, $P(D_2 \mid S_2) = 0.50$
c. $P(D_1 \mid S_3) = 0.8824$, $P(D_2 \mid S_3) = 0.1176$
d. 0.1582 and 0.8418

Chapter 3

1. a. Values: 0, 1, 2, . . . , 20 discrete
b. Values: 0, 1, 2, . . . discrete
c. Values: 0, 1, 2, . . . , 50 discrete
d. Values: $0 \leq x \leq 8$ continuous
e. Values: $x \geq 0$ continuous

2. a. 0.05; probability of a $200,000 profit
b. 0.70
c. 0.40

3. a.

x	$f(x)$
1	3/20 = 0.15
2	5/20 = 0.25
3	8/20 = 0.40
4	4/20 = 0.20
	Total 1.00

b.

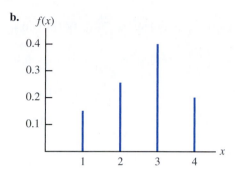

c. $f(x) \geq 0$ for x = 1, 2, 3, 4
$\Sigma f(x) = 1$

4. a.

x	$f(x)$	$xf(x)$
3	0.25	0.75
6	0.50	3.00
9	0.25	2.25
Totals	1.00	6.00

$E(x) = \mu = 6.00$

b.

x	$x - \mu$	$(x - \mu)^2$	$f(x)$	$(x - \mu)^2 f(x)$
3	−3	9	0.25	2.25
6	0	0	0.50	0.00
9	3	9	0.25	2.25
				4.50

$\text{Var}(x) = \sigma^2 = 4.50$

c. $\sigma = \sqrt{4.50} = 2.12$

6. a.

x	$f(x)$
0	0.04
1	0.34
2	0.41
3	0.18
4+	0.04

b. $E(x) = 1.84$; $\text{Var}(x) = 0.79$

c.

y	$f(y)$
0	0.00
1	0.03
2	0.23
3	0.52
4+	0.22

d. $E(y) = 2.93$; $\text{Var}(y) = 0.59$
e. More bedrooms in owner-occupied houses

8. a. Medium 145; large 140; prefer medium
b. Medium 2725; large 12,400; prefer medium

9. a. $f(1) = \binom{2}{1}(0.4)^1(0.6)^1 = \dfrac{2!}{1!1!}(0.4)(0.6) = 0.48$

b. $f(0) = \binom{2}{0}(0.4)^0(0.6)^2 = \dfrac{2!}{0!2!}(1)(0.36) = 0.36$

c. $f(2) = \binom{2}{2}(0.4)^2(0.6)^0 = \dfrac{2!}{2!0!}(0.16)(1) = 0.16$

d. $P(x \geq 1) = f(1) + f(2) = 0.48 + 0.16 = 0.64$

e. $E(x) = np = 2(0.4) = 0.8$
$Var(x) = np(1 - p) = 2(0.4)(0.6) = 0.48$
$\sigma = \sqrt{0.48} = 0.6928$

10. a. $f(0) = 0.3487$
b. $f(2) = 0.1937$
c. 0.9298
d. 0.6513
e. 1
f. $\sigma_2 = 0.9000, \sigma = 0.9487$

12. a. Probability of a defective part being produced must be 0.03 for each trial; trials must be independent.
b. Two outcomes result in exactly one defect.
c. $P(\text{no defects}) = (0.97)(0.97) = 0.9409$
$P(1 \text{ defect}) = 2(0.03)(0.97) = 0.0582$
$P(2 \text{ defects}) = (0.03)(0.03) = 0.0009$

14. a. $f(x) = \dfrac{2^x e^{-2}}{x!}$

b. $\mu = 6$ for 3 time periods

c. $f(x) = \dfrac{6^x e^{-6}}{x!}$

d. $f(2) = \dfrac{2^2 e^{-2}}{2!} = \dfrac{4(0.1353)}{2} = 0.2706$

e. $f(6) = \dfrac{6^6 e^{-6}}{6!} = 0.1606$

f. $f(5) = \dfrac{4^5 e^{-4}}{5!} = 0.1563$

16. a. 0.0009
b. 0.9927
c. 0.0302
d. 0.8271

18. a.

b. $P(x = 1.25) = 0$; the probability of any single point is zero because the area under the curve above any single point is zero.
c. $P(1.0 \leq x \leq 1.25) = 2(0.25) = 0.50$
d. $P(1.2 < x < 1.5) = 2(0.30) = 0.60$

20. a.

b. 0.50
c. 0.30
d. 0.40

21. a. $P(0 \leq z \leq 0.83) = 0.7967 - 0.5000 = 0.2967$
b. $P(-1.57 \leq z \leq 0) = 0.5000 - 0.0582 = 0.4418$
c. $P(z > 0.44) = 1.0000 - 0.6700 = 0.2300$
d. $P(z \geq -0.23) = 1.0000 - 0.4090 = 0.5910$
e. $P(z < 1.20) = 0.8849$
f. $P(z < -0.71) = 0.2389$

22. a. 1.96
b. 1.96
c. 0.61
d. 1.12
e. 0.44
f. 0.44

23. a. Area $= 0.2119 \quad z = -0.80$
b. Area outside the interval 0.0970 must be split between the two tails.
Cumulative probability $= 0.5(0.0970) + 0.9030 = 0.9515 \quad z = 1.66$
c. Area outside the interval 0.7948 must be split between the two tails.
Cumulative probability $= 0.5(0.7948) + 0.2052 = 0.6026 \quad z = 0.26$
d. Area $= 0.9948 \quad z = 2.56$
e. Area $= 1.0000 - 0.6915 = 0.3085 \quad z = -0.50$

24. a. 0.3830
b. 0.1056
c. 0.0062
d. 0.1603

26. a. 0.7745
b. 36.32 days
c. 19%

28. $\mu = 19.23$

29. a. $P(x \leq x_0) = 1 - e^{-x_0/3}$
b. $P(x \leq 2) = 1 - e^{-2/3} = 1 - 0.5134 = 0.4866$
c. $P(x \geq 3) = 1 - P(x \leq 3) = 1 - (1 - e^{-3/3}) = e^{-1} = 0.3679$
d. $P(x \leq 5) = 1 - e^{-5/3} = 1 - 0.1889 = 0.8111$
e. $P(2 \leq x \leq 5) = P(x \leq 5) - P(x \leq 2) = 0.8111 - 0.4866 = 0.3245$

30. a. 0.3935
b. 0.2231
c. 0.3834

31. a.

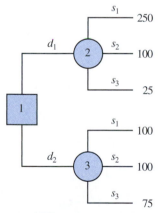

b. $P(x \leq 12) = 1 - e^{-12/12} = 0.6321$

c. $P(x \leq 6) = 1 - e^{-6/12} = 0.3935$

d. $P(x \geq 30) = 1 - P(x < 30) = 1 - (1 - e^{-30/12}) = 0.0821$

32. a. 50 hours

b. 0.3935

c. 0.1353

34. a. 0.5130

b. 0.1655

c. 0.3679

Chapter 4

1. a.

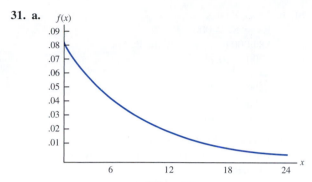

b.

Decision	Maximum Profit	Minimum Profit
d_1	250	25
d_2	100	75

Optimistic approach: Select d_1
Conservative approach: Select d_2
Regret or opportunity loss table:

Decision	s_1	s_2	s_3
d_1	0	0	50
d_2	150	0	0

Maximum regret: 50 for d_1 and 150 for d_2; select d_1

2. a. Optimistic: d_1
Conservative: d_3
Minimax regret: d_3

c. Optimistic: d_1
Conservative: d_2 or d_3
Minimax regret: d_2

3. a. Decision: Choose the best plant size from the two alternatives—a small plant and a large plant.
Chance event: market demand for the new product line with three possible outcomes (states of nature): low, medium, and high

b. Influence Diagram:

c.

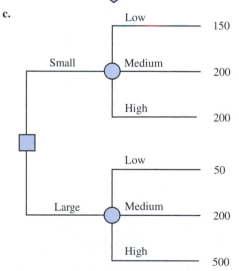

d.

Decision	Maximum Profit	Minimum Profit	Maximum Regret
Small	200	150	300
Large	500	50	100

Optimistic Approach: Large plant
Conservative Approach: Small plant
Minimax Regret: Large plant

4. a. Decision: Which lease option to choose
Chance event: Miles driven

b.

Annual Miles Driven			
	12,000	15,000	18,000
Forno	10,764	12,114	13,464
Midtown	11,160	11,160	12,960
Hopkins	11,700	11,700	11,700

c. Optimistic: Forno Saab
Conservative: Hopkins Automotive
Minimax: Hopkins Automotive
d. Midtown Motors
e. Most likely: $11,160; Probability = 0.9
f. Midtown Motors or Hopkins Automotive

5. a. $EV(d_1) = 0.65(250) + 0.15(100) + 0.20(25) = 182.5$
$EV(d_2) = 0.65(100) + 0.15(100) + 0.20(75) = 95$
The optimal decision is d_1.

6. a. Pharmaceuticals; 3.4%
b. Financial; 4.6%

7. a. EV(own staff) = 0.2(650) + 0.5(650) + 0.3(600) = 635
EV(outside vendor) = 0.2(900) + 0.5(600)
             + 0.3(300) = 570
EV(combination) = 0.2(800) + 0.5(650) + 0.3(500)
             = 635

Optimal decision: hire an outside vendor with an expected cost of $570,000

b.

	Cost	Probability
Own staff	300	0.3
Outside vendor	600	0.5
Combination	900	0.2
		1.0

8. a. $EV(d_1) = p(10) + (1 - p)(1) = 9p + 1$
$EV(d_2) = p(4) + (1 - p)(3) = 1p + 3$

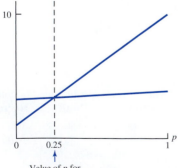

9p + 1 = 1p + 3 and hence p = 0.25
d_2 is optimal for $p \geq 0.25$, d_1 is optimal for $p \geq 0.25$
b. d_2
c. As long as the payoff for $s_1 \geq 2$, then d_2 is optimal.

10. b. Space Pirates
EV = $724,000
$84,000 better than Battle Pacific
c. $200   0.18
$400   0.32
$800   0.30
$1600   0.20
d. P(Competition) > 0.7273

12. a. Decision: Whether to lengthen the runway
Chance Event: The location decisions of Air Express and DRI
Consequence: Annual revenue
b. $255,000
c. $270,000
d. No
e. Lengthen the runway.

14. a. If s_1, then d_1; if s_2, then d_1 or d_2; if s_3, then d_2
b. EvwPI = 0.65(250) + 0.15(100) + 0.20(75) = 192.5
c. From the solution to Problem 5, we know that EV(d_1) = 182.5 and EV(d_2) = 95; thus, recommended decision is d_1; hence, EvwoPI = 182.5.
d. EVPI = EvwPI − EvwoPI = 192.5 − 182.5 = 10

16. a.

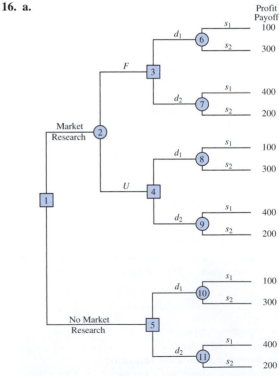

b. EV (node 6) = 0.57(100) + 0.43(300) = 186
EV (node 7) = 0.57(400) + 0.43(200) = 314
EV (node 8) = 0.18(100) + 0.82(300) = 264
EV (node 9) = 0.18(400) + 0.82(200) = 236
EV (node 10) = 0.40(100) + 0.60(300) = 220
EV (node 11) = 0.40(400) + 0.60(200) = 280

EV (node 3) $= \text{Max}(186, 314) = 314 \, d_2$
EV (node 4) $= \text{Max}(264, 236) = 264 \, d_1$
EV (node 5) $= \text{Max}(220, 280) = 280 \, d_2$
EV (node 2) $= 0.56(314) + 0.44(264) = 292$
EV (node 1) $= \text{Max}(292, 280) = 292$
∴ Market Research
    If favorable, decision d_2
    If unfavorable, decision d_1

18. a. $5000 - 200 - 2000 - 150 = 2650$
$3000 - 200 - 2000 - 150 = 650$

b. Expected values at nodes:
    8: 2350   5: 2350   9: 1100
    6: 1150   10: 2000   7: 2000
    4: 1870   3: 2000   2: 1560
    1: 1560

c. Cost would have to decrease by at least $130,000.

d.

Payoff (in millions)	Probability
−$200	0.20
800	0.32
2800	0.48
	1.00

20. b. If Do Not Review, Accept
    If Review and F, Accept
    If Review and U, Accept
    Always Accept

c. Do not review; EVSI = $0
d. $87,500; better method of predicting success

22. a. Order 2 lots; $60,000
b. If E, order 2 lots
    If V, order 1 lot
    EV = $60,500
c. EVPI = $14,000
    EVSI = $500
    Efficiency = 3.6%
    Yes, use consultant.

23.

State of Nature	$P(s_j)$	$P(I/s_j)$	$P(I \cap s_j)$	$P(s_j/I)$
s_1	0.2	0.10	0.020	0.1905
s_2	0.5	0.05	0.025	0.2381
s_3	0.3	0.20	0.060	0.5714
	1.0		$P(I) = 0.105$	1.0000

24. a. 0.695, 0.215, 0.090
    0.98, 0.02
    0.79, 0.21
    0.00, 1.00

c. If C, Expressway
    If O, Expressway
    If R, Queen City
    26.6 minutes

Chapter 5

1. a. $EV(d_1) = 0.40(100) + 0.30(25) + 0.30(0) = 47.5$
$EV(d_2) = 0.40(75) + 0.30(50) + 0.30(25) = 52.5$
$EV(d_3) = 0.40(50) + 0.30(50) + 0.30(50) = 50.0$
The optimal solution is d_2.

b. Using utilities

Decision Maker A	Decision Maker B
$EU(d_1) = 4.9$	$EU(d_1) = 4.45$ Best
$EU(d_2) = 5.9$	$EU(d_2) = 3.75$
$EU(d_1) = 6.0$ Best	$EU(d_1) = 3.00$

c. Difference in attitude toward risk; decision maker A tends to avoid risk, whereas decision maker B tends to take a risk for the opportunity of a large payoff.

2. a. d_2; $EV(d_2) = \$5000$
b. p = probability of a $0 cost
    $1 - p$ = probability of a $200,000 cost
c. d_1; $EV(d_1) = 9.9$
d. Expected utility approach; it avoids risk of large loss.

4. a. Route B; EV = 58.5
b. p = probability of a 45-minute travel time
    $1 - p$ = probability of a 90-minute travel time
c. Route A; EV = 7.6; risk-avoider

5. a.

b. A—risk avoider
    B—risk taker
    C—risk neutral
c. Risk-avoider A, at $20 payoff $p = 0.70$
    ∴ EV(Lottery) $= 0.70(100) + 0.30(-100) = \$40$
    ∴ Will pay $40 - 20 = \$20$
    Risk-taker B, at $20 payoff $p = 0.45$
    ∴ EV(Lottery) $= 0.45(100) + 0.55(-100) = -\$10$
    ∴ Will pay $20 - (-10) = \$30$

6. A: d_1; B: d_2; C: d_2

8. a.

	Win	Lose
Bet	350	−10
Do not bet	0	0

b. d_2
c. Risk takers
d. Between 0 and 0.26

10. a. Western; EV = 26%
    b. p = probability of a 40% show
      $1 - p$ = probability of a 15% show
    c. Musical; risk taker

11.

		Player B		
		b_1 b_2 b_3	**Minimum**
Player A	a_1	8 5 7	⑤
	a_2	2 4 10	2
	Maximum	8 ⑤ 10	

The maximum of the row minimums is 5 and the minimum of the column maximums is 5. The game has a pure strategy. Player A should take strategy a_1 and Player B should take strategy b_2. The value of the game is 5.

12. Pure Strategy
A: a_2 news program
B: b_3 home improvement
Station A gains 6000.

14. a. Strategy a_3 dominated by a_2
      Strategy b_1 dominated by b_2

		Player B	
		b_2	b_3
Player A	a_1	−1	2
	a_2	4	−3

b. Let p = probability of a_1 and $(1 - p)$ = probability of a_2
If b_1, EV = $-1p + 4(1 - p)$
If b_2, EV = $2p - 3(1 - p)$
$$-1p + 4(1 - p) = 2p - 3(1 - p)$$
$$-1p + 4 - 4p = 2p - 3 + 3p$$
$$10p = 7$$
$$p = 0.70$$
$p(a_1) = p = 0.70$
$p(a_2) = 1 - 0.70 = 0.30$
Let q = probability of b_2 and $(1 - q)$ = probability of b_3
If a_1, EV = $-1q + 2(1 - q)$
If a_2, EV = $4q - 3(1 - q)$
$$-1q + 2(1 - q) = 4q - 3(1 - q)$$
$$-1q + 2 - 2q = 4q - 3 + 3q$$
$$10q = 5$$
$$q = 0.50$$
$P(b_2) = q = 0.50$
$P(b_3) = 1 - 0.50 = 0.50$
c. $-1p + 4(1 - p) = -(0.70) + 4(0.30) = +0.50$

16. A: $P(a_3) = 0.80$, $P(a_4) = 0.20$
B: $P(b_1) = 0.40$, $P(b_2) = 0.60$
Value = 2.8

Chapter 6

1. a.

Month	Time Series Value	3-Month Moving Average Forecast	(Error)^2	4-Month Moving Average Forecast	(Error)^2
1	9.5				
2	9.3				
3	9.4				
4	9.6	9.40	0.04		
5	9.8	9.43	0.14	9.45	0.12
6	9.7	9.60	0.01	9.53	0.03
7	9.8	9.70	0.01	9.63	0.03
8	10.5	9.77	0.53	9.73	0.59
9	9.9	10.00	0.01	9.95	0.00
10	9.7	10.07	0.14	9.98	0.08
11	9.6	10.03	0.18	9.97	0.14
12	9.6	9.73	0.02	9.92	0.10
		Totals	1.08		1.09

MSE(3-month) = 1.08/9 = 0.12
MSE(4-month) = 1.09/8 = 0.14
Use a three-month moving average.
b. Forecast = (9.7 + 9.6 + 9.6)/3 = 9.63

2. a.

Month	Time Series Value	4-Week Moving Average Forecast	(Error)^2	5-Week Moving Average Forecast	(Error)^2
1	17				
2	21				
3	19				
4	23				
5	18	20.00	4.00		
6	16	20.25	18.06	19.60	12.96
7	20	19.00	1.00	19.40	0.36
8	18	19.25	1.56	19.20	1.44
9	22	18.00	16.00	19.00	9.00
10	20	19.00	1.00	18.80	1.44
11	15	20.00	25.00	19.20	17.64
12	22	18.75	10.56	19.00	9.00
		Totals	77.18		51.84

b. MSE(4-week) = 77.18/8 = 9.65
MSE(5-week) = 51.84/7 = 7.41
c. For the limited data provided, the five-week moving average provides the smallest MSE.

4.

Week	Time Series Value	Forecast	Error	(Error)^2
1	17			
2	21	17.00	4.00	16.00
3	19	17.40	1.60	2.56
4	23	17.56	5.44	29.59
5	18	18.10	−0.10	0.01
6	16	18.09	−2.09	4.37
7	20	17.88	2.12	4.49
8	18	18.10	−0.10	0.01
9	22	18.09	3.91	15.29
10	20	18.48	1.52	2.31
11	15	18.63	−3.63	13.18
12	22	18.27	3.73	13.91
			Total	101.72

MSE = 101.72/11 = 9.25

$\alpha = 0.2$ provided a lower MSE; therefore, $\alpha = 0.2$ is better than $\alpha = 0.1$.

5. a.

Month	Y_t	3-Month Moving Averages Forecast	(Error)^2	$\alpha = 2$ Forecast	(Error)^2
1	80				
2	82			80.00	4.00
3	84			80.40	12.96
4	83	82.00	1.00	81.12	3.53
5	83	83.00	0.00	81.50	2.25
6	84	83.33	0.45	81.80	4.84
7	85	83.33	2.79	82.24	7.62
8	84	84.00	0.00	82.79	1.46
9	82	84.33	5.43	83.03	1.06
10	83	83.67	0.45	82.83	0.03
11	84	83.00	1.00	82.86	1.30
12	83	83.00	0.00	83.09	0.01
		Totals	11.12		39.06

MSE(3-month) = 11.12/9 = 1.24
MSE($\alpha = 0.2$) = 39.06/11 = 3.55
Use a three-month moving average.
b. (83 + 84 + 83)/3 = 83.3

6. b. The more recent data receive the greater weight or importance in determining the forecast.

8. a. 15.71
b. 15.74
c. 15.51
d. Moving averages; it has the smallest MSE (0.60).

10. a. $\alpha = 0.1$
b. 29.99

12. 3117.01

14. $\sum t = 21; \sum t^2 = 91; \sum Y_t = 117.1;$
$\sum tY_t = 403.7; n = 6$

$$b_1 = \frac{\sum tY_t - (\sum t \sum Y_t)/n}{\sum t^2 - (\sum t)^2/n}$$

$$= \frac{403.7 - (21)(117.1)/6}{91 - (21)^2/6}$$

$$= -0.3514$$

$b_0 = \bar{Y} - b_1\bar{t} = 19.5167 - (-.3514)(3.5) = 20.7466$
$T_t = 20.7466 - 0.3514t$
Conclusion: Enrollment appears to be decreasing by an average of approximately 351 students per year.

16. a. Linear trend appears to be reasonable.
b. $T_t = 19.993 + 1.774t$
Average cost increase of $1.77 per unit per year

18. a. The graph shows a linear trend.
b. $T_t = 60.553 - 1.141t; 1.14\%$
c. 48.0%

20. a. A linear trend appears to exist.
b. $T_t = -5 + 15t$
Average increase in sales is 15 units per year.

22. a. A linear trend appears to be appropriate.
b. $T_t = 6.4564 + 0.5345t$
c. 5.345 million
d. 2001–2002 season: $T_{13} = 6.4564 + 0.5345(12) = 12.87$ million

24. a. Forecast for July is 236.97; forecast for August is 236.97.
b. Forecast for July is 278.88; forecast for August is 297.33.
c. Not fair; it does not account for upward trend in sales.

25. a. Four-quarter moving averages beginning with
(1690 + 940 + 2625 + 2500)/4 = 1938.75
Other moving averages:

1966.25	2002.50
1956.25	2052.50
2025.00	2060.00
1990.00	2123.75

b.

Quarter	Seasonal-Irregular Component Values		Seasonal Index	Adjusted Seasonal Index
1	0.904	0.900	0.9020	0.900
2	0.448	0.526	0.4970	0.486
3	1.344	1.453	1.3985	1.396
4	1.275	1.164	1.2195	1.217
			Total 4.0070	

Note: Adjustment for seasonal index = 4.000/4.007 = 0.9983

c. The largest seasonal effect is in the third quarter, which corresponds to the back-to-school demand during July, August, and September of each year.

26. 0.707, 0.777, 0.827, 0.966, 1.016, 1.305, 1.494, 1.225, 0.976, 0.986, 0.936, 0.787

28. a. Selected centered moving averages for $t = 5, 10, 15,$ and 20 are 11.125, 18.125, 22.875, and 27.000
b. 0.899, 1.362, 1.118, 0.621
c. Quarter 2, prior to summer boating season

30. a. $T_t = 6.329 + 1.055t$
b. 36.92, 37.98, 39.03, 40.09
c. 33.23, 51.65, 43.71, 24.86

32. a. Yes, there is a seasonal effect; seasonal indexes are 1.696, 1.458, 0.711, 0.326, 0.448, 1.362.
b. Forecast for 12–4 is 166,761.13; forecast for 4–8 is 146,052.99

33. a.

Restaurant (i)	x_i	y_i	$x_i y_i$	x_i^2
1	1	19	19	1
2	4	44	176	16
3	6	40	240	36
4	10	52	520	100
5	14	53	742	196
Totals	35	208	1697	349

$$\bar{x} = \frac{35}{5} = 7$$

$$\bar{y} = \frac{208}{5} = 41.6$$

$$b_1 = \frac{\sum x_i y_i - (\sum x_i \sum y_i)/n}{\sum x_i^2 - (\sum x_i)^2/n}$$

$$= \frac{1697 - (35)(208)/5}{349 - (35)^2/5}$$

$$= \frac{241}{104} = 2.317$$

$b_0 = \bar{y} - b_1\bar{x} = 41.6 - 2.317(7) = 25.381$
$\hat{y} = 25.381 + 2.317x$
b. $\hat{y} = 25.381 + 2.317(8) = 43.917$, or \$43,917

34. a. $\hat{y} = 37.666 - 3.222x$
b. \$3444

Chapter 7

1. Parts (a), (b), and (e) are acceptable linear programming relationships.
Part (c) is not acceptable because of $-2x_2^2$.
Part (d) is not acceptable because of $3\sqrt{x_1}$.
Part (f) is not acceptable because of $1x_1x_2$.

Parts (c), (d), and (f) could not be found in a linear programming model because they contain nonlinear terms.

2. a.

b.

c.

6. $7A + 10B = 420$
$6A + 4B = 420$
$4A + 7B = 420$

7.

10.

$$A + 2B = 6 \quad (1)$$
$$5A + 3B = 15 \quad (2)$$

Equation (1) times 5: $\quad 5A + 10B = 30 \quad (3)$
Equation (2) minus equation (3): $\quad -7B = -15$
$$B = 15/7$$
From equation (1): $\quad A = 6 - 2(15/7)$
$$= 6 - 30/7 = 12/7$$

12. a. $A = 3, B = 1.5$; Value of optimal solution $= 13.5$
    b. $A = 0, B = 3$; Value of optimal solution $= 18$
    c. Four: $(0, 0), (4, 0), (3, 1.5),$ and (0.3)

13. a.

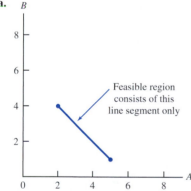

    b. The extreme points are $(5, 1)$ and $(2, 4)$.
    c.

14. a. 540 standard bags, 252 deluxe bags
    b. 7668
    c. 630, 480, 708, 117
    d. 0, 120, 0, 18

16. a. $3S + 9D$
    b. $(0,540)$
    c. 90, 150, 348, 0

17. Max $\quad 5A + 2B + 0s_1 + 0s_2 + 0s_3$
    s.t.

$$1A - 2B + 1s_1 \qquad\qquad = 420$$
$$2A + 3B - \qquad + 1s_2 \qquad = 610$$
$$6A - 1B + \qquad\qquad + 1s_3 = 125$$
$$A, B, s_1, s_2, s_3 \geq 0$$

18. b. $A = 18/7, B = 15/7$
    c. $0, 0, 4/7$

20. b. $A = 3.43, B = 3.43$
    c. $2.86, 0, 1.43, 0$

22. b.

Extreme Point	Coordinates	Profit ($)
1	(0, 0)	0
2	(1700, 0)	8500
3	(1400, 600)	9400
4	(800, 1200)	8800
5	(0, 1680)	6720

Extreme point 3 generates the highest profit.

    c. $A = 1400, C = 600$
    d. Cutting and dyeing constraint and the packaging constraint
    e. $A = 800, C = 1200$; profit $= \$9200$

24. a. Let $R =$ number of units of regular model
           $C =$ number of units of catcher's model

    Max $\quad 5R + 8C$

$$1R + C + 3/2C \leq 900 \quad \text{Cutting and sewing}$$
$$1/2R + \qquad 1/3C \leq 300 \quad \text{Finishing}$$
$$1/8R + \qquad 1/4C \leq 100 \quad \text{Packaging and shipping}$$
$$R, C \geq 0$$

    b.

c. $5(500) + 8(150) = \$3700$

d.

C & S	$1(500) + {}^{3}/_{2}(150) = 725$
F	${}^{1}/_{2}(500) + {}^{1}/_{3}(150) = 300$
P & S	${}^{1}/_{8}(500) + {}^{1}/_{4}(150) = 100$

e.

Department	Capacity	Usage	Slack
Cutting and sewing	900	725	175 hours
Finishing	300	300	0 hours
Packaging and shipping	100	100	0 hours

26. a. Max $50N + 80R$
s.t.
$$
\begin{aligned}
N + R &= 1000 \\
N &\geq 250 \\
R &\geq 250 \\
N - 2R &\geq 0 \\
N, R &\geq 0
\end{aligned}
$$
b. $N = 666.67$, $R = 333.33$; Audience exposure = 60,000

28. a. Max $1W + 1.25M$
  $-$ s.t.
$$
\begin{aligned}
5W + 7M &\leq 4480 \\
3W + 1M &\leq 2080 \\
2W + 2M &\leq 1600 \\
W, M &\geq 0
\end{aligned}
$$
b. $W = 560$, $M = 240$; Profit = 860

30. a. Max $15E + 18C$
s.t.
$$
\begin{aligned}
40E + 25C &\leq 50,000 \\
40E &\geq 15,000 \\
25C &\geq 10,000 \\
25C &\leq 25,000 \\
E, C &\geq 0
\end{aligned}
$$
c. (375, 400); (1000, 400); (625, 1000); (375, 1000)
d. $E = 625$, $C = 1000$
Total return = \$27,375

31.

Optimal solution
$A = 3, B = 1$ $3A + 4B \geq 13$

Objective function value = 13

32.

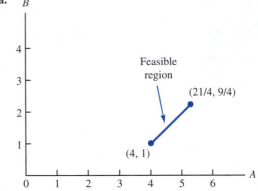

Objective Extreme Points	Function Value	Surplus Demand	Stock Total Production	Processing Time
(250, 100)	800	125	—	—
(125, 225)	925	—	—	125
(125, 350)	1300	—	125	—

34. a.

Feasible region

(21/4, 9/4)

(4, 1)

b. There are two extreme points:

$(A = 4, B = 1)$ and $(A = 21/4, B = 9/4)$

c. The optimal solution [see part (a)] is $A = 4$, $B = 1$.

35. a. Min $6A + 4B + 0s_1 + 0s_2 + 0s_3$
s.t.
$$
\begin{aligned}
2A + 1B - s_1 &= 12 \\
1A + 1B - s_2 &= 10 \\
1B + s_3 &= 4 \\
A, B, s_1, s_2, s_3 &\geq 0
\end{aligned}
$$
b. The optimal solution is $A = 6$, $B = 4$
c. $s_1 = 4$, $s_2 = 0$, $s_3 = 0$

36. a. Min $10,000T + 8000P$
s.t.
$$
\begin{aligned}
T &\geq 8 \\
P &\geq 10 \\
T + P &\geq 25 \\
3T + 2P &\leq 84
\end{aligned}
$$
c. (15, 10); (21.33, 10); (8, 30); (8, 17)
d. $T = 8$, $P = 17$
Total cost = \$216,000

38. a. Min $7.50S + 9.00P$
s.t.
$$
\begin{aligned}
0.10S + 0.30P &\geq 6 \\
0.06S + 0.12P &\leq 3 \\
S + P &= 30 \\
S, P &\geq 0
\end{aligned}
$$
c. The optimal solution is $S = 15$, $P = 15$.

d. No
e. Yes

40. $P_1 = 30$, $P_2 = 25$, Cost = \$55

42.

43.

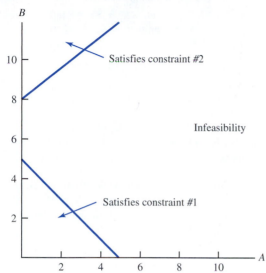

44. a. $A = 30/16$, $B = 30/16$; Value of optimal solution $= {}^{60}/_{16}$

 b. $A = 0$, $B = 3$; Value of optimal solution $= 6$

46. a. 180, 20
 b. Alternative optimal solutions
 c. 120, 80

48. No feasible solution

50. $M = 65.45$, $R = 261.82$; Profit $= \$45,818$

52. $S = 384$, $O = 80$

54. a. Max $160M_1 + 345M_2$
   s.t.
$$
\begin{aligned}
M_1 &\le 15 \\
M_2 &\le 10 \\
M_1 &\ge 5 \\
M_2 &\ge 5 \\
40M_1 + 50M_2 &\le 1000 \\
M_1, M_2 &\ge 0
\end{aligned}
$$

 b. $M_1 = 12.5$, $M_2 = 10$

Chapter 8

1. a.

 b. The same extreme point, $A = 7$ and $B = 3$, remains optimal; Value of the objective function becomes $5(7) + 2(3) = 41$.
 c. A new extreme point, $A = 4$ and $B = 6$, becomes optimal; Value of the objective function becomes $3(4) + 4(6) = 36$.
 d. The objective coefficient range for variable A is 2 to 6; the optimal solution, $A = 7$ and $B = 3$, does not change. The objective coefficient range for variable B is 1 to 3; resolve the problem to find the new optimal solution.

2. a. The feasible region becomes larger with the new optimal solution of $A = 6.5$ and $B = 4.5$.
 b. Value of the optimal solution to the revised problem is $3(6.5) + 2(4.5) = 28.5$; the one-unit increase in the right-hand side of constraint 1 improves the value of the optimal solution by $28.5 - 27 = 1.5$; therefore, the dual price for constraint 1 is 1.5.
 c. The right-hand-side range for constraint 1 is 8 to 11.2; as long as the right-hand side stays within this range, the dual price of 1.5 is applicable
 d. The improvement in the value of the optimal solution will be 0.5 for every unit increase in the right-hand side of constraint 2 as long as the right-hand side is between 18 and 30.

4. a. $X = 2.5$, $Y = 2.5$
 b. -2
 c. 5 to 11
 d. -3 between 9 and 18

5. a. Regular glove = 500; Catcher's mitt = 150; Value = 3700
 b. The finishing, packaging, and shipping constraints are binding; there is no slack
 c. Cutting and sewing = 0
  Finishing = 3
  Packaging and shipping = 28
  Additional finishing time is worth \$3 per unit, and additional packaging and shipping time is worth \$28 per unit.

  d. In the packaging and shipping department, each additional hour is worth $28.

6. a. 4 to 12

3.33 to 10

  b. As long as the profit contribution for the regular glove is between $4.00 and $12.00, the current solution is optimal; as long as the profit contribution for the catcher's mitt stays between $3.33 and $10.00, the current solution is optimal; the optimal solution is not sensitive to small changes in the profit contributions for the gloves.

  c. The dual prices for the resources are applicable over the following ranges:

Constraint	Right-Hand-Side Range
Cutting and sewing	725 to No Upper Limit
Finishing	133.33 to 400
Packaging and shipping	75 to 135

  d. Amount of increase = (28)(20) = $560

8. a. More than $7.00

  b. More than $3.50

  c. None

10. a. $S = 4000, M = 10,000$, Total risk = 62,000

  b.

Variable	Objective Coefficient Range
S	3.75 to No Upper Limit
M	No Lower Limit to 6.4

  c. $5(4000) + 4(10,000) = \$60,000$

  d. $60,000/1,200,000 = 0.05$ or 5%

  e. 0.057 risk units

  f. $0.057(100) = 5.7\%$

12. a. $E = 80, S = 120, D = 0$

Profit = $16,440

  b. Fan motors and cooling coils

  c. Labor-hours; 320 hours available

  d. Objective function coefficient range of optimality

No Lower Limit to 159

Because $150 is in this range, the optimal solution would not change.

13. a. Range of optimality

E 47.5 to 75

S 87 to 126

D No Lower Limit to 159

  b.

Model	Profit	Change	Allowable Increase/Decrease	%
E	$ 63	Increase $6(100)	$75 − $63 = $12	$6/12(100) = 50$
S	$ 95	Decrease $2	$95 − $87 = $8	$2/8(100) = 25$
D	$135	Increase $4	$159 − $135 = $24	$4/24(100) = \dfrac{17}{\underline{}}$
				92

Because changes are 92% of allowable changes, the optimal solution of $E = 80, S = 120, D = 0$ will not change.

The change in total profit will be

$$\begin{array}{lll} E & 80 \text{ units @ } + \$6 = & \$480 \\ S & 120 \text{ units @ } - \$2 = & \underline{-240} \\ & & \$240 \end{array}$$

∴ Profit = $16,440 + $240 = $16,680

  c. Range of feasibility

Constraint 1   160 to 280

Constraint 2   200 to 400

Constraint 3   2080 to No Upper Limit

  d. Yes, Fan motors = 200 + 100 = 300 is outside the range of feasibility; the dual price will change.

14. a. Manufacture 100 cases of A and 60 cases of B, and purchase 90 cases of B; Total cost = $2170

  b. Demand for A, demand for B, assembly time

  c. $-12.25, -9.0, 0, 0.375$

  d. Assembly time constraint

16. a. 100 suits, 150 sport coats

Profit = $40,900

40 hours of cutting overtime

  b. Optimal solution will not change.

  c. Consider ordering additional material.

$34.50 is the maximum price.

  d. Profit will improve by $875.

18. a. The linear programming model is as follows:

$$\text{Min} \quad 30AN + 50AO + 25BN + 40BO$$

$$\begin{array}{rcrcrcrl} AN & + & AO & & & & & \geq 50,000 \\ & & & & BN & + & BO & \geq 70,000 \\ AN & & & + & BN & & & \leq 80,000 \\ & & AO & & & + & BO & \leq 60,000 \\ \end{array}$$

$$AN, AO, BN, BO \geq 0$$

  b. Optimal solution

	New Line	Old Line
Model A	50,000	0
Model B	30,000	40,000

Total cost: $3,850,000

  c. The first three constraints are binding.

  d. Because the dual price is positive, increasing the right-hand side of constraint 3 will *improve* the solution; thus, an increase in capacity for the new production line is desirable.

  e. Because constraint 4 is not a binding constraint, any increase in the production line capacity of the old production line will have no effect on the optimal solution; thus, increasing the capacity of the old production line results in no benefit.

f. The reduced cost for model A made on the old production line is 5; thus, the cost would have to decrease by at least \$5 before any units of model A would be produced on the old production line.

g. The right-hand-side range for constraint 2 shows a lower limit of 30,000; thus, if the minimum production requirement is reduced 10,000 units to 60,000, the dual price of -40 is applicable; thus, total cost would decrease by $10,000(40) = \$400,000$.

20. a. Max $\quad 0.07H + 0.12P + 0.09A$

$$\begin{aligned} H + \quad P + \quad A &= 1,000,000 \\ 0.6H - \quad 0.4P - \quad 0.4A &\geq 0 \\ P - \quad 0.6A &\leq 0 \\ H, P, A &\geq 0 \end{aligned}$$

b. $H = \$400,000$, $P = \$225,000$, $A = \$375,000$
Total annual return $= \$88,750$
Annual percentage return $= 8.875\%$

c. No change

d. Increase of \$890

e. Increase of \$312.50, or 0.031%

22. a. Min $\quad 30L + \quad 25D + \quad 18S$

$$\begin{aligned} L + \quad D + \quad S &= 100 \\ 0.6L - \quad 0.4D &\geq 0 \\ -0.15L - 0.15D + 0.85S &\geq 0 \\ -0.25L - 0.25D + \quad S &\leq 0 \\ L &\leq 50 \\ L, D, S &\geq 0 \end{aligned}$$

b. $L = 48$, $D = 72$, $S = 30$
Total cost $= \$3780$

c. No change

d. No change

24. a. 333.3, 0, 833.3; Risk $= 14,666.7$; Return $= 18,000$, or 9%

b. 1000, 0, 0, 2500; Risk $= 18,000$; Return $= 22,000$, or 11%

c. \$4000

26. a. Let $M_1 =$ units of component 1 manufactured
$M_2 =$ units of component 2 manufactured
$M_3 =$ units of component 3 manufactured
$P_1 =$ units of component 1 purchased
$P_2 =$ units of component 2 purchased
$P_3 =$ units of component 3 purchased

Min $\quad 4.50M_1 + 5.00M_2 + 2.75M_3 + 6.50P_1 + 8.80P_2 + 7.00P_3$
$\quad 2M_1 + \quad 3M_2 + 4M_3 \qquad\qquad\qquad \leq 21,600 \quad$ Production
$\quad 1M_1 + 1.5M_2 + 3M_3 \qquad\qquad\qquad \leq 15,000 \quad$ Assembly
$\quad 1.5M_1 + \quad 2M_2 + 5M_3 \qquad\qquad\qquad \leq 18,000 \quad$ Testing/Packaging
$\quad 1M_1 \qquad\qquad\qquad + 1P_1 \qquad\qquad = \quad 6,000 \quad$ Component 1
$\qquad\qquad 1M_2 \qquad\qquad + 1P_2 \qquad = \quad 4,000 \quad$ Component 2
$\qquad\qquad\qquad 1M_3 \qquad\qquad + 1P_3 = \quad 3,500 \quad$ Component 3
$\quad M_1, M_2, M_3, P_1, P_2, P_3 \geq 0$

b.

Source	Component 1	Component 2	Component 3
Manufacture	2000	4000	1400
Purchase	4000		2100

Total Cost \$73,550

c. Production: \$54.36 per hour
Testing & Packaging: \$7.50 per hour

d. Dual prices $= -\$7.969$; it would cost Benson \$7.969 to add a unit of component 2.

28. b. $G = 120,000$; $S = 30,000$; $M = 150,000$

c. 0.15 to 0.60; No Lower Limit to 0.122; 0.02 to 0.20

d. 4668

e. $G = 48,000$; $S = 192,000$; $M = 60,000$

f. The client's risk index and the amount of funds available

30. a. $L = 3$, $N = 7$, $W = 5$, $S = 5$

b. Each additional minute of broadcast time increases cost by \$100.

c. If local coverage is increased by 1 minute, total cost will increase by \$100.

d. If the time devoted to local and national news is increased by 1 minute, total cost will increase by \$100.

e. Increasing the sports by 1 minute will have no effect because the dual price is 0.

32. a. Let $P_1 =$ number of PT-100 battery packs produced at the Philippines plant
$P_2 =$ number of PT-200 battery packs produced at the Philippines plant
$P_3 =$ number of PT-300 battery packs produced at the Philippines plant
$M_1 =$ number of PT-100 battery packs produced at the Mexico plant
$M_2 =$ number of PT-200 battery packs produced at the Mexico plant
$M_3 =$ number of PT-300 battery packs produced at the Mexico plant

Min $\quad 1.13P_1 + 1.16P_2 + 1.52P_3 + 1.08M_1 + 1.16M_2 + 1.25M_3$
$\quad P_1 \qquad\qquad\qquad + M_1 \qquad\qquad\qquad = 200,000$
$\qquad P_2 \qquad\qquad\qquad + M_2 \qquad\qquad = 100,000$
$\qquad\qquad P_3 \qquad\qquad\qquad + M_3 = 150,000$
$\quad P_1 + \quad P_2 \qquad\qquad\qquad\qquad\qquad \leq 175,000$
$\qquad\qquad\qquad\qquad M_1 + \quad M_2 \qquad \leq 160,000$
$\qquad\qquad P_3 \qquad\qquad\qquad\qquad\qquad \leq 75,000$
$\qquad\qquad\qquad\qquad\qquad\qquad M_3 \leq 100,000$
$\quad P_1, P_2, P_3, M_1, M_2, M_3 \geq 0$

b. The optimal solution is as follows:

	Philippines	Mexico
PT-100	40,000	160,000
PT-200	100,000	0
PT-300	50,000	100,000

Total production and transportation cost is \$535,000.

c. The range of optimality for the objective function coefficient for P_1 shows a lower limit of $1.08; thus, the production and/or shipping cost would have to decrease by at least 5 cents per unit.

d. The range of optimality for the objective function coefficient for M_1 shows a lower limit of $1.11; thus, the production and/or shipping cost would have to decrease by at least 5 cents per unit.

Chapter 9

1. a. Let T = number of television spot advertisements
R = number of radio advertisements
N = number of newspaper advertisements

Max 100,000T + 18,000R + 40,000N
s.t.

$$
\begin{array}{llll}
2{,}000T + & 300R + & 600N \le 18{,}200 & \text{Budget} \\
T & & \le 10 & \text{Max TV} \\
& R & \le 20 & \text{Max Radio} \\
& & N \le 10 & \text{Max News} \\
-0.5T + & 0.5R - & 0.5N \le 0 & \text{Max 50\% Radio} \\
0.9T - & 0.1R - & 0.1N \ge 0 & \text{Min 10\% TV} \\
T, R, N, \ge 0
\end{array}
$$

		Budget \$
Solution:	$T = 4$	\$ 8000
	$R = 14$	4200
	$N = 10$	6000
		\$18,200

Audience = 1,052,000

This information can be obtained from The Management Scientist as follows:

```
OPTIMAL SOLUTION

Objective Function Value =        1052000.000

        Variable              Value           Reduced Costs
     --------------        ------------       ---------------
          T                    4.000               0.000
          R                   14.000               0.000
          N                   10.000               0.000

        Constraint         Slack/Surplus        Dual Prices
     --------------        ------------       ---------------
           1                   0.000              51.304
           2                   6.000               0.000
           3                   6.000               0.000
           4                   0.000           11826.087
           5                   0.000            5217.391
           6                   1.200               0.000

OBJECTIVE COEFFICIENT RANGES

    Variable      Lower Limit     Current Value      Upper Limit
  ------------   -------------   ---------------   ---------------
        T         -18000.000       100000.000        120000.000
        R          15000.000        18000.000      No Upper Limit
        N          28173.913        40000.000      No Upper Limit

RIGHT HAND SIDE RANGES

    Constraint    Lower Limit     Current Value      Upper Limit
  ------------   -------------   ---------------   ---------------
        1          14750.000        18200.000         31999.996
        2              4.000           10.000      No Upper Limit
        3             14.000           20.000      No Upper Limit
        4              0.000           10.000            12.339
        5             -8.050            0.000             2.936
        6         No Lower Limit        0.000             1.200
```

b. The dual price for the budget constraint is 51.30. Thus, a $100 increase in budget should provide an increase in audience coverage of approximately 5,130. The right-hand-side range for the budget constraint will show this interpretation is correct.

2. a. Let x_1 = units of product 1 produced
x_2 = units of product 2 produced

Max $30x_1 + 15x_2$
s.t.

$$x_1 + 0.35x_2 \leq 100 \quad \text{Dept. A}$$
$$0.30x_1 + 0.20x_2 \leq 36 \quad \text{Dept. B}$$
$$0.20x_1 + 0.50x_2 \leq 50 \quad \text{Dept. C}$$
$$x_1, x_2 \leq 0$$

Solution: $x_1 = 77.89$, $x_2 = 63.16$; Profit = 3284.21

b. The dual price for Department A is $15.79; for Department B it is $47.37; and for Department C it is $0.00. Therefore, we would attempt to schedule overtime in Departments A and B. Assuming the current labor available is a sunk cost, we should be willing to pay up to $15.79 per hour in Department A and up to $47.37 in Department B.

c. Let x_A = hours of overtime in Department A
x_B = hours of overtime in Department B
x_C = hours of overtime in Department C

Max $30x_1 + 15x_2 - 18x_A - 22.5x_B - 12x_C$
s.t.

$$x_1 + 0.35x_2 - x_A \leq 100$$
$$0.30x_1 + 0.20x_2 - x_B \leq 36$$
$$0.20x_1 + 0.50x_2 - x_C \leq 50$$
$$x_A \leq 10$$
$$x_B \leq 6$$
$$x_C \leq 8$$

$$x_1, x_2, x_A, x_B, x_C \leq 0$$

$$x_1 = 87.21$$
$$x_2 = 65.12$$
Profit = $3341.34

Overtime	
Department A	10 hours
Department B	3.186 hours
Department C	0 hours

Increase in profit from overtime = $3341.34 − 3284.21 = $57.13

4. a. x_1 = pounds of bean 1
x_2 = pounds of bean 2
x_3 = pounds of bean 3

Max $0.50x_1 + 0.70x_2 + 0.45x_3$
s.t.

$$\frac{75x_1 + 85x_2 + 60x_3}{x_1 + x_2 + x_3} \geq 75$$

or $10x_2 - 15x_3 \geq 0$ Aroma

$$\frac{86x_1 + 88x_2 + 75x_3}{x_1 + x_2 + x_3} \geq 80$$

or

$$6x_1 + 8x_2 - 5x_3 \geq 0 \quad \text{Taste}$$
$$x_1 \leq 500 \quad \text{Bean 1}$$
$$x_2 \leq 600 \quad \text{Bean 2}$$
$$x_3 \leq 400 \quad \text{Bean 3}$$
$$x_1 + x_2 + x_3 = 1000 \quad \text{1000 pounds}$$
$$x_1, x_2, x_3 \geq 0$$

Optimal Solution: $x_1 = 500$, $x_2 = 300$, $x_3 = 200$; Cost: $550

b. Cost per pound = $550/1000 = $0.55

c. Surplus for aroma: $s_1 = 0$; thus, aroma rating = 75
Surplus for taste: $s_2 = 4400$; thus, taste rating = 80 + 4400/1000 lb = 84.4

d. Dual price = −$0.60. Extra coffee can be produced at a cost of $0.60 per pound.

6. Let x_1 = units of product 1
x_2 = units of product 2
b_1 = labor-hours Department A
b_2 = labor-hours Department B

Max $25x_1 + 20x_2 + 0b_1 + 0b_2$
s.t.

$$6x_1 + 8x_2 - 1b_1 = 0$$
$$12x_1 + 10x_2 - 1b_2 = 0$$
$$1b_1 + 1b_2 \leq 900$$
$$x_1, x_2, b_1, b_2 \geq 0$$

Solution: $x_1 = 50$, $x_2 = 0$, $b_1 = 300$, $b_2 = 600$; Profit: $1250

8. Let x_1 = the number of officers scheduled to begin at 8:00 A.M.
x_2 = the number of officers scheduled to begin at noon
x_3 = the number of officers scheduled to begin at 4:00 P.M.
x_4 = the number of officers scheduled to begin at 8:00 P.M.
x_5 = the number of officers scheduled to begin at midnight
x_6 = the number of officers scheduled to begin at 4:00 A.M.

The objective function to minimize the number of officers required is as follows:

Min $x_1 + x_2 + x_3 + x_4 + x_5 + x_6$

The constraints require the total number of officers on duty each of the six 4-hour periods to be at least equal to the minimum officer requirements. The constraints for the six 4-hour periods are as follows:

Time of Day

8:00 A.M.–Noon	$x_1 + x_6 \geq 5$	
Noon–4:00 P.M.	$x_1 + x_2 \geq 6$	
4:00 P.M.–8:00 P.M.	$x_2 + x_3 \geq 10$	
8:00 P.M.–Midnight	$x_3 + x_4 \geq 7$	
Midnight–4:00 A.M.	$x_4 + x_5 \geq 4$	
4:00 A.M.–8:00 A.M.	$x_5 + x_6 \geq 6$	

$$x_1, x_2, x_3, x_4, x_5, x_6 \geq 0$$

Schedule 19 officers as follows:

x_1 = 3 begin at 8:00 A.M.
x_2 = 3 begin at noon
x_3 = 7 begin at 4:00 P.M.
x_4 = 0 begin at 8:00 P.M.
x_5 = 4 begin at midnight
x_6 = 2 begin at 4:00 A.M.

9. a. Let each decision variable, A, P, M, H, and G, represent the fraction or proportion of the total investment placed in each investment alternative.

Max $0.073A + 0.103P + 0.064M + 0.075H + 0.045G$
s.t.

$$
\begin{array}{rrrrrl}
A + & P + & M + & H + & G = & 1 \\
0.5A + & 0.5P - & 0.5M - & 0.5H & & \leq 0 \\
-0.5A - & 0.5P + & 0.5M + & 0.5H & & \leq 0 \\
 & & - 0.25M - & 0.25H + & G \geq & 0 \\
-0.6A + & 0.4P & & & & \leq 0 \\
\end{array}
$$

$A, P, M, H, G \geq 0$

Solution: Objective function = 0.079 with

Atlantic Oil   = 0.178
Pacific Oil   = 0.267

Midwest Oil   = 0.000
Huber Steel   = 0.444
Government Bonds   = 0.111

b. For a total investment of $100,000, we show

Atlantic Oil	= $ 17,800
Pacific Oil	= 26,700
Midwest Oil	= 0.000
Huber Steel	= 44,400
Government Bonds	= 11,100
Total	$100,000

c. Total earnings = $100,000 (0.079) = $7,900
d. Marginal rate of return = 0.079

10. a. Let S = the proportion of funds invested in stocks
B = the proportion of funds invested in bonds
M = the proportion of funds invested in mutual funds
C = the proportion of funds invested in cash

The linear program and optimal solution obtained using The Management Scientist is as follows:

```
MAX 0.1S+0.03B+0.04M+0.01C
  S.T.

1)  1S+1B+1M+1C=1
2)  0.8S+0.2B+0.3M<0.4
3)  1S<0.75
4)  −1B+1M>0
5)  1C>0.1
6)  1C<0.3


OPTIMAL SOLUTION


Objective Function Value =            0.054

        Variable              Value              Reduced Costs
     --------------      ---------------        ----------------
           S                  0.409                  0.000
           B                  0.145                  0.000
           M                  0.145                  0.000
           C                  0.300                  0.000

       Constraint          Slack/Surplus            Dual Prices
     --------------      ---------------        ----------------
           1                  0.000                  0.005
           2                  0.000                  0.118
           3                  0.341                  0.000
           4                  0.000                 -0.001
           5                  0.200                  0.000
           6                  0.000                  0.005
```

```
OBJECTIVE COEFFICIENT RANGES

    Variable         Lower Limit        Current Value        Upper Limit
  ------------     ---------------     ---------------     ---------------
       S                    0.090               0.100      No Upper Limit
       B                    0.028               0.030               0.036
       M           No Lower Limit               0.040               0.042
       C                    0.005               0.010      No Upper Limit


RIGHT HAND SIDE RANGES

   Constraint        Lower Limit        Current Value        Upper Limit
  ------------     ---------------     ---------------     ---------------
       1                    0.800               1.000               1.900
       2                    0.175               0.400               0.560
       3                    0.409               0.750      No Upper Limit
       4                   -0.267               0.000               0.320
       5           No Lower Limit               0.100               0.300
       6                    0.100               0.300               0.500
```

The optimal allocation among the four investment alternatives:

Stocks	40.9%
Bonds	14.5%
Mutual Funds	14.5%
Cash	30.0%

The annual return associated with the optimal portfolio is 5.4%.
Total risk = 0.409(0.8) + 0.145(0.2) + 0.145(0.3) + 0.300(0.0) = 0.4

b. Changing the right-hand-side value for constraint 2 to 0.18 and resolving using The Management Scientist, we obtain the following optimal solution:

Stocks	0.0%
Bonds	36.0%
Mutual Funds	36.0%
Cash	28.0%

The annual return associated with the optimal portfolio is 2.52%.
Total risk = 0.0(0.8) + 0.36(0.2) + 0.36(0.3) + 0.28(0.0) = 0.18

c. Changing the right-hand-side value for constraint 2 to 0.7 and resolving using The Management Scientist, we obtain the following optimal allocation among the four investment alternatives:

Stocks	75.0%
Bonds	0.0%
Mutual Funds	15.0%
Cash	10.0%

The annual return associated with the optimal portfolio is 8.2%.
Total risk = 0.75(0.8) + 0.0(0.2) + 0.15(0.3) + 0.10(0.0) = 0.65

d. Note that a maximum risk of 0.7 was specified for this aggressive investor, but that the risk index for the portfolio is only 0.65. Thus, this investor is willing to take more risk than the solution shown above provides. There are only two ways the investor can become even more aggressive: by increasing the proportion invested in stocks to more than 75% or reducing the cash requirement of at least 10% so that additional cash could be put into stocks. For the data given here, the investor should ask the investment advisor to relax either or both of these constraints.

e. Defining the decision variables as proportions means the investment advisor can use the linear programming model for any investor, regardless of the amount of the investment. All the investor advisor must do is to establish the maximum total risk for the investor and resolve the problem using the new value for maximum total risk.

12. Let B_i = pounds of shrimp bought in week i, i = 1, 2, 3, 4
  S_i = pounds of shrimp sold in week i, i = 1, 2, 3, 4
  I_i = pounds of shrimp held in storage (inventory) in week i

Total purchase cost $= 6.00B_1 + 6.20B_2 + 6.65B_3 + 5.55B_4$
Total sales revenue $= 6.00S_1 + 6.20S_2 + 6.65S_3 + 5.55S_4$
Total storage cost $= 0.15I_1 + 0.15I_2 + 0.15I_3 + 0.15I_4$
Total profit contribution = (total sales revenue) − (total purchase cost) − (total storage cost)
Objective: Maximize total profit contribution subject to balance equations for each week, storage capacity for each week, and ending inventory requirement for week 4.

$$\text{Max} \quad 6.00S_1 + 6.20S_2 + 6.65S_3 + 5.55S_4 - 6.00B_1 - 6.20B_2 - 6.65B_3 - 5.55B_4 - 0.15I_1 - 0.15I_2 - 0.15I_3 - 0.15I_4$$

s.t.

$$
\begin{array}{lll}
20{,}000 + B_1 - S_1 = I_1 & \text{Balance equation—week 1} \\
I_1 + B_2 - S_2 = I_2 & \text{Balance equation—week 2} \\
I_2 + B_3 - S_3 = I_3 & \text{Balance equation—week 3} \\
I_3 + B_4 - S_4 = I_4 & \text{Balance equation—week 4} \\
I_1 \le 100{,}000 & \text{Storage capacity—week 1} \\
I_2 \le 100{,}000 & \text{Storage capacity—week 2} \\
I_3 \le 100{,}000 & \text{Storage capacity—week 3} \\
I_4 \le 100{,}000 & \text{Storage capacity—week 4} \\
I_4 \le 25{,}000 & \text{Required inventory—week 4} \\
\text{all variables} \ge 0
\end{array}
$$

Note that the first four constraints can be written as follows:

$$
\begin{array}{ll}
I_1 - B_1 + S_1 &= 20{,}000 \\
I_1 - I_2 + B_2 - S_2 &= 0 \\
I_2 - I_3 + B_3 - S_3 &= 0 \\
I_3 - I_4 + B_4 - S_4 &= 0
\end{array}
$$

The optimal solution obtained using The Management Scientist follows:

Week (i)	B_i	S_i	I_i
1	80,000	0	100,000
2	0	0	100,000
3	0	100,000	0
4	25,000	0	25,000

Total profit contribution = $12,500
Note, however, ASC started week 1 with 20,000 pounds of shrimp and ended week 4 with 25,000 pounds of shrimp. During the 4-week period, ASC has taken profits to reinvest and build inventory by 5000 pounds in anticipation of future higher prices. The amount of profit reinvested in inventory is ($5.55 + $0.15)(5000) = $28,500. Thus, total profit for the 4-week period including reinvested profit is $12,500 + $28,500 = $41,000.

14. a. Let x_i = number of Classic 2l boats produced in Quarter i; $i = 1, 2, 3, 4$
s_i = ending inventory of Classic 2l boats in Quarter i; $i = 1, 2, 3, 4$

$$\text{Min} \quad 10{,}000x_1 + 11{,}000x_2 + 12{,}100x_3 + 13{,}310x_4 + 250s_1 + 250s_2 + 300s_3 + 300s_4$$

s.t.

$$
\begin{array}{lll}
x_1 - s_1 = 1900 & \text{Quarter 1 demand} \\
s_1 + x_2 - s_2 = 4000 & \text{Quarter 2 demand} \\
s_2 + x_3 - s_3 = 3000 & \text{Quarter 3 demand} \\
s_3 + x_4 - s_4 = 1500 & \text{Quarter 4 demand} \\
s_4 \ge 500 & \text{Ending Inventory} \\
x_1 \le 4000 & \text{Quarter 1 capacity} \\
x_2 \le 3000 & \text{Quarter 2 capacity} \\
x_3 \le 2000 & \text{Quarter 3 capacity} \\
x_4 \le 4000 & \text{Quarter 4 capacity}
\end{array}
$$

b.

Quarter	Production	Ending Inventory	Cost ($)
1	4000	2100	40,525,000
2	3000	1100	33,275,000
3	2000	100	24,230,000
4	1900	500	25,439,000
			$123,469,000

c. The dual prices tell us how much it would cost if demand were to increase by one additional unit. For example, in Quarter 2 the dual price is −$12,760; thus, demand for one more boat in Quarter 2 will increase costs by $12,760.

d. The dual price of 0 for Quarter 4 tells us we have excess capacity in Quarter 4. The positive dual prices in Quarters 1–3 tell us how much increasing the production capacity will improve the objective function. For example, the dual price of $2510 for Quarter 1 tells us that if capacity were increased by 1 unit for this quarter, costs would go down $2510.

15. Let x_{11} = gallons of crude 1 used to produce regular
x_{12} = gallons of crude 1 used to produce high-octane
x_{21} = gallons of crude 2 used to produce regular
x_{22} = gallons of crude 2 used to produce high-octane

$$\text{Min} \quad 0.10x_{11} + 0.10x_{12} + 0.15x_{21} + 0.15x_{22}$$

s.t.

Each gallon of regular must have at least 40% A.

$$
\begin{array}{ll}
x_{11} + x_{21} &= \text{amount of regular produced} \\
0.4(x_{11} + x_{21}) &= \text{amount of A required for regular} \\
0.2x_{11} + 0.50x_{21} &= \text{amount of A in } (x_{11} + x_{21}) \text{ gallons} \\
& \quad \text{of regular gas}
\end{array}
$$

$$\therefore 0.2x_{11} + 0.50x_{21} \ge 0.4x_{11} + 0.40x_{21} \qquad (1)$$
$$\therefore -0.2x_{11} + 0.10x_{21} \ge 0$$

Each gallon of high octane can have at most 50% B.

$$
\begin{array}{ll}
x_{12} + x_{22} &= \text{amount high-octane} \\
0.5(x_{12} + x_{22}) &= \text{amount of B required for high octane} \\
0.60x_{12} + 0.30x_{22} &= \text{amount of B in } (x_{12} + x_{22}) \text{ gallons of high octane.}
\end{array}
$$

$\therefore 0.60x_{12} + 0.30x_{22} \leq 0.5x_{12} + 0.5x_{22}$
$\therefore 0.1x_{12} - 0.2x_{22} \leq 0$ (2)
$x_{11} + x_{21} \geq 800,000$ (3)
$x_{12} + x_{22} \geq 500,000$ (4)
$x_{11}, x_{12}, x_{21}, x_{22} \geq 0$

Optimal Solution: $x_{11} = 266,667$, $x_{12} = 333,333$, $x_{21} = 533,333$, $x_{22} = 166,667$

Cost = $165,000

16. Let x_i = number of 10-inch rolls of paper processed by cutting alternative i; $i = 1, 2, \ldots, 7$

Min $x_1 + x_2 + x_3 + x_4 + x_5 + x_6 + x_7$
s.t.

$6x_1 + 2x_3 + x_5 + x_6 + 4x_7 \geq 1000$ $1\frac{1}{2}$" production
$4x_2 + x_4 + 3x_5 + 2x_6 \geq 2000$ $2\frac{1}{2}$" production
$2x_3 + 2x_4 + x_6 + x_7 \geq 4000$ $3\frac{1}{2}$" production
$x_1, x_2, x_3, x_4, x_5, x_6, x_7 \geq 0$

$x_1 = 0$
$x_2 = 125$
$x_3 = 500$ 2125 Rolls
$x_4 = 1500$
$x_5 = 0$ Production:
$x_6 = 0$ $1\frac{1}{2}$"   1000
$x_7 = 0$ $2\frac{1}{2}$"   2000
       $3\frac{1}{2}$"   4000

Waste: Cut alternative 4 ($\frac{1}{2}$" per roll)
$\therefore$ 750 inches

b. Only the objective function needs to be changed. An objective function minimizing waste production and the new optimal solution are given.

Min $x_1 + 0x_2 + 0x_3 + 0.5x_4 + x_5 + 0x_6 + 0.5x_7$
$x_1 = 0$
$x_2 = 500$
$x_3 = 2000$ 2500 Rolls
$x_4 = 0$
$x_5 = 0$ Production:
$x_6 = 0$ $1\frac{1}{2}$"   4000
$x_7 = 0$ $2\frac{1}{2}$"   2000
       $3\frac{1}{2}$"   4000

Waste is 0; however, we have overproduced the $1\frac{1}{2}$" size by 3000 units. Perhaps these can be inventoried for future use.

c. Minimizing waste may cause you to overproduce. In this case, we used 375 more rolls to generate a 3000 surplus of the $1\frac{1}{2}$" product. Alternative b might be preferred on the basis that the 3000 surplus could be held in inventory for later demand. However, in some trim problems, excess production cannot be used and must be scrapped. If this were the case, the 3000 unit $1\frac{1}{2}$" size would result in 4500 inches of waste, and thus alternative 1 would be the preferred solution.

18. a. Let x_1 = number of Super Tankers purchased
       x_2 = number of Regular Line Tankers purchased
       x_3 = number of Econo-Tankers purchased

Min $550x_1 + 425x_2 + 350x_3$
s.t.

$6700x_1 + 55000x_2 + 4600x_3 \leq 600,000$ Budget
$15(5000)x_1 + 20(2500)x_2 + 25(1000)x_3 \geq 550,000$

or

$75000x_1 + 50000x_2 + 25000x_3 \geq 550,000$ Meet Demand
$x_1 + x_2 + x_3 \leq 15$ Max. Total Vehicles
$x_3 \geq 3$ Min. Econo-Tankers

$x_1 \leq \frac{1}{2}(x_1 + x_2 + x_3)$

or

$\frac{1}{2}x_1 - \frac{1}{2}x_2 - \frac{1}{2}x_3 \leq 0$ No more than 50% Super Tankers
$x_1, x_2, x_3 \geq 0$

Solution: 5 Super Tankers, 2 Regular Tankers, 3 Econo-Tankers

Total Cost: $583,000

Monthly Operating Cost: $4650

b. The last two constraints in the formulation above must be deleted and the problem resolved.

    The optimal solution calls for $7\frac{1}{3}$ Super Tankers at an annual operating cost of $4033. However, because a partial Super Tanker can't be purchased, we must round up to find a feasible solution of 8 Super Tankers with a monthly operating cost of $4400.

    Actually this is an integer programming problem, because partial tankers can't be purchased. We were fortunate in part (a) that the optimal solution turned out integer.

    The true optimal integer solution to part (b) is $x_1 = 6$ and $x_2 = 2$, with a monthly operating cost of $4150. This is 6 Super Tankers and 2 Regular Line Tankers.

19. a. Let x_{11} = amount of men's model in month 1
       x_{21} = amount of women's model in month 1
       x_{12} = amount of men's model in month 2
       x_{22} = amount of women's model in month 2
       s_{11} = inventory of men's model at end of month 1
       s_{21} = inventory of women's model at end of month 1
       s_{12} = inventory of men's model at end of month 2
       s_{22} = inventory of women's model at end of month 2

The model formulation for part (a) is given.

Min $120x_{11} + 90x_{21} + 120x_{12} + 90x_{22} + 2.4s_{11} + 1.8s_{21} + 2.4s_{12} + 1.8s_{22}$
s.t.

$20 + x_{11} - s_{11} = 150$

or

$x_{11} - s_{11} = 130$ Satisfy Demand   (1)
$30 + x_{21} - s_{21} = 125$

or

$x_{21} - s_{21} = 95$ Satisfy Demand   (2)
$s_{11} + x_{12} - s_{12} = 200$ Satisfy Demand   (3)
$s_{21} + x_{22} - s_{22} = 150$ Satisfy Demand   (4)
$s_{12} \geq 25$ Ending Inventory   (5)
$s_{22} \geq 25$ Ending Inventory   (6)

Labor-hours: Men's   = $2.0 + 1.5 = 3.5$
            Women's = $1.6 + 1.0 = 2.6$

$3.5x_{11} + 2.6x_{21} \geq 900$ Labor Smoothing for   (7)
$3.5x_{11} + 2.6x_{21} \leq 1100$ Month 1   (8)
$3.5x_{11} + 2.6x_{21} - 3.5x_{12} - 2.6x_{22} \leq 100$ Labor Smoothing for   (9)
$3.5x_{11} + 2.6x_{21} + 3.5x_{12} + 2.6x_{22} \leq 100$ Month 2   (10)
$x_{11}, x_{12}, x_{21}, x_{22}, s_{11}, s_{12}, s_{21}, s_{22} \geq 0$

The optimal solution is to produce 193 of the men's model in month 1, 162 of the men's model in month 2, 95 units of the women's model in month 1, and 175 of the women's model in month 2. Total Cost = $67,156

Inventory Schedule

Month 1	63 Men's	0 Women's
Month 2	25 Men's	25 Women's

Labor Levels

Previous month	1000.00 hours
Month 1	922.25 hours
Month 2	1022.25 hours

b. To accommodate this new policy the right-hand sides of constraints 7−10 must be changed to 950, 1050, 50, and 50, respectively. The revised optimal solution is given.

$$x_{11} = 201$$
$$x_{21} = 95$$
$$x_{12} = 154$$
$$x_{22} = 175 \quad \text{Total Cost} = \$67,175$$

We produce more men's models in the first month and carry a larger men's model inventory; the added cost however is only $19. This seems to be a small expense to have less drastic labor force fluctuations. The new labor levels are 1000, 950, and 994.5 hours each month. Because the added cost is only $19, management might want to experiment with the labor force smoothing restrictions to enforce even less fluctuations. You may want to experiment yourself to see what happens.

20. Let x_m = number of units produced in month m
I_m = increase in the total production level in month m
D_m = decrease in the total production level in month m
s_m = inventory level at the end of month m

where

$m = 1$ refers to March
$m = 2$ refers to April
$m = 3$ refers to May

Min $1.25 I_1 + 1.25 I_2 + 1.25 I_3 + 1.00 D_1 + 1.00 D_2 + 1.00 D_3$
s.t.
Change in production level in March:

$$x_1 - 10,000 = I_1 - D_1$$

or

$$x_1 - I_1 + D_1 = 10,000$$

Change in production level in April:

$$x_2 - x_1 = I_2 - D_2$$

or

$$x_2 - x_1 - I_2 + D_2 = 0$$

Change in production level in May:

$$x_3 - x_2 = I_3 - D_3$$

or

$$x_3 - x_2 - I_3 + D_3 = 0$$

Demand in March:

$$2500 + x_1 - s_1 = 12,000$$

or

$$x_1 - s_1 = 9500$$

Demand in April:

$$s_1 + x_2 - s_2 = 8000$$

Demand in May:

$$s_2 + x_3 = 15,000$$

Inventory capacity in March:

$$s_1 \leq 3000$$

Inventory capacity in April:

$$s_2 \leq 3000$$

Optimal Solution:

Total cost of monthly production increases and decreases = $2500

$x_1 = 10,250$	$I_1 = 250$	$D_1 = 0$
$x_2 = 10,250$	$I_2 = 0$	$D_2 = 0$
$x_3 = 12,000$	$I_3 = 1750$	$D_3 = 0$
$s_1 = 750$		
$s_2 = 3000$		

22. Let SM_1 = No. of small on machine M_1
SM_2 = No. of small on machine M_2
SM_3 = No. of small on machine M_3
LM_1 = No. of large on machine M_1
LM_2 = No. of large on machine M_2
LM_3 = No. of large on machine M_3
MM_2 = No. of meal on machine M_2
MM_3 = No. of meal on machine M_3

Output from The Management Scientist showing the formulation and solution follows. Note that constraints 1–3 guarantee that next week's schedule will be met and constraints 4–6 enforce machine capacities.

```
LINEAR PROGRAMMING PROBLEM

MIN 20SM1+24SM2+32SM3+15LM1+28LM2+35LM3+18MM2+36MM3

    S.T.

    1)   1SM1+1SM2+1SM3>80000
    2)   +1LM1+1LM2+1LM3>80000
    3)   +1MM2+1MM3>65000
    4)   0.03333SM1+0.04LM1<2100
    5)   +0.02222SM2+0.025LM2+0.03333MM2<2100
    6)   +0.01667SM3+0.01923LM3+0.02273MM3<2400

OPTIMAL SOLUTION

Objective Function Value =    5515886.58866
```

Variable	Value	Reduced Costs
SM1	0.00000	4.66500
SM2	0.00000	4.00000
SM3	80000.00000	0.00000
LM1	52500.00000	0.00000
LM2	0.00000	6.50135
LM3	27500.00000	0.00000
MM2	63006.30063	0.00000
MM3	1993.69937	0.00000

Constraint	Slack/Surplus	Dual Prices
1	0.00000	-32.00000
2	0.00000	-35.00000
3	0.00000	-36.00000
4	0.00000	500.00000
5	0.00000	540.05401
6	492.25821	0.00000

```
OBJECTIVE COEFFICIENT RANGES
```

Variable	Lower Limit	Current Value	Upper Limit
SM1	15.33500	20.00000	No Upper Limit
SM2	20.00000	24.00000	No Upper Limit
SM3	0.00000	32.00000	36.00000
LM1	No Lower Limit	15.00000	20.59856
LM2	21.49865	28.00000	No Upper Limit
LM3	29.40144	35.00000	41.50135
MM2	No Lower Limit	18.00000	24.00000
MM3	30.00000	36.00000	No Upper Limit

```
RIGHT HAND SIDE RANGES
```

Constraint	Lower Limit	Current Value	Upper Limit
1	0.00000	80000.00000	109529.58688
2	52500.00000	80000.00000	105598.45103
3	63006.30063	65000.00000	86656.76257
4	1076.06196	2100.00000	3200.00000
5	1378.18010	2100.00000	2166.45000
6	1907.74179	2400.00000	No Upper Limit

Note that 5,515,887 square inches of waste are generated. Machine 3 has 492 minutes of idle capacity.

24. Let x_1 = proportion of investment A undertaken
x_2 = proportion of investment B undertaken
s_1 = funds placed in savings for period 1
s_2 = funds placed in savings for period 2
s_3 = funds placed in savings for period 3
s_4 = funds placed in savings for period 4
L_1 = funds received from loan in period 1
L_2 = funds received from loan in period 2
L_3 = funds received from loan in period 3
L_4 = funds received from loan in period 4

Objective Function:
In order to maximize the cash value at the end of the four periods, we must consider the value of investment A, the value of investment B, savings income from period 4, and loan expenses for period 4.

Max $3200x_1 + 2500x_2 + 1.1s_4 - 1.18L_4$

Constraints require the *use* of funds to equal the *source* of funds for each period.

Period 1:

$1000x_1 + 800x_2 + s_1 = 1500 + L_1$

or

$1000x_1 + 800x_2 + s_1 - L_1 = 1500$

Period 2:

$800x_1 + 500x_2 + s_2 + 1.18L_1 = 400 + 1.1s_1 + L_2$

or

$800x_1 + 500x_2 - 1.1s_1 + s_2 + 1.18L_1 - L_2 = 400$

Period 3:

$200x_1 + 300x_2 + s_3 + 1.18L_2 = 500 + 1.1s_2 + L_3$

or

$200x_1 + 300x_2 - 1.1s_2 + s_3 + 1.18L_2 - L_3 = 500$

Period 4:

$s_4 + 1.18L_3 = 100 + 200x_1 + 300x_2 + 1.1s_3 + L_4$

or

$-200x_1 - 300x_2 - 1.1s_3 + s_4 + 1.18L_3 - L_4 = 100$

Limits on Loan Funds Available:

$L_1 \leq 200$
$L_2 \leq 200$
$L_3 \leq 200$
$L_4 \leq 200$

Proportion of Investment Undertaken:

$x_1 \leq 1$
$x_2 \leq 1$

Optimal Solution: $4340.40

Investment A $x_1 = 0.458$ or   45.8%
Investment B $x_2 = 1.0$ or   100.0%

Savings/Loan Schedule:

	Period 1	Period 2	Period 3	Period 4
Savings	242.11	—	—	341.04
Loan	—	200.00	127.58	—

Chapter 10

1. The network model is shown:

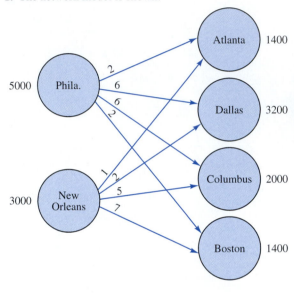

2. a. Let x_{11} = amount shipped from Jefferson City to Des Moines
x_{12} = amount shipped from Jefferson City to Kansas City
.
.
.

Min $14x_{11} + 9x_{12} + 7x_{13} + 8x_{21} + 10x_{22} + 5x_{23}$
s.t.

$$
\begin{aligned}
x_{11} + x_{12} + x_{13} &\leq 30 \\
x_{21} + x_{22} + x_{23} &\leq 20 \\
x_{11} \qquad\qquad + x_{21} \qquad\qquad &= 25 \\
x_{12} \qquad\qquad + x_{22} \qquad &= 15 \\
x_{13} \qquad\qquad + x_{23} &= 10 \\
\end{aligned}
$$
$x_{11}, x_{12}, x_{13}, x_{21}, x_{22}, x_{23} \geq 0$

b. Optimal Solution:

	Amount	Cost
Jefferson City–Des Moines	5	70
Jefferson City–Kansas City	15	135
Jefferson City–St. Louis	10	70
Omaha–Des Moines	20	160
	Total	435

4. a.

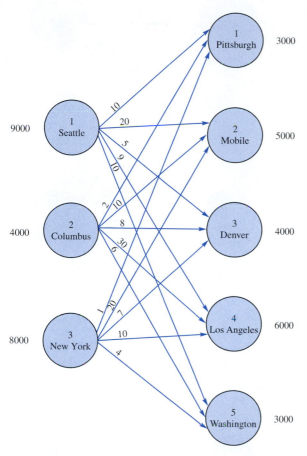

b. The linear programming formulation and optimal solution as printed by The Management Scientist are shown. The first two letters of the variable name identify the "from" node and the second two letters identify the "to" node. Also, The Management Scientist prints "<" for "≤."

```
LINEAR PROGRAMMING PROBLEM

MIN 10SEPI + 20SEMO + 5SEDE + 9SELA + 10SEWA
+ 2COPI + 10COMO + 8CODE + 30COLA + 6COWA +
1NYPI + 20NYMO + 7NYDE + 10NYLA + 4NYWA

S.T.

1) SEPI + SEMO + SEDE + SELA + SEWA < 9000
2) COPI + COMO + CODE + COLA + COWA < 4000
3) NYPI + NYMO + NYDE + NYLA + NYWA < 8000
4) SEPI + COPI + NYPI = 3000
5) SEMO + COMO + NYMO = 5000
6) SEDE + CODE + NYDE = 4000
7) SELA + COLA + NYLA = 6000
8) SEWA + COWA + NYWA = 3000
```

```
OPTIMAL SOLUTION

Objective Function Value =          150000.000

    Variable           Value          Reduced Costs
  ------------      -------------      --------------
      SEPI             0.000              10.000
      SEMO             0.000               1.000
      SEDE          4000.000               0.000
      SELA          5000.000               0.000
      SEWA             0.000               7.000
      COPI             0.000              11.000
      COMO          4000.000               0.000
      CODE             0.000              12.000
      COLA             0.000              30.000
      COWA             0.000              12.000
      NYPI          3000.000               0.000
      NYMO          1000.000               0.000
      NYDE             0.000               1.000
      NYLA          1000.000               0.000
      NYWA          3000.000               0.000
```

c. The new optimal solution actually shows a decrease of $9000 in shipping cost. It is summarized.

Optimal Solution	Units	Cost
Seattle–Denver	4000	$ 20,000
Seattle–Los Angeles	5000	45,000
Columbus–Mobile	5000	50,000
New York–Pittsburgh	4000	4,000
New York–Los Angeles	1000	10,000
New York–Washington	3000	12,000
	Total:	$141,000

6. The network model, the linear programming formulation, and the optimal solution are shown. Note that the third constraint corresponds to the dummy origin. The variables x_{31}, x_{32}, x_{33}, and x_{34} are the amounts shipped out of the dummy origin; they do not appear in the objective function because they are given a coefficient of zero.

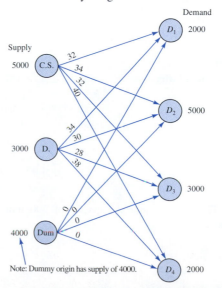

Note: Dummy origin has supply of 4000.

$$\text{Max } 32x_{11} + 34x_{12} + 32x_{13} + 40x_{14} + 34x_{21} + 30x_{22} + 28x_{23} + 38x_{24}$$

s.t.

$$
\begin{array}{llll}
x_{11} + x_{12} + x_{13} + x_{14} & & \le 5000 \\
& x_{21} + x_{22} + x_{23} + x_{24} & & \le 3000 \\
& & x_{31} + x_{32} + x_{33} + x_{34} \le 4000 & \text{Dummy} \\
x_{11} & + x_{21} & + x_{31} & = 2000 \\
\phantom{x_{11}} x_{12} & + x_{22} & + x_{32} & = 5000 \\
\phantom{x_{11}} x_{13} & + x_{23} & + x_{33} & = 3000 \\
\phantom{x_{11}} x_{14} & + x_{24} & + x_{34} & = 2000 \\
\end{array}
$$

$x_{ij} \ge 0 \quad \text{for all } i, j$

Optimal Solution	Units	Cost
Clifton Springs–D_2	4000	$136,000
Clifton Springs–D_4	1000	40,000
Danville–D_1	2000	68,000
Danville–D_4	1000	38,000
	Total Cost	$282,000

Customer 2 demand has a shortfall of 1000.
Customer 3 demand of 3000 is not satisfied.

8. The linear programming formulation and optimal solution are shown:

Let x_{1A} = Units of product A on machine 1
       x_{1B} = Units of product B on machine 1
        .
        .
       x_{3C} = Units of product C on machine 3

$$\text{Min } x_{1A} + 1.2x_{1B} + 0.9x_{1C} + 1.3x_{2A} + 1.4x_{2B} + 1.2x_{2C} + 1.1x_{3A} + x_{3B} + 1.2x_{3C}$$

s.t.

$$
\begin{array}{llll}
x_{1A} + x_{1B} + x_{1C} & & \le 1500 \\
& x_{2A} + x_{2B} + x_{2C} & & \le 1500 \\
& & x_{3A} + x_{3B} + x_{3C} \le 1000 \\
x_{1A} & + x_{2A} & + x_{3A} & = 2000 \\
\phantom{x_{1A}} x_{1B} & + x_{2B} & + x_{3B} & = 500 \\
\phantom{x_{1A}} x_{1C} & + x_{2C} & + x_{3C} & = 1200 \\
\end{array}
$$

$x_{ij} \ge 0 \quad \text{for all } i, j$

Optimal Solution	Units	Cost
1–A	300	$ 300
1–C	1200	1080
2–A	1200	1560
3–A	500	550
3–B	500	500
	Total	$3990

Note: There is an unused capacity of 300 units on machine 2.

9. a.

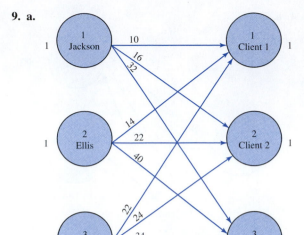

b.

$$\text{Min } 10x_{11} + 16x_{12} + 32x_{13} + 14x_{21} + 22x_{22} + 40x_{23} + 22x_{31} + 24x_{32} + 34x_{33}$$

s.t.

$$
\begin{array}{lll}
x_{11} + x_{12} + x_{13} & & \le 1 \\
& x_{21} + x_{22} + x_{23} & \le 1 \\
& & x_{31} + x_{32} + x_{33} \le 1 \\
x_{11} & + x_{21} & + x_{31} = 1 \\
\phantom{x_{11}} x_{12} & + x_{22} & + x_{32} = 1 \\
\phantom{x_{11}} x_{13} & + x_{23} & + x_{33} = 1 \\
\end{array}
$$

$x_{ij} \ge 0 \quad \text{for all } i, j$

Solution: $x_{12} = 1$, $x_{21} = 1$, $x_{33} = 1$ Total completion time = 64

10. a.

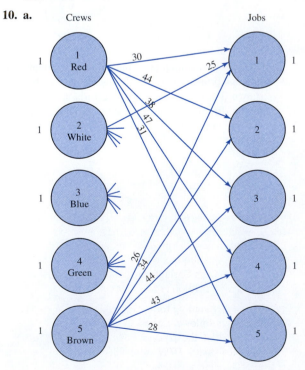

b.

Min $30x_{11} + 44x_{12} + 38x_{13} + 47x_{14} + 31x_{15} + 25x_{21} + \cdots + 28x_{55}$
s.t.

$$
\begin{aligned}
x_{11} + x_{12} + x_{13} + x_{14} + x_{15} &\leq 1 \\
x_{21} + x_{22} + x_{23} + x_{24} + x_{25} &\leq 1 \\
x_{31} + x_{32} + x_{33} + x_{34} + x_{35} &\leq 1 \\
x_{41} + x_{42} + x_{43} + x_{44} + x_{45} &\leq 1 \\
x_{51} + x_{52} + x_{53} + x_{54} + x_{55} &\leq 1 \\
x_{11} + x_{21} + x_{31} + x_{41} + x_{51} &= 1 \\
x_{12} + x_{22} + x_{32} + x_{42} + x_{52} &= 1 \\
x_{13} + x_{23} + x_{33} + x_{43} + x_{53} &= 1 \\
x_{14} + x_{24} + x_{34} + x_{44} + x_{54} &= 1 \\
x_{15} + x_{25} + x_{35} + x_{45} + x_{55} &= 1
\end{aligned}
$$

$x_{ij} \geq 0,\ i = 1, 2, \ldots, 5;\ j = 1, 2, \ldots, 5$

Optimal Solution:

Green to Job 1	$ 26
Brown to Job 2	34
Red to Job 3	38
Blue to Job 4	39
White to Job 5	25
	$162

Because the data is in hundreds of dollars, the total installation cost for the 5 contracts is $16,200.

12. a. This is the variation of the assignment problem in which multiple assignments are possible. Each distribution center may be assigned up to 3 customer zones.

The linear programming model of this problem has 40 variables (one for each combination of distribution center and customer zone). It has 13 constraints. There are 5 supply (≤ 3) constraints and 8 demand ($= 1$) constraints.

The problem can also be solved using the Transportation module of The Management Scientist. The optimal solution is given below:

	Assignments	Cost ($1000s)
Plano	Kansas City, Dallas	34
Flagstaff	Los Angeles	15
Springfield	Chicago, Columbus, Atlanta	70
Boulder	Newark, Denver	97
	Total Cost	$216

b. The Nashville distribution center is not used.

c. All the distribution centers are used. Columbus is switched from Springfield to Nashville. Total cost increases by $11,000 to $227,000.

14. A linear programming formulation of this problem can be developed as follows. Let the first letter of each variable name represent the professor and the second two the course. Note that a DPH variable is not created because the assignment is unacceptable.

Max $2.8AUG + 2.2AMB + 3.3AMS + 3.0APH + 3.2BUG + \cdots + 2.5DMS$
s.t.

$$
\begin{aligned}
AUG + AMB + AMS + APH &\leq 1 \\
BUG + BMB + BMS + BPH &\leq 1 \\
CUG + CMB + CMS + CPH &\leq 1 \\
DUG + DMB + DMS &\leq 1 \\
AUG + BUG + CUG + DUG &= 1 \\
AMB + BMB + CMB + DMB &= 1 \\
AMS + BMS + CMS + DMS &= 1 \\
APH + BPH + CPH &= 1
\end{aligned}
$$

All Variables ≥ 0

Optimal Solution	Rating
A to MS course	3.3
B to Ph.D. course	3.6
C to MBA course	3.2
D to Undergraduate course	3.2
Max Total Rating	13.3

16. a. The total cost is the sum of the purchase cost and the transportation cost. We show the calculation for Division 1–Supplier 1 and present the result for the other Division–Supplier combinations.

Division 1–Supplier 1

Purchase cost (40,000 × $12.60)	$504,000
Transportation Cost (40,000 × $2.75)	110,000
Total Cost:	$614,000

Cost Matrix ($1000s)

	Supplier					
Division	1	2	3	4	5	6
1	614	660	534	680	590	630
2	603	639	702	693	693	630
3	865	830	775	850	900	930
4	532	553	511	581	595	553
5	720	648	684	693	657	747

b. Optimal Solution:

Supplier 1–Division 2	$ 603
Supplier 2–Division 5	648
Supplier 3–Division 3	775
Supplier 5–Division 1	590
Supplier 6–Division 4	553
Total	$3169

17. a. Network Model

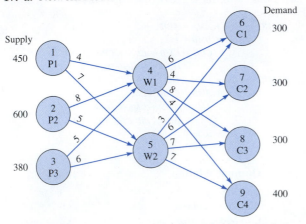

b. & c. The linear programming formulation and solution as printed by The Management Scientist is shown:

```
LINEAR PROGRAMMING PROBLEM

MIN 4X14 + 7X15 + 8X24 + 5X25 + 5X34 + 6X35
+ 6X46 + 4X47 + 8X48 + 4X49 + 3X56 + 6X57
+ 7X58 + 7X59

S.T.

1) X14 + X15 < 450
2) X24 + X25 < 600
3) X34 + X35 < 380
4) X46 + X47 + X48 + X49 − X14 − X24
   − X34 = 0
5) X56 + X57 + X58 + X59 − X15 − X25
   − X35 = 0
6) X46 + X56 = 300
7) X47 + X57 = 300
8) X48 + X58 = 300
9) X49 + X59 = 400


OPTIMAL SOLUTION

Objective Function Value =     11850.000

   Variable        Value         Reduced Costs
 ------------   ------------    ----------------
    X14          450.000          0.000
    X15            0.000          3.000
    X24            0.000          3.000
    X25          600.000          0.000
    X34          250.000          0.000
    X35            0.000          1.000
    X46            0.000          3.000
    X47          300.000          0.000
    X48            0.000          1.000
    X49          400.000          0.000
    X56          300.000          0.000
    X57            0.000          2.000
    X58          300.000          0.000
    X59            0.000          3.000
```

There is an excess capacity of 130 units at plant 3.

18. a. Three arcs must be added to the network model in Problem 23a. The new network is shown:

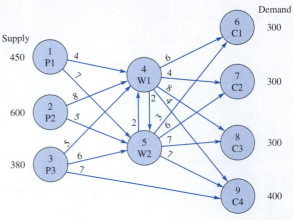

b. & c. The linear programming formulation and optimal solution as printed by The Management Scientist follow:

```
LINEAR PROGRAMMING PROBLEM

MIN 4X14 + 7X15 + 8X24 + 5X25 + 5X34 +
6X35 + 6X46 + 4X47 + 8X48 + 4X49 + 3X56 +
6X57 + 7X58 + 7X59 + 7X39 + 2X45 + 2X54

S.T.

1) X14 + X15 < 450
2) X24 + X25 < 600
3) X34 + X35 + X39 < 380
4) X45 + X46 + X47 + X48 + X49 − X14 − X24
   − X34 − X54 = 0
5) X54 + X56 + X57 + X58 + X59 − X15 − X25
   − X35 − X45 = 0
6) X46 + X56 = 300
7) X47 + X57 = 300
8) X48 + X58 = 300
9) X39 + X49 + X59 = 400


OPTIMAL SOLUTION

Objective Function Value =    11220.000

   Variable        Value         Reduced Costs
 ------------   ------------    ----------------
    X14          320.000          0.000
    X15            0.000          2.000
    X24            0.000          4.000
    X25          600.000          0.000
    X34            0.000          2.000
    X35            0.000          2.000
    X46            0.000          2.000
    X47          300.000          0.000
    X48            0.000          0.000
    X49           20.000          0.000
    X56          300.000          0.000
    X57            0.000          3.000
    X58          300.000          0.000
    X59            0.000          4.000
    X39          380.000          0.000
    X45            0.000          1.000
    X54            0.000          3.000
```

The value of the solution here is $630 less than the value of the solution for Problem 23. The new shipping route from plant 3 to customer 4 has helped ($x_{39} = 380$). There is now excess capacity of 130 units at plant 1.

20.

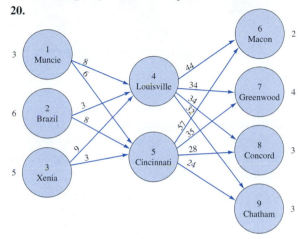

A linear programming model is

$$\text{Min } 8x_{14}+6x_{15}+3x_{24}+8x_{25}+9x_{34}+3x_{35}+44x_{46}+34x_{47}+34x_{48}+32x_{49}+57x_{56}+35x_{57}+28x_{58}+24x_{59}$$

s.t.

$$
\begin{aligned}
x_{14}+\ x_{15} &\le 3 \\
x_{24}+\ x_{25} &\le 6 \\
x_{34}+\ x_{35} &\le 5 \\
-x_{14}\quad -\ x_{24}\quad -\ x_{34}\ +\ x_{46}+\ x_{47}+\ x_{48}+\ x_{49} &= 0 \\
-x_{15}\quad -\ x_{25}\quad -\ x_{35}\qquad\qquad +\ x_{56}+\ x_{57}+\ x_{58}+\ x_{59} &= 0 \\
x_{46}\qquad\qquad +\ x_{56} &= 2 \\
x_{47}\qquad\qquad +\ x_{57} &= 4 \\
x_{48}\qquad\qquad +\ x_{58} &= 3 \\
x_{49}\qquad\qquad +\ x_{59} &= 3
\end{aligned}
$$

$x_{ij} \ge 0$ for all i, j

Optimal Solution	Units Shipped	Cost
Muncie–Cincinnati	1	6
Cincinnati–Concord	3	84
Brazil–Louisville	6	18
Louisville–Macon	2	88
Louisville–Greenwood	4	136
Xenia–Cincinnati	5	15
Cincinnati–Chatham	3	72
		419

Two rail cars must be held at Muncie until a buyer is found.

22. a.

$$\text{Min } 20x_{12} + 25x_{15} + 30x_{25} + 45x_{27} + 20x_{31} + 35x_{36}$$
$$+ 30x_{42} + 25x_{53} + 15x_{54} + 28x_{56} + 12x_{67} + 27x_{74}$$

s.t.

$$
\begin{aligned}
x_{31} - \ x_{12} - \ x_{15} &= 8 \\
x_{25} + \ x_{27} - \ x_{12} - \ x_{42} &= 5 \\
x_{31} + \ x_{36} - \ x_{53} &= 3 \\
x_{54} + \ x_{74} - \ x_{42} &= 3 \\
x_{53} + \ x_{54} + \ x_{56} - \ x_{15} - \ x_{25} &= 2 \\
x_{36} + \ x_{56} - \ x_{67} &= 5 \\
x_{74} - \ x_{27} - \ x_{67} &= 6
\end{aligned}
$$

$x_{ij} \ge 0$ for all i, j

b.

$x_{12} = 0$		$x_{53} = 5$	
$x_{15} = 0$		$x_{54} = 0$	
$x_{25} = 8$		$x_{56} = 5$	
$x_{27} = 0$		$x_{67} = 0$	
$x_{31} = 8$		$x_{74} = 6$	
$x_{36} = 0$		$x_{56} = 5$	
$x_{42} = 3$			

Total cost of redistributing cars = $917

23. Origin—Node 1
Transshipment—Nodes 2–5
Destination—Node 7

The linear program will have 14 variables for the arcs and 7 constraints for the nodes.

Let

$$x_{ij} = \begin{cases} 1 & \text{if the arc from node } i \text{ to node } j \text{ is on the shortest route} \\ 0 & \text{otherwise} \end{cases}$$

$$\text{Min } 7x_{12} + 9x_{13} + 18x_{14} + 3x_{23} + 5x_{25} + 3x_{32} + 4x_{35}$$
$$+ 3x_{46} + 5x_{52} + 4x_{53} + 2x_{56} + 6x_{57} + 2x_{65} + 3x_{67}$$

s.t.

	Flow Out	Flow In	
Node 1	$x_{12} + x_{13} + x_{14}$		$= 1$
Node 2	$x_{23} + x_{25}$	$-x_{12} - x_{32} - x_{52}$	$= 0$
Node 3	$x_{32} + x_{35}$	$-x_{13} - x_{23} - x_{53}$	$= 0$
Node 4	x_{46}	$-x_{14}$	$= 0$
Node 5	$x_{52} + x_{53} + x_{56} + x_{57}$	$-x_{25} - x_{35} - x_{65}$	$= 0$
Node 6	$x_{65} + x_{67}$	$-x_{46} - x_{56}$	$= 0$
Node 7		$+x_{57} + x_{67}$	$= 1$

$x_{ij} \ge 0$ for all i and j

Optimal Solution: $x_{12} = 1, x_{25} = 1, x_{56} = 1$, and $x_{67} = 1$
Shortest Route: 1–2–5–6–7
Length $= 17$

24. The linear program has 13 variables for the arcs and 6 constraints for the nodes. Use the same 6 constraints for the Gorman shortest route problem, as shown in the text. The objective function changes to travel time as follows:

$$\text{Min } 40x_{12} + 36x_{13} + 6x_{23} + 6x_{32} + 12x_{24} + 12x_{42} +$$
$$25x_{26} + 15x_{35} + 15x_{53} + 8x_{45} + 8x_{54} + 11x_{46} + 23x_{56}$$

Optimal Solution: $x_{12} = 1, x_{24} = 1$, and $x_{46} = 1$
Shortest Route: 1–2–4–6
Total Time = 63 minutes

26. Origin—Node 1
Transshipment—Nodes 2–5 and node 7
Destination—Node 6

The linear program will have 18 variables for the arcs and 7 constraints for the nodes.

Let

$$x_{ij} = \begin{cases} 1 & \text{if the arc from node } i \text{ to node } j \text{ is on the shortest route} \\ 0 & \text{otherwise} \end{cases}$$

$$\text{Min } 35x_{12} + 30x_{13} + 20x_{14} + 8x_{23} + 12x_{25} + 8x_{32} + 9x_{34} + 10x_{35}$$
$$+ 20x_{36} + 9x_{43} + 15x_{47} + 12x_{52} + 10x_{53} + 5x_{56} + 20x_{57} + 15x_{74}$$
$$+ 20x_{75} + 5x_{76}$$

s.t.

	Flow Out	Flow In	
Node 1	$x_{12} + x_{13} + x_{14}$		$= 1$
Node 2	$x_{23} + x_{25}$	$-x_{12} - x_{32} - x_{52}$	$= 0$
Node 3	$x_{32} + x_{34} + x_{35} + x_{36}$	$-x_{13} - x_{23} - x_{43} - x_{53}$	$= 0$
Node 4	$x_{43} + x_{47}$	$-x_{14} - x_{34} - x_{74}$	$= 0$
Node 5	$x_{52} + x_{53} + x_{56} + x_{57}$	$-x_{25} - x_{35} - x_{75}$	$= 0$
Node 6		$+x_{36} + x_{56} + x_{76}$	$= 1$
Node 7	$x_{74} + x_{75} + x_{76}$	$-x_{47} - x_{57}$	$= 0$

$$x_{ij} \geq 0 \quad \text{for all } i \text{ and } j$$

Optimal Solution: $x_{14} = 1$, $x_{47} = 1$, and $x_{76} = 1$

Shortest Route: 1–4–7–6

Total Distance = 40 miles

28. Origin—Node 0

Transshipment—Nodes 1 to 3

Destination—Node 4

The linear program will have 10 variables for the arcs and 5 constraints for the nodes.

Let

$$x_{ij} = \begin{cases} 1 & \text{if the arc from node } i \text{ to node } j \text{ is on the minimum cost route} \\ 0 & \text{otherwise} \end{cases}$$

Min $600x_{01} + 1000x_{02} + 2000x_{03} + 2800x_{04} + 500x_{12} + 1400x_{13} + 2100x_{14} + 800x_{23} + 1600x_{24} + 700x_{34}$

s.t.

	Flow Out	Flow In	
Node 0	$x_{01} + x_{02} + x_{03} + x_{04}$		$= 1$
Node 1	$x_{12} + x_{13} + x_{14}$	$-x_{01}$	$= 0$
Node 2	$x_{23} + x_{24}$	$-x_{02} - x_{12}$	$= 0$
Node 3	x_{34}	$-x_{03} - x_{13} - x_{23}$	$= 0$
Node 4		$-x_{04} - x_{14} - x_{24} - x_{34}$	$= 1$

$$x_{ij} \geq 0 \quad \text{for all } i \text{ and } j$$

Optimal Solution: $x_{02} = 1$, $x_{23} = 1$, and $x_{34} = 1$

Shortest Route: 0–2–3–4

Total Cost = $2500

29. The capacitated transshipment problem to solve is given:

Max x_{61}

s.t.

$$x_{12} + x_{13} + x_{14} - x_{61} = 0$$
$$x_{24} + x_{25} - x_{12} - x_{42} = 0$$
$$x_{34} + x_{36} - x_{13} - x_{43} = 0$$
$$x_{42} + x_{43} + x_{45} + x_{46} - x_{14} - x_{24} - x_{34} - x_{54} = 0$$
$$x_{54} + x_{56} - x_{25} - x_{45} = 0$$
$$x_{61} - x_{36} + x_{46} - x_{56} = 0$$

$x_{12} \leq 2$	$x_{13} \leq 6$	$x_{14} \leq 3$
$x_{24} \leq 1$	$x_{25} \leq 4$	
$x_{34} \leq 3$	$x_{36} \leq 2$	
$x_{42} \leq 1$	$x_{43} \leq 3$	$x_{45} \leq 1$ $x_{46} \leq 3$
$x_{54} \leq 1$	$x_{56} \leq 6$	

$$x_{ij} \geq 0 \text{ for all } i, j$$

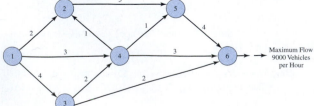

Maximum Flow 9000 Vehicles per Hour

The system cannot accommodate a flow of 10,000 vehicles per hour.

30.

11,000

32. **a.** 10,000 gallons per hour or 10 hours

b. Flow reduced to 9000 gallons per hour; 11.1 hours.

34. Maximal Flow = 23 gallons/minute. Five gallons will flow from node 3 to node 5.

36. **a.** Let R_1, R_2, R_3 represent regular time production in months 1, 2, 3

O_1, O_2, O_3 represent overtime production in months 1, 2, 3

D_1, D_2, D_3 represent demand in months 1, 2, 3

Using these 9 nodes, a network model is shown:

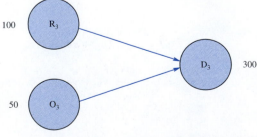

b. Use the following notation to define the variables: The first two letters designate the "from node" and the second two letters designate the "to node" of the arc. For instance, R_1D_1 is amount of regular time production available to satisfy demand in month 1; O_1D_1 is amount of overtime production in month 1 available to satisfy demand in month 1; D_1D_2 is the amount of inventory carried over from month 1 to month 2; and so on.

```
MIN 50R1D1 + 80O1D1 + 20D1D2 + 50R2D2 +
80O2D2 + 20D2D3 + 60R3D3 + 100O3D3

S.T.

  1)  R1D1 ≤ 275
  2)  O1D1 ≤ 100
  3)  R2D2 ≤ 200
  4)  O2D2 ≤ 50
  5)  R3D3 ≤ 100
  6)  O3D3 ≤ 50
  7)  R1D1 + O1D1 − D1D2        = 150
  8)  R2D2 + O2D2 + D1D2 − D2D3 = 250
  9)  R3D3 + O3D3 + D2D3        = 300
```

c. Optimal Solution:

Variable	Value
R1D1	275.000
O1D1	25.000
D1D2	150.000
R2D2	200.000
O2D2	50.000
D2D3	150.000
R3D3	100.000
O3D3	50.000

Value = $46,750

Note: Slack variable for constraint 2 = 75

d. The values of the slack variables for constraints 1 through 6 represent unused capacity. The only nonzero slack variable is for constraint 2; its value is 75. Thus, there are 75 units of unused overtime capacity in month 1.

Chapter 11

2. a.

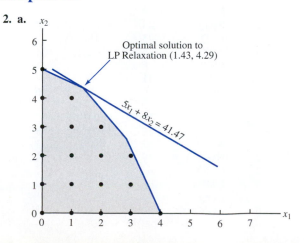

b. The optimal solution to the LP Relaxation is given by $x_1 = 1.43$, $x_2 = 4.29$ with an objective function value of 41.47. Rounding down gives the feasible integer solution $x_1 = 1$, $x_2 = 4$; its value is 37.

c.

The optimal solution is given by $x_1 = 0$, $x_2 = 5$; its value is 40. It is not the same solution as found by rounding down; it provides a 3-unit increase in the value of the objective function.

4. a. $x_1 = 3.67$, $x_2 = 0$; Value = 36.7
Rounded: $x_1 = 3$, $x_2 = 0$; Value = 30
Lower bound = 30; Upper bound = 36.7

b. $x_1 = 3$, $x_2 = 2$; Value = 36

c. Alternative optimal solutions: $-x_1 = 0$, $x_2 = 5$
  $x_1 = 2$, $x_2 = 4$

5. a. The feasible mixed-integer solutions are indicated by the boldface vertical lines in the graph.

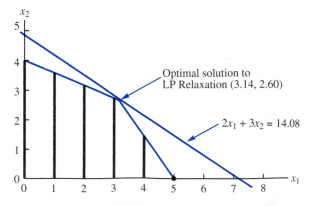

b. The optimal solution to the LP Relaxation is given by $x_1 = 3.14$, $x_2 = 2.60$; its value is 14.08.
Rounding down the value of x_1 to find a feasible mixed-integer solution yields $x_1 = 3$, $x_2 = 2.60$ with a value of 13.8; this solution is clearly not optimal; with $x_1 = 3$, x_2 can be made larger without violating the constraints.

c. The optimal solution to the MILP is given by $x_1 = 3$, $x_2 = 2.67$; its value is 14, as shown in the following figure:

6. b. $x_1 = 1.96$, $x_2 = 5.48$; Value = 7.44
Rounded: $x_1 = 1.96$, $x_2 = 5$; Value = 6.96
Lower bound = 6.96; Upper bound = 7.44
c. $x_1 = 1.29$, $x_2 = 6$; Value = 7.29

7. a. $x_1 + x_3 + x_5 + x_6 = 2$
b. $x_3 - x_5 = 0$
c. $x_1 + x_4 = 1$
d. $x_4 \leq x_1$
$x_4 \leq x_3$
e. $x_4 \leq x_1$
$x_4 \leq x_3$
$x_4 \leq x_1 + x_3 - 1$

8. a. $x_3 = 1$, $x_4 = 1$, $x_6 = 1$; Value = 17,500
b. Add $x_1 + x_2 \leq 1$.
c. Add $x_3 - x_4 = 0$.

10. b. Choose locations B and E.

12. a. $P \leq 15 + 15Y_P$
$D \leq 15 + 15Y_D$
$J \leq 15 + 15Y_J$
$Y_P + Y_D + Y_J \leq 1$
b. $P = 15$, $D = 15$, $J = 30$
$Y_P = 0$, $Y_D = 0$, $Y_J = 1$; Value = 50

13. a. Add the following multiple-choice constraint to the problem:

$y_1 + y_2 = 1$

New optimal solution: $y_1 = 1$, $y_3 = 1$, $x_{12} = 10$, $x_{31} = 30$, $x_{52} = 10$, $x_{53} = 20$
Value = 940
b. Because one plant is already located in St. Louis, it is only necessary to add the following constraint to the model:

$y_3 + y_4 \leq 1$

New optimal solution: $y_4 = 1$, $x_{42} = 20$, $x_{43} = 20$, $x_{51} = 30$
Value = 860

14. b. Modernize plants 1 and 3 or plants 4 and 5.
d. Modernize plants 1 and 3.

16. b. Use all part-time employees.
Bring on as follows: 9:00 A.M.–6, 11:00 A.M.–2, 12:00 noon–6, 1:00 P.M.–1, 3:00 P.M.–6
Cost = \$672
c. Same as in part (b)
d. New solution is to bring on 1 full-time employee at 9:00 A.M., 4 more at 11:00 A.M., and part-time employees as follows:
9:00 A.M.–5, 12:00 noon–5, and 3:00 P.M.–2

18. a. 52, 49, 36, 83, 39, 70, 79, 59
b. Thick crust, cheese blend, chunky sauce, medium sausage. Six of eight consumers will prefer this pizza (75%).

20. a. New objective function: Min $25x_1 + 40x_2 + 40x_3 + 40x_4 + 25x_5$
b. $x_4 = x_5 = 1$; modernize the Ohio and California plants
c. Add the constraint $x_2 + x_3 = 1$.
d. $x_1 = x_3 = 1$

22. $x_1 + x_2 + x_3 = 3y_1 + 5y_2 + 7y_3$
$y_1 + y_2 + y_3 = 1$

24. a. x_{111}, x_{112}, x_{121}
b. $x_{111} + x_{112} + x_{121} \leq 1$
c. $x_{531} + x_{532} + x_{533} + x_{541} + x_{542} + x_{543} + x_{551} + x_{552} + x_{561} \leq 1$
d. Only two screens are available.
e. $x_{222} + x_{231} + x_{422} + x_{431} + x_{531} + x_{532} + x_{533} + x_{631} + x_{632} + x_{633} \leq 2$

Chapter 12

2. a. Flight Leg 1: $8 + 0 + 4 + 4 + 1 + 2 = 19$
Flight Leg 2: $6 + 3 + 2 + 4 + 2 + 1 = 18$
Flight Leg 3: $0 + 1 + 3 + 2 + 4 + 2 = 12$
Flight Leg 4: $4 + 2 + 2 + 1 + 6 + 3 = 18$
b. The calculation of the remaining demand for each ODIF is shown below:

ODIF	ODIF Code	Original Allocation	Seats Sold	Seats Available
1	PCQ	33	25	8
2	PMQ	44	44	0
3	POQ	45	18	27
4	PCY	16	12	4
5	PMY	6	5	1
6	POY	11	9	2
7	NCQ	26	20	6
8	NMQ	56	33	23
9	NOQ	39	37	2
10	NCY	15	11	4
11	NMY	7	5	2
12	NOY	9	8	1
13	CMQ	64	27	37
14	CMY	8	6	2
15	COQ	46	35	11
16	COY	10	7	3

c.

```
OPTIMAL SOLUTION

Objective Function Value = 15730.000

    Variable        Value        Reduced Costs
  ------------   ------------   ----------------
     PCQ          8.000             0.000
     PMQ          1.000             0.000
     POQ          3.000             0.000
     PCY          4.000             0.000
     PMY          1.000             0.000
     POY          2.000             0.000
     NCQ          6.000             0.000
     NMQ          3.000             0.000
     NOQ          2.000             0.000
     NCY          4.000             0.000
     NMY          2.000             0.000
     NOY          1.000             0.000
     CMQ          3.000             0.000
     CMY          2.000             0.000
     COQ          7.000             0.000
     COY          3.000             0.000
```

4. b. 65.7% small-cap growth fund
34.3% of the portfolio in a small-cap value
Expected return = 18.5%

c. 10% foreign stock
50.8% small-cap fund
39.2% of the portfolio in small-cap value
Expected return = 17.178%

6. Using LINGO or Excel Solver, the optimal solution is $X = 2$, $Y = -4$, for an optimal solution value of 0.

8. a. With $1000 being spent on radio and $1000 being spent on direct mail, we substitute those values into the sales function:

$$S = -2R^2 - 10M^2 - 8RM + 18R + 43M$$
$$= -2(2^2) - 10(1^2) - 8(2)(1) + 18(2) + 43(1)$$
$$= 18$$

Sales of $18,000 will be realized with this allocation of the media budget.

b. Add a budget constraint to the sales function that is to be maximized.

max $-2R^2 - 10M^2 - 8RM + 18R + 34M$
s.t.
$$R + M \leq 3$$

c. The optimal solution is to invest $2500 in radio advertising and $500 in direct mail advertising. The total sales generated is $37,000.

10. a. The optimization model is

Max $5L^{.25}C^{.75}$
s.t.
$$25L + 75C \leq 75000$$
$$L, C \geq 0$$

b. The optimal solution to this is $L = 750$ and $C = 750$ for an optimal objective function value of 3750. If Excel Solver is used for this problem, we recommend starting with an initial solution that has $L > 0$ and $C > 0$.

12. a. Let OT be the number of overtime hours scheduled. Then the optimization model is

max $-3x_1^2 + 42x_1 - 3x_2^2 + 48x_2 + 700 - 5OT$
s.t.
$$4x_1 + 6x_2 \leq 24 + OT$$
$$x_1, x_2, OT \geq 0$$

b. The optimal solution is to schedule $OT = 8.66667$ overtime hours and produce $x_1 = 3.66667$ units of product 1 and $x_2 = 3.00000$ units of product 2 for a profit of 887.3333.

13. a. If X is the weekly production volume in thousands of units at the Dayton plant and Y is the weekly production volume in thousands of units at the Hamilton plant, then the optimization model is

min $X^2 - X + 5 + Y^2 + 2Y + 3$
s.t.
$$X + Y = 8$$
$$X, Y \geq 0$$

b. Using LINGO or Excel Solver, the optimal solution is $X = 4.75$ and $Y = 3.25$ for an optimal objective value of 42.875.

14. Define the variables to be the dollars invested in the mutual fund. For example, IB = 500 means that $500 is invested in the Intermediate-Term bond fund. The LINGO formulation is

```
MIN = (1/5)*((R1 - RBAR)^2 + (R2 - RBAR)^2
      + (R3 - RBAR)^2 + (R4 - RBAR)^2 +
      (R5 - RBAR)^2);

.1006*FS + .1764*IB + .3241*LG + .3236*LV
+ .3344*SG + .2456*SV = R1;

.1312*FS + .0325*IB + .1871*LG + .2061*LV
+ .1940*SG + .2532*SV = R2;

.1347*FS + .0751*IB + .3328*LG + .1293*LV
+ .0385*SG - .0670*SV = R3;

.4542*FS - .0133*IB + .4146*LG + .0706*LV
+ .5868*SG + .0543*SV = R4;

-.2193*FS + .0736*IB - .2326*LG - .0537*LV
- .0902*SG + .1731*SV = R5;

FS + IB + LG + LV + SG + SV = 50000;
(1/5)*(R1 + R2 + R3 + R4 + R5) = RBAR;
RBAR > RMIN;
RMIN = 5000;

@FREE(R1);
@FREE(R2);
@FREE(R3);
@FREE(R4);
@FREE(R5);
```

The optimal solution to this model using LINGO is

```
Local optimal solution found.
  Objective value:                    6,784,038
  Total solver iterations:                   19

Model Title: MARKOWITZ

   Variable          Value      Reduced Cost
 ------------   ------------   ---------------
      R1          9478.492        0.000000
     RBAR         5000.000        0.000000
      R2          5756.023        0.000000
      R3          2821.951        0.000000
      R4          4864.037        0.000000
      R5          2079.496        0.000000
      FS          7920.372        0.000000
      IB          26273.98        0.000000
      LG          2103.251        0.000000
      LV          0.000000        208.2068
      SG          0.000000        78.04764
      SV          13702.40        0.000000
      RMIN        5000.000        0.000000
```

Excel Solver will also produce the same optimal solution.

15. The optimal value of α is 0.1743882 and the resulting sum of squared errors is 98.56.

16. The returns appear in Figure 12.13.

18.

```
Model Title: MATCHING S&P INFO TECH RETURNS

   Variable          Value      Reduced Cost
 ------------   ------------   ---------------
      R1         -0.1526620       0.000000
      R2          0.7916129       0.000000
      R3          0.9403282       0.000000
      R4          0.1694353       0.000000
      R5         -0.5132641       0.000000
      R6         -0.4379140       0.000000
      R7          0.2329556       0.000000
      R8         0.3760108E-03    0.000000
      R9         0.1671686E-01    0.000000
      AAPL        0.000000        1.624161
      AMD         0.1014161       0.000000
      ORCL        0.8985839       0.000000
```

20. a. The optimal value is 2.118493.

  b. No, minimizing risk is not the same thing as minimizing VaR. Minimizing σ is not the same thing as maximizing Value at Risk. If we maximize Value at Risk, the objective function is

  Max $\mu - 2.33\sigma$ = Min $2.33\sigma - \mu$

  and the objective has two variables, σ and μ.

  c. If we fix mean return, then it is a constant and

  Max $\mu - 2.33\sigma$ = Min $2.33\sigma - \mu$ = $-\mu$ + Min 2.33σ
  $= -\mu + 2.33$ Min σ

Finally, observe that minimizing σ is the same as minimizing σ^2 because the standard deviation is always non-negative.

22. This is a nonlinear 0-1 integer programming problem. Let $XIJ = 1$ if tanker I is assigned loading dock J and 0 if not. The optimal solution to this model is 10000.00. Tanker 1 should be assigned to dock 2, tanker 2 to dock 1, and tanker 3 to dock 3. Depending on the starting point, Excel Solver will likely get stuck at a local optimum and not the find the optimal solution that LINGO finds.

Chapter 13

2.

3.

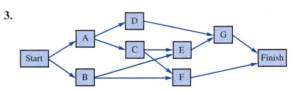

4. a. A–D–G

  b. No; Time = 15 months

  6. a. Critical path: A–D–F–H

  b. 22 weeks

  c. No, it is a critical activity.

  d. Yes, 2 weeks

  e. Schedule for activity E:

Earliest start	3
Latest start	4
Earliest finish	10
Latest finish	11

8. b. B–C–E–F–H

  d. Yes, time = 49 weeks

10. a.

Activity	Optimistic	Most Probable	Pessimistic	Expected Times	Variance
A	4	5.0	6	5.00	0.11
B	8	9.0	10	9.00	0.11
C	7	7.5	11	8.00	0.44
D	7	9.0	10	8.83	0.25
E	6	7.0	9	7.17	0.25
F	5	6.0	7	6.00	0.11

b. Critical activities: B–D–F

Expected project completion time: $9.00 + 8.83 + 6.00 = 23.83$

Variance of projection completion time: $0.11 + 0.25 + 0.11 = 0.47$

12. a. A–D–H–I

b. 25.66 days

c. 0.2578

13.

Activity	Expected Time	Variance
A	5	0.11
B	3	0.03
C	7	0.11
D	6	0.44
E	7	0.44
F	3	0.11
G	10	0.44
H	8	1.78

From Problem 6, A–D–F–H is the critical path, so $E(T) = 5 + 6 + 3 + 8 = 22$

$\sigma^2 = 0.11 + 0.44 + 0.11 + 1.78 = 2.44$.

$$z = \frac{\text{Time} - E(T)}{\sigma} = \frac{\text{Time} - 22}{\sqrt{2.44}}$$

a. Time = 21: $z = -0.64$

Cumulative Probability = 0.2611

$P(21 \text{ weeks}) = 0.2611$

b. Time = 22: $z = 0.00$

Cumulative Probability = 0.5000

$P(22 \text{ weeks}) = 0.5000$

c. Time = 25: $z = +1.92$

Cumulative Probability = 0.9726

$P(25 \text{ weeks}) = 0.9726$

14. a. A–C–E–G–H

b. 52 weeks (1 year)

c. 0.0174

d. 0.0934

e. 10 months—doubtful

13 months—very likely

Estimate 12 months (1 year).

16. a.

$E(T)$	Variance
16	3.92
13	2.03
10	1.27

b. 0.9783, approximately 1.00, approximately 1.00

18. c. A–B–D–G–H–I, 14.17 weeks

d. 0.0951, yes

20. b. Crash B(1 week), D(2 weeks), E(1 week), F(1 week), G(1 week)

Total cost = $2427

c. All activities are critical

21. a.

Activity	Earliest Start	Latest Start	Earliest Finish	Latest Finish	Slack	Critical Activity
A	0	0	3	3	0	Yes
B	0	1	2	3	1	
C	3	3	8	8	0	Yes
D	2	3	7	8	1	
E	8	8	14	14	0	Yes
F	8	10	10	12	2	
G	10	12	12	14	2	

Critical Path: A–C–E

Project completion time $= t_A + t_C + t_E = 3 + 5 + 6 = 14$ days

b. Total cost = $8400

22. a.

Activity	Max. Crash Days	Crash Cost/Day
A	1	600
B	1	700
C	2	400
D	2	400
E	2	500
F	1	400
G	1	500

Min $600Y_A + 700Y_B + 400Y_C + 400Y_D + 500Y_E + 400Y_F + 400Y_G$

s.t.

$$
\begin{aligned}
X_A + Y_A &\geq 3 \\
X_B + Y_B &\geq 2 \\
-X_A + X_C + Y_C &\geq 5 \\
-X_B + X_D + Y_D &\geq 5 \\
-X_C + X_E + Y_E &\geq 6 \\
-X_D + X_E + Y_E &\geq 6 \\
-X_C + X_F + Y_F &\geq 2 \\
-X_D + X_F + Y_F &\geq 2 \\
-X_F + X_G + Y_G &\geq 2 \\
-X_E + X_{FIN} &\geq 0 \\
-X_G + X_{FIN} &\geq 0 \\
X_{FIN} &\leq 12 \\
Y_A &\leq 1 \\
Y_B &\leq 1 \\
Y_C &\leq 2 \\
Y_D &\leq 2 \\
Y_E &\leq 2 \\
Y_F &\leq 1 \\
Y_G &\leq 1
\end{aligned}
$$

All $X, Y \geq 0$

b. Solution of the linear programming model in part (a) shows:

Activity	Crash	Crashing Cost
C	1 day	$400
E	1 day	500
	Total	$900

c. Total cost = Normal cost + Crashing cost
= $8400 + $900 = $9300

24. c. A–B–C–F, 31 weeks
d. Crash A(2 weeks), B(2 weeks), C(1 week), D(1 week), E(1 week)
e. All activities are critical.
f. $112,500

Chapter 14

1. a. $Q^* = \sqrt{\dfrac{2DC_0}{C_h}} = \sqrt{\dfrac{2(3600)(20)}{0.25(3)}} = 438.18$

b. $r = dm = \dfrac{3600}{250}(5) = 72$

c. $T = \dfrac{250Q^*}{D} = \dfrac{250(438.18)}{3600} = 30.43$ days

d. $TC = \dfrac{1}{2}QC_h + \dfrac{D}{Q}C_0$

$= \dfrac{1}{2}(438.18)(0.25)(3) + \dfrac{3600}{438.18}(20) = \$328.63$

2. $164.32 for each; Total cost = $328.64

4. a. 1095.45
b. 240
c. 22.82 days
d. $273.86 for each; Total cost = $547.72

6. a. 15.95
b. $2106
c. 15.04
d. 16.62 days

8. $Q^* = 11.73$, use 12
5 classes per year
$225,200

10. $Q^* = 1414.21$
$T = 28.28$ days
Production runs of 7.07 days

12. a. 1500
b. 4; 3-month cycle time
c. Change to $Q^* = 1500$
d. Savings = $12,510

13. a. $Q^* = \sqrt{\dfrac{2DC_0}{(1 - D/P)C_h}}$

$= \sqrt{\dfrac{2(7200)(150)}{(1 - 7200/25,000)(0.18)(14.50)}} = 1078.12$

b. Number of production runs $= \dfrac{D}{Q^*} = \dfrac{7200}{1078.12} = 6.68$

c. $T = \dfrac{250Q}{D} = \dfrac{250(1078.12)}{7200} = 37.43$ days

d. Production run length $= \dfrac{Q}{P/250}$

$= \dfrac{1078.12}{25,000/250} = 10.78$ days

e. Maximum inventory $= \left(1 - \dfrac{D}{P}\right)Q$

$= \left(1 - \dfrac{7200}{25,000}\right)(1078.12)$

$= 767.62$

f. Holding cost $= \dfrac{1}{2}\left(1 - \dfrac{D}{P}\right)QC_h$

$= \dfrac{1}{2}\left(1 - \dfrac{7200}{25,000}\right)(1078.12)(0.18)(14.50)$

$= \$1001.74$

Ordering cost $= \dfrac{D}{Q}C_0 = \dfrac{7200}{1078.12}(150) = \$1001.74$

Total cost = $2003.48

g. $r = dm = \left(\dfrac{D}{250}\right)m = \dfrac{7200}{250}(15) = 432$

14. New $Q^* = 4509$

15. a. $Q^* = \sqrt{\dfrac{2DC_0}{C_h}\left(\dfrac{C_h + C_b}{C_b}\right)}$

$= \sqrt{\dfrac{2(12,000)(25)}{0.50}\left(\dfrac{0.50 + 5}{0.50}\right)} = 1148.91$

b. $S^* = Q^*\left(\dfrac{C_h}{C_h + C_b}\right) = 1148.91\left(\dfrac{0.50}{0.50 + 5}\right) = 104.45$

c. Max inventory = $Q^* - S^* = 1044.46$

d. $T = \dfrac{250Q^*}{D} = \dfrac{250(1148.91)}{12,000} = 23.94$ days

e. Holding $= \dfrac{(Q - S)^2}{2Q}C_h = \$237.38$

Ordering $= \dfrac{D}{Q}C_0 = \$261.12$

Backorder $= \dfrac{S^2}{2Q}C_b = \$23.74$

Total cost = $522.24
The total cost for the EOQ model in Problem 4 was $547.72; allowing backorders reduces the total cost.

16. 135.55; $r = dm - S$; less than

18. 64, 24.44

20. $Q^* = 100$; Total cost = $3,601.50

21. $Q = \sqrt{\dfrac{2DC_0}{C_h}}$

$Q_1 = \sqrt{\dfrac{2(500)(40)}{0.20(10)}} = 141.42$

$Q_2 = \sqrt{\dfrac{2(500)(40)}{0.20(9.7)}} = 143.59$

Because Q_1 is over its limit of 99 units, Q_1 cannot be optimal (see Problem 23); use $Q_2 = 143.59$ as the optimal order quantity.

Total cost $= \dfrac{1}{2}QC_h + \dfrac{D}{Q}C_0 + DC$

$= 139.28 + 139.28 + 4850.00 = \$5128.56$

22. $Q^* = 300$; Savings = $480

24. a. 500
   b. 580.4

25. a. $c_o = 80 - 50 = 30$
   $c_u = 125 - 80 = 45$

$P(D \le Q^*) = \dfrac{c_u}{c_u + c_o} = \dfrac{45}{45 + 30} = 0.60$

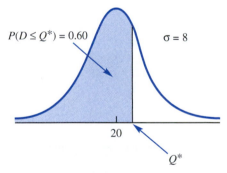

$P(D \le Q^*) = 0.60$ $\sigma = 8$

20   Q^*

For the cumulative standard normal probability 0.60, $z = 0.25$;
$Q^* = 20 + 0.25(8) = 22$.

   b. $P(\text{Sell all}) = P(D \ge Q^*) = 1 - 0.60 = 0.40$

26. a. $150
   b. $240 - \$150 = \$90$
   c. 47
   d. 0.625

28. a. 440
   b. 0.60
   c. 710
   d. $c_u = \$17$

29. a. $r = dm = (200/250)15 = 12$
   b. $\dfrac{D}{Q} = \dfrac{200}{25} = 8$ orders/year

The limit of 1 stock-out per year means that $P(\text{Stock-out/cycle}) = 1/8 = 0.125$.

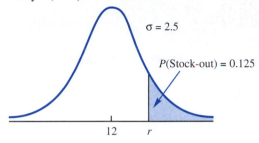

$\sigma = 2.5$

$P(\text{Stock-out}) = 0.125$

12   r

$P(\text{No Stockout/cycle}) = 1 - 0.125 = 0.875$
For cumulative probability 0.875, $z = 1.15$

Thus, $z = \dfrac{r - 12}{2.5} = 1.15$

$r = 12 + 1.15(2.5) = 14.875$ Use 15.
   c. Safety stock = 3 units
   Added cost = 3($5) = \$15/year

30. a. 13.68 (14)
   b. 17.83 (18)
   c. 2, $10; 6, $30

32. a. 31.62
   b. 19.8 (20); 0.2108
   c. 5, $15

33. a. $1/52 = 0.0192$
   b. $P(\text{No Stockout}) = 1 - 0.0192 = 0.9808$
   For cumulative probability 0.9808, $z = 2.07$.

Thus, $z = \dfrac{M - 60}{12} = 2.07$

$M = \mu + z\sigma = 60 + 2.07(12) = 85$
   c. $M = 35 + (0.9808)(85 - 35) = 84$

34. a. 243
   b. 93, $54.87
   c. 613
   d. 163, $96.17
   e. Yes, added cost would be only $41.30 per year.
   f. Yes, added cost would be $4130 per year.

36. a. 40
   b. 62.25; 7.9
   c. 54
   d. 36

Chapter 15

2. a. 0.4512
   b. 0.6988
   c. 0.3012

4. 0.3333, 0.2222, 0.1481, 0.0988; 0.1976

5. a. $P_0 = 1 - \dfrac{\lambda}{\mu} = 1 - \dfrac{10}{12} = 0.1667$

b. $L_q = \dfrac{\lambda^2}{\mu(\mu - \lambda)} = \dfrac{10^2}{12(12 - 10)} = 4.1667$

c. $W_q = \dfrac{L_q}{\lambda} = 0.4167$ hour (25 minutes)

d. $W = W_q + \dfrac{1}{\mu} = 0.5$ hour (30 minutes)

e. $P_w = \dfrac{\lambda}{\mu} = \dfrac{10}{12} = 0.8333$

6. a. 0.3750
b. 1.0417
c. 0.8333 minutes (50 seconds)
d. 0.6250
e. Yes

8. 0.20, 3.2, 4, 3.2, 4, 0.80
Slightly poorer service

10. a. New: 0.3333, 1.3333, 2, 0.6667, 1, 0.6667
Experienced: 0.50, 0.50, 1, 0.25, 0.50, 0.50
b. New \$74; experienced \$50; hire experienced

11. a. $\lambda = 2.5$; $\mu = \dfrac{60}{10} = 6$ customers per hour

$L_q = \dfrac{\lambda^2}{\mu(\mu - \lambda)} = \dfrac{(2.5)^2}{6(6 - 2.5)} = 0.2976$

$L = L_q + \dfrac{\lambda}{\mu} = 0.7143$

$W_q = \dfrac{L_q}{\lambda} = 0.1190$ hours (7.14 minutes)

$W = W_q + \dfrac{1}{\mu} = 0.2857$ hours

$P_w = \dfrac{\lambda}{\mu} = \dfrac{2.5}{6} = 0.4167$

b. No; $W_q = 7.14$ minutes; firm should increase the service rate (μ) for the consultant or hire a second consultant.

c. $\mu = \dfrac{60}{8} = 7.5$ customers per hour

$L_q = \dfrac{\lambda^2}{\mu(\mu - \lambda)} = \dfrac{(2.5)^2}{7.5(7.5 - 2.5)} = 0.1667$

$W_q = \dfrac{L_q}{\lambda} = 0.0667$ hour (4 minutes)

The service goal is being met.

12. a. 0.25, 2.25, 3, 0.15 hours, 0.20 hours, 0.75
b. The service needs improvement.

14. a. 8
b. 0.3750
c. 1.0417
d. 12.5 minutes
e. 0.6250
f. Add a second consultant.

16. a. 0.50
b. 0.50
c. 0.10 hours (6 minutes)
d. 0.20 hours (12 minutes)
e. Yes, $W_q = 6$ minutes is most likely acceptable for a marina.

18. a. $k = 2$; $\lambda/\mu = 5.4/3 = 1.8$; $P_0 = 0.0526$

$L_q = \dfrac{(\lambda/\mu)^2 \lambda\mu}{(k - 1)!(2\mu - \lambda)^2} P_0$

$= \dfrac{(1.8)^2(5.4)(3)}{(2 - 1)!(6 - 5.4)^2}(0.0526) = 7.67$

$L = L_q + \lambda/\mu = 7.67 + 1.8 = 9.47$

$W_q = \dfrac{L_q}{\lambda} = \dfrac{7.67}{5.4} = 1.42$ minutes

$W = W_q + 1/\mu = 1.42 + 0.33 = 1.75$ minutes

$P_w = \dfrac{1}{k!}\left(\dfrac{\lambda}{\mu}\right)^k \left(\dfrac{k\mu}{k\mu - \lambda}\right)P_0$

$= \dfrac{1}{2!}(1.8)^2\left(\dfrac{6}{6 - 5.4}\right)0.0526 = 0.8526$

b. $L_q = 7.67$; Yes
c. $W = 1.75$ minutes

20. a. Use $k = 2$.
$W = 3.7037$ minutes
$L = 4.4444$
$P_w = 0.7111$
b. For $k = 3$
$W = 7.1778$ minutes
$L = 15.0735$ customers
$P_N = 0.8767$
Expand post office.

21. From Problem 11, a service time of 8 minutes has $\mu = 60/8 = 7.5$

$L_q = \dfrac{\lambda^2}{\mu(\mu - \lambda)} = \dfrac{(2.5)^2}{7.5(7.5 - 2.5)} = 0.1667$

$L = L_q + \dfrac{\lambda}{\mu} = 0.50$

Total cost $= \$25L + \$16$
$= 25(0.50) + 16 = \$28.50$
Two channels: $\lambda = 2.5$; $\mu = 60/10 = 6$
With $P_0 = 0.6552$,

$L_q = \dfrac{(\lambda/\mu)^2 \lambda\mu}{1!(2\mu - \lambda)^2} P_0 = 0.0189$

$L = L_q + \dfrac{\lambda}{\mu} = 0.4356$

Total cost $= 25(0.4356) + 2(16) = \$42.89$
Use one consultant with an 8-minute service time.

22.

Characteristic	A	B	C
a. P_0	0.2000	0.5000	0.4286
b. L_q	3.2000	0.5000	0.1524
c. L	4.0000	1.0000	0.9524
d. W_q	0.1333	0.0208	0.0063
e. W	0.1667	0.0417	0.0397
f. P_w	0.8000	0.5000	0.2286

The two-channel System C provides the best service.

24. a. 0.0466, 0.05

    b. 1.4

    c. 11:00 A.M.

25. $\lambda = 4$, $W = 10$ minutes

    a. $\mu = 1/2 = 0.5$

    b. $W_q = W - 1/\mu = 10 - 1/0.5 = 8$ minutes

    c. $L = \lambda W = 4(10) = 40$

26. a. 0.2668, 10 minutes, 0.6667

    b. 0.0667, 7 minutes, 0.4669

    c. \$25.33; \$33.34; one-channel

27. a. $2/8$ hours $= 0.25$ per hour

    b. $1/3.2$ hours $= 0.3125$ per hour

    c.
$$L_q = \frac{\lambda^2 \sigma^2 + (\lambda/\mu)^2}{2(1 - \lambda/\mu)}$$
$$= \frac{(0.25)^2(2)^2 + (0.25/0.3125)^2}{2(1 - 0.25/0.3125)} = 2.225$$

    d. $W_q = \dfrac{L_q}{\lambda} = \dfrac{2.225}{0.25} = 8.9$ hours

    e. $W = W_q + \dfrac{1}{\mu} = 8.9 + \dfrac{1}{0.3125} = 12.1$ hours

    f. Same as $P_w = \dfrac{\lambda}{\mu} = \dfrac{0.25}{0.3125} = 0.80$

    80% of the time the welder is busy.

28. a. 10, 9.6

    b. Design A with $\mu = 10$

    c. 0.05, 0.01

    d. A: 0.5, 0.3125, 0.8125, 0.0625, 0.1625, 0.5
B: 0.4792, 0.2857, 0.8065, 0.0571, 0.1613, 0.5208

    e. Design B has slightly less waiting time.

30. a. $\lambda = 42$; $\mu = 20$

i	$(\lambda/\mu)^i/i!$
0	1.0000
1	2.1000
2	2.2050
3	1.5435
Total	6.8485

j	P_j	
0	1/6.8485	$= -0.1460$
1	2.1/6.8485	$= -0.3066$
2	2.2050/6.8485	$= -0.3220$
3	1.5435/6.8485	$= -0.2254$
		1.0000

    b. 0.2254

    c. $L = \lambda/\mu(1 - P_k) = 42/20(1 - 0.2254) = 1.6267$

    d. Four lines will be necessary; the probability of denied access is 0.1499.

32. a. 31.03%

    b. 27.59%

    c. 0.2759, 0.1092, 0.0351

    d. 3, 10.92%

34. $N = 5$; $\lambda = 0.025$; $\mu = 0.20$; $\lambda/\mu = 0.125$

    a.

n	$\dfrac{N!}{(N-n)!}\left(\dfrac{\lambda}{\mu}\right)^n$
0	1.0000
1	0.6250
2	0.3125
3	0.1172
4	0.0293
5	0.0037
Total	2.0877

$$P_0 = 1/2.0877 = 0.4790$$

    b. $L_q = N - \left(\dfrac{\lambda + \mu}{\lambda}\right)(1 - P_0)$

$$= 5 - \left(\frac{0.225}{0.025}\right)(1 - 0.4790) = 0.3110$$

    c. $L = L_q + (1 - P_0) = 0.3110 + (1 - 0.4790) = 0.8321$

    d. $W_q = \dfrac{L_q}{(N - L)\lambda} = \dfrac{0.3110}{(5 - 0.8321)(0.025)}$

$$= 2.9854 \text{ minutes}$$

    e. $W = W_q + \dfrac{1}{\mu} = 2.9854 + \dfrac{1}{0.20} = 7.9854$ minutes

    f. Trips/day $= (8 \text{ hours})(60 \text{ minutes/hour})(\lambda)$
$= (8)(60)(0.025) = 12$ trips
Time at copier: $12 \times 7.9854 = 95.8$ minutes/day
Wait time at copier: $12 \times 2.9854 = 35.8$ minutes/day

    g. Yes, five assistants $\times$ 35.8 = 179 minutes (3 hours/day), so 3 hours per day are lost to waiting.
$(35.8/480)(100) = 7.5\%$ of each assistant's day is spent waiting for the copier.

Chapter 16

2. a. c = variable cost per unit
x = demand
Profit = $(50 - c)x - 30,000$
b. Base: Profit = $(50 - 20)1200 - 30,000 = 6000$
Worst: Profit = $(50 - 24)300 - 30,000 = -22,200$
Best: Profit = $(50 - 16)2100 - 30,000 = 41,400$
c. Simulation will be helpful in estimating the probability of a loss.

4. a.

Number of New Accounts	Interval
0	0.00 but less than 0.01
1	0.01 but less than 0.05
2	0.05 but less than 0.15
3	0.15 but less than 0.40
4	0.40 but less than 0.80
5	0.80 but less than 0.95
6	0.95 but less than 1.00

b. 4, 3, 3, 5, 2, 6, 4, 4, 4, 2
37 new accounts
c. First-year commission = $185,000
Cost of 10 seminars = $35,000
Yes

5. a.

Stock Price Change	Interval
−2	0.00 but less than 0.05
−1	0.05 but less than 0.15
0	0.15 but less than 0.40

Stock Price Change	Interval
+1	0.40 but less than 0.60
+2	0.60 but less than 0.80
+3	0.80 but less than 0.90
+4	0.90 but less than 1.00

b. Beginning price $39
0.1091 indicates −1 change; $38
0.9407 indicates +4 change; $42
0.1941 indicates 0 change; $42
0.8083 indicates +3 change; $45 (ending price)

6. a. 0.00–0.83, 0.83–0.89, 0.89–0.94, 0.94–0.96, 0.96–0.98, 0.98–0.99, 0.99–1.00
b. 4 claims paid; Total = $22,000

8. a. Atlanta wins each game if random number is in interval 0.00–0.60, 0.00–0.55, 0.00–0.48, 0.00–0.45, 0.00–0.48, 0.00–0.55, 0.00–0.50.
b. Atlanta wins games 1, 2, 4, and 6.
Atlanta wins series, 4 to 2.
c. Repeat many times; record % of Atlanta wins.

9. a. Base-case based on most likely;
Time = 6 + 5 + 14 + 8 = 33 weeks
Worst: Time = 8 + 7 + 18 + 10 = 43 weeks
Best: Time = 5 + 3 + 10 + 8 = 26 weeks

b. 0.1778 for A: 5 weeks
0.9617 for B: 7 weeks
0.6849 for C: 14 weeks
0.4503 for D: 8 weeks; Total = 34 weeks
c. Simulation will provide an estimate of the probability of 35 weeks or less.

10. a.

Hand Value	Interval
17	0.0000 but less than 0.1654
18	0.1654 but less than 0.2717
19	0.2717 but less than 0.3780
20	0.3780 but less than 0.4797
21	0.4797 but less than 0.5769
Broke	0.5769 but less than 1.0000

b, c, & d. Dealer wins 13 hands, player wins 5, 2 pushes.
e. Player wins 7, dealer wins 13.

12. a. $7, $3, $12
b. Purchase: 0.00–0.25, 0.25–0.70, 0.70–1.00
Labor: 0.00–0.10, 0.10–0.35, 0.35–0.70, 0.70–1.00
Transportation: 0.00–0.75, 0.75–1.00
c. $5
d. $7
e. Provide probability profit less than $5/unit

14. Selected cell formulas for the worksheet shown in Figure G16.14 are as follows:

Cell	Formula
B13	=$C$7+RAND()*($C$8−$C$7)
C13	=NORMINV(RAND(),$G$7,$G$8)
D13	=($C$3−B13)*C13−$C$4

a. The mean profit should be approximately $6000; simulation results will vary with most simulations having a mean profit between $5500 and $6500.
b. 120 to 150 of the 500 simulation trials should show a loss; thus, the probability of a loss should be between 0.24 and 0.30.
c. This project appears too risky.

16. a. About 36% of simulation runs will show $130,000 as the winning bid.
b. $150,000; $10,000
c. Recommended $140,000

18. Selected cell formulas for the worksheet shown in Figure G16.18 are as follows:

Cell	Formula
B11	=$C$4+RAND()*($C$5−$C$4)
C11	=NORMINV(RAND(),$H$4,$H$5)
D11	=MAX(B11:C11)
G11	=COUNTIF(D11:D1010,"<750")
H11	=G11/COUNT(D11:D1010)

FIGURE G16.14   WORKSHEET FOR THE MADEIRA MANUFACTURING COMPANY

	A	B	C	D	E	F	G	H
1	**Madeira Manufacturing Company**							
2								
3	Selling Price per Unit		$50					
4	Fixed Cost		$30,000					
5								
6	**Variable Cost (Uniform Distribution)**				**Demand (Normal Distribution)**			
7	Smallest Value		$16		Mean		1200	
8	Largest Value		$24		Standard Deviation		300	
9								
10	**Simulation trials**							
11		Variable						
12	Trial	Cost per Unit	Demand	Profit				
13	1	$17.81	788	($4,681)				
14	2	$18.86	1078	$3,580				
15								

FIGURE G16.18   WORKSHEET FOR THE CONTRACTOR BIDDING

	A	B	C	D	E	F	G	H	I
1	**Contractor Bidding**								
2									
3	**Contractor A (Uniform Distribution)**					**Contractor B (Normal Distribution)**			
4	Smallest Value		$600			Mean		$700	
5	Largest Value		$800			Standard Deviation		$50	
6									
7									
8									
9									
10	**Simulation**					**Results**			
11		Contractor	Contractor	Highest		Contractor's	Number	Probability	
12	Trial	A's Bid	B's Bid	Bid		Bid	of Wins	of Winning	
13	1	$673.00	$720	$720		750	629	0.629	
14	2	$757.00	$655	$757		775	824	0.824	
15	3	$706	$791	$791		785	887	0.887	
16	4	$638	$677	$677					
17									

a. $750,000 should win roughly 600 to 650 of the 1000 times; the probability of winning the bid should be between 0.60 and 0.65.

b. The probability of $775,000 winning should be roughly 0.82, and the probability of $785,000 winning should be roughly 0.88; a contractor's bid of $775,000 is recommended.

20. a. Results vary with each simulation run.
Approximate results: 50,000 provided $230,000
60,000 provided $190,000
70,000 less than $100,000

b. Recommend 50,000 units

c. Roughly 0.75

22. Very poor operation; some customers wait 30 minutes or more.

24. b. Waiting time approximately 0.8 minutes
   c. 30% to 35% of customers have to wait.

Chapter 17

2. a. 0.82
   b. $\pi_1 = 0.5$, $\pi_2 = 0.5$
   c. $\pi_1 = 0.6$, $\pi_2 = 0.4$

3. a. 0.10 as given by the transition probability
   b. $\pi_1 = 0.90\pi_1 + 0.30\pi_2$ (1)
   $\pi_2 = 0.10\pi_1 + 0.70\pi_2$ (2)
   $\pi_1 + \pi_2 = 1$ (3)
   Using (1) and (3),
   $$0.10\pi_1 - 0.30\pi_2 = 0$$
   $$0.10\pi_1 - 0.30(1 - \pi_1) = 0$$
   $$0.10\pi_1 - 0.30 + 0.30\pi_1 = 0$$
   $$0.40\pi_1 = 0.30$$
   $$\pi_1 = 0.75$$
   $$\pi_2 = (1 - \pi_1) = 0.25$$

4. a. $\pi_1 = 0.92$, $\pi_2 = 0.08$
   b. $85

6. a.

	City	Suburbs
City	0.98	0.02
Suburbs	0.01	0.99

   b. $\pi_1 = 0.333$, $\pi_2 = 0.667$
   c. City will decrease from 40% to 33%; suburbs will increase from 60% to 67%.

7. a. $\pi_1 = 0.85\pi_1 + 0.20\pi_2 + 0.15\pi_3$ (1)
   $\pi_2 = 0.10\pi_1 + 0.75\pi_2 + 0.10\pi_3$ (2)
   $\pi_3 = 0.05\pi_1 + 0.05\pi_2 + 0.75\pi_3$ (3)
   $\pi_1 + \pi_2 + \pi_3 = 1$ (4)
   Using (1), (2), and (4) provides three equations with three unknowns; solving provides $\pi_1 = 0.548$, $\pi_2 = 0.286$, and $\pi_3 = 0.166$.
   b. 16.6% as given by π_3
   c. Quick Stop should take
   $$667 - 0.548(1000) = 119 \text{ Murphy's customers}$$
   $$\text{and } 333 - 0.286(1000) = \underline{47} \text{ Ashley's customers}$$
   $$\text{Total} \quad 166 \text{ Quick Stop customers}$$
   It will take customers from Murphy's and Ashley's.

8. a. MDA
   b. $\pi_1 = 1/3$, $\pi_2 = 2/3$

10. $3 - 1(0.59)$, $4 - 1(0.52)$

11. $I = \begin{bmatrix} 1 & 0 \\ 0 & 1 \end{bmatrix}$ $Q = \begin{bmatrix} 0.25 & 0.25 \\ 0.05 & 0.25 \end{bmatrix}$

$(I - Q) = \begin{bmatrix} 0.75 & -0.25 \\ -0.05 & 0.75 \end{bmatrix}$

$N = (I - Q)^{-1} = \begin{bmatrix} 1.3636 & 0.4545 \\ 0.0909 & 1.3636 \end{bmatrix}$

$NR = \begin{bmatrix} 1.3636 & 0.4545 \\ 0.0909 & 1.3636 \end{bmatrix}\begin{bmatrix} 0.5 & 0.0 \\ 0.5 & 0.2 \end{bmatrix} = \begin{bmatrix} 0.909 & 0.091 \\ 0.727 & 0.273 \end{bmatrix}$

$BNR = \begin{bmatrix} 4000 & 5000 \end{bmatrix}\begin{bmatrix} 0.909 & 0.091 \\ 0.727 & 0.273 \end{bmatrix} = \begin{bmatrix} 7271 & 1729 \end{bmatrix}$

Estimate $1729 in bad debts.

12. 3580 will be sold eventually; 1420 will be lost.

14. a. Graduate and drop out
   b. $P(\text{Drop Out}) = 0.15$, $P(\text{Sophomore}) = 0.10$, $P(\text{Junior}) = 0.75$
   c. 0.706, 0.294
   d. Yes; $P(\text{Graduate}) = 0.54$
   $P(\text{Drop Out}) = 0.46$
   e. 1479 (74%) will graduate

Appendix A

2. =F6*$F$3

4.

	A	B
1	**Nowlin Plastics**	
2		
3	**Fixed Cost**	$3,000.00
4		
5	**Variable Cost Per Unit**	$2.00
6		
7	**Selling Price Per Unit**	$5.00
8		
9	**Capacity**	1500
10		
11	**Forecasted Demand**	1200
12		
13	**Model**	
14		
15	**Production Volume**	1200
16		
17	**Total Cost**	$5,400.00
18		
19	**Total Revenue**	$6,000.00
20		
21	**Total Profit (Loss)**	$600.00
22		

14		
15	**Production Volume**	=IF(B11<B9,B11,B9)
16		
17	**Total Cost**	=B3+B5*B15
18		
19	**Total Revenue**	=B7*B15
20		
21	**Total Profit (Loss)**	=B19-B17
22		

6.

Cell	Formula
D14	=C14*$B$3
E14	=C14*$B$7
F14	=C14*$B$9
G14	=$B$5
H14	=SUM(E14:G14)
I14	=D14-H14

	A	B	C	D	E	F	G	H	I
1	Cox Electric Break even Analysis								
2									
3	Revenue per Unit	$0.63							
4									
5	Fixed Costs	$10,000.00							
6									
7	Material Cost per Unit	$0.15							
8									
9	Labor Cost per Unit	$0.10							
10									
11									
12	Model								
13			Volume	Total Revenue	Material Cost	Labor Cost	Fixed Cost	Total Cost	Profit
14			10000	$6,300.00	$1,500.00	$1,000.00	$10,000.00	$12,500.00	−$6,200.00
15			20000	$12,600.00	$3,000.00	$2,000.00	$10,000.00	$15,000.00	−$2,400.00
16			30000	$18,900.00	$4,500.00	$3,000.00	$10,000.00	$17,500.00	$1,400.00
17									

8.

Grade	Count
F	1
D	2
C−	1
C−	1
C+	0
B−	2
B	1
B+	0
A−	1
A	3

10. Error in Sumproduct range in cell B17
Cell A23 should be Lexington.

Index

X

Z